The Wadsworth Anthology of

poetry

JAY PARINI
Middlebury College

THOMSON
———————✳———————™
WADSWORTH

United States • Australia • Canada • Mexico • Singapore • Spain • United Kingdom

THOMSON
WADSWORTH

The Wadsworth Anthology of Poetry
Jay Parini

Publisher: **Michael Rosenberg**
Acquisitions Editor: **Aron Keesbury**
Development Editor: **Meg Botteon**
Assistant Editor: **Marita Sermolins**
Editorial Assistant: **Cheryl Forman**
Senior Technology Project Manager:
Cara Douglass-Graff
Marketing Manager: **Mary Jo Southern**
Marketing Assistant: **Dawn Giovanniello**
Advertising Project Manager:
Patrick Rooney

Senior Project Manager, Editorial Production:
Lianne Ames
Senior Print Buyer: **Mary Beth Hennebury**
Permissions Editor: **Karyn Morrison**
Production Service: **Kathy Smith**
Text Designer: **Garry Harman**
Cover Designer: **Tenazas Design**
Cover Printer: **Webcom Ltd**
Compositor: **Publishers' Design & Production
Services, Inc.**
Printer: **Webcom, Ltd.**

**Thomson Higher Education
25 Thomson Place
Boston, MA 02210-1202
USA**

Asia (including India)
Thomson Learning
5 Shenton Way
#01-01 UIC Building
Singapore 068808

Australia/New Zealand
Thomson Learning Australia
102 Dodds Street
Southbank, Victoria 3006
Australia

Canada
Thomson Nelson
1120 Birchmount Road
Toronto, Ontario M1K 5G4
Canada

UK/Europe/Middle East/Africa
Thomson Learning
High Holborn House
50–51 Bedford Road
London WC1R 4LR
United Kingdom

Latin America
Thomson Learning
Seneca, 53
Colonia Polanco
11560 Mexico
D.F. Mexico

Spain (including Portugal)
Thomson Paraninfo
Calle Magallanes, 25
28015 Madrid, Spain

Library of Congress Control Number:
20055921983

ISBN 1-4130-0473-3

CONTENTS

3 "Once Upon a Midnight Dreary": An Anthology of Narrative Poetry 256

Section II THEMES   975

15 "Love's Austere and Lonely Offices": An Anthology of Poems about Family 977

Section III CONTEXTS   1487

23 "Doom Is Dark and Deeper": An Anthology of Alliterative Verse 1489

24 "Behold Her, Single in the Field!": An Anthology of Meditative Poetry 1523

25 "This Is Just to Say": An Anthology of Poets in Dialogue 1544

PREFACE FOR INSTRUCTORS

For a long time now, it has struck me that classrooms lacked a proper teaching anthology, one that introduced students to poems not only as a march of poets through history but as poets in conversation, poets listening and reacting to the work of the poets who went before them, even anticipating those who come after. I was eager to create an anthology of voices alive on the page, in argument and assent, in fury, fondness, and gentle remorse. To create what would become the book you now hold in your hand, I put aside the usual arrangement of anthologies by chronology and, instead, arranged the poems according to criteria that poets themselves actually use when writing poems, when trying to find an appropriate form for the strong feelings they wish to express or explore.

An Anthology of Anthologies

The Wadsworth Anthology of Poetry collects 25 "mini-anthologies" that will help students understand poetry as poets themselves often do. These shorter sections (each usually fewer than 50 poems) include anthologies of epics, elegies, odes, ballads, monologues, short lyrics, sonnets, and sestinas, for example, or collections of poems about families, love and longing, war, politics, first and last things, nature, animals, and poetry itself.

The 25 mini-anthologies (chapters, in and of themselves) in *The Wadsworth Anthology of Poetry* are collected in three over-arching sections: "The Shape of the Poem," "Themes," and "Contexts." The groupings are meant to introduce students to the most elementary types of poetry, the thematic concerns of poems, and the conversations in which poets have engaged through the ages. Brief historical and descriptive introductions precede each chapter, and after many chapter introductions, I suggest poems from elsewhere in the book that would fit in the chapter, making the point that none of these categories is exclusive. A poem can be, for example, an elegy and also be written in heroic couplets. An ode will almost certainly be written in stanzas. Blank verse is a common form of narrative poetry and was commonly used for epics. In other words, the student should not feel that any of these categories corral meaning and expression under a specific rubric. This is never the case. The literary tradition is broad and deep, and there are, of course, many ways to arrange poems that speak to some aspect of their form.

Chronology is still, of course, important, since poets themselves have a deep sense of historical development and of an evolving canon, and so the anthology includes a full chronological table of contents to illustrate the deep sense of poetic history, and to facilitate chronological approaches in class. Furthermore, within each grouping of poems, the work is arranged according to the birth date of the poet, so that readers will have a sense of development within each type of form, theme, or subject.

Shape, Theme, and Context

In the first section, "The Shape of the Poem," the poems cluster according to their type or specific form. By type, I refer to traditional types of poetry, such as epic, elegy, ode, or ballad, as well as poems that adhere to a specific tradition, such as narrative poetry or dramatic poetry. This section also includes particular forms of poetry, such as the sonnet and sestina, the villanelle, heroic couplets, blank verse, and various stanza forms. The lyric tradition, which is fairly generic, has a cluster of its own, as does free verse, which has become the most common form of poetry in the past century.

The second major section gathers poems according to specific themes, such as poems about family, love, war, politics, nature, animals, and so forth. I think of this book as an anthology of anthologies, and this section makes that point rather emphatically. One could go into any bookstore and buy a book of poems about love or nature or war. I've made an attempt here to gather some of the most beloved poems on the major themes, and to add to each theme a number of lesser known poems, often by contemporary poets or poets who, for one reason or another, have been overlooked by critics. Among my favorite chapters here is the one called "Ars Poetica," the "art of poetry." Poets often write a poem, or several poems, that deal explicitly with poetry itself, that express their own principles for writing poems. In this chapter, I include poems that might be regarded as the poet's artistic credo.

In the third section, "Contexts," students will find poets responding to specific poems or poetic traditions, either explicitly or implicitly. One could, indeed, have made several volumes of poems arranged according to this principle. Teachers, I think, will find a good deal to talk about here. It's often surprising to see how poets react to an earlier poem, adding their turn of the screw, objecting to some point, or simply by attempting to rewrite the poem in their own voice. This section makes the point that poetry remains a living tradition, one in constant development, and one that depends on the work that has gone before.

The Poems Themselves (Readable and Teachable)

The great question for any anthologist is what to include and what to exclude. One cannot include every good example, or hope to reprint every major poem in the English language. In all cases, I have opted for poems that seemed, to me, highly readable. This means that many fine poems have been excluded because they seemed too difficult for readers who are just beginning to study poetry. It was important to represent all major voices, from the anonymous author of *Beowulf* through

Chaucer, Shakespeare, Milton, Pope, Wordsworth, Keats, Dickinson, Tennyson, Yeats, Eliot, Frost, and Bishop, and the classic poems by the major poets are, for the most part, included here. It is on the margins that, as an anthologist, one has some fun, and I've tried to include a fair number of the poems that, over thirty years of teaching, I have found useful or entertaining for students. Many of these poems will not be familiar to teachers, and I ask that you give them due consideration. I think you will enjoy them.

Of course I've made an effort to include a generous sampling of poems by women and poems by writers coming from minority traditions. The great discovery of the past decades for critics is that these traditions have been overlooked, and that the best work in each compares favorably with the poems by previously established (usually white male) authors. I make no apologies for any poem included in this book. Every poem in this anthology has, in my view and the view of my editorial board, passed the test of excellence.

The Elements of Poetry

Most anthologies such as this have only a brief introduction. *The Wadsworth Anthology*, by contrast, offers a comprehensive introduction to reading and appreciation of poetry. This includes, for example, discussions of the nature of poetic language, the use of imagery, metaphor, and symbol, the employment of poetic forms, including meter and rhyme, and the various ways that critics approach the reading of poems. A good deal of what the beginning student needs to start reading poems with some sophistication is, I hope, included here in an accessible format and style.

In addition, a glossary of poetic terms appears at the back of the book as an index. It includes not only those terms used in the general introduction of the book, or the chapter introductions that follow, but also those covered more extensively on the introduction to prosody included on the *Poetry21* CD-ROM. Students interested in enhancing their study with interactive, or animated exercises should turn to the *Poetry21* CD-ROM.

The Editorial Board

Throughout the process of selecting, re-selecting, organizing, and re-organizing the poems that now make up *The Wadsworth Anthology of Poetry*, I've enjoyed the generous help, and have relied heavily on my editorial board of advisors—an unrivaled collection of poets, scholars, and friends. Because of them, I may be confident that the selections in the book and the chapter breakdowns meet the very high standard of their excellence. Thanks to Julia Alvarez, William Cook, Greg Delanty, Sandra M. Gilbert, Henry Hart, William H. Pritchard, Alastair Reid, Charles Simic, Ellen Bryant Voigt, and Charles Wright. These advisors have all been hugely supportive, and without them this book would not exist.

Poetry21 CD-ROM

Integrated with the anthology and bound into every copy, *Poetry21* contains 130 poems read aloud (mostly by the poets themselves), an interactive timeline that puts every poet in historical context, poetry pages and biographies for more than 250 poets, an interactive video anthology on slam poetry, and Wadsworth's *The Explicator*—a poetry analysis tool that guides students through close readings and helps them create notes for their papers. Designed by poets and teachers, *Poetry21* provides resources and activities that students will actually find useful.

Instructor's Manual

An instructor's manual, prepared by my colleague at Middlebury College, Pauls Toutonghi, offers teachers additional ideas and resources for using *The Wadsworth Anthology of Poetry*. We designed the manual so that teachers would have something interesting or surprising about *every* poem to take to class and start a conversation. You will find sample syllabi for different kinds of poetry courses (upper-level literary studies, creative writing courses, and general introduction courses among them); suggestions for moving among and between the little anthologies; brief essays providing a teacher's perspective on each chapter, and lists of additional resources about the teaching of poetry.

Acknowledgments

It would be ludicrous to claim this work as anything like my own. First, I must thank my research assistants, Dimiter Kenarov and Jacob Risinger. Their energetic help, which went way beyond the usual work of assistants, is gratefully acknowledged here. In particular, Dimiter—a poet himself—gave me countless suggestions, large and small, that have improved this book.

I have also had a good deal of help from my editors at Wadsworth. Thanks to Aron Keesbury, who, as Acquisitions Editor, offered me the opportunity to do such a book, and Meg Botteon, who developed the project from top to bottom. I'm grateful to them for their enthusiastic attention to this manuscript. Thanks to Assistant Editor Marita Sermolins, who, with the help of Wadsworth's Technology Project Manager, Cara Douglass-Graff, and the folks at X-Plana, realized the extraordinary *Poetry21* that accompanies this book. Thanks as well to Bill Coyle at Salem State College for his contributions to the disk, and to Editorial Assistants Dawn Giovanniello and Cheryl Forman for the work they did behind the scenes on the disk and the book. Finally, thanks to Karyn Morrison for clearing permissions to reprint the poems, to Katrina Byrd and Mary Jo Southern for marketing the book, to Kathy Smith for her detailed and precise coordination of manuscript to pages, to Publishers' Design and Production Services for their nearly instantaneous production of pages, and to Lianne Ames, the manuscript's cool-headed shepherd through production.

In addition, many instructors have helped me throughout the process, offering suggestions and criticisms through thorough reviews. Without their help, this project would not be the same. My thanks to:

Laurel Amtower
San Diego State University

Amittai Aviram
University of South Carolina

Dorothy Baker
University of Houston

Stephen Bernstein
University of Michigan—Flint

Laura Berry
University of Arizona

Tina Blue
University of Kansas

Mark Boren
University of North Carolina at Wilmington

Leslie Brisman
Yale University

Stephen Burt
Macalester College

Charles Cantalupo
Penn State University

Elizabeth Cooley
Gonzaga University

Sharon Cumberland
Seattle University

Stephen Evans
University of Kansas

Norman Finkelstein
Xavier University

Mark Forrester
University of Maryland

August Gering
University of Illinois at Urbana-Champaign

Sheryl Gifford
Florida Atlantic University

Naomi Guttman
Hamilton College

Robert Habich
Ball State University

Lynne Hahn
Florida Atlantic University

Mark Jarman
Vanderbilt University

Kari Kalve
Earlham College

Philip Kelly
Gannon University

William Linn
University of Michigan

Marilyn McEntyre
Westmont College

Peter Melville
Cornell University

Berwyn Moore
Gannon University

Roger Moore
Vanderbilt University

Kimberly Myers
Montana State University

Ann Neelon
Murray State University

Channa Newman
Point Park University

Oliver de la Paz
Utica College of Syracuse University

Mary Pollock
Stetson University

Joseph Scallorns
Louisiana State University

Richard Schrader
Boston College

Louis Schwartz
University of Richmond

Edward Shannon
Ramapo College of New Jersey

Martin Shichtman
Eastern Michigan University

John Shoptaw
University of California—Berkeley

Jenita Smith
Athens State University

Margaret Songe
Louisiana State University

Tony Spicer
Eastern Michigan University

Mircea Tomus
Kirkwood Community College

Edward Walkiewicz
Oklahoma State University

Leon Weinmann
Fitchburg State College

Margaret Whitt
University of Denver

R L Widmann
University of Colorado at Boulder

Anita Willsie Kerr
North Carolina State University

Rosemary Winslow
Catholic University of America

Steven Yao
Hamilton College

WHAT IS POETRY?

Poetry is a language adequate to one's experience. In a deep and true way, this language reflects the complexities of human experience in words suitable to these complexities, enhanced by many techniques and conventions associated with the art of poetry. This language entails thought and feeling, expressing the wide range of both: "What oft' was thought, but ne'er so well expressed," as the English poet, Alexander Pope, once wrote. At its best, the language of poetry pushes to the farthest edges of this experience, marking its borders, even suggesting what lies beyond.

The consequences of not having a language adequate to one's experience are severe, even though most readers will not realize this until late in life, when the importance of having such a language becomes apparent. People often, without being quite aware of it, go to psychiatrists and therapists because the language that they hear in their head, the soft voice that speaks to them when they are falling asleep, does not accurately or usefully reflect their experience. Popular magazines and the broadcasting media are full of language, but this language is quite often false: cliché-ridden, silly, unreal. It's quite easy to fall into a false sense of the world, a false view of oneself. Poetry brings us back to experience in lively, exhilarating, harsh, and beautiful ways. It refreshes our sense of the spoken and written word. It brings us closer to ourselves and our communities. It reinvigorates our faith in ourselves, in the greater powers of the universe, in the possibilities for humankind. Without poetry, we become very poor indeed, detached from those around us, separated from our truest selves. Poetry is, in the finest sense of that word, a cure for detachment, a way beyond the illness that seems to afflict the world at large, a relief from the buzzing, unreal, flashy, foolish noise of contemporary life.

Poetry matters. As Wallace Stevens, the American poet, once wrote: "The soldier is poor without the poet's lines." Nevertheless, the soldier who has poetry with him, who possesses a language that reflects his or her experience, "lives on the bread of faithful speech." This "bread of faithful speech" is what we present in this anthology, which offers a wide range of poetic examples, from short lyrics to longer narrative poems, from poems that use intricate forms—sonnets, villanelles, complex stanzas—to lyrics that employ less intricate forms but still manage to provide sustenance to the reader and to address complex issues or reflect complex realities.

One can define poetry in many different ways, and each of these will have some validity. Robert Frost famously defined poetry as "a momentary stay against confusion." The two operative words in his definition are *momentary* and *confusion*. Life, for most of us, is confusing. Moving through our lives is like walking through a dense forest. It's very difficult to see our way through this dark wood. But once in a while, we happen onto a clearing: a bright, clear circle, where the blue sky shines overhead, and where one sees, briefly, the forest for the trees. While reading a poem, or even writing one, a certain clarity occurs, a brief but wonderful sense of wholeness. "Drink and be whole beyond confusion," Frost wrote at the end of a poem called "Directive," asking readers to dip into the clear stream of his verse. He invited us into his poetry, into the world of poetry overall, as a move toward sanity, recognizing that one acquired this sanity while immersed in the poem itself. All else was, potentially, confusion.

A further definition that seems useful to readers was made by W. H. Auden, the modern English poet who referred to poetry as "memorable language." That is, poetry stays in the mind—long after the reader has closed the book. In the early twentieth century and before, generations of schoolchildren were asked to memorize well-known poems. It seems a pity that we have lost this tradition, and it may prove valuable to readers of this anthology to commit several poems included here—the ones that strike an appealing note—to memory. It is quite easy to do, in part because poets have chosen to write in memorable ways, picking words that seem especially appropriate, using techniques such as rhyme and meter, imagery and various sound combinations, to create a language that hovers in the mind.

Finally, the American poet Ezra Pound once defined poetry as "news that stays news." That is, the news that appears in newspapers each day is ephemeral. The various crises of the moment pass. Without doubt, the human stories told in those pages can be riveting, but they quickly become yesterday's stories, old news. The various crises of the moment pass because the language used to communicate them is simple, even mundane. Readers look for new stories to replace them. This is not true of poems. The poets bring us information about our lives in resonant, extraordinary language that stays fresh from year to year, even century to century. The language of poets from past eras may seem difficult to read, but (with a little help and study) these difficulties are quickly overcome. The core meaning of the poetry stays fresh, informing the lives of readers, explaining things that will always need explaining, showing things that must be shown, embodying feelings and ideas in ways that always remain unique, relevant, and moving.

THE STUDY OF POETRY: SHAPE, THEME, AND CONTEXT

It's one thing to read poetry in a casual way and quite another thing to *study* it. This anthology is arranged in ways that will enhance your study of poems, putting them in helpful contexts, sorting them in useful and interesting ways. The essential ways that we organize poems here are by their shape, by their theme, and by their context. In this, we move somewhat away from chronology—the organizing principle of most other anthologies—looking instead at the traditions that a poet chooses for a poem, how that tradition affects the subject or theme of the poem, and how poets write with both their predecessors and posterity in mind.

Needless to say, chronology—another word for history—is deeply important in the study of literature, since the language of poetry, much like the language of everyday speech, evolves in time. There are always new words and expressions, new contexts for speech, new allusions, new ways of plucking the strings of language to produce different, more "modern" sounds. So in this volume we have not dispensed totally with chronology: each section tracks the evolution of a particular type of poem, form, or theme as it moves through successive eras. In this way, readers can observe the transformations in language that make for the transformations of poetry. In the sections that follow, we examine these broad concepts of shape, content, and context. Let us first turn our attention to the language of poetry.

The Language of Poetry

Poetry and language are, of course, intimately bound. Poetic language, which is different from the language of newspapers or ordinary speech, even different from the language of philosophy or most academic subjects, is usually concrete and concise. It contains **images,** or mental pictures, which bring into focus a range of thought and feeling. Ralph Waldo Emerson, the American essayist and poet, once noted that "all language is fossil poetry," in that many words, in their original form, contained concrete images. The tendency of language is to move toward abstraction, with words pulling away from the concreteness they once owned. The words *right* and *wrong*, for example, in their Anglo-Saxon root-meanings, meant "straight" and "crooked." In other words, one could take the right or the straight path to a destination or the roundabout way, the crooked way, the wrong way. Take a word like *understand*. It means to "stand under" an idea, hence to possess it, to comprehend it. Many Latinate words, such as *supercilious*, have a concrete image buried in their syllables. A supercilious person is someone who snickers at others, raising an eyebrow at what other people do. In Latin, *super* means "above," while *cilia* refers to the little hairs that make up one's eyebrow. So the word is a tiny poem, meaning "raising one's eyebrow."

Poets understand the root-meanings of language. When Robert Frost uses the word *appall* in a poem called "Design," for instance (p. 1259), he knows that the Latin meaning of the word is "to make white." (Modern descendents of that Latin word are *pallid* and *pale*.) In the context of the Frost poem, this meaning adheres with an almost eerie specificity, adding wonderful dimensions. Roots are crucial to words, since words keep adding new meanings, fresh layers; nevertheless, words retain a tint or tincture of their original meaning. Every word is, in a sense, a history lesson, and one can understand the evolution of consciousness by looking carefully at words and the way they add layers of meaning.

It's important to remember that poetry is a form of thought, and that poets are thinkers, though not in the same way as philosophers or scientists or historians. Thought in poetry is usually indirect, and it commonly takes the form of metaphorical or analogical thinking. That is, poets often compare one thing with another, creating analogues. Analogical thinking is crucial to all students, in all disciplines, and one of the best ways to develop a good sense of analogy and its possibilities is through the reading of poems.

The main form of comparison that poets employ is **metaphor,** a term (or **figure of speech,** as rhetoricians say) which comes from a Greek word signifying to carry meaning over from one thing to another, effecting a transfer of content by association. Metaphor is, in a way, a more complex figure of speech than its cousin, **simile,** where the words *like* or *as* come into play as a way of making the comparison explicit. "My love is like a red, red rose" wrote the Scottish poet Robert Burns in a famous poem (p. 1063). In writing this, he made a simple comparison, creating a simile, holding up a flower beside his beloved, asking the reader to connect them. But in what ways can we compare a rose with a woman?

One thing is like another in certain respects, yet unlike in other respects. "My love" may be sweet and attractive, fresh and beautiful— like a rose, as the poet insists. But one hopes that "my love" is not thorny like a rose or subject to seasonal shifts, withering in the fall. Would any-body want a "thorny" love who crumpled when the weather turned cold? A rose is, for all its beauty, rooted in one place, incapable of being moved without a good deal of fuss. The metaphor invites comparison, and metaphorical thinking involves trying to decide how far you can go with a metaphor and where that metaphor lets off, breaks down, becomes less useful or downright unhelpful as a point of comparison. Knowing exactly how far you can take a metaphor is, in fact, a sign of being well educated. (Robert Frost once said that people not educated in metaphorical thinking were not safe to be let loose in the world.)

A literary **symbol** is metaphorical, but not specific in the same way that a metaphor is specific. In the Robert Burns line, we regard the two parts of the metaphor quite explicitly, seeing the rose and the poet's love side by side (these are called the **tenor** and the **vehicle** of the simile). The vehicle, like a car, "carries" the meaning of the tenor, which is the primary subject. William Blake wrote a highly symbolic poem called "The Sick Rose," wherein he does not make any specific links to "reality." So we never really can know what the rose stands in for:

> O rose, thou art sick. The invisible worm
> That flies in the night, in the howling storm
> Has found out thy bed of crimson joy,
> And his dark, secret love does thy life destroy.

What on earth is Blake saying here? What is the point of his peculiar comparison? In the compass of a short lyric, we get a "sick" rose and an "invisible worm" going after it. We've got a howling storm, too. The rose represents "crimson joy," which is rather sensual, even dangerously so. Blake even creates a "bed of crimson joy." The flying worm, whatever it represents, seems definitely phallic, flying toward the "secret" folds of the rose. But the analogy is tied to no particular thing in nature: no "real" rose—one found in the natural world—fits this description. The reader is left to wonder about the meaning of this symbol, to allow associations to multiply. *This is the nature of the literary symbol.* It cannot be pinned down, tied up, linked without doubt to something specific, as in the lines from Burns. Yet because of this lack of specificity, a literary symbol is free-ranging in its applicability; its meaning is multiple, various, and therefore full of potential. The reader's job is that of interpreting the symbol, trying to discover—from the context, from the meaning of the words—what the symbol means, and how far its meaning can be extended without threatening rationality itself. This is part of the adventure of reading poetry. The writer invites the reader to think within a circumscribed field. Meaning flows from the center of the symbol. Much like a pebble thrown into a pond, concentric circles expand from the first splash, and eventually the widest ring—a slight ripple—laps the shore. But the possibilities for meaning are not unlimited: a symbol has the effect of limiting meaning to some extent. The rose in Blake's poem cannot mean just anything. The literary symbol gets the reader thinking in certain directions; it opens possibilities.

All symbols arise from images, acquiring their specificity from the concreteness of the image. The Blake poem creates a complex image of the storm, the flying worm, the sick rose. The mind can conjure up this picture quite easily. But imagery is complex, and it often involves more than simply the physical or mental picture presented by the language. An image is a complex emotional unit, involving the whole of the reader's mind. It compels attention by its sound as well as its visual elements. It conjoins thought and emotion, making a unified impression. In the very best poems, images lodge deep in the mind, where they cannot easily be removed. In many poems, a poet develops one deep image throughout the poem, adding to its complexity stanza by stanza. In other poems, an array of images occur, each of them adding to the elaborate tapestry of the poem, which might be considered a sequence of images.

Sometimes a poet will develop a complex image or metaphor over several lines or stanzas, even throughout a whole poem, as in the following poem by John Donne, "A Valediction, Forbidding Mourning":

> As virtuous men pass mildly away,
>   And whisper to their souls to go,
> Whilst some of their sad friends do say
>   The breath goes now, and some say, No.
>
> 5   So let us melt, and make no noise,
>   No tear-floods, nor sigh-tempests move,
> 'Twere profanation of our joys
>   To tell the laity our love.
>
> Moving of th' earth brings harms and fears,
> 10   Men reckon what it did and meant;
> But trepidation of the spheres,
>   Though greater far, is innocent.
>
> Dull sublunary lovers' love
>   (Whose soul is sense) cannot admit
> 15 Absence, because it doth remove
>   Those things which elemented it.
>
> But we by a love so much refined
>   That our selves know not what it is,
> Inter-assuréd of the mind,
> 20   Care less, eyes, lips, and hands to miss.
>
> Our two souls therefore, which are one,
>   Though I must go, endure not yet
> A breach, but an expansion,
>   Like gold to airy thinness beat.
>
> 25   If they be two, they are two so
>   As stiff twin compasses are two;
> Thy soul, the fixed foot, makes no show
>   To move, but doth, if th' other do.
>
> And though it in the center sit,
> 30   Yet when the other far doth roam,

It leans and harkens after it,
   And grows erect, as that comes home.

Such wilt thou be to me, who must
   Like th' other foot, obliquely run;
35   Thy firmness makes my circle just,
   And makes me end where I begun.

Donne compares two lovers to the arms of a compass, a drawing tool familiar to all students of geometry—and useful for making circles, a symbol of perfection (as suggested in the last lines of the poem). If one part of the couple departs, straying from his or her mate, the other follows, leaning in the lover's direction. Ingeniously, Donne develops the analogy over several stanzas. The poem is witty and suggestive. It's even funny, with that pun on "grows erect" in the next-to-last stanza. Notice that the comparison is well developed, carried to extraordinary length. This sort of extended comparison is called a **conceit.** Donne and poets like him make a point of drawing elaborate conceits; they are often called Metaphysical poets, since their work has a certain philosophical air about it, an atmosphere of concentrated thought.

    Two well-known forms that metaphorical thinking can take are represented by the terms **metonymy** and **synecdoche,** which are figures of speech that depend on metaphor. In metonymy, the metaphor is drawn from the context, as in the following sentence: "The kettle is boiling." The kettle had better *not* be boiling! The water in the kettle is boiling. So the word *kettle* stands in for the word *water,* meaning is carried over from one term to another. In the related term, synecdoche, a little piece of something stands in for something larger. In its crudest form, synecdoche occurs in a sentence such as the following: "Let us count noses." The nose-counting is really people-counting, of course. The nose stands in for the whole person. In a very real way, all poetry is synecdochal, with little bits of reality suggesting vast stretches of reality. A good example of this is "Fragmentary Blue" by Robert Frost:

Why make so much of fragmentary blue
In here and there a bird, or butterfly,
Or flower or wearing-stone, or open eye,
When heaven presents in sheets the solid hue?

5   Since earth is earth, perhaps, not heaven (as yet)—
Though some savants make earth include the sky;
And blue so far above us comes so high,
It only gives our wish for blue a whet.

Frost, more than most poets, understood the potential for synecdoche. In this poem, he asks the reader why he or she "makes so much" about bits of blue, when there is so much blue overhead. The fragments

of blue found in blue eyes or gems ("wearing-stones") or flowers represent a piece of blueness, which represents heaven itself. The part stands
in for the whole, once again. Indeed, Frost wrote in a letter to a friend,
"If I must be classified as a poet, I might be called a Synecdochist, for I
prefer the synecdoche in poetry—that figure of speech in which we use
a part for the whole."

He took this idea even further when he wrote: "The height of all
poetic thinking is that attempt to say matter in terms of spirit and spirit in
terms of matter." Poets are, it seems, always translating meaning, changing one term for another, making substitutions, extending thought, trying
to open up the possibilities of thought and meaning by creating a world
of analogies. So that little bit of blue in the bluebird flying across the
window is important because it stands in for the whole of sky, the whole
of heaven. The part makes it possible to comprehend a whole that, as
mere mortals, we cannot fully comprehend.

The study of poetry means taking in the implications of metaphor
or analogical thinking, reading and rereading a poem, uncovering its
symbols, contemplating ways to extend the meaning of these symbols,
understanding how far you can go and how far you cannot. It means
always reading the poem on two levels: the **literal** level, where we
understand exactly what is meant (without bothering too much about
the implications of a symbol or metaphor), then moving to the **figurative** level, where all points of comparison come into play, and where the
suggestive nature of metaphor applies.

The Poem's Shape: Types and Forms

Poems fall into various categories that may be divided into "types" and
"forms" or, more simply, "shapes," although these are all loose terms.
Some of the major types of poetry collected in this anthology are, for
example, **epic, elegy, narrative verse, ode, dramatic poetry,** and
the **short lyric.** These are considered **genres**—or literary modes. Poets
usually write in one mode or another, although these types of poetry are
hardly exclusive; indeed, they often blend or cross over. For example, a
poem could be written in dramatic form, with lots of dialogue (as in
"Home Burial" by Robert Frost [p. 348]), but also be called a narrative
poem, a poem that tells a story. In fact, almost all dramatic poems tell a
story, so dramatic poems might well be considered a kind of narrative.
Nevertheless, the dramatic poem has certain **conventions**—consistent
elements, with historical roots—that recur. The epic is often narrative,
too. Yet there are obvious conventions—the sweep or scope of the
poem being one of them, as well as its attempt to represent a culture at
large—that turn epic into a recognizable type all by itself.

Each of the major types of poetry evolves in time, its usefulness
shifting as fresh generations come along. Homer's epics, *The Iliad* and
The Odyssey (p. 34), told stories that were central to Greek culture.

These stories of the Trojan War and its aftermath were mythic in their sweep and meaning, and the ancient Greeks used them as mirrors in which they could see their own hopes for themselves—their individual and collective lives—reflected. In a similar way, the elegy and the ode shifted, functioning in different ways for different generations. Few of the great classical elegies, for example, were laments for the death of someone; they were usually love poems. But the elegy took on new dimensions in later periods. Today, one thinks of elegies as poems about the death of someone important—to the poet, personally, or to the nation in general. For contemporary poets, the elegy is often simply a poem about loss, which can be regarded in many different ways.

Epics tell stories, as do narrative and dramatic poems. The element of overlap here is worth considering for a moment. The epic is really a subgenre of the narrative poem, with specific requirements. Dramatic poetry features dialogue or, sometimes—as in the dramatic monologue—it features a single voice. The context of a dramatic poem is significant, too, as the speaker or speakers are caught by the poet in a situation that has dramatic qualities. The context only gradually emerges as the poem proceeds. In the case of the dramatic monologue, there is often an implied listener, someone in addition to the reader of the poem. So when the duke in Robert Browning's "My Last Duchess" (p. 579) explains "That's my last duchess" in the painting on the wall, he addresses a silent courtier who descends a staircase with him; the courtier represents a young woman who will become the new duchess. There is a sly element of menace in the poem, although readers only gradually come to understand this element. Like most good poems, it should be read again and again. Once through is hardly enough to comprehend the meaning of a complex, artfully composed, poem. *It might even be said that a poem cannot be read; it can only be reread.*

The most common type of poetry is, and also has been, the short lyric. In ancient Greece, poems were originally songs composed for accompaniment by the lyre, a kind of harp. The ancient poet recited or sang the poem to crowds, large or small. As a result, short lyrics are often musical in some way, employing satisfying sounds, finding a particular "tune." The poet may use rhyme and meter to create certain effects, or may write in what is called **free verse,** which is notable for its absence of requirements, although poets have always noted that no verse is really "free." (When asked if he ever wrote free verse, Robert Frost famously replied that it would be like playing tennis with the net down.) The speaker is usually the "I" of the poem, the lyric I, *who is not the poet.* Poetry is, of course, a form of fiction; this means that the speaker of the poem should never be identified with the author of the poem, even if the poet tries hard to make this connection.

Poems may also be defined by the specific **form** of the poem, and this form may affect the nature of the line, the pattern of rhyme, the absence of rhyme, or a particular stanza shape. "After great pain, a formal feeling comes," wrote Emily Dickinson in one poem. What this line suggests is that when poets feel a very strong emotion, they may want to "formalize" the feeling, to contain it, to find the limits of this experience within a particular poetic form, such as the **sonnet**—the most famous of all specific forms, known for its number of lines (fourteen) and the various patterns of rhyming and stanza shapes that one associates with the sonnet. In fact, there are many forms that poets can choose among as they attempt to create a poem adequate to the experience they hope to embody in language.

The form a poem takes can depend on its rhythmical structure, rhyme scheme, stanza format, or some combination of these. Myriad possibilities exist for rhyme, meter, and stanza pattern—all of which affect the shape of a poem. In fact, attentive readers will usually discover patterns of one kind or another, even within supposedly "free" verse: elements that work together to create a poetic effect. (Free verse lines always have a rhythm of some kind, and one can often be very specific about the nature of that rhythm.) It would be the rare poem indeed that did not have some linking devices, given that a poem is "a system of linked sounds," as the English poet Thomas Campion once said.

Two of the obvious ways that sounds can be linked are **alliteration** (chiming on consonants, as when "less" connects with "loss") and **rhyme** (chiming on vowels, as when "house" is rhymed with "mouse"). Rhyming can, it should be remembered, occur within lines as well as at the ends of lines. If the chiming is within the lines themselves, on vowels, this device is called **assonance.** Rhymes can also be subtle, as when the word "stone" is rhymed with the word "stain" or "receiver" with "Land Rover." This device is called **slant rhyme,** and poets have been incredibly ingenious in finding rhymes in words that, at first, seem quite distinct. One sometimes sees a rhyme rather than hears it, as when the word "move" is rhymed with "love." This **sight rhyme** may have occurred because of pronunciation changes over time; or the poet may have intended it to work like that. Rhyming is a great mnemonic device as well: a way of remembering the language, as word calls out to word. Usually poets keep a pattern of rhyming from stanza to stanza, and this is called a **rhyme scheme,** and one talks about a rhyme scheme by attaching letters to the rhymes. An Italian sonnet, for example, rhymes like this: ABBA ABBA CDCDCD. The last words in each line might be something like this:

doom/hat/cat/broom
tomb/bat/rat/gloom
ghost/grave/host/cave/frost/brave.

That Italian sonnet would almost certainly be about Halloween! (Notice that I rhymed "ghost" and "host" with "frost." Frost would be a sight rhyme there, since the words don't chime in any exact way.)

The earliest English poets wrote in a form called **alliterative verse.** Old English, which is also called Anglo-Saxon, was the original language of English poetry, and many of the great works of this period—from roughly the sixth through the twelfth centuries—appeared during that time. The most famous English epic, *Beowulf* (p. 46), dates from the early eighth century, and it was written anonymously in the most common form that alliterative verse takes: a four-beat line, with a pause called a **caesura** in the middle of the line. Some historians of literature speculate that during recitations of Anglo-Saxon poems, a harp was struck during the pause; if so, this would have added to the drama of the performance.

The verse unit here is the line itself, since there are no rhymes that link a particular line with other lines (except in very late Anglo-Saxon verse, where rhymes begin to occur). Anglo-Saxon poetry is also called **stressed verse,** meaning that what makes up a line are a certain number of beats or stresses. In *Beowulf* and other poems of this era, a four-beat line is commonly used. What links the sounds in the line are alliteration and patterns of stress. "In a summer season when soft was the sun" is the first line, for example, of *Piers Plowman,* another well-known Anglo-Saxon poem with a four-beat line. Hence, the chiming on the consonant "s" becomes the organizing principle of the line.

In the English language, poetry does not need to rhyme; indeed, much poetry that you will find in this book does not rhyme. Rhyme emerges in Middle English verse, which runs from the twelfth through the fifteenth centuries. This era is known for the importation of forms from Italy and France, and other continental European countries, where elaborate rhyming and stanza patterns were common. This is especially true of Italian poetry, where—a benefit of the language itself—rhymes are easily found. When the Norman French conquered Britain in 1066, French-speaking soldiers brought with them a huge vocabulary of words with Latin roots, thus expanding the storehouse of words in English and adding to the possibilities of English syntax. Rhyming became possible on a grand scale, although it should still be noted that English poetry has only rarely depended on rhyme.

The evolution from the four-beat Anglo-Saxon line was gradual, and a Middle English poem such as *Sir Gawain and the Green Knight* (p. 1489) still retains many elements of stressed, alliterative poetry. With Geoffrey Chaucer and *The Canterbury Tales* (p. 683), a five-beat, ten-syllable line came into vogue; this line forms the basis for modern iambic pentameter, which became popular during the Renaissance. Indeed, the most common form of English verse is blank verse, which is unrhymed iambic pentameter, as in the following line: "Along the ridge a raging windstorm blew." Lines are not linked by rhymes, as no end-rhymes occur. There are no regular stanza breaks either, although the poet may choose to create breaks here and there, creating the equivalent of paragraphs in prose.

The lines themselves fill up to five beats; hence the "penta" (the Greek number five) in pentameter. The verse foot—one stressed syllable surrounded by any number of unstressed syllables equals a poetic "foot"—is iambic, a pattern in which an unstressed syllable is followed by a stressed syllable within the single poetic foot. Such a line may be **scanned** or measured out as follows, with notations to indicate stressed and unstressed elements of each foot: "Alóng/ the rídge/ a rág/ ing wínd/ storm bléw/."

Blank verse was often used by William Shakespeare in his plays, by John Milton in *Paradise Lost* (p. 54), by William Wordsworth in *The Prelude* (p. 1432), and by many modern poets, including Wallace Stevens and Robert Frost. It is still a serviceable form, attracting a range of contemporary poets. In some ways, blank verse can be regarded as the most basic form of English poetry, although there are many other prevalent forms. When more intricate forms were imported from the Continent, other elements—such as stanza shape and rhyme pattern—were added to iambic pentameter. The sonnet, a poem of fourteen lines written in iambic pentameter with a certain rhyme scheme or pattern, came from Italy, for example. Other complicated forms, such as the villanelle and the sestina, also employ iambic pentameter.

It should be observed here that poetry in English is essentially **stressed poetry,** counting "beats," as in Anglo-Saxon alliterative verse. In Latin poetry, by contrast, poets created patterns in verse by taking note of long and short vowels. The notation used for scanning English verse derives from Latin scansion. Unfortunately, English metrics are extremely casual, based on the throb of the line, or the "beat." (The number of syllables is rarely the determining factor in lines of English poetry, except when **syllabics** becomes the determining form.) What makes stressed poetry difficult to scan is the obvious fact that no two readers have ever read a line of verse with exactly the same intonation. The implications of this point are large. When we say, for example, that a poem is written in iambic pentameter, it should be noticed that this is only the abstract idea upon which the reality of the poetry settles. A poem written in very strict meter, with every foot iambic (ta-tum, ta-tum, ta-tum, ta-tum, ta-tum) would quickly become boring, even unreadable. "Most arts," as Ezra Pound, the American poet, once wrote, "achieve their effect by using a fixed element and a variable."

If you look at *Paradise Lost,* the epic by Milton written in blank verse (p. 54), you soon discover a wide variation in the way the poet plays the line. The number of syllables will vary from ten, which would be the norm, to as few as five syllables or as many as fourteen, depending on the stresses and where they fall. Milton generally keeps to the decasyllabic line, comprising ten syllables, but the variations are important, and they make the poem flexible and appealing to the ear.

It's crucial that readers of poetry keep in mind that the poetry in a line is always a product of the speaking voice as it plays against the abstract version of the line. The abstract pattern underpins the music of the line; the voice runs over this, to some degree controlled and shaped by the abstract potential of the ideal line. The first line of Frost's "Mending Wall," for example, runs like this: "Something there is that doesn't love a wall." This line, abstractly, would be read with the stresses falling like this: Some-thíng there ís that doés-n't lóve a wáll. Think how odd that would sound. Read the line again, and see where the speaking voice naturally plays over the line, where the stresses fall. The *poetry* in the line is the difference between the two possibilities.

Gerard Manley Hopkins, the nineteenth century English poet, once defined poetry as "the common language heightened." Meter is one of the important tools that poets have for heightening the common language, for making it seem more permanent, more memorable, for giving it a "tune." A serious student of poetry must get a gut feel for poetic rhythms, acquiring a basic knowledge of meter and rhythm. What follows is a very elementary guide to English poetic rhythm and meter.

Rhythm and Meter   There are only a few basic metrical possibilities in English verse. A foot may be **iambic** (ta-tum), **trochaic** (tum-ta), **dactyllic** (tum-ta-ta), or **anapestic** (ta-ta-tum). When the stresses in a foot are essentially equal, this is a **spondaic** foot. The noun forms of each of these are as follows: iamb, trochee, dactyl, anapest, and spondee. Other feet, of course, exist, based (as always) on Greek and Latin meters. For the most part, readers need only keep the above feet in mind. Again: one foot of verse equals one stress plus any number of unstressed syllables. So when you scan a line, you are looking for the number of feet in the line, the number of stressed syllables. You will rather quickly find yourself able to isolate the feet, and determine the basic movement of the line. Then you will be able to find the variations in the feet. If you are trying to scan a line, put a slash (/) between feet, after the stressed syllable, as in the following line: "The cúr/ few tólls/ the knéll/ of pár/ ting dáy/."

Readers are often stumped when trying to figure out what metrical pattern a poet has chosen because of the way even stresses are often counted as unstressed beats, for the purposes of abstract scansion. Here is the first line of a poem by Ben Jonson that might be confusing in this way: "Slow, slow, fresh fount, keep time with my salt tears." This is iambic pentameter, in theory. The first foot would, abstractly, be scanned as follows: "Slow, slów, fresh foúnt." But if anyone read the poem in that way, it would seem distorted and unreal. Nobody ever spoke like that. "Salt tears" is certainly a spondee—the foot allows for equal weight on both words.

The number of feet per line determines the name for the meter, as in pentameter being a five-foot line. Here are the names of the meters, going from one through eight feet per line: **monometer, dimeter, trimeter, tetrameter, pentameter, hexameter, heptameter,** and

octometer. English poetry usually stays within the three- to seven-foot range, although the free verse line will vary pretty wildly from poet to poet.

Poetry is written in lines (except in the case of prose poems, which are relatively rare), so when you quote a poem, always use a slash (/) to indicate the line break. When thinking about lines, it should also be noted that many lines are **end-stopped,** which means that the sense of the line, grammatically or rhythmically, comes to a halt at the end of a line. If the sense of the line spills over onto the next line, the line is said to be **enjambed.** Enjambment is common in poetry, and gives the work a fluid, conversational quality. The reader's eye and ear do not like being pulled up abruptly at the end of each line. So when Milton begins *Paradise Lost,* we see an example of heavy enjambent:

> Of Man's First Disobedience and the Fruit
> Of that Forbidden Tree, whose mortal taste
> Brought Death into the World, and all our woe,
> With loss of Eden, till one greater Man
> 5   Restore us, and regain the blissful Seat . . .

As we see here, the sense of the line spills over onto the next line again and again. By contrast, consider the first stanza of "I Knew A Woman" by Theodore Roethke. It is heavily end-stopped, in that the sense of the line comes to a fairly abrupt halt at the end of each line:

> I knew a woman, lovely in her bones.
> When small birds sighed, she would sigh back at them;
> Ah, when she moved, she moved more ways than one:
> The shapes a bright container can contain!
> 5   Of her choice virtues only gods should speak,
> Or English poets who grew up on Greek
> (I'd have them sing in chorus, cheek to cheek).

When you hold a poem at arm's length, blurring your eyes slightly, you will see that it makes a shape on the page. Once you get familiar with the possibilities for poetic shapes, you will quickly note that the poem is, for example, written in blank verse, free verse, or even ballad form. Sonnets, villanelles, sestinas, and other "fancy" shapes catch the eye at once. If the poem has lots of quotation marks, it may well be a "dramatic" poem, with characters talking among themselves or addressing the reader. Once you begin to read the poem, its rhyming patterns will become clear, as will its adherence to older traditions, for example, as in the epic, the elegy, or the ode. Many of the well-known shapes that a poem can take are represented in the pages of this book, and it should prove useful, informative, and stimulating to make comparisons, to see how the shapes of poetry have changed as poets responded, in highly inventive ways, to the realities of their lives and times.

The Poem's Theme: Subjects and Senses

"A poet's subject is his sense of the world," wrote Wallace Stevens. This is true enough, but poets also fit the subject to their immediate needs, skimming the world for objects upon which they can focus their imagination. They write poems because they have a compelling reason to write them: to celebrate a military victory or lament a defeat, to memorialize a relative or friend, to declare themselves in love, to praise friends or family, to hurl abuse at someone who has annoyed them, to castigate society or complain about an injustice, to speculate about the nature of life or death, or to respond to the natural world, in joy or despair. Many good poems are, indeed, about the creative process itself—poems on the theme of **ars poetica** or "the art of poetry."

The possibilities for thematic anthologies are endless. You can go into any bookstore and find collections dealing with all kinds of themes. These may be quite specific, as in a book that contains sonnets about erotic love. There are gatherings of poems about dogs or cats, about birds, about insects. There are volumes of poems about God, about death, about almost any philosophical inclination imaginable. Poems often have a specific subject, but fit a larger category. For example, a poet may well write a poem about a specific battle in a particular war. That poem may be classified as a "war" poem or even an "antiwar" poem. But, as with the overlap of forms, there are thematic overlaps. A love poem may also be an antiwar poem. A poem on the subject of foxes may, in fact, really be a poem about smart choices or craftiness or, as in "The Thought-Fox" by Ted Hughes (p. 1457), a poem about the creative process itself. When discussing the theme of any particular poem, think about the range of possibilities, and make comparisons with similar poems. Always think about the **literal** level—the most basic subject or theme of the poem—and possible extensions of that theme, its metaphorical or **figurative** levels.

It is essential to recognize that form and content are inseparable, especially in work of the highest quality. A good poem acquires its meaning from its shape (its form, its generic type, its literal or figurative pattern) as well as the subject it addresses. Ideally, the form contributes to the meaning by enhancing or sharpening its viewpoint. For instance, the wittiness of "The Rape of the Lock" by Alexander Pope (p. 64) owes a good deal to its form, the heroic couplet, which assists the poet in making ironic contrasts and amusing juxtapositions. Shakespeare's sonnets benefit from their closing couplets, which lock a certain "moral" into place, summarizing the thematic aspect of the poem, often creating a **totalizing image,** one that gathers the thematic elements of the poem into a single image. The ferocious narrative drive of John Milton's *Paradise Lost* (p. 54) is made especially vivid by his use of blank verse, which gives the poem a rolling and thunderous quality. The free verse of T. S. Eliot's *The Waste Land* (p. 102) contributes to its disjunctions and dislocations; these effects all play into the overall meaning of the poem. Similarly, Whitman's expansiveness in "Song of Myself" (p. 84) is amplified by the long length of his free verse lines. Emily Dickinson's shrewd, caustic, ironic, gnomic wit are wonderfully amplified by her tight form, called **common measure**—a form that writers of hymns such as "Amazing Grace" often favored.

Poets do not "choose" a theme. The thematic aspects of the poem arise, naturally, from the music of the poem, from the poet's angle of vision, from the original purpose of the poem and its enactment in actual language, in whatever form it acquires in the course of this enactment. So, when studying poems, always try to figure out how the form of the poem contributes to or enhances thematic elements of the poem. There is a good deal of mutual interplay between "form" and "content," and a solid analysis of a poem depends on making connections between these two aspects.

"A poem should not mean but be," wrote Archibald MacLeish. This is all well and good, but a poem *does mean something*. It may simply tell a story or express a feeling; but it may have an argument. It will certainly have a **point of view,** so the first thing to notice when reading a poem is the nature of the speaker. Who is talking here? What is the context of this speech? In most lyrics, the speaker is "I," the poet— a fictional first-person narrator, as noted above. *Never mistake the speaker in a poem for the poet.* That is an elementary rule. If you wish to talk about the poem, say something like this: "The speaker in this poem notices that. . . ." This will free you from an error that seems to plague most beginning readers of poetry.

A poem is fiction, a piece of shaped reality (going back to the Latin word, *fictio*). This means that some bits of reality are left out, that alterations have been made to create certain effects and impressions. The "I" of the lyric is an invention, a persona, a mask, through which the speaker's voice emerges. (*Per/sona* is also a Latin word, meaning "sounding through," as in the voice that pushes through the mask.) The poet, in a lyric poem, strikes an attitude, an angle toward the world; he or she creates a voice that is artful, or artificial.

Close reading involves a careful examination of a poem, its language, its form, its themes, its literary and historical context. This kind of reading is demanding, as it requires paying attention to subtleties of diction, to shifts of meaning, and to changes in **tone,** which may be defined as *the speaker's attitude toward the subject in the poem*. Let's take one example here, a beloved poem by Robert Frost called "The Road Not Taken."

Two roads diverged in a yellow wood
And sorry I could not travel both
And be one traveler, long I stood
And looked down one as far as I could
5   To where it bent in the undergrowth;

Then took the other, as just as fair,
And having perhaps the better claim,
Because it was grassy and wanted wear;
Though as for that the passing there
10   Had worn them really about the same,

And both that morning equally lay
In leaves no step had trodden black.
Oh, I kept the first for another day!
Yet knowing how way leads on to way,
15   I doubted if I should ever come back.

I shall be telling this with a sigh
Somewhere ages and ages hence:
Two roads diverged in a wood, and I—
I took the road less traveled by,
20   And that has made all the difference.

I recall a teacher of mine who framed the last two lines and hung them above her desk, saying: "Class, remember to take the advice of Robert Frost. Be an original. March to the beat of a different drummer. Don't be afraid to take the road less traveled. It will make all the difference." It was an inspiring notion. But I read the poem more carefully in subsequent years and discovered that Frost was not saying anything quite so simple as what my teacher had suggested. Indeed, if you go back to the actual text, reading carefully, you will notice that Frost spends a good deal of time in making the point firmly that these two roads in the yellow wood are pretty much equal.

   When Frost wrote this poem he had in mind a very indecisive friend, and he writes here from that friend's viewpoint. The speaker looks down one road, then the other, "as just as fair." Indeed, the passing there had worn these paths "really about the same." In case the reader still doesn't get it, the third stanza opens with a flat statement: "And both that morning equally lay / In leaves no step had trodden black." So what on earth is the speaker talking about at the end?

   That sigh, which opens the final stanza, is a pregnant sigh, a sigh of regret, a sigh of admission. The speaker knows that when he becomes an old man, he will insist that he took "the one less traveled" of two roads that were "really about the same." Why would he do this? We must speculate here. Perhaps Frost understands that most of us want to believe that we took the less traveled road, that we operate as courageous and independent-minded people. The poem is, as much as anything, about how we often hesitate before a major fork in the road, and how—after a choice of direction is made—we cast our choice in the best possible light. Not surprisingly, this version of the poem, its "meaning," is more interesting and complex than the simpler one, which in any case makes absolutely no sense in the context of the poem.

The theme of the poem, then, is both indecision and the need that people have to frame their choices in a rosy light. Frost finds a form that easily accommodates, and enhances, the theme of the poem—a rhyming stanza of five lines, written in iambic tetrameter, with a rhyme scheme that runs ABAAB. (There are new rhymes in each stanza. Throughout, rhyme leads on to rhyme much as "way leads onto way." There is really no turning back.) In a sense, there are two possible rhymes in each stanza, and the speaker has to try one, then the other, much like a man at a crossroads who steps one way, retreats, steps another way, retreats, and so forth. The lines are heavily enjambed, so that the speaking voice flows gently forward, the sense of most lines spilling onto the next, except where Frost wants to make a point emphatically, as in the opening of the third stanza: "And both that morning equally lay / In leaves no step had trodden black."

The situation itself is plainly symbolic, representing alternative paths or choices. Nothing could be more simple or more symbolic. The traveler is the speaker, and the road is the choice of a way of life. This is a symbol because the image itself is open-ended; it means lots of things. Frost develops this single image in a deep and thoroughly sophisticated way, moving sinuously through the poem in language that concretely summons and embodies the theme of the poem. This is remarkably sure-footed work by a master-poet.

Not all poems are as "clever" as this poem, which seems to mean one thing while, in reality, suggesting another. Frost was a canny fellow and a wily poet, and he invites us—the reader—back into the poem by complicating its meaning. Yet few good poems will not benefit from close reading, from a careful and systematic exploration of the text, with attention to the language of the poem, its shape, its thematic development, and the use of such well-tried techniques as symbolism and metaphor.

The Poem's Context: Reflections and Responses

Poets write with other poems in mind. They are vividly alert to traditions. They understand that no poem, however wonderful, exists by itself. Poems grow from poems, attaching themselves to various lines of development, and these alliances may take the shape of formal alliances or thematic alliances. In his essay "Tradition and the Individual Talent,"

T. S. Eliot memorably observed that "No poet, no artist of any art, has his complete meaning alone. His significance, his appreciation is the appreciation of his relation to the dead poets and artists. You cannot value him alone; you must set him, for contrast and comparison, among the dead." Eliot thought deeply about the meaning of the word *tradition,* which he regarded as no dead thing but as a living organism. He argued that all poems written in the past form a kind of "ideal order" among themselves, and that when new work is added, the whole shifts, however slightly. The past is therefore altered, modified, by the present.

In all of the sections of this anthology, we consider poems in relation to other poems, especially those that have come before. More specifically, in the third major section—Contexts—we explore connections, hoping to provoke comparisons, to get you thinking about the poetic tradition as a living organism, which grows and changes in such a way that each modification or extension affects the whole.

Two of the many traditions (or lines of influence) have been singled out for special attention. One of them is the tradition of **alliterative verse,** which has its origins in the poetry of the Anglo-Saxon era but which continues to the present day, finding new expression in poets like Ted Hughes and Seamus Heaney. These poets, and others like them, have studied the strong poetry of Old English carefully. Heaney has even translated *Beowulf* himself, creating a splendid text in which his own muscular voice attaches itself to that of the *Beowulf* author. Early in the twentieth century, Ezra Pound attached himself to *The Seafarer* (p. 1505), another masterwork of Anglo-Saxon verse, translating it with a unique vivacity. The way these alliterative poems interact, as a body of writing, is worth considering.

In a section on **meditative poetry,** we examine a fairly major but often hidden strain of poetry that—in its modern form—grew out of the traditions of formal prayer and the meditative practices of Christianity as they arose during the Renaissance. In fact, the wider meditative tradition has its roots deep in the ancient world, especially in the East, where Hindu and Buddhist monks had long been interested in techniques that focus the mind. A work of art, as English writer D. H. Lawrence once noted, might be called an "act of attention," and there are numerous ways to focus the attention of the artist. One of those ways is explored here, where we look in particular at English and American religious poems of the seventeenth century and see how their meditative styles influenced later poets, such as William Wordsworth and Gerard Manley Hopkins. The aftershocks of meditative poetry can still be felt among such poets as Louise Glück and Robert Hass, among others.

The Wadsworth Anthology also includes a chapter called "Poets in Dialogue." The point being made here, by example, is that poets often rewrite the work of their predecessors. They may self-consciously exploit an earlier poem, commenting on it, or they may simply appropriate a context or theme and revisit it. Poets often parody earlier work, creating poems that mock their source; but parody is a form of homage, too, and some of the great works—Pope's "The Rape of the Lock" (p. 64) is a good example—were written to mimic and mock an earlier work or form. Sometimes poets simply write to contradict something said in an earlier poem, supplanting the earlier vision with their own. Most often, they write with a firm sense of a previous example in mind. They are, as we say, **influenced** by the previous poem.

A great poem is like a power plant. Poets coming after it may attach cables to that plant, getting an energetic charge from it. They may also, as the critic Harold Bloom has argued, engage in mortal combat with the earlier poem, rewriting it to repossess and redefine it. They may well misconstrue the earlier poem, exhibiting an "anxiety of influence," as Bloom says. But most often they will simply acknowledge, in subtle ways, their debt to their ancestor and, in their own way, attempt to reha-bilitate or revise the subject, adding the tincture of their own imagina-tion to the imagination of the earlier poet or poem.

The "Poets in Dialogue" chapter illuminates, in a definitive way, the point made by all of the selections here, which are chosen to suggest that poetry is a living tradition, and that poets write with an acute aware-ness of their place in this tradition. The study of poetry demands from the efficient and well-trained reader an understanding of literary tradi-tions, including the forms and themes that have evolved throughout the centuries.

Originality is not called into question here. Beginning students often make the mistake of thinking that if a poet has not invented the form and subject of a poem from scratch, he or she is not an original poet. This is nonsense, in fact. Originality in poetry has to do with uniqueness of expression, with subtle modifications of voice, with inter-esting and fresh ways of engaging the literary traditions. Poets wrestle with the poets who come before them, objecting to their vision, or—in most cases—simply revising their vision, adding a fresh layer of meaning. Great poets do not invent anything. They modify and extend traditions that have gone before them. Their originality lies in their revi-sionary powers.

This is not to say that, in the course of many centuries, a few voices that seem wildly fresh and bravely new do not occur. Homer, Dante, Chaucer, Shakespeare, Milton, Blake, Wordsworth, Dickinson, Whit-man—just to name a few obvious examples—seemed to emerge from nowhere, to create a whole world in their poetry. Yet in each case, one finds the poets working within established traditions. Milton, for exam-ple, modifies and extends the great epic tradition of the Greeks and Romans by working with Judeo-Christian subject matter. He was attempting to "justify the ways of God to man"—but this was not Homer's God he was talking about. Shakespeare, the most luminously original of the English poets, robbed and plundered, taking plots for his plays from a variety of sources, well-known and obscure. He was unabashed in doing so. He assumed that poets are always free to take whatever they need, as long as they provide a new context for the material they appropriate, giving it fresh life.

SCHOOLS AND MOVEMENTS

Critics and historians of literature often place poets into schools or literary movements of one kind of another, although relatively few poets in the history of the world have ever tried to write a poem that would fit into a category. There would be something terribly artificial about that, and "movements" are usually identified long after the fact by historians of literature. They can be useful to a limited degree in helping to group poets, compare types of poetry, and spot trends. But it's important to remember how limited this way of thinking is. One does not experience a poem as an example of a movement or school. The text itself should *be* an experience. What follows is a brief chronological overview of major schools and movements in English-language poetry; for additional context and information, see the disk *Poetry 21*.

A general sense of major movements and schools is useful for understanding how poets are influenced by other poets and poems. The **classical poets** were those who wrote in ancient Greece and Rome. Not surprisingly, countless schools of poetry arose within the classical period, and many different genres of poetry evolved, including the brief lyric (as practiced by Sappho, who lived and wrote on the isle of Lesbos) and, of course, the major epic, including *The Iliad* and *The Odyssey*— poems that evolved over many decades, if not centuries, and were recited aloud on public occasions. One notable movement in ancient Greece and Rome was **pastoral verse,** a highly stylized poetry written about country and rural life, often with shepherds speaking to each other. These poems were also called **eclogues.** Theocritus in Greece and Virgil in Rome were two of the most widely admired of the pastoral poets, and their work provided models for future writers of eclogues and paved the way for what is now called "nature poetry." Many of the great forms— **ode** and **elegy** being two of the most prominent—evolved during the classical period, too, and poets of the **Neoclassical Movement** (which had various spurts of activity from the time of the Renaissance through the nineteenth century) are those who hark back to classical forms, attitudes, and values. This movement reached its height during the eighteenth century in England, when classical values—such as reason and balance—were especially esteemed. (It should be noted that these poets chose to value a particular vein of classical writing. Not all classical poets were rational or balanced. Most schools of poetry are based on distorted or partial versions of literary history.)

The Renaissance was marked, even defined, by a revival of interest in the Greeks and Romans. The English poets of this period certainly looked back to poets like Homer and Horace for models, and their work is full of allusions or references to classical poets. Horace, perhaps the greatest of the Roman poets next to Virgil, was a mild-mannered, well-balanced, intensely refined poet who wrote many well-known odes and **epistles** (poems written as letters). He lived in the Roman countryside on a farm that had been given to him by his powerful friend Maecenas. His influence on poets, from Sir Philip Sidney and Ben Jonson to Andrew Marvell, John Milton, Alexander Pope, and John Dryden, has been widely observed by critics.

The literary movement known generally as **Romanticism** had its beginning in the eighteenth century in Germany and France. William Blake was the first of the great Romantics to write in English, followed by Wordsworth, Coleridge, Keats, Shelley, Byron, and a host of others, moving through the mid-nineteenth century. These poets had very little in common, although—as historians of literature have noticed—they were all interested in *poetry as self-expression*. They were intensely interested in feeling. The German poet Schiller wrote to his compatriot Goethe in 1801, "Each one who is in a position to put his state of feeling into an object so that this object compels me to pass over into that state of feeling . . . I call a poet, a maker." One sees this line of thinking recurring through poetry of the nineteenth and twentieth centuries, as in e.e. cummings' poem, which begins "since feeling is first. . . ."

Romanticism might be considered a cluster of related ideas or notions. One of these was the notion of a poem as an organism, a living thing that develops from a seed, growing into a unique design—its form. This concept dates from the eighteenth century in Germany. Another idea was that poetry was a form of social critique. Romantic poets often identified with revolutionary movements, siding with the poor, the downtrodden. These poets developed the idea of symbolism in ways different from earlier poets, valuing the human imagination above all else. In a sense, the Romantics were writing in a vein that one critic (M. H. Abrams) has identified as "natural supernaturalism," meaning that the Romantic poets were largely secular, making poetry into a kind of religion, elevating its purpose a good deal. The creation of a poem was regarded as a divine activity, with the poem seen as a kind of second universe, having a life of its own.

The Romantic poet was not so much a craftsman, somebody who—like a well-educated carpenter—gathers the materials of the poem and builds it. He or she is a divinely inspired magician, a genius, as the German Romantic poet A. W. Schlegel noted when he said that true genius "is precisely the most intimate union of unconscious and self-conscious activity in the human spirit, of instinct and purpose, of freedom and necessity." Certainly the Germans regarded their great poet Goethe as the supreme genius of their language, and they revered Shakespeare as the ultimate genius of the English language. English poets like Blake and Wordsworth valued the notion of creative genius, and saw themselves as vessels of a sort, mouthpieces for the Muse. This concept of the Romantic genius has continued to our day, although the conception is not without its many eloquent critics, who (especially in the last decades) look on the notion of the individual genius with a good deal of skepticism, believing that the culture itself plays a huge role in the creation of the "genius" who speaks for the masses.

The classical poets tended to see art (including poetry) as an imitation of life, as a mirror reflecting human activity and the natural world. This theory of art is called **mimesis,** and it has never been without its adherents. The Romantics turned the tables on mimesis. They thought of poetry as having a life of its own, not imitating or reflecting life, but *creating* life. The mirror of the poem became a kind of lamp, burning from within, shining a light outward on the world. The Romantic poet tended to see himself or herself as a priest, a visionary, preaching a new way of being as well as a new way of seeing. A poet like William Blake, for example, created a vast mythology of his own, a kind of pseudo-religion. Many of the key Romantic ideas found their way into American poetry through Ralph Waldo Emerson, the philosopher and poet who brought these notions to the new world, inspiring a range of poets, including Walt Whitman and Emily Dickinson. An echo of Romantic theory ultimately sounded in the Beat poets, in the political poetry of the sixties, and in the work (and self-conception) of many rock stars.

Modernism was itself an extension of Romanticism, placing many of the same tenets and assumptions about literature into a fresh perspective. Modernism encompassed a large international movement across the arts, with many smaller schools and ancillary movements, such as **Imagism**, a school of poetry that focused on the creation of a single, deep image within a poem. The Modernist poets began in earnest around the time of the First World War. T. S. Eliot, Wallace Stevens, and Ezra Pound were leading poets in this movement, comparable to novelists like James Joyce or Gertrude Stein and painters like Pablo Picasso. **Cubism,** in painting, was a school within the Modernist movement that emphasized a multi-layered, fractionated viewpoint; indeed, Picasso defined Cubism as "a dance around the object."

Modernism stressed a fragmented narrative and multiple viewpoints. Modernist poets emphasized the uniqueness of the individual vision, but understood that an individual vision is limited. T. S. Eliot's *The Waste Land* (p. 102) stands at the center of this poetic movement, with its many voices. Eliot creates a dark and foreboding atmosphere in this poem, an aura of dislocation and emptiness. The traditional symbols of religion were viewed, by Eliot, as bankrupt of meaning. His poem was an effort to find the speech of his time, to reflect the agony and disorientation that beset Europe in the face of a devastating war in which millions of people had died; its theme is the search for meaning in an apparently meaningless world. With its density and difficulty, its countless allusions to other and prior texts, its sense of alienation, and its nerve-wracking, endlessly shifting perspectives, it remains a central text of Modernism.

Nowadays, one often hears of **Postmodernism,** a movement that represents an extension of Modernism more than a reaction against it. The critic and novelist Malcolm Bradbury notes that "What Modernism and Postmodernism share in common is a single adversary which is, to put it crudely, realism or naïve mimesis. Both are forms of post-Realism. They likewise share in common a practice based on avant-garde and movement tactics and a sense of modern culture as a field of anxious stylistic formation." This is extremely useful. Modernist and postmodernist artists share a desire to create art that does not reflect life, at least not in the simple way that a mirror reflects life. The distortions of art are regarded by Modernist and Postmodernist artists alike as a way toward comprehending reality in a higher sense. The strategies used by many Modernist artists in particular have been called **avant-garde** or **experimentalist.** This is to say, their work dispenses with the easy realism of already familiar work; their work becomes "difficult," as in *The Waste Land,* which requires a huge amount of intellectual effort to comprehend.

The movement called *Postmodernism* has attracted a fairly wide array of contemporary poets, including John Ashbery, Paul Muldoon, and Jorie Graham—poets who self-consciously reflect on the nature of art while making art. There is often a parodic element to their work, too—a sassiness, a refusal to follow the "normal" passages of logic. Postmodernist artists borrow freely from unlikely sources, creating a collage effect. In many ways, the Postmodernist work of art separates from the Modernist only by its savage detachment, its drive toward parody, its love of wit. (One thinks of Modernist art as having a certain gravity, as in *The Waste Land,* although elements of parody certainly begin to emerge quite early in Joyce and Stein, in Picasso, and in others. In a sense, Modernism is a house that adds a wing called Postmodernism. The wing eventually becomes the main house.)

Other important movements arose from Modernism, including the **Beat Movement,** which began in New York and was, according to Allen Ginsberg, associated with a particular "frame of mind" that arose in the late 1940s and looked at American society "from the underside." One associates such poets as Ginsberg and Gregory Corso from the East Coast and Lawrence Ferlinghetti, Gary Snyder, and Kenneth Rexroth with the West Coast wing of the Beats. Sex and drugs, jazz, and radical politics found a unique mix in the work of these writers. In San Francisco, younger poets such as Robert Duncan and Jack Spicer soon attracted attention, adding to what is often called the **San Francisco Poetry Renaissance.**

As much as anything, the Beat Movement was born in resistance to Formalism. This eclectic group of poets opposed the Formalist tendencies commonly found in mainstream poets of the 1940s and 1950s. They disliked the establishment politics that seemed part and parcel of **Formalism**—an extremely influential movement that flourished in the postwar era of American and British poetry. W. H. Auden, John Crowe Ransom, Allen Tate, Robert Penn Warren, Robert Lowell, Randall Jarrell, Elizabeth Bishop, Theodore Roethke, Richard Wilbur, Philip Larkin, and James Merrill could all be regarded as Formalists, although none of these gave much thought to belonging to any "school" known as *Formalism*. In the years after World War I, some of these poets (the Southerners) had belonged to the **Fugitive Movement,** centered on John Crowe Ransom, a professor at Vanderbilt who taught Warren and Jarrell. This group was a spin-off of the Southern Agrarian Movement, a larger political movement that had a strong regional and conservative aspect. Formalists quite often wrote poems in traditional forms, without any special political attachments or even aesthetic dogmas. Lowell, Roethke, and Warren certainly broke with strict formalism after their earlier years. James Wright and Adrienne Rich—a generation behind Lowell and Roethke—began as a formalists, but quickly moved in other directions.

Indeed, Lowell himself, with *Life Studies* in 1959, set in motion what is called the **Confessional School** of poetry. Poets identified with this school, including Sylvia Plath, John Berryman, Anne Sexton, and W. D. Snodgrass, wrote poems in free verse (for the most part) that were nakedly autobiographical, often revealing an anguished sense of the world. Once again, none of these poets thought of themselves as belonging to any school of poetry; their work evolved, perhaps, in relation to other poets like themselves, but there was no official doctrine of any kind. Confessional poetry has continued to flourish, becoming a dominant mode of writing among contemporary poets, such as Sharon Olds and Julia Alvarez, who write urgently and frankly about their own lives.

Many recent schools of poetry are identified with a particular city or part of the country. **The New York School** arose in the 1950s and 1960s, with a mode of poetry that seemed witty, disjunctive, and distinctly postmodern in its jazzy free verse forms. Frank O'Hara, James Schuyler, and John Ashbery are associated with this kind of poetry. Various movements on the West Coast grew out of Postmodernism, including the so-called **Language Poets,** who were descendents of Ezra Pound and Louis Zukofsy. One of many offshoots of the Beat Movement was the **Black Mountain School** of poetry, centered on a cluster of poets who happened to gather at a particular place and time and who looked back, for inspiration, to poets like William Carlos Williams and Ezra Pound. In England in the 1980s arose the **Martian School** of poets, a group loosely gathered around the poet Craig Raine. These so-called schools have come and gone, with the central figures in each school or movement often changing stripes, writing in a new mode, repudiating his or her former style or aesthetic.

The **New Formalism** was a movement that began in the 1980s; this school of poets self-consciously wrote in traditional forms, eschewing free verse. Some of the poets associated with the New Formalism are Dana Gioia, Brad Leithauser, David Mason, Richard Kenney, and Mary Jo Salter. These poets have looked fondly on various Formalist poets of the previous generation, such as Richard Wilbur, X. J. Kennedy, and Anne Stevenson.

In the 1920s, there was a revival of African American poetry and prose in Harlem, called the **Harlem Renaissance.** One associates Langston Hughes, Claude McKay, Countee Cullen, and Melvin B. Tolson, among others, with this group of poets who drew heavily on black culture, jazz, and earlier African American poets. An offshoot school of this group, the **Black Arts Movement** of the 1960s, is associated with Gwendolyn Brooks, LeRoi Jones (later Imamu Amiri Baraka), Sonia Sanchez, and Nikki Giovanni. This later movement stressed a heightened political consciousness and a revolutionary zeal. Black poets, said Brooks at the time, "are becoming increasingly aware of themselves and their blackness." The sense of what was "good poetry" was shifting. A new aesthetic began to evolve, in direct contrast to the Formalists, but with roots in African American dialect and culture. These poets looked to Malcolm X for political inspiration, and to jazz virtuosos like John Coltrane and Miles Davis for aesthetic inspiration. They attempted to blur the boundaries between poems and songs, between readings of poems and musical performances. This movement has led directly to the kind of **performance poetry** and **slams** that are popular today.

Countless movements and schools of poets have come and gone. Often they represent a conscious effort of an underclass or minority, or an isolated group to affiliate in order to raise their profile or celebrate their own aesthetic. Sometimes the "group" remains unidentified until critics come along—usually after the movement has evaporated—and write about the group as a movement or school. It is usually difficult to see what the poets of any particular school or movement have in common, poem by poem; but there are broad categories, theories about what makes a good poem, notions about the relationship between the poet and society or, in some cases, the poet and language itself.

Students of poetry need to think about all of these things, to reflect on the kinds of poetry that appear and disappear, and attempt to see the lines of development and the continuities that exist between poets of the past and the present.

REMAKING THE CANON: JUDGMENT AND TASTE

There has been a lot of talk in recent years about the literary **canon,** the body of literature that in any given period seems to represent the best work produced over the centuries. This canon shifts and evolves decade by decade, even year by year. For example, what a maker of anthologies such as this one believed to be the essential poems thirty years ago will look rather different from what we present here.

Feminist criticism, which began in earnest in the early 1970s, has added considerably to our understanding of women poets, and feminist scholars have rediscovered a wide range of poets, from ancient to modern times, who have been neglected or overlooked because of their gender. Readers will find many excellent poems by women from all centuries and traditions represented here. **Multiculturalism** has also been influential in reshaping the canon, and one will find in these pages a healthy complement of poems by African Americans, Hispanics, Chinese Americans, and other poets from ethnic or cultural traditions barely represented in earlier anthologies. The vibrancy of these poems is undeniable, and poets from mainstream traditions have often looked to this work for inspiration. Gay and lesbian poetry is also well-represented in these pages.

Finally, it should be said that all that really matters is what you, the reader, think and feel when you read a poem. You must test its inherent value on your pulse. Does the poem express what seems to you an important aspect of experience? Does it "ring true" or feel right? As you read poetry over the years, your taste will necessarily grow and change. It is rare for a person age twenty to have a favorite poet who remains the favorite decade after decade. But important or "great" poems are those that speak to many people over time. Most of the poems in this anthology have already met the test of time, having found grateful readers over many decades or centuries. Your job is to read closely, to read again, and to listen to the words as they fall into place in your mind. Certain lines will stay with you, as will whole poems. Robert Frost once said that he hoped to "lodge a few poems where they can't be gotten rid of easily." We hope this book manages just that: to lodge a few poems in your mind. As your experience of poetry expands, that place will contain more and more poems in time. These poems will, in the end, help you to live your life more fully, more sanely, with a deeper sense of where and who you are.

The Shape of the Poem

poetry

SING, HEAVENLY MUSE
—John Milton
An Anthology of Epic Poetry

The epic is one of the major genres. The term is rather flexible, and it often refers loosely to works written on a grand scale with heroic dimensions. Tolstoy's *War and Peace* and Melville's *Moby-Dick,* for example, are often called "epic novels," in large part because of their ambition and scope. But the term has a more specific meaning in poetry, usually referring back to ancient epics, such as *The Iliad* and *The Odyssey* by Homer.

An **epic poem** is often defined as a long poem written about heroic adventures. It will frequently have an elevated style, and will sometimes conform to the conventions of the epic as established by Homer. *The Iliad* and *The Odyssey* are both poems related to the Trojan War. The former takes place during the war, the latter follows a warrior, Odysseus, on his way home after the battles have ended. This very ancient war centered on a conflict between the Greeks and the citizens of Troy, perhaps around the thirteenth century B.C. The Homeric epics are hardly historical documents, however. The Trojan War could be regarded as a national myth; the heroic figures of these epics acquire legendary status in the course of the narratives. The epics were written sometime during the eighth century B.C., and may have been the work of several generations of poets whose work finally was established under the name of Homer.

It should be noted that Greek literature existed in oral form long before the Greeks possessed an alphabet and therefore a means of writing down their legends and stories. With the Homeric epics, Greek literature essentially came into view for the first time. Whether or not one poet, called Homer, really wrote down these epics remains uncertain, although nobody doubts that whoever wrote down the poem was working from an established body of myth, and that parts of these stories had long been in circulation.

The Homeric poems were oral verse, recited at banquets and on public occasions by traveling bards. In character with most oral literature, the poems have certain conventions that aided the memory of the bards who recited them. Certain adjective combinations, for example, were often used; hence, the sea is often described as "the wine-dark sea." These combinations are called **heroic epithets.** Extended similes (or **epic similes**) are also common to these works. The style itself is elevated, oratorical. One can easily imagine a bard declaiming these tales from a platform.

Epics, in the Greek mode, tell heroic stories about great men who become representative of the culture. These works thus help to define a culture, to teach a nation about its own values, its heroic past, its high ideals. Aware that the task before him was daunting, Homer began each epic with an invocation of the muse, calling on the gods for help in telling such an important story. The invocation of the muse is now widely associated with epics in the Homeric tradition.

Epic texts are, in a sense, religious texts as well. They explain to a people their relationship with the heavens, their place in the world, and their need to subject their own wills to those of the gods, who control their fate. While the heroes and heroines of epic poems are not necessarily models for ordinary men and women, they provide some point of reference in the historic past, and they address subjects that concern everyone: the quest for love, the need for control over one's life, the agonies of war, and the painfulness of death. There is often a patriotic element to the great epics, too; these tales help to explain to a nation something about its own divinely ordered purpose.

The original epics, which are also called **traditional epics** or **primary epics,** became foundational texts for later writers. Even before Homer, there was the *Epic of Gilgamesh,* written a thousand or more years before *The Iliad,* in the fertile valleys of the Tigris and Euphrates Rivers of Mesopotamia, which is now Iraq. This poem tells the story of a lonely king in Babylon trying to come to terms with his own power, his situation in life. It's a story of heroic struggle and survival, and remains a work of considerable literary power.

The ancient Indians also had epic tales, such as *The Mahabharata* and *The Ramayana.* The former is an epic work that, like most ancient epics, evolved over time, accumulating bits and pieces from oral history and legend. The original text may date back to many centuries before Christ, although the present text probably came together around 400 B.C. *The Mahabharata* is a rambling text, part mythic, part historical. Eight times as long as *The Iliad* and *The Odyssey* combined, it defies characterization. It is enough that it can be described as a *foundational text,* a long poem in an elevated style that gathers together many of the central myths of Indian civilization. *The Ramayana* is more focused, telling the story of the great prince, Rama, and his heroic struggles to overcome evil and discover virtue. It, too, has ancient roots and evolved over time, coming into various written forms in the period 400 B.C.–200 B.C. There is no definitive single text of *The Ramayana,* however; it survives in multiple forms, often with local inflections, and might be considered a tradition of storytelling as much as a single epic work.

One of the founding or primary epics for English is *Beowulf,* written sometime between the eighth and the tenth centuries (only one manuscript survives). Composed in Anglo-Saxon, a language spoken by one of the many Scandinavian tribes that inhabited what we now know as England, it tells the story of a Scandinavian king during the sixth century; his heroic struggles are recounted in brilliant alliterative verse. This epic poem has fascinated readers for centuries, and was recently a best-selling work in the translation of Seamus Heaney, the Irish poet.

The **literary epic** or **secondary epic** defines an epic poem written in imitation of an earlier epic. John Milton's seventeenth-century masterwork, *Paradise Lost,* is a prime example of this type of epic, a poem about Adam and Eve and their banishment from the Garden of Eden. It represents Milton's attempt to "justify the ways of God to man." A deeply learned man, Milton drew heavily on previous epics and classical works, including those of Homer and Virgil, the Roman author of the *Aeneid,* another great epic from the ancient world.

Later epics include the "mock-epic" of Alexander Pope, in which he makes fun of the epic conventions, turning the tables on them in a way that entertained a highly sophisticated audience in the eighteenth century. In the nineteenth century, in the United States, Walt Whitman turned the tables again, writing *Song of Myself,* a huge personal epic that redefines a nation for itself, seeing the American republic as a place where the individual matters greatly. Whitman celebrates the self, seeing himself as a representative person, someone who speaks for the nation. It's a vivid, tempestuous, brave, unlikely poem; Whitman included it in all the various editions of *Leaves of Grass,* his ongoing project, to which he regularly added poems throughout his life.

Two of the prominent Modernist poets in English, T. S. Eliot and Ezra Pound, both attempted poems on an epic scale. *The Waste Land* (1922) represents a highly original attempt to identify the mind of Europe in the wake of World War I, an immensely devastating war. "I will show you fear in a handful of dust," writes Eliot. He does so, describing a world in which the traditional symbols have all become bankrupt. Eliot rummages through the literature of the past, in many languages, finding fragments only, bits and pieces that he uses to shore himself up. This is a quest poem, like the primary epics, but the quest is oblique and inconclusive. Eliot draws on a host of primary works, creating a text from other texts, a strange but compelling work that has all the reading difficulty one expects from a defining work of Modernist poetry.

Eliot's friend and mentor, Ezra Pound, began writing *The Cantos* in the late 1920s and continued writing them until his death in 1972. This magnificent, frequently obscure, unlikely poem gathers fragments from eastern and western culture, quoting works (often) in their original languages, creating many dazzling and many frustrating passages. Whether or not the whole is better than its parts is a question that has occupied critics for a very long time, and the question will never be solved. In any case, Pound's contribution to the epic form seems beyond dispute.

Pound certainly influenced his friend, H. D. (as Hilda Doolittle called herself). She began writing short poems in the Imagist manner; she ended with long poems, such as *Helen in Egypt* (1961), her rewriting of the myth of Helen of Troy. This is a strong, engaging poem that redefines Helen—the woman about whom the Trojan War was supposedly fought—as a tough, independent person, no passive agent. This epic has long been overlooked by most readers, but it deserves a place in any anthology devoted to epic forms and epic transformations.

Finally, there is *Omeros* (1990), the last poem in the epic samples that follow. It's a brilliant reinvention of Homer's *Odyssey* by Derek Walcott, a Caribbean poet who won the Nobel Prize for Literature. Walcott retells the old story of the wandering and suffering hero (or several heroes, in fact) on the way home. His main wanderer finds a lyrical contemporary embodiment in his fluid stanzas. This long tale, which draws on the conventions of the epic in subtle ways, reflects on all lost and isolated wanderers who have been dispossessed by history. With its powerful theme, the poem defines postcolonial studies—that branch of critical thinking and scholarship devoted to former colonies, the ruins of empires. *Omeros* stands as one of the finest texts inspired by the epic poetry of Homer, and it merits close reading.

HOMER (ca. 850 B.C.)
trans. Richmond Lattimore (1906–1984)

from The Odyssey, Book XI (trans. 1965)

'Now when we had gone down again to the sea and our vessel,
first of all we dragged the ship down into the bright water,
and in the black hull set the mast in place, and set sails,
and took the sheep and walked them aboard, and ourselves also
5   embarked, but sorrowful, and weeping big tears. Circe[1]
of the lovely hair, the dread goddess who talks with mortals,
sent us an excellent companion, a following wind, filling
the sails, to carry from astern the ship with the dark prow.
We ourselves, over all the ship making fast the running gear,
10   sat still, and let the wind and the steersman hold her steady.
All day long her sails were filled as she went through the water,
and the sun set, and all the journeying-ways were darkened.
    'She made the limit, which is of the deep-running Ocean.
There lie the community and city of Kimmerian people,

---

[1] **Circe:** Daughter of the sun, known for her ability to turn men into animals. Odysseus lived with Circe on Aiaia for over a year.

15   hidden in fog and cloud, nor does Helios,[2] the radiant
        sun, ever break through the dark, to illuminate them with his shining,
        neither when he climbs up into the starry heaven,
        nor when he wheels to return again from heaven to earth,
        but always a glum night is spread over wretched mortals.
20   Making this point, we ran the ship ashore, and took out
        the sheep, and ourselves walked along by the stream of the Ocean
        until we came to that place of which Circe had spoken.
          'There Perimedes and Eurylochos[3] held the victims
        fast, and I, drawing from beside my thigh my sharp sword,
25   dug a pit, of about a cubit in each direction,
        and poured it full of drink offerings for all the dead, first
        honey mixed with milk, and the second pouring was sweet wine,
        and the third, water, and over it all I sprinkled white barley.
        I promised many times to the strengthless heads of the perished
30   dead that, returning to Ithaka,[4] I would slaughter a barren
        cow, my best, in my palace, and pile the pyre with treasures,
        and to Teiresias[5] apart would dedicate an all-black
        ram, the one conspicuous in all our sheep flocks.
        Now when, with sacrifices and prayers, I had so entreated
35   the hordes of the dead, I took the sheep and cut their throats
        over the pit, and the dark-clouding blood ran in, and the souls
        of the perished dead gathered to the place, up out of Erebos,[6]
        brides, and young unmarried men, and long-suffering elders,
        virgins, tender and with the sorrows of young hearts upon them,
40   and many fighting men killed in battle, stabbed with brazen
        spears, still carrying their bloody armor upon them.
        These came swarming around my pit from every direction
        with inhuman clamor, and green fear took hold of me.
        Then I encouraged my companions and told them, taking
45   the sheep that were lying by, slaughtered with the pitiless
        bronze, to skin these, and burn them, and pray to the divinities,
        to Hades the powerful, and to revered Persephone,[7]
        while I myself, drawing from beside my thigh my sharp sword,
        crouched there, and would not let the strengthless heads of the perished
50   dead draw nearer to the blood, until I had questioned Teiresias.
          'But first there came the soul of my companion, Elpenor[8]

---

[2] **Helios:** Greek god of the sun.
[3] **Perimedes and Eurylochos:** Eurylochos is Odysseus's second-in-command during his travels, and Perimedes is another of his crew.
[4] **Ithaka:** Island home of Odysseus.
[5] **Teiresias:** Blind prophet who encounters Odysseus in the land of the dead.
[6] **Erebos:** Land of the dead.
[7] **Hades . . . Persephone:** Hades is lord of the underworld, and Persephone is goddess of the underworld.
[8] **Elpenor:** Friend of Odysseus, who fell off Circe's palace while drunk.

for he had not yet been buried under earth of the wide ways,
since we had left his body behind in Circe's palace,
unburied and unwept, with this other errand before us.
55   I broke into tears at the sight of him, and my heart pitied him,
and so I spoke aloud to him and addressed him in winged words:
"Elpenor, how did you come here beneath the fog and the darkness?
You have come faster on foot than I could in my black ship."
'So I spoke, and he groaned aloud and spoke and answered:
60   "Son of Laertes and seed of Zeus, resourceful Odysseus,
the evil will of the spirit and the wild wine bewildered me.
I lay down on the roof of Circe's palace, and never thought,
when I went down, to go by way of the long ladder,
but blundered straight off the edge of the roof, so that my neck bone
65   was broken out of its sockets, and my soul went down to Hades'.
But now I pray you, by those you have yet to see, who are not here,
by your wife, and by your father, who reared you when you were little,
and by Telemachos[9] whom you left alone in your palace;
for I know that after you leave this place and the house of Hades
70   you will put back with your well-made ship to the island, Aiaia;
there at that time, my lord, I ask that you remember me,
and do not go and leave me behind unwept, unburied,
when you leave, for fear I might become the gods' curse upon you;
but burn me there with all my armor that belongs to me,
75   and heap up a grave mound beside the beach of the gray sea,
for an unhappy man, so that those to come will know of me.
Do this for me, and on top of the grave mound plant the oar
with which I rowed when I was alive and among my companions."
'So he spoke, and I in turn spoke to him in answer:
80   "All this, my unhappy friend, I will do for you as you ask me."
'So we two stayed there exchanging our sad words, I on
one side holding my sword over the blood, while opposite
me the phantom of my companion talked long with me.
'Next there came to me the soul of my dead mother,
85   Antikleia, daughter of great-hearted Autolykos,
whom I had left alive when I went to sacred Illion.°   Troy
I broke into tears at the sight of her and my heart pitied her,
but even so, for all my thronging sorrow, I would not
let her draw near the blood until I had questioned Teiresias.
90   'Now came the soul of Teiresias the Theban, holding
a staff of gold, and he knew who I was, and spoke to me:
"Son of Laertes and seed of Zeus, resourceful Odysseus,
how is it then, unhappy man, you have left the sunlight
and come here, to look on dead men, and this place without pleasure?
95   Now draw back from the pit, and hold your sharp sword away from me,

---

[9] **Telemachos:** Son of Odysseus and Penelope, left behind on Ithaka during his father's long absence.

so that I can drink of the blood and speak the truth to you."
  'So he spoke, and I, holding away the sword with the silver
nails, pushed it back in the sheath, and the flawless prophet,
after he had drunk the blood, began speaking to me.
100 "Glorious Odysseus, what you are after is sweet homecoming,
but the god will make it hard for you. I think you will not
escape the Shaker of the Earth,[10] who holds a grudge against you
in his heart, and because you blinded his dear son, hates you.
But even so and still you might come back, after much suffering,
105 if you can contain your own desire, and contain your companions',
at that time when you first put in your well-made vessel
at the island Thrinakia,[11] escaping the sea's blue water,
and there discover pasturing the cattle and fat sheep
of Helios, who sees all things, and listens to all things.
110 Then, if you keep your mind on homecoming, and leave these unharmed,
you might all make your way to Ithaka, after much suffering;
but if you do harm them, then I testify to the destruction
of your ship and your companions, but if you yourself get clear,
you will come home in bad case, with the loss of all your companions,
115 in someone else's ship, and find troubles in your household,
insolent men, who are eating away your livelihood
and courting your godlike wife and offering gifts to win her.
You may punish the violences of these men, when you come home.
But after you have killed these suitors in your own palace,
120 either by treachery, or openly with the sharp bronze,
then you must take up your well-shaped oar and go on a journey
until you come where there are men living who know nothing
of the sea, and who eat food that is not mixed with salt, who never
have known ships whose cheeks are painted purple, who never
125 have known well-shaped oars, which act for ships as wings do.
And I will tell you a very clear proof, and you cannot miss it.
When, as you walk, some other wayfarer happens to meet you,
and says you carry a winnow-fan on your bright shoulder,
then you must plant your well-shaped oar in the ground, and render
130 ceremonies sacrifice to the lord Poseidon,
one ram and one bull, and a mounter of sows, a boar pig,
and make your way home again and render holy hecatombs
to the immortal gods who hold the wide heaven, all
of them in order. Death will come to you from the sea, in
135 some altogether unwarlike way, and it will end you
in the ebbing time of a sleek old age. Your people
about you will be prosperous. All this is true that I tell you."

---

[10] **Shaker of the Earth:** Poseidon, the god of the sea. Earlier in Homer's epic, Odysseus blinded
Poseidon's son Polyphemos.
[11] **Thrinakia:** Island on which Helios's cattle grazed.

'So he spoke, but I in turn said to him in answer:
"All this, Teiresias, surely must be as the gods spun it.
140   But come now, tell me this and give me an accurate answer.
I see before me now the soul of my perished mother,
but she sits beside the blood in silence, and has not yet deigned
to look directly at her own son and speak a word to me.
Tell me, lord, what will make her know me, and know my presence?"
145   'So I spoke, and he at once said to me in answer:
"Easily I will tell you and put it in your understanding.
Any one of the perished dead you allow to come up
to the blood will give you a true answer, but if you begrudge this
to any one, he will return to the place where he came from."
150   'So speaking, the soul of the lord Teiresias went back into
the house of Hades, once he had uttered his prophecies, while I
waited steadily where I was standing, until my mother
came and drank the dark-clouding blood, and at once she knew me,
and full of lamentation she spoke to me in winged words:
155   "My child, how did you come here beneath the fog and the darkness
and still alive? All this is hard for the living to look on,
for in between lie the great rivers and terrible waters
that flow, Ocean first of all, which there is no means of crossing
on foot, not unless one has a well-made ship. Are you
160   come now to this place from Troy, with your ship and your companions,
after wandering a long time, and have you not yet come
to Ithaka, and there seen your wife in your palace?"
'So she spoke, and I in turn said to her in answer:
"Mother, a duty brought me here to the house of Hades.
165   I had to consult the soul of Teiresias the Theban.
For I have not yet been near Achaian[12] country, nor ever
set foot on our land, but always suffering I have wandered
since the time I first went along with great Agamemnon[13]
to Ilion, land of good horses, and the battle against the Trojans.
170   But come now, tell me this, and give me an accurate answer.
What doom of death that lays men low has been your undoing?
Was it a long sickness, or did Artemis[14] of the arrows
come upon you with her painless shafts, and destroy you?
And tell me of my father and son whom I left behind. Is
175   my inheritance still with them, or does some other
man hold them now, and thinks I will come no more? Tell me
about the wife I married, what she wants, what she is thinking,
and whether she stays fast by my son, and guards everything,

---

[12] **Achaian:** A member of one of the four divisions of ancient Greeks.
[13] **Agamemnon:** Leader of the Greek forces during the Trojan War.
[14] **Artemis:** Daughter of Zeus, twin sister of Apollo. Considered the goddess of wilderness, hunting, and fertility. Known to be an excellent archer.

or if she has married the best man among the Achaians."
180   'So I spoke, and my queenly mother answered me quickly:
"All too much with enduring heart she does wait for you
there in your own palace, and always with her the wretched
nights and the days also waste her away with weeping.
No one yet holds your fine inheritance, but in freedom
185   Telemachos administers your allotted lands, and apportions
the equal feasts, work that befits a man with authority
to judge, for all call him in. Your father remains, on the estate
where he is, and does not go to the city. There is no bed there
nor is there bed clothing nor blankets nor shining coverlets,
190   but in the winter time he sleeps in the house, where the thralls do,
in the dirt next to the fire, and with foul clothing upon him;
but when the summer comes and the blossoming time of harvest,
everywhere he has places to sleep on the ground, on fallen
leaves in piles along the rising ground of his orchard,
195   and there he lies, grieving, and the sorrow grows big within him
as he longs for your homecoming, and harsh old age is on him.
And so it was with me also and that was the reason I perished,
nor in my palace did the lady of arrows, well-aiming,
come upon me with her painless shafts, and destroy me,
200   nor was I visited by sickness, which beyond other
things takes the life out of the body with hateful weakness,
but, shining Odysseus, it was my longing for you, your cleverness
and your gentle ways, that took the sweet spirit of life from me."
'So she spoke, but I, pondering it in my heart, yet wished
205   to take the soul of my dead mother in my arms. Three times
I started toward her, and my heart was urgent to hold her,
and three times she fluttered out of my hands like a shadow
or a dream, and the sorrow sharpened at the heart within me,
and so I spoke to her and addressed her in winged words, saying:
210   "Mother, why will you not wait for me, when I am trying
to hold you, so that even in Hades' with our arms embracing
we can both take the satisfaction of dismal mourning?
Or are you nothing but an image that proud Persephone
sent my way, to make me grieve all the more for sorrow?"
215   'So I spoke, and my queenly mother answered me quickly:
"Oh my child, ill-fated beyond all other mortals,
this is not Persephone, daughter of Zeus, beguiling you,
but it is only what happens, when they die, to all mortals.
The sinews no longer hold the flesh and the bones together,
220   and once the spirit has left the white bones, all the rest
of the body is made subject to the fire's strong fury,
but the soul flitters out like a dream and flies away. Therefore
you must strive back toward the light again with all speed; but remember
these things for your wife, so you may tell her hereafter."

225   'Now when chaste Persephone had scattered the female
souls of the women, driving them off in every direction,
there came the soul of Agamemnon, the son of Atreus,
grieving, and the souls of the other men, who died with him
and met their doom in the house of Aigisthos,[15] were gathered
            around him.

230   He knew me at once, when he drank the dark blood, and fell to
lamentation loud and shrill, and the tears came springing,
and threw himself into my arms, meaning so to embrace me,
but there was no force there any longer, nor any juice left
now in his flexible limbs, as there had been in time past.

235   I broke into tears at the sight of him and my heart pitied him,
and so I spoke aloud to him and addressed him in winged words:
"Son of Atreus, most lordly and king of men, Agamemnon,
what doom of death that lays men low has been your undoing?
Was it with the ships, and did Poseidon, rousing a stormblast

240   of battering winds that none would wish for, prove your undoing?
Or was it on the dry land, did men embattled destroy you
as you tried to cut out cattle and fleecy sheep from their holdings,
or fighting against them for the sake of their city and women?"
    'So I spoke, and he in turn said to me in answer:

245   "Son of Laertes and seed of Zeus, resourceful Odysseus,
not in the ships, nor did Poseidon, rousing a stormblast
of battering winds that none would wish for, prove my destruction,
nor on dry land did enemy men destroy me in battle;
Aigisthos, working out my death and destruction, invited

250   me to his house, and feasted me, and killed me there, with the help
of my sluttish wife, as one cuts down an ox at his manger.
So I died a most pitiful death, and my other companions
were killed around me without mercy, like pigs with shining
tusks, in the house of a man rich and very powerful,

255   for a wedding, or a festival, or a communal dinner.
You have been present in your time at the slaughter of many
men, killed singly, or in the strong encounters of battle;
but beyond all others you would have been sorry at heart
for this scene, how we lay sprawled by the mixing bowl and the loaded

260   tables, all over the palace, and the whole floor was steaming
with blood; and most pitiful was the voice I heard of Priam's
daughter Kassandra,[16] killed by treacherous Klytaimestra

---

[15] **Aigisthos:** While Agamemnon was away at Troy, Aigisthos initiated an affair with his wife Queen
Klytaimestra. Aigisthos helped kill Agamemnon upon his return to Troy.
[16] **Priam's . . . Kassandra:** Priam was the King of Troy, killed by Achilles' son in the battle of Troy. His
daughter, Kassandra, was given to Agamemnon as a war prize after Troy's defeat. Blessed with the gift
of prophecy, she attempted to warn Agamemnon about his unfortunate fate upon their return to
Greece. He would not listen, and both Agamemnon and Kassandra were killed by Aigisthos and
Klytaimestra.

over me; but I lifted my hands and with them beat on
the ground as I died upon the sword, but the sluttish woman
265 turned away from me and was so hard that her hands would not
press shut my eyes and mouth though I was going to Hades'.
So there is nothing more deadly or more vile than a woman
who stores her mind with acts that are of such sort, as this one
did when she thought of this act of dishonor, and plotted
270 the murder of her lawful husband. See, I had been thinking
that I would be welcome to my children and thralls of my household
when I came home, but she with thoughts surpassingly grisly
splashed the shame on herself and the rest of her sex, on women
still to come, even on the one whose acts are virtuous."
275   'So he spoke, and I again said to him in answer:
"Shame it is, how most terribly Zeus of the wide brows
from the beginning has been hateful to the seed of Atreus
through the schemes of women. Many of us died for the sake of Helen,
and when you were far, Klytaimestra plotted treason against you."
280   'So I spoke, and he in turn said to me in answer:
"So by this, do not be too easy even with your wife,
nor give her an entire account of all you are sure of.
Tell her part of it, but let the rest be hidden in silence.
And yet you, Odysseus, will never be murdered by your wife.
285 The daughter of Ikarios,[17] circumspect Penelope,
is all too virtuous and her mind is stored with good thoughts.
Ah well. She was only a young wife when we left her
and went off to the fighting, and she had an infant child then
at her breast. That child now must sit with the men and be counted.
290 Happy he! For his dear father will come back, and see him,
and he will fold his father in his arms, as is right. My wife
never even let me feed my eyes with the sight of
my own son, but before that I myself was killed by her.
And put away in your heart this other thing that I tell you.
295 When you bring your ship in to your own dear country, do it
secretly, not in the open. There is no trusting in women.
But come now, tell me this and give me an accurate answer;
tell me if you happened to hear that my son was still living,
whether perhaps in Orchomenos, or in sandy Pylos,
300 or perhaps with Menelaos in wide Sparta; for nowhere
upon the earth has there been any death of noble Orestes.[18]
     'So he spoke, and I again said to him in answer:
"Son of Atreus, why do you ask me that? I do not know
if he is alive or dead. It is bad to babble emptily."

---

[17] **Ikarios:** Father of Penelope. He offered his daughter's hand in marriage to anyone who could beat
him in a running race; Odysseus won.
[18] **Orestes:** Son of Agamemnon, exiled after his father was murdered by his mother Klytaimestra.

305   'So we two stood there exchanging our sad words, grieving
      both together and shedding the big tears. After this,
      there came to us the soul of Peleus' son, Achilleus,
      and the soul of Patroklos and the soul of stately Antilochos,
      and the soul of Aias, who for beauty and stature was greatest
310   of all the Danaans, next to the stately son of Peleus.
      The soul of swift-footed Achilleus,[19] scion of Aiakos, knew me,
      and full of lamentation he spoke to me in winged words:
      "Son of Laertes and seed of Zeus, resourceful Odysseus,
      hard man, what made you think of this bigger endeavor, how could you
315   endure to come down here to Hades' place, where the senseless
      dead men dwell, mere imitations of perished mortals?"
        'So he spoke, and I again said to him in answer:
      "Son of Peleus, far the greatest of the Achaians, Achilleus,
      I came for the need to consult Teiresias, if he might tell me
320   some plan by which I might come back to rocky Ithaka;
      for I have not yet been near Achaian country, nor ever
      set foot on my land, but always I have troubles. Achilleus,
      no man before has been more blessed than you, nor ever
      will be. Before, when you were alive, we Argives[20] honored you
325   as we did the gods, and now in this place you have great authority
      over the dead. Do not grieve, even in death, Achilleus."
        'So I spoke, and he in turn said to me in answer:
      "O shining Odysseus, never try to console me for dying.
      I would rather follow the plow as thrall to another
330   man, one with no land allotted him and not much to live on,
      than be a king over all the perished dead. But come now,
      tell me anything you have heard of my proud son, whether
      or not he went along to war to fight as a champion;
      and tell me anything you have heard about stately Peleus,[21]
335   whether he still keeps his position among the Myrmidon[22]
      hordes, or whether in Hellas° and Phthia[23] they have diminished   Greece
      his state, because old age constrains his hands and feet, and I
      am no longer there under the light of the sun to help him,
      not the man I used to be once, when in the wide Troad[24]
340   I killed the best of their people, fighting for the Argives. If only
      for a little while I could come like that to the house of my father,
      my force and my invincible hands would terrify such men
      as use force on him and keep him away from his rightful honors."

---

[19] **Achilleus:** Half-mortal, half-god, Achilleus was Greece's most distinguished warrior in the battle of
Troy, defeating Priam's son Hector before being wounded by Hector's brother Paris.
[20] **Argives:** One who lives in the Greek city Argos, near Sparta.
[21] **Peleus:** Father of Achilleus, he was a mortal who married the Nereid Thetis.
[22] **Myrmidon:** Greeks who once inhabited the island of Aegina, where the father of Peleus was king.
[23] **Phthia:** Homeland of the Myrmidon Greeks after a plague struck the island of Aegina.
[24] **Troad:** Ancient region in Asia Minor, near Troy.

'So he spoke, and I again said to him in answer:

345 "I have no report to give you of stately Peleus,
but as for your beloved son Neoptolemos,[25] I will
tell you, since you ask me to do it, all the true story;
for I myself, in the hollow hull of a balanced ship, brought him
over from Skyros, to join the strong-greaved Achaians. Whenever

350 we, around the city of Troy, talked over our counsels,
he would always speak first, and never blunder. In speaking
only godlike Nestor[26] and I were better than he was.
And when we Achaians fought in the Trojan plain, he never
would hang back where there were plenty of other men, nor stay with

355 the masses, but run far out in front, giving way to no man
for fury, and many were those he killed in the terrible fighting.
I could not tell over the number of all nor name all
the people he killed as he fought for the Argives, but what a great man
was one, the son of Telephos he slew with the brazen

360 spear, the hero Eurypylos, and many Keteian
companions were killed about him, by reason of womanish presents.
Next to great Memnon,[27] this was the finest man I ever
saw. Again, when we who were best of the Argives entered
the horse that Epeios[28] made, and all the command was given

365 to me, to keep close hidden inside, or sally out from it,
the other leaders of the Danaans and men of counsel
were wiping their tears away and the limbs were shaking under
each man of them; but never at any time did I see him
losing his handsome color and going pale, or wiping

370 the tears off his face, but rather he implored me to let him
sally out of the horse; he kept feeling for his sword hilt
and spear weighted with bronze, full of evil thoughts for the Trojans.
But after we had sacked the sheer citadel of Priam,
with his fair share and a princely prize of his own, he boarded

375 his ship, unscathed; he had not been hit by thrown and piercing
bronze, nor stabbed in close-up combat, as often happens
in fighting. The War God rages at all, and favors no man."
   'So I spoke, and the soul of the swift-footed scion of Aiakos
stalked away in long strides across the meadow of asphodel,[29]

380 happy for what I had said of his son, and how he was famous.
   'Now the rest of the souls of the perished dead stood near me
grieving, and each one spoke to me and told of his sorrows.

---

[25] **Neoptolemos:** Only son of Achilleus, killed King Priam in the battle of Troy.
[26] **Nestor:** Oldest Greek hero to participate in the battle against Troy.
[27] **Memnon:** In the war, he fought on the side of Troy, killing Nestor's son Antilochus before being mortally wounded by Achilleus.
[28] **Epeios:** Greek solider who constructed the Trojan Horse.
[29] **asphodel:** Flower which covers the plains of Hades.

Only the soul of Telamonian Aias[30] stood off
at a distance from me, angry still over that decision
385 I won against him, when beside the ships we disputed
our cases for the arms of Achilleus. His queenly mother
set them as prize, and the sons of the Trojans, with Pallas Athene,
judged; and I wish I had never won in a contest like this,
so high a head has gone under the ground for the sake of that armor,
390 Aias, who for beauty and for achievement surpassed
all the Danaans next to the stately son of Peleus.°   Achilleus
So I spoke to him now in words of conciliation:
"Aias, son of stately Telamon, could you then never
even in death forget your anger against me, because of
395 that cursed armor? The gods made it to pain the Achaians,
so great a bulwark were you, who were lost to them. We Achaians
grieved for your death as incessantly as for Achilleus
the son of Peleus at his death, and there is no other
to blame, but Zeus; he, in his terrible hate for the army
400 of Danaan spearmen, visited this destruction upon you.
Come nearer, my lord, so you can hear what I say and listen
to my story; suppress your anger and lordly spirit."
   'So I spoke. He gave no answer, but went off after
the other souls of the perished dead men, into the darkness.
405 There, despite his anger, he might have spoken, or I might
have spoken to him, but the heart in my inward breast wanted
still to see the souls of the other perished dead men.
   'There I saw Minos,[31] the glorious son of Zeus, seated,
holding a golden scepter and issuing judgments among
410 the dead, who all around the great lord argued their cases,
some sitting and some standing, by the wide-gated house of Hades.
   'After him I was aware of gigantic Orion[32]
in the meadow of asphodel, rounding up and driving together
wild animals he himself had killed in the lonely mountains,
415 holding in his hands a brazen club, forever unbroken.
   'And I saw Tityos,[33] Earth's glorious son, lying
in the plain, and sprawled over nine acres. Two vultures,
sitting one on either side, were tearing his liver,
plunging inside the caul. With his hands he could not beat them

---

[30] **Telamonian Aias:** (also, Telamonian Ajax) One of Greece's strongest warriors in the Trojan War; after Achilles death, competed against Odysseus for Achilles' armor and lost. Aias was driven mad by his defeat, eventually committing suicide.

[31] **Minos:** Son of Zeus, husband of Pasiphae, the daughter of the sun god.

[32] **Orion:** Son of Poseidon the sea god, a physically imposing deity known for his hunting.

[33] **Tityos:** Illegitimate son of Zeus by Elara. After Tityos attempted to rape Leto, he was killed by Artemis and Apollo. As punishment, his body was stretched out in Hades, where two vultures constantly feed on his liver.

420 away. He had manhandled Leto,[34] the honored consort
of Zeus, as she went through spacious Panopeus, toward Pytho.
'And I saw Tantalos[35] also, suffering hard pains, standing
in lake water that came up to his chin, and thirsty
as he was, he tried to drink, but could capture nothing;
425 for every time the old man, trying to drink, stooped over,
the water would drain away and disappear, and the black earth
showed at his feet, and the divinity dried it away. Over
his head trees with lofty branches had fruit like a shower descending,
pear trees and pomegranate trees and apple trees with fruit shining,
430 and figs that were sweet and olives ripened well, but each time
the old man would straighten up and reach with his hands for them,
the wind would toss them away toward the clouds overhanging.
'Also I saw Sisyphos.[36] He was suffering strong pains,
and with both arms embracing the monstrous stone, struggling
435 with hands and feet alike, he would try to push the stone upward
to the crest of the hill, but when it was on the point of going
over the top, the force of gravity turned it backward,
and the pitiless stone rolled back down to the level. He then
tried once more to push it up, straining hard, and sweat ran
440 all down his body, and over his head a cloud of dust rose.
'After him I was aware of powerful Herakles,[37]
his image, that is, but he himself among the immortal
gods enjoys their festivals, married to sweet-stepping
Hebe, child of great Zeus and Hera of the golden sandals.
445 All around him was a clamor of the dead as of birds scattering
scared in every direction; but he came on, like dark night,
holding his bow bare with an arrow laid on the bowstring,
and forever looking, as one who shot, with terrible glances.
There was a terrible belt crossed over his chest, and a golden
450 baldrick, with marvelous works of art that figured upon it,
bears, and lions with glaring eyes, and boars of the forests,
the battles and the quarrels, the murders and the manslaughters.
May he who artfully designed them, and artfully put them
upon that baldrick, never again do any designing.
455 He recognized me at once as soon as his eyes had seen me,
and full of lamentation he spoke to me in winged words:

---

[34] **Leto:** Lover of Zeus, mother of Artemis and Apollo.
[35] **Tantalos:** Mortal son of Zeus, Tantalos was the king of Sipylos. He was invited to share the food of the gods, but abused the privilege. As a result, he was punished with eternal hunger.
[36] **Sisyphos:** Founder of Corinth, known for his evil and treachery. After he betrayed the secrets of the gods and chained the god of death, he was sentenced to Hades, where he was forced to roll a stone up a steep hill for eternity.
[37] **Herakles:** Son of Zeus and Alcmene, known for his strength. Driven mad by Hera, he killed his own children. After their death, he consulted the oracle of Apollo, who advised him to complete twelve labors, one of which was bringing the three-headed dog from Hades to the surface world.

"Son of Laertes and seed of Zeus, resourceful Odysseus,
unhappy man, are you too leading some wretched destiny
such as I too pursued when I went still in the sunlight?
460   For I was son of Kronian Zeus, but I had an endless
spell of misery. I was made bondman to one who was far worse
than I, and he loaded my difficult labors on me. One time
he sent me here to fetch the dog back, and thought there could be
no other labor to be devised more difficult than that
465   one, but I brought the dog up and led him from the realm of Hades,
and Hermes saw me on my way, with Pallas Athene."
  'So he spoke, and went back into the realm of Hades,
but I stayed fast in place where I was, to see if some other
one of the generation of heroes who died before me
470   would come; and I might have seen men earlier still, whom I wanted
to see, Perithoös and Theseus, gods' glorious children;
but before that the hordes of the dead men gathered about me
with inhuman clamor, and green fear took hold of me
with the thought that proud Persephone might send up against me
475   some gorgonish head of a terrible monster up out of Hades'.
So, going back on board my ship, I told my companions
also to go aboard, and to cast off the stern cables;
and quickly they went aboard the ship and sat to the oarlocks,
and the swell of the current carried her down the Ocean river
480   with rowing at first, but after that on a fair wind following.

ANONYMOUS
trans. Seamus Heaney (1939–   )

from Beowulf (trans. 2000)

Then down the brave man lay with his bolster°   pillow
under his head and his whole company
of sea-rovers at rest beside him.
None of them expected he would ever see
5   his homeland again or get back
to his native place and the people who reared him.
They knew too well the way it was before,
how often the Danes had fallen prey
to death in the mead-hall. But the Lord was weaving
10   a victory on His war-loom for the Weather-Geats.
Through the strength of one they all prevailed;

they would crush their enemy and come through
in triumph and gladness. The truth is clear:
Almighty God rules over mankind
15 and always has.
                          Then out of the night
came the shadow-stalker, stealthy and swift;
the hall-guards were slack, asleep at their posts,
all except one; it was widely understood
20 that as long as God disallowed it,
the fiend could not bear them to his shadow-bourne.
One man, however, was in fighting mood,
awake and on edge, spoiling for action.

In off the moors, down through the mist bands
25 God-cursed Grendel came greedily loping.
The bane of the race of men roamed forth,
hunting for a prey in the high hall.
Under the cloud-murk he moved towards it
until it shone above him, a sheer keep
30 of fortified gold. Nor was that the first time
he had scouted the grounds of Hrothgar's[1] dwelling—
although never in his life, before or since,
did he find harder fortune or hall-defenders.
Spurned and joyless, he journeyed on ahead
35 and arrived at the bawn. The iron-braced door
turned on its hinge when his hands touched it.
Then his rage boiled over, he ripped open
the mouth of the building, maddening for blood,
pacing the length of the patterned floor
40 with his loathsome tread, while a baleful light,
flame more than light, flared from his eyes.
He saw many men in the mansion, sleeping,
a ranked company of kinsmen and warriors
quartered together. And his glee was demonic,
45 picturing the mayhem: before morning
he would rip life from limb and devour them,
feed on their flesh; but his fate that night
was due to change, his days of ravening
had come to an end.
50   Mighty and canny,
Hygelac's kinsman° was keenly watching   Beowulf
for the first move the monster would make.

---

[1] **Hrothgar's:** King of the Danes. Beowulf leaves his homeland to defend Hrothgar's hall from the monster Grendel.

Nor did the creature keep him waiting
but struck suddenly and started in;
55   he grabbed and mauled a man on his bench,
bit into his bone-lappings, bolted down his blood
and gorged on him in lumps, leaving the body
utterly lifeless, eaten up
hand and foot. Venturing closer,
60   his talon was raised to attack Beowulf
where he lay on the bed; he was bearing in
with open claw when the alert hero's
comeback and armlock forestalled him utterly.
The captain of evil discovered himself
65   in a handgrip harder than anything
he had ever encountered in any man
on the face of the earth. Every bone in his body
quailed and recoiled, but he could not escape.
He was desperate to flee to his den and hide
70   with the devil's litter, for in all his days
he had never been clamped or cornered like this.
Then Hygelac's trusty retainer recalled
his bedtime speech, sprang to his feet
and got a firm hold. Fingers were bursting,
75   the monster back-tracking, the man overpowering.
The dread of the land was desperate to escape,
to take a roundabout road and flee
to his lair in the fens.° The latching power   marsh
in his fingers weakened; it was the worst trip
80   the terror-monger had taken to Heorot.°   King Hrothgar's hall
And now the timbers trembled and sang,
a hall-session that harrowed every Dane
inside the stockade: stumbling in fury,
the two contenders crashed through the building.
85   The hall clattered and hammered, but somehow
survived the onslaught and kept standing:
it was handsomely structured, a sturdy frame
braced with the best of blacksmith's work
inside and out. The story goes
90   that as the pair struggled, mead-benches were smashed
and sprung off the floor, gold fittings and all.
Before then, no Shielding[2] elder would believe
there was any power or person upon earth
capable of wrecking their horn-rigged hall
95   unless the burning embrace of a fire

---

[2] **Shielding:** A subject of King Hrothgar's kingdom.

engulf it in flame. Then an extraordinary
wail arose, and bewildering fear
came over the Danes. Everyone felt it
who heard that cry as it echoed off the wall,
100 a God-cursed scream and strain of catastrophe,
the howl of the loser, the lament of the hell-serf
keening his wound. He was overwhelmed,
manacled tight by the man who of all men
was foremost and strongest in the days of this life.

105 But the earl-troop's leader was not inclined
to allow his caller to depart alive:
he did not consider that life of much account
to anyone anywhere. Time and again,
Beowulf's warriors worked to defend
110 their lord's life, laying about them
as best they could with their ancestral blades.
Stalwart in action, they kept striking out
on every side, seeking to cut
straight to the soul. When they joined the struggle
115 there was something they could not have known at the time,
that no blade on earth, no blacksmith's art
could ever damage their demon opponent.
He had conjured the harm from the cutting edge
of every weapon. But his going away
120 out of this world and the days of his life
would be agony to him, and his alien spirit
would travel far into fiends' keeping.

Then he who had harrowed the hearts of men
with pain and affliction in former times
125 and had given offence also to God
found that his bodily powers failed him.
Hygelac's kinsman kept him helplessly
locked in a handgrip. As long as either lived,
he was hateful to the other. The monster's whole
130 body was in pain, a tremendous wound
appeared on his shoulder. Sinews split
and the bone-lappings burst. Beowulf was granted
the glory of winning; Grendel was driven
under the fen-banks, fatally hurt,
135 to his desolate lair. His days were numbered,
the end of his life was coming over him,
he knew it for certain; and one bloody clash
had fulfilled the dearest wishes of the Danes.
The man who had lately landed among them,

140   proud and sure, had purged the hall,
        kept it from harm; he was happy with his nightwork
        and the courage he had shown. The Geat captain
        had boldly fulfilled his boast to the Danes:
        he had healed and relieved a huge distress,
145   unremitting humiliations,
        the hard fate they'd been forced to undergo,
        no small affliction. Clear proof of this
        could be seen in the hand the hero displayed
        high up near the roof: the whole of Grendel's
150   shoulder and arm, his awesome grasp.

        Then morning came and many a warrior
        gathered, as I've heard, around the gift-hall,
        clan-chiefs flocking from far and near
        down wide-ranging roads, wondering greatly
155   at the monster's footprints. His fatal departure
        was regretted by no-one who witnessed his trail,
        the ignominious marks of his flight
        where he'd skulked away, exhausted in spirit
        and beaten in battle, bloodying the path,
160   hauling his doom to the demons' mere.°   small pond
        The bloodshot water wallowed and surged,
        there were loathsome upthrows and overturnings
        of waves and gore and wound-slurry.
        With his death upon him, he had dived deep
165   into his marsh-den, drowned out his life
        and his heathen soul: hell claimed him there.
        With high hearts they headed away
        along footpaths and trails through the fields,
        roads that they knew, each of them wrestling
170   with the head they were carrying from the lakeside cliff,
        men kingly in their courage and capable
        of difficult work. It was a task for four
        to hoist Grendel's head on a spear
        and bear it under strain to the bright hall.
175   But soon enough they neared the place,
        fourteen Geats in fine fettle,°   health
        striding across the outlying ground
        in a delighted throng around their leader.

        In he came then, the thane's commander,
180   the arch-warrior, to address Hrothgar:
        his courage was proven, his glory was secure.
        Grendel's head was hauled by the hair,
        dragged across the floor where the people were drinking,

a horror for both queen and company to behold.
185 They stared in awe. It was an astonishing sight.

Beowulf, son of Ecgtheow, spoke:
"So, son of Halfdane, prince of the Shieldings,
we are glad to bring this booty from the lake.
It is a token of triumph and we tender it to you.
190 I barely survived the battle under water.
It was hard-fought, a desperate affair
that could have gone badly; if God had not helped me,
the outcome would have been quick and fatal.
Although Hrunting is hard-edged,
195 I could never bring it to bear in battle.
But the Lord of Men allowed me to behold—
for He often helps the unbefriended—
an ancient sword shining on the wall,
a weapon made for giants, there for the wielding.
200 Then my moment came in the combat and I struck
the dwellers in that den. Next thing the damascened
sword blade melted; it bloated and it burned
in their rushing blood. I have wrested the hilt
from the enemies' hand, avenged the evil
205 done to the Danes; it is what was due.
And this I pledge, O prince of the Shieldings:
you can sleep secure with your company of troops
in Heorot Hall. Never need you fear
for a single thane° of your sept° or nation,   feudal lord / family line
210 young warriors or old, that laying waste of life
that you and your people endured of yore."

Then the gold hilt was handed over
to the old lord, a relic from long ago
for the venerable ruler. That rare smithwork
215 was passed on to the prince of the Danes
when those devils perished; once death removed
that murdering, guilt-steeped, God-cursed fiend,
eliminating his unholy life
and his mother's as well, it was willed to that king
220 who of all the lavish gift-lords of the north
was the best regarded between the two seas.

Hrothgar spoke; he examined the hilt,
that relic of old times. It was engraved all over
and showed how war first came into the world
225 and the flood destroyed the tribe of giants.
They suffered a terrible severance from the Lord;

the Almighty made the waters rise,
drowned them in the deluge for retribution.
In pure gold inlay on the sword-guards
230   there were rune-markings correctly incised,
stating and recording for whom the sword
had been first made and ornamented
with its scrollworked hilt. Then everyone hushed
as the son of Halfdane spoke this wisdom.
235   "A protector of his people, pledged to uphold
truth and justice and to respect tradition,
is entitled to affirm that this man
was born to distinction. Beowulf, my friend,
your fame has gone far and wide,
240   you are known everywhere. In all things you are even-tempered,
prudent and resolute. So I stand firm by the promise of friendship
we exchanged before. Forever you will be
your people's mainstay and your own warriors'
helping hand.
245   Heremod was different,
the way he behaved to Ecgwala's sons.
His rise in the world brought little joy
to the Danish people, only death and destruction.
He vented his rage on men he caroused with,
250   killed his own comrades, a pariah king
who cut himself off from his own kind,
even though Almighty God had made him
eminent and powerful and marked him from the start
for a happy life. But a change happened,
255   he grew bloodthirsty, gave no more rings
to honour the Danes. He suffered in the end
for having plagued his people for so long:
his life lost happiness.
                    So learn from this
260   and understand true values. I who tell you
have wintered into wisdom.
                    It is a great wonder
how Almighty God in His magnificence
favours our race with rank and scope
265   and the gift of wisdom; His sway is wide.
Sometimes He allows the mind of a man
of distinguished birth to follow its bent,
grants him fulfilment and felicity on earth
and forts to command in his own country.
270   He permits him to lord it in many lands
until the man in his unthinkingness
forgets that it will ever end for him.

He indulges his desires; illness and old age
mean nothing to him; his mind is untroubled
275   by envy or malice or the thought of enemies
with their hate-honed swords. The whole world
conforms to his will, he is kept from the worst
until an element of overweening
enters him and takes hold
280   while the soul's guard, its sentry, drowses,
grown too distracted. A killer stalks him,
an archer who draws a deadly bow.
And then the man is hit in the heart,
the arrow flies beneath his defences,
285   the devious promptings of the demon start.
His old possessions seem paltry to him now.
He covets and resents; dishonours custom
and bestows no gold; and because of good things
that the Heavenly Powers gave him in the past
290   he ignores the shape of things to come.
Then finally the end arrives
when the body he was lent collapses and falls
prey to its death; ancestral possessions
and the goods he hoarded are inherited by another
295   who lets them go with a liberal hand.

"O flower of warriors, beware of that trap.
Choose, dear Beowulf, the better part,
eternal rewards. Do not give way to pride.
For a brief while your strength is in bloom
300   but it fades quickly; and soon there will follow
illness or the sword to lay you low,
or a sudden fire or surge of water
or jabbing blade or javelin from the air
or repellent age. Your piercing eye
305   will dim and darken; and death will arrive,
dear warrior, to sweep you away.

"Just so I ruled the Ring-Danes' country
for fifty years, defended them in wartime
with spear and sword against constant assaults
310   by many tribes: I came to believe
my enemies had faded from the face of the earth.
Still, what happened was a hard reversal
from bliss to grief. Grendel struck
after lying in wait. He laid waste to the land
315   and from that moment my mind was in dread
of his depredations. So I praise God

in His heavenly glory that I lived to behold
this head dripping blood and that after such harrowing
I can look upon it in triumph at last.
320 Take your place, then, with pride and pleasure
and move to the feast. To-morrow morning
our treasure will be shared and showered upon you."

JOHN MILTON   (1608–1674)

from **Paradise Lost, Book I**   (1667)

Of man's first disobedience, and the fruit
Of that forbidden tree, whose mortal taste
Brought death into the world, and all our woe,
With loss of Eden, till one greater Man
5   Restore us, and regain the blissful seat,
Sing Heav'nly Muse, that on the secret top
Of Oreb, or of Sinai, didst inspire
That shepherd,[1] who first taught the chosen seed,
In the beginning how the heav'ns and earth
10 Rose out of chaos: or if Sion hill
Delight thee more, and Siloa's brook that flowed
Fast by the oracle of God,[2] I thence
Invoke thy aid to my advent'rous song,
That with no middle flight intends to soar
15 Above th' Aonian mount,[3] while it pursues
Things unattempted yet in prose or rhyme.
And chiefly thou O Spirit, that dost prefer
Before all temples th' upright heart and pure,
Instruct me, for thou know'st; thou from the first
20 Wast present, and with mighty wings outspread
Dove-like sat'st brooding on the vast abyss
And mad'st it pregnant: what in me is dark
Illumine, what is low raise and support;

---

[1] **Sing . . . shepherd:** Following the tradition of epic poetry, Milton invokes the aid of a muse before beginning his story. Unlike his predecessors, however, Milton's muse springs from the Judeo-Christian tradition, the same Muse who inspired Moses when he received the ten commandments on Mount Horeb or Mount Sinai.
[2] **Sion . . . God:** By referring to Mount Zion in Jerusalem, near Siloa's brook, Milton associates his Muse with the nine Greek Muses who preferred to dwell on mountains with nearby waterways.
[3] **Aonian mount:** Mount Helicon, residence of the Greek Muses.

That to the highth of this great argument
25 I may assert Eternal Providence,
And justify the ways of God to men.

JOHN MILTON (1608–1674)

from **Paradise Lost, Book II** (1667)

High on a throne of royal state, which far
Outshone the wealth of Ormus and of Ind,[1]
Or where the gorgeous East with richest hand
Show'rs on her kings barbaric pearl and gold,
5   Satan exalted sat, by merit raised
To that bad eminence; and from despair
Thus high uplifted beyond hope, aspires
Beyond thus high, insatiate to pursue
Vain war with Heav'n, and by success° untaught   outcome
10 His proud imaginations thus displayed.
    "Powers and Dominions, deities of heaven,
For since no deep within her gulf can hold
Immortal vigor, though oppressed and fall'n,
I give not heav'n for lost. From this descent
15 Celestial Virtues rising, will appear
More glorious and more dread than from no fall,
And trust themselves to fear no second fate:
Me though just right, and the fixed laws of heav'n
Did first create your leader, next, free choice,
20 With what besides, in counsel or in fight,
Hath been achieved of merit, yet this loss
Thus far at least recovered, hath much more
Established in a safe unenvied throne
Yielded with full consent. The happier state
25 In heaven, which follows dignity, might draw
Envy from each inferior; but who here
Will envy whom the highest place exposes
Foremost to stand against the thunderer's aim
Your bulwark, and condemns to greatest share
30 Of endless pain? Where there is then no good
For which to strive, no strife can grow up there
From faction; for none sure will claim in hell
Precédence, none, whose portion is so small

[1] **Ormus and of Ind:** Hormuz, a wealthy trading town at the mouth of the Persian Gulf, and India.

Of present pain, that with ambitious mind
35   Will covet more. With this advantage then
To union, and firm faith, and firm accord,
More than can be in heav'n, we now return
To claim our just inheritance of old,
Surer to prosper than prosperity
40   Could have assured us; and by what best way,
Whether of open war or covert guile,
We now debate; who can advise, may speak."
    He ceas'd, and next him Moloch, sceptered king
Stood up, the strongest and the fiercest Spirit
45   That fought in heav'n; now fiercer by despair:
His trust was with th' Eternal to be deemed
Equal in strength, and rather than be less
Cared not to be at all; with that care lost
Went all his fear: of God, or hell, or worse
50   He recked° not, and these words thereafter spake.   took heed
    "My sentence° is for open war: of wiles,   opinion
More unexpert, I boast not: them let those
Contrive who need, or when they need, not now.
For while they sit contriving, shall the rest,
55   Millions that stand in arms, and longing wait
The signal to ascend, sit lingering here
Heav'n's fugitives, and for their dwelling-place
Accept this dark opprobrious den of shame,
The prison of his tyranny who reigns
60   By our delay? No, let us rather choose
Armed with hell flames and fury all at once
O'er heav'n's high tow'rs to force resistless way,
Turning our tortures into horrid arms
Against the torturer; when to meet the noise
65   Of his almighty engine he shall hear
Infernal thunder, and for lightning see
Black fire and horror shot with equal rage
Among his angels; and his throne itself
Mixed with Tartarean² sulfur, and strange fire,
70   His own invented torments. But perhaps
The way seems difficult and steep to scale
With upright wing against a higher foe.
Let such bethink them, if the sleepy drench
Of that forgetful lake³ benumb not still,
75   That in our proper motion we ascend

---

² **Tartarean:** Tartarean is derived from Tartarus, a place of torment where the most guilty are punished in Hades.
³ **forgetful lake:** The River Lethe in Hades, whose waters move the dead to forget their life on earth.

Up to our native seat: descent and fall
To us is adverse. Who but felt of late
When the fierce foe hung on our broken rear
Insulting, and pursued us through the deep,
80   With what compulsion and laborious flight
We sunk thus low? Th' ascent is easy then;
Th' event° is feared; should we again provoke   outcome
Our stronger, some worse way his wrath may find
To our destruction: if there be in hell
85   Fear to be worse destroyed: what can be worse
Than to dwell here, driven out from bliss, condemned
In this abhorrèd deep to utter woe;
Where pain of unextinguishable fire
Must exercise us without hope of end
90   The vassals° of his anger, when the scourge   slaves
Inexorably, and the torturing hour
Calls us to penance? More destroyed than thus
We should be quite abolished and expire.
What fear we then? What doubt we to incense
95   His utmost ire? which to the highth enraged,
Will either quite consume us, and reduce
To nothing this essential,° happier far   essence
Than miserable to have eternal being:
Or if our substance be indeed divine,
100   And cannot cease to be, we are at worst
On this side nothing; and by proof we feel
Our power sufficient to disturb his heav'n,
And with perpetual inroads to alarm,
Though inaccessible, his fatal throne:
105   Which if not victory is yet revenge."
    He ended frowning, and his look denounced
Desperate revenge, and battle dangerous
To less than gods. On th' other side up rose
Belial, in act more graceful and humane;
110   A fairer person lost not heav'n; he seemed
For dignity composed and high exploit:
But all was false and hollow; though his tongue
Dropped manna, and could make the worse appear
The better reason, to perplex and dash
115   Maturest counsels: for his thoughts were low;
To vice industrious, but to nobler deeds
Timorous and slothful: yet he pleased the ear,
And with persuasive accent thus began.
    "I should be much for open war, O Peers,
120   As not behind in hate; if what was urged
Main reason to persuade immediate war,

Did not dissuade me most, and seem to cast
Ominous conjecture on the whole success:
When he who most excels in fact of arms,
125   In what he counsels and in what excels
Mistrustful, grounds his courage on despair
And utter dissolution, as the scope
Of all his aim, after some dire revenge.
First, what revenge? The tow'rs of heav'n are filled
130   With armèd watch, that render all access
Impregnable; oft on the bordering deep
Encamp their legions, or with óbscure wing
Scout far and wide into the realm of Night,
Scorning surprise. Or could we break our way
135   By force, and at our heels all hell should rise
With blackest insurrection, to confound
Heav'n's purest light, yet our great enemy
All incorruptible would on his throne
Sit unpolluted, and th' ethereal mold[4]
140   Incapable of stain would soon expel
Her mischief, and purge off the baser fire
Victorious. Thus repulsed, our final hope
Is flat despair: we must exasperate
Th' almighty victor to spend all his rage,
145   And that must end us, that must be our cure,
To be no more; sad cure; for who would lose,
Though full of pain, this intellectual being,
Those thoughts that wander[5] through eternity,
To perish rather, swallowed up and lost
150   In the wide womb of uncreated night,
Devoid of sense and motion? And who knows,
Let this be good, whether our angry foe
Can give it, or will ever? How he can
Is doubtful; that he never will is sure.
155   Will he, so wise, let loose at once his ire,
Belike through impotence, or unaware,
To give his enemies their wish, and end
Them in his anger, whom his anger saves
To punish endless? 'Wherefore cease we then?'
160   Say they who counsel war, 'We are decreed,
Reserved and destined to eternal woe;
Whatever doing, what can we suffer more,
What can we suffer worse?' Is this then worst,

---

[4] **ethereal mold:** Heavenly substance, i.e., celestial fire.
[5] **wander:** By using *wander,* a word that also means "to stray" or "err," Milton portrays Belial as inadvertently ironic.

Thus sitting, thus consulting, thus in arms?
165 What when we fled amain,° pursued and strook   with full speed
With Heav'n's afflicting thunder, and besought
The deep to shelter us? This hell then seemed
A refuge from those wounds: or when we lay
Chained on the burning lake? That sure was worse.
170 What if the breath that kindled those grim fires
Awaked should blow them into sevenfold rage
And plunge us in the flames? Or from above
Should intermitted° vengeance arm again   suspended
His red right hand[6] to plague us? What if all
175 Her stores were opened, and this firmament
Of hell should spout her cataracts of fire,
Impendent horrors, threat'ning hideous fall
One day upon our heads; while we perhaps
Designing or exhorting glorious war,
180 Caught in a fiery tempest shall be hurled
Each on his rock transfixed, the sport and prey
Of racking whirlwinds, or for ever sunk
Under yon boiling ocean, wrapped in chains;
There to converse with everlasting groans,
185 Unrespited, unpitied, unreprieved,
Ages of hopeless end; this would be worse.
War therefore, open or concealed, alike
My voice dissuades; for what can force or guile
With him, or who deceive his mind, whose eye
190 Views all things at one view? He from heav'n's highth
All these our motions vain, sees and derides;
Not more almighty to resist our might
Than wise to frustrate all our plots and wiles.
Shall we then live thus vile, the race of heav'n
195 Thus trampled, thus expelled to suffer here
Chains and these torments? Better these than worse
By my advice; since fate inevitable
Subdues us, and omnipotent decree,
The victor's will. To suffer, as to do,
200 Our strength is equal,[7] nor the law unjust
That so ordains: this was at first resolved,
If we were wise, against so great a foe
Contending, and so doubtful what might fall.
I laugh, when those who at the spear are bold

---

[6] **red right hand:** The Roman lyric poet Horace refers to Jupiter, who throws thunderbolts, as having a
"red right hand."
[7] **To suffer . . . equal:** In other words, we are able to withstand as much suffering as we are able to
inflict.

²⁰⁵   And vent'rous, if that fail them, shrink and fear
        What yet they know must follow, to endure
        Exile, or ignominy, or bonds, or pain,
        The sentence of their conqueror: This is now
        Our doom; which if we can sustain and bear,
²¹⁰   Our Súpreme foe in time may much remit
        His anger, and perhaps thus far removed
        Not mind us not offending, satisfied
        With what is punished; whence these raging fires
        Will slacken, if his breath stir not their flames.
²¹⁵   Our purer essence then will overcome
        Their noxious vapor, or inured° not feel,   used to
        Or changed at length, and to the place conformed
        In temper and in nature, will receive
        Familiar the fierce heat, and void of pain;
²²⁰   This horror will grow mild, this darkness light,
        Besides what hope the never-ending flight
        Of future days may bring, what chance, what change
        Worth waiting, since our present lot appears
        For happy[8] though but ill, but ill not worst,
²²⁵   If we procure not to ourselves more woe."
            Thus Belial with words clothed in reason's garb
        Counseled ignoble ease, and peaceful sloth,
        Not peace: and after him thus Mammon spake.
            "Either to disenthrone the King of heav'n
²³⁰   We war, if war be best, or to regain
        Our own right lost: him to unthrone we then
        May hope when everlasting fate shall yield
        To fickle chance, and Chaos judge the strife:
        The former vain to hope argues as vain
²³⁵   The latter: for what place can be for us
        Within heav'n's bound, unless heav'n's Lord supreme
        We overpower? Suppose he should relent
        And publish grace to all, on promise made
        Of new subjection; with what eyes could we
²⁴⁰   Stand in his presence humble, and receive
        Strict laws imposed, to celebrate his throne
        With warbled hymns, and to his Godhead sing
        Forced hallelujahs;° while he lordly sits   songs of praise
        Our envied Sovran, and his altar breathes
²⁴⁵   Ambrosial° odors and ambrosial flowers,   worthy of the gods
        Our servile offerings. This must be our task
        In heav'n, this our delight; how wearisome

---

[8] **for happy:** In other words, from the perspective of happiness.

Eternity so spent in worship paid
To whom we hate. Let us not then pursue
250 By force impossible, by leave obtained
Unácceptable, though in heav'n, our state
Of splendid vassalage, but rather seek
Our own good from ourselves, and from our own
Live to ourselves, though in this vast recess,
255 Free, and to none accountable, preferring
Hard liberty before the easy yoke
Of servile pomp. Our greatness will appear
Then most conspicuous, when great things of small,
Useful of hurtful, prosperous of adverse
260 We can create, and in what place soe'er
Thrive under evil, and work ease out of pain
Through labor and endurance. This deep world
Of darkness do we dread? How oft amidst
Thick clouds and dark doth heav'n's all-ruling Sire
265 Choose to reside, his glory unobscured,
And with the majesty of darkness round
Covers his throne; from whence deep thunders roar
Must'ring their rage, and heav'n resembles hell?
As he our darkness, cannot we his light
270 Imitate when we please? This desert soil
Wants° not her hidden luster, gems and gold;   lacks
Nor want we skill or art, from whence to raise
Magnificence; and what can heav'n show more?
Our torments also may in length of time
275 Become our elements, these piercing fires
As soft as now severe, our temper changed
Into their temper; which must needs remove
The sensible° of pain. All things invite   physical part
To peaceful counsels, and the settled state
280 Of order, how in safety best we may
Compose our present evils,° with regard   misfortunes
Of what we are and where, dismissing quite
All thoughts of war: ye have what I advise."
  He scarce had finished, when such murmur filled
285 Th' assembly, as when hollow rocks retain
The sound of blust'ring winds, which all night long
Had roused the sea, now with hoarse cadence lull
Seafaring men o'erwatched, whose bark° by chance   ship
Or pinnace° anchors in a craggy bay   boat
290 After the tempest: such applause was heard
As Mammon ended, and his sentence pleased,
Advising peace: for such another field
They dreaded worse than hell: so much the fear

Of thunder and the sword of Michaël[9]

295 Wrought still within them; and no less desire
     To found this nether empire, which might rise
     By policy, and long process of time,
     In emulation opposite to heav'n.
     Which then Beëlzebub perceived, than whom,

300 Satan except, none higher sat, with grave
     Aspect he rose, and in his rising seemed
     A pillar of state; deep on his front° engraven   face
     Deliberation sat and public care;
     And princely counsel in his face yet shone,

305 Majestic though in ruin: sage he stood
     With Atlantean shoulders fit to bear
     The weight of mightiest monarchies,[10] his look
     Drew audience and attention still as night
     Or summer's noontide air, while thus he spake.

310   "Thrones and imperial Powers, offspring of heav'n,
     Ethereal Virtues; or these titles now
     Must we renounce, and changing style be called
     Princes of hell? for so the popular vote
     Inclines, here to continue, and build up here

315 A growing empire; doubtless; while we dream,
     And know not that the King of heav'n hath doomed
     This place our dungeon, not our safe retreat
     Beyond his potent arm, to live exempt
     From Heav'n's high jurisdiction, in new league

320 Banded against his throne, but to remain
     In strictest bondage, though thus far removed,
     Under th' inevitable curb, reserved
     His captive multitude: for he, be sure,
     In highth or depth, still first and last will reign

325 Sole king, and of his kingdom lose no part
     By our revolt, but over hell extend
     His empire, and with iron scepter rule
     Us here, as with his golden those in heav'n.
     What sit we then projecting peace and war?

330 War hath determined° us, and foiled with loss   put an end to
     Irreparable; terms of peace yet none
     Vouchsafed or sought; for what peace will be giv'n
     To us enslaved, but custody severe,
     And stripes, and arbitrary punishment

335 Inflicted? And what peace can we return,

---

[9] **Michaël:** An archangel who is loyal to God and an enemy of Satan.
[10] **Atlantean . . . monarchies:** In Greek mythology, a Titan whose punishment after leading an unsuccessful revolt was to carry the heavens upon his shoulders.

But to° our power hostility and hate,   to the extreme of
Untamed reluctance, and revenge though slow,
Yet ever plotting how the conqueror least
May reap his conquest, and may least rejoice
340   In doing what we most in suffering feel?
Nor will occasion want,° nor shall we need   be lacking
With dangerous expedition to invade
Heav'n, whose high walls fear no assault or siege,
Or ambush from the deep. What if we find
345   Some easier enterprise? There is a place
(If ancient and prophetic fame° in heav'n   rumor
Err not) another world, the happy seat
Of some new race called Man, about this time
To be created like to us, though less
350   In power and excellence, but favored more
Of him who rules above; so was his will
Pronounced among the gods, and by an oath,
That shook heav'n's whole circumference, confirmed.
Thither let us bend all our thoughts, to learn
355   What creatures there inhabit, of what mold,
Or substance, how endued,° and what their power,   gifted
And where their weakness, how attempted° best,   tempted
By force or subtlety: though heav'n be shut,
And heav'n's high arbitrator sit secure
360   In his own strength, this place may lie exposed
The utmost border of his kingdom, left
To their defense who hold it: here perhaps
Some advantageous act may be achieved
By sudden onset, either with hell fire
365   To waste his whole creation, or possess
All as our own, and drive as we were driven,
The puny° habitants, or if not drive,   created later
Seduce them to our party, that their God
May prove their foe, and with repenting hand
370   Abolish his own works. This would surpass
Common revenge, and interrupt his joy
In our confusion, and our joy upraise
In his disturbance; when his darling sons
Hurled headlong to partake with us, shall curse
375   Their frail original,[11] and faded bliss,
Faded so soon. Advise if this be worth
Attempting, or to sit in darkness here
Hatching vain empires." Thus Beëlzebub

---

[11] **Their frail original:** Likely refers to Adam, the first man.

Pleaded his devilish counsel, first devised
380 By Satan, and in part proposed: for whence,
But from the author of all ill could spring
So deep a malice, to confound° the race   spoil
Of mankind in one root, and earth with hell
To mingle and involve, done all to spite
385 The great Creator? But their spite still serves
His glory to augment. The bold design
Pleased highly those infernal States,° and joy   statesmen
Sparkled in all their eyes; with full assent
They vote: whereat his speech he thus renews.
390   "Well have ye judged, well ended long debate,
Synod of gods, and like to what ye are,
Great things resolved, which from the lowest deep
Will once more lift us up, in spite of fate,
Nearer our ancient seat; perhaps in view
395 Of those bright confines, whence with neighboring arms
And opportune excursion we may chance
Re-enter heav'n; or else in some mild zone
Dwell not unvisited of heav'n's fair light
Secure, and at the bright'ning orient beam
400 Purge off this gloom; the soft delicious air,
To heal the scar of these corrosive fires
Shall breathe her balm.

ALEXANDER POPE (1688–1744)

The Rape of the Lock (1712)
An Heroi-Comical Poem[1]

> Nolueram, Belinda, tuos violare capillos; sed juvat hoc precibus
> me tribuisse tuis.[2]
>
> —MARTIAL

Canto I

What dire offense from amorous causes springs,
What mighty contests rise from trivial things,

---

[1] **An Heroi-Comical Poem:** John Caryll asked his friend Alexander Pope to write this mock-epic
poem after Lord Petre, Caryll's relative, casually cut off a lock of Miss Arabella Fermor's hair. The theft
of the lock in 1711 initiated a family feud, and Caryll hoped that Pope's poetical jest might ease the
tensions between the two families.
[2] **Nolueram . . . tuis:** From Latin: "I did not want, Belinda, to violate your locks, but it pleases me to
have paid this tribute to your prayers."

I sing—This verse to Caryll, Muse! is due:
This, even Belinda may vouchsafe to view:
5 Slight is the subject, but not so the praise,
If she inspire, and he approve my lays.
  Say what strange motive, Goddess! could compel
A well-bred lord to assault a gentle belle?
Oh, say what stranger cause, yet unexplored,
10 Could make a gentle belle reject a lord?
In tasks so bold can little men engage,
And in soft bosoms dwells such mighty rage?
  Sol through white curtains shot a timorous ray,
And oped those eyes that must eclipse the day.
15 Now lapdogs give themselves the rousing shake,
And sleepless lovers just at twelve awake:
Thrice rung the bell,³ the slipper knocked the ground,
And the pressed watch returned a silver sound.
Belinda still her downy pillow pressed,
20 Her guardian Sylph⁴ prolonged the balmy rest:
'Twas he had summoned to her silent bed
The morning dream that hovered o'er her head.
A youth more glittering than a birthnight beau⁵
(That even in slumber caused her cheek to glow)
25 Seemed to her ear his winning lips to lay,
And thus in whispers said, or seemed to say:
  "Fairest of mortals, thou distinguished care
Of thousand bright inhabitants of air!
If e'er one vision touched thy infant thought,
30 Of all the nurse and all the priest have taught,
Of airy elves by moonlight shadows seen,
The silver token, and the circled green,⁶
Or virgins visited by angel powers,
With golden crowns and wreaths of heavenly flowers,
35 Hear and believe! thy own importance know,
Nor bound thy narrow views to things below.
Some secret truths, from learned pride concealed,
To maids alone and children are revealed:
What though no credit doubting wits may give?
40 The fair and innocent shall still believe.
Know, then, unnumbered spirits round thee fly,
The light militia of the lower sky:

---

³ **Thrice . . . bell:** Belinda's call to her maid employs the triple repetition commonly present in epic poetry.
⁴ **Sylph:** A spirit of the air.
⁵ **birthnight beau:** Attendant dressed for a royal birthday extravaganza.
⁶ **silver . . . green:** The silver token is a coin left behind by fairies or elves, and a circled green is a circle of dark grass supposedly left behind where fairies have danced.

These, though unseen, are ever on the wing,
Hang o'er the box, and hover round the Ring.[7]
45 Think what an equipage thou hast in air,
And view with scorn two pages and a chair.
As now your own, our beings were of old,
And once enclosed in woman's beauteous mold;
Thence, by a soft transition, we repair
50 From earthly vehicles to these of air.
Think not, when woman's transient breath is fled,
That all her vanities at once are dead:
Succeeding vanities she still regards,
And though she plays no more, o'erlooks the cards.
55 Her joy in gilded chariots,° when alive,   carriages
And love of ombre,° after death survive.   a card game
For when the Fair in all their pride expire,
To their first elements their souls retire:[8]
The sprites of fiery termagants in flame
60 Mount up, and take a Salamander's name.
Soft yielding minds to water glide away,
And sip, with Nymphs, their elemental tea.
The graver prude sinks downward to a Gnome,
In search of mischief still on earth to roam.
65 The light coquettes in Sylphs aloft repair,
And sport and flutter in the fields of air.
    "Know further yet; whoever fair and chaste
Rejects mankind, is by some Sylph embraced:
For spirits, freed from mortal laws, with ease
70 Assume what sexes and what shapes they please.
What guards the purity of melting maids,
In courtly balls, and midnight masquerades,
Safe from the treacherous friend, the daring spark,
The glance by day, the whisper in the dark,
75 When kind occasion prompts their warm desires,
When music softens, and when dancing fires?
'Tis but their Sylph, the wise Celestials know,
Though Honor is the word with men below.
    "Some nymphs[9] there are, too conscious of their face,
80 For life predestined to the Gnomes' embrace.
These swell their prospects and exalt their pride,
When offers are disdained, and love denied:

---

[7] **Hang . . . Ring:** Here, the box is a theater box, and the Ring is a circular driveway in London's Hyde
Park, often visited by fashionable women.
[8] **first . . . retire:** The four elements suggested by the Rosicrucian myths from which Pope borrows
part of his cosmology: fire, water, earth, and air.
[9] **nymphs:** Here used in the sense of maidens.

Then gay ideas crowd the vacant brain,
While peers, and dukes, and all their sweeping train,
85   And garters, stars, and coronets[10] appear,
And in soft sounds, 'your Grace' salutes their ear.
'Tis these that early taint the female soul,
Instruct the eyes of young coquettes to roll,
Teach infant cheeks a bidden blush to know,
90   And little hearts to flutter at a beau.
   "Oft, when the world imagine women stray,
The Sylphs through mystic mazes guide their way,
Through all the giddy circle they pursue,
And old impertinence expel by new.
95   What tender maid but must a victim fall
To one man's treat, but for another's ball?
When Florio speaks what virgin could withstand,
If gentle Damon did not squeeze her hand?
With varying vanities, from every part,
100   They shift the moving toyshop of their heart;
Where wigs with wigs, with sword-knots sword-knots strive,[11]
Beaux banish beaux, and coaches coaches drive.
This erring mortals levity may call;
Oh, blind to truth! the Sylphs contrive it all.
105   "Of these am I, who thy protection claim,
A watchful sprite, and Ariel is my name.
Late, as I ranged the crystal wilds of air,
In the clear mirror of thy ruling star
I saw, alas! some dread event impend,
110   Ere to the main this morning sun descend,
But Heaven reveals not what, or how, or where:
Warned by the Sylph, O pious maid, beware!
This to disclose is all thy guardian can:
Beware of all, but most beware of Man!"
115   He said; when Shock,[12] who thought she slept too long,
Leaped up, and waked his mistress with his tongue.
'Twas then, Belinda, if report say true
Thy eyes first opened on a billet-doux;°   love letter
Wounds, charms, and ardors were no sooner read,
120   But all the vision vanished from thy head.
   And now, unveiled, the toilet stands displayed,
Each silver vase in mystic order laid.
First, robed in white, the nymph intent adores,
With head uncovered, the cosmetic powers.

---

[10] **garters . . . coronets:** Symbols of court standing and rank.
[11] **sword-knots:** Ribbons tied to the hilt of a sword.
[12] **Shock:** A small, furry lapdog; Pope employs a pun on the usual meaning of the word.

125 A heavenly image in the glass appears,[13]
To that she bends, to that her eyes she rears.
The inferior priestess, at her altar's side,
Trembling begins the sacred rites of pride.
Unnumbered treasures ope at once, and here
130 The various offerings of the world appear;
From each she nicely culls with curious toil,
And decks the goddess with the glittering spoil.
This casket India's glowing gems unlocks,
And all Arabia breathes from yonder box.
135 The tortoise here and elephant unite,
Transformed to combs, the speckled and the white.
Here files of pins extend their shining rows,
Puffs, powders, patches, Bibles, billet-doux.
Now awful Beauty put on all its arms;
140 The fair each moment rises in her charms,
Repairs her smiles, awakens every grace,
And calls forth all the wonders of her face;
Sees by degrees a purer blush arise,
And keener lightnings quicken in her eyes.
145 The busy Sylphs surround their darling care,
These set the head, and those divide the hair,
Some fold the sleeve, whilst others plait the gown;
And Betty's praised for labors not her own.

Canto II

Not with more glories, in the ethereal plain,
The sun first rises o'er the purpled main,
Than, issuing forth, the rival of his beams[14]
Launched on the bosom of the silver Thames.
5 Fair nymphs and well-dressed youths around her shone,
But every eye was fixed on her alone.
On her white breast a sparkling cross she wore,
Which Jews might kiss, and infidels adore.
Her lively looks a sprightly mind disclose,
10 Quick as her eyes, and as unfixed as those:
Favors to none, to all she smiles extends;
Oft she rejects, but never once offends.
Bright as the sun, her eyes the gazers strike,
And, like the sun, they shine on all alike.
15 Yet graceful ease, and sweetness void of pride,

---

[13] **A heavenly . . . appears:** The following scene parallels a ritual where Belinda's image in the glass becomes an object of worship, with Betty (the maid) as an "inferior priestess." The scene is also suggestive of an epic hero preparing for battle.
[14] **the rival of his beams:** Belinda travels on the river Thames from London to Hampton Court.

Might hide her faults, if belles had faults to hide:
If to her share some female errors fall,
Look on her face, and you'll forget 'em all.
  This nymph, to the destruction of mankind,
20 Nourished two locks which graceful hung behind
In equal curls, and well conspired to deck
With shining ringlets the smooth ivory neck.
Love in these labyrinths his slaves detains,
And mighty hearts are held in slender chains.
25 With hairy springes° we the birds betray,   traps
Slight lines of hair surprise the finny prey,
Fair tresses man's imperial race ensnare,
And beauty draws us with a single hair.
  The adventurous Baron the bright locks admired,
30 He saw, he wished, and to the prize aspired.
Resolved to win, he meditates the way,
By force to ravish, or by fraud betray;
For when success a lover's toil attends,
Few ask if fraud or force attained his ends.
35 For this, ere Phoebus[15] rose, he had implored
Propitious Heaven, and every power adored,
But chiefly Love—to Love an altar built,
Of twelve vast French romances, neatly gilt.
There lay three garters, half a pair of gloves,
40 And all the trophies of his former loves.
With tender billet-doux he lights the pyre,
And breathes three amorous sighs to raise the fire.
Then prostrate falls, and begs with ardent eyes
Soon to obtain, and long possess the prize:
45 The powers gave ear, and granted half his prayer,
The rest the winds dispersed in empty air.
  But now secure the painted vessel glides,
The sunbeams trembling on the floating tides,
While melting music steals upon the sky,
50 And softened sounds along the waters die.
Smooth flow the waves, the zephyrs gently play,
Belinda smiled, and all the world was gay.
All but the Sylph—with careful thoughts oppressed,
The impending woe sat heavy on his breast.
55 He summons straight his denizens° of air;   inhabitants
The lucid squadrons round the sails repair:
Soft o'er the shrouds aërial whispers breathe
That seemed but zephyrs to the train beneath.

---

[15] **Phoebus:** In Greek mythology, Apollo, god of the sun.

Some to the sun their insect-wings unfold,
60   Waft on the breeze, or sink in clouds of gold.
Transparent forms too fine for mortal sight,
Their fluid bodies half dissolved in light,
Loose to the wind their airy garments flew,
Thin glittering textures of the filmy dew,
65   Dipped in the richest tincture of the skies,
Where light disports in ever-mingling dyes,
While every beam new transient colors flings,
Colors that change whene'er they wave their wings.
Amid the circle, on the gilded mast,
70   Superior by the head was Ariel placed;
His purple pinions opening to the sun,
He raised his azure wand, and thus begun:
   "Ye Sylphs and Sylphids, to your chief give ear!¹⁶
Fays, Fairies, Genii, Elves, and Daemons, hear!
75   Ye know the spheres and various tasks assigned
By laws eternal to the aërial kind.
Some in the fields of purest ether play,
And bask and whiten in the blaze of day.
Some guide the course of wandering orbs on high,
80   Or roll the planets through the boundless sky.
Some less refined, beneath the moon's pale light
Pursue the stars that shoot athwart the night,
Or suck the mists in grosser air below,
Or dip their pinions in the painted bow,°   rainbow
85   Or brew fierce tempests on the wintry main,
Or o'er the glebe° distill the kindly rain.   land
Others on earth o'er human race preside,
Watch all their ways, and all their actions guide:
Of these the chief the care of nations own,
90   And guard with arms divine the British Throne.
   "Our humbler province is to tend the Fair,
Not a less pleasing, though less glorious care:
To save the powder from too rude a gale,
Nor let the imprisoned essences exhale;
95   To draw fresh colors from the vernal flowers;
To steal from rainbows e'er they drop in showers
A brighter wash; to curl their waving hairs,
Assist their blushes, and inspire their airs;
Nay oft, in dreams invention we bestow,
100   To change a flounce, or add a furbelow.°   decorative pleat
   "This day black omens threat the brightest fair,

---

¹⁶ **Ye Sylphs . . . ear:** A sylphid is a female air spirit. In this address, Pope parodies Satan's addresses
in Milton's *Paradise Lost.*

That e'er deserved a watchful spirit's care;
Some dire disaster, or by force or slight,
But what, or where, the Fates have wrapped in night:
105 Whether the nymph shall break Diana's law,[17]
Or some frail china jar receive a flaw,
Or stain her honor or her new brocade,
Forget her prayers, or miss a masquerade,
Or lose her heart, or necklace, at a ball;
110 Or whether Heaven has doomed that Shock must fall.
Haste, then, ye spirits! to your charge repair:
The fluttering fan be Zephyretta's care;
The drops° to thee, Brillante, we consign;   earrings
And, Momentilla, let the watch be thine;
115 Do thou, Crispissa,[18] tend her favorite Lock;
Ariel himself shall be the guard of Shock.
    "To fifty chosen Sylphs, of special note,
We trust the important charge, the petticoat;
Oft have we known that sevenfold fence to fail,
120 Though stiff with hoops, and armed with ribs of whale.
Form a strong line about the silver bound,
And guard the wide circumference around.
    "Whatever spirit, careless of his charge,
His post neglects, or leaves the fair at large,
125 Shall feel sharp vengeance soon o'ertake his sins,
Be stopped in vials, or transfixed with pins,
Or plunged in lakes of bitter washes lie,
Or wedged whole ages in a bodkin's eye;
Gums and pomatums shall his flight restrain,
130 While clogged he beats his silken wings in vain,
Or alum styptics with contracting power
Shrink his thin essence like a riveled° flower: wrinkled
Or, as Ixion[19] fixed, the wretch shall feel
The giddy motion of the whirling mill,°   cocoa mill
135 In fumes of burning chocolate shall glow,
And tremble at the sea that froths below!"
    He spoke; the spirits from the sails descend;
Some, orb in orb, around the nymph extend;
Some thread the mazy ringlets of her hair;
140 Some hang upon the pendants of her ear:
With beating hearts the dire event they wait,
Anxious, and trembling for the birth of Fate.

---

[17] **Diana's law:** Diana was the Roman goddess of chastity and the moon.
[18] **Crispissa:** To "crisp" is to curl one's hair.
[19] **Ixion:** As punishment in Hades, Ixion was tied to a constantly spinning, fiery wheel.

Canto III

Close by those meads, forever crowned with flowers,
Where Thames with pride surveys his rising towers,
There stands a structure of majestic frame,[20]
Which from the neighboring Hampton takes its name.
5   Here Britain's statesmen oft the fall foredoom
Of foreign tyrants and of nymphs at home;
Here thou, great Anna! whom three realms obey,
Dost sometimes counsel take—and sometimes tea.
   Hither the heroes and the nymphs resort,
10   To taste awhile the pleasures of a court;
In various talk the instructive hours they passed,
Who gave the ball, or paid the visit last;
One speaks the glory of the British Queen,
And one describes a charming Indian screen;
15   A third interprets motions, looks, and eyes;
At every word a reputation dies.
Snuff, or the fan, supply each pause of chat,
With singing, laughing, ogling, and all that.
   Meanwhile, declining from the noon of day,
20   The sun obliquely shoots his burning ray;
The hungry judges soon the sentence sign,
And wretches hang that jurymen may dine;
The merchant from the Exchange° returns in peace,   stock market
And the long labors of the toilet cease.
25   Belinda now, whom thirst of fame invites,
Burns to encounter two adventurous knights,
At ombre[21] singly to decide their doom,
And swells her breast with conquests yet to come.
Straight the three bands prepare in arms to join,
30   Each band the number of the sacred nine.
Soon as she spreads her hand, the aërial guard
Descend, and sit on each important card:
First Ariel perched upon a Matadore,
Then each according to the rank they bore;
35   For Sylphs, yet mindful of their ancient race,
Are, as when women, wondrous fond of place.
   Behold, four Kings in majesty revered,
With hoary whiskers and a forky beard;
And four fair Queens whose hands sustain a flower,
40   The expressive emblem of their softer power;

---

[20] **structure . . . frame:** Hampton Court, one of Queen Anne's palaces.
[21] **ombre:** A card game, resembling a combination of three-handed bridge and poker. Lines 27–100 narrate Belinda's game against the Baron in mock-epic style.

Four Knaves in garbs succinct, a trusty band,
Caps on their heads, and halberts° in their hand;   weapons
And parti-colored troops, a shining train,
Draw forth to combat on the velvet plain.
45   The skillful nymph reviews her force with care;
"Let Spades be trumps!" she said, and trumps they were
    Now move to war her sable Matadores,
In show like leaders of the swarthy Moors.
Spadillio first, unconquerable lord!
50   Led off two captive trumps, and swept the board.
As many more Manillio forced to yield,
And marched a victor from the verdant field.
Him Basto followed, but his fate more hard
Gained but one trump and one plebeian card.
55   With his broad saber next, a chief in years,
The hoary Majesty of Spades appears,
Puts forth one manly leg, to sight revealed,
The rest his many-colored robe concealed.
The rebel Knave,° who dares his prince engage,   jack
60   Proves the just victim of his royal rage.
Even mighty Pam, that kings and queens o'erthrew
And mowed down armies in the fights of loo,
Sad chance of war! now destitute of aid,
Falls undistinguished by the victor Spade.
65   Thus far both armies to Belinda yield;
Now to the Baron fate inclines the field.
His warlike amazon her host invades,
The imperial consort of the crown of Spades.
The Club's black tyrant first her victim died,
70   Spite of his haughty mien and barbarous pride.
What boots the regal circle on his head,
His giant limbs, in state unwieldy spread?
That long behind he trails his pompous robe.
And of all monarchs only grasps the globe?
75   The Baron now his Diamonds pours apace;
The embroidered King who shows but half his face,
And his refulgent Queen, with powers combined
Of broken troops an easy conquest find.
Clubs, Diamonds, Hearts, in wild disorder seen,
80   With throngs promiscuous strew the level green.
Thus when dispersed a routed army runs,
Of Asia's troops, and Afric's sable sons,
With like confusion different nations fly,
Of various habit,° and of various dye,°   dress / color
85   The pierced battalions disunited fall
In heaps on heaps; one fate o'erwhelms them all.

    The Knave of Diamonds tries his wily arts,
And wins (oh, shameful chance!) the Queen of Hearts.
At this, the blood the virgin's cheek forsook,
90   A livid paleness spreads o'er all her look;
She sees, and trembles at the approaching ill,
Just in the jaws of ruin, and Codille,
And now (as oft in some distempered state)
On one nice trick depends the general fate.
95   An Ace of Hearts steps forth: the King unseen
Lurked in her hand, and mourned his captive Queen.
He springs to vengeance with an eager pace,
And falls like thunder on the prostrate Ace.
The nymph exulting fills with shouts the sky,
100   The walls, the woods, and long canals reply.
    O thoughtless mortals! ever blind to fate,
Too soon dejected, and too soon elate:
Sudden these honors shall be snatched away,
And cursed forever this victorious day.
105   For lo! the board with cups and spoons is crowned,
The berries crackle, and the mill turns round;[22]
On shining altars of Japan[23] they raise
The silver lamp; the fiery spirits blaze:
From silver spouts the grateful liquors glide,
110   While China's earth° receives the smoking tide.   China cups
At once they gratify their scent and taste,
And frequent cups prolong the rich repast.
Straight hover round the fair her airy band;
Some, as she sipped, the fuming liquor fanned,
115   Some o'er her lap their careful plumes displayed,
Trembling, and conscious of the rich brocade.
Coffee (which makes the politician wise,
And see through all things with his half-shut eyes)
Sent up in vapors to the Baron's brain
120   New stratagems, the radiant Lock to gain.
Ah, cease, rash youth! desist ere 'tis too late,
Fear the just Gods, and think of Scylla's fate![24]
Changed to a bird, and sent to flit in air,
She dearly pays for Nisus' injured hair!
125   But when to mischief mortals bend their will,
How soon they find fit instruments of ill!

---

[22] **The berries . . . round:** Coffee beans are roasted and ground.

[23] **On shining altars of Japan:** Black, glossy tables.

[24] **Scylla's fate:** In Greek mythology, Scylla promised her lover Minos that she would steal a lock of her father's hair upon which his life depended. For this offense, she was transformed into a seabird and pursued by her father in the shape of an eagle.

Just then, Clarissa drew with tempting grace
A two-edged weapon from her shining case:
So ladies in romance assist their knight,
130 Present the spear, and arm him for the fight.
He takes the gift with reverence, and extends
The little engine on his fingers' ends;
This just behind Belinda's neck he spread,
As o'er the fragrant steams she bends her head.
135 Swift to the Lock a thousand sprites repair,
A thousand wings, by turns, blow back the hair,
And thrice they twitched the diamond in her ear,
Thrice she looked back, and thrice the foe drew near.
Just in that instant, anxious Ariel sought
140 The close recesses of the virgin's thought;
As on the nosegay° in her breast reclined,   bouquet
He watched the ideas rising in her mind,
Sudden he viewed, in spite of all her art,
An earthly lover lurking at her heart.
145 Amazed, confused, he found his power expired,
Resigned to fate, and with a sigh retired.
    The Peer now spreads the glittering forfex° wide,   scissors
To enclose the Lock; now joins it, to divide.
Even then, before the fatal engine closed,
150 A wretched Sylph too fondly interposed;
Fate urged the shears, and cut the Sylph in twain
(But airy substance soon unites again):
The meeting points the sacred hair dissever
From the fair head, forever, and forever!
155   Then flashed the living lightning from her eyes,
And screams of horror rend the affrighted skies.
Not louder shrieks to pitying heaven are cast,
When husbands, or when lapdogs breathe their last;
Or when rich china vessels fallen from high,
160 In glittering dust and painted fragments lie!
"Let wreaths of triumph now my temples twine,"
The victor cried, "the glorious prize is mine!
While fish in streams, or birds delight in air,
Or in a coach and six the British Fair,
165 As long as *Atalantis*[25] shall be read,
Or the small pillow grace a lady's bed,
While visits shall be paid on solemn days,
When numerous wax-lights in bright order blaze,
While nymphs take treats, or assignations give,

---

[25] **Atalantis:** *The New Atlantis,* written by Mrs. Manley in 1709, contained an account of scandal in high life.

170 So long my honor, name, and praise shall live!
    What Time would spare, from Steel receives its date,°   end
    And monuments, like men, submit to fate!
    Steel could the labor of the Gods destroy,
    And strike to dust the imperial towers of Troy,[26]
175 Steel could the works of mortal pride confound,
    And hew triumphal arches to the ground.
    What wonder then, fair nymph! thy hairs should feel,
    The conquering force of unresisted Steel?"

Canto IV

    But anxious cares the pensive nymph oppressed,
    And secret passions labored in her breast.
    Not youthful kings in battle seized alive,
    Not scornful virgins who their charms survive,
5   Not ardent lovers robbed of all their bliss,
    Not ancient ladies when refused a kiss,
    Not tyrants fierce that unrepenting die,
    Not Cynthia when her manteau's° pinned awry,   cloak's
    E'er felt such rage, resentment, and despair,
10 As thou, sad virgin! for thy ravished hair.
       For, that sad moment, when the Sylphs withdrew
    And Ariel weeping from Belinda flew,
    Umbriel, a dusky, melancholy sprite
    As ever sullied the fair face of light,
15 Down to the central earth, his proper scene,
    Repaired to search the gloomy Cave of Spleen.[27]
       Swift on his sooty pinions flits the Gnome,
    And in a vapor reached the dismal dome.
    No cheerful breeze this sullen region knows,
20 The dreaded east is all the wind that blows.
    Here in a grotto, sheltered close from air,
    And screened in shades from day's detested glare,
    She sighs forever on her pensive bed,
    Pain at her side, and Megrim° at her head.   migraine
25   Two handmaids wait the throne: alike in place,
    But differing far in figure and in face.
    Here stood Ill-Nature like an ancient maid,
    Her wrinkled form in black and white arrayed;
    With store of prayers for mornings, nights, and noons,
30 Her hand is filled; her bosom with lampoons.°   ridicule
       There Affectation, with a sickly mien,

---

[26] **Steel could . . . Troy:** Troy was built by Apollo, god of the sun, and Posiedon, god of the sea.
[27] **Cave of Spleen:** In Elizabethan time, the spleen was the source of the fashionable disease melancholy, also known as the "vapors."

Shows in her cheek the roses of eighteen,
Practiced to lisp, and hang the head aside,
Faints into airs, and languishes with pride,
35   On the rich quilt sinks with becoming woe,
Wrapped in a gown, for sickness and for show.
The fair ones feel such maladies as these,
When each new nightdress gives a new disease.
   A constant vapor o'er the palace flies,
40   Strange phantoms rising as the mists arise;
Dreadful as hermit's dreams in haunted shades,
Or bright as visions of expiring maids.
Now glaring fiends, and snakes on rolling spires,°   spirals
Pale specters, gaping tombs, and purple fires;
45   Now lakes of liquid gold, Elysian scenes,
And crystal domes, and angels in machines.[28]
   Unnumbered throngs on every side are seen
Of bodies changed to various forms by Spleen.
Here living teapots stand, one arm held out,
50   One bent: the handle this, and that the spout:
A pipkin° there, like Homer's tripod, walks;   earthen pot
Here sighs a jar, and there a goose pie talks;
Men prove with child, as powerful fancy works,
And maids, turned bottles, call aloud for corks.
55   Safe passed the Gnome through this fantastic band,
A branch of healing spleenwort[29] in his hand.
Then thus addressed the Power: "Hail, wayward Queen!
Who rule the sex to fifty from fifteen:
Parent of vapors and of female wit,
60   Who give the hysteric or poetic fit,
On various tempers act by various ways,
Make some take physic,° others scribble plays;   medicine
Who cause the proud their visits to delay,
And send the godly in a pet to pray.
65   A nymph there is that all thy power disdains,
And thousands more in equal mirth maintains.
But oh! if e'er thy Gnome could spoil a grace,
Or raise a pimple on a beauteous face,
Like citron-waters° matrons' cheeks inflame,   orange brandy
70   Or change complexions at a losing game;
If e'er with airy horns I planted heads,
Or rumpled petticoats, or tumbled beds,
Or caused suspicion when no soul was rude,

---

[28] **Now glaring . . . machines:** These images suggest the hallucinations resulting from melancholy.
[29] **spleenwort:** A fern believed to cure ailments of the spleen, and suggestive of the gold bough that allowed Aeneas to enter Hades in *The Aeneid.*

Or discomposed the headdress of a prude,
75   Or e'er to costive° lapdog gave disease,   constipated
Which not the tears of brightest eyes could ease,
Hear me, and touch Belinda with chagrin:°   embarrassment
That single act gives half the world the spleen."
       The Goddess with a discontented air
80   Seems to reject him though she grants his prayer.
A wondrous bag with both her hands she binds,
Like that where once Ulysses held the winds;[30]
There she collects the force of female lungs,
Sighs, sobs, and passions, and the war of tongues.
85   A vial next she fills with fainting fears,
Soft sorrows, melting griefs, and flowing tears.
The Gnome rejoicing bears her gifts away,
Spreads his black wings, and slowly mounts to day.
       Sunk in Thalestris'[31] arms the nymph he found,
90   Her eyes dejected and her hair unbound.
Full o'er their heads the swelling bag he rent,
And all the Furies issued at the vent.
Belinda burns with more than mortal ire,
And fierce Thalestris fans the rising fire.
95   "O wretched maid!" she spreads her hands, and cried
(While Hampton's echoes, "Wretched maid!" replied),
"Was it for this you took such constant care
The bodkin,° comb, and essence to prepare?   hairpin
For this your locks in paper durance bound,
100   For this with torturing irons wreathed around?
For this with fillets° strained your tender head,   headbands
And bravely bore the double loads of lead?[32]
Gods! shall the ravisher display your hair,
While the fops envy, and the ladies stare!
105   Honor forbid! at whose unrivaled shrine
Ease, pleasure, virtue, all, our sex resign.
Methinks already I your tears survey,
Already hear the horrid things they say,
Already see you a degraded toast,
110   And all your honor in a whisper lost!
How shall I, then, your helpless fame defend?
'Twill then be infamy to seem your friend!
And shall this prize, the inestimable prize,
Exposed through crystal to the gazing eyes,

---

[30] **Like . . . winds:** In *The Odyssey*, Aeolus, the wind god, permits Odysseus to hold back all adverse
wind save the west wind that would carry his ship home.
[31] **Thalestris':** An Amazon, or aggressive woman.
[32] **double loads of lead:** Lead strips held Belinda's curlers in place.

115 And heightened by the diamond's circling rays,
     On that rapacious hand forever blaze?
     Sooner shall grass in Hyde Park Circus grow,
     And wits take lodgings in the sound of Bow;[33]
     Sooner let earth, air, sea, to chaos fall,
120 Men, monkeys, lapdogs, parrots, perish all!"
        She said; then raging to Sir Plume repairs,
     And bids her beau demand the precious hairs
     (Sir Plume of amber snuffbox justly vain,
     And the nice° conduct of a clouded cane).   exact
125 With earnest eyes, and round unthinking face,
     He first the snuffbox opened, then the case,
     And thus broke out—"My Lord, why, what the devil!
     Zounds! damn the lock! 'fore Gad, you must be civil!
     Plague on't! 'tis past a jest—nay prithee, pox!
130 Give her the hair"—he spoke, and rapped his box.
        "It grieves me much," replied the Peer again,
     "Who speaks so well should ever speak in vain.
     But by this Lock, this sacred Lock I swear
     (Which never more shall join its parted hair;
135 Which never more its honors shall renew,
     Clipped from the lovely head where late it grew),
     That while my nostrils draw the vital air,
     This hand, which won it, shall forever wear."
     He spoke, and speaking, in proud triumph spread
140 The long-contended honors of her head.
        But Umbriel, hateful Gnome, forbears not so;
     He breaks the vial whence the sorrows flow.
     Then see! the nymph in beauteous grief appears,
     Her eyes half languishing, half drowned in tears;
145 On her heaved bosom hung her drooping head,
     Which with a sigh she raised, and thus she said:
        "Forever cursed be this detested day,
     Which snatched my best, my favorite curl away!
     Happy! ah, ten times happy had I been,
150 If Hampton Court these eyes had never seen!
     Yet am not I the first mistaken maid,
     By love of courts to numerous ills betrayed.
     Oh, had I rather unadmired remained
     In some lone isle, or distant northern land;
155 Where the gilt chariot never marks the way,
     Where none learn ombre, none e'er taste bohea!°   black tea
     There kept my charms concealed from mortal eye,

---

[33] **Bow:** St. Mary Le Bow, a church in London's unfashionable mercantile section.

Like roses that in deserts bloom and die.
What moved my mind with youthful lords to roam?
160   Oh, had I stayed, and said my prayers at home!
'Twas this the morning omens seemed to tell,
Thrice from my trembling hand the patch box fell;
The tottering china shook without a wind,
Nay, Poll sat mute, and Shock was most unkind!
165   A Sylph too warned me of the threats of fate,
In mystic visions, now believed too late!
See the poor remnants of these slighted hairs!
My hands shall rend what e'en thy rapine spares.
These in two sable ringlets taught to break,
170   Once gave new beauties to the snowy neck;
The sister lock now sits uncouth, alone,
And in its fellow's fate foresees its own;
Uncurled it hands, the fatal shears demands,
And tempts once more thy sacrilegious hands.
175   Oh, hadst thou, cruel! been content to seize
Hairs less in sight, or any hairs but these!"

Canto V

She said: the pitying audience melt in tears.
But Fate and Jove had stopped the Baron's ears.
In vain Thalestris with reproach assails,
For who can move when fair Belinda fails?
5   Not half so fixed the Trojan could remain,
While Anna begged and Dido raged in vain.[34]
Then grave Clarissa graceful waved her fan;
Silence ensued, and thus the nymph began:
"Say why are beauties praised and honored most,
10   The wise man's passion, and the vain man's toast?
Why decked with all that land and sea afford,
Why angels called, and angel-like adored?
Why round our coaches crowd the white-gloved beaux,
Why bows the side box[35] from its inmost rows?
15   How vain are all these glories, all our pains,
Unless good sense preserve what beauty gains;
That men may say when we the front box grace,
'Behold the first in virtue as in face!'
Oh! if to dance all night, and dress all day,
20   Charmed the smallpox, or chased old age away,
Who would not scorn what housewife's cares produce,

---

[34] **Not half . . . vain:** In *The Aeneid,* Dido and her sister Anna plead with Aeneas to remain in Carthage.
[35] **Why bows the side box:** At the theater, gentlemen sat in side-boxes, while ladies sat in front-boxes.

Or who would learn one earthly thing of use?
To patch, nay ogle, might become a saint,
  Nor could it sure be such a sin to paint.°   wear cosmetics
25 But since, alas! frail beauty must decay,
Curled or uncurled, since locks will turn to gray;
Since painted, or not painted, all shall fade,
And she who scorns a man must die a maid;
What then remains but well our power to use,
30 And keep good humor still whate'er we lose?
And trust me, dear, good humor can prevail
When airs, and flights, and screams, and scolding fail.
Beauties in vain their pretty eyes may roll;
Charms strike the sight, but merit wins the soul."
35   So spoke the dame, but no applause ensued;
Belinda frowned, Thalestris called her prude.
"To arms, to arms!" the fierce virago° cries,   fierce woman
And swift as lightning to the combat flies.
All side in parties, and begin the attack;
40 Fans clap, silks rustle, and tough whalebones crack;
Heroes' and heroines' shouts confusedly rise,
And bass and treble voices strike the skies.
No common weapons in their hands are found,
Like Gods they fight, nor dread a mortal wound.
45   So when bold Homer makes the Gods engage,
And heavenly breasts with human passions rage;
'Gainst Pallas, Mars; Latona, Hermes arms;
And all Olympus rings with loud alarms:
Jove's thunder roars, heaven trembles all around,
50 Blue Neptune storms,[36] the bellowing deeps resound:
Earth shakes her nodding towers, the ground gives way,
And the pale ghosts start at the flash of day!
    Triumphant Umbriel on a sconce's° height   candlestick's
Clapped his glad wings, and sat to view the fight:
55 Propped on the bodkin spears, the sprites survey
The growing combat, or assist the fray.
    While through the press enraged Thalestris flies,
And scatters death around from both her eyes,
A beau and witling perished in the throng,
60 One died in metaphor, and one in song.
"O cruel nymph! a living death I bear,"
Cried Dapperwit, and sunk beside his chair.
A mournful glance Sir Fopling upwards cast,
"Those eyes are made so killing"—was his last.

---

[36] **'Gainst . . . storms:** In *The Iliad,* Mars fights against Pallas, and Hermes against Latona. In Roman mythology, Neptune is the god of the sea.

65 Thus on Maeander's flowery margin[37] lies
    The expiring swan, and as he sings he dies.
       When bold Sir Plume had drawn Clarissa down,
    Chloe stepped in, and killed him with a frown;
    She smiled to see the doughty hero slain,
70 But, at her smile, the beau revived again.
       Now Jove suspends his golden scales in air,
    Weighs the men's wits against the lady's hair;
    The doubtful beam long nods from side to side;
    At length the wits mount up, the hairs subside.
75   See, fierce Belinda on the Baron flies,
    With more than usual lightning in her eyes;
    Nor feared the chief the unequal fight to try,
    Who sought no more than on his foe to die.[38]
       But this bold lord with manly strength endued,
80 She with one finger and a thumb subdued:
    Just where the breath of life his nostrils drew,
    A charge of snuff the wily virgin threw;
    The Gnomes direct, to every atom just,
    The pungent grains of titillating dust.
85 Sudden, with starting tears each eye o'erflows,
    And the high dome re-echoes to his nose.
       "Now meet thy fate," incensed Belinda cried,
    And drew a deadly bodkin from her side.
    (The same, his ancient personage to deck,
90 Her great-great-grandsire wore about his neck,
    In three seal rings; which after, melted down,
    Formed a vast buckle for his widow's gown:
    Her infant grandame's whistle next it grew,
    The bells she jingled, and the whistle blew;
95 Then in a bodkin graced her mother's hairs,
    Which long she wore, and now Belinda wears.)
       "Boast not my fall," he cried, "insulting foe!
    Thou by some other shalt be laid as low.
    Nor think to die dejects my lofty mind:
100 All that I dread is leaving you behind!
    Rather than so, ah, let me still survive,
    And burn in Cupid's flames—but burn alive."
       "Restore the Lock!" she cries; and all around
    "Restore the Lock!" the vaulted roofs rebound.
105 Not fierce Othello in so loud a strain
    Roared for the handkerchief that caused his pain.
    But see how oft ambitious aims are crossed,

---

[37] **Maeander's flowery margin:** A wandering river in Asia Minor.
[38] **foe to die:** In other words, to feel sexual pleasure.

And chiefs contend till all the prize is lost!
The lock, obtained with guilt, and kept with pain,
110   In every place is sought, but sought in vain:
With such a prize no mortal must be blessed,
So Heaven decrees! with Heaven who can contest?
   Some thought it mounted to the lunar sphere,
Since all things lost on earth are treasured there.
115   There heroes' wits are kept in ponderous vases,
And beaux' in snuffboxes and tweezer cases.
There broken vows and deathbed alms are found,
And lovers' hearts with ends of riband bound,
The courtier's promises, and sick man's prayers,
120   The smiles of harlots, and the tears of heirs,
Cages for gnats, and chains to yoke a flea,
Dried butterflies, and tomes of casuistry.
   But trust the Muse—she saw it upward rise,
Though marked by none but quick, poetic eyes
125   (So Rome's great founder to the heavens withdrew,
To Proculus alone confessed in view),[39]
A sudden star, it shot through liquid air,
And drew behind a radiant trail of hair
Not Berenice's locks first rose so bright,[40]
130   The heavens bespangling with disheveled light.
The Sylphs behold it kindling as it flies,
And pleased pursue its progress through the skies.
   This the beau monde shall from the Mall survey,
And hail with music its propitious ray.
135   This the blest lover shall for Venus take,
And send up vows from Rosamonda's Lake.[41]
This Partridge soon shall view in cloudless skies,
When next he looks through Galileo's eyes;[42]
And hence the egregious wizard shall foredoom
140   The fate of Louis, and the fall of Rome.
   Then cease, bright nymph! to mourn thy ravished hair,
Which adds new glory to the shining sphere!
Not all the tresses that fair head can boast,
Shall draw such envy as the Lock you lost.
145   For, after all the murders of your eye,

[39] **So Rome's . . . view:** Romulus disappeared in a thunderstorm and later ascended to Heaven in the presence of Proculus.
[40] **Not Berenice's . . . bright:** The Egyptian queen Bernice dedicated a lock to her husband's safe return; the lock was later turned into the constellation *Coma Berenices.*
[41] **the Mall . . . Lake:** In St. James's Park, a fashionable walk. Rosamonda's Lake is a pond in the same park.
[42] **This Partridge . . . eyes:** Looking through his telescope, the British astronomer John Partridge (1644–1751) predicted disaster for the enemies of England.

When, after millions slain, yourself shall die:
When those fair suns shall set, as set they must,
And all those tresses shall be laid in dust,
This Lock the Muse shall consecrate to fame,
150   And 'midst the stars inscribe Belinda's name.

WALT WHITMAN (1819–1892)

from **Song of Myself** (1855)

I

I celebrate myself, and sing myself,
And what I assume you shall assume,
For every atom belonging to me as good belongs to you.

I loafe and invite my soul,
5   I lean and loafe at my ease observing a spear of summer grass.

My tongue, every atom of my blood, form'd from this soil, this air,
Born here of parents born here from parents the same, and their
            parents the same,
I, now thirty-seven years old in perfect health begin,
Hoping to cease not till death.

10   Creeds and schools in abeyance,
Retiring back a while sufficed at what they are, but never forgotten,
I harbor for good or bad, I permit to speak at every hazard,
Nature without check with original energy.

7

Has any one supposed it lucky to be born?
15   I hasten to inform him or her it is just as lucky to die, and I know it.

I pass death with the dying and birth with the new-wash'd babe,
            and am not contain'd between my hat and boots,
And peruse manifold objects, no two alike and every one good,
The earth good and the stars good, and their adjuncts all good.

I am not an earth nor an adjunct of an earth,
20   I am the mate and companion of people, all just as immortal and
            fathomless as myself,
(They do not know how immortal, but I know.)

Every kind for itself and its own, for me mine male and female,
For me those that have been boys and that love women,
For me the man that is proud and feels how it stings to be slighted,
25 For me the sweet-heart and the old maid, for me mothers and the
    mothers of mothers,
For me lips that have smiled, eyes that have shed tears,
For me children and the begetters of children.

Undrape! you are not guilty to me, nor stale nor discarded,
I see through the broadcloth and gingham whether or no,
30 And am around, tenacious, acquisitive, tireless, and cannot be
    shaken away.

8

The little one sleeps in its cradle,
I lift the gauze and look a long time, and silently brush away flies
    with my hand.
The youngster and the red-faced girl turn aside up the bushy hill,
I peeringly view them from the top.

35 The suicide sprawls on the bloody floor of the bedroom,
I witness the corpse with its dabbled hair, I note where the pistol
    has fallen.
The blab of the pave, tires of carts, sluff of boot-soles, talk of the
    promenaders,
The heavy omnibus, the driver with his interrogating thumb, the
    clank of the shod horses on the granite floor,
The snow-sleighs, clinkink, shouted jokes, pelts of snow-balls,
40 The hurrahs for popular favorites, the fury of rous'd mobs,
The flap of the curtain'd litter, a sick man inside borne to the hospital,
The meeting of enemies, the sudden oath, the blows and fall,
The excited crowd, the policeman with his star quickly working
    his passage to the centre of the crowd,
The impassive stones that receive and return so many echoes,
45 What groans of over-fed or half-starv'd who fall sunstruck or in fits,
What exclamations of women taken suddenly who hurry home
    and give birth to babes,
What living and buried speech is always vibrating here, what
    howls restrain'd by decorum,
Arrests of criminals, slights, adulterous offers made, acceptances,
    rejections with convex lips,
I mind them or the show or resonance of them—I come and I depart.

9

50 The big doors of the country barn stand open and ready,
The dried grass of the harvest-time loads the slow-drawn wagon,

The clear light plays on the brown gray and green intertinged,
The armfuls are pack'd to the sagging mow.

I am there, I help, I came stretch'd atop of the load,
55   I felt its soft jolts, one leg reclined on the other,
I jump from the cross-beams and seize the clover and timothy,
And roll head over heels and tangle my hair full of wisps.

10

Alone far in the wilds and mountains I hunt,
Wandering amazed at my own lightness and glee,
60   In the late afternoon choosing a safe spot to pass the night,
Kindling a fire and broiling the fresh-kill'd game,
Falling asleep on the gather'd leaves with my dog and gun by my side.
The Yankee clipper is under her sky-sails, she cuts the sparkle and
        scud,
My eyes settle the land, I bend at her prow or shout joyously from
        the deck.

65   The boatmen and clam-diggers arose early and stopt for me,
I tuck'd my trowser-ends in my boots and went and had a good time;
You should have been with us that day round the chowder-kettle.

I saw the marriage of the trapper in the open air in the far west,
        the bride was a red girl,
Her father and his friends sat near cross-legged and dumbly
        smoking, they had moccasins to their feet and large
        thick blankets hanging from their shoulders,
70   On a bank lounged the trapper, he was drest mostly in skins, his
        luxuriant beard and curls protected his neck, he held
        his bride by the hand,
She had long eyelashes, her head was bare, her coarse straight
        locks descended upon her voluptuous limbs and
        reach'd to her feet.

The runaway slave came to my house and stopt outside,
I heard his motions crackling the twigs of the woodpile,
Through the swung half-door of the kitchen I saw him limpsy and weak,
75   And went where he sat on a log and led him in and assured him,
And brought water and fill'd a tub for his sweated body and bruis'd feet,
And gave him a room that enter'd from my own, and gave him some
        coarse clean clothes,
And remember perfectly well his revolving eyes and his awkwardness,
And remember putting plasters on the galls of his neck and ankles;
80   He staid with me a week before he was recuperated and pass'd north,
I had him sit next me at table, my fire-lock lean'd in the corner.

11

Twenty-eight young men bathe by the shore,
Twenty-eight young men and all so friendly;
Twenty-eight years of womanly life and all so lonesome.

85 She owns the fine house by the rise of the bank,
She hides handsome and richly drest aft the blinds of the window.

Which of the young men does she like the best?
Ah the homeliest of them is beautiful to her.

Where are you off to, lady? for I see you,
90 You splash in the water there, yet stay stock still in your room.

Dancing and laughing along the beach came the twenty-ninth bather,
The rest did not see her, but she saw them and loved them.

The beards of the young men glisten'd with wet, it ran from their
            long hair,
Little streams pass'd all over their bodies.

95 An unseen hand also pass'd over their bodies,
It descended tremblingly from their temples and ribs.

The young men float on their backs, their white bellies bulge to
            the sun, they do not ask who seizes fast to them,
They do not know who puffs and declines with pendant and
            bending arch,
They do not think whom they souse with spray.

21

100 I am the poet of the Body and I am the poet of the Soul,
The pleasures of heaven are with me and the pains of hell are with me,
The first I graft and increase upon myself, the latter I translate into
            a new tongue.

I am the poet of the woman the same as the man,
And I say it is as great to be a woman as to be a man,
105 And I say there is nothing greater than the mother of men.

I chant the chant of dilation or pride,
We have had ducking and deprecating about enough,
I show that size is only development.

Have you outstript the rest? are you the President?
110 It is a trifle, they will more than arrive there every one, and still pass on.

I am he that walks with the tender and growing night,
I call to the earth and sea half-held by the night.

Press close bare-bosom'd night—press close magnetic nourishing night!
Night of south winds—night of the large few stars!
115 Still nodding night—mad naked summer night.

Smile O voluptuous cool-breath'd earth!
Earth of the slumbering and liquid trees!
Earth of departed sunset—earth of the mountains misty-topt!
Earth of the vitreous pour of the full moon just tinged with blue!
120 Earth of shine and dark mottling the tide of the river!
Earth of the limpid gray of clouds brighter and clearer for my sake!
Far-swooping elbow'd earth—rich apple-blossom'd earth!
Smile, for your lover comes.

Prodigal, you have given me love—therefore I to you give love!
125 O unspeakable passionate love.

24

Walt Whitman, a kosmos, of Manhattan the son,
Turbulent, fleshy, sensual, eating, drinking and breeding,
No sentimentalist, no stander above men and women or apart from
        them,
No more modest than immodest.

130 Unscrew the locks from the doors!
Unscrew the doors themselves from their jambs!

Whoever degrades another degrades me,
And whatever is done or said returns at last to me.

Through me the afflatus surging and surging, through me the
        current and index.

135 I speak the pass-word primeval, I give the sign of democracy,
By God! I will accept nothing which all cannot have their
        counterpart of on the same terms.

Through me many long dumb voices,
Voices of the interminable generations of prisoners and slaves,
Voices of the diseas'd and despairing and of thieves and dwarfs,
140 Voices of cycles of preparation and accretion,
And of the threads that connect the stars, and of wombs and of
        the father-stuff,

And of the rights of them the others are down upon,
Of the deform'd, trivial, flat, foolish, despised,
Fog in the air, beetles rolling balls of dung.

145   Through me forbidden voices,
Voices of sexes and lusts, voices veil'd and I remove the veil,
Voices indecent by me clarified and transfigur'd.

I do not press my fingers across my mouth,
I keep as delicate around the bowels as around the head and heart,
150   Copulation is no more rank to me than death is.

I believe in the flesh and the appetites,
Seeing, hearing, feeling, are miracles, and each part and tag of me
          is a miracle.

Divine am I inside and out, and I make holy whatever I touch or
          am touch'd from,
The scent of these arm-pits aroma finer than prayer,
155   This head more than churches, bibles, and all the creeds.

If I worship one thing more than another it shall be the spread of
          my own body, or any part of it,
Translucent mould of me it shall be you!
Shaded ledges and rests it shall be you!
Firm masculine colter¹ it shall be you!
160   Whatever goes to the tilth° of me it shall be you!   cultivated land
You my rich blood! your milky stream pale strippings of my life!
Breast that presses against other breasts it shall be you!
My brain it shall be your occult convolutions!
Root of wash'd sweet-flag! timorous pond-snipe! nest of guarded
          duplicate eggs! it shall be you!
165   Mix'd tussled hay of head, beard, brawn, it shall be you!
Trickling sap of maple, fibre of manly wheat, it shall be you!
Sun so generous it shall be you!
Vapors lighting and shading my face it shall be you!
You sweaty brooks and dews it shall be you!
170   Winds whose soft-tickling genitals rub against me it shall be you!
Broad muscular fields, branches of live oak, loving lounger in my
          winding paths, it shall be you!
Hands I have taken, face I have kiss'd, mortal I have ever touch'd,
          it shall be you.

---

¹ **colter:** A sharp steel wedge attached to a plow.

I dote on myself, there is that lot of me and all so luscious,
Each moment and whatever happens thrills me with joy,
175 I cannot tell how my ankles bend, nor whence the cause of my
          faintest wish,
Nor the cause of the friendship I emit, nor the cause of the
          friendship I take again.

That I walk up my stoop, I pause to consider if it really be,
A morning-glory at my window satisfies me more than the
          metaphysics of books.

To behold the day-break!
180 The little light fades the immense and diaphanous shadows,
The air tastes good to my palate.

Hefts of the moving world at innocent gambols silently rising,
          freshly exuding,
Scooting obliquely high and low.

Something I cannot see puts upward libidinous prongs,
185 Seas of bright juice suffuse heaven.

The earth by the sky staid with, the daily close of their junction,
The heav'd challenge from the east that moment over my head,
The mocking taunt, See then whether you shall be master!

31

I believe a leaf of grass is no less than the journey-work of the stars,
190 And the pismire° is equally perfect, and a grain of sand, and the   ant
          egg of the wren,
And the tree-toad is a chef-d'œuvre for the highest,
And the running blackberry would adorn the parlors of heaven,
And the narrowest hinge in my hand puts to scorn all machinery,
And the cow crunching with depress'd head surpasses any statue,
195 And a mouse is miracle enough to stagger sextillions of infidels.

I find I incorporate gneiss, coal, long-threaded moss, fruits, grains,
          esculent roots,
And am stucco'd with quadrupeds and birds all over,
And have distanced what is behind me for good reasons,
But call any thing back again when I desire it.

200 In vain the speeding or shyness,
In vain the plutonic rocks send their old heat against my approach,
In vain the mastodon retreats beneath its own powder'd bones,

In vain objects stand leagues off and assume manifold shapes,
In vain the ocean settling in hollows and the great monsters lying low,
205   In vain the buzzard houses herself with the sky,
In vain the snake slides through the creepers and logs,
In vain the elk takes to the inner passes of the woods,
In vain the razor-bill'd auk sails far north to Labrador,
I follow quickly, I ascend to the nest in the fissure of the cliff.

46

210   I know I have the best of time and space, and was never measured
       and never will be measured.

I tramp a perpetual journey, (come listen all!)
My signs are a rain-proof coat, good shoes, and a staff cut from the
       woods,
No friend of mine takes his ease in my chair,
I have no chair, no church, no philosophy,
215   I lead no man to a dinner-table, library, exchange,
But each man and each woman of you I lead upon a knoll,
My left hand hooking you round the waist,
My right hand pointing to landscapes of continents and the public
       road.

Not I, not any one else can travel that road for you,
220   You must travel it for yourself.

It is not far, it is within reach,
Perhaps you have been on it since you were born and did not know,
Perhaps it is everywhere on water and on land.

Shoulder your duds° dear son, and I will mine, and let us hasten   clothes
       forth,
225   Wonderful cities and free nations we shall fetch as we go.

If you tire, give me both burdens, and rest the chuff of your hand
       on my hip,
And in due time you shall repay the same service to me,
For after we start we never lie by again.

This day before dawn I ascended a hill and look'd at the crowded
       heaven,
230   And I said to my spirit *When we become the enfolders of those orbs,*
       and the pleasure and knowledge of every thing in them,
       shall we be fill'd and satisfied then?
And my spirit said *No, we but level that lift to pass and continue*
       beyond.

You are also asking me questions and I hear you,
I answer that I cannot answer, you must find out for yourself.

Sit a while dear son,
235   Here are biscuits to eat and here is milk to drink,
But as soon as you sleep and renew yourself in sweet clothes, I kiss
      you with a good-by kiss and open the gate for your
      egress hence.

Long enough have you dream'd contemptible dreams,
Now I wash the gum from your eyes,
You must habit yourself to the dazzle of the light and of every
      moment of your life.

240   Long have you timidly waded holding a plank by the shore,
Now I will you to be a bold swimmer,
To jump off in the midst of the sea, rise again, nod to me, shout,
      and laughingly dash with your hair.

52

The spotted hawk swoops by and accuses me, he complains of my
      gab and my loitering.

I too am not a bit tamed, I too am untranslatable,
245   I sound my barbaric yawp over the roofs of the world.

The last scud of day holds back for me,
It flings my likeness after the rest and true as any on the shadow'd
      wilds,
It coaxes me to the vapor and the dusk.

I depart as air, I shake my white locks at the runaway sun,
250   I effuse my flesh in eddies, and drift it in lacy jags.

I bequeath myself to the dirt to grow from the grass I love,
If you want me again look for me under your boot-soles.

You will hardly know who I am or what I mean,
But I shall be good health to you nevertheless,
255   And filter and fibre your blood.

Failing to fetch me at first keep encouraged,
Missing me one place search another,
I stop somewhere waiting for you.

EZRA POUND   (1885–1972)

from **The Cantos**   (1921; 1930)

I[1]

And then went down to the ship,
Set keel to breakers, forth on the godly sea, and
We set up mast and sail on that swart° ship,   dark
Bore sheep aboard her, and our bodies also
5   Heavy with weeping, and winds from sternward
Bore us out onward with bellying canvas,
Circe's[2] this craft, the trim-coifed goddess.
Then sat we amidships, wind jamming the tiller,
Thus with stretched sail, we went over sea till day's end.
10   Sun to his slumber, shadows o'er all the ocean,
Came we then to the bounds of deepest water,
To the Kimmerian lands,[3] and peopled cities
Covered with close-webbed mist, unpierced ever
With glitter of sun-rays
15   Nor with stars stretched, nor looking back from heaven
Swartest night stretched over wretched men there.
The ocean flowing backward, came we then to the place
Aforesaid by Circe.
Here did they rites, Perimedes and Eurylochus,[4]
20   And drawing sword from my hip
I dug the ell-square pitkin;°   trench
Poured we libations unto each the dead,
First mead[5] and then sweet wine, water mixed with white flour.
Then prayed I many a prayer to the sickly death's-heads;
25   As set in Ithaca, sterile bulls of the best
For sacrifice, heaping the pyre with goods,
A sheep to Tiresias only, black and a bell-sheep.[6]
Dark blood flowed in the fosse,°   ditch
Souls out of Erebus,[7] cadaverous dead, of brides

---

[1] **I:** In the first canto of Pound's epic, he translates book 11 of Homer's *Odyssey* (lines 1–67). The book narrates Odysseus's trip to the land of the dead to consult Tiresias, a blind Theban prophet.
[2] **Circe's:** Daughter of the sun, known for her ability to turn men into animals. Odysseus lived with Circe on Aiaia for over a year.
[3] **Kimmerian lands:** The Cimmerians were a legendary people who lived on the farthest edges of the known world.
[4] **Perimedes and Eurylochus:** Eurylochus is Odysseus's second-in-command during his travels, and Perimedes is another member of his crew.
[5] **mead:** Drink made of fermented water and honey.
[6] **bell-sheep:** A sheep that guides its herd.
[7] **Erebus:** Land of the dead.

30   Of youths and of the old who had borne much;
      Souls stained with recent tears, girls tender,
      Men many, mauled with bronze lance heads,
      Battle spoil, bearing yet dreory° arms,   bloody
      These many crowded about me; with shouting,
35   Pallor upon me, cried to my men for more beasts;
      Slaughtered the herds, sheep slain of bronze;
      Poured ointment, cried to the gods,
      To Pluto the strong, and praised Proserpine,[8]
      Unsheathed the narrow sword,
40   I sat to keep off the impetuous impotent dead,
      Till I should hear Tiresias.
      But first Elpenor[9] came, our friend Elpenor,
      Unburied, cast on the wide earth,
      Limbs that we left in the house of Circe,
45   Unwept, unwrapped in sepulchre, since toils urged other.
      Pitiful spirit. And I cried in hurried speech:
      "Elpenor, how art thou come to this dark coast?
      "Cam'st thou afoot, outstripping seamen?"
              And he in heavy speech:
50   "Ill fate and abundant wine. I slept in Circe's ingle.°   nook
      "Going down the long ladder unguarded,
      "I fell against the buttress,
      "Shattered the nape-nerve, the soul sought Avernus.[10]
      "But thou, O King, I bid remember me, unwept, unburied,
55   "Heap up mine arms, be tomb by sea-bord, and inscribed:
      A man of no fortune, and with a name to come.
      "And set my oar up, that I swung mid fellows."

      And Anticlea[11] came, whom I beat off, and then Tiresias Theban,
      Holding his golden wand, knew me, and spoke first:
60   "A second time? why? man of ill star,
      "Facing the sunless dead and this joyless region?
      "Stand from the fosse,° leave me my bloody bever°   trench / beverage
      "For soothsay."
              And I stepped back,
65   And he strong with the blood, said then: "Odysseus
      "Shalt return through spiteful Neptune, over dark seas,

---

[8] **To Pluto . . . Proserpine:** Pluto is god of the underworld, and Proserpine (Persephone) is his queen.
[9] **Elpenor:** Friend of Odysseus, who fell off Circe's palace while drunk.
[10] **Avernus:** Lake believed to be the entrance to the land of the dead.
[11] **Anticlea:** The mother of Odysseus.

"Lose all companions." And then Anticlea came.
Lie quiet Divus. I mean, that is Andreas Divus,
In officina Wecheli, 1538, out of Homer.[12]
70   And he sailed, by Sirens and thence outward and away
And unto Circe.
              Venerandam,[13]
In the Cretan's phrase, with the golden crown, Aphrodite,
Cypri munimenta sortita est, mirthful, oricalchi,[14] with golden
75   Girdles and breast bands, thou with dark eyelids
Bearing the golden bough of Argicida.[15] So that:

XIII

Kung[16] walked
              by the dynastic temple
and into the cedar grove,
              and then out by the lower river,
5   And with him Khieu, Tchi
              and Tian the low speaking
And "we are unknown," said Kung,
"You will take up charioteering?
              Then you will become known,
10   "Or perhaps I should take up charioteering, or archery?
"Or the practice of public speaking?"
And Tseu-lou said, "I would put the defences in order,"
And Khieu said, "If I were lord of a province
I would put it in better order than this is."
15   And Tchi said, "I would prefer a small mountain temple,
"With order in the observances,
              with a suitable performance of the ritual,"
And Tian said, with his hand on the strings of his lute
The low sounds continuing
20   after his hand left the strings,
And the sound went up like smoke, under the leaves,
And he looked after the sound:

---

[12] **Andreas . . . Homer:** Andreas Divus was a sixteenth-century Italian who published a translation of the *Odyssey* in Chrétien Wechel's Paris publishing house in 1538. Pound's first Canto is based on his translation.

[13] **Venerandam:** In Latin, "worthy of worship," applied to Aphrodite, the goddess of love and beauty.

[14] **In the . . . oricalchi:** Lines from a Latin hymn to Aphrodite, that read, "Reverend golden-crowned beautiful Aphrodite / I shall sing, who has received as her lot the citadels of all sea-grit Cyprus . . ."

[15] **Argicida:** An epithet for Hermes, "slayer of Argos." In Greek mythology, Hermes was a messenger of the gods, and Argos was a many-eyed herdsman.

[16] **Kung:** K'ung-fu-tze, or Confucius.

"The old swimming hole,
"And the boys flopping off the planks,
25 "Or sitting in the underbrush playing mandolins."
              And Kung smiled upon all of them equally.
And Thseng-sie desired to know:
              "Which had answered correctly?"
And Kung said, "They have all answered correctly,
30 "That is to say, each in his nature."
And Kung raised his cane against Yuan Jang,
              Yuan Jang being his elder,
For Yuan Jang sat by the roadside pretending to
              be receiving wisdom.
35 And Kung said
              "You old fool, come out of it,
Get up and do something useful."
              And Kung said
"Respect a child's faculties
40 "From the moment it inhales the clear air,
"But a man of fifty who knows nothing
              Is worthy of no respect."
And "When the prince has gathered about him
"All the savants and artists, his riches will be fully employed."
45 And Kung said, and wrote on the bo leaves:[17]
              If a man have not order within him
He can not spread order about him;
And if a man have not order within him
His family will not act with due order;
50   And if the prince have not order within him
He can not put order in his dominions.
And Kung gave the words "order"
and "brotherly deference"
And said nothing of the "life after death."
55 And he said
              "Anyone can run to excesses,
It is easy to shoot past the mark,
It is hard to stand firm in the middle."

And they said: If a man commit murder
60   Should his father protect him, and hide him?
And Kung said:
              He should hide him.

---

[17] **bo leaves:** Leaves of the sacred Bodhi tree, often used as paper.

And Kung gave his daughter to Kong-Tch'ang
       Although Kong-Tch'ang was in prison.
65   And he gave his niece to Nan-Young
       although Nan-Young was out of office.
And Kung said "Wang ruled with moderation,
       In his day the State was well kept,
And even I can remember
70   A day when the historians left blanks in their writings,
I mean for things they didn't know,
But that time seems to be passing."
And Kung said, "Without character you will
       be unable to play on that instrument
75   Or to execute the music fit for the Odes.
The blossoms of the apricot
       blow from the east to the west,
And I have tried to keep them from falling."

H. D. (HILDA DOOLITTLE) (1886–1961)

from Helen in Egypt
(*from* Leuké—Book One)

[1]

Why Leuké?[1] *Because here, Achilles is said to have married Helen
who bore him a son, Euphorion. Helen in Egypt did not taste of
Lethe, forgetfulness, on the other hand; she was in an ecstatic or
semi-trance state. Though she says, "I am awake, no trance," yet
she confesses, "I move as one in a dream." Now, it is as if momen-
tarily, at any rate, the dream is over. Remembrance is taking its
place. She immediately reminds us of her "first rebellion" and the so
far suppressed memory and unspoken name—Paris.*

I am not nor mean to be
the Daemon they made of me;
going forward, my will was the wind,

(or the will of Aphrodite[2]
5   filled the sail, as the story told
of my first rebellion;

---

[1] **Leuké:** One of the Greek Islands.
[2] **Aphrodite:** Daughter of Zeus, the goddess of love and beauty.

the sail, they said,
was the veil of Aphrodite),
and I am tired of the memory of battle,

10   I remember a dream that was real;
let them sing Helena for a thousand years,
let them name and re-name Helen,

I can not endure the weight of eternity,
they will never understand
15   how, a second time, I am free;

he was banished, as his mother dreamed
that he (Paris) would cause war,
and war came.

[2]

And now she is back with the old dilemma—who caused the war?
She has been blamed, Paris has been blamed but, fundamentally, it
was the fault of Thetis, the mother of Achilles. There is the old
argument regarding mésalliance, *a goddess marries a mortal,*
some social discord is sure to arise. The traditional uninvited guest
introduces the fatal apple of discord. But Helen outlives, as it were,
her own destiny and "Helen's epiphany in Egypt."

Was it Paris who caused the war?
20   or was it Thetis? the goddess
married a mortal, Peleus,[3]

the banquet, the wedding-feast
lacked nothing, only one uninvited guest,
Eris,[4] so the apple was cast,

25   so the immortals woke to petty strife
over the challenge, *to the fairest;*
surely, the gods knew

that Thetis was fairer than Helen,
but the balance swayed
30   and Thetis was a goddess,

---

[3] **Peleus:** Father of Achilleus, he was a mortal who married the Nereid Thetis.
[4] **Eris:** Sister of Ares, the goddess of discord.

and Helen, half of earth,
out-lived the goddess Helen
and Helen's epiphany in Egypt.

[3]

> *There is more to it. She would have taken the "wisdom of Thoth"*[5]
> *or of Egypt "back to the islands." Now on Leuké, l'isle blanche, she*
> *would reconstruct the Greek past. Thetis had said, "Achilles waits,"*
> *but he must wait a little longer. He was given to her with the mys-*
> *tery, the miracle, in another dimension, in Egypt. But there is this*
> *world of which Thetis had spoken, of forest-trees, involuted sea-*
> *shells, snow. Helen had lived here before. In the light of her inheri-*
> *tance as neophyte or initiate, she would re-assess that first*
> *experience. It is true that Love "let fly the dart" that had sent*
> *Achilles to her, but it was Paris who was the agent, medium or*
> *intermediary of Love and of Troy's great patron, Apollo, the god of*
> *Song.*

He would set the Towers a-flame;
35   Hecuba's[6] second son would undo
the work of his father, Priam,

and of his brother, the valiant
first-born, Hector;
was this, was this not true?

40   they met, Hector and Achilles,
and Achilles slew Hector,
but later, a bowman from the Walls

let fly the dart;
some said it was Apollo,
45   but I, Helena, knew it was Love's arrow;

it was Love, it was Apollo, it was Paris;
I knew and I did not know this,
while I slept in Egypt.

[4]

> *Surely, her former state was perfect, but now the temple or the*
> *tomb, the infinite is reduced to a finite image, a "delicate sea-shell."*
> *It is Thetis who has given this image to her, "a simple spiral-shell*
> *may tell a tale more ancient than these mysteries."*

---

[5] **Thoth:** An Egyptian moon deity, Thoth is the god of wisdom, learning, and the arts.
[6] **Hecuba's:** Hecuba was King Priam of Troy's wife, mother of Paris and Hector.

O the tomb, delicate sea-shell,
50   rock-cut but frail,
the thousand, thousand Greeks

fallen before the Walls,
were as one soul, one pearl;
I was asleep,

55   part of the infinite,
but there is another,
resilient as fire—Paris? Achilles?

[5]

*But Thetis? She has summoned Helen out of Egypt with "Achilles
waits." But Helen is back in time, in memory. While "Achilles
waits," she reconstructs the early story of—"Eros.[7] Eris?"*

What is Achilles without war?
it was Thetis, his mother,
60   who planned this (bridal and rest),

but even the gods' plans
are shaped by another—
Eros? Eris?

[6]

*What boat, what "skiff" has brought Helen here? And how was she
brought? Was it in a dream? It seems so, for she says, "I woke to
familiar fragrance."*

A sharp sword divides me from the past,
65   yet no glaive,° this;   sharp sword
how did I cross?

coast from coast, they are separate;
I can recall the skiff,
the stars' countless host,

70   but I would only remember
how I woke to familiar fragrance,
late roses, bruised apples;

reality opened before me,
I had come back;
75   I retraced the thorny path

---

[7] **Eros:** Son of Aphrodite, the god of love.

but the thorns of rancour and hatred
were gone—Troy? Greece?
they were one and I was one,

I was laughing with Paris;
80 so we cheated the past,
I had escaped—Achilles.

[7]

*Now Helen's concern is anxiety about the Sea-goddess. This is her
island. Helen has been recalled from Egypt to a Greek union, marriage or mystery, by Thetis' "Achilles waits, and life." But for the
moment, her overwhelming experience in Egypt must be tempered
or moderated, if, "in life," she is to progress at all. It was Paris, in
the first instance, Helen says, who "had lured me from Sparta."
Now again, Paris lures her from Sparta or from her dedication to the
Spartan ideal. She is laughing with Paris, there are roses. She is
running away, as in the scene of her "first rebellion," to "hide
among the apple-trees."*

And Thetis? she of the many forms
had manifested as Choragus,[8]
Thetis, lure-of-the-sea;

85 will she champion?
will she reject me?
we will hide,

a hooded cloak was thrown over me,
now it is dark upon Leuké;
90 the same whisper had lured me from Sparta,

we will hide among the apple-trees . . .
so it was his arrow that had given me Achilles—
it was his arrow that set me free.

[8]

*Now Paris would remind us of his early life as shepherd and "Wolf-
slayer." It was his recall to Troy, (after years of banishment and
obscurity) as Prince, second only to great Hector, that had caused
his death. "Death dwells in the city," he tells us. He does not seem
to blame this death on Helen.*

---

[8] **Choragus:** In ancient Greece, leader of a festival or chorus.

Learn of me (this is Paris)—
95 leave obelisks and cities,
pylons and fortresses;

my dart was named Saviour,
Ida's shepherds called me
defence and protector, Wolf-slayer;

100 I unsheathed my long-spear,
a staff rather, thonged with a hunting-knife;
hail Saviour, farewell,

(they knew the blight),
Death awaits you
105 was in the herdsman's farewell,

Death dwells in the city
whispered the hail,
warned the farewell.

T. S. ELIOT (1888–1965)

The Waste Land (1922)

"Nam Sibyllam quidem Cumis ego ipse oculis meis vidi in ampulla
pendere, et cum illi pueri dicerent: Σίβυλλα τί θέλεις;
respondebat illa: ἀποθανεῖν θέίλω." [1]

For Ezra Pound
il miglior fabbro. [2]

I. The Burial of the Dead

April is the cruellest month, breeding
Lilacs out of the dead land, mixing
Memory and desire, stirring
Dull roots with spring rain.
5   Winter kept us warm, covering
Earth in forgetful snow, feeding
A little life with dried tubers.

---

[1] **Nam Sibyllam . . . :** From the *Satyricon* of Petronius (d. 66 A.D.). "For indeed I myself have seen,
with my own eyes, the Sibyl hanging in a bottle at Cumae, and when those boys would say to her:
'Sibyl, what do you want?' she replied, 'I want to die.'"
[2] **il miglior fabbro:** Italian: "the better craftsman."

Summer surprised us, coming over the Starnbergersee
With a shower of rain; we stopped in the colonnade,
10   And went on in sunlight, into the Hofgarten,[3]
And drank coffee, and talked for an hour.
Bin gar keine Russin, stamm' aus Litauen, echt deutsch.[4]
And when we were children, staying at the arch-duke's,
My cousin's, he took me out on a sled,
15   And I was frightened. He said, Marie,
Marie, hold on tight. And down we went.
In the mountains, there you feel free.
I read, much of the night, and go south in the winter.

What are the roots that clutch, what branches grow
20   Out of this stony rubbish? Son of man,
You cannot say, or guess, for you know only
A heap of broken images, where the sun beats,
And the dead tree gives no shelter, the cricket no relief,
And the dry stone no sound of water. Only
25   There is shadow under this red rock,
(Come in under the shadow of this red rock),[5]
And I will show you something different from either
Your shadow at morning striding behind you
Or your shadow at evening rising to meet you;
30   I will show you fear in a handful of dust.
                    Frisch weht der Wind
                    Der Heimat zu
                    Mein Irisch Kind,
                    Wo weilest du?[6]
35   "You gave me hyacinths first a year ago;
"They called me the hyacinth girl."
—Yet when we came back, late, from the Hyacinth garden,
Your arms full, and your hair wet, I could not
Speak, and my eyes failed, I was neither
40   Living nor dead, and I knew nothing,
Looking into the heart of light, the silence.
Oed' und leer das Meer.[7]

---

[3] **Starnbergersee . . . Hofgarten:** A lake south of Munich, in Germany. The Hofgarten is a public garden in Munich.

[4] **Bin . . . deutsch:** "I am no Russian, I come from Lithuania, true German."

[5] **(Come . . . red rock):** Interpretations of the red rock vary. From Isaiah 32.1–3: "Behold, a king shall reign in righteousness, and princes shall rule in judgment. And a man shall be as a hiding place from the wind, and a covert from the tempest; as rivers of water in a dry place, as the shadow of a great rock in a weary land." For others, the rock represents Peter, the rock on whom Christ intended to build his church.

[6] **Frisch . . . du?:** "The wind blow fresh / toward land of home: / My Irish child, / where do you roam?" From the opera *Tristan und Isolde* by Richard Wagner.

[7] **Oed' . . . Meer:** Again, from Wagner: "Bleak and bare the sea."

Madame Sosostris,[8] famous clairvoyante,
Had a bad cold, nevertheless
45   Is known to be the wisest woman in Europe,
With a wicked pack of cards.° Here, said she,   tarot cards
Is your card, the drowned Phoenician Sailor,
(Those are pearls that were his eyes. Look!)
Here is Belladonna,[9] the Lady of the Rocks,
50   The lady of situations.
Here is the man with three staves, and here the Wheel,
And here is the one-eyed merchant, and this card,
Which is blank, is something he carries on his back,
Which I am forbidden to see. I do not find
55   The Hanged Man. Fear death by water.
I see crowds of people, walking round in a ring.
Thank you. If you see dear Mrs. Equitone,
Tell her I bring the horoscope myself:
One must be so careful these days.

60   Unreal City,
Under the brown fog of a winter dawn,
A crowd flowed over London Bridge, so many,
I had not thought death had undone so many.
Sighs, short and infrequent, were exhaled,
65   And each man fixed his eyes before his feet.
Flowed up the hill and down King William Street,
To where Saint Mary Woolnoth kept the hours
With a dead sound on the final stroke of nine.[10]
There I saw one I knew, and stopped him, crying: "Stetson!
70   "You who were with me in the ships at Mylae![11]
"That corpse you planted last year in your garden,
"Has it begun to sprout? Will it bloom this year?
"Or has the sudden frost disturbed its bed?
"Oh keep the Dog far hence, that's friend to men,
75   "Or with his nails he'll dig it up again!
"You! hypocrite lecteur!—mon semblable,—mon frère!"[12]

II. A Game of Chess

The Chair she sat in, like a burnished throne,
Glowed on the marble, where the glass

---

[8] **Madame Sosostris:** A fortune teller in Aldous Huxley's *Chrome Yellow.*
[9] **Belladonna:** Italian: "fair lady." Also the name of a poisonous plant.
[10] **King William Street . . . nine:** All landmarks from London's business district.
[11] **Mylae:** In Sicily, site of the battle of Mylae, in which the Carthaginians were defeated by the Romans in 260 B.C.
[12] **You! . . . frère!:** From Baudelaire's *To The Reader: "Hypocrite reader!—my likeness,—my brother!"*

Held up by standards wrought with fruited vines
80   From which a golden Cupidon peeped out
(Another hid his eyes behind his wing)
Doubled the flames of sevenbranched candelabra
Reflecting light upon the table as
The glitter of her jewels rose to meet it,
85   From satin cases poured in rich profusion;
In vials of ivory and coloured glass
Unstoppered, lurked her strange synthetic perfumes,
Unguent,° powdered, or liquid—troubled, confused   ointment
And drowned the sense in odours; stirred by the air
90   That freshened from the window, these ascended
In fattening the prolonged candle-flames,
Flung their smoke into the laquearia,°   ceiling
Stirring the pattern on the coffered ceiling.
Huge sea-wood fed with copper
95   Burned green and orange, framed by the coloured stone,
In which sad light a carvéd dolphin swam.
Above the antique mantel was displayed
As though a window gave upon the sylvan scene[13]
The change of Philomel, by the barbarous king[14]
100   So rudely forced; yet there the nightingale
Filled all the desert with inviolable voice
And still she cried, and still the world pursues,
"Jug Jug"[15] to dirty ears.
And other withered stumps of time
105   Were told upon the walls; staring forms
Leaned out, leaning, hushing the room enclosed.
Footsteps shuffled on the stair.
Under the firelight, under the brush, her hair
Spread out in fiery points
110   Glowed into words, then would be savagely still.

"My nerves are bad to-night. Yes, bad. Stay with me.
"Speak to me. Why do you never speak. Speak.
    "What are you thinking of? What thinking? What?
"I never know what you are thinking. Think."

115   I think we are in rats' alley
Where the dead men lost their bones.

---

[13] **sylvan scene:** Description of Eden from Satan's perspective in Milton's *Paradise Lost,* book IV.
[14] **Philomel:** Tereus raped his sister-in-law Philomela. In revenge, his wife Pronce killed her son and fed him to an unsuspecting Tereus. He tried to chase the two women, but all three morphed into birds. Philomela became a nightingale.
[15] **Jug Jug:** Obscene noise.

"What is that noise?"
          The wind under the door.
"What is that noise now? What is the wind doing?"
120   Nothing again nothing.
            "Do
"You know nothing? Do you see nothing? Do you remember
"Nothing?"

   I remember
Those are pearls that were his eyes.
125   "Are you alive, or not? Is there nothing in your head?"

                            But

O O O O that Shakespeherian Rag[16]—
It's so elegant
So intelligent
130   "What shall I do now? What shall I do?"
"I shall rush out as I am, and walk the street
"With my hair down, so. What shall we do tomorrow?
"What shall we ever do?"
                The hot water at ten.
135   And if it rains, a closed car at four.
And we shall play a game of chess,
Pressing lidless eyes and waiting for a knock upon the door.

     When Lil's husband got demobbed,[17] I said—
I didn't mince my words, I said to her myself,
140   HURRY UP PLEASE ITS TIME
Now Albert's coming back, make yourself a bit smart.
He'll want to know what you done with that money he gave you
To get yourself some teeth. He did, I was there.
You have them all out, Lil, and get a nice set,
145   He said, I swear, I can't bear to look at you.
And no more can't I, I said, and think of poor Albert,
He's been in the army four years, he wants a good time,
And if you don't give it him, there's others will, I said.
Oh is there, she said. Something o' that, I said.
150   Then I'll know who to thank, she said, and give me a straight look.
HURRY UP PLEASE ITS TIME
If you don't like it you can get on with it, I said.
Others can pick and choose if you can't.
But if Albert makes off, it won't be for lack of telling.
155   You ought to be ashamed, I said, to look so antique.

---

[16] **Shakespeherian Rag:** Popular song in the United States in 1912.
[17] **demobbed:** Demobilized from military service following the conclusion of World War I.

(And her only thirty-one.)
I can't help it, she said, pulling a long face,
It's them pills I took, to bring it off, she said.
(She's had five already, and nearly died of young George.)
160   The chemist° said it would be all right, but I've never been   pharmacist
           the same.
You *are* a proper fool, I said.
Well, if Albert won't leave you alone, there it is, I said,
What you get married for if you don't want children?
HURRY UP PLEASE ITS TIME
165   Well, that Sunday Albert was home, they had a hot gammon,°   smoked ham
And they asked me in to dinner, to get the beauty of it hot—
HURRY UP PLEASE ITS TIME
HURRY UP PLEASE ITS TIME
Goonight Bill. Goonight Lou. Goonight May. Goonight.
170   Ta ta. Goonight. Goonight.
Good night, ladies, good night, sweet ladies, good night, good night.[18]

III. The Fire Sermon

   The river's tent is broken: the last fingers of leaf
Clutch and sink into the wet bank. The wind
175   Crosses the brown land, unheard. The nymphs are departed
Sweet Thames,[19] run softly, till I end my song.
The river bears no empty bottles, sandwich papers,
Silk handkerchiefs, cardboard boxes, cigarette ends
Or other testimony of summer nights. The nymphs are departed.
180   And their friends, the loitering heirs of city directors;
Departed, have left no addresses.
By the waters of Leman[20] I sat down and wept . . .
Sweet Thames, run softly till I end my song,
Sweet Thames, run softly, for I speak not loud or long.
185   But at my back in a cold blast I hear
The rattle of the bones, and chuckle spread from ear to ear.
A rat crept softly through the vegetation
Dragging its slimy belly on the bank
While I was fishing in the dull canal
190   On a winter evening round behind the gashouse
Musing upon the king my brother's wreck
And on the king my father's death before him.
White bodies naked on the low damp ground
And bones cast in a little low dry garret,
195   Rattled by the rat's foot only, year to year.

---

[18] **Good . . . night:** From Shakespeare's *Hamlet*, Ophelia's farewell before drowning herself.
[19] **Sweet Thames:** The Thames is a river that runs through London.
[20] **Leman:** Leman is the Lake of Geneva, near where Eliot wrote much of *The Waste Land*.

But at my back from time to time I hear
The sound of horns and motors, which shall bring
Sweeney to Mrs. Porter in the spring.
O the moon shone bright on Mrs. Porter
200   And on her daughter
They wash their feet in soda water
Et O ces voix d'enfants, chantant dans la coupole![21]

Twit twit twit
Jug jug jug jug jug jug
205   So rudely forc'd.
Tereu[22]

    Unreal City
Under the brown fog of a winter noon
Mr. Eugenides, the Smyrna merchant
210   Unshaven, with a pocket full of currants
C.i.f. London: documents at sight,
Asked me in demotic° French   simplified
To luncheon at the Cannon Street Hotel
Followed by a weekend at the Metropole.[23]

215   At the violet hour, when the eyes and back
Turn upward from the desk, when the human engine waits
Like a taxi throbbing waiting,
I Tiresias,[24] though blind, throbbing between two lives,
Old man with wrinkled female breasts, can see
220   At the violet hour, the evening hour that strives
Homeward, and brings the sailor home from sea,
The typist home at teatime, clears her breakfast, lights
Her stove, and lays out food in tins.
Out of the window perilously spread
225   Her drying combinations° touched by the sun's last rays,   underwear
On the divan are piled (at night her bed)
Stockings, slippers, camisoles, and stays.
I Tiresias, old man with wrinkled dugs°   breasts
Perceived the scene, and foretold the rest—
230   I too awaited the expected guest.
He, the young man carbuncular,° arrives,   with acne
A small house agent's clerk, with one bold stare,

---

[21] **Et . . . coupole!:** From Verlaine's sonnet "Parsifal": "And, O those children's voices singing in the dome!"
[22] **Tereu:** An attempt of Elizabethan poets to represent the song of the nightingale, as well as a reference to Tereus.
[23] **Metropole:** A large hotel in Brighton, a beach town in southern England.
[24] **Tiresias:** Blind prophet and famous soothsayer of ancient Greece.

One of the low on whom assurance sits
As a silk hat on a Bradford[25] millionaire.
235   The time is now propitious, as he guesses,
The meal is ended, she is bored and tired,
Endeavours to engage her in caresses
Which still are unreproved, if undesired.
Flushed and decided, he assaults at once;
240   Exploring hands encounter no defence;
His vanity requires no response,
And makes a welcome of indifference.
(And I Tiresias have foresuffered all
Enacted on this same divan or bed;
245   I who have sat by Thebes below the wall
And walked among the lowest of the dead.)
Bestows one final patronizing kiss,
And gropes his way, finding the stairs unlit . . .

She turns and looks a moment in the glass,
250   Hardly aware of her departed lover;
Her brain allows one half-formed thought to pass:
"Well now that's done: and I'm glad it's over."
When lovely woman stoops to folly and
Paces about her room again, alone,
255   She smoothes her hair with automatic hand,
And puts a record on the gramophone.

"This music crept by me upon the waters"
And along the Strand,[26] up Queen Victoria Street.
O City city, I can sometimes hear
260   Beside a public bar in Lower Thames Street,
The pleasant whining of a mandolin
And a clatter and a chatter from within
Where fishmen lounge at noon: where the walls
Of Magnus Martyr[27] hold
265   Inexplicable splendour of Ionian white and gold.

The river sweats
Oil and tar
The barges drift
With the turning tide
270   Red sails

---

[25] **Bradford:** Industrial town in Yorkshire, England, which was prosperous during World War I.
[26] **the Strand:** Street in west central London, famous for its hotels, theaters, and tourism.
[27] **Magnus Martyr:** Saint Magnus Martyr, famous church in London, formerly at the head of London Bridge. It was designed by Sir Christopher Wren (1632–1723).

Wide
To leeward, swing on the heavy spar.
The barges wash
Drifting logs
275   Down Greenwich reach
Past the Isle of Dogs. [28]
       Weialala leia
       Wallala leialala

Elizabeth and Leicester[29]
280   Beating oars
The stern was formed
A gilded shell
Red and gold
The brisk swell
285   Rippled both shores
Southwest wind
Carried down stream
The peal of bells
White towers
290   Weialala leia
       Wallala leialala

'Trams and dusty trees.
Highbury bore me. Richmond and Kew[30]
Undid me. By Richmond I raised my knees
295   Supine on the floor of a narrow canoe.'

"My feet are at Moorgate,[31] and my heart
Under my feet. After the event
He wept. He promised 'a new start.'
I made no comment. What should I resent?"

300   "On Margate Sands.[32]
I can connect
Nothing with nothing.
The broken fingernails of dirty hands.

---

[28] **Isle of Dogs:** Stretch of land that extends into the Thames near Greenwich.
[29] **Elizabeth and Leicester:** Queen Elizabeth favored Sir Robert Dudley (1532?–1588), the earl of Leicester.
[30] **Highbury . . . Kew:** Highbury is a suburb of London, Richmond is a village north of London, and Kew is a town near London known for its botanical gardens.
[31] **Moorgate:** East London slum.
[32] **Margate Sands:** Seaside resort near Kent, where the Thames opens into the English Channel.

My people humble people who expect
305   Nothing."
                    la la
        To Carthage then I came[33]
        Burning burning burning burning
        O Lord Thou pluckest me out
310   O Lord Thou pluckest

        burning

IV. Death by Water

Phlebas the Phoenician,[34] a fortnight dead,
Forgot the cry of gulls, and the deep sea swell
And the profit and loss.
315   A current under sea
Picked his bones in whispers. As he rose and fell
He passed the stages of his age and youth
Entering the whirlpool.
                    Gentile or Jew
320   O you who turn the wheel and look to windward,
        Consider Phlebas, who was once handsome and tall as you.

V. What the Thunder Said

After the torchlight red on sweaty faces
After the frosty silence in the gardens
After the agony in stony places
325   The shouting and the crying
Prison and palace and reverberation
Of thunder of spring over distant mountains
He who was living is now dead
We who were living are now dying
330   With a little patience

Here is no water but only rock
Rock and no water and the sandy road
The road winding above among the mountains
Which are mountains of rock without water
335   If there were water we should stop and drink
Amongst the rock one cannot stop or think
Sweat is dry and feet are in the sand
If there were only water amongst the rock

---

[33] **Carthage:** Ancient city-state in Northern Africa, near modern-day Tunis. St. Augustine addressed Carthage in his *Confessions*.
[34] **Phlebas the Phoenician:** Likely the drowned Phoenician sailor from line 47.

Dead mountain mouth of carious° teeth that cannot spit   rotted
340 Here one can neither stand nor lie nor sit
There is not even silence in the mountains
But dry sterile thunder without rain
There is not even solitude in the mountains
But red sullen faces sneer and snarl
345 From doors of mudcracked houses
                                        If there were water

      And no rock
      If there were rock
      And also water
350   And water
      A spring
      A pool among the rock
      If there were the sound of water only
      Not the cicada
355   And dry grass singing
      But sound of water over a rock
      Where the hermit-thrush sings in the pine trees
      Drip drop drip drop drop drop drop
      But there is no water

360   Who is the third who walks always beside you?
      When I count, there are only you and I together
      But when I look ahead up the white road
      There is always another one walking beside you
      Gliding wrapt in a brown mantle, hooded
365   I do not know whether a man or a woman
      —But who is that on the other side of you?

      What is that sound high in the air
      Murmur of maternal lamentation
      Who are those hooded hordes swarming
370   Over endless plains, stumbling in cracked earth
      Ringed by the flat horizon only
      What is the city over the mountains
      Cracks and reforms and bursts in the violet air
      Falling towers
375   Jerusalem Athens Alexandria
      Vienna London
      Unreal

      A woman drew her long black hair out tight
      And fiddled whisper music on those strings
380   And bats with baby faces in the violet light
      Whistled, and beat their wings

And crawled head downward down a blackened wall
And upside down in air were towers
Tolling reminiscent bells, that kept the hours
385   And voices singing out of empty cisterns and exhausted wells.

    In this decayed hole among the mountains
In the faint moonlight, the grass is singing
Over the tumbled graves, about the chapel
There is the empty chapel, only the wind's home.
390   It has no windows, and the door swings,
Dry bones can harm no one.
Only a cock stood on the rooftree
Co co rico co co rico [35]
In a flash of lightning. Then a damp gust
395   Bringing rain

    Ganga was sunken, and the limp leaves
Waited for rain, while the black clouds
Gathered far distant, over Himavant. [36]
The jungle crouched, humped in silence.
400   Then spoke the thunder
DA
Datta: [37] what have we given?
My friend, blood shaking my heart
The awful daring of a moment's surrender
405   Which an age of prudence can never retract
By this, and this only, we have existed
Which is not to be found in our obituaries
Or in memories draped by the beneficent spider
Or under seals broken by the lean solicitor
410   In our empty rooms
DA
Dayadhvam: I have heard the key
Turn in the door once and turn once only
We think of the key, each in his prison
415   Thinking of the key, each confirms a prison
Only at nightfall, ethereal rumours
Revive for a moment a broken Coriolanus [38]

---

[35] **Cock . . . rico:** See Matthew 26.75: "Immediately a rooster crowed. Then Peter remembered the word Jesus had spoken: 'Before the rooster crows, you will disown me three times.' And he went outside and wept bitterly." Also, a cock's crow was known to scare away ghosts and spirits.
[36] **Ganga . . . Himavant:** In Sanskrit, the River Ganges. According to Hindu tradition, bathing in the Ganges results in personal renewal. Himavant, "snowy mountain," refers to a sacred mountain in the Himalayas.
[37] **Datta:** From the legend of thunder in the *Brhad-aranyaka Upanisad:* "Datta, dayadhvam, damyata."—"Give, sympathize, control." The commands reflect the duty of gods, humans, and demons.
[38] **Coriolanus:** Coriolanus (ca. fifth century B.C.), Roman patrician and hero who later turned against Rome when he lost support of the people.

DA
Damyata: The boat responded
420 Gaily, to the hand expert with sail and oar
The sea was calm, your heart would have responded
Gaily, when invited, beating obedient
To controlling hands

                              I sat upon the shore
425 Fishing, with the arid plain behind me
Shall I at least set my lands in order?
London Bridge is falling down falling down falling down
Poi s'ascose nel foco che gli affina[39]
Quando fiam uti chelidon[40]—O swallow swallow
430 *Le Prince d'Aquitaine à la tour abolie*[41]
These fragments I have shored against my ruins
Why then Ile fit you. Hieronymo's mad againe.[42]
Datta. Dayadhvam. Damyata.
                   Shantih   shantih   shantih[43]

T. S. Eliot (1888–1965)
Original Footnotes to *The Waste Land*

NOTES

Not only the title, but the plan and a good deal of the incidental symbolism of the poem were suggested by Miss Jessie L. Weston's book on the Grail legend: *From Ritual to Romance* (Macmillan). Indeed, so deeply am I indebted, Miss Weston's book will elucidate the difficulties of the poem much better than my notes can do; and I recommend it (apart from the great interest of the book itself) to any who think such elucidation of the poem worth the trouble. To another work of anthropology I am indebted in general, one which has influenced our generation profoundly; I mean *The Golden Bough*; I have used especially the two volumes *Adonis, Attis, Osiris*. Anyone who is acquainted with these works will immediately recognize in the poem certain references to vegetation ceremonies.

    I. THE BURIAL OF THE DEAD
Line 20 Cf. Ezekiel 2:7.
  23. Cf. Ecclesiastes 12:5.
  31. *V. Tristan und Isolde*, i, verses 5–8.

---

[39] **Poi . . . affina:** From Dante's *Purgatorio*: "Then he hid himself in the fire that purifies them."
[40] **Quando . . . chelidon:** From *The Vigil of Venus*: "When shall I become like the swallow."
[41] **Le Prince . . . abolie:** From Gerard de Neval's sonnet *El Desdichado*: "The prince of Aquitania in the ruined tower."
[42] **Hieronymo's mad againe:** In Thomas Kyd's *The Spanish Tragedy*, Hieronymo goes insane after his son Horatio is murdered.
[43] **Shantih:** "The peace which passeth understanding."

42. Id. iii, verse 24.

46. I am not familiar with the exact constitution of the Tarot pack of cards, from which I have obviously departed to suit my own convenience. The Hanged Man, a member of the traditional pack, fits my purpose in two ways: because he is associated in my mind with the Hanged God of Frazer, and because I associate him with the hooded figure in the passage of the disciples to Emmaus in Part V. The Phoenician Sailor and the Merchant appear later; also the 'crowds of people', and Death by Water is executed in Part IV. The Man with Three Staves (an authentic member of the Tarot pack) I associate, quite arbitrarily, with the Fisher King himself.

60. Cf. Baudelaire:

>Fourmillante cité, cité pleine de rêves,
>
>Où le spectre en plein jour raccroche le passant.

63. Cf. *Inferno*, iii. 55–7:

>si lunga tratta
>
>di gente, ch'io non avrei mai creduto
>
>che morte tanta n'avesse disfatta.

64. Cf. *Inferno*, iv. 25–27:

>Quivi, secondo che per ascoltare,
>
>non avea pianto, ma' che di sospiri,
>
>che l'aura eterna facevan tremare.

68. A phenomenon which I have often noticed.

74. Cf. the Dirge in Webster's *White Devil*.

76. *V.* Baudelaire, Preface to *Fleurs du Mal*.

II. A GAME OF CHESS

77. Cf. *Antony and Cleopatra*, II. ii. 190.

92. Laquearia. *V. Aeneid*, I. 726:

>dependent lychni laquearibus aureis incensi, et noctem flammis
>>funalia vincunt.

98. Sylvan scene. *V.* Milton, *Paradise Lost*, iv. 140.

99. *V.* Ovid, *Metamorphoses*, vi, Philomela.

100. Cf. Part III, l. *204*.

115. Cf. Part III, l. *195*.

118. Cf. Webster: 'Is the wind in that door still?'

126. Cf. Part I, l. *37, 48*.

138. Cf. the game of chess in Middleton's *Women beware Women*.

III. THE FIRE SERMON

176. *V.* Spenser, *Prothalamion*.

192. Cf. *The Tempest*, I. ii.

196. Cf. Marvell, *To His Coy Mistress*.

197. Cf. Day, *Parliament of Bees*:

> When of the sudden, listening, you shall hear,
>
> A noise of horns and hunting, which shall bring
>
> Actaeon to Diana in the spring,
>
> Where all shall see her naked skin . . .

199. I do not know the origin of the ballad from which these lines are taken: it was reported to me from Sydney, Australia.

202. V. Verlaine, *Parsifal.*

210. The currants were quoted at a price 'carriage and insurance free to London'; and the Bill of Lading, etc., were to be handed to the buyer upon payment of the sight draft.

218. Tiresias, although a mere spectator and not indeed a 'character', is yet the most important personage in the poem, uniting all the rest. Just as the one-eyed merchant, seller of currants, melts into the Phoenician Sailor, and the latter is not wholly distinct from Ferdinand Prince of Naples, so all the women are one woman, and the two sexes meet in Tiresias. What Tiresias *sees,* in fact, is the substance of the poem. The whole passage from Ovid is of great anthropological interest:

> . . . Cum Iunone iocos et 'maior vestra profecto est
>
> Quam, quae contingit maribus', dixisse, 'voluptas.'
>
> Illa negat; placuit quae sit sententia docti
>
> Quaerere Tiresiae: venus huic erat utraque nota.
>
> Nam duo magnorum viridi coeuntia silva
>
> Corpora serpentum baculi violaverat ictu
>
> Deque viro factus, mirabile, femina septem
>
> Egerat autumnos; octavo rursus eosdem
>
> Vidit et 'est vestrae si tanta potentia plagae',
>
> Dixit 'ut auctoris sortem in contraria mutet,
>
> Nunc quoque vos feriam!' percussis anguibus isdem
>
> Forma prior rediit genetivaque venit imago.
>
> Arbiter hic igitur sumptus de lite iocosa
>
> Dicta Iovis firmat; gravius Saturnia iusto
>
> Nec pro materia fertur doluisse suique
>
> Iudicis aeterna damnavit lumina nocte,
>
> At pater omnipotens (neque enim licet inrita cuiquam
>
> Facta dei fecisse deo) pro lumine adempto
>
> Scire futura dedit poenamque levavit honore.

221. This may not appear as exact as Sappho's lines, but I had in mind the 'longshore' or 'dory' fisherman, who returns at nightfall.

253. V. Goldsmith, the song in *The Vicar of Wakefield.*

257. V. *The Tempest,* as above.

264. The interior of St. Magnus Martyr is to my mind one of the finest among Wren's interiors. See *The Proposed Demolition of Nineteen City Churches* (P. S. King & Son, Ltd.).

266. The Song of the (three) Thames-daughters begins here. From line 292 to 306 inclusive they speak in turn. *V. Götterdammerung*, III. i: The Rhine-daughters.

279. *V.* Froude, *Elizabeth*, vol. I, ch. iv, letter of De Quadra to Philip of Spain:

> In the afternoon we were in a barge, watching the games on the river. (The queen) was alone with Lord Robert and myself on the poop, when they began to talk nonsense, and went so far that Lord Robert at last said, as I was on the spot there was no reason why they should not be married if the queen pleased.

293. Cf. *Purgatorio*, V. 133:

> 'Ricorditi di me, che son la Pia;
> Siena mi fe', disfecemi Maremma.'

307. *V.* St. Augustine's *Confessions:* 'to Carthage then I came, where a cauldron of unholy loves sang all about mine ears'.

308. The complete text of the Buddha's Fire Sermon (which corresponds in importance to the Sermon on the Mount) from which these words are taken, will be found translated in the late Henry Clarke Warren's *Buddhism in Translation* (Harvard Oriental Series). Mr. Warren was one of the great pioneers of Buddhist studies in the Occident.

309. From St. Augustine's *Confessions* again. The collocation of these two representatives of eastern and western asceticism, as the culmination of this part of the poem, is not an accident.

V. WHAT THE THUNDER SAID

In the first part of Part V three themes are employed: the journey to Emmaus, the approach to the Chapel Perilous (see Miss Weston's book), and the present decay of eastern Europe.

357. This is *Turdus aonalaschkae pallasii,* the hermit-thrush which I have heard in Quebec County. Chapman says (*Handbook of Birds in Eastern North America*) 'it is most at home in secluded woodland and thickety retreats . . . . Its notes are not remarkable for variety or volume, but in purity and sweetness of tone and exquisite modulation they are unequalled.' Its 'water-dripping song' is justly celebrated.

360. The following lines were stimulated by the account of one of the Antarctic expeditions (I forget which, but I think one of Shackleton's): it was related that the party of explorers, at the extremity of their strength, had the constant delusion that there was *one more member* than could actually be counted.

367–77. Cf. Hermann Hesse, *Blick ins Chaos:*

> Schon ist halb Europa, schon ist zumindest der halbe Osten Europas auf dem Wege zum Chaos, fährt betrunken im heiligen Wahn am Abgrund entlang und singt dazu, singt betrunken und hymnisch wie Dmitri Karamasoff sang. Ueber diese Lieder lacht der Bürger beleidigt, der Heilige und Seher hört sie mit Tränen.

401. 'Datta, dayadhvam, damyata' (Give, sympathize, control). The fable of the meaning of the Thunder is found in the *Brihadaranyaka—Upanishad*, 5, 1. A translation is found in Deussen's *Sechzig Upanishads des Veda*, p. 489.

407. Cf. Webster, *The White Devil*, V, vi:

>   . . . they'll remarry
> Ere the worm pierce your winding-sheet, ere the spider
> Make a thin curtain for your epitaphs.

411. Cf. *Inferno*, xxxiii. 46:

> ed io sentii chiavar l'uscio di sotto
> all'orribile torre.

Also F. H. Bradley, *Appearance and Reality*, p. 346:

> My external sensations are no less private to myself than are my thoughts
> or my feelings. In either case my experience falls within my own circle, a circle
> closed on the outside; and, with all its elements alike, every sphere is opaque
> to the others which surround it . . . . In brief, regarded as an existence which
> appears in a soul, the whole world for each is peculiar and private to that soul.

424. V. Weston, *From Ritual to Romance;* chapter on the Fisher King.

427. V. *Purgatorio*, xxvi. 148.

> 'Ara vos prec per aquella valor
> 'que vos guida al som de l'escalina,
> 'sovegna vos a temps de ma dolor.'
> Poi s'ascose nel foco che gli affina.

428. V. *Pervigilium Veneris*. Cf. Philomela in Parts II and III.

429. V. Gerard de Nerval, Sonnet *El Desdichado*.

431. V. Kyd's *Spanish Tragedy*.

433. Shantih. Repeated as here, a formal ending to an *Upanishad*. 'The Peace which passeth understanding' is a feeble translation of the conduct of this word.

DEREK WALCOTT (1930–   )

from Omeros [1]

Chapter I

I

"This is how, one sunrise, we cut down them canoes."
Philoctete smiles for the tourists, who try taking
his soul with their cameras. "Once wind bring the news

---

[1] **Omeros:** In *Omeros*, Derek Walcott examines the fusion of his native St. Lucian culture and British imperialism. *Omeros* is the Greek name for the poet Homer, and Walcott uses the characters and themes found in Homer's *Iliad* to articulate both the beauty and the complexity of St. Lucia's native culture. The epic is a convergence of several plots: Achille and Hector fight over the beautiful island girl Helen, a retired British Major and his wife adjust to St. Lucia's local culture, and Philoctete attempts to recover from a wound that is both physical and spiritual. The opening section printed here puts the contrast between traditional and modern culture in balance.

to the *laurier-cannelles*,° their leaves start shaking   cinnamon-laurel
5   the minute the axe of sunlight hit the cedars,
because they could see the axes in our own eyes.

Wind lift the ferns. They sound like the sea that feed us
fishermen all our life, and the ferns nodded 'Yes,
the trees have to die.' So, fists jam in our jacket,

10   cause the heights was cold and our breath making feathers
like the mist, we pass the rum. When it came back, it
give us the spirit to turn into murderers.

I lift up the axe and pray for strength in my hands
to wound the first cedar. Dew was filling my eyes,
15   but I fire one more white rum. Then we advance."

For some extra silver, under a sea-almond,
he shows them a scar made by a rusted anchor,
rolling one trouser-leg up with the rising moan

of a conch. It has puckered like the corolla
20   of a sea-urchin. He does not explain its cure.
"It have some things"—he smiles—"worth more than a dollar."

He has left it to a garrulous waterfall
to pour out his secret down La Sorcière,[2] since
the tall laurels fell, for the ground-dove's mating call

25   to pass on its note to the blue, tacit mountains
whose talkative brooks, carrying it to the sea,
turn into idle pools where the clear minnows shoot

and an egret stalks the reeds with one rusted cry
as it stabs and stabs the mud with one lifting foot.
30   Then silence is sawn in half by a dragonfly

as eels sign their names along the clear bottom-sand,
when the sunrise brightens the river's memory
and waves of huge ferns are nodding to the sea's sound.

Although smoke forgets the earth from which it ascends,
35   and nettles guard the holes where the laurels were killed,
an iguana hears the axes, clouding each lens

---

[2] **La Sorcière:** "The Sorceress," a great mountain in St. Lucia rumored to possess supernatural powers.

over its lost name, when the hunched island was called
"Iounalao," "Where the iguana is found."
But, taking its own time, the iguana will scale

40   the rigging of vines in a year, its dewlap fanned,
its elbows akimbo, its deliberate tail
moving with the island. The slit pods of its eyes

ripened in a pause that lasted for centuries,
that rose with the Aruacs'[3] smoke till a new race
45   unknown to the lizard stood measuring the trees.

These were their pillars that fell, leaving a blue space
for a single God where the old gods stood before.
The first god was a gommier.[4] The generator

began with a whine, and a shark, with sidewise jaw,
50   sent the chips flying like mackerel over water
into trembling weeds. Now they cut off the saw,

still hot and shaking, to examine the wound it
had made. They scraped off its gangrenous moss, then ripped
the wound clear of the net of vines that still bound it

55   to this earth, and nodded. The generator whipped
back to its work, and the chips flew much faster as
the shark's teeth gnawed evenly. They covered their eyes

from the splintering nest. Now, over the pastures
of bananas, the island lifted its horns. Sunrise
60   trickled down its valleys, blood splashed on the cedars,

and the grove flooded with the light of sacrifice.
A gommier was cracking. Its leaves an enormous
tarpaulin with the ridgepole gone. The creaking sound

made the fishermen leap back as the angling mast
65   leant slowly towards the troughs of ferns; then the ground
shuddered under the feet in waves, then the waves passed.

---

[3] **Aruacs':** Indian tribe native to the Caribbean region that was basically eliminated as a result of colonization and exploration.
[4] **gommier:** Found in St. Lucia and Dominica, the gommier tree secretes a waterproof resin that makes its wood perfect material from which to fashion a canoe.

II

Achille looked up at the hole the laurel had left.
He saw the hole silently healing with the foam
of a cloud like a breaker. Then he saw the swift

70   crossing the cloud-surf, a small thing, far from its home,
confused by the waves of blue hills. A thorn vine gripped
his heel. He tugged it free. Around him, other ships

were shaping from the saw. With his cutlass he made
a swift sign of the cross, his thumb touching his lips
75   while the height rang with axes. He swayed back the blade,

and hacked the limbs from the dead god, knot after knot,
wrenching the severed veins from the trunk as he prayed:
"Tree! You can be a canoe! Or else you cannot!"

The bearded elders endured the decimation
80   of their tribe without uttering a syllable
of that language they had uttered as one nation,

the speech taught their saplings: from the towering babble
of the cedar to green vowels of *bois-campêche*.°   logwood
The *bois-flot* held its tongue with the *laurier-cannelle*,°   sea hibiscus

85   the red-skinned logwood endured the thorns in its flesh,
while the Aruacs' patois[5] crackled in the smell
of a resinous bonfire that turned the leaves brown

with curling tongues, then ash, and their language was lost.
Like barbarians striding columns they have brought down,
90   the fishermen shouted. The gods were down at last.

Like pygmies they hacked the trunks of wrinkled giants
for paddles and oars. They were working with the same
concentration as an army of fire-ants.

But vexed by the smoke for defaming their forest,
95   blow-darts of mosquitoes kept needling Achille's trunk.
He frotted white rum on both forearms that, at least,

---

[5] **patois:** Unwritten regional dialect of a language, especially French.

those that he flattened to asterisks would die drunk.
They went for his eyes. They circled them with attacks
that made him weep blindly. Then the host retreated

100   to high bamboo like the archers of Aruacs
running from the muskets of cracking logs, routed
by the fire's banner and the remorseless axe

hacking the branches. The men bound the big logs first
with new hemp and, like ants, trundled them to a cliff
105   to plunge through tall nettles. The logs gathered that thirst

for the sea which their own vined bodies were born with.
Now the trunks in eagerness to become canoes
ploughed into breakers of bushes, making raw holes

of boulders, feeling not death inside them, but use—
110   to roof the sea, to be hulls. Then, on the beach, coals
were set in their hollows that were chipped with an adze.°   edging tool

A flat-bed truck had carried their rope-bound bodies.
The charcoals, smouldering, cored the dugouts for days
till heat widened the wood enough for ribbed gunwales.

115   Under his tapping chisel Achille felt their hollows
exhaling to touch the sea, lunging towards the haze
of bird-printed islets, the beaks of their parted bows.

Then everything fit. The pirogues[6] crouched on the sand
like hounds with sprigs in their teeth. The priest
120   sprinkled them with a bell, then he made the swift's sign.

When he smiled at Achille's canoe, *In God We Troust,*
Achille said: "Leave it! Is God' spelling and mine."
After Mass one sunrise the canoes entered the troughs

of the surpliced shallows, and their nodding prows
125   agreed with the waves to forget their lives as trees;
one would serve Hector and another, Achilles.

---

[6] **pirogues:** A canoe made by hollowing out a large log.

III

Achille peed in the dark, then bolted the half-door shut.
It was rusted from sea-blast. He hoisted the fishpot
with the crab of one hand; in the hole under the hut

130   he hid the cinder-block step. As he neared the depot,
the dawn breeze salted him coming up the grey street
past sleep-tight houses, under the sodium bars

of street-lamps, to the dry asphalt scraped by his feet;
he counted the small blue sparks of separate stars.
135   Banana fronds nodded to the undulating

anger of roosters, their cries screeching like red chalk
drawing hills on a board. Like his teacher, waiting,
the surf kept chafing at his deliberate walk.

By the time they met at the wall of the concrete shed
140   the morning star had stepped back, hating the odour
of nets and fish-guts; the light was hard overhead

and there was a horizon. He put the net by the door
of the depot, then washed his hands in its basin.
The surf did not raise its voice, even the ribbed hounds

145   around the canoes were quiet; a flask of l'absinthe
was passed by the fishermen, who made smacking sounds
and shook at the bitter bark from which it was brewed.

This was the light that Achille was happiest in.
When, before their hands gripped the gunwales, they stood
150   for the sea-width to enter them, feeling their day begin.

Chapter II

I

Hector was there. Theophile also. In this light,
they have only Christian names. Placide, Pancreas,
Chrysostom, Maljo, Philoctete with his head white

as the coiled surf. They shipped the lances of oars,
155   placed them parallel in the grave of the gunwales
like man and wife. They scooped the leaf-bilge from the planks,

loosened knots from the bodies of flour-sack sails,
while Hector, at the shallows' edge, gave a quick thanks,
with the sea for a font, before he waded, thigh-in.

160   The rest walked up the sand with identical stride
except for foam-haired Philoctete. The sore on his shin
still unhealed, like a radiant anemone. It had come

from a scraping, rusted anchor. The pronged iron
peeled the skin in a backwash. He bent to the foam,
165   sprinkling it with a salt hiss. Soon he would run,

hobbling, to the useless shade of an almond,
with locked teeth, then wave them off from the shame
of his smell, and once more they would leave him alone

under its leoparding light. This sunrise the same
170   damned business was happening. He felt the sore twitch
its wires up to his groin. With his hop-and-drop

limp, hand clutching one knee, he left the printed beach
to crawl up the early street to Ma Kilman's shop.
She would open and put the white rum within reach.

175   His shipmates watched him, then they hooked hands like anchors
under the hulls, rocking them; the keels sheared dry sand
till the wet sand resisted, rattling the oars

that lay parallel amidships; then, to the one sound
of curses and prayers at the logs jammed as a wedge,
180   one after one, as their tins began to rattle,

the pirogues slid to the shallows' nibbling edge,
towards the encouraging sea. The loose logs swirled
in surf, face down, like warriors from a battle

lost somewhere on the other shore of the world.
185   They were dragged to a place under the manchineels
to lie there face upward, the sun moving over their brows

with the stare of myrmidons[7] hauled up by the heels
high up from the tide-mark where the pale crab burrows.
The fishermen brushed their palms. Now all the canoes

---

[7] **myrmidons:** A man who follows orders without question, but also, in Greek mythology, a warrior who followed Achilles in the battle against Troy.

190 were riding the pink morning swell. They drew their bows
gently, the way grooms handle horses in the sunrise,
flicking the ropes like reins, pinned them by the nose—

Praise Him, Morning Star, St. Lucia, Light of My Eyes,
threw bailing tins in them, and folded their bodies across
195 the tilting hulls, then sculled one oar in the slack

of the stern. Hector rattled out his bound canvas
to gain ground with the gulls, hoping to come back
before that conch-coloured dusk low pelicans cross.

II

Seven Seas rose in the half-dark to make coffee.
200 Sunrise was heating the ring of the horizon
and clouds were rising like loaves. By the heat of the

glowing iron rose he slid the saucepan's base onto the ring and anchored it there. The saucepan shook
from the weight of water in it, then it settled.

205 His kettle leaked. He groped for the tin chair and took
his place near the saucepan to hear when it bubbled.
It would boil but not scream like a bosun's° whistle   boatswain's

to let him know it was ready. He heard the dog's
morning whine under the boards of the house, its tail
210 thudding to be let in, but he envied the pirogues

already miles out at sea. Then he heard the first breeze
washing the sea-almond's wares; last night there had been
a full moon white as his plate. He saw with his ears.

He warmed with the roofs as the sun began to climb.
215 Since the disease had obliterated vision,
when the sunset shook the sea's hand for the last time—

and an inward darkness grew where the moon and sun
indistinctly altered—he moved by a sixth sense,
like the moon without an hour or second hand,

220 wiped clean as the plate that he now began to rinse
while the saucepan bubbled; blindness was not the end.
It was not a palm-tree's dial on the noon sand.

He could feel the sunlight creeping over his wrists.
The sunlight moved like a cat along the palings
225 of a sandy street; he felt it unclench the fists

of the breadfruit tree in his yard, run the railings
of the short iron bridge like a harp, its racing
stick rippling with the river; he saw the lagoon

behind the church, and in it, stuck like a basin,
230 the rusting enamel image of the full moon.
He lowered the ring to sunset under the pan.

The dog scratched at the kitchen door for him to open
but he made it wait. He drummed the kitchen table
with his fingers. Two blackbirds quarrelled at breakfast.

235 Except for one hand he sat as still as marble,
with his egg-white eyes, fingers recounting the past
of another sea, measured by the stroking oars.

O open this day with the conch's moan, Omeros,
as you did in my boyhood, when I was a noun
240 gently exhaled from the palate of the sunrise.

A lizard on the sea-wall darted its question
at the waking sea, and a net of golden moss
brightened the reef, which the sails of their far canoes

avoided. Only in you, across centuries
245 of the sea's parchment atlas, can I catch the noise
of the surf lines wandering like the shambling fleece

of the lighthouse's flock, that Cyclops whose blind eye
shut from the sunlight. Then the canoes were galleys
over which a frigate sawed its scythed wings slowly.

250 In you the seeds of grey almonds guessed a tree's shape,
and the grape leaves rusted like serrated islands,
and the blind lighthouse, sensing the edge of a cape,

paused like a giant, a marble cloud in its hands,
to hurl its boulder that splashed into phosphorous
255 stars; then a black fisherman, his stubbled chin coarse

as a dry sea-urchin's, hoisted his flour-sack
sail on its bamboo spar, and scanned the opening line
of our epic horizon; now I can look back

to rocks that see their own feet when light nets the waves,
260 as the dugouts set out with ebony captains,
since it was your light that startled our sunlit wharves

where schooners swayed idly, moored to their cold capstans.
A wind turns the harbour's pages back to the voice
that hummed in the vase of a girl's throat: "Omeros."

THE FORGETFUL KINGDOM OF DEATH

CHAPTER 2

—John Crowe Ransom

An Anthology of the Elegy

Elegy has been central to poetry since the times of ancient Greece and Rome, although the nature of elegy itself has changed significantly over the centuries. The word itself derives from a Greek word that means "a poem written in couplets." It has a secondary meaning of, quite simply, "song." The word can also mean, in Greek, "a mournful song." The adjectival form of the word, *elegiac*, originally meant a poem written in couplets, although it has come to mean "mournful" or "solemn and stately." The Greeks and Romans, however, did not usually write elegies lamenting the death of someone. That came with the English elegy, in the sixteenth century. The great classical elegies were usually love poems or war poems, and some of them had a pastoral setting.

The first elegies emerged in the seventh century B.C., and were songs written for men going into battle. Among the earliest fragments are those by Callinus, Archilochus, Tyrtaeus, and Mimnermus. The notion that an army, poised for battle, would pause to listen to a poet may seem peculiar, but it has been recorded that in the fourth century B.C., as the Spartans were about to set off for war, they were forced to gather before the king's residence and listen to recitals from the work of Tyrtaeus, himself a Spartan.

Historians of Greek literature believe that these poems were accompanied by musical instruments, such as pipes or drums. Later elegists included Solon (very little of his work survives, and he was better known as a statesman) and Callimachus. The latter was a librarian at the famous library in Alexandria, Egypt. In general, the Greek elegists influenced the great Roman elegists, such as Catullus, Tibullus, Propertius, and Ovid. As with the Greeks, the Roman elegists almost never wrote poems lamenting the death of someone. Their elegies were characterized by strong emotion, however. In the case of Catullus, these were intensely erotic poems. What made them elegies was their poetic form: a couplet or distich, with a hexameter line followed by a pentameter line. It was Propertius who brought this form to a kind of perfection, with his fluid movement from couplet to couplet, his dexterous alteration of rhythms as he moved from the hexameter to the pentameter line.

During the Renaissance in England, interest in Greek and Roman literature flourished, and poets began to write what they called elegies: poems of lament, usually celebrating a departed hero or friend. Among the earliest writers of elegy in English was George Gascoigne, who called his famous "Complaint of Philomene" an elegy or "sorrowful song," as he defined it in his preface to the poem, which appeared in 1576. Soon the elegy became known as a poem of considerable length that mourned the loss of someone or dwelled with some melancholic grandeur on feelings of regret.

During the seventeenth and eighteenth centuries, the form flourished, with elegant examples of the elegy entering the canon. These include Milton's *Lycidas* (p. 142) and Thomas Gray's "Elegy Written in a Country Churchyard" (p. 153). This latter poem extends the form considerably, in that the subject was not the death of a particular person (as with Milton's poem), but a general lament for the mortality of human beings. It was, in fact, written during a period when the poet was grieving for a recently deceased friend, Richard West, who died in 1742, but this is never mentioned. Gray's poem conjures a "solemn stillness," its main setting (emerging in the fourth stanza) being a village graveyard under elms and yew trees. It is a place where "The rude forefathers of the hamlet sleep." The poem is also a pastoral poem, evoking imagery of rural life, thus referring back to the Greek and Roman pastoral elegy— one of the classic modes of the form.

Gray's elegy contrasts the simple life of poor country folks with that of the wealthy and powerful who have been corrupted by these adornments. His speaker in the poem, however, is not himself; in keeping with neoclassical tradition, the speaker is identified as someone "mindful of the unhonor'd dead" who relates this "artful tale." In other words, the poem should not be misconstrued as the expression of deep feeling by the poet himself, speaking *as* himself.

That will come later, with Romantic poets like Wordsworth, Keats, and Shelley. The centerpiece of the elegy during the Romantic period, in the nineteenth century, was Shelley's *Adonais* (p. 161), a poem on the death of his close friend Keats. It's a work of huge ambition, strong feeling, and masterful construction. Alfred, Lord Tennyson, wrote *In Memoriam* (p. 179) during the Victorian era, and it remains one of the important poems of the latter half of the century. An elegiac poem of great length, it might be considered a string of elegies. Indeed, the poem consists of 133 poems, strung elegantly together, all lamenting the death of a friend, Arthur Hallem, who was engaged to be married to the poet's sister.

Among the central American elegies is Walt Whitman's lament for the death of Abraham Lincoln, "When Lilacs Last in the Dooryard Bloom'd" (p. 187). One can hardly imagine a poem of greater intensity of feeling or one written in a more original and noble style. "O powerful

western fallen star!" cried Whitman. He is speaking as himself here, decry-
ing the assassination of a man who had meant so much to his country.
The poem is a funeral dirge: a poem of ritual. Whitman brilliantly and
with striking beauty associates the recently deceased president with the
cycles of the natural world. Nature, as ever, is reborn in the spring. The
poet understands this, and the great consolation for writers of elegies is
always the hope of renewal.

Human beings are always moved by the death of someone personally beloved, or by the loss of a statesman or artist whom they
revered. In a masterful elegy by Auden, "In Memory of W. B. Yeats"
(p. 219), the poet uses the occasion of the death of an older poet to meditate on the role of poet in society and on the fate of poetry itself in a
dark historical time. Auden composed this elegy in 1939, as the clouds
of war were gathering over Europe. He ponders the hard fact that
"poetry makes nothing happen." He asks earth to receive her "honored
guest" in the form of Yeats's body. Now this vessel, the poet's dead body,
lies "emptied of its poetry." The poem, in the end, celebrates freedom
and song, the art of poetry itself, which Auden raises up against the barking dogs of war.

The form of the elegy is immensely flexible, and might even be
extended to include a poem such as Wallace Stevens's "The Emperor of
Ice-Cream" (p. 207), which celebrates the triumph of life over death in
the context of a house where the corpse of a woman lies barely covered. The poet says: "Let be be finale of seem." That is, let the reader
and the characters in the poem praise the living, the sensuous and
sensate. Ice cream, for the poet, represents everything that is alive
and well.

Perhaps the least attractive but undeniably vivid elegy in the selections that follow is that by Sylvia Plath called "Daddy" (p. 234). It's a
poem written from a frankly autobiographical viewpoint. It's also a
poem devoid of sweetness, devoid of human sympathy. The poet writes
about her deceased father without attempting to whitewash his dark
side, his anger, his vindictiveness, his ferocity. The poet herself writes
fiercely, without an ounce of remorse for her castigation, turning him
into a Nazi killer. However distasteful, it's a powerful elegy, one that
turns the tradition of elegy sharply on its head. Its insistent rhythms and
compulsive rhyming make it sound like a war poem, one that the
ancient Greeks might have recited marching into battle. In this, Plath
returns us to the elegy as a poem of battle, a poem of anger.

In all, the elegy takes countless forms in English over five centuries.
Poets are always drawn to the possibilities of the form for its elemental
expressiveness. Loss is part of life, and poetry often dwells on the sensations of loss, especially in relation to human mortality. In many ways, the
elegy is a poetic tradition devoted to the feelings of loss that inevitably
arise in the course of any human life. We lose so much every day, every

year. The elegy helps us to account for these losses, to give them form, to make sense of them.

ADDITIONAL EXAMPLES OF THE ELEGY IN THIS BOOK

- Ben Jonson, "To the Memory of My Beloved, the Author William Shakespeare" (p. 1422)

- John Milton, "On his Dead Wife" (p. 980)

- Edgar Allen Poe, "Annabel Lee" (p. 495)

- Gerard Manley Hopkins, "Spring and Fall" (p. 1535)

- Thomas Hardy, "Neutral Tones" (p. 1068)

- Wilfred Owen, "Anthem for Doomed Youth" (p. 824)

- Allen Tate, "Ode to the Confederate Dead" (p. 1612)

- Dylan Thomas, "Do Not Go Gentle into That Good Night" (p. 842)

- Robert Hayden, "Those Winter Sundays" (p. 990)

- Robert Lowell, "The Quaker Graveyard in Nantucket" (p. 1511)

- Donald Justice, "In Memory of the Unknown Poet, Robert Boardman Vaughn" (p. 844)

- Seamus Heaney, "Sunlight" (p. 1519)

BION (ca. second century B.C.)
trans. John Addington Symonds

Lament for Adonis [1]

Wail, wail, Ah for Adonis! He is lost to us, lovely Adonis!
Lost is lovely Adonis! The Loves respond with lamenting.

Nay, no longer in robes of purple recline, Aphrodite:
Wake from thy sleep, sad queen, black-stoled, rain blows on thy bosom;
5   Cry to the listening world, *He is lost to us, lovely Adonis!*

Wail, wail, Ah for Adonis! The Loves respond with lamenting.
Lovely Adonis is lying, sore hurt in his thigh, on the mountains,
Hurt in his thigh with the tusk, while grief consumes Aphrodite:
Slowly he droops toward death, and the black blood drips from his
        fair flesh,
10   Down from his snow-white skin; his eyes wax dull 'neath the eyelids,
Yea and the rose hath failed his lips, and around them the kisses
Die and wither, the kisses that Kupris [2] will not relinquish:
Still, though he lives no longer, a kiss consoles Aphrodite;
But he knows not, Adonis, she kissed him while he was dying.
15   Wail, wail, Ah for Adonis! The Loves respond with lamenting.
Cruel, cruel the wound in the thigh that preys on Adonis:
But in her heart Cytherea [3] hath yet worse wounds to afflict her.
Round him his dear hounds bay, they howl in their grief to the heavens;
Nymphs of the woodlands wail: but she, the Queen Aphrodite,
20   Loosing her locks to the air, roams far and wide through the forest,
Drowned in grief, dishevelled, unsandalled, and as she flies onward,
Briars stab at her feet and cull the blood of the goddess.

She with shrill lamentation thro' glen and thro' glade is carried,
Calling her Syrian lord, [4] demanding him back, and demanding.
25   But where he lies, dark blood wells up and encircles the navel;
Blood from the gushing thighs empurples the breast; and the snow-white
Flank that was once so fair, is now dyed red for Adonis.

Wail, wail, Ah, Cytherea! The Loves respond with lamenting.
She then hath lost her lord, and with him hath lost her celestial

---

[1] **Adonis:** According to the myth, Adonis was a man of rare beauty, dearly loved by Aphrodite, the
Greek goddess of love (Venus in the Roman tradition). While on a hunt, he was attacked and killed
by a wild boar. Aphrodite rushed to save him, but was too late. However, a drop of Adonis' blood fell
on a flower, an anemone, which became known as a symbol of resurrection. This poem by the Greek
pastoral poet Bion (ca. second century B.C.) is considered one of the earliest examples of elegiac
verse. The Greek poet Theocritus and the Roman poet Virgil also wrote famous elegies.
[2] **Kupris:** I.e., the isle of Cyprus, where Aphrodite was born.
[3] **Cytherea:** Another name of Aphrodite, derived from her birthplace Cyprus.
[4] **Syrian lord:** I.e., Adonis.

30 Beauty; for fair was he, and fair, while he lived, Aphrodite:
    Now in his death her beauty hath died. *Ah, Ah, Cytherea!*
    Now in the oak-woods cease to lament for thy lord, Aphrodite.
    No proper couch is this which the wild leaves strew for Adonis.
    Let him thy own bed share, Cytherea, the corpse of Adonis;
35 E'en as a corpse he is fair, fair corpse as fallen aslumber.
    Now lay him soft to sleep, sleep well in the wool of the bedclothes,
    Where with thee through the night in holy dreams he commingled,
    Stretched on a couch all gold, that yearns for him stark though he
        now be.
    Shower on him garlands, flowers: all fair things died in his dying;
40 Yea, as he faded away, so shrivel and wither the blossoms.
    Syrian spikenard° scatter, anoint him with myrrh and with unguents: an herbal oil
    Perish perfumes all, since he, thy perfume, is perished.
        Wail, wail, Ah for Adonis! The Loves respond with lamenting.
    Lapped in his purple robes is the delicate form of Adonis.
45 Round him weeping Loves complain and moan in their anguish,
    Clipping their locks for Adonis: and one of them treads on his arrows,
    One of them breaks his bow, and one sets heel on the quiver;
    One hath loosed for Adonis the latchet of sandals, and some bring
    Water to pour in an urn; one laves the wound in his white thigh;
50 One from behind with his wings keeps fanning dainty Adonis.
        Wail, wail, Ah for Adonis! The Loves respond with lamenting.

        Wail, wail, Ah, Cytherea! The Loves respond with lamenting.

    Every torch at the doors hath been quenched by thy hand,
        Hymenaeus;[5]
    Every bridal wreath hath been torn to shreds; and no longer,
55 Hymen, Hymen no more is the song, but a new song of sorrow,
    Woe, woe! and *Ah for Adonis!* resounds in lieu of the bridesong.
    This the Graces are shrilling, the son of Cinyras[6] hymning,
    Lost is lovely Adonis! in loud antiphonal accents.
    Woe, woe! sharply repeat, far more than the praises of Paion,°   a tribe from the
60 *Woe!* and *Ah for Adonis!* the Muses who wail for Adonis,   Balkan peninsula
    Chaunt their charms to Adonis.—But he lists not to their singing;
    Not that he wills not to hear, but the Maiden doth not release him.

    Cease from moans, Cytherea, today refrain from the death-songs:
    Thou must lament him again, and again shed tears in a new year.

---

[5] **Hymenaeus:** I.e., Hymen, the Greek goddess of marriage.
[6] **Cinyras:** In Ovid's *Metamorphoses*, Myrrha was madly in love with her father Cyniras, the king of
Cyrus. Under the cloak of night, she managed to seduce him, but one night he brought in a lamp and
unveiled her identity. Banished from her home, Myrrha, already pregnant, prayed the gods that she
neither live nor die. In response, she was turned into a myrrh tree and from its bark was born Adonis.

SIR WALTER RALEGH (ca. 1552–1618)

"Fortune hath taken thee away, my love" (ca. 1589)

Fortune hath taken thee away, my love,
My life's soul and my soul's heaven above;
Fortune hath taken thee away, my princess;
My only light and my true fancy's mistress.

5   Fortune hath taken all away from me,
Fortune hath taken all by taking thee.
Dead to all joy, I only live to woe,
So fortune now becomes my mortal foe.

In vain your eyes, your eyes do waste your tears,
10 In vain your sighs do smoke forth my despairs,
In vain you search the earth and heaven above,
In vain you search, for fortune rules in love.

Thus now I leave my love in fortune's hands,
Thus now I leave my love in fortune's bands,
15 And only love the sorrows due to me;
Sorrow henceforth it shall my princess be.

I joy in this, that fortune conquers kings;
Fortune that rules on earth and earthly things
Hath taken my love in spite of Cupid's might;[1]
20 So blind a dame[2] did never Cupid right.

With wisdom's eyes had but blind Cupid seen,
Then had my love my love for ever been;
But love farewell; though fortune conquer thee,
No fortune base shall ever alter me.

---

[1] **Cupid's might:** In Roman mythology, the god of love and son of Venus, often depicted with a bow and a quiver of arrows. Eros in Greek mythology.
[2] **blind a dame:** Fortune was often represented as a blindfolded woman.

ANNE HOWARD   (1557–1630)

from The Good Shepherd's Sorrow for the Death of His Beloved Son[1]   (1631)

In sad and ashy weeds
    I sigh, I pine, I grieve, I mourn;
My oats and yellow reeds
    I now to jet° and ebon turn.   deep black
5   My urgèd° eyes,   burning
      Like winter skies,
My furrowed cheeks o'erflow
    All heaven knows why
    Men mourn as I,
10 And who can blame my woe?

In sable robes of night
    My days of joy appareled be:
My sorrows see no light:
    My light through sorrows nothing see;
15   For now my son
      His date hath run,
And from his sphere doth go
    To endless bed
    Of folded lead;
20 And who can blame my woe?

My flocks I now forsake,
    That silly sheep my griefs may know,
And lilies loathe to take
    That since his fall presumed to grow.
25   I envy air,
      Because it dare
Still breathe, and he not so;
    Hate earth, that doth
    Entomb his youth;
30 And who can blame my woe?

Not I, poor lad alone
    (Alone how can this sorrow be?):
Not only men make moan,

---

[1] **The Good . . . Son:** The pastoral, a type of poem which originated in ancient Greece, took as its subject the rural life and manners of shepherds. During the Renaissance, many elegies, including this one by Anne Howard, employed the style and conventions of the traditional pastoral. For more examples, see Milton's "Lycidas," Shelley's "Adonais," and Matthew Arnold's "Thyrsis" in this chapter.

But more than men make moan with me:
35   The gods of greens,
   The mountain queens,
The fairy circle's row,
   The Muses nine,
   The nymphs divine,
40   Do all condole my woe.

CHIDIOCK TICHBORNE (ca. 1558–1586)

Elegy (1586)

My prime of youth is but a frost of cares,
   My feast of joy is but a dish of pain,
My crop of corn is but a field of tares,
   And all my good is but vain hope of gain;
5   The day is past, and yet I saw no sun,
   And now I live, and now my life is done.

My tale was heard and yet it was not told,
   My fruit is fallen and yet my leaves are green,
My youth is spent and yet I am not old,
10   I saw the world and yet I was not seen;
   My thread is cut and yet it is not spun,
   And now I live, and now my life is done.

I sought my death and found it in my womb,
   I looked for life and saw it was a shade,
15   I trod the earth and knew it was my tomb,
   And now I die, and now I was but made;
   My glass is full, and now my glass is run,
   And now I live, and now my life is done.

WILLIAM SHAKESPEARE (1564–1616)

from The Tempest
Act I, Scene 2 (1611; 1623)
"Ariel's Song"—"Full fathom five"

Full fathom five thy father lies;
   Of his bones are coral made;
Those are pearls that were his eyes:

Nothing of him that doth fade,
5   But doth suffer a sea-change
Into something rich and strange:
Sea nymphs hourly ring his knell.
            Ding-dong!
      Hark! now I hear them,
10   Ding-dong, bell!

JOHN DONNE (1572–1631)

The Relic[1]   (1633)

When my grave is broke up again
Some second guest to entertain,[2]
(For graves have learned that woman-head
To be to more than one a bed)
5   And he that digs it, spies
A bracelet of bright hair about the bone,
            Will he not let us alone,
And think that there a loving couple lies
Who thought that this device might be some way
10   To make their souls, at the last busy day,
Meet at this grave, and make a little stay?

If this fall in a time, or land,
Where mis-devotion doth command,
Then he that digs us up will bring
15   Us to the Bishop and the King,
            To make us relics; then
Thou shalt be a Mary Magdalen,[3] and I
            A something else thereby;
All women shall adore us, and some men;
20   And since at such times miracles are sought,
I would that age were by this paper taught
What miracles we harmless lovers wrought.

---

[1] **The Relic:** Refers to the practice of the Catholic Church to consecrate the bodily remains (relics) of dead saints, such as bones or locks of hair.
[2] **some . . . entertain:** In the seventeenth century, it was not an uncommon practice to reuse graves after a period of seven years. The remains of the previous occupant were usually transferred to charnel houses.
[3] **Mary Magdalen:** In Luke 7:37–50, a woman whose sins are forgiven by Christ. Traditionally associated with the repentant prostitute.

> First, we loved well and faithfully,
> Yet knew not what we loved, nor why;
25 Difference of sex no more we knew
> Than our guardian angels do;
> Coming and going we
> Perchance might kiss, but not between those meals;[4]
> Our hands ne'er touched the seals,
30 Which nature, injured by late law, sets free:
> These miracles we did; but now alas,
> All measure, and all language, I should pass,
> Should I tell what a miracle she was.

BEN JONSON (1572–1637)

On My First Son (1616)

> Farewell, thou child of my right hand,[1] and joy;
> My sin was too much hope of thee, loved boy.
> Seven years thou wert lent to me, and I thee pay,
> Exacted by thy fate, on the just day.[2]
5 Oh, could I lose all father, now! For why
> Will man lament the state he should envy?
> To have so soon scaped world's and flesh's rage,
> And, if no other misery, yet age!
> Rest in soft peace, and, asked, say here doth lie
10 Ben Jonson his best piece of poetry;
> For whose sake, henceforth, all his vows be such,
> As what he loves may never like too much.

BEN JONSON (1572–1637)

On My First Daughter (1616)

> Here lies, to each her parents' ruth,°   sorrow
> Mary, the daughter of their youth:
> Yet, all heaven's gifts being heaven's due,

---

[4] **between those meals:** I.e., kisses between meeting and parting.
[1] **child . . . hand:** A literal translation of the Hebrew *Benjamin*, the name of Jonson's son.
[2] **the just day:** The boy died on his seventh birthday.

It makes the father less to rue.
5   At six months' end she parted hence
With safety of her innocence;
Whose soul heaven's queen (whose name she bears),[1]
In comfort of her mother's tears,
Hath placed amongst her virgin train:
10   Where, while that severed doth remain,[2]
This grave partakes the fleshly birth;
Which cover lightly, gentle earth.

THOMAS CAREW (ca. 1594–1640)

An Elegy Upon the Death of the Dean of Paul's, Dr. John Donne[1] (1640)

    Can we not force from widowed poetry,
Now thou art dead, great Donne, one elegy
To crown thy hearse? Why yet did we not trust,
Though with unkneaded dough-bak'd prose, thy dust,
5   Such as the unscissor'd lect'rer from the flower
Of fading rhetoric, short-lived as his hour,
Dry as the sand° that measures it, might lay   hourglass
Upon the ashes on the funeral day?
Have we nor tune, nor voice? Didst thou dispense
10   Through all our language both words and sense?
'Tis a sad truth. The pulpit may her plain
And sober Christian precepts still retain;
Doctrines it may, and wholesome uses frame,
Grave homilies and lectures; but the flame
15   Of thy brave soul, that shot such heat and light
As burnt our earth and made our darkness bright,
Committed holy rapes upon our will,
Did through the eye the melting heart distil,
And the deep knowledge of dark truths so teach
20   As sense might judge what fancy could not reach,
Must be desir'd forever. So the fire
That fills with spirit and heat the Delphic choir,[2]

---

[1] **heaven's queen . . . bears:** I.e., the Virgin Mary.
[2] **that severed doth remain:** I.e., the severance of soul from the body.
[1] **An Elegy . . . Donne:** The poet John Donne died in 1631.
[2] **Delphic choir:** I.e., poets; the shrine of Apollo, the god of poetry, was at Delphi.

Which, kindled first by thy Promethean breath,[3]
Glow'd here a while, lies quenched now in thy death.
25   The Muses' garden, with pedantic weeds
O'erspread, was purg'd by thee; the lazy seeds
Of servile imitation thrown away,
And fresh invention planted; thou didst pay
The debts of our penurious bankrupt age:
30   Licentious thefts, that make poetic rage
A mimic fury, when our souls must be
Possess'd, or with Anacreon's ecstasy,
Or Pindar's,[4] not their own. The subtle cheat
Of sly exchanges, and the juggling feat
35   Of two-edg'd words, or whatsoever wrong
By ours was done the Greek or Latin tongue,
Thou hast redeem'd, and open'd us a mine
Of rich and pregnant fancy, drawn a line
Of masculine expression, which had good
40   Old Orpheus[5] seen, or all the ancient brood
Our superstitious fools admire, and hold
Their lead more precious than thy burnish'd gold,
Thou hadst been their exchequer, and no more
They in each other's dung had raked for ore.
45   Thou shalt yield no precedence, but of time
And the blind fate of language, whose tuned chime
More charms the outward sense; yet thou mayest claim
From so great disadvantage greater fame,
Since to the awe of thy imperious wit
50   Our troublesome language bends, made only fit
With her tough thick-ribb'd hoops, to gird about
Thy giant fancy, which had prov'd too stout
For their soft melting phrases. As in time
They had the start, so did they cull the prime
55   Buds of invention many a hundred year,
And left the rifled fields, besides the fear
To touch their harvest; yet from those bare lands
Of what is only thine, thy only hands
(And that their smallest work) have gleaned more

---

[3] **Promethean breath:** Prometheus stole fire from the gods and offered it to the mortals. The gods
grew angry with him and as a punishment bound him to a rock with an eagle pecking at his liver.
[4] **Anacreon's . . . Pindar's:** Anacreon and Pindar were Greek poets, most famous for their odes.
[5] **Orpheus:** In Greek mythology, a singer of songs who descended to the underworld to plead for the
release of his dead wife Eurydice. He is also the archetypical poet.

60   Than all those times and tongues could reap before.
      But thou art gone, and thy strict laws will be
   Too hard for libertines in poetry.
   They will repeal the goodly exiled train
   Of gods and goddesses, which in thy just reign
65   Were banish'd nobler poems; now with these
   The silenced tales in the *Metamorphoses*[6]
   Shall stuff their lines and swell the windy page,
   Till verse, refin'd by thee in this last Age,
   Turn ballad-rhyme, or those old idols be
70   Ador'd again with new apostasy.
      O pardon me, that break with untun'd verse
   The reverend silence that attends thy hearse,
   Whose awful solemn murmurs were to thee,
   More than these faint lines, a loud elegy,
75   That did proclaim in a dumb eloquence
   The death of all the Arts, whose influence,
   Grown feeble, in these panting numbers lies
   Gasping short-winded accents, and so dies:
   So doth the swiftly turning wheel not stand
80   In th' instant we withdraw the moving hand,
   But some small time retain a faint weak course
   By virtue of the first impulsive force:
   And so whilst I cast on thy funeral pile
   Thy crown of bays,° oh, let it crack awhile   *laurel wreath*
85   And spit disdain, till the devouring flashes
   Suck all the moisture up, then turn to ashes.
      I will not draw the envy to engross°   *to enumerate*
   All thy perfections, or weep all the loss;
   Those are too numerous for one elegy,
90   And this too great to be express'd by me.
   Let others carve the rest; it shall suffice
   I on thy grave this epitaph incise:

   Here lies a king, that rul'd as he thought fit,
   The universal monarchy of wit;
95   *Here lie two flamens, and both those the best,*
   Apollo's° first, at last the true God's priest.   *god of love*

---

[6] **Metamorphoses:** The most famous of Ovid's long works and perhaps the most influential book in Western literature after the Bible.

JOHN MILTON (1608–1674)

Lycidas[1] (1638)

Yet once more, O ye laurels, and once more
Ye myrtles brown, with ivy never sere,°   withered; dry
I come to pluck your berries harsh and crude,
And with forced fingers rude
5   Shatter your leaves before the mellowing year.
Bitter constraint and sad occasion dear
Compels me to disturb your season due;
For Lycidas is dead, dead ere his prime,
Young Lycidas, and hath not left his peer:
10   Who would not sing for Lycidas? He knew
Himself to sing, and build the lofty rhyme.
He must not float upon his watery bier
Unwept, and welter to the parching wind,
Without the meed of some melodious tear.
15   Begin then, sisters of the sacred well,
That from beneath the seat of Jove doth spring;
Begin, and somewhat loudly sweep the string.
Hence with denial vain and coy excuse;
So may some gentle Muse
20   With lucky words favour my destined urn,
And as he passes turn,
And bid fair peace be to my sable shroud.
For we were nursed upon the self-same hill,
Fed the same flock; by fountain, shade, and rill.
25   Together both, ere the high lawns appeared
Under the opening eyelids of the morn,
We drove a-field, and both together heard
What time the grey-fly winds her sultry horn,
Battening our flocks with the fresh dews of night
30   Oft till the star that rose, at evening, bright
Toward heaven's descent had sloped his westering wheel.
Meanwhile the rural ditties were not mute,
Tempered to the oaten flute,
Rough satyrs danced, and fauns with cloven heel
35   From the glad sound would not be absent long,
And old Damaetas[2] loved to hear our song.
    But oh the heavy change, now thou art gone,
Now thou art gone, and never must return!

[1] **Lycidas:** Milton wrote this poem on the death of his friend Edward King, a scholar and poet whose ship foundered at sea in August 1637. When Milton published the poem in 1645, he added the following headnote: *In This Monody the Author Bewails a Learned Friend, Unfortunately Drowned in His Passage from Chester in the Irish Seas, 1637. And by Occasion Foretells the Ruin of Our Corrupted Clergy, Then in Their Height.*
[2] **Damaetas:** A common pastoral name.

Thee shepherd, thee the woods and desert caves,
40 With wild thyme and the gadding° vine o'ergrown,   wandering
And all their echoes mourn.
The willows and the hazel copses green
Shall now no more be seen,
Fanning their joyous leaves to thy soft lays.
45 As killing as the canker to the rose,
Or taint-worm to the weanling herds that graze,
Or frost to flowers that their gay wardrobe wear
When first the white-thorn blows:
Such, Lycidas, thy loss to shepherd's ear.
50   Where were ye nymphs when the remorseless deep
Closed o'er the head of your loved Lycidas?
For neither were ye playing on the steep,
Where your old bards, the famous Druids, lie,
Nor on the shaggy top of Mona high,
55 Nor yet where Deva spreads her wizard stream;[3]
Ay me, I fondly dream!
Had ye been there . . . for what could that have done?
What could the Muse herself that Orpheus bore,
The Muse herself for her enchanting son
60 Whom universal nature did lament,
When by the rout that made the hideous roar,
His gory visage down the stream was sent,
Down the swift Hebrus to the Lesbian shore.
     Alas! What boots it with uncessant care
65 To tend the homely slighted shepherd's trade,
And strictly meditate the thankless Muse;
Were it not better done as others use,
To sport with Amaryllis in the shade,
Or with the tangles of Neaera's hair?[4]
70 Fame is the spur that the clear spirit doth raise
(That last infirmity of noble mind)
To scorn delights and live laborious days;
But the fair guerdon° when we hope to find,   reward
And think to burst out into sudden blaze,
75 Comes the blind Fury with th' abhorrèd shears,
And slits the thin-spun life. 'But not the praise,'
Phoebus replied, and touched my trembling ears:[5]
'Fame is no plant that grows on mortal soil,
Nor in the glistering foil

---

[3] **Mona . . . stream:** Mona (the Isle of Anglesay) and Deva (the river Dee, whose "wizard" course was believed to have the power to foretell the country's future) are both sites near the Irish sea, where King drowned.
[4] **Amaryllis . . . Neaera's hair:** Both Amaryllis and Neaera are common female names in pastoral erotic poetry.
[5] **But not . . . ears:** In Virgil's *Eclogues* (6.3–4) Phoebus Apollo, god of poetic inspiration, touches Virgil's ears to remind him that praise does not end with death.

80   Set off to the world, nor in broad rumour lies,
        But lives and spreads aloft by those pure eyes
        And perfect witness of all-judging Jove;
        As he pronounces lastly on each deed,
        Of so much fame in heaven expect thy meed.'
85   O fountain Arethuse,[6] and thou honoured flood,
        Smooth-sliding Mincius,[7] crowned with vocal reeds,
        That strain I heard was of a higher mood;
        But now my oat proceeds,
        And listens to the herald of the sea
90   That came in Neptune's plea.[8]
        He asked the waves, and asked the felon winds,
        What hard mishap hath doomed this gentle swain,
        And questioned every gust of rugged wings
        That blows from off each beakèd promontory:
95   They knew not of his story,
        And sage Hippotades[9] their answer brings,
        That not a blast was from his dungeon strayed,
        The air was calm, and on the level brine
        Sleek Panope[10] with all her sisters played.
100   It was that fatal and perfidious bark,
        Built in the eclipse and rigged with curses dark,
        That sunk so low that sacred head of thine.
            Next Camus,[11] reverend sire, went footing slow,
        His mantle hairy, and his bonnet sedge,
105   Inwrought with figures dim, and on the edge
        Like to that sanguine flower inscribed with woe.[12]
        'Ah; who hath reft,' quoth he, 'my dearest pledge?'
        Last came, and last did go,
        The pilot of the Galilean lake;[13]
110   Two massy keys he bore of metals twain,
        (The golden opes,° the iron shuts amain°).   opens / vehemently
        He shook his mitred locks, and stern bespake,

---

[6] **Arethuse:** A spring in Sicily symbolizing Greek pastoral poetry and the *Idylls* of Theocritus in particular.
[7] **Mincius:** An Italian river running round Mantua, the place of Virgil's birth. Here, it is the symbol of Latin pastoral poetry.
[8] **herald . . . plea:** Neptune, the god of seas and oceans, pleaded Triton ("the herald of the sea") to exculpate him for the death of Lycidas, by calling attention to the calm weather.
[9] **Hippotades:** Son of Hippotes and the guardian of the winds.
[10] **Panope:** One of the sea-nymphs (Nereids) oftentimes invoked by Roman sailors as she was associated with calm weather.
[11] **Camus:** The genius of Cam and a representative here of Cambridge University, where Milton and King first met as students.
[12] **that sanguine flower . . . woe:** The hyacinth flower, which appears in Ovid's *Metamorphoses* (X, 174–217). Hyacinth, a friend and lover of the god Apollo, was accidentally killed by a discus. His blood dripped on a Lily and on its petals Apollo inscribed *ai, ai*—a sign of his inconsolable grief.
[13] **pilot of the Galilean lake:** I.e., St. Peter.

'How well could I have spared for thee, young swain,
Enow of such as for their bellies' sake
115 Creep and intrude and climb into the fold!
Of other care they little reckoning make
Than how to scramble at the shearers' feast,
And shove away the worthy bidden guest;
Blind mouths! that scarce themselves know how to hold
120 A sheep-hook, or have learned aught else the least
That to the faithful herdman's art belongs!
What recks it them? What need they? They are sped;
And when they list, their lean and flashy songs
Grate on their scrannel° pipes of wretched straw,   meager
125 The hungry sheep look up, and are not fed,
But swollen with wind and the rank mist they draw
Rot inwardly, and foul contagion spread;
Besides what the grim wolf with privy paw
Daily devours apace,° and nothing said;   quickly
130 But that two-handed engine at the door
Stands ready to smite once, and smite no more.
    Return Alpheus,[14] the dread voice is past
That shrunk thy streams; return Sicilian Muse,
And call the vales, and bid them hither cast
135 Their bells and flowrets of a thousand hues.
Ye valleys low where the mild whispers use
Of shades and wanton winds and gushing brooks,
On whose fresh lap the swart star[15] sparely looks,
Throw hither all your quaint enamelled eyes,
140 That on the green turf suck the honied showers,
And purple all the ground with vernal flowers.
Bring the rathe° primrose that forsaken dies;   early
The tufted crow-toe and pale jessamine,
The white pink and the pansy freaked with jet,
145 The glowing violet,
The musk-rose and the well-attired woodbine,
With cowslips wan that hang the pensive head,
And every flower that sad embroidery wears:
Bid amaranthus all his beauty shed,
150 And daffadillies fill their cups with tears,
To strew the laureate hearse where Lycid lies.
For so to interpose a little ease

---

[14] **Alpheus:** In Ovid's *Metamorphoses,* Alpheus, a river god, pursues the nymph Arethuse (see note 6), whom Diana helps escape by transforming her into a spring. Both Alpheus and Arethuse symbolize pastoral poetry.
[15] **swart star:** Sirius, or the dog-star, which rises in August, was believed to possess a wicked influence.

Let our frail thoughts dally with false surmise.
Ay me! Whilst thee the shores and sounding seas
155   Wash far away, where'er thy bones are hurled:
Whether beyond the stormy Hebrides,[16]
Where thou perhaps under the whelming tide
Visitst the bottom of the monstrous world;
Or whether thou, to our moist vows denied,
160   Sleepst by the fable of Bellerus old,[17]
Where the great vision of the guarded mount
Looks toward Namancos and Bayona's hold; [18]
Look homeward angel now, and melt with ruth.
And, O ye dolphins, waft the hapless youth.[19]
165   Weep no more, woeful shepherds weep no more,
For Lycidas your sorrow is not dead,
Sunk though he be beneath the watery floor;
So sinks the day-star in the ocean bed,
And yet anon repairs his drooping head,
170   And tricks his beams, and with new spangled ore
Flames in the forehead of the morning sky:
So Lycidas sunk low, but mounted high,
Through the dear might of him that walked the waves;
Where other groves, and other streams along,
175   With nectar pure his oozy locks he laves,°   bathes
And hears the unexpressive nuptial song,
In the blest kingdoms meek of joy and love.
There entertain him all the saints above,
In solemn troops and sweet societies
180   That sing, and singing in their glory move,
And wipe the tears for ever from his eyes.
Now Lycidas the shepherds weep no more;
Henceforth thou art the genius of the shore,
In thy large recompense, and shalt be good
185   To all that wander in that perilous flood.
   Thus sang the uncouth swain to the oaks and rills;
While the still morn went out with sandals grey,
He touched the tender stops of various quills,
With eager thought warbling his Doric lay:

---

[16] **stormy Hebrides:** Islands off the west coast of Scotland.
[17] **Bellerus old:** Possibly a reference to the *Bellerium*, the Roman name of Cornwall.
[18] **mount . . . hold:** The "mount" here is a reference to St. Michaels Mount, a rock off the south coast of Cornwall guarded by the archangel Gabriel from the traditional enemy Spain, metonymically represented here by the district of Namancos and the castle of Bayona.
[19] **dolphins, waft the hapless youth:** Possibly a reference to the poet Arion, who was rescued by a dolphin.

190   And now the sun had stretched out all the hills,
      And now was dropped into the western bay;
      At last he rose, and twitched his mantle blue:
      Tomorrow to fresh woods, and pastures new.

JOHN DRYDEN (1631–1700)

To the Memory of Mr Oldham[1] (1684)

      Farewell, too little and too lately known,
      Whom I began to think and call my own;
      For sure our souls were near allied, and thine
      Cast in the same poetic mould with mine.
5   One common note on either lyre did strike,
      And knaves and fools we both abhorred alike;
      To the same goal did both our studies drive,
      The last set out the soonest did arrive.
      Thus Nisus[2] fell upon the slippery place,
10   While his young friend performed and won the race.
      O early ripe! To thy abundant store
      What could advancing age have added more?
      It might (what nature never gives the young)
      Have taught the numbers of thy native tongue;
15   But satire needs not those, and wit will shine
      Through the harsh cadence of a rugged line.
      A noble error, and but seldom made,
      When poets are by too much force betrayed.
      Thy generous fruits, though gathered ere their prime,
20   Still showed a quickness; and maturing time
      But mellows what we write to the dull sweets of rhyme.
      Once more, hail and farewell; farewell thou young,
      But ah too short, Marcellus[3] of our tongue;
      Thy brows with ivy and with laurels bound,
25   But fate and gloomy night encompass thee around.

---

[1] **Mr Oldham:** John Oldham, a verse satirist and a contemporary of Dryden, died at the age of thirty.
[2] **Nisus:** The legend of Nisus recounts how he slipped in a puddle of blood and fell while running a race. Then, in order to ensure the win of his friend, he rolled in the way of a rival contestant.
[3] **Marcellus:** The son-in-law and nephew of the Roman emperor Augustus, who passed away at an early age.

KATHERINE FOWLER PHILIPS (1631–1664)

Epitaph on Her Son Hector Philips (ca. 1660)

What on Earth deserves our trust?
Youth and beauty both are dust.
Long we gathering are with pain,
What one moment calls again.
5   Seven years childless, marriage past,
A son, a son is born at last;
So exactly limb'd and fair,
Full of good spirits, mien, and air,
As a long life promised;
10   Yet, in less then six weeks, dead.
Too promising, too great a mind
In so small room to be confin'd:
Therefore, fit in Heav'n to dwell,
He quickly broke the prison shell.
15   So the subtle alchemist,
Can't with Hermes' seal[1] resist
The powerful spirit's subtler flight,
But 'twill bid him long good night.
And so the sun, if it arise
20   Half so glorious as his eyes,
Like this infant, takes a shroud,
Buried in a morning cloud.

APHRA BEHN (1640–1689)

On the Death of the Late Earl of Rochester[1] (1685)

Mourn, mourn, ye Muses, all your loss deplore,
The young, the noble *Strephon*[2] is no more.
Yes, yes, he fled quick as departing light,
And ne'er shall rise from Death's eternal night,
5   So rich a prize the *Stygian*[3] gods ne'er bore,

---

[1] **Hermes' seal:** I.e., hermetically sealed, as a coffin.
[1] **Earl of Rochester:** John Wilmot, the second Earl of Rochester, was a leading poet and satirist at the court of Charles II. During his lifetime, he was notorious for his extravagant behavior and libertine mores.
[2] **Strephon:** A traditional pastoral name.
[3] **Stygian:** Referring to Styx, the underworld river of forgetfulness, over which Charon ferried the souls of the dead. In Greek mythology, the god Hades and his wife Persephone (Pluto and Proserpina in the Roman tradition) presided over the underworld.

Such wit, such beauty, never graced their shore.
He was but lent this duller world t' improve
In all the charms of poetry, and love;
Both were his gift, which freely he bestowed,
10 And like a god, dealt to the wond'ring crowd.
Scorning the little vanity of fame,
Spight° of himself attained a glorious name.   *in spite of*
But oh! in vain was all his peevish pride,
The sun as soon might his vast luster hide,
15 As piercing, pointed, and more lasting bright,
As suffering no vicissitudes of night.
    Mourn, mourn, ye Muses, all your loss deplore,
    The young, the noble *Strephon* is no more.

Now uninspired upon your banks[4] we lie,
20 Unless when we would mourn his elegy;
His name's a genius[5] that would wit dispense,
And give the theme a soul, the words a sense.
But all fine thought that ravisht when it spoke,
With the soft youth eternal leave has took;
25 Uncommon wit that did the soul o'ercome,
Is buried all in *Strephon's* worshiped tomb;
Satire has lost its art, its sting is gone,
The Fop and Cully[6] now may be undone;
That dear instructing rage is now allayed,
30 And no sharp pen dares tell 'em how they've strayed;
Bold as a god was ev'ry lash he took,
But kind and gentle the chastizing stroke.
    Mourn, mourn, ye youths, whom fortune has betrayed,
    The last reproacher of your vice is dead.

35 Mourn, all ye beauties, put your *Cyprus*[7] on,
The truest swain° that e're adored you's gone;   *lover, also shepherd*
Think how he loved, and writ, and sighed, and spoke,
Recall his mien, his fashion, and his look.
By what dear arts the soul he did surprise,
40 Soft as his voice, and charming as his eyes.
Bring garlands all of never-dying flowers,
Bedewed with everlasting falling showers;
Fix your fair eyes upon your victimed slave,

---

[4] **banks:** The nine Muses, according to Greek mythology, lived on mount Helicon and sang on the banks of the Hippocrene spring.
[5] **genius:** I.e., a spirit able to influence (inspire) the fortunes or character of a person.
[6] **Fop and Cully:** I.e., a fool, a gullible person.
[7] **Cyprus:** A transparent fabric used at funerals. Also, the Cyprus tree was a symbol of mourning.

Sent gay and young to his untimely grave.
45 See where the noble swain extended lies,
Too sad a triumph of your victories;
Adorned with all the graces Heaven e'er lent, ⎫
All that was great, soft, lovely, excellent   ⎬
You've laid into his early monument.   ⎭
50   Mourn, mourn, ye beauties, your sad loss deplore,
The young, the charming *Strephon* is no more.

Mourn, all ye little gods of love, whose darts
Have lost their wonted power of piercing hearts;
Lay by the gilded quiver and the bow,
55 The useless toys can do no mischief now,
Those eyes that all your arrows' points inspired,
Those lights that gave ye fire are now retired,
Cold as his tomb, pale as your mother's doves; [8]
Bewail him then oh all ye little loves,
60 For you the humblest votary° have lost   devotee
That ever your divinities could boast;
Upon your hands your weeping heads decline,
And let your wings encompass round his shrine;
In stead of flowers your broken arrows strow,
65 And at his feet lay the neglected bow.
Mourn, all ye little gods, your loss deplore,
The soft, the charming *Strephon* is no more.

Large was his fame, but short his glorious race,
Like young *Lucretius* [9] lived and died apace.
70 So early roses fade, so over all
They cast their fragrant scents, then softly fall,
While all the scattered perfumed leaves declare,
How lovely 'twas when whole, how sweet, how fair.
Had he been to the Roman Empire known,
75 When great *Augustus* [10] filled the peaceful throne;
Had he the noble wond'rous poet seen,
And known his genius, and surveyed his mien,
(When wits, and heroes graced divine abodes),
He had increased the number of their gods;

---

[8] **your mother's doves:** I.e., Venus, the goddess of love and mother of Cupid, who was oftentimes accompanied by flocks of doves.

[9] **Lucretius:** The Roman poet Lucretius lived in the first century B.C. His most famous work *De Rerum Natura* (On the Nature of Things) dealt with questions of death and the afterlife. Some reports claim that he committed suicide.

[10] **Augustus:** The first Roman emperor, who led his country to the greatest political and cultural expansion.

80   The royal judge[11] had temples rear'd to's° name,   to his
     And made him as immortal as his fame;
     In love and verse his *Ovid* he'ad out-done,
     And all his laurels, and his *Julia*[12] won.
          Mourn, mourn, unhappy world, his loss deplore,
85   The great, the charming *Strephon* is no more.

JONATHAN SWIFT (1667–1745)

A Satirical Elegy on the Death of a Late Famous General[1] (1722)

     His Grace! impossible! what dead!
     Of old age too, and in his bed!
     And could that mighty warrior fall?
     And so inglorious, after all!
5   Well, since he's gone, no matter how,
     The last loud trump[2] must wake him now:
     And, trust me, as the noise grows stronger,
     He'd wish to sleep a little longer.
     And could he be indeed so old
10   As by the newspapers we're told?
     Threescore,° I think, is pretty high;   sixty years
     'Twas time in conscience he should die.
     This world he cumbered long enough;
     He burnt his candle to the snuff;
15   And that's the reason, some folks think,
     He left behind so great a s- - -k.
     Behold his funeral appears,
     Nor widow's sighs, nor orphan's tears,
     Wont° at such times each heart to pierce,   accustomed
20   Attend the progress of his hearse.
     But what of that, his friends may say,
     He had those honors in his day.
     True to his profit and his pride,
     He made them weep before he died.
25   Come hither, all ye empty things,

---

[11] **royal judge:** I.e., Augustus.
[12] **Ovid . . . Julia:** Perhaps the finest lyric poet of the Augustan Age. His poem *Ars Amatoria* (The Art of Love) and his alleged involvement with the daughter of Augustus Julia led to his fall from favor and eventual banishment from Rome.
[1] **Famous General:** The Duke of Marlborough died in 1722.
[2] **last loud trump:** According to *Revelation*, the day when the dead will be raised for judgment (Judgment Day) will be announced by seven trumpets.

Ye bubbles raised by breath of kings;
Who float upon the tide of state,
Come hither, and behold your fate.
Let pride be taught by this rebuke,
30 How very mean a thing's a Duke;
From all his ill-got honors flung,
Turned to that dirt from whence he sprung.

SAMUEL JOHNSON (1709–1784)

On the Death of Mr. Robert Levet
A Practiser in Physic[1] (1783)

Condemned to Hope's delusive mine,
    As on we toil from day to day,
By sudden blasts or slow decline
    Our social comforts drop away.

5 Well tried through many a varying year,
    See Levet to the grave descend;
Officious, innocent, sincere,
    Of every friendless name the friend.

Yet still he fills affection's eye,
10   Obscurely wise and coarsely kind;
Nor, lettered Arrogance, deny
    Thy praise to merit unrefined.

When fainting nature called for aid,
    And hovering death prepared the blow,
15 His vigorous remedy displayed
    The power of art without the show.

In Misery's darkest cavern known,
    His useful care was ever nigh,
Where hopeless Anguish poured his groan,
20   And lonely Want retired to die.

No summons mocked by chill delay,
    No petty gain disdained by pride;

---

[1] **On the death . . . physic:** Robert Levet, a personal friend of Johnson's, practiced among the poor as an unlicensed physician.

The modest wants of every day
    The toil of every day supplied.

25 His virtues walked their narrow round,
        Nor made a pause, nor left a void;
    And sure the Eternal Master found
        The single talent well employed.

    The busy day, the peaceful night,
30   Unfelt, uncounted, glided by;
    His frame was firm—his powers were bright,
        Though now his eightieth year was nigh.

    Then with no fiery throbbing pain,
        No cold gradations of decay,
35 Death broke at once the vital chain,
        And freed his soul the nearest way.

THOMAS GRAY (1716–1771)

Elegy Written in a Country Churchyard (1751)

    The curfew tolls the knell of parting day,
    The lowing herd wind slowly o'er the lea,
    The ploughman homeward plods his weary way,
    And leaves the world to darkness and to me.

5   Now fades the glimmering landscape on the sight,
    And all the air a solemn stillness holds,
    Save where the beetle wheels his droning flight,
    And drowsy tinklings lull the distant folds;

    Save that from yonder ivy-mantled tow'r
10 The moping owl does to the moon complain
    Of such as, wand'ring near her secret bow'r,
    Molest her ancient solitary reign.

    Beneath those rugged elms, that yew-tree's shade,
    Where heaves the turf in many a mould'ring heap,
15 Each in his narrow cell for ever laid,
    The rude forefathers of the hamlet sleep.

    The breezy call of incense-breathing morn,
    The swallow twitt'ring from the straw-built shed,

The cock's shrill clarion or the echoing horn,
20   No more shall rouse them from their lowly bed.

For them no more the blazing hearth shall burn,
Or busy housewife ply her evening care:
No children run to lisp their sire's return,
Or climb his knees the envied kiss to share.

25   Oft did the harvest to their sickle yield,
Their furrow oft the stubborn glebe° has broke;   earth
How jocund did they drive their team afield!
How bowed the woods beneath their sturdy stroke!

Let not Ambition mock their useful toil,
30   Their homely joys and destiny obscure;
Nor Grandeur hear, with a disdainful smile,
The short and simple annals of the poor.

The boast of heraldry, the pomp of pow'r,
And all that beauty, all that wealth e'er gave,
35   Awaits alike the inevitable hour.
The paths of glory lead but to the grave.

Nor you, ye Proud, impute to these the fault,
If Mem'ry o'er their tomb no trophies raise,
Where through the long-drawn aisle and fretted vault
40   The pealing anthem swells the note of praise.

Can storied urn or animated bust
Back to its mansion call the fleeting breath?
Can Honour's voice provoke the silent dust,
Or Flatt'ry soothe the dull cold ear of Death?

45   Perhaps in this neglected spot is laid
Some heart once pregnant with celestial fire;
Hands that the rod of empire might have swayed,
Or waked to ecstasy the living lyre.

But Knowledge to their eyes her ample page
50   Rich with the spoils of time did ne'er unroll;
Chill Penury repressed their noble rage,
And froze the genial current of the soul.

Full many a gem of purest ray serene
The dark unfathomed caves of ocean bear:

55   Full many a flower is born to blush unseen
    And waste its sweetness on the desert air.

    Some village-Hampden[1] that with dauntless breast
    The little tyrant of his fields withstood;
    Some mute inglorious Milton here may rest,
60   Some Cromwell guiltless of his country's blood.

    Th' applause of list'ning senates to command,
    The threats of pain and ruin to despise,
    To scatter plenty o'er a smiling land,
    And read their hist'ry in a nation's eyes,

65   Their lot forbade: nor circumscribed alone
    Their growing virtues, but their crimes confined;
    Forbade to wade through slaughter to a throne,
    And shut the gates of mercy on mankind,

    The struggling pangs of conscious truth to hide,
70   To quench the blushes of ingenuous shame,
    Or heap the shrine of Luxury and Pride
    With incense kindled at the Muse's flame.

    Far from the madding crowd's ignoble strife
    Their sober wishes never learned to stray;
75   Along the cool sequestered vale of life
    They kept the noiseless tenor of their way.

    Yet ev'n these bones from insult to protect
    Some frail memorial still erected nigh,
    With uncouth rhymes and shapeless sculpture decked,
80   Implores the passing tribute of a sigh.

    Their name, their years, spelt by th' unlettered muse,
    The place of fame and elegy supply:
    And many a holy text around she strews,
    That teach the rustic moralist to die.

85   For who to dumb Forgetfulness a prey,
    This pleasing anxious being e'er resigned,
    Left the warm precincts of the cheerful day,
    Nor cast one longing ling'ring look behind?

---

[1] **Hampden:** John Hampden (ca. 1595–1643) was a statesman and leader of the English revolution in its earlier stages.

On some fond breast the parting soul relies,
90   Some pious drops the closing eye requires;
Ev'n from the tomb the voice of Nature cries,
Ev'n in our ashes live their wonted fires.

For thee who, mindful of th' unhonoured dead,
Dost in these lines their artless tale relate;
95   If chance, by lonely Contemplation led,
Some kindred spirit shall inquire thy fate,

Haply some hoary-headed swain may say,
'Oft have we seen him at the peep of dawn
Brushing with hasty steps the dews away
100 To meet the sun upon the upland lawn.

'There at the foot of yonder nodding beech
That wreathes its old fantastic roots so high,
His listless length at noontide would he stretch,
And pore upon the brook that babbles by.

105 'Hard by yon wood, now smiling as in scorn,
Muttering his wayward fancies he would rove,
Now drooping, woeful wan, like one forlorn,
Or crazed with care, or crossed in hopeless love.

'One morn I missed him on the customed hill,
110 Along the heath and near his fav'rite tree;
Another came; nor yet beside the rill,
Nor up the lawn, nor at the wood was he;

'The next with dirges due in sad array
Slow through the church-way path we saw him borne.
115 Approach and read (for thou canst read) the lay,
Graved on the stone beneath yon aged thorn.'

The Epitaph

Here rests his head upon the lap of earth
A youth to fortune and to fame unknown.
Fair Science frowned not on his humble birth,
120 *And Melancholy marked him for her own.*

Large was his bounty and his soul sincere,
Heaven did a recompense as largely send:
He gave to Mis'ry all he had, a tear,
He gained from heav'n ('twas all he wished) a friend.

125   *No farther seek his merits to disclose,*
      Or draw his frailties from their dread abode
      (There they alike in trembling hope repose),
      The bosom of his Father and his God.

CHARLOTTE SMITH (1749–1806)

To the Shade of Burns[1] (1797)

Mute is thy wild harp, now, O Bard sublime!
   Who, amid Scotia's° mountain solitude,   Scotland's
Great Nature taught to "build the lofty rhyme,"[2]
   And even beneath the daily pressure, rude,
5   Of laboring Poverty, thy generous blood,
Fired with the love of freedom—Not subdued
   Wert thou by thy low fortune: But a time
   Like this we live in, when the abject chime
Of echoing Parasite is best approved,
10   Was not for thee—Indignantly is fled
Thy noble Spirit; and no longer moved
   By all the ills o'er which thine heart has bled,
   Associate worthy of the illustrious dead,
Enjoys with them "the Liberty it loved."[3]

PHILLIS WHEATLEY (1753–1784)

On the Death of the Rev. Mr. George Whitefield[1] (1770)

Hail, happy saint, on thine immortal throne,
Possest of glory, life, and bliss unknown;
We hear no more the music of thy tongue,
Thy wonted auditories cease to throng.
5   Thy sermons in unequall'd accents flow'd,

---

[1] **Burns:** The Scottish poet Robert Burns died in 1796, at the age of thirty-seven.
[2] **build the lofty rhyme:** From Milton's "Lycidas" (line 11).
[3] **the Liberty it loved:** From Alexander Pope's "Epitaph on Sir William Trumbull" (line 12).
[1] **Rev. Mr. George Whitefield:** A Methodist minister (1714–1770), one of the most prominent revivalists of the eighteenth century.

And ev'ry bosom with devotion glow'd;
Thou didst in strains of eloquence refin'd
Inflame the heart, and captivate the mind.
Unhappy we the setting sun deplore,
10 So glorious once, but ah! it shines no more.

Behold the prophet in his tow'ring flight!
He leaves the earth for heav'n's unmeasur'd height,
And worlds unknown receive him from our sight.
There *Whitefield* wings with rapid course his way,
15 And sails to *Zion*[2] through vast seas of day.
Thy pray'rs, great saint, and thine incessant cries
Have pierc'd the bosom of thy native skies.
Thou moon hast seen, and all the stars of light,
How he has wrestled with his God by night.

20 He pray'd that grace in ev'ry heart might dwell,
He long'd to see *America* excel;
He charg'd its youth that ev'ry grace divine
Should with full lustre in their conduct shine;
That Saviour, which his soul did first receive,
25 The greatest gift that ev'n a God can give,
He freely offer'd to the num'rous throng,
That on his lips with list'ning pleasure hung.

"Take him, ye wretched, for your only good,
"Take him ye starving sinners, for your food;
30 "Ye thirsty, come to this life-giving stream,
"Ye preachers, take him for your joyful theme;
"Take him my dear *Americans*, he said.
"Be your complaints on his kind bosom laid:
"Take him, ye *Africans*, he longs for you,
35 "*Impartial Saviour* is his title due:
"Wash'd in the fountain of redeeming blood,
"You shall be sons, and kings, and priests to God."

Great *Countess*,[3] we *Americans* revere
Thy name, and mingle in thy grief sincere;
40 *New England* deeply feels, the *Orphans* mourn,
Their more than father will no more return.

But, though arrested by the hand of death,
Whitefield no more exerts his lab'ring breath,

---

[2] **Zion:** An idealized world, utopia. Also, the city of God.
[3] **Great Countess:** "The Countess of Huntingdon, to whom Mr. Whitefield was Chaplain" [Wheatley's note].

Yet let us view him in th' eternal skies,
45   Let ev'ry heart to this bright vision rise;
While the tomb safe retains its sacred trust,
Till life divine re-animates his dust.

WILLIAM WORDSWORTH (1770–1850)

Elegiac Stanzas[1] (1807)

*Suggested by a Picture of Peele Castle, in a Storm,
painted by Sir George Beaumont*

I was thy Neighbour once, thou rugged Pile!
Four summer weeks I dwelt in sight of thee:
I saw thee every day; and all the while
Thy Form was sleeping on a glassy sea.

5   So pure the sky, so quiet was the air!
So like, so very like, was day to day!
Whene'er I look'd, thy Image still was there;
It trembled, but it never pass'd away.

How perfect was the calm! it seem'd no sleep;
10   No mood, which season takes away, or brings:
I could have fancied that the mighty Deep
Was even the gentlest of all gentle Things.

Ah! then, if mine had been the Painter's hand,
To express what then I saw; and add the gleam,
15   The light that never was, on sea or land,
The consecration, and the Poet's dream;

I would have planted thee, thou hoary Pile!
Amid a world how different from this!
Beside a sea that could not cease to smile;
20   On tranquil land, beneath a sky of bliss:

Thou shouldst have seem'd a treasure-house, a mine
Of peaceful years; a chronicle of heaven:—

---

[1] **Elegiac Stanzas:** Composed in memory of Wordsworth's younger brother, Captain John
Wordsworth, whose ship foundered in February 1805.

Of all the sunbeams that did ever shine
The very sweetest had to thee been given.

25 A Picture had it been of lasting ease,
Elysian quiet, without toil or strife;
No motion but the moving tide, a breeze,
Or merely silent Nature's breathing life.

Such, in the fond delusion of my heart,
30 Such Picture would I at that time have made:
And seen the soul of truth in every part;
A faith, a trust, that could not be betray'd.

So once it would have been,—'tis so no more;
I have submitted to a new controul:
35 A power is gone, which nothing can restore;
A deep distress hath humaniz'd my Soul.

Not for a moment could I now behold
A smiling sea and be what I have been:
The feeling of my loss will ne'er be old;
40 This, which I know, I speak with mind serene.

Then, Beaumont, Friend! who would have been the Friend,
If he had lived, of Him whom I deplore,
This Work of thine I blame not, but commend;
This sea in anger, and that dismal shore.

45 Oh 'tis a passionate Work!—yet wise and well;
Well chosen is the spirit that is here;
That Hulk which labours in the deadly swell,
This rueful sky, this pageantry of fear!

And this huge Castle, standing here sublime,
50 I love to see the look with which it braves,
Cased in the unfeeling armour of old time,
The light'ning, the fierce wind, and trampling waves.

Farewell, farewell the Heart that lives alone,
Hous'd in a dream, at distance from the Kind!
55 Such happiness, wherever it be known,
Is to be pitied; for 'tis surely blind.

But welcome fortitude, and patient chear,
And frequent sights of what is to be borne!

Such sights, or worse, as are before me here.—
60   Not without hope we suffer and we mourn.

PERCY BYSSHE SHELLEY (1792–1822)

Adonais[1] (1821)
An Elegy on the Death of John Keats[2]

Αστήρ πρὶν μὲν ἐλαμπες ενι ζῶοισιν εῶος.
Νυν δε θανῶν, λαμπεις ἔοπερος εν φθίμενοις.[3]
                                   PLATO

I

I weep for Adonais—he is dead!
O, weep for Adonais! though our tears
Thaw not the frost which binds so dear a head!
And thou, sad Hour, selected from all years
5   To mourn our loss, rouse thy obscure compeers,°   equals
And teach them thine own sorrow, say: with me
Died Adonais; till the Future dares
Forget the Past, his fate and fame shall be
An echo and a light unto eternity!

II

10   'Where wert thou mighty Mother,[4] when he lay,
When thy Son lay, pierced by the shaft which flies
In darkness? where was lorn Urania
When Adonais died? With veiled eyes,
'Mid listening Echoes, in her Paradise
15   She sate, while one, with soft enamoured breath,
Rekindled all the fading melodies,
With which, like flowers that mock the corse° beneath,   corpse
He had adorned and hid the coming bulk of death.

---

[1] **Adonais:** This name is a derivation of Adonis, the youth who, according to the Greek myth, was slain by a boar and mourned by his lover, the goddess Venus.
[2] **An Elegy . . . Keats:** The poet John Keats died of consumption in Rome, on February 23, 1821. Shelley, who had met Keats in England, wrote and published his elegy later that year.
[3] **Ancient Greek epigraph:** "Thou wert the morning star among the living, / Ere thy fair light had fled; / Now, having died, thou art as Hesperus, giving / New splendour to the dead" [Shelley's translation]. Venus is both the morning star and the evening star (Hesperus).
[4] **Mother:** Here, Urania, the muse of astronomy, whom Milton also invokes in *Paradise Lost* (1.6–16). In the elegy, Shelley associates her with Venus and the mother of Adonis.

III

O, weep for Adonais—he is dead!
20 Wake, melancholy Mother, wake and weep!
Yet wherefore? Quench within their burning bed
Thy fiery tears, and let thy loud heart keep
Like his, a mute and uncomplaining sleep;
For he is gone, where all things wise and fair
25 Descend;—oh, dream not that the amorous Deep
Will yet restore him to the vital air;
Death feeds on his mute voice, and laughs at our despair.

IV

Most musical of mourners, weep again!
Lament anew, Urania!—He died,
30 Who was the Sire of an immortal strain,
Blind, old, and lonely, when his country's pride,
The priest, the slave, and the liberticide,
Trampled and mocked with many a loathed rite
Of lust and blood; he went, unterrified,
35 Into the gulf of death; but his clear Sprite
Yet reigns o'er earth; the third among the sons of light.[5]

V

Most musical of mourners, weep anew!
Not all to that bright station dared to climb;
And happier they their happiness who knew,
40 Whose tapers yet burn through that night of time
In which suns perished, others more sublime,
Struck by the envious wrath of man or God,
Have sunk, extinct in their refulgent prime;
And some yet live, treading the thorny road,
45 Which leads, through toil and hate, to Fame's serene abode.

VI

But now, thy youngest, dearest one, has perished
The nursling of thy widowhood, who grew,
Like a pale flower by some sad maiden cherished,
And fed with true love tears, instead of dew;
50 Most musical of mourners, weep anew!
Thy extreme hope, the loveliest and the last,
The bloom, whose petals nipt before they blew

---

[5] **He died . . . sons of light:** In this stanza, Shelley alludes to the blind poet Milton and his two great predecessors, Homer and Dante.

Died on the promise of the fruit, is waste;
The broken lily lies—the storm is overpast.

VII

55 To that high Capital,[6] where kingly Death
Keeps his pale court in beauty and decay,
He came; and bought, with price of purest breath,
A grave among the eternal.—Come away!
Haste, while the vault of blue Italian day
60 Is yet his fitting charnel-roof! while still
He lies, as if in dewy sleep he lay;
Awake him not! surely he takes his fill
Of deep and liquid rest, forgetful of all ill.

VIII

He will awake no more, oh, never more!—
65 Within the twilight chamber spreads apace,
The shadow of white Death, and at the door
Invisible Corruption waits to trace
His extreme way to her dim dwelling-place;
The eternal Hunger sits, but pity and awe
70 Soothe her pale rage, nor dares she to deface
So fair a prey, till darkness, and the law
Of mortal change, shall fill the grave which is her maw.

IX

O, weep for Adonais!—The quick Dreams,
The passion-winged Ministers of thought,
75 Who were his flocks, whom near the living streams
Of his young spirit he fed, and whom he taught
The love which was its music, wander not,—
Wander no more, from kindling brain to brain,
But droop there, whence they sprung; and mourn their lot
80 Round the cold heart, where, after their sweet pain,
They ne'er will gather strength, or find a home again.

X

And one with trembling hands clasps his cold head,
And fans him with her moonlight wings, and cries;
'Our love, our hope, our sorrow, is not dead;
85 See, on the silken fringe of his faint eyes,
Like dew upon a sleeping flower, there lies

---

[6] **Capital:** The city of Rome, where Keats passed away.

A tear some Dream has loosened from his brain.'
Lost Angel of a ruined Paradise!
She knew not 'twas her own; as with no stain
90   She faded, like a cloud which had outwept its rain.

XI

One from a lucid urn of starry dew
Washed his light limbs as if embalming them;
Another clipt her profuse locks, and threw
The wreath upon him, like an anadem,°   a wreath, garland
95   Which frozen tears instead of pearls begem;
Another in her wilful grief would break
Her bow and winged reeds, as if to stem
A greater loss with one which was more weak;
And dull the barbed fire against his frozen cheek.

XII

100 Another Splendour on his mouth alit,
That mouth, whence it was wont to draw the breath
Which gave it strength to pierce the guarded wit,
And pass into the panting heart beneath
With lightning and with music the damp death
105 Quenched its caress upon his icy lips;
And, as a dying meteor stains a wreath
Of moonlight vapour, which the cold night clips,°   encompasses
It flushed through his pale limbs, and past to its eclipse.

XIII

And others came . . . Desires and Adorations,
110 Winged Persuasions and veiled Destinies,
Splendours, and Glooms, and glimmering Incarnations
Of hopes and fears, and twilight Phantasies;
And Sorrow, with her family of Sighs,
And Pleasure, blind with tears, led by the gleam
115 Of her own dying smile instead of eyes,
Came in slow pomp;—the moving pomp might seem
Like pageantry of mist on an autumnal stream.

XIV

All he had loved, and moulded into thought,
From shape, and hue, and odour, and sweet sound,
120 Lamented Adonais. Morning sought
Her eastern watchtower, and her hair unbound,
Wet with the tears which should adorn the ground,
Dimmed the aerial eyes that kindle day;

Afar the melancholy thunder moaned,
125   Pale Ocean in unquiet slumber lay,
And the wild winds flew round, sobbing in their dismay.

XV

Lost Echo[7] sits amid the voiceless mountains,
And feeds her grief with his remembered lay,
And will no more reply to winds or fountains,
130   Or amorous birds perched on the young green spray,
Or herdsman's horn, or bell at closing day;
Since she can mimic not his lips, more dear
Than those for whose disdain she pined away
Into a shadow of all sounds:—a drear
135   Murmur, between their songs, is all the woodmen hear.

XVI

Grief made the young Spring wild, and she threw down
Her kindling buds, as if she Autumn were,
Or they dead leaves; since her delight is flown
For whom should she have waked the sullen year?
140   To Phœbus was not Hyacinth[8] so dear
Nor to himself Narcissus,[9] as to both
Thou Adonais: wan they stand and sere
Amid the drooping comrades of their youth,
With dew all turned to tears; odour, to sighing ruth.

XVII

145   Thy spirit's sister, the lorn nightingale[10]
Mourns not her mate with such melodious pain;
Not so the eagle, who like thee could scale
Heaven, and could nourish in the sun's domain
Her mighty youth with morning, doth complain,
150   Soaring and screaming round her empty nest,
As Albion wails for thee: the curse of Cain
Light on his head who pierced thy innocent breast,
And scared the angel soul that was its earthly guest![11]

---

[7] **Echo:** The story of Echo and Narcissus is recounted by Ovid in his *Metamorphoses*. The nymph Echo fell madly in love with Narcissus and pined away until all that was left of her was a voice.
[8] **Hyacinth:** A youth loved by Apollo who was accidentally killed by a discus thrown by the god.
[9] **Narcissus:** In the Greek myth, Narcissus falls in love with himself after seeing his own reflection on the surface of a pool. He eventually drowns attempting to embrace his image. See also note 7.
[10] **nightingale:** See Keats's "Ode to a Nightingale" in Chapter 21.
[11] **who pierced . . . guest:** It was believed by some, Shelley among others, that Keats contracted the illness which eventually led to his premature death after an anonymous reviewer wrote a vicious attack of his newly published poem *Endymion* (see an excerpt from the poem in Chapter 9).

XVIII

Ah woe is me! Winter is come and gone,
155   But grief returns with the revolving year;
The airs and streams renew their joyous tone;
The ants, the bees, the swallows reappear;
Fresh leaves and flowers deck the dead Seasons' bier;
The amorous birds now pair in every brake,
160   And build their mossy homes in field and brere;
And the green lizard, and the golden snake,
Like unimprisoned flames, out of their trance awake.

XIX

Through wood and stream and field and hill and Ocean
A quickening life from the Earth's heart has burst
165   As it has ever done, with change and motion,
From the great morning of the world when first
God dawned on Chaos; in its steam immersed
The lamps of Heaven flash with a softer light;
All baser things pant with life's sacred thirst;
170   Diffuse themselves; and spend in love's delight,
The beauty and the joy of their renewed might.

XX

The leprous corpse touched by this spirit tender
Exhales itself in flowers of gentle breath;
Like incarnations of the stars, when splendour
175   Is changed to fragrance, they illumine death
And mock the merry worm that wakes beneath;
Nought we know, dies. Shall that alone which knows
Be as a sword consumed before the sheath
By sightless lightning?—th' intense atom glows
180   A moment, then is quenched in a most cold repose.

XXI

Alas! that all we loved of him should be,
But for our grief, as if it had not been,
And grief itself be mortal! Woe is me!
Whence are we, and why are we? of what scene
185   The actors or spectators? Great and mean
Meet massed in death, who lends what life must borrow.
As long as skies are blue, and fields are green,
Evening must usher night, night urge the morrow,
Month follow month with woe, and year wake year to sorrow.

XXII

190 *He* will awake no more, oh, never more!
'Wake thou,' cried Misery, 'childless Mother, rise
Out of thy sleep, and slake, in thy heart's core,
A wound more fierce than his with tears and sighs.'
And all the Dreams that watched Urania's eyes,
195 And all the Echoes whom their sister's song
Had held in holy silence, cried: 'Arise!'
Swift as a Thought by the snake Memory stung,
From her ambrosial rest the fading Splendour sprung.

XXIII

She rose like an autumnal Night, that springs
200 Out of the East, and follows wild and drear
The golden Day, which, on eternal wings,
Even as a ghost abandoning a bier,
Had left the Earth a corpse. Sorrow and fear
So struck, so roused, so rapt Urania;
205 So saddened round her like an atmosphere
Of stormy mist; so swept her on her way
Even to the mournful place where Adonais lay.

XXIV

Out of her secret Paradise she sped,
Through camps and cities rough with stone, and steel,
210 And human hearts, which to her aery tread
Yielding not, wounded the invisible
Palms of her tender feet where'er they fell:
And barbed tongues, and thoughts more sharp than they
Rent the soft Form they never could repel,
215 Whose sacred blood, like the young tears of May,
Paved with eternal flowers that undeserving way.

XXV

In the death chamber for a moment Death
Shamed by the presence of that living Might
Blushed to annihilation, and the breath
220 Revisited those lips, and life's pale light
Flashed through those limbs, so late her dear delight.
'Leave me not wild and drear and comfortless,
As silent lightning leaves the starless night!
Leave me not!' cried Urania: her distress
225 Roused Death: Death rose and smiled, and met her vain caress.

XXVI

'Stay yet awhile! speak to me once again;
Kiss me, so long but as a kiss may live;
And in my heartless breast and burning brain
That word, that kiss shall all thoughts else survive,
230   With food of saddest memory kept alive,
Now thou art dead, as if it were a part
Of thee, my Adonais! I would give
All that I am to be as thou now art!
But I am chained to Time, and cannot thence depart!

XXVII

235   'Oh gentle child, beautiful as thou wert,
Why didst thou leave the trodden paths of men
Too soon, and with weak hands though mighty heart
Dare the unpastured dragon in his den?
Defenceless as thou wert, oh where was then
240   Wisdom the mirrored shield, or scorn the spear?
Or hadst thou waited the full cycle, when
Thy spirit should have filled its crescent sphere,
The monsters of life's waste had fled from thee like deer.

XXVIII

'The herded wolves, bold only to pursue;
245   The obscene ravens, clamorous oer the dead;
The vultures to the conqueror's banner true
Who feed where Desolation first has fed,
And whose wings rain contagion;—how they fled,
When like Apollo, from his golden bow,
250   The Pythian of the age one arrow sped
And smiled!—The spoilers tempt no second blow,
They fawn on the proud feet that spurn them as they go.[12]

XXIX

'The sun comes forth, and many reptiles spawn;
He sets, and each ephemeral insect then
255   Is gathered into death without a dawn,
And the immortal stars awake again;
So is it in the world of living men:

---

[12] **The herded wolves . . . they go:** In this stanza, the literary critics of the time are likened to "herded wolves" and "obscene ravens." Keats was not the only one to suffer from their condemnations. *Hours of Idleness* by Byron (depicted here as "Pythion of the age") was also subject to their harsh criticism. The poet swiftly retaliated with his scathing book *English Bards and Scotch Reviewers*.

A godlike mind soars forth, in its delight
Making earth bare and veiling heaven, and when
260   It sinks, the swarms that dimmed or shared its light
Leave to its kindred lamps the spirit's awful night.'

XXX

Thus ceased she: and the mountain shepherds came
Their garlands sere, their magic mantles rent;
The Pilgrim of Eternity,[13] whose fame
265   Over his living head like Heaven is bent,
An early but enduring monument,
Came, veiling all the lightnings of his song
In sorrow; from her wilds Ierne° sent   Ireland
The sweetest lyrist of her saddest wrong,
270   And love taught grief to fall like music from his tongue.

XXXI

Midst others of less note, came one frail Form,
A phantom among men; companionless
As the last cloud of an expiring storm
Whose thunder is its knell; he, as I guess,
275   Had gazed on Nature's naked loveliness,
Actæon-like,[14] and now he fled astray
With feeble steps o'er the world's wilderness,
And his own thoughts, along that rugged way,
Pursued, like raging hounds, their father and their prey.

XXXII

280   A pardlike° Spirit beautiful and swift—   leopardlike
A Love in desolation masked;—a Power
Girt round with weakness;—it can scarce uplift
The weight of the superincumbent hour;
It is a dying lamp, a falling shower,
285   A breaking billow;—even whilst we speak
Is it not broken? On the withering flower
The killing sun smiles brightly: on a cheek
The life can burn in blood, even while the heart may break.

---

[13] **Pilgrim of Eternity:** I.e., Byron.
[14] **Actæon-like:** According to the Greek myth as recounted by Ovid, Actæon was a hunter who was transformed by Diana into a stag and devoured by his own hounds as a punishment for seeing the goddess naked.

XXXIII

His head was bound with pansies overblown,
290   And faded violets, white, and pied, and blue;
And a light spear topped with a cypress cone,
Round whose rude shaft dark ivy tresses grew [15]
Yet dripping with the forest's noonday dew,
Vibrated, as the ever-beating heart
295   Shook the weak hand that grasped it; of that crew
He came the last, neglected and apart;
A herd-abandoned deer struck by the hunter's dart.

XXXIV

All stood aloof, and at his partial moan
Smiled through their tears; well knew that gentle band
300   Who in another's fate now wept his own;
As in the accents of an unknown land,
He sung new sorrow; sad Urania scanned
The Stranger's mien, and murmured: 'who art thou?'
He answered not, but with a sudden hand
305   Made bare his branded and ensanguined brow,
Which was like Cain's or Christ's—Oh! that it should be so!

XXXV

What softer voice is hushed over the dead?
Athwart what brow is that dark mantle thrown?
What form leans sadly o'er the white death-bed,
310   In mockery of monumental stone,
The heavy heart heaving without a moan?
If it be He,[16] who, gentlest of the wise,
Taught, soothed, loved, honoured the departed one,
Let me not vex, with inharmonious sighs
315   The silence of that heart's accepted sacrifice.

XXXVI

Our Adonais has drunk poison—oh!
What deaf and, viperous murderer could crown
Life's early cup with such a draught of woe?
The nameless worm[17] would now itself disown:
320   It felt, yet could escape the magic tone

---

[15] **a light spear . . . tresses grew:** The emblem of Dionysus, the Greek god of revelry and wine.
[16] **He:** Leigh Hunt (1784–1859) was a poet and friend of both Shelley and Keats.
[17] **nameless worm:** The anonymous reviewer.

Whose prelude held all envy, hate, and wrong,
But what was howling in one breast alone,
Silent with expectation of the song,
Whose master's hand is cold, whose silver lyre unstrung.

XXXVII

325 Live thou, whose infamy is not thy fame!
Live! fear no heavier chastisement from me,
Thou noteless blot on a remembered name!
But be thyself, and know thyself to be!
And ever at thy season be thou free
330 To spill the venom when thy fangs o'er flow:
Remorse and Self-contempt shall cling to thee;
Hot Shame shall burn upon thy secret brow,
And like a beaten hound tremble thou shalt—as now.

XXXVIII

Nor let us weep that our delight is fled
335 Far from these carrion kites that scream below;
He wakes or sleeps with the enduring dead;
Thou canst not soar where he is sitting now.—
Dust to the dust! but the pure spirit shall flow
Back to the burning fountain whence it came,
340 A portion of the Eternal, which must glow
Through time and change, unquenchably the same,
Whilst thy cold embers choke the sordid hearth of shame.

XXXIX

Peace, peace! he is not dead, he doth not sleep—
He hath awakened from the dream of life—
345 'Tis we, who lost in stormy visions, keep
With phantoms an unprofitable strife,
And in mad trance, strike with our spirit's knife
Invulnerable nothings.—*We* decay
Like corpses in a charnel; fear and grief
350 Convulse us and consume us day by day,
And cold hopes swarm like worms within our living clay.

XL

He has outsoared the shadow of our night;
Envy and calumny and hate and pain,
And that unrest which men miscall delight,
355 Can touch him not and torture not again;
From the contagion of the world's slow stain

He is secure, and now can never mourn
A heart grown cold, a head grown grey in vain;
Nor, when the spirit's self has ceased to burn,
360   With sparkless ashes load an unlamented urn.

XLI

He lives, he wakes—'tis Death is dead, not he;
Mourn not for Adonais.—Thou young Dawn
Turn all thy dew to splendour, for from thee
The spirit thou lamentest is not gone;
365   Ye caverns and ye forests, cease to moan!
Cease ye faint flowers and fountains, and thou Air
Which like a mourning veil thy scarf hadst thrown
O'er the abandoned Earth, now leave it bare
Even to the joyous stars which smile on its despair!

XLII

370   He is made one with Nature: there is heard
His voice in all her music, from the moan
Of thunder, to the song of night's sweet bird;
He is a presence to be felt and known
In darkness and in light, from herb and stone,
375   Spreading itself where'er that Power may move
Which has withdrawn his being to its own;
Which wields the world with never wearied love,
Sustains it from beneath, and kindles it above.

XLIII

He is a portion of the loveliness
380   Which once he made more lovely: he doth bear
His part, while the one Spirit's plastic stress
Sweeps through the dull dense world, compelling there,
All new successions to the forms they wear;
Torturing th'unwilling dross that checks its flight
385   To its own likeness, as each mass may bear;
And bursting in its beauty and its might
From trees and beasts and men into the Heaven's light.

XLIV

The splendours of the firmament of time
May be eclipsed, but are extinguished not;
390   Like stars to their appointed height they climb
And death is a low mist which cannot blot
The brightness it may veil. When lofty thought

Lifts a young heart above its mortal lair,
And love and life contend in it, for what
395   Shall be its earthly doom, the dead live there
And move like winds of light on dark and stormy air.

XLV

The inheritors of unfulfilled renown
Rose from their thrones, built beyond mortal thought,
Far in the Unapparent. Chatterton
400   Rose pale, his solemn agony had not
Yet faded from him; Sidney, as he fought
And as he fell and as he lived and loved
Sublimely mild, a Spirit without spot,
Arose; and Lucas,[18] by his death approved:
405   Oblivion as they rose shrank like a thing reproved.

XLVI

And many more, whose names on Earth are dark
But whose transmitted effluence cannot die
So long as fire outlives the parent spark,
Rose, robed in dazzling immortality.
410   'Thou art become as one of us', they cry,
'It was for thee yon kingless sphere has long
Swung blind in unascended majesty,
Silent alone amid an Heaven of song.
Assume thy winged throne, thou Vesper of our throng!'

XLVII

415   Who mourns for Adonais? oh come forth
Fond wretch! and know thyself and him aright.
Clasp with thy panting soul the pendulous Earth;
As from a centre, dart thy spirit's light
Beyond all worlds, until its spacious might
420   Satiate the void circumference: then shrink
Even to a point within our day and night;
And keep thy heart light lest it make thee sink
When hope has kindled hope, and lured thee to the brink.

---

[18] **Chatterton . . . Lucas:** Chatterton, Sidney, and Lucas were all poets of considerable talent, who, like Keats, died in their early age.

XLVIII

Or go to Rome, which is the sepulchre
425 O, not of him, but of our joy: 'tis nought
That ages, empires, and religions there.
Lie buried in the ravage they have wrought;
For such as he can lend,—they borrow not
Glory from those who made the world their prey;
430 And he is gathered to the kings of thought
Who waged contention with their time's decay,
And of the past are all that cannot pass away.

XLIX

Go thou to Rome,—at once the Paradise,
The grave, the city, and the wilderness;
435 And where its wrecks like shattered mountains rise,
And flowering weeds, and fragrant copses dress
The bones of Desolation's nakedness
Pass, till the Spirit of the spot shall lead
Thy footsteps to a slope of green access
440 Where, like an infant's smile, over the dead,
A light of laughing flowers along the grass is spread.

L

And gray walls moulder round, on which dull Time
Feeds, like slow fire upon a hoary brand;
And one keen pyramid with wedge sublime,
445 Pavilioning the dust of him who planned
This refuge for his memory, doth stand
Like flame transformed to marble; and beneath,
A field is spread, on which a newer band
Have pitched in Heaven's smile their camp of death
450 Welcoming him we lose with scarce extinguished breath.

LI

Here pause: these graves are all too young as yet
To have outgrown the sorrow which consigned
Its charge to each; and if the seal is set,
Here, on one fountain of a mourning mind,
455 Break it not thou! too surely shalt thou find
Thine own well full, if thou returnest home,
Of tears and gall. From the world's bitter wind
Seek shelter in the shadow of the tomb.
What Adonais is, why fear we to become?

LII

460 The One remains, the many change and pass;
 Heaven's light forever shines, Earth's shadows fly;
 Life, like a dome of many-coloured glass,
 Stains the white radiance of Eternity,
 Until Death tramples it to fragments.—Die,
465 If thou wouldst be with that which thou dost seek!
 Follow where all is fled!—Rome's azure sky,
 Flowers, ruins, statues, music, words, are weak
 The glory they transfuse with fitting truth to speak.

LIII

 Why linger, why turn back, why shrink, my Heart?
470 Thy hopes are gone before: from all things here
 They have departed; thou shouldst now depart!
 A light is past from the revolving year,
 And man, and woman; and what still is dear
 Attracts to crush, repels to make thee wither.
475 The soft sky smiles,—the low wind whispers near:
 'Tis Adonais calls! oh, hasten thither,
 No more let Life divide what Death can join together.

LIV

 That Light whose smile kindles the Universe,
 That Beauty in which all things work and move,
480 That Benediction which the eclipsing Curse
 Of birth can quench not, that sustaining Love
 Which through the web of being blindly wove
 By man and beast and earth and air and sea,
 Burns bright or dim, as each are mirrors of
485 The fire for which all thirst; now beams on me,
 Consuming the last clouds of cold mortality.

LV

 The breath whose might I have invoked in song
 Descends on me; my spirit's bark° is driven,   ship
 Far from the shore, far from the trembling throng
490 Whose sails were never to the tempest given;
 The massy earth and sphered skies are riven!
 I am borne darkly, fearfully, afar;
 Whilst burning through the inmost veil of Heaven,
 The soul of Adonais, like a star,
495 Beacons from the abode where the Eternal are.

FELICIA DOROTHEA HEMANS (1793–1835)

England's Dead (1822)

Son of the ocean isle!
Where sleep your mighty dead?
Show me what high and stately pile
Is rear'd o'er Glory's bed.

5   Go, stranger! track the deep,
Free, free the white sail spread!
Wave may not foam, nor wild wind sweep,
Where rest not England's dead.

On Egypt's burning plains,
10   By the pyramid o'ersway'd,
With fearful power the noonday reigns,
And the palm trees yield no shade.

But let the angry sun
From heaven look fiercely red,
15   Unfelt by those whose task is done!—
There slumber England's dead.

The hurricane hath might
Along the Indian shore,
And far by Ganges' banks at night,
20   Is heard the tiger's roar.

But let the sound roll on!
It hath no tone of dread,
For those that from their toils are gone;—
There slumber England's dead.

25   Loud rush the torrent floods
The western wilds among,
And free, in green Columbia's woods,
The hunter's bow is strung.

But let the floods rush on!
30   Let the arrow's flight be sped!
Why should *they* reck whose task is done?—
There slumber England's dead!

The mountain storms rise high
In the snowy Pyrenees,
35   And toss the pine boughs through the sky,
Like rose leaves on the breeze.

But let the storm rage on!
Let the fresh wreaths be shed!
For the Roncesvalles' field [1] is won,—
40   *There* slumber England's dead.

On the frozen deep's repose
'Tis a dark and dreadful hour,
When round the ship the ice-fields close,
     And the northern night clouds lower.

45   But let the ice drift on!
Let the cold-blue desert spread!
Their course with mast and flag is done,—
     Even there sleep England's dead.

The warlike of the isles,
50   The men of field and wave!
Are not the rocks their funeral piles,
     The seas and shores their grave?

Go, stranger! track the deep,
Free, free the white sail spread!
55   Wave may not foam, nor wild wind sweep,
     Where rest not England's dead.

HENRY WADSWORTH LONGFELLOW   (1807–1882)

The Jewish Cemetery at Newport [1]   (1852)

How strange it seems! These Hebrews in their graves,
     Close by the street of this fair seaport town,
Silent beside the never-silent waves,
     At rest in all this moving up and down!

5   The trees are white with dust, that o'er their sleep
     Wave their broad curtains in the southwind's breath,
While underneath these leafy tents they keep
     The long, mysterious Exodus [2] of Death.

---

[1] **Roncesvalles' field:** During the 1813 battle of Roncesvalles, in the Pyrenees, the French forces defeated the Anglo-Portuguese.
[1] **Newport:** Newport, Rhode Island, is the site of the oldest Jewish cemetery in the United States.
[2] **Exodus:** A book in the Bible describing the flight of the Israelites from Egypt in search of the Promised Land.

And these sepulchral stones, so old and brown,
10   That pave with level flags their burial-place,
Seem like the tablets of the Law, thrown down
      And broken by Moses at the mountain's base.[3]

The very names recorded here are strange,
      Of foreign accent, and of different climes;
15   Alvares and Rivera[4] interchange
      With Abraham and Jacob of old times.[5]

"Blessed be God! for he created Death!"
      The mourners said, "and Death is rest and peace;"
Then added, in the certainty of faith,
20   "And giveth Life that nevermore shall cease."

Closed are the portals of their Synagogue,
      No Psalms of David now the silence break,
No Rabbi reads the ancient Decalogue°   Ten Commandments
      In the grand dialect the Prophets spake.

25   Gone are the living, but the dead remain,
      And not neglected; for a hand unseen,
Scattering its bounty, like a summer rain,
      Still keeps their graves and their remembrance green.

How came they here? What burst of Christian hate,
30   What persecution, merciless and blind,
Drove o'er the sea—that desert desolate—
      These Ishmaels and Hagars of mankind?[6]

They lived in narrow streets and lanes obscure,
      Ghetto and Judenstrass,[7] in mirk and mire;
35   Taught in the school of patience to endure
      The life of anguish and the death of fire.

All their lives long, with the unleavened bread
      And bitter herbs of exile and its fears,

---

[3] **tablets . . . mountain's base:** Moses broke the tablets with God's Ten Commandments in his rage over the sins of the Israelites.
[4] **Alvares and Rivera:** The first Jewish immigrants in America arrived from Spain and Portugal; thus, the names Alvares and Rivera.
[5] **Abraham and Jacob:** Jacob was the son of Abraham. God promised Abraham that his heirs would be the Chosen People, i.e., the Israelites.
[6] **Ishmaels and Hagars:** Hagar, Abraham's servant and concubine, was banished with her son Ishmael (also the son of Abraham) into the desert, where she was saved by an angel.
[7] **Ghetto and Judenstrass:** The ghetto was originally a city quarter to which Jews were confined. *Judenstrasse:* German, literally "Street of Jews."

The wasting famine of the heart they fed,
40   And slaked its thirst with marah[8] of their tears.

Anathema maranatha![9] was the cry
    That rang from town to town, from street to street;
At every gate the accursed Mordecai[10]
    Was mocked and jeered, and spurned by Christian feet.

45 Pride and humiliation hand in hand
    Walked with them through the world where'er they went;
Trampled and beaten were they as the sand,
    And yet unshaken as the continent.

For in the background figures vague and vast
50   Of patriarchs and of prophets rose sublime,
And all the great traditions of the Past
    They saw reflected in the coming time.

And thus forever with reverted look
    The mystic volume of the world they read,
55 Spelling it backward, like a Hebrew book,[11]
    Till life became a Legend of the Dead.

But ah! what once has been shall be no more!
    The groaning earth in travail and in pain
Brings forth its races, but does not restore,
60   And the dead nations never rise again.

ALFRED, LORD TENNYSON (1809–1892)

from In Memoriam A. H. H. (18–29) (1850)

II

Old Yew, which graspest at the stones
    That name the under-lying dead,
    Thy fibres net the dreamless head,
Thy roots are wrapt about the bones.

---

[8] **marah:** Hebrew for "bitterness." Refers to the undrinkable ("bitter") water the wandering Jews found in the desert. Like unleavened bread and bitter herbs, marah is part of the Passover fast.
[9] **Anathema maranatha:** A curse of excommunication among Jews. Its literal meaning is "given over to destruction" and "at the Lord's coming."
[10] **Mordecai:** Mordecai and the rest of the Jews were persecuted by Haman, the advisor to the king of Persia, Ahasuerus.
[11] **Spelling . . . Hebrew book:** Hebrew is read from right to left.

5   The seasons bring the flower again,
         And bring the firstling to the flock;
         And in the dusk of thee, the clock
     Beats out the little lives of men.

     O not for thee the glow, the bloom,
10   Who changest not in any gale,
         Nor branding summer suns avail
     To touch thy thousand years of gloom:

     And gazing on thee, sullen tree,
         Sick for thy stubborn hardihood,
15   I seem to fail from out my blood
     And grow incorporate° into thee.   united

                        VII

     Dark house, by which once more I stand
         Here in the long unlovely street,
         Doors, where my heart was used to beat
20   So quickly, waiting for a hand,

     A hand that can be clasp'd no more—
         Behold me, for I cannot sleep,
         And like a guilty thing I creep
     At earliest morning to the door.

25   He is not here; but far away
         The noise of life begins again,
         And ghastly thro' the drizzling rain
     On the bald street breaks the blank day.

                        XI

     Calm is the morn without a sound,
30   Calm as to suit a calmer grief,
         And only thro' the faded leaf
     The chestnut pattering to the ground:

     Calm and deep peace on this high wold,°   deforested hill
         And on these dews that drench the furze,
35   And all the silvery gossamers
     That twinkle into green and gold:

     Calm and still light on yon great plain
         That sweeps with all its autumn bowers,

And crowded farms and lessening towers,
40 To mingle with the bounding main:°   mainland

Calm and deep peace in this wide air,
    These leaves that redden to the fall;
    And in my heart, if calm at all,
If any calm, a calm despair:

45 Calm on the seas, and silver sleep,
    And waves that sway themselves in rest,
    And dead calm in that noble breast
Which heaves but with the heaving deep.

L

Be near me when my light is low,
50   When the blood creeps, and the nerves prick
    And tingle; and the heart is sick,
And all the wheels of Being slow.

Be near me when the sensuous frame
    Is rack'd with pangs that conquer trust;
55   And Time, a maniac scattering dust,
And Life, a Fury slinging flame

Be near me when my faith is dry,
    And men the flies of latter spring,
    That lay their eggs, and sting and sing
60 And weave their petty cells and die.

Be near me when I fade away,
    To point the term of human strife,
    And on the low dark verge of life
The twilight of eternal day.

LIV

65 Oh yet we trust that somehow good
    Will be the final goal of ill,
    To pangs of nature, sins of will,
Defects of doubt, and taints of blood;

That nothing walks with aimless feet;
70   That not one life shall be destroy'd,
    Or cast as rubbish to the void,
When God hath made the pile complete;

That not a worm is cloven in vain;
  That not a moth with vain desire
75   Is shrivell'd in a fruitless fire,
Or but subserves another's gain.

Behold, we know not anything;
  I can but trust that good shall fall
  At last—far off—at last, to all,
80 And every winter change to spring.

So runs my dream: but what am I?
  An infant crying in the night:
  An infant crying for the light:
And with no language but a cry.

LV

85 The wish, that of the living whole
  No life may fail beyond the grave,
  Derives it not from what we have
The likest God within the soul?

Are God and Nature then at strife,
90 That Nature lends such evil dreams?
  So careful of the type she seems,
So careless of the single life;

That I, considering everywhere
  Her secret meaning in her deeds,
95 And finding that of fifty seeds
She often brings but one to bear,

I falter where I firmly trod,
  And falling with my weight of cares
  Upon the great world's altar-stairs
100 That slope thro' darkness up to God,

I stretch lame hands of faith, and grope,
  And gather dust and chaff, and call
  To what I feel is Lord of all,
And faintly trust the larger hope.

LVI

105 'So careful of the type?' but no.
  From scarped cliff and quarried stone
  She cries, 'A thousand types are gone:
I care for nothing, all shall go.

'Thou makest thine appeal to me:
110 I bring to life, I bring to death:
 The spirit does but mean the breath:
I know no more.' And he, shall he,

Man, her last work, who seem'd so fair,
 Such splendid purpose in his eyes,
115 Who roll'd the psalm to wintry skies,
Who built him fanes of fruitless prayer,

Who trusted God was love indeed
 And love Creation's final law—
 Tho' Nature, red in tooth and claw
120 With ravine, shriek'd against his creed—

Who loved, who suffer'd countless ills,
 Who battled for the True, the Just,
 Be blown about the desert dust,
Or seal'd within the iron hills?

125 No more? A monster then, a dream,
 A discord. Dragons of the prime,
 That tare each other in their slime,
Were mellow music match'd with him.

O life as futile, then, as frail!
130 O for thy voice to soothe and bless!
 What hope of answer, or redress?
Behind the veil, behind the veil.

LXX

I cannot see the features right,
 When on the gloom I strive to paint
135 The face I know; the hues are faint
And mix with hollow masks of night;

Cloud-towers by ghostly masons wrought,
 A gulf that ever shuts and gapes,
 A hand that points, and palled shapes
140 In shadowy thoroughfares of thought;

And crowds that stream from yawning doors,
 And shoals of pucker'd faces drive;
 Dark bulks that tumble half alive,
And lazy lengths on boundless shores;

145 Till all at once beyond the will
        I hear a wizard music roll,
        And thro' a lattice on the soul
Looks thy fair face and makes it still.

LXXXIII

Dip down upon the northern shore,
150   O sweet new-year delaying long;
        Thou doest expectant nature wrong;
Delaying long, delay no more.

What stays thee from the clouded noons,
        Thy sweetness from its proper place?
155   Can trouble live with April days,
Or sadness in the summer moons?

Bring orchis, bring the foxglove spire,
        The little speedwell's darling blue,
        Deep tulips dash'd with fiery dew,
160 Laburnums, dropping-wells of fire.

O thou, new-year, delaying long,
        Delayest the sorrow in my blood,
        That longs to burst a frozen bud
And flood a fresher throat with song.

XCV

165 By night we linger'd on the lawn,
        For underfoot the herb was dry;
        And genial warmth; and o'er the sky
The silvery haze of summer drawn;

And calm that let the tapers burn
170   Unwavering: not a cricket chirr'd:
        The brook alone far-off was heard,
And on the board the fluttering urn:

And bats went round in fragrant skies,
        And wheel'd or lit the filmy shapes
175   That haunt the dusk, with ermine capes
And woolly breasts and beaded eyes;

While now we sang old songs that peal'd
        From knoll to knoll, where, couch'd at ease,
        The white kine° glimmer'd, and the trees   cows
180 Laid their dark arms about the field.

But when those others, one by one,
    Withdrew themselves from me and night,
    And in the house light after light
Went out, and I was all alone,

185   A hunger seized my heart; I read
    Of that glad year which once had been,
    In those fall'n leaves which kept their green,
The noble letters of the dead:

And strangely on the silence broke
190   The silent-speaking words, and strange
    Was love's dumb cry defying change
To test his worth; and strangely spoke

The faith, the vigour, bold to dwell
    On doubts that drive the coward back,
195   And keen thro' wordy snares to track
Suggestion to her inmost cell.

So word by word, and line by line,
    The dead man touch'd me from the past,
    And all at once it seem'd at last
200   The living soul was flash'd on mine,

And mine in this was wound, and whirl'd
    About empyreal heights of thought,
    And came on that which is, and caught
The deep pulsations of the world,

205   Æonian° music measuring out   eternal, everlasting
    The steps of Time—the shocks of Chance—
    The blows of Death. At length my trance
Was cancell'd, stricken thro' with doubt.

Vague words! but ah, how hard to frame
210   In matter-moulded forms of speech,
    Or ev'n for intellect to reach
Thro' memory that which I became:

Till now the doubtful dusk reveal'd
    The knolls once more where, couch'd at ease,
215   The white kine glimmer'd, and the trees
Laid their dark arms about the field:

And suck'd from out the distant gloom
    A breeze began to tremble o'er
    The large leaves of the sycamore,
220 And fluctuate all the still perfume,

And gathering freshlier overhead,
    Rock'd the full foliaged elms, and swung
    The heavy-folded rose, and flung
The lilies to and fro, and said

225 'The dawn, the dawn,' and died away;
    And East and West, without a breath,
    Mixt their dim lights, like life and death,
To broaden into boundless day.

CXV

Now fades the last long streak of snow,
230   Now burgeons every maze of quick
    About the flowering squares, and thick
By ashen roots the violets blow.

Now rings the woodland loud and long,
    The distance takes a lovelier hue,
235   And drown'd in yonder living blue
The lark becomes a sightless song.

Now dance the lights on lawn and lea,
    The flocks are whiter down the vale,
    And milkier every milky sail
240 On winding stream or distant sea;

Where now the seamew° pipes, or dives   seagulls
    In yonder greening gleam, and fly
    The happy birds, that change their sky
To build and brood; that live their lives

245 From land to land; and in my breast
    Spring wakens too; and my regret
    Becomes an April violet,
And buds and blossoms like the rest.

CXXIII

There rolls the deep where grew the tree.
250   O earth, what changes hast thou seen!
    There where the long street roars, hath been
The stillness of the central sea.

The hills are shadows, and they flow
     From form to form, and nothing stands;
255   They melt like mist, the solid lands,
Like clouds they shape themselves and go.

But in my spirit will I dwell,
     And dream my dream, and hold it true;
     For tho' my lips may breathe adieu,
260   I cannot think the thing farewell.

WALT WHITMAN (1819–1892)

When Lilacs Last in the Dooryard Bloom'd[1] (1866; 1881)

1

When lilacs last in the dooryard bloom'd,
And the great star early droop'd in the western sky in the night,
I mourn'd, and yet shall mourn with ever-returning spring.
Ever-returning spring, trinity sure to me you bring,
5   Lilac blooming perennial and drooping star in the west,
And thought of him I love.

2

O powerful western fallen star!
O shades of night—O moody, tearful night!
O great star disappear'd—O the black murk that hides the star!
10   O cruel hands that hold me powerless—O helpless soul of me!
O harsh surrounding cloud that will not free my soul.

3

In the dooryard fronting an old farm-house near the white-wash'd
      palings,°   fence pickets
Stands the lilac-bush tall-growing with heart-shaped leaves of
      rich green,
With many a pointed blossom rising delicate, with the perfume
      strong I love,
15   With every leaf a miracle—and from this bush in the dooryard,
With delicate-color'd blossoms and heart-shaped leaves of rich green,
A sprig with its flower I break.

----

[1] **When Lilacs . . . Bloom'd:** Whitman composed this poem as an elegy to Abraham Lincoln, who was assassinated on April 14, 1865 in the Ford Theatre, Washington DC.

4

In the swamp in secluded recesses,
A shy and hidden bird is warbling a song.

20   Solitary the thrush,
The hermit withdrawn to himself, avoiding the settlements,
Sings by himself a song.

Song of the bleeding throat,
Death's outlet song of life, (for well dear brother I know,
25   If thou wast not granted to sing thou would'st surely die.)

5

Over the breast of the spring, the land, amid cities,
Amid lanes and through old woods, where lately the violets peep'd
            from the ground, spotting the gray debris,
Amid the grass in the fields each side of the lanes, passing the
            endless grass,
Passing the yellow-spear'd wheat, every grain from its shroud in
            the dark-brown fields uprisen,
30   Passing the apple-tree blows of white and pink in the orchards,
Carrying a corpse to where it shall rest in the grave,
Night and day journeys a coffin.

6

Coffin that passes through lanes and streets,[2]
Through day and night with the great cloud darkening the land,
35   With the pomp of the inloop'd flags with the cities draped in black,
With the show of the States themselves as of crape-veil'd women
            standing,
With processions long and winding and the flambeaus° of the night,   torches
With the countless torches lit, with the silent sea of faces and the
            unbared heads,
With the waiting depot, the arriving coffin, and the sombre faces,
40   With dirges through the night, with the thousand voices rising
            strong and solemn,
With all the mournful voices of the dirges pour'd around the coffin,
The dim-lit churches and the shuddering organs—where amid
            these you journey,
With the tolling tolling bells' perpetual clang,
Here, coffin that slowly passes,
45   I give you my sprig of lilac.

---

[2] **Coffin . . . streets:** Lincoln's funeral cortege started in Washington DC and ended in Springfield, Illinois.

7

(Nor for you, for one alone,
Blossoms and branches green to coffins all I bring,
For fresh as the morning, thus would I chant a song for you O sane
        and sacred death.

All over bouquets of roses,
50 O death, I cover you over with roses and early lilies,
But mostly and now the lilac that blooms the first,
Copious I break, I break the sprigs from the bushes,
With loaded arms I come, pouring for you,
For you and the coffins all of you O death.)

8

55 O western orb sailing the heaven,
Now I know what you must have meant as a month since I walk'd,
As I walk'd in silence the transparent shadowy night,
As I saw you had something to tell as you bent to me night after
        night,
As you droop'd from the sky low down as if to my side, (while the
        other stars all look'd on,)
60 As we wander'd together the solemn night, (for something I know
        not what kept me from sleep,)
As the night advanced, and I saw on the rim of the west how full you
        were of woe,
As I stood on the rising ground in the breeze in the cool transparent
        night,
As I watch'd where you pass'd and was lost in the netherward black
        of the night,
As my soul in its trouble dissatisfied sank, as where you sad orb,
65 Concluded, dropt in the night, and was gone.

9

Sing on there in the swamp,
O singer bashful and tender, I hear your notes, I hear your call,
I hear, I come presently, I understand you,
But a moment I linger, for the lustrous star has detain'd me,
70 The star my departing comrade holds and detains me.

10

O how shall I warble myself for the dead one there I loved?
And how shall I deck my song for the large sweet soul that has gone?
And what shall my perfume be for the grave of him I love?

Sea-winds blown from east and west,
75   Blown from the Eastern sea and blown from the Western sea, till
                  there on the prairies meeting,
These and with these and the breath of my chant,
I'll perfume the grave of him I love.

11

O what shall I hang on the chamber walls?
And what shall the pictures be that I hang on the walls,
80   To adorn the burial-house of him I love?

Pictures of growing spring and farms and homes,
With the Fourth-month eve at sundown, and the gray smoke
                  lucid and bright,
With floods of the yellow gold of the gorgeous, indolent, sinking sun,
                  burning, expanding the air,
With the fresh sweet herbage under foot, and the pale green leaves
                  of the trees prolific,
85   In the distance the flowing glaze, the breast of the river, with a
                  wind-dapple here and there,
With ranging hills on the banks, with many a line against the sky,
                  and shadows,
And the city at hand with dwellings so dense, and stacks of chimneys,
And all the scenes of life and the workshops, and the workmen
                  homeward returning.

12

Lo, body and soul—this land,
90   My own Manhattan with spires, and the sparkling and hurrying tides,
                  and the ships,
The varied and ample land, the South and the North in the light,
                  Ohio's shores and flashing Missouri,
And ever the far-spreading prairies cover'd with grass and corn.

Lo, the most excellent sun so calm and haughty,
The violet and purple morn with just-felt breezes,
95   The gentle soft-born measureless light,
The miracle spreading bathing all, the fulfill'd noon,
The coming eve delicious, the welcome night and the stars,
Over my cities shining all, enveloping man and land.

13

Sing on, sing on you gray-brown bird,
100   Sing from the swamps, the recesses, pour your chant from the bushes,
Limitless out of the dusk, out of the cedars and pines.

Sing on dearest brother, warble your reedy song,
Loud human song, with voice of uttermost woe.

O liquid and free and tender!
105   O wild and loose to my soul— O wondrous singer!
You only I hear— yet the star holds me, (but will soon depart,)
Yet the lilac with mastering odor holds me.

14

Now while I sat in the day and look'd forth,
In the close of the day with its light and the fields of spring, and the
        farmers preparing their crops,
110   In the large unconscious scenery of my land with its lakes and forests,
In the heavenly aerial beauty, (after the perturb'd winds and the
        storms,)
Under the arching heavens of the afternoon swift passing, and the
        voices of children and women,
The many-moving sea-tides, and I saw the ships how they sail'd,
And the summer approaching with richness, and the fields all busy
        with labor,
115   And the infinite separate houses, how they all went on, each with its
        meals and minutia of daily usages,
And the streets how their throbbings throbb'd, and the cities pent—
        lo, then and there,
Falling upon them all and among them all, enveloping me with the
        rest,
Appear'd the cloud, appear'd the long black trail,
And I knew death, its thought, and the sacred knowledge of death.

120   Then with the knowledge of death as walking one side of me,
And the thought of death close-walking the other side of me,
And I in the middle as with companions, and as holding the hands
        of companions,
I fled forth to the hiding receiving night that talks not,
Down to the shores of the water, the path by the swamp in the
        dimness,
125   To the solemn shadowy cedars and ghostly pines so still.

And the singer so shy to the rest receiv'd me,
The gray-brown bird I know receiv'd us comrades three,
And he sang the carol of death, and a verse for him I love.

From deep secluded recesses,
130   From the fragrant cedars and the ghostly pines so still,
Came the carol of the bird.

And the charm of the carol rapt me,
As I held as if by their hands my comrades in the night,
And the voice of my spirit tallied the song of the bird.

135 *Come lovely and soothing death,*
Undulate round the world, serenely arriving, arriving,
In the day, in the night, to all, to each,
Sooner or later delicate death.

Prais'd be the fathomless universe,
140 *For life and joy, and for objects and knowledge curious,*
And for love, sweet love— but praise! praise! praise!
For the sure-enwinding arms of cool-enfolding death.

Dark mother always gliding near with soft feet,
Have none chanted for thee a chant of fullest welcome?
145 *Then I chant it for thee, I glorify thee above all,*
I bring thee a song that when thou must indeed come, come
            unfalteringly.

Approach strong deliveress,
When it is so, when thou hast taken them I joyously sing the dead,
Lost in the loving floating ocean of thee,
150 *Laved in the flood of thy bliss O death.*

From me to thee glad serenades,
Dances for thee I propose saluting thee, adornments and feastings for thee,
And the sights of the open landscape and the high-spread sky are fitting,
And life and the fields, and the huge and thoughtful night.

155 *The night in silence under many a star,*
The ocean shore and the husky whispering wave whose voice I know,
And the soul turning to thee O vast and well-veil'd death,
And the body gratefully nestling close to thee.

Over the tree-tops I float thee a song,
160 *Over the rising and sinking waves, over the myriad fields and the*
            prairies wide,
Over the dense-pack'd cities all and the teeming wharves and ways,
I float this carol with joy, with joy to thee O death.

15

To the tally of my soul,
Loud and strong kept up the gray-brown bird,
165 With pure deliberate notes spreading filling the night.

Loud in the pines and cedars dim,
Clear in the freshness moist and the swamp-perfume,
And I with my comrades there in the night.

While my sight that was bound in my eyes unclosed,
170   As to long panoramas of visions.

And I saw askant the armies,
I saw as in noiseless dreams hundreds of battle-flags,
Borne through the smoke of the battles and pierc'd with missiles I
              saw them,
And carried hither and yon through the smoke, and torn and bloody,
175   And at last but a few shreds left on the staffs, (and all in silence,)
And the staffs all splinter'd and broken.

I saw battle-corpses, myriads of them,
And the white skeletons of young men, I saw them,
I saw the debris and debris of all the slain soldiers of the war,
180   But I saw they were not as was thought,
They themselves were fully at rest, they suffer'd not,
The living remain'd and suffer'd, the mother suffer'd,
And the wife and the child and the musing comrade suffer'd,
And the armies that remain'd suffer'd.

16

185   Passing the visions, passing the night,
Passing, unloosing the hold of my comrades' hands,
Passing the song of the hermit bird and the tallying song of my soul,
Victorious song, death's outlet song, yet varying ever-altering song,
As low and wailing, yet clear the notes, rising and falling, flooding
              the night,
190   Sadly sinking and fainting, as warning and warning, and yet again
              bursting with joy,
Covering the earth and filling the spread of the heaven,
As that powerful psalm in the night I heard from recesses,
Passing, I leave thee lilac with heart-shaped leaves,
I leave thee there in the door-yard, blooming, returning with spring.

195   I cease from my song for thee,
From my gaze on thee in the west, fronting the west, communing
              with thee,
O comrade lustrous with silver face in the night.

Yet each to keep and all, retrievements out of the night,
The song, the wondrous chant of the gray-brown bird,

200   And the tallying chant, the echo arous'd in my soul,
        With the lustrous and drooping star with the countenance full of woe,
        With the holders holding my hand nearing the call of the bird,
        Comrades mine and I in the midst, and their memory ever to keep,
                for the dead I loved so well,
        For the sweetest, wisest soul of all my days and lands—and this for
                his dear sake,
205   Lilac and star and bird twined with the chant of my soul,
        There in the fragrant pines and the cedars dusk and dim.

MATTHEW ARNOLD (1822–1888)

Thyrsis[1] (1866)

A Monody, to commemorate the author's friend,
Arthur Hugh Clough, who died at Florence, 1861

How changed is here each spot man makes or fills!
    In the two Hinkseys[2] nothing keeps the same;
        The village street its haunted mansion lacks,
    And from the sign is gone Sibylla's[3] name,
5   And from the roofs the twisted chimney-stacks—
           Are ye too changed, ye hills?
    See, 'tis no foot of unfamiliar men
        To-night from Oxford up your pathway strays!
        Here came I often, often, in old days—
10   Thyrsis and I; we still had Thyrsis then.

Runs it not here, the track by Childsworth Farm,
    Past the high wood, to where the elm-tree crowns
        The hill behind whose ridge the sunset flames?
    The signal-elm, that looks on Ilsley Downs,
15   The Vale, the three lone weirs, the youthful Thames?—
           This winter-eve is warm,
    Humid the air! leafless, yet soft as spring,
        The tender purple spray on copse and briers!
        And that sweet city with her dreaming spires,
20   She needs not June for beauty's heightening,

---

[1] **Thyrsis:** A traditional pastoral name. Arnold's elegy, like Milton's "Lycidas" and Shelley's "Adonais,"
employs many of the conventions of pastoral poetry.
[2] **two Hinkseys:** I.e., North and South Hinksey, villages near Oxford.
[3] **Sibylla's:** Sybilla Kerr was the proprietor of a tavern at the time Arnold and Clough were classmates
at Oxford.

Lovely all times she lies, lovely to-night!—
   Only, methinks, some loss of habit's power
     Befalls me wandering through this upland dim.
   Once passed I blindfold here, at any hour;
25   Now seldom come I, since I came with him.
       That single elm-tree bright
   Against the west—I miss it! is it gone?
     We prized it dearly; while it stood, we said,
     Our friend, the Gipsy-Scholar,[4] was not dead;
30   While the tree lived, he in these fields lived on.

Too rare, too rare, grow now my visits here,
   But once I knew each field, each flower, each stick;
     And with the country-folk acquaintance made
   By barn in threshing-time, by new-built rick.
35   Here, too, our shepherd-pipes we first assayed.
       Ah me! this many a year
   My pipe is lost, my shepherd's holiday!
     Needs must I lose them, needs with heavy heart
     Into the world and wave of men depart;
40   But Thyrsis of his own will went away.

It irked him to be here, he could not rest.
   He loved each simple joy the country yields,
     He loved his mates; but yet he could not keep,
   For that a shadow loured on the fields,
45   Here with the shepherds and the silly sheep.
       Some life of men unblest
   He knew, which made him droop, and filled his head.
     He went; his piping took a troubled sound
     Of storms that rage outside our happy ground;
50   He could not wait their passing, he is dead.

So, some tempestuous morn in early June,
   When the year's primal burst of bloom is o'er,
     Before the roses and the longest day—
   When garden-walks and all the grassy floor
55   With blossoms red and white of fallen May
       And chestnut-flowers are strewn—
   So have I heard the cuckoo's parting cry,
     From the wet field, through the vext garden-trees,
     Come with the volleying rain and tossing breeze:
60   *The bloom is gone, and with the bloom go I!*

---

[4] **Gipsy-Scholar:** See Arnold's poem "The Scholar Gypsy" in Chapter 13.

Too quick despairer, wherefore wilt thou go?
   Soon will the high Midsummer pomps come on,
      Soon will the musk carnations break and swell,
   Soon shall we have gold-dusted snapdragon,
65   Sweet-William with his homely cottage-smell,
         And stocks in fragrant blow;
   Roses that down the alleys shine afar,
      And open, jasmine-muffled lattices,
      And groups under the dreaming garden-trees,
70   And the full moon, and the white evening-star.

He hearkens not! light comer, he is flown!
   What matters it? next year he will return,
      And we shall have him in the sweet spring-days,
   With whitening hedges, and uncrumpling fern,
75   And blue-bells trembling by the forest-ways,
         And scent of hay new-mown.
   But Thyrsis never more we swains shall see;
      See him come back, and cut a smoother reed,
      And blow a strain the world at last shall heed—
80   For Time, not Corydon,[5] hath conquered thee!

Alack, for Corydon no rival now!—
   But when Sicilian shepherds lost a mate,
      Some good survivor with his flute would go,
   Piping a ditty sad for Bion's[6] fate;
85   And cross the unpermitted ferry's flow,
         And relax Pluto's brow,
   And make leap up with joy the beauteous head
      Of Proserpine, among whose crowned hair
      Are flowers first opened on Sicilian air,
90   And flute his friend, like Orpheus, from the dead.[7]

O easy access to the hearer's grace
   When Dorian[8] shepherds sang to Proserpine!

---

[5] **Corydon:** As Arnold calls Clough Thyrsis in the poem, likewise he names himself Corydon.
[6] **Bion:** A Greek pastoral poet and author of the elegy "Lament for Adonis." Another elegy, "Lament for Bion" was purportedly written by his pupil Moschus. Both Bion and Moschus resided in Sicily.
[7] **And cross the unpermitted . . . dead:** According to the Greek myth, Orpheus was an exquisite singer who resided in Thrace. When his wife Eurydice died of snakebite, Orpheus was so disconsolate that he decided to seek her out in the underworld. He used his music to charm Pluto and Proserpina, the rulers of the underworld, who allowed him to take Eurydice back to the land of the living, on condition that he never looked back. However, Orpheus could not resist the temptation and glanced behind his shoulder, only to see his wife disappearing once again into the netherworld.
[8] **Dorian:** A Greek mode marked by clarity and simplicity.

For she herself had trod Sicilian fields,
She knew the Dorian water's gush divine,
95   She knew each lily white which Enna yields,
          Each rose with blushing face;
She loved the Dorian pipe, the Dorian strain.
       But ah, of our poor Thames she never heard!
       Her foot the Cumner cowslips never stirred;
100   And we should tease her with our plaint in vain!

Well! wind-dispersed and vain the words will be,
      Yet, Thyrsis, let me give my grief its hour
        In the old haunt, and find our tree-topped hill!
      Who, if not I, for questing here hath power?
105   I know the wood which hides the daffodil,
        I know the Fyfield tree,
I know what white, what purple fritillaries°   flowers
        The grassy harvest of the river-fields,
        Above by Ensham, down by Sandford, yields,
110   And what sedged brooks are Thames's tributaries;

I know these slopes; who knows them if not I?—
      But many a dingle on the loved hill-side,
        With thorns once studded, old, white-blossomed trees,
      Where thick the cowslips grew, and far descried
115   High towered the spikes of purple orchises,
        Hath since our day put by
The coronals of that forgotten time;
        Down each green bank hath gone the ploughboy's team,
        And only in the hidden brookside gleam
120   Primroses, orphans of the flowery prime.

Where is the girl, who by the boatman's door,
      Above the locks, above the boating throng,
        Unmoored our skiff when through the Wytham flats,
      Red loosestrife and blond meadow-sweet among
125   And darting swallows and light water-gnats,
        We tracked the shy Thames shore?
Where are the mowers, who, as the tiny swell
        Of our boat passing heaved the river-grass,
        Stood with suspended scythe to see us pass?—
130   They all are gone, and thou art gone as well!

Yes, thou art gone! and round me too the night
      In ever-nearing circle weaves her shade.
        I see her veil draw soft across the day,
      I feel her slowly chilling breath invade

135 The cheek grown thin, the brown hair sprent with grey;
  I feel her finger light
  Laid pausefully upon life's headlong train;—
   The foot less prompt to meet the morning dew,
   The heart less bounding at emotion new,
140 And hope, once crushed, less quick to spring again.

 And long the way appears, which seemed so short
  To the less practised eye of sanguine youth;
   And high the mountain-tops, in cloudy air,
  The mountain-tops where is the throne of Truth,
145 Tops in life's morning-sun so bright and bare!
   Unbreachable the fort
  Of the long-battered world uplifts its wall;
   And strange and vain the earthly turmoil grows,
   And near and real the charm of thy repose,
150 And night as welcome as a friend would fall.

 But hush! the upland hath a sudden loss
  Of quiet!—look, adown the dusk hill-side,
   A troop of Oxford hunters going home,
  As in old days, jovial and talking, ride!
155 From hunting with the Berkshire hounds they come.
   Quick! let me fly, and cross
  Into yon farther field!—'Tis done; and see,
   Backed by the sunset, which doth glorify
   The orange and pale violet evening-sky,
160 Bare on its lonely ridge, the Tree! the Tree!

 I take the omen! Eve lets down her veil,
  The white fog creeps from bush to bush about,
   The west unflushes, the high stars grow bright,
  And in the scattered farms the lights come out.
165 I cannot reach the signal-tree to-night,
   Yet, happy omen, hail!
  Hear it from thy broad lucent Arno-vale,[9]
   (For there thine earth-forgetting eyelids keep
   The morningless and unawakening sleep
170 Under the flowery oleanders pale),

---

[9] **Arno-vale:** The river Arno flows through Florence, where Arthur Clough was buried.

Hear it, O Thyrsis, still our tree is there!—
  Ah, vain! These English fields, this upland dim,
    These brambles pale with mist engarlanded,
  That lone, sky-pointing tree, are not for him;
175   To a boon southern country he is fled,
      And now in happier air,
  Wandering with the great Mother's[10] train divine
    (And purer or more subtle soul than thee,
    I trow, the mighty Mother doth not see)
180   Within a folding of the Apennine,

Thou hearest the immortal chants of old!—
  Putting his sickle to the perilous grain
    In the hot cornfield of the Phrygian king,
  For thee the Lityerses-song again
185   Young Daphnis with his silver voice doth sing;[11]
     Sings his Sicilian fold,
  His sheep, his hapless love, his blinded eyes—
    And how a call celestial round him rang,
    And heavenward from the fountain-brink he sprang,
190   And all the marvel of the golden skies.

There thou art gone, and me thou leavest here
  Sole in these fields! yet will I not despair.
    Despair I will not, while I yet descry
  'Neath the mild canopy of English air
195   That lonely tree against the western sky.
     Still, still these slopes, 'tis clear,
  Our Gipsy-Scholar haunts, outliving thee!
    Fields where soft sheep from cages pull the hay,
    Woods with anemonies in flower till May,
200   Know him a wanderer still; then why not me?

---

[10] **great Mother's:** Nature.
[11] **Young Daphnis . . . sing:** "Daphnis, the ideal Sicilian shepherd of Greek pastoral poetry, was said to have followed into Phrygia his mistress Piplea, who had been carried off by robbers, and to have found her in the power of the King of Phrygia, Lityerses. Lityerses used to make strangers try a contest with him in reaping corn, and to put them to death if he overcame them. Hercules arrived in time to save Daphnis, took upon him the reaping contest with Lityerses, overcame him and slew him. The Lityerses song connected with the tradition was, like the Linus-song, one of the early plaintive strains of Greek popular poetry, and used to be sung by corn reapers. Other traditions represent Daphnis as beloved by a nymph, who exacted from him an oath to love no one else. He fell in love with a princess and was struck blind by the jealous nymph. Mercury, who was his father, raised him to heaven, and made a fountain spring up in the place from which he ascended. At this fountain the Sicilians offered yearly sacrifices." [Arnold's note]

A fugitive and gracious light he seeks,
   Shy to illumine; and I seek it too.
     This does not come with houses or with gold,
   With place, with honour, and a flattering crew;
205   'Tis not in the world's market bought and sold—
        But the smooth-slipping weeks
   Drop by, and leave its seeker still untired;
     Out of the heed of mortals he is gone,
     He wends unfollowed, he must house alone;
210   Yet on he fares, by his own heart inspired.

Thou too, O Thyrsis, on like quest wast bound;
   Thou wanderedst with me for a little hour!
     Men gave thee nothing; but this happy quest,
   If men esteemed thee feeble, gave thee power,
215   If men procured thee trouble, gave thee rest.
        And this rude Cumner ground,
   Its fir-topped Hurst, its farms, its quiet fields,
     Here cam'st thou in thy jocund youthful time,
     Here was thine height of strength, thy golden prime!
220   And still the haunt beloved a virtue yields.

What though the music of thy rustic flute
   Kept not for long its happy, country tone;
     Lost it too soon, and learnt a stormy note
   Of men contention-tost, of men who groan,
225   Which tasked thy pipe too sore, and tired thy throat—
        It failed, and thou wast mute!
   Yet hadst thou alway visions of our light,
     And long with men of care thou couldst not stay,
     And soon thy foot resumed its wandering way,
230   Left human haunt, and on alone till night.

Too rare, too rare, grow now my visits here!
   'Mid city-noise, not, as with thee of yore,
     Thyrsis! in reach of sheep-bells is my home.
   —Then through the great town's harsh, heart-wearying roar,
235   Let in thy voice a whisper often come,
        To chase fatigue and fear:
   Why faintest thou? I wandered till I died.
     Roam on! The light we sought is shining still.
     Dost thou ask proof? Our tree yet crowns the hill,
240   *Our Scholar travels yet the loved hill-side.*

THOMAS HARDY (1840–1928)

The Convergence of the Twain (1912)
(Lines on the Loss of the *Titanic*)[1]

     In a solitude of the sea
     Deep from human vanity,
And the Pride of Life that planned her, stilly couches she.

     Steel chambers, late the pyres
5   Of her salamandrine fires,
Cold currents thrid,° and turn to rhythmic tidal lyres.   thread

     Over the mirrors meant
     To glass the opulent
The sea-worm crawls—grotesque, slimed, dumb, indifferent.

10   Jewels in joy designed
     To ravish the sensuous mind
Lie lightless, all their sparkles bleared and black and blind.

     Dim moon-eyed fishes near
     Gaze at the gilded gear
15   And query: "What does this vaingloriousness down here?" . . .

     Well: while was fashioning
     This creature of cleaving wing,
The Immanent Will that stirs and urges everything

     Prepared a sinister mate
20   For her—so gaily great—
A Shape of Ice, for the time far and dissociate.

     And as the smart ship grew
     In stature, grace, and hue,
In shadowy silent distance grew the Iceberg too.

25   Alien they seemed to be:
     No mortal eye could see
The intimate welding of their later history,

---

[1] ***Titanic:*** The *Titanic*, a luxurious sea-liner, collided with an iceberg on April 15, 1912. Some 1500 passengers were drowned.

Or sign that they were bent
By paths coincident
30 On being anon twin halves of one august event,

Till the Spinner of the Years
Said "Now!" And each one hears,
And consummation comes, and jars two hemispheres.

A. E. HOUSMAN (1859–1936)

To an Athlete Dying Young (1896)

The time you won your town the race
We chaired you through the market-place;
Man and boy stood cheering by,
And home we brought you shoulder-high.

5 Today, the road all runners come,
Shoulder-high we bring you home,
And set you at your threshold down,
Townsman of a stiller town.

Smart lad, to slip betimes away
10 From fields where glory does not stay
And early though the laurel grows
It withers quicker than the rose.

Eyes the shady night has shut
Cannot see the record cut,
15 And silence sounds no worse than cheers
After earth has stopped the ears:

Now you will not swell the rout
Of lads that wore their honours out,
Runners whom renown outran
20 And the name died before the man.

So set, before its echoes fade,
The fleet foot on the sill of shade,
And hold to the low lintel up
The still-defended challenge-cup.

25 And round that early-laurelled head
Will flock to gaze the strengthless dead,

And find unwithered on its curls
The garland briefer than a girl's.

WILLIAM BUTLER YEATS (1865–1939)

In Memory of Major Robert Gregory[1] (1919)

1

Now that we're almost settled in our house
I'll name the friends that cannot sup with us
Beside a fire of turf in the ancient tower,
And having talked to some late hour
5   Climb up the narrow winding stair to bed:
Discoverers of forgotten truth
Or mere companions of my youth,
All, all are in my thoughts to-night, being dead.

2

Always we'd have the new friend meet the old,
10   And we are hurt if either friend seem cold,
And there is salt to lengthen out the smart
In the affections of our heart,
And quarrels are blown up upon that head;
But not a friend that I would bring
15   This night can set us quarrelling,
For all that come into my mind are dead.

3

Lionel Johnson[2] comes the first to mind,
That loved his learning better than mankind,
Though courteous to the worst; much falling he
20   Brooded upon sanctity
Till all his Greek and Latin learning seemed
A long blast upon the horn that brought
A little nearer to his thought
A measureless consummation that he dreamed.

---

[1] **Major Robert Gregory:** The son of Lady Gregory, Yeats's close friend and patron, served as a pilot during the First World War. He was killed in action in 1918. See also "An Irish Airman Foresees His Death" in Chapter 6.
[2] **Lionel Johnson:** An English poet (1867–1902), member of the Rhymers Club, and a close friend of Yeats. Johnson died of alcoholism.

4

25   And that enquiring man John Synge[3] comes next,
     That dying chose the living world for text
     And never could have rested in the tomb
     But that, long travelling, he had come
     Towards nightfall upon certain set apart
30   In a most desolate stony place,
     Towards nightfall upon a race
     Passionate and simple like his heart.

5

     And then I think of old George Pollexfen,[4]
     In muscular youth well known to Mayo men[5]
35   For horsemanship at meets or at racecourses,
     That could have shown how purebred horses
     And solid men, for all their passion, live
     But as the outrageous stars incline
     By opposition, square and trine;
40   Having grown sluggish and contemplative.

6

     They were my close companions many a year,
     A portion of my mind and life, as it were,
     And now their breathless faces seem to look
     Out of some old picture-book;
45   I am accustomed to their lack of breath,
     But not that my dear friend's dear son,
     Our Sidney[6] and our perfect man,
     Could share in that discourtesy of death.

7

     For all things the delighted eye now sees
50   Were loved by him; the old storm-broken trees
     That cast their shadows upon road and bridge;
     The tower set on the stream's edge;
     The ford where drinking cattle make a stir
     Nightly, and startled by that sound

---

[3] **John Synge:** An Irish musician and playwright (1871–1909), who traveled widely in Europe. In 1899, he met Yeats, and the two men lived together for a while on the Aran Islands. As a result, Synge published his diary from that time, *The Aran Islands* (1907), which received some critical acclaim.
[4] **George Pollexfen:** Yeats's uncle and close friend.
[5] **Mayo men:** A reference to county Mayo in Ireland.
[6] **Sidney:** Robert Gregory was a true Renaissance man, who, among other things, wrote verse. Thus, Yeats compares him to the Elizabethan poet Sidney.

55   The water-hen must change her ground;
     He might have been your heartiest welcomer.

                              8

     When with the Galway foxhounds he would ride
     From Castle Taylor to the Roxborough side
     Or Esserkelly plain, few kept his pace;
60   At Mooneen[7] he had leaped a place
     So perilous that half the astonished meet
     Had shut their eyes, and where was it
     He rode a race without a bit?
     And yet his mind outran the horses' feet.

                              9

65   We dreamed that a great painter had been born
     To cold Clare rock and Galway rock[8] and thorn,
     To that stern colour and that delicate line
     That are our secret discipline
     Wherein the gazing heart doubles her might.
70   Soldier, scholar, horseman, he,
     And yet he had the intensity
     To have published all to be a world's delight.

                             10

     What other could so well have counselled us
     In all lovely intricacies of a house
75   As he that practised or that understood
     All work in metal or in wood,
     In moulded plaster or in carven stone?
     Soldier, scholar, horseman, he,
     And all he did done perfectly
80   As though he had but that one trade alone.

                             11

     Some burn damp fagots, others may consume
     The entire combustible world in one small room
     As though dried straw, and if we turn about
     The bare chimney is gone black out
85   Because the work had finished in that flare.
     Soldier, scholar, horseman, he,
     As 'twere all life's epitome.
     What made us dream that he could comb grey hair?

---

[7] **Galway . . . Mooneen:** The places described here are all in Ireland.
[8] **Clare rock and Galway rock:** Sites in Ireland.

12

I had thought, seeing how bitter is that wind
90   That shakes the shutter, to have brought to mind
All those that manhood tried, or childhood loved,
Or boyish intellect approved,
With some appropriate commentary on each;
Until imagination brought
95   A fitter welcome; but a thought
Of that late death took all my heart for speech.

JAMES D. CORROTHERS (1869–1917)

Paul Laurence Dunbar[1] (1912)

He came, a dark youth, singing in the dawn
    Of a new freedom, glowing o'er his lyre,
    Refining, as with great Apollo's[2] fire,
    His people's gift of song. And, thereupon,
5   This Negro singer, come to Helicon,[3]
    Constrained the masters, listening, to admire,
    And roused a race to wonder and aspire,
    Gazing which way their honest voice was gone,
With ebon face uplit of glory's crest.
10   Men marveled at the singer, strong and sweet,
    Who brought the cabin's mirth, the tuneful night,
But faced the morning, beautiful with light,
    To die while shadows yet fell toward the west,
    And leave his laurels at his people's feet.

15   Dunbar, no poet wears your laurels now;
    None rises, singing, from your race like you.
    Dark melodist, immortal, though the dew
    Fell early on the bays upon your brow,
And tinged with pathos every halcyon vow
20   And brave endeavor. Silence o'er you threw
    Flowerets of love. Or, if an envious few
    Of your own people brought no garlands, how
Could Malice smite him whom the gods had crowned?

---

[1] **Paul Laurence Dunbar:** An African-American poet (1872–1906).
[2] **Apollo:** According to some sources, Apollo was the Greek god of poetry.
[3] **Helicon:** The mountain, home of the Muses.

If, like the meadow-lark, your flight was low,
25   Your flooded lyrics half the hilltops drowned;
A wide world heard you, and it loved you so
   It stilled its heart to list the strains you sang,
   And o'er your happy songs its plaudits rang.

PAUL LAURENCE DUNBAR (1872–1906)

Douglass[1] (1903)

Ah, Douglass, we have fall'n on evil days,
   Such days as thou, not even thou didst know,
   When thee, the eyes of that harsh long ago
Saw, salient, at the cross of devious ways,
5   And all the country heard thee with amaze.
   Not ended then, the passionate ebb and flow,
   The awful tide that battled to and fro;
We ride amid a tempest of dispraise.

Now, when the waves of swift dissension swarm,
10   And Honor, the strong pilot, lieth stark,
Oh, for thy voice high-sounding o'er the storm,
   For thy strong arm to guide the shivering bark,
The blast-defying power of thy form,
   To give us comfort through the lonely dark.

WALLACE STEVENS (1879–1955)

The Emperor of Ice-Cream (1923)

Call the roller of big cigars,
The muscular one, and bid him whip
In kitchen cups concupiscent° curds.   libidinous; lustful
Let the wenches dawdle in such dress
5   As they are used to wear, and let the boys
Bring flowers in last month's newspapers.
Let be be finale of seem.
The only emperor is the emperor of ice-cream.

---

[1] **Douglass:** I.e., Frederick Douglass, the nineteenth century writer and abolitionist. His acclaimed
autobiography, *The Narrative of the Life of Frederick Douglass* (1845), described the author's flight
from the inhuman conditions of slavery.

Take from the dresser of deal.
10 Lacking the three glass knobs, that sheet
On which she embroidered fantails once
And spread it so as to cover her face.
If her horny feet protrude, they come
To show how cold she is, and dumb.
15 Let the lamp affix its beam.
The only emperor is the emperor of ice-cream.

WILLIAM CARLOS WILLIAMS (1883–1963)

An Elegy for D. H. Lawrence[1] (1935)

Green points on the shrub
and poor Lawrence dead.
The night damp and misty
and Lawrence no more in the world
5 to answer April's promise
with a fury of labor
against waste, waste and life's
coldness.

Once he received a letter—
10 he never answered it—
praising him: so English
he had thereby raised himself
to an unenglish greatness.
Dead now and it grows clearer
15 what bitterness drove him.

This is the time.
The serpent in the grotto
water dripping from the stone
into a pool.
20 Mediterranean evenings. Ashes
of Cretan fires. And to the north
forsythia hung with
yellow bells in the cold.

---

[1] **D. H. Lawrence:** An acclaimed British essayist, poet, and novelist (1885–1930), whose controversial works offered a direct and frank treatment of sexuality. An opponent of repressive Victorian mores and bourgeois decorum, Lawrence advocated the liberation of the human mind and emotions. He traveled widely, visiting Australia, Italy, Mexico, and the United States, among other countries. Lawrence died of tuberculosis in France at the age of forty-five.

Poor Lawrence
25 worn with a fury of sad labor
to create summer from
spring's decay. English
women. Men driven not to love
but to the ends of the earth.
30 The serpent turning his
stone-like head,
the fixed agate eyes turn also.

And unopened jonquils
hang their folded heads. No
35 summer. But for Lawrence
full praise in this
half cold half season—
before trees are in leaf and
tufted grass stars
40 unevenly the bare ground.

Slowly the serpent leans
to drink by the tinkling water
the forked tongue alert,
Then fold after fold,
45 glassy strength, passing
a given point,
as by desire drawn
forward bodily, he glides
smoothly in.

50 To stand by the sea or walk
again along a river's bank and talk
with a companion, to halt
watching where the edge of water
meets and lies upon
55 the unmoving shore—
Flood waters rise, and will rise,
rip the quiet valley
trap the gypsy and the girl
She clings drowning to
60 a bush in flower.

Remember, now, Lawrence dead.
Blue squills in bloom—to
the scorched aridity of
the Mexican plateau. Or baked
65 public squares in the cities of
Mediterranean islands

where one waits for busses and
boats come slowly along the water
arriving.

70   But the sweep of spring over
temperate lands, meadows and woods
where the young walk and talk
incompletely,
straining to no summer,
75   hearing the frogs, speaking of
birds and insects—

Febrile° spring moves not to heat   feverish
but always more slowly,
burdened by a weight of leaves.
80   Nothing now
to burst the bounds—
remains confined by them. Heat,
heat! Unknown. Poor Lawrence,
dead and only the drowned
85   fallen dancing from the deck
of a pleasure boat
unfading desire.

Rabbits, imaginings, the
drama, literature, satire.
90   The serpent cannot move
his stony eyes, scarcely sees
but touching the air
with his forked tongue surmises
and his body which dipped
95   into the cold water
is gone.

Violently the satiric sun
that leads April not to
the panting dance but to stillness
100   in, into the brain, dips
and is gone also.
And sisters return
through the dusk
to the measured rancor
105   of their unbending elders.

Greep, greep, greep the cricket
chants where the snake

with agate eyes leaned to the water.
Sorrow to the young
110   that Lawrence has passed
unwanted from England.
And in the gardens forsythia
and in the woods
now the crinkled spice-bush
115   in flower.

T. S. ELIOT (1888–1965)

The Hollow Men (1925)

> Mistah Kurtz—he dead.[1]
>
> A penny for the Old Guy[2]

I

We are the hollow men
We are the stuffed men
Leaning together
Headpiece filled with straw. Alas!
5   Our dried voices, when
We whisper together
Are quiet and meaningless
As wind in dry grass
Or rats' feet over broken glass
10   In our dry cellar

Shape without form, shade without colour,
Paralysed force, gesture without motion;

Those who have crossed
With direct eyes, to death's other Kingdom
15   Remember us—if at all—not as lost
Violent souls, but only

---

[1] **Mistah Kurtz—he dead:** From Joseph Conrad's *Heart of Darkness*, a novel exploring, among other things, the rise of nihilistic morality and the barrenness of the human spirit.
[2] **A penny for the Old Guy:** A children's saying in England when soliciting money for fireworks to commemorate the foiling of Guy Fawkes's "gun-powder plot." In 1605, Guy Fawkes conspired to blow up the Houses of Parliament in London. Eliot's epigraph could also allude to Charon, the ferryman who demanded a coin in order to carry the dead across Lethe, the river of forgetfulness in Greek mythology and Dante's *Inferno*.

As the hollow men
The stuffed men.

II

Eyes I dare not meet in dreams
20   In death's dream kingdom
These do not appear:
There, the eyes are
Sunlight on a broken column
There, is a tree swinging
25   And voices are
In the wind's singing
More distant and more solemn
Than a fading star.

Let me be no nearer
30   In death's dream kingdom
Let me also wear
Such deliberate disguises
Rat's coat, crowskin, crossed staves
In a field
35   Behaving as the wind behaves
No nearer—

Not that final meeting
In the twilight kingdom

III

This is the dead land
40   This is cactus land
Here the stone images
Are raised, here they receive
The supplication of a dead man's hand
Under the twinkle of a fading star.

45   Is it like this
In death's other kingdom
Waking alone
At the hour when we are
Trembling with tenderness
50   Lips that would kiss
Form prayers to broken stone.

IV

The eyes are not here
There are no eyes here
In this valley of dying stars
55 In this hollow valley
This broken jaw of our lost kingdoms

In this last of meeting places
We grope together
And avoid speech
60 Gathered on this beach of the tumid river

Sightless, unless
The eyes reappear
As the perpetual star
Multifoliate rose
65 Of death's twilight kingdom
The hope only
Of empty men.

V

Here we go round the prickly pear
Prickly pear prickly pear
70 *Here we go round the prickly pear*
At five o'clock in the morning.[3]

Between the idea
And the reality
Between the motion
75 And the act
Falls the Shadow
                    For Thine is the Kingdom [4]

Between the conception
And the creation
80 Between the emotion
And the response
Falls the Shadow
                    Life is very long

---

[3] **Here we go . . . morning:** Eliot's parody of the nursery rhyme "The Mulberry Bush."
[4] **For Thine is the Kingdom:** From the Lord's Prayer (Matthew 6:13 and Luke 11:2–4).

Between the desire
85 And the spasm
Between the potency
And the existence
Between the essence
And the descent
90 Falls the Shadow

    For Thine is the Kingdom

For Thine is
Life is
For Thine is the

95 *This is the way the world ends*
This is the way the world ends
This is the way the world ends
Not with a bang but a whimper.

JOHN CROWE RANSOM (1888–1974)

Bells for John Whiteside's Daughter (1924)

There was such speed in her little body,
And such lightness in her footfall,
It is no wonder that her brown study°   lost in thought; absorbed in
Astonishes us all.   serious concentration

5 Her wars were bruited° in our high window.   displayed; also clamor
We looked among orchard trees and beyond,
Where she took arms against her shadow,
Or harried unto the pond

The lazy geese, like a snow cloud
10 Dripping their snow on the green grass,
Tricking and stopping, sleepy and proud,
Who cried in goose, Alas,

For the tireless heart within the little
Lady with rod that made them rise
15 From their noon apple dreams, and scuttle
Goose-fashion under the skies!

But now go the bells, and we are ready;
In one house we are sternly stopped
To say we are vexed at her brown study,
20   Lying so primly propped.

JOHN CROWE RANSOM   (1888–1974)

Janet Waking   (1927)

Beautifully Janet slept
Till it was deeply morning. She woke then
And thought about her dainty-feathered hen,
To see how it had kept.

5   One kiss she gave her mother,
Only a small one gave she to her daddy
Who would have kissed each curl of his shining baby;
No kiss at all for her brother.

"Old Chucky, Old Chucky!" she cried,
10   Running on little pink feet upon the grass
To Chucky's house, and listening. But alas,
Her Chucky had died.

It was a transmogrifying bee
Came droning down on Chucky's old bald head
15   And sat and put the poison. It scarcely bled,
But how exceedingly

And purply did the knot
Swell with the venom and communicate
Its rigour! Now the poor comb stood up straight
20   But Chucky did not.

So there was Janet
Kneeling on the wet grass, crying her brown hen
(Translated far beyond the daughters of men)
To rise and walk upon it.

25   And weeping fast as she had breath
Janet implored us, "Wake her from her sleep!"
And would not be instructed in how deep
Was the forgetful kingdom of death.

E. E. CUMMINGS (1894–1962)

"my father moved through dooms of love" (1940)

my father moved through dooms of love
through sames of am through haves of give,
singing each morning out of each night
my father moved through depths of height

5   this motionless forgetful where
turned at his glance to shining here;
that if(so timid air is firm)
under his eyes would stir and squirm

newly as from unburied which
10   floats the first who,his april touch
drove sleeping selves to swarm their fates
woke dreamers to their ghostly roots

and should some why completely weep
my father's fingers brought her sleep:
15   vainly no smallest voice might cry
for he could feel the mountains grow.

Lifting the valleys of the sea
my father moved through griefs of joy;
praising a forehead called the moon
20   singing desire into begin

joy was his song and joy so pure
a heart of star by him could steer
and pure so now and now so yes
the wrists of twilight would rejoice

25   keen as midsummer's keen beyond
conceiving mind of sun will stand,
so strictly(over utmost him
so hugely)stood my father's dream

his flesh was flesh his blood was blood:
30   no hungry man but wished him food;
no cripple wouldn't creep one mile
uphill to only see him smile.

Scorning the pomp of must and shall
my father moved through dooms of feel;
35 his anger was as right as rain
his pity was as green as grain

septembering arms of year extend
less humbly wealth to foe and friend
than he to foolish and to wise
40 offered immeasurable is

proudly and(by octobering flame
beckoned)as earth will downward climb,
so naked for immortal work
his shoulders marched against the dark

45 his sorrow was as true as bread:
no liar looked him in the head;
if every friend became his foe
he'd laugh and build a world with snow.

My father moved through theys of we,
50 singing each new leaf out of each tree
(and every child was sure that spring
danced when she heard my father sing)

then let men kill which cannot share,
let blood and flesh be mud and mire,
55 scheming imagine,passion willed,
freedom a drug that's bought and sold

giving to steal and cruel kind,
a heart to fear,to doubt a mind,
to differ a disease of same,
60 conform the pinnacle of am

though dull were all we taste as bright,
bitter all utterly things sweet,
maggoty minus and dumb death
all we inherit,all bequeath

65 and nothing quite so least as truth
—i say though hate were why men breathe—
because my father lived his soul
love is the whole and more than all

HART CRANE (1899–1932)

At Melville's Tomb[1]   (1926)

Often beneath the wave, wide from this ledge
The dice of drowned men's bones he saw bequeath
An embassy. Their numbers as he watched,
Beat on the dusty shore and were obscured.

5   And wrecks passed without sound of bells,
The calyx of death's bounty giving back
A scattered chapter, livid hieroglyph,
The portent wound in corridors of shells.

Then in the circuit calm of one vast coil,
10   Its lashings charmed and malice reconciled,
Frosted eyes there were that lifted altars;
And silent answers crept across the stars.

Compass, quadrant and sextant[2] contrive
No farther tides . . . High in the azure steeps
15   Monody[3] shall not wake the mariner.
This fabulous shadow only the sea keeps.

COUNTEE CULLEN (1903–1946)

In Memory of Colonel Charles Young[1]   (1925)

Along the shore the tall, thin grass
That fringes that dark river,
While sinuously soft feet pass,
Begins to bleed and quiver.

5   The great dark voice breaks with a sob
Across the womb of night;

---

[1] **Melville's Tomb:** Herman Melville (1819–1891), an American novelist and poet, author of *Moby-Dick* among other works.
[2] **quadrant and sextant:** Instruments formerly used in the navigation of ships, particularly for the measurement of latitude and longitude.
[3] **Monody:** A dirge or elegy sung by a single voice.
[1] **Colonel Charles Young:** The son of former slaves, Charles Young graduated from West Point. He soon embarked on a brilliant military career and became the first African American to reach the rank of Colonel in the U.S. army.

Above your grave the tom-toms throb,
And the hills are weird with light.

The great dark heart is like a well
10   Drained bitter by the sky,
And all the honeyed lies they tell
Come there to thirst and die.

No lie is strong enough to kill
The roots that work below;
15   From your rich dust and slaughtered will
A tree with tongues will grow.

W. H. AUDEN   (1907–1973)

In Memory of W. B. Yeats [1]   (1939)

(d. Jan. 1939)

I

He disappeared in the dead of winter:
The brooks were frozen, the airports almost deserted,
And snow disfigured the public statues;
The mercury sank in the mouth of the dying day.
5   What instruments we have agree
The day of his death was a dark cold day.

Far from his illness
The wolves ran on through the evergreen forests,
The peasant river was untempted by the fashionable quays;
10   By mourning tongues
The death of the poet was kept from his poems.

But for him it was his last afternoon as himself,
An afternoon of nurses and rumours;
The provinces of his body revolted,
15   The squares of his mind were empty,
Silence invaded the suburbs,
The current of his feeling failed; he became his admirers.

Now he is scattered among a hundred cities
And wholly given over to unfamiliar affections,

---

[1] **In Memory of W. B. Yeats:** The Irish poet and playwright William Butler Yeats passed away on January 28, 1939.

20 To find his happiness in another kind of wood
And be punished under a foreign code of conscience.
The words of a dead man
Are modified in the guts of the living.

But in the importance and noise of to-morrow
25 When the brokers are roaring like beasts on the floor of the Bourse,[2]
And the poor have the sufferings to which they are fairly accustomed,
And each in the cell of himself is almost convinced of his freedom,
A few thousand will think of this day
As one thinks of a day when one did something slightly unusual.

30 What instruments we have agree
The day of his death was a dark cold day.

II

You were silly like us; your gift survived it all:
The parish of rich women, physical decay,
Yourself. Mad Ireland hurt you into poetry.
35 Now Ireland has her madness and her weather still,
For poetry makes nothing happen: it survives
In the valley of its making where executives
Would never want to tamper, flows on south
From ranches of isolation and the busy griefs,
40 Raw towns that we believe and die in; it survives,
A way of happening, a mouth.

III

Earth, receive an honoured guest:
William Yeats is laid to rest.
Let the Irish vessel lie
45 Emptied of its poetry.[3]

In the nightmare of the dark
All the dogs of Europe bark,
And the living nations wait,
Each sequestered in its hate;

50 Intellectual disgrace
Stares from every human face,

---

[2] **Bourse:** The stock exchange.
[3] At this place, an earlier version of the poem included three additional stanzas, which Auden eventually expurgated for ideological reasons. The stanzas read: "Time that is intolerant / To the brave and innocent, / And indifferent in a week / To a beautiful physique, // Worships language and forgives / Everyone by who it leaves; / Pardons cowardice, conceit / Lays the honor at their feet, // Time that with this strange excuse / Pardoned Kipling and his views, / And will pardon Paul Claudel, / Pardons him for writing well."

And the seas of pity lie
Locked and frozen in each eye.

55 Follow, poet, follow right
To the bottom of the night,
With your unconstraining voice
Still persuade us to rejoice;

With the farming of a verse
Make a vineyard of the curse,
60 Sing of human unsuccess
In a rapture of distress;

In the deserts of the heart
Let the healing fountain start,
In the prison of his days
65 Teach the free man how to praise.

THEODORE ROETHKE (1908–1963)

Elegy for Jane (1953)
My Student, Thrown by a Horse

I remember the neckcurls, limp and damp as tendrils;
And her quick look, a sidelong pickerel smile;
And how, once startled into talk, the light syllables leaped for her,
And she balanced in the delight of her thought,
5 A wren, happy, tail into the wind,
Her song trembling the twigs and small branches.
The shade sang with her;
The leaves, their whispers turned to kissing;
And the mold sang in the bleached valleys under the rose.

10 Oh, when she was sad, she cast herself down into such a pure depth,
Even a father could not find her:
Scraping her cheek against straw;
Stirring the clearest water.

My sparrow, you are not here,
15 Waiting like a fern, making a spiny shadow.
The sides of wet stones cannot console me,
Nor the moss, wound with the last light.

If only I could nudge you from this sleep,
My maimed darling, my skittery pigeon.

20 Over this damp grave I speak the words of my love:
    I, with no rights in this matter,
    Neither father nor lover.

PAULI MURRAY (1910–1985)

For Mack C. Parker (1959)

> *Victim of lynching in Mississippi, 1959*
> In the hour of death,
> In the day of judgment,
>
>> *Good Lord, deliver us!*
>> —*THE BOOK OF COMMON PRAYER*

The cornered and trapped,
The bludgeoned and crushed,
The hideously slain,
Freed from the dreaded waiting,
5   The tortured body's pain,
On death's far shore cast mangled shrouds
To clothe the damned whose fear
Decreed a poisoned harvest,
Garnered a bitter grain.
10 For these who wear the cloak of shame
Must eat the bread of gall,
Each vainly rubbing the 'cursed spot
Which brands him Cain.

JOHN BERRYMAN (1914–1972)

An Elegy for W. C. W.,[1] the lovely man (1968)

Henry[2] in Ireland to Bill underground:
Rest well, who worked so hard, who made a good sound
constantly, for so many years:

---

[1] **W. C. W.:** William Carlos Williams (1873–1963), an American poet, whose groundbreaking innovations in style and technique became a major landmark in twentieth century American literature. This elegy is part of a long sequence of eighteen-line poems called *Dream Songs*.
[2] **Henry:** The main character in Berryman's *Dream Songs* and a hypothetical alter ego of the author.

your high-jinks delighted the continents & our ears:
5 you had so many girls your life was a triumph
and you loved your one wife.

At dawn you rose & wrote—the books poured forth—
you delivered infinite babies, in one great birth—[3]
and your generosity
10 to juniors made you deeply loved, deeply:
if envy was a Henry trademark, he would envy you,
especially the being through.

Too many journeys lie for him ahead,
too many galleys & page-proofs to be read,
15 he would like to lie down
in your sweet silence, to whom was not denied
the mysterious late excellence which is the crown
of our trials & our last bride.

WELDON KEES (1914–1955)

For My Daughter (1943)

Looking into my daughter's eyes I read
Beneath the innocence of morning flesh
Concealed, hintings of death she does not heed.
Coldest of winds have blown this hair, and mesh
5 Of seaweed snarled these miniatures of hands;
The night's slow poison, tolerant and bland.
Has moved her blood. Parched years that I have seen
That may be hers appear: foul, lingering
Death in certain war, the slim legs green.
10 Or, fed on hate, she relishes the sting
Of others' agony; perhaps the cruel
Bride of a syphilitic or a fool.
These speculations sour in the sun.
I have no daughter. I desire none.

---

[3] **you delivered . . . birth:** William Carlos Williams was also an obstetrician.

DYLAN THOMAS (1914–1953)

A Refusal to Mourn the Death, by Fire,
of a Child in London[1] (1946)

Never until the mankind making
Bird beast and flower
Fathering and all humbling darkness
Tells with silence the last light breaking
5   And the still hour
Is come of the sea tumbling in harness

And I must enter again the round
Zion of the water bead
And the synagogue of the ear of corn
10   Shall I let pray the shadow of a sound
Or sow my salt seed
In the least valley of sackcloth to mourn

The majesty and burning of the child's death.
I shall not murder
15   The mankind of her going with a grave truth
Nor blaspheme down the stations of the breath
With any further
Elegy of innocence and youth.

Deep with the first dead lies London's daughter,
20   Robed in the long friends,
The grains beyond age, the dark veins of her mother,
Secret by the unmourning water
Of the riding Thames.
After the first death, there is no other.

PHILIP LARKIN (1922–1985)

An Arundel Tomb (1956)

Side by side, their faces blurred,
The earl and countess lie in stone,
Their proper habits vaguely shown

---

[1] **Death . . . London:** This elegy refers to the firebombing of London by the Germans during World War II.

As jointed armour, stiffened pleat,
5   And that faint hint of the absurd—
The little dogs under their feet.

Such plainness of the pre-baroque
Hardly involves the eye, until
It meets his left-hand gauntlet, still
10   Clasped empty in the other; and
One sees, with a sharp tender shock,
His hand withdrawn, holding her hand.

They would not think to lie so long.
Such faithfulness in effigy
15   Was just a detail friends would see:
A sculptor's sweet commissioned grace
Thrown off in helping to prolong
The Latin names around the base.

They would not guess how early in
20   Their supine stationary voyage
The air would change to soundless damage,
Turn the old tenantry away;
How soon succeeding eyes begin
To look, not read. Rigidly they

25   Persisted, linked, through lengths and breadths
Of time. Snow fell, undated. Light
Each summer thronged the glass. A bright
Litter of birdcalls strewed the same
Bone-riddled ground. And up the paths
30   The endless altered people came,

Washing at their identity.
Now, helpless in the hollow of
An unarmorial age, a trough
Of smoke in slow suspended skeins
35   Above their scrap of history,
Only an attitude remains:

Time has transfigured them into
Untruth. The stone fidelity
They hardly meant has come to be
40   Their final blazon, and to prove
Our almost-instinct almost true:
What will survive of us is love.

ALLEN GINSBERG (1926–1997)

To Aunt Rose (1961)

Aunt Rose—now—might I see you
    with your thin face and buck tooth smile and pain
          of rheumatism—and a long black heavy shoe
             for your bony left leg
5   limping down the long hall in Newark on the running carpet
           past the black grand piano
           in the day room
              where the parties were
    and I sang Spanish loyalist[1] songs
10   in a high squeaky voice
              (hysterical) the committee listening
          while you limped around the room
           collected the money—
Aunt Honey, Uncle Sam, a stranger with a cloth arm
15   in his pocket
            and huge young bald head
              of Abraham Lincoln Brigade[2]

—your long sad face
        your tears of sexual frustration
20   (what smothered sobs and bony hips
                 under the pillows of Osborne Terrace)
—the time I stood on the toilet seat naked
      and you powdered my thighs with calamine
         against the poison ivy—my tender
25   and shamed first black curled hairs
what were you thinking in secret heart then
         knowing me a man already—
and I an ignorant girl of family silence on the thin pedestal
        of my legs in the bathroom—Museum of Newark.

30   Aunt Rose
Hitler is dead, Hitler is in Eternity; Hitler is with
        Tamburlane and Emily Brontë[3]

---

[1] **Spanish loyalist:** Refers to the Spanish Civil War (1936–1939). Ginsberg's family and other people with left-wing views sympathized with the Loyalist cause.
[2] **Abraham Lincoln Brigade:** A unit of American volunteers, who traveled to Spain to fight on the side of the Loyalists.
[3] **Tamburlane and Emily Brontë:** Tamburlane: A military commander of the twelfth century, who was the "scourge" of Central Asia and the Middle East. Also, the hero in Christopher Marlowe's play *Tamburlaine the Great* (1588). Emily Brontë: English poet and novelist (1818–1848).

Though I see you walking still, a ghost on Osborne Terrace
                 down the long dark hall to the front door
35   limping a little with a pinched smile
                   in what must have been a silken
                              flower dress
welcoming my father, the Poet, on his visit to Newark
                 —see you arriving in the living room
40   dancing on your crippled leg
                   and clapping hands his book
                      had been accepted by Liveright[4]

Hitler is dead and Liveright's gone out of business
The Attic of the Past and *Everlasting Minute*[5] are out of print
45   Uncle Harry sold his last silk stocking
             Claire quit interpretive dancing school
                   Buba sits a wrinkled monument in Old
                         Ladies Home blinking at new babies

last time I saw you was the hospital
50   pale skull protruding under ashen skin
                      blue veined unconscious girl
                         in an oxygen tent
             the war in Spain has ended long ago
                      Aunt Rose

FRANK O'HARA (1926–1966)

The Day Lady Died (1964)

It is 12:20 in New York a Friday
three days after Bastille day,[1] yes
it is 1959 and I go get a shoeshine
because I will get off the 4:19 in Easthampton
5   at 7:15 and then go straight to dinner
and I don't know the people who will feed me

I walk up the muggy street beginning to sun
and have a hamburger and a malted and buy

---

[4] **Liveright:** An American publishing house in the 1920s and 1930s, now a subsidiary of W.W. Norton & Co.
[5] ***The Attic . . . Minute:*** These are titles of poetry collections by Louis Ginsberg, Allen Ginsberg's father. Both books were published by Liveright Publishing Corporation.
[1] **Bastille Day:** The French National Holiday, July 14.

an ugly NEW WORLD WRITING to see what the poets
10   in Ghana are doing these days
                I go on to the bank
and Miss Stillwagon (first name Linda I once heard)
doesn't even look up my balance for once in her life
and in the GOLDEN GRIFFIN I get a little Verlaine
15   for Patsy with drawings by Bonnard although I do
think of Hesiod, trans. Richmond Lattimore or
Brendan Behan's new play or *Le Balcon* or *Les Nègres*
of Genet,[2] but I don't, I stick with Verlaine
after practically going to sleep with quandariness

20   and for Mike I just stroll into the PARK LANE
Liquor Store and ask for a bottle of Strega and
then I go back where I came from to 6th Avenue
and the tobacconist in the Ziegfeld Theatre and
casually ask for a carton of Gauloises and a carton
25   of Picayunes, and a NEW YORK POST with her[3] face on it

and I am sweating a lot by now and thinking of
leaning on the john door in the 5 SPOT
while she whispered a song along the keyboard
to Mal Waldron[4] and everyone and I stopped breathing

ANNE SEXTON   (1928–1974)

Elizabeth Gone   (1960)

1.

You lay in the nest of your real death,
Beyond the print of my nervous fingers
Where they touched your moving head;
Your old skin puckering, your lungs' breath
5   Grown baby short as you looked up last
At my face swinging over the human bed,
And somewhere you cried, *let me go let me go.*

---

[2] **Verlaine . . . Genet:** Paul Verlaine (1844–1896), French poet; Pierre Bonnard (1867–1947), French painter. Hesiod (eighth century B.C.), Greek poet and author of *Works and Days*. Brendan Behan (1923–1964), Irish playwright. Jean Genet (1910–1986), French playwright, notoriously famous for his plays *The Balcony* (1956) and *The Blacks* (1958).
[3] **her:** Billie Holiday (1915–1959), jazz singer, also known as "Lady Day."
[4] **Mal Waldron:** (1925–2002), pianist and Billie Holiday's accompanist.

You lay in the crate of your last death,
But were not you, not finally you.
10   They have stuffed her cheeks, I said;
This clay hand, this mask of Elizabeth
Are not true. From within the satin
And the suede of this inhuman bed,
Something cried, *let me go let me go.*

2.

15   They gave me your ash and bony shells,
Rattling like gourds in the cardboard urn,
Rattling like stones that their oven had blest.
I waited you in the cathedral of spells
And I waited you in the country of the living,
20   Still with the urn crooned to my breast,
When something cried, *let me go let me go.*

So I threw out your last bony shells
And heard me scream for the look of you,
Your apple face, the simple crèche [1]
25   Of your arms, the August smells
Of your skin. Then I sorted your clothes
And the loves you had left, Elizabeth,
Elizabeth, until you were gone.

IAIN CRICHTON SMITH (1928–1998)

At the Scott[1] Exhibition, Edinburgh Festival (1972)

(1)

He will outlast us, churning out his books,
advocate and historian, his prose
earning him Abbotsford[2] with its borrowed gates,
its cheap mementos from the land he made.
5   Walking the room together in this merciless
galaxy of manuscripts and notes
I am exhausted by such energy.
I hold your hand for guidance. Over your brow

---

[1] **crèche:** A representation of the Nativity scene with figurines. Here, possibly, the likening of the hands to a cradle.
[1] **Scott:** Sir Walter Scott (1771–1832), a Scottish poet and novelist, famous for his historical romances.
[2] **Abbotsford:** A castle, which Scott built as his residence.

the green light falls from tall and narrow windows.
10   His style is ignorant of this tenderness,
the vulnerable angle of your body
below the Raeburn[3] with its steady gaze.

(II)

It was all in his life, not in his books
"Oh I am dying, take me home to Scotland
15   *where I can breathe though that breath were my last."*[4]
He limped through an Edinburgh being made anew.
He worked his way through debts, past a dead wife.
My dear, we love each other in our weakness
as he with white grave face diminishing through
20   stroke after stroke down to the unpaid room.
We know what we are but know not what we will be.
I tremble in this factory of books.
What love he must have lost to write so much.

THOM GUNN (1929–2004)

The Missing (1987; 1992)

Now as I watch the progress of the plague,[1]
The friends surrounding me fall sick, grow thin,
And drop away. Bared, is my shape less vague
—Sharply exposed and with a sculpted skin?

5   I do not like the statue's chill contour,
Not nowadays. The warmth investing me
Let outward through mind, limb, feeling, and more
In an involved increasing family.

Contact of friend led to another friend,
10   Supple entwinement through the living mass
Which for all that I knew might have no end,
Image of an unlimited embrace.

I did not just feel ease, though comfortable:
Aggressive as in some ideal of sport,

---

[3] **Raeburn:** Sir Henry Raeburn (1756–1923) was a Scottish artist, who painted a celebrated portrait of Sir Walter Scott.
[4] **"Oh I am dying . . . last":** A quotation from Scott.
[1] **plague:** The AIDS epidemic.

15   With ceaseless movement thrilling through the whole,
     Their push kept me as firm as their support.

     But death—Their deaths have left me less defined:
     It was their pulsing presence made me clear.
     I borrowed from it, I was unconfined,
20   Who tonight balance unsupported here,

     Eyes glaring from raw marble, in a pose
     Languorously part-buried in the block,
     Shins perfect and no calves, as if I froze
     Between potential and a finished work.

25   —Abandoned incomplete, shape of a shape,
     In which exact detail shows the more strange,
     Trapped in unwholeness, I find no escape
     Back to the play of constant give and change.

THOM GUNN (1929–2004)

My Sad Captains (1961)

     One by one they appear in
     the darkness: a few friends, and
     a few with historical
     names. How late they start to shine!
5   but before they fade they stand
     perfectly embodied, all

     the past lapping them like a
     cloak of chaos. They were men
     who, I thought, lived only to
10   renew the wasteful force they
     spent with each hot convulsion.
     They remind me, distant now.

     True, they are not at rest yet,
     but now that they are indeed
15   apart, winnowed from failures,
     they withdraw to an orbit
     and turn with disinterested
     hard energy, like the stars.

X. J. KENNEDY (1929–)

Little Elegy (1960)
For a Child Who Skipped Rope

Here lies resting, out of breath,
Out of turns, Elizabeth
Whose quicksilver toes not quite
Cleared the whirring edge of night.

5   Earth whose circles round us skim
Till they catch the lightest limb,
Shelter now Elizabeth
And for her sake trip up Death.

LINDA PASTAN (1932–)

The Five Stages of Grief (1982)

The night I lost you
someone pointed me towards
the Five Stages of Grief.
Go that way, they said,
5   it's easy, like learning to climb
stairs after the amputation.
And so I climbed.
Denial was first.
I sat down at breakfast
10   carefully setting the table
for two. I passed you the toast—
you sat there. I passed
you the paper—you hid
behind it.
15   *Anger* seemed more familiar.
I burned the toast, snatched
the paper and read the headlines myself.
But they mentioned your departure,
and so I moved on to

20 *Bargaining.* What could I exchange
for you? The silence
after storms? My typing fingers?
Before I could decide, *Depression*
came puffing up, a poor relation
25 its suitcase tied together
with string. In the suitcase
were bandages for the eyes
and bottles of sleep. I slid
all the way down the stairs
30 feeling nothing.
And all the time Hope
flashed on and off
in defective neon.
Hope was a signpost pointing
35 straight in the air.
Hope was my uncle's middle name,
he died of it.
After a year I am still climbing,
though my feet slip
40 on your stone face.
The treeline
has long since disappeared;
green is a color
I have forgotten.
45 But now I see what I am climbing
towards: *Acceptance*
written in capital letters,
a special headline:
Acceptance,
50 its name is in lights.
I struggle on,
waving and shouting.
Below, my whole life spreads its surf,
all the landscapes I've ever known
55 or dreamed of. Below
a fish jumps: the pulse
in your neck.
Acceptance. I finally
reach it.
60 But something is wrong.
Grief is a circular staircase.
I have lost you.

SYLVIA PLATH (1932–1963)

Daddy (1962)

You do not do, you do not do
Any more, black shoe
In which I have lived like a foot
For thirty years, poor and white,
5   Barely daring to breathe or Achoo.

Daddy, I have had to kill you.
You died before I had time——
Marble-heavy, a bag full of God,
Ghastly statue with one gray toe [1]
10   Big as a Frisco seal

And a head in the freakish Atlantic [2]
Where it pours bean green over blue
In the waters off beautiful Nauset. [3]
I used to pray to recover you.
15   Ach, du. [4]

In the German tongue, in the Polish town
Scraped flat by the roller
Of wars, wars, wars.
But the name of the town is common.
20   My Polack friend

Says there are a dozen or two.
So I never could tell where you
Put your foot, your root,
I never could talk to you.
25   The tongue stuck in my jaw.

It stuck in a barb wire snare.
Ich, ich, ich, ich, [5]
I could hardly speak.
I thought every German was you.
30   And the language obscene

---

[1] **gray toe:** Plath's father, Otto Plath, died of gangrene which first developed in his toe.
[2] **Frisco seal . . . Atlantic:** "Frisco seal" possibly refers to an entomological study "Muscid Larvae of the San Francisco Bay Region Which Sucks Blood of Nesting Birds" published by Otto Plath. Thus the "ghastly statue" (the colossus) of the father stretches across America, from the West to the East coast.
[3] **Nauset:** A beach on Cape Cod, in eastern Massachusetts.
[4] **Du:** You (German).
[5] **Ich:** I (German).

An engine, an engine
Chuffing me off like a Jew.
A Jew to Dachau, Auschwitz, Belsen.[6]
I began to talk like a Jew.
35   I think I may well be a Jew.

The snows of the Tyrol,[7] the clear beer of Vienna
Are not very pure or true.
With my gipsy ancestress and my weird luck
And my Taroc pack[8] and my Taroc pack
40   I may be a bit of a Jew.

I have always been scared of *you,*
With your Luftwaffe,[9] your gobbledygoo.[10]
And your neat mustache
And your Aryan eye, bright blue.
45   Panzer-man, panzer-man,[11] O You——

Not God but a swastika
So black no sky could squeak through.
Every woman adores a Fascist,
The boot in the face, the brute
50   Brute heart of a brute like you.

You stand at the blackboard, daddy,
In the picture I have of you,
A cleft in your chin instead of your foot
But no less a devil for that, no not
55   Any less the black man who

Bit my pretty red heart in two.
I was ten when they buried you.
At twenty I tried to die
And get back, back, back to you.
60   I thought even the bones would do.

But they pulled me out of the sack,
And they stuck me together with glue.[12]

---

[6] **Dachau, Auschwitz, Belsen:** Nazi concentration camps, where millions of Jews were systematically exterminated during World War II.
[7] **Tyrol:** An area in the Austrian Alps.
[8] **Taroc pack:** A version of Tarot Pack, a deck of cards used to tell fortunes.
[9] **Luftwaffe:** A reference to the German air force during World War II.
[10] **gobbledygoo:** Plath's derivation from the word gobbledygook, i.e., incomprehensible jargon of scientists.
[11] **Panzer:** A German armored vehicle, such as tank, during World War II.
[12] **At twenty . . . glue:** While an undergraduate at Smith College, Plath made her first attempt to commit suicide.

And then I knew what to do.
I made a model of you,
65   A man in black with a Meinkampf[13] look

And a love of the rack and the screw.
And I said I do, I do.
So daddy, I'm finally through.
The black telephone's off at the root,
70   The voices just can't worm through.

If I've killed one man, I've killed two——
The vampire who said he was you
And drank my blood for a year,
Seven years, if you want to know.
75   Daddy, you can lie back now.

There's a stake in your fat black heart
And the villagers never liked you.
They are dancing and stamping on you.
They always *knew* it was you.
80   Daddy, daddy, you bastard, I'm through.

AMIRI BARAKA   (1934–   )

A Poem for Black Hearts   (1969)

For Malcolm's[1] eyes, when they broke
the face of some dumb white man, For
Malcolm's hands raised to bless us
all black and strong in his image
5   of ourselves, For Malcolm's words
fire darts, the victor's tireless
thrusts, words hung above the world
change as it may, he said it, and
for this he was killed, for saying,
10   and feeling, and being///change, all
collected hot in his heart, For Malcolm's
heart, raising us above our filthy cities,
for his stride, and his beat, and his address

---

[13] **Meinkampf:** A reference to Adolf Hitler's book *Mein Kampf* (My Struggle).
[1] **Malcolm's:** Malcolm X, a black militant leader who advocated the concepts of black pride and black nationalism. He was shot to death in 1965.

to the grey monsters of the world, For Malcolm's
15   pleas for your dignity, black men, for your life,
black man, for the filling of your minds
with righteousness, For all of him dead and
gone and vanished from us, and all of him which
clings to our speech black god of our time.
20   For all of him, and all of yourself, look up,
black man, quit stuttering and shuffling, look up,
black man, quit whining and stooping, for all of him,
For Great Malcolm a prince of the earth, let nothing in us rest
until we avenge ourselves for his death, stupid animals
25   that killed him, let us never breathe a pure breath if
we fail, and white men call us faggots till the end of
the earth.

MARK STRAND (1934–   )

In Memory of Joseph Brodsky [1]   (2001)

It could be said, even here, that what remains of the self
Unwinds into a vanishing light, and thins like dust, and heads
To a place where knowing and nothing pass into each other, and
          through;
5   That it moves, unwinding still, beyond the vault of brightness ended,
And continues to a place which may never be found, where the
          unsayable,
Finally, once more is uttered, but lightly, quickly, like random rain
That passes in sleep, that one imagines passes in sleep.
10   What remains of the self unwinds and unwinds, for none
Of the boundaries holds—neither the shapeless one between us,
Nor the one that falls between your body and your voice. Joseph,
Dear Joseph, those sudden reminders of your having been—the
          places
15   And times whose greatest life was the one you gave them—now appear
Like ghosts in your wake. What remains of the self unwinds
Beyond us, for whom time is only a measure of meanwhile
And the future no more than et cetera et cetera . . . but fast and
20   forever.

---

[1] **Joseph Brodsky:** A Russian-American poet (1940–1996). He was forcefully exiled from the USSR in
1972 and settled in the United States.

LUCILLE CLIFTON (1936–   )

malcolm[1] (1972)

nobody mentioned war
but doors were closed
black women shaved their heads
black men rustled in the alleys like leaves
5   prophets were ambushed as they spoke
and from their holes black eagles flew
screaming through the streets

SANDRA M. GILBERT (1938–   )

Elegy

The pages of history open. The dead enter.
It is winter in the spine of the book
where they land, inexplicable texts,
and a small rain falling, a mist of promises,
5   disjointed sentences, woes, failures.

The dead are puzzled:
was it for this they left
the land of grammar, the syntax of their skin?
We turn the pages. We read.
10   Sometimes, in moments of vertigo,

we notice that they're speaking.
Tiny whinings and murmurings arise,
as of insects urging their rights, their dissatisfactions,
invisible insects dwelling uncomfortably
15   in the margins, in the white spaces around words.

---

[1] **malcolm:** I.e., Malcolm X, a black militant leader who advocated the concepts of black pride and black nationalism. He was shot to death in 1965.

MICHAEL S. HARPER (1938–   )

Double Elegy (1985)

Whatever city or country road
you two are on
there are nettles,
and the dark invisible
5   elements cling to your skin
though you do not cry
and you do not scratch
your arms at forty-five degree angles
as the landing point of a swan
10   in the Ohio, the Detroit River;

at the Paradise Theatre
you named the cellist
with the fanatical fingers
of the plumber, the exorcist,
15   and though the gimmicky at wrist
and kneecaps could lift the seance
table, your voice was real
in the gait and laughter of Uncle
Henry, who could dance on either
20   leg, wooden or real, to the sound
of the troop train, megaphone,
catching the fine pitch of a singer
on the athletic fields of Virginia.

At the Radisson Hotel,
25   we once took a fine angel
of the law to the convention center,
and put her down as an egret
in the subzero platform of a friend—
this is Minneapolis, the movies
30   are all of strangers, holding themselves
in the delicacy of treading water,
while they wait for the trumpet
of the 20th Century Limited [1]
over the bluff or cranny.
35   You two men like to confront.
the craters of history and spillage,
our natural infections of you

---

[1] **20th Century Limited:** America's famous luxurious train from New York to Chicago.

innoculating blankets and fur,
ethos of cadaver and sunflower.

40 I hold the dogwood blossom,
eat the pear, and watch the nettle
swim up in the pools
of the completed song
of Leadbelly and Little Crow [2]
45 crooning the buffalo and horse
to the changes and the bridge
of a twelve-string guitar,
the melody of "Irene"; [3]
this is really goodbye—
50 I can see the precious stones
of embolism [4] and consumption
on the platinum wires of the mouth:
in the flowing rivers, in the public baths
of Ohio and Michigan.

STEPHEN DUNN (1939–   )

That Saturday Without a Car (1981)

for Ellen Dunn (1910–1969)

Five miles to my mother's house,
a distance I'd never run.
"I *think* she's dead"
my brother said, and hung up

5 as if with death
language should be mercifully approximate,
should keep the fact
that would forever be fact

at bay. I understood,
10 and as I ran wondered what words
I might say, and to whom.
I saw myself opening the door—

---

[2] **Leadbelly and Little Crow:** Leadbelly (1888–1949), an itinerant blues musician. Little Crow (1810–1863), a Sioux Indian chief.
[3] **Irene:** A famous song by Leadbelly, which was covered by various artists in subsequent years.
[4] **embolism:** An obstruction of a blood vessel by an embolus (a small particle).

my brother, both of us, embarrassed
by the sudden intimacy we'd feel.
15   We had expected it
but we'd expected it every year

for ten: her heart was the best
and worst of her—every kindness
fought its way through damage,
20   her breasts disappeared

as if the heart itself, for comfort,
had sucked them in.
And I was running better
than I ever had. How different it was

25   from driving, the way I'd gone
to other deaths—
my body fighting it all off, my heart,
this adequate heart, getting me there.

SEAMUS HEANEY (1939–   )

Mid-Term Break   (1966)

I sat all morning in the college sick bay
Counting bells knelling classes to a close.
At two o'clock our neighbours drove me home.

In the porch I met my father crying—
5   He had always taken funerals in his stride—
And Big Jim Evans saying it was a hard blow.

The baby cooed and laughed and rocked the pram
When I came in, and I was embarrassed
By old men standing up to shake my hand

10   And tell me they were 'sorry for my trouble'.
Whispers informed strangers I was the eldest,
Away at school, as my mother held my hand

In hers and coughed out angry tearless sighs.
At ten o'clock the ambulance arrived
15   With the corpse, stanched and bandaged by the nurses.

Next morning I went up into the room. Snowdrops
And candles soothed the bedside; I saw him
For the first time in six weeks. Paler now,

Wearing a poppy bruise on his left temple,
20   He lay in the four-foot box as in his cot.
No gaudy scars, the bumper knocked him clear.

A four-foot box, a foot for every year.

MARILYN HACKER (1942–   )

Elegy for a Soldier (2003)
June Jordan, 1936–2002[1]

I.

The city where I knew you was swift.
A lover cabbed to Brooklyn
(broke, but so what) after the night shift
in a Second Avenue
5   diner. The lover was a Quaker,
a poet, an anti-war
activist. Was blonde, was twenty-four.
Wet snow fell on the access
road to the Manhattan Bridge. I was
10   neither lover, slept uptown.
But the arteries, streetlights, headlines,
phonelines, feminine plural
links ran silver through the night city
as dawn and the yellow cab
15   passed on the frost-blurred bridge, headed for
that day's last or first coffee.

The city where I knew you was rich
in bookshops, potlucks, ad hoc
debates, demos, parades and picnics.
20   There were walks I liked to take.
I was on good terms with two rivers.
You turned, burned, flame-wheel of words
lighting the page, good neighbor on your

---

[1] **June Jordan:** An American poet (1936–2002) famous for her outspoken position on the rights of women.

homely street in Park Slope,[2] whose
25 Russian zaydes,[3] Jamaican grocers,
dyke vegetarians, young
gifted everyone, claimed some changes
—at least a new food co-op.
In the laundromat, ordinary
30 women talked revolution.
We knew we wouldn't live forever
but it seemed as if we could.

The city where I knew you was yours
and mine by birthright: Harlem,
35 the Bronx. Separately we left it
and came separately back.
There's no afterlife for dialogue,
divergences we never
teased apart to weave back together.
40 Death slams down in the midst of
all your unfinished conversations.
Whom do I address when I
address you, larger than life as you
always were, not alive now?
45 Words are not you, poems are not you,
ashes on the Pacific
tide, you least of all. I talk to myself to keep the line open.

The city where I knew you is gone.
50 Pink icing roses spelled out
PASSION[4] on a book-shaped chocolate cake.
The bookshop's a sushi bar
now, and PASSION is long out of print.
Would you know the changed street that
55 cab swerved down toward you through cold white mist?
We have a Republican
mayor. Threats keep citizens in line:
anthrax; suicide attacks.[5]
A scar festers where towers once were;
60 dissent festers unexpressed.
You are dead of a woman's disease.[6]
Who gets to choose what battle

---

[2] **Park Slope:** A part of Brooklyn in New York City.
[3] **zaydes:** Grandfathers (from Hebrew).
[4] **PASSION:** A volume of poetry by June Jordan (1980).
[5] **anthrax; suicide attacks:** i.e., the September 11th attacks on the United States.
[6] **dead of a woman's disease:** June Jordan died of breast cancer.

takes her down? Down to the ocean, friends
mourn you, with no time to mourn.

II.

65   You, who stood alone in the tall bay window
of a Brooklyn brownstone, conjuring morning
with free-flying words, knew the power, terror
in words, in flying;

knew the high of solitude while the early
70   light prowled Seventh Avenue, lupine, hungry
like you, your spoils raisins and almonds, ballpoint
pen, yellow foolscap.

You, who stood alone in your courage, never
hesitant to underline the connections
75   (between rape, exclusion and occupation . . .)
and separations

were alone and were not alone when morning
blotted the last spark of you out, around you
voices you no longer had voice to answer,
80   eyes you were blind to.

All your loves were singular: you scorned labels.
Claimed *black; woman*, and for the rest eluded
limits, quicksilver (Caribbean), staked out
self-definition.

85   Now your death, as if it were "yours": your house, your
dog, your friends, your son, your serial lovers.
Death's not "yours," what's yours are a thousand poems
alive on paper,

in the present tense of a thousand students'
90   active gaze at printed pages and blank ones
which you gave permission to blacken into
outrage and passion.

You, at once an optimist, a Cassandra,
Lilith in the wilderness of her lyric,[7]

---

[7] **Cassandra, / Lilith . . . lyric:** Cassandra was the clairvoyant daughter of Priam, the king of Troy. However, her prophesies were never believed. Lilith: according to Hebrew folklore, Lilith was the first woman and wife of Adam, before Eve was created.

95 were a black American, born in Harlem,
    citizen soldier

    If you had to die—and I don't admit it—
    who dared "What if, each time they kill a black man/
    we kill a cop?" couldn't you take down with you
100 a few prime villains

    in the capitol, who are also mortal?
    June, you should be living, the states are bleeding.
    Leaden words like "Homeland" translate abandoned
    dissident discourse.

105 Twenty years ago, you denounced the war crimes
    still in progress now, as Jenin, Ramallah[8]
    dominate, then disappear from the headlines.
    Palestine: your war.

    "To each nation, its Jews," wrote Primo Levi.[9]
110 "Palestinians are Jews to Israelis."
    Afterwards, he died in despair, or so we
    infer, despairing.

    To each nation its Jews, its blacks, its Arabs,
    Palestinians, immigrants, its women.
115 From each nation, its poets: Mahmoud Darwish,
    Kavanagh, Sháhid

    (who, beloved witness for silenced Kashmir,
    cautioned, shift the accent, and he was "martyr"),
    Audre Lorde, Neruda, Amichai, Senghor,[10]
120 and you, June Jordan.

---

[8] **Jenin, Ramallah:** Palestinian cities in the Israeli-occupied West Bank.
[9] **Primo Levi:** A Jewish-Italian writer and chemist (1919–1987), who was sent to Auschwitz by the Nazis during World War II and later recounted his harrowing experiences in the autobiographical story *Se Questo È Un Umo* (1947, *If This Is a Man*).
[10] **Mahmoud Darwish . . . Senghor:** Mahmoud Darwish, a Palestinian poet and journalist. Patrick Kavanagh (1904–1967), an Irish poet. Agha Sháhid Ali (1949–2001), a Kashmiri-American poet. Audre Lorde (1934–1992), an African-American poet. Pablo Neruda (1904–1973), a Chilean poet. Yehuda Amichai (1924–2000), an Israeli poet. Léopold Sédar Senghor (1906–2001), a poet and statesman, elected as the first president of Senegal. All of poets listed above explored, in one way or another, the connection between art and politics.

WILLIAM MATTHEWS (1942–1997)

An Elegy for Bob Marley[1] (1984)

In an elegy for a musician,
one talks a lot about music,
which is a way to think about time
instead of death or Marley,

5   and isn't poetry itself about time?
But death is about death and not time.
Surely the real fuel for elegy
is anger to be mortal.

No wonder Marley sang so often
10   of an ever-arriving future, that verb tense
invented by religion and political rage.
Soon come. Readiness is all,

and not enough. From the urinous
dust and sodden torpor
15   of Trenchtown,[2] from the fruitpeels
and imprecations, from cunning,

from truculence, from the luck
to be alive, however, cruelly,
Marley made a brave music—
20   a rebel music, he called it,

though music calls us together,
however briefly—and a fortune.
One is supposed to praise the dead
in elegies for leaving us their songs,

25   though they had not choice; nor could
the dead bury the dead if we could pay
them to. This is something else we can't
control, another loss, which is, as someone

said in hope of consolation,
30   only temporary, though the same phrase

---

[1] **Bob Marley:** A famous reggae singer and composer from Jamaica.
[2] **Trenchtown:** A housing scheme in Kingston (Jamaica) built after a 1951 hurricane destroyed the area's squatter camps. During Marley's time, it was considered one of the poorest and most violent quarters of the city.

could be used of our lives and bodies
and all that we hope survives them.

JAMES TATE (1943–   )

The Lost Pilot (1978)

for my father, 1922–1944

Your face did not rot
like the others—the co-pilot,
for example, I saw him

yesterday. His face is corn-
5   mush: his wife and daughter,
the poor ignorant people, stare

as if he will compose soon.
He was more wronged than Job.[1]
But your face did not rot

10   like the others—it grew dark,
and hard like ebony;
the features progressed in their

distinction. If I could cajole
you to come back for an evening,
15   down from your compulsive

orbiting, I would touch you,
read your face as Dallas,
your hoodlum gunner, now,

with the blistered eyes, reads
20   his braille editions. I would
touch your face as a disinterested

scholar touches an original page.
However frightening, I would
discover you, and I would not

---

[1] **Job:** The Biblical prophet, whose faith and righteousness God decided to test by submitting him to numerous afflictions.

25 turn you in; I would not make
you face your wife, or Dallas,
or the co-pilot, Jim. You

could return to your crazy
orbiting, and I would not try
30 to fully understand what

it means to you. All I know
is this: when I see you,
as I have seen you at least

once every year of my life,
35 spin across the wilds of the sky
like a tiny, African god,

I feel dead. I feel as if I were
the residue of a stranger's life,
that I should pursue you.

40 My head cocked toward the sky,
I cannot get off the ground,
and, you, passing over again,

fast, perfect, and unwilling
to tell me that you are doing
45 well, or that it was mistake

that placed you in that world,
and me in this; or that misfortune
placed these worlds in us.

CAROL MUSKE-DUKES (1945–   )

The Call (2003)

When I heard the voice on the telephone
telling me there'd been an accident,
I repeated my question twice
without receiving an answer.

5 I was given another number
and at that number I asked again

without response. At last someone took
pity on me. That nurse in a distant blazing room

beginning to take shape before my eyes
10   paused, then put my question back to me.
Did I want to be told what was happening to you?
I looked at my daughter poised next to me, waiting,

her hand over her mouth. She inclined her head.
I do, I said, like a bride. And then the professional
15   voice, rising only slightly, called out to me, step by step,
precisely how your body failed—as she watched it fail

before her. I held the phone to my ear, repeating each
of these answers to my question, so that images of you,
disappearing, appeared in the air. Our kitchen, the dishes
20   in the sink, the stove, that shocked gaze meeting mine—

then yours superimposed over hers—your eyes wide
in that other room where you lay, rapidly dying
beyond the open receiver. The shouting technicians
hovering over your body as that other sound, unearthly,

25   spoke quietly beyond the monotone in my ear: blood
pressure, pulse rate, respiration. The soul, its heraldic
voice, murmuring other answers—then images, startled
one by one, from faith, from terror, from all that we
                              ever sought to know about you.

NEIL POWELL (1948–   )

Coda (1982)
Thelonious Monk, d. 17 February 1982[1]

Goat-bearded, crazy-hatted old wrong-noter:
Your half-tones filled the gaps of adolescence,
When all brave young aficionados claimed
To know what you were up to: shameless bluff, -
5   Until one day we woke to find it true.

---

[1] **Thelonious Monk:** A virtuoso jazz piano player and composer.

Thus now hands, aimless on a keyboard, fall
Into 'Round Midnight'[2]—haunted, audible
Through the sizzling of a Riverside LP
Those twenty years ago, the sheet music
10   Ordered from a baffled small-town shop:

Both still possessed, with later images
Of one March night in London, '65,
Prancing before a South Bank audience.
Within the pauses and abrasive chords,
15   *Misterioso*[3]—hermit or buffoon?

No need to choose. I couldn't understand
Then how defences crowd about the self;
How, hedged around with paradox, we lose
The centre we defend; so couldn't know
20   Why you fragmented sentimental songs,

Invented notes for dislocated moods,
Evaded easy treasonable concord.
I'd hope but daren't believe at last you rest,
Beyond our life's perverse cacophony,
25   If not in peace, at least in harmony.

DANA GIOIA (1950–   )

Guide to the Other Gallery   (1991)

This is the hall of broken limbs
Where splintered marble athletes lie
Beside the arms of cherubim.
Nothing is ever thrown away.

5   These butterflies are set in rows.
So small and gray inside their case
They look alike now. I suppose
Death makes most creatures commonplace.

These portraits here of the unknown
10   Are hung three high, frame piled on frame.
Each potent soul who craved renown,
Immortalized without a name.

---

[2] **"Round Midnight":** A famous composition by Monk.
[3] **Misterioso:** A 1963 live performance by Monk in New York City, later distributed as a record.

Here are the shelves of unread books,
Millions of pages turning brown.
15   Visitors wander through the stacks,
But no one ever takes one down.

I wish I were a better guide.
There's so much more that you should see.
Rows of bottles with nothing inside.
20   Displays of locks which have no key.

You'd like to go? I wish you could.
This room has such a peaceful view.
Look at that case of antique wood
Without a label. It's for you.

PAUL MULDOON (1951–   )

Milkweed and Monarch (1994)

As he knelt by the grave of his mother and father
the taste of dill, or tarragon—
he could barely tell one from the other—

filled his mouth. It seemed as if he might smother.
5   Why should he be stricken
with grief, not for his mother and father,

but a woman slinking from the fur of a sea-otter
in Portland, Maine, or, yes, Portland, Oregon—
he could barely tell one from the other—

10   and why should he now savour
the tang of her, her little pickled gherkin,
as he knelt by the grave of his mother and father?

He looked about. He remembered her palaver
on how both earth and sky would darken—
15   "You could barely tell one from the other"—

while the Monarch butterflies passed over
in their milkweed-hunger: "A wing-beat, some reckon,
may trigger off the mother and father

of all storms, striking your Irish Cliffs of Moher
20   with the force of a hurricane."
Then: "Milkweed and Monarch 'invented' each other."

He looked about. Cow's-parsley in a samovar.[1]
He'd mistaken his mother's name, "Regan", for "Anger":
as he knelt by the grave of his mother and father
25   he could barely tell one from the other.

RITA DOVE (1952–   )

David Walker (1785–1830)[1] (1980)

Free to travel, he still couldn't be shown how lucky
he was: *They strip and beat and drag us about*
like rattlesnakes. Home on Brattle Street, he took in the sign
on the door of the slop shop. All day at the counter—
5   white caps, ale-stained pea coats. Compass: needles,
eloquent as tuning forks, shivered, pointing north.
Evenings, the ceiling fan sputtered like a second pulse.
Oh Heaven! I am full!! I can hardly move my pen!!!

On the faith of an eye-wink, pamphlets were stuffed
10   into trouser pockets. Pamphlets transported
in the coat linings of itinerant seamen, jackets
ringwormed with salt traded drunkenly to pursers
in the Carolinas, pamphlets ripped out, read aloud:
Men of colour, who are also of sense.
15   Outrage. Incredulity. Uproar in state legislatures.

We are the most wretched, degraded and abject set
of beings that ever lived since the world began.
The jewelled canaries in the lecture halls tittered,
pressed his dark hand between their gloves.
20   Every half-step was no step at all.
Every morning, the man on the corner strung a fresh
bunch of boots from his shoulders. "I'm happy!" he said.
"I never want to live any better or happier than
when I can get a-plenty of boots and shoes to clean!"

---

[1] **samovar:** A metal urn-like container used for boiling water for tea, originally used in Russia.
[1] **David Walker:** a militant abolitionist, who lived in Boston. In his best known work, *Appeal in Four Articles* (1829), he urged blacks to revolt against their enslavers. He was purportedly poisoned in 1830 by his enemies.

25   A second edition. A third.
    The abolitionist press is *perfectly appalled.*
    Humanity, kindness and the fear of the Lord
    does not consist in protecting devils. A month—
    his person (is that all?) found face-down
30   in the doorway at Brattle Street,
    his frame slighter than friends remembered.

ALBERTO RÍOS (1952–   )

Mi Abuelo[1] (1982)

    Where my grandfather is is in the ground
    where you can hear the future
    like an Indian with his ear at the tracks.
    A pipe leads down to him so that sometimes
5   he whispers what will happen to a man
    in town or how he will meet the best
    dressed woman tomorrow and how the best
    man at her wedding will chew the ground
    next to her. Mi abuelo is the man
10   who speaks through all the mouths in my house.
    An echo of me hitting the pipe sometimes
    to stop him from saying *my hair is a*
    sieve is the only other sound. It is a phrase
    that among all others is the best,
15   he says, and *my hair is a sieve* is sometimes
    repeated for hours out of the ground
    when I let him, which is not often.
    An abuelo should be much more than a man
    like you! He stops then, and speaks: *I am a man*
20   *who has served ants with the attitude*
    of a waiter, who has made each smile as only
    an ant who is fat can, and they liked me best,
    but there is nothing left. Yet I know he ground
    green coffee beans as a child, and sometimes
25   he will talk about his wife, and sometimes
    about when he was deaf and a man
    cured him by mail and he heard groundhogs
    talking, or about how he walked with a cane
    he chewed on when he got hungry.

[1] **Mi Abuelo:** My grandfather (Spanish).

30   At best, mi abuelo is a liar.
     I see an old picture of him at nani's with an
     off-white yellow center mustache and sometimes
     that's all I know for sure. He talks best
     about these hills, *slowest waves*, and where this man
35   is going, and I'm convinced his hair is a sieve,
     that his fever is cooled now underground.
     Mi abuelo is an ordinary man.
     I look down the pipe, sometimes, and see a
     ripple-topped stream in its best suit, in the ground.

MARK DOTY (1953–   )

Tiara (1990)

Peter died in a paper tiara
cut from a book of princess paper dolls;
he loved royalty, sashes

and jewels. *I don't know,*
5   he said, when he woke in the hospice,
I was watching the Bette Davis[1] *film festival*

on Channel 57 and then—
At the wake, the tension broke
when someone guessed

10   the casket closed because
he was *in there in a big wig
and heels*, and someone said,

*You know he's always late,
he probably isn't here yet—*
15   *he's still fixing his makeup.*

And someone said he asked for it.
Asked for it—
when all he did was go down

---

[1] **Bette Davis:** An American movie actress (1908–1989).

into the salt tide
20   of wanting as much as he wanted,
giving himself over so drunk

or stoned it almost didn't matter who,
though they were beautiful,
stampeding into him in the simple,

25   ravishing music of their hurry.
I think heaven is perfect stasis
poised over the realms of desire,

where dreaming and waking men lie
on the grass while wet horses
30   roam among them, huge fragments

of the music we die into
in the body's paradise.
Sometimes we wake not knowing

how we came to lie here,
35   or who has crowned us with these temporary,
precious stones. And given

the world's perfectly turned shoulders,
the deep hollows blued by longing,
given the irreplaceable silk

40   of horses rippling in orchards,
fruit thundering and chiming down,
given the ordinary marvels of form

and gravity, what could he do,
what could any of us ever do
45   but ask for it.

CHAPTER 3

ONCE UPON A MIDNIGHT DREARY
—Edgar Allan Poe

An Anthology of Narrative Poetry

Narrative poems tell a story. This is the simple defini-tion, and it remains useful, although the term is broad and could be used to talk about many different kinds of poems that, in fact, belong to a more specific tradition. For example, ballads and epics are narrative poems, but we have isolated these forms in this anthology so that their generic aspects will stand out.

It could be argued that most poems have a narrative aspect. One of the first things you ask when you read a poem is: Who is speaking here? What is the situation of this person? Even a brief lyric often catch-es a speaker in a situation of some kind: in passionate love, in despair over a love gone sour, in excitement about some natural scene, in sorrow over a death or loss. In each of these situations, a narrative ele-ment contributes to the effect of the poem on the reader.

In each of the poems in Chapter 3, the poet attempts to create a larger narrative pattern, employing all of the elements of poetry—includ-ing rhythm, meter, sound effects, imagery, analogy, and symbolism—to enhance the story. Each of these poems has a sense of gathering action, of movement rising toward a point of climax, a feeling of release after the action has been fulfilled. There is also present in these poems that curious thing called narrative momentum. That is, the reader is drawn through the story, lured by techniques that are ancient in origin. In most cases, a narrative poem will have an element of suspense, so that the reader wonders: What happens next? How will this turn out?

Telling stories is part of what it means to be human. Stories define a culture, explaining the culture to those who live within its boundaries. Stories enable readers to live vicariously, to imagine situations of some relevance, experiencing the passions without enduring the travails. This is one of the functions of narrative: to provide a simulacrum, a "made-up" space in which life is experienced from a certain aesthetic distance, and thereby shaped and made explicable.

In a place and time without written language, people depended on storytellers for the transmission of lore; for passing on information and cultural history; for all of the things one now gets from books, tele-vision, newspapers, and magazines. The ancient Greeks, for example, experienced centuries of storytelling before the eighth century B.C., when they first learned alphabetic writing from the Phoenicians. Songs, legends, myths, historical facts, and stories had been passed from person to person by word of mouth. Rather suddenly, it was possible to possess written forms of the great myths and stories, and so *The Iliad* and *The Odyssey*, among other traditional stories, found written expression.

Not surprisingly, the narratives of ancient civilizations—such as those of the Indians, Greeks, Hebrews, and Romans—functioned in those cultures much as narratives do for us today. They entertained and enchanted, scolded, informed, and united those who encountered these works. There was often a religious or moral element and didactic purpose to ancient narratives—they were meant to teach people lessons about how to behave. This was certainly true of the Old and New Testaments (which were not poems, although they contain poetic passages and, in the case of *The Psalms* and a few other places in the Bible, have a poetic form as well). To this day, narrative poetry retains a certain instructive feel, an ethical edge.

The epic and the ballad are two of the oldest forms of narrative poetry, and each has a separate chapter in this anthology. But the poems gathered here in Chapter 3 are part of the wider tradition of narrative verse, reaching back to the ancient Romans, whose poets often wrote in narrative form. For example, Ovid wrote *The Metamorphoses* in order to put into verse ancient myths from an oral tradition. He shaped these tales in his own fashion, giving them a vivid narrative structure.

The great Anglo-Saxon epic, *Beowulf*, was a founding narrative poem of considerable consequence for English poetry; we have included excerpts from it in Chapter 1 (p. 46). During the Renaissance in England, Edmund Spenser published *The Faerie Queene* in installments between 1590 and 1609. It became a central poem of the period, and it remains one of the great narrative poems of all time. The poem (which could have been included in the epic section as well) celebrates a Protestant nation that has only recently become a world power in its own right. The shape of the poem represents a blending of the Italian romantic epic with the allegorical poetry popular during the Middle Ages. As you will note, Spenser devised a stanza form that is commonly referred to as the **Spenserian stanza,** a rhyming stanza in nine lines. We have included here (p. 264) the first (and perhaps most famous) of the six books that Spenser completed (he had originally hoped to write twelve books).

A wide range of well-known examples of narrative poetry are included in this chapter, from Blake's soaring mythology in "The Book of Thel" (p. 283) to Wordsworth's down-to-earth "Michael" (p. 293) to Poe's well-known and popular narrative, "The Raven" (p. 318), as well as some splendid modern examples of the genre. In "The Moose" by Elizabeth Bishop (p. 354) and "Cherrylog Road" by James Dickey (p. 364), one sees modern poets reaching back to storytelling as a primary function of the poet, bending the form to their own purposes.

In essence, this chapter is about stories, and about poets who have been moved to tell stories. They naturally use the same techniques that storytellers have always counted on, including conflict, characterization, suspense, and dialogue. Sometimes the narrative begins in the midst of the action (*in medias res* is the literary term for this), as in Frost's haunting poem, "Home Burial" (p. 348), about a young couple who (one gradually realizes) have lost their infant child. The whole poem takes place on a stairwell in the lonely farmhouse of this couple, and it becomes, in effect, a little play with two characters.

Frost could have chosen to write this story in prose, but the advantages of the form he selected should be evident to the reader: it moves with a strange, stately pace, controlled by the poet's expert command of blank verse, which is used here to approximate the speaking voice of the characters, who are simple farmers. The poem lingers in the mind, its lines beautifully shaped and phrased. The imagery is vivid throughout. The metaphors are subtle. There is a muscular quality to the language that would seem out of place in prose.

The narrative poem is an ancestor of modern novels and films. Narrative poems have continued to flourish in the age of prose and film, in part because poems have a strong musical element, an aspect of compression, and a quality of linguistic intensity (heightened by the conventions of poetry, such as rhyme and meter). These qualities are difficult for writers to achieve in prose narratives. Rock and folk singers as well as hip-hop performers know this, and their work falls quite directly in the ancient tradition of sung narrative. In many ways, the rock, folk, and hip-hop traditions in music, which in some ways have cornered the market on narrative poetry, dip repeatedly into the deep well from the which the poems that follow are drawn—the great tradition of narrative verse.

ADDITIONAL EXAMPLES OF NARRATIVE POEMS IN THIS BOOK

- Homer, from *The Odyssey* (p. 34)
- Anonymous, from *Beowulf* (p. 46)
- Anonymous, "Lord Randal" (p. 452)
- Anonymous, "Bonny Barbara Allan" (p. 454)
- Anonymous, "Sir Patrick Spens" (p. 455)
- Geoffrey Chaucer, *The Pardoner's Prologue and Tale* (p. 531)
- Alexander Pope, "The Rape of the Lock" (p. 64)
- William Wordsworth, "Nutting" (p. 1290)
- Robert Browning, "My Last Duchess" (p. 579)
- Robert Frost, " 'Out, Out—' " (p. 985)
- Robert W. Service, "The Cremation of Sam McGee" (p. 1602)
- Audre Lorde, "Ballad from Childhood" (p. 526)
- Bob Dylan, "The Lonesome Death of Hattie Carol" (p. 527)

OVID (43 B.C.–17 A.D.)
trans. Ted Hughes

Actaeon (8 A.D.)
from The Metamorphoses

Destiny, not guilt, was enough
For Actaeon.[1] It is no crime
To lose your way in a dark wood.

It happened on a mountain where hunters
5   Had slaughtered so many animals
The slopes were patched red with the butchering places.

When shadows were shortest and the sun's heat hardest
Young Actaeon called a halt:
"We have killed more than enough for the day.

10   "Our nets are stiff with blood,
Our spears are caked, and our knives
Are clogged in their sheaths with the blood of a glorious hunt.

"Let's be up again in the grey dawn—
Back to the game afresh. This noon heat
15   Has baked the stones too hot for a human foot."

All concurred. And the hunt was over for the day.
A deep cleft at the bottom of the mountain
Dark with matted pine and spiky cypress

Was known as Gargaphie, sacred to Diana,[2]
20   Goddess of the hunt.
In the depths of this goyle was the mouth of a cavern

That might have been carved out with deliberate art
From the soft volcanic rock.
It half-hid a broad pool, perpetually shaken

25   By a waterfall inside the mountain,
Noisy but hidden. Often to that grotto,
Aching and burning from her hunting,

---

[1] **Actaeon:** In Greek myth, he was the hunter who surprised Diana in the woods as she was bathing.
[2] **Diana:** Roman goddess of fertility, childbirth, and nature. Diana was closely identified with the Greek goddess Artemis.

Diana came
To cool the naked beauty she hid from the world.
30   All her nymphs would attend her.

One held her javelin,
Her quiverful of arrows and her unstrung bow.
Another folded her cape.

Two others took off her sandals, while Crocale[3]
35   The daughter of Ismenus
Whose hands were the most artful, combing out

The goddess' long hair, that the hunt had tangled,
Bunched it into a thick knot,
Though her own hair stayed as the hunt had scattered it.

40   Five others, Nephele, Hyale, Phiale
Psecas and Rhanis, filled great jars with water
And sluiced it over Diana's head and shoulders.

The goddess was there, in her secret pool,
Naked and bowed
45   Under those cascades from the mouths of jars

In the fastness of Gargaphie, when Actaeon,
Making a beeline home from the hunt
Stumbled on this gorge. Surprised to find it,

He pushed into it, apprehensive, but
50   Steered by a pitiless fate—whose nudgings he felt
Only as surges of curiosity.

So he came to the clearing. And saw ripples
Flocking across the pool out of the cavern.
He edged into the cavern, under ferns

55   That dripped with spray. He peered
Into the gloom to see the waterfall—
But what he saw were nymphs, their wild faces

Screaming at him in a commotion of water.
And as his eyes adjusted, he saw they were naked,
60   Beating their breasts as they screamed at him.

---

[3] **Crocale:** An attendant nymph of Diana/Artemis. Nephele, Hyale, Phiale, Psecas, and Rhanis were
also Diana's attendant nymphs.

And he saw they were crowding together
To hide something from him. He stared harder.
Those nymphs could not conceal Diana's whiteness,

The tallest barely reached her navel. Actaeon
65   Stared at the goddess, who stared at him.
She twisted her breasts away, showing him her back.

Glaring at him over her shoulder
She blushed like a dawn cloud
In that twilit grotto of winking reflections,

70   And raged for a weapon—for her arrows
To drive through his body.
No weapon was to hand—only water.

So she scooped up a handful and dashed it
Into his astonished eyes, as she shouted:
75   "Now, if you can, tell how you saw me naked."

That was all she said, but as she said it
Out of his forehead burst a rack of antlers.
His neck lengthened, narrowed, and his ears

Folded to whiskery points, his hands were hooves,
80   His arms long slender legs. His hunter's tunic
Slid from his dappled hide. With all this

The goddess
Poured a shocking stream of panic terror
Through his heart like blood. Actaeon

85   Bounded out across the cave's pool
In plunging leaps, amazed at his own lightness.
And there

Clear in the bulging mirror of his bow-wave
He glimpsed his antlered head,
90   And cried: "What has happened to me?"

No words came. No sound came but a groan.
His only voice was a groan.
Human tears shone on his stag's face

From the grief of a mind that was still human.
95   He veered first this way, then that.
Should he run away home to the royal palace?

Or hide in the forest? The thought of the first
Dizzied him with shame. The thought of the second
Flurried him with terrors.

100   But then, as he circled, his own hounds found him.
The first to give tongue were Melampus
And the deep-thinking Ichnobates.

Melampus a Spartan, Ichnobates a Cretan.
The whole pack piled in after.
105   It was like a squall crossing a forest.

Dorceus, Pamphagus and Oribasus—
Pure Arcadians. Nebrophonus,
Strong as a wild boar, Theras, as fierce.

And Laelaps never far from them. Pterelas
110   Swiftest in the pack, and Agre
The keenest nose. And Hylaeus

Still lame from the rip of a boar's tusk.
Nape whose mother was a wolf, and Poemenis—
Pure sheep-dog. Harpyia with her grown pups,

115   Who still would never leave her.
The lanky hound Ladon, from Sicyon,
With Tigris, Dromas, Canace, Sticte and Alce,

And Asbolus, all black, and all-white Leuca.
Lacon was there, with shoulders like a lion.
120   Aello, who could outrun wolves, and Thous,

Lycise, at her best in a tight corner,
Her brother Cyprius, and black Harpalus
With a white star on his forehead.

Lachne, like a shaggy bear-cub. Melaneus
125   And the Spartan-Cretan crossbreeds
Lebros and Agriodus. Hylactor,

With the high, cracked voice, and a host of others,
Too many to name.[4] The strung-out pack,
Locked onto their quarry,

---

[4] **his own hounds . . . to name:** Actaeon's hunting dogs attack their own transformed master.

130 Flowed across the landscape, over crags,
Over cliffs where no man could have followed,
Through places that seemed impossible.

Where Actaeon had so often strained
Every hound to catch and kill the quarry,
135 Now he strained to shake the same hounds off—

His own hounds. He tried to cry out:
"I am Actaeon—remember your master,"
But his tongue lolled wordless, while the air

Belaboured his ears with hounds' voices.
140 Suddenly three hounds appeared, ahead,
Raving towards him. They had been last in the pack.

But they had thought it out
And made a short cut over a mountain.
As Actaeon turned, Melanchaetes

145 The ringleader of this breakaway trio
Grabbed a rear ankle
In the trap of his jaws. Then the others,

Theridamus and Oristrophus, left and right,
Caught a foreleg each, and he fell.
150 These three pinned their master, as the pack

Poured onto him like an avalanche.
Every hound filled its jaws
Till there was hardly a mouth not gagged and crammed

With hair and muscle. Then began the tugging and the ripping.
155 Actaeon's groan was neither human
Nor the natural sound of a stag.

Now the hills he had played on so happily
Toyed with the echoes of his death-noises.
His head and antlers reared from the heaving pile.

160 And swayed—like the signalling arm
Of somebody drowning in surf.
But his friends, who had followed the pack

To this unexpected kill,
Urged them to finish the work. Meanwhile they shouted
165 For Actaeon—over and over for Actaeon

To hurry and witness this last kill of the day—
And such a magnificent beast—
As if he were absent. He heard his name

And wished he were as far off as they thought him.
170   He wished he were among them
Not suffering this death but observing

The terrible method
Of his murderers, as they knotted
Muscles and ferocity to dismember

175   Their own master.
Only when Actaeon's life
Had been torn from his bones, to the last mouthful,

Only then
Did the remorseless anger of Diana,
180   Goddess of the arrow, find peace.

EDMUND SPENSER (ca. 1552–1599)

from The Faerie Queene[1] (1590)
The First Booke

> *Contayning*
> *The Legende of the*
> *Knight of the Red Crosse,*
> *or*
> *Of Holinesse*

1

Lo I the man, whose Muse[2] whilome° did maske,	previously
As time her taught, in lowly Shepheards weeds,°	garments
Am now enforst a far unfitter taske,	
For trumpets sterne to chaunge mine Oaten reeds,[3]	
5 And sing of Knights and Ladies gentle deeds;	
Whose prayses having slept in silence long,	
Me, all too meane, the sacred Muse areeds°	commands
To blazon broad emongst her learned throng:	
Fierce warres and faithfull loves shall moralize my song.	

---

[1] **The Faerie Queene:** The title references both to Gloriana, the poem's Fairy Queen, and to England's Queen Elizabeth I, who ruled from 1558 to 1603.
[2] **Muse:** One of the nine daughters of Zeus and Mnemosyne, protectors of arts and science.
[3] **For . . . reeds:** The trumpet is a symbol of epic poetry, while oaten reeds, or pipes, represent pastoral poetry.

2

10 Helpe then, O holy Virgin chiefe of nine,
     Thy weaker Novice to performe thy will,
     Lay forth out of thine everlasting scryne°   shrine
     The antique rolles, which there lye hidden still,
     Of Faerie knights and fairest Tanaquill,[4]
15   Whom that most noble Briton Prince° so long   Arthur
     Sought through the world, and suffered so much ill,
     That I must rue his undeservèd wrong:
  O helpe thou my weake wit, and sharpen my dull tong.

3

  And thou most dreaded impe[5] of highest Jove,
20   Faire Venus sonne, that with thy cruell dart
     At that good knight so cunningly didst rove,°   shoot
     That glorious fire it kindled in his hart,
     Lay now thy deadly Heben° bow apart,   ebony
     And with thy mother milde come to mine ayde:
25   Come both, and with you bring triumphant Mart,[6]
     In loves and gentle jollities arrayd,
  After his murdrous spoiles and bloudy rage allayd.

4

  And with them eke, O Goddesse heavenly bright,
     Mirrour of grace and Majestie divine,
30   Great Lady of the greatest Isle, whose light
     Like Phoebus lampe[7] throughout the world doth shine,
     Shed thy faire beames into my feeble eyne,
     And raise my thoughts too humble and too vile,
     To thinke of that true glorious type of thine,
35   The argument of mine afflicted stile:°   human pen
  The which to heare, vouchsafe, O dearest dred a-while.

Canto 1

The Patron of true Holinesse,
Foule Errour doth defeate:
Hypocrisie him to entrappe,
40   *Doth to his home entreate.*

---

[4] **Tanaquill:** The wife of Tarquin I, a legendary king of Rome. Here Spenser uses Tanaquill as a reference to Gloriana, the Fairy Queen.
[5] **dreaded impe:** Cupid, the god of love, whose mother was Venus, the goddess of love and beauty.
[6] **Mart:** Mars, the god of war.
[7] **Like Phoebus lampe:** The sun; here, Spenser refers to Phoebus Apollo, the Greek god of the sun.

1

A Gentle Knight was pricking° on the plaine,   galloping
    Ycladd in mightie armes and silver shielde,
    Wherein old dints of deepe wounds did remaine,
    The cruell markes of many a bloudy fielde;
45   Yet armes till that time did he never wield:
    His angry steede did chide his foming bitt,
    As much disdayning to the curbe to yield:
    Full jolly knight he seemd, and faire did sitt,
As one for knightly giusts° and fierce encounters fitt.   jousts

2

50 But on his brest a bloudie Crosse he bore,
    The deare remembrance of his dying Lord,
    For whose sweete sake that glorious badge he wore,
    And dead as living ever him ador'd:
    Upon his shield the like was also scor'd,
55   For soveraine hope, which in his helpe he had:
    Right faithfull true he was in deede and word,
    But of his cheere did seeme too solemne sad;
Yet nothing did he dread, but ever was ydrad.°   dreaded

3

Upon a great adventure he was bond,°   bound
60   That greatest Gloriana to him gave,
    That greatest Glorious Queene of Faerie lond,
    To winne him worship, and her grace to have,
    Which of all earthly things he most did crave;
    And ever as he rode, his hart did earne°   yearn
65   To prove his puissance° in battell brave   power
    Upon his foe, and his new force to learne;
Upon his foe, a Dragon horrible and stearne.

4

A lovely Ladie rode him faire beside,
    Upon a lowly Asse more white then snow,
70   Yet she much whiter, but the same did hide
    Under a vele, that wimpled° was full low,   wrinkled
    And over all a blacke stole she did throw,
    As one that inly° mourned: so was she sad,   internally
    And heavie sat upon her palfrey slow:
75   Seemèd in heart some hidden care she had,
And by her in a line a milke white lambe she lad.

5

So pure an innocent, as that same lambe,
 She was in life and every vertuous lore,°   doctrine
 And by descent from Royall lynage came
80 Of ancient Kings and Queenes, that had of yore
 Their scepters stretcht from East to Westerne shore,
 And all the world in their subjection held;
 Till that infernall feend with foule uprore°   rebellion
 Forwasted all their land, and them expeld:
85 Whom to avenge, she had this Knight from far compeld.°   called

6

Behind her farre away a Dwarfe did lag,
 That lasie seemd in being ever last,
 Or wearied with bearing of her bag
 Of needments at his backe. Thus as they past,
90 The day with cloudes was suddeine overcast,
 And angry Jove an hideous storme of raine
 Did poure into his Lemans lap so fast,[8]
 That every wight° to shrowd° it did constrain,   being / take cover
And this faire couple eke to shroud themselves were fain.

7

95 Enforst to seeke some covert nigh at hand,
 A shadie grove not far away they spide,
 That promist ayde the tempest to withstand:
 Whose loftie trees yclad with sommers pride,
 Did spred so broad, that heavens light did hide,
100 Not perceable° with power of any starre: penetrable
 And all within were pathes and alleies wide,
 With footing worne, and leading inward farre:
Faire harbour that them seemes; so in they entred arre.

8

And foorth they passe, with pleasure forward led,
105 Joying to heare the birdes sweete harmony,
 Which therein shrouded from the tempest dred,
 Seemd in their song to scorne the cruell sky.
 Much can they prayse the trees so straight and hy,
 The sayling Pine, the Cedar proud and tall,
110 The vine-prop Elme, the Poplar never dry,

---

[8] **And angry . . . fast:** Jove ruled classical gods. Here, Spenser alludes to "his Lemans" or lover, the earth.

The builder Oake, sole king of forrests all,
The Aspine good for staves, the Cypresse funerall.

9

The Laurell, meed° of mightie Conquerours   prize
    And Poets sage, the Firre that weepeth still,
115   The Willow worne of forlorne Paramours,
    The Eugh obedient to the benders will,
    The Birch for shaftes, the Sallow for the mill,
    The Mirrhe sweete bleeding in the bitter wound,
    The warlike Beech, the Ash for nothing ill,
120   The fruitful Olive, and the Platane round,
The carver Holme, the Maple seeldom inward sound.

10

Led with delight, they thus beguile the way,
    Untill the blustring storme is overblowne;
    When weening° to returne, whence they did stray,   meaning
125   They cannot finde that path, which first was showne,
    But wander too and fro in wayes unknowne,
    Furthest from end then, when they neerest weene.
    That makes them doubt, their wits be not their owne:
    So many pathes, so many turnings seene,
130   That which of them to take, in diverse doubt they been.

11

At last resolving forward still to fare,
    Till that some end they finde or in or out,
    That path they take, that beaten seemd most bare,
    And like to lead the labyrinth about;°   out of
135   Which when by tract they hunted had throughout,
    At length it brought them to a hollow cave,
    Amid the thickest woods. The Champion stout
    Eftsoones° dismounted from his courser° brave,   forthwith / horse
And to the Dwarfe a while his needlesse spere he gave.

12

140   Be well aware, quoth then that Ladie milde,
    Least suddaine mischiefe° ye too rash provoke: misfortune
    The danger hid, the place unknowne and wilde,
    Breedes dreadfull doubts: Oft fire is without smoke,
    And perill without show: therefore your stroke
145   Sir knight with-hold, till further triall made.
    Ah Ladie (said he) shame were to revoke
    The forward footing for an hidden shade:
Vertue gives her selfe light, through darkenesse for to wade.

13

Yea but (quoth she) the perill of this place
150   I better wot° then you, though now too late   know
To wish you backe returne with foule disgrace,
Yet wisedome warnes, whilest foot is in the gate,
To stay the steppe, ere forcèd to retrate.
This is the wandring wood, this Errours den,
155   A monster vile, whom God and man does hate:
Therefore I read° beware. Fly fly (quoth then   recommend
The fearefull Dwarfe:) this is no place for living men.

14

But full of fire and greedy hardiment,°   courage
The youthfull knight could not for ought be staide,
160   But forth unto the darksome hole he went,
And lookèd in: his glistring° armor made   glistening
A litle glooming light, much like a shade,
By which he saw the ugly monster plaine,
Halfe like a serpent horribly displaide,
165   But th' other halfe did womans shape retaine,
Most lothsom, filthie, foule, and full of vile disdaine.

15

And as she lay upon the durtie ground,
Her huge long taile her den all overspred,
Yet was in knots and many boughtes° upwound,   coils
170   Pointed with mortall sting. Of her there bred
A thousand yong ones, which she dayly fed,
Sucking upon her poisonous dugs, eachone
Of sundry shapes, yet all ill favorèd:
Soone as that uncouth° light upon them shone,   unknown
175   Into her mouth they crept, and suddain all were gone.

16

Their dam upstart, out of her den effraide,°   distressed
And rushèd forth, hurling her hideous taile
About her cursèd head, whose folds displaid°   extended
Were stretcht now forth at length without entraile.°   twisting
180   She lookt about, and seeing one in mayle
Armèd to point,[9] sought backe to turne againe;
For light she hated as the deadly bale,°   evil
Ay wont in desert darknesse to remaine,
Where plaine none might her see, nor she see any plaine.

---

[9] **Armèd to point:** Well-armed.

17

185 Which when the valiant Elfe[10] perceiv'd, he lept
   As Lyon fierce upon the flying pray,
   And with his trenchand° blade her boldly kept   sharp
   From turning backe, and forcèd her to stay:
   Therewith enrag'd she loudly gan to bray,
190 And turning fierce, her speckled taile advaunst,
   Threatning her angry sting, him to dismay:
   Who nough aghast, his mightie hand enhaunst:°   raised
The stroke down from her head unto her shoulder glaunst.

18

   Much daunted with that dint, her sence was dazd,
195 Yet kindling rage, her selfe she gathered round,
   And all attonce her beastly body raizd
   With doubled forces high above the ground:
   Tho° wrapping up her wrethèd sterne arownd,   then
   Lept fierce upon his shield, and her huge traine°   tail
200 All suddenly about his body wound,
   That hand or foot to stirre he strove in vaine:
God helpe the man so wrapt in Errours endlesse traine.

19

   His Lady sad to see his sore constraint,
   Cride out, Now now Sir knight, shew what ye bee,
205 Add faith unto your force, and be not faint:
   Strangle her, else she sure will strangle thee.
   That when he heard, in great perplexitie,
   His gall[11] did grate for griefe and high disdaine,
   And knitting all his force got one hand free,
210 Wherewith he grypt her gorge° with so great paine,   throat
That soone to loose her wicked bands did her constraine.

20

   Therewith she spewd out of her filthy maw
   A floud of poyson horrible and blacke,
   Full of great lumpes of flesh and gobbets° raw,   chunks of food
215 Which stunck so vildly, that it forst him slacke
   His grasping hold, and from her turne him backe:

---

[10] **Elfe:** A knight from the fairy land.
[11] **His gall:** Source of deep and bitter anger.

Her vomit full of bookes and papers was,[12]
    With loathly frogs and toades, which eyes did lacke,
    And creeping sought way in the weedy gras:
220 Her filthy parbreake° all the place defilèd has.   *vomit*

21

As when old father Nilus [13] gins to swell
    With timely pride above the Aegyptian vale,
    His fattie° waves do fertile slime outwell,   *abundant*
    And overflow each plaine and lowly dale:
225 But when his later spring gins to avale,°   *recede*
    Huge heapes of mudd he leaves, wherein there breed
    Ten thousand kindes of creatures, partly male
    And partly female of his fruitfull seed;
Such ugly monstrous shapes elswhere may no man reed.

22

230 The same so sore annoyèd has the knight,
    That welnigh chokèd with the deadly stinke,
    His forces faile, ne can no longer fight.
    Whose corage when the feend perceived to shrinke,
    She pourèd forth out of her hellish sinke°   *mouth*
235 Her fruitfull cursèd spawne of serpents small,
    Deformèd monsters, fowle, and blacke as inke,
    Which swarming all about his legs did crall,
And him encombred sore, but could not hurt at all.

23

As gentle Shepheard in sweete even-tide,
240 When ruddy Phoebus gins to welke° in west,   *descend*
    High on an hill, his flocke to vewen wide,
    Markes which do byte their hasty supper best;
    A cloud of combrous° gnattes do him molest,   *encumbering*
    All striving to infixe their feeble stings,
245 That from their noyance he no where can rest,
    But with his clownish hands their tender wings
He brusheth oft, and oft doth mar their murmurings.

24

Thus ill bestedd,° and fearfull more of shame,   *positioned*
    Then of the certaine perill he stood in,

---

[12] **Her vomit . . . was:** Possibly a reference to Catholic publications that attacked Queen Elizabeth, who was a Protestant.
[13] **old father Nilus:** The Nile River.

250   Halfe furious unto his foe he came,
      Resolv'd in minde all suddenly to win,
      Or soone to lose, before he once would lin;°   finish
      And strooke at her with more then manly force,
      That from her body full of filthie sin
255   He raft° her hatefull head without remorse;   severed
      A streame of cole black bloud forth gushèd from her corse.

                                    25

      Her scattred brood, soone as their Parent deare
         They saw so rudely falling to the ground,
         Groning full deadly, all with troublous feare,
260   Gathred themselves about her body round,
         Weening their wonted entrance to have found
         At her wide mouth: but being there withstood
         They flockèd all about her bleeding wound,
         And suckèd up their dying mothers blood,
265   Making her death their life, and eke her hurt their good.

                                    26

      That detestable sight him much amazde,
         To see th' unkindly Impes° of heaven accurst,   offspring
         Devoure their dam; on whom while so he gazd,
         Having all satisfide their bloudy thurst,
270   Their bellies swolne he saw with fulnesse burst,
         And bowels gushing forth: well worthy end
         Of such as drunke her life, the which them nurst;
         Now needeth him no lenger labour spend,
      His foes have slaine themselves, with whom he should contend.

                                    27

275   His Ladie seeing all, that chaunst, from farre
         Approcht in hast to greet his victorie,
         And said, Faire knight, borne under happy° starre,   favorable
         Who see your vanquisht foes before you lye:
         Well worthy be you of that Armorie,°   armor
280   Wherein ye have great glory wonne this day,
         And proov'd your strength on a strong enimie,
         Your first adventure: many such I pray,
      And henceforth ever wish, that like succeed it may.

                                    28

      Then mounted he upon his Steede againe,
285   And with the Lady backward sought to wend;
         That path he kept, which beaten was most plaine,
         Ne ever would to any by-way bend,

But still did follow one unto the end,
The which at last out of the wood them brought
290 So forward on his way (with God to frend)°   as a friend
He passèd forth, and new adventure sought;
Long way he travellèd, before he heard of ought.

29

At length they chaunst to meet upon the way
An aged Sire, in long blacke weedes° yclad,°   garments / dressed
295 His feete all bare, his beard all hoarie° gray,   ancient
And by his belt his booke he hanging had;
Sober he seemde, and very sagely sad,
And to the ground his eyes were lowly bent,
Simple in shew, and voyde of malice bad,
300 And all the way he prayèd, as he went,
And often knockt his brest, as one that did repent.

30

He faire the knight saluted, louting° low,   bowing
Who faire him quited,° as that courteous was: responded
305 And after askèd him, if he did know
Of straunge adventures, which abroad did pas.
Ah my deare Sonne (quoth he) how should, alas,
Silly old man, that lives in hidden cell,
Bidding his beades [14] all day for his trespas,
310 Tydings of warre and worldly trouble tell?
With holy father sits not with such things to mell.°   meddle

31

But if of daunger which hereby doth dwell,
And homebred evill ye desire to heare,
Of a straunge man I can you tidings tell,
315 That wasteth all this countrey farre and neare.
Of such (said he) I chiefly do inquere,
And shall you well reward to shew the place,
In which that wicked wight his dayes doth weare:
For to all knighthood it is foule disgrace,
320 That such a cursed creature lives so long a space.

32

Far hence (quoth he) in wastfull° wildernesse   bleak
His dwelling is, by which no living wight
May ever passe, but thorough great distresse.
Now (sayd the Lady) draweth toward night,

---

[14] **Bidding his beades:** Counting his rosary beads, a form of Catholic prayer.

325 And well I wote, that of your later fight
Ye all forwearied be: for what so strong,
But wanting rest will also want of might?
The Sunne that measures heaven all day long,
At night doth baite° his steedes the Ocean waves emong.   feed

33

330 Then with the Sunne take Sir, your timely rest,
And with new day new worke at once begin:
Untroubled night they say gives counsell best.
Right well Sir knight ye have advisèd bin,
(Quoth then that aged man;) the way to win
335 Is wisely to advise:° now day is spent;   consider
Therefore with me ye may take up your In
For this same night. The knight was well content:
So with that godly father to his home they went.

34

A little lowly Hermitage it was,
340 Downe in a dale, hard by a forests side,
Far from resort of people, that did pas
In travell to and froe: a little wyde
There was an holy Chappell edifyde,°   built
Wherein the Hermite dewly wont to say
345 His holy things each morne and eventyde:
Thereby a Christall streame did gently play,
Which from a sacred fountaine wellèd forth alway.

35

Arrivèd there, the little house they fill,
Ne looke for entertainement, where none was:
350 Rest is their feast, and all things at their will;
The noblest mind the best contentment has.
With faire discourse the evening so they pas:
For that old man of pleasing wordes had store,
And well could file his tongue as smooth as glas;
355 He told of Saintes and Popes, and evermore
He strowd an Ave-Mary[15] after and before.

36

The drouping Night thus creepeth on them fast,
And the sad humour loading their eye liddes,

---

[15] **Ave-Mary:** Latin, "Hail Mary," a Catholic prayer directed to Mary, the virgin mother of Christ.

As messenger of Morpheus[16] on them cast
360   Sweet slombring deaw, the which to sleepe them biddes.
Unto their lodgings then his guestes he riddes:
Where when all drownd in deadly sleepe[17] he findes,
He to his study goes, and there amiddes
His Magick bookes and artes of sundry kindes,
365   He seekes out mighty charmes, to trouble sleepy mindes.

37

Then choosing out few wordes most horrible,
  (Let none them read) thereof did verses frame,
With which and other spelles like terrible,
He bade awake blacke Plutoes griesly Dame,[18]
370   And cursèd heaven, and spake reprochfull shame
Of highest God, the Lord of life and light;
A bold bad man, that dared to call by name
Great Gorgon,[19] Prince of darknesse and dead night,
At which Cocytus quakes, and Styx is put to flight.

38

375   And forth he cald out of deepe darknesse dred
Legions of Sprights, the which like little flyes
Fluttring about his ever damnèd hed,
A-waite whereto their service he applyes,
To aide his friends, or fray° his enimies: scare
380   Of those he chose out two, the falsest twoo,
And fittest for to forge true-seeming lyes;
The one of them he gave a message too,
The other by him selfe staide other worke to doo.

39

He making speedy way through spersèd° ayre,   dispersed
385   And through the world of waters wide and deepe,
To Morpheus house doth hastily repaire.
Amid the bowels of the earth full steepe,
And low, where dawning day doth never peepe,
His dwelling is; there Tethys[20] his wet bed
390   Doth ever wash, and Cynthia[21] still doth steepe

---

[16] **Morpheus:** The Roman god of sleep and dreams.
[17] **deadly sleepe:** Sleep that resembles death.
[18] **blacke Plutoes griesly Dame:** Proserpina, goddess of the underworld.
[19] **Great Gorgon:** Demogorgon, a demon so powerful that the invocation of his name caused the rivers in hell to shake.
[20] **Tethys:** Goddess of the sea.
[21] **Cynthia:** Goddess of the moon.

In silver deaw his ever-drouping hed,
Whiles sad Night over him her mantle black doth spred.

40

Whose double gates he findeth lockèd fast,
   The one faire fram'd of burnisht Yvory,
395   The other all with silver overcast;
   And wakefull dogges before them farre do lye,
   Watching to banish Care their enimy,
   Who oft is wont° to trouble gentle Sleepe.   accustomed
   By them the Sprite doth passe in quietly,
400   And unto Morpheus comes, whom drownèd deepe,
In drowsie fit he findes: of nothing he takes keepe.

41

And more, to lulle him in his slumber soft,
   A trickling streame from high rocke tumbling downe
   And ever-drizling raine upon the loft,
405   Mixt with a murmuring winde, much like the sowne°   sound
   Of swarming Bees, did cast him in a swowne:
   No other noyse, nor peoples troublous cryes,
   As still° are wont t'annoy the wallèd towne,   always
   Might there be heard: but carelesse Quiet lyes,
410 Wrapt in eternall silence farre from enemyes.

42

The messenger approaching to him spake,
   But his wast° wordes returnd to him in vaine: wasted
   So sound he slept, that nought mought° him awake.   might
   Then rudely he him thrust, and pusht with paine,
415   Whereat he gan to stretch: but he againe
   Shooke him so hard, that forced him to speake.
   As one then in a dreame, whose dryer braine
   Is tost with troubled sights and fancies weake,
He mumbled soft, but would not all his silence breake.

43

420 The Sprite then gan more boldly him to wake,
   And threatned unto him the dreaded name
   Of Hecate:[22] whereat he gan to quake,
   And lifting up his lumpish head, with blame
   Halfe angry askèd him, for what he came.
425   Hither (quoth he) me Archimago° sent,   chief deceiver

---

[22] **Hecate:** In Greek mythology, the three-headed goddess of witchcraft and sorcery.

He that the stubborne Sprites can wisely tame,
He bids thee to him send for his intent
A fit false dreame, that can delude the sleepers sent.°   senses

44

The God obayde, and calling forth straight way
430 A diverse° dreame out of his prison darke,   confusing
Delivered it to him, and downe did lay
His heavie head, devoide of carefull carke,°   concerns
Whose sences all were straight benumbd and starke.
He backe returning by the Yvorie dore,
435 Remounted up as light as chearefull Larke,
And on his litle winges the dreame he bore
In hast unto his Lord, where he him left afore.

45

Who all this while with charmes and hidden artes,
Had made a Lady of that other Spright,
440 And fram'd of liquid ayre her tender partes
So lively, and so like in all mens sight,
That weaker sence it could have ravisht quight:
The maker selfe for all his wondrous witt,
Was nigh beguilèd with so goodly sight:
445 Her all in white he clad, and over it
Cast a blacke stole, most like to seeme for Una [23] fit.

46

Now when that ydle dreame was to him brought,
Unto that Elfin knight he bad him fly,
Where he slept soundly void of evill thought,
450 And with false shewes abuse his fantasy,
In sort as he him schoolèd privily:
And that new creature borne without her dew,[24]
Full of the makers guile, with usage sly
He taught to imitate that Lady trew,
455 Whose semblance she did carrie under feignèd hew.

47

Thus well instructed, to their worke they hast
And comming where the knight in slomber lay
The one upon his hardy head him plast,
And made him dreame of loves and lustfull play,

---

[23] **Una:** Latin, "one" or "unity."
[24] **borne without her dew:** Born unnaturally.

460   That nigh his manly hart did melt away,
      Bathèd in wanton blis and wicked joy:
      Then seemèd him his Lady by him lay,
      And to him playnd, how that false wingèd boy,[25]
   Her chast hart had subdewd, to learne Dame pleasures toy.[26]

48

465   And she her selfe of beautie soveraigne Queene
      Faire Venus seemde unto his bed to bring
      Her, whom he waking evermore did weene°   think
      To be the chastest flowre, that ay did spring
      On earthly braunch, the daughter of a king,
470   Now a loose Leman° to vile service bound: lover
      And eke the Graces seemèd all to sing,
      Hymen iō Hymen, dauncing all around,
   Whilst freshest Flora[27] her with Yvie girlond crownd.

49

   In this great passion of unwonted° lust,   unfamiliar
475   Or wonted feare of doing ought amis,
      He started up, as seeming to mistrust
      Some secret ill, or hidden foe of his:
      Lo there before his face his Lady is,
      Under blake stole hyding her bayted hooke,
480   And as halfe blushing offred him to kis,
      With gentle blandishment and lovely looke,
   Most like that virgin true, which for her knight him took.

50

   All cleane dismayd to see so uncouth° sight,   strange
      And halfe enragèd at her shamelesse guise,
485   He thought have slaine her in his fierce despight:°   outrage
      But hasty heat tempring with sufferance wise,
      He stayede his hand, and gan himselfe advise
      To prove his sense, and tempt her faignèd truth.
      Wringing her hands in wemens pitteous wise,
490   Tho can she weepe, to stirre up gentle ruth,°   pity
   Both for her noble bloud, and for her tender youth.

51

   And said Ah Sir, my liege Lord and my love,
      Shall I accuse the hidden cruell fate,

---

[25] **false wingèd boy:** Cupid.
[26] **Dame pleasures toy:** The lustful play of Venus.
[27] **Hymen . . . Flora:** Hymen is the god of marriage, and Flora is the flower goddess.

And mightie causes wrought in heaven above,
495   Or the blind God, that doth me thus amate,°   alarm
    For hopèd love to winne me certaine hate?
    Yet thus perforce he bids me do, or die.
    Die is my dew: yet rew my wretched state
    You, whom my hard avenging destinie
500 Hath made judge of my life or death indifferently.

52

Your owne deare sake forst me at first to leave
    My Fathers kingdome, There she stopt with teares;
    Her swollen hart her speach seemd to bereave,
    And then againe begun, My weaker yeares
505   Captiv'd to fortune and frayle worldly feares,
    Fly to your faith for succour and sure ayde:
    Let me not dye in languor° and long teares.   sorrow
    Why Dame (quoth he) what hath ye thus dismayd?
What frayes° ye, that were wont to comfort me affrayd?   scares

53

510 Love of your selfe, she said, and deare constraint
    Lets me not sleepe, but wast the wearie night
    In secret anguish and unpittied plaint,
    Whiles you in carelesse sleepe are drownèd quight.
    Her doubtfull words made that redoubted knight
515   Suspect her truth: yet since no untruth he knew,
    Her fawning love with foule disdainefull spight
    He would not shend,° but said, Deare dame I rew,   reject
That for my sake unknowne such griefe unto you grew.

54

Assure your selfe, it fell not all to ground;
520   For all so deare as life is to my hart,
    I deeme your love, and hold me to you bound;
    Ne let vaine feares procure your needlesse smart,
    Where cause is none, but to your rest depart.
    Not all content, yet seemd she to appease
525   Her mournefull plaintes, beguilèd° of her art,   deprived
    And fed with words, that could not chuse but please,
So slyding softly forth, she turnd as to her ease.

55

Long after lay he musing at her mood,
    Much griev'd to thinke that gentle Dame so light,°   unchaste
530   For whose defence he was to shed his blood.

At last dull wearinesse of former fight
Having yrockt a sleepe his irkesome spright,
That troublous dreame gan freshly tosse his braine,
With bowres, and beds, and Ladies deare delight:
535   But when he saw his labour all was vaine,
With that misformèd spright he backe returnd againe.

JONATHAN SWIFT (1667–1745)

The Lady's Dressing Room (1730)

Five hours, (and who can do it less in?)
By haughty Celia[1] spent in dressing;
The goddess from her chamber issues,
Arrayed in lace, brocades and tissues.[2]
5   Strephon, who found the room was void,
And Betty otherwise employed,
Stole in, and took a strict survey,
Of all the litter as it lay;
Whereof, to make the matter clear,
10   An inventory follows here.
        And first a dirty smock appeared,
Beneath the armpits well besmeared.
Strephon, the rogue,° displayed it wide,   rascal
And turned it round on every side.
15   On such a point few words are best,
And Strephon bids us guess the rest,
But swears how damnably the men lie,
In calling Celia sweet and cleanly.
Now listen while he next produces
20   The various combs for various uses,
Filled up with dirt so closely fixt,
No brush could force a way betwixt.
A paste of composition rare,
Sweat, dandruff, powder, lead[3] and hair;
25   A forehead cloth with oil upon't
To smooth the wrinkles on her front;
Here alum flower[4] to stop the steams,

---

[1] **Celia:** Celia and Strephon were names conventionally employed in pastoral poetry.
[2] **lace, brocades and tissues:** Rich, luxurious fabrics.
[3] **lead:** At the time, employed to make hair shiny.
[4] **alum flower:** Medicinal salt.

Exhaled from sour unsavory streams,
There night-gloves made of Tripsy's hide,
30   Bequeathed by Tripsy when she died,
With puppy water,[5] beauty's help
Distilled from Tripsy's darling whelp;
Here gallypots and vials placed,
Some filled with washes, some with paste,
35   Some with pomatum,° paints and slops,   fragrant ointment
And ointments good for scabby chops.
Hard by a filthy basin stands,
Fouled with the scouring of her hands;
The basin takes whatever comes
40   The scrapings of her teeth and gums,
A nasty compound of all hues,
For here she spits, and here she spews.
But oh! it turned poor Strephon's bowels,
When he beheld and smelled the towels,
45   Begummed, bemattered, and beslimed
With dirt, and sweat, and earwax grimed.
No object Strephon's eye escapes,
Here petticoats in frowzy° heaps;   unkempt
Nor be the handkerchiefs forgot
50   All varnished o'er with snuff and snot.
The stockings why should I expose,
Stained with the marks of stinking toes;
Or greasy coifs and pinners[6] reeking,
Which Celia slept at least a week in?
55   A pair of tweezers next he found
To pluck her brows in arches round,
Or hairs that sink the forehead low,
Or on her chin like bristles grow.
      The virtues we must not let pass,
60   Of Celia's magnifying glass.
When frighted Strephon cast his eye on't
It showed visage of a giant
A glass that can to sight disclose,
The smallest worm° in Celia's nose,   abscess
65   And faithfully direct her nail
To squeeze it out from head to tail;
For catch it nicely by the head,
It must come out alive or dead.
      Why Strephon will you tell the rest?
70   And must you needs describe the chest?°   chamber pot

_____

[5] **puppy water:** A dog's urine, applied as a cosmetic.
[6] **coifs and pinners:** Hair accessories.

That careless wench! no creature warn her
To move it out from yonder corner;
But leave it standing full in sight
For you to exercise your spite.
75 In vain the workman showed his wit
With rings and hinges counterfeit
To make it seem in this disguise
A cabinet to vulgar eyes;
For Strephon ventured to look in,
80 Resolved to go through thick and thin;
He lifts the lid, there needs no more,
He smelled it all the time before.
As from within Pandora's box,
When Epimetheus op'd the locks,
85 A sudden universal crew
Of human evils upwards flew,[7]
He still was comforted to find
That Hope at last remained behind;
So Strephon lifting up the lid,
90 To view what in the chest was hid.
The vapors flew from out the vent,
But Strephon cautious never meant
The bottom of the pan to grope,
And foul his hands in search of Hope.
95 O never may such vile machine
Be once in Celia's chamber seen!
O may she better learn to keep
Those "secrets of the hoary deep!"
    As mutton cutlets, prime of meat,
100 Which though with art you salt and beat
As laws of cookery require,
And toast them at the clearest fire;
If from adown the hopeful chops
The fat upon a cinder drops,
105 To stinking smoke it turns the flame
Pois'ning the flesh from whence it came,
And up exhales a greasy stench,
For which you curse the careless wench;
So things, which must not be expressed,
110 When plumped° into the reeking chest,   dropped
Send up an excremental smell
To taint the parts from whence they fell.
The petticoats and gown perfume,

---

[7] **As from . . . evils upwards flew:** Epimetheus was the husband of Pandora, the first woman created by the gods. The gods gave Pandora a box that, when opened, released all human ills into the world.

Which waft a stink round every room.
115   Thus finishing his grand survey,
Disgusted Strephon stole away
Repeating in his amorous fits,
Oh! Celia, Celia, Celia shits!
       But Vengeance, goddess never sleeping
120   Soon punished Strephon for his peeping;
His foul imagination links
Each Dame he sees with all her stinks:
And, if unsavory odors fly,
Conceives a lady standing by:
125   All women his description fits,
And both ideas jump° like wits: match
By vicious fancy coupled fast,
And still appearing in contrast.
I pity wretched Strephon blind
130   To all the charms of female kind;
Should I the queen of love refuse,
Because she rose from stinking ooze?
To him that looks behind the scene,
Satira's[8] but some pocky° quean.   pox-infected
135   When Celia in her glory shows,
If Strephon would but stop his nose
(Who now so impiously blasphemes
Her ointments, daubs, and paints and creams,
Her washes, slops, and every clout,°   cloth
140   With which he makes so foul a rout°)   fuss
He soon would learn to think like me,
And bless his ravished sight to see
Such order from confusion sprung,
Such gaudy tulips raised from dung.

WILLIAM BLAKE   (1757–1827)

The Book of Thel[1]   (1791)
Thel's Motto

Does the Eagle know what is in the pit?
Or wilt thou go ask the Mole?

---

[8] **Satira's:** Likely Statira, a wife of Alexander the Great in the tragedy *Rival Queens* (1677) by Nathaniel Lee.
[1] **Thel:** The name Thel appears to be derived from the Greek root meaning "desire." All the proper names in the poem, however, spring from Blake's imagination.

Can Wisdom be put in a silver rod?
Or Love in a golden bowl?

1

5 The daughters of Mne Seraphim led round their sunny flocks,
All but the youngest; she in paleness sought the secret air,
To fade away like morning beauty from her mortal day;
Down by the river of Adona her soft voice is heard,
And thus her gentle lamentation falls like morning dew:

10 "O life of this our spring! why fades the lotus of the water?
Why fade these children of the spring? born but to smile & fall.
Ah! Thel is like a watry bow, and like a parting cloud,
Like a reflection in a glass, like shadows in the water,
Like dreams of infants, like a smile upon an infant's face,
15 Like the dove's voice, like transient day, like music in the air.
Ah! gentle may I lay me down, and gentle rest my head,
And gentle sleep the sleep of death and gentle hear the voice
Of him that walketh in the garden in the evening time."

The Lilly of the valley, breathing in the humble grass,
20 Answer'd the lovely maid and said: "I am a watry weed,
And I am very small, and love to dwell in lowly vales;
So weak, the gilded butterfly scarce perches on my head;
Yet I am visited from heaven, and he that smiles on all
Walks in the valley and each morn over me spreads his hand,
25 Saying: 'Rejoice, thou humble grass, thou new-born lilly flower,
Thou gentle maid of silent valleys and of modest brooks;
For thou shalt be clothed in light, and fed with morning manna,
Till summer's heat melts thee beside the fountains and the springs
To flourish in eternal vales.' Then why should Thel complain?

30 Why should the mistress of the vales of Har utter a sigh?"

She ceasd & smild in tears, then sat down in her silver shrine.

Thel answerd: "O thou little virgin of the peaceful valley,
Giving to those that cannot crave, the voiceless, the o'ertired;
Thy breath doth nourish the innocent lamb, he smells thy milky garments,
35 He crops thy flowers, while thou sittest smiling in his face,
Wiping his mild and meekin[2] mouth from all contagious taints.
Thy wine doth purify the golden honey; thy perfume,
Which thou dost scatter on every little blade of grass that springs,

---

[2] **meekin:** Likely describes a lamb's slightly wrinkled mouth.

Revives the milkéd cow, & tames the fire-breathing steed.
40   But Thel is like a faint cloud kindled at the rising sun:
I vanish from my pearly throne, and who shall find my place?"
"Queen of the vales," the Lilly answered, "ask the tender cloud,
And it shall tell thee why it glitters in the morning sky,
And why it scatters its bright beauty thro' the humid air.
45   Descend, O little cloud, & hover before the eyes of Thel."

The Cloud descended, and the Lilly bowd her modest head,
And went to mind her numerous charge among the verdant grass.

2

"Oh little Cloud," the virgin said, "I charge thee tell to me,
Why thou complainest not when in one hour thou fade away:
50   Then we shall seek thee but not find; ah, Thel is like to Thee.
I pass away, yet I complain, and no one hears my voice."

The Cloud then shew'd his golden head & his bright form emerg'd,
Hovering and glittering on the air before the face of Thel.

"O virgin, know'st thou not our steeds drink of the golden springs
55   Where Luvah[3] doth renew his horses? Look'st thou on my youth,
And fearest thou, because I vanish and am seen no more,
Nothing remains? O maid, I tell thee, when I pass away,
It is to tenfold life, to love, to peace, and raptures holy:
Unseen descending, weigh my light wings upon balmy flowers,
60   And court the fair eyed dew, to take me to her shining tent;
The weeping virgin trembling kneels before the risen sun,
Till we arise link'd in a golden band, and never part,
But walk united, bearing food to all our tender flowers."

"Dost thou O little Cloud? I fear that I am not like thee;
65   For I walk through the vales of Har and smell the sweetest flowers,
But I feed not the little flowers; I hear the warbling birds,
But I feed not the warbling birds; they fly and seek their food;
But Thel delights in these no more, because I fade away,
And all shall say, 'Without a use this shining woman liv'd,
70   Or did she only live to be at death the food of worms?'"

The Cloud reclind upon his airy throne and answer'd thus:

"Then if thou are the food of worms, O virgin of the skies,
How great thy use, how great thy blessing! Every thing that lives

---

[3] **Luvah:** A sun god of love in Blake's personal mythology.

Lives not alone, nor for self; fear not, and I will call
75 The weak worm from its lowly bed, and thou shalt hear its voice.
Come forth, worm of the silent valley, to thy pensive queen."

The helpless worm arose, and sat upon the Lilly's leaf,
And the bright Cloud saild on, to find his partner in the vale.

3

Then Thel astonish'd view'd the Worm upon its dewy bed.

80 "Art thou a Worm? Image of weakness, art thou but a Worm?
I see thee like an infant wrapped in the Lilly's leaf;
Ah, weep not, little voice, thou can'st not speak, but thou can'st weep.
Is this a Worm? I see thee lay helpless & naked, weeping,
And none to answer, none to cherish thee with mother's smiles."

85 The Clod of Clay heard the Worm's voice, & raisd her pitying head;
She bow'd over the weeping infant, and her life exhal'd
In milky fondness; then on Thel she fix'd her humble eyes.

"O beauty of the vales of Har! we live not for ourselves;
Thou seest me the meanest thing, and so I am indeed.
90 My bosom of itself is cold, and of itself is dark;

But he that loves the lowly, pours his oil upon my head,
And kisses me, and binds his nuptial bands around my breast,
And says: 'Thou mother of my children, I have lovéd thee,
And I have given thee a crown that none can take away.'
95 But how this is, sweet maid, I know not, and I cannot know;
I ponder, and I cannot ponder; yet I live and love."

The daughter of beauty wip'd her pitying tears with her white veil,
And said: "Alas! I knew not this, and therefore did I weep.
That God would love a Worm, I knew, and punish the evil foot
100 That, wilful, bruis'd its helpless form; but that he cherish'd it
With milk and oil I never knew; and therefore did I weep,
And I complaind in the mild air, because I fade away,
And lay me down in thy cold bed, and leave my shining lot."

"Queen of the vales," the matron Clay answerd, "I heard thy sighs,
105 And all thy moans flew o'er my roof, but I have call'd them down.
Wilt thou, O Queen, enter my house? 'Tis given thee to enter
And to return; fear nothing, enter thy virgin feet."

4

The eternal gates' terrific porter lifted the northern bar:[4]
Thel enter'd in & saw the secrets of the land unknown.
110 She saw the couches of the dead, & where the fibrous roots
Of every heart on earth infixes deep its restless twists:
A land of sorrows & of tears where never smile was seen.

She wanderd in the land of clouds thro' valleys dark, listning
Dolours & lamentations; waiting oft beside a dewy grave,
115 She stood in silence, listning to the voices of the ground,
Till to her own grave plot she came, & there she sat down,
And heard this voice of sorrow breathéd from the hollow pit:

"Why cannot the Ear be closed to its own destruction?
Or the glistning Eye to the poison of a smile?
120 Why are Eyelids stord with arrows ready drawn,
Where a thousand fighting men in ambush lie?
Or an Eye of gifts & graces, show'ring fruits & coinéd gold?
Why a Tongue impress'd with honey from every wind?
Why an Ear, a whirlpool fierce to draw creations in?
125 Why a Nostril wide inhaling terror, trembling, & affright?
Why a tender curb upon the youthful burning boy?
Why a little curtain of flesh on the bed of our desire?"

The Virgin started from her seat, & with a shriek
Fled back unhinderd till she came into the vales of Har.

THE END

ROBERT BURNS   (1759–1796)

Tam O' Shanter   (late 1790; publ. 1791)

Of Brownyis and of Bogillis full is this Buke.[1]
(GAVIN DOUGLAS, *ENEADOS*)

When chapman° billies° leave the street,	peddler / fellows
And drouthy° neebors neebors meet;	thirsting
As market-days are wearing late,	
An' folk begin to tak the gate;°	road

---

[4] **northern bar:** Likely the gate between the worlds of life and death.
[1] **Of Brownyis . . . Buke:** From Gavin Douglas' translation of the *Aeneid* into Scottish dialect: "Brownies are unfriendly goblins and bogles unfriendly."

5   While we sit bousing° at the nappy,°   boozing / ale
An' getting fou and unco happy,
We think na on the lang Scots miles,
The mosses,° waters, slaps,° and styles,   bogs / hedge gaps
That lie between us and our hame,
10 Whare sits our sulky, sullen dame,
Gathering her brows like gathering storm,
Nursing her wrath to keep it warm!
This truth fand honest Tam o' Shanter,
As he frae Ayr ae night did canter—
15 Auld Ayr, wham ne'er a town surpasses,
For honest men and bonnie lasses.
     Oh Tam, hadst thou but been sae wise
As taen thy ain wife Kate's advice!
She tauld thee weel thou was a skellum,°   good-for-nothing
20 A blethering, blustering, drunken blellum°—   babbler
That frae November till October,
Ae market-day thou was nae sober;
That ilka melder° wi' the miller,   meal-grinding
Thou sat as lang as thou had siller;
25 That ev'ry naig° was caed° a shoe on,   horse / driven
The smith and thee gat roaring fou on;
That at the Lord's house, even on Sunday,
Thou drank wi' Kirkton Jean till Monday.
She prophesied, that, late or soon,
30 Thou would be found deep drowned in Doon,
Or catched wi' warlocks in the mirk°   dark
By Alloway's auld, haunted kirk.[2]
Ah! gentle dames, it gars° me greet°   makes / cry
To think how monie counsels sweet,
35 How monie lengthened, sage advices
The husband frae the wife despises!
     But to our tale! Ae market-night,
Tam had got planted unco° right,   uncommonly
Fast by an ingle,° bleezing finely,   hearth
40 Wi' reaming° swats,° that drank divinely   frothing / ale
And at his elbow Souter° Johnie,   cobbler
His ancient, trusty, drouthy cronie:
(Tam loved him like a very brither—
They had been fou for weeks thegither).
45 The night drave on wi' sangs and clatter,
And ay the ale was growing better!
The landlady and Tam grew gracious

---

[2] **By Alloway's . . . kirk:** Ruins of a church near Burns' residence.

Wi' secret favours, sweet and precious;
The Souter tauld his queerest stories;
50   The landlord's laugh was ready chorus;
The storm without might rair° and rustle,   roar
Tam did na mind the storm a whistle.
Care, mad to see a man sae happy,
E'en drowned himsel amang the nappy!
55   As bees flee hame wi' lades o' treasure,
The minutes winged their way wi' pleasure—
Kings may be blest, but Tam was glorious,
O'er a' the ills o' life victorious!
       But pleasures are like poppies spread—
60   You seize the flower, its bloom is shed—
Or like the snow falls in the river,
A moment white, then melts for ever;
Or like the borealis race,
That flit ere you can point their place;
65   Or like the rainbow's lovely form
Evanishing amid the storm.
Nae man can tether time or tide—
The hour approaches Tam maun° ride—   must
That hour, o' night's black arch the key-stane,
70   That dreary hour Tam mounts his beast in,
And sic a night he taks the road in
As ne'er poor sinner was abroad in.
The wind blew as 'twad blawn its last;
The rattling showers rose on the blast;
75   The speedy gleams the darkness swallowed;
Loud, deep, and lang the thunder bellowed—
That night, a child might understand,
The Deil° had business on his hand!   Devil
Weel mounted on his grey mare Meg
80   (Better never lifted leg)
Tam skelpit° on through dub° and mire,   clattered / puddle
Despising wind, and rain, and fire;
Whiles holding fast his guid blue bonnet,
Whiles crooning o'er some auld Scots sonnet,
85   Whiles glow'ring round wi' prudent cares,
Lest bogles° catch him unawares!   spirits
Kirk-Alloway was drawing nigh,
Whare ghaists and houlets° nightly cry.   owls
       By this time he was cross the ford,
90   Whare in the snaw the chapman smoored;
And past the birks° and meikle° stane,   birches / great
Whare drunken Charlie brak's neck-bane;
And through the whins,° and by the cairn,   shrubs

Whare hunters fand the murdered bairn;
95 And near the thorn, aboon the well,
Whare Mungo's mither hanged hersel.
Before him Doon pours all his floods;
The doubling storm roars through the woods;
The lightning's flash from pole to pole;
100 Near and more near the thunders roll—
When, glimmering through the groaning trees,
Kirk-Alloway seemed in a bleeze:
Through ilka bore° the beams were glancing,   hole
And loud resounded mirth and dancing.
105 Inspiring bold John Barleycorn,
What dangers thou canst make us scorn!
Wi' tippenny,° we fear nae evil;   two-penny ale
Wi' usquabae,° we'll face the Devil!   whiskey
The swats° sae reamed in Tammie's noddle,   ale
110 Fair play, he cared na deils a boddle.
    But Maggie stood, right sair astonished,
Till, by the heel and hand admonished,
She ventured forward on the light,
And, wow, Tam saw an unco sight!—
115 Warlocks and witches in a dance—
Nae cotillion,° brent new frae France,   dance
But hornpipes, jigs, strathspeys° and reels,   Highland dances
Put life and mettle in their heels.
A winnock-bunker° in the east,   window-sill
120 There sat Auld Nick, in shape o'beast
(A tousie° tyke,° black, grim, and large)—   shaggy / dog
To gie them music was his charge.
He screwed the pipes and gart° them skirl,°   made / shriek
Till roof and rafters a' did dirl.°   resonate
125 Coffins stood round, like open presses,
That shawed the dead in their last dresses;
And, by some devilish cantraip° sleight,   magic
Each in its cauld hand held a light—
By which heroic Tam was able
130 To note upon the haly table,
A murderer's banes, in gibbet-airns;°   -irons
Twa span-lang, wee, unchristened bairns;°   children
A thief new-cutted frae a rape
(Wi' his last gasp his gab did gape);
135 Five tomahawks wi' bluid red-rusted;
Five scymitars wi' murder crusted;
A garter which a babe had strangled;
A knife a father's throat had mangled,
Whom his ain son o' life bereft—

140   The grey-hairs yet stack to the heft!—
      Wi' mair of horrible and awefu',
      Which even to name wad be unlawfu'.
          As Tammie glowred, amazed and curious,
      The mirth and fun grew fast and furious;
145   The piper loud and louder blew,
      The dancers quick and quicker flew,
      They reeled, they set, they crossed, they cleekit.°   held hands
      Till ilka carlin° swat° and reekit,°   witch / sweat / steamed
      And coost her duddies° to the wark,   clothes
150   And linket° at it in her sark!°   tripped / shirt
      Now Tam, oh Tam—had thae been queans,
      A' plump and strapping in their teens—
      Their sarks, instead o' creeshie° flannen,   greasy
      Been snaw-white seventeen-hunder linen,
155   Thir breeks° o' mine (my only pair   breeches
      That ance were plush, o' guid blue hair),
      I wad hae gi'en them off my hurdies°   buttocks
      For ae blink o' the bonnie burdies.°   girls
      But withered beldams, auld and droll,
      Rigwoodie° hags wad spean a foal,   scrawny
160   Louping° and flinging on a crummock,°   leaping / cane
      I wonder did na turn thy stomach!
          But Tam kend what was what fu' brawlie:°   well
      There was ae winsome wench and wawlie°   choice
      That night enlisted in the core,
165   Lang after kend on Carrick shore³—
      For monie a beast to dead she shot,
      An' perished monie a bonnie boat,
      And shook baith meikle° corn and bear,°   much / barley
      And kept the country-side in fear!
170   Her cutty° sark, o' Paisley harn,   short
      That while a lassie she had worn,
      In longitude though sorely scanty,
      It was her best, and she was vauntie.°   proud
      Ah, little kend thy reverend grannie,
175   That sark she coft° for her wee Nannie,   bought
      Wi' twa pund Scots ('twas a' her riches),
      Wad ever graced a dance of witches!
          But here my Muse her wing maun° cour,°   must / stoop
      Sic flights are far beyond her power—
180   To sing how Nannie lap and flang
      (A souple jade she was and strang),

---

³ **Carrick shore:** Carrick is a district of Ayrshire, Scotland.

And how Tam stood like ane bewitched,
And thought his very een enriched!
Even Satan glowred, and fidged° fu' fain,°   fidgeted / happy
185   And hotched° and blew wi' might and main;   jerked
Till—first ae caper, syne° anither—   then
Tam tint his reason a' thegither,
And roars out: 'Weel done, Cutty-sark!'
And in an instant all was dark;
190   And scarcely had he Maggie rallied,
When out the hellish legion sallied.
As bees bizz out wi' angry fyke,°   agitation
When plundering herds assail their byke,°   hive
As open pussie's° mortal foes,   hare's
195   When, pop! she starts before their nose;
As eager runs the market-crowd,
When 'Catch the thief!' resounds aloud—
So Maggie runs; the witches follow,
Wi' monie an eldritch° skriech and hollo!   unearthly
200   Ah, Tam! Ah, Tam! thou'll get thy fairin°—   reward
In hell they'll roast thee like a herrin!
In vain thy Kate awaits thy comin—
Kate soon will be a woefu' woman!
Now, do thy speedy utmost, Meg,
205   And win the key-stane of the brig;°   bridge
There, at them thou thy tail may toss,
A running stream they dare na cross!
But ere the key-stane she could make,
The fient a° tail she had to shake—   devil a
210   For Nannie, far before the rest,
Hard upon noble Maggie prest,
And flew at Tam wi' furious ettle!°   endeavor
But little wist she Maggie's mettle—
Ae spring brought off her master hale,°   whole
215   But left behind her ain grey tail:
The carlin° claught her by the rump,   old woman
And left poor Maggie scarce a stump!
    Now, wha this tale o' truth shall read,
Ilk man, and mother's son, take heed:
220   Whene'er to drink you are inclined,
Or cutty sarks run in your mind,
Think, ye may buy the joys o'er dear—
Remember Tam o' Shanter's mare!

WILLIAM WORDSWORTH (1770–1850)

Michael: A Pastoral Poem (1800)

If from the public way you turn your steps
Up the tumultuous brook of Greenhead Gill,[1]
    You will suppose that with an upright path
    Your feet must struggle; in such bold ascent
5   The pastoral mountains front you, face to face.
    But, courage! for around that boisterous brook
    The mountains have all opened out themselves,
    And made a hidden valley of their own.
    No habitation can be seen; but they
10   Who journey thither find themselves alone
    With a few sheep, with rocks and stones, and kites
    That overhead are sailing in the sky.
    It is in truth an utter solitude;
    Nor should I have made mention of this Dell
15   But for one object which you might pass by,
    Might see and notice not. Beside the brook
    Appears a straggling heap of unhewn stones!
    And to that simple object appertains
    A story—unenriched with strange events,
20   Yet not unfit, I deem, for the fireside,
    Or for the summer shade. It was the first
    Of those domestic tales that spake to me
    Of Shepherds, dwellers in the valleys, men
    Whom I already loved;—not verily
25   For their own sakes, but for the fields and hills
    Where was their occupation and abode.
    And hence this Tale, while I was yet a Boy
    Careless of books, yet having felt the power
    Of Nature, by the gentle agency
30   Of natural objects, led me on to feel
    For passions that were not my own, and think
    (At random and imperfectly indeed)
    On man, the heart of man, and human life.
    Therefore, although it be a history
35   Homely and rude, I will relate the same
    For the delight of a few natural hearts;
    And, with yet fonder feeling, for the sake

---

[1] **Greenhead Gill:** A gill signifies a narrow valley through which a stream passes. Greenhead Gill rises eastward from Grasmere, in England's Lake District.

Of youthful Poets, who among these hills
Will be my second self when I am gone.

40   Upon the forest-side in Grasmere Vale
There dwelt a Shepherd, Michael was his name;
An old man, stout of heart, and strong of limb.
His bodily frame had been from youth to age
Of an unusual strength: his mind was keen,
45   Intense, and frugal, apt for all affairs,
And in his shepherd's calling he was prompt
And watchful more than ordinary men.
Hence had he learned the meaning of all winds,
Of blasts of every tone; and oftentimes,
50   When others heeded not, he heard the South
Make subterraneous music, like the noise
Of bagpipers on distant Highland hills.
The Shepherd, at such warning, of his flock
Bethought him, and he to himself would say,
55   "The winds are now devising work for me!"
And, truly, at all times, the storm, that drives
The traveller to a shelter, summoned him
Up to the mountains: he had been alone
Amid the heart of many thousand mists,
60   That came to him, and left him, on the heights.
So lived he till his eightieth year was past.
And grossly that man errs, who should suppose
That the green valleys, and the streams and rocks,
Were things indifferent to the Shepherd's thoughts.
65   Fields, where with cheerful spirits he had breathed
The common air; hills, which with vigorous step
He had so often climbed; which had impressed
So many incidents upon his mind
Of hardship, skill or courage, joy or fear;
70   Which, like a book, preserved the memory
Of the dumb animals, whom he had saved,
Had fed or sheltered, linking to such acts
The certainty of honourable gain;
Those fields, those hills—what could they less? had laid
75   Strong hold on his affections, were to him
A pleasurable feeling of blind love,
The pleasure which there is in life itself.

His days had not been passed in singleness.
His Helpmate was a comely matron, old—
80   Though younger than himself full twenty years.
She was a woman of a stirring life,

Whose heart was in her house: two wheels she had
Of antique form; this large, for spinning wool;
That small, for flax; and, if one wheel had rest,
85   It was because the other was at work.
The Pair had but one inmate in their house,
An only Child, who had been born to them
When Michael, telling o'er his years, began
To deem that he was old,—in shepherd's phrase,
90   With one foot in the grave. This only Son,
With two brave sheep-dogs tried in many a storm,
The one of an inestimable worth,
Made all their household. I may truly say,
That they were as a proverb in the vale
95   For endless industry. When day was gone,
And from their occupations out of doors
The Son and Father were come home, even then,
Their labour did not cease; unless when all
Turned to the cleanly supper-board, and there,
100   Each with a mess of pottage and skimmed milk,
Sat round the basket piled with oaten cakes,
And their plain home-made cheese. Yet when the meal
Was ended, Luke (for so the Son was named)
And his old Father both betook themselves
105   To such convenient work as might employ
Their hands by the fireside; perhaps to card
Wool for the Housewife's spindle, or repair
Some injury done to sickle, flail, or scythe,
Or other implement of house or field.

110   Down from the ceiling, by the chimney's edge,
That in our ancient uncouth country style
With huge and black projection overbrowed
Large space beneath, as duly as the light
Of day grew dim the Housewife hung a lamp,
115   An aged utensil, which had performed
Service beyond all others of its kind.
Early at evening did it burn—and late,
Surviving comrade of uncounted hours,
Which, going by from year to year, had found,
120   And left the couple neither gay perhaps
Nor cheerful, yet with objects and with hopes,
Living a life of eager industry.
And now, when Luke had reached his eighteenth year,
There by the light of this old lamp they sate,
125   Father and Son, while far into the night
The Housewife plied her own peculiar work,

Making the cottage through the silent hours
Murmur as with the sound of summer flies.
This light was famous in its neighbourhood,
130   And was a public symbol of the life
That thrifty Pair had lived. For, as it chanced,
Their cottage on a plot of rising ground
Stood single, with large prospect, north and south,
High into Easedale, up to Dunmail-Raise,[2]
135   And westward to the village near the lake;
And from this constant light, so regular
And so far seen, the House itself, by all
Who dwelt within the limits of the vale,
Both old and young, was named The Evening Star.

140   Thus living on through such a length of years,
The Shepherd, if he loved himself, must needs
Have loved his Helpmate; but to Michael's heart
This son of his old age was yet more dear—
Less from instinctive tenderness, the same
145   Fond spirit that blindly works in the blood of all—
Than that a child, more than all other gifts
That earth can offer to declining man,
Brings hope with it, and forward-looking thoughts,
And stirrings of inquietude, when they
150   By tendency of nature needs must fail.
Exceeding was the love he bare to him,
His heart and his heart's joy! For oftentimes
Old Michael, while he was a babe in arms,
Had done him female service, not alone
155   For pastime and delight, as is the use
Of fathers, but with patient mind enforced
To acts of tenderness; and he had rocked
His cradle, as with a woman's gentle hand.

          And, in a later time, ere yet the Boy
160   Had put on boy's attire, did Michael love,
Albeit of a stern unbending mind,
To have the Young-one in his sight, when he
Wrought in the field, or on his shepherd's stool
Sate with a fettered sheep before him stretched
165   Under the large old oak, that near his door
Stood single, and, from matchless depth of shade,
Chosen for the Shearer's covert from the sun,

---

[2] **Dunmail-Raise:** Pass from Grasmere to Keswick.

Thence in our rustic dialect was called
The Clipping Tree, a name which yet it bears.
170 There, while they two were sitting in the shade,
With others round them, earnest all and blithe,
Would Michael exercise his heart with looks
Of fond correction and reproof bestowed
Upon the Child, if he disturbed the sheep
175 By catching at their legs, or with his shouts
Scared them, while they lay still beneath the shears.

And when by Heaven's good grace the boy grew up
A healthy Lad, and carried in his cheek
Two steady roses that were five years old;
180 Then Michael from a winter coppice cut
With his own hand a sapling, which he hooped
With iron, making it throughout in all
Due requisites a perfect shepherd's staff,
And gave it to the Boy; wherewith equipt
185 He as a watchman oftentimes was placed
At gate or gap, to stem or turn the flock;
And, to his office prematurely called,
There stood the urchin, as you will divine,
Something between a hindrance and a help,
190 And for this cause not always, I believe,
Receiving from his Father hire of praise;
Though nought was left undone which staff, or voice,
Or looks, or threatening gestures, could perform.

But soon as Luke, full ten years old, could stand
195 Against the mountain blasts; and to the heights,
Not fearing toil, nor length of weary ways,
He with his Father daily went, and they
Were as companions, why should I relate
That objects which the Shepherd loved before
200 Were dearer now? that from the Boy there came
Feelings and emanations—things which were
Light to the sun and music to the wind;
And that the old Man's heart seemed born again?

Thus in his Father's sight the Boy grew up:
205 And now, when he had reached his eighteenth year,
He was his comfort and his daily hope.

While this good household thus were living on
From day to day, to Michael's ear there came
Distressful tidings. Long before the time

210 Of which I speak, the shepherd had been bound
     In surety for his brother's son, a man
     Of an industrious life and ample means,
     But unforeseen misfortunes suddenly
     Had pressed upon him, and old Michael now
215 Was summoned to discharge the forfeiture—
     A grievous penalty, but little less
     Than half his substance. This unlooked-for claim,
     At the first hearing, for a moment took
     More hope out of his life than he supposed
220 That any old man ever could have lost.
     As soon as he had gathered so much strength
     That he could look his trouble in the face,
     It seemed that his sole refuge was to sell
     A portion of his patrimonial fields.
225 Such was his first resolve; he thought again,
     And his heart failed him.
                              'Isabel', said he,
     Two evenings after he had heard the news,
     'I have been toiling more than seventy years,
230 And in the open sunshine of God's love
     Have we all lived, yet if these fields of ours
     Should pass into a stranger's hands, I think
     That I could not lie quiet in my grave.
     Our lot is a hard lot; the sun itself
235 Has scarcely been more diligent than I,
     And I have lived to be a fool at last
     To my own family. An evil man
     That was, and made an evil choice, if he
     Were false to us; and if he were not false,
240 There are ten thousand to whom loss like this
     Had been no sorrow. I forgive him—but
     'Twere better to be dumb than to talk thus!
     When I began, my purpose was to speak
     Of remedies and of a cheerful hope.
245 Our Luke shall leave us, Isabel; the land
     Shall not go from us, and it shall be free—
     He shall possess it, free as is the wind
     That passes over it. We have, thou knowest,
     Another kinsman; he will be our friend
250 In this distress. He is a prosperous man,
     Thriving in trade, and Luke to him shall go
     And with his kinsman's help and his own thrift
     He quickly will repair this loss, and then
     May come again to us. If here he stay,

255   What can be gained?'
                      At this the old man paused,
      And Isabel sat silent, for her mind
      Was busy looking back into past times:
      'There's Richard Bateman', thought she to herself,
260   'He was a parish-boy—at the church-door
      They made a gathering for him, shillings, pence
      And halfpennies, wherewith the neighbours bought
      A basket, which they filled with pedlar's wares,
      And with this basket on his arm the lad
265   Went up to London, found a master there,
      Who out of many chose the trusty boy
      To go and overlook his merchandise
      Beyond the seas, where he grew wondrous rich
      And left estates and moneys to the poor,
270   And at his birthplace built a chapel, floored
      With marble which he sent from foreign lands.'
          These thoughts, and many others of like sort,
      . Passed quickly through the mind of Isabel,
      And her face brightened. The old man was glad,
275   And thus resumed: 'Well, Isabel, this scheme
      These two days has been meat and drink to me:
      Far more than we have lost is left us yet.
      We have enough—I wish indeed that I
      Were younger, but this hope is a good hope.
280   Make ready Luke's best garments; of the best
      Buy for him more, and let us send him forth
      Tomorrow, or the next day, or tonight—
      If he could go, the boy should go tonight!'
          Here Michael ceased, and to the fields went forth
285   With a light heart. The housewife for five days
      Was restless morn and night, and all day long
      Wrought on with her best fingers to prepare
      Things needful for the journey of her son.
      But Isabel was glad when Sunday came
290   To stop her in her work; for when she lay
      By Michael's side, she for the two last nights
      Heard him, how he was troubled in his sleep;
      And when they rose at morning she could see
      That all his hopes were gone. That day at noon
295   She said to Luke, while they two by themselves
      Were sitting at the door: 'Thou must not go,
      We have no other child but thee to lose,
      None to remember—do not go away,
      For if thou leave thy father he will die.'

300   The lad made answer with a jocund° voice,   high-spirited
       And Isabel, when she had told her fears,
       Recovered heart. That evening her best fare
       Did she bring forth, and all together sat
       Like happy people round a Christmas fire.
305   Next morning Isabel resumed her work,
       And all the ensuing week the house appeared
       As cheerful as a grove in spring. At length
       The expected letter from their kinsman came,
       With kind assurances that he would do
310   His utmost for the welfare of the boy—
       To which requests were added that forthwith
       He might be sent to him. Ten times or more
       The letter was read over; Isabel
       Went forth to show it to the neighbours round;
315   Nor was there at that time on English land
       A prouder heart than Luke's. When Isabel
       Had to her house returned the old man said,
       'He shall depart tomorrow.' To this word
       The housewife answered, talking much of things
320   Which, if at such short notice he should go,
       Would surely be forgotten—but at length
       She gave consent, and Michael was at ease.
           Near the tumultuous brook of Greenhead Gill
       In that deep valley, Michael had designed
325   To build a sheepfold, and before he heard
       The tidings of his melancholy loss
       For this same purpose he had gathered up
       A heap of stones, which close to the brook-side
       Lay thrown together, ready for the work.
330   With Luke that evening thitherward he walked,
       And soon as they had reached the place he stopped,
       And thus the old man spake to him: 'My son,
       Tomorrow thou wilt leave me. With full heart
       I look upon thee, for thou art the same
335   That wert a promise to me ere thy birth,
       And all thy life hast been my daily joy,
       I will relate to thee some little part
       Of our two histories—'twill do thee good
       When thou art from me, even if I should speak
340   Of things thou canst not know of.
                                        After thou
       First camest into the world, as it befalls
       To newborn infants, thou didst sleep away
       Two days, and blessings from thy father's tongue
345   Then fell upon thee. Day by day passed on,

And still I loved thee with increasing love
Never to living ear came sweeter sounds
Than when I heard thee by our own fireside
First uttering without words a natural tune—
350 When thou, a feeding babe, didst in thy joy
Sing at thy mother's breast. Month followed month,
And in the open fields my life was passed,
And in the mountains, else I think that thou
Hadst been brought up upon thy father's knees!
355 But we were playmates, Luke: among these hills,
As well thou knowest, in us the old and young
Have played together!—nor with me didst thou
Lack any pleasure which a boy can know.'
  Luke had a manly heart; but at these words
360 He sobbed aloud. The old man grasped his hand,
And said, 'Nay, do not take it so—I see
That these are things of which I need not speak.
Even to the utmost have I been to thee
A kind and a good father; and herein
365 I but repay a gift which I myself
Received at others' hands, for though now old
Beyond the common life of man I still
Remember them who loved me in my youth.
Both of them sleep together—here they lived
370 As all their forefathers had done; and when
At length their time was come, they were not loath
To give their bodies to the family mould.
  I wished that thou shouldst live the life they lived;
But 'tis a long time to look back, my son,
375 And see so little gain from sixty years.
These fields were burdened when they came to me:
Till I was forty years of age, not more
Than half of my inheritance was mine.
I toiled and toiled—God blest me in my work,
380 And till these three weeks past the land was free.
I looks as if it never could endure
Another master! Heaven forgive me, Luke,
If I judge ill for thee, but it seems good
That thou shouldst go.'
385   At this the old man paused,
Then, pointing to the stones near which they stood,
Thus after a short silence he resumed:
'This was a work for us, and now, my son,
It is a work for me! But, lay one stone—
390 There, lay it for me, Luke, with thine own hands—
I for the purpose brought thee to this place.

Nay, boy, be of good hope, we both may live
To see a better day! At eighty-four
I still am strong and stout: do thou thy part,
395   I will do mine. I will begin again
With many tasks that were resigned to thee:
Up to the heights, and in among the storms,
Will I without thee go again, and do
All works which I was wont to do alone
400   Before I knew thy face.
                            Heaven bless thee,
Thy heart these two weeks has been beating fast
With many hopes. It should be so—yes, yes—
I knew that thou couldst never have a wish
405   To leave me, Luke. Thou hast been bound to me
Only by links of love! When thou art gone
What will be left to us?—but I forget
My purposes. Lay now the corner-stone
As I requested, and hereafter, Luke,
410   When thou art gone away, should evil men
Be thy companions, let this sheepfold be
Thy anchor and thy shield. Amid all fear,
And all temptation, let it be to thee
An emblem of the life thy fathers lived,
415   Who, being innocent, did for that cause
Bestir them in good deeds. Now, fare thee well.
When thou returnst, thou in this place wilt see
A work which is not here. A covenant
'Twill be between us—but whatever fate
420   Befall thee, I shall love thee to the last,
And bear thy memory with me to the grave.'
    The shepherd ended here, and Luke stooped down
And, as his father had requested, laid
The first stone of the sheepfold. At the sight
425   The old man's grief broke from him. To his heart
He pressed his son; he kissed him and he wept,
And to the house together they returned.
Next morning, as had been resolved, the boy
Began his journey; and when he had reached
430   The public way he put on a bold face,
And all the neighbours as he passed their doors
Came forth with wishes and with farewell prayers
That followed him till he was out of sight.
    A good report did from their kinsman come
435   Of Luke and his well-doing; and the boy
Wrote loving letters, full of wondrous news,
Which, as the housewife phrased it, were throughout

The prettiest letters that were ever seen!
Both parents read them with rejoicing hearts.
440 So many months passed on, and once again
The shepherd went about his daily work
With confident and cheerful thoughts; and now
Sometimes when he could find a leisure hour
He to that valley took his way, and there
445 Wrought at the sheepfold. Meantime Luke began
To slacken in his duty, and at length
He in the dissolute city gave himself
To evil courses. Ignominy and shame
Fell on him, so that he was driven at last
450 To seek a hiding-place beyond the seas.
    There is a comfort in the strength of love,
'Twill make a thing endurable which else
Would break the heart—old Michael found it so.
I have conversed with more than one who well
455 Remember the old man, and what he was
Years after he had heard this heavy news.
His bodily frame had been from youth to age
Of an unusual strength. Among the rocks
He went, and still looked up upon the sun
460 And listened to the wind, and, as before,
Performed all kinds of labour for his sheep
And for the land, his small inheritance.
And to that hollow dell from time to time
Did he repair, to build the fold of which
465 His flock had need. 'Tis not forgotten yet
The pity which was then in every heart
And the old man, and 'tis believed by all
That many and many a day he thither went,
And never lifted up a single stone.
470   There by the sheepfold sometimes was he seen
Sitting alone, with that his faithful dog
(Then old) beside him, lying at his feet.
The length of full seven years from time to time
He at the building of this sheepfold wrought,
475 And left the work unfinished when he died.
Three years, or little more, did Isabel
Survive her husband; at her death the estate
Was sold, and went into a stranger's hand.
The cottage which was named the Evening Star
480 Is gone; the ploughshare has been through the ground
On which it stood. Great changes have been wrought
In all the neighbourhood; yet the oak is left
That grew beside their door, and the remains

Of the unfinished sheepfold may be seen
485   Beside the boisterous brook of Greenhead Gill.

JOHN KEATS (1795–1821)

The Eve of St Agnes (1813; 1820)

1

St Agnes' Eve[1]—ah, bitter chill it was!
The owl, for all his feathers, was a-cold;
The hare limped trembling through the frozen grass,
And silent was the flock in woolly fold;
5   Numb were the Beadsman's[2] fingers, while he told
His rosary, and while his frosted breath,
Like pious incense from a censer old,
Seemed taking flight for Heaven, without a death,
Past the sweet Virgin's picture, while his prayer he saith.

2

10   His prayer he saith, this patient holy man;
Then takes his lamp, and riseth from his knees,
And back returneth, meagre, barefoot, wan,
Along the chapel-aisle by slow degrees.
The sculptured dead, on each side, seem to freeze,
15   Imprisoned in black, purgatorial rails:
Knights, ladies, praying in dumb oratories,[3]
He passeth by, and his weak spirit fails
To think how they may ache in icy hoods and mails.

3

Northward he turneth through a little door,
20   And scarce three steps, ere music's golden tongue
Flattered to tears this agéd man and poor;
But no—already had his deathbell rung;

---

[1] **St Agnes' Eve:** St. Agnes, holding herself to be the wife of Christ, was martyred on January 21 (in the fourth century A.D.) when she would not marry an unbeliever. St. Agnes' Eve occurs on January 20, a night when virgins might see a vision of their future husband if they observe certain rites.
[2] **Beadsman's:** An impoverished person paid to pray for his benefactor.
[3] **oratories:** Small chapel within a church.

The joys of all his life were said and sung—
His was harsh penance on St Agnes' Eve!
25   Another way he went, and soon among
Rough ashes sat he for his soul's reprieve,
And all night kept awake, for sinners' sake to grieve.

4

That ancient Beadsman heard the prelude soft—
And so it chanced, for many a door was wide
30   From hurry to and fro. Soon, up aloft,
The silver snarling trumpets gan to chide;
The level chambers, ready with their pride,
Were glowing to receive a thousand guests;
The carvéd angels, ever eager-eyed,
35   Stared, where upon their heads the cornice rests,
With hair blown back, and wings put cross-wise on their breasts.

5

At length burst in the argent revelry,
With plume, tiara, and all rich array,
Numerous as shadows haunting fairily
40   The brain, new stuffed in youth with triumphs gay
Of old romance. These let us wish away,
And turn, sole-thoughted, to one lady there,
Whose heart had brooded all that wintry day
On love, and winged St Agnes' saintly care—
45   As she had heard old dames full many times declare.

6

They told her how upon St Agnes' Eve
Young virgins might have visions of delight,
And soft adorings from their loves receive
Upon the honeyed middle of the night,
50   If ceremonies due they did aright—
As, supperless to bed they must retire,
And couch supine° their beauties, lily white;   lying face upward
Nor look behind, nor sideways, but require
Of Heaven with upward eyes for all that they desire.

7

55   Full of this whim was thoughtful Madeline:
The music, yearning like a god in pain,
She scarcely heard; her maiden eyes divine,
Fixed on the floor, saw many a sweeping train
Pass by—she heeded not at all. In vain

60 Came many a tiptoe amorous cavalier,
   And back retired—not cooled by high disdain,
   But she saw not. Her heart was otherwhere:
   She sighed for Agnes' dreams, the sweetest of the year.

8

   She danced along with vague regardless eyes,
65 Anxious her lips, her breathing quick and short.
   The hallowed hour was near at hand—she sighs
   Amid the timbrels,° and the thronged resort   hand drums
   Of whisperers in anger, or in sport,
   Mid looks of love, defiance, hate, and scorn,
70 Hoodwinked with faery fancy—all amort,°   indifferent
   Save to St Agnes and her lambs unshorn,
   And all the bliss to be before tomorrow morn.

9

   So, purposing each moment to retire,
   She lingered still. Meantime, across the moors
75 Had come young Porphyro, with heart on fire
   For Madeline. Beside the portal-doors,
   Buttressed from moonlight, stands he and implores
   All saints to give him sight of Madeline
   But for one moment in the tedious hours,
80 That he might gaze and worship all unseen—
   Perchance speak, kneel, touch, kiss! In sooth such things have been.

10

   He ventures in! Let no buzzed whisper tell—
   All eyes be muffled, or a hundred swords
   Will storm his heart, love's feverous citadel.
85 For him, those chambers held barbarian hordes,
   Hyena foemen and hot-blooded lords,
   Whose very dogs would execrations howl
   Against his lineage. Not one breast affords
   Him any mercy in that mansion foul,
90 Save one old beldame,° weak in body and in soul.   old woman

11

   Ah, happy chance—the agéd creature came,
   Shuffling along with ivory-headed wand,
   To where he stood, hid from the torch's flame
   Behind a broad hall-pillar, far beyond
95 The sound of merriment and chorus bland.°   blended
   He startled her; but soon she knew his face

And grasped his fingers in her palsied hand,
Saying, 'Mercy, Porphyro! Hie thee from this place—
They are all here to-night, the whole bloodthirsty race!

12

100 Get hence! Get hence! There's dwarfish Hildebrand;
     He had a fever late, and in the fit
     He curséd thee and thine, both house and land—
     Then there's that old Lord Maurice, not a whit
     More tame for his grey hairs! Alas me, flit!
105 Flit like a ghost away!' 'Ah, Gossip dear,
     We're safe enough—here in this armchair sit,
     And tell me how—' 'Good saints not here, not here!
Follow me, child, or else these stones will be thy bier.'°   coffin

13

     He followed through a lowly archéd way,
110 Brushing the cobwebs with his lofty plume,
     And as she muttered, 'Well-a—well-a-day!'
     He found him in a little moonlight room,
     Pale, latticed, chill, and silent as a tomb.
     'Now tell me where is Madeline', said he,
115 'Oh tell me, Angela, by the holy loom
     Which none but secret sisterhood may see,
When they St Agnes' wool are weaving piously.'

14

     'St Agnes? Ah, it is St Agnes' Eve—
     Yet men will murder upon holy days:
120 Thou must hold water in a witch's sieve,
     And be liege-lord of all the elves and fays,
     To venture so! It fills me with amaze
     To see thee, Porphyro! St Agnes' Eve!
     God's help! My lady fair the conjuror plays[4]
125 This very night—good angels her deceive!
But let me laugh awhile, I've mickle° time to grieve.'   much

15

     Feebly she laugheth in the languid moon,
     While Porphyro upon her face doth look,
     Like puzzled urchin on an agéd crone

---

[4] **My lady . . . plays:** I.e., is attempting magic spells.

130   Who keepeth closed a wondrous riddle-book,
      As spectacled she sits in chimney nook.
      But soon his eyes grew brilliant, when she told
      His lady's purpose; and he scarce could brook°   hold back
      Tears at the thought of those enchantments cold,
135 And Madeline asleep in lap of legends old.

                              16

      Sudden a thought came like a full-blown rose,
      Flushing his brow, and in his painéd heart
      Made purple riot. Then doth he propose
      A stratagem that makes the beldame start:
140   'A cruel man and impious thou art!
      Sweet lady, let her pray, and sleep, and dream
      Alone with her good angels, far apart
      From wicked men like thee. Go, go!—I deem
Thou canst not surely be the same that thou didst seem.'

                              17

145   'I will not harm her, by all saints I swear',
      Quoth Porphyro. 'Oh may I ne'er find grace
      When my weak voice shall whisper its last prayer,
      If one of her soft ringlets I displace,
      Or look with ruffian passion in her face!
150   Good Angela, believe me by these tears;
      Or I will, even in a moment's space,
      Awake, with horrid shout, my foemen's ears,
      And beard° them, though they be more fanged than wolves and   challenge
            bears.'

                              18

      'Ah, why wilt thou affright a feeble soul—
155   A poor, weak, palsy-stricken, churchyard thing,[5]
      Whose passing-bell may ere the midnight toll,
      Whose prayers for thee each morn and evening
      Were never missed?' Thus plaining,° doth she bring   complaining
      A gentler speech from burning Porphyro,
160   So woeful, and of such deep sorrowing,
      That Angela gives promise she will do
Whatever he shall wish, betide her weal or woe—

---

[5] **churchyard thing:** In other words, close to death.

19

Which was, to lead him in close secrecy
Even to Madeline's chamber, and there hide
165   Him in a closet of such privacy
That he might see her beauty unespied,
And win perhaps that night a peerless bride,
While legioned fairies paced the coverlet
And pale enchantment held her sleepy-eyed.
170   Never on such a night have lovers met,
Since Merlin[6] paid his demon all the monstrous debt!

20

'It shall be as thou wishest', said the dame,
All cates° and dainties shall be storéd there   delicacies
Quickly on this feast-night—by the tambour-frame°   embroidery frame
175   Her own lute thou wilt see—no time to spare
For I am slow and feeble, and scarce dare
On such a catering trust my dizzy head!
Wait here, my child, with patience; kneel in prayer
The while. Ah! thou must needs the lady wed,
180   Or may I never leave my grave among the dead!'

21

So saying, she hobbled off with busy fear.
The lover's endless minutes slowly passed;
The dame returned, and whispered in his ear
To follow her—with agéd eyes aghast
185   From fright of dim espial. Safe at last,
Through many a dusky gallery, they gain
The maiden's chamber, silken, hushed, and chaste;
Where Porphyro took covert, pleased amain—
His poor guide hurried back with agues° in her brain.   chills

22

190   Her faltering hand upon the balustrade,°   railing
Old Angela was feeling for the stair,
When Madeline, St Agnes' charméd maid,
Rose, like a missioned spirit, unaware.
With silver taper's light, and pious care,
195   She turned, and down the agéd gossip led
To a safe level matting. Now prepare,

---

[6] **Merlin:** Great magician of Arthurian legends and son of a demon.

Young Porphyro, for gazing on that bed—
She comes, she comes again, like ring-dove frayed° and fled.   afraid

23

Out went the taper as she hurried in—
200   Its little smoke in pallid moonshine died—
She closed the door, she panted, all akin
To spirits of the air, and visions wide.
No uttered syllable (or, woe betide!)
But to her heart, her heart was voluble,
205   Paining with eloquence her balmy side,
As though a tongueless nightingale should swell
Her throat in vain, and die, heart-stifled, in her dell.

24

A casement high and triple-arched there was,
All garlanded with carven imageries
210   Of fruits, and flowers, and bunches of knot-grass,
And diamonded with panes of quaint device,
Innumerable of stains and splendid dyes
As are the tiger-moth's deep-damasked wings;
And in the midst, 'mong thousand heraldries,
215   And twilight saints, and dim emblazonings,
A shielded scutcheon blushed with blood of queens and kings.[7]

25

Full on this casement shone the wintry moon,
And threw warm gules[8] on Madeline's fair breast
As down she knelt for Heaven's grace and boon;
220   Rose-bloom fell on her hands, together prest,
And on her silver cross soft amethyst,
And on her hair a glory,° like a saint: halo
She seemed a splendid angel, newly drest,
Save wings, for Heaven—Porphyro grew faint:
225   She knelt, so pure a thing, so free from mortal taint.

26

Anon his heart revives. Her vespers done,
Of all its wreathéd pearls her hair she frees,
Unclasps her warméd jewels one by one,
Loosens her fragrant bodice—by degrees
230   Her rich attire creeps rustling to her knees.

---

[7] **shielded . . . kings:** A coat of arms marked by royal ancestry.
[8] **gules:** Heraldic term for red, cast here as the moon shines through stained glass.

Half-hidden, like a mermaid in sea-weed,
Pensive awhile she dreams awake, and sees,
In fancy, fair St Agnes in her bed,
But dares not look behind, or all the charm is fled.

27

235   Soon, trembling in her soft and chilly nest,
In sort of wakeful swoon, perplexed she lay,
Until the poppied warmth of sleep oppressed
Her soothéd limbs, and soul fatigued away—
Flown, like a thought, until the morrow-day;
240   Blissfully havened both from joy and pain;
Clasped like a missal° where swart Paynims° pray;   prayer book / Pagans
Blinded alike from sunshine and from rain,
As though a rose should shut, and be a bud again!

28

Stolen to this paradise, and so entranced,
245   Porphyro gazed upon her empty dress
And listened to her breathing, if it chanced
To wake into a slumberous tenderness—
Which when he heard, that minute did he bless,
And breathed himself; then from the closet crept,
250   Noiseless as fear in a wide wilderness,
And over the hushed carpet, silent, stepped
And 'tween the curtains peeped, where, lo—how fast she slept!

29

Then by the bedside, where the faded moon
Made a dim silver twilight, soft he set
255   A table, and, half anguished, threw thereon
A cloth of woven crimson, gold, and jet—
Oh for some drowsy Morphean amulet![9]
The boisterous, midnight, festive clarion,
The kettle-drum and far-heard clarionet,
260   Affray his ears, though but in dying tone:
The hall door shuts again, and all the noise is gone.

30

And still she slept an azure-liddéd sleep,
In blanchéd linen, smooth and lavendered,
While he from forth the closet brought a heap

---

[9] **Morphean amulet:** An object wielding the power of Morpheus, the roman god of sleep and dreams.

265 Of candied apple, quince, and plum, and gourd;
  With jellies soother than the creamy curd,
  And lucent syrops, tinct with cinnamon;
  Manna and dates, in argosy transferred
  From Fez;° and spicéd dainties, every one,   *Moroccan city*
270 From silken Samarcand to cedared Lebanon.[10]

31

  These delicates he heaped with glowing hand
  On golden dishes and in baskets bright
  Of wreathéd silver—sumptuous they stand
  In the retiréd quiet of the night,
275 Filling the chilly room with perfume light:
  'And now, my love, my seraph fair, awake!
  Thou art my Heaven, and I thine eremite.°   *hermit*
  Open thine eyes, for meek St Agnes' sake,
Or I shall drowse beside thee, so my soul doth ache.'

32

280 Thus whispering, his warm, unnervéd arm
  Sank in her pillow. Shaded was her dream
  By the dusk curtains—'twas a midnight charm
  Impossible to melt as icéd stream!
  The lustrous salvers° in the moonlight gleam;   *serving platters*
285 Broad golden fringe upon the carpet lies:
  It seemed he never, never could redeem
  From such a stedfast spell his lady's eyes,
So mused awhile, entoiled in wooféd° fantasies.   *intricate*

33

  Awakening up, he took her hollow lute
290 Tumultuous, and, in chords that tenderest be,
  He played an ancient ditty, long since mute,
  In Provence called *La Belle Dame Sans Mercy*,[11]
  Close to her ear touching the melody.
  Wherewith disturbed, she uttered a soft moan—
295 He ceased—she panted quick—and suddenly
  Her blue affrayéd eyes wide open shone:
Upon his knees he sank, pale as smooth-sculptured stone.

---

[10] **Samarcand . . . Lebanon:** Ancient places associated with opulence and wealth.
[11] **Provence . . . Mercy:** Provence was a province in southeastern France. The tune, in French, translates as "The lady beautiful but without mercy."

34

Her eyes were open, but she still beheld,
Now wide awake, the vision of her sleep.
300   There was a painful change, that nigh expelled
The blisses of her dream so pure and deep—
At which fair Madeline began to weep,
And moan forth witless words with many a sigh,
While still her gaze on Porphyro would keep;
305   Who knelt, with joinéd hands and piteous eye,
Fearing to move or speak, she looked so dreamingly.

35

'Ah, Porphyro!' said she, 'but even now
Thy voice was at sweet tremble in mine ear,
Made tuneable with every sweetest vow,
310   And those sad eyes were spiritual and clear.
How changed thou art! How pallid, chill, and drear!
Give me that voice again, my Porphyro,
Those looks immortal, those complainings dear—
Oh leave me not in this eternal woe,
315 For if thou diest, my love, I know not where to go.'

36

Beyond a mortal man impassioned far
At these voluptuous accents, he arose,
Ethereal, flushed, and, like a throbbing star
Seen mid the sapphire heaven's deep repose,
320   Into her dream he melted, as the rose
Blendeth its odour with the violet—
Solution sweet! Meantime the frost-wind blows
Like love's alarum pattering the sharp sleet
Against the window-panes. St Agnes' moon hath set.

37

325   'Tis dark—quick pattereth the flaw-blown° sleet: wind-blown
'This is no dream, my bride, my Madeline!'
'Tis dark—the icéd gusts still rave and beat:
'No dream, alas! alas! and woe is mine!
Porphyro will leave me here to fade and pine—
330   Cruel! What traitor could thee hither bring?
I curse not, for my heart is lost in thine,
Though thou forsakest a deceivéd thing,
A dove forlorn and lost with sick unprunéd wing.'

38

'My Madeline! Sweet dreamer! Lovely bride!
335   Say, may I be for aye thy vassal blest—
        Thy beauty's shield, heart-shaped and vermeil° dyed?   vermilion
        Ah, silver shrine, here will I take my rest
        After so many hours of toil and quest,
        A famished pilgrim saved by miracle!
340   Though I have found, I will not rob thy nest,
        Saving of thy sweet self—if thou thinkst well
    To trust, fair Madeline, to no rude infidel.

39

Hark! 'Tis an elfin-storm from faery land,
        Of haggard° seeming, but a boon indeed!   wild
345   Arise, arise! The morning is at hand—
        The bloated wassaillers° will never heed—   drunk rioters
        Let us away, my love, with happy speed!
        There are no ears to hear, or eyes to see,
        Drowned all in Rhenish and the sleepy mead.[12]
350   Awake! Arise, my love, and fearless be,
    For o'er the southern moors I have a home for thee!'

40

She hurried at his words, beset with fears,
        For there were sleeping dragons all around,
        At glaring watch, perhaps with ready spears;
355   Down the wide stairs a darkling way they found.
        In all the house was heard no human sound:
        A chain-drooped lamp was flickering by each door;
        The arras,° rich with horseman, hawk, and hound,   tapestries
        Fluttered in the besieging wind's uproar;
360   And the long carpets rose along the gusty floor.

41

They glide, like phantoms, into the wide hall—
        Like phantoms, to the iron porch, they glide—
        Where lay the porter, in uneasy sprawl,
        With a huge empty flagon by his side!
365   The wakeful bloodhound rose, and shook his hide,
        But his sagacious eye an inmate owns;
        By one, and one, the bolts full easy slide,
        The chains lie silent on the footworn stones;
    The key turns, and the door upon its hinges groans,

---

[12] **Rhenish . . . mead:** Rhine wine, and a fermented mixture of honey and water.

42

370 And they are gone—aye, ages long ago
These lovers fled away into the storm!
That night the Baron dreamt of many a woe,
And all his warrior-guests, with shade and form
Of witch, and demon, and large coffin-worm,
375 Were long be-nightmared. Angela the old
Died palsy-twitched, with meagre face deform;
The Beadsman, after thousand avés° told,   prayers
For aye unsought for, slept among his ashes cold.

HENRY WADSWORTH LONGFELLOW (1807–1882)

Paul Revere's Ride (1863)

Listen, my children, and you shall hear
Of the midnight ride of Paul Revere,
On the eighteenth of April, in Seventy-five;
Hardly a man is now alive
5   Who remembers that famous day and year.

He said to his friend, 'If the British march
By land or sea from the town tonight,
Hang a lantern aloft in the belfry arch
Of the North Church tower as a signal light—
10 One, if by land, and two, if by sea;
And I on the opposite shore will be,
Ready to ride and spread the alarm
Through every Middlesex[1] village and farm,
For the country folk to be up and to arm.'

15 Then he said 'Good night!' and with muffled oar
Silently rowed to the Charlestown shore,
Just as the moon rose over the bay,
Where swinging wide at her moorings lay
The *Somerset*, British man-of-war;
20 A phantom ship, with each mast and spar
Across the moon like a prison bar,
And a huge black hulk, that was magnified
By its own reflection in the tide.

---

[1] **Middesex:** County outside of Boston, Massachusetts, where the Revolutionary War began on April 18, 1775. The villages mentioned in the poem are all a part of Middlesex County.

Meanwhile, his friend, through alley and street,
25   Wanders and watches with eager ears,
Till in the silence around him he hears
The muster of men at the barrack door,
The sound of arms, and the tramp of feet,
And the measured tread of the grenadiers°   infantry men
30   Marching down to their boats on the shore.

Then he climbed the tower of the Old North Church,
By the wooden stairs, with stealthy tread,
To the belfry chamber overhead,
And startled the pigeons from their perch
35   On the sombre rafters, that round him made
Masses and moving shapes of shade—
By the trembling ladder, steep and tall,
To the highest window in the wall,
Where he paused to listen and look down
40   A moment on the roofs of the town,
And the moonlight flowing over all.

Beneath, in the churchyard, lay the dead,
In their night-encampment on the hill,
Wrapped in silence so deep and still
45   That he could hear, like a sentinel's tread,
The watchful night-wind, as it went
Creeping along from tent to tent,
And seeming to whisper, 'All is well!'
A moment only he feels the spell
50   Of the place and the hour, and the secret dread
Of the lonely belfry and the dead;
For suddenly all his thoughts are bent
On a shadowy something far away,
Where the river widens to meet the bay—
55   A line of black that bends and floats
On the rising tide, like a bridge of boats.

Meanwhile, impatient to mount and ride,
Booted and spurred, with a heavy stride
On the opposite shore walked Paul Revere.
60   Now he patted his horse's side,
Now gazed at the landscape far and near,
Then, impetuous, stamped the earth,
And turned and tightened his saddle-girth;
But mostly he watched with eager search
65   The belfry-tower of the Old North Church,
As it rose above the graves on the hill,
Lonely and spectral and sombre and still.

And lo! as he looks, on the belfry's height
A glimmer, and then a gleam of light!
70   He springs to the saddle, the bridle he turns,
But lingers and gazes, till full on his sight
A second lamp in the belfry burns!

A hurry of hoofs in a village street,
A shape in the moonlight, a bulk in the dark,
75   And beneath, from the pebbles, in passing, a spark
Struck out by a steed flying fearless and fleet:
That was all! And yet, through the gloom and the light,
The fate of a nation was riding that night;
And the spark struck out by that steed, in his flight,
80   Kindled the land into flame with its heat.

He has left the village and mounted the steep,
And beneath him, tranquil and broad and deep,
Is the Mystic,[2] meeting the ocean tides;
And under the alders, that skirt its edge,
85   Now soft on the sand, now loud on the ledge,
Is heard the tramp of his steed as he rides.

It was twelve by the village clock
When he crossed the bridge into Medford town.
He heard the crowing of the cock,
90   And the barking of the farmer's dog,
And felt the damp of the river fog,
That rises after the sun goes down.

It was one by the village clock,
When he galloped into Lexington.
95   He saw the gilded weathercock
Swim in the moonlight as he passed,
And the meeting-house windows, blank and bare,
Gaze at him with a spectral glare,
As if they already stood aghast
100   At the bloody work they would look upon.

It was two by the village clock,
When he came to the bridge in Concord town.
He heard the bleating of the flock,
And the twitter of birds among the trees,
105   And felt the breath of the morning breeze
Blowing over the meadows brown.

---

[2] **Mystic:** The Mystic River runs southeastward toward the Boston Harbor.

And one was safe and asleep in his bed
Who at the bridge would be first to fall,
Who that day would be lying dead,
110 Pierced by a British musket-ball.

You know the rest. In the books you have read,
How the British Regulars fired and fled,
How the farmers gave them ball for ball,
From behind each fence and farmyard wall;
115 Chasing the red-coats down the lane,
Then crossing the fields to emerge again
Under the trees at the turn of the road,
And only pausing to fire and load.

So through the night rode Paul Revere;
120 And so through the night went his cry of alarm
To every Middlesex village and farm—
A cry of defiance and not of fear,
A voice in the darkness, a knock at the door,
And a word that shall echo for evermore!
125 For, borne on a night-wind of the Past,
Through all our history, to the last,
In the hour of darkness and peril and need,
The people will waken and listen to hear
The hurrying hoof-beats of that steed,
130 And the midnight message of Paul Revere.

EDGAR ALLAN POE (1809–1849)

The Raven (1845)

Once upon a midnight dreary, while I pondered, weak and weary,
Over many a quaint and curious volume of forgotten lore—
While I nodded, nearly napping, suddenly there came a tapping,
As of some one gently rapping, rapping at my chamber door.
5 " 'Tis some visiter," I muttered, "tapping at my chamber door—
Only this and nothing more."

Ah, distinctly I remember it was in the bleak December;
And each separate dying ember wrought its ghost upon the floor.
Eagerly I wished the morrow;—vainly I had sought to borrow
10 From my books surcease of sorrow—sorrow for the lost Lenore—
For the rare and radiant maiden whom the angels name Lenore—
Nameless *here* for evermore.

And the silken, sad, uncertain rustling of each purple curtain
Thrilled me—filled me with fantastic terrors never felt before;
15 So that now, to still the beating of my heart, I stood repeating
" 'Tis some visiter entreating entrance at my chamber door—
Some late visiter entreating entrance at my chamber door;—
                              This it is and nothing more."

Presently my soul grew stronger; hesitating then no longer,
20 "Sir," said I, "or Madam, truly your forgiveness I implore;
But the fact is I was napping, and so gently you came rapping,
And so faintly you came tapping, tapping at my chamber door,
That I scarce was sure I heard you"—here I opened wide the door;—
                              Darkness there and nothing more.

25 Deep into that darkness peering, long I stood there wondering, fearing,
Doubting, dreaming dreams no mortal ever dared to dream before;
But the silence was unbroken, and the stillness gave no token,
And the only word there spoken was the whispered word, "Lenore?"
This I whispered, and an echo murmured back the word, "Lenore!"
30   Merely this and nothing more.

Back into the chamber turning, all my soul within me burning,
Soon again I heard a tapping somewhat louder than before.
"Surely," said I, "surely that is something at my window lattice;
Let me see, then, what the threat is, and this mystery explore—
35 Let my heart be still a moment and this mystery explore;—
                              'Tis the wind and nothing more!"

Open here I flung the shutter, when, with many a flirt and flutter,
In there stepped a stately Raven of the saintly days of yore;
Not the least obeisance made he; not a minute stopped or stayed he;
40 But, with mien of lord or lady perched above my chamber door—
Perched upon a bust of Pallas[1] just above my chamber door—
                              Perched, and sat, and nothing more.

Then this ebony bird beguiling my sad fancy into smiling,
By the grave and stern decorum of the countenance it wore,
45 "Though thy crest be shorn and shaven, thou," I said, "art sure no craven,
Ghastly grim and ancient Raven wandering from the Nightly shore—
Tell me what thy lordly name is on the Night's Plutonian shore!"[2]
                              Quoth the Raven "Nevermore."

---

[1] **Pallas:** In Greek mythology, the goddess of wisdom and the arts.
[2] **Night's Plutonian shore:** In Greek mythology, Pluto was the god of the underworld.

Much I marvelled this ungainly fowl to hear discourse so plainly,
50   Though its answer little meaning—little relevancy bore;
For we cannot help agreeing that no living human being
Ever yet was blessed with seeing bird above his chamber door—
Bird or beast upon the sculptured bust above his chamber door,
                              With such name as "Nevermore."

55   But the Raven, sitting lonely on the placid bust, spoke only
That one word, as if his soul in that one word he did outpour.
Nothing farther then he uttered—not a feather then he fluttered—
Till I scarcely more than muttered "Other friends have flown before—
On the morrow *he* will leave me, as my Hopes have flown before."
60   Then the bird said "Nevermore."

Startled at the stillness broken by reply so aptly spoken,
"Doubtless," said I, "what it utters is its only stock and store
Caught from some unhappy master whom unmerciful Disaster
Followed fast and followed faster till his songs one burden bore—
65   Till the dirges of his Hope that melancholy burden bore
                              Of 'Never—nevermore.' "

But the Raven still beguiling my sad fancy into smiling,
Straight I wheeled a cushioned seat in front of bird, and bust and door;
Then, upon the velvet sinking, I betook myself to linking
70   Fancy unto fancy, thinking what this ominous bird of yore—
What this grim, ungainly, ghastly, gaunt, and ominous bird of yore
                              Meant in croaking "Nevermore."

This I sat engaged in guessing, but no syllable expressing
To the fowl whose fiery eyes now burned into my bosom's core;
75   This and more I sat divining, with my head at ease reclining
On the cushion's velvet lining that the lamp-light gloated o'er,
But whose velvet-violet lining with the lamp-light gloating o'er,
                              She shall press, ah, nevermore!

Then, methought, the air grew denser, perfumed from an unseen censer
80   Swung by seraphim whose foot-falls tinkled on the tufted floor.
"Wretch," I cried, "thy God hath lent thee—by these angels he hath sent
          thee
Respite—respite and nepenthe³ from thy memories of Lenore;
Quaff, oh quaff this kind nepenthe and forget this lost Lenore!"
                              Quoth the Raven "Nevermore."

---

³ **nepenthe:** Ancient drug used to relieve pain and sorrow.

85 "Prophet!" said I, "thing of evil!—prophet still, if bird or devil!—
Whether Tempter sent, or whether tempest tossed thee here ashore,
Desolate yet all undaunted, on this desert land enchanted—
On this home by Horror haunted—tell me truly, I implore—
Is there—*is* there balm in Gilead?[4]—tell me—tell me, I implore!"
90   Quoth the Raven "Nevermore."

"Prophet!" said I, "thing of evil!—prophet still, if bird or devil!
By that Heaven that bends above us—by that God we both adore—
Tell this soul with sorrow laden if, within the distant Aidenn,°   Eden
It shall clasp a sainted maiden whom the angels name Lenore—
95 Clasp a rare and radiant maiden whom the angels name Lenore."
          Quoth the Raven "Nevermore."

"Be that word our sign of parting, bird or fiend!" I shrieked, upstarting—
"Get thee back into the tempest and the Night's Plutonian shore!
Leave no black plume as a token of that lie thy soul hath spoken!
100 Leave my loneliness unbroken!—quit the bust above my door!
Take thy beak from out my heart, and take thy form from off my door!"
          Quoth the Raven "Nevermore."

And the Raven, never flitting, still is sitting, *still* is sitting
On the pallid bust of Pallas just above my chamber door;
105 And his eyes have all the seeming of a demon's that is dreaming,
And the lamp-light o'er him streaming throws his shadow on the floor;
And my soul from out that shadow that lies floating on the floor
          Shall be lifted—nevermore!

ALFRED, LORD TENNYSON (1809–1892)

The Lady of Shalott (1842)

Part I

On either side the river lie
Long fields of barley and of rye,
That clothe the wold° and meet the sky;   plain
And through the field the road runs by
5 To many-towered Camelot,[1]
And up and down the people go,

---

[4] **balm in Gilead:** See Jeremiah 8.22: "Is there no balm in Gilead; is there no physician there?"
[1] **Camelot:** Castle of King Arthur.

Gazing where the lilies blow
Round an island there below,
        The island of Shalott.

10 Willows whiten, aspens quiver,
Little breezes dusk and shiver
Through the wave that runs for ever
By the island in the river
        Flowing down to Camelot.
15 Four gray walls, and four gray towers,
Overlook a space of flowers,
And the silent isle imbowers
        The Lady of Shalott.

By the margin, willow-veiled,
20 Slide the heavy barges trailed
By slow horses; and unhailed
The shallop flitteth° silken-sailed   open boat
        Skimming down to Camelot:
But who hath seen her wave her hand?
25 Or at the casement seen her stand?
Or is she known in all the land,
        The Lady of Shalott?

Only reapers, reaping early
In among the bearded barley,
30 Hear a song that echoes cheerly
From the river winding clearly,
        Down to towered Camelot:
And by the moon the reaper weary,
Piling sheaves in uplands airy,
35 Listening, whispers ' 'Tis the fairy
        Lady of Shalott.'

Part II

There she weaves by night and day
A magic web with colours gay.
She has heard a whisper say,
40 A curse is on her if she stay
        To look down to Camelot.
She knows not what the curse may be,
And so she weaveth steadily,
And little other care hath she,
45   The Lady of Shalott.

And moving through a mirror clear
That hangs before her all the year,
Shadows of the world appear.
There she sees the highway near
50   Winding down to Camelot:
There the river eddy whirls,
And there the surly village-churls,
And the red cloaks of market girls,
        Pass onward from Shalott.

55 Sometimes a troop of damsels glad,
An abbot on an ambling pad,°   horse
Sometimes a curly shepherd-lad,
Or long-haired page in crimson clad,
        Goes by to towered Camelot;
60 And sometimes through the mirror blue
The knights come riding two and two:
She hath no loyal knight and true,
        The Lady of Shalott.

But in her web she still delights
65 To weave the mirror's magic sights,
For often through the silent nights
A funeral, with plumes and lights
        And music, went to Camelot:
Or when the moon was overhead,
70 Came two young lovers lately wed;
'I am half sick of shadows,' said
        The Lady of Shalott.

Part III

A bow-shot from her bower-eaves,
He rode between the barley-sheaves,
75 The sun came dazzling through the leaves,
And flamed upon the brazen greaves
        Of bold Sir Lancelot.
A red-cross knight for ever kneeled
To a lady in his shield,
80 That sparkled on the yellow field,
        Beside remote Shalott.

The gemmy bridle glittered free,
Like to some branch of stars we see
Hung in the golden Galaxy.
85 The bridle bells rang merrily

As he rode down to Camelot:
And from his blazoned baldric slung
A mighty silver bugle hung,
And as he rode his armour rung,
90　　　Beside remote Shalott.

All in the blue unclouded weather
Thick-jewelled shone the saddle-leather,
The helmet and the helmet-feather
Burned like one burning flame together,
95　　　As he rode down to Camelot.
As often through the purple night,
Below the starry clusters bright,
Some bearded meteor, trailing light,
　　　Moves over still Shalott.

100　His broad clear brow in sunlight glowed;
On burnished hooves his war-horse trode;
From underneath his helmet flowed
His coal-black curls as on he rode,
　　　As he rode down to Camelot.
105　From the bank and from the river
He flashed into the crystal mirror,
'Tirra lirra,' by the river
　　　Sang Sir Lancelot.

She left the web, she left the loom,
110　She made three paces through the room,
She saw the water-lily bloom,
She saw the helmet and the plume,
　　　She looked down to Camelot.
Out flew the web and floated wide;
115　The mirror cracked from side to side;
'The curse is come upon me,' cried
　　　The Lady of Shalott.

Part IV

In the stormy east-wind straining,
The pale yellow woods were waning,
120　The broad stream in his banks complaining,
Heavily the low sky raining
　　　Over towered Camelot;
Down she came and found a boat
Beneath a willow left afloat,
125　And round about the prow she wrote
　　　The Lady of Shalott.

And down the river's dim expanse
Like some bold seër in a trance,
Seeing all his own mischance—
130   With a glassy countenance
  Did she look to Camelot.
And at the closing of the day
She loosed the chain, and down she lay;
The broad stream bore her far away,
135   The Lady of Shalott.

Lying, robed in snowy white
That loosely flew to left and right—
The leaves upon her falling light—
Through the noises of the night
140   She floated down to Camelot:
And as the boat-head wound along
The willowy hills and fields among,
They heard her singing her last song,
  The Lady of Shalott.

145   Heard a carol, mournful, holy,
Chanted loudly, chanted slowly,
Till her blood was frozen slowly,
And her eyes were darkened wholly,
  Turned to towered Camelot.
150   For ere she reached upon the tide
The first house by the water-side,
Singing in her song she died,
  The Lady of Shalott.

Under tower and balcony,
155   By garden-wall and gallery,
A gleaming shape she floated by,
Dead-pale between the houses high,
  Silent into Camelot.
Out upon the wharfs they came,
160   Knight and burgher, lord and dame,
And round the prow they read her name,
  The Lady of Shalott.

Who is this? and what is here?
And in the lighted palace near
165   Died the sound of royal cheer;
And they crossed themselves for fear,
  All the knights at Camelot:
But Lancelot mused a little space;

He said, 'She has a lovely face;
170   God in his mercy lend her grace,
      The Lady of Shalott.'

ROBERT BROWNING   (1812–1889)

'Childe Roland to the Dark Tower Came'[1]   (1855)
(*See Edgar's song in* 'Lear')

I

My first thought was, he lied in every word,
    That hoary cripple, with malicious eye
    Askance to watch the working of his lie
On mine, and mouth scarce able to afford
5   Suppression of the glee, that pursed and scored
    Its edge, at one more victim gained thereby.

II

What else should he be set for, with his staff?
    What, save to waylay with his lies, ensnare
    All travellers who might find him posted there,
10   And ask the road? I guessed what skull-like laugh
Would break, what crutch 'gin write my epitaph
    For pastime in the dusty thoroughfare,

III

If at his counsel I should turn aside
    Into that ominous tract which, all agree,
15   Hides the Dark Tower. Yet acquiescingly
I did turn as he pointed: neither pride
Nor hope rekindling at the end descried,
    So much as gladness that some end might be.

IV

For, what with my whole world-wide wandering,
20   What with my search drawn out thro' years, my hope
    Dwindled into a ghost not fit to cope
With that obstreperous joy success would bring,—

---

[1] **Childe . . . Came:** A candidate for knighthood. For the origin of the title line, see Shakespeare's *King Lear* 2.4.

I hardly tried now to rebuke the spring
    My heart made, finding failure in its scope.

V

25 As when a sick man very near to death
    Seems dead indeed, and feels begin and end
    The tears and takes the farewell of each friend,
And hears one bid the other go, draw breath
Freelier outside, ('since all is o'er,' he saith,
30   'And the blow fallen no grieving can amend;')

VI

While some discuss if near the other graves
    Be room enough for this, and when a day
    Suits best for carrying the corpse away,
With care about the banners, scarves and staves:
35 And still the man hears all, and only craves
    He may not shame such tender love and stay.

VII

Thus, I had so long suffered in this quest,
    Heard failure prophesied so oft, been writ
    So many times among 'The Band'—to wit,
40 The knights who to the Dark Tower's search addressed
Their steps—that just to fail as they, seemed best,
    And all the doubt was now—should I be fit?

VIII

So, quiet as despair, I turned from him,
    That hateful cripple, out of his highway
45   Into the path he pointed. All the day
Had been a dreary one at best, and dim
Was settling to its close, yet shot one grim
    Red leer to see the plain catch its estray.[2]

IX

For mark! no sooner was I fairly found
50   Pledged to the plain, after a pace or two,
    Than, pausing to throw backward a last view
O'er the safe road, 't was gone; grey plain all round:
Nothing but plain to the horizon's bound.
    I might go on; nought else remained to do.

---

[2] **estray:** A stray, domestic animal.

X

55   So, on I went. I think I never saw
         Such starved ignoble nature; nothing throve:
         For flowers—as well expect a cedar grove!
     But cockle, spurge,[3] according to their law
     Might propagate their kind, with none to awe,
60   You'd think; a burr had been a treasure-trove.

XI

     No! penury,° inertness and grimace,   extreme poverty
         In some strange sort, were the land's portion. 'See
         'Or shut your eyes,' said Nature peevishly,
     'It nothing skills: I cannot help my case:
65   ''T is the Last Judgment's fire must cure this place,
         'Calcine° its clods and set my prisoners free.'   burn to dust

XII

     If there pushed any ragged thistle-stalk
         Above its mates, the head was chopped; the bents°   reeds
         Were jealous else. What made those holes and rents
70   In the dock's[4] harsh swarth leaves, bruised as to baulk
     All hope of greenness? 't is a brute must walk
         Pashing° their life out, with a brute's intents.   crushing

XIII

     As for the grass, it grew as scant as hair
         In leprosy; thin dry blades pricked the mud
75   Which underneath looked kneaded up with blood.
     One stiff blind horse, his every bone a-stare,
     Stood stupefied, however he came there:
         Thrust out past service from the devil's stud!

XIV

     Alive? he might be dead for aught I know,
80   With that red gaunt and colloped neck a-strain,
         And shut eyes underneath the rusty mane;
     Seldom went such grotesqueness with such woe;
     I never saw a brute I hated so;
         He must be wicked to deserve such pain.

---

[3] **cockle, spurge:** A cockle is a weed that grows among wheat, and a spurge is a plant with small flowers.
[4] **the dock's:** A weed.

XV

85 I shut my eyes and turned them on my heart,
　　As a man calls for wine before he fights,
　　I asked one draught of earlier, happier sights,
Ere fitly I could hope to play my part,
Think first, fight afterwards—the soldier's art:
90 　　One taste of the old time sets all to rights.

XVI

Not it! I fancied Cuthbert's⁵ reddening face
　　Beneath its garniture of curly gold,
　　Dear fellow, till I almost felt him fold
An arm in mine to fix me to the place,
95 That way he used. Alas, one night's disgrace!
　　Out went my heart's new fire and left it cold.

XVII

Giles then, the soul of honour—there he stands
　　Frank as ten years ago when knighted first.
　　What honest man should dare (he said) he durst.
100 Good—but the scene shifts—faugh! what hangman-hands
Pin to his breast a parchment? His own bands
　　Read it. Poor traitor, spit upon and curst!

XVIII

Better this present than a past like that;
　　Back therefore to my darkening path again!
105 　　No sound, no sight as far as eye could strain.
Will the night send a howlet° or a bat?　　　　　　　　　owl
I asked: when something on the dismal flat
　　Came to arrest my thoughts and change their train.

XIX

A sudden little river crossed my path
110 　　As unexpected as a serpent comes.
　　No sluggish tide congenial to the glooms;
This, as it frothed by, might have been a bath
For the fiend's glowing hoof—to see the wrath
　　Of its black eddy bespate° with flakes and spumes.　　　spattered

---

⁵ **Cuthbert's:** Saint Cuthbert (ca. 635–687 A.D.), once a soldier, became Bishop of Lindisfarne, a tidal island in England.

XX

115 So petty yet so spiteful! All along,
      Low scrubby alders kneeled down over it;
      Drenched willows flung them headlong in a fit
Of mute despair, a suicidal throng:
The river which had done them all the wrong,
120   Whate'er that was, rolled by, deterred no whit.

XXI

Which, while I forded,—good saints, how I feared
      To set my foot upon a dead man's cheek,
      Each step, or feel the spear I thrust to seek
For hollows, tangled in his hair or beard!
125 —It may have been a water-rat I speared,
      But, ugh! it sounded like a baby's shriek.

XXII

Glad was I when I reached the other bank.
      Now for a better country. Vain presage!
      Who were the strugglers, what war did they wage,
130 Whose savage trample thus could pad the dank
Soil to a plash? Toads in a poisoned tank,
      Or wild cats in a red-hot iron cage—

XXIII

The fight must so have seemed in that fell cirque.°   steep-walled basin
      What penned them there, with all the plain to choose?
135   No foot-print leading to that horrid mews,°   stabling area
None out of it. Mad brewage set to work
Their brains, no doubt, like galley-slaves the Turk
      Pits for his pastime, Christians against Jews.

XXIV

And more than that—a furlong on—why, there!
140   What bad use was that engine for, that wheel,
      Or brake,[6] not wheel—that harrow fit to reel
Men's bodies out like silk? with all the air
Of Tophet's° tool, on earth left unaware,   Hell's
      Or brought to sharpen its rusty teeth of steel.

---

[6] **brake:** Here, a tool used for breaking up flax into fibers.

XXV

145 Then came a bit of stubbed ground, once a wood,
       Next a marsh, it would seem, and now mere earth
       Desperate and done with; (so a fool finds mirth,
   Makes a thing and then mars it, till his mood
   Changes and off he goes!) within a rood—
150   Bog, clay and rubble, sand and stark black dearth.

XXVI

   Now blotches rankling,° coloured gay and grim,   festering
       Now patches where some leanness of the soil's
       Broke into moss or substances like boils;
   Then came some palsied oak, a cleft in him
155   Like a distorted mouth that splits its rim
       Gaping at death, and dies while it recoils.

XXVII

   And just as far as ever from the end!
       Nought in the distance but the evening, nought
       To point my footstep further! At the thought,
160   A great black bird, Apollyon's[7] bosom-friend,
   Sailed past, nor beat his wide wing dragon-penned[8]
       That brushed my cap—perchance the guide I sought.

XXVIII

   For, looking up, aware I somehow grew,
       'Spite of the dusk, the plain had given place
165   All round to mountains—with such name to grace
   Mere ugly heights and heaps now stolen in view.
   How thus they had surprised me,—solve it, you!
       How to get from them was no clearer case.

XXIX

   Yet half I seemed to recognize some trick
170   Of mischief happened to me, God knows when—
       In a bad dream perhaps. Here ended, then,
   Progress this way. When, in the very nick
   Of giving up, one time more, came a click
       As when a trap shuts—you're inside the den!

---

[7] **Apollyon's:** In *The Revelation,* the angel of the bottomless pit.
[8] **dragon-penned:** With wings like a dragon.

XXX

175 Burningly it came on me all at once,
    This was the place! those two hills on the right,
    Crouched like two bulls locked horn in horn in fight;
While to the left, a tall scalped mountain . . . Dunce,
Dotard, a-dozing at the very nonce,°   present occasion
180   After a life spent training for the sight!

XXXI

What in the midst lay but the Tower itself?
    The round squat turret, blind as the fool's heart,
    Built of brown stone, without a counterpart
In the whole world. The tempest's mocking elf
185 Points to the shipman thus the unseen shelf
    He strikes on, only when the timbers start.

XXXII

Not see? because of night perhaps?—why, day
    Came back again for that! before it left,
    The dying sunset kindled through a cleft:
190 The hills, like giants at a hunting, lay,
Chin upon hand, to see the game at bay,—
    'Now stab and end the creature—to the heft!'°   handle of a knife

XXXIII

Not hear? when noise was everywhere! it tolled
    Increasing like a bell. Names in my ears
195   Of all the lost adventurers my peers,—
How such a one was strong, and such was bold,
And such was fortunate, yet each of old
    Lost, lost! one moment knelled the woe of years.

XXXIV

There they stood, ranged along the hill-sides, met
200   To view the last of me, a living frame
    For one more picture! in a sheet of flame
I saw them and I knew them all. And yet
Dauntless the slug-horn[9] to my lips I set,
    And blew. *'Childe Roland to the Dark Tower came.'*

---

[9] **slug-horn:** Rough instrument fashioned from the horn of an ox or cow.

FRANCES E. W. HARPER (1825–1911)

Eliza Harris[1] (1853)

Like a fawn from the arrow, startled and wild,
A woman swept by us, bearing a child;
In her eye was the night of a settled despair,
And her brow was o'ershaded with anguish and care.

5   She was nearing the river—in reaching the brink,
She heeded no danger, she paused not to think!
For she is a mother—her child is a slave—
And she'll give him his freedom, or find him a grave!

It was a vision to haunt us, that innocent face—
10   So pale in its aspect, so fair in its grace;
As the tramp of the horse and the bay of the hound,
With the fetters that gall, were trailing the ground!

She was nerv'd by despair, and strengthened by woe,
As she leap'd o'er the chasms that yawn'd from below;
15   Death howl'd in the tempest, and rav'd in the blast,
But she heard not the sound till the danger was past.

Oh! how shall I speak of my proud country's shame?
Of the stains on her glory, how give them their name?
How say that her banner in mockery waves—
20   Her "star spangled banner"—o'er millions of slaves?

How say that the lawless may torture and chase
A woman whose crime is the hue of her face?
How the depths of the forest may echo around
With the shrieks of despair, and the bay of the hound?

25   With her step on the ice, and her arm on her child,
The danger was fearful, the pathway was wild;
But, aided by Heaven, she gained a free shore,
Where the friends of humanity open'd their door.

So fragile and lovely, so fearfully pale,
30   Like a lily that bends to the breath of the gale,
Save the heave of her breast, and the sway of her hair,
You'd have thought her a statue of fear and despair.

---

[1] **Eliza Harris:** Like Stowe's *Uncle Tom's Cabin*, Harper's narrative is based on an actual event that occurred in Cincinnati, Ohio.

In agony close to her bosom she press'd
The life of her heart, the child of her breast:—
35   Oh! love from its tenderness gathering might,
Had strengthen'd her soul for the dangers of flight.

But she's free—yes, free from the land where the slave
From the hand of oppression must rest in the grave;
Where bondage and torture, where scourges and chains,
40   Have plac'd on our banner indelible stains.

Did a fever e'er burning through bosom and brain,
Send a lava-like flood through every vein,
Till it suddenly cooled 'neath a healing spell,
And you knew, oh! the joy! you knew you were well?

45   So felt this young mother, as a sense of the rest
Stole gently and sweetly o'er *her* weary breast,
As her boy looked up, and, wondering, smiled
On the mother whose love had freed her child.

The bloodhounds have miss'd the scent of her way;
50   The hunter is rifled and foil'd of his prey;
Fierce jargon and cursing, with clanking of chains,
Make sounds of strange discord on Liberty's plains.

With the rapture love and fulness of bliss,
She plac'd on his brow a mother's fond kiss:—
55   Oh! poverty, danger and death she can brave,
For the child of her love is no longer a slave!

CHRISTINA G. ROSSETTI (1830–1894)

Goblin Market (1859; 1862)

Morning and evening
Maids heard the goblins cry.
'Come buy our orchard fruits,
Come buy, come buy:
5   Apples and quinces,
Lemons and oranges,
Plump unpecked cherries,
Melons and raspberries,
Bloom-down-cheeked peaches,

10 Swart-headed mulberries,
    Wild free-born cranberries,
    Crab-apples, dewberries,
    Pine-apples, blackberries,
    Apricots, strawberries;—
15 All ripe together
    In summer weather,—
    Morns that pass by,
    Fair eves that fly;
    Come buy, come buy:
20 Our grapes fresh from the vine,
    Pomegranates full and fine,
    Dates and sharp bullaces,
    Rare pears and greengages,
    Damsons and bilberries,
25 Taste them and try:
    Currants and gooseberries,
    Bright-fire-like barberries,
    Figs to fill your mouth,
    Citrons from the South,
30 Sweet to tongue and sound to eye;
    Come buy, come buy.'

    Evening by evening
    Among the brookside rushes,
    Laura bowed her head to hear,
35 Lizzie veiled her blushes:
    Crouching close together
    In the cooling weather,
    With clasping arms and cautioning lips,
    With tingling cheeks and finger tips.
40 'Lie close,' Laura said,
    Pricking up her golden head:
    'We must not look at goblin men,
    We must not buy their fruits:
    Who knows upon what soil they fed
45 Their hungry thirsty roots?'
    'Come buy' call the goblins
    Hobbling down the glen.
    'Oh,' cried Lizzie, 'Laura, Laura,
    You should not peep at goblin men.'
50 Lizzie covered up her eyes,
    Covered close lest they should look;
    Laura reared her glossy head,
    And whispered like the restless brook:
    'Look, Lizzie, look, Lizzie,

55   Down the glen tramp little men.
      One hauls a basket,
      One bears a plate,
      One lugs a golden dish
      Of many pounds weight.
60   How fair the vine must grow
      Whose grapes are so luscious;
      How warm the wind must blow
      Thro' those fruit bushes.'
      'No,' said Lizzie: 'No, no, no;
65   Their offers should not charm us,
      Their evil gifts would harm us.'
      She thrust a dimpled finger
      In each ear, shut eyes and ran:
      Curious Laura chose to linger
70   Wondering at each merchant man.
      One had a cat's face,
      One whisked a tail,
      One tramped at a rat's pace,
      One crawled like a snail,
75   One like a wombat prowled obtuse and furry,
      One like a ratel° tumbled hurry skurry   badger
      She heard a voice like voice of doves
      Cooking all together:
      They sounded kind and full of loves
80   In the pleasant weather.

      Laura stretched her gleaming neck
      Like a rush-imbedded swan,
      Like a lily from the beck,
      Like a moonlit poplar branch,
85   Like a vessel at the launch
      When its last restraint is gone.
      Backwards up the mossy glen
      Turned and trooped the goblin men,
      With their shrill repeated cry,
90   'Come buy, come buy.'
      When they reached where Laura was
      They stood stock still upon the moss,
      Leering at each other,
      Brother with queer brother;
95   Signalling each other,
      Brother with sly brother.
      One set his basket down,
      One reared his plate;
      One began to weave a crown

100   Of tendrils, leaves and rough nuts brown
      (Men sell not such in any town);
      One heaved the golden weight
      Of dish and fruit to offer her:
      'Come buy, come buy,' was still their cry.

105   Laura stared but did not stir,
      Longed but had no money:
      The whisk-tailed merchant bade her taste
      In tones as smooth as honey,
      The cat-faced purr'd,
110   The rat-paced spoke a word
      Of welcome, and the snail-paced even was heard;
      One parrot-voiced and jolly
      Cried 'Pretty Goblin' still for 'Pretty Polly;'—
      One whistled like a bird.

115   But sweet-tooth Laura spoke in haste:
      'Good folk, I have no coin;
      To take were to purloin:
      I have no copper in my purse,
      I have no silver either,
120   And all my gold is on the furze¹
      That shakes in windy weather
      Above the rusty heather.'
      'You have much gold upon your head,'
      They answered all together:
125   'Buy from us with a golden curl.'
      She clipped a precious golden lock,
      She dropped a tear more rare than pearl,
      Then sucked their fruit globes fair or red:
      Sweeter than honey from the rock,
130   Stronger than man-rejoicing wine,
      Clearer than water flowed that juice;
      She never tasted such before,
      How should it cloy° with length of use?   enjoy to excess
      She sucked and sucked and sucked the more
135   Fruits which that unknown orchard bore;
      She sucked until her lips were sore;
      Then flung the emptied rinds away
      But gathered up one kernel-stone,
      And knew not was it night or day
140   As she turned home alone.

---

¹ **furze:** Thick evergreen shrub with golden-yellow flowers.

Lizzie met her at the gate
Full of wise upbraidings:
'Dear, you should not stay so late,
Twilight is not good for maidens;
145   Should not loiter in the glen
In the haunts of goblin men.
Do you not remember Jeanie,
How she met them in the moonlight,
Took their gifts both choice and many,
150   Ate their fruits and wore their flowers
Plucked from bowers
Where summer ripens at all hours?
But ever in the noonlight
She pined and pined away;
155   Sought them by night and day,
Found them no more but dwindled and grew grey;
Then fell with the first snow,
While to this day no grass will grow
Where she lies low:
160   I planted daisies there a year ago
That never blow.°   bloom
You should not loiter so.'
'Nay, hush,' said Laura:
'Nay, hush, my sister:
165   I ate and ate my fill,
Yet my mouth waters still;
Tomorrow night I will
Buy more:' and kissed her:
'Have done with sorrow;
170   I'll bring you plums tomorrow
Fresh on their mother twigs,
Cherries worth getting;
You cannot think what figs
My teeth have met in,
175   What melons icy-cold
Piled on a dish of gold
Too huge for me to hold,
What peaches with a velvet nap,
Pellucid° grapes without one seed: transparent
180   Odorous indeed must be the mead
Whereon they grow, and pure the wave they drink
With lilies at the brink,
And sugar-sweet their sap.'

Golden head by golden head,
185   Like two pigeons in one nest

Folded in each other's wings,
They lay down in their curtained bed:
Like two blossoms on one stem,
Like two flakes of new-fall'n snow,
190 Like two wands of ivory
Tipped with gold for awful kings.
Moon and stars gazed in at them,
Wind sang to them lullaby,
Lumbering owls forbore to fly,
195 Not a bat flapped to and fro
Round their rest:
Cheek to cheek and breast to breast
Locked together in one nest.

Early in the morning
200 When the first cock crowed his warning,
Neat like bees, as sweet and busy,
Laura rose with Lizzie:
Fetched in honey, milked the cows,
Aired and set to rights the house,
205 Kneaded cakes of whitest wheat,
Cakes for dainty mouths to eat,
Next churned butter, whipped up cream,
Fed their poultry, sat and sewed;
Talked as modest maidens should:
210 Lizzie with an open heart,
Laura in an absent dream,
One content, one sick in part;
One warbling for the mere bright day's delight,
One longing for the night.

215 At length slow evening came:
They went with pitchers to the reedy brook;
Lizzie most placid in her look,
Laura most like a leaping flame.
They drew the gurgling water from its deep;
220 Lizzie plucked purple and rich golden flags,[2]
Then turning homewards said: 'The sunset flushes
Those furthest loftiest crags;
Come, Laura, not another maiden lags,
No wilful squirrel wags,
225 The beasts and birds are fast asleep.'
But Laura loitered still among the rushes
And said the bank was steep.

---

[2] **flags:** A plant with sword-shaped leaves, stiff stalks, and bright flowers.

And said the hour was early still,
The dew not fall'n, the wind not chill:
230 Listening ever, but not catching
The customary cry,
'Come buy, come buy,'
With its iterated jingle
Of sugar-baited words:
235 Not for all her watching
Once discerning even one goblin
Racing, whisking, tumbling, hobbling;
Let alone the herds
That used to tramp along the glen,
240 In groups or single,
Of brisk fruit-merchant men.
Till Lizzie urged, 'O Laura, come;
I hear the fruit-call but I dare not look:
You should not loiter longer at this brook:
245 Come with me home.
The stars rise, the moon bends her arc,
Each glowworm winks her spark,
Let us get home before the night grows dark:
For clouds may gather
250 Tho' this is summer weather,
Put out the lights and drench us thro';
Then if we lost our way what should we do?'

Laura turned cold as stone
To find her sister heard that cry alone,
255 That goblin cry,
'Come buy our fruits, come buy.'
Must she then buy no more such dainty fruit?
Must she no more such succous° pasture find,   juicy
Gone deaf and blind?
260 Her tree of life drooped from the root:
She said not one word in her heart's sore ache;
But peering thro' the dimness, nought discerning,
Trudged home, her pitcher dripping all the way;
So crept to bed, and lay
265 Silent till Lizzie slept;
Then sat up in a passionate yearning,
And gnashed her teeth for baulked desire, and wept
As if her heart would break.

Day after day, night after night,
270 Laura kept watch in vain
In sullen silence of exceeding pain.

She never caught again the goblin cry:
'Come buy, come buy;'—
She never spied the goblin men
275 Hawking their fruits along the glen:
But when the noon waxed bright
Her hair grew thin and gray;
She dwindled, as the fair full moon doth turn
To swift decay and burn
280 Her fire away.

One day remembering her kernel-stone
She set it by a wall that faced the south;
Dewed it with tears, hoped for a root,
Watched for a waxing shoot,
285 But there came none;
It never saw the sun,
It never felt the trickling moisture run:
While with sunk eyes and faded mouth
She dreamed of melons, as a traveller sees
290 False waves in desert drouth
With shade of leaf-crowned trees,
And burns the thirstier in the sandful breeze.

She no more swept the house,
Tended the fowls or cows,
295 Fetched honey, kneaded cakes of wheat,
Brought water from the brook:
But sat down listless in the chimney-nook
And would not eat.

Tender Lizzie could not bear
300 To watch her sister's cankerous care
Yet not to share.
She night and morning
Caught the goblins' cry:
'Come buy our orchard fruits,
305 Come buy, come buy;'—
Beside the brook, along the glen,
She heard the tramp of goblin men,
The voice and stir
Poor Laura could not hear;
310 Longed to buy fruit to comfort her,
But feared to pay too dear.
She thought of Jeanie in her grave,
Who should have been a bride;
But who for joys brides hope to have

315   Fell sick and died
     In her gay prime,
     In earliest Winter time,
     With the first glazing rime,°   frost
     With the first snow-fall of crisp Winter time.

320   Till Laura dwindling
     Seemed knocking at Death's door:
     Then Lizzie weighed no more
     Better and worse;
     But put a silver penny in her purse,
325   Kissed Laura, crossed the heath with clumps of furze
     At twilight, halted by the brook:
     And for the first time in her life
     Began to listen and look.

     Laughed every goblin
330   When they spied her peeping:
     Came towards her hobbling,
     Flying, running, leaping,
     Puffing and blowing,
     Chuckling, clapping, crowing,
335   Clucking and gobbling,
     Mopping and mowing,
     Full of airs and graces,
     Pulling wry faces,
     Demure grimaces,
340   Cat-like and rat-like,
     Ratel- and wombat-like,
     Snail-paced in a hurry,
     Parrot-voiced and whistler,
     Helter skelter, hurry skurry,
345   Chattering like magpies,
     Fluttering like pigeons,
     Gliding like fishes,—
     Hugged her and kissed her,
     Squeezed and caressed her:
350   Stretched up their dishes,
     Panniers, and plates:
     'Look at our apples
     Russet and dun,
     Bob at our cherries,
355   Bite at our peaches,
     Citrons and dates,
     Grapes for the asking,
     Pears red with basking

Out in the sun,
360   Plums on their twigs;
Pluck them and suck them,
Pomegranates, figs.'—

'Good folk,' said Lizzie,
Mindful of Jeanie:
365   'Give me much and many:'—
Held out her apron,
Tossed them her penny.
'Nay, take a seat with us,
Honour and eat with us,'
370   They answered grinning:
'Our feast is but beginning.
Night yet is early,
Warm and dew-pearly,
Wakeful and starry:
375   Such fruits as these
No man can carry;
Half their bloom would fly,
Half their dew would dry,
Half their flavour would pass by.
380   Sit down and feast with us,
Be welcome guest with us,
Cheer you and rest with us.'—
'Thank you,' said Lizzie: 'But one waits
At home alone for me:
385   So without further parleying,
If you will not sell me any
Of your fruits tho' much and many,
Give me back my silver penny
I tossed you for a fee.'—
390   They began to scratch their pates,
No longer wagging, purring,
But visibly demurring,
Grunting and snarling.
One called her proud,
395   Cross-grained, uncivil;
Their tones waxed loud,
Their looks were evil.
Lashing their tails
They trod and hustled her,
400   Elbowed and jostled her,
Clawed with their nails,
Barking, mewing, hissing, mocking,
Tore her gown and soiled her stocking,

Twitched her hair out by the roots,
405   Stamped upon her tender feet,
Held her hands and squeezed their fruits
Against her mouth to make her eat.

White and golden Lizzie stood,
Like a lily in a flood,—
410   Like a rock of blue-veined stone
Lashed by tides obstreperously°—   *attracting attention*
Like a beacon left alone
In a hoary roaring sea,
Sending up a golden fire,—
415   Like a fruit-crowned orange-tree
White with blossoms honey-sweet
Sore beset by wasp and bee,—
Like a royal virgin town
Topped with gilded dome and spire
420   Close beleaguered° by a fleet   *besieged*
Mad to tug her standard down.

One may lead a horse to water,
Twenty cannot make him drink.
Tho' the goblins cuffed and caught her,
425   Coaxed and fought her,
Bullied and besought her,
Scratched her, pinched her black as ink,
Kicked and knocked her,
Mauled and mocked her,
430   Lizzie uttered not a word;
Would not open lip from lip
Lest they should cram a mouthful in:
But laughed in heart to feel the drip
Of juice that syrupped all her face,
435   And lodged in dimples of her chin,
And streaked her neck which quaked like curd.
At last the evil people
Worn out by her resistance
Flung back her penny, kicked their fruit
440   Along whichever road they took,
Not leaving root or stone or shoot;
Some writhed into the ground,
Some dived into the brook
With ring and ripple,
445   Some scudded on the gale without a sound,
Some vanished in the distance.

In a smart, ache, tingle,
Lizzie went her way;
Knew not was it night or day;
450 Sprang up the bank, tore thro' the furze,
Threaded copse and dingle,[3]
And heard her penny jingle
Bouncing in her purse,
Its bounce was music to her ear.
455 She ran and ran
As if she feared some goblin man
Dogged her with gibe or curse
Or something worse:
But not one goblin skurried after,
460 Nor was she pricked by fear;
The kind heart made her windy-paced
That urged her home quite out of breath with haste
And inward laughter.

She cried 'Laura,' up the garden,
465 'Did you miss me?
Come and kiss me.
Never mind my bruises,
Hug me, kiss me, suck my juices
Squeezed from goblin fruits for you,
470 Goblin pulp and goblin dew.
Eat me, drink me, love me;
Laura, make much of me:
For your sake I have braved the glen
And had to do with goblin merchant men.'

475 Laura started from her chair,
Flung her arms up in the air,
Clutched her hair:
'Lizzie, Lizzie, have you tasted
For my sake the fruit forbidden?
480 Must your light like mine be hidden,
Your young life like mine be wasted,
Undone in mine undoing
And ruined in my ruin,
Thirsty, cankered, goblin-ridden?'—
485 She clung about her sister,
Kissed and kissed and kissed her:

---

[3] **copse and dingle:** A copse is a thick growth of bushes, while a dingle is a small wooded hollow.

Tears once again
Refreshed her shrunken eyes,
Dropping like rain
490 After long sultry drouth;
Shaking with aguish fear, and pain,
She kissed and kissed her with a hungry mouth.

Her lips began to scorch,
That juice was wormwood [4] to her tongue,
495 She loathed the feast:
Writhing as one possessed she leaped and sung,
Rent all her robe, and wrung
Her hands in lamentable haste,
And beat her breast.
500 Her locks streamed like the torch
Borne by a racer at full speed,
Or like the mane of horses in their flight,
Or like an eagle when she stems the light
Straight toward the sun,
505 Or like a caged thing freed,
Or like a flying flag when armies run.

Swift fire spread thro' her veins, knocked at her heart,
Met the fire smouldering there
And overbore its lesser flame;
510 She gorged on bitterness without a name:
Ah! fool, to choose such part
Of soul-consuming care!
Sense failed in the mortal strife:
Like the watch-tower of a town
515 Which an earthquake shatters down,
Like a lightning-stricken mast,
Like a wind-uprooted tree
Spun about,
Like a foam-topped waterspout
520 Cast down headlong in the sea,
She fell at last;
Pleasure past and anguish past,
Is it death or is it life?

Life out of death.
525 That night long Lizzie watched by her,

---

[4] **wormwood:** A bitter herb, used by wet-nurses to wean infants from their mother's breast.

Counted her pulse's flagging stir,
Felt for her breath,
Held water to her lips, and cooled her face
With tears and fanning leaves:
530 But when the first birds chirped about their eaves,
And early reapers plodded to the place
Of golden sheaves,
And dew-wet grass
Bowed in the morning winds so brisk to pass,
535 And new buds with new day
Opened of cup-like lilies on the stream,
Laura awoke as from a dream,
Laughed in the innocent old way,
Hugged Lizzie but not twice or thrice;
540 Her gleaming locks showed not one thread of grey,
Her breath was sweet as May
And light danced in her eyes.

Days, weeks, months, years
Afterwards, when both were wives
545 With children of their own;
Their mother-hearts beset with fears,
Their lives bound up in tender lives;
Laura would call the little ones
And tell them of her early prime,
550 Those pleasant days long gone
Of not-returning time:
Would talk about the haunted glen,
The wicked, quaint fruit-merchant men,
Their fruits like honey to the throat
555 But poison in the blood;
(Men sell not such in any town:)
Would tell them how her sister stood
In deadly peril to do her good,
And win the fiery antidote:
560 Then joining hands to little hands
Would bid them cling together,
'For there is no friend like a sister
In calm or stormy weather;
To cheer one on the tedious way,
565 To fetch one if one goes astray,
To lift one if one totters down,
To strengthen whilst one stands.'

ROBERT FROST (1874–1963)

Home Burial (1914)

He saw her from the bottom of the stairs
Before she saw him. She was starting down,
Looking back over her shoulder at some fear.
She took a doubtful step and then undid it
5   To raise herself and look again. He spoke
Advancing toward her: "What is it you see
From up there always?—for I want to know."
She turned and sank upon her skirts at that,
And her face changed from terrified to dull.
10   He said to gain time: "What is it you see?"
Mounting until she cowered under him.
"I will find out now—you must tell me, dear."
She, in her place, refused him any help,
With the least stiffening of her neck and silence.
15   She let him look, sure that he wouldn't see,
Blind creature; and awhile he didn't see.
But at last he murmured, "Oh," and again, "Oh."

"What is it—what?" she said.

                       "Just that I see."

20   "You don't," she challenged. "Tell me what it is."

"The wonder is I didn't see at once.
I never noticed it from here before.
I must be wonted to it—that's the reason.
The little graveyard where my people are!
25   So small the window frames the whole of it.
Not so much larger than a bedroom, is it?
There are three stones of slate and one of marble,
Broad-shouldered little slabs there in the sunlight
On the sidehill. We haven't to mind *those*.
30   But I understand: it is not the stones,
But the child's mound—"

                    "Don't, don't, don't,
     don't," she cried.

She withdrew, shrinking from beneath his arm
35   That rested on the banister, and slid downstairs;

And turned on him with such a daunting look,
He said twice over before he knew himself:
"Can't a man speak of his own child he's lost?"

"Not you!—Oh, where's my hat? Oh, I don't need it!
40 I must get out of here. I must get air.—
I don't know rightly whether any man can."

"Amy! Don't go to someone else this time.
Listen to me. I won't come down the stairs."
He sat and fixed his chin between his fists.
45 "There's something I should like to ask you, dear."

"You don't know how to ask it."

                        "Help me, then."

Her fingers moved the latch for all reply.

"My words are nearly always an offense.
50 I don't know how to speak of anything
So as to please you. But I might be taught,
I should suppose. I can't say I see how.
A man must partly give up being a man
With womenfolk. We could have some arrangement
55 By which I'd bind myself to keep hands off
Anything special you're a-mind to name.
Though I don't like such things 'twixt those that love.
Two that don't love can't live together without them.
But two that do can't live together with them."
60 She moved the latch a little. "Don't—don't go.
Don't carry it to someone else this time.
Tell me about it if it's something human.
Let me into your grief. I'm not so much
Unlike other folks as your standing there
65 Apart would make me out. Give me my chance.
I do think, though, you overdo it a little.
What was it brought you up to think it the thing
To take your mother-loss of a first child
So inconsolably—in the face of love.
70 You'd think his memory might be satisfied—"

"There you go sneering now!"

                        "I'm not, I'm not!

You make me angry. I'll come down to you.
God, what a woman! And it's come to this,
75   A man can't speak of his own child that's dead."

"You can't because you don't know how to speak.
If you had any feelings, you that dug
With your own hand—how could you?—his little grave;
I saw you from that very window there,
80   Making the gravel leap and leap in air,
Leap up, like that, like that, and land so lightly
And roll back down the mound beside the hole.
I thought, Who is that man? I didn't know you.
And I crept down the stairs and up the stairs
85   To look again, and still your spade kept lifting.
Then you came in. I heard your rumbling voice
Out in the kitchen, and I don't know why,
But I went near to see with my own eyes.
You could sit there with the stains on your shoes
90   Of the fresh earth from your own baby's grave
And talk about your everyday concerns.
You had stood the spade up against the wall
Outside there in the entry, for I saw it."

"I shall laugh the worst laugh I ever laughed.
95   I'm cursed. God, if I don't believe I'm cursed."

"I can repeat the very words you were saying:
'Three foggy mornings and one rainy day
Will rot the best birch fence a man can build.'
Think of it, talk like that at such a time!
100   What had how long it takes a birch to rot
To do with what was in the darkened parlor?
You *couldn't* care! The nearest friends can go
With anyone to death, comes so far short
They might as well not try to go at all.
105   No, from the time when one is sick to death,
One is alone, and he dies more alone.
Friends make pretense of following to the grave,
But before one is in it, their minds are turned
And making the best of their way back to life
110   And living people, and things they understand.
But the world's evil. I won't have grief so
If I can change it. Oh, I won't, I won't!"

"There, you have said it all and you feel better.
You won't go now. You're crying. Close the door.

115 The heart's gone out of it: why keep it up?
    Amy! There's someone coming down the road!"

    "*You*—oh, you think the talk is all. I must go—
    Somewhere out of this house. How can I make you——"

    "If—you—do!" She was opening the door wider.
120 "Where do you mean to go? First tell me that.
    I'll follow and bring you back by force. I *will*!—"

E. E. CUMMINGS (1894–1962)

"anyone lived in a pretty how town" (1940)

anyone lived in a pretty how town
(with up so floating many bells down)
spring summer autumn winter
he sang his didn't he danced his did

5 Women and men(both little and small)
cared for anyone not at all
they sowed their isn't they reaped their same
sun moon stars rain

children guessed(but only a few
10 and down they forgot as up they grew
autumn winter spring summer)
that noone loved him more by more

when by now and tree by leaf
she laughed his joy she cried his grief
15 bird by snow and stir by still
anyone's any was all to her

someones married their everyones
laughed their cryings and did their dance
(sleep wake hope and then)they
20 said their nevers they slept their dream

stars rain sun moon
(and only the snow can begin to explain
how children are apt to forget to remember
with up so floating many bells down)

25   one day anyone died i guess
(and noone stooped to kiss his face)
busy folk buried them side by side
little by little and was by was

all by all and deep by deep
30   and more by more they dream their sleep
noone and anyone earth by april
wish by spirit and if by yes.

Women and men(both dong and ding)
summer autumn winter spring
35   reaped their sowing and went their came
sun moon stars rain

LANGSTON HUGHES (1902–1967)

Theme for English B (1951)

The instructor said,

    Go home and write
    a page tonight.
    And let that page come out of you—
5   *Then, it will be true.*

I wonder if it's that simple?
I am twenty-two, colored, born in Winston-Salem.
I went to school there, then Durham, then here
to this college on the hill above Harlem.
10   I am the only colored student in my class.
The steps from the hill lead down into Harlem,
through a park, then I cross St. Nicholas,
Eighth Avenue, Seventh, and I come to the Y,
the Harlem Branch Y, where I take the elevator.
15   up to my room, sit down, and write this page:

It's not easy to know what is true for you or me
at twenty-two, my age. But I guess I'm what
I feel and see and hear, Harlem, I hear you:
hear you, hear me—we two—you, me, talk on this page.
20   (I hear New York, too.) Me—who?
Well, I like to eat, sleep, drink, and be in love.

I like to work, read, learn, and understand life.
I like a pipe for a Christmas present,
or records—Bessie,[1] bop, or Bach.
25   I guess being colored doesn't make me *not* like
the same things other folks like who are other races.
So will my page be colored that I write?
Being me, it will not be white.
But it will be
30   a part of you, instructor.
You are white—
yet a part of me, as I am a part of you.
That's American.
Sometimes perhaps you don't want to be a part of me.
35   Nor do I often want to be a part of you.
But we are, that's true!
I guess you learn from me—
although you're older—and white—
and somewhat more free.

40   This is my page for English B.

THEODORE ROETHKE   (1908–1963)

Big Wind   (1948)

Where were the greenhouses going,
Lunging into the lashing
Wind driving water
So far down the river
5   All the faucets stopped?—
So we drained the manure-machine
For the steam plant,
Pumping the stale mixture
Into the rusty boilers,
10   Watching the pressure gauge
Waver over to red,
As the seams hissed
And the live steam
Drove to the far
15   End of the rose-house,
Where the worst wind was,

---

[1] **Bessie:** Bessie Smith (ca. 1894–1937), a blues singer.

Creaking the cypress window-frames,
Cracking so much thin glass
We stayed all night,
20   Stuffing the holes with burlap;
But she rode it out,
That old rose-house,
She hove into the teeth of it,
The core and pith of that ugly storm,
25   Ploughing with her stiff prow,
Bucking into the wind-waves
That broke over the whole of her,
Flailing her sides with spray,
Flinging long strings of wet across the roof-top,
30   Finally veering, wearing themselves out, merely
Whistling thinly under the wind-vents;
She sailed until the calm morning,
Carrying her full cargo of roses.

ELIZABETH BISHOP   (1911–1979)

The Moose   (1976)
For Grace Bulmer Bowers

From narrow provinces[1]
of fish and bread and tea,
home of the long tides
where the bay leaves the sea
5   twice a day and takes
the herrings long rides,

where if the river
enters or retreats
in a wall of brown foam
10   depends on if it meets
the bay coming in,
the bay not at home;

---

[1] **From narrow provinces:** The geography of the poem belongs to Canada, especially the towns and coastline of Nova Scotia, where Bishop was born, and New Brunswick.

where, silted red,
sometimes the sun sets
15 facing a red sea,
and others, veins the flats'
lavender, rich mud
in burning rivulets;

on red, gravelly roads,
20 down rows of sugar maples,
past clapboard farmhouses
and neat, clapboard churches,
bleached, ridged as clamshells,
past twin silver birches,

25 through late afternoon
a bus journeys west,
the windshield flashing pink,
pink glancing off of metal,
brushing the dented flank
30 of blue, beat-up enamel;

down hollows, up rises,
and waits, patient, while
a lone traveller gives
kisses and embraces
35 to seven relatives
and a collie supervises.

Goodbye to the elms,
to the farm, to the dog.
The bus starts. The light
40 grows richer; the fog,
shifting, salty, thin,
comes closing in.

Its cold, round crystals
form and slide and settle
45 in the white hens' feathers,
in gray glazed cabbages,
on the cabbage roses
and lupins like apostles;

the sweet peas cling
50 to their wet white string
on the whitewashed fences;
bumblebees creep

inside the foxgloves,
and evening commences.

55   One stop at Bass River.
Then the Economies—
Lower, Middle, Upper;
Five Islands, Five Houses,
where a woman shakes a tablecloth
60   out after supper.

A pale flickering. Gone.
The Tantramar[2] marshes
and the smell of salt hay.
An iron bridge trembles
65   and a loose plank rattles
but doesn't give way.

On the left, a red light
swims through the dark:
a ship's port lantern.
70   Two rubber boots show,
illuminated, solemn.
A dog gives one bark.

A woman climbs in
with two market bags,
75   brisk, freckled, elderly.
"A grand night. Yes, sir,
all the way to Boston."
She regards us amicably.

Moonlight as we enter
80   the New Brunswick woods,
hairy, scratchy, splintery;
moonlight and mist
caught in them like lamb's wool
on bushes in a pasture.

85   The passengers lie back.
Snores. Some long sighs.
A dreamy divagation°   digression
begins in the night,
a gentle, auditory,
90   slow hallucination. . . .

---

[2] **Tantramar:** The Tantramar River in New Brunswick pours into the Bay of Fundy.

In the creakings and noises,
an old conversation
—not concerning us,
but recognizable, somewhere,
95   back in the bus:
Grandparents' voices

uninterruptedly
talking, in Eternity:
names being mentioned,
100   things cleared up finally;
what he said, what she said,
who got pensioned;

deaths, deaths and sicknesses;
the year he remarried;
105   the year (something) happened.
She died in childbirth.
That was the son lost
when the schooner foundered.

He took to drink. Yes.
110   She went to the bad.
When Amos began to pray
even in the store and
finally the family had
to put him away.

115   "Yes . . ." that peculiar
affirmative. "Yes . . ."
A sharp, indrawn breath,
half groan, half acceptance,
that means "Life's like that.
120   We know *it* (also death)."

Talking the way they talked
in the old featherbed,
peacefully, on and on,
dim lamplight in the hall,
125   down in the kitchen, the dog
tucked in her shawl.

Now, it's all right now
even to fall asleep
just as on all those nights.
130   —Suddenly the bus driver

stops with a jolt,
turns off his lights.

A moose has come out of
the impenetrable wood
135 and stands there, looms, rather,
in the middle of the road.
It approaches; it sniffs at
the bus's hot hood.

Towering, antlerless,
140 high as a church,
homely as a house
(or, safe as houses).
A man's voice assures us
"Perfectly harmless. . . ."

145 Some of the passengers
exclaim in whispers,
childishly, softly,
"Sure are big creatures."
"It's awful plain."
150 "Look! It's a she!"

Taking her time,
she looks the bus over,
grand, otherworldly.
Why, why do we feel
155 (we all feel) this sweet
sensation of joy?

"Curious creatures,"
says our quiet driver,
rolling his *r*'s.
160 "Look at that, would you."
Then he shifts gears.
For a moment longer,

by craning backward,
the moose can be seen
165 on the moonlit macadam;
then there's a dim
smell of moose, an acrid
smell of gasoline.

ROBERT HAYDEN (1913–1982)

Middle Passage[1] (1962)

I

Jesús, Estrella, Esperanza, Mercy:[2]

   Sails flashing to the wind like weapons,
   sharks following the moans the fever and the dying:
   horror the corposant and compass rose.

   Middle Passage:
5   voyage through death
           to life upon these shores.

   "10 April 1800—
   Blacks rebellious. Crew uneasy. Our linguist says
   their moaning is a prayer for death,
10   ours and their own. Some try to starve themselves.
   Lost three this morning leaped with crazy laughter
   to the waiting sharks, sang as they went under."

Desire, Adventure, Tartar, Ann:

   Standing to America, bringing home
15   black gold, black ivory, black seed.

       Deep in the festering hold thy father lies,
       of his bones New England pews are made,
       those are altar lights that were his eyes.

   Jesus Saviour Pilot Me
20   Over Life's Tempestuous Sea[3]

   We pray that Thou wilt grant, O Lord,
   safe passage to our vessels bringing
   heathen souls unto Thy chastening.

   Jesus Saviour

25   "8 bells. I cannot sleep, for I am sick
       with fear, but writing eases fear a little
       since still my eyes can see these words take shape

---

[1] **Middle Passage:** Voyage across the Atlantic Ocean aboard slave ships.
[2] **Jesús . . . Mercy:** Names of slave ships. "Estrella," in Spanish, means star. "Esperanza" means hope.
[3] **Jesus . . . Sea:** Lyrics from a Protestant hymn.

upon the page & so I write, as one
would turn to exorcism. 4 days scudding,
30   but now the sea is calm again. Misfortune
follows in our wake like sharks (our grinning
tutelary gods). Which one of us
has killed an albatross?[4] A plague among
our blacks—Ophthalmia: blindness—& we
35   have jettisoned the blind to no avail.
It spreads, the terrifying sickness spreads.
Its claws have scratched sight from the Capt.'s eyes
& there is blindness in the fo'c'sle[5]
& we must sail 3 weeks before we come
40   to port."

What port awaits us, Davy Jones'
or home? I've heard of slavers drifting, drifting,
playthings of wind and storm and chance, their crews
gone blind, the jungle hatred
45   *crawling up on deck.*

Thou Who Walked On Galilee

"Deponent further sayeth *The Bella J*
left the Guinea Coast
with cargo of five hundred blacks and odd
50   for the barracoons° of Florida: slave quarters

"That there was hardly room 'tween-decks for half
the sweltering cattle stowed spoon-fashion there;
that some went mad of thirst and tore their flesh
and sucked the blood:

55   "That Crew and Captain lusted with the comeliest
of the savage girls kept naked in the cabins;
that there was one they called The Guinea Rose
and they cast lots and fought to lie with her:

"That when the Bo's'n° piped all hands, the flames   boatswain
60   spreading from starboard already were beyond
control, the negroes howling and their chains
entangled with the flames:

---

[4] **Which one . . . albatross:** In Coleridge's "Rime of the Ancient Mariner," a ship is lost at sea when a
member of the crew kills an albatross, typically considered to be an omen of good luck.
[5] **fo'c'sle:** The forecastle, or sailors' quarters on a ship.

"That the burning blacks could not be reached,
that the Crew abandoned ship,
65   leaving their shrieking negresses behind,
that the Captain perished drunken with the wenches:

"Further Deponent sayeth not."

Pilot Oh Pilot Me

II

Aye, lad, and I have seen those factories,
70   Gambia, Rio Pongo, Calabar;[6]
have watched the artful mongos° baiting traps   *Africans*
of war wherein the victor and the vanquished

Were caught as prizes for our barracoons.
Have seen the nigger kings whose vanity
75   and greed turned wild black hides of Fellatah,
Mandingo, Ibo, Kru[7] to gold for us.

And there was one—King Anthracite° we named him—   *coal*
fetish face beneath French parasols
of brass and orange velvet, impudent mouth
80   whose cups were carven skulls of enemies:

He'd honor us with drum and feast and conjo°   *dance*
and palm-oil-glistening wenches deft in love,
and for tin crowns that shone with paste,
red calico and German-silver trinkets

85   Would have the drums talk war and send
his warriors to burn the sleeping villages
and kill the sick and old and lead the young
in coffles° to our factories.   *slave gangs*

Twenty years a trader, twenty years,
90   for there was wealth aplenty to be harvested
from those black fields, and I'd be trading still
but for the fevers melting down my bones.

---

[6] **Gambia . . . Calabar:** Gambia is a country in western Africa, and the Rio Pongo is an African
waterway. Calabar is a city in Nigeria.
[7] **Fellatah . . . Kru:** African tribes.

III

Shuttles in the rocking loom of history,
the dark ships move, the dark ships move,
95   their bright ironical names
like jests of kindness on a murderer's mouth;
plough through thrashing glister toward
fata morgana's° lucent melting shore,   a mirage
weave toward New World littorals° that are   coasts
100   mirage and myth and actual shore.

Voyage through death,
                     voyage whose chartings are unlove.

A charnel stench, effluvium of living death
spreads outward from the hold,
105   where the living and the dead, the horribly dying,
lie interlocked, lie foul with blood and excrement.

    Deep in the festering hold thy father lies,
    the corpse of mercy rots with him,
    rats eat love's rotten gelid° eyes.   frigid

110   *But, oh, the living look at you*
    with human eyes whose suffering accuses you,
    whose hatred reaches through the swill of dark
    to strike you like a leper's claw.

    You cannot stare that hatred down
115   *or chain the fear that stalks the watches*
    and breathes on you its fetid scorching breath;
    cannot kill the deep immortal human wish,
    the timeless will.

    "But for the storm that flung up barriers
120   of wind and wave, *The Amistad*,[8] señores,
    would have reached the port of Principe in two,
    three days at most; but for the storm we should
    have been prepared for what befell.
    Swift as the puma's leap it came. There was

---

[8] **The Amistad:** Spanish: "friendship." The Spanish ship carried slaves obtained illegally near Cuba in 1839. The slaves, led by Cinquez, rebelled, killing the captain and taking over the ship. After two months, the Amistad and its mutineers were captured near Long Island. In a landmark Supreme Court Case, the Africans were defended by former U.S. President John Quincy Adams; ruling in their favor, the surviving Africans were absolved of charges and returned to Africa.

125 that interval of moonless calm filled only
 with the water's and the rigging's usual sounds,
 then sudden movement, blows and snarling cries
 and they had fallen on us with machete
 and marlinspike. It was as though the very
130 air, the night itself were striking us.
 Exhausted by the rigors of the storm,
 we were no match for them. Our men went down
 before the murderous Africans. Our loyal
 Celestino ran from below with gun
135 and lantern and I saw, before the cane-
 knife's wounding flash, Cinquez,
 that surly brute who calls himself a prince,
 directing, urging on the ghastly work.
 He hacked the poor mulatto down, and then
140 he turned on me. The decks were slippery
 when daylight finally came. It sickens me
 to think of what I saw, of how these apes
 threw overboard the butchered bodies of
 our men, true Christians all, like so much jetsam
145 Enough, enough. The rest is quickly told:
 Cinquez was forced to spare the two of us
 you see to steer the ship to Africa,
 and we like phantoms doomed to rove the sea
 voyaged east by day and west by night,
150 deceiving them, hoping for rescue,
 prisoners on our own vessel, till
 at length we drifted to the shores of this
 your land, America, where we were freed
 from our unspeakable misery. Now we
155 demand, good sirs, the extradition of
 Cinquez and his accomplices to La
 Havana. And it distresses us to know
 there are so many here who seem inclined
 to justify the mutiny of these blacks.
160 We find it paradoxical indeed
 that you whose wealth, whose tree of liberty
 are rooted in the labor of your slaves
 should suffer the august John Quincy Adams
 to speak with so much passion of the right
165 of chattel slaves to kill their lawful masters
 and with his Roman rhetoric weave a hero's
 garland for Cinquez. I tell you that
 we are determined to return to Cuba
 with our slaves and there see justice done. Cinquez—
170 or let us say 'the Prince'—Cinquez shall die."

The deep immortal human wish,
the timeless will:

Cinquez its deathless primaveral[9] image,
life that transfigures many lives.

175   Voyage through death
                        to life upon these shores.

JAMES DICKEY (1923–1997)

Cherrylog Road (1963)

Off Highway 106
At Cherrylog Road I entered
The '34 Ford without wheels,
Smothered in kudzu,[1]
5   With a seat pulled out to run
Corn whiskey down from the hills,

And then from the other side
Crept into an Essex
With a rumble seat of red leather
10   And then out again, aboard
A blue Chevrolet, releasing
The rust from its other color,

Reared up on three building blocks.
None had the same body heat;
15   I changed with them inward, toward
The weedy heart of the junkyard,
For I knew that Doris Holbrook
Would escape from her father at noon

And would come from the farm
20   To seek parts owned by the sun
Among the abandoned chassis,
Sitting in each in turn
As I did, leaning forward
As in a wild stock-car race

---

[9] **primaveral:** Spanish: "springlike."
[1] **kudzu:** Fast-growing vine common in the southern United States.

25   In the parking lot of the dead.
      Time after time, I climbed in
      And out the other side, like
      An envoy or movie star
      Met at the station by crickets.
30   A radiator cap raised its head,

      Become a real toad or a kingsnake
      As I neared the hub of the yard,
      Passing through many states,
      Many lives, to reach
35   Some grandmother's long Pierce-Arrow [2]
      Sending platters of blindness forth

      From its nickel hubcaps
      And spilling its tender upholstery
      On sleepy roaches,
40   The glass panel in between
      Lady and colored driver
      Not all the way broken out,

      The back-seat phone
      Still on its hook.
45   I got in as though to exclaim,
      "Let us go to the orphan asylum,
      John; I have some old toys
      For children who say their prayers."

      I popped with sweat as I thought
50   I heard Doris Holbrook scrape
      Like a mouse in the southern-state sun
      That was eating the paint in blisters
      From a hundred car tops and hoods.
      She was tapping like code,

55   Loosening the screws,
      Carrying off headlights,
      Sparkplugs, bumpers,
      Cracked mirrors and gear-knobs,
      Getting ready, already,
60   To go back with something to show

      Other than her lips' new trembling
      I would hold to me soon, soon,

---

[2] **Pierce-Arrow:** United States company that manufactured luxury cars from 1901 to 1938.

Where I sat in the ripped back seat
Talking over the interphone,
65   Praying for Doris Holbrook
To come from her father's farm

And to get back there
With no trace of me on her face
To be seen by her red-haired father
70   Who would change, in the squalling barn,
Her back's pale skin with a strop,
Then lay for me

In a bootlegger's roasting car
With a string-triggered 12-gauge shotgun
75   To blast the breath from the air.
Not cut by the jagged windshields,
Through the acres of wrecks she came
With a wrench in her hand,

Through dust where the blacksnake dies
80   Of boredom, and the beetle knows
The compost has no more life.
Someone outside would have seen
The oldest car's door inexplicably
Close from within:

85   I held her and held her and held her,
Convoyed at terrific speed
By the stalled, dreaming traffic around us,
So the blacksnake, stiff
With inaction, curved back
90   Into life, and hunted the mouse

With deadly overexcitement,
The beetles reclaimed their field
As we clung, glued together,
With the hooks of the seat springs
95   Working through to catch us red-handed
Amidst the gray, breathless batting

That burst from the seat at our backs.
We left by separate doors
Into the changed, other bodies
100   Of cars, she down Cherrylog Road
And I to my motorcycle
Parked like the soul of the junkyard

Restored, a bicycle fleshed
With power, and tore off
105 Up Highway 106, continually
Drunk on the wind in my mouth,
Wringing the handlebar for speed,
Wild to be wreckage forever.

WOLE SOYINKA (1934–   )

Telephone Conversation (1962)

The price seemed reasonable, location
Indifferent. The landlady swore she lived
Off premises. Nothing remained
But self-confession. "Madam," I warned,
5   "I hate a wasted journey—I am African."
Silence. Silenced transmission of
Pressurized good-breeding. Voice, when it came,
Lipstick coated, long gold-rolled
Cigarette-holder pipped. Caught I was, foully.
10   "HOW DARK?" . . . I had not misheard . . . "ARE YOU LIGHT
OR VERY DARK?" Button B. Button A.[1] Stench
Of rancid breath of public hide-and-speak.
Red booth. Red pillar-box. Red double-tiered
Omnibus squelching tar. It *was* real! Shamed
15   By ill-mannered silence, surrender
Pushed dumbfoundment to beg simplification.
Considerate she was, varying the emphasis—
"ARE YOU DARK? OR VERY LIGHT?" Revelation came.
"You mean—like plain or milk chocolate?"
20   Her assent was clinical, crushing in its light
Impersonality. Rapidly, wave-length adjusted,
I chose. "West African sepia"—and as afterthought,
"Down in my passport." Silence for spectroscopic
Flight of fancy, till truthfulness clanged her accent
25   Hard on the mouthpiece. "WHAT'S THAT?" conceding
"DON'T KNOW WHAT THAT IS." "Like brunette."
"THAT'S DARK, ISN'T IT?" "Not altogether.
Facially, I am brunette, but, madam, you should see
The rest of me. Palm of my hand, soles of my feet

---

[1] **Button B. Button A.:** Buttons found on old British pay phones.

30 Are a peroxide blond. Friction, caused—
    Foolishly, madam—by sitting down, has turned
    My bottom raven black—One moment, madam!"—sensing
    Her receiver rearing on the thunderclap
    About my ears—"Madam," I pleaded, "wouldn't you rather
35 See for yourself?"

JORIE GRAHAM (1950–   )

The Hiding Place (1991)

        The last time I saw it was 1968.
    Paris, France. The time of the *disturbances*.
        We had claims. Schools shut down.
    A million *workers* and *students* on strike.

5   Marches, sit-ins, helicopters, gas.
    They stopped you at gunpoint asking for papers.

        I spent 11 nights sleeping in the halls. Arguments. *Negotiations*.
    Hurrying in the dawn looking for a certain leader
        I found his face above an open streetfire.
10 *No* he said, tell them *no concessions*.
        His voice above the fire as if there were no fire—

    language floating everywhere above the sleeping bodies;
            and crates of fruit donated in secret;
    and torn sheets (for tear gas) tossed down from shuttered windows;
15   and bread; and blankets, stolen from the firehouse.

    The CRS[1] (the government police) would swarm in around dawn
            in small blue vans and round us up.
    Once I watched the searchbeams play on some flames.
            The flames push up into the corridor of light.

20 In the cell we were so crowded no one could sit or lean.
            People peed on each other. I felt a girl
    vomiting gently onto my back.
            I found two Americans rounded up by chance,
    their charter left that morning they screamed, what were they going to do?

---

[1] **CRS:** Compagnie Républicaine de Sécurité, the riot control forces of the French National Police.

25   Later a man in a uniform came in with a stick.
      Started beating here and there, found the girl in her eighth month.
              He beat her frantically over and over.
      He pummeled her belly. Screaming aren't you ashamed?

              I remember the cell vividly
30   but is it from a photograph? I think the shadows as I
              see them still—the slatted brilliant bits
      against the wall—I think they're true—but are they from a photograph?
              Do I see it from inside now—his hands, her face—or

      is it from the new account?
35   The strangest part of getting out again was *streets*.
      The light running down them.
              Everything spilling whenever the wall breaks.
      And the air—thick with dwellings—the air filled—doubled—
              as if the open

40   had been made to render—
              The open squeezed for space until the hollows spill out,
      story upon story of them
              starting to light up as I walked out.
      How thick was the empty meant to be?
45   What were we finding in the air?

              What were we meant to find?
      I went home slowly sat in my rented room.
              Sat for a long time the window open,

              watched the white gauze curtain sluff this way then that
50   a bit—
              watched the air suck it out, push it back in. Lung
      of the room with streetcries in it. Watched until the lights
              outside made it gold, pumping gently.
      Was I meant to get up again? I was inside. The century clicked by.
55   The woman below called down *not to forget the*

              loaf. Crackle of helicopters. Voice on a loudspeaker issuing
      warnings.
              They made agreements we all returned to work.
      The government fell but then it was all right again.
60   The man above the fire, listening to my question,

      the red wool shirt he wore: where is it? who has it?
              He looked straight back into the century: no concessions.
      I took the message back.

The look in his eyes—shoving out—into the open—
65   expressionless with thought:
   no—tell them *no*—

DAVID MASON (1954–   )

Spooning (1991)

After my grandfather died I went back home
to help my mother sell his furniture:
the old chair he did his sitting on,
the kitchen things. Going through his boxes
5   I found letters, cancelled checks, the usual
old photographs of relatives I hardly knew
and grandmother, clutching an apron in both hands.
And *her.* There was an old publicity still
taken when she wore her hair like a helmet,
10   polished black. Posed before a cardboard shell
and painted waves, she seemed unattainable,
as she was meant to.

                    For years we thought he lied
about his knowing her when he was young,
15   but grandfather was a man who hated liars,
a man who worshipped all the tarnished virtues,
when daily to his shop at eight, until
the first of three strokes forced him to retire.

He liked talking. Somebody had to listen,
20   so I was the listener for hours after school
until my parents called me home for dinner.
We'd sit on his glassed-in porch where he kept a box
of apples wrapped in newsprint.

He told me about the time he lost a job
25   at the mill. Nooksack[1] seemed to kill its young
with boredom even then, but he owned a car,
a '24 Ford. He drove it east to see
America, got as far as Spokane's desert,
sold the car and worked back on the railroad.

---

[1] **Nooksack:** Nooksack is a town in northwestern Washington; Spokane lies at the eastern border of that state.

30 Sometimes he asked me what I liked to do.
I told him about the drive-in movies where
my brother, Billy, took me if I paid.
In small towns everyone goes to the movies.
Not grandfather. He said they made them better when
35 nobody talked, and faces told it all.
"I knew Lydia Truman Gates," he said,
"back when she was plain old Lydia Carter
down on Water Street. One time her old man
caught us spooning out to the railroad tracks.
40 Nearly tanned my hide. He was a fisherman—
that is, till she moved her folks to Hollywood."

I don't know why, but I simply couldn't ask
what spooning was. He seemed to talk then
more to his chair's abrasions on the floor,
45 more to the pale alders outside his window.
The way he said her name I couldn't ask
who was Lydia Truman Gates.

*

                    "Nonsense,"
was all my mother said at dinner. "His mind
50 went haywire in the hospital. He's old.
He makes things up and can't tell the difference."

I think my father's smile embarrassed her
when he said, "The poor guy's disappointed.
Nothing went right for him, so he daydreams."

55 "Nonsense," my mother said. "And anyway
no Lydia Truman Gates ever came
from a town like this."

    "It's not so bad a place."
I make a pretty decent living here."

60 My mother huffed. While I stared past my plate
Billy asked, "Who is Lydia Truman Gates?"

*

It wasn't long before we all found out.
The papers ran a story on her. How
she was famous in the twenties for a while,
65 married the oil billionaire, Gates, and retired.
She was coming back home to Nooksack. The mayor

would give a big award and ask her help
to renovate our landmark theatre.

Our mother said we had better things to spend
70 our money on than some old movie house,
though she remembered how it used to look.
She said that people living in the past
wouldn't amount to much.
Billy and I pretended we didn't care.
75 We didn't tell our parents where we went
that night, riding our bikes in a warm wind
past the fishhouses on the Puget Sound,
and up Grant Street to the Hiawatha.

Inside, Billy held my hand, and showed me
80 faded paintings of Indians on the walls
and dark forest patterns in the worn carpet.
The place smelled stale like old decaying clothes
shut up in a trunk for twenty years,
but Nooksack's best were there, some in tuxes,
85 and women stuffed into their evening gowns.
We sat in the balcony looking down
on bald heads, high hair-dos and jewels.
Near the stage they had a twenty-piece band—
I still remember when the lights went out
90 the violins rose like a flock of birds
all at once. The drums sounded a shudder.

We saw *Morocco Gold, The Outlaw, Colonel Clay*
and the comic short, *A Bird in the Hand,*
flickering down to the screen
95 where Lydia Truman Gates arose in veils,
in something gossamer
astonishing even in 1965.
Lydia Truman Gates was like a dream
of lithe attention, her dark eyes laughing
100 at death, at poverty or a satin bed.
And when they brought her on the stage, applause
rising and falling like a tidal wave,
I had to stand up on my seat to see
a frail old woman assisted by two men,
105 tiny on that distant stage.

                    My brother
yanked me past what seemed like a hundred pairs
of knees for all the times I said, "Excuse us."

We ran out where the chauffeur
110 waited by her limousine, his face painted
green by the light from Heilman's Piano Store,
breathing smoke. "You guys keep your distance."

"Is she coming out?"

                    He crushed his cigarette:
115 "No, she's gonna die in there. What do you think?"

More people joined us, pacing in the alley,
watching the chauffeur smoke by the door propped
open with a cinderblock.
And then the door half-opened, sighed back,
120 opened at last on the forearm of a man.

Behind him, Lydia Truman Gates stepped out
with her cane—hardly the woman I had seen
enduring all the problems of the world
with such aplomb. She stared down at the pavement,
125 saying, "Thank you, I can see it clearly now."

"Mrs. Gates," Billy stuttered. "Mrs. Gates."

The chauffeur tried to block us, but she said,
"That's all right, Andrew. They're just kids. I'm safe."

"Our grandpa says hello," I blurted out.

130 She paused for half a beat, glanced at Billy,
then peered at me as if to study terror,
smiling. "Well I'll be damned. And who's he?"

"Don't listen to him," Billy said. "He's nuts."

"George McCracken," I said, "the one you spooned with
135 down by the railroad tracks."

                    "George McCracken."
She straightened, looked up at the strip of sky.
"Spooned. Well, that's one way to talk about it."
She laughed from deep down in her husky lungs.
140 "Old Georgie McCracken. Is he still alive?
Too scared to come downtown and say hello?"
She reached out from her furs and touched my hair.
"Thanks for the message, little man. I knew him.

I knew he'd never get out of this town.
145   You tell your grampa Hi from Liddy Carter."

The man at her elbow said they had to leave.
She nodded, handing her award and purse
to the chauffeur.

                 Then flashbulbs started popping.
150   I saw her face lit up, then pale and caving
back into the darkness. "Christ," she whispered,
"get me out of here."

                  I stumbled, or was pushed.
My eyes kept seeing her exploding at me,
155   a woman made entirely of light
beside the smaller figure who was real.
Two men tipped her into the limousine
and it slid off like a shark, parting the crowd.

                  *

A picture ran in the next day's *Herald*—
160   the great actress touches a local boy.
For two weeks everybody talked about me,
but I kept thinking, "Is he still alive?
Too scared to come downtown and say hello?"

I thought of her decaying on a screen,
165   her ribs folding like a silk umbrella's rods,
while all the men who gathered around her
clutched at the remnants of her empty dress.

CHAPTER 4

OH! BLESSED RAGE FOR ORDER

—Wallace Stevens

An Anthology of the Ode

One of the more ancient forms of poetry is the ode, which may be defined as a poem of considerable length that takes up fairly serious themes in an elevated style, and is usually written in some kind of stanzas. The shape and manner of the ode has varied over time, and each age has demanded something different from this form, which has proved unusually flexible. Poets have responded to these demands in fascinating ways, finding something in the form itself to inspire them and continually refreshing the possibilities of the ode.

In the classical era, two ancient poets stood out as practitioners of the ode: Pindar and Horace. Each defined the form in his own way, and each generated a tradition of ode writing. The great revival of the ode during the early nineteenth century in England—Wordsworth, Keats, and Shelley were masters of the form—seems to have drawn on both of these traditions.

Pindar stood out as one of the great lyric poets of the fifth century, B.C. In fact, he is one of the first lyric poets whose texts survive intact. He was much revered in his time as an innovative poet who loved complex stanza forms and extremely rich language. His odes derived from choral song, which in ancient Greece was used to celebrate public occasions, such as victories in war or athletic events. Pindar became popular among English poets beginning in the sixteenth century. Some of the greatest lyric poems in English belong to this tradition, including the "Pindaric Ode" (also called the "Cary/Morison Ode") of Ben Jonson (p. 382), Milton's "Nativity Ode" (p. 384), Dryden's "Alexander's Feast" (p. 396), Wordsworth's "Intimations of Immortality" (409), and Hopkins's "Wreck of the Deutschland" (p. 427).

Following the choral form made popular by Greek drama, in his odes, Pindar adhered closely to a three-part or triadic structure in which a stanza called a **strophe** is followed by one called an **antistrophe,** which in turn is followed by a stanza called an **epode.** In a Greek play, the chorus danced to the left when singing the strophe; they danced to the right when singing the antistrophe. During the epode, they stood still. In later poetry in English, these three movements were often called "turn," "counterturn," and "stand."

Pindaric odes often begin and end with a similar kind of language or thematic material, giving them a sense of unity or completion; this approach to shaping a poem is called **ring composition.** This material may be personal to the poet, whereas the main body of the poem will treat a larger theme, celebrate a victory, or describe a mythic event. An interesting adaptation of ring composition, for example, is Hopkins's "The Wreck of the Deutschland" (p. 427), where the opening and closing segments refer to the poet's own religious conversion; the middle and main section depicts the sinking of a ship and the death of five nuns aboard that ship.

Pindar was an aristocrat from Boeotia, part of ancient Greece, and his odes often celebrate victory in athletic contests or chariot races. These are not usually thought of as weighty subjects, but in the hands of a poet like Pindar, such contests become an occasion for elaborate reflections of a highly religious or philosophical character. Athletic contests were often staged in honor of some god, and so the ode acquired a ceremonial aspect. The victory was often compared to some great myth, placing the momentary success of athletes in a timeless space and giving a sense of permanence to the event. Pindar liked to moralize as well, so his odes became vehicles for serious ethical reflection, a fact that influenced later poets writing in the Pindaric mode, from Ben Jonson through Wordsworth and Hopkins.

It is easy to see why the English poets of the Romantic period were drawn to Pindar; he loved to seek out the spiritual implications of physical events and images. He was drawn to moments of extreme beauty that have a lasting effect, and he was a consummate artist, reveling in complex stanza patterns. But there is always in Pindar a strong sense of unity, a fusion of elements. His odes make a unified and definite impression.

The Roman poet, Horace, was utterly different in temperament from Pindar, although he shared with his Greek ancestor a love of elaborate stanzas. Horatian odes often are meditations on history or historical events, and they are usually **homostrophic:** written in stanzas of equal length, with (in the English ode) a similar rhyme scheme, as in Keats's "Ode on a Grecian Urn" (p. 421). The Horatian ode is usually quiet, meditative, and restrained in tone, in contrast to the Pindaric ode, which is visionary and expansive. A fine example of the influence of Horace on the English ode is found in the famous "Horatian Ode upon Cromwell's Return from Ireland" (p. 392) written by Andrew Marvell in 1650. But almost any of the odes by Keats reflect this tradition as well.

All definitions of the ode are suitably vague, as so many different kinds of poem may be included in this category. What links all of them is that the poets writing them identified with a particular tradition. They were always serious, addressing important subjects or themes in a formal manner. They assumed that a poet must—or should attempt to—

treat important material in this extended lyric form. However, there is often—especially in the nineteenth and twentieth centuries—a sense of failure in the poem as well, as the poet stands up to his or her theme without confidence, sensing a gap between the language used and the events described.

From Marvell's "Horatian Ode" (p. 392) through the magnificent "Nativity Ode" of Milton (p. 384) and "Alexander's Feast" by Dryden (p. 396), one will notice the poet again and again adapting the form to fit his own purposes. This adaptability is the key to the survival of the form, which has yielded some magnificent work in modern and contemporary poetry, including "The Idea of Order at Key West" by Wallace Stevens (p. 436) and Robert Creeley's "America" (p. 442). In each case, the poet will be seen to address a lofty subject and deal with the material with a certain ferocity of attention, always looking for larger philosophical or moral or aesthetic points. The poem itself will twist, with a wild, associational logic, from stanza to stanza, accumulating power as it proceeds, always harking back—explicitly or inexplicitly—to the grand tradition of the ode itself.

ADDITIONAL EXAMPLES OF THE ODE IN THIS BOOK

Horace, from Odes Book III, *Exegi Monumentum* (trans. by James Michie) (p. 1411)

Richard Lovelace, "The Grasshopper: To My Noble Friend, Mr. Charles Cotton: Ode" (p. 1343)

Percy Bysshe Shelley, "To a Skylark" (p. 1347)

John Keats, "Ode to a Nightingale" (p. 1352)

John Keats, "To Autumn" (p. 1584)

William Cullen Bryant, "To a Waterfowl" (p. 1351)

Robert Frost, "After Apple-Picking" (p. 1585)

Allen Tate, "Ode to the Confederate Dead" (p. 1612)

Robert Lowell, "For the Union Dead" (p. 1614)

William Wordsworth, "Lines Written a Few Miles above Tintern Abbey" (p. 1576)

Robert Hass, "Meditation at Lagunitas" (p. 1464)

Billy Collins, "Lines Composed Over Three Thousand Miles from Tintern Abbey" (p. 1580)

PINDAR (522 B.C.–438 B.C.)
trans. Richmond Lattimore

Olympia 12

Daughter of Zeus who sets free, I beseech you, Fortune,
lady of salvation, guard the wide strength of Himera.[1]
By your power are steered fleet ships on the sea,
sudden wars by land, the gatherings heavy
5   with counsel. Men's hopes, oft in the air,
downward rock again as they shear a heaving sea of lies.

Never yet has a man who walks upon earth
found from God sure sign of the matter to come.
Perception of future goes blind.
10   Many things fall counter to judgment, sometimes
against delight, yet others that encountered evil
gales win in a moment depth of grandeur for pain.

Son of Philanor,[2] like a cock that fights at home
by his own hearth, even so the splendor
15   of your feet might have dropped to obscurity, had not
strife that sets men at odds cost you your homeland, Knossos.
Now, Ergoteles, garlanded at Olympia,
twice at Pytho, at the Isthmos, here at your new home,
Himera, you magnify in fame the Bathing Place of the Nymphs.

HORACE (65 B.C.–8 B.C.)
trans. James Michie

from Odes, Book I (23 B.C.)

II

Enough the ordeal now, the snow- and hail-storms
God has unleashed on earth, whose red right hand hurled
Bolts at the Capitol's[1] sacred summits, spreading
   Fear in the City streets,

---

[1] **Himera:** A region in Greece.
[2] **Son of Philanor:** A young athlete called Ergoteles who fled Knosses, on the island of Crete in ancient Greece, when a revolution broke out. It was as a citizen of Himera that he twice won long footraces in the Olympics.
[1] **Capitol's:** Temple of Jupiter in Rome, named Capitol (from Latin *caput,* "head") after workers uncovered a bloody head near its foundation, viewed as a sign that Rome would be the "head" on an empire.

5   Fear among nations lest the age of horror
     Should come again when Pyrrha[2] gasped at strange sights:
     Old Proteus[3] herding his whole sea-zoo uphill,
         Visiting mountain-tops,

     And the fish people, tangled in the elm-trees,
10   Floundering among the ancient haunts of pigeons,
     And deer in terror struggling through the new-spread
         Fields of a world-wide flood.

     We watched the Tiber's tawny water, wrenched back
     Hard from the Tuscan side,[4] go raging forward
15   To Vesta's[5] temple and King Numa's palace,[6]
         Threatening their overthrow.

     Wild, love-lorn river god! He saw himself as
     Avenger of his long-lamenting Ilia,[7]
     And trespassed left across his banks, thus crossing
20   Jupiter's[8] wishes too.

     The old have erred; survivors of those errors,
     Thinned ranks, the young shall hear how brothers sharpened
     Against each other swords that should have carried
         Death to the Parthian[9] pest.

25   Which of the gods now shall the people summon
     To prop Rome's reeling sovereignty? What prayer
     Shall the twelve Virgins use to reach the ear of
         Vesta, who grows each day

     Deafer to litanies? Whom shall the Father
30   Appoint as instrument of our atonement?
     Come, augur god, Apollo,[10] come, we pray thee,
         Glittering shoulders hid

---

[2] **Pyrrha:** Along with her husband Deucalion, Pyrrha was the sole survivor of a flood sent by Zeus to destroy all the evil creatures on the earth.

[3] **Proteus:** In Greek mythology, god of the sea capable of shifting his shape at will.

[4] **We watched . . . side:** The Tiber is the second longest river in Italy, and Tuscan refers to a region in central Italy.

[5] **Vesta's:** In Roman mythology, Vesta was the goddess of home and hearth.

[6] **King Numa's palace:** According to legend, Numa Pompilius was the second king of Rome, known for his piety to the gods.

[7] **Ilia:** Mother of Romulus, a founder and first king of Rome.

[8] **Jupiter's:** In classical mythology, Jupiter was the supreme god of the Romans.

[9] **Parthian:** Refers to Parthia, an ancient country in Asia near the Caspian Sea. Parthia dominated Asia from 100 B.C. to 200 A.D.

[10] **augur God, Apollo:** In ancient Rome, an augur was one who could interpret omens to guide public policy. Apollo was the god of light.

In cloud; or thou, gay goddess of Mount Eryx,[11]
Desire and Laughter fluttering in attendance;
35   Or thou, great parent of our race, grown tired of
          Relishing war, that long,

Sad game, the battle-cries, the flashing helmets,
The bloodsoaked legionary, the Moor's ferocious
Glare as they meet—O Mars,[12] if still regarding
40   Us, thy neglected sons,

Come; or else thou, winged boy of gentle Maia,[13]
Put on the mortal shape of a young Roman,
Descend and, well contented to be known as
          Caesar's avenger, stay

45   Gladly and long with Romulus's people,
Delaying late thy homeward, skybound journey,
And may no whirlwind prematurely snatch thee,
          Wrath with our sins, away.

Rather on earth enjoy resplendent triumphs;
50   Be Prince, be Father—titles to rejoice in;
And let no Parthian raider ride unscathed while
          Caesar has charge of Rome.

HORACE (65 B.C.–8 B.C.)
trans. James Michie

from Odes, Book II (23 B.C.)

VII

Pompeius, chief of all my friends, with whom
I often ventured to the edge of doom
          When Brutus[1] led our line,
          With whom, aided by wine

---

[11] **Mount Eryx:** In Sicily, mountain named for Eryx, legendary king of the Elimi and son of Venus (the Roman goddess of love).
[12] **Mars:** The Roman god of war.
[13] **Maia:** One of the seven daughters of Atlas and Pleione, Zeus entrusted her to care for his son Arcas.
[1] **Pompeius . . . Brutus:** Sextus Pompeius Magnus Pius was a Roman general who opposed the second triumvirate of Julius Caesar along with the Roman politician Brutus.

5   And garlands and Arabian spikenard,°   ointment
    I killed those afternoons that died so hard—
        Who has new-made you, then,
        A Roman citizen

    And given you back your native gods and weather?
10 We two once beat a swift retreat together
        Upon Philippi's field,[2]
        When I dumped my poor shield,

    And courage cracked, and the strong men who frowned
    Fiercest were felled, chins to the miry ground.
15   But I, half-dead with fear,
        Was wafted, airborne, clear

    Of the enemy lines, wrapped in a misty blur
    By Mercury,[3] not sucked back, as you were,
        From safety and the shore
20   By the wild tide of war.

    Pay Jove his feast, then. In my laurel's shade
    Stretch out the bones that long campaigns have made
        Weary. Your wine's been waiting
        For years: no hesitating!

25 Fill up the polished goblets to the top
    With memory-drowning Massic! Slave, unstop
        The deep-mouthed shells that store
        Sweet-smelling oil and pour!

    Who'll run to fit us out with wreaths and find
30 Myrtle and parsley, damp and easily twined?
        Who'll win the right to be
        Lord of the revelry

    By dicing highest? I propose to go
    As mad as a Thracian.[4] It's a joy to throw
35   Sanity overboard
        When a dear friend's restored.

---

[2] **Philippi's field:** In 42 B.C., the final battle between Brutus's forces and those of Marc Antony and Octavian, which led to Brutus's defeat.

[3] **Mercury:** The Roman god of commerce.

[4] **Thracian:** Inhabitant of Thrace, a region to the north of ancient Greece.

BEN JONSON (1572–1637)

from A Pindaric Ode   (1629; 1640)

> *To the Immortal Memory and Friendship of That Noble Pair*
> *Sir Lucius Cary and Sir H. Morison* [1]

It is not growing like a tree
In bulk, doth make man better be;
Or standing long an oak, three hundred year,
To fall a log at last, dry, bald, and sear:
5   A lily of a day
      Is fairer far, in May,
    Although it fall and die that night;
    It was the plant and flower of light.
In small proportions we just beauties see,
10 And in short measures life may perfect be.

BEN JONSON (1572–1637)

An Ode. To Himself   (1640)

Where dost thou careless lie,
    Buried in ease and sloth?
Knowledge that sleeps doth die;
And this security,
5   It is the common moth,
That eats on wits, and arts, and oft destroys them both.

Are all the Aonian springs
    Dried up? Lies Thespia waste?[1]
Doth Clarius'[2] harp want strings,
10 That not a nymph now sings?
    Or droop they, as disgraced
To see their seats and bowers by chattering pies[3] defaced?

---

[1] **To . . . Morison:** Sir Lucius Cary (1610–1643) was a wealthy patron of men of letters (including Jonson) who died at Newbury in the English Civil War. His friend, Sir Henry Morison (1608–1629) was knighted in 1627.
[1] **Are all . . . waste?:** Aonia, a region of Greece home to Mount Helicon and the nine Muses of artistic inspiration. Thespia is a town in that region.
[2] **Clarius':** Apollo, the god of poetry and music, who takes his name from his temple at Clarus.
[3] **pies:** After the daughters of King Pierus challenged the primacy of the Muses in poetry, they were transformed into magpies.

If hence thy silence be,
    As 'tis too just a cause,
15 Let this thought quicken thee:
Minds that are great and free
    Should not on fortune pause;
'Tis crown enough to virtue still, her own applause.

What though the greedy fry°   youth
20   Be taken with false baits
Of worded balladry,
And think it poesy?°   poetry
    They die with their conceits,
And only piteous scorn upon their folly waits.

25 Then take in hand thy lyre,
    Strike in thy proper strain;
With Japhet's line, aspire
Sol's chariot for new fire
    To give the world again;[4]
30 Who aided him, will thee, the issue of Jove's brain.[5]

And since our dainty age
    Cannot endure reproof,
Make not thyself a page
To that strumpet, the stage;
35   But sing high and aloof,
Safe from the wolf's black jaw, and the dull ass's hoof.

ROBERT HERRICK (1591–1674)

An Ode for Him [*Ben Jonson*] (1648)

    Ah Ben![1]
Say how, or when
    Shall we thy guests
Meet at those lyric feasts
5   Made at the Sun,
The Dog, the Triple Tun?[2]
Where we such clusters° had   drinks

---

[4] **Japhet's line . . . again:** Japhet (Prometheus) stole fire from the gods and brought it to mortals for their use.
[5] **the issue of Jove's brain:** Minerva, Roman goddess of warriors and wisdom, emerged from the brain of her father Jove.
[1] **Ben!:** Ben Jonson (1572–1637), Elizabethan dramatist and poet.
[2] **the Sun . . . Tun:** Inns in London.

As made us nobly wild, not mad;
   And yet each verse of thine
10 Outdid the meat, outdid the frolic wine.

    My Ben,
    Or come again,
    Or send to us
  Thy wits' great overplus;
15   But teach us yet
    Wisely to husband it,
    Lest we that talent spend,
  And having once brought to an end
    That precious stock, the store
20 Of such a wit the world should have no more.

JOHN MILTON (1608–1674)

On the Morning of Christ's Nativity (1629; 1645)

1

This is the month, and this the happy morn,
Wherein the Son of Heaven's Eternal King,
Of wedded maid and virgin mother born,
Our great redemption from above did bring;
5 For so the holy sages° once did sing,   *prophets*
  That he our deadly forfeit[1] should release,
And with his Father work us a perpetual peace.

2

That glorious form, that light unsufferable,
And that far-beaming blaze of majesty,
10 Wherewith he wont at Heaven's high council-table
To sit the midst of Trinal° Unity,   *three-fold*
He laid aside, and, here with us to be,
  Forsook the courts of everlasting day,
And chose with us a darksome house of mortal clay.[2]

---

[1] **deadly forfeit:** The penalty of death, incurred by Adam as a result of the original sin in Genesis.
[2] **house of mortal clay:** In Genesis, the first man was made from the dust of the ground in Eden. The house of mortal clay refers to the human body.

3

15 Say, Heavenly Muse,[3] shall not thy sacred vein
    Afford a present to the Infant God?
    Hast thou no verse, no hymn, or solemn strain,
    To welcome him to this his new abode,
    Now while the heaven, by the Sun's team untrod,
20   Hath took no print of the approaching light,
    And all the spangled host[4] keep watch in squadrons bright?

4

    See how from far upon the eastern road
    The star-led wizards[5] haste with odors sweet!
    Oh run, prevent° them with thy humble ode,   anticipate
25 And lay it lowly at his blessèd feet;
    Have thou the honor first thy Lord to greet,
       And join thy voice unto the angel choir
    From out his secret altar touched with hallowed fire.

The Hymn

1

       It was the winter wild,
30   While the heaven-born child
    All meanly wrapt in the rude manger lies;
          Nature, in awe to him,
          Had doffed° her gaudy trim,   removed
    With her great Master so to sympathize:
35 It was no season then for her
    To wanton with the Sun, her lusty paramour.°   lover

2

       Only with speeches fair
       She woos the gentle air
    To hide her guilty front with innocent snow,
40   And on her naked shame,
          Pollute with sinful blame,
    The saintly veil of maiden white to throw;
    Confounded,° that her Maker's eyes   ashamed
    Should look so near upon her foul deformities.

---

[3] **Heavenly Muse:** In Greek mythology, one of the nine daughters of Zeus responsible for inspiring
artists. Milton's muse, however, springs from the Judeo-Christian tradition, the same Muse who
inspired Moses when he received the ten commandments on Mount Horeb or Mount Sinai.
[4] **spangled host:** The angels.
[5] **star-led wizards:** The "wise men from the east" (*Matthew* 2).

3

45   But he, her fears to cease,
            Sent down the meek-eyed Peace:
         She, crowned with olive green, came softly sliding
            Down through the turning sphere,
            His ready harbinger,°   messenger
50   With turtle° wing the amorous clouds dividing;   dove
         And, waving wide her myrtle wand,[6]
         She strikes a universal peace through sea and land.

4

            No war, or battle's sound,
            Was heard the world around;
55   The idle spear and shield were high uphung;
            The hookèd chariot stood,
            Unstained with hostile blood;
         The trumpet spake not to the armèd throng;
         And kings sat still with awful eye,[7]
60   As if they surely knew their sovran Lord was by.

5

            But peaceful was the night
            Wherein the Prince of Light
         His reign of peace upon the earth began.
            The winds, with wonder whist,
65   Smoothly the waters kissed,
         Whispering new joys to the mild Ocean,
         Who now hath quite forgot to rave,
         While birds of calm[8] sit brooding on the charmèd wave.

6

            The stars, with deep amaze,°   amazement
70   Stand fixed in steadfast gaze,
         Bending one way their precious influence,
            And will not take their flight,
            For all the morning light,
         Or Lucifer[9] that often warned them thence;

---

[6] **She, crowned . . . wand:** The olive branch and dove are traditional symbols of peace, and the turtledove and myrtle are symbols of love.
[7] **with awful eye:** In other words, with eyes of awe and astonishment.
[8] **birds of calm:** Halcyons, or kingfishers, were traditionally thought to hatch their offspring at sea, calming the waves during the incubation of their eggs in early winter.
[9] **Lucifer:** Here, the morning star thought to be the guardian of the heavens.

75   But in their glimmering orbs[10] did glow,
     Until their Lord himself bespake, and bid them go.

                              7

     And, though the shady gloom
     Had given day her room,
     The Sun himself withheld his wonted° speed,   typical
80   And hid his head for shame,
     As his inferior flame
     The new-enlightened world no more should need:
     He saw a greater Sun appear
     Than his bright throne or burning axletree[11] could bear.

                              8

85   The shepherds on the lawn,
     Or ere the point of dawn,
     Sat simply chatting in a rustic row;
     Full little thought they than
     That the mighty Pan[12]
90   Was kindly come to live with them below:
     Perhaps their loves, or else their sheep,
     Was all that did their silly° thoughts so busy keep.   simple

                              9

     When such music sweet
     Their hearts and ears did greet
95   As never was by mortal finger strook,
     Divinely-warbled voice
     Answering the stringéd noise,
     As all their souls in blissful rapture took:
     The air, such pleasure loth to lose,
100 With thousand echoes still prolongs each heavenly close.°   cadence

                             10

     Nature, that heard such sound
     Beneath the hollow round
     Of Cynthia's seat[13] the airy region thrilling,

---

[10] **glimmering orbs:** In Ptolemy's astronomical scheme, the earth was surrounded by concentric
spheres ("glimmering orbs"), each of which contained a heavenly body such as the moon, a planet,
or the stars. According to Ptolemy, these orbs revolved around the earth, making harmonious music.
[11] **burning axletree:** In other words, the sun's chariot.
[12] **Pan:** The Greek god of shepherds, often associated with Christ, the Good Shepherd, in Renaissance
poetry.
[13] **Cynthia's seat:** In Greek mythology, Cynthia was goddess of the moon. Here Milton refers to the
earth below the sphere of the moon.

Now was almost won
105   To think her part was done,
And that her reign had here its last fulfilling:
She knew such harmony alone
Could hold all Heaven and Earth in happier uniòn.

11

At last surrounds their sight
110   A globe of circular light,
That with long beams the shamefaced Night arrayed;
The helmèd cherubim
And sworded seraphim
Are seen in glittering ranks with wings displayed,
115   Harping loud and solemn quire,°   choir
With unexpressive° notes, to Heaven's new-born Heir.   ineffable

12

Such music (as 'tis said)
Before was never made,
But when of old the sons of morning sung,[14]
120   While the Creator great
His constellations set,
And the well-balanced world on hinges hung,
And cast the dark foundations deep,
And bid the weltering waves their oozy channel keep.

13

125   Ring out, ye crystal spheres,
Once bless our human ears,
If ye have power to touch our senses so;
And let your silver chime
Move in melodious time;
130   And let the bass of heaven's deep organ blow;
And with your ninefold harmony
Make up full consort to th' angelic symphony.

14

For, if such holy song
Enwrap our fancy long,
135   Time will run back and fetch the age of gold;[15]

---

[14] **sons of morning sung:** Job speaks of the creation of the earth in Job 38.7: "When the morning stars sang together, and all the sons of God shouted for joy."
[15] **the age of gold:** In the cyclical view of Greek history, the earliest era was a Golden Age of happiness and innocence. According to this scheme, history grows progressively worse until the Golden Age is once again ushered in.

And speckled vanity
   Will sicken soon and die;
And leprous sin will melt from earthly mold,
And Hell itself will pass away,
140   And leave her dolorous mansions to the peering day.

                          15

Yea, Truth and Justice then
   Will down return to men,
Orbed in a rainbow; and, like glories wearing,
   Mercy will sit between,
145   Throned in celestial sheen,
With radiant feet the tissued clouds down steering;
And Heaven, as at some festival,
Will open wide the gates of her high palace-hall.

                          16

But wisest Fate[16] says no,
150   This must not yet be so;
The Babe lies yet in smiling infancy
   That on the bitter cross
   Must redeem our loss,
So both himself and us to glorify:
155   Yet first, to those ychained in sleep,[17]
The wakeful trump of doom must thunder through the deep,

                          17

With such a horrid clang
   As on Mount Sinai rang,[18]
While the red fire and smoldering clouds outbrake:
160   The aged Earth, aghast,
   With terror of the blast,
Shall from the surface to the center shake,
When, at the world's last sessiòn,
The dreadful Judge in middle air shall spread his throne.

                          18

165   And then at last our bliss
   Full and perfect is,
But now begins; for from this happy day

---

[16] **wisest Fate:** I.e., the will of God.
[17] **those ychained in sleep:** I.e., those who are dead.
[18] **Mount Sinai rang:** Mt. Sinai, where Moses received the Ten Commandments. See Exodus 19.

> Th' old Dragon° under ground,   Satan
>   In straiter limits bound,
> 170 Not half so far casts his usurpèd sway,
> And, wroth to see his kingdom fail,
> Swinges the scaly horror of his folded tail.

19

>   The Oracles are dumb;
>   No voice or hideous hum
> 175 Runs through the archéd roof in words deceiving.
>   Apollo from his shrine
>   Can no more divine,
> With hollow shriek the steep of Delphos leaving! [19]
> No nightly trance, or breathéd spell,
> 180 Inspires the pale-eyed priest from the prophetic cell.

20

>   The lonely mountains o'er,
>   And the resounding shore,
> A voice of weeping heard and loud lament;
>   From haunted spring, and dale
> 185   Edged with poplar pale,
> The parting genius° is with sighing sent;   local spirit
> With flower-inwoven tresses torn
> The Nymphs in twilight shade of tangled thickets mourn.

21

>   In consecrated earth,
> 190   And on the holy hearth,
> The Lars and Lemures [20] moan with midnight plaint;
>   In urns and altars round,
>   A drear and dying sound
> Affrights the flamens° at their service quaint;°   priests / intricate
> 195 And the chill marble seems to sweat,
> While each peculiar power forgoes his wonted seat.

22

>   Peor and Baalim [21]
>   Forsake their temples dim,

---

[19] **Oracles . . . leaving:** Plutarch asserted that Christ's birth left the ancient oracles (such as Apollo's oracle at Delphi) silent.
[20] **Lars and Lemures:** Lars were Roman household gods, and lemures were unfriendly spirits of the unburied dead.
[21] **Peor and Baalim:** Peor was a manifestation of the Phoenician sun god Baal. Baalim were other manifestations of Baal.

With that twice-battered God of Palestine;[22]
200   And moonèd Ashtaroth,[23]
            Heaven's queen and mother both,
         Now sits not girt° with tapers' holy shine: surrounded
         The Libyc Hammon[24] shrinks his horn;
         In vain the Tyrian maids their wounded Thammuz mourn.[25]

                                23

205   And sullen Moloch,[26] fled,
            Hath left in shadows dread
         His burning idol all of blackest hue;
            In vain with cymbals' ring
            They call the grisly king,
210   In dismal dance about the furnace blue;
         The brutish gods of Nile as fast,
         Isis, and Orus, and the dog Anubis, haste.

                                24

         Nor is Osiris seen
            In Memphian grove or green,[27]
215   Trampling the unshowered grass with lowings loud;
            Nor can he be at rest
            Within his sacred chest;
         Nought but profoundest Hell can be his shroud;
         In vain, with timbreled anthems dark,
220   The sable-stolèd sorcerers bear his worshipped ark.

                                25

         He feels from Juda's land[28]
            The dreaded Infant's hand;
         The rays of Bethlehem blind his dusky eyn;°   eyes
            Nor all the gods beside
225   Longer dare abide,
         Not Typhon[29] huge ending in snaky twine:
         Our Babe, to show his Godhead true,
         Can in his swaddling bands control the damnèd crew.

---

[22] **God of Palestine:** Dagon, whose statue fell twice before the ark of the Lord. See Samuel 5.

[23] **Ashtaroth:** Astarte, Phoenician goddess of the moon.

[24] **The Libyc Hammon:** The Egyptian god Ammon had the head of a ram and was worshipped in the Libyan desert.

[25] **Thammuz mourn:** The Phoenician (Tyrian) women mourned the death of Thammuz, Ashtaroth's lover, whose death was a sign of the coming of winter.

[26] **Moloch:** God of the Ammonites who demanded the sacrifice of children.

[27] **brutish gods . . . green:** The gods of ancient Egypt were associated with animals: Isis a cow, Orus a hawk, Anubis a dog, and Osiris (who had a shrine at Memphis) a bull.

[28] **Juda's land:** Christ was a descendant of the Hebrew tribe of Judah.

[29] **Typhon:** In Greek mythology, a serpent monster with one hundred heads whom Zeus destroyed.

26

So, when the sun in bed,
230   Curtained with cloudy red,
Pillows his chin upon an orient° wave,   eastern
The flocking shadows pale
Troop to th' infernal jail;
Each fettered ghost slips to his several° grave,   separate
235 And the yellow-skirted fays°   fairies
Fly after the night-steeds, leaving their moon-loved maze.°   woods

27

But see! the Virgin blest
Hath laid her Babe to rest.
Time is our tedious song should here have ending:
240   Heaven's youngest-teemèd star
Hath fixed her polished car,
Her sleeping Lord with handmaid lamp attending;
And all about the courtly stable
Bright-harnessed angels sit in order serviceable.

ANDREW MARVELL (1621–1678)

An Horatian Ode[1] upon Cromwell's[2] Return From Ireland (1650; 1681)

The forward youth that would appear
Must now forsake his Muses[3] dear,
Nor in the shadows sing
His numbers° languishing.   verses
5 'Tis time to leave the books in dust,
And oil the unusèd armour's rust;
Removing from the wall
The corslet° of the hall.   armor
So restless Cromwell could not cease

---

[1] **Horatian Ode:** Unlike the glorified praise of Pindar's (ca. 522 B.C.–ca. 438 B.C.) odes, the Horatain ode, based on the writing of the Roman poet Horace (65 B.C.–8 B.C.), offers a calm balanced judgment.
[2] **Cromwell's:** Oliver Cromwell (1599–1658) was lord protector of England following the English civil war and overthrow of the monarchy. After conquering Ireland, Cromwell returned to England in May of 1650, just ten months after the execution of Charles I.
[3] **Muses:** In Greek mythology, the nine goddesses thought to inspire artists.

10   In the inglorious arts of peace,
       But through adventurous war
       Urgèd his active star.
     And, like the three-forked lightning, first
     Breaking the clouds where it was nursed,
15   Did thorough his own side
       His fiery way divide.[4]
     For 'tis all one to courage high
     The emulous or enemy;
       And with such to inclose
20   Is more than to oppose
     Then burning through the air he went,
     And palaces and temples rent;
       And Caesar's head at last
       Did through his laurels blast.[5]
25   'Tis madness to resist or blame
     The force of angry heaven's flame:
       And, if we would speak true,
       Much to the man is due,
     Who, from his private gardens, where
30   He lived reservèd and austere,
       As if his highest plot
       To plant the bergamot,°   pear
     Could by industrious valour climb
     To ruin the great work of time,
35   And cast the kingdoms old
       Into another mould.[6]
     Though justice against fate complain,
     And plead the ancient rights in vain:
       But those do hold or break
40   As men are strong or weak.
     Nature, that hateth emptiness,
     Allows of penetration[7] less:
       And therefore must make room
       Where greater spirits come.
45   What field of all the civil wars,

---

[4] **And, like . . . divide:** Here Marvell refers to Zeus ("the three-forked lightning"), whose daughter Minerva sprang fully grown from his head.
[5] **Caesar's head . . . blast:** Charles I ("Caesar") was beheaded in January 1649. Ancient rulers wore laurels as crowns because they were rumored to protect the wearer from lightning, which represented the jealousy of the gods.
[6] **Into another mould:** I.e., the shift from a monarchy to a republic form of government.
[7] **penetration:** I.e., two bodies simultaneously in the same place.

Where his were not the deepest scars?
  And Hampton shows what part
  He had of wiser art,
Where, twining subtile fears with hope,
50 He wove a net of such a scope
    That Charles himself might chase
    To Caresbrook's narrow case:[8]
That thence the royal actor born
The tragic scaffold might adorn:
55   While round the armèd bands
    Did clap their bloody hands.
He° nothing common did or mean   Charles I
Upon that memorable scene;
    But with his keener eye
60   The axe's edge did try:
Nor called the gods with vulgar spite
To vindicate his helpless right;
    But bowed his comely head
    Down as upon a bed.
65 This was that memorable hour
Which first assured the forcèd power.
    So when they did design
    The capitol's first line,
A bleeding head where they begun
70 Did fright the architects to run;
    And yet in that the state
    Foresaw its happy fate.[9]
And now the Irish are ashamed
To see themselves in one year tamed:
75   So much one man can do,
    That does both act and know.
They can affirm his praises best,
And have, though overcome, confessed
    How good he is, how just,
80   And fit for highest trust:
Nor yet grown stiffer with command,
But still in the republic's hand:

---

[8] **Hampton . . . case:** Cromwell was rumored to have allowed Charles I to escape from Hampton Court to Caresbrook Castle so that Cromwell could persuade Parliament that his execution was necessary. Contemporary historians doubt this claim.

[9] **So when . . . fate:** When a bloody head was uncovered during the construction of the temple of Jupiter in Rome, the workers were persuaded to view it as a sign that Rome would be "head" of an empire. From that point forward, the temple was called "the Capitol," from the Latin *caput,* "head."

How fit he is to sway
That can so well obey.
85 He to the Commons' feet presents
A kingdom,° for his first year's rents: Ireland
   And, what he may, forbears
   His fame, to make it theirs:
And has his sword and spoils ungirt,
90 To lay them at the public's skirt.
   So when the falcon high
   Falls heavy from the sky,
She, having killed, no more does search
But on the next green bough to perch,
95   Where, when he first does lure,
   The falc'ner has her sure.
What may not then our isle presume
While victory his crest does plume?
   What may not others fear
100 If thus he crown each year?
A Caesar, he, ere long to Gaul,
To Italy an Hannibal,[10]
   And to all states not free
   Shall climactéric[11] be.
105 The Pict° no shelter now shall find   The Scots
Within his party-coloured mind,
   But from this valour sad
   Shrink underneath the plaid:
Happy, if in the tufted brake°   bushes
110 The English hunter him mistake,
   Nor lay his hounds in near
   The Caledonian° deer.   Scottish
But thou, the wars' and fortune's son,
March indefatigably on,
115   And for the last effect
   Still keep thy sword erect:
Besides the force it has to fright
The spirits of the shady night,[12]
   The same arts that did gain
120 A power must it maintain.

---

[10] **A Caesar . . . Hannibal:** Gaius Julius Caesar (100 B.C.–44 B.C.) conquered Gaul, and Hannibal of Carthage (247? B.C.–183 B.C.) conquered Italy.
[11] **climactéric:** I.e., launching a new era.
[12] **Besides . . . night:** In classical mythology, the spirits of the underworld feared cold iron.

JOHN DRYDEN (1631–1700)

Alexander's Feast[1] (1697)

I

'Twas at the royal feast, for Persia won
    By Philip's warlike son:[2]
    Aloft in awful state
    The godlike hero sate
5   On his imperial throne;
    His valiant peers were plac'd around;
Their brows with roses and with myrtles bound:
    (So should desert in arms be crown'd.)
The lovely Thais,[3] by his side,
10 Sate like a blooming Eastern bride
In flow'r of youth and beauty's pride.
    Happy, happy, happy pair!
    None but the brave,
    None but the brave,
15   None but the brave deserves the fair.

CHORUS

    Happy, happy, happy pair!
    None but the brave,
    None but the brave,
    None but the brave deserves the fair.

II

20   Timotheus, plac'd on high
    Amid the tuneful choir,
    With flying fingers touch'd the lyre:
    The trembling notes ascend the sky,
    And heav'nly joys inspire.
25 The song began from Jove,[4]
Who left his blissful seats above,
(Such is the pow'r of mighty love.)
A dragon's fiery form belied the god:

---

[1] **Alexander's Feast:** In the poem, Alexander the Great celebrates his defeat over Darius, the King of Persia, in 331 B.C., while Timotheus, a famous flute-player, entertains his guests.
[2] **Philip's warlike son:** Alexander the Great (365 B.C.–323 B.C.), king of Macedon who united the warring Greek city-states and conquered Persia and Egypt.
[3] **Thais:** Sophisticated Greek hataera—or female companion—the mistress of Alexander the Great.
[4] **Jove:** Jupiter, leader of the Roman gods. This stanza refers to Alexander's visit to Jupiter's shrine in Egypt, where he was informed that he was the son of Jupiter.

Sublime on radiant spires he rode,
30   When he to fair Olympia press'd;
        And while he sought her snowy breast:
Then, round her slender waist he curl'd,
And stamp'd an image of himself, a sov'reign of the world.
The list'ning crowd admire the lofty sound,
35 "A present deity," they shout around:
"A present deity," the vaulted roofs rebound.
        With ravish'd ears
        The monarch hears,
        Assumes the god,
40   Affects to nod,
    And seems to shake the spheres.

CHORUS

        With ravish'd ears
        The monarch hears,
        Assumes the god,
45   Affects to nod,
    And seems to shake the spheres.

III

The praise of Bacchus[5] then the sweet musician sung,
    Of Bacchus ever fair and ever young:
        The jolly god in triumph comes;
50   Sound the trumpets; beat the drums;
        Flush'd with a purple grace
        He shews his honest° face: handsome
Now give the hautboys° breath; he comes, he comes.   oboes
        Bacchus, ever fair and young
55   Drinking joys did first ordain;
        Bacchus' blessings are a treasure,
        Drinking is the soldier's pleasure;
        Rich the treasure,
        Sweet the pleasure,
60   Sweet is pleasure after pain.

CHORUS

        Bacchus' blessings are a treasure,
        Drinking is the soldier's pleasure;
        Rich the treasure,

---

[5] **Bacchus:** The Roman god of wine.

Sweet the pleasure,
65 Sweet is pleasure after pain.

IV

Sooth'd with the sound, the king grew vain;
  Fought all his battles o'er again;
And thrice he routed all his foes; and thrice he slew the slain.
The master saw the madness rise,
70 His glowing cheeks, his ardent eyes;
And, while he heav'n and earth defied,
Chang'd his hand, and check'd his pride.
    He chose a mournful Muse,
    Soft pity to infuse;
75 He sung Darius great and good,
    By too severe a fate,
Fallen, fallen, fallen, fallen,
    Fallen from his high estate,
    And welt'ring in his blood;
80 Deserted, at his utmost need
By those his former bounty fed;
On the bare earth expos'd he lies,
With not a friend to close his eyes.
With downcast looks the joyless victor sate,
85   Revolving in his alter'd soul
    The various turns of chance below;
  And, now and then, a sigh he stole,
    And tears began to flow.

CHORUS

    Revolving in his alter'd soul
90   The various turns of chance below;
  And, now and then, a sigh he stole,
    And tears began to flow.

V

The mighty master smil'd to see
That love was in the next degree;
95 'T was but a kindred sound to move,
For pity melts the mind to love.
    Softly sweet, in Lydian [6] measures,
    Soon he sooth'd his soul to pleasures.
    "War," he sung, "is toil and trouble;
100 Honour, but an empty bubble.

---

[6] **Lydian:** In ancient Greece, a mode of music suited for tender themes.

Never ending, still beginning,
　Fighting still, and still destroying:
　　If the world be worth thy winning,
　Think, O think it worth enjoying.
105　　　Lovely Thais sits beside thee,
　　Take the good the gods provide thee."
The many rend the skies with loud applause;
So Love was crown'd, but Music won the cause.
　The prince, unable to conceal his pain,
110　　Gaz'd on the fair
　　Who caus'd his care,
　　And sigh'd and look'd, sigh'd and look'd,
Sigh'd and look'd, and sigh'd again:
At length, with love and wine at once oppress'd,
115　The vanquish'd victor sunk upon her breast.

CHORUS

　The prince, unable to conceal his pain,
　Gaz'd on the fair
　Who caus'd his care,
　And sigh'd and look'd, sigh'd and look'd,
120　Sigh'd and look'd, and sigh'd again:
At length, with love and wine at once oppress'd,
The vanquish'd victor sunk upon her breast.

VI

　Now strike the golden lyre again:
　A louder yet, and yet a louder strain.
125　Break his bands of sleep asunder,
　And rouse him, like a rattling peal of thunder.
　　　Hark, hark, the horrid sound
　　　Has rais'd up his head:
　　　As wak'd from the dead,
130　　　And amaz'd, he stares around.
"Revenge, revenge!" Timotheus cries,
　"See the Furies[7] arise!
　See the snakes that they rear,
　How they hiss in their hair,
135　And the sparkles that flash from their eyes!
　　Behold a ghastly band,
　　Each a torch in his hand!
Those are Grecian ghosts, that in battle were slain,
　　　And unburied remain

---

[7] **Furies:** Female personifications of vengeance.

140   Inglorious on the plain:
         Give the vengeance due
         To the valiant crew.
      Behold how they toss their torches on high,
         How they point to the Persian abodes,
145   And glitt'ring temples of their hostile gods!"
      The princes applaud, with a furious joy;
      And the king seiz'd a flambeau° with zeal to destroy;   torch
         Thais led the way,
         To light him to his prey,
150   And, like another Helen, fir'd another Troy.

CHORUS

      And the king seiz'd a flambeau with zeal to destroy;
         Thais led the way,
            To light him to his prey,
      And, like another Helen, fir'd another Troy.

                                    VII

155   Thus long ago,
         Ere heaving bellows learn'd to blow,
            While organs yet were mute;
         Timotheus, to his breathing flute,
            And sounding lyre,
160   Could swell the soul to rage, or kindle soft desire.
         At last, divine Cecilia came,
         Inventress of the vocal frame;
      The sweet enthusiast, from her sacred store,
         Enlarg'd the former narrow bounds,
165   And added length to solemn sounds,
      With nature's mother wit, and arts unknown before.
        Let old Timotheus yield the prize,
           Or both divide the crown:
        He rais'd a mortal to the skies;
170   She drew an angel down.

GRAND CHORUS

         At last, divine Cecilia came,
         Inventress of the vocal frame;
      The sweet enthusiast, from her sacred store,
         Enlarg'd the former narrow bounds,
175   And added length to solemn sounds,
      With nature's mother wit, and arts unknown before.
        Let old Timotheus yield the prize,

Or both divide the crown:
He rais'd a mortal to the skies;
180   She drew an angel down.

ANNE FINCH, COUNTESS OF WINCHILSEA
(1661–1720)

The Spleen: A Pindaric Poem[1]   (1701)

What art thou, spleen, which everything dost ape?
Thou Proteus[2] to abused mankind,
Who never yet thy real cause could find,
Or fix thee to remain in one continued shape.
5   Still varying they perplexing form,
Now a Dead Sea[3] thou'lt represent,
A calm of stupid° discontent;   unemotional
Then, dashing on the rocks, wilt rage into a storm.
Trembling sometimes thou dost appear
10   Dissolved into a panic fear;
On sleep intruding dost thy shadows spread
Thy gloomy terrors round the silent bed,
And crowd with boding dreams the melancholy head;
Or, when the midnight hour is told,
15   And drooping lids thou still dost waking hold,
Thy fond delusions cheat the eyes:
Before them antic° spectres dance,   strange
Unusual fires their pointed heads advance,
And airy phantoms rise.
20   Such was the monstrous vision seen,
When Brutus (now beneath his cares oppressed,
And all Rome's fortunes rolling in his breast,
Before Philippi's latest field,
Before his fate did to Octavius lead[4])
25   Was vanquished by the spleen.
Falsely, the mortal part we blame
Of our depressed and ponderous° frame,   awkward
Which, till the first degrading sin

---

[1] **The Spleen: A Pindaric Poem:** The Spleen was a strange illness, a form of depression and melancholy, attributed mainly to women, lovers, and poets. Pindar (ca. 522 B.C.–ca. 438 B.C.) was a Greek poet who experimented with the ode form of poetry.
[2] **Proteus:** In Greek mythology, a god of the sea capable of shifting his shape at will.
[3] **Dead Sea:** Between Israel and Jordan, the salt lake is thought to be "dead" because it contains no visible flora or fauna.
[4] **When Brutus . . . lead:** Brutus saw the ghost of Caesar before the Battle of Philippi (42 B.C.), where he was defeated by Marc Antony and Caesar's nephew Octavius.

Let thee, its dull attendant, in,
30   Still with the other did comply,
Nor clogged the active soul disposed to fly
And range the mansions of its native sky.
Nor, whilst in his own heaven he dwelt,
Whilst man his paradise possessed,
35   His fertile garden in the fragrant east,
And all united odours smelt,
No armèd sweets, until thy reign,
Could shock the sense, or in the face
A flushed, unhandsome colour place.
40   Now the jonquil o'ercomes the feeble brain:
We faint beneath the aromatic pain,
Till some offensive scent thy powers appease,
And pleasure we resign for short and nauseous ease.[5]
   In everyone thou dost possess,
45   New are thy motions° and thy dress: effects
Now in some grove a listening friend
Thy false suggestions must attend,
Thy whispered griefs, thy fancied sorrows hear,
Breathed in a sigh and witnessed by a tear;
50   Whilst in the light and vulgar crowd[6]
Thy slaves, more clamorous and loud,
By laughters unprovoked, thy influence too confess.
In the imperious wife thou vapours[7] art,
Which from o'erheated passions rise
55   In clouds to the attractive brain,
Until, descending thence again,
Through the o'ercast and showering eyes,
Upon her husband's softened heart,
He the disputed point must yield,
60   Something resign of the contested field;
Till lordly man, born to imperial sway,
Compounds° for peace, to make that right away,   negotiates
And woman, armed with spleen, does servilely obey.
   The fool, to imitate the wits,
65   Complains of thy pretended fits,
And dullness, born with him, would lay
Upon thy accidental sway;
Because, sometimes, thou dost presume
Into the ablest heads to come,

---

[5] **Now the jonquil . . . ease:** The poet suggests that pleasant odors cause "spleen," while unpleasant odors soothe the disease.
[6] **light and vulgar crowd:** Frivolous, uncultivated persons who might fake symptoms of "spleen."
[7] **vapours:** A disease associated with "spleen," marked by depression, hysteria, and anxiety.

70 That often men of thoughts refined,
    Impatient of unequal sense,
    Such slow returns where they so much dispense,
    Retiring from the crowd, are to thy shades inclined.[8]
    O'er me, alas! thou dost too much prevail:
75 I feel thy force, whilst I against thee rail;
    I feel my verse decay, and my cramped numbers° fail.   verses
    Through thy black jaundice I all objects see
    As dark and terrible as thee,
    My lines decried, and my employment thought
80 An useless folly or presumptuous fault:
    Whilst in the Muses'[9] paths I stray,
    Whilst in their groves and by their secret springs
    My hand delights to trace° unusual things,   write
    And deviates from the known and common way,
85 Nor will in fading silks compose
    Faintly th' inimitable rose,
    Fill up an ill-drawn bird, or paint on glass
    The sovereign's blurred and undistinguished face,
    The threatening angel, and the speaking ass.
90   Patron thou art to every gross abuse:
    The sullen husband's feigned excuse,
    When the ill humour with his wife he spends,
    And bears recruited° wit and spirits to his friends.   bolstered
    The son of Bacchus[10] pleads thy power,
95 As to the glass he still repairs,
    Pretends but to remove thy cares,
    Snatch from thy shades one gay and smiling hour,
    And drown thy kingdom in a purple shower.
    When the coquette,° whom every fool admires,   seductive woman
100 Would in variety be fair,
    And, changing hastily the scene
    From light, impertinent, and vain,
    Assumes a soft, a melancholy air,
    And of her eyes rebates° the wandering fires,   reduces
105 The careless posture, and the head reclined;
    The thoughtful and composèd face
    Proclaiming the withdrawn, the absent mind,
    Allows the fop° more liberty to gaze,   foolish dandy
    Who gently for the tender cause inquires:

---

[8] **ablest heads . . . inclined:** In *Anatomy of Melancholy* (1621), Robert Burton associates "spleen" with a love of knowledge.
[9] **the Muses':** In Greek mythology, the nine goddesses who inspire artists.
[10] **son of Bacchus:** In Roman mythology, Bacchus is the god of wine. A "son of Bacchus" is one who overindulges in alcohol.

110　The cause, indeed, is a defect in sense;
　　　Yet is the spleen alleged,° and still the dull pretence.　　　　　　　　blamed
　　　But these are thy fantastic harms,
　　　The tricks of thy pernicious stage,
　　　Which do the weaker sort engage;
115　Worse are the dire effects of thy more powerful charms.
　　　By thee religion, all we know
　　　That should enlighten here below,
　　　Is veiled in darkness, and perplexed
　　　With anxious doubts, with endless scruples vexed,
120　And some restraint implied from each perverted text; [11]
　　　Whilst 'touch not', 'taste not' what is freely given
　　　Is but thy niggard° voice, disgracing bounteous heaven.　　　　　　　miserly
　　　From speech restrained by thy deceits abused,
　　　To deserts banished, or in cells reclused,
125　Mistaken vot'ries° to the powers divine,　　　　　　　　　　　　　devotees
　　　Whilst they a purer sacrifice design,
　　　Do but the spleen obey, and worship at thy shrine.
　　　In vain to chase thee every art we try,
　　　In vain all remedies apply,
130　In vain the Indian leaf° infuse,　　　　　　　　　　　　　　　　tea
　　　Or the parched eastern berry° bruise;　　　　　　　　　　　　　coffee
　　　Some pass, in vain, those bounds, and nobler liquors use.
　　　Now harmony, in vain, we bring:
　　　Inspire the flute, and touch the string.
135　From harmony no help is had;
　　　Music but soothes thee, if too sweetly sad,
　　　And if too light, but turns thee gaily mad.
　　　Though the physician's greatest gains,
　　　Although his growing wealth he sees
140　Daily increased by ladies' fees,
　　　Yet dost thou baffle all his studious pains.
　　　Not skilful Lower [12] thy source could find,
　　　Or through the well-dissected body trace
　　　The secret, the mysterious ways
145　By which thou dost surprise and prey upon the mind.
　　　Though in the search, too deep for human thought,
　　　With unsuccessful toil he wrought,
　　　Till thinking thee to have catched, himself by thee was caught,
　　　Retained thy prisoner, thy acknowledged slave,
150　And sunk beneath thy chain to a lamented grave.

---

[11] **And . . . perverted text:** I.e., some "restraint" created by misinterpreting biblical texts. Repressive, Puritanical enthusiasm was considered another symptom of "spleen."
[12] **skilful Lower:** Richard Lower (1631–1691), British physician and author of *Treatise on the Heart* (1669).

ALEXANDER POPE (1688–1744)

Ode on Solitude (1717)

Happy the man whose wish and care
A few paternal acres bound,
Content to breathe his native air,
    In his own ground.

5 Whose herds with milk, whose fields with bread,
Whose flocks supply him with attire,
Whose trees in summer yield him shade,
    In winter fire.

Blest! who can unconcernedly find
10 Hours, days, and years slide soft away,
In health of body, peace of mind,
    Quiet by day,

Sound sleep by night; study and ease
Together mixed; sweet recreation
15 And innocence, which most does please,
    With meditation.

Thus let me live, unseen, unknown;
Thus unlamented let me die;
Steal from the world, and not a stone
20   Tell where I lie.

THOMAS GRAY (1716–1771)

Ode on the Death of a Favourite Cat,
Drowned in a Tub of Gold Fishes (1748)

'Twas on a lofty vase's side,
Where China's gayest art had dyed
    The azure flowers, that blow;
Demurest of the tabby kind,
5 The pensive Selima reclined,
    Gazed on the lake below.

Her conscious tail her joy declared;
The fair round face, the snowy beard,

      The velvet of her paws,
10 Her coat that with the tortoise vies,
      Her ears of jet and emerald eyes,
         She saw; and purred applause.

      Still had she gazed; but 'midst the tide
      Two angel forms were seen to glide,
15   The genii of the stream:
      Their scaly armour's Tyrian hue[1]
      Through richest purple to the view
         Betrayed a golden gleam.

      The hapless nymph with wonder saw:
20 A whisker first and then a claw,
         With many an ardent wish,
      She stretched in vain to reach the prize.
      What female heart can gold despise?
         What cat's averse to fish?

25 Presumptuous maid! with looks intent
      Again she stretched, again she bent,
         Nor knew the gulf between
      (Malignant Fate sat by and smiled)
      The slipp'ry verge her feet beguiled,
30   She tumbled headlong in.

      Eight times emerging from the flood
      She mewed to every watry god,
         Some speedy aid to send.
      No dolphin came, no Nereid° stirred: sea-nymph
35 Nor cruel Tom nor Susan heard.
         A fav'rite has no friend!

      From hence, ye beauties, undeceived,
      Know, one false step is ne'er retrieved,
         And be with caution bold.
40 Not all that tempts your wand'ring eyes
      And heedless hearts is lawful prize;
         Nor all that glisters gold.

---

[1] **Tyrian hue:** Purple, from Tyre in Phoenicia, which was famous for its purple dyes. "Tyrian" covered
a wide color spectrum that included crimson as well as purple.

WILLIAM COLLINS (1721–1759)

Ode on the Poetical Character (1746)

1

As once, if not with light regard
I read aright that gifted bard
(Him whose school above the rest
His loveliest Elfin Queen has blessed),[1]
5 One, only one, unrivalled fair
Might hope the magic girdle[2] wear,
At solemn tourney hung on high,
The wish of each love-darting eye;
Lo! to each other nymph in turn applied,
10   As if, in air unseen, some hov'ring hand,
Some chaste and angel-friend to virgin fame,
    With whispered spell had burst the starting band,
It left unblest her loathed, dishonoured side;
    Happier, hopeless fair, if never
15   Her baffled hand with vain endeavour
Had touched that fatal zone to her denied!
Young Fancy thus, to me divinest name,
    To whom, prepared and bathed in heav'n,
    The cest of amplest pow'r is giv'n,
20   To few the godlike gift assigns,
    To gird their blest prophetic loins,
And gaze her visions wild, and feel unmixed her flame!

2

The band, as fairy legends say,
Was wove on that creating day,
25 When He, who called with thought to birth
Yon tented sky, this laughing earth,
And dressed with springs and forests tall,
And poured the main engirting all,
Long by the loved Enthusiast[3] wooed,
30 Himself in some diviner mood,
Retiring, sat with her alone,

---

[1] **Him . . . blessed:** The "gifted bard" is Edmund Spenser (ca. 1552–1599), whose poem the *Faerie Queene* is considered his best work.
[2] **magic girdle:** A restraint that in *Faerie Queene* 4.5 "gave the virtue of chaste love and wifehood to all that did it bear." For Collins, the magic girdle seems to represent the poetical character.
[3] **Enthusiast:** Literally, one inspired by god. Collins suggests that the union of the Deity and imagination results in the creation of the world and the poetical character.

And placed her on his sapphire throne;
The whiles, the vaulted shrine around,
Seraphic wires were heard to sound,
35 Now sublimest triumph swelling,
Now on love and mercy dwelling,
And she, from out the veiling cloud,
Breathed her magic notes aloud:
And thou, thou rich-haired youth of morn,[4]
40 And all thy subject life was born!
The dang'rous Passions kept aloof,
Far from the sainted growing woof;[5]
But near it sat ecstatic Wonder,
List'ning the deep applauding thunder;
45 And Truth, in sunny vest arrayed,
By whose the tarsel's° eyes were made,   falcon's
All the shad'wy tribes of Mind,
In braided dance their murmurs joined,
And all the bright uncounted pow'rs
50 Who feed on heaven's ambrosial flow'rs.
Where is the bard whose soul can now
Its high presuming hopes avow?
Where he who thinks, with rapture blind,
This hallowed work for him designed?

3

55 High on some cliff,[6] to heav'n up-piled,
Of rude access, of prospect wild,
Where, tangled round the jealous steep,
Strange shades o'erbrow the valleys deep,
And holy genii guard the rock,
60 Its glooms embrown, its springs unlock,
While on its rich ambitious head,
An Eden, like his own, lies spread;
I view that oak, the fancied glades among,
    By which as Milton lay, his ev'ning ear,
65 From many a cloud that dropped ethereal dew,
    Nigh sphered in heav'n, its native strains could hear,
On which that ancient trump° he reached was hung: trumpet
    Thither oft, his glory greeting,
    From Waller's myrtle[7] shades retreating,

---

[4] **youth of morn:** Apollo, Greek god of the sun.
[5] **woof:** Fabric of the magic girdle.
[6] **High on some cliff:** The cliff is symbolic of John Milton's (1608–1674) poetry.
[7] **Waller's myrtle:** Edmund Waller (1605–1687), the lyric poet. Myrtle is a symbol of love.

70   With many a vow from hope's aspiring tongue,
     My trembling feet his guiding steps pursue:
          In vain—such bliss to one alone
          Of all the sons of soul was known;
          And Heav'n and Fancy, kindred pow'rs,
75   Have now o'erturned th' inspiring bow'rs,
     Or curtained close such scene from ev'ry future view.

WILLIAM WORDSWORTH (1770–1850)

Ode (1807)
[*Intimations of Immortality*]

There was a time when meadow, grove, and stream,
The earth, and every common sight,
          To me did seem
          Apparelled in celestial light,
5   The glory and the freshness of a dream.
It is not now as it has been of yore;—
          Turn wheresoe'er I may,
          By night or day,
The things which I have seen I now can see no more.

10   The Rainbow comes and goes,
          And lovely is the Rose,
          The Moon doth with delight
     Look round her when the heavens are bare;
          Waters on a starry night
15   Are beautiful and fair;
     The sunshine is a glorious birth;
     But yet I know, where'er I go,
That there hath passed away a glory from the earth.

Now, while the Birds thus sing a joyous song,
20   And while the young Lambs bound
          As to the tabor's° sound,   drum's
To me alone there came a thought of grief:
A timely utterance gave that thought relief,
          And I again am strong.
25   The Cataracts blow their trumpets from the steep,
     No more shall grief of mine the season wrong;
     I hear the Echoes through the mountains throng,
     The Winds come to me from the fields of sleep,

And all the earth is gay,
30   Land and sea
Give themselves up to jollity,
        And with the heart of May
Doth every Beast keep holiday,
        Thou Child of Joy
35   Shout round me, let me hear thy shouts, thou happy Shepherd Boy!

Ye blessed Creatures, I have heard the call
       Ye to each other make; I see
The heavens laugh with you in your jubilee;
       My heart is at your festival,
40   My head hath its coronal,[1]
The fullness of your bliss, I feel—I feel it all.
       Oh evil day! if I were sullen
       While the Earth herself is adorning,
          This sweet May-morning,
45   And the Children are pulling,
           On every side,
       In a thousand vallies far and wide,
       Fresh flowers; while the sun shines warm,
And the Babe leaps up on his mother's arm:—
50   I hear, I hear, with joy I hear!
       —But there's a Tree, of many one,
A single Field which I have looked upon,
Both of them speak of something that is gone:
        The Pansy at my feet
55   Doth the same tale repeat:
Whither is fled the visionary gleam?
Where is it now, the glory and the dream?

Our birth is but a sleep and a forgetting:
The Soul that rises with us, our life's Star,
60   Hath had elsewhere its setting,
          And cometh from afar:
       Not in entire forgetfulness,
       And not in utter nakedness,
But trailing clouds of glory do we come
65   From God, who is our home:
Heaven lies about us in our infancy!
Shades of the prison-house begin to close
        Upon the growing Boy,
But He beholds the light, and whence it flows,

---

[1] **coronal:** A garland of flowers often worn by shepherds in pastoral poetry.

70   He sees it in his joy;
       The Youth, who daily farther from the East
           Must travel, still is Nature's Priest,
               And by the vision splendid
               Is on his way attended;
75   At length the Man perceives it die away,
       And fade into the light of common day.

       Earth fills her lap with pleasures of her own;
       Yearnings she hath in her own natural kind,
       And, even with something of a Mother's mind,
80   And no unworthy aim,
           The homely Nurse doth all she can
       To make her Foster-child, her Inmate Man,
           Forget the glories he hath known,
       And that imperial palace whence he came.
85   Behold the Child among his new-born blisses,
       A four year's Darling of a pigmy size!
       See, where 'mid work of his own hand he lies,
       Fretted by sallies of his Mother's kisses,
       With light upon him from his Father's eyes!
90   See, at his feet, some little plan or chart,
       Some fragment from his dream of human life,
       Shaped by himself with newly-learned art;
               A wedding or a festival,
               A mourning or a funeral;
95   And this hath now his heart,
           And unto this he frames his song:
               Then will he fit his tongue
       To dialogues of business, love, or strife;
               But it will not be long
100   Ere this be thrown aside,
           And with new joy and pride
       The little Actor cons another part,
       Filling from time to time his 'humorous stage' [2]
       With all the Persons, down to palsied Age,
105   That Life brings with her in her Equipage;°   group of servants
               As if his whole vocation
               Were endless imitation.

       Thou, whose exterior semblance doth belie
               Thy Soul's immensity;
110   Thou best Philosopher, who yet dost keep

---

[2] **"humorous stage"**: I.e., taking on the traits of other dispositions, called "humors" in the Elizabethan period. The quotation is from Samuel Daniel's (1562–1619) dedicatory sonnet in *Musophilus*.

Thy heritage, thou Eye among the blind,
That, deaf and silent, read'st the eternal deep,
Haunted for ever by the eternal mind,—
           Mighty Prophet! Seer blest!
115   On whom those truths do rest,
Which we are toiling all our lives to find;
Thou, over whom thy Immortality
Broods like the Day, a Master o'er a Slave,
A Presence which is not to be put by;
120   To whom the grave
Is but a lonely bed without the sense or sight
           Of day or the warm light,
A place of thought where we in waiting lie;
Thou little Child, yet glorious in the might
125 Of untamed pleasures, on thy Being's height,
Why with such earnest pains dost thou provoke
The Years to bring the inevitable yoke,
Thus blindly with thy blessedness at strife?
Full soon thy Soul shall have her earthly freight,
130 And custom lie upon thee with a weight,
Heavy as frost, and deep almost as life!

           O joy! that in our embers
           Is something that doth live,
           That nature yet remembers
135   What was so fugitive!
The thought of our past years in me doth breed
Perpetual benedictions: not indeed
For that which is most worthy to be blest;
Delight and liberty, the simple creed
140 Of Childhood, whether fluttering or at rest,
With new-born hope for ever in his breast:—
               Not for these I raise
               The song of thanks and praise;
145   But for those obstinate questionings
           Of sense and outward things,
           Fallings from us, vanishings;
           Blank misgivings of a Creature
Moving about in worlds not realized,
150 High instincts, before which our mortal Nature
Did tremble like a guilty Thing surprized:
           But for those first affections,
           Those shadowy recollections,
               Which, be they what they may,
155 Are yet the fountain light of all our day,
Are yet a master light of all our seeing;

Uphold us, cherish us, and make
Our noisy years seem moments in the being
Of the eternal Silence: truths that wake,
160   To perish never;
Which neither listlessness, nor mad endeavour,
         Nor Man nor Boy,
Nor all that is at enmity with joy,
Can utterly abolish or destroy!
165   Hence, in a season of calm weather,
         Though inland far we be,
Our Souls have sight of that immortal sea
          Which brought us hither,
         Can in a moment travel thither,
170 And see the Children sport upon the shore,
And hear the mighty waters rolling evermore.

Then, sing ye Birds, sing, sing a joyous song!
         And let the young Lambs bound
         As to the tabor's sound!
175 We in thought will join your throng,
         Ye that pipe and ye that play,
         Ye that through your hearts today
         Feel the gladness of the May!
What though the radiance which was once so bright
180 Be now for ever taken from my sight,
        Though nothing can bring back the hour
Of splendour in the grass, of glory in the flower;
         We will grieve not, rather find
         Strength in what remains behind,
185   In the primal sympathy
         Which having been must ever be,
         In the soothing thoughts that spring
         Out of human suffering,
         In the faith that looks through death,
190 In years that bring the philosophic mind.

And oh ye Fountains, Meadows, Hills, and Groves,
Think not of any severing of our loves!
Yet in my heart of hearts I feel your might;
I only have relinquished one delight
195 To live beneath your more habitual sway.
I love the Brooks which down their channels fret,
Even more than when I tripped lightly as they;
The innocent brightness of a new-born Day
         Is lovely yet;
200 The Clouds that gather round the setting sun

Do take a sober colouring from an eye
That hath kept watch o'er man's mortality;
Another race hath been, and other palms are won.
Thanks to the human heart by which we live,
205   Thanks to its tenderness, its joys, and fears,
To me the meanest° flower that blows can give   most ordinary
Thoughts that do often lie too deep for tears.

SAMUEL TAYLOR COLERIDGE (1772–1834)

Dejection: An Ode (1802)

> Late, late yestreen I saw the new moon,
> With the old moon in her arms,
> And I fear, I fear, my Master dear,
> We shall have a deadly storm.
>
> (BALLAD OF SIR PATRICK SPENS)

I

Well, if the bard was weather-wise, who made
    The grand old ballad of Sir Patrick Spens,
    This night, so tranquil now, will not go hence
Unroused by winds, that ply a busier trade
5   Than those which mould you cloud in lazy flakes,
Or the dull sobbing draught, that drones and rakes
Upon the strings of this Eolian lute,[1]
        Which better far were mute.
    For lo! the new moon, winter-bright
10   And overspread with phantom light—
    With swimming phantom light o'erspread,
    But rimmed and circled by a silver thread—
I see the old moon in her lap, foretelling
    The coming-on of rain and squally blast.
15   And oh, that even now the gust were swelling,
    And the slant night-shower driving loud and fast!
Those sounds which oft have raised me, while they awed,
        And sent my soul abroad,
    Might now perhaps their wonted° impulse give,   usual
20   Might startle this dull pain, and make it move and live!

---

[1] **Eolian lute:** Named for Eolus, god of the wind, the Eolian lute was designed with strings that res-onate and produce sound as the wind passes through.

II

A grief without a pang, void, dark, and drear,
    A stifled, drowsy, unimpassioned grief,
    Which finds no natural outlet, no relief,
        In word or sigh, or tear—
25   Oh Edmund,[2] in this wan and heartless mood,
To other thoughts by yonder throstle wooed,
    All this long eve, so balmy and serene,
Have I been gazing on the western sky,
    And its peculiar tint of yellow-green—
30   And still I gaze—and with how blank an eye!
And those thin clouds above, in flakes and bars,
That give away their motion to the stars;
Those stars, that glide behind them or between,
Now sparkling, now bedimmed, but always seen;
35   Yon crescent moon, as fixed as if it grew
In its own cloudless, starless lake of blue—
A boat becalmed, a lovely sky-canoe!
I see them all, so excellently fair,
I *see*, not *feel*, how beautiful they are!

III

40   My genial spirits fail;
    And what can these avail
To lift the smothering weight from off my breast?
    It were a vain endeavour,
    Though I should gaze for ever
45   On that green light that lingers in the west:
I may not hope from outward forms to win
The passion and the life, whose fountains are within.

IV

Oh Edmund, we receive but what we give,
And in *our* life alone does Nature live:
50   Ours is her wedding garment, ours her shroud!
    And would we aught behold of higher worth
Than that inanimate cold world allowed
To the poor loveless ever-anxious crowd,
    Ah! from the soul itself must issue forth
55   A light, a glory, a fair luminous cloud
        Enveloping the earth—
And from the soul itself must there be sent

---

[2] **Oh Edmund:** The poet likely addresses his friend William Wordsworth (1770–1850).

A sweet and potent voice, of its own birth,
Of all sweet sounds the life and element.

60 Oh pure of heart, thou needst not ask of me
What this strong music in the soul may be—
What, and wherein it doth exist,
This light, this glory, this fair luminous mist,
This beautiful and beauty-making power.
65   Joy, virtuous Edmund—joy that ne'er was given,
Save to the pure, and in their purest hour—
Joy, Edmund, is the spirit and the power
Which, wedding Nature to us, gives in dower
      A new Earth and new Heaven,
70 Undreamt of by the sensual and the proud!
Joy is the sweet voice, joy the luminous cloud—
        We, we ourselves, rejoice!
And thence flows all that charms or ear or sight—
      All melodies the echoes of that voice,
75 All colours a suffusion from that light.

V

Yes, dearest Edmund, yes,
There was a time when, though my path was rough,
      This joy within me dallied with distress,
And all misfortunes were but as the stuff
80 Whence fancy made me dreams of happiness;
For hope grew round me like the twining vine,
And fruits and foliage not my own, seemed mine!
But now afflictions bow me down to earth—
Nor care I that they rob me of my mirth,
85   But oh, each visitation
Suspends what Nature gave me at my birth,
      My shaping spirit of imagination!

VI

Oh, wherefore did I let it haunt my mind,
      This dark distressful dream?
90 I turn from it and listen to the wind,
      Which long has raved unnoticed. What a scream
Of agony, by torture lengthened out,
That lute sent forth! Thou wind, that ravest without!
      Bare crag, or mountain-tairn,° or blasted tree,   pool
95 Or pine-grove whither woodman never clomb,
Or lonely house, long held the witches' home,
      Methinks were fitter instruments for thee,

Mad lutanist, who in this month of showers,
Of dark-brown gardens, and of peeping flowers,
100　Makest devils' yule,[3] with worse than wintry song
The blossoms, buds, and timorous leaves among.
　　Thou actor, perfect in all tragic sounds!
　　　Thou mighty poet, even to frenzy bold!
What tellest thou now about?
105　'Tis of the rushing of an host in rout,
　　　　With many groans of men with smarting wounds—
　　　　　At once they groan with pain, and shudder with the cold!
But hush, there is a pause of deepest silence!
　　And all that noise, as of a rushing crowd,
110　　With groans and tremulous shudderings—all is over!
　　It tells another tale, with sounds less deep and loud,
　　　　A tale of less affright
　　　　And tempered with delight,
As Edmund's self had framed the tender lay.
115　　　'Tis of a little child
　　　Upon a lonesome wild
Not far from home, but she has lost her way
And now moans low in utter grief and fear,
And now screams loud, and hopes to make her mother hear!

VII

120　'Tis midnight, and small thoughts have I of sleep—
Full seldom may my friend such vigils keep!
Visit him, gentle sleep, with wings of healing,
　　And may this storm be but a mountain-birth,
May all the stars hang bright above his dwelling,
125　　Silent as though they watched the sleeping Earth!
　　　With light heart may he rise,
　　　Gay fancy, cheerful eyes,
And sing his lofty song, and teach me to rejoice!
Oh Edmund, friend of my devoutest choice,
130　Oh, raised from anxious dread and busy care
By the immenseness of the good and fair
Which thou seest everywhere—
Joy lifts thy spirit, joy attunes thy voice;
To thee do all things live, from pole to pole,
135　Their life the eddying of thy living soul!
Oh simple spirit, guided from above;
Oh lofty poet, full of light and love;
Brother and friend of my devoutest of my choice,
Thus mayst thou ever, evermore rejoice!

---

[3] **Makest devils' yule:** A winter storm in the spring, or a Christmas for the devil.

THOMAS CAMPBELL (1777–1844)

Ye Mariners of England[1]

Ye Mariners of England
    That guard our native seas!
Whose flag has braved a thousand years
    The battle and the breeze!
5   Your glorious standard launch again
      To match another foe;
And sweep through the deep,
    While the stormy winds do blow!
While the battle rages loud and long
10   And the stormy winds do blow.

The spirits of your fathers
    Shall start from every wave—
For the deck it was their field of fame,
    And Ocean was their grave:
15   Where Blake and mighty Nelson fell
      Your manly hearts shall glow,
As ye sweep through the deep,
    While the stormy winds do blow!
While the battle rages loud and long
20   And the stormy winds do blow.

Britannia needs no bulwarks,
    No towers along the steep;
Her march is o'er the mountain-waves,
    Her home is on the deep.
25   With thunders from her native oak
      She quells the floods below,
As they roar on the shore,
    When the stormy winds do blow!
When the battle rages loud and long,
30   And the stormy winds do blow.

The meteor flag of England
    Shall yet terrific burn;
Till danger's troubled night depart
    And the star of peace return.
35   Then, then, ye ocean-warriors!
      Our song and feast shall flow

---

[1] **Ye Mariners of England:** This poem uses a ballad stanza but has many odelike qualities.

To the fame of your name,
   When the storm has ceased to blow!
When the fiery fight is heard no more,
40   And the storm has ceased to blow.

PERCY BYSSHE SHELLEY (1792–1822)

Ode to the West Wind[1] (1820)

I

O Wild West Wind, thou breath of Autumn's being
   Thou from whose unseen presence the leaves dead
Are driven like ghosts from an enchanter fleeing,

   Yellow, and black, and pale, and hectic red,
5 Pestilence-stricken multitudes! O thou
   Who chariotest to their dark wintry bed

The wingèd seeds, where they lie cold and low,
   Each like a corpse within its grave, until
Thine azure sister of the Spring shall blow

10 Her clarion° o'er the dreaming earth, and fill   trumpet-call
   (Driving sweet buds like flocks to feed in air)
     With living hues and odours plain and hill;

Wild Spirit, which art moving everywhere;
Destroyer and preserver; hear, O hear!

II

15 Thou on whose stream, 'mid the steep sky's commotion,
   Loose clouds like earth's decaying leaves are shed,
Shook from the tangled boughs of heaven and ocean,

   Angels of rain and lightning! there are spread
On the blue surface of thine airy surge,
20   Like the bright hair uplifted from the head

---

[1] "This poem was conceived and chiefly written in a wood that skirts the Arno, near Florence, and on a day when that tempestuous wind, whose temperature is at once mild and animating, was collecting the vapours which pour down the autumnal rains. They began, as I foresaw, at sunset with a violent tempest of hail and rain, attended by that magnificent thunder and lightning peculiar to the Cisalpine regions" [Shelley's note]. The Cisalpine region refers to the Italian side of the Alps.

Of some fierce Mænad,² even from the dim verge
  Of the horizon to the zenith's height,
The locks of the approaching storm. Thou dirge

  Of the dying year, to which this closing night
25 Will be the dome of a vast sepulchre,
    Vaulted with all thy congregated might

Of vapours, from whose solid atmosphere
Black rain, and fire, and hail, will burst: O hear!

III

Thou who didst waken from his summer dreams
30   The blue Mediterranean, where he lay,
Lull'd by the coil of his crystàlline streams,

  Beside a pumice isle in Baiæ's bay,³
And saw in sleep old palaces and towers
    Quivering within the wave's intenser day,

35 All overgrown with azure moss, and flowers
  So sweet, the sense faints picturing them! Thou
For whose path the Atlantic's level powers

  Cleave themselves into chasms, while far below
The sea-blooms and the oozy woods which wear
40   The sapless foliage of the ocean, know

Thy voice, and suddenly grow gray with fear,
And tremble and despoil themselves: O hear!

IV

If I were a dead leaf thou mightest bear;
  If I were a swift cloud to fly with thee;
45 A wave to pant beneath thy power, and share

  The impulse of thy strength, only less free
Than thou, O uncontrollable! if even
    I were as in my boyhood, and could be

The comrade of thy wanderings over heaven,
50   As then, when to outstrip thy skiey speed
Scarce seem'd a vision—I would ne'er have striven

---

² **Mænad:** Greek: "frenzied dancer." Mænads were votaries of Dionysus, the Greek god of wine and fertility.
³ **Baiæ's bay:** A region near Naples, Italy, formerly a favorite resort for Roman emperors.

As thus with thee in prayer in my sore need.
O! lift me as a wave, a leaf, a cloud!
  I fall upon the thorns of life! I bleed!

55 A heavy weight of hours has chain'd and bow'd
One too like thee—tameless, and swift, and proud.

V

Make me thy lyre,[4] even as the forest is:
  What if my leaves are falling like its own?
The tumult of thy mighty harmonies

60   Will take from both a deep autumnal tone,
Sweet though in sadness. Be thou, Spirit fierce,
  My spirit! Be thou me, impetuous one!

Drive my dead thoughts over the universe,
  Like wither'd leaves, to quicken a new birth;
65 And, by the incantation of this verse,

  Scatter, as from an unextinguish'd hearth
Ashes and sparks, my words among mankind!
  Be through my lips to unawaken'd earth

The trumpet of a prophecy! O Wind,
70 If Winter comes, can Spring be far behind?

JOHN KEATS (1795–1821)

Ode on a Grecian Urn (1820)

I

Thou still unravished bride of quietness,
  Thou foster-child of silence and slow time,
Sylvan historian, who canst thus express
  A flowery tale more sweetly than our rhyme!
5 What leaf-fringed legend haunts about thy shape,
  Of deities or mortals, or of both,

---

[4] **thy lyre:** Shelley likely refers to the Eolian lyre, designed with strings that resonate and produce sound as the wind passes through.

In Tempe or the dales of Arcady? [1]
What men or gods are these? What maidens loath?
What mad pursuit? What struggle to escape?
10   What pipes and timbrels? What wild ecstasy?

II

Heard melodies are sweet, but those unheard
    Are sweeter; therefore, ye soft pipes, play on—
Not to the sensual ear, but, more endeared,
    Pipe to the spirit ditties of no tone.
15 Fair youth, beneath the trees, thou canst not leave
    Thy song, nor ever can those trees be bare;
        Bold lover, never, never canst thou kiss,
Though winning near the goal—yet, do not grieve:
    She cannot fade, though thou hast not thy bliss,
20   For ever wilt thou love, and she be fair!

III

Ah, happy, happy boughs! that cannot shed
    Your leaves, nor ever bid the spring adieu;
And, happy melodist, unweariéd,
    For ever piping songs for ever new!
25 More happy love! more happy, happy love!
    For ever warm and still to be enjoyed,
        For ever panting, and for ever young—
All breathing human passion far above,
    That leaves a heart high-sorrowful and cloyed,
30   A burning forehead, and a parching tongue.

IV

Who are these coming to the sacrifice?
    To what green altar, oh mysterious priest,
Leadst thou that heifer lowing at the skies,
    And all her silken flanks with garlands drest?
35 What little town by river or sea shore,
    Or mountain-built with peaceful citadel,
        Is emptied of this folk, this pious morn?
And, little town, thy streets for evermore
    Will silent be; and not a soul to tell
40   Why thou art desolate, can e'er return.

---

[1] **Tempe . . . Arcady:** Traditional symbols of pastoral beauty in Greece.

V

Oh Attic° shape! Fair attitude! with brede°   Athenian / braid
    Of marble men and maidens overwrought,
With forest branches and the trodden weed—
    Thou, silent form, dost tease us out of thought
45   As doth eternity. Cold pastoral!
      When old age shall this generation waste
        Thou shalt remain, in midst of other woe
Than ours, a friend to man, to whom thou sayst,
    'Beauty is truth, truth beauty—that is all
50   Ye know on earth, and all ye need to know.'

JOHN KEATS (1795–1821)

Ode on Melancholy (1819)

1

No, no, go not to Lethe, neither twist
    Wolfsbane, tight-rooted, for its poisonous wine;
Nor suffer thy pale forehead to be kissed
    By nightshade,[1] ruby grape of Proserpine;[2]
5   Make not your rosary of yew-berries,[3]
    Nor let the beetle, nor the death-moth be
      Your mournful Psyche, nor the downy owl[4]
A partner in your sorrow's mysteries;
    For shade to shade will come too drowsily,
10   And drown the wakeful anguish of the soul.

2

But when the melancholy fit shall fall
    Sudden from heaven like a weeping cloud,
That fosters the droop-headed flowers all,
    And hides the green hill in an April shroud;
15   Then glut thy sorrow on a morning rose,
    Or on the rainbow of the salt sand-wave,

---

[1] **Lethe . . . nightshade:** Lethe was the river of forgetting in Hades. Wolfsbane and nightshade are poisonous herbs. Keats implies that these standard symbols have little to do with actual melancholy.
[2] **Proserpine:** Wife of Pluto, god of the underworld.
[3] **yew-berries:** Often found in cemeteries, a symbol of mourning.
[4] **Nor let . . . owl:** The Beetle, or Egyptian scarab, was often placed in coffins. A death-moth was named for the skull-like markings on its wings. Along with owls, both are traditional symbols of death and darkness. Psyche ("soul") is often symbolized by a butterfly.

Or on the wealth of globéd peonies;
Or if thy mistress some rich anger shows,
    Imprison her soft hand, and let her rave,
20   And feed deep, deep upon her peerless eyes.

3

She[5] dwells with Beauty—Beauty that must die;
    And Joy, whose hand is ever at his lips
Bidding adieu; and aching Pleasure nigh,
    Turning to Poison while the bee-mouth sips:
25 Aye, in the very temple of Delight
    Veiled Melancholy has her sov'reign shrine,
        Though seen of none save him whose strenuous tongue
Can burst Joy's grape against his palate fine;
His soul shall taste the sadness of her might,
30   And be among her cloudy trophies hung.

RALPH WALDO EMERSON (1803–1882)

Ode (1847)

Inscribed to W. H. Channing [1]

Though loath to grieve
The evil time's sole patriot,
I cannot leave
My honied thought
5 For the priest's cant,
Or statesman's rant.

If I refuse
My study for their politique,
Which at the best is trick,
10 The angry Muse
Puts confusion in my brain.

But who is he that prates
Of the culture of mankind,
Of better arts and life?
15 Go, blindworm, go,
Behold the famous States

---

[5] **She:** Here, the goddess of melancholy.
[1] **W. H. Channing:** William Henry Channing (1810–1884), a minister and abolitionist.

Harrying Mexico
With rifle and with knife![2]

Or who, with accent bolder,
20   Dare praise the freedom-loving mountaineer?
I found by thee, O rushing Contoocook![3]
And in thy valleys, Agiochook![4]
The jackals of the negro-holder.

The God who made New Hampshire
25   Taunted the lofty land
With little men;—
Small bat and wren
House in the oak:—
If earth-fire cleave
30   The upheaved land, and bury the folk,
The southern crocodile would grieve.
Virtue palters;° Right is hence;   is evasive
Freedom praised, but hid;
Funeral eloquence
35   Rattles the coffin-lid.

What boots° thy zeal,   powers
O glowing friend,
That would indignant rend
The northland from the south?
40   Wherefore? to what good end?
Boston Bay and Bunker Hill[5]
Would serve things still;—
Things are of the snake.

The horseman serves the horse
45   The neatherd° serves the neat,°   cowherd / cow
The merchant serves the purse,
The eater serves his meat;
'Tis the day of the chattel,
Web to weave, and corn to grind;
50   Things are in the saddle,
And ride mankind.

---

[2] **Behold . . . knife:** Emerson disagreed with the war between the United States and Mexico
(1846–1848), holding that a United States victory would serve only to extend slave-holding territory.
[3] **Contoocook:** A section of the Merrimack River in New Hampshire.
[4] **Agiochook:** New Hampshire's White Mountains.
[5] **Boston Bay and Bunker Hill:** The Boston Tea Party (December 16, 1773) and the Battle of Bunker
Hill (June 17, 1775) were central events in the American Revolution.

There are two laws discrete,
Not reconciled,—
Law for man, and law for things;
55 The last builds town and fleet,
But it runs wild,
And doth the man unking.

'Tis fit the forest fall,
The steep be graded,
60 The mountain tunnelled,
The sand shaded,
The orchard planted,
The glebe tilled,
The prairie granted,
65 The steamer built.

Let man serve law for man;
Live for friendship, live for love,
For truth's and harmony's behoof;°   sake
The state may follow how it can,
70 As Olympus follows Jove.⁶

Yet do not I implore
The wrinkled shopman to my surrounding woods,
Nor bid the unwilling senator
Ask votes of thrushes in the solitudes.
75 Every one to his chosen work;—
Foolish hands may mix and mar;
Wise and sure the issues are.
Round they roll till dark is light,
Sex to sex, and even to odd;—
80 The over-god
Who marries Right to Might,
Who peoples, unpeoples,—
He who exterminates
Races by stronger races,
85 Black by white faces,—
Knows to bring honey
Out of the lion;⁷
Grafts gentlest scion
On pirate and Turk.

---

⁶ **As Olympus follows Jove:** Mt. Olympus was the home of the Greek pantheon and Jove (Zeus), their ruler.
⁷ **Out of the lion:** In Judges 14, Samson killed a lion and returned to find its carcass filled with honey.

90   The Cossack eats Poland,[8]
     Like stolen fruit;
     Her last noble is ruined,
     Her last poet mute:
     Straight, into double band
95   The victors divide;
     Half for freedom strike and stand;—
     The astonished Muse finds thousands at her side.

GERARD MANLEY HOPKINS (1844–1889)

The Wreck of the Deutschland[1]   (1876; 1918)

To the
happy memory of five Franciscan nuns
exiled by the Falck Laws[2]
drowned between midnight and morning of
Dec. 7th, 1875

Part the First

1

     Thou mastering me
    God! giver of breath and bread;
   World's strand, sway of the sea;
    Lord of living and dead;
5   Thou hast bound bones and veins in me, fastened me flesh,
And after it almost unmade, what with dread,
     Thy doing: and dost thou touch me afresh?
Over again I feel thy finger and find thee.

2

     I did say yes
10   O at lightning and lashed rod;
   Thou heardst me truer than tongue confess
    Thy terror, O Christ, O God;
Thou knowest the walls, altar and hour and night:
The swoon of a heart that the sweep and the hurl of thee trod

---

[8] **The Cossack eats Poland:** In 1846, an uprising challenged Russian military tyranny in Poland.
[1] **Deutschland:** "Germany," the name of the ship.
[2] **Falck Laws:** From 1873–1875, Albert Falck, the Prussian minister of culture and education, passed several laws diminishing the power of the Roman Catholic Church and abolishing most religious orders.

15   Hard down with a horror of height:
And the midriff astrain with leaning of, laced with fire of stress.

3

The frown of his face
Before me, the hurtle of hell
Behind, where, where was a, where was a place?
20   I whirled out wings that spell
And fled with a fling of the heart to the heart of the Host.
My heart, but you were dovewinged, I can tell,
Carrier-witted,[3] I am bold to boast,
To flash from the flame to the flame then, tower from the grace
to the grace.

4

I am soft sift
25   In an hourglass—at the wall
Fast, but mined with a motion, a drift,
And it crowds and it combs to the fall;
I steady as a water in a well, to a poise, to a pane,
30   But roped with, always, all the way down from the tall
Fells or flanks of the voel,° a vein   mountain
Of the gospel proffer, a pressure, a principle, Christ's gift.

5

I kiss my hand
To the stars, lovely-asunder
35   Starlight, wafting him out of it; and
Glow, glory in thunder;
Kiss my hand to the dappled-with-damson[4] west:
Since, tho' he is under the world's splendour and wonder,
His mystery must be instressed,° stressed;   recognized
40   For I greet him the days I meet him, and bless when I understand.

6

Not out of his bliss
Springs the stress felt
Nor first from heaven (and few know this)
Swings the stroke dealt—
45   Stroke and a stress that stars and storms deliver,
That guilt is hushed by, hearts are flushed by and melt—

---

[3] **carrier-witted:** With the wit of a carrier pigeon.
[4] **damson:** A dark-purple plum.

But it rides time like riding a river
(And here the faithful waver, the faithless fable and miss).

7

50
It dates from day
            Of his going in Galilee;
      Warm-laid grave of a womb-life grey;
            Manger, maiden's knee;
      The dense and the driven Passion, and frightful sweat:
      Thence the discharge° of it, there its swelling to be,   manifestation
55
            Though felt before, though in high flood yet—
What none would have known of it, only the heart, being hard at bay,

8

            Is out with it! Oh,
            We lash with the best or worst
      Word last! How a lush-kept plush-capped sloe°   berry
60
            Will, mouthed to flesh-burst,
      Gush!—flush the man, the being with it, sour or sweet,
      Brim, in a flash, full!—Hither then, last or first,
            To hero of Calvary,[5] Christ's, feet—
Never ask if meaning it, wanting it, warned of it—men go.

9

65
            Be adored among men,
            God, three-numberèd form;
      Wring thy rebel, dogged in den,
            Man's malice, with wrecking and storm.
      Beyond saying sweet, past telling of tongue,
70
      Thou art lightning and love, I found it, a winter and warm;
            Father and fondler of heart thou hast wrung:
Hast thy dark descending and most art merciful then.

10

            With an anvil-ding
            And with fire in him forge thy will
75
            Or rather, rather then, stealing as Spring
            Through him, melt him but master him still:
      Whether at once, as once at a crash Paul,
      Or as Austin, a lingering-out swéet skíll,[6]

---

[5] **Calvary:** Hill near Jerusalem where Jesus was crucified.
[6] **Whether . . . skíll:** The sudden nature of Paul's conversion near Damascus is compared to the gradual, meditative conversion of Augustine.

Make mercy in all of us, out of us all
80   Mastery, but be adored, but be adored King.

Part the Second

11

'Some find me a sword; some
The flange and the rail; flame,
Fang, or flood' goes Death on drum,
And storms bugle his fame.
85   But wé dream we are rooted in earth—Dust!
Flesh falls within sight of us, we, though our flower the same,
Wave with the meadow, forget that there must
The sour scythe cringe, and the blear share come.

12

On Saturday sailed from Bremen,
90   American-outward-bound,
Take settler and seamen, tell men with women,
Two hundred souls in the round—
O Father, not under thy feathers[7] nor ever as guessing
The goal was a shoal, of a fourth the doom to be drowned;
95   Yet did the dark side of the bay of thy blessing
Not vault them, the million of rounds of thy mercy not reeve°   fasten
even them in?

13

Into the snows she sweeps,
Hurling the haven behind,
The Deutschland, on Sunday; and so the sky keeps,
100   For the infinite air is unkind,
And the sea flint-flake, black-backed in the regular blow,
Sitting Eastnortheast, in cursed quarter, the wind;
Wiry and white-fiery and whirlwind-swivellèd snow
Spins to the widow-making unchilding unfathering deeps.

14

105   She drove in the dark to leeward,
She struck—not a reef or a rock
But the combs of a smother of sand: night drew her
Dead to the Kentish Knock,[8]

---

[7] **under thy feathers:** See Matthew 23.37: "O Jerusalem, Jerusalem, thou that killest the prophets, and stonest them which are sent unto thee, how often would I have gathered thy children together, even as a hen gathereth her chickens under her wings, and ye would not!"
[8] **Kentish Knock:** A sandbar near the mouth of the Thames River, in England.

And she beat the bank down with her bows and the ride of her keel:
110   The breakers rolled on her beam with ruinous shock;
        And canvas and compass, the whorl and the wheel
Idle for ever to waft her or wind her with, these she endured.

15

      Hope had grown grey hairs,
      Hope had mourning on,
115   Trenched with tears, carved with cares,
      Hope was twelve hours gone;
And frightful a nightfall folded rueful a day
Nor rescue, only rocket and lightship, shone,
     And lives at last were washing away:
120 To the shrouds they took,—they shook in the hurling and horrible airs.

16

     One stirred from the rigging to save
     The wild woman-kind below,
With a rope's end round the man, handy and brave—
     He was pitched to his death at a blow,
125 For all his dreadnought breast and braids of thew:
They could tell him for hours, dandled the to and fro
     Through the cobbled foam-fleece. What could he do
With the burl° of the fountains of air, buck and the flood of the wave?   vortex

17

     They fought with God's cold—
130   And they could not and fell to the deck
(Crushed them) or water (and drowned them) or rolled
     With the sea-romp over the wreck.
Night roared, with the heart-break hearing a heart-broke rabble,
The woman's wailing, the crying of child without check—
135   Till a lioness arose breasting the babble,
A prophetess towered in the tumult, a virginal tongue told.

18

     Ah, touched in your bower of bone,
     Are you! turned for an exquisite smart,
Have you! make words break from me here all alone,
140   Do you!—mother of being in me, heart.
O unteachably after evil, but uttering truth,
Why, tears! is it? tears; such a melting, a madrigal start!
     Never-eldering revel and river of youth,
What can it be, this glee? the good you have there of your own?

19

145 Sister, a sister calling
A master, her master and mine!—
And the inboard seas run swirling and hawling;
The rash smart sloggering brine
Blinds her; but she that weather sees one thing, one;
150 Has one fetch⁹ in her: she rears herself to divine
Ears, and the call of the tall nun
To the men in the tops and the tackle rode over the storm's brawling.

20

She was first of a five and came
Of a coifèd sisterhood.
155 (O Deutschland, double a desperate name!
O world wide of its good!
But Gertrude, lily, and Luther, are two of a town,¹⁰
Christ's lily and beast of the waste wood:
From life's dawn it is drawn down,
160 Abel is Cain's brother and breasts they have sucked the same.)

21

Loathed for a love men knew in them,
Banned by the land of their birth,
Rhine refused them, Thames would ruin them;
Surf, snow, river and earth
165 Gnashed: but thou art above, thou Orion of light;
Thy unchancelling° poising palms were weighing the worth,   exiling
Thou martyr-master: in thy sight
Storm flakes were scroll-leaved flowers, lily showers—sweet
heaven was astrew in them.

22

Five!¹¹ the finding and sake
170 And cipher of suffering Christ.
Mark, the mark is of man's make
And the word of it Sacrificed.
But he scores it in scarlet himself on his own bespoken,
Before-time-taken, dearest prizèd and priced—
175 Stigma, signal, cinquefoil¹² token
For lettering of the lamb's fleece, ruddying of the rose-flake.

---

⁹ **fetch:** Here, the miracle of the nun's sacrifice.
¹⁰ **Gertrude . . . town:** St. Gertrude lived in Saxony near the birthplace of Martin Luther, a Catholic heretic.
¹¹ **Five!:** In stanzas 22 and 23, Hopkins links the five nuns with the five wounds of Christ and the stigmata of St. Francis.
¹² **cinquefoil:** A flower with five leaves.

23

Joy fall to thee, father Francis,
Drawn to the Life that died;
With the gnarls of the nails in thee, niche of the lance, his
180   Lovescape crucified
And seal of his seraph-arrival! and these thy daughters
And five-livèd and leavèd favour and pride,
Are sisterly sealed in wild waters,
To bathe in his fall-gold mercies, to breathe in his all-fire glances.

24

185   Away in the loveable west,
On a pastoral forehead of Wales,
I was under a roof here, I was at rest,
And they the prey of the gales;
She to the black-about air, to the breaker, the thickly
190   Falling flakes, to the throng that catches and quails
Was calling 'O Christ, Christ, come quickly':
To cross to her she calls Christ to her, christens her wild-worst° Best.   death

25

The majesty! what did she mean?
Breathe, arch and original Breath.°   the Holy Spirit
195   Is it love in her of the being as her lover had been?
Breathe, body of lovely Death.
They were else-minded then, altogether, the men
Woke thee with a *We are perishing* in the weather
of Gennesareth.°   Jesus Christ
Or is it that she cried for the crown then,
200   The keener to come at the comfort for feeling the combating keen?

26

For how to the heart's cheering
The down-dugged ground-hugged grey
Hovers off, the jay-blue heavens appearing
Of pied and peeled May!
205   Blue-beating and hoary-glow height; or night, still higher,
With belled fire and the moth-soft Milky Way,
What by your measure is the heaven of desire,
The treasure never eyesight got, nor was ever guessed what for
the hearing?

27

No, but it was not these.
210   The jading and jar of the cart,
Time's tasking, it is fathers that asking for ease

Of the sodden-with-its-sorrowing heart,
Not danger, electrical horror; then further it finds
The appealing of the Passion is tenderer in prayer apart:
215   Other, I gather, in measure her mind's
Burden, in wind's burly and beat of endragonèd seas.

28

But how shall I . . . make me room there:
Reach me a . . . Fancy, come faster—
Strike you the sight of it? look at it loom there,
220   Thing that she . . . There then! the Master,
Ipse,° the only one, Christ, King, Head: Himself
He was to cure the extremity where he had cast her;
Do, deal, lord it with living and dead;
Let him ride, her pride, in his triumph, despatch and have done
with his doom there.

29

225   Ah! there was a heart right!
There was single eye!
Read the unshapeable shock night
And knew the who and the why;
Wording it how but by him that present and past,
230   Heaven and earth are word of, worded by?—
The Simon Peter[13] of a soul! to the blast
Tarpeïan[14]-fast, but a blown beacon of light.

30

Jesu, heart's light,
Jesu, maid's son,
235   What was the feast followed the night
Thou hadst glory of this nun?—[15]
Feast of the one woman without stain.
For so conceivèd, so to conceive thee is done;
But here was heart-throe, birth of a brain,
240   Word, that heard and kept thee and uttered thee outright.

31

Well, she has thee for the pain, for the
Patience; but pity of the rest of them!

---

[13] **Simon Peter:** The apostle Peter, chosen by Christ to form his church.

[14] **Tarpeïan:** Peak in Rome from which criminals were tossed to their death.

[15] **What was . . . nun?:** Hopkins draws parallels between the nun's death and the Feast of Immaculate Conception of the Virgin Mary on December 8th, the day following the wreck of the Deutschland.

Heart, go and bleed at a bitterer vein for the
Comfortless unconfessed of them—
245   No not uncomforted: lovely-felicitous Providence
Finger of a tender of, O of a feathery delicacy, the breast of the
Maiden could obey so, be a bell to, ring of it,[16] and
Startle the poor sheep back! is the shipwrack then a harvest, does
tempest carry the grain for thee?

32

I admire thee, master of the tides,
250   Of the Yore-flood,[17] of the year's fall;
The recurb and the recovery of the gulf's sides,[18]
The girth of it and the wharf of it and the wall;
Stanching, quenching ocean of a motionable mind;
Ground of being, and granite of it: past all
255   Grasp God, throned behind
Death with a sovereignty that heeds but hides, bodes but abides;

33

With a mercy that outrides
The all of water, an ark
For the listener; for the lingerer with a love glides
260   Lower than death and the dark;
A vein for the visiting of the past-prayer, pent in prison,
The-last-breath penitent spirits—the uttermost mark
Our passion-plungèd giant risen,
The Christ of the Father compassionate, fetched in the storm of
his strides.

34

265   Now burn, new born to the world,
Double-naturèd name,[19]
The heaven-flung, heart-fleshed, maiden-furled
Miracle-in-Mary-of-flame,
Mid-numberèd he in three of the thunder-throne.[20]
270   Not a dooms-day dazzle in his coming nor dark as he came;
Kind, but royally reclaiming his own;
A released shower, let flash to the shire, not a lightning of fire
hard-hurled.

---

[16] **ring of it:** The nun is like a bell who summons others to God.
[17] **Yore-flood:** Hopkins likely refers to the primal waters or massive flood in Genesis.
[18] **recurb . . . sides:** The ebb and flow of the tide.
[19] **Double-naturèd name:** Christ is considered to be both God and man.
[20] **Mid-numberèd . . . throne:** Christ is in the middle of the Trinity: the Father, the Son, and the Holy Ghost.

35

Dame, at our door
Drowned, and among our shoals,
275   Remember us in the roads, the heaven-haven of the reward:
Our King back, Oh, upon English souls!
Let him easter in us, be a dayspring to the dimness of us, be a
crimson-cresseted east,
More brightening her, rare-dear Britain, as his reign rolls,
Pride, rose, prince, hero of us, high-priest,
280   Our heart's charity's hearth's fire, our thoughts' chivalry's throng's Lord.

WALLACE STEVENS (1879–1955)

The Idea of Order at Key West (1935)

She sang beyond the genius of the sea.
The water never formed to mind or voice,
Like a body wholly body, fluttering
Its empty sleeves; and yet its mimic motion
5   Made constant cry, caused constantly a cry,
That was not ours although we understood,
Inhuman, of the veritable ocean.

The sea was not a mask. No more was she.
The song and water were not medleyed sound
10   Even if what she sang was what she heard,
Since what she sang was uttered word by word.
It may be that in all her phrases stirred
The grinding water and the gasping wind;
But it was she and not the sea we heard.
15   For she was the maker of the song she sang.
The ever-hooded, tragic-gestured sea
Was merely a place by which she walked to sing.
Whose spirit is this? we said, because we knew
It was the spirit that we sought and knew
20   That we should ask this often as she sang.

If it was only the dark voice of the sea
That rose, or even colored by many waves;

If it was only the outer voice of sky
And cloud, of the sunken coral water-walled,
25 However clear, it would have been deep air,
The heaving speech of air, a summer sound
Repeated in a summer without end
And sound alone. But it was more than that,
More even than her voice, and ours, among
30 The meaningless plungings of water and the wind,
Theatrical distances, bronze shadows heaped
On high horizons, mountainous atmospheres
Of sky and sea.
                    It was her voice that made
35 The sky acutest at its vanishing.
She measured to the hour its solitude.
She was the single artificer of the world
In which she sang. And when she sang, the sea,
Whatever self it had, became the self
40 That was her song, for she was the maker. Then we,
As we beheld her striding there alone,
Knew that there never was a world for her
Except the one she sang and, singing, made.

Ramon Fernandez,[1] tell me, if you know,
45 Why, when the singing ended and we turned
Toward the town, tell why the glassy lights,
The lights in the fishing boats at anchor there,
As the night descended, tilting in the air,
Mastered the night and portioned out the sea,
50 Fixing emblazoned zones and fiery poles,
Arranging, deepening, enchanting night.

Oh! Blessed rage for order, pale Ramon,
The maker's rage to order words of the sea,
Words of the fragrant portals, dimly-starred,
55 And of ourselves and of our origins,
In ghostlier demarcations, keener sounds.

---

[1] **Ramon Fernandez:** According to Stevens, a combination of two common Spanish names, not an actual historical figure.

PABLO NERUDA (1904–1973)
trans. Nathaniel Tarn

Ode to a Beautiful Nude (1954)

With a chaste heart,
with pure eyes,
I celebrate your beauty
holding the leash of blood
5   so that it might leap out
and trace your outline
where
you lie down in my ode
as in a land of forests, or in surf:
10   in aromatic loam
or in sea-music.

Beautiful nude:
equally beautiful
your feet
15   arched by primeval tap
of wind or sound;
your ears
small shells
of the splendid American sea;
20   your breasts
of level plenitude full-
filled by living light;
your flying
eyelids of wheat
25   revealing
or enclosing
the two deep countries of your eyes.

The line your shoulders
have divided
30   into pale regions
loses itself and blends
into the compact halves
of an apple,
continues separating
35   your beauty down
into two columns
of burnished gold, fine alabaster,
to sink into the two grapes of your feet,

where your twin symmetrical tree
40 burns again and rises:
flowering fire, open chandelier,
a swelling fruit
over the pact of sea and earth.

From what materials—
45 agate, quartz, wheat—
did your body come together,
swelling like baking bread
to signal silvered
hills,
50 the cleavage of one petal,
sweet fruits of a deep velvet,
until alone remained,
astonished,
the fine and firm feminine form?

55 It is not only light that falls
over the world,
spreading inside your body
its suffocated snow,
so much as clarity
60 taking its leave of you
as if you were
on fire within.

The moon lives in the lining of your skin.

W. H. AUDEN   (1907–1973)

In Praise of Limestone   (1951)

If it form the one landscape that we, the inconstant ones,
      Are consistently homesick for, this is chiefly
Because it dissolves in water. Mark these rounded slopes
      With their surface fragrance of thyme and, beneath,
5   A secret system of caves and conduits; hear the springs
      That spurt out everywhere with a chuckle,
Each filling a private pool for its fish and carving
      Its own little ravine whose cliffs entertain
The butterfly and the lizard; examine this region

10   Of short distances and definite places:
        What could be more like Mother or a fitter background
            For her son, the flirtatious male who lounges
        Against a rock in the sunlight, never doubting
            That for all his faults he is loved; whose works are but
15   Extensions of his power to charm? From weathered outcrop
            To hilltop temple, from appearing waters to
        Conspicuous fountains, from a wild to a formal vineyard,
            Are ingenious but short steps that a child's wish
        To receive more attention than his brothers, whether
20   By pleasing or teasing, can easily take.

        Watch, then, the band of rivals as they climb up and down
            Their steep stone gennels° in twos and threes, at times   channels
        Arm in arm, but never, thank God, in step; or engaged
            On the shady side of a square at midday in
25   Voluble discourse, knowing each other too well to think
            There are any important secrets, unable
        To conceive a god whose temper tantrums are moral
            And not to be pacified by a clever line
        Or a good lay: for, accustomed to a stone that responds,
30   They have never had to veil their faces in awe
        Of a crater whose blazing fury could not be fixed;
            Adjusted to the local needs of valleys
        Where everything can be touched or reached by walking,
            Their eyes have never looked into infinite space
35   Through the latticework of a nomad's comb; born lucky,
            Their legs have never encountered the fungi
        And insects of the jungle, the monstrous forms and lives
            With which we have nothing, we like to hope, in common.
        So, when one of them goes to the bad, the way his mind works
40   Remains comprehensible: to become a pimp
        Or deal in fake jewelry or ruin a fine tenor voice
            For effects that bring down the house, could happen to all
        But the best and the worst of us . . .
                                        That is why, I suppose,
45   The best and worst never stayed here long but sought
        Immoderate soils where the beauty was not so external,
            The light less public and the meaning of life
        Something more than a mad camp. "Come!" cried the granite wastes,
            "How evasive is your humour, how accidental
50   Your kindest kiss, how permanent is death." (Saints-to-be
            Slipped away sighing.) "Come!" purred the clays and gravels.

"On our plains there is room for armies to drill; rivers
    Wait to be tamed and slaves to construct you a tomb
In the grand manner: soft as the earth is mankind and both
55   Need to be altered." (Intendant Caesars rose and
Left, slamming the door.) But the really reckless were fetched
    By an older colder voice, the oceanic whisper:
"I am the solitude that asks and promises nothing;
    That is how I shall set you free. There is no love;
60   There are only the various envies, all of them sad."
    They were right, my dear, all those voices were right
And still are; this land is not the sweet home that it looks,
    Nor its peace the historical calm of a site
Where something was settled once and for all: A backward
65   And dilapidated province, connected
To the big busy world by a tunnel, with a certain
    Seedy appeal, is that all it is now? Not quite:
It has a worldly duty which in spite of itself
    It does not neglect, but calls into question
70   All the Great Powers assume; it disturbs our rights. The poet,
    Admired for his earnest habit of calling
The sun the sun, his mind Puzzle, is made uneasy
    By these marble statues which so obviously doubt
His antimythological myth; and these gamins,°   homeless children
75   Pursuing the scientist down the tiled colonnade
With such lively offers, rebuke his concern for Nature's
    Remotest aspects: I, too, am reproached, for what
And how much you know. Not to lose time, not to get caught,
    Not to be left behind, not, please! to resemble
80   The beasts who repeat themselves, or a thing like water
    Or stone whose conduct can be predicted, these
Are our Common Prayer, whose greatest comfort is music
    Which can be made anywhere, is invisible,
And does not smell. In so far as we have to look forward
85   To death as a fact, no doubt we are right: But if
Sins can be forgiven, if bodies rise from the dead,
    These modifications of matter into
Innocent athletes and gesticulating fountains,
    Made solely for pleasure, make a further point:
90   The blessed will not care what angle they are regarded from,
    Having nothing to hide. Dear, I know nothing of
Either, but when I try to imagine a faultless love
    Or the life to come, what I hear is the murmur
Of underground streams, what I see is a limestone landscape.

ROBERT CREELEY (1926–   )

America (1969)

America, you ode for reality!
Give back the people you took.

Let the sun shine again
on the four corners of the world

5   you thought of first but do not
own, or keep like a convenience.

People are your own word, you
invented that locus and term.

Here, you said and say, is
10 where we are. Give back

what we are, these people you made,
us, and nowhere but you to be.

FRANK O'HARA (1926–1966)

Ode to Joy (1960)

We shall have everything we want and there'll be no more dying
    on the pretty plains or in the supper clubs
for our symbol we'll acknowledge vulgar materialistic laughter
    over an insatiable sexual appetite
5   and the streets will be filled with racing forms
and the photographs of murderers and narcissists and movie stars
    will swell from the walls and books alive in steaming rooms
    to press against our burning flesh not once but interminably
as water flows down hill into the full-lipped basin
10 and the adder dives for the ultimate ostrich egg
and the feather cushion preens beneath a reclining monolith
    that's sweating with post-exertion visibility and sweetness
    near the grave of love

                                No more dying

15 We shall see the grave of love as a lovely sight and temporary
          near the elm that spells the lovers' names in roots
      and there'll be no more music but the ears in lips and no more wit
          but tongues in ears and no more drums but ears to thighs
      as evening signals nudities unknown to ancestors' imaginations
20   and the imagination itself will stagger like a tired paramour of ivory
          under the sculptural necessities of lust that never falters
          like a six-mile runner from Sweden or Liberia covered with gold
      as lava flows up and over the far-down somnolent° city's abdication   drowsy
      and the hermit always wanting to be lone is lone at last
25   and the weight of external heat crushes the heat-hating Puritan
          whose self-defeating vice becomes a proper sepulchre at last
          that love may live

      Buildings will go up into the dizzy air as love itself goes in
          and up the reeling life that it has chosen for once or all
30   while in the sky a feeling of intemperate fondness will excite the birds
          to swoop and veer like flies crawling across absorbed limbs
      that weep a pearly perspiration on the sheets of brief attention
      and the hairs dry out that summon anxious declaration of the organs
          as they rise like buildings to the needs of temporary neighbors
35   pouring hunger through the heart to feed desire in intravenous ways
      like the ways of gods with humans in the innocent combination of light
      and flesh or as the legends ride their heroes through the dark to found
      great cities where all life is possible to maintain as long as time
          which wants us to remain for cocktails in a bar and after dinner
40   lets us live with it
                                        No more dying

J. D. McCLATCHY   (1945–   )

Late Night Ode   (1998)

Horace IV. i [1]

It's over, love. Look at me pushing fifty now,
     Hair like grave-grass growing in both ears,
The piles and boggy prostate, the crooked penis,
     The sour taste of each day's first lie,

---

[1] **Horace IV.i:** In this section, Horace both laments and fears old age.

5   And that recurrent dream of years ago pulling
         A swaying bead-chain of moonlight,
    Of slipping between the cool sheets of dark
         Along a body like my own, but blameless.

    What good's my cut-glass conversation now,
10   Now I'm so effortlessly vulgar and sad?
    You get from life what you can shake from it?
         For me, it's g and t's all day and CNN.

    Try the blond boychick lawyer, entry level
         At eighty grand, who pouts about the overtime,
15   Keeps Evian and a beeper in his locker at the gym,
         And hash in tinfoil under the office fern.

    There's your hound from heaven, with buccaneer
         Curls and perfumed war-paint on his nipples.
    His answering machine always has room for one more
20   Slurred, embarrassed call from you-know-who.

    Some nights I've laughed so hard the tears
         Won't stop. Look at me now. Why *now*?
    I long ago gave up pretending to believe
         Anyone's memory will give as good as it gets.

25   So why these stubborn tears? And why do I dream
         Almost every night of holding you again,
    Or at least of diving after you, my long-gone,
         Through the bruised unbalanced waves?

GARY SOTO (1952–   )

Ode to the Yard Sale (1985)

    A toaster,
    A plate
    Of pennies,
    A plastic rose
5   Staring up
    To the sky
    It's Saturday
    And two friends,
    Merchants of
10   The salvageable heart,
    Are throwing

Things onto
The front lawn—
A couch,
15   A beanbag,
A table to clip
Poodles on,
Drawers of
Potato mashers,
20   Spoons, knives
That signaled
To the moon
For help.
Rent is due.
25   It's somewhere
On this lawn,
Somewhere among
The shirts we've
Looked good in,
30   Taken off before
We snuggled up
To breasts
That almost made
Us gods.
35   It'll be a good
Day, because
There's much
To sell,
And the pitcher
40   Of water
Blue in the shade,
Clear in the
Light, with
The much-handled
45   Scotch the color
Of leaves
Falling at our
Shoes, will
Get us through
50   The afternoon
Rush of old
Ladies, young women
On their way
To becoming nurses,
55   Bachelors of
The twice-dipped
Tea bag. It's

An eager day:
Wind in the trees,
60 Laughter of
Children behind
Fences. Surely
People will arrive
With handbags
65 And wallets,
To open up coffee
Pots and look
In, weigh pans
In each hand,
70 And prop hats
On their heads
And ask, "How do
I look?" (foolish
To most,
75 Beautiful to us).
And so they
Come, poking
At the clothes,
Lifting salt
80 And pepper shakers
For their tiny music,
Thumbing through
Old magazines
For someone
85 They know,
As we sit with
Our drinks
And grow sad
That the ashtray
90 Has been sold,
A lamp, a pillow,
The fry pans
That were action
Packed when
95 We cooked,
Those things
We threw so much
Love on, day
After day,
100 Sure they would
Mean something
When it came
To this.

MARY JO SALTER

Home Movies: A Sort of Ode   (1999)

Because it hadn't seemed enough,
after a while, to memorialize
more Christmases, the three-layer cakes
ablaze with birthday candles, the blizzard
5   Billy took a shovel to,
Phil's lawn mower tour of the yard,
the tree forts, the shoot-'em-ups
between the boys in new string ties
and cowboy hats and holsters,
10   or Mother sticking a bow as big
as Mouseketeer ears in my hair,

my father sometimes turned the gaze
of his camera to subjects more
artistic or universal:
15   rapt close-ups of a rose's face;
a real-time sunset (nearly an hour);
what one assumes were brilliant autumn
leaves before their colors faded
to dry beige on the aging film;
20   a great deal of pacing, at the zoo,
by polar bears and leopards caged,
he seemed to say, like him.

What happened between him and her
is another story. And just as well
25   we have no movie of it, only
some unforgiving scowls she gave
through terrifying, ticking silence
when he must have asked her (no
sound track) for a smile.
30   Yet the scenes I keep reversing to
are private: not those generic cherry
blossoms at the full, or the brave
daffodil after a snowfall;

instead, it's the re-run surprise
35   of the unshuttered, prefab blanks
of windows at the back of the house,
and how the lines of aluminum
siding are scribbled on with meaning

only for us who lived there.
40 It's the pair of elephant bookends
I'd forgotten, with the upraised trunks
like handles, and the books they sought
to carry in one block to a future
that scattered all of us.

45 And look: it's the stoneware mixing bowl
figured with hand-holding dancers
handed down so many years
ago to my own kitchen, still
valueless, unbroken. Here
50 she's happy, teaching us to dye
some Easter eggs in it, a Grecian
urn of sorts[1] near which—a foster
child of silence and slow time
myself—I smile because she does,
55 and patiently await my turn.

---

[1] **Grecian urn of sorts:** In "Ode on a Grecian Urn," John Keats describes an urn that remains static through constantly shifting time, comparing the urn to "a foster-child of silence and slow time."

LET ME TELL YOU A LITTLE STORY

CHAPTER 5

—W. H. Auden

An Anthology of the Ballad

The **ballad,** like the epic, has its origins in oral poetry, with roots deep in western European history. Like many forms of spoken poetry, it employs a regular, rhyming stanza format as a mnemonic device (an aid to memory). In the ballad, one hears a good deal of repetition. Refrains (repeating lines) are common, and even certain words and phrases are often repeated to create interesting effects. A ballad has a certain swing, a mood, a sway, telling a story in a dramatic fashion, using description and (sometimes) dialogue.

The rhythmical and rhyming structures of the ballad stanza are simple, usually consisting of four or six lines. In the four-line stanza, the second and fourth lines rhyme. In the six-line stanza, the first, fourth, and sixth lines rhyme, although poets will sometimes vary the pattern. The lines generally alternate between a four-beat line (tetrameter) and a three-beat line (trimeter), and there is often an iambic throb to each line, although lots of anapests will occur, as in the famous opening of "Sir Patrick Spens" (p. 455):

> The King sits in Dunfermline town,
> Drinking the blood-red wine;
> "O where shall I get a skeely skipper
> To sail this ship of mine?"

Ballad, as a term, refers broadly to any poem or song that tells a story, but in the poetic tradition the form is identified by its characteristic stanza and rhythmical pattern. The word *ballad* itself derives from an Italian word (*ballare*), meaning "to dance," and a ballad should move with the simple briskness and regularity of a folk dance.

Folk ballads in the medieval period were usually anonymous, passed on in various forms from generation to generation by word of mouth. In some countries, ballads celebrated great victories on the battlefield, and these were often woven into an epic tapestry. In Britain, a tradition of so-called **border ballads** arose: cycles of ballads that commemorated the skirmishes on the border between Scotland and England. Many folk myths, such as the tales of Robin Hood and his merry men in Sherwood Forest, were also enshrined in ballad form.

The folk ballad form had somewhat died out by the eighteenth century, when it was revived by Bishop Percy's *Reliques of Ancient English Poetry* (1765). This brought the form to the attention of the early Romantics, such as Wordsworth and Coleridge, who took eagerly to its appealing folk elements. During the nineteenth century, collections of anonymous ballads from earlier times were extremely popular with readers.

Folk ballads have many elements in common. For a start, they always tell a story. This story often begins abruptly and moves along at a rapid pace, without time wasted in exposition. The narrator cannot be identified in most cases; this gives the folk ballad a feeling of impersonality. There is frequently a sad, even tragic, aspect to the events described in the ballad, and sometimes these events have a sensational element—except in the case of the **comic ballad,** which is a minor subgenre. There will often be refrains or repeating elements, although these repetitions may vary from stanza to stanza.

The thematic material of the folk ballad normally draws on historical or political events or legends of a quasi-historical nature. Ballads tell stories of daring action, endurance, perseverance, betrayal, or divine intervention in human affairs. Many relate tales of loves won or lost. There is a sense of yearning in many ballads that makes them an ideal type of poem for folk musicians, and both the rhythms and themes of ballads are recognizable in country and western music as well as bluegrass.

The basic ballad form was modified slightly by writers of hymns, so that the rhyme scheme shifted from ABCB to ABAB, adding an element of regularity that was useful for performances by church choirs. Poets like Emily Dickinson and A. E. Housman adapted this modified form, known as **common measure**, for their own poetry. (It's the form used in "Amazing Grace," one of the most popular hymns of all time.)

Ballads were sometimes printed on one sheet of paper and sold in the streets. These were called **broadside ballads,** and might be considered an early form of tabloid journalism. They often had a strong political slant, siding with the working man against his bosses, and frequently recounted or satirized contemporary events. These broadside ballads led, in due course, to the modern political ballad, as seen in Dudley Randall's "Ballad of Birmingham" (p. 523), a remarkable poem about the bombing of a black church by white supremacists in Birmingham, Alabama, in which four little girls were killed. Of course, Randall took certain poetic liberties, such as limiting the victim to one child, who was much younger than the girls who were actually killed. This was a wise choice on his part, giving the poem a unity and compression it might otherwise have lacked.

The **literary ballad** was a later development, pioneered by Coleridge and Keats, who self-consciously developed their own, more elaborate, ballad stanzas, adding a level of complexity to the text not commonly found in earlier ballads. "The Rime of the Ancient Mariner" by Coleridge (p. 471) and "La Belle Dame Sans Merci" by Keats (p. 491) are splendid examples of the literary ballad in its renewed format.

Coleridge and Oscar Wilde (in "Ballad of the Reading Gaol," p. 506) expanded the usual four-line stanza to six or more lines, increasing the level of textual density. Coleridge manages this stanza rather deftly, playing with cleverly variable feet in each line:

> An orphan's curse would drag to hell
> A spirit from on high;
> But oh! more horrible than that
> Is the curse in a dead man's eye!
> 5   Seven days, seven nights, I saw that curse,
> And yet I could not die.

The ballad form also appealed to modernists such as W. H. Auden. "Miss Gee" (p. 518) is one of his most sardonic poems, a lively turn on the old form. The ballad also appeals to a wide range of contemporary poets, from Muriel Rukeyser and Anne Sexton to Audre Lorde. In each case, the poet has used this ancient form, with its folk echoes and affiliations, to tell a fresh story in ways that lend an aura of permanence to the material. A ballad always sounds as though it has been there for centuries, written by Anonymous, the greatest poet of them all!

There is a lively urban poetry today, heard in rap music, in poetry slams, and on the street corners of major cities, that owes much to the ballad format, which has always been used by ordinary people to convey information, create tribal myths, debunk those in power, and pass on legends as well as historical facts. This writing falls directly in the line of folk ballads, where the form has often been employed to celebrate cultural heroes and rebels. In the 1920s and 1930s, the form was used by union members to protest corporate misdeeds and to celebrate successes. In the 1960s, it was adopted by singers like Bob Dylan and Joan Baez to promote social justice.

In all its varied forms and incarnations, the ballad remains one of the liveliest and shrewdest traditions of poetry written in English. It shows no sign of losing its value in the twenty-first century.

GEOFFREY CHAUCER (ca. 1343–1400)

To Rosemounde (ca. 1380; 1891)

Madame, ye ben of alle beaute shryne
As fer as cercled is the mapamounde,[1]
For as the cristall glorious ye shyne,
And lyke ruby ben your chekes rounde.
5   Therwyth ye ben so mery and so jocounde
That at a revell whan that I se you daunce,
It is an oynement unto my wounde,
Thogh ye to me ne do no daliaunce.°   encouragement

For thogh I wepe of teres ful a tyne,°   tub
10   Yet may that wo myn herte nat confounde.
Your semy° voys,° that ye so small out twyne,[2]   small / voice
Maketh my thoght in joy and blys habounde.°   abound
So curtaysly I go, with love bounde,
That to myself I sey, in my penaunce,
15   "Suffyseth me to love you, Rosemounde,
Thogh ye to me ne do no daliaunace."

Nas never pyk walwed in galauntyne[3]
As I in love am walwed and iwounde,
For whych ful ofte I of myself devyne
20   That I am trewe Tristam[4] the secounde.
My love may not refreyde° nor affounde;°   cool / chill
I brenne° ay in an amorouse plesaunce.   burn
Do what you lyst; I wyl your thral° be founde,   slave
Thogh ye to me ne do no daliaunce.

ANONYMOUS

Lord Randal (eighteenth cent.; 1803)

1

"O where ha' you been, Lord Randal, my son?
And where ha' you been, my handsome young man?"

---

[1] **As fer . . . mapamounde:** I.e., the farthest circles (circumference) of the map of the world.
[2] **ye so small . . . twyne:** I.e., that you so deftly spin out.
[3] **Nas never . . . galauntyne:** Pike rolled in galantine sauce.
[4] **Tristam:** According to the myth, the famous, unwavering lover of Isolde.

"I ha' been at the greenwood; mother, mak my bed soon,
For I'm wearied wi' huntin', and fain wad° lie down."   would

2

5   "And wha° met ye there, Lord Randal, my son?   who
    And wha met you there, my handsome young man?"
    "O I met wi' my true-love; mother, mak my bed soon,
    For I'm wearied wi' huntin', and fain wad lie down."

3

    "And what did she give you, Lord Randal, my son?
10 And what did she give you, my handsome young man?"
    "Eels fried in a pan; mother, mak my bed soon,
    For I'm wearied wi' huntin', and fain wad lie down."

4

    "And wha gat your leavin's, Lord Randal, my son?
    And wha gat your leavin's, my handsome young man?"
15 "My hawks and my hounds; mother, mak my bed soon,
    For I'm wearied wi' huntin', and fain wad lie down."

5

    "And what becam of them, Lord Randal, my son?
    And what becam of them, my handsome young man?"
    "They stretched their legs out and died; mother, mak my bed soon,
20 For I'm wearied wi' huntin', and fain wad lie down."

6

    "O I fear you are poisoned, Lord Randal, my son!
    I fear you are poisoned, my handsome young man!"
    "O yes, I am poisoned; mother, mak my bed soon,
    For I'm sick at the heart, and I fain wad lie down."

7

25 "What d' ye leave to your mother, Lord Randal, my son?
    What d'ye leave to your mother, my handsome young man?"
    "Four and twenty milk kye;° mother, mak my bed soon,   cattle
    For I'm sick at the heart, and I fain wad lie down."

8

    "What d' ye leave to your sister, Lord Randal, my son?
30 What d' ye leave to your sister, my handsome young man?"
    "My gold and my silver; mother, mak my bed soon,
    For I'm sick at the heart, and I fain wad lie down."

9

"What d' ye leave to your brother, Lord Randal, my son?
What d' ye leave to your brother, my handsome young man?"
35   "My houses and my lands; mother, mak my bed soon,
For I'm sick at the heart, and I fain wad lie down."

10

"What d' ye leave to your true-love, Lord Randal, my son?
What d' ye leave to your true-love, my handsome young man?"
"I leave her hell and fire; mother, mak my bed soon,
40   For I'm sick at the heart, and I fain wad lie down."

ANONYMOUS

Bonny Barbara Allan   (1763 pub.)

1

It was in and about the Martinmas[1] time,
    When the green leaves were a falling,
That Sir John Græme, in the West Country,
    Fell in love with Barbara Allan.

2

5   He sent his man down through the town,
    To the place where she was dwelling:
"O haste and come to my master dear,
    Gin° ye be Barbara Allan."   *if*

3

O hooly,° hooly rose she up,   *slowly*
10   To the place where he was lying,
And when she drew the curtain by:
    "Young man, I think you're dying."

4

"O it's I'm sick, and very, very sick,
    And 'tis a' for Barbara Allan."

---

[1] **Martinmas:** The feast of St. Martin, November 11.

15 "O the better for me ye s'° never be,   ye shall
        Though your heart's blood were a-spilling.

                                    5

"O dinna° ye mind, young man," said she,   don't
        "When ye was in the tavern a drinking,
That ye made the healths gae° round and round,   go
20   And slighted Barbara Allan?"

                                    6

He turned his face unto the wall,
        And death was with him dealing:
"Adieu, adieu, my dear friends all,
        And be kind to Barbara Allan."

                                    7

25 And slowly, slowly raise she up,
        And slowly, slowly left him,
And sighing said, she could not stay,
        Since death of life had reft him.

                                    8

She had not gane a mile but twa,
30   When she heard the dead-bell ringing,
And every jow° that the dead-bell geid,°   stroke / gave
        It cried, "Woe to Barbara Allan!"

                                    9

"O mother, mother, make my bed!
        O make it saft and narrow!
35 Since my love died for me to-day,
        I'll die for him to-morrow."

ANONYMOUS

Sir Patrick Spens (1763 pub.)

                                    1

The king sits in Dumferling town,
        Drinking the blude-reid° wine: blood-red

"O whar will I get guid sailor,
　　To sail this ship of mine?"

2

5　Up and spak an eldern knicht,
　　　Sat at the king's richt knee:
　"Sir Patrick Spens is the best sailor
　　　That sails upon the sea."

3

　The king has written a braid° letter   long
10　　And signed it wi' his hand,
　And sent it to Sir Patrick Spens,
　　　Was walking on the sand.

4

　The first line that Sir Patrick read,
　　　A loud lauch° lauched he,   laugh
15　The next line that Sir Patrick read,
　　　The tear blinded his ee.°   eye

5

　"O wha is this has done this deed,
　　　This ill deed done to me,
　To send me out this time o' the year,
20　　　To sail upon the sea?

6

　"Mak haste, mak haste, my mirry men all,
　　　Our guid ship sails the morn."
　"O say na sae,° my master dear,   so
　　　For I fear a deadly storm.

7

25　"Late, late yestre'en I saw the new moon
　　　Wi' the auld moon in hir arm,
　And I fear, I fear, my dear master,
　　　That we will come to harm."

8

　O our Scots nobles were richt laith°   loath
30　　To weet° their cork-heeled shoon,°   wet / shoes
　But lang or° a' the play were played   before
　　　Their hats they swam aboon.°   above

9

O lang, lang may their ladies sit,
   Wi' their fans into their hand,
35 Or ere they see Sir Patrick Spens
   Come sailing to the land.

10

O lang, lang may the ladies stand
   Wi' their gold kems° in their hair,   combs
Waiting for their ain dear lords,
40   For they'll see them na mair.°   more

11

Half o'er, half o'er to Aberdour
   It's fifty fadom deep,
And there lies guid Sir Patrick Spens
   Wi' the Scots lords at his feet.

ANNE ASKEW (1521–1546)

The Ballad Which Anne Askewe Made and Sang When She Was in Newgate[1] (1546 pub.)

Like as the armèd knight
Appointed to the field,
With this world will I fight
And faith shall be my shield.
5   Faith is that weapon strong
Which will not fail at need;
My foes therefore among
Therewith will I proceed.
    As it is had in strength
10 And force of Christ's way,
It will prevail at length
Though all the devils say nay.
    Faith in the father's old

---

[1] **The Ballad . . . Newgate:** Anne Askew was arrested and imprisoned at Newgate prison for heresy in 1546. After being subjected to torture, she was burned at the stake in July of the same year. The Protestant Bishop John Bale included this ballad along with other accounts of her examination and death.

Obtainèd rightwiseness
15 Which make me very bold
To fear no world's distress.
        I now rejoice in heart
And hope bid me do so,
For Christ will take my part
20 And ease me of my woe.
        Thou sayst lord, who so kneck,°   knock
To them wilt thou attend;
Undo therefore the lock
And thy strong power send.
25   More enemies now I have
Than hairs upon my head
Let them not me deprave,
But fight thou in my stead.
        On thee my care I cast
30 For all their cruel spite
I set not by their haste,
For thou art my delight.
        I am not she that list°   chooses
My anchor to let fall
35 For every drizzling mist
My ship substantial.
        Not oft use I to write
In prose nor yet in rhyme,
Yet will I show one sight
40 That I saw in my time.
        I saw a royal throne
Where Justice should have sit,
But in her stead was one
Of modie° cruel wit.   wrathful
45   Absorbed was rightwiseness
As of the raging flood;
Satan in his excess
Sucked up the guiltless blood.
        Then thought I, Jesus lord,
50 When thou shalt judge us all,
Hard is it to record
On these men what will fall.
        Yet lord I thee desire
For that they do to me,
55 Let them not taste the hire°   reward
Of their iniquity.

MICHAEL DRAYTON (1563–1631)

His Ballad of Agincourt[1] (1606; 1619)

Fair stood the wind for France,
When we our sails advance,
Nor now to prove our chance
Longer will tarry;
5   But putting to the main,
At Caux, the mouth of Seine,
With all his martial train,
Landed King Harry.[2]

And taking many a fort,
10   Furnished in warlike sort,
Marcheth towards Agincourt
In happy hour;
Skirmishing day by day
With those that stopped his way
15   Where the French general lay,
With all his power.

Which in his height of pride,
King Henry to deride,
His ransom to provide
20   To the king sending;
Which he neglects the while,
As from a nation vile,
Yet with an angry smile
Their fall portending.

25   And turning to his men,
Quoth our brave Henry then,
"Though they to one be ten,
Be not amazèd.
Yet have we well begun;
30   Battles so bravely won
Have ever to the sun
By fame been raisèd.

---

[1] **Agincourt:** Agincourt, in France, was the site of a major battle (1415), in which the English forces of Henry V defeated the French.
[2] **King Harry:** I.e., King Henry V.

"And for myself," quoth he,
"This my full rest shall be;
35   England ne'er mourn for me,
Nor more esteem me.
Victor I will remain,
Or on this earth lie slain;
Never shall she sustain
40   Loss to redeem me.

"Poitiers and Crécy[3] tell
When most their pride did swell,
Under our swords they fell;
No less our skill is,
45   Than when our grandsire great,
Claiming the regal seat,
By many a warlike feat
Lopped the French lilies."

The Duke of York so dread
50   The eager vaward° led;   vanguard
With the main Henry sped
Amongst his henchmen.
Exeter[4] had the rear,
A braver man not there;
55   O Lord, how hot they were
On the false Frenchmen!

They now to fight are gone,
Armour on armour shone,
Drum now to drum did groan,
60   To hear was wonder;
That with the cries they make
The very earth did shake;
Trumpet to trumpet spake,
Thunder to thunder.

65   Well it thine age became,
O noble Erpingham,[5]
Which didst the signal aim
To our hid forces;
When from a meadow by,

---

[3] **Poitiers and Crécy:** Sites of earlier battles in the Hundred Years' War between England and France.
[4] **Exeter:** I.e., the Duke of Exeter.
[5] **Erpingham:** Sir Thomas Erpingham, one of the leaders of the English army. Also a character in Shakespeare's *Henry V.*

70   Like a storm suddenly,
     The English archery
     Struck the French horses.

     With Spanish yew so strong,
     Arrows a cloth-yard long
75   That like to serpents stung,
     Piercing the weather,
     None from his fellow starts,
     But playing manly parts,
     And like true English hearts,
80   Stuck close together.

     When down their bows they threw,
     And forth their bilboes[6] drew,
     And on the French they flew,
     Not one was tardy;
85   Arms were from shoulders sent,
     Scalps to the teeth were rent,
     Down the French peasants went;
     Our men were hardy.

     This while our noble king,
90   His broad sword brandishing,
     Down the French host did ding,
     As to o'erwhelm it;
     And many a deep wound lent,
     His arms with blood besprent,
95   And many a cruel dent
     Bruisèd his helmet.

     Gloucester, that duke so good,
     Next of the royal blood,
     For famous England stood,
100 With his brave brother;
     Clarence, in steel so bright,
     Though but a maiden knight,
     Yet in that furious fight
     Scarce such another.

105 Warwick in blood did wade,
     Oxford the foe invade,
     And cruel slaughter made

---

[6] **bilboes:** I.e., fine swords from Bilboa, Spain.

Still as they ran up;
Suffolk his axe did ply,
110   Beaumont and Willoughby
Bare them right doughtily,
Ferrers and Fanhope.[7]

Upon Saint Crispin's day [8]
Fought was this noble fray,
115   Which fame did not delay
To England to carry;
O, when shall English men
With such acts fill a pen,
Or England breed again
120   Such a King Harry?

SIR JOHN SUCKLING (1609–1642)

A Ballad upon a Wedding[1] (ca. 1641)

I tell thee, Dick, where I have been,
Where I the rarest things have seen,
   Oh, things without compare!
Such sights again cannot be found
5   In any place on English ground,
   Be it at wake° or fair.   funeral

At Charing Cross,[2] hard by the way
Where we (thou know'st) do sell our hay,
   There is a house with stairs;
10   And there did I see coming down
Such folk as are not in our town,
   Forty, at least, in pairs.

Amongst the rest, one pest'lent fine
(His beard no bigger, though, than thine)
15   Walked on before the rest.

---

[7] **Gloucester . . . Fanhope:** All the names in these two stanzas belong to noblemen fighting on the side of the English.
[8] **Saint Crispin's day:** October 25, 1415. See *Henry V* (III, iv).
[1] **A Ballad upon a Wedding:** This ballad by John Suckling can be taken as a parody of the epithalamion, a poem in celebration of marriage characterized by complex prosody and ornate language. See "Epithalamion" by Edmund Spenser in Chapter 13.
[2] **Charing Cross:** A busy site in the center of London near Haymarket. King Edward (1239–1307) once had a stone cross erected there in memory of his wife, Queen Eleanor.

Our landlord looks like nothing to him;
The king (God bless him!), 'twould undo him
    Should he go still so dressed.

At course-a-park,[3] without all doubt,
20   He should have first been taken out
    By all the maids i' th' town,
Though lusty Roger there had been,
Or little George upon the Green,
    Or Vincent of the Crown.

25   But wot° you what? the youth was going   know
To make an end of all his wooing;
    The parson for him stayed.
Yet by his leave, for all his haste,
He did not so much wish all past,
30   Perchance, as did the maid.

The maid (and thereby hangs a tale),
For such a maid no Whitsun-ale[4]
    Could ever yet produce;
No grape, that's kindly ripe, could be
35   So round, so plump, so soft as she,
    Nor half so full of juice.

Her finger was so small the ring
Would not stay on, which they did bring;
    It was too wide a peck:[5]
40   And to say truth (for out it must),
It looked like the great collar (just)
    About our young colt's neck.

Her feet beneath her petticoat,
Like little mice, stole in and out,
45   As if they feared the light;
But oh, she dances such a way,
No sun upon an Easter day
    Is half so fine a sight!

He would have kissed her once or twice,
50   But she would not, she was so nice,
    She would not do 't in sight;

---

[3] **course-a-park:** A rural game in which a girl chooses a boy to chase her.
[4] **Whitsun-ale:** A church festival at Whitsuntide during which a lot of ale was consumed.
[5] **peck:** A measure of capacity.

And then she looked as who should say,
"I will do what I list today;
    And you shall do 't at night."

55 Her cheeks so rare a white was on,
No daisy makes comparison
    (Who sees them is undone),
For streaks of red were mingled there,
Such as are on a Catherine pear[6]
60   (The side that's next the sun).

Her lips were red, and one was thin
Compared to that was next her chin
    (Some bee had stung it newly);
But, Dick, her eyes so guard her face
65 I durst no more upon them gaze
    Than on the sun in July.

Her mouth so small, when she does speak,
Thou 'dst swear her teeth her words did break,
    That they might passage get;
70 But she so handled still the matter,
They came as good as ours, or better,
    And are not spent a whit.

If wishing should be any sin,
The parson himself had guilty been
75   (She looked that day so purely);
And did the youth so oft the feat
At night, as some did in conceit,°   *imagination*
    It would have spoiled him, surely.

Passion o' me, how I run on!
80 There's that that would be thought upon,
    I trow,° besides the bride.   *suppose*
The business of the kitchen's great,
For it is fit that man should eat,
    Nor was it there denied.

85 Just in the nick the cook knocked thrice,
And all the waiters in a trice
    His summons did obey;
Each serving-man, with dish in hand,
Marched boldly up, like our trained band,°   *militia*
90   Presented, and away.

---

[6] **Catherine pear:** A variety of pear.

When all the meat was on the table,
What man of knife or teeth was able
    To stay to be entreated?
And this the very reason was,
95   Before the parson could say grace,
    The company was seated.

Now hats fly off, and youths carouse;
Healths first go round, and then the house;
    The bride's came thick and thick:
100   And when 'twas named another's health,
Perhaps he made it hers by stealth;
    And who could help it, Dick?

O' th' sudden up they rise and dance;
Then sit again and sigh and glance;
105   Then dance again and kiss.
Thus several ways the time did pass,
Till every woman wished her place,
    And every man wished his!

By this time all were stolen aside
110   To counsel and undress the bride,
    But that he must not know;
But yet 'twas thought he guessed her mind,
And did not mean to stay behind
    Above an hour or so.

115   When in he came, Dick, there she lay
Like new-fallen snow melting away
    ('Twas time, I trow, to part);
Kisses were now the only stay,
Which soon she gave, as who would say,
120   "God b' w' ye, with all my heart."

But just as heaven would have, to cross it,
In came the bridesmaids with the posset.[7]
    The bridegroom ate in spite,
For had he left the women to 't,
125   It would have cost two hours to do 't,
    Which were too much that night.

At length the candle's out, and now
All that they had not done, they do.

---

[7] **posset:** An alcoholic drink with spiced milk and ale.

What that is, who can tell?
130 But I believe it was no more
Than thou and I have done before
With Bridget and with Nell.

WILLIAM CONGREVE (1670–1729)

Doris (1710)

Doris, a nymph of riper age,
   Has every grace and art
A wise observer to engage,
   Or wound a heedless heart.
5 Of native blush and rosy dye
   Time has her cheek bereft,
Which makes the prudent nymph supply
   With paint th' injurious theft.
Her sparkling eyes she still retains,
10   And teeth in good repair,
And her well-furnished front disdains
   To grace with borrowed hair.
Of size, she is not short nor tall,
   And does to fat incline
15 No more than what the French would call
   Aimable embonpoint.[1]
Farther her person to disclose
   I leave—let it suffice,
She has few faults but what she knows,
20   And can with skill disguise.
She many lovers has refused,
   With many more complied,
Which, like her clothes, when little used
   She always lays aside.
25 She's one who looks with great contempt
   On each affected creature,
Whose nicety would seem exempt
   From appetites of nature.
She thinks they want of health or sense,
30   Who want an inclination;

---

[1] **Aimable embonpoint:** Literally, pleasant plumpness (French).

And therefore never takes offence
    At him who pleads his passion.
Whom she refuses she treats still
    With so much sweet behaviour,
35 That her refusal, through her skill,
    Looks almost like a favour.
Since she this softness can express
    To those whom she rejects,
She must be very fond, you'll guess,
40   Of such whom she affects.
But here our Doris far outgoes
    All that her sex have done;
She no regard for custom knows,
    Which reason bids her shun.
45 By reason, her own reason's meant,
    Or, if you please, her will:
For when this last is discontent,
    The first is served but ill.
Peculiar therefore is her way;
50   Whether by nature taught,
I shall not undertake to say,
    Or by experience bought.
But who o'er-night obtained her grace,
    She can next day disown,
55 And stare upon the strange man's face
    As one she ne'er had known
So well she can the truth disguise,
    Such artful wonder frame,
The lover or distrusts his eyes,
60   Or thinks 'twas all a dream.
Some censure this as lewd and low,
    Who are to bounty blind;
For to forget what we bestow
    Bespeaks a noble mind.
65 Doris our thanks nor asks nor needs,
    For all her favours done:
From her love flows, as light proceeds
    Spontaneous from the sun.
On one or other still her fires
70   Display their genial force;
And she, like Sol,[2] alone retires
    To shine elsewhere of course.

---

[2] **Sol:** In Roman mythology, the god of the sun (equivalent to the Greek god Helios).

HENRY CAREY (ca. 1687–1743)

The Ballad of Sally in Our Alley (ca. 1715)

Of all the girls that are so smart
    There's none like pretty Sally;
She is the darling of my heart,
    And she lives in our alley.
5   There is no lady in the land
    Is half so sweet as Sally;
She is the darling of my heart,
    And she lives in our alley.

Her father he makes cabbage-nets,
10   And through the streets does cry 'em;
Her mother she sells laces long
    To such as please to buy 'em;
But sure such folks could ne'er beget
    So sweet a girl as Sally!
15   She is the darling of my heart,
    And she lives in our alley.

When she is by I leave my work
    (I love her so sincerely);
My master comes like any Turk
20   And bangs me most severely;
But let him bang his bellyfull,
    I'll bear it all for Sally;
She is the darling of my heart,
    And she lives in our alley.

25   Of all the days that's in the week
    I dearly love but one day,
And that's the day that comes betwixt
    A Saturday and Monday;
For then I'm dressed all in my best
30   To walk abroad with Sally;
She is the darling of my heart,
    And she lives in our alley.

My master carries me to church,
    And often am I blamed
35   Because I leave him in the lurch
    As soon as text is named;
I leave the church in sermon time
    And slink away to Sally;
She is the darling of my heart,
40   And she lives in our alley.

When Christmas comes about again,
    O then I shall have money;
I'll hoard it up, and box and all
    I'll give it to my honey;
45 And would it were ten thousand pounds,
    I'd give it all to Sally;
She is the darling of my heart,
    And she lives in our alley.

My master and the neighbours all
50   Make game of me and Sally;
And, but for her, I'd better be
    A slave and row a galley;
But when my seven long years are out,[1]
    O, then I'll marry Sally!
55 O then we'll wed, and then we'll bed,
    But not in our alley.

WILLIAM WORDSWORTH (1770–1850)

Lucy Gray (1800)

Oft I had heard of Lucy Gray,
And when I cross'd the Wild,
I chanc'd to see at break of day
The solitary Child.

5 No Mate, no comrade Lucy knew;
She dwelt on a wild Moor,
The sweetest Thing that ever grew
Beside a human door!

You yet may spy the Fawn at play,
10 The Hare upon the Green;
But the sweet face of Lucy Gray
Will never more be seen.

'To-night will be a stormy night,
You to the Town must go,
15 And take a lantern, Child, to light
Your Mother thro' the snow.'

---

[1] **when my seven . . . out:** I.e., when I'm through with my seven years of apprenticeship.

'That, Father! will I gladly do;
'Tis scarcely afternoon—
The Minster-clock has just struck two,
20   And yonder is the Moon.'

At this the Father rais'd his hook
And snapp'd a faggot-band;[1]
He plied his work, and Lucy took
The lantern in her hand.

25   Not blither is the mountain roe,
With many a wanton stroke
Her feet disperse the powd'ry snow
That rises up like smoke.

The storm came on before its time,
30   She wander'd up and down,
And many a hill did Lucy climb
But never reach'd the Town.

The wretched Parents all that night
Went shouting far and wide;
35   But there was neither sound nor sight
To serve them for a guide.

At day-break on a hill they stood
That overlook'd the Moor;
And thence they saw the Bridge of Wood
40   A furlong from their door.

And now they homeward turn'd, and cry'd
'In Heaven we all shall meet!'
When in the snow the Mother spied
The print of Lucy's feet.

45   Then downward from the steep hill's edge
They track'd the footmarks small;
And through the broken hawthorn-hedge,
And by the long stone-wall;

And then an open field they cross'd,
50   The marks were still the same;
They track'd them on, nor ever lost,
And to the Bridge they came.

---

[1] **rais'd his hook . . . faggot-band:** Here, the father is perhaps involved in yard work, moving bundles of branches (faggot-band).

They follow'd from the snowy bank
The footmarks, one by one,
55   Into the middle of the plank,
And further there were none.

Yet some maintain that to this day
She is a living Child,
That you may see sweet Lucy Gray
60   Upon the lonesome Wild.

O'er rough and smooth she trips along,
And never looks behind;
And sings a solitary song
That whistles in the wind.

SAMUEL TAYLOR COLERIDGE (1772–1834)

The Rime of the Ancient Mariner (1798; 1817)
In Seven Parts

Facile credo, plures esse Naturas invisibles quam visibiles in
rerum universitate. Sed horum [sic] omnium familiam quis nobis
enarrabit? et gradus et cognationes et discrimina et singulorum
munera? Quid agunt? quae loca habitant? Harum rerum notitiam
semper ambivit ingenium humanum, nunquam attigit. Juvat,
interea, non diffiteor, quandoque in animo, in tabulâ, majoris et
melioris mundi imaginem contemplari: ne mens assuefacta
hodiernae vitae minutiis se contrahat nimis, et tota subsidat in
pusillas cogitationes. Sed veritati interea invigilandum est,
modusque servandus, ut certa ab incertis, diem a nocte,
distinguamus.

                                        —T. BURNET[1]

---

[1] **Epigraph:** From Thomas Burnet's *Archaeologiae Philosophicae.* "I can easily believe, that there are
more Invisible than Visible Beings in the Universe; but who will declare to us the Family of all these,
and acquaint us with the Agreements, Differences, and peculiar Talents which are to be found
among them? What do they do and where do they live? It is true, human Wit has always desired a
Knowledge of these Things, though it has never yet attained it. I will own that it is very profitable,
sometimes to contemplate in the Mind, as in a Draught, the Image of the greater and better World;
lest the Soul being accustomed to the Trifles of this present Life, should contract itself too much, and
altogether rest in mean Cogitations; but, in the mean Time, we must take Care to keep to the Truth,
and observe Moderation, that we may distinguish certain Things, and Day from Night."

Part I

<table>
<tr>
<td>

An ancient
Mariner meeteth
three Gallants
bidden to a
wedding feast, and
detaineth one.
</td>
<td>

It is an ancient Mariner
And he stoppeth one of three.
—"By thy long gray beard and glittering eye,
Now wherefore stopp'st thou me?
</td>
</tr>
</table>

The Bridegroom's doors are opened wide,   5
And I am next of kin;
The guests are met, the feast is set:
May'st hear the merry din."

He holds him with his skinny hand,
"There was a ship," quoth he.   10
"Hold off! unhand me, graybeard loon!"
Eftsoons° his hand dropped he.   straightway

The Wedding
• Guest is spell-
bound by the eye
of the old sea-
faring man, and
constrained to
hear his tale.

He holds him with his glittering eye—
The Wedding Guest stood still,
And listens like-a-three years' child: 15
The Mariner hath his will.

The Wedding Guest sat on a stone:
He cannot choose but hear;
And thus spake on that ancient man,
The bright-eyed Mariner.   20

"The ship was cheered, the harbor cleared,
Merrily did we drop
Below the kirk,° below the hill,   church
Below the lighthouse top.

The Mariner tells
how the ship
sailed southward
with a good wind
and fair weather,
till it reached the
line.

The Sun came up upon the left,   25
Out of the sea came he!
And he shone bright, and on the right
Went down into the sea.

Higher and higher every day,
Till over the mast at noon—"   30
The Wedding Guest here beat his breast,
For he heard the loud bassoon.

The Wedding
Guest heareth the
bridal music; but
the Mariner contin-
ueth his tale.

The bride hath paced into the hall,
Red as a rose is she;
Nodding their heads before her goes   35
The merry minstrelsy.

The Wedding Guest he beat his breast,
Yet he cannot choose but hear;
And thus spake on that ancient man,
The bright-eyed Mariner.   40

The ship driven by
a storm toward the
South Pole.

"And now the STORM-BLAST came, and he
Was tyrannous and strong;
He struck with his o'ertaking wings,
And chased us south along.

With sloping masts and dipping prow,   45
As who pursued with yell and blow
Still treads the shadow of his foe,
And forward bends his head,
The ship drove fast, loud roared the blast,
And southward aye we fled.   50

And now there came both mist and snow,
And it grew wondrous cold:
And ice, mast-high, came floating by,
As green as emerald.

The land of ice,
and of fearful
sounds where no
living thing was to
be seen.

And through the drifts the snowy clifts°   55   cliffs
Did send a dismal sheen:
Nor shapes of men nor beasts we ken—
The ice was all between.

The ice was here, the ice was there,
The ice was all around: 60
It cracked and growled, and roared and howled,
Like noises in a swound!

Till a great sea
bird, called the
Albatross, came
through the snow-
fog, and was
received with great
joy and hospitality.

At length did cross an Albatross,
Thorough the fog it came;
As if it had been a Christian soul,   65
We hailed it in God's name.

It ate the food it ne'er had eat,
And round and round it flew.
The ice did split with a thunder-fit;
The helmsman steered us through!   70

And lo! the Alba-
tross proveth a
bird of good omen,
and followeth the
ship as it returned
northward through
fog and floating ice.

And a good south wind sprung up behind;
The Albatross did follow,
And every day, for food or play,
Came to the mariners' hollo!

In mist or cloud, on mast or shroud,   75
It perched for vespers nine;
Whiles all the night, through fog-smoke white,
Glimmered the white Moon-shine."

The ancient Mariner inhospitably killeth the pious bird of good omen.

"God save thee, ancient Mariner!
From the fiends, that plague thee thus!—   80
Why look'st thou so?"—With my crossbow
I shot the ALBATROSS.

Part II

The Sun now rose upon the right:
Out of the sea came he,
Still hid in mist, and on the left   85
Went down into the sea.

And the good south wind still blew behind,
But no sweet bird did follow,
Nor any day for food or play
Came to the mariners' hollo!   90

His shipmates cry out against the ancient Mariner, for killing the bird of good luck.

And I had done a hellish thing,
And it would work 'em woe:
For all averred, I had killed the bird
That made the breeze to blow.
Ah wretch! said they, the bird to slay,   95
That made the breeze to blow!

But when the fog cleared off, they justify the same, and thus make themselves accomplices in the crime.

Nor dim nor red, like God's own head,
The glorious Sun uprist:
Then all averred, I had killed the bird
That brought the fog and mist.   100
'Twas right, said they, such birds to slay,
That bring the fog and mist.

The fair breeze continues; the ship enters the Pacific Ocean, and sails northward, even till it reaches the Line.

The fair breeze blew, the white foam flew,
The furrow followed free;
We were the first that ever burst   105
Into that silent sea.

The ship hath been suddenly becalmed.

Down dropped the breeze, the sails dropped down,
'Twas sad as sad could be;
And we did speak only to break
The silence of the sea!   110

All in a hot and copper sky,
The bloody Sun, at noon,
Right up above the mast did stand,
No bigger than the Moon.

Day after day, day after day,   115
We stuck, nor breath nor motion;
As idle as a painted ship
Upon a painted ocean.

And the Albatross   Water, water, everywhere,
begins to be   And all the boards did shrink;   120
avenged.   Water, water, everywhere,
Nor any drop to drink.

The very deep did rot: O Christ!
That ever this should be!
Yea, slimy things did crawl with legs   125
Upon the slimy sea.

About, about, in reel and rout
The death-fires danced at night;
The water, like a witch's oils,
Burnt green, and blue and white.   130

A Spirit had   And some in dreams assuréd were
followed them;   Of the Spirit that plagued us so;
one of the invisi-   Nine fathom deep he had followed us
ble inhabitants of   From the land of mist and snow.
this planet, neither
departed souls
nor angels; concerning whom the learned Jew, Josephus, and the Platonic Constantinopolitan, Michael
Psellus, may be consulted. They are very numerous, and there is no climate or element without one or more.

And every tongue, through utter drought,   135
Was withered at the root;
We could not speak, no more than if
We had been choked with soot.

The shipmates, in   Ah! well-a-day! what evil looks
their sore distress,   Had I from old and young!   140
would fain throw   Instead of the cross, the Albatross
the whole guilt on   About my neck was hung.
the ancient Mari-
ner: in sign where-
of they hang the   *Part III*
dead sea bird
round his neck.   There passed a weary time. Each throat
Was parched, and glazed each eye.

A weary time! a weary time!   145
How glazed each weary eye,
When looking westward, I beheld
A something in the sky.

The ancient Mari-
ner beholdeth a
sign in the element
afar off.

At first it seemed a little speck,
And then it seemed a mist;   150
It moved and moved, and took at last
A certain shape, I wist.

A speck, a mist, a shape, I wist!
And still it neared and neared:
As if it dodged a water sprite,   155
It plunged and tacked and veered.

As its nearer
approach, it
seemeth him to be
a ship; and at a
dear ransom he
freeth his speech
from the bonds of
thirst.

With throats unslaked, with black lips baked,
We could nor laugh nor wail;
Through utter drought all dumb we stood!
I bit my arm, I sucked the blood,   160
And cried, A sail! a sail!

A flash of joy;

With throats unslaked, with black lips baked,
Agape they heard me call:
Gramercy!° they for joy did grin,   thank heaven
And all at once their breath drew in,   165
As they were drinking all.

And horror follows.
For can it be a
ship that comes
onward without
wind or tide?

See! see! (I cried) she tacks no more!
Hither to work us weal;
Without a breeze, without a tide,
She steadies with upright keel!   170

The western wave was all aflame.
The day was well nigh done!
Almost upon the western wave
Rested the broad bright Sun;
When that strange shape drove suddenly   175
Betwixt us and the Sun.

It seemeth him but
the skeleton of
a ship.

And straight the Sun was flecked with bars,
(Heaven's Mother send us grace!)
As if through a dungeon grate he peered
With broad and burning face.   180

And its ribs are seen
as bars on the face
of the setting Sun.

Alas! (thought I, and my heart beat loud)
How fast she nears and nears!

Are those *her* sails that glance in the Sun,
Like restless gossameres?

Are those *her* ribs through which the Sun   185
Did peer, as through a grate?
And is that Woman all her crew?
Is that a DEATH? and are there two?
Is DEATH that woman's mate?

Her lips were red, *her* looks were free,   190
Her locks were yellow as gold:
Her skin was as white as leprosy,
The Nightmare LIFE-IN-DEATH was she,
Who thicks man's blood with cold.

The naked hulk alongside came,   195
And the twain were casting dice;
"The game is done! I've won! I've won!"
Quoth she, and whistles thrice.

The Sun's rim dips; the stars rush out:
At one stride comes the dark;   200
With far-heard whisper, o'er the sea,
Off shot the specter-bark.

We listened and looked sideways up!
Fear at my heart, as at a cup,
My lifeblood seemed to sip!   205
The stars were dim, and thick the night,
The steersman's face by his lamp gleamed white;
From the sails the dew did drip—
Till clomb° above the eastern bar   climb
The hornéd Moon, with one bright star   210
Within the nether tip.

One after one, by the star-dogged Moon,
Too quick for groan or sigh,
Each turned his face with ghastly pang,
And cursed me with his eye.   215

Four times fifty living men,
(And I heard nor sigh nor groan)
With heavy thump, a lifeless lump,
They dropped down one by one.

The souls did from their bodies fly—   220
They fled to bliss or woe!

And every soul, it passed me by,
Like the whizz of my cross-bow!

Part IV

"I fear thee, ancient Mariner!
I fear thy skinny hand!   225
And thou art long, and lank, and brown,
As is the ribbed sea-sand.

I fear thee and thy glittering eye,
And thy skinny hand, so brown."—

Fear not, fear not, thou Wedding Guest!   230
This body dropped not down.

Alone, alone, all, all alone,
Alone on a wide wide sea!
And never a saint took pity on
My soul in agony.   235

The many men, so beautiful!
And they all dead did lie:
And a thousand thousand slimy things
Lived on; and so did I.

I looked upon the rotting sea,   240
And drew my eyes away;
I looked upon the rotting deck,
And there the dead men lay.

I looked to heaven, and tried to pray;
But or ever a prayer had gushed,   245
A wicked whisper came, and made
My heart as dry as dust.

I closed my lids, and kept them close,
And the balls like pulses beat,
For the sky and the sea, and the sea and the sky   250
Lay like a load on my weary eye,
And the dead were at my feet.

The cold sweat melted from their limbs,
Nor rot nor reek did they:
The look with which they looked on me   255
Had never passed away.

An orphan's curse would drag to hell
A spirit from on high;

But oh! more horrible than that
Is the curse in a dead man's eye!   260
Seven days, seven nights, I saw that curse,
And yet I could not die.

The moving Moon went up the sky,
And nowhere did abide:
In his loneliness Softly she was going up,   265
and fixedness he And a star or two beside—
yearneth towards
the journeying
Moon, and the Her beams bemocked the sultry main,
stars that still Like April hoar-frost spread;
sojourn, yet still But where the ship's huge shadow lay,
move onward; The charméd water burnt alway   270
and everywhere
the blue sky A still and awful red.
belongs to them,
and is their
appointed rest, and their native country and their own natural homes, which they enter unannounced,
as lords that are certainly expected and yet there is a silent joy at their arrival.

By the light of Beyond the shadow of the ship,
the Moon he I watched the water snakes:
beholdeth God's
creatures of the They moved in tracks of shining white,
great calm. And when they reared, the elfish light   275
Fell off in hoary flakes.

Within the shadow of the ship
I watched their rich attire:
Blue, glossy green, and velvet black,
They coiled and swam; and every track   280
Was a flash of golden fire.

Their beauty and O happy living things! no tongue
their happiness. Their beauty might declare:
A spring of love gushed from my heart,
He blesseth them And I blessed them unaware: 285
in his heart. Sure my kind saint took pity on me,
And I blessed them unaware.

The spell begins The self-same moment I could pray;
to break. And from my neck so free
The Albatross fell off, and sank   290
Like lead into the sea.

Part V

Oh sleep! it is a gentle thing,
Beloved from pole to pole!
To Mary Queen the praise be given!

She sent the gentle sleep from Heaven,   295
That slid into my soul.

By grace of the
holy Mother, the
ancient Mariner is
refreshed with
rain. The silly buckets on the deck,
That had so long remained,
I dreamt that they were filled with dew;
And when I awoke, it rained.   300

My lips were wet, my throat was cold,
My garments all were dank;
Sure I had drunken in my dreams,
And still my body drank.

I moved, and could not feel my limbs: 305
I was so light—almost
I thought that I had died in sleep,
And was a blessèd ghost.

He heareth
sounds and seeth
strange sights and
commotions in
the sky and the
element. And soon I heard a roaring wind:
It did not come anear;   310
But with its sound it shook the sails,
That were so thin and sere.°   dry

The upper air burst into life!
And a hundred fire-flags sheen,
To and fro they were hurried about!   315
And to and fro, and in and out,
The wan stars danced between.

And the coming wind did roar more loud,
And the sails did sigh like sedge;
And the rain poured down from one black cloud;   320
The Moon was at its edge.

The thick black cloud was cleft, and still
The Moon was at its side:
Like waters shot from some high crag,
The lightning fell with never a jag,   325
A river steep and wide.

The bodies of the
ship's crew are
inspirited, and the
ship moves on; The loud wind never reached the ship,
Yet now the ship moved on!
Beneath the lightning and the Moon
The dead men gave a groan.   330

They groaned, they stirred, they all uprose,
Nor spake, nor moved their eyes;

It had been strange, even in a dream,
To have seen those dead men rise.

The helmsman steered, the ship moved on;   335
Yet never a breeze up-blew;
The mariners all 'gan work the ropes,
Where they were wont to do;
They raised their limbs like lifeless tools—
We were a ghastly crew.   340

The body of my brother's son
Stood by me, knee to knee:
The body and I pulled at one rope,
But he said nought to me.

*But not by the
souls of the men,
nor by demons of
earth or middle
air, but by a
blessèd troop of
angelic spirits,
sent down by the
invocation of the
guardian saint.*

"I fear thee, ancient Mariner!"   345
Be calm, thou Wedding Guest!
'Twas not those souls that fled in pain,
Which to their corses° came again,   corpses
But a troop of spirits blest:

For when it dawned—they dropped their arms,   350
And clustered round the mast;
Sweet sounds rose slowly through their mouths,
And from their bodies passed.

Around, around, flew each sweet sound,
Then darted to the Sun;   355
Slowly the sounds came back again,
Now mixed, now one by one.

Sometimes a-dropping from the sky
I heard the sky-lark sing;
Sometimes all little birds that are,   360
How they seemed to fill the sea and air
With their sweet jargoning!

And now 'twas like all instruments,
Now like a lonely flute;
And now it is an angel's song,   365
That makes the heavens be mute.

It ceased; yet still the sails made on
A pleasant noise till noon,
A noise like of a hidden brook
In the leafy month of June,   370
That to the sleeping woods all night
Singeth a quiet tune.

Till noon we quietly sailed on,
Yet never a breeze did breathe:
Slowly and smoothly went the ship,   375
Moved onward from beneath.

Under the keel nine fathom deep,
From the land of mist and snow,
The spirit slid: and it was he
That made the ship to go.   380
The sails at noon left off their tune,
And the ship stood still also.

The Sun, right up above the mast,
Had fixed her to the ocean:
But in a minute she 'gan stir,
With a short uneasy motion—   385
Backwards and forwards half her length
With a short uneasy motion.

Then like a pawing horse let go,
She made a sudden bound:
It flung the blood into my head,   390
And I fell down in a swound.

How long in that same fit I lay,
I have not to declare;
But ere my living life returned,
I heard and in my soul discerned   395
Two voices in the air.

"Is it he?" quoth one, "Is this the man?
By him who died on cross,
With his cruel bow he laid full low
The harmless Albatross.   400

The spirit who bideth by himself
In the land of mist and snow,
He loved the bird that loved the man
Who shot him with his bow."

The other was a softer voice,   405
As soft as honey-dew:
Quoth he, "The man hath penance done,
And penance more will do."

Part VI

First Voice

"But tell me, tell me! speak again,
Thy soft response renewing—   410
What makes that ship drive on so fast?
What is the ocean doing?"

Second Voice

"Still as a slave before his lord,
The ocean hath no blast;
His great bright eye most silently   415
Up to the Moon is cast—

If he may know which way to go;
For she guides him smooth or grim.
See, brother, see! how graciously
She looketh down on him."   420

First Voice

The Mariner hath
been cast into a
trance; for the
angelic power
causeth the vessel
to drive northward
faster than human
life could endure.

"But why drives on that ship so fast,
Without or wave or wind?"

Second Voice

"The air is cut away before,
And closes from behind.

Fly, brother, fly! more high, more high!   425
Or we shall be belated:
For slow and slow that ship will go,
When the Mariner's trance is abated."

The supernatural
motion is retard-
ed; the Mariner
awakes, and his
penance begins
anew.

I woke, and we were sailing on
As in a gentle weather: 430
'Twas night, calm night, the moon was high;
The dead men stood together.

All stood together on the deck,
For a charnel-dungeon fitter:
All fixed on me their stony eyes,   435
That in the Moon did glitter.

The pang, the curse, with which they died,
Had never passed away:

I could not draw my eyes from theirs,
Nor turn them up to pray.   440

The curse is finally
expiated. And now this spell was snapped: once more
I viewed the ocean green,
And looked far forth, yet little saw
Of what had else been seen—

Like one, that on a lonesome road   445
Doth walk in fear and dread,
And having once turned round walks on,
And turns no more his head;
Because he knows, a frightful fiend
Doth close behind him tread.   450

But soon there breathed a wind on me,
Nor sound nor motion made:
Its path was not upon the sea,
In ripple or in shade.

It raised my hair, it fanned my cheek   455
Like a meadow-gale of spring—
It mingled strangely with my fears,
Yet it felt like a welcoming.

Swiftly, swiftly flew the ship,
Yet she sailed softly too: 460
Sweetly, sweetly blew the breeze—
On me alone it blew.

And the ancient
Mariner beholdeth
his native country. Oh! dream of joy! is this indeed
The lighthouse top I see?
Is this the hill? Is this the kirk?   465
Is this mine own countree?

We drifted o'er the harbor-bar,
And I with sobs did pray—
O let me be awake, my God
Or let me sleep alway.   470

The harbor-bay was clear as glass,
So smoothly it was strewn!
And on the bay the moonlight lay,
And the shadow of the Moon.

The rock shone bright, the kirk no less,   475
That stands above the rock:

The moonlight steeped in silentness
The steady weathercock.

The angelic spirits
leave the dead
bodies,

And the bay was white with silent light,
Till rising from the same,   480
Full many shapes, that shadows were,
In crimson colors came.

A little distance from the prow
Those crimson shadows were:

And appear in
their own forms
of light.

I turned my eyes upon the deck—   485
Oh, Christ! what saw I there!

Each corse lay flat, lifeless and flat,
And, by the holy rood!
A man all light, a seraph-man,
On every corse there stood.   490

This seraph-band, each waved his hand:
It was a heavenly sight!
They stood as signals to the land,
Each one a lovely light;

This seraph-band, each waved his hand,   495
No voice did they impart—
No voice; but oh! the silence sank
Like music on my heart.

But soon I heard the dash of oars,
I heard the Pilot's cheer;   500
My head was turned perforce away
And I saw a boat appear.

The Pilot and the Pilot's boy,
I heard them coming fast:
Dear Lord in Heaven! it was a joy   505
The dead men could not blast.

I saw a third—I heard his voice:
It is the Hermit good!
He singeth loud his godly hymns
That he makes in the wood.   510
He'll shrieve² my soul, he'll wash away
The Albatross's blood.

---

² **shrieve:** I.e., free from sin.

Part VII

This Hermit good lives in that wood
Which slopes down to the sea.
How loudly his sweet voice he rears!   515
He loves to talk with marineres
That come from a far countree.

He kneels at morn, and noon, and eve—
He hath a cushion plump:
It is the moss that wholly hides   520
The rotted old oak stump.

The skiff-boat neared: I heard them talk,
"Why, this is strange, I trow!
Where are those lights so many and fair,
That signal made but now?"   525

"Strange, by my faith!" the Hermit said—
"And they answered not our cheer!
The planks looked warped! and see those sails,
How thin they are and sere!
I never saw aught like to them,   530
Unless perchance it were

Brown skeletons of leaves that lag
My forest-brook along;
When the ivy tod° is heavy with snow,   bushy clump
And the owlet whoops to the wolf below,   535
That eats the she-wolf's young."

"Dear Lord! it hath a fiendish look,"
The Pilot made reply,
"I am a-feared"—"Push on, push on!"
Said the Hermit cheerily.   540

The boat came closer to the ship,
But I nor spake nor stirred;
The boat came close beneath the ship,
And straight a sound was heard.

Under the water it rumbled on,   545
Still louder and more dread:
It reached the ship, it split the bay;
The ship went down like lead.

The ancient
Mariner is saved in
the Pilot's boat.

Stunned by that loud and dreadful sound,
Which sky and ocean smote,   550
Like one that hath been seven days drowned
My body lay afloat;
But swift as dreams, myself I found
Within the Pilot's boat.

Upon the whirl, where sank the ship,   555
The boat spun round and round;
And all was still, save that the hill
Was telling of the sound.

I moved my lips—the Pilot shrieked
And fell down in a fit;   560
The holy Hermit raised his eyes,
And prayed where he did sit.

I took the oars: the Pilot's boy,
Who now doth crazy go,
Laughed loud and long, and all the while   565
His eyes went to and fro.
"Ha! ha!" quoth he, "full plain I see,
The Devil knows how to row."

And now, all in my own countree,
I stood on the firm land!   570
The Hermit stepped forth from the boat,
And scarcely he could stand.

The ancient
Mariner earnestly
entreateth the
Hermit to shrieve
him; and the
penance of life
falls on him.

"O shrieve me, shrieve me, holy man!"
The Hermit crossed his brow.
"Say quick," quoth he, "I bid thee say—   575
What manner of man art thou?"

Forthwith this frame of mine was wrenched
With a woeful agony,
Which forced me to begin my tale;
And then it left me free.   580

And ever and
anon throughout
his future life an
agony con-
straineth him to
travel from land
to land;

Since then, at an uncertain hour,
That agony returns:
And till my ghastly tale is told,
This heart within me burns.

I pass, like night, from land to land;   585
I have strange power of speech;

That moment that his face I see,
I know the man that must hear me:
To him my tale I teach.

What loud uproar bursts from that door!   590
The wedding guests are there:
But in the garden-bower the bride
And bridemaids singing are:
And hark the little vesper bell,
Which biddeth me to prayer!   595

O Wedding Guest! this soul hath been
Alone on a wide wide sea:
So lonely 'twas, that God himself
Scarce seeméd there to be.

O sweeter than the marriage feast,   600
'Tis sweeter far to me,
To walk together to the kirk
With a goodly company!

To walk together to the kirk,
And all together pray,   605
While each to his great Father bends,
Old men, and babes, and loving friends
And youths and maidens gay!

And to teach, by   Farewell, farewell! but this I tell
his own example,   To thee, thou Wedding Guest!   610
love and rever-
ence to all things He prayeth well, who loveth well
that God made   Both man and bird and beast.
and loveth.

He prayeth best, who loveth best
All things both great and small;
For the dear God who loveth us,   615
He made and loveth all.

The Mariner, whose eye is bright,
Whose beard with age is hoar,
Is gone: and now the Wedding Guest
Turned from the bridegroom's door.   620

He went like one that hath been stunned,
And is of sense forlorn:
A sadder and a wiser man,
He rose the morrow morn.

ROBERT SOUTHEY (1774–1843)

The Battle of Blenheim[1]

It was a summer evening,
   Old Kaspar's work was done,
And he before his cottage door
   Was sitting in the sun,
5 And by him sported on the green
His little grandchild Wilhelmine.

She saw her brother Peterkin
   Roll something large and round
That he beside the rivulet
10   In playing there had found;
He came to ask what he had found
That was so large, and smooth, and round.

Old Kaspar took it from the boy
   Who stood expectant by,
15 And then the old man shook his head
   And with a natural sigh,
' 'Tis some poor fellow's skull', said he,
'Who fell in the great victory.

I find them in the garden for
20   There's many here about,
And often when I go to plough
   The ploughshare turns them out—
For many thousand men', said he,
'Were slain in the great victory.'

25 'Now tell us what 'twas all about',
   Young Peterkin he cries,
And little Wilhelmine looks up
   With wonder-waiting eyes,
'Now tell us all about the war
30 And what they killed each other for.'

---

[1] **Battle of Blenheim:** An important battle of the War of the Spanish Succession. On August 13, 1704, the allied Anglo-Austrian armies under the command of John Churchill, Duke of Marlborough, and Prince Eugene of Savoy defeated the French and Bavarian forces near the village of Blenheim in Bavaria.

'It was the English', Kaspar cried,
    'That put the French to rout,
But what they killed each other for
    I could not well make out.
35 But everybody said', quoth he,
    'That 'twas a famous victory.

My father lived at Blenheim then,
    Yon little stream hard by—
They burnt his dwelling to the ground
40   And he was forced to fly;
So with his wife and child he fled,
Nor had he where to rest his head.

With fire and sword the country round
    Was wasted far and wide,
45 And many a childing mother then
    And new-born infant died.
But things like that, you know, must be
At every famous victory.

They say it was a shocking sight
50   After the field was won,
For many thousand bodies here
    Lay rotting in the sun —
But things like that you know must be
After a famous victory.

55 Great praise the Duke of Marlborough won,
    And our good Prince Eugene.'
'Why 'twas a very wicked thing!'
    Said little Wilhelmine.
'Nay, nay, my little girl', quoth he,
60 'It was a famous victory,

And everybody praised the Duke
    Who such a fight did win.'
'But what good came of it at last?'
    Quoth little Peterkin.
65 'Why that I cannot tell', said he,
    'But 'twas a famous victory!'

JOHN KEATS (1795–1821)

La Belle Dame Sans Merci[1] (1819; 1820)

'Oh, what can ail thee, knight-at-arms,
    Alone and palely loitering?
The sedge is withered from the lake,
    And no birds sing!

5   Oh, what can ail thee, knight-at-arms,
    So haggard and so woe-begone?
The squirrel's granary is full,
    And the harvest's done.

I see a lily on thy brow,
10   With anguish moist and fever-dew,
And on thy cheek a fading rose
    Fast withereth too.'

'I met a lady in the meads
    Full beautiful, a fairy's child;
15   Her hair was long, her foot was light,
    And her eyes were wild.

I made a garland for her head,
    And bracelets too, and fragrant zone;
She looked at me as she did love,
20   And made sweet moan.

I set her on my pacing steed,
    And nothing else saw all day long;
For sidelong would she bend, and sing
    A fairy's song.

25   She found me roots of relish sweet,
    And honey wild, and manna-dew;
And sure in language strange she said,
    'I love thee true.'

She took me to her elfin grot,
30   And there she wept, and sighed full sore,
And there I shut her wild wild eyes
    With kisses four.

---

[1] **La Belle . . . Merci:** "The beautiful lady without mercy" (French).

And there she lulléd me asleep
    And there I dreamed, ah woe betide!
35   The latest dream I ever dreamed
    On the cold hill side.

I saw pale kings, and princes too,
    Pale warriors—death-pale were they all—
Who cried: 'La belle Dame sans merci
40   Thee hath in thrall!'

I saw their starved lips in the gloam
    With horrid warning gapéd wide,
And I awoke, and found me here
    On the cold hill's side.

45   And this is why I sojourn here
    Alone and palely loitering,
Though the sedge is withered from the lake,
    And no birds sing.'

JAMES HENRY (1798–1876)

"Two hundred men and eighteen killed"[1] (1862; 1866)

Two hundred men and eighteen killed
    For want of a second door!
Ay, for with two doors, each ton coal
    Had cost one penny more.

5   And what is it else makes England great,
    At home, by land, by sea,

---

[1] **Two hundred . . . eighteen killed:** "At ten o'clock on the morning of Thursday, January 16, 1862, the great iron beam of the steam-engine which worked the pumps of the Hester coal pit near Hartley in Northumberland, snapped across, and a portion of the beam, 40 tons in weight, fell into the shaft tearing away the boarded lining so that the earthly sides collapsed and fell in, filling up the shaft in such a manner as not only to cut off all communication between the interior of the pit and the outer world, but entirely to obstruct all passage of pure air into, and of foul air out of, the pit. All of the persons who were at work below at the time, two hundred and eighteen in number, were of course suffocated, nor was it until the seventh day after the accident that access could be had to the interior of the pit, or anything, beyond the mere fact of their entombment, ascertained concerning the helpless and unfortunate victims of that 'aura sacra fames' [the accursed hunger for gold] which so generally, so heartlessly, so pertinaciously refuses the poor workers in the coal mines of England, even the sad resource of a second staple or air shaft. See the *Illustrated London News* of Jan. 25, and Febr. 1, 1862." [author's note]

But her cheap coal, and eye's tail turned
    Toward strict economy?

But if a slate falls off the roof
10   And kills a passer-by,
Or if a doctor's dose too strong
    Makes some half-dead man die,

We have coroners and deodands [2]
    And inquests, to no end,
15 And every honest Englishman's
    The hapless sufferer's friend,

And householder's or doctor's foe,
    For he has nought to lose,
And fain will, if he can, keep out
20   Of that poor dead man's shoes.

But if of twice a hundred men,
    And eighteen more, the breath
Is stopped at once in a coal pit,
    It's quite a natural death;

25 For, God be praised! the chance is small
    That either you or I
Should come, for want of a second door,
    In a coal pit to die.

Besides, 'twould cost a thousand times
30   As much, or something more,
To make to every pit of coal
    A second, or safety door,

As all the shrouds and coffins cost
    For those who perish now
35 For want of a second door, and that's
    No trifle, you'll allow;

And trade must live, though now and then
    A man or two may die;
So merry sing 'God bless the Queen,'
40   And long live you and I;

---

[2] **deodands:** A piece of movable property that has caused the death of a person and for that reason has been given to God, i.e., confiscated by the Crown. For example, if a car runs over a person, the car is confiscated as a deodand. This legal concept existed only in England and was abolished in 1846.

And, Jenny, let each widow have
  A cup of congo strong,°   black tea
And every orphan half a cup,
  And so I end my song,

45 With prayer to God to keep coal cheap,
    Both cheap and plenty too,
And if the pit's a whole mile deep,
    What is it to me or you?

For though we're mortal too, no doubt,
50   And Death for us his scythe
Has ready still, the chance is small
    We ever die of stithe.[3]

And if we do, our gracious Queen
    Will, sure, a telegram send,
55 To say how sore she grieves for us
    And our untimely end;

And out of her own privy purse
    A sovereign down will pay,
To have us decently interred
60   And put out of the way;

And burial service shall for us
    In the churchyard be read,
And more bells rung and more hymns sung
    Than if we had died in bed:

65 For such an accident as this
    May never occur again,
And till it does, one door's enough
    For pumps, air, coal, and men;

And should it occur—which God forbid!—
70   And stifle every soul,
Remember well, good Christians all,
    Not one whit worse the coal.

---

[3] **stithe:** Perhaps "stythe," a mining term for choke damp.

EDGAR ALLAN POE (1809–1849)

Annabel Lee (1849)

It was many and many a year ago,
      In a kingdom by the sea,
That a maiden there lived whom you may know
      By the name of Annabel Lee;
5 And this maiden she lived with no other thought
      Than to love and be loved by me.

She was a child and *I* was a child,
      In this kingdom by the sea,
But we loved with a love that was more than love—
10   I and my Annabel Lee—
With a love that the wingéd seraphs of Heaven
      Coveted her and me.

And this was the reason that, long ago,
      In this kingdom by the sea,
15 A wind blew out of a cloud by night
      Chilling my Annabel Lee;
So that her highborn kinsmen came
      And bore her away from me,
To shut her up in a sepulchre
20   In this kingdom by the sea.

The angels, not half so happy in Heaven,
      Went envying her and me:
Yes! that was the reason (as all men know,
      In this kingdom by the sea)
25 That the wind came out of the cloud, chilling
      And killing my Annabel Lee.

But our love it was stronger by far than the love
      Of those who were older than we—
      Of many far wiser than we—
30 And neither the angels in Heaven above
      Nor the demons down under the sea,
Can ever dissever my soul from the soul
      Of the beautiful Annabel Lee:

For the moon never beams without bringing me dreams
35   Of the beautiful Annabel Lee;
And the stars never rise but I see the bright eyes

Of the beautiful Annabel Lee;
And so, all the night-tide, I lie down by the side
Of my darling, my darling, my life and my bride,
40   In her sepulchre there by the sea—
           In her tomb by the side of the sea.

EDWARD LEAR (1812–1888)

The Owl and the Pussy-Cat (1871 pub.)

1

The Owl and the Pussy-cat went to sea
    In a beautiful pea-green boat,
They took some honey, and plenty of money,
    Wrapped up in a five-pound note.
5   The Owl looked up to the stars above,
    And sang to a small guitar,
"O lovely Pussy! O Pussy, my love,
    What a beautiful Pussy you are,
            You are,
10   You are!
    What a beautiful Pussy you are!"

2

Pussy said to the Owl, "You elegant fowl!
    How charmingly sweet you sing!
O let us be married! too long we have tarried:
15   But what shall we do for a ring?"
They sailed away, for a year and a day,
    To the land where the Bong-tree grows
And there in a wood a Piggy-wig stood
    With a ring at the end of his nose,
20   His nose,
            His nose,
    With a ring at the end of his nose.

3

"Dear Pig, are you willing to sell for one shilling
    Your ring?" Said the Piggy, "I will."
25 So they took it away, and were married next day
    By the Turkey who lives on the hill.
They dined on mince, and slices of quince,

Which they ate with a runcible[1] spoon;
And hand in hand, on the edge of the sand,
30   They danced by the light of the moon,
The moon,
The moon,
They danced by the light of the moon.

ARTHUR HUGH CLOUGH (1819–1861)

There Is No God (1850; 1865)

'There is no God,' the wicked saith,
'And truly it's a blessing,
For what he might have done with us
It's better only guessing.'

5   'There is no God,' a youngster thinks,
'Or really, if there may be,
He surely didn't mean a man
Always to be a baby.'

'There is no God, or if there is,'
10   The tradesman thinks, ''twere funny
If he should take it ill in me
To make a little money.'

'Whether there be,' the rich man says,
'It matters very little,
15   For I and mine, thank somebody,
Are not in want of victual.'

Some others, also, to themselves
Who scarce so much as doubt it,
Think there is none, when they are well,
20   And do not think about it.

But country folks who live beneath
The shadow of the steeple;
The parson and the parson's wife,
And mostly married people;

---

[1] **runcible:** A nonsense word coined by Lear.

25 Youths green and happy in first love,
        So thankful for illusion;
    And men caught out in what the world
        Calls guilt, in first confusion;

    And almost every one when age,
30   Disease, or sorrows strike him,
    Inclines to think there is a God,
        Or something very like Him.

FRANCES E. W. HARPER (1825–1911)

The Slave Mother (1854 pub.)

    Heard you that shriek? It rose
        So wildly on the air,
    It seemed as if a burden'd heart
        Was breaking in despair.

5   Saw you those hands so sadly clasped—
        The bowed and feeble head—
    The shuddering of that fragile form—
        That look of grief and dread?

    Saw you the sad, imploring eye?
10   Its every glance was pain,
    As if a storm of agony
        Were sweeping through the brain.

    She is a mother, pale with fear,
        Her boy clings to her side,
15 And in her kirtle° vainly tries   loose gown
        His trembling form to hide.

    He is not hers, although she bore
        For him a mother's pains;
    He is not hers, although her blood
20   Is coursing through his veins!

    He is not hers, for cruel hands
        May rudely tear apart
    The only wreath of household love
        That binds her breaking heart.

25 His love has been a joyous light
    That o'er her pathway smiled,
A fountain gushing ever new,
    Amid life's desert wild.

His lightest word has been a tone
30   Of music round her heart,
Their lives a streamlet blent in one—
    Oh, Father! must they part?

They tear him from her circling arms,
    Her last and fond embrace.
35 Oh! never more may her sad eyes
    Gaze on his mournful face.

No marvel, then, these bitter shrieks
    Disturb the listening air:
She is a mother, and her heart
40   Is breaking in despair.

DANTE GABRIEL ROSSETTI (1828–1882)

The Blessed Damozel[1] (1847; 1850)

The blessed damozel leaned out
    From the gold bar of Heaven;
Her eyes were deeper than the depth
    Of waters stilled at even;
5 She had three lilies in her hand,
    And the stars in her hair were seven.

Her robe, ungirt from clasp to hem,
    No wrought flowers did adorn,
But a white rose of Mary's gift,
10   For service meetly worn;
Her hair that lay along her back
    Was yellow like ripe corn.

Her seemed she scarce had been a day
    One of God's choristers;

---

[1] **Damozel:** A young, unmarried woman.

15 The wonder was not yet quite gone
        From that still look of hers;
    Albeit, to them she left, her day
        Had counted as ten years.

    (To one, it is ten years of years.
20   . . . Yet now, and in this place,
    Surely she leaned o'er me—her hair
        Fell all about my face . . .
    Nothing: the autumn-fall of leaves.
        The whole year sets apace.)

25 It was the rampart of God's house
        That she was standing on;
    By God built over the sheer depth
        The which is Space begun;
    So high, that looking downward thence
30   She scarce could see the sun.

    It lies in Heaven, across the flood
        Of ether, as a bridge.
    Beneath, the tides of day and night
        With flame and darkness ridge
35 The void, as low as where this earth
        Spins like a fretful midge.°   biting insect

    Around her, lovers, newly met
        'Mid deathless love's acclaims,
    Spoke evermore among themselves
40   Their heart-remembered names;
    And the souls mounting up to God
        Went by her like thin flames.

    And still she bowed herself and stooped
        Out of the circling charm;
45 Until her bosom must have made
        The bar she leaned on warm,
    And the lilies lay as if asleep
        Along her bended arm.

    From the fixed place of Heaven she saw
50   Time like a pulse shake fierce
    Through all the worlds. Her gaze still strove
        Within the gulf to pierce
    Its path; and now she spoke as when
        The stars sang in their spheres.

55   The sun was gone now; the curled moon
     Was like a little feather
Fluttering far down the gulf; and now
     She spoke through the still weather.
Her voice was like the voice the stars
60   Had when they sang together.

    (Ah sweet! Even now, in that bird's song,
     Strove not her accents there,
Fain to be hearkened? When those bells
     Possessed the mid-day air,
65   Strove not her steps to reach my side
     Down all the echoing stair?)

    'I wish that he were come to me,
     For he will come,' she said.
'Have I not prayed in Heaven?—on earth,
70   Lord, Lord, has he not pray'd?
Are not two prayers a perfect strength?
     And shall I feel afraid?

    'When round his head the aureole clings,
     And he is clothed in white,
75   I'll take his hand and go with him
     To the deep wells of light;
As unto a stream we will step down,
     And bathe there in God's sight.

    'We two will stand beside that shrine,
80   Occult, withheld, untrod,
Whose lamps are stirred continually
     With prayer sent up to God;
And see our old prayers, granted, melt
     Each like a little cloud.

85   'We two will lie i' the shadow of
     That living mystic tree
Within whose secret growth the Dove
     Is sometimes felt to be,
While every leaf that His plumes touch
90   Saith His Name audibly.

    'And I myself will teach to him,
     I myself, lying so,
The songs I sing here; which his voice
     Shall pause in, hushed and slow,

95 And find some knowledge at each pause,
        Or some new thing to know.'

    (Alas! we two, we two, thou say'st!
        Yea, one wast thou with me
    That once of old. But shall God lift
100   To endless unity
    The soul whose likeness with thy soul
        Was but its love for thee?)

    'We two,' she said, 'will seek the groves
        Where the lady Mary is,
105 With her five handmaidens, whose names
        Are five sweet symphonies,
    Cecily, Gertrude, Magdalen,
        Margaret and Rosalys.

    'Circlewise sit they, with bound locks
110   And foreheads garlanded;
    Into the fine cloth white like flame
        Weaving the golden thread,
    To fashion the birth-robes for them
        Who are just born, being dead.

115 'He shall fear, haply, and be dumb:
        Then will I lay my cheek
    To his, and tell about our love,
        Not once abashed or weak:
    And the dear Mother will approve
120   My pride, and let me speak.

    'Herself shall bring us, hand in hand,
        To Him round whom all souls
    Kneel, the clear-ranged unnumbered heads
        Bowed with their aureoles:
125 And angels meeting us shall sing
        To their citherns and citoles.

    'There will I ask of Christ the Lord
        Thus much for him and me:—
    Only to live as once on earth
130   With Love,—only to be,
    As then awhile, for ever now
        Together, I and he.'

She gazed and listened and then said,
    Less sad of speech than mild,—
135 'All this is when he comes.' She ceased.
    The light thrilled towards her, fill'd
With angels in strong level flight.
    Her eyes prayed, and she smil'd.

(I saw her smile.) But soon their path
140   Was vague in distant spheres:
And then she cast her arms along
    The golden barriers,
And laid her face between her hands,
    And wept. (I heard her tears.)

LEWIS CARROLL (1832–1898)
from *The Hunting of the Snark*

Fit the First—The Landing (1876 pub.)

"Just the place for a Snark!" the Bellman cried,
As he landed his crew with care;
Supporting each man on the top of the tide
By a finger entwined in his hair.

5   "Just the place for a Snark! I have said it twice:
That alone should encourage the crew.
Just the place for a Snark! I have said it thrice:
What I tell you three times is true."

The crew was complete: it included a Boots—
10   A maker of Bonnets and Hoods—
A Barrister, brought to arrange their disputes—
And a Broker, to value their goods.

A Billiard-maker, whose skill was immense,
Might perhaps have won more than his share—
15   But a Banker, engaged at enormous expense,
Had the whole of their cash in his care.

There was also a Beaver, that paced on the deck,
Or would sit making lace in the bow:
And had often (the Bellman said) saved them from wreck,
20   Though none of the sailors knew how.

There was one who was famed for the number of things
He forgot when he entered the ship:
His umbrella, his watch, all his jewels and rings,
And the clothes he had bought for the trip.

25   He had forty-two boxes, all carefully packed,
With his name painted clearly on each:
But, since he omitted to mention the fact,
They were all left behind on the beach.

The loss of his clothes hardly mattered, because
30   He had seven coats on when he came,
With three pairs of boots—but the worst of it was,
He had wholly forgotten his name.

He would answer to "Hi!" or to any loud cry,
Such as "Fry me!" or "Fritter my wig!"
35   To "What-you-may-call-um!" or "What-was-his-name!"
But especially "Thing-um-a-jig!"

While, for those who preferred a more forcible word,
He had different names from these:
His intimate friends called him "Candle-ends,"
40   And his enemies "Toasted-cheese."

"His form is ungainly—his intellect small—"
(So the Bellman would often remark)
"But his courage is perfect! And that, after all,
Is the thing that one needs with a Snark."

45   He would joke with hyenas, returning their stare
With an impudent wag of the head:
And he once went a walk, paw-in-paw, with a bear,
"Just to keep up its spirits," he said.

He came as a Baker: but owned, when too late—
50   And it drove the poor Bellman half-mad—
He could only bake Bridecake—for which, I may state,
No materials were to be had.

The last of the crew needs especial remark,
Though he looked an incredible dunce:

55   He had just one idea—but, that one being "Snark,"
      The good Bellman engaged him at once.

      He came as a Butcher: but gravely declared,
      When the ship had been sailing a week,
      He could only kill Beavers. The Bellman looked scared,
60   And was almost too frightened to speak:

      But at length he explained, in a tremulous tone,
      There was only one Beaver on board;
      And that was a tame one he had of his own,
      Whose death would be deeply deplored.

65   The Beaver, who happened to hear the remark,
      Protested, with tears in its eyes,
      That not even the rapture of hunting the Snark
      Could atone for that dismal surprise!

      It strongly advised that the Butcher should be
70   Conveyed in a separate ship:
      But the Bellman declared that would never agree
      With the plans he had made for the trip:

      Navigation was always a difficult art,
      Though with only one ship and one bell:
75   And he feared he must really decline, for his part,
      Undertaking another as well.

      The Beaver's best course was, no doubt, to procure
      A second-hand dagger-proof coat—
      So the Baker advised it—and next, to insure
80   Its life in some Office of note:

      This the Banker suggested, and offered for hire
      (On moderate terms), or for sale,
      Two excellent Policies, one Against Fire,
      And one Against Damage From Hail.

85   Yet still, ever after that sorrowful day,
      Whenever the Butcher was by,
      The Beaver kept looking the opposite way,
      And appeared unaccountably shy.

OSCAR WILDE (1854–1900)

from The Ballad of Reading Gaol° (1897; 1898)   jail

I

He did not wear his scarlet coat,
    For blood and wine are red,
And blood and wine were on his hands
    When they found him with the dead,
5 The poor dead woman whom he loved,
    And murdered in her bed.

He walked amongst the Trial Men
    In a suit of shabby gray;
A cricket cap was on his head,
10   And his step seemed light and gay;
But I never saw a man who looked
    So wistfully at the day.

I never saw a man who looked
    With such a wistful eye
15 Upon that little tent of blue
    Which prisoners call the sky,
And at every drifting cloud that went
    With sails of silver by.

I walked, with other souls in pain,
20   Within another ring,
And was wondering if the man had done
    A great or little thing,
When a voice behind me whispered low,
    '*That fellow's got to swing.*'

25 Dear Christ! the very prison walls
    Suddenly seemed to reel,
And the sky above my head became
    Like a casque of scorching steel;
And, though I was a soul in pain,
30   My pain I could not feel.

I only knew what hunted thought
    Quickened his step, and why
He looked upon the garish day
    With such a wistful eye;

35   The man had killed the thing he loved,
    And so he had to die.

      . . . . . .

    Yet each man kills the thing he loves,
      By each let this be heard,
    Some do it with a bitter look,
40   Some with a flattering word,
    The coward does it with a kiss,
      The brave man with a sword!

    Some kill their love when they are young,
      And some when they are old;
45   Some strangle with the hands of Lust,
      Some with the hands of Gold:
    The kindest use a knife, because
      The dead so soon grow cold.

    Some love too little, some too long,
50   Some sell, and others buy;
    Some do the deed with many tears,
      And some without a sigh;
    For each man kills the thing he loves,
      Yet each man does not die.

55   He does not die a death of shame
      On a day of dark disgrace,
    Nor have a noose about his neck,
      Nor a cloth upon his face,
    Nor drop feet foremost through the floor
60   Into an empty space.

      . . . . . .

    He does not sit with silent men
      Who watch him night and day;
    Who watch him when he tries to weep,
      And when he tries to pray;
65   Who watch him lest himself should rob
      The prison of its prey.

    He does not wake at dawn to see
      Dread figures throng his room,
    The shivering Chaplain robed in white,
70   The Sheriff stern with gloom,
    And the Governor all in shiny black,
      With the yellow face of Doom.

He does not rise in piteous haste
  To put on convict-clothes,
75 While some coarse-mouthed Doctor gloats, and notes
  Each new and nerve-twitched pose,
Fingering a watch whose little ticks
  Are like horrible hammer-blows.

He does not know that sickening thirst
80   That sands one's throat, before
The hangman with his gardener's gloves
  Slips through the padded door,
And binds one with three leathern thongs,
  That the throat may thirst no more.

85 He does not bend his head to hear
  The Burial Office read,
Nor, while the terror of his soul
  Tells him he is not dead,
Cross his own coffin, as he moves
90   Into the hideous shed.

He does not stare upon the air
  Through a little roof of glass:
He does not pray with lips of clay
  For his agony to pass;
95 Nor feel upon his shuddering cheek
  The kiss of Caiaphas.[1]

III

In Debtors' Yard the stones are hard,
  And the dripping wall is high,
So it was there he took the air
100   Beneath the leaden sky,
And by each side a Warder walked,
  For fear the man might die.

Or else he sat with those who watched,
  His anguish night and day;
105 Who watched him when he rose to weep,
  And when he crouched to pray;
Who watched him lest himself should rob
  Their scaffold of its prey.

---

[1] **Caiaphas:** A Jewish high priest who accused Jesus of blasphemy and handed him over for trial to the Roman authorities. Here, he is equated with Judas, the disciple who betrayed Jesus by kissing him on the cheek.

The Governor was strong upon
110   The Regulations Act:
The Doctor said that Death was but
        A scientific fact:
And twice a day the Chaplain called,
        And left a little tract.

115   And twice a day he smoked his pipe,
        And drank his quart of beer:
His soul was resolute, and held
        No hiding-place for fear;
He often said that he was glad
120   The hangman's hands were near.

But why he said so strange a thing
        No Warder dared to ask:
For he to whom a watcher's doom
        Is given as his task,
125   Must set a lock upon his lips,
        And make his face a mask.

Or else he might be moved, and try
        To comfort or console:
And what should Human Pity do
130   Pent up in Murderers' Hole?
What word of grace in such a place
        Could help a brother's soul?

·   ·   ·   ·   ·   ·

With slouch and swing around the ring
        We trod the Fools' Parade!
135   We did not care: we knew we were
        The Devil's Own Brigade:
And shaven head and feet of lead
        Make a merry masquerade.

We tore the tarry rope to shreds
140   With blunt and bleeding nails;
We rubbed the doors, and scrubbed the floors,
        And cleaned the shining rails:
And, rank by rank, we soaped the plank,
        And clattered with the pails.

145   We sewed the sacks, we broke the stones,
        We turned the dusty drill:

We banged the tins, and bawled the hymns,
　　And sweated on the mill:
But in the heart of every man
150　　Terror was lying still.

So still it lay that every day
　　Crawled like a weed-clogged wave:
And we forgot the bitter lot
　　That waits for fool and knave,
155　Till once, as we tramped in from work,
　　We passed an open grave.

With yawning mouth the yellow hole
　　Gaped for a living thing;
The very mud cried out for blood
160　　To the thirsty asphalte ring:
And we knew that ere one dawn grew fair
　　Some prisoner had to swing.

Right in we went, with soul intent
　　On Death and Dread and Doom:
165　The hangman, with his little bag,
　　Went shuffling through the gloom:
And each man trembled as he crept
　　Into his numbered tomb.

　　　　·　·　·　·　·　·

That night the empty corridors
170　　Were full of forms of Fear,
And up and down the iron town
　　Stole feet we could not hear,
And through the bars that hide the stars
　　White faces seemed to peer.

175　He lay as one who lies and dreams
　　In a pleasant meadow-land,
The watchers watched him as he slept,
　　And could not understand
How one could sleep so sweet a sleep
180　　With a hangman close at hand.

But there is no sleep when men must weep
　　Who never yet have wept:
So we—the fool, the fraud, the knave—
　　That endless vigil kept,

185 And through each brain on hands of pain
          Another's terror crept.

    Alas! it is a fearful thing
          To feel another's guilt!
    For, right within, the sword of Sin
190   Pierced to its poisoned hilt,
    And as molten lead were the tears we shed
          For the blood we had not spilt.

    The Warders with their shoes of felt
          Crept by each padlocked door,
195 And peeped and saw, with eyes of awe,
          Grey figures on the floor,
    And wondered why men knelt to pray
          Who never prayed before.

    All through the night we knelt and prayed,
200   Mad mourners of a corpse!
    The troubled plumes of midnight were
          The plumes upon a hearse:
    And bitter wine upon a sponge
          Was the savour of Remorse.

                    .   .   .   .   .   .

205 The grey cock crew, the red cock crew,
          But never came the day:
    And crooked shapes of Terror crouched,
          In the corners where we lay:
    And each evil sprite that walks by night
210   Before us seemed to play.

    They glided past, they glided fast,
          Like travellers through a mist:
    They mocked the moon in a rigadoon [2]
          Of delicate turn and twist,
215 And with formal pace and loathsome grace
          The phantoms kept their tryst.

    With mop and mow, we saw them go,
          Slim shadows hand in hand:
    About, about, in ghostly rout

---

[2] **rigadoon:** A lively dance of the seventeenth and eighteenth centuries; also, the music for this dance.

220   They trod a saraband: [3]
     And the damned grotesques made arabesques,
       Like the wind upon the sand!

     With the pirouettes of marionettes,
       They tripped on pointed tread:
225   But with flutes of Fear they filled the ear,
       As their grisly masque they led,
     And loud they sang, and long they sang,
       For they sang to wake the dead.

     '*Oho!*' they cried, '*The world is wide,*
230   *But fettered limbs go lame!*
     And once, or twice, to throw the dice
       Is a gentlemanly game,
     But he does not win who plays with Sin
       In the secret House of Shame.'

235   No things of air these antics were,
       That frolicked with such glee:
     To men whose lives were held in gyves,°   shackles
       And whose feet might not go free,
     Ah! wounds of Christ! they were living things,
240   Most terrible to see.

     Around, around, they waltzed and wound;
       Some wheeled in smirking pairs;
     With the mincing step of a demirep°   reprobate
       Some sidled up the stairs:
245   And with subtle sneer, and fawning leer,
       Each helped us at our prayers.

     The morning wind began to moan,
       But still the night went on:
     Through its giant loom the web of gloom
250   Crept till each thread was spun:
     And, as we prayed, we grew afraid
       Of the Justice of the Sun.

     The moaning wind went wandering round
       The weeping prison-wall:
255   Till like a wheel of turning steel
       We felt the minutes crawl:

---

[3] **saraband:** Another dance of the same period.

O moaning wind! what had we done
    To have such a seneschal?[4]

At last I saw the shadowed bars,
260   Like a lattice wrought in lead,
Move right across the whitewashed wall
    That faced my three-plank bed,
And I knew that somewhere in the world
    God's dreadful dawn was red.

265   At six o'clock we cleaned our cells,
    At seven all was still,
But the sough and swing of a mighty wing
    The prison seemed to fill,
For the Lord of Death with icy breath
270   Had entered in to kill.

He did not pass in purple pomp,
    Nor ride a moon-white steed.
Three yards of cord and a sliding board
    Are all the gallows' need:
275   So with rope of shame the Herald came
    To do the secret deed.

We were as men who through a fen
    Of filthy darkness grope:
We did not dare to breathe a prayer,
280   Or to give our anguish scope:
Something was dead in each of us,
    And what was dead was Hope.

For Man's grim Justice goes its way,
    And will not swerve aside:
285   It slays the weak, it slays the strong,
    It has a deadly stride:
With iron heel it slays the strong,
    The monstrous parricide!

We waited for the stroke of eight:
290   Each tongue was thick with thirst:
For the stroke of eight is the stroke of Fate
    That makes a man accursed,

---

[4] **seneschal:** A steward in a medieval home in charge of domestic arrangements; an overseer.

And Fate will use a running noose
    For the best man and the worst.

295 We had no other thing to do,
        Save to wait for the sign to come:
    So, like things of stone in a valley lone,
        Quiet we sat and dumb:
    But each man's heart beat thick and quick,
300   Like a madman on a drum!

    With sudden shock the prison-clock
        Smote on the shivering air,
    And from all the gaol rose up a wail
        Of impotent despair,
305 Like the sound that frightened marshes hear
        From some leper in his lair.

    And as one sees most fearful things
        In the crystal of a dream,
    We saw the greasy hempen rope
310   Hooked to the blackened beam,
    And heard the prayer the hangman's snare
        Strangled into a scream.

    And all the woe that moved him so
        That he gave that bitter cry,
315 And the wild regrets, and the bloody sweats,
        None knew so well as I:
    For he who lives more lives than one
        More deaths than one must die.

A. E. HOUSMAN (1859–1936)

from **A Shropshire Lad** (1887)

XL

Into my heart an air that kills
    From yon far country blows:
What are those blue remembered hills,
    What spires, what farms are those?

5 That is the land of lost content,
    I see it shining plain,

The happy highways where I went
    And cannot come again.

WILLIAM BUTLER YEATS (1865–1939)

The Stolen Child (1889)

Where dips the rocky highland
Of Sleuth Wood in the lake,
There lies a leafy island
Where flapping herons wake
5   The drowsy water-rats;
There we've hid our faery vats,
Full of herries
And of reddest stolen cherries.
Come away, O human child!
10   *To the waters and the wild*
With a faery, hand in hand,
For the world's more full of weeping than you can understand.

Where the wave of moonlight glosses
The dim grey sands with light,
15   Far off by furthest Rosses
We foot it all the night,
Weaving olden dances,
Mingling hands and mingling glances
Till the moon has taken flight;
20   To and fro we leap
And chase the frothy bubbles,
While the world is full of troubles
And is anxious in its sleep.
Come away, O human child!
25   *To the waters and the wild*
With a faery, hand in hand,
For the world's more full of weeping than you can understand.

Where the wandering water gushes
From the hills above Glen-Car,
30   In pools among the rushes
That scarce could bathe a star,
We seek for slumbering trout
And whispering in their ears
Give them unquiet dreams;

35 Leaning softly out
From ferns that drop their tears
Over the young streams.
Come away, O human child!
To the waters and the wild
40 *With a faery, hand in hand,*
For the world's more full of weeping than you can understand.

Away with us he's going,
The solemn-eyed:
He'll hear no more the lowing
45 Or the calves on the warm hillside
Or the kettle on the hob
Sing peace into his breast,
Or see the brown mice bob
Round and round the oatmeal-chest.
50 *For he comes, the human child!*
To the waters and the wild
With a faery, hand in hand,
From a world more full of weeping than he can understand.

EDWIN ARLINGTON ROBINSON (1869–1935)

Miniver Cheevy (1907)

Miniver Cheevy, child of scorn,
    Grew lean while he assailed the seasons;
He wept that he was ever born,
    And he had reasons.

5 Miniver loved the days of old
    When swords were bright and steeds were prancing;
The vision of a warrior bold
    Would set him dancing.

Miniver sighed for what was not,
10   And dreamed, and rested from his labors;
He dreamed of Thebes and Camelot,
    And Priam's neighbors.

Miniver mourned the ripe renown
    That made so many a name so fragrant;
15 He mourned Romance, now on the town,
    And Art, a vagrant.

Miniver loved the Medici,
    Albeit he had never seen one;
He would have sinned incessantly
20   Could he have been one.

Miniver cursed the commonplace
    And eyed a khaki suit with loathing;
He missed the mediaeval grace
    Of iron clothing.

25 Miniver scorned the gold he sought,
    But sore annoyed was he without it;
Miniver thought, and thought, and thought,
    And thought about it.

Miniver Cheevy, born too late,
30   Scratched his head and kept on thinking;
Miniver coughed, and called it fate,
    And kept on drinking.

LANGSTON HUGHES (1902–1967)

Ballad of the Landlord (1940; 1955)

Landlord, landlord,
My roof has sprung a leak.
Don't you 'member I told you about it
Way last week?

5 Landlord, landlord,
These steps is broken down.
When you come up yourself
It's a wonder you don't fall down.

Ten Bucks you say I owe you?
10 Ten Bucks you say is due?
Well, that's Ten Bucks more'n I'll pay you
Till you fix this house up new.

What? You gonna get eviction orders?
You gonna cut off my heat?
15 You gonna take my furniture and
Throw it in the street?

Um-huh! You talking high and mighty.
Talk on—till you get through.
You ain't gonna be able to say a word
20 If I land my fist on you.

Police! Police!
Come and get this man!
He's trying to ruin the government
And overturn the land!

25 Copper's whistle!
Patrol bell!
Arrest.

Precinct Station.
Iron cell.
30 Headlines in press:

MAN THREATENS LANDLORD

TENANT HELD NO BAIL

JUDGE GIVES NEGRO 90 DAYS IN COUNTY JAIL

W. H. AUDEN (1907–1973)

Miss Gee (1937)

Let me tell you a little story
    About Miss Edith Gee;
She lived in Clevedon Terrace
    At Number 83.

5 She'd a slight squint in her left eye,
    Her lips they were thin and small,
She had narrow sloping shoulders
    And she had no bust at all.

She'd a velvet hat with trimmings,
10   And a dark grey serge costume;
She lived in Clevedon Terrace
    In a small bed-sitting room.

She'd a purple mac for wet days,
    A green umbrella too to take,
15   She'd a bicycle with shopping basket
    And a harsh back-pedal brake.

The Church of Saint Aloysius
    Was not so very far;
She did a lot of knitting,
20   Knitting for that Church Bazaar.

Miss Gee looked up at the starlight
    And said, "Does anyone care
That I live in Clevedon Terrace
    On one hundred pounds a year?"

25   She dreamed a dream one evening
    That she was the Queen of France
And the Vicar of Saint Aloysius
    Asked Her Majesty to dance.

But a storm blew down the palace,
30   She was biking through a field of corn,
And a bull with the face of the Vicar
    Was charging with lowered horn.

She could feel his hot breath behind her,
    He was going to overtake;
35   And the bicycle went slower and slower
    Because of that back-pedal brake.

Summer made the trees a picture,
    Winter made them a wreck;
She bicycled to the evening service
40   With her clothes buttoned up to her neck.

She passed by the loving couples,
    She turned her head away;
She passed by the loving couples
    And they didn't ask her to stay.

45   Miss Gee sat down in the side-aisle,
    She heard the organ play;
And the choir it sang so sweetly
    At the ending of the day.

Miss Gee knelt down in the side-aisle,
50   She knelt down on her knees;
"Lead me not into temptation
       But make me a good girl, please."

The days and nights went by her
       Like waves round a Cornish wreck;
55   She bicycled down to the doctor
       With her clothes buttoned up to her neck.

She bicycled down to the doctor,
       And rang the surgery bell;
"O, doctor, I've a pain inside me,
60   And I don't feel very well."

Doctor Thomas looked her over,
       And then he looked some more;
Walked over to his wash-basin,
       Said, "Why didn't you come before?"

65   Doctor Thomas sat over his dinner,
       Though his wife was waiting to ring,
Rolling his bread into pellets;
       Said, "Cancer's a funny thing.

"Nobody knows what the cause is,
70   Though some pretend they do;
It's like some hidden assassin
       Waiting to strike at you.

"Childless women get it,
       And men when they retire;
75   It's as if there had to be some outlet
       For their foiled creative fire."

His wife she rang for the servant,
       Said, "Don't be so morbid, dear";
He said: "I saw Miss Gee this evening
80   And she's a goner, I fear."

They took Miss Gee to the hospital,
       She lay there a total wreck,
Lay in the ward for women
       With the bedclothes right up to her neck.

85 They laid her on the table,
        The students began to laugh;
    And Mr Rose the surgeon
        He cut Miss Gee in half.

    Mr Rose he turned to his students,
90   Said, "Gentlemen, if you please,
    We seldom see a sarcoma
        As far advanced as this."

    They took her off the table,
        They wheeled away Miss Gee
95 Down to another department
        Where they study Anatomy.

    They hung her from the ceiling,
        Yes, they hung up Miss Gee;
    And a couple of Oxford Groupers
100   Carefully dissected her knee.

MURIEL RUKEYSER (1913–1980)

Ballad of Orange and Grape (1973 pub.)

    After you finish your work
    after you do your day
    after you've read your reading
    after you've written your say—
5   you go down the street to the hot dog stand,
    one block down and across the way.
    On a blistering afternoon in East Harlem in the twentieth century.

    Most of the windows are boarded up,
    the rats run out of a sack—
10 sticking out of the crummy garage
    one shiny long Cadillac;
    at the glass door of the drug-addiction center,
    a man who'd like to break your back.
    But here's a brown woman with a little girl dressed in rose and pink, too.

15 Frankfurters frankfurters sizzle on the steel
where the hot-dog-man leans—
nothing else on the counter
but the usual two machines,
the grape one, empty, and the orange one, empty,
20 I face him in between.
A black boy comes along, looks at the hot dogs, goes on walking.

I watch the man as he stands and pours
in the familiar shape
bright purple in the one marked ORANGE
25 orange in the one marked GRAPE,
the grape drink in the machine marked ORANGE
and orange drink in the GRAPE
Just the one word large and clear, unmistakable, on each
          machine.

I ask him : How can we go on reading
30 and make sense out of what we read?—
How can they write and believe what they're writing,
the young ones across the street,
while you go on pouring grape into ORANGE
and orange into the one marked GRAPE—?
35 (How are we going to believe what we read and we write and
          we hear and we say and we do?)

He looks at the two machines and he smiles
and he shrugs and smiles and pours again.
It could be violence and nonviolence
40 it could be white and black   women and men
it could be war and peace or any
binary system, love and hate, enemy, friend.
Yes and no, be and not-be, what we do and what we don't do.

On a corner in East Harlem
45 garbage, reading, a deep smile, rape,
forgetfulness, a hot street of murder,
misery, withered hope,
a man keeps pouring grape into ORANGE
and orange into the one marked GRAPE,
50 pouring orange into GRAPE and grape into ORANGE forever.

DUDLEY RANDALL   (1914–2000)

Ballad of Birmingham   (1969)

(On the bombing of a church in Birmingham, Alabama, 1963)[1]

"Mother dear, may I go downtown
Instead of out to play,
And march the streets of Birmingham
In a Freedom March today?"

5   "No, baby, no, you may not go,
For the dogs are fierce and wild,
And clubs and hoses, guns and jails
Aren't good for a little child."

"But, mother, I won't be alone.
10   Other children will go with me,
And march the streets of Birmingham
To make our country free."

"No, baby, no, you may not go,
For I fear those guns will fire.
15   But you may go to church instead
And sing in the children's choir."

She has combed and brushed her night-dark hair,
And bathed rose petal sweet,
And drawn white gloves on her small brown hands,
20   And white shoes on her feet.

The mother smiled to know her child
Was in the sacred place,
But that smile was the last smile
To come upon her face.

25   For when she heard the explosion,
Her eyes grew wet and wild.
She raced through the streets of Birmingham
Calling for her child.

---

[1] **On the bombing . . . 1963:** Carried out by members of the Ku Klux Klan, the 1963 bombing of a Baptist church in Birmingham killed four African-American girls.

She clawed through bits of glass and brick,
30   Then lifted out a shoe.
"O, here's the shoe my baby wore,
But, baby, where are you?"

LOUIS SIMPSON (1923–   )

Early in the Morning (1955)

Early in the morning
The dark Queen[1] said,
"The trumpets are warning
There's trouble ahead."
5   Spent with carousing,
With wine-soaked wits,
Antony drowsing
Whispered, "It's
Too cold a morning
10   To get out of bed."

The army's retreating.
The fleet has fled,
Caesar is beating
His drums through the dead.
15   "Antony, horses!
We'll get away,
Gather our forces
For another day . . ."
"It's a cold morning,"
20   Antony said.

Caesar Augustus
Cleared his phlegm.
"Corpses disgust us.
Cover them."

---

[1] **The dark Queen:** I.e., Cleopatra, queen of Egypt. After the assassination of Julius Caesar in 44 B.C., the Roman Empire was torn by intermittent civil wars, with Cicero's forces fighting the alliance of Octavian (Caesar Augustus) and Antony. The latter prevailed and subsequently divided the empire in two, Octavian ruling in the west and Antony in the east. When Antony forged a union with Cleopatra and became her lover, however, Octavian felt threatened and declared war on Egypt. In the decisive naval battle at Actium (31 B.C.), Antony's and Cleopatra's forces were defeated. The two of them fled to Alexandria, where, upon witnessing the inexorable military advance of Octavian, they committed suicide.

25   Caesar Augustus
     In his time lay
     Dying, and just as
     Cold as they,
     On the cold morning
30   Of a cold day.

ANNE SEXTON (1928–1974)

The Ballad of the Lonely Masturbator (1969)

     The end of the affair is always death.
     She's my workshop. Slippery eye,
     out of the tribe of myself my breath
     finds you gone. I horrify
5   those who stand by. I am fed.
     At night, alone, I marry the bed.

     Finger to finger, now she's mine.
     She's not too far. She's my encounter.
     I beat her like a bell. I recline
10   in the bower where you used to mount her.
     You borrowed me on the flowered spread.
     At night, alone, I marry the bed.

     Take for instance this night, my love,
     that every single couple puts together
15   with a joint overturning, beneath, above,
     the abundant two on sponge and feather,
     kneeling and pushing, head to head.
     At night, alone, I marry the bed.

     I break out of my body this way,
20   an annoying miracle. Could I
     put the dream market on display?
     I am spread out. I crucify.
     My little plum is what you said.
     At night, alone, I marry the bed.

25   Then my black-eyed rival came.
     The lady of water, rising on the beach,
     a piano at her fingertips, shame
     on her lips and a flute's speech.

And I was the knock-kneed broom instead.
30 At night, alone, I marry the bed.

She took you the way a woman takes
a bargain dress off the rack
and I broke the way a stone breaks.
I give back your books and fishing tack.
35 Today's paper says that you are wed.
At night, alone, I marry the bed.

The boys and girls are one tonight.
They unbutton blouses. They unzip flies.
They take off shoes. They turn off the light.
40 The glimmering creatures are full of lies.
They are eating each other. They are overfed.
At night, alone, I marry the bed.

AUDRE LORDE (1934–1992)

Ballad from Childhood (1974)

Mommy mommy come and see
what the strawmen left for me
in our land of ice and house of snow
I have found a seed to grow
5 Mommy may I plant a tree?

What the eyes don't see the heart don't hurt.

But mommy look the seed has wings
my tree might call a bird that sings . . .
true, the strawmen left no spade no earth
10 and ice will not bring my seed to birth—
but what if I dig beneath these things?

Watch the birds forget but the trap doesn't.

Please mommy do not beat me so!
yes I will learn to love the snow!
15 yes I want neither seed nor tree!
yes ice is quite enough for me!
who knows what trouble-leaves might grow!

I don't fatten frogs to feed snakes.

BOB DYLAN (1941–   )

The Lonesome Death of Hattie Carroll (1964)

William Zanzinger killed poor Hattie Carroll
With a cane that he twirled around his diamond ring finger
At a Baltimore hotel society gath 'rin'.
And the cops were called in and his weapon took from him
5   As they rode him in custody down to the station
And booked William Zanzinger for first-degree murder.
But you who philosophize disgrace and criticize all fears,
Take the rag away from your face.
Now ain't the time for your tears.

10   William Zanzinger, who at twenty-four years
Owns a tobacco farm of six hundred acres
With rich wealthy parents who provide and protect him
And high office relations in the politics of Maryland,
Reacted to his deed with a shrug of his shoulders
15   And swear words and sneering, and his tongue it was snarling,
In a matter of minutes on bail was out walking.
But you who philosophize disgrace and criticize all fears,
Take the rag away from your face.
Now ain't the time for your tears.

20   Hattie Carroll was a maid of the kitchen.
She was fifty-one years old and gave birth to ten children
Who carried the dishes and took out the garbage
And never sat once at the head of the table
And didn't even talk to the people at the table
25   Who just cleaned up all the food from the table
And emptied the ashtrays on a whole other level,
Got killed by a blow, lay slain by a cane
That sailed through the air and came down through the room,
Doomed and determined to destroy all the gentle.
30   And she never done nothing to William Zanzinger.
But you who philosophize disgrace and criticize all fears,
Take the rag away from your face.
Now ain't the time for your tears.

In the courtroom of honor, the judge pounded his gavel
35   To show that all's equal and that the courts are on the level
And that the strings in the books ain't pulled and persuaded
And that even the nobles get properly handled
Once that the cops have chased after and caught 'em

And that the ladder of law has no top and no bottom,
40 Stared at the person who killed for no reason
Who just happened to be feelin' that way without warnin'.
And he spoke through his cloak, most deep and distinguished,
And handed out strongly, for penalty and repentance,
William Zanzinger with a six-month sentence.
45 Oh, but you who philosophize disgrace and criticize all fears,
Bury the rag deep in your face
For now's the time for your tears.

WYATT PRUNTY (1947–   )

Ballad of the Several Past (1982)

Here is a man, his ticket stamped.
Alone in line and looking down,
this time he boards an all-night train,
finding a seat and stretching out;
5 uninterrupted movement helps him sleep,
he thinks, then leans his head against the glass:

With gentle roll and rhythmic tick
the rails suggest an open-ended trip
through moonlit fields of grain,
10 a metronomic land where harvest yields
old quantities required or stored
for travelers regaining rest.

A jolt. His head snaps back; he starts awake
then slips again:
15   *Revolving scenes,*
selecting one,
                  a room where dinner cools,
his parents laughing until their eyes tear,
napkins used as handkerchiefs,
20 *a family joke they value for the telling.*

That room again, the sun igniting dust
on dark veneer and no one there.
                                  Outside,
houses recede across successive fields
25 as trains unwind along rails.
The miles consume wide fields,
transporting harvest dry as death.

CHAPTER 6

SPEAK TO ME, SPEAK. WHY DO YOU NEVER SPEAK?

—T. S. Eliot

An Anthology of Monologue and Dramatic Poetry

Dramatic literature has a long and vivid tradition, going back to the ancient Greeks, whose major playwrights, such as Aeschylus, Sophocles, and Euripides, remain among the touchstones of Western literature. In English literature, beginning with the medieval mystery plays, dramatic literature has a rich and evolving tradition. But dramatic literature, in English, rose to an early apogee in the work of the great Elizabethan and Jacobean dramatists, who wrote in the sixteenth and early seventeenth centuries. At the white-hot center of this literature stands William Shakespeare, the premiere poet and dramatist of the language.

In a Shakespearean play, one finds riveting theatrical moments when a major character steps forward from the shadows to speak his mind. One thinks immediately of Hamlet as he ponders: "To be or not to be, that is the question." One thinks of King Lear on the heath, old and abandoned, powerless, defying the universe in his great monologues. Or Othello when he considers what an error he has made in killing his own beloved wife. These are called **soliloquies,** and they remain a centerpiece of English poetry: a speaker in a situation of crisis, in a dramatic context, talking to himself. The audience, in a sense, overhears the soliloquy; it is rather like dropping in on somebody's private thoughts.

The verse form called the **dramatic monologue** developed from the soliloquy. In most cases, there is an implied listener, someone present on the scene. A very early version of the dramatic monologue—one that predates the soliloquy—can be found in the tales of the various pilgrims in Chaucer's *Canterbury Tales* (p. 531). Each of these tales might be considered dramatic monologues. They are lively, single-person narratives. The audience is a gang of fellow pilgrims, and centuries of grateful readers. These tales are, by turns, comic and sad, rueful and elevating. Each is told with a purpose in mind: to teach a lesson of some kind.

The dramatic monologue slipped from view for many centuries, only acquiring major status in the Victorian era. Not incidentally, the rise of the dramatic monologue in the nineteenth century seems intimately related to the decline of playwriting during this period. Soon the monologue found eager practitioners in two of the best poets of the era, Alfred, Lord Tennyson and Robert Browning. These poets rediscovered and refashioned the form, giving it new life. Browning's "My Last Duchess" (p. 579) remains the most famous example of this type of poem—a splendidly realized work of art.

The dramatic monologue has two main characteristics. First of all, the speaker is always a character or *persona*, not the poet himself or herself. In Browning's poem, for instance, the speaker is a duke who had his last wife murdered. Second, there is usually an implied listener within the dramatic context of the poem. In this case, the listener is a courtier who has brought a new bride for the duke. Much of the fun of reading Browning's poem lies in measuring the subtle modulations of the duke's tone of voice as he talks to the courtier, keying him into the drama of his former marriage and its brutal conclusion. Needless to say, there is a threatening aspect in the duke's speech that could well be missed on first reading. The full dramatic context of the poem only gradually becomes clear, as detail is added to detail. The context deepens with the addition of every line.

In the twentieth century, poets often created forms of dramatic poetry, sometimes harking back to Browning. In "An Irish Airman Foresees His Death" (p. 581), Yeats speaks from the point of view of a pilot whose plane is about to crash on the Western Front during the first World War. There is no implied listener, no gradually developing dramatic situation; the poem is simply a dramatic lyric, with a speaker who is a character—someone who is definitely *not* the poet. Robert Frost, who aspired to be a playwright early in his career, wrote poems such as "Home Burial" (p. 348) with a dramatic situation and characters speaking. In effect, his poem is a little play in verse, using the dialect of New England farmers but magically transforming that dialect into a remarkably pure form of poetry. In essence, Frost understood that poetry was intimately connected with the speaking voice. Many of his finest poems have an intensely dramatic quality, and quite a few are written in dialogue form.

T. S. Eliot was fascinated by both the theater and dramatic poems. In an essay called "The Possibility of a Poetic Drama," he noted that most poets "hanker for the stage" and that "a not negligible public appears to want verse plays. Surely there is some legitimate craving, not restricted to a few persons, which only the verse play can satisfy." Eliot wrote several plays, including *Murder in the Cathedral*, but most of his impulse toward dramatic literature was channeled into his poems. His innovative monologue, "The Love Song of J. Alfred Prufrock" (p. 581) is really a soliloquy, not a dramatic monologue as defined by Browning; the character in the poem, a frustrated man in middle age, speaks more to himself than to anyone else. Rather intriguingly, the poem opens: "Let us go then, you and I." One might well assume there is another person in the poem, an implied listener; this would make the poem seem like a dramatic monologue in the Browning mold. But, in fact, Prufrock is arguing with himself here, and the opening line represents his divided self. The poem mirrors his unintegrated world, his schizophrenic existence.

Modern poets from Langston Hughes to Wanda Coleman and Anne Carson have experimented with poems that incorporate elements of dramatic speech or dramatic situations. Dialogue itself has become a mainstay of contemporary poetry, and readers often expect a dramatic element in a poem: a situation of crisis, one that evolves. Poetic drama, as practiced by Shakespeare and revived by Yeats, Eliot, and others during the early and middle years of the twentieth century, has largely faded from the scene. What survives of that impulse endures in dramatic poems, which continue to bristle with life.

GEOFFREY CHAUCER (ca. 1343–1400)

The Pardoner's Prologue and Tale[1]
from The Canterbury Tales
(late fourteenth century)

*The Introduction: The Wordes of the Host
to the Phisicien and the Pardoner*

	Oure Hoste gan to swere as he were wood;°	mad
	"Harrow,"° quod he, "by nailes and by blood,	help
	This was a fals cherl and a fals justice.	
	As shameful deeth as herte may devise	
5	Come to thise juges and hir advocats.	
	Algate° this sely° maide is slain, allas!	anyway / innocent
	Allas, too dere boughte she beautee!	
	Wherfore I saye alday° that men may see	always
	The yiftes° of Fortune and of Nature	gifts
10	Been cause of deeth to many a creature.	
	As bothe yiftes that I speke of now,	
	Men han ful ofte more for harm than prow.°	advantage
	"But trewely, myn owene maister dere,	
	This is a pitous tale for to heere.	
15	But nathelees, passe over, is no fors:	
	I praye to God so save thy gentil cors,°	body

---

[1] **The Pardoner's . . . Tale:** In medieval times, a pardoner was commissioned by the Pope to collect money for charitable ventures controlled by the church. In recognition of contributions to the church, the pardoner issued indulgence, or official remission of sins through the power of the Pope. In reality, a pardoner often exceeded the bounds of his office, promising indulgence that exceeded his power and using church money for personal profit.

And eek thine urinals and thy jurdones,
Thyn ipocras and eek thy galiones,[2]
And every boiste° ful of thy letuarye°—   box / medicines
20   God blesse hem, and oure lady Sainte Marye.
So mote I theen, thou art a propre man,
And lik a prelat, by Saint Ronian!
Saide I nat wel? I can nat speke in terme.[3]
But wel I woot,° thou doost myn herte to erme°   know / grieve
25   That I almost have caught a cardinacle.[4]
By corpus bones, but if I have triacle.°   medicine
Or elles a draughte of moiste° and corny° ale,   fresh / malty
Or but I here anoon° a merye tale,   at once
Myn herte is lost for pitee of this maide.
30   "Thou bel ami,° thou Pardoner," he saide,   fair friend
"Tel us som mirthe or japes° right anoon."   jokes
     "It shal be doon," quod he, "by Saint Ronion.
But first," quod he, "here at this ale-stake°   tavern sign
I wol bothe drinke and eten of a cake."
35   And right anoon thise gentils gan to crye,
"Nay, lat him telle us of no ribaudye.°   ribaldry
Tel us som moral thing that we may lere,°   learn
Som wit, and thanne wol we gladly heere."
     "I graunte, ywis,"° quod he, "but I moot° thinke   certainly / must
40   Upon som honeste° thing whil that I drinke.   decent

The Prologue

     Lordinges—quod he—in chirches whan I preche;
I paine me° to han an hautein° speeche,   take pains / loud
And ringe it out as round as gooth a belle,
For I can al by rote that I telle.
45   My theme is alway oon,° and evere was: always the same
Radix malorum est cupiditas.[5]
First I pronounce whennes that I come,
And thanne my bulles[6] shewe I alle and some:°   one and all
Oure lige lordes seel on my patente,[7]

---

[2] **And eek . . . galiones:** "Urinals" are containers for examining urine, while "jurdones" (jordans) are champer pots. "Ipocras" is a medicine named after the eminent Greek physician Hippocrates, while "galiones" is medicine (fabricated by the Host) named after the Greek physician Galen. In these lines, the Host demonstrates that his medical knowledge is less than advanced.
[3] **speke in terme:** Speak in technical jargon.
[4] **caught a cardinacle:** In another faux paux, the host confuses a cardiac condition with a cardinal.
[5] **Radix malorum est cupiditas:** A varice is the root of all evil. (1 Timothy 6.10).
[6] **my bulles shewe:** Papal bulls, or writs of indulgence for sin.
[7] **Oure . . . patente:** The bishop's seal on my papal license.

50	That shewe I first, my body to warente,°	authorize
	That no man be so bold, ne preest ne clerk,	
	Me to destourbe of Cristes holy werk.	
	And after that thanne telle I forth my tales—	
	Bulles of popes and of cardinales,	
55	Of patriarkes and bisshopes I shewe,	
	And in Latin I speke a wordes fewe,	
	To saffron with my predicacioun,[8]	
	And for to stire hem to devocioun.	
	Thanne shewe I forth my longe crystal stones,°	glass cases
60	Ycrammed ful of cloutes° and of bones—	rags
	Relikes been they, as weenen they eechoon.[9]	
	Thanne have I in laton° a shulder-boon	brass
	Which that was of an holy Jewes sheep.	
	"Goode men," I saye, "take of my wordes keep:	
65	If that this boon be wasshe in any welle,	
	If cow, or calf, or sheep, or oxe swelle,	
	That any worm hath ete or worm ystonge,[10]	
	Take water of that welle and wassh his tonge,	
	And it is hool° anoon. And ferthermoor,	healed
70	Of pokkes° and of scabbe and every soor	pox
	Shal every sheep be hool that of this welle	
	Drinketh a draughte. Take keep eek° that I telle:	also
	If that the goode man that the beestes oweth°	owns
	Wol every wike, er° that the cok him croweth,	before
75	Fasting drinken of this welle a draughte—	
	As thilke° holy Jew oure eldres taughte—	that same
	His beestes and his stoor° shal multiplye.	stock
	"And sire, also it heleth jalousye:	
	For though a man be falle in jalous rage,	
80	Lat maken with this water his potage,°	stew
	And nevere shal he more his wif mistriste,	
	Though he the soothe of hir defaute wiste,[11]	
	Al hadde she taken preestes two or three.	
	"Here is a mitein° eek that ye may see:	mitten
85	He that his hand wol putte in this mitein	
	He shal have multiplying of his grain,	
	Whan he hath sowen, be it whete or otes—	
	So that he offre pens or elles grotes.[12]	

---

[8] **To saffron . . . predicacioun:** To add seasoning to my preaching. (Saffron is a yellow spice.)

[9] **Relikes . . . eechoon:** They are [saint's] relics, or so they all suppose.

[10] **That . . . ystonge:** That has eaten any worm or been bitten by a snake.

[11] **soothe . . . wiste:** Knew the truth of her adultery.

[12] **offre . . . grotes:** Offer pennies, or else groats. (A groat is a silver coin.)

"Goode men and wommen, oo thing warne I you:

90 If any wight be in this chirche now

That hath doon sinne horrible, that he

Dar nat for shame of it yshriven° be,   pardoned

Or any womman, be she yong or old,

That hath ymaked hir housbonde cokewold,

95 Swich folk shal have no power ne no grace

To offren to my relikes in this place;

And whoso findeth him out of swich blame,

He wol come up and offre in Goddes name,

And I assoile° him by the auctoritee   absolve

100 Which that by bulle ygraunted was to me."

By this gaude° have I wonne, yeer by yeer,   ploy

An hundred mark sith I was pardoner.

I stonde like a clerk in my pulpet,

And whan the lewed peple is down yset,

105 I preche so as ye han herd bifore,

And telle an hundred false japes° more.   jokes

Thanne paine I me to strecche forth the nekke,

And eest and west upon the people I bekke°   nod

As dooth a douve, sitting on a berne;

110 Mine handes and my tonge goon so yerne°   fast

That it is joye to see my bisinesse.

Of avarice and of swich cursednesse°   sin

Is al my preching, for to make hem free

To yiven hir pens, and namely unto me,

115 For myn entente is nat but for to winne,

And no thing for correccion of sinne:

I rekke° nevere whan that they been beried   care

Though that hir soules goon a-blakeberied.[13]

For certes, many a predicacioun°   sermon

120 Comth ofte time of yvel entencioun:

Som for plesance of folk and flaterye,

To been avaunced by ypocrisye,

And som for vaine glorye, and som for hate;

For whan I dar noon otherways debate,

125 Thanne wol I stinge him with my tonge smerte

In preching, so that he shal nat asterte

To been defamed falsly, if that he

Hath trespassed to my bretheren or to me.

For though I telle nought his propre name,

130 Men shal wel knowe that it is the same

---

[13] **goon a-blakeberied:** Go blackberrying. Figuratively, go to hell.

By signes and by othere circumstaunces.
Thus quite I folk that doon us displeasunces;
Thus spete° I out my venim under hewe°   spit / false colors
Of holinesse, to seeme holy and trewe.
135 But shortly myn entente I wol devise:
I preche of no thing but for coveitise;°   covetousness
Therfore my theme is yit and evere was
Radix malorum est cupiditas
Thus can I preche again° that same vice   against
140 Which that I use, and that is avarice.
But though myself be gilty in that sinne,
Yit can I make other folk to twinne°   part
From avarice, and sore to repente—
But that is nat my principal entente:
145 I preche no thing but for coveitise.
Of this matere it oughte ynough suffise.
Thanne telle I hem ensamples° many oon   examples
Of olde stories longe time agoon,
For lewed° peple loven tales olde—   ignorant
150 Swiche thinges can they wel reporte and holde.
What, trowe° ye that whiles I may preche,   believe
And winne gold and silver for I teche,
That I wol live in poverte wilfully?
Nay, nay, I thoughte it nevere, trewely,
155 For I wol preche and begge in sondry landes;
I wol nat do no labour with mine handes,
Ne make baskettes and live therby,
By cause I wol nat beggen idelly.°   without revenue
I wol none of the Apostles countrefete:°   imitate
160 I wol have moneye, wolle, cheese, and whete,
Al were it yiven of the pooreste page,
Or of the pooreste widwe in a village—
Al sholde hir children sterve for famine.[14]
Nay, I wol drinke licour of the vine
165 And have a joly wenche in every town.
But herkneth, lordinges, in conclusioun,
Youre liking is that I shal telle a tale:
Now have I dronke a draughte of corny ale,
By God, I hope I shal you telle a thing
170 That shal by reson been at youre liking;
For though myself be a ful vicious man,
A moral tale yit I you telle can,

---

[14] **Al sholde . . . famine:** Even if her children should die from hunger.

Which I am wont° to preche for to winne.   used to
Now holde youre pees, my tale I wol biginne.

The Tale

175 In Flandres whilom° was a compaignye   once
Of yonge folk that haunteden folye—
As riot, hasard,° stewes,° and tavernes,   gambling / brothels
Wher as with harpes, lutes, and giternes
They daunce and playen at dees° bothe day and night,   dice
180 And ete also and drinke over hir might,
Thurgh which they doon the devel sacrifise
Within that develes temple in cursed wise
By superfluitee° abhominable.   excess
Hir othes been so grete and so dampnable
185 That it is grisly for to heere hem swere:
Oure blessed Lordes body they totere°—   tear apart
Hem thoughte that Jewes rente° him nought ynough.   tore
And eech of hem at otheres sinne lough.°   laughed
And right anoon thanne comen tombesteres,°   female dancers
190 Fetis and smale, and yonge frutesteres,°   fruit-vending girls
Singeres with harpes, bawdes, wafereres°—   cake-vending girls
Whiche been the verray develes officeres,
To kindle and blowe the fir of lecherye
That is annexed unto glotonye:
195 The Holy Writ take I to my witnesse
That luxure° is in win and dronkenesse.   lechery
Lo, how that dronken Lot unkindely°   unnaturally
Lay by his doughtres two unwitingly:
So dronke he was he niste° what he wroughte.   knew not
200 Herodes, who so wel the stories soughte,
Whan he of win was repleet at his feeste,
Right at his owene table he yaf his heeste
To sleen° the Baptist John, ful giltelees.   slay
Senek¹⁵ saith a good word doutelees:
205 He saith he can no difference finde
Bitwixe a man that is out of his minde
And a man which that is dronkelewe,
But that woodnesse,° yfallen in a shrewe,°   madness / miserable man
Persevereth lenger than dooth dronkenesse.
210 O glotonye, ful of cursednesse!
O cause first of oure confusioun!
O original of oure dampnacioun,°   damnation
Til Crist hadde bought us with his blood again!

---

¹⁵ **Senek:** Seneca (circa 4 B.C.–65 A.D.), Roman statesman, philosopher, and playwright.

Lo, how dere, shortly for to sayn,
215   Abought was thilke° cursed vilainye;°   that same / evil deed
Corrupt was al this world for glotonye:
Adam oure fader and his wif also
Fro Paradis to labour and to wo
Were driven for that vice, it is no drede.°   doubt
220   For whil that Adam fasted, as I rede,
He was in Paradis; and whan that he
Eet of the fruit defended° on a tree,   prohibited
Anoon he was out cast to wo and paine.
O glotonye, on thee wel oughte us plaine!°   complain
225   O, wiste a man how manye maladies
Folwen of excesse and of glotonies,
He wolde been the more mesurable°   temperate
Of his diete, sitting at his table.
Allas, the shorte throte, the tendre mouth,
230   Maketh that eest and west and north and south,
In erthe, in air, in water, men to swinke,°   toil
To gete a gloton daintee mete° and drinke.   meat
Of this matere, O Paul, wel canstou trete:
"Mete unto wombe,° and wombe eek unto mete,   stomach
235   Shal God destroyen bothe," as Paulus saith.
Allas, a foul thing is it, by my faith,
To saye this word, and fouler is the deede
Whan man so drinketh of the white and rede
That of his throte he maketh his privee°   privy
240   Thurgh thilke cursed superfluitee.
The Apostle [16] weeping saith ful pitously,
"Ther walken manye of which you told have I—
I saye it now weeping with pitous vois—
They been enemies of Cristes crois,°   cross
245   Of whiche the ende is deeth—wombe is hir god!"
O wombe, O bely, O stinking cod,°   bag
Fulfilled of dong and of corrupcioun!
At either ende of thee foul is the soun.°   sound
How greet labour and cost is thee to finde!
250   Thise cookes, how they stampe and straine and grinde,
And turnen substance into accident
To fulfillen al thy likerous talent!°   lecherous appetite
Out of the harde bones knokke they
The mary,° for they caste nought away   marrow
255   That may go thurgh the golet° softe and soote.   gullet
Of spicerye° of leef and bark and roote   spices

---

[16] **The Apostle:** Saint Paul.

Shal been his sauce ymaked by delit,
To make him yit a newer appetit.
But certes, he that haunteth swiche delices°   delights
260   Is deed whil that he liveth in tho vices.
        A lecherous thing is win, and dronkenesse
Is ful of striving° and of wrecchednesse.   arguing
O dronke man, disfigured is thy face!
Sour is thy breeth, foul artou to embrace!
265   And thurgh thy dronke nose seemeth the soun
As though thou saidest ay, "Sampsoun, Sampsoun."
And yit, God woot,° Sampson drank nevere win.[17]   knows
Thou fallest as it were a stiked swin;°   stuck pig
Thy tonge is lost, and al thyn honeste cure,°   care for decency
270   For dronkenesse is verray sepulture°   tomb
Of mannes wit and his discrecioun.
In whom that drinke hath dominacioun
He can no conseil° keepe, it is no drede.   secrets
Now keepe you fro the white and fro the rede—
275   And namely fro the white win of Lepe
That is to selle in Fisshstreete or in Chepe:[18]
The win of Spaine creepeth subtilly
In othere wines growing faste by,
Of which ther riseth swich fumositee°   fumes
280   That whan a man hath dronken draughtes three
And weeneth that he be at hoom in Chepe,
He is in Spaine, right at the town of Lepe,
Nat at The Rochele ne at Burdeux town;[19]
And thanne wol he sayn, "Sampsoun, Sampsoun."
285   But herkneth, lordinges, oo word I you praye,
That alle the soverein actes, dar I saye,
Of victories in the Olde Testament,
Thurgh verray God that is omnipotent,
Were doon in abstinence and in prayere:
290   Looketh the Bible and ther ye may it lere.°   learn
        Looke Attila,[20] the grete conquerour,
Deide in his sleep with shame and dishonour,
Bleeding at his nose in dronkenesse:
A capitain sholde live in sobrenesse.

---

[17] **Sampson drank nevere win:** Before Samson's birth, an angel informed his mother that he would be
a Nazarite, a member of the Jewish sect that abstained from alcohol consumption.
[18] **white . . . Chepe:** Lepe is a town in Spain, and Fishstreet and Cheapside are found in London's
marketplace.
[19] **Nat . . . town:** Here, the Pardoner speaks of diluting fine wines from Bordeaux and La Rochelle
with less exquisite Spanish wines.
[20] **Attila:** Leader of the Huns who died of a nosebleed—the result of excessive alcohol consumption.

295 And overal this, aviseth you right wel
      What was comanded unto Lamuel[21]—
      Nat Samuel, but Lamuel, saye I—
      Redeth the Bible and finde it expresly,
      Of win-yiving to hem that han° justise: handles
300 Namore of this, for it may wel suffise.
          And now that I have spoken of glotonye,
      Now wol I you defende° hasardrye:°   forbid / gambling
      Hasard is verray moder° of lesinges,°   mother / lies
      And of deceite and cursed forsweringes,
305 Blaspheme of Crist, manslaughtre, and wast also
      Of catel° and of time; and ferthermo,   possessions
      It is repreve and contrarye of honour
      For to been holden a commune hasardour,°   gambler
      And evere the hyer he is of estat
310 The more is he holden desolat.
      If that a prince useth hasardrye,
      In alle governance and policye
      He is, as by commune opinioun,
      Yholde the lasse in reputacioun
315   Stilbon, that was a wis embassadour,
      Was sent to Corinthe in ful greet honour
      Fro Lacedomye° to make hir alliaunce,   Sparta
      And whan he cam him happede parchaunce
      That alle the gretteste that were of that lond
320 Playing at the hasard he hem foond,
      For which as soone as it mighte be
      He stal him° hoom again to his contree,   stole away
      And saide, "Ther wol I nat lese° my name,   lose
      N'I wol nat take on me so greet defame
325 You to allye unto none hasardours:
      Sendeth othere wise embassadours,
      For by my trouthe, me were levere die°   I would rather die
      Than I you sholde to hasardours allye.
      For ye that been so glorious in honours
330 Shal nat allye you with hasardours
      As by my wil, ne as by my tretee."
      This wise philosophre, thus saide he.
          Looke eek that to the king Demetrius
      The King of Parthes, as the book[22] saith us,
335 Sente him a paire of dees of gold in scorn,

---

[21] **Lamuel:** In Proverbs 31, Lemuel's mother advises him that kings should avoid alcohol.
[22] **the book:** John Salisbury's *Policraticus*, which contains the story of Demetrius as well as the Stilbon's preceding story.

For he hadde used hasard therbiforn,
For which he heeld his glorye or his renown
At no value or reputacioun.
Lordes may finden other manere play
340   Honeste ynough to drive the day away.
    Now wol I speke of othes false and grete
A word or two, as olde bookes trete:
    Greet swering is a thing abhominable
And fals swering is yit more reprevable.°   reproachable
345   The hye God forbad swering at al—
Witnesse on Mathew. But in special
Of swering saith the holy Jeremie,
"Thou shalt swere sooth° thine othes and nat lie,   truly
And swere in doom° and eek in rightwisnesse,°   justice / righteousness
350   But idel swering is a cursedness."
    Biholde and see that in the firste Table
Of hye Goddes heestes° honorable   commandments
How that the seconde heeste of him is this:
"Take nat my name in idel or amis."
355   Lo, rather° he forbedeth swich swering   earlier
Than homicide, or many a cursed thing.
I saye that as by ordre thus it stondeth—
This knoweth that his heestes understondeth [23]
How that the seconde heeste of God is that.
360   And fertherover, I wol thee telle al plat°   flatly
That vengeance shal nat parten° from his hous   part
That of his othes is too outrageous.
"By Goddes precious herte!" and "By his nailes!"
And "By the blood of Crist that is in Hailes,[24]
365   Sevene is my chaunce, and thyn is cink° and traye!"°   five / three
"By Goddes armes, if thou falsly playe
This daggere shal thurghout thyn herte go!"
This fruit cometh of the bicche bones° two—   cursed dice
Forswering, ire, falsnesse, homicide.
370   Now for the love of Crist that for us dyde,
Lete youre othes bothe grete and smale.
But sires, now wol I telle forth my tale.
    Thise riotoures° three of whiche I telle,   rioters
Longe erst er prime° ronge of any belle,   9 A.M.
375   Were set hem in a taverne to drinke,
And as they sat they herde a belle clinke
Biforn a cors° was caried to his grave.   corpse

---

[23] **This . . . understondeth:** He knows this, who understands His commandments.
[24] **Hailes:** An abbey in Gloucestershire, thought to possess, as a relic, some of Christ's blood.

That oon of hem gan callen to his knave:
"Go bet,"° quod he, "and axe redily°   go quickly / ask promptly
380   What cors is this that passeth heer forby,
And looke that thou reporte his name weel."
        "Sire," quod this boy, "it needth neveradeel:°   it isn't a bit necessary
It was me told er ye cam heer two houres.
He was, pardee,° an old felawe of youres,   by God
385   And sodeinly he was yslain tonight,
Fordronke as he sat on his bench upright;
Ther cam a privee° thief men clepeth° Deeth,   secret / called
That in this contree al the people sleeth,°   slays
And with his spere he smoot his herte atwo,
390   And he wente his way withouten wordes mo.
He hath a thousand slain this pestilence.°   during this plague
And maister, er ye come in his presence,
Me thinketh that it were necessarye
For to be war of swich an adversarye;
395   Beeth redy for to meete him everemore:
Thus taughte me my dame. I saye namore."
        "By Sainte Marye," saide this taverner,
"The child saith sooth, for he hath slain this yeer,
Henne over a mile, within a greet village,
400   Bothe man and womman, child and hine° and page.   laborer
I trowe° his habitacion be there.   believe
To been avised greet wisdom it were
Er that he dide a man a dishonour."
        "Ye, Goddes armes," quod this riotour,
405   "Is it swich peril with him for to meete?
I shal him seeke by way and eek by streete,
I make avow to Goddes digne° bones.   worthy
Herkneth, felawes, we three been alle ones:°   of one mind
Lat eech of us holde up his hand to other
410   And eech of us bicome otheres brother,
And we wol sleen this false traitour Deeth.
He shal be slain, he that so manye sleeth,
By Goddes dignitee, er it be night."
        Togidres° han thise three hir trouthes plight²⁵   together
415   To live and dien eech of hem with other,
As though he were his owene ybore brother.
And up they sterte, al dronken in this rage,
And forth they goon towardes that village
Of which the taverner hadde spoke biforn,
420   And many a grisly ooth thanne han they sworn,

---

²⁵ **hir trouthes plight:** Their troths pledged.

And Cristes blessed body they torente:°   *tore apart*
Deeth shal be deed if that they may him hente.°   *catch*
    Whan they han goon nat fully half a mile,
Right as they wolde han treden over a stile,
425   An old man and a poore with hem mette;
This olde man ful mekely hem grette,°   *greeted them*
And saide thus, "Now lordes, God you see."°   *God protect you*
    The pruddeste° of thise riotoures three   *proudest*
Answerde again, "What, carl° with sory grace,   *churl*
430   Why artou al forwrapped save thy face?
Why livestou so longe in so greet age?"
    This olde man gan looke in his visage,
And saide thus, "For I ne can nat finde
A man, though that I walked into Inde,°   *India*
435   Neither in citee ne in no village,
That wolde chaunge his youthe for myn age;
And therfore moot I han myn age stille,
As longe time as it is Goddes wille.
    "Ne Deeth, allas, ne wol nat have my lif.
440   Thus walke I lik a resteless caitif,°   *captive*
And on the ground which is my modres° gate   *mother's*
I knokke with my staf both erly and late,
And saye, 'Leve° moder, leet me in: *dear*
Lo, how I vanisshe, flessh and blood and skin.
445   Allas, whan shal my bones been at reste?
Moder, with you wolde I chaunge my cheste
That in my chambre longe time hath be,
Ye, for an haire-clout° to wrappe me.'   *hair cloth (for burial)*
But yit to me she wol nat do that grace,
450   For which ful pale and welked° is my face.   *withered*
But sires, to you it is no curteisye
To speken to an old man vilainye,
But he trespasse in word or elles in deede.
In Holy Writ ye may yourself wel rede,
455   'Agains an old man, hoor upon his heed,
Ye shal arise.' Wherfore I yive you reed,°   *advice*
Ne dooth unto an old man noon harm now,
Namore than that ye wolde men dide to you
In age, if that ye so longe abide.
460   And God be with you wher ye go or ride:
I moot go thider as I have to go."
    "Nay, olde cherl, by God thou shalt nat so,"
Saide this other hasardour anoon.
"Thou partest nat so lightly, by Saint John!
465   Thou speke right now of thilke traitour Deeth,
That in this contree alle oure freendes sleeth:

Have here my trouthe, as thou art his espye,° spy
Tel wher he is, or thou shalt it abye,° pay for
By God and by the holy sacrament!
470 For soothly thou art oon of his assent° of his party
To sleen us yonge folk, thou false thief."
　　"Now sires," quod he, "if that ye be so lief° eager
To finde Deeth, turne up this crooked way,
For in that grove I lafte him, by my fay,° faith
475 Under a tree, and ther he wol abide:
Nat for youre boost° he wol him no thing hide. boast
See ye that ook?° Right ther ye shal him finde. oak
God save you, that boughte again mankinde,
And you amende." Thus saide this olde man.
480 　　And everich of thise riotoures ran
Til he cam to that tree, and ther they founde
Of florins° fine of gold ycoined rounde coins
Wel neigh an eighte busshels as hem thoughte—
Ne lenger thanne after Deeth they soughte,
485 But eech of hem so glad was of the sighte,
For that the florins been so faire and brighte,
That down they sette hem by this precious hoord.
The worste of hem he spak the firste word:
　　"Bretheren," quod he, "take keep° what that I saye: heed
490 My wit is greet though that I bourde° and playe. tease
This tresor hath Fortune unto us yiven
In mirthe and jolitee oure lif to liven,
And lightly as it cometh so wol we spende.
Ey, Goddes precious dignitee, who wende° would have supposed?
495 Today that we sholde han so fair a grace?
But mighte this gold be caried fro this place
Hoom to myn hous—or elles unto youres—
For wel ye woot that al this gold is oures—
Thanne were we in heigh felicitee.
500 But trewely, by daye it mighte nat be:
Men wolde sayn that we were theves stronge,° flagrant
And for oure owene tresor doon us honge.° have us hanged
This tresor moste ycaried be by nighte,
As wisely and as slyly as it mighte.
505 Therfore I rede° that cut° amonges us alle suggest / straws
Be drawe, and lat see wher the cut wol falle;
And he that hath the cut with herte blithe
Shal renne° to the town, and that ful swithe,° run / quickly
And bringe us breed and win ful prively;
510 And two of us shal keepen subtilly
This tresor wel, and if he wol nat tarye,
Whan it is night we wol this tresor carye

By oon assent wher as us thinketh best."

That oon of hem the cut broughte in his fest°   fist

515 And bad hem drawe and looke wher it wol falle;

And it fil on the yongeste of hem alle,

And forth toward the town he wente anoon.

And also soone as that he was agoon,

That oon of hem spak thus unto that other:

520 "Thou knowest wel thou art my sworen brother;

Thy profit wol I telle thee anoon:

Thou woost wel that oure felawe is agoon,

And here is gold, and that ful greet plentee,

That shal departed° been among us three.   divided

525 But nathelees, if I can shape it so

That it departed were among us two,

Hadde I nat doon a freendes turn to thee?"

That other answerde, "I noot° how that may be: don't know

He woot that the gold is with us twaye.

530 What shal we doon? What shal we to him saye?"

"Shal it be conseil?" saide the firste shrewe.

"And I shal telle in a wordes fewe

What we shul doon, and bringe it wel aboute."

"I graunte," quod that other, "out of doute,

535 That by my trouthe I wol thee nat biwraye."°   betray

"Now," quod the firste, "thou woost wel we be twaye,

And two of us shal strenger° be than oon: stronger

Looke whan that he is set that right anoon

Aris as though thou woldest with him playe,

540 And I shal rive° him thurgh the sides twaye,   stab

Whil that thou strugelest with him as in game,

And with thy daggere looke thou do the same;

And thanne shal al this gold departed be,

My dere freend, bitwixe thee and me.

545 Thanne we may bothe oure lustes° al fulfille,   desires

And playe at dees right at oure owene wille."

And thus accorded been thise shrewes twaye

To sleen the thridde, as ye han herd me saye.

This yongeste, which that wente to the town,

550 Ful ofte in herte he rolleth up and down

The beautee of thise florins newe and brighte.

"O Lord," quod he, "if so were that I mighte

Have al this tresor to myself allone,

Ther is no man that liveth under the trone°   throne

555 Of God that sholde live so merye as I."

And at the laste the feend oure enemy°   Satan

Putte in his thought that he sholde poison beye,°   buy

With which he mighte sleen his felawes twaye—

Forwhy° the feend foond him in swich livinge   Because
560 That he hadde leve° him to sorwe bringe: [26]   permission
For this was outrely his fulle entente,
To sleen hem bothe, and nevere to repente.
        And forth he gooth—no lenger wolde he tarye—
Into the town unto a pothecarye,°   apothecary
565 And prayed him that he him wolde selle
Som poison that he mighte his rattes quelle,°   kill
And eek ther was a polcat° in his hawe°   weasel / house
That, as he saide, his capons hadde yslawe,
And fain he wolde wreke him° if he mighte   avenge himself
570 On vermin that destroyed him by nighte.
        The pothecarye answerde, "And thou shalt have
A thing that, also° God my soule save,   so
In al this world there is no creature
That ete or dronke hath of this confiture°—   mixture
575 Nat but the mountance° of a corn° of whete—   amount / kernel
That he ne shal his lif anoon forlete.°   lose
Ye, sterve° he shal, and that in lasse while   die
Than thou wolt goon a paas° nat but a mile,   walk
The poison is so strong and violent."
580 This cursed man hath in his hand yhent°   held
This poison in a box and sith he ran
Into the nexte streete unto a man
And borwed of him large botels three,
And in the two his poison poured he—
585 The thridde he kepte clene for his drinke,
For al the night he shoop him° for to swinke°   was preparing himself / work
In carying of the gold out of that place.
And whan this riotour with sory grace
Hadde filled with win his grete botels three,
590 To his felawes again repaireth he.
        What needeth it to sermone of it more?
For right as they had cast° his deeth bifore,   planned
Right so they han him slain, and that anoon.
And whan that this was doon, thus spak that oon:
595 "Now lat us sitte and drinke and make us merye,
And afterward we wol his body berye."
And with that word it happed him par cas°   by chance
To take the botel ther the poison was,
And drank, and yaf his felawe drinke also,
600 For which anoon they storven° bothe two.   died

---

[26] **Forwhy . . . bringe:** According to Christian doctrine, the devil cannot tempt people without God's permission.

But certes I suppose that Avicen
Wroot nevere in no canon ne in no *fen*[27]
Mo wonder signes of empoisoning
Than hadde thise wrecches two er hir ending:
605   Thus ended been thise homicides two,
And eek the false empoisonere also.
    O cursed sinne of alle cursednesse!
O traitours homicide, O wikkednesse!
O glotonye, luxure,° and hasardrye!   lechery
610   Thou blasphemour of Crist with vilainye
And othes grete of usage and of pride!
Allas, mankinde, how may it bitide
That to thy Creatour which that thee wroughte,
And with his precious herte blood thee boughte,
615   Thou art so fals and so unkinde,° allas?   unnatural
    Now goode men, God foryive you youre trespas,
And ware° you fro the sinne of avarice: protect
Myn holy pardon may you alle warice°—   save
So that ye offre nobles or sterlinges,[28]
620   Or elles silver brooches, spoones, ringes.
Boweth your heed under this holy bulle!
Cometh up, ye wives, offreth of youre wolle!
Youre name I entre here in my rolle: anoon
Into the blisse of hevene shul ye goon.
625   I you assoile° by myn heigh power—   absolve
Ye that wol offre—as clene and eek as cleer
As ye were born.—And lo, sires, thus I preche.
And Jesu Crist that is oure soules leeche°   healer
So graunte you his pardon to receive,
630   For that is best—I wol you nat deceive.

The Epilogue

"But sires, oo word forgat I in my tale:
I have relikes and pardon in my male
As faire as any man in Engelond,
Whiche were me yiven by the Popes hond.
635   If any of you wol of devocioun
Offren and han myn absolucioun,
Come forth anoon, and kneeleth here adown,
And mekely receiveth my pardoun,

---

[27] **Avicen . . . fen:** Avicenna's *Canon of Medicine*, written in the eleventh century, was divided into segments called "fens."
[28] **So that . . . sterlinges:** As long as you offer nobles or sterlings (valuable coins).

Or elles taketh pardon as ye wende,°   *travel*
640   Al newe and fressh at every miles ende—
     So that ye offre alway newe and newe°   *over and over*
     Nobles or pens whiche that be goode and trewe.
     It is an honour to everich° that is heer   *everyone*
     That ye have a suffisant pardoner
645   T' assoile you in contrees as ye ride,
     For aventures whiche that may bitide:
     Paraventure° ther may falle oon or two   *By chance*
     Down of his hors and breke his nekke atwo;
     Looke which a suretee° is it to you alle   *safety*
650   That I am in youre felaweshipe yfalle
     That may assoile you, bothe more and lasse,
     Whan that the soule shal fro the body passe.
     I rede° that oure Hoste shal biginne,   *advise*
     For he is most envoluped in sinne.
655   Com forth, sire Host, and offre first anoon,
     And thou shalt kisse the relikes everichoon,
     Ye, for a grote: unbokele° anoon thy purs."   *unbuckle*
        "Nay, nay," quod he, "thanne have I Cristes curs!
     Lat be," quod he, "it shal nat be, so theech!°   *I hope to prosper*
660   Thou woldest make me kisse thyn olde breech°   *breeches*
     And swere it were a relik of a saint,
     Though it were with thy fundament° depeint.°   *anus / stained*
     But, by the crois which that Sainte Elaine foond,[29]
     I wolde I hadde thy coilons° in myn hond,   *testicles*
665   In stede of relikes or of saintuarye.°   *holy things*
     Lat cutte hem of: I wol thee helpe hem carye.
     They shal be shrined in an hogges tord."°   *turd*
        This Pardoner answerde nat a word:
     So wroth he was no word ne wolde he saye.
670   "Now," quod oure Host, "I wol no lenger playe
     With thee, ne with noon other angry man."
        But right anoon the worthy Knight bigan,
     Whan that he sawgh that al the peple lough,
     "Namore of this, for it is right ynough.
675   Sire Pardoner, be glad and merye of cheere,
     And ye, sire Host that been to me so dere,
     I praye you that ye kisse the Pardoner,
     And Pardoner, I praye thee, draw thee neer,
     And as we diden lat us laughe and playe."
680   Anoon they kiste and riden forth hir waye.

---

[29] **Sainte Elaine foond:** St. Helena, mother of the Roman emperor Constantine, was rumored to have discovered the True Cross.

WILLIAM SHAKESPEARE (1564–1616)

from Hamlet
Act I, Scene 2 (Hamlet) (ca. 1600)

O! that this too too solid flesh would melt,
Thaw and resolve° itself into a dew;   dissolve
Or that the Everlasting had not fix'd
His canon° 'gainst self-slaughter! O God! O God!   law
5   How weary, stale, flat, and unprofitable
Seem to me all the uses of this world.
Fie on't! O fie! 'tis an unweeded garden,
That grows to seed; things rank and gross in nature
Possess it merely.° That it should come to this!   wholly
10 But two months dead: nay, not so much, not two:
So excellent a king; that was, to this,
Hyperion to a satyr;[1] so loving to my mother
That he might not beteem° the winds of heaven   allow
Visit her face too roughly. Heaven and earth!
15 Must I remember? why, she would hang on him,
As if increase of appetite had grown
By what it fed on; and yet, within a month,
Let me not think on't: Frailty, thy name is woman!
A little month; or ere those shoes were old
20 With which she follow'd my poor father's body,
Like Niobe,[2] all tears; why she, even she, —
O God! a beast, that wants discourse of reason,
Would have mourn'd longer, —married with mine uncle,
My father's brother, but no more like my father
25 Than I to Hercules: within a month,
Ere yet the salt of most unrighteous tears
Had left the flushing in her galled° eyes,   irritated
She married. O! most wicked speed, to post
With such dexterity to incestuous sheets.
30 It is not nor it cannot come to good;
But break, my heart, for I must hold my tongue!

---

[1] **Hyperion . . . satyr:** In Greek mythology, Hyperion was the Titan sun-god. A satyr is half-man, half-goat.
[2] **Niobe:** In Greek mythology, mother of fourteen children who were killed by Apollo and Artemis after she boasted about them. In her grief, Zeus transformed her into a stone that constantly wept tears.

WILLIAM SHAKESPEARE (1564–1616)

from Julius Caesar
Act III, Scene 2 (Antony) (1599; 1623)

Friends, Romans, countrymen, lend me your ears;
I come to bury Cæsar, not to praise him.
The evil that men do lives after them,
The good is oft interred with their bones;
5   So let it be with Cæsar. The noble Brutus
Hath told you Cæsar was ambitious;
If it were so, it was a grievous fault,
And grievously hath Cæsar answered it.
Here, under leave° of Brutus and the rest,—   by consent
10 For Brutus is an honourable man;
So are they all, all honourable men, —
Come I to speak in Cæsar's funeral.
He was my friend, faithful and just to me:
But Brutus says he was ambitious;
15 And Brutus is an honourable man.
He hath brought many captives home to Rome,
Whose ransoms did the general coffers° fill: public treasury
Did this in Cæsar seem ambitious?
When that the poor have cried, Cæsar hath wept;
20 Ambition should be made of sterner stuff:
Yet Brutus says he was ambitious;
And Brutus is an honourable man.
You all did see that on the Lupercal[1]
I thrice presented him a kingly crown,
25 Which he did thrice refuse: was this ambition?
Yet Brutus says he was ambitious;
And, sure, he is an honourable man.
I speak not to disprove what Brutus spoke,
But here I am to speak what I do know.
30 You all did love him once, not without cause:
What cause withholds you then to mourn for him?
O judgment! thou art fled to brutish beasts,
And men have lost their reason. Bear with me;
My heart is in the coffin there with Cæsar,
35 And I must pause till it come back to me.

---

[1] **Lupercal:** Roman holiday held on February 15th in honor of the God of Fertility, *Lupercus*, "the one who wards off the wolf."

WILLIAM SHAKESPEARE (1564–1616)

from Othello
Act I, Scene 3 (Othello) (1604)

Her father lov'd me; oft invited me;
Still° question'd me the story of my life   constantly
From year to year, the battles, sieges, fortunes
That I have pass'd.
5   I ran it through, even from my boyish days
To the very moment that he bade me tell it;
Wherein I spake of most disastrous° chances,   unlucky
Of moving accidents by flood and field,[1]
Of hair-breadth 'scapes i' the imminent deadly breach,[2]
10   Of being taken by the insolent foe
And sold to slavery, of my redemption thence
And portance in my travel's history;
Wherein of antres° vast and desarts idle,   caves
Rough quarries, rocks and hills whose heads touch heaven,
15   It was my hint° to speak, such was the process;   opportunity
And of the Cannibals that each other eat,
The Anthropophagi,° and men whose heads   man-eaters
Do grow beneath their shoulders. This to hear
Would Desdemona seriously incline;
20   But still the house-affairs would draw her thence;
Which ever as she could with haste dispatch,
She'd come again, and with a greedy ear
Devour up my discourse. Which I observing,
Took once a pliant° hour, and found good means   opportune
25   To draw from her a prayer of earnest heart
That I would all my pilgrimage dilate,°   convey
Whereof by parcels she had something heard,
But not intentively: I did consent;
And often did beguile her of her tears,
30   When I did speak of some distressful stroke
That my youth suffer'd. My story being done,
She gave me for my pains a world of sighs:
She swore, in faith, 'twas strange, 'twas passing strange;
'Twas pitiful, 'twas wondrous pitiful:
35   She wish'd she had not heard it, yet she wish'd
That heaven had made her such a man; she thank'd me,
And bade me, if I had a friend that lov'd her,
I should but teach him how to tell my story,

---

[1] **by . . . field:** By sea and land.
[2] **i' . . . breach:** Refers to gaps in a defense fortification that will result in immediate death.

And that would woo her. Upon this hint I spake:
40   She lov'd me for the dangers I had pass'd,
And I lov'd her that she did pity them.
This only is the witchcraft I have us'd:

EDWARD WARD   (1667–1731)

Dialogue between a Squeamish Cotting[1] Mechanic and his Sluttish Wife, in the Kitchen   (1710 pub.)

Husband   Is the fish ready? You're a tedious while;
Take care the butter does not turn to oil:
Lay on more coals, and hang the pot down low'r,
Or 'twill not boil with such a fire this hour.
Is that, my dear, the saucepan you design   5
To stew the shrimps and melt the butter in?
Nouns!° withinside as nasty it appears   Nonsense
As if't had ne'er been scoured this fifty years.
Rare, hussifs!° how confounded black it looks!   housewife
God sends us meat, the devil sends us cooks.   10
Wife   Why, how now, cot! Must I be taught by you?
Sure I without you know what I've to do.
Prithee go mind your shop, attend your trade,
And leave the kitchen to your wife and maid.
O'erlook your 'prentices, you cot, and see   15
They do their work, leave cookery to me.
Is't fit a man, you contradicting sot,
Should mind the kettle or the porridge-pot,
And run his nose in ev'ry dirty hole,
To see what platter's clean, what dish is foul?   20
Be gone, you prating ninny, whilst you're well,
Or, faith, I'll pin the dish-clout° to your tail.   cloth
Husband   I'll not be poisoned by a sluttish quean.
Hussy,° I say, go scour the saucepan clean.   woman adulterer
What though your mistress is a careless beast,   25
I love to have my victuals cleanly dressed!
Cot me no cots, I'll not be bound to eat
Such dirty sauce to good and wholesome meat.
I will direct and govern, since I find
You're both to so much nastiness inclined.   30

---

[1] **Cotting:** Refers to a man who completes domestic chores typically reserved for women.

I'd have you know I neither fear or matter
Your threatened dish-clouts or your scalding water.

Wife   Stand by, you prating fool, you damned provoker,
Or, by my soul, I'll burn you with the poker.
Must I be thus abused, as if your maid,   35
And called a slut before a saucy jade?[2]
Gad, speak another word and, by my troth,
I'll spoil the fish and scald you with the broth.
The kitchen fire, alas! don't burn to please ye;
The saucepan is, forsooth, too foul and greasy.   40
Minx, touch it not, I say it's clean enough:
Your scouring rubs the tin withinside off;
I'll have no melted butter taste of brass
To please the humour of a squeamish ass.
If cot-comptroller does not like its looks,   45
Let him spend sixpence at his nasty cook's,
Where rotten mutton, beef that's turnip-fed,
Lean measly pork on London muck-hills bred,
Will please the fool much better than the best
Of meat by his own wife or servant dressed.   50
Why don't you thither go before you dine,
Where you may see, perhaps, a noble loin
Of a bull-calf lie sweating at the fire,
Beneath fat pork, nursed up in t—d and mire,
And under that a chump of Suffolk beef,   55
Thrice roasted for some hungry clown's relief,
Till black as soot that from the chimney falls,
And hard as Severn salmon[3] dried in Wales,
All basted with a flux of mingled fat,
Which greasily distils from this and that?   60
Such nice tid cleanly bits would please my dear,
Prithee go thither, do not plague us here.

Husband   Hussy, what I direct you ought to do;
I'm lord and master of this house and you.
Do you not know that wise and noble prince,   65
King 'Hasuerus,[4] made a law long since
That ev'ry husband should the ruler be
Of his own wife, as well as family?
How dare you then control my lawful sway,

---

[2] **saucy jade:** Like "minx" and "hussy," jade implies a female adulterer, yet is often used in a playful connotation.

[3] **Severn salmon:** Salmon from the Severn River, the longest river in Great Britain.

[4] **King 'Hasuerus:** Known in the Bible as Ahasuerus, Xerxes I was king of Egypt from 485 B.C.–465 B.C.

When Scripture tells you woman should obey?   70
Therefore, I say, I'll have my fish well dressed,
After such manner as shall please me best,
Or, hussy, by this ladle, if I han't,
I'll make you show good reason why I shan't.
I'll have more coals upon the fire, I tell ye,   75
And have the saucepan cleaned, aye marry will I,
Or I'll acquaint your teacher, Mr. Blunder,
That all the art of man can't keep you under.

Wife   Here, hussy, fetch some coals, 'tis long of you
That we have ev'ry day all this to do.   80
Pray clean the saucepan, you forgetful trull,
I must confess it looks a little dull.
You shall not say I love this jarring life,
You shall have no complaints against your wife.
But prithee, husband, leave us and be easy,   85
Ne'er doubt but I will cook your fish to please ye.
When men o'erlook us, we proceed in fear,
And ne'er can do so well when they are near;
Therefore I hope, my dear, you will not mind
A woman's passion, words you know are wind.   90
I would not for the world have Mr. Blunder
Know that we jar; the good old man would wonder
That you and I, who've been so long his hearers,
Should now want grace, and fall into such errors.

Husband   Since you repent your failings, I'll be gone,   95
But prithee let the fish be nicely done.
I buy the best and, whether roast or boiled,
You know I hate to have my victuals spoiled.

Wife   My dear, I'll take such care, that you shall find
It shall be rightly ordered to your mind.   100
I'm glad he's gone. Pox° take him for a cot;   *small pox*
What wife would humour such a snarling sot?
Here, Kather'n, take my keys, slip gently by
The Fox, and fetch a dram° for thee and I.   *medicinal liquor*
Lay down the saucepan; poh! it's clean enough   105
For such an old, ill-natured, stingy cuff.
Prithee ne'er value what thy master says;
You should not mind his cross-grained, foolish ways;
But when I bid you, hussy, you must run.
Now his back's turned, the kitchen is our own.   110
Bless me! how eas'ly can a woman blind
And cheat a husband, if he proves unkind:
He thinks, poor cuckold, that he bears the rule,
When heaven knows I do but gull the fool.

ELIZABETH BARRETT BROWNING (1806–1861)

from **Aurora Leigh** (1853; 1857)
from **First Book**

Of writing many books there is no end;
And I who have written much in prose and verse
For others' uses, will write now for mine,—
Will write my story for my better self,
5   As when you paint your portrait for a friend,
Who keeps it in a drawer and looks at it
Long after he had ceased to love you, just
To hold together what he was and is.
I, writing thus, am still what men call young;
10   I have not so far left the coasts of life
To travel inward, that I cannot hear
That murmur of the outer Infinite
Which unweaned babies smile at in their sleep
When wondered at for smiling; not so far,
15   But still I catch my mother at her post
Beside the nursery door, with finger up,
'Hush, hush—here's too much noise!' while her sweet eyes
Leap forward, taking part against her word
In the child's riot. Still I sit and feel
20   My father's slow hand, when she had left us both,
Stroke out my childish curls across his knee,
And hear Assunta's daily jest (she knew
He liked it better than a better jest)
Inquire how many golden scudi° went   coins
25   To make such ringlets. O my father's hand,
Stroke heavily, heavily the poor hair down,
Draw, press the child's head closer to thy knee!
I'm still too young, too young, to sit alone.

I write. My mother was a Florentine,
30   Whose rare blue eyes were shut from seeing me
When scarcely I was four years old, my life
A poor spark snatched up from a failing lamp
Which went out therefore. She was weak and frail;
She could not bear the joy of giving life,
35   The mother's rapture slew her. If her kiss
Had left a longer weight upon my lips
It might have steadied the uneasy breath,
And reconciled and fraternised my soul
With the new order. As it was, indeed,
40   I felt a mother-want about the world,

And still went seeking, like a bleating lamb
Left out at night in shutting up the fold,—
As restless as a nest-deserted bird
Grown chill through something being away, though what
45 It knows not. I, Aurora Leigh, was born
To make my father sadder, and myself
Not overjoyous, truly. Women know
The way to rear up children (to be just),
They know a simple, merry, tender knack
50 Of tying sashes, fitting baby-shoes,
And stringing pretty words that make no sense,
And kissing full sense into empty words,
Which things are corals to cut life upon,
Although such trifles: children learn by such,
55 Love's holy earnest in a pretty play
And get not over-early solemnised,
But seeing, as in a rose-bush, Love's Divine
Which burns and hurts not,—not a single bloom,—
Become aware and unafraid of Love.
60 Such good do mothers. Fathers love as well
—Mine did, I know,—but still with heavier brains,
And wills more consciously responsible,
And not as wisely, since less foolishly;
So mothers have God's license to be missed.

65 My father was an austere Englishman,
Who, after a dry lifetime spent at home
In college-learning, law, and parish talk,
Was flooded with a passion unaware,
His whole provisioned and complacent past
70 Drowned out from him that moment. As he stood
In Florence, where he had come to spend a month
And note the secret of Da Vinci's drains,
He musing somewhat absently perhaps
Some English question . . . whether men should pay
75 The unpopular but necessary tax
With left or right hand—in the alien sun
In that great square of the Santissima[1]
There drifted past him (scarcely marked enough
To move his comfortable island scorn)
80 A train of priestly, banners, cross and psalm,
The white-veiled rose-crowned maidens holding up
Tall tapers, weighty for such wrists, aslant

---

[1] **Santissima:** The Santissima Annunziata, a thirteenth century gothic cathedral in Florence.

To the blue luminous tremor of the air,
And letting drop the white wax as they went
85   To eat the bishop's wafer at the church;
From which long trail of chanting priests and girls,
A face flashed like a cymbal on his face
And shook with silent clangour brain and heart,
Transfiguring him to music. Thus, even thus,
90   He too received his sacramental gift
With eucharistic meanings; for he loved.

And thus beloved, she died. I've heard it said
That but to see him in the first surprise
Of widower and father, nursing me,
95   Unmothered little child of four years old,
His large man's hands afraid to touch my curls,
As if the gold would tarnish,—his grave lips
Contriving such a miserable smile
As if he knew needs must, or I should die,
100   And yet 'twas hard,—would almost make the stones
Cry out for pity. There's a verse he set
In Santa Croce[2] to her memory,—
'Weep for an infant too young to weep much
When death removed this mother'—stops the mirth
105   To-day on women's faces when they walk
With rosy children hanging on their gowns,
Under the cloister to escape the sun
That scorches in the piazza. After which
He left our Florence and made haste to hide
110   Himself, his prattling child, and silent grief,
Among the mountains above Pelago;[3]
Because unmothered babes, he thought, had need
Of mother nature more than others use,
And Pan's white goats, with udders warm and full
115   Of mystic contemplations, come to feed
Poor milkless lips of orphans like his own—
Such scholar-scraps he talked, I've heard from friends,
For even prosaic men who wear grief long
Will get to wear it as a hat aside
120   With a flower stuck in't. Father, then, and child,
We lived among the mountains many years,
God's silence on the outside of the house,
And we who did not speak too loud within,

---

[2] **Santa Croce:** The Basilica of Santa Croce, a gothic cathedral in Florence that houses the tombs of Michelangelo and Galileo.
[3] **Pelago:** A small village to the east of Florence.

And old Assunta to make up the fire,
125 Crossing herself whene'er a sudden flame
Which lightened from the firewood, made alive
That picture of my mother on the wall.
The painter drew it after she was dead,
And when the face was finished, throat and hands,
130 Her cameriera° carried him, in hate   maid
Of the English-fashioned shroud, the last brocade
She dressed in at the Pitti;[4] 'he should paint
No sadder thing than that,' she swore, 'to wrong
Her poor signora.' Therefore very strange
135 The effect was. I, a little child, would crouch
For hours upon the floor with knees drawn up,
And gaze across them, half in terror, half
In adoration, at the picture there,—
That swan-like supernatural white life
140 Just sailing upward from the red stiff silk
Which seemed to have no part in it nor power
To keep it from quite breaking out of bounds.
For hours I sat and stared. Assunta's awe
And my poor father's melancholy eyes
145 Still pointed that way. That way went my thoughts
When wandering beyond sight. And as I grew
In years, I mixed, confused, unconsciously,
Whatever I last read or heard or dreamed,
Abhorrent, admirable, beautiful,
150 Pathetical, or ghastly, or grotesque,
With still that face . . . which did not therefore change,
But kept the mystic level of all forms,
Hates, fears, and admirations, was by turns
Ghost, fiend, and angel, fairy, witch, and sprite,
155 A dauntless Muse who eyes a dreadful Fate,
A loving Psyche who loses sight of Love,
A still Medusa with mild milky brows
All curdled and all clothed upon with snakes
Whose slime falls fast as sweat will; or anon
160 Our Lady of the Passion, stabbed with swords
Where the Babe sucked; or Lamia[5] in her first
Moonlighted pallor, ere she shrunk and blinked
And shuddering wriggled down to the unclean;
Or my own mother, leaving her last smile

---

[4] **Pitti:** Great palace in Florence, home of Italy's ruling dynasties since 1550.
[5] **Lamia:** In Greek mythology, daughter of Belus and lover of Zeus. When Hera, the wife of Zeus, learned of Lamia's affair with her husband, she killed Lamia's children. Destroyed by grief, Lamia became a monster, hunting down and eating the children of other mothers.

165 In her last kiss upon the baby-mouth
My father pushed down on the bed for that,—
Or my dead mother, without smile or kiss,
Buried at Florence. All which images,
Concentred on the picture, glassed themselves
170 Before my meditative childhood, as
The incoherencies of change and death
Are represented fully, mixed and merged,
In the smooth fair mystery of perpetual Life.
And while I stared away my childish wits
175 Upon my mother's picture (ah, poor child!),
My father, who through love had suddenly
Thrown off the old conventions, broken loose
From chin-bands of the soul, like Lazarus,
Yet had no time to learn to talk and walk
180 Or grow anew familiar with the sun,—
Who had reached to freedom, not to action, lived,
But lived as one entranced, with thoughts, not aims,—
Whom love had unmade from a common man
But not completed to an uncommon man,—
185 My father taught me what he had learnt the best
Before he died and left me,—grief and love.
And, seeing we had books among the hills,
Strong words of counselling souls confederate
With vocal pines and waters,—out of books
190 He taught me all the ignorance of men,
And how God laughs in heaven when any man
Says 'Here I'm learned; this, I understand;
In that, I am never caught at fault or doubt.'
He sent the schools to school, demonstrating
195 A fool will pass for such through one mistake,
While a philosopher will pass for such,
Through said mistakes being ventured in the gross
And heaped up to a system.
                    I am like,
They tell me, my dear father. Broader brows
200 Howbeit, upon a slenderer undergrowth
Of delicate features,—paler, near as grave;
But then my mother's smile breaks up the whole,
And makes it better sometimes than itself.
So, nine full years, our days were hid with God
205 Among his mountains: I was just thirteen,
Still growing like the plants from unseen roots
In tongue-tied Springs,—and suddenly awoke
To full life and life's needs and agonies
With an intense, strong, struggling heart beside

210   A stone-dead father. Life, struck sharp on death,
Makes awful lightning. His last word was 'Love—'
'Love, my child, love, love!'—(then he had done with grief)
'Love, my child.' Ere I answered he was gone,
And none was left to love in all the world.

215   There, ended childhood. What succeeded next
I recollect as, after fevers, men
Thread back the passage of delirium,
Missing the turn still, baffled by the door;
Smooth endless days, notched here and there with knives,
220   A weary, wormy darkness, spurred i' the flank
With flame, that it should eat and end itself
Like some tormented scorpion. Then at last
I do remember clearly how there came
A stranger with authority, not right
225   (I thought not), who commanded, caught me up
From old Assunta's neck; how, with a shriek,
She let me go,—while I, with ears too full
Of my father's silence to shriek back a word,
In all a child's astonishment at grief
230   Stared at the wharf-edge where she stood and moaned,
My poor Assunta, where she stood and moaned!
The white walls, the blue hills, my Italy,
Drawn backward from the shuddering steamer-deck,
Like one in anger drawing back her skirts
235   Which suppliants catch at. Then the bitter sea
Inexorably pushed between us both
And, sweeping up the ship with my despair,
Threw us out as a pasture to the stars,

Ten nights and days we voyaged on the deep;
240   Ten nights and days without the common face
Of any day or night; the moon and sun
Cut off from the green reconciling earth,
To starve into a blind ferocity
And glare unnatural; the very sky
245   (Dropping its bell-net down upon the sea,
As if no human heart should 'scape alive)
Bedraggled with the desolating salt;
Until it seemed no more that holy heaven
To which my father went. All new and strange;
250   The universe turned stranger, for a child.

Then, land!—then, England! oh, the frosty cliffs
Looked cold upon me. Could I find a home

Among those mean red houses through the fog?
And when I heard my father's language first
255 From alien lips which had no kiss for mine
I wept aloud, then laughed, then wept, then wept,
And some one near me said the child was mad
Through much sea-sickness. The train swept us on:
Was this my father's England? the great isle?
260 The ground seemed cut up from the fellowship
Of verdure,° field from field, as man from man;   green foliage
The skies themselves looked low and positive,
As almost you could touch them with a hand,
And dared to do it they were so far off
265 From God's celestial crystals; all things blurred
And dull and vague. Did Shakespeare and his mates
Absorb the light here?—not a hill or stone
With heart to strike a radiant colour up
Or active outline on the indifferent air.

270 I think I see my father's sister stand
Upon the hall-step of her country-house
To give me welcome. She stood straight and calm,
Her somewhat narrow forehead braided tight
As if for taming accidental thoughts
275 From possible pulses; brown hair pricked with gray
By frigid use of life (she was not old,
Although my father's elder by a year),
A nose drawn sharply, yet in delicate lines;
A close mild mouth, a little soured about
280 The ends, through speaking unrequited loves
Or peradventure° niggardly half-truths;   by chance
Eyes of no colour,—once they might have smiled,
But never, never have forgot themselves
In smiling; cheeks, in which was yet a rose
285 Of perished summers, like a rose in a book,
Kept more for ruth than pleasure,—if past bloom,
Past fading also.
                         She had lived, we'll say,
A harmless life, she called a virtuous life,
A quiet life, which was not life at all
290 (But that, she had not lived enough to know),
Between the vicar and the county squires,
The lord-lieutenant looking down sometimes
From the empyrean to assure their souls
Against chance vulgarisms, and, in the abyss,
295 The apothecary, looked on once a year
To prove their soundness of humility.

The poor-club exercised her Christian gifts
Of knitting stockings, stitching petticoats,
Because we are of one flesh, after all,
300   And need one flannel (with a proper sense
Of difference in the quality)—and still
The book-club, guarded from your modern trick
Of shaking dangerous questions from the crease,
Preserved her intellectual. She had lived
305   A sort of cage-bird life, born in a cage,
Accounting that to leap from perch to perch
Was act and joy enough for any bird.
Dear heaven, how silly are the things that live
In thickets, and eat berries!
                                      I, alas,
310   A wild bird scarcely fledged, was brought to her cage,
And she was there to meet me. Very kind.
Bring the clean water, give out the fresh seed.

She stood upon the steps to welcome me,
Calm, in black garb. I clung about her neck,—
315   Young babes, who catch at every shred of wool
To draw the new light closer, catch and cling
Less blindly. In my ears my father's word
Hummed ignorantly, as the sea in shells,
'Love, love, my child.' She, black there with my grief,
320   Might feel my love—she was his sister once—
I clung to her. A moment she seemed moved,
Kissed me with cold lips, suffered me to cling,
And drew me feebly through the hall into
The room she sat in.
                                 There, with some strange spasm
325   Of pain and passion, she wrung loose my hands
Imperiously, and held me at arm's length,
And with two grey-steel naked-bladed eyes
Searched through my face,—ay, stabbed it through and through,
Through brows and cheeks and chin, as if to find
330   A wicked murderer in my innocent face,
If not here, there perhaps. Then, drawing breath,
She struggled for her ordinary calm—
And missed it rather,—told me not to shrink,
As if she had told me not to lie or swear,—
335   'She loved my father and would love me too
As long as I deserved it.' Very kind.

I understood her meaning afterward;
She thought to find my mother in my face,

And questioned it for that. For she, my aunt,
340 Had loved my father truly, as she could,
And hated, with the gall of gentle souls,
My Tuscan mother who had fooled away
A wise man from wise courses, a good man
From obvious duties, and, depriving her,
345 His sister, of the household precedence,
Had wronged his tenants, robbed his native land,
And made him mad, alike by life and death,
In love and sorrow. She had pored for years
What sort of woman could be suitable
350 To her sort of hate, to entertain it with,
And so, her very curiosity
Became hate too, and all the idealism
She ever used in life was used for hate,
Till hate, so nourished, did exceed at last
355 The love from which it grew, in strength and heat,
And wrinkled her smooth conscience with a sense
Of disputable virtue (say not, sin)
When Christian doctrine was enforced at church.

And thus my father's sister was to me
360 My mother's hater. From that day she did
Her duty to me (I appreciate it
In her own word as spoken to herself).
Her duty, in large measure, well pressed out
But measured always. She was generous, bland,
365 More courteous than was tender, gave me still
The first place,—as if fearful that God's saints
Would look down suddenly and say 'Herein
You missed a point, I think, through lack of love.'
Alas, a mother never is afraid
370 Of speaking angerly to any child,
Since love, she knows, is justified of love.

And I, I was a good child on the whole,
A meek and manageable child. Why not?
I did not live, to have the faults of life:
375 There seemed more true life in my father's grave
Than in all England. Since *that* threw me off
Who fain would cleave (his latest will, they say,
Consigned me to his land), I only thought
Of lying quiet there where I was thrown
380 Like sea-weed on the rocks, and suffering her
To prick me to a pattern with her pin,
Fibre from fibre, delicate leaf from leaf,

And dry out from my drowned anatomy
The last sea-salt left in me.
                              So it was.
385   I broke the copious curls upon my head
In braids, because she liked smooth-ordered hair.
I left off saying my sweet Tuscan words
Which still at any stirring of the heart
Came up to float across the English phrase
390   As lilies (*Bene* or *Che che*),[6] because
She liked my father's child to speak his tongue.
I learnt the collects and the cathecism,
The creeds, from Athanasius back to Nice,[7]
The Articles, the Tracts *against* the times
395   (By no means Buonaventure's 'Prick of Love'),[8]
And various popular synopses of
Inhuman doctrines never taught by John,
Because she liked instructed piety.
I learnt my complement of classic French
400   (Kept pure of Balzac and neologism)[9]
And German also, since she liked a range
Of liberal education,—tongues, not books.
I learnt a little algebra, a little
Of the mathematics,—brushed with extreme flounce°   quick movement
405   The circle of the sciences, because
She misliked women who are frivolous.
I learnt the royal genealogies
Of Oviedo, the internal laws
Of the Burmese empire,—by how many feet
410   Mount Chimborazo outsoars Teneriffe.
What navigable river joins itself
To Lara, and what census of the year five
Was taken at Klagenfurt,—because she liked
A general insight into useful facts.[10]
415   I learnt much music,—such as would have been
As quite impossible in Johnson's day

---

[6] (***Bene* or *Che che***): Italian: "well" and "who who."
[7] **Athanasius . . . Nice:** Athanasius (293–373 A.D.), Greek patriarch of Alexandria who supported orthodox Christianity. Nice likely refers to Nicaea, a city in Asia Minor where a formal creed of Christian beliefs was articulated in 325 A.D.
[8] **Buonaventure . . . Love:** St. Bonaventure (1221–1274) wrote *The Prick of Love,* a popular devotional text during the Middle Ages that focused on both the death of Christ and the necessity of compassion.
[9] **Balzac . . . neologism:** Honoré Balzac (1799–1850), French novelist whose writing addressed the complexity of French society. A neologism is a newly invented word.
[10] **I learnt . . . facts:** Oviedo is a city in northwestern Spain, while "Burmese empire" refers to Burma, an Asian republic near the Bay of Bengal, known in contemporary culture as Myanmar. Mount Chimborazo is in the Andes range of Ecuador, while Teneriffe, the highest point in Spain, is the largest of the seven Canary Islands. Klagenfurt is a city in Austria.

As still it might be wished—fine sleights of hand
And unimagined fingering, shuffling off
The hearer's soul through hurricanes of notes
420   To a noisy Tophet;[11] and I drew . . . costumes
From French engravings, nereids[12] neatly draped
(With smirks of simmering godship): I washed in
Landscapes from nature (rather say, washed out).
I danced the polka and Cellarius,[13]
425   Spun glass, stuffed birds, and modelled flowers in wax,
Because she liked accomplishments in girls.
I read a score of books on womanhood
To prove, if women do not think at all,
They may teach thinking (to a maiden aunt
430   Or else the author),—books that boldly assert
Their right of comprehending husband's talk
When not too deep, and even of answering
With pretty 'may it please you,' or 'so it is,'—
Their rapid insight and fine aptitude,
435   Particular worth and general missionariness,
As long as they keep quiet by the fire
And never say 'no' when the world says 'ay',
For that is fatal,—their angelic reach
Of virtue, chiefly used to sit and darn,
440   And fatten household sinners,—their, in brief,
Potential faculty in everything
Of abdicating power in it: she owned
She liked a woman to be womanly,
And English women, she thanked God and sighed
445   (Some people always sigh in thanking God)
Were models to the universe. And last
I learnt cross-stitch, because she did not like
To see me wear the night with empty hands
A-doing nothing. So, my shepherdess
450   Was something after all (the pastoral saints
Be praised for't), leaning lovelorn with pink eyes
To match her shoes, when I mistook the silks;
Her head uncrushed by that round weight of hat
So strangely similar to the tortoise-shell
455   Which slew the tragic poet.
                                        By the way,
The works of women are symbolical.
We sew, sew, prick our fingers, dull our sight,

---

[11] **Tophet:** Region lying southeast of Jerusalem, often an alternative name for hell.
[12] **nereids:** Sea-nymph daughters of the sea god Nereus.
[13] **Cellarius:** Famous dance composed by Henri Cellarius in mid-nineteenth century Paris.

Producing what? A pair of slippers, sir,
To put on when you're weary—or a stool
460 To stumble over and vex you . . . 'curse that stool!'
Or else at best, a cushion, where you lean
And sleep, and dream of something we are not
But would be for your sake. Alas, alas!
This hurts most, this—that, after all, we are paid
465 The worth of our work, perhaps.

                        In looking down
Those years of education (to return)
I wonder if Brinvilliers[14] suffered more
In the water-torture . . . flood succeeding flood
To drench the incapable throat and split the veins . . .
470 Than I did. Certain of your feebler souls
Go out in such a process; many pine
To a sick, inodorous light; my own endured:
I had relations in the Unseen, and drew
The elemental nutriment and heat
475 From nature, as earth feels the sun at nights,
Or as a babe sucks surely in the dark.
I kept the life thrust on me, on the outside
Of the inner life with all its ample room
For heart and lungs, for will and intellect,
480 Inviolable by conventions. God,
I thank thee for that grace of thine!

                        At first
I felt no life which was not patience,—did
The thing she bade me, without heed to a thing
Beyond it, sat in just the chair she placed,
485 With back against the window, to exclude
The sight of the great lime-tree on the lawn,
Which seemed to have come on purpose from the woods
To bring the house a message,—ay, and walked
Demurely in her carpeted low rooms,
490 As if I should not, hearkening my own steps,
Misdoubt I was alive. I read her books,
Was civil to her cousin, Romney Leigh,
Gave ear to her vicar, tea to her visitors,
And heard them whisper, when I changed a cup
495 (I blushed for joy at that),—'The Italian child,
For all her blue eyes and her quiet ways,
Thrives ill in England: she is paler yet

---

[14] **Brinvilliers:** Marquise de Brinvilliers, a French woman beheaded in 1676 for poisoning her father, two brothers, and a sister. Her story was later captured by Alexandre Dumas in *Celebrated Crimes*.

Than when we came the last time; she will die.'

'Will die.' My cousin, Romney Leigh, blushed too,
500   With sudden anger, and approaching me
Said low between his teeth, 'You're wicked now?
You wish to die and leave the world a-dusk
For others, with your naughty light blown out?'
I looked into his face defyingly;
505   He might have known that, being what I was,
'Twas natural to like to get away
As far as dead folk can: and then indeed
Some people make no trouble when they die.
He turned and went abruptly, slammed the door,
510   And shut his dog out.
                                    Romney, Romney Leigh.
I have not named my cousin hitherto,
And yet I used him as a sort of friend;
My elder by few years, but cold and shy
And absent . . . tender, when he thought of it,
515   Which scarcely was imperative, grave betimes,
As well as early master of Leigh Hall,
Whereof the nightmare sat upon his youth,
Repressing all its seasonable delights,
And agonising with a ghastly sense
520   Of universal hideous want and wrong
To incriminate possession. When he came
From college to the country, very oft
He crossed the hill on visits to my aunt,
With gifts of blue grapes from the hothouses,
525   A book in one hand,—mere statistics (if
I chanced to lift the cover), count of all
The goats whose beards grow sprouting down toward hell
Against God's separative judgment-hour.
And she, she almost loved him,—even allowed
530   That sometimes he should seem to sigh my way;
It made him easier to be pitiful,
And sighing was his gift. So, undisturbed,
At whiles she let him shut my music up
And push my needles down, and lead me out
535   To see in that south angle of the house
The figs grow black as if by a Tuscan rock,
On some light pretext. She would turn her head
At other moments, go to fetch a thing,
And leave me breath enough to speak with him,
540   For his sake; it was simple.
                                    Sometimes too

He would have saved me utterly, it seemed,
He stood and looked so.
                Once, he stood so near,
He dropped a sudden hand upon my head
Bent down on woman's work, as soft as rain—
545   But then I rose and shook it off as fire,
The stranger's touch that took my father's place
Yet dared seem soft.
              I used him for a friend
Before I ever knew him for a friend.
'Twas better, 'twas worse also, afterward:
550   We came so close, we saw our differences
Too intimately. Always Romney Leigh
Was looking for the worms, I for the gods.
A godlike nature his; the gods look down,
Incurious of themselves; and certainly
555   'Tis well I should remember, how, those days,
I was a worm too, and he looked on me.

A little by his act perhaps, yet more
By something in me, surely not my will,
I did not die. But slowly, as one in swoon,
560   To whom life creeps back in the form of death,
With a sense of separation, a blind pain
Of blank obstruction, and a roar i' the ears
Of visionary chariots which retreat
As earth grows clearer . . . slowly, by degrees;
565   I woke, rose up . . . where was I? in the world;
For uses therefore I must count worth while.

ALFRED, LORD TENNYSON (1809–1892)

Ulysses[1] (1842)

It little profits that an idle king,
By this still hearth, among these barren crags,
Matched with an agèd wife, I mete and dole
Unequal laws unto a savage race,
5   That hoard, and sleep, and feed, and know not me.

---

[1] Based on the figure of Ulysses in Dante's *Inferno* 26, Tennyson's Ulysses has felt the adventure and anxiety of war and is restless in his domestic life in Ithaca. Tennyson wrote *Ulysses* after the death of his friend, the English poet Arthur Hallam.

I cannot rest from travel: I will drink
Life to the lees: all times I have enjoyed
Greatly, have suffered greatly, both with those
That loved me, and alone; on shore, and when
10   Through scudding drifts the rainy Hyades[2]
Vext the dim sea: I am become a name;
For always roaming with a hungry heart
Much have I seen and known; cities of men
And manners, climates, councils, governments,
15   Myself not least, but honoured of them all;
And drunk delight of battle with my peers,
Far on the ringing plains of windy Troy.

I am a part of all that I have met;
Yet all experience is an arch wherethrough
20   Gleams that untravelled world, whose margin fades
For ever and for ever when I move.
How dull it is to pause, to make an end,
To rust unburnished, not to shine in use!
As though to breathe were life. Life piled on life
25   Were all too little, and of one to me
Little remains: but every hour is saved
From that eternal silence, something more,
A bringer of new things; and vile it were
For some three suns to store and hoard myself,
30   And this gray spirit yearning in desire
To follow knowledge like a sinking star,
Beyond the utmost bound of human thought.

This is my son, mine own Telemachus,[3]
To whom I leave the sceptre and the isle—
35   Well-loved of me, discerning to fulfil
This labour, by slow prudence to make mild
A rugged people, and through soft degrees
Subdue them to the useful and the good.
Most blameless is he, centred in the sphere
40   Of common duties, decent not to fail
In offices of tenderness, and pay
Meet adoration to my household gods,
When I am gone. He works his work, I mine.

---

[2] **Hyades:** V-shaped cluster of stars in the constellation Taurus that supposedly foretold the coming of rain if they rose with the sun.
[3] **Telemachus:** In Homer's *Odyssey*, the son of Odysseus and Penelope.

	There lies the port; the vessel puffs her sail:
45	There gloom the dark broad seas. My mariners,
	Souls that have toiled, and wrought, and thought with me—
	That ever with a frolic welcome took
	The thunder and the sunshine, and opposed
	Free hearts, free foreheads—you and I are old;
50	Old age hath yet his honour and his toil;
	Death closes all: but something ere the end,
	Some work of noble note, may yet be done,
	Not unbecoming men that strove with Gods.
	The lights begin to twinkle from the rocks:
55	The long day wanes: the slow moon climbs: the deep
	Moans round with many voices. Come, my friends,
	'Tis not too late to seek a newer world.
	Push off, and sitting well in order smite
	The sounding furrows; for my purpose holds
60	To sail beyond the sunset, and the baths
	Of all the western stars, until I die.
	It may be that the gulfs will wash us down:
	It may be we shall touch the Happy Isles,[4]
	And see the great Achilles, whom we knew.
65	Though much is taken, much abides; and though
	We are not now that strength which in old days
	Moved earth and heaven; that which we are, we are;
	One equal temper of heroic hearts,
	Made weak by time and fate, but strong in will
70	To strive, to seek, to find, and not to yield.

ROBERT BROWNING (1812–1889)

Fra Lippo Lippi[1] (1855 pub.)

	I am poor brother Lippo, by your leave!
	You need not clap your torches to my face.
	Zooks, what's to blame? you think you see a monk!
	What, 'tis past midnight, and you go the rounds,
5	And here you catch me at an alley's end

---

[4] **the Happy Isles:** The Happy Isles, or Elysium, were the destination for those favored by the gods (such as Achilles) after death. In mythology, Elysium was located beyond the western edge of the known world.

[1] **Fra Lippo Lippi:** Although Browning would have been familiar with Fra Filippo di Tommaso Lippi's (1406–1469) paintings from his time in Florence, Browning uses Vasari's account of Lippo's life from *Lives of the Most Eminent Painters, Sculptors, and Architects*.

Where sportive ladies leave their doors ajar?
The Carmine's my cloister:[2] hunt it up,
Do—harry out, if you must show your zeal,
Whatever rat, there, haps on his wrong hole,
10 And nip each softling of a wee white mouse,
Weke, weke, that's crept to keep him company!
Aha, you know your betters! Then, you'll take
Your hand away that's fiddling on my throat,
And please to know me likewise. Who am I?
15 Why, one, sir, who is lodging with a friend
Three streets off—he's a certain . . . how d'ye call?
Master—a . . . Cosimo of the Medici,[3]
I' the house that caps the corner. Boh! you were best!
Remember and tell me, the day you're hanged,
20 How you affected such a gullet's-gripe!°   grip on my throat
But you, sir, it concerns you that your knaves
Pick up a manner nor discredit you:
Zooks, are we pilchards,° that they sweep the streets   fish
And count fair prize what comes into their net?
25 He's Judas to a tittle, that man is!
Just such a face! Why, sir, you make amends.
Lord, I'm not angry! Bid your hangdogs go
Drink out this quarter-florin to the health
Of the munificent House that harbors me
30 (And many more beside, lads! more beside!)
And all's come square again. I'd like his face—
His, elbowing on his comrade in the door
With the pike and lantern—for the slave that holds
John Baptist's head a-dangle by the hair
35 With one hand ("Look you, now," as who should say)
And his weapon in the other, yet unwiped!
It's not your chance to have a bit of chalk,
A wood-coal or the like? or you should see!
Yes, I'm the painter, since you style me so.
40 What, brother Lippo's doings, up and down,
You know them and they take you? like enough!
I saw the proper twinkle in your eye—
'Tell you, I liked your looks at very first.
Let's sit and set things straight now, hip to haunch.
45 Here's spring come, and the nights one makes up bands

---

[2] **The Carmine's my cloister:** Fra Lippo entered the Carmelite monestary while still a boy, giving up his monastic vows in 1421 at the age of 15.
[3] **Cosimo of the Medici:** Cosimo de'Medici (1389–1464), ruler of Florence, supporter of the arts, and Fra Lippo's prosperous patron.

To roam the town and sing out carnival,
And I've been three weeks shut within my mew,°   quarters
A-painting for the great man, saints and saints
And saints again. I could not paint all night—
50   Ouf! I leaned out of window for fresh air.
There came a hurry of feet and little feet,
A sweep of lute-strings, laughs, and whiffs of song—
Flower o' the broom,
Take away love, and our earth is a tomb!
55   *Flower o' the quince,*
I let Lisa go, and what good in life since?
Flower o' the thyme—and so on. Round they went.
Scarce had they turned the corner when a titter
Like the skipping of rabbits by moonlight—three slim shapes,
60   And a face that looked up . . . zooks, sir, flesh and blood,
That's all I'm made of! Into shreds it went,
Curtain and counterpane and coverlet,
All the bed-furniture—a dozen knots,
There was a ladder! Down I let myself,
65   Hands and feet, scrambling somehow, and so dropped,
And after them. I came up with the fun
Hard by Saint Laurence,[4] hail fellow, well met—
Flower o' the rose,
If I've been merry, what matter who knows?
70   And so as I was stealing back again
To get to bed and have a bit of sleep
Ere I rise up to-morrow and go work
On Jerome[5] knocking at his poor old breast
With his great round stone to subdue the flesh,
75   You snap me of the sudden. Ah, I see!
Though your eye twinkles still, you shake your head—
Mine's shaved—a monk, you say—the sting's in that!
If Master Cosimo announced himself,
Mum's the word naturally; but a monk!
80   Come, what am I a beast for? tell us, now!
I was a baby when my mother died
And father died and left me in the street.
I starved there, God knows how, a year or two
On fig-skins, melon-parings, rinds and shucks,
85   Refuse and rubbish. One fine frosty day,
My stomach being empty as your hat,

---

[4] **Saint Laurence:** The church of San Lorenzo, close to Fra Lippo's quarters and now famous for the tombs of the Medici.
[5] **Jerome:** Church Father known for translating the Bible into Latin and living a life of extreme asceticism.

The wind doubled me up and down I went.
Old Aunt Lapaccia trussed me with one hand,
(Its fellow was a stinger as I knew)
90 And so along the wall, over the bridge,
By the straight cut to the convent. Six words there,
While I stood munching my first bread that month:
"So, boy, you're minded," quoth the good fat father
Wiping his own mouth, 't was refection-time—
95 "To quit this very miserable world?
"Will you renounce" . . . "the mouthful of bread?" thought I;
By no means! Brief, they made a monk of me;
I did renounce the world, its pride and greed,
Palace, farm, villa, shop and banking-house,
100 Trash, such as these poor devils of Medici
Have given their hearts to—all at eight years old.
Well, sir, I found in time, you may be sure,
'T was not for nothing—the good bellyful;
The warm serge and the rope that goes all round,
105 And day-long blessed idleness beside!
"Let's see what the urchin's fit for"—that came next.
Not overmuch their way, I must confess.
Such a to-do! They tried me with their books:
Lord, they'd have taught me Latin in pure waste!
110 *Flower o' the clove,*
All the Latin I construe is, "amo" I love!
But, mind you, when a boy starves in the streets
Eight years together, as my fortune was,
Watching folk's faces to know who will fling
115 The bit of half-stripped grape-bunch he desires,
And who will curse or kick him for his pains—
Which gentleman processional and fine,
Holding a candle to the Sacrament,
Will wink and let him lift a plate and catch
120 The droppings of the wax to sell again,
Or holla for the Eight [6] and have him whipped—
How say I? nay, which dog bites, which lets drop
His bone from the heap of offal in the street—
Why, soul and sense of him grow sharp alike,
125 He learns the look of things, and none the less
For admonition from the hunger-pinch.
I had a store of such remarks, be sure,
Which, after I found leisure, turned to use.
I drew men's faces on my copy-books,

---

[6] **the Eight:** Magistrates of Florence.

130   Scrawled them within the antiphonary's[7] marge,°   margins
       Joined legs and arms to the long music-notes,
       Found eyes and nose and chin for A's and B's,
       And made a string of pictures of the world
       Betwixt the ins and outs of verb and noun,
135   On the wall, the bench, the door. The monks looked black.
       "Nay," quoth the Prior, "turn him out, d'ye say?
       "In no wise. Lose a crow and catch a lark.
       "What if at last we get our man of parts,
       "We Carmelites, like those Camaldolese
140   "And Preaching Friars,[8] to do our church up fine
       "And put the front on it that ought to be!"
       And hereupon he bade me daub away.
       Thank you! my head being crammed, the walls a blank,
       Never was such prompt disemburdening.
145   First, every sort of monk, the black and white,
       I drew them, fat and lean: then, folk at church,
       From good old gossips waiting to confess
       Their cribs° of barrel-droppings, candle-ends—   petty thefts
       To the breathless fellow at the altar-foot,
150   Fresh from his murder, safe and sitting there
       With the little children round him in a row
       Of admiration, half for his beard and half
       For that white anger of his victim's son
       Shaking a fist at him with one fierce arm,
155   Signing himself with the other because of Christ
       (Whose sad face on the cross sees only this
       After the passion of a thousand years)
       Till some poor girl, her apron o'er her head,
       (Which the intense eyes looked through) came at eve
160   On tiptoe, said a word, dropped in a loaf,
       Her pair of earrings and a bunch of flowers
       (The brute took growling), prayed, and so was gone.
       I painted all, then cried " 'Tis ask and have;
       "Choose, for more's ready!"—laid the ladder flat,
165   And showed my covered bit of cloister-wall.
       The monks closed in a circle and praised loud
       Till checked, taught what to see and not to see,
       Being simple bodies— "That's the very man!
       "Look at the boy who stoops to pat the dog!
170   "That woman's like the Prior's niece who comes

---

[7] **antiphonary's:** Book of responses to the chanted liturgy.
[8] **Camaldolese . . . Friars:** The Camaldolese belonged to a religious order in Camaldoli, and the Preaching Friars refers to the Dominican order.

"To care about his asthma: it's the life!"
But there my triumph's straw-fire flared and funked;°   ended in smoke
Their betters took their turn to see and say:
The Prior and the learned pulled a face
175 And stopped all that in no time. "How? what's here?
"Quite from the mark of painting, bless us all!
"Faces, arms, legs and bodies like the true
"As much as pea and pea! it's devil's-game!
"Your business is not to catch men with show,
180 "With homage to the perishable clay,
"But lift them over it, ignore it all,
"Make them forget there's such a thing as flesh.
"Your business is to paint the souls of men—
"Man's soul, and it's a fire, smoke . . . no, it's not . . .
185 "It's vapor done up like a new-born babe—
"(In that shape when you die it leaves your mouth)
"It's . . . well, what matters talking, it's the soul!
"Give us no more of body than shows soul!
"Here's Giotto,[9] with his Saint a-praising God,
190 "That sets us praising—why not stop with him?
"Why put all thoughts of praise out of our head
"With wonder at lines, colors, and what not?
"Paint the soul, never mind the legs and arms!
"Rub all out, try at it a second time.
195 "Oh, that white smallish female with the breasts,
"She's just my niece . . . Herodias,[10] I would say—
"Who went and danced and got men's heads cut off!
"Have it all out!" Now, is this sense, I ask?
A fine way to paint soul, by painting body
200 So ill, the eye can't stop there, must go further
And can't fare worse! Thus, yellow does for white
When what you put for yellow's simply black,
And any sort of meaning looks intense
When all beside itself means and looks nought.
205 Why can't a painter lift each foot in turn,
Left foot and right foot, go a double step,
Make his flesh liker and his soul more like,
Both in their order? Take the prettiest face,
The Prior's niece . . . patron-saint—is it so pretty
210 You can't discover if it means hope, fear,
Sorrow or joy? won't beauty go with these?
Suppose I've made her eyes all right and blue,

---

[9] **Giotto:** Giotto di Bondone (1267–1337), Florentine painter.
[10] **Herodias:** King Herod's sister-in-law, who demanded that John the Baptist be jailed. Her daughter
Salome asked for John's head on a platter.

Can't I take breath and try to add life's flash,
And then add soul and heighten them threefold?
215   Or say there's beauty with no soul at all—
(I never saw it—put the case the same—)
If you get simple beauty and nought else,
You get about the best thing God invents:
That's somewhat: and you'll find the soul you have missed,
220   Within yourself, when you return him thanks.
"Rub all out!" Well, well, there's my life, in short,
And so the thing has gone on ever since.
I'm grown a man no doubt, I've broken bounds:
You should not take a fellow eight years old
225   And make him swear to never kiss the girls.
I'm my own master, paint now as I please—
Having a friend, you see, in the Corner-house!
Lord, it's fast holding by the rings in front—
Those great rings serve more purposes than just
230   To plant a flag in, or tie up a horse!
And yet the old schooling sticks, the old grave eyes
Are peeping o'er my shoulder as I work,
The heads shake still— "It's art's decline, my son!
"You're not of the true painters, great and old;
235   "Brother Angelico's the man, you'll find;
"Brother Lorenzo[11] stands his single peer:
"Fag on at flesh, you'll never make the third!"
Flower o' the pine,
You keep your mistr . . . manners, and I'll stick to mine!
240   I'm not the third, then: bless us, they must know!
Don't you think they're the likeliest to know,
They with their Latin? So, I swallow my rage,
Clench my teeth, suck my lips in tight, and paint
To please them—sometimes do and sometimes don't;
245   For, doing most, there's pretty sure to come
A turn, some warm eve finds me at my saints—
A laugh, a cry, the business of the world—
(Flower o' the peach,
Death for us all, and his own life for each!)
250   And my whole soul revolves, the cup runs over,
The world and life's too big to pass for a dream,
And I do these wild things in sheer despite,
And play the fooleries you catch me at,
In pure rage! The old mill-horse, out at grass
255   After hard years, throws up his stiff heels so,

---

[11] **Brother Angelico . . . Lorenzo:** Fra Angelico (1387–1455) and Fra Lorenzo Monaco (1370–1425).

Although the miller does not preach to him
The only good of grass is to make chaff.
What would men have? Do they like grass or no—
May they or mayn't they? all I want's the thing
260   Settled for ever one way. As it is,
You tell too many lies and hurt yourself:
You don't like what you only like too much,
You do like what, if given you at your word,
You find abundantly detestable.
265   For me, I think I speak as I was taught;
I always see the garden and God there
A-making man's wife: and, my lesson learned,
The value and significance of flesh,
I can't unlearn ten minutes afterwards.

270   You understand me: I'm a beast, I know.
But see, now—why, I see as certainly
As that the morning-star's about to shine,
What will hap some day. We've a youngster here
Comes to our convent, studies what do,
275   Slouches and stares and lets no atom drop:
His name is Guidi [12]—he'll not mind the monks—
They call him Hulking Tom, he lets them talk—
He picks my practice up—he'll paint apace,
I hope so—though I never live so long,
280   I know what's sure to follow. You be judge!
You speak no Latin more than I, belike;
However, you're my man, you've seen the world
—The beauty and the wonder and the power,
The shapes of things, their colors, lights and shades,
285   Changes, surprises—and God made it all!
—For what? Do you feel thankful, ay or no,
For this fair town's face, yonder river's line,
The mountain round it and the sky above,
Much more the figures of man, woman, child,
290   These are the frame to? What's it all about?
To be passed over, despised? or dwelt upon,
Wondered at? oh, this last of course!—you say.
But why not do as well as say, paint these
Just as they are, careless what comes of it?
295   God's works—paint anyone, and count it crime
To let a truth slip. Don't object, "His works

---

[12] **Guidi:** Tommaso Guidi (1401–1428) painted a set of well-known frescoes in Florence's Santa Maria del Carmine, and was likely an influence on Fra Lippo, not his pupil as is suggested here.

"Are here already; nature is complete:
"Suppose you reproduce her (which you can't)
"There's no advantage! you must beat her, then."
300 For, don't you mark? we're made so that we love
First when we see them painted, things we have passed
Perhaps a hundred times nor cared to see,
And so they are better, painted—better to us,
Which is the same thing. Art was given for that;
305 God uses us to help each other so,
Lending our minds out. Have you noticed, now,
Your cullion's° hanging face? A bit of chalk,   scoundrel's
And trust me but you should, though! How much more,
If I drew higher things with the same truth!
310 That were to take the Prior's pulpit-place,
Interpret God to all of you! Oh, oh,
It makes me mad to see what men shall do
And we in our graves! This world's no blot for us,
Nor blank; it means intensely, and means good:
315 To find its meaning is my meat and drink.
"Ay, but you don't so instigate to prayer!"
Strikes in the Prior: "when your meaning's plain
"It does not say to folk—remember matins,
"Or, mind you fast next Friday!" Why, for this
320 What need of art at all? A skull and bones,
Two bits of stick nailed crosswise, or, what's best,
A bell to chime the hour with, does as well.
I painted a Saint Laurence six months since
At Prato,[13] splashed the fresco in fine style:
325 "How looks my painting, now the scaffold's down?"
I ask a brother: "Hugely," he returns—
"Already not one phiz° of your three slaves   face
"Who turn the Deacon off his toasted side,
"But's scratched and prodded to our heart's content,
330 "The pious people have so eased their own
"With coming to say prayers there in a rage:
"We get on fast to see the bricks beneath.
"Expect another job this time next year,
"For pity and religion grow i' the crowd—
335 "Your painting serves its purpose!" Hang the fools!

     —That is—you'll not mistake an idle word
Spoke in a huff by a poor monk, God wot,
Tasting the air this spicy night which turns

---

[13] **Prato:** Small town near Florence.

The unaccustomed head like Chianti wine!
340 Oh, the church knows! don't misreport me, now!
It's natural a poor monk out of bounds
Should have his apt word to excuse himself:
And hearken how I plot to make amends.
I have bethought me: I shall paint a piece
345 . . . There's for you! Give me six months, then go, see
Something in Sant' Ambrogio's![14] Bless the nuns!
They want a cast o' my office. I shall paint
God in the midst, Madonna and her babe,
Ringed by a bowery flowery angel-brood,
350 Lilies and vestments and white faces, sweet
As puff on puff of grated orris-root
When ladies crowd to Church at midsummer.
And then i' the front, of course a saint or two—
Saint John,[15] because he saves the Florentines,
355 Saint Ambrose, who puts down in black and white
The convent's friends and gives them a long day,
And Job, I must have him there past mistake,
The man of Uz (and Us without the z,
Painters who need his patience). Well, all these
360 Secured at their devotion, up shall come
Out of a corner when you least expect,
As one by a dark stair into a great light,
Music and talking, who but Lippo! I!
Mazed, motionless and moonstruck—I'm the man!
365 Back I shrink—what is this I see and hear?
I, caught up with my monk's-things by mistake,
My old serge gown and rope that goes all round,
I, in this presence, this pure company!
Where's a hole, where's a corner for escape?
370 Then steps a sweet angelic slip of a thing
Forward puts out a soft palm—"Not so fast!"
—Addresses the celestial presence, "nay—
"He made you and devised you, after all,
"Though he's none of you! Could Saint John there draw—
375 "His camel-hair make up a painting-brush?
"We come to brother Lippo for all that,
"*Iste perfecit opus!*"[16] So, all smile—
I shuffle sideways with my blushing face

---

[14] **Something in Sant' Ambrogio's:** Fra Lippo's masterpiece, the *Coronation of the Virgin*, was painted for the altar of Sant' Ambrogio in 1447.
[15] **Saint John:** John the Baptist is the patron saint of Florence.
[16] *Iste perfecit opus!*: Latin: "This man accomplished the work."

Under the cover of a hundred wings
380   Thrown like a spread of kirtles° when you're gay   gowns
And play hot cockles,[17] all the doors being shut,
Till, wholly unexpected, in there pops
The hothead husband! Thus I scuttle off
To some safe bench behind, not letting go
385   The palm of her, the little lily thing
That spoke the good word for me in the nick,
Like the Prior's niece . . . Saint Lucy, I would say.
And so all's saved for me, and for the church
A pretty picture gained. Go, six months hence!
390   Your hand, sir, and good-bye: no lights, no lights!
The street's hushed, and I know my own way back,
Don't fear me! there's the gray beginning. Zooks!

ROBERT BROWNING (1812–1889)

My Last Duchess (1842)
Ferrara[1]

That's my last Duchess painted on the wall,
Looking as if she were alive. I call
That piece a wonder, now: Frà Pandolf's[2] hands
Worked busily a day, and there she stands.
5   Will't please you sit and look at her? I said
'Frà Pandolf' by design, for never read
Strangers like you that pictured countenance,
The depth and passion of its earnest glance,
But to myself they turned (since none puts by
10   The curtain I have drawn for you, but I)
And seemed as they would ask me, if they durst,
How such a glance came there; so, not the first
Are you to turn and ask thus. Sir, 't was not
Her husband's presence only, called that spot
15   Of joy into the Duchess' cheek: perhaps
Frà Pandolf chanced to say 'Her mantle laps

---

[17] **hot cockles:** Game in which an individual is blindfolded and must deduce who has hit him in the dark.
[1] **Ferrara:** Browning likely refers to Alfonso II, the fifth duke of northern Italy's Ferrara from 1559 to 1597. Alfonso married his first wife, and then abandoned her for a two-year period before seeking another mistress only three days after their wedding.
[2] **Frà Pandolf's:** A painter formulated by Browning's imagination, not a figure from actual history.

'Over my lady's wrist too much,' or 'Paint
'Must never hope to reproduce the faint
'Half-flush that dies along her throat:' such stuff
20   Was courtesy, she thought, and cause enough
For calling up that spot of joy. She had
A heart—how shall I say?—too soon made glad,
Too easily impressed; she liked whate'er
She looked on, and her looks went everywhere.
25   Sir, 't was all one! My favour³ at her breast,
The dropping of the daylight in the West,
The bough of cherries some officious fool
Broke in the orchard for her, the white mule
She rode with round the terrace—all and each
30   Would draw from her alike the approving speech,
Or blush, at least. She thanked men,—good! but thanked
Somehow—I know not how—as if she ranked
My gift of a nine-hundred-years-old name
With anybody's gift. Who'd stoop to blame
35   This sort of trifling? Even had you skill
In speech—(which I have not)—to make your will
Quite clear to such an one, and say, 'Just this
'Or that in you disgusts me; here you miss,
'Or there exceed the mark'—and if she let
40   Herself be lessoned⁴ so, nor plainly set
Her wits to yours, forsooth,° and made excuse,   *in truth*
—E'en then would be some stooping; and I choose
Never to stoop. Oh sir, she smiled, no doubt,
Whene'er I passed her; but who passed without
45   Much the same smile? This grew; I gave commands;
Then all smiles stopped together. There she stands
As if alive. Will't please you rise? We'll meet
The company below, then. I repeat,
The Count your master's known munificence
50   Is ample warrant that no just pretence
Of mine for dowry will be disallowed;
Though his fair daughter's self, as I avowed
At starting, is my object. Nay, we'll go
Together down, sir. Notice Neptune, though,
55   Taming a sea-horse, thought a rarity,
Which Claus of Innsbruck⁵ cast in bronze for me!

---

³ **My favour:** A love-gift, such as a ribbon. Also, a sexual innuendo.
⁴ **lessoned:** Instructed, but also a pun on "lessened."
⁵ **Neptune . . . Innsbruck:** Neptune was the Roman god of the sea. Claus of Innsbruck, again, was a
figure from Browning's imagination.

WILLIAM BUTLER YEATS (1865–1939)

An Irish Airman Foresees His Death[1]   (1919)

I know that I shall meet my fate
Somewhere among the clouds above;
Those that I fight I do not hate,
Those that I guard I do not love;
5   My country is Kiltartan Cross,[2]
My countrymen Kiltartan's poor,
No likely end could bring them loss
Or leave them happier than before.
Nor law, nor duty bade me fight,
10   Nor public men, nor cheering crowds,
A lonely impulse of delight
Drove to this tumult in the clouds;
I balanced all, brought all to mind,
The years to come seemed waste of breath,
15   A waste of breath the years behind
In balance will this life, this death.

T. S. ELIOT (1888–1965)

The Love Song of J. Alfred Prufrock (1917)

S'io credessi che mia risposta fosse
A persona che mai tornasse al mondo,
Questa fiamma staria senza più scosse.
Ma per cio che giammai di questo fondo
Non tornò viva alcun, s'i'odo il vero,
Senza tema d'infamia ti rispondo.[1]

Let us go then, you and I,
When the evening is spread out against the sky
Like a patient etherised upon a table;

---

[1] **An Irish . . . Death:** The airman in this poem is Major Robert Gregory, who was killed in combat in Italy in 1918.
[2] **Kiltartan Cross:** Near the Gregory estate, Kiltartan Cross is a village in County Galway, western Ireland.
[1] **S'io credessi . . . rispondo:** From Dante's *Inferno* 27: "If I thought my answer were given / to anyone who would ever return to the world, / this flame would stand still without moving any further. / But since never from this abyss / has anyone ever returned alive, if what I hear is true, / without fear of infamy I answer you." The quotation belongs to Guido da Montefeltro, a false counselor who encounters Dante and Virgil as a spirit housed within a flame.

Let us go, through certain half-deserted streets,
5 The muttering retreats
Of restless nights in one-night cheap hotels
And sawdust restaurants with oyster-shells:
Streets that follow like a tedious argument
Of insidious intent
10 To lead you to an overwhelming question . . .
Oh, do not ask, 'What is it?'
Let us go and make our visit.

    In the room the women come and go
Talking of Michelangelo.

15   The yellow fog that rubs its back upon the window-panes,
The yellow smoke that rubs its muzzle on the window-panes,
Licked its tongue into the corners of the evening,
Lingered upon the pools that stand in drains,
Let fall upon its back the soot that falls from chimneys,
20 Slipped by the terrace, made a sudden leap,
And seeing that it was a soft October night,
Curled once about the house, and fell asleep.

    And indeed there will be time
For the yellow smoke that slides along the street
25 Rubbing its back upon the window-panes;
There will be time, there will be time
To prepare a face to meet the faces that you meet;
There will be time to murder and create,
And time for all the works and days[2] of hands
30 That lift and drop a question on your plate;
Time for you and time for me,
And time yet for a hundred indecisions,
And for a hundred visions and revisions,
Before the taking of a toast and tea.

35   In the room the women come and go
Talking of Michelangelo.

    And indeed there will be time
To wonder, 'Do I dare?' and, 'Do I dare?'
Time to turn back and descend the stair,
40 With a bald spot in the middle of my hair—

---

[2] **works and days:** Here Eliot makes reference to the Greek poet Hesoid (eighth century, B.C.), whose poem *Works and Days* depicted the domestic life of that era.

(They will say: 'How his hair is growing thin!')
My morning coat, my collar mounting firmly to the chin,
My necktie rich and modest, but asserted by a simple pin—
(They will say: 'But how his arms and legs are thin!')
45 Do I dare
Disturb the universe?
In a minute there is time
For decisions and revisions which a minute will reverse.

        For I have known them all already, known them all—
50 Have known the evenings, mornings, afternoons,
I have measured out my life with coffee spoons;
I know the voices dying with a dying fall
Beneath the music from a farther room.
        So how should I presume?

55   And I have known the eyes already, known them all—
The eyes that fix you in a formulated phrase,
And when I am formulated, sprawling on a pin,
When I am pinned and wriggling on the wall,
Then how should I begin
60 To spit out all the butt-ends of my days and ways?
        And how should I presume?

        And I have known the arms already, known them all—
Arms that are braceleted and white and bare
(But in the lamplight, downed with light brown hair!)
65 Is it perfume from a dress
That makes me so digress?
Arms that lie along a table, or wrap about a shawl.
        And should I then presume?
        And how should I begin?

                    . . . . .

70   Shall I say, I have gone at dusk through narrow streets
And watched the smoke that rises from the pipes
Of lonely men in shirt-sleeves, leaning out of windows? . . .

        I should have been a pair of ragged claws
Scuttling across the floors of silent seas.

                    . . . . .

75   And the afternoon, the evening, sleeps so peacefully!
Smoothed by long fingers,
Asleep . . . tired . . . or it malingers,

Stretched on the floor, here beside you and me.
Should I, after tea and cakes and ices,
80   Have the strength to force the moment to its crisis?
But though I have wept and fasted, wept and prayed,
Though I have seen my head (grown slightly bald) brought in upon
            a platter,[3]
I am no prophet—and here's no great matter;
I have seen the moment of my greatness flicker,
85   And I have seen the eternal Footman hold my coat, and snicker,
And in short, I was afraid.

      And would it have been worth it, after all,
After the cups, the marmalade, the tea,
Among the porcelain, among some talk of you and me,
90   Would it have been worth while,
To have bitten off the matter with a smile,
To have squeezed the universe into a ball
To roll it toward some overwhelming question,
To say: 'I am Lazarus, come from the dead,
95   Come back to tell you all, I shall tell you all'—
If one, settling a pillow by her head,
        Should say: 'That is not what I meant at all.
        That is not it, at all.'

      And would it have been worth it, after all,
100   Would it have been worth while,
After the sunsets and the dooryards and the sprinkled streets,
After the novels, after the teacups, after the skirts that trail along
            the floor—
And this, and so much more?—
It is impossible to say just what I mean!
105   But as if a magic lantern threw the nerves in patterns on a screen:
Would it have been worth while
If one, settling a pillow or throwing off a shawl,
And turning toward the window, should say:
        'That is not it at all.
110   That is not what I meant, at all.'

                  .   .   .   .   .

      No! I am not Prince Hamlet, nor was meant to be;
Am an attendant lord, one that will do

---

[3] **my head . . . platter:** King Herod presented the head of John the Baptist to Salome in Matthew 14.

To swell a progress,[4] start a scene or two,
Advise the prince; no doubt, an easy tool,
115   Deferential, glad to be of use,
Politic, cautious, and meticulous;
Full of high sentence, but a bit obtuse;
At times, indeed, almost ridiculous—
Almost, at times, the Fool.

120   I grow old . . . I grow old . . .
I shall wear the bottoms of my trousers rolled.

Shall I part my hair behind? Do I dare to eat a peach?
I shall wear white flannel trousers, and walk upon the beach.
I have heard the mermaids singing, each to each.

125   I do not think that they will sing to me.

I have seen them riding seaward on the waves
Combing the white hair of the waves blown back
When the wind blows the water white and black.

We have lingered in the chambers of the sea
130   By sea-girls wreathed with seaweed red and brown
Till human voices wake us, and we drown.

ROBERT GRAVES (1895–1985)

Welsh Incident (1929)

'But that was nothing to what things came out
From the sea-caves of Criccieth[1] yonder.'
'What were they? Mermaids? dragons? ghosts?'
'Nothing at all of any things like that.'
5   'What where they, then?'
                          'All sorts of queer things,
Things never seen or heard or written about,
Very strange, un-Welsh, utterly peculiar
Things. Oh, solid enough they seemed to touch,
Had anyone dared it. Marvellous creation,

---

[4] **progress:** The procession of a royal prince through the English countryside with his accompanying convoy of servants and possessions.
[1] **Criccieth:** Town on the Llyn Peninsula in Northwest Wales.

10   All various shapes and sizes, and no sizes,
     All new, each perfectly unlike his neighbour,
     Though all came moving slowly out together.'
     'Describe just one of them.'
                    'I am unable.'
     'What were their colours?'
                    'Mostly nameless colours,

15   Colours you'd like to see; but one was puce°   *purplish brown*
     Or perhaps more like crimson, but not purplish.
     Some had no colour.'
               'Tell me, had they legs?'
     'Not a leg nor foot among them that I saw.'
     'But did these things come out in any order?

20   What o'clock was it? What was the day of the week?
     Who else was present? How was the weather?'
     'I was coming to that. It was half-past three
     On Easter Tuesday last. The sun was shining.
     The Harlech Silver Band [2] played *Marchog Jesu*

25   On thirty-seven shimmering instruments,
     Collecting for Carnarvon's (Fever) Hospital Fund.
     The populations of Pwllheli, Criccieth,
     Portmadoc, Borth, Tremadoc, Penrhyndeudraeth,[3]
     Were all assembled. Criccieth's mayor addressed them

30   First in good Welsh and then in fluent English,
     Twisting his fingers in his chain of office,
     Welcoming the things. They came out on the sand,
     Not keeping time to the band, moving seaward
     Silently at a snail's pace. But at last

35   The most odd, indescribable thing of all,
     Which hardly one man there could see for wonder
     Did something recognizably a something.'
     'Well, what?'
               'It made a noise.'
                     'A frightening noise?'
     'No, no.'
             'A musical noise? A noise of scuffling?'

40   'No, but a very loud, respectable noise—
     Like groaning to oneself on Sunday morning
     In Chapel, close before the second psalm.'
     'What did the mayor do?'
                'I was coming to that.'

---

[2] **Harlech Silver Band:** Harlech, a small Welsh village overlooking the Llyn Peninsula, is home to a world-famous brass band.
[3] **Pwllheli . . . Penrhyndeudraeth:** All towns near the Llyn Peninsula in Wales.

LANGSTON HUGHES (1902–1967)

The Black Clown   (1932)

A dramatic monologue to be spoken by a pure-blooded Negro in the white suit and hat of a clown, to the music of a piano, or an orchestra.

THE MOOD	THE POEM	
A gay and	You laugh	
low-down blues.	Because I'm poor and black and funny—	
Comic entrance	Not the same as you—	
like the clowns	Because my mind is dull	
in the circus.	And dice instead of books will do	5
Humorous	For me to play with	
defiance.	When the day is through.	
Melancholy		
jazz. Then	I am the fool of the whole world.	
defiance again	Laugh and push me down.	
followed by	Only in song and laughter	10
loud joy.	I rise again—a black clown.	
A burst of	Strike up the music.	
music. Strutting	Let it be gay.	
and dancing.	Only in joy	
Then sudden	Can a clown have his day.	15
sadness again.		
Back bent as	Three hundred years	
in the fields.	In the cotton and the cane,	
The slow step.	Plowing and reaping	
The bowed head.	With no gain—	
"Nobody knows	Empty handed as I began.	20
de trouble I've		
had."	A slave—under the whip,	
Flinching	Beaten and sore.	
under the whip.	God! Give me laughter	
The spiritual	That I can stand more.	
syncopated.		
Determined to	God! Give me the spotted	25
laugh.	Garments of a clown	
A bugle call.	So that the pain and the shame	
Gay, martial	Will not pull me down.	
music. Walking		
proudly, almost	Freedom!	
prancing.	Abe Lincoln done set me free—	30
But gradually	One little moment	
subdued to a	To dance with glee.	

*slow, heavy
pace. "Some-
times I feel
like a mother-
less chile."
Turning futilely
from one side
to the other.
But now a harsh
and bitter note
creeps into
the music.
Over-burdened.
Backing away
angrily.
Frantic
with
humiliation
and helpless-
ness.
The music
is like
a mourn-
ful tom-tom
in the dark!
But out of
sadness
it rises to
defiance
and determina-
tion. A hymn
of faith
echoes the
fighting
"Marseillaise."* [1]
*Tearing off
his clown's
suit, throwing*

Then sadness again—
No land, no house, no job,
No place to go.   35
Black—in a white world
Where cold winds blow.
The long struggle for life:
No schools, no work—
Not wanted here; not needed there—   40
Black—you can die.
Nobody will care—

Yet clinging to the ladder,
Round by round,
Trying to climb up,   45
Forever pushed down.

Day after day
White spit in my face—
Worker and clown am I
For the "civilized" race.   50

Nigger! Nigger! Nigger!
Scorn crushing me down.
Laugh at me! Laugh at me!
Just a black clown!

Laugh at me then,   55
All the world round—
From Africa to Georgia
I'm only a clown!

But no! Not forever
Like this will I be: 60
Here are my hands
That can really make me free!

Suffer and struggle.
Work, pray, and fight.
Smash my way through   65
To Manhood's true right.

Say to all foemen:
You can't keep me down!

---

[1] **Marseillaise:** The French National Anthem, adopted internationally by many left-wing political groups.

*down the hat
of a fool,
and standing
forth,
straight
and strong,
in the clothes
of a modern
man, he proclaims
himself.*

Tear off the garments
That make me a clown!   70

Rise from the bottom,
Out of the slime!
Look at the stars yonder
Calling through time!

Cry to the world   75
That all might understand:
I was once a black clown
But now—
I'm a man!

JOHN ASHBERY (1927–   )

Thoughts of a Young Girl (1957)

"It is such a beautiful day I had to write you a letter
From the tower, and to show I'm not mad:
I only slipped on the cake of soap of the air
And drowned in the bathtub of the world.
5   You were too good to cry much over me.
And now I let you go. Signed, The Dwarf."

I passed by late in the afternoon
And the smile still played about her lips
As it has for centuries. She always knows
10   How to be utterly delightful. Oh my daughter,
My sweetheart, daughter of my late employer, princess,
May you not be long on the way!

PHILIP LEVINE (1928–   )

Angel Butcher (1972)

At sun up I am up
hosing down the outdoor abattoir°   slaughterhouse
getting ready. The water
steams and hisses on the white stones
5   and the air pales to a

thin blue.
                    Today it is
Christophe. I don't see him
come up the long climb or
know he's here until I hear
10   my breathing double
and he's beside me smiling
like a young girl.
                       He asks
me the names of all
the tools and all
15   their functions, he lifts
and weighs and
balances, and runs a long
forefinger down the tongue
of each blade.
                    He asks
20   me how I came to this place and
this work, and I tell him how
I began with animals, and
he tells me how
he began with animals. We
25   talk about growing up and losing
the strange things we never
understood and settling.
                         I help
him with his robes; he
has a kind of modesty and sits
30   on the stone table with
the ends of the gown crossed
in his lap.
                 He wants to die
like a rabbit, and he wants me
to help him. I hold
35   his wrist; it's small, like
the throat of a young hen, but
cool and dry. He holds
mine and I can feel the
blood thudding in the ring
40   his fingers make.
                 He helps me, he
guides my hand at first. I can
feel my shoulders settle and
the bones take the weight, I can
feel my lungs flower as the
45   swing begins. He smiles again
with only one side of his mouth

and looks down to the
dark valley where the cities
burn. When I hit
50   him he comes apart like a
perfect puzzle or an
old flower.
                    And my legs
dance and twitch for hours.

MARGARET ATWOOD (1939–   )

At the Tourist Center in Boston   (1968)

There is my country under glass,
a white relief-
map with red dots for the cities,
reduced to the size of a wall

5   and beside it 10 blownup snapshots
one for each province,
in purple-browns and odd reds,
the green of the trees dulled;
all blues however
10   of an assertive purity.

Mountains and lakes and more lakes
(though Quebec is a restaurant and Ontario the empty
interior of the parliament buildings),
with nobody climbing the trails and hauling out
15   the fish and splashing in the water

but arrangements of grinning tourists—
look here, Saskatchewan
is a flat lake, some convenient rocks
where two children pose with a father
20   and the mother is cooking something
in immaculate slacks by a smokeless fire,
her teeth white as detergent.

Whose dream is this, I would like to know:
is this a manufactured
25   hallucination, a cynical fiction, a lure
for export only?

I seem to remember people,
at least in the cities, also slush,
machines and assorted garbage. Perhaps
30   that was my private mirage
which will just evaporate
when I go back. Or the citizens will be gone,
run off to the peculiarly-
green forests
35   to wait among the brownish mountains
for the platoons of tourists
and plan their odd red massacres.

Unsuspecting
window lady, I ask you:

40   Do you see nothing
watching you from under the water?

Was the sky ever that blue?

Who really lives there?

WANDA COLEMAN (1946–   )

African Sleeping Sickness (1990)

for Anna Halprin

even my dreams have dreams

1

four centuries of sleep they say
i've no memory
say they say they i talked quite coherently
i don't remember
5   four centuries gone

i walk eternal night/the curse of ever-dreaming

sing me a lullaby

2

my father hoists me over his shoulder, holds me
snug to him. i cannot walk

10   we move thru the sea of stars in blue
      i love my father's strength
      i love how blue the blue is
      and the coolness of stars against my face
      he sings me "my blue heaven"

                          3

15   i am tied hand and foot
      astraddle the gray county hospital bed on the basement floor
      my scream smothered in 4 × 4 adhesive
      nothing on but the too short too thin cotton gown
      above a naked saffron bulb in socket
20   nothing else in the ward but empty beds row upon row
      and barred windows

      i do not know why i'm here or who i am
      i see my wounds
      they belong to the black child

                          4

25   giant green leech-dinosaurs invade the city
      superman flies to rescue but weakened by kryptonite
      can't stop the havoc
      the slug creatures destroy the city, ooze into the Sierras/
      along my back into my spinal cord leaving a trail
30   of upper Jurassic slime

      (it gets down to skin and bones, skin/the body's last line
      of defense. when awakened the impulse to become—a
      cavernous hunger unfillable unsated

                          bones/the minimal elements
                          of survival)

35   "who am i?"
      the physician observes my return to consciousness
      the petite white man with sable hair and clark kents
      makes note. he is seated in front of a panorama
      hills and A-frames sloping to the sea

40   "who am i," i ask again
      "who do you think you are?" he asks
      "i'm not myself," i say

                          5

      the encephalopathy° of slavery—trauma to racial cortices   brain disorder
      resulting in herniated ego/loss of self

45   rupture of the socio-eco spleen and
      intellectual thrombosis

      (terminal)

      sing me rivers the anthem of blue waters the hymn of
      genesis

                              6

      lift up your voice and

50   the tympanic reverberation of orgasmic grunt
                      ejaculatio praecox[1]
      traumatized. infected. abrupt behavioral changes
                      the vomitus/love-stuff

      he watches me masturbating with the Jamaican dancer
55   whose hand is up my womb to the elbow
      and starts to cry

      the weight swells my heart/cardiopulmonary edema
      doubled in size it threatens to pop

      i ask the doctor why things are so distorted

60   "we've given you morphine
      for the pain of becoming"

                              7

      chills. sing to me fever. sing to me. myalgia.° sing to me   muscle pain
      delirium. sing to me. fluid filled lungs
      i walk eternal night

65   in the room done in soft maroon warm mahogany amber gold
      we disrobe to the dom-dom-dom a heady blues suite

      i pity the man his 4-inch penis
      then am horrified as it telescopes upward becoming a
      2-quart bottle of Coca-Cola

70   i talk quite coherently they say

---

[1] **ejaculatio praecox:** Premature ejaculation.

8

fucking in the early dark of evening
mid-stroke he's more interested in being overheard
i go back into my trance as we resume the
6 o'clock news

75   the car won't start. the mechanic is drunk
            i can't break his snore. the engine whines sputters
            clunks shutters in the uncanny stillness
            they're coming for me. i've got to escape
            angry, i lash out at the steering wheel, strike
80   my somnambulate° lover in his chest   sleep-walking
            he jumps out of bed yelling
            "what's wrong?"

the curse of ever-dreaming

sing to me, i say. sing to me of rivers

ANNE CARSON (1950–   )

TV Men: Lazarus (2000)

Director of Photography: Voiceover

Yes I admit a degree of unease about my
motives in making
this documentary.
Mere prurience of a kind that is all too common nowadays
5   in public catastrophes. I was listening

to a peace negotiator for the Balkans talk
about his vocation
on the radio the other day.
"We drove down through this wasteland and I didn't know
10   much about the area but I was

fascinated by the horrors of it. I had never
seen a thing like this.
I videotaped it.
Then sent a 13-page memo to the UN with my suggestions."
15   This person was a member

of the International Rescue Committee,
not a man of TV.

But you can see
how the pull is irresistible. The pull to handle horrors
20   and to have a theory of them.

But now I see my assistant producer waving her arms
at me to get
on with the script.
The name Lazarus is an abbreviated form of Hebrew *'El'azar*,
25   meaning "God has helped."

I have long been interested in those whom God has helped.
It seems often to be the case,
e.g. with saints or martyrs,
that God helps them to far more suffering than they would have
30   without God's help. But then you get

someone like Lazarus, a man of no
particular importance,
on whom God bestows
the ultimate benevolence, without explanation, then abandons
35   him again to his nonentity.

We are left wondering, *Why Lazarus?*
My theory is
God wants us to wonder this.
After all, if there were some quality that Lazarus possessed,
40   some criterion of excellence

by which he was chosen to be called
back
from death,
then we would all start competing to achieve this.
45   But if

God's gift is simply random, well
for one thing
it makes a
more interesting TV show. God's choice can be seen emerging
50   from the dark side of reason

like a new planet. No use being historical
about this planet,
it is just an imitation.
As Lazarus is an imitation of Christ. As TV is an imitation of
55   Lazarus. As you and I are an imitation of

TV. Already you notice that
although I am merely
a director of photography,
I have grasped certain fundamental notions first advanced by Plato,
60   e.g. that our reality is just a TV set

inside a TV set inside a TV set, with nobody watching
but Sokrates,
who changed
the channel in 399 B.C.[1] But my bond with Lazarus goes deeper, indeed
65   nausea overtakes me when faced with

the prospect of something simply beginning all over again.
Each time I have to
raise my slate and say
"Take 12!" or "Take 13!" and then "Take 14!"
70   I cannot restrain a shudder.

Repetition is horrible. Poor Lazarus cannot have known
he was an
imitation Christ,
but who can doubt he realized, soon after being ripped out of his
75   warm little bed in the ground,

his own epoch of repetition just beginning.
Lazarus Take 2!
Poor drop.
As a bit of salt falls back down the funnel. Or maybe my pity
80   is misplaced. Some people think Lazarus lucky,

like Samuel Beckett[2] who calls him "Happy Larry" or Rilke[3]
who speaks of
that moment in a game
when "the pure too-little flips over into the empty too-much."
85   Well I am now explaining why my documentary

focuses entirely on this moment, the flip-over moment.
Before and after
don't interest me.

---

[1] **Sokrates . . . 399 B.C.:** Socrates, an Athenian philosopher and teacher of Plato, died in 399 B.C.
[2] **Samuel Beckett:** Samuel Beckett (1906–1989), Irish novelist and playwright whose work focused on human suffering and survival. Beckett received the Nobel Prize for Literature in 1969.
[3] **Rilke:** Rainer Maria Rilke (1875–1926), German poet known for his imagery and mystic lyricism.

You won't be seeing any clips from home videos of Lazarus
90   in short pants racing his sisters up a hill.

No footage of Mary and Martha side by side on the sofa
discussing how they manage
at home
with a dead one sitting down to dinner. No panel of experts
95   debating who was really the victim here.

Our sequence begins and ends with that moment of complete
innocence
and sport—
when Lazarus licks the first drop of afterlife off the nipple
100   of his own old death.

I put tiny microphones all over the ground
to pick up
the magic
of the vermin in his ten fingers and I stand back to wait
105   for the miracle.

CHAPTER 7

MY OWN VOICE, OROTUND SWEEPING AND FINAL
—Walt Whitman
An Anthology of the Short Lyric

The **short lyric** must be considered the primary form of poetry in all languages. The term itself refers back to the short "lyric" poems of ancient Greece, which were sung to the accompaniment of a lyre, an instrument resembling a harp. This association continues to inform our basic notion of lyric, which might be defined as a poem that has a musical flow and conveys a strong emotion—what one might expect from a song.

Lyrics come in all shapes and sizes, in many different forms, some intricate, some quite simple. One of the earliest Western lyrics was by Sappho, who lived on the island of Lesbos around the year 600 B.C. Here is an example of her work, among the earliest Western examples of the genre:

> Some call a fleet of ships, a cavalry,
>   Or rows of men in battle gear
> The finest sight in all the world; but I say no.
>
> I believe the sight of one's beloved
> 5   Is a finer sight. It should be easy
> To defend this view. Just think of Helen,
>
> Who abandoned her fond lover,
>   Sailing off to Troy without a thought
> For her dear child, her adoring parents.
>
> 10 She deserted them, lured off by *eros*,
>   Which is strong, unbending,
> Which ensnares the heart like nothing else.
>
> This makes me think of Anactoria.
>   I would rather see her glide
> 15 Down glassy halls, a shimmer on her face,
>
> Than see a fleet of ships or horses
>   In array, a glittering of great Lydian
> Armaments, all bows and spears.
>   (Translated by Jay Parini)

The subject matter here is love, the allure of *eros*. Sappho writes from the point of view that has been called "the lyric I." This first-person viewpoint must never be mistaken for the voice of the poet. The poet invents a person, a **persona;** that is, the poet takes on a mask, speaking through this mask. In many ways, the "I" of a lyric poem is as much the "eye" of the audience, who regards the material of the poem from a personal angle, having been lured into the vortex of the poem by the poet's voice, which becomes the reader's voice as he or she recites the poem.

The ancient Chinese poets (pp. 601–603) also found the brief lyric an attractive form, writing poems about nature or love or war that retain their freshness and beauty after many centuries. Their power is such that, even in translation, they retain their clean edges, their fierce concentration. In most of these poems, the poet develops a simple, deep image. The images burn their way into the reader's mind, creating a unified impression that is part of the power of any good lyric.

Many of the great poems of the English language, from the anonymous lyrics of the Middle Ages through the short lyrics of Shakespeare, William Blake, and William Wordsworth, fall into the category of the short lyric. What is notable about them is their brevity, their intensity of feeling, and the musical aspects of their language. They are poems that, quite literally, one could sing. (The examples of lyric from Shakespeare, on pages 611–614, were songs embedded in the plays; they were often sung to familiar Elizabethan tunes.)

Several of the poems in the following selection trace their lineage back to the ancient **epigram,** a brief poem that compresses a good deal of wisdom into a very short space. In Greece, the epigram flourished quite early, in the form of poems inscribed on slabs of stones and intended to commemorate the dead or memorialize a certain battle or historical moment. (Inscriptions on tombstones are still a familiar epigrammatic genre.) Soon these poems took on a quality of their own, and were not just meant for the purposes of inscription. Anthologies of epigrams became quite popular among the ancient Greeks, and these gatherings of lyrics (mostly anonymous) were usually about fallen heroes or lost loves.

A. E. Housman, an English poet from the early twentieth century, was himself a classical scholar, and he wrote poems that have a distinctly epigrammatic quality. These short lyrics, written in simple meters and rhymes, blaze with a certain archaic quality. "When I was one-and-twenty" (p. 635), included here, is a fine example of his lyric style. Not surprisingly, Housman has been among the most widely read of all the modern poets, attracting an audience of readers beyond the usual circle who read poetry on a regular basis.

Another popular poet who worked in the epigrammatic tradition was Robert Frost. He wrote several brief lyrics that capture tremendous wisdom within a few deceptively simple lines. "Fire and Ice" (p. 636) and "Nothing Gold Can Stay" (p. 636), for example, are miracles of compression and eloquence. Such poems stay in the mind, fitting W. H. Auden's definition of poetry as "memorable language."

Almost every poet has tried his or her hand at the lyric, and contemporary poetry is rich in examples. Some, like "To a Poor Old Woman" by William Carlos Williams (p. 639) or "Sadie and Maud" by Gwendolyn Brooks (p. 644), have an almost journalistic feel to them. Others, such as "Aubade" by Philip Larkin (p. 1265) or "Snow" by Philip Levine (p. 649), are deeply nostalgic. A few of them, such as "Fork" by Charles Simic (p. 653), take the form in fresh directions, adding an element of surrealism. In every case, the short lyric attracts poets who want to express a strong and distinct feeling. The goal of the lyric poet is to create in a brief, musical poem a fiery moment in which the language itself catches fire, flames, then flares out like a match struck in the dark.

CH'U CH'UANG I (early eighth century)
trans. Kenneth Rexroth

A Mountain Spring

> There is a brook in the mountains,
> Nobody I ask knows its name.
> It shines on the earth like a piece
> Of the sky. It falls away
> 5   In waterfalls, with a sound
> Like rain. It twists between rocks
> And makes deep pools. It divides
> Into islands. It flows through
> Calm reaches. It goes its way
> 10   With no one to mind it. The years
> Go by, its clear depths never change.

CH'U CH'UANG I (early eighth century)
trans. Kenneth Rexroth

Evening in the Garden Clear After Rain

> Fifth month, golden plums are ripe;
> The horizon is hazy; the evening dewfall heavy;
> The grass along the lane is bright green.
> The sun sets in burning clouds.
> 5   The old gardener is glad the rains are over.
> He puts the damp mats out to dry
> And sets to work repairing the collapsed mud walls.

Twilight, the sky is crystal clear.
The children dance with joy.
10   They shout and splash in the puddles.
All the world has been made new.
I walk in the garden without a coat.
The hedges are still wet and glittering.
The pond shimmers with a thousand rippling images.
15   They no sooner appear than
They are erased and appear again.
The beautiful trees are like my heart,
Swelling with boundless happiness.

WANG WEI (701–761)
trans. Kenneth Rexroth

Autumn Twilight in the Mountains

In the empty mountains after the new rain
The evening is cool. Soon it will be Autumn.
The bright moon shines between the pines.
The crystal stream flows over the pebbles.
5   Girls coming home from washing in the river
Rustle through the bamboo grove.
Lotus leaves dance behind the fisherman's boat.
The perfumes of Spring have vanished
But my guests will long remember them.

WANG WEI (701–761)
trans. Jay Parini

Twilight in the Garden

Dusk arrives. The monastery garden
glows, but dimly, in the shade of trees.
Woodcutters cross the broad fields, singing.
Monks chant back an answer from their wood,
5   as small birds flicker, limb to limb,
and drink from basins hidden among flowers.
In a nearby copse of bamboo trees,
someone plays softly on a reedy flute.
I'm not an old man yet myself,
10   but how I'd like to live the hermit's life.

TU FU (712–770)
trans. Kenneth Rexroth

Spring Rain

A good rain knows its season.
It comes at the edge of Spring.
It steals through the night on the breeze
Noiselessly wetting everything.
5   Dark night, the clouds black as the roads,
Only a light on a boat gleaming.
In the morning, thoroughly soaked with water,
The flowers hang their heavy heads.

ANONYMOUS (thirteenth century)

How Death Comes

Wanne mine eyhnen° misten,°   eyes / get misty
And mine heren° sissen,°   ears / hiss
And my nose coldet,
And my tunge foldet,
5   And my rude° slaket,   face
And mine lippes blaken,
And my muth grennet,°   grins
And my spotel° rennet,   spittle
And mine her° riset,   hair
10   And mine herte griset,°   trembles
And mine honden° bivien,°   hands / shake
And mine fet° stivien°—   feet / stiffen
Al to late! al to late!
Wanne the bere° is ate gate.   bier

15   Thanne I schel flutte°   pass
From bedde to flore,
From flore to here,°   shroud
From here to bere,
From bere to putte,°   grave
20   And te putt fordut.°   will be closed
Thanne lyd mine hus° uppe° mine nose.   house / rests
Of al this world ne give I it a pese! [1]

---

[1] **Of al this . . . pese:** I.e., I don't give a jot for this world.

ANONYMOUS (early fourteenth century)

I Am from Ireland

      Ich° am of Irlaunde,   I

      And of the holy londe

      Of Irlande.

      Gode sire, pray ich thee,

5   For of° sainte° charite,   sake of / holy

      Come and daunce wit me

      In Irlaunde.

ANONYMOUS (late fifteenth century)

Bring Us in Good Ale

      Bring us in good ale, and bring us in good ale,

      Fore our blessed Lady sak, bring us in good ale.

      Bring us in no browne bred, fore that is mad of brane;°   chaff

      Nor bring us in no whit bred, fore therin is no game:

5   But bring us in good ale.

      Bring us in no befe, for ther is many bones;

      But bring us in good ale, for that goth downe at ones,

      And bring us in good ale.

      Bring us in no bacon, for that is passing fat;

10   But bring us in good ale, and give us inought° of that,   enough

      And bring us in good ale.

      Bring us in no mutton, for that is ofte lene;

      Nor bring us in no tripes,° for they be seldom clene: entrails

      But bring us in good ale.

15   Bring us in no egges, for ther ar many shelles;

      But bring us in good ale, and give us nothing elles,

      And bring us in good ale.

      Bring us in no butter, for therin ar many heres;

      Nor bring us in no pigges flesh, for that will mak us bores:

20   But bring us in good ale.

Bring us in no podinges,° for therin is all gotes blod;   puddings
Nor bring us in no venison, for that is not for our good:
But bring us in good ale.

Bring us in no capon's° flesh, for that is ofte der;   rooster
25   Nor bring us in no dokes° flesh for they slobber in the mer:°   duck / pond
But bring us in good ale.

JOHN SKELTON   (1460–1529)

To Mistress Margaret Hussey[1]   (1522)

     Merry Margaret,
         As midsummer flower,
     Gentle as falcon
     Or hawk of the tower:[2]
5   With solace and gladness,
     Much mirth and no madness,
     All good and no badness;
         So joyously,
         So maidenly,
10   So womanly
         Her demeaning°   demeanor
         In every thing,
         Far, far passing
         That I can indite,°   compose
15   Or suffice to write
     Of Merry Margaret
         As midsummer flower,
     Gentle as falcon
     Or hawk of the tower.
20   As patient and still
     And as full of good will
     As fair Isaphill,[3]
     Coriander,
     Sweet pomander,[4]

---

[1] **Mistress Margaret Hussey:** Perhaps the daughter of Simon Blount of Magotsfield and a lady to the countess of Surrey. Mistress was a title for an upper-class married woman.
[2] **hawk of the tower:** A hawk, which has been trained to fly high.
[3] **Isaphill:** According to the Greek myth, Isaphill (Hypsipyle) saved her father, when the women of Lemnos killed all the men. She was married to Jason and bore him two sons, but was later deserted by him.
[4] **pomander:** A mixture of aromatic substances.

25 Good Cassander,[5]
    Steadfast of thought,
    Well made, well wrought,
    Far may be sought
    Ere that ye can find
30 So courteous, so kind
    As Merry Margaret,
        This midsummer flower,
    Gentle as falcon
    Or hawk of the tower.

THOMAS WYATT (1503–1542)

Is It Possible

            Is it possible
        That so high debate,
    So sharp, so sore, and of such rate,
    Should end so soon and was begun so late?
5   Is it possible?

            Is it possible
        So cruel intent,
        So hasty heat and so soon spent,
    From love to hate, and thence for to relent?
10   Is it possible?

            Is it possible
        That any may find
    Within one heart so diverse mind,
    To change or turn as weather and wind?
15   Is it possible?

            Is it possible
        To spy it in an eye
    That turns as oft as chance on die?
    The troth° whereof can any try?   truth; faith
20   Is it possible?

---

[5] **Cassander:** Cassandra, the daughter of Priam (the king of Troy), whose prophesies were fated by Apollo never to be believed.

It is possible
For to turn so oft,
To bring that lowest that was most aloft,
And to fall highest yet to light soft?
25   It is possible.

All is possible,
Whoso list° believe;   cares to
Trust therefore first, and after preve:°   proof
As men wed ladies by license and leave,
30   All is possible.

THOMAS WYATT (1503–1542)

What Once I Was (early sixteenth century)

Ons° in your grace I knowe I was,   once
Even as well as now is he;
Tho Fortune so hath torned my case
That I am downe and he full hye°—   high
5   Yet ons I was.

Ons I was he that did you please
So well that nothing did I dobte,
And tho that nowe ye thinke it ease
To take him in and throw me out—
10 Yet ons I was.

Ons I was he in tims past
That as your owne ye did retaine:
And tho ye have me nowe out cast,
Shoing untruthe in you to raigne,
15 Yet ons I was.

Ons I was he that knit the knot
The whiche ye swore not to unknit,
And tho ye faine it now forgot,
In usinge° your newfangled wit,   use
20 Yet ons I was.

Ons I was he to whome ye said,
'Welcomm! my joy, my whole delight.'
And tho ye ar nowe well apayd
Of me, your owne, to clame ye quit—
25 Yet ons I was.

Ons I was he to whome ye spake,
'Have here my hart! It is thy owne.'
And tho thes wordes ye now forsake,
Saying therof my part is none,
30   Yet ons I was.

Ons I was he before reherst,
And nowe am he that nedes must die.
And tho I die, yet, at the lest,
In your remembrance let it lie
35   That ons I was.

SIR WALTER RALEGH (ca. 1552–1618)

The Lie (1608)

Go, soul, the body's guest,
Upon a thankless errand;
Fear not to touch the best;
The truth shall be thy warrant.
5   Go, since I needs must die,
And give the world the lie.[1]

Say to the court, it glows
And shines like rotten wood;
Say to the church, it shows
10   What's good, and doth no good.
If church and court reply,
Then give them both the lie.

Tell potentates, they live
Acting by others' action;
15   Not loved unless they give,
Not strong but by a faction.
If potentates reply,
Give potentates the lie.

Tell men of high condition,
20   That manage the estate,
Their purpose is ambition,
Their practice only hate.

---

[1] **give the world the lie:** The expression "to give the lie" means to contradict, to expose.

And if they once reply,
Then give them all the lie.

25 Tell them that brave it most,
They beg for more by spending,
Who, in their greatest cost,
Seek nothing but commending.
And if they make reply,
30 Then give them all the lie.

Tell zeal it wants devotion;
Tell love it is but lust;
Tell time it is but motion;
Tell flesh it is but dust.
35 And wish them not reply,
For thou must give the lie.

Tell age it daily wasteth;
Tell honor how it alters;
Tell beauty how she blasteth;°   withers
40 Tell favor how it falters.
And as they shall reply,
Give every one the lie.

Tell wit how much it wrangles
In tickle points of niceness;
45 Tell wisdom she entangles
Herself in overwiseness.
And when they do reply,
Straight give them both the lie.

Tell physic° of her boldness;   medicine
50 Tell skill it is pretension;
Tell charity of coldness;
Tell law it is contention.
And as they do reply,
So give them still the lie.

55 Tell fortune of her blindness;
Tell nature of decay;
Tell friendship of unkindness;
Tell justice of delay.
And if they will reply,
60 Then give them all the lie.

Tell arts they have no soundness,
But vary by esteeming;

Tell schools they want profoundness,
And stand too much on seeming.
65 If arts and schools reply,
Give arts and schools the lie.

Tell faith it's fled the city;
Tell how the country erreth;
Tell manhood shakes off pity;
70 Tell virtue least preferreth.
And if they do reply,
Spare not to give the lie.

So when thou hast, as I
Commanded thee, done blabbing—
75 Although to give the lie
Deserves no less than stabbing—
Stab at thee he that will,
No stab the soul can kill.

JOHN LYLY (1554–1606)

Oh, for a Bowl of Fat Canary[1] (1640)

Oh, for a bowl of fat Canary,
Rich Palermo, sparkling Sherry,
Some nectar else, from Juno's dairy;[2]
Oh, these draughts would make us merry!

5 Oh, for a wench (I deal in faces,
And in other daintier things);
Tickled am I with her embraces,
Fine dancing in such fairy rings.[3]

Oh, for a plump fat leg of mutton,
10 Veal, lamb, capon, pig, and coney;[4]
None is happy but a glutton,
None an ass but who wants money.

---

[1] **Canary:** A light sweet wine. The adjective "fat" means strong, well-bodied.
[2] **Juno's dairy:** Juno was the wife of Jove (Jupiter), the most powerful of all the Roman gods (Hera and Zeus are their equivalents in Greek mythology). "Dairy" perhaps refers to Nectar, the drink of the gods.
[3] **fairy rings:** Rings on the grass, supposedly left over from dancing fairies.
[4] **capon . . . coney:** Capon is a rooster fattened for food; coney: a rabbit.

Wines indeed and girls are good,
But brave victuals feast the blood;
15   For wenches, wine, and lusty cheer,
Jove would leap down to surfeit here.

GEORGE PEELE (1557–1596)

Hot Sun, Cool Fire (pub. 1599)

Hot sun, cool fire, tempered with sweet air,
Black shade, fair nurse, shadow my white hair.
Shine, sun; burn, fire; breathe, air, and ease me;
Black shade, fair nurse, shroud me and please me.
5   Shadow, my sweet nurse, keep me from burning;
Make not my glad cause cause of mourning.
    Let not my beauty's fire
    Inflame unstaid desire,
    Nor pierce any bright eye
10   That wandereth lightly.

WILLIAM SHAKESPEARE (1564–1616)

"Under the greenwood tree" (ca. 1599; 1623)

Under the greenwood tree
Who loves to lie with me,
    And turn his merry note
    Unto the sweet bird's throat,
5   Come hither, come hither, come hither:
        Here shall he see
        No enemy
But winter and rough weather.

    Who doth ambition shun
10   And loves to live i' the sun,
    Seeking the food he eats,
    And pleased with what he gets,
Come hither, come hither, come hither:
        Here shall he see
15   No enemy
But winter and rough weather.

WILLIAM SHAKESPEARE (1564–1616)

"Blow, blow, thou winter wind" (ca. 1599)

> Blow, blow, thou winter wind,
> Thou art not so unkind
>   As man's ingratitude;
> Thy tooth is not so keen,
> 5   Because thou art not seen,
>   Although thy breath be rude.
> Heigh-ho! sing, heigh-ho! unto the green holly:
> Most friendship is feigning, most loving mere folly.
>   Then heigh-ho! the holly!
> 10   This life is most jolly.
>
> Freeze, freeze, thou bitter sky,
> That dost not bite so nigh
>   As benefits forgot:
> Though thou the waters warp,
> 15   Thy sting is not so sharp
>   As friend remembered not.
> Heigh-ho! sing, heigh-ho! unto the green holly:
> Most friendship is feigning, most loving mere folly.
>   Then heigh-ho! the holly!
> 20   This life is most jolly.

WILLIAM SHAKESPEARE (1564–1616)

"It was a lover and his lass" (ca. 1599)

> It was a lover and his lass,
>   With a hey, and a ho, and a hey nonino,
> That o'er the green corn-field did pass,
>   In spring time, the only pretty ring time,
> 5   When birds do sing, hey ding a ding, ding;
> Sweet lovers love the spring.
>
> Between the acres of the rye,
>   With a hey, and a ho, and a hey nonino,
> Those pretty country folks would lie,
> 10   In spring time, the only pretty ring time,

When birds do sing, hey ding a ding, ding;
Sweet lovers love the spring.

This carol they began that hour,
    With a hey, and a ho, and a hey nonino,
15 How that a life was but a flower
        In spring time, the only pretty ring time,
    When birds do sing, hey ding a ding, ding;
    Sweet lovers love the spring.

And therefore take the present time,
20   With a hey, and a ho, and a hey nonino;
    For love is crowned with the prime
        In spring time, the only pretty ring time,
    When birds do sing, hey ding a ding, ding;
    Sweet lovers love the spring.

WILLIAM SHAKESPEARE (1564–1616)

"Fear no more the heat o' the sun" (ca. 1610)

Fear no more the heat o' the sun,
    Nor the furious winter's rages;
Thou thy worldly task hast done,
    Home art gone, and ta'en thy wages.
5   Golden lads and girls all must,
As chimney-sweepers, come to dust.

Fear no more the frown o' the great,
    Thou art past the tyrant's stroke;
Care no more to clothe and eat,
10   To thee the reed is as the oak.
The sceptre, learning, physic, must
All follow this, and come to dust.

Fear no more the lightning-flash,
    Nor the all-dreaded thunder-stone;
15 Fear not slander, censure rash;
    Thou hast finished joy and moan.
All lovers young, all lovers must
Consign to thee, and come to dust.

No exorciser harm thee!
20   Nor no witchcraft charm thee!
Ghost unlaid forbear thee!
Nothing ill come near thee!
Quiet consummation have,
And renownèd be thy grave!

THOMAS CAMPION (1567–1620)

When to Her Lute Corinna Sings (1601)

When to her lute Corinna sings,
Her voice revives the leaden strings,
And doth in highest notes appear
As any challenged echo clear;
5   But when she doth of mourning speak,
Ev'n with her sighs the strings do break.

And as her lute doth live or die,
Led by her passion, so must I:
For when of pleasure she doth sing,
10   My thoughts enjoy a sudden spring,
But if she doth of sorrow speak,
Ev'n from my heart the strings do break.

JOHN DONNE (1572–1631)

Song (1633)

Go and catch a falling star,
    Get with child a mandrake root,[1]
Tell me where all past years are,
    Or who cleft the Devil's foot;
5   Teach me to hear mermaids singing,
    Or to keep off envy's stinging,
            And find
            What wind
Serves to advance an honest mind.

---

[1] **mandrake root:** The root of an herb, used as a narcotic or love potion.

10   If thou beest born to strange sights,
        Things invisible to see,
    Ride ten thousand days and nights
        Till Age snow white hairs on thee;
    Thou, when thou return'st, wilt tell me
15   All strange wonders that befell thee,
            And swear
            No where
    Lives a woman true and fair.

    If thou find'st one, let me know;
20   Such a pilgrimage were sweet.
    Yet do not; I would not go,
        Though at next door we might meet.
    Though she were true when you met her,
    And last till you write your letter,
25   Yet she
           Will be
    False, ere I come, to two or three.

BEN JONSON (1572–1637)

Song: To Celia (I) *(from Volpone)* (1616)

    Come, my Celia, let us prove,
    While we can, the sports of love;
    Time will not be ours forever;
    He at length our good will sever.
5   Spend not then his gifts in vain.
    Suns that set may rise again;
    But if once we lose this light,
    'Tis with us perpetual night.
    Why should we defer our joys?
10   Fame and rumor are but toys.
    Cannot we delude the eyes
    Of a few poor household spies,
    Or his easier ears beguile,
    So removèd by our wile?
15   'Tis no sin love's fruit to steal;
    But the sweet thefts to reveal,
    To be taken, to be seen,
    These have crimes accounted been.

My Own Voice / The Short Lyric

BEN JONSON (1572–1637)

Song: To Celia (II) (1616)

Drink to me only with thine eyes,
And I will pledge with mine;
Or leave a kiss but in the cup,
And I'll not look for wine.
5   The thirst that from the soul doth rise,
Doth ask a drink divine:
But might I of Jove's nectar[1] sup,
I would not change for thine.
I sent thee late a rosy wreath,
10   Not so much honoring thee,
As giving it a hope, that there
It could not withered be.
But thou thereon did'st only breathe,
And sent'st it back to me;
15   Since when it grows and smells, I swear,
Not of itself, but thee.

ROBERT HERRICK (1591–1674)

To His Conscience (1648)

Can I not sin, but thou wilt be
My private protonotary?[1]
Can I not woo thee to pass by
A short and sweet iniquity?
5   I'll cast a mist and cloud upon
My delicate transgression,
So utter dark, as that no eye
Shall see the hugged impiety.
Gifts blind the wise, and bribes do please,
10   And wind° all other witnesses;   corrupt
And wilt not thou, with gold, be tied
To lay thy pen and ink aside?

---

[1] **Jove's nectar:** The drink of the gods. Jove (Jupiter) was the most powerful of the Roman deities.
[1] **protonotary:** The principal clerk in a court of law.

That in the murk and tongueless night,
Wanton I may, and thou not write?
15   It will not be; and therefore now,
For times to come, I'll make this vow:
From aberrations to live free;
So I'll not fear the judge or thee.

THOMAS CAREW (ca. 1598–ca. 1640)

Mediocrity in Love Rejected (1640)

Give me more love, or more disdain;
   The torrid or the frozen zone
Bring equal ease unto my pain;
   The temperate affords me none:
5   Either extreme, of love or hate,
Is sweeter than a calm estate.

Give me a storm; if it be love,
   Like Danae in that golden shower,[1]
I swim in pleasure; if it prove
10   Disdain, that torrent will devour
My vulture hopes; and he's possessed
Of heaven that's but from hell released.
   Then crown my joys, or cure my pain;
   Give me more love, or more disdain.

EDMUND WALLER (1606–1687)

Song (1645)

   Go, lovely rose!
Tell her that wastes her time and me
   That now she knows,
When I resemble° her to thee,   compare
5   How sweet and fair she seems to be.

---

[1] **Danae in that golden shower:** According to Ovid's *Metamorphoses*, Danae was the daughter of the king of Argos. Because of a prophecy that her son would kill him, he imprisoned Danae in a tower, but Jove came down upon her in a shower of gold and she conceived a son, Perseus.

Tell her that's young,
And shuns to have her graces spied,
That, hadst thou sprung
In deserts where no men abide,
10   Thou must have uncommended died.

Small is the worth
Of beauty from the light retired;
Bid her come forth,
Suffer herself to be desired,
15   And not blush so to be admired.

Then die; that she
The common fate of all things rare
May read in thee:
How small a part of time they share
20   That are so wondrous sweet and fair!

ANDREW MARVELL (1621–1678)

The Definition of Love   (1681 pub.)

My Love is of a birth as rare
As 'tis, for object, strange and high;
It was begotten by Despair
Upon Impossibility.

5   Magnanimous Despair alone
Could show me so divine a thing,
Where feeble Hope could ne'er have flown
But vainly flapped its tinsel wing.

And yet I quickly might arrive
10   Where my extended soul is fixed;
But Fate does iron wedges drive,
And always crowds itself betwixt.

For Fate with jealous eye does see
Two perfect loves, nor lets them close;
15   Their union would her ruin be,
And her tyrannic power depose.

And therefore her decrees of steel
Us as the distant poles have placed
(Though Love's whole world on us doth wheel),
20   Not by themselves to be embraced,

Unless the giddy heaven fall,
And earth some new convulsion tear,
And, us to join, the world should all
Be cramped into a planisphere.[1]

25   As lines, so loves oblique may well
Themselves in every angle greet;
But ours, so truly parallel,
Though infinite, can never meet.

Therefore the love which us doth bind,
30   But Fate so enviously debars,
Is the conjunction of the mind,
And opposition of the stars.

EDWARD TAYLOR (ca. 1642–1729)

Upon a Spider Catching a Fly (ca. 1680; 1939)

Thou sorrow, venom elf:
    Is this thy ploy,
To spin a web out of thyself
    To catch a fly?
5   For why?

I saw a pettish° wasp   peevish
    Fall foul therein,
Whom yet thy whorl-pins did not clasp
    Lest he should fling
10   His sting.

---

[1] **planisphere:** A chart formed when a sphere (e.g., globe) is projected on a plane.

But as afraid, remote
    Didst stand hereat
And with thy little fingers stroke
    And gently tap
15   His back.

Thus gently him didst treat
    Lest he should pet,°   take offense
And in a froppish,° waspish heat   fretful
    Should greatly fret
20   Thy net.

Whereas the silly fly,
    Caught by its leg
Thou by the throat tookst hastily
    And hind the head
25   Bite dead.

This goes to pot, that not[;]
    Nature doth call.
Strive not above what strength hath got
    Lest in the brawl
30   Thou fall.

This fray seems thus to us.
    Hell's spider gets
His entrails spun to whip-cords thus,
    And wove to nets
35   And sets.

To tangle Adam's race
    In's strategems
To their destructions, spoiled, made base
    By venom things,
40   Damned sins.

But mighty, gracious Lord
    Communicate
Thy grace to break the cord, afford
    Us glory's gate
45   And state.

We'll nightingale sing like
    When perched on high
In glory's cage, thy glory, bright,
    And thankfully,
50   For joy.

JOHN WILMOT, EARL OF ROCHESTER (1648–1680)

Love and Life: A Song (1680)

All my past life is mine no more:
    The flying hours are gone
Like transitory dreams given o'er,
Whose images are kept in store
5   By memory alone.

Whatever is to come is not;
    How can it then be mine?
The present moment's all my lot,
And that as fast as it is got,
10   Phillis, is wholly thine.

Then talk not of inconstancy,
    False hearts, and broken vows:
If I by miracle can be,
    This livelong minute, true to thee,
15   'Tis all that heaven allows.

ISAAC WATTS (1674–1748)

Our God, Our Help[1] (1719)

Our God, our help in ages past,
    Our hope for years to come,
Our shelter from the stormy blast,
    And our eternal home:

5   Under the shadow of thy throne
    Thy saints have dwelt secure;
Sufficient is thine arm alone,
    And our defense is sure.

Before the hills in order stood
10   Or earth received her frame,
From everlasting thou art God,
    To endless years the same.

---

[1] **Our God, Our Help:** This poem is based on Psalm 90.

Thy word commands our flesh to dust,
    "Return, ye sons of men";
15 All nations rose from earth at first,
    And turn to earth again.

A thousand ages in thy sight
    Are like an evening gone;
Short as the watch that ends the night
20   Before the rising sun.

The busy tribes of flesh and blood,
    With all their lives and cares,
Are carried downwards by thy flood,
    And lost in following years.

25 Time, like an ever-rolling stream,
    Bears all its sons away;
They fly forgotten, as a dream
    Dies at the opening day.

Like flowery fields the nations stand,
30   Pleased with the morning light;
The flowers beneath the mower's hand
    Lie withering e'er 'tis night.

Our God, our help in ages past,
    Our hope for years to come,
35 Be thou our guard while troubles last,
    And our eternal home.

WILLIAM BLAKE (1757–1827)

The Lamb (1789)

Little Lamb who made thee?
    Dost thou know who made thee?
Gave thee life & bid thee feed.
By the stream & o'er the mead;
5 Gave thee clothing of delight,
Softest clothing wooly bright;
Gave thee such a tender voice,
Making all the vales rejoice!

Little Lamb who made thee
10   Dost thou know who made thee

Little Lamb I'll tell thee,
Little Lamb I'll tell thee!
He is called by thy name.[1]
For he calls himself a Lamb:
15   He is meek & he is mild,
He became a little child:
I a child & thou a lamb,
We are called by his name.
Little Lamb God bless thee.
20   Little Lamb God bless thee.

WILLIAM BLAKE (1757–1827)

The Little Boy Lost (1789)

"Father, father, where are you going?
O do not walk so fast.
Speak father, speak to your little boy
Or else I shall be lost."

5   The night was dark, no father was there,
The child was wet with dew.
The mire was deep, & the child did weep,
And away the vapor flew.

WILLIAM BLAKE (1757–1827)

The Little Boy Found (1789)

The little boy lost in the lonely fen,
Led by the wand'ring light,

---

[1] **He is called by thy name:** I.e., Christ.

Began to cry, but God ever nigh
Appeard like his father in white.

5   He kissed the child & by the hand led
And to his mother brought,
Who in sorrow pale, thro' the lonely dale,
Her little boy weeping sought.

WILLIAM BLAKE (1757–1827)

The Sick Rose (1794)

O Rose thou art sick.
The invisible worm,
That flies in the night
In the howling storm:

5   Has found out thy bed
Of crimson joy:
And his dark secret love
Does thy life destroy.

WILLIAM BLAKE (1757–1827)

A Poison Tree (1794)

I was angry with my friend;
I told my wrath, my wrath did end.
I was angry with my foe:
I told it not, my wrath did grow.

5   And I waterd it in fears,
Night & morning with my tears:
And I sunned it with smiles,
And with soft deceitful wiles.

And it grew both day and night,
10   Till it bore an apple bright;
And my foe beheld it shine,
And he knew that it was mine,

And into my garden stole,
When the night had veild the pole;
15 In the morning glad I see;
My foe outstretchd beneath the tree.

WILLIAM BLAKE (1757–1827)

Ah! Sun-Flower (1794)

Ah Sun-flower! weary of time,
Who countest the steps of the Sun:
Seeking after that sweet golden clime
Where the travellers journey is done.

5 Where the Youth pined away with desire,
And the pale Virgin shrouded in snow:
Arise from their graves and aspire,
Where my Sun-flower wishes to go.

ROBERT BURNS (1759–1796)

Bonie Doon (1791; 1792)

Ye flowery banks o' bonie Doon,
　　How can ye blume sae fair?
How can ye chant, ye little birds,
　　And I sae fu' o' care?

5 Thou'll break my heart, thou bonie bird,
　　That sings upon the bough;
Thou minds me o' the happy days,
　　When my fause° luve was true.　　　　　　　　　　　　　false

Thou'll break my heart, thou bonie bird,
10　　That sings beside thy mate;
For sae I sat, and sae I sang,
　　And wist° na o' my fate.　　　　　　　　　　　　　　know

Aft hae I roved by bonie Doon
　　To see the wood-bine twine,

15   And ilka° bird sang o' its luve,   every
        And sae did I o' mine.

     Wi' lightsome heart I pu'd° a rose   plucked
        Frae° aff its thorny tree;   from
     And my fause luver staw° my rose   stole
20   But left the thorn wi' me.

WILLIAM WORDSWORTH (1770–1850)

"My heart leaps up" (1807)

My heart leaps up when I behold
   A Rainbow in the sky:
So was it when my life began;
So is it now I am a Man;
5   So be it when I shall grow old,
      Or let me die!
The Child is Father of the Man;
And I could wish my days to be
Bound each to each by natural piety.

WILLIAM WORDSWORTH (1770–1850)

"I wandered lonely as a Cloud" (1807)

I wandered lonely as a Cloud
That floats on high o'er Vales and Hills,
When all at once I saw a crowd
A host of dancing Daffodils;
5   Along the Lake, beneath the trees,
Ten thousand dancing in the breeze.

The waves beside them danced, but they
Outdid the sparkling waves in glee:—
A Poet could not but be gay
10   In such a laughing company:
I gazed—and gazed—but little thought
What wealth the shew to me had brought:

For oft when on my couch I lie
In vacant or in pensive mood,

15 They flash upon that inward eye
Which is the bliss of solitude,
And then my heart with pleasure fills,
And dances with the Daffodils.

SAMUEL TAYLOR COLERIDGE (1772–1834)

Ne Plus Ultra[1] (ca. 1826)

Sole Positive of Night!
Antipathist of Light!
Fate's only essence! primal scorpion rod—
The one permitted opposite of God!—
5 Condensed blackness and abysmal storm
Compacted to one sceptre
Arms the Grasp enorm—
The Intercepter—
The Substance that still casts the shadow Death!—
10 The Dragon foul and fell—
The unrevealable,
And hidden one, whose breath
Gives wind and fuel to the fires of Hell!
Ah! sole despair
15 Of both th' eternities in Heaven!
Sole interdict of all-bedewing prayer,
The all-compassionate!
Save to the Lampads Seven[2]
Reveal'd to none of all th' Angelic State,
20 Save to the Lampads Seven,
That watch the throne of Heaven!

THOMAS MOORE (1779–1852)

Oft, in the Stilly Night (1815)
Scotch Air

Oft, in the stilly night,
Ere Slumber's chain has bound me,

---

[1] **Ne Plus Ultra:** The highest point of something, as of achievement. Also, the most refined, ultimate state.
[2] **Lampads Seven:** I.e., the seven planets known in ancient times, which Aristotle believed to be the only pure and incorruptible substance of the visible world.

Fond Memory brings the light
    Of other days around me;
5   The smiles, the tears,
        Of boyhood's years,
    The words of love then spoken;
        The eyes that shone,
        Now dimmed and gone,
10   The cheerful hearts now broken!
Thus, in the stilly night,
    Ere Slumber's chain has bound me,
Sad Memory brings the light
    Of other days around me.

15 When I remember all
    The friends, so linked together,
I've seen around me fall,
    Like leaves in wintry weather;
        I feel like one
20   Who treads alone
Some banquet hall deserted,
        Whose lights are fled,
        Whose garlands dead,
And all but he departed!
25 Thus, in the stilly night,
    Ere Slumber's chain has bound me,
Sad Memory brings the light
    Of other days around me.

GEORGE GORDON, LORD BYRON (1788–1824)

We'll Go No More a-Roving (1817)

So, we'll go no more a-roving
    So late into the night,
Though the heart be still as loving,
    And the moon be still as bright.

5 For the sword outwears its sheath,
    And the soul wears out the breast,
And the heart must pause to breathe,
    And love itself have rest.

Though the night was made for loving,
10   And the day returns too soon,

Yet we'll go no more a-roving
　　By the light of the moon.

JOHN CLARE (1793–1864)

The Peasant Poet (ca. 1842)

He loved the brook's soft sound,
　　The swallow swimming by
He loved the daisy-covered ground,
　　The cloud-bedappled sky.
5　To him the dismal storm appeared
　　The very voice of God;
And when the evening rock was reared
　　Stood Moses with his rod.[1]
And everything his eyes surveyed,
10　The insects i' the brake,
Were creatures God Almighty made,
　　He loved them for his sake—
A silent man in life's affairs,
　　A thinker from a boy,
15　A peasant in his daily cares,
　　A poet in his joy.

THOMAS LOVELL BEDDOES (1803–1849)

If Thou Wilt Ease Thine Heart (ca. 1826; 1850)

If thou wilt ease thine heart
Of love and all its smart,
　　　Then sleep, dear, sleep;
And not a sorrow
5　　Hang any tear on your eyelashes;
　　　Lie still and deep,
　　Sad soul, until the sea-wave washes
The rim o' the sun tomorrow,
　　　In eastern sky.

---

[1] **Moses with his rod:** Moses was a Biblical prophet, who led the Jews out of Egypt. As a sign of his divine mission, God gave him a rod, which would turn into a snake when tossed on the ground.

10   But wilt thou cure thine heart
        Of love and all its smart,
                Then die, dear, die;
        'Tis deeper, sweeter,
            Than on a rose bank to lie dreaming
15   With folded eye;
            And then alone, amid the beaming
        Of love's stars, thou'lt meet her
                In eastern sky.

ALFRED, LORD TENNYSON (1809–1892)

"Break, break, break" (1842)

Break, break, break,
    On thy cold gray stones, O Sea!
And I would that my tongue could utter
    The thoughts that arise in me.

5   O well for the fisherman's boy,
        That he shouts with his sister at play!
    O well for the sailor lad,
        That he sings in his boat on the bay!

    And the stately ships go on
10   To their haven under the hill;
    But O for the touch of a vanished hand,
        And the sound of a voice that is still!

    Break, break, break,
        At the foot of thy crags, O Sea!
15 But the tender grace of a day that is dead
        Will never come back to me.

EMILY JANE BRONTË (1818–1848)

"Come, walk with me" (1844; 1902)

Come, walk with me;
There's only thee
To bless my spirit now;
We used to love on winter nights

5   To wander through the snow.
    Can we not woo back old delights?
    The clouds rush dark and wild;
    They fleck with shade our mountain heights
    The same as long ago,
10 And on the horizon rest at last
    In looming masses piled;
    While moonbeams flash and fly so fast
    We scarce can say they smiled.

    Come, walk with me—come, walk with me;
15 We were not once so few;
    But Death has stolen our company
    As sunshine steals the dew:
    He took them one by one, and we
    Are left, the only two;
20 So closer would my feelings twine,
    Because they have no stay but thine.

    'Nay, call me not; it may not be;
    Is human love so true?
    Can Friendship's flower droop on for years
25 And then revive anew?
    No; though the soil be wet with tears,
    How fair soe'er it grew;
    The vital sap once perishèd
    Will never flow again;
30 And surer than that dwelling dread,
    The narrow dungeon of the dead,
    Time parts the hearts of men.'

WALT WHITMAN (1819–1892)

I Saw in Louisiana a Live-Oak Growing (1860; 1867)

I saw in Louisiana a live-oak growing,
All alone stood it and the moss hung down from the branches,
Without any companion it grew there uttering joyous leaves of
        dark green,
And its look, rude, unbending, lusty, made me think of myself,
5   But I wonder'd how it could utter joyous leaves standing alone
        there without its friend near, for I knew I could not,
And I broke off a twig with a certain number of leaves upon it,
        and twined around it a little moss,

And brought it away, and I have placed it in sight in my room,
It is not needed to remind me as of my own dear friends,
(For I believe lately I think of little else than of them,)

10   Yet it remains to me a curious token, it makes me think of manly love;
For all that, and though the live-oak glistens there in Louisiana
            solitary in a wide flat space,
Uttering joyous leaves all its life without a friend a lover near,
I know very well I could not.

WILLIAM ALLINGHAM   (1824–1889)

"Everything passes and vanishes"   (1882)

Everything passes and vanishes;
    Everything leaves its trace;
And often you see in a footstep
    What you could not see in a face.

EMILY DICKINSON   (1830–1886)

"Much Madness is divinest Sense—"   (ca. 1862; 1890)

Much Madness is divinest Sense—
To a discerning Eye—
Much Sense—the starkest Madness—
'Tis the Majority

5   In this, as All, prevail—
Assent—and you are sane—
Demur—you're straightway dangerous—
And handled with a Chain—

EMILY DICKINSON   (1830–1886)

"I dwell in Possibility"   (ca. 1862; 1929)

I dwell in Possibility—
A fairer House than Prose—
More numerous of Windows—
Superior—for Doors—

5   Of Chambers as the Cedars—
        Impregnable of Eye—
        And for an Everlasting Roof
        The Gambrels of the Sky—

        Of Visitors—the fairest—
10   For Occupation—This—
        The spreading wide my narrow Hands
        To gather Paradise—

CHRISTINA G. ROSSETTI (1830–1894)

Song (1849; 1850)

        Oh roses for the flush of youth,
           And laurel for the perfect prime;
        But pluck an ivy branch for me
           Grown old before my time.

5   Oh violets for the grave of youth,
           And bay for those dead in their prime;
        Give me the withered leaves I chose
           Before in the old time.

CHRISTINA G. ROSSETTI (1830–1894)

May (1855; 1862)

        I cannot tell you how it was;
        But this I know: it came to pass
        Upon a bright and breezy day
        When May was young; ah pleasant May!
5   As yet the poppies were not born
        Between the blades of tender corn;
        The last eggs had not hatched as yet,
        Nor any bird foregone its mate.

        I cannot tell you what it was;
10   But this I know: it did but pass.
        It passed away with sunny May,
        With all sweet things it passed away,
        And left me old, and cold, and grey.

ROBERT BRIDGES (1844–1930)

"The evening darkens over" (1890)

The evening darkens over.
After a day so bright
The windcapt waves discover
That wild will be the night.
5   There's sound of distant thunder.

The latest sea-birds hover
Along the cliff's sheer height;
As in the memory wander
Last flutterings of delight,
10   White wings lost on the white.

There's not a ship in sight;
And as the sun goes under
Thick clouds conspire to cover
The moon that should rise yonder.
15   Thou art alone, fond lover.

ROBERT LOUIS STEVENSON (1850–1894)

Requiem (ca. 1884; 1887)

Under the wide and starry sky,
Dig the grave and let me lie.
Glad did I live and gladly die,
    And I laid me down with a will.

5   This be the verse you grave for me:
Here he lies where he longed to be;
Home is the sailor, home from sea,
    And the hunter home from the hill.

E. KEARY (ca. 1857–ca. 1882)

Old Age (1874)

Such a wizened creature,
    Sitting alone;
    Every kind of ugliness thrown
Into each feature.

5   'I wasn't always so,'
      Said the wizened
      One; 'sweet motions unimprisoned
Were mine long ago.'

      And again, 'I shall be—
10   At least something
      Out of this outside me, shall wing
Itself fair and free.'

A. E. HOUSMAN (1859–1936)

"When I was one-and-twenty" (1896)

When I was one-and-twenty
    I heard a wise man say,
"Give crowns and pounds and guineas
    But not your heart away;
5   Give pearls away and rubies
    But keep your fancy free."
But I was one-and-twenty,
    No use to talk to me.

When I was one-and-twenty
10   I heard him say again,
"The heart out of the bosom
    Was never given in vain;
'Tis paid with sighs a plenty
    And sold for endless rue."
15   And I am two-and-twenty,
    And oh, 'tis true, 'tis true.

EDWIN ARLINGTON ROBINSON (1869–1935)

Richard Cory (1897)

Whenever Richard Cory went down town,
We people on the pavement looked at him:
He was a gentleman from sole to crown,
Clean favored, and imperially slim.

5   And he was always quietly arrayed,
And he was always human when he talked;

But still he fluttered pulses when he said,
"Good-morning," and he glittered when he walked.

And he was rich—yes, richer than a king—
10   And admirably schooled in every grace:
In fine, we thought that he was everything
To make us wish that we were in his place.

So on we worked, and waited for the light,
And went without the meat, and cursed the bread;
15   And Richard Cory, one calm summer night,
Went home and put a bullet through his head.

ROBERT FROST (1874–1963)

Fire and Ice (1923)

Some say the world will end in fire,
Some say in ice.
From what I've tasted of desire
I hold with those who favor fire.
5   But if it had to perish twice,
I think I know enough of hate
To say that for destruction ice
Is also great
And would suffice.

ROBERT FROST (1874–1963)

Nothing Gold Can Stay (1923)

Nature's first green is gold,
Her hardest hue to hold.
Her early leaf's a flower;
But only so an hour.
5   Then leaf subsides to leaf.
So Eden sank to grief,
So dawn goes down to day.
Nothing gold can stay.

ROBERT FROST   (1874–1963)

Dust of Snow   (1923)

The way a crow
Shook down on me
The dust of snow
From a hemlock tree

5   Has given my heart
A change of mood
And saved some part
Of a day I had rued.

JOHN MASEFIELD   (1878–1967)

Sea-Fever   (1900; 1902)

I must go down to the seas again, to the lonely sea and the sky,
And all I ask is a tall ship and a star to steer her by,
And the wheel's kick and the wind's song and the white sail's
            shaking,
And a grey mist on the sea's face and a grey dawn breaking.

5   I must go down to the seas again, for the call of the running tide
Is a wild call and a clear call that may not be denied;
And all I ask is a windy day with the white clouds flying,
And the flung spray and the blown spume and the sea-gulls crying.

I must go down to the seas again to the vagrant gypsy life,
10   To the gull's way and the whale's way where the wind's like a
            whetted knife;
And all I ask is a merry yarn from a laughing fellow-rover,
And quiet sleep and a sweet dream when the long trick's over.

EDWARD THOMAS   (1878–1917)

Adlestrop   (1915; 1917)

Yes, I remember Adlestrop—
The name, because one afternoon

Of heat the express-train drew up there
Unwontedly. It was late June.

5   The steam hissed. Someone cleared his throat.
No one left and no one came
On the bare platform. What I saw
Was Adlestrop—only the name

And willows, willow-herb, and grass,
10   And meadowsweet, and haycocks dry,
No whit less still and lonely fair
Than the high cloudlets in the sky.

And for that minute a blackbird sang
Close by, and round him, mistier,
15   Farther and farther, all the birds
Of Oxfordshire and Gloucestershire.

WALLACE STEVENS (1879–1955)

Nomad Exquisite (1923)

As the immense dew of Florida
Brings forth
The big-finned palm
And green vine angering for life,

5   As the immense dew of Florida
Brings forth hymn and hymn
From the beholder,
Beholding all these green sides
And gold sides of green sides,

10   And blessed mornings,
Meet for the eye of the young alligator,
And lightning colors
So, in me, come flinging
Forms, flames, and the flakes of flames.

WILLIAM CARLOS WILLIAMS (1883–1963)

Willow Poem (1921)

It is a willow when summer is over,
a willow by the river
from which no leaf has fallen nor
bitten by the sun
5   turned orange or crimson.
The leaves cling and grow paler,
swing and grow paler
over the swirling waters of the river
as if loath to let go,
10   they are so cool, so drunk with
the swirl of the wind and of the river—
oblivious to winter,
the last to let go and fall
into the water and on the ground.

WILLIAM CARLOS WILLIAMS (1883–1963)

To a Poor Old Woman (1935)

munching a plum on
the street a paper bag
of them in her hand

They taste good to her
5   They taste good
to her. They taste
good to her

You can see it by
the way she gives herself
10   to the one half
sucked out in her hand

Comforted
a solace of ripe plums
seeming to fill the air
15   They taste good to her

EZRA POUND (1885–1972)

In a Station of the Metro (1916)

The apparition of these faces in the crowd;
Petals on a wet, black bough.

LOUISE BOGAN (1897–1970)

M., Singing (1937)

Now, innocent, within the deep
Night of all things you turn the key,
Unloosing what we know in sleep.
In your fresh voice they cry aloud
5   Those beings without heart or name.

Those creatures both corrupt and proud,
Upon the melancholy words
And in the music's subtlety,
Leave the long harvest which they reap
10 In the sunk land of dust and flame
And move to space beneath our sky.

GWENDOLYN B. BENNETT (1902–1981)

To a Dark Girl (1927)

I love you for your brownness
And the rounded darkness of your breast.
I love you for the breaking sadness in your voice
And shadows where your wayward eye-lids rest.

5   Something of old forgotten queens
Lurks in the lithe abandon of your walk,
And something of the shackled slave
Sobs in the rhythm of your talk.

Oh, little brown girl, born for sorrow's mate,
10 Keep all you have of queenliness,

Forgetting that you once were slave,
And let your full lips laugh at Fate!

ARNA BONTEMPS   (1902–1973)

A Black Man Talks of Reaping   (1927)

I have sown beside all waters in my day.
I planted deep, within my heart the fear
That wind or fowl would take the grain away.
I planted safe against this stark, lean year.

5   I scattered seed enough to plant the land
In rows from Canada to Mexico
But for my reaping only what the hand
Can hold at once is all that I can show.

Yet what I sowed and what the orchard yields
10   My brother's sons are gathering stalk and root,
Small wonder then my children glean in fields
They have not sown, and feed on bitter fruit.

STEVIE SMITH   (1902–1971)

Not Waving But Drowning   (1957)

Nobody heard him, the dead man,
But still he lay moaning:
I was much further out than you thought
And not waving but drowning.

5   Poor chap, he always loved larking
And now he's dead
It must have been too cold for him his heart gave way,
They said.

Oh, no no no, it was too cold always
10   (Still the dead one lay moaning)
I was much too far out all my life
And not waving but drowning.

W. H. AUDEN (1907–1973)

Hell (1939)

Hell is neither here nor there,
Hell is not anywhere,
Hell is hard to bear.

It is so hard to dream posterity
5   Or haunt a ruined century
And so much easier to be.

Only the challenge to our will,
Our pride in learning any skill,
Sustains our effort to be ill.

10   To talk the dictionary through
Without a chance word coming true
Is more than Darwin's apes could do.

Yet pride alone could not insist
Did we not hope, if we persist,
15   That one day Hell might actually exist.

In time, pretending to be blind
And universally unkind
Might really send us out of our mind.

If we were really wretched and asleep
20   It would be then *de trop°* to weep,   excessive
It would be natural to lie,
There'd be no living left to die.

THEODORE ROETHKE (1908–1963)

Cuttings (1948)

Sticks-in-a-drowse droop over sugary loam,
Their intricate stem-fur dries;
But still the delicate slips keep coaxing up water;
The small cells bulge;

5   One nub of growth
Nudges a sand-crumb loose,
Pokes through a musty sheath
Its pale tendrilous horn.

THEODORE ROETHKE   (1909–1963)

Cuttings   (1948)
(later)

This urge, wrestle, resurrection of dry sticks,
Cut stems struggling to put down feet,
What saint strained so much,
Rose on such lopped limbs to a new life?

5   I can hear, underground, that sucking and sobbing,
In my veins, in my bones I feel it,—
The small waters seeping upward,
The tight grains parting at last.
When sprouts break out,
10   Slippery as fish,
I quail, lean to beginnings, sheath-wet.

JOSEPHINE MILES   (1911–1985)

On Inhabiting an Orange   (1935)

All our roads go nowhere.
Maps are curled
To keep the pavement definitely
On the world.

5   All our footsteps, set to make
Metric advance,
Lapse into arcs in deference
To circumstance.

All our journeys nearing Space
10   Skirt it with care,
Shying at the distances
Present in air.

Blithely travel-stained and worn,
Erect and sure,
15   All our travelers go forth,
Making down the roads of Earth
Endless detour.

GWENDOLYN BROOKS (1917–2000)

Sadie and Maud (1945)

Maud went to college.
Sadie stayed at home.
Sadie scraped life
With a fine-tooth comb.

5   She didn't leave a tangle in.
Her comb found every strand.
Sadie was one of the livingest chits
In all the land.

Sadie bore two babies
10   Under her maiden name.
Maud and Ma and Papa
Nearly died of shame.

When Sadie said her last so-long
Her girls struck out from home.
15   (Sadie had left as heritage
Her fine-tooth comb.)

Maud, who went to college,
Is a thin brown mouse.
She is living all alone
20   In this old house.

ROBERT DUNCAN (1919–1988)

Often I Am Permitted to Return to a Meadow (1960)

as if it were a scene made-up by the mind,
that is not mine, but is a made place,

that is mine, it is so near to the heart,
an eternal pasture folded in all thought
5   so that there is a hall therein

that is a made place, created by light
wherefrom the shadows that are forms fall.

Wherefrom fall all architectures I am
I say are likeness of the First Beloved
10   whose flowers are flames lit to the Lady.

She it is Queen Under The Hill[1]
whose hosts are a disturbance of words within words
that is a field folded.

It is only a dream of the grass blowing
15   east against the source of the sun
in an hour before the sun's going down

whose secret we see in a children's game
of ring a round of roses told.

Often I am permitted to return to a meadow
as if it were a given property of the mind
20   that certain bounds hold against chaos,

that is a place of first permission,
everlasting omen of what is.

JACK GILBERT (1925–   )

Explicating the Twilight (1994)

The rat makes her way up
the mulberry tree, the branches
getting thin and risky up close
to the fruit, and she slows.
5   The berry she is after is so ripe,
there is almost no red. Prospero
thinks of Christopher Smart[1] saying
purple is black blooming. She lifts
her mouth to the berry, stretching.
10   The throat is an elegant gray.
A thousand shades, Christopher wrote
among the crazy people. A thousand
colors from white to silver.

[1] **Queen Under The Hill:** I.e., Persephone, the wife of Hades and queen of the underworld.
[1] **Prospero thinks of Christopher Smart:** Prospero, a character from Shakespeare's *The Tempest*, is the exiled Duke of Milan and a sorcerer (an archetypical poet) living on an enchanted island. Christopher Smart (1722–1771) was an English poet and the author of the visionary works *Song to David* and *Jubilate Agno*. Late in his life he developed a religious mania and was confined to an institution for the mentally ill.

A. R. AMMONS (1926–2001)

So I Said I Am Ezra (1955)

So I said I am Ezra
and the wind whipped my throat
gaming for the sounds of my voice
      I listened to the wind
5   go over my head and up into the night
Turning to the sea I said
        I am Ezra
but there were no echoes from the waves
The words were swallowed up
10   in the voice of the surf
or leaping over swells
lost themselves oceanward
      Over the bleached and broken fields
I moved my feet and turning from the wind
15   that ripped sheets of sand
       from the beach and threw them
       like seamists across the dunes
swayed as if the wind were taking me away
and said
20   I am Ezra
As a word too much repeated
falls out of being
so I Ezra went out into the night
like a drift of sand
25   and splashed among the windy oats
that clutch the dunes
of unremembered seas

ROBERT CREELEY (1926–   )

The Rain (1962)

All night the sound had
come back again,
and again falls
this quiet, persistent rain.

5   What am I to myself
that must be remembered,

insisted upon
so often? Is it

that never the ease,
10   even the hardness,
of rain falling
will have for me

something other than this,
something not so insistent—
15   am I to be locked in this
final uneasiness.

Love, if you love me,
lie next to me.
Be for me, like rain,
20   the getting out

of the tiredness, the fatuousness, the semi-
lust of intentional indifference.
Be wet
with a decent happiness.

JAMES MERRILL (1926–1995)

The Kimono (1976)

When I returned from lovers' lane
My hair was white as snow.
Joy, incomprehension, pain
I'd seen like seasons come and go.
5   How I got home again
Frozen half dead, perhaps you know.

You hide a smile and quote a text:
Desires ungratified
Persist from one life to the next.
10   Hearths we strip ourselves beside
Long, long ago were x'd
On blueprints of "consuming pride."

Times out of mind, the bubble-gleam
To our charred level drew

15   April back. A sudden beam . . .
    —Keep talking while I change into
    The pattern of a stream
    Bordered with rushes white on blue.

JOHN ASHBERY (1927–   )

At North Farm (1984)

Somewhere someone is traveling furiously toward you,
At incredible speed, traveling day and night,
Through blizzards and desert heat, across torrents, through narrow passes.
But will he know where to find you,
5 Recognize you when he sees you,
Give you the thing he has for you?

Hardly anything grows here,
Yet the granaries are bursting with meal,
The sacks of meal piled to the rafters.
10 The streams run with sweetness, fattening fish;
Birds darken the sky. Is it enough
That the dish of milk is set out at night,
That we think of him sometimes,
Sometimes and always, with mixed feelings?

W. S. MERWIN (1927–   )

For the Anniversary of My Death (1967)

Every year without knowing it I have passed the day
When the last fires will wave to me
And the silence will set out
Tireless traveller
5 Like the beam of a lightless star

Then I will no longer
Find myself in life as in a strange garment
Surprised at the earth
And the love of one woman
10 And the shamelessness of men
As today writing after three days of rain

Hearing the wren sing and the falling cease
And bowing not knowing to what

JAMES WRIGHT (1927–1980)

Lying in a Hammock at William Duffy's Farm in Pine Island, Minnesota (1963)

Over my head, I see the bronze butterfly,
Asleep on the black trunk,
Blowing like a leaf in green shadow.
Down the ravine behind the empty house,
5   The cowbells follow one another
Into the distances of the afternoon.
To my right,
In a field of sunlight between two pines,
The droppings of last year's horses
10   Blaze up into golden stones.
I lean back, as the evening darkens and comes on.
A chicken hawk floats over, looking for home.
I have wasted my life.

PHILIP LEVINE (1928–   )

Snow (1979)

Today the snow is drifting
on Belle Isle,[1] and the ducks
are searching for some opening
to the filthy waters of their river.
5   On Grand River Avenue, which is not
in Venice but in Detroit, Michigan,
the traffic has slowed to a standstill
and yet a sober man has hit a parked car
and swears to the police he was
10   not guilty. The bright squads of children
on their way to school howl
at the foolishness of the world

---

[1] **Belle Isle:** An island on the Detroit River and a Detroit city park.

they will try not to inherit.
Seen from inside a window,
15   even a filthy one like those
at Automotive Supply Company, the snow
which has been falling for hours
is more beautiful than even the spring
grass which once unfurled here
20   before the invention of steel and fire,
for spring grass is what the earth sang
in answer to the new sun, to
melting snow, and the dark rain
of spring nights. But snow is nothing.
25   It has no melody or form, it
is as though the tears of all
the lost souls rose to heaven
and were finally heard and blessed
with substance and the power of flight
30   and given their choice chose then
to return to earth, to lay their
great pale cheek against the burning
cheek of earth and say, There, there, child.

ADRIENNE RICH (1929–   )

In the Evening

Three hours chain-smoking words
and you move on. We stand in the porch,
two archaic figures: a woman and a man.

The old masters, the old sources,
5   haven't a clue what we're about,
shivering here in the half-dark 'sixties.

Our minds hover in a famous impasse
and cling together. Your hand
grips mine like a railing on an icy night.

10   The wall of the house is bleeding. Firethorn!
The moon, cracked every-which-way,
pushes steadily on.

GARY SNYDER (1930–   )

Mid-August at Sourdough Mountain[1] Lookout (1965)

Down valley a smoke haze
Three days heat, after five days rain
Pitch glows on the fir-cones
Across rocks and meadows
5   Swarms of new flies.

I cannot remember things I once read
A few friends, but they are in cities.
Drinking cold snow-water from a tin cup
Looking down for miles
10   Through high still air.

GARY SNYDER (1930–   )

The Snow on Saddle Mountain[1]

The only thing that can be relied on
is the snow on Kurakake Mountain.[2]
fields and woods
thawing, freezing, and thawing,
5   totally untrustworthy.
it's true, a great fuzzy windstorm
like yeast up there today, still
the only faint source of hope
is the snow on Kurakake mountain.

---

[1] **Sourdough Mountain:** A mountain, part of the North Cascades Range, Washington State.
[1] **Saddle Mountain:** A mountain in the state of Oregon.
[2] **Kurakake Mountain:** A mountain in Japan.

SYLVIA PLATH (1932–1963)

Morning Song (1961)

Love set you going like a fat gold watch.
The midwife slapped your footsoles, and your bald cry
Took its place among the elements.

Our voices echo, magnifying your arrival. New statue.
5   In a drafty museum, your nakedness
Shadows our safety. We stand round blankly as walls.

I'm no more your mother
Than the cloud that distills a mirror to reflect its own slow
Effacement at the wind's hand.

10   All night your moth-breath
Flickers among the flat pink roses. I wake to listen:
A far sea moves in my ear.

One cry, and I stumble from bed, cow-heavy and floral
In my Victorian nightgown.
15   Your mouth opens clean as a cat's. The window square

Whitens and swallows its dull stars. And now you try
Your handful of notes;
The clear vowels rise like balloons.

ANNE STEVENSON (1933–   )

In the Orchard

Black bird, black voice,
almost the shadow of a voice,
so kind to this tired summer sky,
a rim of night around it,
5   yet almost an echo of today,
all the days since that first
soft guttural disaster
gave us "apple" and "tree"
and all that transpired thereafter
10   in the city of the tongue.

Blackbird, so old, so young,
happy to be stricken with a song
you can never choose away from.

N. SCOTT MOMADAY (1934–   )

Carriers of the Dream Wheel (1975)

This is the Wheel of Dreams
Which is carried on their voices,
By means of which their voices turn
And center upon being.
5   It encircles the First World,
This powerful wheel.
They shape their songs upon the wheel
And spin the names of the earth and sky,
The aboriginal names.
10   They are old men, or men
Who are old in their voices,
And they carry the wheel among the camps,
Saying: Come, come,
Let us tell the old stories,
15   Let us sing the sacred songs.

CHARLES SIMIC (1938–   )

Fork (1971)

This strange thing must have crept
Right out of hell.
It resembles a bird's foot
Worn around the cannibal's neck.

5   As you hold it in your hand,
As you stab with it into a piece of meat,
It is possible to imagine the rest of the bird:
Its head which like your fist
Is large, bald, beakless and blind.

GARY SOTO (1952–   )

Field Poem (1977)

When the foreman whistled
My brother and I
Shouldered our hoes,
Leaving the field.
5 We returned to the bus
Speaking
In broken English, in broken Spanish
The restaurant food,
The tickets to a dance
10 We wouldn't buy with our pay.

From the smashed bus window,
I saw the leaves of cotton plants
Like small hands waving good-bye.

CHAPTER 8

WHEN I SEE BIRCHES BEND TO LEFT AND RIGHT
—Robert Frost

An Anthology of Blank Verse

Blank verse, which may succinctly but somewhat too rigidly be defined as unrhymed iambic pentameter, is probably the most common and influential form that English poetry has taken since the sixteenth century, when it first came into view as a popular vehicle for poetry. Since then, it has been deployed in countless ways, creating a wide range of effects.

One of the earliest examples of blank verse was by Henry Howard, Earl of Surrey, who found it appropriate for his translation of Virgil's *Aeneid*. This made a good deal of sense, as in many ways the form approximates the unrhymed poetry commonly used in Latin and Greek epic poetry. Surrey was, perhaps, imitating Continental translators of Virgil, such as Francesco Maria Molza, who used an Italian form of blank verse in his 1514 version of *The Aeneid*.

Blank verse was the medium preferred by most of the great Elizabethan and Jacobean playwrights, including Christopher Marlowe and William Shakespeare, both of whose immensely inventive contributions to the form extended its range. Both moved away from counting syllables and evolved a form of blank verse that depends on five strong beats per line. One sees the form at its dramatic height in Shakespeare's famous tragedies and late romances. Yet keep in mind what T. S. Eliot said: "Every writer who has written any blank verse worth saving has produced particular tones which his verse and no other's is capable of rendering." That is, the form must be reinvented each time a poet chooses to employ it.

Given that blank verse often has a different sound in the voice of different poets, it might well be better to think of the form as a gesture in a certain poetical direction. One can usually identify the meter easily by looking at the line length, sounding out roughly five strong beats per line (and sometimes ten syllables), then looking for that characteristic flow, which seems to mimic conversational English—which is why the Elizabethan playwrights found it such a convenient meter for verse drama.

John Milton was the first major poet to use the form at great length in *nondramatic* poetry. His epic, *Paradise Lost* (pp. 657–660), employs a kind of blank verse that is immensely flexible in its rhythms. Like Shakespeare and Marlowe in their plays, Milton in his poetry allowed himself to vary the rhythmical flow quite radically from line to line, as in the memorable opening of his epic:

> Of Man's first disobedience, and the fruit
> Of that forbidden tree whose mortal taste
> Brought death into the World, and all our woe,
> With loss of Eden, till one greater Man
> 5   Restore us, and regain the blissful seat,
> Sing, Heavenly Muse. . . .

There is tremendous fluidity here, as in the first line, where the stresses fall on "Man's" as well as "first" in the opening two feet, disrupting the iambic flow from the outset. The last foot ("and the fruit") is really an anapestic foot (*ta-ta-tum*), and the line is heavily enjambed, with a strong stress on "that" in the second line. Notice that the third line begins: "Brought death. . . ." Here the stress falls equally on both words. In fact, one cannot easily see how the rhythm can be described as iambic pentameter: *ta-tum, ta-tum, ta-tum, ta-tum, ta-tum*. Indeed, Milton—like all intelligent poets—took liberties with his blank verse, letting the rhythm flow so that it gathers rhetorical steam as the poem moves along.

When talking about poetic meters, one must always note that the set meter is simply an abstract idea, a kind of (usually unrealized) potential for the line. The speaking voice plays over this abstract possibility, creating fresh effects, approximating conversation wherever possible. This is especially true with modern poets, such as Robert Frost, who in "Birches" (p. 666) creates a wonderfully casual speaking voice that appeals to the ear and seems to mimic easy conversation, as in the opening lines:

> When I see birches bend to left and right
> Across the lines of straighter darker trees,
> I like to think some boy's been swinging them.
> But swinging doesn't bend them down to stay
> 5   As ice storms do. Often you must have seen them
> Loaded with ice a sunny winter morning
> After a rain. They click upon themselves
> As the breeze rises, and turn many-colored
> As the stir cracks and crazes their enamel.

Frost shows himself more than capable of producing those "particular tones" that make any poet's verse sound fresh and distinct, and he wrote a good deal of poetry in blank verse. He seems to have looked back more to Wordsworth than to Milton in the development of his fairly conversational and low-keyed blank verse. *The Prelude* (p. 660) is certainly a fine example of the use of blank verse in a book-length poem.

The language surges and meanders with the poet's thoughts, tracking his every turn of mind, his every pulse of feeling. In Wordsworth's hands, blank verse becomes an almost philosophical instrument, rich in tonal possibilities, equally capable of expressing abstract ideas and concrete imagery.

Not surprisingly, contemporary poets have also found the form useful. The essential five-beat structure of the line seems endlessly flexible, capable of subtle variations. Just as the French poets most often fall back upon a six-beat line, poets writing in English fall naturally into a five-beat line; the underlying meter is usually iambic because the language itself tends in the direction of iambic meter, with a light stress preceding a heavier stress. The poetic possibilities within this metrical system are vast, and they have been realized in countless ways by poets over the past five centuries.

JOHN MILTON   (1608–1674)

from Paradise Lost, Book IV: 207–318   (1667)
Paradise

In narrow room nature's whole wealth, yea more,
A heaven on Earth, for blissful paradise
Of God the garden was, by him in the east
Of Eden planted; Eden stretched her line
5   From Auran eastward to the royal towers
Of great Seleucia,[1] built by Grecian kings,
Or where the sons of Eden long before
Dwelt in Telassar:° in this pleasant soil   Mesopotamia
His far more pleasant garden God ordained;
10   Out of the fertile ground he caused to grow
All trees of noblest kind for sight, smell, taste;
And all amid them stood the tree of life,
High eminent, blooming ambrosial[2] fruit
Of vegetable gold; and next to life
15   Our death the tree of knowledge grew fast by,
Knowledge of good bought dear by knowing ill.
Southward through Eden went a river large,
Nor changed his course, but through the shaggy hill
Passed underneath ingulfed; for God had thrown

---

[1] **Auran . . . Seleucia:** Cities in or near Mesopotamia, an ancient kingdom in the Middle East.
[2] **ambrosial:** Fragrant like ambrosia, a favorite drink of the gods.

20   That mountain as his garden mould high raised
     Upon the rapid current, which through veins
     Of porous earth with kindly thirst up drawn,
     Rose a fresh fountain, and with many a rill
     Watered the garden; thence united fell
25   Down the steep glade, and met the nether flood,
     Which from his darksome passage now appears,
     And now divided into four main streams
     Runs diverse, wandering many a famous realm
     And country whereof here needs no account;
30   But rather to tell how, if art could tell,
     How from that sapphire fount the crispèd° brooks,   rippling
     Rolling on orient pearl and sands of gold,
     With mazy error under pendant shades
     Ran nectar, visiting each plant, and fed
35   Flowers worthy of paradise which not nice art
     In beds and curious knots, but nature boon
     Poured forth profuse on hill and dale and plain,
     Both where the morning sun first warmly smote
     The open field, and where the unpierced shade
40   Embrowned° the noontide bowers; thus was this place   darkened
     A happy rural seat of various view:
     Groves whose rich trees wept odorous gums and balm,
     Others whose fruit burnished with golden rind
     Hung amiable, Hesperian fables[3] true,
45   If true, here only, and of delicious taste;
     Betwixt them lawns, or level downs, and flocks
     Grazing the tender herb, were interposed,
     Or palmy hillock, or the flowery lap
     Of some irriguous° valley spread her store,   watered
50   Flowers of all hue, and without thorn the rose;
     Another side, umbrageous grots° and caves   shadowy woods
     Of cool recess, o'er which the mantling vine
     Lays forth her purple grape, and gently creeps
     Luxuriant; meanwhile murmuring waters fall
55   Down the slope hills, dispersed, or in a lake,
     That to the fringèd bank with myrtle crowned
     Her crystal mirror holds, unite their streams.
     The birds their choir apply; airs, vernal airs,
     Breathing the smell of field and grove, attune
60   The trembling leaves, while universal Pan°   God of nature

---

[3] **Hesperian fables:** Stories concerning the gardens of the Hesperides, where golden apples were guarded by a dragon.

Knit with the Graces[4] and the Hours[5] in dance
Led on the eternal spring. Not that fair field
Of Enna, where Proserpine gathering flowers
Herself a fairer flower by gloomy Dis
65   Was gathered, which cost Ceres[6] all that pain
To seek her through the world; nor that sweet grove
Of Daphne by Orontes, and the inspired
Castalian spring,[7] might with this paradise
Of Eden strive; nor that Nyseian isle
70   Girt with the river Triton, where old Cham,
Whom gentiles Ammon call and Libyan Jove,
Hid Amalthea and her florid son
Young Bacchus from his stepdame Rhea's eye;[8]
Nor where Abássin kings their issue guard,
75   Mount Amara,[9] though this by some supposed
True paradise under the Ethiop line°   the equator
By Nilus' head,° enclosed with shining rock,   head of the Nile
A whole day's journey high, but wide remote
From this Assyrian garden,° where the fiend   paradise
80   Saw undelighted all delight, all kind
Of living creatures new to sight and strange:
Two of far nobler shape erect and tall,
Godlike erect, with native honour clad
In naked majesty seemed lords of all,
85   And worthy seemed, for in their looks divine
The image of their glorious maker shone,
Truth, wisdom, sanctitude severe and pure,
Severe but in true filial freedom placed;
Whence true authority in men; though both
90   Not equal, as their sex not equal seemed;
For contemplation he and valour formed,
For softness she and sweet attractive grace,
He for God only, she for God in him:

---

[4] **Graces:** Three goddesses—Euphrosyne, Aglaia, and Thalia—who represent the pleasures of life.
[5] **the Hours:** Goddesses representing the seasons of the year.
[6] **Proserpine . . . Ceres:** Prosperine was goddess of springtime fertility. She was captured in Sicily at Enna by Dis (Pluto), god of the underworld (Ovid, *Metamorphoses*, V, 385–91). Ceres, her mother, searched for her throughout the earth.
[7] **Daphne . . . Castalian spring:** The gardens of Daphne on the river Orontes in Syria contained a spring named after the Castalian spring on Mt. Parnassus in Greece, the source of poetic inspiration.
[8] **Nyseian isle . . . Rhea's eye:** Nysa was a beautiful isle in the river Triton in Tunisia. There the son of Ammon, called Bacchus, was concealed by the nymph Amalthea and thus protected from the jealous rage of Rhea, Ammon's wife. The Egyptian god Ammon was thought to relate to the Egyptian deity and was known as Zeus-Arnmon or Jupiter-Ammon (hence "Libyan Jove"), and Christian tradition identified him with Ham (Cham), the second son of Noah, who (according to myth) settled in Africa after the Flood.
[9] **Mount Amara:** A remote place where the Abyssinian kings were sent to be educated.

His fair large front° and eye sublime declared   forehead
95   Absolute rule; and hyacinthine° locks   dark
     Round from his parted forelock manly hung
     Clustering, but not beneath his shoulders broad:
     She as a veil down to the slender waist
     Her unadornèd golden tresses wore
100 Dishevelled, but in wanton° ringlets waved   wild, unrestrained
     As the vine curls her tendrils; which implied
     Subjection, but required with gentle sway,
     And by her yielded, by him best received,
     Yielded with coy submission, modest pride,
105 And sweet reluctant amorous delay.
     Nor those mysterious parts were then concealed,
     Then was not guilty shame, dishonest shame
     Of nature's works, honour dishonourable–
     Sin-bred, how have ye troubled all mankind
110 With shows instead, mere shows of seeming pure,
     And banished from man's life his happiest life,
     Simplicity and spotless innocence.

WILLIAM WORDSWORTH (1770–1850)
from The Prelude

London Images (1805; 1850)
(Book VII. 594–740)

     How often in the overflowing Streets,
     Have I gone forward with the Crowd, and said
     Unto myself, the face of every one
     That passes by me is a mystery.
5   Thus have I look'd, nor ceas'd to look, oppress'd
     By thoughts of what, and whither, when and how
     Until the shapes before my eyes became
     A second-sight procession, such as glides
     Over still mountains, or appears in dreams;
10   And all the ballast of familiar life,
     The present, and the past; hope, fear; all stays,
     All laws of acting, thinking, speaking man
     Went from me, neither knowing me, nor known.
     And once, far-travell'd in such mood, beyond
15   The reach of common indications, lost

Amid the moving pageant, 'twas my chance
Abruptly to be smitten with the view
Of a blind Beggar, who, with upright face,
Stood propp'd against a Wall, upon his Chest
20   Wearing a written paper, to explain
The story of the Man, and who he was.
My mind did at this spectacle turn round
As with the might of waters, and it seemed
To me that in this Label was a type,
25   Or emblem, of the utmost that we know,
Both of ourselves and of the universe;
And, on the shape of the unmoving man,
His fixèd face and sightless eyes, I look'd
As if admonish'd from another world.
30   Though rear'd upon the base of outward things,
These, chiefly, are such structures as the mind
Builds for itself. Scenes different there are,
Full-form'd, which take, with small internal help,
Possession of the faculties; the peace
35   Of night, for instance, the solemnity
Of nature's intermediate hours of rest,
When the great tide of human life stands still,
The business of the day to come unborn,
Of that gone by, lock'd up as in the grave;
40   The calmness, beauty, of the spectacle,
Sky, stillness, moonshine, empty streets, and sounds
Unfrequent as in desarts; at late hours
Of winter evenings when unwholesome rains
Are falling hard, with people yet astir,
45   The feeble salutation from the voice
Of some unhappy Woman, now and then
Heard as we pass; when no one looks about,
Nothing is listen'd to. But these, I fear,
Are falsely catalogu'd, things that are, are not,
50   Even as we give them welcome, or assist,
Are prompt, or are remiss. What say you then,
To times, when half the City shall break out
Full of one passion, vengeance, rage, or fear,
To executions, to a Street on fire,
55   Mobs, riots, or rejoicings? From these sights
Take one, an annual Festival, the Fair
Holden where Martyrs suffer'd in past time,
And named of Saint Bartholomew; there see
A work that's finish'd to our hands, that lays,
60   If any spectacle on earth can do,

The whole creative powers of man asleep!
For once the Muse's help will we implore,
And she shall lodge us, wafted on her wings,
Above the press and danger of the Crowd,
65 Upon some Showman's platform; what a hell
For eyes and ears! what anarchy and din
Barbarian and infernal! 'tis a dream,
Monstrous in colour, motion, shape, sight, sound.
Below, the open space, through every nook
70 Of the wide area, twinkles, is alive
With heads; the midway region and above
Is throng'd with staring pictures, and huge scrolls,
Dumb proclamations of the prodigies;
And chattering monkeys dangling from their poles.
75 And children whirling in their roundabouts;
With those that stretch the neck, and strain the eyes.
And crack the voice in rivalship, the crowd
Inviting; with buffoons against buffoons
Grimacing, writhing, screaming; him who grinds
80 The hurdy-gurdy, at the fiddle weaves;
Rattles the salt-box, thumps the kettle-drum,
And him who at the trumpet puffs his cheeks,
The silver-collar'd Negro with his timbrel,
Equestrians, Tumblers, Women, Girls, and Boys,
85 Blue-breech'd, pink-vested, and with towering plumes.
—All moveables of wonder from all parts,
Are here, Albinos, painted Indians, Dwarfs,
The Horse of Knowledge, and the learned Pig,
The Stone-eater, the Man that swallows fire,
90 Giants, Ventriloquists, the Invisible Girl,
The Bust that speaks, and moves its goggling eyes,
The Wax-work, Clock-work, all the marvellous craft
Of modern Merlins, wild Beasts, Puppet-shows,
All out-o'-the-way, far-fetch'd, perverted things,
95 All freaks of Nature, all Promethean thoughts
Of Man; his dulness, madness, and their feats,
All jumbled up together to make up
This Parliament of Monsters. Tents and Booths
Meanwhile, as if the whole were one vast Mill,
100 Are vomiting, receiving, on all sides,
Men, Women, three-years' Children, Babes in arms.

    Oh, blank confusion! and a type not false
Of what the mighty City is itself

To all except a Straggler here and there,
105 To the whole Swarm of its inhabitants;
An undistinguishable world to men,
The slaves unrespited of low pursuits,
Living amid the same perpetual flow
Of trivial objects, melted and reduced
110 To one identity, by differences
That have no law, no meaning, and no end;
Oppression under which even highest minds
Must labour, whence the strongest are not free;
But though the picture weary out the eye,
115 By nature an unmanageable sight,
It is not wholly so to him who looks
In steadiness, who hath among least things
An under-sense of greatest; sees the parts
As parts, but with a feeling of the whole.
120 This, of all acquisitions first, awaits
On sundry and most widely different modes
Of education; nor with least delight
On that through which I pass'd. Attention comes,
And comprehensiveness and memory,
125 From early converse with the works of God
Among all regions; chiefly where appear
Most obviously simplicity and power.
By influence habitual to the mind
The mountain's outline and its steady form
130 Gives a pure grandeur, and its presence shapes
The measure and the prospect of the soul
To majesty; such virtue have the forms
Perennial of the ancient hills; nor less
The changeful language of their countenances
135 Gives movement to the thoughts, and multitude,
With order and relation. This, if still,
As hitherto, with freedom I may speak,
And the same perfect openness of mind,
Not violating any just restraint,
140 As I would hope, of real modesty,
This did I feel in that vast receptacle.
The Spirit of Nature was upon me here;
The Soul of Beauty and enduring life
Was present as a habit, and diffused,
145 Through meagre lines and colours, and the press
Of self-destroying, transitory things
Composure and ennobling Harmony.

SAMUEL TAYLOR COLERIDGE (1772–1834)

Frost at Midnight (1798)

The frost performs its secret ministry,
Unhelped by any wind. The owlet's cry
Came loud—and hark, again—loud as before!
The inmates of my cottage, all at rest,
5   Have left me to that solitude which suits
Abstruser musings—save that at my side
My cradled infant slumbers peacefully.
'Tis calm indeed—so calm that it disturbs
And vexes meditation with its strange
10   And extreme silentness. Sea, hill, and wood,
This populous village—sea, and hill, and wood,
With all the numberless goings-on of life,
Inaudible as dreams! The thin blue flame
Lies on my low-burnt fire, and quivers not.
15   Only that film, which fluttered on the grate,
Still flutters there, the sole unquiet thing!
      Methinks, its motion in this hush of Nature
Gives it dim sympathies with me who live,
Making it a companionable form,
20   With which I can hold commune. Idle thought!
But still the living spirit in our frame,
That loves not to behold a lifeless thing,
Transfuses into all its own delights,
Its own volition, sometimes with deep faith,
25   And sometimes with fantastic playfulness.
Ah me! amused by no such curious toys,
How often in my early schoolboy days,
With most believing superstitious wish
Presageful, have I gazed upon the bars
30   To watch the *stranger* there!
                              And oft, belike,
With unclosed lids, already had I dreamt
Of my sweet birth-place, and the old church-tower,
Whose bells, the poor man's only music, rang
35   From morn to evening, all the hot Fair-day,
So sweetly, that they stirred and haunted me
With a wild pleasure, falling on mine ear
Most like articulate sounds of things to come.
So gazed I, till the soothing things I dreamt
40   Lulled me to sleep, and sleep prolonged my dreams!
And so I brooded all the following morn,

Awed by the stern preceptor's face, mine eye
Fixed with mock study on my swimming book;
Save if the door half opened, and I snatched
45 A hasty glance—and still my heart leapt up,
For still I hoped to see the *stranger's* face,
Townsman, or aunt, or sister more beloved,
My play-mate when we both were clothed alike!
 Dear babe, that sleepest cradled by my side,
50 Whose gentle breathings, heard in this dead calm,
Fill up the intersperséd vacancies
And momentary pauses of the thought!
My babe so beautiful, it thrills my heart
With tender gladness, thus to look at thee,
55 And think that thou shalt learn far other lore,
And in far other scenes! For I was reared
In the great city, pent mid cloisters dim,
And saw nought lovely but the sky and stars.
But thou, my babe, shalt wander like a breeze
60 By lakes and sandy shores, beneath the crags
Of ancient mountain, and beneath the clouds,
Which image in their bulk both lakes and shores
And mountain-crags. So shalt thou see and hear
The lovely shapes and sounds intelligible
65 Of that eternal language which thy God
Utters, who from eternity doth teach
Himself in all, and all things in himself.
Great universal Teacher—he shall mould
Thy spirit, and by giving make it ask!
70 Therefore all seasons shall be sweet to thee,
Whether the summer clothe the general earth
With greenness, or the redbreast sit and sing
Betwixt the tufts of snow on the bare branch
Of mossy apple-tree, while all the thatch
75 Smokes in the sun-thaw; whether the eave-drops fall
Heard only in the trances of the blast,
Or whether the secret ministry of cold
Shall hang them up in silent icicles,
Quietly shining to the quiet moon—
80 Like those, my babe, which, ere tomorrow's warmth
Have capped their sharp keen points with pendulous drops,
Will catch thine eye, and with their novelty
Suspend thy little soul, then make thee shout
And stretch and flutter from thy mother's arms
85 As thou wouldst fly for very eagerness.

ROBERT FROST (1874–1963)

Birches (1916)

When I see birches bend to left and right
Across the lines of straighter darker trees,
I like to think some boy's been swinging them.
But swinging doesn't bend them down to stay
5   As ice storms do. Often you must have seen them
Loaded with ice a sunny winter morning
After a rain. They click upon themselves
As the breeze rises, and turn many-colored
As the stir cracks and crazes their enamel.
10   Soon the sun's warmth makes them shed crystal shells
Shattering and avalanching on the snow crust—
Such heaps of broken glass to sweep away
You'd think the inner dome of heaven had fallen.
They are dragged to the withered bracken by the load,
15   And they seem not to break; though once they are bowed
So low for long, they never right themselves:
You may see their trunks arching in the woods
Years afterwards, trailing their leaves on the ground
Like girls on hands and knees that throw their hair
20   Before them over their heads to dry in the sun.
But I was going to say when Truth broke in
With all her matter-of-fact about the ice-storm
I should prefer to have some boy bend them
As he went out and in to fetch the cows—
25   Some boy too far from town to learn baseball,
Whose only play was what he found himself,
Summer or winter, and could play alone.
One by one he subdued his father's trees
By riding them down over and over again
30   Until he took the stiffness out of them,
And not one but hung limp, not one was left
For him to conquer. He learned all there was
To learn about not launching out too soon
And so not carrying the tree away
35   Clear to the ground. He always kept his poise
To the top branches, climbing carefully
With the same pains you use to fill a cup
Up to the brim, and even above the brim.
Then he flung outward, feet first, with a swish,
40   Kicking his way down through the air to the ground.

So was I once myself a swinger of birches.
And so I dream of going back to be.
It's when I'm weary of considerations,
And life is too much like a pathless wood
45   Where your face burns and tickles with the cobwebs
Broken across it, and one eye is weeping
From a twig's having lashed across it open.
I'd like to get away from earth awhile
And then come back to it and begin over.
50   May no fate willfully misunderstand me
And half grant what I wish and snatch me away
Not to return. Earth's the right place for love:
I don't know where it's likely to go better.
I'd like to go by climbing a birch tree,
55   And climb black branches up a snow-white trunk
Toward heaven, till the tree could bear no more,
But dipped its top and set me down again.
That would be good both going and coming back.
One could do worse than be a swinger of birches.

ROBERT FROST (1874–1963)

Directive (1947)

Back out of all this now too much for us,
Back in a time made simple by the loss
Of detail, burned, dissolved, and broken off
Like graveyard marble sculpture in the weather,
5   There is a house that is no more a house
Upon a farm that is no more a farm
And in a town that is no more a town.
The road there, if you'll let a guide direct you
Who only has at heart your getting lost,
10   May seem as if it should have been a quarry—
Great monolithic knees the former town
Long since gave up pretense of keeping covered.
And there's a story in a book about it:
Besides the wear of iron wagon wheels
15   The ledges show lines ruled southeast-northwest,
The chisel work of an enormous Glacier
That braced his feet against the Arctic Pole.

You must not mind a certain coolness from him
Still said to haunt this side of Panther Mountain.
20 Nor need you mind the serial ordeal
Of being watched from forty cellar holes
As if by eye pairs out of forty firkins.°   barrels
As for the woods' excitement over you
That sends light rustle rushes to their leaves,
25 Charge that to upstart inexperience.
Where were they all not twenty years ago?
They think too much of having shaded out
A few old pecker-fretted apple trees.
Make yourself up a cheering song of how
30 Someone's road home from work this once was,
Who may be just ahead of you on foot
Or creaking with a buggy load of grain.
The height of the adventure is the height
Of country where two village cultures faded
35 Into each other. Both of them are lost.
And if you're lost enough to find yourself
By now, pull in your ladder road behind you
And put a sign up CLOSED to all but me.
Then make yourself at home. The only field
40 Now left's no bigger than a harness gall.
First there's the children's house of make-believe,
Some shattered dishes underneath a pine,
The playthings in the playhouse of the children.
Weep for what little things could make them glad.
45 Then for the house that is no more a house,
But only a belilaced° cellar hole,   covered with lilacs
Now slowly closing like a dent in dough.
This was no playhouse but a house in earnest.
Your destination and your destiny's
50 A brook that was the water of the house,
Cold as a spring as yet so near its source,
Too lofty and original to rage.
(We know the valley streams that when aroused
Will leave their tatters hung on barb and thorn.)
55 I have kept hidden in the instep arch
Of an old cedar at the waterside
A broken drinking goblet like the Grail
Under a spell so the wrong ones can't find it,
So can't get saved, as Saint Mark° says they mustn't.   Gospel of Mark
60 (I stole the goblet from the children's playhouse.)
Here are your waters and your watering place.
Drink and be whole again beyond confusion.

WALLACE STEVENS (1879–1955)

Sunday Morning (1923)

I

Complacencies of the peignoir,° and late   nightgown
Coffee and oranges in a sunny chair,
And the green freedom of a cockatoo
Upon a rug mingle to dissipate
5   The holy hush of ancient sacrifice.
She dreams a little, and she feels the dark
Encroachment of that old catastrophe,
As a calm darkens among water-lights.
The pungent oranges and bright, green wings
10   Seem things in some procession of the dead,
Winding across wide water, without sound.
The day is like wide water, without sound,
Stilled for the passing of her dreaming feet
Over the seas, to silent Palestine,
15   Dominion of the blood and sepulchre.

II

Why should she give her bounty to the dead?
What is divinity if it can come
Only in silent shadows and in dreams?
Shall she not find in comforts of the sun,
20   In pungent fruit and bright, green wings, or else
In any balm or beauty of the earth,
Things to be cherished like the thought of heaven?
Divinity must live within herself:
Passions of rain, or moods in falling snow;
25   Grievings in loneliness, or unsubdued
Elations when the forest blooms; gusty
Emotions on wet roads on autumn nights;
All pleasures and all pains, remembering
The bough of summer and the winter branch.
30   These are the measures destined for her soul.

III

Jove in the clouds had his inhuman birth.
No mother suckled him, no sweet land gave
Large-mannered motions to his mythy mind
He moved among us, as a muttering king,
35   Magnificent, would move among his hinds,

Until our blood, commingling, virginal,
With heaven, brought such requital to desire
The very hinds discerned it, in a star.
Shall our blood fail? Or shall it come to be
40   The blood of paradise? And shall the earth
Seem all of paradise that we shall know?
The sky will be much friendlier then than now,
A part of labor and a part of pain,
And next in glory to enduring love,
45   Not this dividing and indifferent blue.

IV

She says, "I am content when wakened birds,
Before they fly, test the reality
Of misty fields, by their sweet questionings;
But when the birds are gone, and their warm fields
50   Return no more, where, then, is paradise?"
There is not any haunt of prophecy,
Nor any old chimera of the grave,
Neither the golden underground, nor isle
Melodious, where spirits gat them home,
55   Nor visionary south, nor cloudy palm
Remote on heaven's hill, that has endured
As April's green endures; or will endure
Like her remembrance of awakened birds,
Or her desire for June and evening, tipped
60   By the consummation of the swallow's wings.

V

She says, "But in contentment I still feel
The need of some imperishable bliss."
Death is the mother of beauty; hence from her,
Alone, shall come fulfilment to our dreams
65   And our desires. Although she strews the leaves
Of sure obliteration on our paths,
The path sick sorrow took, the many paths
Where triumph rang its brassy phrase, or love
Whispered a little out of tenderness,
70   She makes the willow shiver in the sun
For maidens who were wont to sit and gaze
Upon the grass, relinquished to their feet.
She causes boys to pile new plums and pears
On disregarded plate. The maidens taste
75   And stray impassioned in the littering leaves.

VI

Is there no change of death in paradise?
Does ripe fruit never fall? Or do the boughs
Hang always heavy in that perfect sky,
Unchanging, yet so like our perishing earth,
80 With rivers like our own that seek for seas
They never find, the same receding shores
That never touch with inarticulate pang?
Why set the pear upon those river-banks
Or spice the shores with odors of the plum?
85 Alas, that they should wear our colors there,
The silken weavings of our afternoons,
And pick the strings of our insipid lutes!
Death is the mother of beauty, mystical,
Within whose burning bosom we devise
90 Our earthly mothers waiting, sleeplessly.

VII

Supple and turbulent, a ring of men
Shall chant in orgy on a summer morn
Their boisterous devotion to the sun,
Not as a god, but as a god might be,
95 Naked among them, like a savage source.
Their chant shall be a chant of paradise,
Out of their blood, returning to the sky;
And in their chant shall enter, voice by voice,
The windy lake wherein their lord delights,
100 The trees, like serafin, and echoing hills,
That choir among themselves long afterward.
They shall know well the heavenly fellowship
Of men that perish and of summer morn.
And whence they came and whither they shall go
105 The dew upon their feet shall manifest.

VIII

She hears, upon that water without sound,
A voice that cries, "The tomb in Palestine
Is not the porch of spirits lingering.
It is the grave of Jesus, where he lay."
110 We live in an old chaos of the sun,
Or old dependency of day and night,
Or island solitude, unsponsored, free,
Of that wide water, inescapable.
Deer walk upon our mountains, and the quail

115   Whistle about us their spontaneous cries;
      Sweet berries ripen in the wilderness;
      And, in the isolation of the sky,
      At evening, casual flocks of pigeons make
      Ambiguous undulations as they sink,
120   Downward to darkness, on extended wings.

DELMORE SCHWARTZ (1913–1966)

In the Naked Bed, in Plato's Cave

In the naked bed, in Plato's cave,[1]
Reflected headlights slowly slid the wall,
Carpenters hammered under the shaded window,
Wind troubled the window curtains all night long,
5   A fleet of trucks strained uphill, grinding,
Their freights covered, as usual.
The ceiling lightened again, the slanting diagram
Slid slowly forth.
                     Hearing the milkman's chop,
10   His striving up the stair, the bottle's chink,
I rose from bed, lit a cigarette,
And walked to the window. The stony street
Displayed the stillness in which buildings stand,
The street-lamp's vigil and the horse's patience.
15   The winter sky's pure capital
Turned me back to bed with exhausted eyes.

Strangeness grew in the motionless air. The loose
Film grayed. Shaking wagons, hooves' waterfalls,
Sounded far off, increasing, louder and nearer.
20   A car coughed, starting. Morning, softly
Melting the air, lifted the half-covered chair
From underseas, kindled the looking-glass,
Distinguished the dresser and the white wall.
The bird called tentatively, whistled, called,
25   Bubbled and whistled, so! Perplexed, still wet

---

[1] **Plato's cave:** Schwartz refers to Plato's "Allegory of the Cave" in Book VII of *The Republic,* in which he likens human beings to people trapped in a cave who mistake the shadows on the walls of the cave for reality, unaware that reality burns brightly outside of the cave.

With sleep, affectionate, hungry and cold. So, so,
O son of man, the ignorant night, the travail
Of early morning, the mystery of beginning
Again and again,
                      while History is unforgiven.

HOWARD NEMEROV (1920–1991)

The Town Dump (1958)

"*The art of our necessities is strange,*
That can make vile things precious."

A mile out in the marshes, under a sky
Which seems to be always going away
In a hurry, on that Venetian land threaded
With hidden canals, you will find the city
5   Which seconds ours (so cemeteries, too,
Reflect a town from hillsides out of town),
Where Being most Becomingly ends up
Becoming some more. From cardboard tenements,
Windowed with cellophane, or simply tenting
10   In paper bags, the angry mackerel eyes
Glare at you out of stove-in, sunken heads
Far from the sea; the lobster, also, lifts
An empty claw in his most minatory
Of gestures; oyster, crab, and mussel shells
15   Lie here in heaps, savage as money hurled
Away at the gate of hell. If you want results,
These are results.
                      Objects of value or virtue,
However, are also to be picked up here,
20   Though rarely, lying with bones and rotten meat,
Eggshells and mouldy bread, banana peels
No one will skid on, apple cores that caused
Neither the fall of man nor a theory
Of gravitation. People do throw out
25   The family pearls by accident, sometimes,
Not often; I've known dealers in antiques
To prowl this place by night, with flashlights, on
The off-chance of somebody's having left
Derelict chairs which will turn out to be
30   By Hepplewhite, a perfect set of six
Going to show, I guess, that in any sty

Someone's heaven may open and shower down
Riches responsive to the right dream; though
It is a small chance, certainly, that sends
35 The ghostly dealer, heavy with fly-netting
Over his head, across these hills in darkness,
Stumbling in cut-glass goblets, lacquered cups,
And other products of his dreamy midden
Penciled with light and guarded by the flies.

40 For there are flies, of course. A dynamo
Composed, by thousands, of our ancient black
Retainers, hums here day and night, steady
As someone telling beads, the hum becoming
A high whine at any disturbance; then,
45 Settled again, they shine under the sun
Like oil-drops, or are invisible as night,
By night.
       All this continually smoulders,
Crackles, and smokes with mostly invisible fires
50 Which, working deep, rarely flash out and flare,
And never finish. Nothing finishes;
The flies, feeling the heat, keep on the move.

Among the flies, the purefying fires,
The hunters by night, acquainted with the art
55 Of our necessities, and the new deposits
That each day wastes with treasure, you may say
There should be ratios. You may sum up
The results, if you want results. But I will add
That wild birds, drawn to the carrion and flies,
60 Assemble in some numbers here, their wings
Shining with light, their flight enviably free,
Their music marvelous, though sad, and strange.

AMY CLAMPITT (1920–1994)

From a Clinic Waiting Room (1985)

I write from the denser enclave of the stricken,
eight stories up, a prairie *gratte-ciel.*°   skyscraper
Above the valley floor, the bell tower
of a displaced Italian hill town listens, likewise
5 attentive to the mysteries of one Body.
If the two salute, it must be as monks do,

without gesture, eyes lowered
by the force of gravity. Between them,
down among the car parks, tree shapes
10   stripped twig-bare appear to bruise
with tenderness, illusory as sea anemones.
There is no wind. For days
the geese that winter in the bottomland
have been the one thing always on the move,
15   in swags of streaming fronds, chiaroscuro
sea blooms, their wavering V-signs
following the turnings of one body.
Where are they going?
                         Down in the blood bank
20   the centrifuge, its branched transparent siphons
stripping the sap of Yggdrasil°   mythical world tree
from the slit arm of the donor, skims
the spinning corpuscles, cream-white
from hectic red. Below the pouched pack
25   dangled like a gout of mistletoe, the tubing
drips, drips from valve to valve to enter,
in a gradual procession, the cloistered
precincts of another body.
                         Sunset, its tinctured
30   layerings vivid as delirium, astonishing
as merely to be living, stains the cold
of half a hemisphere. The old
moon's dark corpus, its mysteries
likewise halfway illusory, tonight sleeps slumped
35   on the phosphorescent threshold of the new.

RICHARD WILBUR (1921–   )

Love Calls Us to the Things of This World (1956)

The eyes open to a cry of pulleys,
And spirited from sleep, the astounded soul
Hangs for a moment bodiless and simple
As false dawn.
5   Outside the open window
The morning air is all awash with angels.

Some are in bed-sheets, some are in blouses,
Some are in smocks: but truly there they are.
Now they are rising together in calm swells

10   Of halcyon feeling, filling whatever they wear
     With the deep joy of their impersonal breathing;

       Now they are flying in place, conveying
     The terrible speed of their omnipresence, moving
     And staying like white water; and now of a sudden
15   They swoon down into so rapt a quiet
     That nobody seems to be there.
                         The soul shrinks

       From all that it is about to remember,
     From the punctual rape of every blessèd day,
20   And cries,
              "Oh, let there be nothing on earth but laundry,
     Nothing but rosy hands in the rising steam
     And clear dances done in the sight of heaven."

       Yet, as the sun acknowledges
     With a warm look the world's hunks and colors,
25   The soul descends once more in bitter love
     To accept the waking body, saying now
     In a changed voice as the man yawns and rises,

       "Bring them down from their ruddy gallows;
     Let there be clean linen for the backs of thieves;
30   Let lovers go fresh and sweet to be undone,
     And the heaviest nuns walk in a pure floating
     Of dark habits,
                keeping their difficult balance."

PHILIP LEVINE (1928–   )

Belle Isle, 1949

     We stripped in the first warm spring night
     and ran down into the Detroit River
     to baptize ourselves in the brine
     of car parts, dead fish, stolen bicycles,
5   melted snow. I remember going under
     hand in hand with a Polish highschool girl
     I'd never seen before, and the cries
     our breath made caught at the same time
     on the cold, and rising through the layers
10   of darkness into the final moonless atmosphere

that was this world, the girl breaking
the surface after me and swimming out
on the starless waters towards the lights
of Jefferson Ave. and the stacks
15   of the old stove factory unwinking.
Turning at last to see no island at all
but a perfect calm dark as far
as there was sight, and then a light
and another riding low out ahead
20   to bring us home, ore boats maybe, or smokers
walking alone. Back panting
to the gray coarse beach we didn't dare
fall on, the damp piles of clothes,
and dressing side by side in silence
25   to go back where we came from.

ANNE SEXTON   (1928–1974)

Wanting to Die   (1966)

Since you ask, most days I cannot remember.
I walk in my clothing, unmarked by that voyage.
Then the almost unnameable lust returns.

Even then I have nothing against life.
5   I know well the grass blades you mention,
the furniture you have placed under the sun.

But suicides have a special language.
Like carpenters they want to know *which tools*.
They never ask *why build*.

10   Twice I have so simply declared myself,
have possessed the enemy, eaten the enemy,
have taken on his craft, his magic.

In this way, heavy and thoughtful,
warmer than oil or water,
15   I have rested, drooling at the mouth-hole.

I did not think of my body at needle point.
Even the cornea and the leftover urine were gone.
Suicides have already betrayed the body.

Still-born, they don't always die,
20   but dazzled, they can't forget a drug so sweet
that even children would look on and smile.

To thrust all that life under your tongue!—
that, all by itself, becomes a passion.
Death's a sad bone; bruised, you'd say,

25   and yet she waits for me, year after year,
to so delicately undo an old wound,
to empty my breath from its bad prison.

Balanced there, suicides sometimes meet,
raging at the fruit, a pumped-up moon,
30   leaving the bread they mistook for a kiss,

leaving the page of the book carelessly open,
something unsaid, the phone off the hook
and the love, whatever it was, an infection.

JAY PARINI (1948–   )

The Function of Winter (1988)

I'm for it, as the last leaves shred
or powder on the floor, as sparrows find
the driest footing, and November rains
fall hard as salt sprayed over roads.
5   The circulating spores take cover
where they can, and light runs level
to the ground again: no more the vertical
blond summer sheen that occupies a day,
but winter flatness—light as part of things,
10   not things themselves. My heart's in storage
for the six-month siege we're in for here,
laid up for use a little at a time
like hardtack on a polar expedition,
coveted though stale. Ideas, which in
15   summer hung a crazy jungle in my head,
subside now, separate and gleam in parts;
I braid them for display on winter walls
like garlic tails or onions, crisp bay wreaths.
One by one, I'll pluck them into spring.

20   If truth be told, I find it easier
      to live this way: the fructifying boom
      of summer over, wild birds gone, and wind
      along the ground where cuffs can feel it.
      Everything's in reach or neatly labeled
25   on my basement shelves. I'm ready to begin
      to see what happened when my heart was hot,
      my head too dazzled by itself to think.

GARRETT KAORU HONGO (1951–   )

Yellow Light (1982)

      One arm hooked around the frayed strap
      of a tar-black, patent-leather purse,
      the other cradling something for dinner:
      fresh bunches of spinach from a J-Town *yaoya*,°   market
5   sides of split Spanish mackerel from Alviso's,
      maybe a loaf of Langendorf;° she steps   wheat bread
      off the hissing bus at Olympic and Fig,
      begins the three-block climb up the hill,
      passing gangs of schoolboys playing war,
10   Japs against Japs, Chicanas chalking sidewalks
      with the holy double-yoked crosses of hopscotch,
      and the Korean grocer's wife out for a stroll
      around this neighborhood of Hawaiian apartments
      just starting to steam with cooking
15   and the anger of young couples coming home
      from work, yelling at kids, flicking on
      TV sets for the Wednesday Night Fights.

      If it were May, hydrangeas and jacaranda
      flowers in the streetside trees would be
20   blooming through the smog of late spring.
      Wisteria in Masuda's front yard would be
      shaking out the long tresses of its purple hair.
      Maybe mosquitoes, moths, a few orange butterflies
      settling on the lattice of monkey flowers
25   tangled in chain-link fences by the trash.

      But this is October, and Los Angeles
      seethes like a billboard under twilight.
      From used-car lots and the movie houses uptown,
      long silver sticks of light probe the sky.

30 From the Miracle Mile, whole freeways away,
    a brilliant fluorescence breaks out
    and makes war with the dim squares
    of yellow kitchen light winking on
    in all the side streets of the Barrio.

35 She climbs up the two flights of flagstone
    stairs to 201-B, the spikes of her high heels
    clicking like kitchen knives on a cutting board,
    props the groceries against the door,
    fishes through memo pads, a compact,
40 empty packs of chewing gum, and finds her keys.

    The moon then, cruising from behind
    a screen of eucalyptus across the street,
    covers everything, everything in sight,
    in a heavy light like yellow onions.

MAJOR JACKSON (1968–   )

Indian Song (2002)

    Freddie Hubbard's playing the cassette deck
    Forty miles outside Hays and I've looked at
    This Kansas sunset for three hours now,
    Almost bristling as big rigs bounce and grumble
5 Along I-70. At this speed cornfields come
    In splotches, murky yellows and greens abutting
    The road's shoulder, the flat wealth of the nation whirring by.
    It's a kind of ornamentation I've gotten used to—
    As in a dream. Espaliered against the sky's blazing—
10 Cloud-luffs cascade lacelike darkening whole fields.
    30,000 feet above someone is buttering a muffin.
    Someone stares at a SKYPHONE, and momentarily—
    A baby cries in pressurized air. Through double-paned squares
    Someone squints: fields crosshatched by asphalt-strips.
15 It is said Cézanne looked at a landscape so long he felt
    As if his eyes were bleeding. No matter that. I'm heading west.
    It's all so redolent, this wailing music, by my side—
    You fingering fields of light, sunflowers over earth,
    Miles traveled, a patchwork of good-byes.

PROUD AS A PEERESS, PROUDER AS A PUNK

CHAPTER 9

—Alexander Pope

An Anthology of Heroic Couplets

The essential shape of the **heroic couplet** is a pair of rhyming lines of iambic pentameter. Couplets may consist of lines with any number of stresses or beats (iambs) per line, but the traditional heroic couplet counts five feet, hence, "pentameter." In English poetry, the form rose to prominence in the seventeenth and eighteenth centuries, when it became quite popular. In fact, the heroic couplet played a dominant role in the eighteenth century. But the form has its origins in the work of Geoffrey Chaucer, who is often called "the father of English poetry."

Chaucer, who wrote in the fourteenth century, seems to have invented the form. In the mid-1380s, he published his "The Legend of Good Woman." One of the prologues to that poem opens:

> A thousand times have I heard men tell
> That there is joy in heaven and pain in hell,
> And I accord well that it is so;
> Yet natheless, yet wot I well also
> 5   That there is none dwelling in this country
> That either hath in heaven or hell y-be,
> Ne may of hit none other wayes witten
> But as he hath heard said or found it written.

(This is Middle English, wherein "natheless" means *nonetheless,* "wot" and "witten" mean *understand,* and "hit" means *it*; "y-be" means *there have been.*)

The rhythm of Chaucer's line is not strictly or even mostly iambic. "A thousand times have I heard men tell" has an anapest, "have I heard," in the third foot, giving the line a tripping motion. (It should also be noted that, in Middle English, the "e" could have been sounded, although historians of the language disagree about the extent to which the "e" was sounded.) The second line is more strictly iambic pentameter: "That there is joy in heaven and pain in hell." The third line, oddly, has nine syllables, although Chaucer is not counting syllables but stresses, and one can discover five stresses in the line: "And I accord well that it is so."

One finds the couplet in use through the sixteenth and seventeenth centuries, often in a fairly "rough" or stressed line, although Ben Jonson made good use of the form, as in his elegy for his son (p. 138):

> Farewell, thou child of my right hand, and joy;
> My sin was too much hope of thee, loved boy,
> Seven years thou wert lent to me, and I thee pay
> Exacted by thy fate, on the just day.

This is elegant verse, with the couplet used quite effectively to contain the powerful emotion within strict boundaries, lending power to the feeling.

The form achieved its most typical aspect in the hands of eighteenth century masters of the form, including John Dryden, Jonathan Swift, and Alexander Pope. For Pope, it was nearly the only form worth using, and his witty, long, intellectually rigorous and amusing poems, such as the "Epistle to a Lady: Of the Characters of Women" (p. 724), use the form brilliantly. The rhyming of the couplet provided a delicious opportunity for Pope to show off his wit and high intelligence.

Poets in the nineteenth and twentieth centuries only occasionally used the form, although often they did so to great effect, as in Wilfred Owen's "Strange Meeting" (p. 776), which uses slant rhyme and enjambment to create a unique sound and feel. That poem opens fluidly, with hardly a sense of the rhyme except as a kind of distant echo:

> It seemed that out of battle I escaped
> Down some profound dull tunnel, long since scooped
> Through granites which titanic wars had groined.
> Yet also there encumbered sleepers groaned,
> 5   Too fast in thought or death to be bestirred.
> Then, as I probed them, one sprang up, and stared
> With piteous recognition in fixed eyes,
> Lifting distressful hands as if to bless.
> And by his smile I knew that sullen hall,
> 10 By his dead smile I knew we stood in Hell.

The form is put to quite a test by Robert Lowell in "To Speak of Woe That Is in Marriage" (p. 787), which is also a sonnet—or, at least, fits the sonnet's conventional fourteen lines. This all suggests that the form is capable of considerable flexibility.

The heroic couplet is artful, even artificial, and calls attention to itself as a self-consciously "made" thing. The speech patterns of contemporary English are so informal that the form can hardly accommodate its modalities without seeming archaic and constrained. But the form has enough range and flexibility to serve poets in a certain mood, and it often attracts poets who want to play with the language in witty and intelligent ways.

ADDITIONAL EXAMPLES OF HEROIC COUPLETS IN THIS BOOK

- Geoffrey Chaucer, "The Pardoner's Prologue and Tale" (p. 531)
- Ben Jonson, "On My First Son" and "On My First Daughter" (p. 138)
- Alexander Pope, "The Rape of the Lock" (p. 64)
- Robert Browning, "My Last Duchess" (p. 579)

GEOFFREY CHAUCER (ca. 1343–1400)
from The Canterbury Tales

The General Prologue (ca. 1387; 1478)

	Whan that Aprill with his° shoures sote°	its / sweet
	The droghte of Marche hath perced to the rote,	
	And bathed every veyne in swich° licour,°	such / liquid
	Of which vertu° engendred is the flour;	also
5	Whan Zephirus° eek with his swete breeth	West Wind
	Inspired hath in every holt° and heeth°	bower / field
	The tendre croppes,° and the yonge sonne	shoots
	Hath in the Ram his halfe cours y-ronne;	
	And smale fowles maken melodye,	
10	That slepen al the night with open ye°—	eye
	So priketh hem Nature in hir corages°—	hearts
	Than longen folk to goon° on pilgrimages,	go
	And palmeres for to seken straunge strondes,	
	To ferne halwes,° couthe° in sondry londes;	distant shrines / known
15	And specially, from every shires ende	
	Of Engelond to Caunterbury they wende,	
	The holy blisful martir[1] for to seke,	
	That hem hath holpen, whan that they were seke.	
	Bifel° that, in that seson on a day,	It befell
20	In Southwerk at the Tabard[2] as I lay	
	Redy to wenden on my pilgrimage	
	To Caunterbury with ful devout corage,	
	At night was come into that hostelrye°	hostel
	Wel nyne and twenty in a companye	

---

[1] **The holy blisful martir:** St. Thomas à Becket was murdered because of his faith in Canterbury Cathedral in 1170.
[2] **Southwerk . . . Tabard:** The Tabard Inn was in the Southwark part of London.

25 Of sondry folk, by aventure° y-falle°   by chance / fallen
    In felawshipe, and pilgrims were they alle,
    That toward Caunterbury wolden° ryde.   would
    The chambres and the stables weren wyde,
    And wel we weren esed° atte beste.°   put up / in the best way
30 And shortly, whan the sonne was to reste,°   had set
    So hadde I spoken with hem everichon°   everyone
    That I was of hir felawshipe anon,
    And made forward° erly for to ryse,   an agreement
    To take oure wey, ther as I yow devyse.°   describe
35   But natheles,° whyl I have tyme and space,   nevertheless
    Er that I ferther in this tale pace,
    Me thinketh it acordaunt to resoun
    To telle yow al the condicioun
    Of ech of hem, so as it semed me,
40 And whiche they weren, and of what degree,
    And eek in what array that they were inne;
    And at a knight than wol° I first biginne.   then will
         A KNIGHT ther was, and that a worthy man,
    That fro° the tyme that he first bigan   from
45 To ryden out, he loved chivalrye,
    Trouthe and honour, fredom and curteisye.
    Ful worthy was he in his lordes werre,°   war
    And therto hadde he riden, no man ferre,°   further
    As wel in Cristendom as in hethenesse,°   heathen places
50 And evere honoured for his worthinesse.
         At Alisaundre° he was whan it was wonne;   Alexandria
    Ful ofte tyme he hadde the bord bigonne
    Aboven alle naciouns in Pruce.
    In Lettow hadde he reysed° and in Ruce,   campaigned
55 No Cristen man so ofte of his degree.
    In Gernade at the sege° eek hadde he be   siege
    Of Algezir, and riden in Belmarye.
    At Lyeys was he and at Satalye,
    Whan they were wonne; and in the Grete See[3]
60 At many a noble armee hadde he be.
    At mortal batailles° hadde he been fiftene,   battles
    And foughten for oure feith at Tramissene
    In listes thryes,° and ay slayn his foo.°   attacks thrice / foes
    This ilke° worthy knight hadde been also   same
65 Somtyme with the lord of Palatye,[4]

---

[3] **Alisaundre . . . Grete See:** The knight has fought many battles against pagans and taken part in some famous battles between England and France.
[4] **lord of Palatye:** A pagan with whom Crusaders often made strategic alliances.

Ageyn° another hethen in Turkye;   against
And everemore he hadde a sovereyn prys.°   renown
And though that he were worthy, he was wys,°   wise
And of his port° as meke as is a mayde.   manner
70 He nevere yet no vileinye° ne sayde   vileness
In al his lyf, unto no maner wight.
He was a verray,° parfit,° gentil° knight.   true / perfect / gentle
But for to tellen yow of his array,
His hors° were gode, but he was nat gay.   horses
75 Of fustian° he wered° a gipoun,°   cloth / wore / tunic
Al bismotered° with his habergeoun,°   soiled / coat of mail
For he was late y-come from his viage,°   voyage
And wente for to doon his pilgrimage.
    With him ther was his sone, a young SQUYER,
80 A lovyere, and a lusty bacheler,
With lokkes crulle,° as they were leyd in presse.   curly hair
Of twenty yeer of age he was, I gesse.
Of his stature he was of evene lengthe,°   moderate height
And wonderly delivere, and of greet strengthe.
85 And he hadde been somtyme in chivachye
In Flaundres, in Artoys, and Picardye,
And born him wel, as of so litel space,
In hope to stonden° in his lady° grace.   stands / lady's
Embrouded° was he, as it were a mede°   embroidered / meadow
90 Al ful of fresshe floures, whyte and rede.
Singinge he was, or floytinge,° al the day;   whistling
He was as fresh as is the month of May.
Short was his gowne, with sleves longe and wyde.
Wel coude he sitte on hors, and faire ryde.
95 He coude songes make and wel endyte,°   create
Juste° and eek daunce, and wel purtreye° and wryte.   joust / portray or sketch
So hote° he lovede that by nightertale°   hotly / night
He sleep namore° than dooth a nightingale.   no more
Curteys he was, lowly, and servisable,
100 And carf° biforn his fader° at the table.   carve / food; meat
    A YEMAN hadde he, and servaunts namo°   no more
At that tyme, for him liste ryde so;
And he was clad in cote and hood of grene.
A sheef of pecok-arwes° brighte and kene   peacock arrows
105 Under his belt he bar° ful thriftily.°   bore / shrewdly
Wel coude he dresse° his takel° yemanly: tend / his gear
His arwes drouped noght with fetheres lowe,
And in his hand he bar a mighty bowe.
A not-heed° hadde he, with a broun visage.   knot-head
110 Of wodecraft wel coude he al the usage.
Upon his arm he bar a gay bracer,°   wrist guard

And by his syde a swerd and a bokeler,°   shield
And on that other syde a gay daggere,
Harneised° wel, and sharp as point of spere;   mounted
115   A Cristofre° on his brest of silver shene.°   St. Christopher / shone
An horn he bar, the bawdrik° was of grene;   strap
A forster° was he, soothly, as I gesse.   forester
     Ther was also a Nonne, a PRIORESSE,
That of hir smyling was ful simple and coy—
120   Hir gretteste ooth was but by Seynte Loy°—   Eloi
And she was cleped° madame Eglentyne.   called
Ful wel she song the service divyne,
Entuned in hir nose ful semely;
And Frensh she spak ful faire and fetisly,
125   After the scole of Stratford atte Bowe,⁵
For Frensh of Paris was to hire unknowe.
At mete° wel y-taught was she with alle: meals
She leet° no morsel from hir lippes falle,   let
Ne wette hir fingres in hir sauce depe.°   deep
130   Wel coude she carie a morsel, and wel kepe
That no drope ne fille° upon hire brest.   should fall
In curteisye was set ful muchel hir lest.
Hir over-lippe wyped she so clene,
That in hir coppe° was no ferthing° sene°   cup / drop / seen
135   Of grece,° whan she dronken hadde hir draughte.   grease
Ful semely after hir mete she raughte,°   reached
And sikerly° she was of greet disport,°   certainly / good cheer
And ful plesaunt, and amiable of port,°   mien
And peyned hire to countrefete chere
140   Of court, and to been estatlich° of manere,   dignified
And to ben holden digne° of reverence.   worthy
But, for to speken of hire conscience,
She was so charitable and so pitous,
She wolde wepe, if that she sawe a mous°   mouse
145   Caught in a trappe, if it were deed or bledde.
Of° smale houndes hadde she, that she fedde   Some
With rosted flesh, or milk and wastel-breed.
But sore wepte she if oon of hem were deed,
Or if men smoot it with a yerde° smerte;°   rod / sharply
150   And al was conscience and tendre herte.
Ful semely hir wimpel° pinched° was,   hood / wrinkled
Hir nose tretys,° hir eyen greye as glas,   well-shaped
Hir mouth ful smal, and therto softe and reed.
But sikerly° she hadde a fair forheed—   certainly

---

⁵ **scole of Stratford atte Bowe:** A school where poor French was apparently taught.

155   It was almost a spanne° brood, I trowe°—   span (of a hand) / believe
     For hardily° she was nat undergrowe.°   assuredly / thin
     Ful fetis° was hir cloke, as I was war.°   handsome / aware
     Of smal coral aboute hire arm she bar
     A peire of bedes, gauded al with grene;[6]
160   And theron heng a broche of gold ful shene,
     On which ther was first write a crowned A,[7]
     And after, *Amor vincit omnia.*[8]
        Another NONNE with hire hadde she,
     That was hir chapeleyne,° and PREESTES three.   assistant
165   A MONK ther was, a fair for the maistrye,°   a terrific fellow
     An outrydere that lovede venerye:[9]
     A manly man, to been an abbot able.
     Ful many a deyntee° hors hadde he in stable,   fine
     And whan he rood, men mighte his brydel here
170   Ginglen° in a whistling wind als clere   jingling
     And eek as loude as dooth the chapel belle,
     Ther as this lord was kepere of the celle.
     The reule of Seint Maure or of Seint Beneit,[10]
     By cause that it was old and somdel streit,°   somewhat strict
175   This ilke° monk leet olde thinges pace,°   same / pass
     And held after the newe world the space.[11]
     He yaf nat of that text a pulled hen,[12]
     That seith that hunters ben° nat holy men,   are
     Ne that a monk, whan he is reccheless,°   reckless
180   Is lykned til° a fish that is waterlees   to
     (This is to seyn,° a monk out of his cloistre);   say
     But thilke° text held he nat worth an oistre.°   that same / oyster
     And I seyde his opinioun was good:
     What sholde he studie, and make himselven wood,°   dull
185   Upon a book in cloistre alwey to poure,°   pour
     Or swinken° with his handes, and laboure,   work
     As Austin bit?[13] How shal the world be served?
     Lat Austin have his swink to him reserved!
     Therfore he was a pricasour° aright: hard rider
190   Grehoundes he hadde, as swifte as fowel in flight;
     Of priking° and of hunting for the hare   riding

---

[6] **smal coral . . . grene:** She wore a nice bracelet and green prayer beads, a special rosary.
[7] **a crowned A:** An A with a special crown on it for decoration.
[8] ***Amor vincit omnia:*** Latin: Love conquers all.
[9] **An outrydere . . . venerye:** A monk who rode around the periphery of the monastery property to supervise activity.
[10] **Seint Maure . . . Beneit:** St. Maurus and St. Benedict each established monastic rules for their orders.
[11] **held . . . space:** That is, he favors the present world.
[12] **yaf . . . hen:** He didn't give a plucked hen for that text.
[13] **As Austin bit:** As St. Augustine bids.

	Was al his lust,° for no cost wolde he spare.	desire
	I seigh° his sleves purfiled° at the hond	saw / fur-lined
	With grys,° and that the fyneste of a lond;°	fur / land
195	And, for to festne° his hood under his chin,	fasten
	He hadde of gold y-wroght° a ful curious pin:	made
	A love-knotte in the gretter° ende ther was.	greater
	His heed was balled,° that shoon as any glas,	bald
	And eek his face, as he had been anoint.	
200	He was a lord ful fat and in good point:°	shape
	His eyen stepe,° and rollinge in his heed,	eyes protruding
	That stemed as a forneys of a leed;[14]	
	His bootes souple,° his hors in greet estat°—	supple / fine condition
	Now certeinly he was a fair prelat.	
205	He was nat pale as a forpyned goost;°	wasted ghost
	A fat swan loved he best of any roost.	
	His palfrey° was as broun as is a berye.°	saddle horse / bear
	A FRERE° ther was, a wantowne and a merye,	friar
	A limitour,[15] a ful solempne man.	
210	In alle the ordres foure° is noon that can°	four orders / know
	So muchel of daliaunce and fair langage.	
	He hadde maad° ful many a mariage	created
	Of yonge wommen, at his owne cost.	
	Unto his ordre he was a noble post.°	pillar
215	Ful wel biloved and famulier was he	
	With frankeleyns over al in his contree,[16]	
	And eek with worthy wommen of the toun;	
	For he hadde power of confessioun,	
	As seyde himself, more than a curat,°	curate or priest
220	For of his ordre he was licentiat.[17]	
	Ful swetely herde he confessioun,	
	And plesaunt was his absolucioun;	
	He was an esy man to yeve° penaunce	give
	Ther as he wiste to have a good pitaunce.°	donation
225	For unto a povre° ordre for to yive°	poor / give
	Is signe that a man is wel y-shrive°—	forgiven
	For if he yaf, he dorste make avaunt,°	a boast
	He wiste° that a man was repentaunt.	wishes
	For many a man so hard is of his herte,	
230	He may nat wepe al-thogh hym sore smerte:°	sorely grieved
	Therfore, in stede of wepinge and preyeres,	
	Men moot° yeve silver to the povre° freres.	may / poor

---

[14] **stemed . . . leed:** That steamed like a stove with a lead pot upon it.
[15] **limitour:** One who is licensed to beg for the Church.
[16] **frankeleyns . . . contree:** He was known and beloved by franklins everywhere.
[17] **licentiat:** He was licensed to hear confessions.

His tipet° was ay farsed° ful of knyves   scarf / packed

And pinnes, for to yeven° faire wyves.   impress

235   And certeinly he hadde a murye° note;   merry

Wel coude he singe and pleyen on a rote;°   fiddle

Of yeddinges he bar outrely the prys.[18]

His nekke whyt was as the flour-de-lys;°   lily

Therto° he strong was as a champioun.   Therefore

240   He knew the tavernes wel in every toun,

And everich hostiler° and tappestere°   innkeeper / barmaid

Bet than a lazar or a beggestere,°   female beggar

For unto swich° a worthy man as he   such

Acorded nat, as by his facultee,°   position

245   To have with seke lazars° aqueyntaunce: lepers

It is nat honest,° it may nat avaunce°   dignified / profit

For to delen with no swich poraille,°   poor folks

But al with riche and selleres of vitaille.°   food

And over al, ther as profit sholde aryse,

250   Curteys he was, and lowely of servyse.

Ther nas° no man nowher so vertuous.°   never / shrewd

He was the beste beggere in his hous,

[And yaf a certeyn ferme for the graunt:[19]

Noon of his bretheren cam ther in his haunt.]

255   For thogh a widwe° hadde noght a sho,°   widow / shoe

So pleasaunt was his *In principio,*°   In the beginning

Yet wolde he have a ferthing,° er he wente.   coin

His purchas was wel bettre than his rente.[20]

And rage he coude, as it were right a whelpe;°   puppy

260   In love-dayes ther coude he muchel helpe,[21]

For there he was nat lyk a cloisterer,°   monk

With a thredbare cope,° as is a povre scoler.   cape

But he was lyk a maister° or a pope: great scholar

Of double worsted was his semi-cope,°   short gown

265   That rounded as a belle out of the presse.

Somwhat he lipsed, for his wantownesse,°   affectation

To make his English swete upon his tonge;

And in his harping, whan that he hadde songe,

His eyen twinkled in his heed aright

270   As doon the sterres° in the frosty night.   stars

This worthy limitour was cleped° Huberd.   called

    A MARCHANT was ther with a forked berd,°   beard

---

[18] **Of yeddinges . . . prys:** He took the prize for his ballads.

[19] **And yaf . . . graunt:** He paid a fee for the right to beg, so others didn't dare to come into the region that he had paid to canvas.

[20] **rente:** The money he received through this activity exceeded his regular income.

[21] **love-dayes . . . helpe:** On days appointed for settling lawsuits out of court.

In mottelee,° and hye° on horse he sat;   motley / high
Upon his heed a Flaundrish° bever° hat,   Flemish / beaver
275 His bootes clasped faire and fetisly.°   fashionably
His resons° he spak ful solempnely,   opinions
Souninge° alway th'encrees of his winning.   sounding
He wolde the see were kept for any thing
Bitwixe Middelburgh and Orewelle.
280 Wel coude he in eschaunge sheeldes selle.²²
This worthy man ful wel his wit bisette:°   employed
Ther wiste no wight that he was in dette,
So estatly° was he of his governaunce,°   dignified / self-governance
With his bargaynes and with his chevisaunce.°   borrowing
285 For sothe he was a worthy man with alle,
But sooth to seyn, I noot how men him calle.
      A CLERK ther was of Oxenford° also,   Oxford University
That unto logik hadde longe y-go.
As leene° was his hors as is a rake,   lean
290 And he nas nat right fat, I undertake,
But loked holwe,° and therto soberly.   hollow
Ful thredbar was his overest courtepy,°   overcoat
For he hadde geten him yet no benefyce,
Ne was so worldly for to have offyce;
295 For him was levere° have at his beddes heed   rather
Twenty bokes, clad in blak or reed,
Of Aristotle and his philosophye,
Than robes riche, or fithele,° or gay sautrye.°   fiddle / harp
But al be that he was philosophre,
300 Yet hadde he but litel gold in cofre;°   coffer
But al that he mighte of his freendes hente,°   take
On bokes and on lerninge he it spente,
And bisily gan for the soules preye
Of hem that yaf him wherwith to scoleye.°   study
305 Of studie took he most cure° and most hede.°   care / heed
Noght o° word spak he more than was nede,   one
And that was seyd in forme° and reverence,   with decorum
And short and quik, and ful of hy sentence.
Souninge° in moral vertu was his speche,   Resounding
310 And gladly wolde he lerne, and gladly teche.
      A SERGEANT OF THE LAWE,° war° and wys,°   judge / wary / wise
That often hadde been at the Parvys,²³
Ther was also, ful riche of excellence.

---

²² **He wolde . . . sheeldes selle:** The sea passage between Middleburgh (in the Netherlands) and
Orwell (in England) was important for the Merchant's trade in wool.
²³ **Parvys:** The "Paradise" was a place where clients meet with their lawyers.

Discreet he was and of greet reverence:
315 He semed swich, his wordes weren so wyse.
Justyce he was ful often in assyse,°   circuit courts
By patente° and by pleyn° commissioun;   warrant / full
For his science° and for his heigh renoun,   knowledge
Of fees and robes hadde he many oon.°   owned
320 So greet a purchasour° was nowher noon:°   land speculator / known
Al was fee simple to him in effect;
His purchasing mighte nat been infect.[24]
Nowher so bisy a man as he ther nas;
And yet he semed bisier than he was.
325 In termes hadde he caas and domes alle,[25]
That from the tyme of King William were falle.
Therto he coude endyte,° and make a thing,°   draw up / deed
Ther coude no wight pinche at° his wryting,   cavil at
And every statut coude° he pleyn by rote.°   knew / by heart
330 He rood but hoomly° in a medlee° cote,   homey / coat of mixed colors
Girt with a ceint of silk, with barres smale;
Of his array telle I no lenger tale.
     A FRANKELEYN[26] was in his companye.
Whyt was his berd as is the dayesye;°   daisy
335 Of his complexioun he was sangwyn.°   flushed
Wel loved he by the morwe a sop in wyn.[27]
To liven in delyt was evere his wone,°   wish
For he was Epicurus[28] owene sone,
That heeld opinioun that pleyn° delyt   full
340 Was verray felicitee parfyt.
An housholdere, and that a greet, was he;
Seint Julian[29] he was in his contree.
His breed, his ale, was alweys after oon;[30]
A bettre envyned° man was nowher noon.   wine-stocked
345 Withoute bake mete was nevere his hous,
Of fish and flesh, and that so plentevous
It snewed° in his hous of met° and drinke.   showed / meat
Of alle deyntees that men coude thinke,
After the sondry sesons of the yeer,
350 So chaunged he his mete and his soper.
Ful many a fat partrich hadde he in mewe,°   cage

---

[24] **infect:** Invalidated on a technical point of law.
[25] **caas . . . alle:** Law cases and decisions all.
[26] **Frankeleyn:** A Franklin was a prosperous country man.
[27] **morwe . . . wyn:** Bread soaked in wine.
[28] **Epicurus:** Greek philosopher who (by tradition) suggested pleasure was the goal of life.
[29] **Julian:** Patron saint of hospitality.
[30] **oon:** Always of the same high quality.

And many a breem° and many a luce° in stewe.°   carp / pike / stew
Wo was his cook, but if his sauce were
Poynaunt° and sharp, and redy al his gere.   pungent
355   His table dormant in his halle alway
Stood redy covered al the longe day.[31]
At sessiouns ther was he lord and sire;
Ful ofte tyme he was knight of the shire.
An anlas° and a gipser° al of silk   dagger / purse
360   Heng at his girdel, whyt as morne milk.
A shirreve° hadde he been, and a countour;°   sheriff / auditor
Was nowher such a worthy vavasour.°   gentleman
       An HABERDASSHER and a CARPENTER,
A WEBBE,° a DYERE, and a TAPICER,°   weaver / maker of tapestries
365   Were with us eek, clothed in o liveree
Of a solempne and greet fraternitee.
Ful fresh and newe hir gere apyked° was;   polished
Hir knyves were chaped noght with bras,
But al with silver; wroght ful clene and weel
370   Hire girdles and hire pouches everydeel.°   altogether
Wel semed ech of hem a fair burgeys°   burgher
To sitten in a yeldhallo° on a deys.°   guildhall / dias
Everich, for the wisdom that he can,
Was shaply° for to been an alderman.   suitable
375   For catel° hadde they ynogh and rente,°   property / income
And eek hir wyves wolde it wel assente;
And elles certein were they to blame.
It is ful fair to been y-clept "*Madame,*"
And goon to vigilyës al bifore,[32]
380   And have a mantel royalliche y-bore.°   royally carried
       A COOK they hadde with hem for the nones,°   occasion
To boille the chiknes with the mary-bones°   marrow bones
And poudre-marchant tart and galingale.[33]
Wel coude he knowe a draughte of London ale.
385   He coude roste, and sethe, and broille, and frye,
Maken mortreux,° and wel bake a pye.   stews
But greet harm was it, as it thoughte° me,   seemed to
That on his shine° a mormal° hadde he.   face / ulcer
For blankmanger,° that made he with the beste.   stew
390   A SHIPMAN was ther, woninge fer by weste:[34]

---

[31] **His table . . . day:** Tables were commonly dismantled when not in use. The Franklin kept his up
and set ("covered"), and so "dormant."
[32] **goon . . . bifore:** They went to feasts on the eves of saints' days and were always ("al bifore") at the
head of the procession.
[33] **poudre-marchant . . . galingale:** These are flavoring substances used in cooking.
[34] **woninge . . . weste:** Dwelling in the west.

For aught I woot,° he was of Dertemouthe.°   know / Dartmouth
He rood upon a rouncy, as he couthe,[35]
In a gowne of falding° to the knee.   wool
A daggere hanginge on a laas° hadde he   strap
395 Aboute his nekke, under his arm adoun.
The hote somer hadde maad his hewe al broun;
And certeinly he was a good felawe.
Ful many a draughte of wyn had he y-drawe°   stolen
Fro Burdeux-ward, whyl that the chapman sleep.[36]
400 Of nyce conscience took he no keep.
If that he faught, and hadde the hyer hond,
By water he sente hem hoom to every lond.
But of his craft, to rekene wel his tydes,°   tides
His stremes° and his daungers him bisydes,°   currents / hazards
405 His herberwe° and his mone,° his lodemenage,°   anchorage / moon / pilotage
Ther nas noon swich from Hulle to Cartage.[37]
Hardy he was, and wys to undertake;
With many a tempest hadde his berd been shake.
He knew wel alle the havenes,° as they were,   harbors
410 From Gootlond to the cape of Finistere,
And every cryke in Britayne and in Spayne;[38]
His barge y-cleped° was the Maudelayne.   was called
        With us ther was a DOCTOUR OF PHISYK;°   medicine
In al this world ne was ther noon him lyk
415 To speke of phisik and of surgerye,
For he was grounded in astronomye.
He kepte his pacient a ful greet deel
In houres, by his magik naturel.
Wel coude he fortunen the ascendent
420 Of his images for his pacient.
He knew the cause of everich maladye,
Were it of hoot or cold, or moiste, or drye,
And where engendred, and of what humour;
He was a verrey parfit practisour.°   practitioner
425 The cause y-knowe, and of his harm the roote,
Anon he yaf the seke man his boote.°   remedy
Ful redy hadde he his apothecaries,°   pharmacists
To sende him drogges and his letuaries,°   medicines
For ech of hem made other for to winne;
430 Hir frendschipe nas nat newe to biginne.

---

[35] **rouncy . . . couthe:** A stolen nag.
[36] **Burdeux-ward . . . sleep:** Wine from Bordeaux. Chapman was a wine merchant.
[37] **Hulle to Cartage:** Hull, a city in England, to Cartagena, in Spain.
[38] **Gootlond . . . Spayne:** Gootland is an island in the Baltic Sea. Finisterre is in Spain. A "cryke" is an inlet.

Wel knew he the olde Esculapius,
And Deiscorides, and eek Rufus,
Old Ypocras, Haly, and Galien,
Serapion, Razis, and Avicen,
435 Averrois, Damascien, and Constantyn,
Bernard, and Gatesden, and Gilbertyn.[39]
Of his diete mesurable° was he,   moderate
For it was of no superfluitee,
But of greet norissing and digestible.
440 His studie was but litel on the Bible.
In sangwin° and in pers° he clad was al,   blood-red / blue
Lyned with taffata and with sendal;°   silk
And yet he was but esy of dispence.°   cost
He kepte that he wan in pestilence,
445 For gold in phisik is a cordial;°   stimulant
Therefore he lovede gold in special.
     A good WYF was ther of bisyde BATHE,
But she was somdel° deef, and that was scathe.°   somewhat / a pity
Of clooth-making she hadde swiche an haunt,
450 She passed hem of Ypres and of Gaunt.[40]
In al the parisshe wyf ne was ther noon
That to the offringe° bifore hir sholde goon;   alms
And if ther dide, certeyn so wrooth° was she,   wrath
That she was out of alle charitee.
455 Hir coverchiefs ful fyne were of ground;°   texture
I dorste° swere they weyeden° ten pound   dare / weighed
That on a Sonday weren upon hir heed.
Hir hosen° weren of fyn scarlet reed,   hose
Ful streite y-teyd,° and shoos ful moiste° and newe.   laced / unworn
460 Bold was hir face, and fair, and reed of hewe.
She was a worthy womman al hir lyve:
Housbondes at chirche dore she hadde fyve,
Withouten other companye in youthe—
But therof nedeth nat to speke as nouthe°—   how
465 And thryes° hadde she been at Jerusalem.   thrice
She hadde passed many a straunge streem:°   river
At Rome she hadde been, and at Boloigne,
In Galice at Seint Jame, and at Coloigne;[41]
She coude° muchel of wandringe by the weye.°   knew / way
470 Gat-tothed° was she, soothly for to seye.   gap-toothed
Upon an amblere° esily° she sat,   horse / easily

---

[39] **Esculapius . . . Gilbertyn:** All famous authors on medical topics.
[40] **Ypres . . . Gaunt:** Flemish cloth-making towns.
[41] **Rome . . . Coloigne:** Sites of pilgrimage: Rome, Boulogne (France); St. James (Compostella, Spain); Cologne (Germany).

Y-wimpled° wel, and on hir heed an hat   *veiled*
As brood as is a bokeler or a targe; [42]
A foot-mantel° aboute hir hipes large,   *riding skirt*
475   And on hir feet a paire of spores° sharpe.   *spurs*
In felawschipe wel coude she laughe and carpe.°   *talk*
Of remedyes of love she knew per chaunce,°   *perchance*
For she coude of that art the olde daunce.[43]
     A good man was ther of religioun,
480   And was a povre PERSOUN° of a toun,   *parson*
But riche he was of holy thoght and werk.
He was also a lerned man, a clerk,
That Cristes gospel trewely wolde preche;
His parisshens° devoutly wolde he teche.   *parishioners*
485   Benigne° he was, and wonder° diligent,   *kind / wonderfully*
And in adversitee ful pacient,
And swich he was y-preved° ofte sythes.°   *proved /times*
Ful looth° were him to cursen° for his tithes,   *loath / condemn*
But rather wolde he yeven,° out of doute,°   *given / doubt*
490   Unto his povre parisshens aboute
Of his offring, and eek of his substaunce.°   *property*
He coude in litel thing han suffisaunce.°   *sufficiency*
Wyd was his parisshe, and houses fer asonder,
But he ne lafte° nat, for reyn ne thonder,   *neglected*
495   In siknes nor in meschief, to visyte
The ferreste° in his parisshe, muche and lyte,   *farthest*
Upon his feet, and in his hand a staf.
This noble ensample to his sheep he yaf,
That first he wroghte, and afterward he taughte.
500   Out of the gospel he tho° wordes caughte,°   *those / took*
And this figure he added eek therto,
That if gold ruste, what shal iren° do?   *iron*
For if a preest be foul,° on whom we truste,   *fool*
No wonder is a lewed° man to ruste;   *uneducated*
505   And shame it is, if a preest take keep,°   *heed*
A shiten° shepherde and a clene sheep.   *filthy*
Wel oghte a preest ensample for to yive,°   *give*
By his clennesse, how that his sheep sholde live.
He sette nat his benefice to hyre,°   *hire*
510   And leet° his sheep encombred in the myre,   *let*
And ran to London unto Seynte Poules°   *St. Paul's Cathedral*
To seken him a chaunterie for soules,
Or with a bretherhed to been withholde,

---

[42] **bokeler . . . targe:** Small shields.
[43] **coude . . . daunce:** That is, she understood the tricks of the trade.

But dwelte at hoom, and kepte wel his folde,
515 So that the wolf ne made it nat miscarie;
He was a shepherde and noght a mercenarie.
And though he holy were, and vertuous,
He was to sinful men nat despitous,°   scornful
Ne of his speche daungerous ne digne,°   superior
520 But in his teching discreet and benigne.
To drawen folk to heven by fairnesse,
By good ensample, this was his bisinesse;
But it were° any persone obstinat,   if there were
What so he were, of heigh or lough estat,
525 Him wolde he snibben° sharply for the nones.°   scold / occasion
A bettre preest I trowe° that nowher noon is.   trust
He wayted after° no pompe and reverence,   expected
Ne maked him a spyced conscience,°   overly fastidious conscience
But Cristes lore,° and his apostles twelve,   teaching
530 He taughte, and first he folwed it himselve.
     With him ther was a PLOWMAN, was his brother,
That hadde y-lad° of dong° ful many a fother.°   carried / dung / load
A trewe swinkere° and a good was he,   worker
Livinge in pees° and parfit charitee.   peace
535 God loved he best with al his hole° herte   whole
At alle tymes, thogh him gamed or smerte,°   pleased or grieved
And thanne his neighebour right as himselve.
He wolde thresshe, and therto dyke° and delve,°   dig / shovel
For Cristes sake, for every povre wight,
540 Withouten hyre, if it lay in his might.
His tythes payed he ful faire and wel,
Bothe of his propre swink° and his catel.°   work / property
In a tabard° he rood upon a mere.°   coat / mare
     Ther was also a Reve [44] and a Millere,
545 A Somnour and a Pardoner also,
A Maunciple, and myself—ther were namo.°   no more
     The MILLERE was a stout carl° for the nones;°   fellow / occasion
Ful big he was of brawn, and eek of bones—
That proved wel, for over al ther he cam,
550 At wrastling he wolde have alwey the ram. [45]
He was short-sholdred, brood, a thikke knarre:°   bully
Ther nas no dore that he nolde heve of harre, [46]
Or breke it at a renning° with his heed.   running

---

[44] **Reve:** A reeve is an estate manager. A miller grinds grain for bread. A "somnour" or summoner serves ecclesiastical summonses. A pardoner dispenses pardons from the Vatican. A maunciple is a steward.

[45] **ram:** A ram was often given as a prize to wrestlers.

[46] **nolde . . . harre:** Would not heave off its hinges.

His berd as any sowe or fox was reed,
555   And therto brood, as though it were a spade.
      Upon the cop right° of his nose he hade   right ridge
      A werte,° and theron stood a tuft of herys,   wart
      Reed as the bristles of a sowes erys;°   ears
      His nosethirles° blake were and wyde.   nostrils
560   A swerd and a bokeler° bar he by his syde.   shield
      His mouth as greet was as a greet forneys;°   furnace
      He was a janglere° and a goliardeys,°   juggler / storyteller
      And that was most of sinne and harlotryes.
      Wel coude he stelen corn, and tollen thryes,[47]
565   And yet he hadde a thombe of gold, pardee.°   by heaven
      A whyt cote and a blew hood wered° he.   wore
      A baggepype wel coude he blowe and sowne,°   sound
      And therwithal he broghte us out of towne.
         A gentil MAUNCIPLE was ther of a temple,
570   Of which achatours° mighte take exemple   purchasers of food
      For to be wyse in bying of vitaille,°   provisions
      For whether that he payde, or took by taille,°   on credit
      Algate he wayted so in his achat°   purchasing
      That he was ay biforn° and in good stat.   ahead of the game
575   Now is nat that of God a ful fair grace,
      That swich a lewed° mannes wit shal pace°   ignorant / surpass
      The wisdom of an heep of lerned men?
      Of maistres hadde he mo° than thryes ten   more
      That weren of lawe expert and curious,
580   Of which ther were a doseyn in that hous
      Worthy to been stiwardes of rente and lond°   land
      Of any lord that is in Engelond,°   England
      To make him live by his propre good°   his own money
      In honour, dettelees, but he were wood,[48]
585   Or live as scarsly as him list desire,°   it pleases him
      And able for to helpen al a shire
      In any cas° that mighte falle or happe;   case
      And yit this maunciple sette hir aller cappe.[49]
         The REVE was a sclendre colerik man.
590   His berd was shave as ny° as ever he can;   close
      His heer was by his eres° ful round y-shorn;°   ears / shorn
      His top was dokked° lyk a preest biforn.°   styled / of old
      Ful longe were his legges, and ful lene,
      Y-lyk° a staf; ther was no calf y-sene.°   like / seen

---

[47] **stelen . . . thryes:** Could steal and take thrice the toll.
[48] **dettelees . . . wood:** Out of debt, unless he were a madman.
[49] **yit . . . cappe:** And yet this manciple made fools of them all.

595   Wel coude he kepe a gerner° and a binne—   grainary
      Ther was noon auditour coude on him winne.[50]
      Wel wiste° he by the droghte and by the reyn   knew
      The yeldinge of his seed and of his greyn.
      His lordes sheep, his neet,° his dayerye,°   cattle / dairy
600   His swyn, his hors, his stoor,° and his pultrye,°   stock / poultry
      Was hoolly in this reves governinge,
      And by his covenaunt yaf the rekeninge,
      Sin that his lord was twenty yeer of age.
      Ther coude no man bringe him in arrerage.°   arrears
605   Ther nas baillif, ne herde, ne other hyne,
      That he ne knew his sleighte and his covyne;[51]
      They were adrad° of him as of the deeth.°   afraid / death
      His woning° was ful fair upon an heeth;   dwelling
      With grene trees shadwed was his place.
610   He coude bettre than his lord purchace.
      Ful riche he was astored prively;°   privately stocked
      His lord wel coude he plesen subtilly,
      To yeve and lene him of his owne good,
      And have a thank, and yet a cote and hood.
615   In youthe he hadde lerned a good mister:°   occupation
      He was a wel good wrighte,° a carpenter.   wheelwright
      This reve sat upon a ful good stot°   stallion
      That was al pomely° grey and highte° Scot.   dappled / named
      A long surcote° of pers° upon he hade,   overcoat / blue
620   And by his syde he bar° a rusty blade.   bore
      Of Northfolk was this reve of which I tell,
      Bisyde° a toun men clepen° Baldeswelle.   beside / called
      Tukked° he was as is a frere° aboute;   clothed / friar
      And evere he rood the hindreste of oure route.[52]
625   A SOMONOUR° was ther with us in that place,   summoner
      That hadde a fyr-reed cherubinnes face,
      For sawcefleem° he was, with eyen narwe.   acne-covered
      As hoot° he was and lecherous as a sparwe,°   hot / sparrow
      With scalled° browes blake, and piled berd;°   scaly / beard
630   Of his visage° children were aferd.°   look / afraid
      Ther nas quik-silver, litarge, ne brimstoon,
      Boras, ceruce, ne oille of tartre noon,[53]
      Ne oynement that wolde clense and byte,°   bite
      That him mighte helpen of his whelkes° whyte,   blotches

---

[50] **auditour . . . winne:** No auditor could fault his finances.
[51] **nas baillif . . . covyne:** There was no foreman, no shepherd, no other farm worker whose slyness
and tricks he didn't know.
[52] **rood . . . route:** Rode at the back of our pack.
[53] **quik-silver . . . noon:** These are all ointments for bad skin, possibly of venereal origin.

635	Nor of the knobbes° sittinge on his chekes.	bumps
	Wel loved he garleek, oynons, and eek leckes,	
	And for to drinken strong wyn, reed as blood.	
	Thanne wolde he speke, and crye as he were wood,°	mad
	And whan that he wel dronken hadde the wyn,	
640	Thanne wolde he speke no word but Latyn.°	Latin
	A fewe termes hadde he, two or three,	
	That he had lerned out of som decree—	
	No wonder is, he herde it al the day;	
	And eek ye knowen wel, how that a jay°	parrot
645	Can clepen "Watte" as well as can the Pope.[54]	
	But whoso coude in other thing him grope,°	grope for
	Thanne hadde he spent al his philosophye;	
	Ay "*Questio quid iuris*"[55] wolde he crye.	
	He was a gentil harlot° and a kinde;	rascal
650	A bettre felawe° sholde men noght finde:	fellow
	He wolde suffre, for a quart of wyn,	
	A good felawe to have his concubyn	
	A twelf-month, and excuse him atte fulle;°	fully
	Ful prively a finch eek coude he pulle.[56]	
655	And if he fond° owher° a good felawe,	found / anywhere
	He wolde techen him to have non awe	
	In swich cas of the erchedeknes curs,°	archdeacon's curse
	But-if° a mannes soule were in his purs,	unless
	For in his purs he sholde y-punisshed be.	
660	"Purs is the erchedeknes helle," seyde he.	
	But wel I woot° he lyed right in dede:	suspect
	Of cursing oghte ech gilty man him drede—	
	For curs wol slee, right as assoilling saveth—	
	And also war him of a *significavit*.[57]	
665	In daunger hadde he at his owene gyse°	disposal
	The yonge girles of the diocyse,	
	And knew hir counseil,° and was al hir reed.°	secrets / under her domination
	A gerland° hadde he set upon his heed,	garland or flag
	As greet as it were for an ale-stake;[58]	
670	A bokeler° hadde he maad him of a cake.	shield
	With him ther rood a gentil PARDONER	
	Of Rouncival[59] his freend and his compeer,°	comrade

---

[54] **clepen "Watte"** . . . **Pope:** Parrots cried "Wally" (as we say "Polly").

[55] **"*Questio* . . . *iuris*":** "What is the legal question here?"

[56] **finch . . . pulle:** "To pull a finch" means to have sex with a woman.

[57] **significavit:** Also one should beware of getting a *significat,* a writ of punishment transferred from church to secular authorities.

[58] **gerland . . . ale-stake:** A pub or tavern had a pole out front, with a garland or flag hanging from it.

[59] **Pardoner of Rouncival:** This pardoner said he was collecting money for a hospital based in Rouncival, Spain, but which had a branch in London.

That streight was comen fro the court of Rome.
Ful loude he song, "Com hider, love, to me."
675 This somnour bar to him a stif burdoun,° .... burden
Was nevere trompe° of half so greet a soun.° .... trumpet / sound
This pardoner hadde heer° as yelow as wex,° .... hair / wax
But smothe it heng,° as dooth a strike of flex;° .... hung / flax
By ounces° henge his lokkes that he hadde, ... strands
680 And therwith he his shuldres overspradde;° .... overspread
But thinne it lay, by colpons° oon and oon;° .... strands / one by one
But hood, for jolitee, wered he noon,
For it was trussed up in his walet.° .... knapsack
Him thoughte he rood al of the newe jet;° .... fashion
685 Dischevele, save his cappe, he rood al bare.
Swiche glaringe eyen hadde he as an hare.
A vernicle⁶⁰ hadde he sowed on his cappe.
His walet lay biforn him in his lappe,
Bretful of pardoun comen from Rome al hoot.° .... hot
690 A voys he hadde as smal as hath a goot.° .... goat
No berd hadde he, ne nevere sholde have,
As smothe it was as it were late shave:
I trowe° he were a gelding or a mare. .... trust
But of his craft, fro Berwik into Ware,⁶¹
695 Ne was ther swich another pardoner.
For in his male° he hadde a pilwe-beer,° .... bag / pillowcase
Which that he seyde was Oure Lady veyl.° .... veil
He seyde he hadde a gobet° of the seyl° .... piece / sail
That seynt Peter hadde, whan that he wente
700 Upon the see,° til Jesu Crist him hente.° .... sea / seized
He hadde a croys° of latoun,° ful of stones, ... cross / brass
And in a glas he hadde pigges bones.
But with thise relikes,° whan that he fond .... relics
A povre person dwellinge upon lond,° .... land
705 Upon a day he gat him more moneye
Than that the person gat in monthes tweye.° .... twice
And thus, with feyned flaterye and japes,° .... jokes
He made the person and the peple his apes.° .... dupes
But trewely to tellen, atte laste,° .... at the last
710 He was in chirche a noble ecclesiaste.° .... priest
Wel coude he rede a lessoun or a storie,° .... religious story
But alderbest° he song an offertorie; .... best of all
For wel he wiste,° whan that song was songe, ... knew
He moste preche, and wel affyle° his tonge .... sharpen

⁶⁰ **vernicle:** A picture of Christ's head.
⁶¹ **Berwik . . . Ware:** Towns near London.

715   To winne silver, as he ful wel coude—

      Therefore he song the murierly° and loude.   *merrily*

         Now have I told you soothly, in a clause,°   *in a short space*

      Th'estaat, th'array, the nombre, and eek the cause

      Why that assembled was this compaignye

720   In Southwerk, at this gentil hostelrye,

      That highte the Tabard, faste° by the Belle.°   *close / a tavern*

      But now is tyme to yow for to telle

      How that we baren us° that ilke° night,   *bore ourselves / same*

      Whan we were in that hostelrye alight;

725   And after wol I telle of our viage,°   *trip*

      And al the remenaunt of oure pilgrimage.

      But first I pray yow, of youre curteisye,

      That ye n'arette it nat my vileinye,[62]

      Though that I pleynly speke in this matere,

730   To tell yow hir° wordes and hir chere,°   *her / behavior*

      Ne thogh I speke hir wordes properly.

      For this ye knowen al so wel as I:

      Whoso shal telle a tale after a man,

      He moot reherce° as ny° as evere he can   *must repeat / high*

735   Everich a word, if it be in his charge,

      Al speke he never so rudeliche and large;°   *rudely and coarsely*

      Or elles he moot telle his tale untrewe,

      Or feyne thing, or finde wordes newe.

      He may nat spare, althogh he were his brother;

740   He moot as wel seye o word as another.

      Crist spak himself ful brode° in Holy Writ,   *broadly*

      And wel ye woot, no vileinye is it.

      Eek Plato seith, whoso can him rede,

      The wordes mote be cosin° to the dede.   *cousin*

745   Also I prey yow to foryeve° it me,   *forgive*

      Al have I nat set folk in hir degree

      Here in this tale, as that they sholde stonde;

      My wit is short, ye may wel understonde.

         Greet chere made oure Hoste us everichon,

750   And to the soper sette he us anon;

      He served us with vitaille° at the beste.   *food*

      Strong was the wyn, and wel to drinke us leste.°   *pleased*

      A semely° man oure hoste was withalle   *pleasant*

      For to been a marshal in an halle; [63]

755   A large man he was with eyen stepe°—   *prominent*

---

[62] **ye n'arette . . . vileinye:** That you won't blame my lack of manners.
[63] **marshal . . . halle:** A marshall was in charge of banquets.

A fairer burgeys was ther noon in Chepe.[64]
Bold of his speche, and wys, and wel y-taught,
And of manhod him lakkede° right naught.   lacked
Eek therto he was right a mery man,
760   And after soper pleyen he bigan,
And spak of mirthe amonges othere thinges—
Whan that we hadde maad oure rekeninges°—   reckonings
And seyde thus: "Now, lordinges, trewely,
Ye been to me right welcome hertely.°   heartily
765   For by my trouthe, if that I shal nat lye,
I saugh nat this yeer so mery a compaignye
Atones° in this herberwe° as is now.   at once / inn
Fayn wolde I doon yow mirthe, wiste I how,
And of a mirthe I am right now bithout,
770   To doon yow ese,° and it shal coste noght.   ease
      Ye goon° to Caunterbury—God yow spede;   going
The blisful martir quyte° yow your mede.°   pay for / reward
And wel I woot, as ye goon by the weye,
Ye shapen yow to talen and to pleye;
775   For trewely, confort ne mirthe is noon
To ryde by the weye doumb as a stoon;°   stone
And therefore wol I maken yow disport,
As I seyde erst,° and doon yow som confort.   erstwhile
And if yow lyketh° alle, by oon° assent,   like / one
780   Now for to stonden at° my jugement,   abide by
And for to werken as I shal yow seye,
To-morwe, when ye ryden by the weye—
Now by my fader° soule that is deed—   father's
But° ye be merye, I wol yeve yow myn heed.°   unless / head
785   Hold up youre hondes, withouten more speche."
      Oure counseil was nat longe for to seche;°   seek
Us thoughte it was noght worth to make it wys,°   an issue
And graunted him withouten more avys,°   deliberation
And bad him seye his voirdit° as him leste.°   verdict / pleased
790   "Lordinges," quod he, "now herkneth for the beste,
But tak it nought, I prey yow, in desdeyn.°   disdain
This is the poynt, to speken short and pleyn:
That ech of yow, to shorte with oure weye,
In this viage° shal telle tales tweye,°   journey / two
795   To Caunterbury-ward,° I mene it so,   toward Canterbury
And homward he shal tellen othere two,
Of aventures that whylom° han bifalle.   once upon a time
And which of yow that bereth him best of alle,

---

[64] **burgeys . . . Chepe:** A burgher from Cheapside, a rather fashionable part of London.

That is to seyn, that telleth in this cas°   case
800 Tales of best sentence° and most solas,°   intent / solace
Shal have a soper at oure aller cost [65]
Here in this place, sittinge by this post,
Whan that we come agayn fro Caunterbury.
And for to make yow the more mery,°   merry
805 I wol myselven goodly° with yow ryde,   kindly
Right at myn owne cost, and be youre gyde.
And whoso wole my jugement withseye°   oppose
Shal paye al that we spenden by the weye.
And if ye vouchesauf° that it be so,   swear
810 Tel me anon, withouten wordes mo,°   more
And I wol erly shape me° therfore."   prepare myself
        This thing was graunted, and oure othes swore
With ful glad herte, and preyden° him also   prayed
That he wolde vouchesauf for to do so,
815 And that he wolde been oure governour
And of oure tales juge and reportour,°   accountant
And sette a soper at a certeyn prys;°   price
And we wol reuled been at his devys°   disposal
In heigh and lowe; and thus, by oon assent,
820 We been acorded to his jugement.
And therupon the wyn was fet° anon;°   fetched / at once
We dronken, and to reste wente echon,
Withouten any lenger° taryinge.°   longer / tarrying
        Amorwe,° whan that day bigan to springe,   in the morning
825 Up roos oure Host and was oure aller cok,°   rooster
And gadrede° us togidre,° alle in a flok;   guided / together
And forth we riden,° a litel more than pas,°   ride / pass or step
Unto the watering of Seint Thomas,[66]
And there oure Host bigan his hors areste,°   halt
830 And seyde, "Lordinges, herkneth, if yow leste.°   please
Ye woot youre forward,° and I it yow recorde.°   agreement / recall
If even-song and morwe-song° acorde,   morning song
Lat se° now who shal telle the firste tale.   see
As evere mote I drinke wyn or ale,
835 Whoso be rebel to my jugement
Shal paye for al that by the weye is spent.
Now draweth cut,° er that we ferrer twinne;°   lots / go farther
He which that hath the shortest shal biginne.
Sire Knight," quod he, "my maister and my lord,
840 Now draweth cut, for that is myn acord.°   will

---

[65] **at oure . . . cost:** At our expense.
[66] **Seint Thomas:** A bar near Southwark, in London.

Cometh neer,"° quod he, "my lady Prioresse;   near
And ye, sire Clerk, lat be youre shamfastnesse,°   modesty
Ne studieth noght. Ley hond to, every man!"
Anon to drawen every wight bigan,
845   And shortly for to tellen as it was,
Were it by aventure,° or sort,° or cas,°   luck / fate / chance
The sothe° is this, the cut fil° to the Knight,   truth / fell
Of which ful blythe and glad was every wight;
And telle he moste° his tale, as was resoun,°   must / reasonable
850   By forward° and by composicioun,°   agreement / compact
As ye han herd. What nedeth wordes mo?°   more
And whan this gode man saugh it was so,
As he that wys was and obedient
To kepe his forward by his free assent,
855   He seyde: "Sin° I shal biginne the game,   Since
What, welcome be the cut, a Goddes° name!   God's
Now lat us ryde, and herkneth what I seye."
And with that word we riden° forth oure weye;   rode
And he bigan with right a mery chere°   bearing
860   His tale anon, and seyde as ye may heere.

HOMER
trans. George Chapman (1559–1634)

from The Odyssey (ca. 1614)
Ulysses Describes His Visit to the Underworld[1]

Translated from the Odyssey, *Book XI*

When to the powers beneath,
The sacred nation that survives with Death,
My prayers and vows had done devotions fit,
I took the offerings, and upon the pit
5   Bereft their lives. Out gushed the sable blood,
And round about me fled out of the flood
The souls of the deceased. There clustered then
Youths, and their wives, much suffering agèd men,

---

[1] This is a famous translation of the Homeric epic into English. This passage is about the descent of
the hero, Ulysses, into the underworld of Hades to find his father. Note that John Keats wrote about
this translation in his poem, "On First Looking into Chapman's Homer."

Soft tender virgins that but new came there
10   By timeless death, and green their sorrows were.
There men at arms, with armours all imbrued,
Wounded with lances and with falchions hewed,
In numbers up and down the ditch did stalk,
And threw unmeasured cries about their walk,
15   So horrid that a bloodless fear surprised
My daunted spirits. Straight then I advised
My friends to flay the slaughtered sacrifice,
Put them in fire, and to the Deities,
Stern Pluto and Persephone [2] apply
20   Exciteful prayers. Then drew I from my thigh
My well-edged sword, stepped in, and firmly stood
Betwixt the press of shadows and the blood,
And would not suffer any one to dip
Within our offering his unsolid lip
25   Before Tiresias, that did all control.
The first that pressed in was Elpenor's soul,[3]
His body in the broad-wayed earth as yet
Unmourned, unburied by us since we sweat
With other urgent labours. Yet his smart
30   I wept to see, and rued it from my heart,
Enquiring how he could before me be
That came by ship? He, mourning, answered me:
'In Circe's house, the spite some spirit did bear
And the unspeakable good liquor there
35   Hath been my bane. For being to descend
A ladder much in height, I did not tend
My way well down, but forwards made a proof
To tread the rounds, and from the very roof
Fell on my neck and brake it. And this made
40   My soul thus visit this infernal shade.
And here, by them that next thyself are dear,
Thy wife and father, that a little one
Gave food to thee, and by thy only son
At home behind thee left, Telemachus,
45   Do not depart by stealth and leave me thus,
Unmourned, unburied, lest neglected I
Bring on thyself th'incensèd Deity.

---

[2] **Pluto and Persephone:** The god and goddess who ruled the underworld, called Hades.
[3] **Tiresias . . . Elpenor's soul:** Tiresias was a blind prophet who had been at the Trojan War. Elpenor had been a young member of Ulysses' crew. Ulysses sees them in Hades.

I know that, sailed from hence, thy ship must touch
On th'Isle Aeaea, where vouchsafe thus much,
50 Good king, that, landed, thou wilt instantly
Bestow on me thy royal memory,
To this grace, that my body, arms and all,
May rest consumed in fiery funeral.
And on the foamy shore a sepulchre
55 Erect to me, that after times may hear
Of one so hapless. Let me these implore,
And fix upon my sepulchre the oar
With which alive I shook the agèd seas,
And had of friends the dear societies.'
60   I told the wretched soul I would fulfil
And execute to th'utmost point his will;
And all the time we sadly talked, I still
My sword above the blood held, when aside
The idol of my friend still amplified
65 His plaint, as up and down the shades he erred.
Then my deceasèd mother's soul appeared,
Fair daughter of Autolycus the Great,[4]
Grave Anticlea, whom, when forth I set
For sacred Ilion,° I had left alive.   site of Trojan War
70 Her sight much moved me, and to tears did drive
My note of her decease; and yet not she
(Though in my ruth she held the highest degree)
Would I admit to touch the sacred blood
Till from Tiresias I had understood
75 What Circe[5] told me. At the length did land
Theban Tiresias' soul, and in his hand
Sustained a golden sceptre, knew me well,
And said: 'Oh man unhappy, why to hell
Admit'st thou dark arrival and the light
80 The sun gives leav'st, to have the horrid sight
Of this black region and the shadows here?
Now sheath thy sharp sword and the pit forbear,
That I the blood may taste, and then relate
The truth of those acts that affect thy Fate.'

---

[4] **Autolycus the Great:** The son of Hermes, considered a master thief.
[5] **Circe:** Sorceress who detained Ulysses on her island and turned his men into swine.

WILLIAM SHAKESPEARE (1564–1616)

from Romeo and Juliet
Act I, Scene 5 (Romeo) (ca. 1591)

O, she doth teach the torches to burn bright!
    It seems she hangs upon the cheek of night
    Like a rich jewel in an Ethiope's° ear;   *Ethiopian's*
    Beauty too rich for use, for earth too dear!
5   So shows a snowy dove trooping with crows,
    As yonder lady o'er her fellows shows.
    The measure done, I'll watch her place of stand,
    And, touching hers, make blessed my rude hand.
    Did my heart love till now? forswear it, sight!
10   For I ne'er saw true beauty till this night.

CHRISTOPHER MARLOWE (1564–1593)

from Hero and Leander (1598)

(i)

Love at First Sight

On this feast day, oh, cursèd day and hour!
    Went Hero thorough Sestos,[1] from her tower
    To Venus'° temple, where unhappily,   *goddess of love*
    As after chanced, they did each other spy.
5   So fair a church as this had Venus none;
    The walls were of discoloured jasper stone,
    Wherein was Proteus[2] carvèd, and o'erhead
    A lively vine of green sea-agate spread,
    Where by one hand light-headed Bacchus hung,
10   And with the other wine from grapes out-wrung.
    Of crystal shining fair the pavement was;
    The town of Sestos called it Venus' glass.
    There might you see the gods in sundry shapes,
    Committing heady riots, incest, rapes:
15   For know that underneath this radiant floor
    Was Danae's[3] statue in a brazen tower;

---

[1] **Sestos:** An ancient town of the Thracian Chersonese, the modern Gallipoli peninsula.
[2] **Proteus:** A god who changes his shape easily and often.
[3] **Danae:** The daughter of Acrsius, the king of Argos.

Jove slyly stealing from his sister's bed
To dally with Idalian Ganymede,
And for his love Europa bellowing loud,
20 And tumbling with the rainbow in a cloud;
Blood-quaffing Mars heaving the iron net
Which limping Vulcan and his Cyclops set;
Love kindling fire to burn such towns as Troy;
Silvanus weeping for the lovely boy
25 That now is turned into a cypress tree,
Under whose shade the wood-gods love to be.[4]
And in the midst a silver altar stood;
There Hero sacrificing turtles' blood,
Vailed to the ground, veiling her eyelids close,
30 And modestly they opened as she rose:
Thence flew love's arrow with the golden head,
And thus Leander was enamourèd.
Stone-still he stood, and evermore he gazed,
Till with the fire that from his countenance blazed
35 Relenting Hero's gentle heart was strook;
Such force and virtue hath an amorous look.

      It lies not in our power to love or hate,
For will in us is over-ruled by fate.
When two are stripped, long ere the course begin,
40 We wish that one should lose, the other win;
And one especially do we affect
Of two gold ingots, like in each respect.
The reason no man knows; let it suffice,
What we behold is censured by our eyes.
45 Where both deliberate, the love is slight;
Who ever loved, that loved not at first sight?

(ii)

Amorous Neptune°   sea god

With that he stripped him to the ivory skin,
And crying, 'Love, I come', leaped lively in.
Whereat the sapphire-visaged god grew proud,
50 And made his capering Triton sound aloud,
Imagining that Ganymede,[5] displeased,
Had left the heavens; therefore on him he seized.

---

[4] **Jove . . . be:** These are all examples of erotic passion and its consequences from Greek myth.
[5] **Ganymede:** He was a beautiful young prince from Troy whom Zeus (or Jove, the Roman name for Zeus) abducted after falling in love with him. He was made the immortal cup-bearer of the gods on Mount Olympus. He was also put among the constellations of the heavens under the sign of Aquarius.

Leander strived; the waves about him wound,
And pulled him to the bottom, where the ground
55   Was strewed with pearl, and in low coral groves
Sweet singing mermaids sported with their loves
On heaps of heavy gold, and took great pleasure
To spurn in careless sort the shipwreck treasure:
For here the stately azure palace stood,
60   Where kingly Neptune and his train abode.
The lusty god embraced him, called him love,
And swore he never should return to Jove.
But when he knew it was not Ganymede,
For under water he was almost dead,
65   He heaved him up, and looking on his face,
Beat down the bold waves with his triple mace,
Which mounted up, intending to have kissed him,
And fell in drops like tears, because they missed him.
Leander, being up, began to swim,
70   And looking back, saw Neptune follow him;
Whereat aghast, the poor soul 'gan to cry:
'O! let me visit Hero ere I die!'
The god put Helle's bracelet on his arm,
And swore the sea should never do him harm.
75   He clapped his plump cheeks, with his tresses played,
And smiling wantonly, his love bewrayed.
He watched his arms, and as they opened wide,
At every stroke betwixt them would he slide,
And steal a kiss, and then run out and dance,
80   And as he turned, cast many a lustful glance,
And threw him gaudy toys to please his eye,
And dive into the water, and there pry
Upon his breast, his thighs, and every limb,
And up again, and close beside him swim,
85   And talk of love. Leander made reply:
'You are deceived, I am no woman, I.'
Thereat smiled Neptune, and then told a tale,
How that a shepherd, sitting in a vale,
Played with a boy so lovely fair and kind,
90   As for his love both earth and heaven pined;
That of the cooling river durst not drink
Lest water-nymphs should pull him from the brink;
And when he sported in the fragrant lawns,
Goat-footed satyrs and up-staring fauns
95   Would steal him thence. Ere half this tale was done,
'Ay me!' Leander cried, 'the enamoured sun,
That now should shine on Thetis' glassy bower,
Descends upon my radiant Hero's tower.

O! that these tardy arms of mine were wings!'
100   And as he spake, upon the waves he springs.

AEMILIA LANYER (1569–1645)

The Description of Cooke-ham[1] (1611)

Farewell (sweet *Cooke-ham*) where I first obtained
Grace[2] from that grace where perfect grace remained;
And where the muses gave their full consent,
I should have power the virtuous to content;
5   Where princely palace willed me to indite,°   proclaim
The sacred story of the soul's delight.
Farewell (sweet place) where virtue then did rest,
And all delights did harbor in her breast;
Never shall my sad eyes again behold
10   Those pleasures which my thoughts did then unfold.
Yet you (great Lady) Mistress° of that place,   Margaret Clifford
From whose desires did spring this work of grace;
Vouchsafe to think upon those pleasures past,
As fleeting worldly joys that could not last,
15   Or, as dim shadows of celestial° pleasures,   heavenly
Which are desired above all earthly treasures.
Oh how (methought) against you thither came,
Each part did seem some new delight to frame!
The house received all ornaments to grace it,
20   And would endure no foulness to deface it.
And walks put on their summer liveries,°   adornments
And all things else did hold like similes.
The trees with leaves, with fruits, with flowers clad,
Embraced each other, seeming to be glad,
25   Turning themselves to beauteous Canopies,
To shade the bright sun from your brighter eyes;
The crystal streams with silver spangles graced,
While by the glorious sun they were embraced;
The little birds in chirping notes did sing,
30   To entertain both you and that sweet spring.
And *Philomela*° with her sundry lays,   the nightingale
Both you and that delightful place did praise.

---

[1] **Cooke-ham:** The country seat of the poet's friend and partroness, who was Margaret Clifford, the Countess of Cumberland.
[2] **Grace:** In the religious sense, redemption. In a more secular way, a sense of release.

Oh how me thought each plant, each flower, each tree
Set forth their beauties then to welcome thee!
35   The very hills right humbly did descend,
When you to tread on them did intend.
And as you set your feet, they still did rise,
Glad that they could receive so rich a prize.
The gentle winds did take delight to be
40   Among those woods that were so graced by thee,
And in sad murmur uttered pleasing sound,
That pleasure in that place might more abound.
The swelling banks delivered all their pride
When such a *Phoenix*³ once they had espied.
45   Each arbor, bank, each seat, each stately tree,
Thought themselves honored in supporting thee.
The pretty birds would oft come to attend thee,
Yet fly away for fear they should offend thee;
The little creatures in the burrough° by   area
50   Would come abroad to sport them in your eye,
Yet fearful of the bow in your fair hand.
Would run away when you did make a stand.
Now let me come unto that stately tree,
Wherein such goodly prospects you did see;
55   That oak that did in height his fellows pass,
As much as lofty trees, low growing grass,
Much like a comely cedar straight and tall,
Whose beauteous stature far exceeded all.
How often did you visit this fair tree,
60   Which seeming joyful in receiving thee,
Would like a palm tree spread his arms abroad,
Desirous that you there should make abode;
Whose fair green leaves much like a comely° veil,   modest
Defended *Phoebus*° when he would assail;   sun-god
65   Whose pleasing boughs did yield a cool fresh air,
Joying his happiness when you were there.
Where being seated, you might plainly see
Hills, vales, and woods, as if on bended knee
They had appeared, your honor to salute,
70   Or to prefer some strange unlooked-for suit;
All interlaced with brooks and crystal springs,
A prospect fit to please the eyes of kings.
And thirteen shires appeared all in your sight,
Europe could not afford much more delight.
75   What was there then but gave you all content,

---

³ **Phoenix:** A bird that rises from its ashes.

While you the time in meditation spent
Of their Creator's power, which there you saw,
In all his creatures held a perfect law;
And in their beauties did you plain descry
80 His beauty, wisdom, grace, love, majesty.
In these sweet woods how often did you walk,
With Christ and his Apostles there to talk;
Placing his holy Writ in some fair tree
To meditate what you therein did see.
85 With *Moses*° you did mount his holy hill   great prophet
To know his pleasure, and perform his will.
With lowly *David*° you did often sing   great King of Israel
His holy hymns to Heaven's eternal King.
And in sweet music did your soul delight
90 To sound his praises, morning, noon, and night.
With blessed *Joseph*[4] you did often feed
Your pined brethren, when they stood in need.
And that sweet Lady sprung from *Clifford's* race,[5]
Of noble *Bedford's* blood,[6] fair stem of grace,
95 To honorable *Dorset*[7] now espoused,
In whose fair breast true virtue then was housed,
Oh what delight did my weak spirits find
In those pure parts of her well framèd mind.
And yet it grieves me that I cannot be
100 Near unto her, whose virtues did agree
With those fair ornaments of outward beauty,
Which did enforce from all both love and duty.
Unconstant Fortune, thou art most to blame,
Who casts us down into so low a frame
105 Where our great friends we cannot daily see,
So great a difference is there in degree.
Many are placed in those orbs of state,
Parters in honor, so ordained by Fate,
Nearer in show, yet farther off in love,
110 In which, the lowest always are above.
But whither am I carried in conceit,
My wit too weak to conster° of the great.   construe
Why not? although we are but born of earth.

---

[4] **Joseph:** He was sold into slavery in Egypt by his brothers. He rose to power in Egypt, and later his brothers came seeking grain. He refused to take their money, placing it in their grain sacks; he invited them to dinner.
[5] **Clifford's race:** Refers to the lineage of the Countess of Cumberland.
[6] **Bedford's blood:** Margaret Clifford was born Lady Margaret Russell, third daughter of Francis, second earl of Bedford.
[7] **Dorset:** Refers to the husband of Lady Anne, the Earl of Dorset.

We may behold the heavens, despising death;
115 And loving heaven that is so far above,
May in the end vouchsafe us entire love.
Therefore sweet memory do thou retain
Those pleasures past, which will not turn again:
Remember beauteous *Dorset's* former sports,
120 So far from being touched by ill reports,
Wherein myself did always bear a part,
While reverend love presented my true heart.
Those recreations let me bear in mind,
Which her sweet youth and noble thoughts did find,
125 Whereof deprived, I evermore must grieve,
Hating blind Fortune, careless to relieve.
And you sweet Cooke-ham, whom these ladies leave,
I now must tell the grief you did conceive
At their departure, when they went away,
130 How everything retained a sad dismay.
Nay long before, when once an inkling came,
Methought each thing did unto sorrow frame:
The trees that were so glorious in our view,
Forsook both flowers and fruit, when once they knew
135 Of your depart, their very leaves did wither,
Changing their colors as they grew together.
But when they saw this had no power to stay you,
They often wept, though, speechless, could not pray you,
Letting their tears in your fair bosoms fall,
140 As if they said, Why will ye leave us all?
This being vain, they cast their leaves away
Hoping that pity would have made you stay:
Their frozen tops, like age's hoary° hairs,   gray
Shows their disasters, languishing in fears.
145 A swarthy riveled rind all over spread,
Their dying bodies half alive, half dead.
But your occasions called you so away
That nothing there had power to make you stay.
Yet did I see a noble grateful mind
150 Requiting° each according to their kind,   satisfying
Forgetting not to turn and take your leave
Of these sad creatures, powerless to receive
Your favor, when with grief you did depart,
Placing their former pleasures in your heart,
155 Giving great charge to noble memory
There to preserve their love continually.
But specially the love of that fair tree,
That first and last you did vouchsafe to see,
In which it pleased you oft to take the air

160   With noble *Dorset,* then a virgin fair,
      Where many a learned book was read and scanned,
      To this fair tree, taking me by the hand,
      You did repeat the pleasures which had passed,
      Seeming to grieve they could no longer last.
165   And with a chaste, yet loving kiss took leave,
      Of which sweet kiss I did it soon bereave,
      Scorning a senseless creature should possess
      So rare a favor, so great happiness.
      No other kiss it could receive from me,
170   For fear to give back what it took of thee,
      So I ungrateful creature did deceive it
      Of that which you in love vouchsafed° to leave it.   sworn
      And though it oft had given me much content,
      Yet this great wrong I never could repent;
175   But of the happiest made it most forlorn,
      To show that nothing's free from Fortune's scorne,
      While all the rest with this most beauteous tree
      Made their sad consort sorrow's harmony.
      The flowers that on the banks and walks did grow,
180   Crept in the ground, the grass did weep for woe.
      The winds and waters seemed to chide together
      Because you went away they knew not whither;
      And those sweet brooks that ran so fair and clear,
      With grief and trouble wrinkled did appear.
185   Those pretty birds that wonted° were to sing,   desired
      Now neither sing, nor chirp, nor use their wing,
      But with their tender feet on some bare spray,
      Warble forth sorrow, and their own dismay.
      Fair *Philomela* leaves her mournful ditty,°   song
190   Drowned in deep sleep, yet can procure no pity.
      Each arbor, bank, each seat, each stately tree
      Looks bare and desolate now for want of thee,
      Turning green tresses° into frosty gray,   hair/branches
      While in cold grief they wither all away.
195   The sun grew weak, his beams no comfort gave,
      While all green things did make the earth their grave.
      Each brier, each bramble, when you went away
      Caught fast your clothes, thinking to make you stay;
      Delightful Echo[8] wonted to reply
200   To our last words, did now for sorrow die;

---

[8] **Echo:** A nymph. She was cursed to speak only when spoken to, in repetition of others. Echo's love, Narcissus, disliked her because she only repeated his words. In her grief, Echo wasted away to a shadow, leaving only her voice.

The house cast off each garment that might grace it,
Putting on dust and cobwebs to deface it.
All desolation then there did appear,
When you were going whom they held so dear.
205   This last farewell to *Cooke-ham* here I give,
When I am dead thy name in this may live,
Wherein I have performed her noble hest
Whose virtues lodge in my unworthy breast,
And ever shall, so long as life remains,
210   Tying my life to her by those rich chains.

BEN JONSON   (1572–1637)

Inviting a Friend to Supper   (1616)

Tonight, grave Sir, both my poor house and I
    Do equally desire your company:
Not that we think us worthy such a guest,
    But that your worth will dignify our feast
5   With those that come; whose grace may make that seem
    Something, which else could hope for no esteem.
It is the fair acceptance, Sir, creates
    The entertainment perfect: not the cates.°   food
Yet shall you have, to rectify your palate,
10   An olive, capers, or some better salad,
Ushering the mutton; with a short-legged hen,
    If we can get her, full of eggs, and then
Lemons, and wine for sauce; to these a cony°   rabbit
    Is not to be despaired of for our money;
15   And though fowl now be scarce, yet there are clerks,
    The sky not falling, think we may have larks.[1]
I'll tell you of more, and lie, so you will come:
    Of partridge, pheasant, wood-cock, of which some
May yet be there; and godwit,° if we can;   sandpiper
20   Knot, rail and ruff too. How so ere, my man
Shall read a piece of Virgil, Tacitus,
    Livy,° or of some better book to us,   Roman authors
Of which we'll speak our minds, amidst our meat;
    And I'll profess no verses to repeat:
25   To this, if ought appear which I not know of,

---

[1] **we may have larks:** An old proverb runs like this: "When the sky falls, we shall have larks." Note that the rhyme is with "clerks," pronounced as "clarks."

That will the pastry, not my paper show of.
Digestive[2] cheese and fruit there sure will be;
    But that which most doth take my Muse and me
Is a pure cup of rich Canary wine,
30   Which is the Mermaid's° now, but shall be mine;   *a tavern*
Of which had Horace° or Anacreon° tasted,   *Roman poet / Greek poet*
    Their lives, as do their lines, till now had lasted.
Tobacco, nectar, or the Thespian spring
    Are all but Luther's beer,° to this I sing.   *German beer*
35 Of this we will sup free, but moderately,
    And we will have no Pooly or Parrot[3] by;
Nor shall our cups make any guilty men,
    But at our parting we will be as when
We innocently met. No simple word
40   That shall be uttered at our mirthful board
Shall make us sad next morning, or affright
    The liberty that we'll enjoy tonight.

BEN JONSON (1572–1637)

from The Forest (159–162) (1616)
To Penshurst[1]

Thou art not, Penshurst, built to envious show,
Of touch or marble, nor canst boast a row
Of polished pillars, or a roof of gold;
Thou hast no lantern whereof tales are told,
5 Or stair, or courts; but standst an ancient pile,
And these grudged at, art reverenced the while.
Thou joy'st in better marks, of soil, of air,
Of wood, of water; therein thou art fair.
Thou hast thy walks for health as well as sport:
10 Thy Mount, to which the dryads do resort,
Where Pan and Bacchus[2] their high feasts have made
Beneath the broad beech and the chestnut shade;

---

[2] **Digestive:** And so aiding in digestion.
[3] **Pooly or Parrot:** Robert Pooly and Henry Parrot were spies. Pooly stood by when the poet Christopher Marlowe was killed in a tavern in 1593. Note that Jonson plays on the word "polly," which is what parrots say.
[1] **Penshurst:** A stately home that was the birthplace of Sir Philip Sidney. It was owned by the Sidney family in Kent. Jonson uses the country house to represent the state as well as the human body.
[2] **dryads . . . Bacchus:** Dryads are tree-dwelling spirits; Pan and Bacchus were gods of nature and revelry.

That taller tree, which of a nut was set
At his great birth, where all the Muses met.
15 There, in the writhèd bark, are cut the names
Of many a sylvan, taken with his flames;
And thence the ruddy satyrs oft provoke
The lighter fauns to reach thy lady's oak.
Thy copse,° too, named of Gamage,³ thou hast there,   woodland park
20 That never fails to serve thee seasoned deer
When thou wouldst feast or exercise thy friends.
The lower land, that to the river bends,
Thy sheep, thy bullocks, kine and calves do feed;
The middle grounds thy mares and horses breed.
25 Each bank doth yield thee conies, and the tops,
Fertile of wood, Ashour and Sidney's copse,⁴
To crown thy open table, doth provide
The purpled pheasant with the speckled side;
The painted partridge lies in every field,
30 And for thy mess is willing to be killed.
And if the high-swoll'n Medway⁵ fail thy dish,
Thou hast thy ponds that pay thee tribute fish:
Fat, agéd carps, that run into thy net;
And pikes, now weary their own kind to eat,
35 As loth the second draught or cast to stay,
Officiously, at first, themselves betray;
Bright eels, that emulate them, and leap on land
Before the fisher, or into his hand.
Then hath thy orchard fruit, thy garden flowers,
40 Fresh as the air and new as are the Hours:
The early cherry, with the later plum,
Fig, grape and quince, each in his time doth come;
The blushing apricot and woolly peach
Hang on thy walls, that every child may reach.
45 And though thy walls be of the country stone,
They're reared with no man's ruin, no man's groan;
There's none that dwell about them wish them down,
But all come in, the farmer and the clown,
And no one empty-handed, to salute
50 Thy lord and lady, though they have no suit.
Some bring a capon, some a rural cake,
Some nuts, some apples; some that think they make

---

³ **Gamage:** Lady Barbara Gamage used to feed deer there, at the entrance to the estate.
⁴ **Ashour and Sidney's copse:** Names of particular wooded areas.
⁵ **Medway:** A stream.

The better cheeses, bring them; or else send
By their ripe daughters, whom they would commend
55 This way to husbands; and whose baskets bear
An emblem of themselves, in plum or pear.
But what can this (more than express their love)
Add to thy free provisions, far above
The need of such? whose liberal board doth flow,
60 With all that hospitality doth know!
Where comes no guest but is allowed to eat
Without his fear, and of thy lord's own meat;
Where the same beer and bread and self-same wine
That is his lordship's shall be also mine;
65 And I not fain to sit (as some, this day,
At great men's tables) and yet dine away.
Here no man tells my cups, nor, standing by,
A waiter, doth my gluttony envy,
But gives me what I call, and lets me eat;
70 He knows below he shall find plenty of meat,
Thy tables hoard not up for the next day.
Nor, when I take my lodging, need I pray
For fire or lights or livery: all is there,
As if thou then wert mine, or I reigned here;
75 There's nothing I can wish, for which I stay.
That found King James, when, hunting late this way
With his brave son, the prince, they saw thy fires
Shine bright on every hearth, as the desires
Of thy Penates had been set on flame
80 To entertain them; or the country came
With all their zeal to warm their welcome here.
What (great, I will not say, but) sudden cheer
Didst thou then make them! And what praise was heaped
On thy good lady then! who therein reaped
85 The just reward of her high huswifery:
To have her linen, plate, and all things nigh,
When she was far; and not a room but dressed
As if it had expected such a guest!
These, Penshurst, are thy praise, and yet not all.
90 Thy lady's noble, fruitful, chaste withal;
His children thy great lord may call his own,
A fortune in this age but rarely known.
They are and have been taught religion; thence
Their gentler spirits have sucked innocence.
95 Each morn and even they are taught to pray
With the whole household, and may every day
Read in their virtuous parents' noble parts

The mysteries of manners, arms and arts.
Now, Penshurst, they that will proportion thee
100   With other edifices, when they see
Those proud, ambitious heaps, and nothing else,
May say, their lords have built, but thy lord dwells.

JOHN DONNE (1572–1631)

Good Friday,[1] 1613. Riding Westward   (1633)

Let man's soul be a sphere, and then, in this,
The intelligence that moves, devotion is;
And as the other spheres, by being grown
Subject to foreign motions, lose their own,
5   And being by others hurried every day,
Scarce in a year their natural form obey:
Pleasure or business, so, our souls admit
For their first mover, and are whirled by it.[2]
Hence is't that I am carried towards the west
10   This day, when my soul's form bends to the east.
There I should see a sun by rising set,[3]
And by that setting endless day beget;
But that Christ on this cross did rise and fall,
Sin had eternally benighted all.
15   Yet dare I' almost be glad I do not see
That spectacle of too much weight for me.
Who sees God's face, that is self life, must die;
What a death were it then to see God die?[4]
It made his own lieutenant nature shrink,
20   It made his footstool crack, and the sun wink.[5]
Could I behold those hands which span the poles,

---

[1] **Good Friday:** Refers to the Friday before Easter, the day that Christ was crucified.
[2] **whirled by it:** Outside powers deflect planets from their orbits in much the same way as our souls are diverted by "pleasure or business." Donne refers to theories of astronomy long in place, as construed by Ptolemy, the Greek astronomer, who argued that planets move in their own "spheres" or orbits but are influenced by "foreign motions" from other planets as well as by God, the prime mover, as referred to in line 8.
[3] **a sun by rising set:** Donne is punning on Son of God, Jesus.
[4] **God die:** In Exodus 33:20: "Thou can not see my face: for there shall no man see me and live."
[5] **sun wink:** At the death of Christ, there was an earthquake and an eclipse of the sun.

And turn all spheres at once, pierced with those holes?
Could I behold that endless height which is
Zenith to us, and our antipodes,[6]
25   Humbled below us? or that blood which is
The seat of all our souls, if not of his,
Made dirt of dust, or that flesh which was worn
By God, for his apparel, ragged and torn?
If on these things I durst not look, durst I
30   Upon his miserable mother cast mine eye,
Who was God's partner here, and furnished thus
Half of that sacrifice which ransomed us?
Though these things, as I ride, be from mine eye,
They are present yet unto my memory,
35   For that looks towards them; and thou lookst towards me,
O Saviour, as thou hangst upon the tree;
I turn my back to thee but to receive
Corrections, till thy mercies bid thee leave.°   discontinue
Oh think me worth thine anger, punish me,
40   Burn off my rusts and my deformity,
Restore thine image so much, by thy grace,
That thou mayst know me, and I'll turn my face.

ANNE BRADSTREET (ca. 1612–1672)

A Letter to Her Husband, Absent upon Public Employment[1] (1678)

My head, my heart, mine eyes, my life, nay, more,
My joy, my magazine° of earthly store,   storehouse
If two be one, as surely thou and I,
How stayest thou there, whilst I at Ipswich[2] lie?
5   So many steps, head from the heart to sever,
If but a neck, soon should we be together.
I, like the Earth this season, mourn in black,
My Sun is gone so far in's zodiac,
Whom whilst I 'joyed, nor storms, nor frost I felt,
10   His warmth such frigid colds did cause to melt.

---

[6] **antipodes:** The opposite pole from the zenith, or the point above anyone's head in the heavens.
[1] The poet's husband, Simon, had gone south to Boston to assist in discussions about combining several colonies into the United Colonies of New England.
[2] **Ipswich:** A town north of Boston.

My chillèd limbs now numbèd lie forlorn;
Return; return, sweet Sol, from Capricorn;[3]
In this dead time, alas, what can I more
Than view those fruits[4] which through thy heat I bore?
15   Which sweet contentment yield me for a space,
True living pictures of their father's face.
O strange effect! now thou art southward[5] gone,
I weary grow the tedious day so long;
But when thou northward to me shalt return,
20   I wish my Sun may never set, but burn
Within the Cancer[6] of my glowing breast,
The welcome house of him my dearest guest.
Where ever, ever stay, and go not thence,
Till nature's sad decree shall call thee hence;
25   Flesh of thy flesh, bone of thy bone,[7]
I here, thou there, yet both but one.

MARGARET CAVENDISH, DUCHESS OF NEWCASTLE (1623–1673)

Of Many Worlds in This World (1668)

Just like as in a nest of boxes round,
Degrees of sizes in each box are found:
So, in this world, may many others be
Thinner and less, and less still by degree:
5   Although they are not subject to our sense,
A world may be no bigger than two-pence.
Nature is curious,° and such works may shape,   clear
Which our dull senses easily escape:
For creatures, small as atoms, may be there,
10   If every one a creature's figure bear.
If atoms four, a world can make, then see
What several worlds might in an ear-ring be:
For, millions of those atoms may be in
The head of one small, little, single pin.

---

[3] **Capricorn:** Sign of the zodiac representing winter. "Sol" is the sun.
[4] **those fruits:** She refers to their children.
[5] **southward:** Toward Boston.
[6] **Cancer:** Sign of the zodiac representing summer.
[7] **bone of thy bone:** Refers to Genesis 2:23: "This is now bone of my bones, and flesh of my flesh."
Adam says this of Eve, delighted by her creation.

15 And if thus small, then ladies may well wear
    A world of worlds, as pendents in each ear.

APHRA BEHN   (ca. 1640–1689)

To the Fair Clarinda, Who Made Love[1] to Me, Imagined More Than Woman   (1688)

By Mrs. B.

Fair lovely maid, or if that title be
Too weak, too feminine for nobler thee,
Permit a name that more approaches truth:
And let me call thee, lovely charming youth.°   young man
5   This last will justify my soft complaint,[2]
While they may serve to lessen my constraint;
And without blushes I the youth pursue,
When so much beauteous woman is in view.
Against thy charms we struggle but in vain
10 With thy deluding form thou giv'st us pain,
While the bright nymph betrays us to the swain.[3]
In pity to our sex sure thou wer't sent,
That we might love, and yet be innocent:
For sure no crime with thee we can commit;
15 Or if we should—thy form excuses it.
For who, that gathers fairest flowers believes
A snake lies hid beneath the fragrant leaves.

    Thou beauteous wonder of a different kind,
    Soft *Cloris* with the dear *Alexis* [4] joined;
20 When e'r the manly part of thee, would plead
    Thou tempts us with the image of the maid,
    While we the noblest passions do extend
    The love to *Hermes, Aphrodite* [5] the friend.

---

[1] **Made Love:** In other words, paid attention to in a loving way. Clarinda is a stock name, employed by the poet to refer to one of her contemporaries.

[2] **complaint:** A standard type of poem in which a poet anguishes over the absence of a lover.

[3] **swain:** Swains and nymphs are stock figures in pastoral verse. A swain is a shepherd boy or rustic young man. A nymph is a female shepherd or country woman.

[4] **Cloris with the dear Alexis:** Stock pastoral characters.

[5] **Hermes, Aphrodite:** Hermaphrodites was the child of Hermes and Aphrodite, the Greek gods, thus male and female in one body, as in the term *hermaphrodite*, meaning one who combines both sexes.

JONATHAN SWIFT (1667–1745)

A Description of a City Shower (1710)

	Careful observers may foretell the hour	
	(By sure prognostics) when to dread a shower:	
	While rain depends,° the pensive cat gives o'er	threatens
	Her frolics, and pursues her tail no more.	
5	Returning home at night, you'll find the sink°	sewer
	Strike your offended sense with double stink.	
	If you be wise, then go not far to dine;	
	You'll spend in coach hire more than save in wine.	
	A coming shower your shooting corns presage,	
10	Old achès throb, your hollow tooth will rage.	
	Sauntering in coffeehouse is Dulman° seen;	dull man
	He damns the climate and complains of spleen.°	irritability
	Meanwhile the South,° rising with dabbled° wings,	wind / dappled
	A sable cloud athwart the welkin flings,	
15	That swilled more liquor than it could contain,	
	And, like a drunkard, gives it up again.	
	Brisk Susan whips her linen from the rope,	
	While the first drizzling shower is borne aslope.°	slanting
	Such is that sprinkling which some careless quean°	saucy woman
20	Flirts° on you from her mop, but not so clean:	splashes
	You fly, invoke the gods; then turning, stop	
	To rail; she singing, still whirls on her mop.	
	Not yet the dust had shunned the unequal strife,	
	But, aided by the wind, fought still for life,	
25	And wafted with its foe by violent gust,	
	'Twas doubtful which was rain and which was dust.	
	Ah! where must needy poet seek for aid,	
	When dust and rain at once his coat invade?	
	Sole coat, where dust cemented by the rain	
30	Erects the nap,° and leaves a mingled stain.	texture
	Now in contiguous drops the flood comes down,	
	Threatening with deluge this devoted° town.	overwhelmed
	To shops in crowds the daggled° females fly,	splashed
	Pretend to cheapen° goods, but nothing buy.	consider the price of
35	The Templar spruce,° while every spout's abroach,°	law student / running
	Stays till 'tis fair, yet seems to call a coach.	
	The tucked-up sempstress° walks with hasty strides,	seamstress
	While streams run down her oiled umbrella's sides.	
	Here various kinds, by various fortunes led,	
40	Commence acquaintance underneath a shed.	

Triumphant Tories and desponding Whigs[1]
Forget their feuds, and join to save their wigs.
Boxed in a chair the beau impatient sits,
While spouts run clattering o'er the roof by fits,
45 And ever and anon with frightful din
The leather sounds; he trembles from within.
So when Troy chairmen bore the wooden steed,
Pregnant with Greeks impatient to be freed
(Those bully Greeks, who, as the moderns do,
50 Instead of paying chairmen, run them through),
Laocoön struck the outside with his spear,
And each imprisoned hero quaked for fear.[2]
    Now from all parts the swelling kennels° flow,   gutters
And bear their trophies with them as they go:
55 Filth of all hues and odors seem to tell
What street they sailed from, by their sight and smell.
They, as each torrent drives with rapid force,
From Smithfield or St. Pulchre's shape their course,
And in huge confluence joined at Snow Hill ridge,
60 Fall from the conduit prone to Holborn Bridge.[3]
Sweepings from butchers' stalls, dung, guts, and blood,
Drowned puppies, stinking sprats,° all drenched in mud,   herring
Dead cats, and turnip tops, come tumbling down the flood.

ALEXANDER POPE (1688–1744)

Epistle to a Lady: Of the Characters of Women (1735)

Nothing so true as what you once let fall:
'Most women have no characters at all.'
Matter too soft a lasting mark to bear,
And best distinguished by black, brown, or fair.
5   How many pictures of one nymph we view,
All how unlike each other, all how true!

-----

[1] **Tories . . . Whigs:** Tories and Whigs were opposing political parties in Swift's time. He belonged to the Tory Party, which had just come into power.
[2] **Laocoön . . . fear:** In Virgil's *Aeneid*, Laocoön hit the sides of the Trojan horse, scaring the Greeks who hid within it.
[3] **Smithfield . . . Bridge:** There was a famous cattle market at Smithfield; the scraps or offal from that market would be swept downward toward the Fleet Ditch, which ran below Holborn Bridge. Garbage running down from a stream called Snow Hill merged there, making quite a stench. St. Sepulchre's was a church in Holborn.

Arcadia's Countess, here, in ermined pride,
Is there, Pastora by a fountain side.
Here Fannia, leering on her own good man,
10   And there, a naked Leda with a swan.
Let then the fair one beautifully cry
In Magdalen's loose hair and lifted eye,
Or dressed in smiles of sweet Cecilia shine,[1]
With simp'ring angels, palms, and harps divine;
15   Whether the charmer sinner it, or saint it,
If folly grows romantic, I must paint it.
        Come then, the colours and the ground prepare!
Dip in the rainbow, trick her off in air,
Choose a firm cloud before it fall, and in it
20   Catch, ere she change, the Cynthia° of this minute.   Queen Elizabeth I
        Rufa,° whose eye quick-glancing o'er the park   redhead
Attracts each light gay meteor of a spark,
Agrees as ill with Rufa studying Locke,[2]
As Sappho's[3] diamonds with her dirty smock,
25   Or Sappho at her toilet's greasy task,
With Sappho fragrant at an evening mask:
So morning insects, that in muck begun,
Shine, buzz, and fly-blow in the setting sun.
        How soft is Silia! fearful to offend,
30   The frail one's advocate, the weak one's friend:
To her, Calista[4] proved her conduct nice,
And good Simplicius[5] asks of her advice.
Sudden, she storms! she raves! You tip the wink,
But spare your censure—Silia does not drink.
35   All eyes may see from what the change arose,
All eyes may see—a pimple on her nose.
        Papillia,[6] wedded to her doting spark,
Sighs for the shades—'How charming is a park!'
A park is purchased, but the fair he sees
40   All bathed in tears—'Oh odious, odious trees!'
        Ladies, like variegated tulips, show,
'Tis to their changes that their charms we owe;
Their happy spots the nice admirer take,

---

[1] **Arcadia's Countess . . . Cecilia shine:** These are all composite type; that is, they are imaginary figures drawn loosely from women Pope may have known.
[2] **Locke:** John Locke (1632–1704) was an English philosopher.
[3] **Sappho:** Lady Mary Whortley Montagu.
[4] **Calista:** The name means "fairness." The name also suggests Callisto, a wood nymph made pregnant by Zeus.
[5] **Simplicius:** The name suggests a woman who is simple-minded.
[6] **Papillia:** The name means "butterfly" in Latin (*papilo*).

Fine by defect, and delicately weak.
45   'Twas thus Calypso[7] once each heart alarmed,
     Awed without virtue, without beauty charmed;
     Her tongue bewitched as oddly as her eyes,
     Less wit than mimic, more a wit than wise;
     Strange graces still, and stranger flights she had,
50   Was just not ugly, and was just not mad;
     Yet ne'er so sure our passion to create,
     As when she touched the brink of all we hate.
         Narcissa's nature, tolerably mild,[8]
     To make a wash° would hardly stew a child,   hair lotion
55   Has ev'n been proved to grant a lover's pray'r,
     And paid a tradesman once to make him stare;
     Gave alms at Easter, in a Christian trim,
     And made a widow happy for a whim.
     Why then declare good-nature is her scorn,
60   When 'tis by that alone she can be borne?
     Why pique all mortals, yet affect a name?
     A fool to pleasure, and a slave to fame:
     Now deep in Taylor and the Book of Martyrs,[9]
     Now drinking citron with his Grace and Chartres.[10]
65   Now conscience chills her, and now passion burns;
     And atheism and religion take their turns;
     A very heathen in the carnal part,
     Yet still a sad, good Christian at her heart.
         See sin in state, majestically drunk,
70   Proud as a peeress, prouder as a punk;°   whore
     Chaste to her husband, frank to all beside,
     A teeming mistress, but a barren bride.
     What then? let blood and body bear the fault,
     Her head's untouched, that noble seat of thought:
75   Such this day's doctrine—in another fit
     She sins with poets through pure love of wit.
     What has not fired her bosom or her brain?
     Caesar and Tall-boy, Charles and Charlemagne.[11]

---

[7] **Calypso:** The nymph who kept Odysseus on her island for eight years. The name means "one who conceals something."

[8] **Narcissa:** From Narcissus, the youth with whom Echo fell fatally in love.

[9] **Taylor . . . Martyrs:** Jeremy Taylor's *Holy Living and Holy Dying* was a popular seventeenth-century devotional manual. *Book of Martyrs* refers to John Foxe's *Actes and Monuments,* another popular book of the day.

[10] **citron . . . Chartres:** Citron water was flavoured with brandy and a peel of citron or lemon. His Grace was any duke, although sometimes identified with Philip, Duke of Wharton. Chartres was Francis Chartres, a gambler condemned for rape on two infamous occasions.

[11] **Caesar . . . Charlemagne:** Here Pope contrasts Julius Caesar and Charlemagne, two grand rulers, with idiots, represented by the names Tall-boy and Charles. Charles was usually the name of a footman.

As Helluo,° late dictator of the feast,   glutton
80   The nose of *haut-goût*° and the tip of taste,   fancy taste
Critiqued your wine, and analysed your meat,
Yet on plain pudding deigned at home to eat;
So Philomedé,° lect'ring all mankind   laughter-loving
On the soft passion, and the taste refined,
85   Th' address, the delicacy—stoops at once,
And makes her hearty meal upon a dunce.
      Flavia's a wit, has too much sense to pray;
To toast our wants and wishes is her way;
Nor asks of God, but of her stars, to give
90   The mighty blessing, 'while we live, to live.'
Then all for death, that opiate of the soul!
Lucretia's dagger, Rosamonda's bowl.
Say, what can cause such impotence of mind?
A spark too fickle, or a spouse too kind.
95   Wise wretch! with pleasures too refined to please,
With too much spirit to be e'er at ease,
With too much quickness ever to be taught,
With too much thinking to have common thought:
Who purchase pain with all that joy can give,
100   And die of nothing but a rage to live.
      Turn then from wits; and look on Simo's° mate,   old man
No ass so meek, no ass so obstinate;
Or her that owns her faults, but never mends,
Because she's honest, and the best of friends;
105   Or her whose life the church and scandal share,
For ever in a passion, or a pray'r;
Or her who laughs at hell, but (like her Grace)[12]
Cries, 'Ah! how charming if there's no such place!';
Or who in sweet vicissitude appears
110   Of mirth and opium, ratafie and tears,
The daily anodyne, and nightly draught,
To kill those foes to fair ones, time and thought.
Woman and fool are two hard things to hit,
For true no-meaning puzzles more than wit.
115   But what are these to great Atossa's mind? [13]
Scarce once herself, by turns all womankind!
Who, with herself, or others, from her birth
Finds all her life one warfare upon earth:

---

[12] **her Grace:** Any duchess.
[13] **Atossa's mind:** Atossa was a daughter of Cyrus and Cambyses, rulers in ancient Babylon. Pope applies the portrait generally, but it is developed from the figure of Katherine, Duchess of Buckinghamshire (1682–1743), an arrogant, argumentative woman who nevertheless was highly intelligent and accomplished.

Shines in exposing knaves and painting fools,
120   Yet is whate'er she hates and ridicules.
No thought advances, but her eddy brain
Whisks it about, and down it goes again.
Full sixty years the world has been her trade,
The wisest fool much time has ever made.
125   From loveless youth to unrespected age,
No passion gratified except her rage,
So much the fury still outran the wit,
The pleasure missed her, and the scandal hit.
Who breaks with her, provokes revenge from hell,
130   But he's a bolder man who dares be well:
Her ev'ry turn with violence pursued,
Nor more a storm her hate than gratitude.
To that each passion turns, or soon or late;
Love, if it makes her yield, must make her hate:
135   Superiors? death! and equals? what a curse!
But an inferior not dependant? worse.
Offend her, and she knows not to forgive;
Oblige her, and she'll hate you while you live:
But die, and she'll adore you—then the bust
140   And temple rise—then fall again to dust.
Last night, her lord was all that's good and great,
A knave this morning, and his will a cheat.
Strange! by the means defeated of the ends,
By spirit robbed of pow'r, by warmth of friends,
145   By wealth of follow'rs! without one distress,
Sick of herself through very selfishness!
Atossa, cursed with ev'ry granted pray'r,
Childless with all her children, wants an heir.
To heirs unknown descends th' unguarded store,
150   Or wanders, heav'n-directed, to the poor.
      Pictures like these, dear Madam, to design,
Asks no firm hand, and no unerring line;
Some wand'ring touch, or some reflected light,
Some flying stroke alone can hit 'em right:
155   For how should equal colours do the knack?
Chameleons who can paint in white and black?
      'Yet Cloe sure was formed without a spot.'—
Nature in her then erred not, but forgot.
'With every pleasing, every prudent part,
160   Say, what can Cloe want?'—She wants a heart.
She speaks, behaves, and acts, just as she ought,
But never, never reached one gen'rous thought.
Virtue she finds too painful an endeavour,
Content to dwell in decencies for ever.

165   So very reasonable, so unmoved,
     As never yet to love, or to be loved.
     She, while her lover pants upon her breast,
     Can mark the figures on an Indian chest;
     And when she sees her friend in deep despair,
170   Observes how much a chintz exceeds mohair.
     Forbid it, heav'n, a favour or a debt
     She e'er should cancel—but she may forget.
     Safe is your secret still in Cloe's ear;
     But none of Cloe's shall you ever hear.
175   Of all her dears she never slandered one,
     But cares not if a thousand are undone.
     Would Cloe know if you're alive or dead?
     She bids her footman put it in her head.
     Cloe is prudent—would you too be wise?
180   Then never break your heart when Cloe dies.
        One certain portrait may (I grant) be seen,
     Which heav'n has varnished out,° and made a Queen: [14]   erased
     The same for ever! and described by all
     With truth and goodness, as with crown and ball.
185   Poets heap virtues, painters gems, at will,
     And show their zeal, and hide their want of skill.
     'Tis well—but artists! who can paint or write,
     To draw the naked is your true delight:
     That robe of quality so struts and swells,
190   None see what parts of nature it conceals.
     Th' exactest traits of body or of mind,
     We owe to models of an humble kind.
     If Queensberry [15] to strip there's no compelling,
     'Tis from a handmaid we must take a Helen.
195   From peer or bishop 'tis no easy thing
     To draw the man who loves his God or King:
     Alas! I copy (or my draught would fail)
     From honest Mah'met, or plain Parson Hale.[16]
        But grant, in public men sometimes are shown,
200   A woman's seen in private life alone:
     Our bolder talents in full light displayed,
     Your virtues open fairest in the shade.
     Bred to disguise, in public 'tis you hide;
     There, none distinguish 'twixt your shame or pride,

---

[14] **a Queen:** Refers to Queen Caroline (1683–1737), a strong Whig supporter.
[15] **Queensberry:** The Duchess of Queensbury (1700–1777), a very beautiful woman.
[16] **Mah'met . . . Hale:** Mah'met was a well-known personal servant of King George I; Dr. Stephen Hale was a physician and friend of the poet.

205   Weakness or delicacy; all so nice,
      That each may seem a virtue or a vice.
            In men we various ruling passions find,
      In women, two almost divide the kind;
      Those, only fixed, they first or last obey,
210   The love of pleasure, and the love of sway.
            That, nature gives; and where the lesson taught
      Is but to please, can pleasure seem a fault?
      Experience, this; by man's oppression cursed,
      They seek the second not to lose the first.
215   Men, some to bus'ness, some to pleasure take;
      But ev'ry woman is at heart a rake:
      Men, some to quiet, some to public strife;
      But ev'ry lady would be queen for life.
            Yet mark the fate of a whole sex of queens!
220   Pow'r all their end, but beauty all the means.
      In youth they conquer with so wild a rage,
      As leaves them scarce a subject in their age:
      For foreign glory, foreign joy, they roam;
      No thought of peace or happiness at home.
225   But wisdom's triumph is well-timed retreat,
      As hard a science to the fair as great!
      Beauties, like tyrants, old and friendless grown,
      Yet hate to rest, and dread to be alone,
      Worn out in public, weary ev'ry eye,
230   Nor leave one sigh behind them when they die.
            Pleasures the sex, as children birds, pursue,
      Still out of reach, yet never out of view;
      Sure, if they catch, to spoil the toy at most,
      To covet flying, and regret when lost:
235   At last, to follies youth could scarce defend,
      'Tis half their age's prudence to pretend;
      Ashamed to own they gave delight before,
      Reduced to feign it, when they give no more:
      As hags hold sabbaths, less for joy than spite,
240   So these their merry, miserable night;
      Still round and round the ghosts of beauty glide,
      And haunt the places where their honour died.
            See how the world its veterans rewards!
      A youth of frolics, an old age of cards;
245   Fair to no purpose, artful to no end,
      Young without lovers, old without a friend;
      A fop their passion, but their prize a sot,
      Alive, ridiculous, and dead, forgot!
            Ah, friend! to dazzle let the vain design;
250   To raise the thought and touch the heart be thine!

That charm shall grow, while what fatigues the Ring
Flaunts and goes down, an unregarded thing.
So when the sun's broad beam has tired the sight,
All mild ascends the moon's more sober light;
255 Serene in virgin modesty she shines,
And unobserved the glaring orb declines.
    Oh! blessed with temper, whose unclouded ray
Can make tomorrow cheerful as today;
She who can love a sister's charms, or hear
260 Sighs for a daughter with unwounded ear;
She who ne'er answers till a husband cools,
Or, if she rules him, never shows she rules;
Charms by accepting, by submitting sways,
Yet has her humour most when she obeys;
265 Lets fops or fortune fly which way they will;
Disdains all loss of tickets, or codille;
Spleen, vapours, or small-pox, above them all,
And mistress of herself, though china fall.
    And yet, believe me, good as well as ill,
270 Woman's at best a contradiction still.
Heav'n, when it strives to polish all it can
Its last best work, but forms a softer man;
Picks from each sex, to make its fav'rite blest,
Your love of pleasure, our desire of rest,
275 Blends, in exception to all gen'ral rules,
Your taste of follies, with our scorn of fools,
Reserve with frankness, art with truth allied,
Courage with softness, modesty with pride,
Fixed principles, with fancy ever new;
280 Shakes all together, and produces—you.
    Be this a woman's fame; with this unblest,
Toasts live a scorn, and queens may die a jest.
This Phoebus° promised (I forget the year)   Apollo
When those blue eyes first opened on the sphere;
285 Ascendant Phoebus watched that hour with care,
Averted half your parents' simple pray'r,
And gave you beauty, but denied the pelf
Which buys your sex a tyrant o'er itself.
The gen'rous god, who wit and gold refines,
290 And ripens spirits as he ripens mines,[17]
Kept dross for duchesses, the world shall know it,
To you gave sense, good-humour, and a poet.

---

[17] **he ripens mines:** Ripened minds, as god of the sun; the analogy is with the sun ripening grapes for wine.

ALEXANDER POPE (1688–1744)

from An Essay on Criticism (1711)

Of all the causes which conspire to blind
Man's erring judgement, and misguide the mind,
What the weak head with strongest bias rules,
Is pride, the never-failing vice of fools.
5 Whatever nature has in worth denied,
She gives in large recruits of needless pride;
For as in bodies, thus in souls we find
What wants in blood and spirits, swelled with wind;
Pride, where wit fails, steps in to our defence,
10 And fills up all the mighty void of sense!
If once right reason drives that cloud away,
Truth breaks upon us with resistless day.
Trust not yourself; but your defects to know,
Make use of ev'ry friend—and ev'ry foe.
15 A little learning is a dang'rous thing;
Drink deep, or taste not the Pierian spring:[1]
There shallow draughts intoxicate the brain,
And drinking largely sobers us again.
Fired at first sight with what the Muse imparts,
20 In fearless youth we tempt the heights of arts,
While from the bounded level of our mind,
Short views we take, nor see the lengths behind;
But more advanced, behold with strange surprise
New, distant scenes of endless science rise!
25 So pleased at first the tow'ring Alps we try,
Mount o'er the vales, and seem to tread the sky;
Th' eternal snows appear already past,
And the first clouds and mountains seem the last:
But, those attained, we tremble to survey
30 The growing labours of the lengthened way,
Th' increasing prospect tires our wand'ring eyes,
Hills peep o'er hills, and Alps on Alps arise!
A perfect judge will read each work of wit
With the same spirit that its author writ,
35 Survey the whole, nor seek slight faults to find,
Where nature moves, and rapture warms the mind;
Nor lose, for that malignant dull delight,
The gen'rous pleasure to be charmed with wit.

---

[1] **Pierian spring:** A spring sacred to the Muses, near Mount Olympus.

But in such lays as neither ebb nor flow,
40 Correctly cold, and regularly low,[2]
That shunning faults, one quiet tenor keep;
We cannot blame indeed—but we may sleep.
In wit, as nature, what affects our hearts
Is not th' exactness of peculiar parts;
45 'Tis not a lip, or eye, we beauty call,
But the joint force and full result of all.
Thus when we view some well-proportioned dome,[3]
(The world's just wonder, and ev'n thine, O Rome!)
No single parts unequally surprise,
50 All comes united to th' admiring eyes;
No monstrous height, or breadth, or length appear;
The whole at once is bold and regular.

. . . .

Some to conceit alone their taste confine,
And glitt'ring thoughts struck out at ev'ry line;
55 Pleased with a work where nothing's just or fit,
One glaring chaos and wild heap of wit.
Poets, like painters, thus, unskilled to trace
The naked nature and the living grace,
With gold and jewels cover every part,
60 And hide with ornaments their want of art.
True wit is nature to advantage dressed,
What oft was thought, but ne'er so well expressed;
Something, whose truth convinced at sight we find,
That gives us back the image of our mind:
65 As shades more sweetly recommend the light,
So modest plainness sets off sprightly wit:
For works may have more wit than does 'em good,
As bodies perish through excess of blood.
Others for language all their care express,
70 And value books, as women men, for dress:
Their praise is still,—the style is excellent;
The sense, they humbly take upon content.
Words are like leaves; and where they most abound,
Much fruit of sense beneath is rarely found.
75 False eloquence, like the prismatic glass,
Its gaudy colours spreads on ev'ry place;
The face of nature we no more survey,
All glares alike, without distinction gay:

---

[2] **regularly low:** In keeping with the rules, but nevertheless mediocre.
[3] **dome:** A nicely proportioned dome, as the dome of St. Peter's Cathedral in Rome.

But true expression, like th' unchanging sun,
80 Clears and improves whate'er it shines upon,
It gilds all objects, but it alters none.
Expression is the dress of thought, and still
Appears more decent as more suitable;
A vile conceit in pompous words expressed
85 Is like a clown in regal purple dressed;
For diff'rent styles with diff'rent subjects sort,
As several garbs with country, town and court.
Some by old words to fame have made pretence,
Ancients in phrase, mere moderns in their sense!
90 Such laboured nothings, in so strange a style,
Amaze th' unlearned, and make the learned smile.
Unlucky as Fungoso[4] in the play,
These sparks with awkward vanity display
What the fine gentleman wore yesterday!
95 And but so mimic ancient wits at best,
As apes our grandsires, in their doublets dressed.
In words, as fashions, the same rule will hold,
Alike fantastic, if too new, or old;
Be not the first by whom the new are tried,
100 Nor yet the last to lay the old aside.
    But most by numbers judge a poet's song,
And smooth or rough, with them, is right or wrong:
In the bright Muse though thousand charms conspire,
Her voice is all these tuneful fools admire,
105 Who haunt Parnassus but to please their ear,
Not mend their minds; as some to church repair,
Not for the doctrine, but the music there.
These equal syllables alone require,
Though oft the ear the open vowels tire,
110 While expletives their feeble aid *do* join,
And ten low words oft creep in one dull line,
While they ring round the same unvaried chimes,
With sure returns of still expected rhymes.
Where'er you find 'the cooling western breeze',
115 In the next line, it 'whispers through the trees';
If crystal streams 'with pleasing murmurs creep',
The reader's threatened (not in vain) with 'sleep'.
Then, at the last and only couplet fraught
With some unmeaning thing they call a thought,
120 A needless Alexandrine[5] ends the song,

---

[4] **Fungoso:** An unlucky character in *Every Man in His Humour,* a play by Ben Jonson.
[5] **Alexandrine:** A line of six poetic feet.

That, like a wounded snake, drags its slow length along.
Leave such to tune their own dull rhymes, and know
What's roundly smooth, or languishingly slow;
And praise the easy vigour of a line,
125   Where Denham's strength and Waller's sweetness join.[6]
True ease in writing comes from art, not chance,
As those move easiest who have learned to dance.
'Tis not enough no harshness gives offence,
The sound must seem an echo to the sense.
130   Soft is the strain when Zephyr° gently blows,   the West Wind
And the smooth stream in smoother numbers flows;
But when loud surges lash the sounding shore,
The hoarse, rough verse should like the torrent roar.
When Ajax[7] strives some rock's vast weight to throw,
135   The line too labours, and the words move slow:
Not so, when swift Camilla[8] scours the plain,
Flies o'er th' unbending corn, and skims along the main.

SAMUEL JOHNSON   (1709–1784)

The Vanity of Human Wishes. The Tenth Satire of Juvenal[1] Imitated   (1749)

Let observation with extensive view
Survey mankind from China to Peru;
Remark each anxious toil, each eager strife,
And watch the busy scenes of crowded life;
5   Then say how hope and fear, desire and hate,
O'erspread with snares the clouded maze of fate,
Where wav'ring man, betrayed by vent'rous pride
To tread the dreary paths without a guide,
As treach'rous phantoms in the mist delude,
10   Shuns fancied ills, or chases airy good.
How rarely reason guides the stubborn choice,
Rules the bold hand, or prompts the suppliant voice;
How nations sink, by darling schemes oppressed,

---

[6] **Denham's . . . join:** Sir John Denham (1615–1669) was a poet and playwright known for his simple, clear writing. Edmund Waller (1606–1687) was a poet and politician who was known for his highly polished and sweet-sounding verse.
[7] **Ajax:** A hero in Homer's *Iliad* (Book VII) who picks up a stone in a battle with Hector.
[8] **Camilla:** A female warrior in Virgil's *Aeneid* (Book VII).
[1] **Juvenal:** A Roman satirist from the first century, A.D.

When vengeance listens to the fool's request.
15 Fate wings with ev'ry wish th' afflictive dart,°   arrow
Each gift of nature, and each grace of art;
With fatal heat impetuous courage glows,
With fatal sweetness elocution flows,
Impeachment stops the speaker's pow'rful breath,
20 And restless fire precipitates on° death.   hastens
  But scarce observed, the knowing and the bold
Fall in the gen'ral massacre of gold;
Wide-wasting pest! that rages unconfined,
And crowds with crimes the records of mankind;
25 For gold his sword the hireling ruffian draws,
For gold the hireling judge distorts the laws;
Wealth heaped on wealth nor truth nor safety buys,
The dangers gather as the treasures rise.
  Let hist'ry tell where rival kings command,
30 And dubious title shakes the madded land,
When statutes glean the refuse of the sword,
How much more safe the vassal than the lord;
Low skulks the hind° beneath the rage of pow'r,   peasant
And leaves the wealthy traitor in the Tow'r,[2]
35 Untouched his cottage, and his slumbers sound,
Though confiscation's vultures hover round.
  The needy traveller, serene and gay,
Walks the wild heath, and sings his toil away.
Does envy seize thee? crush th' upbraiding joy,
40 Increase his riches and his peace destroy;
Now fears in dire vicissitude invade,
The rustling brake° alarms, and quiv'ring shade,   thicket
Nor light nor darkness bring his pain relief,
One shows the plunder, and one hides the thief.
45   Yet still one gen'ral cry the skies assails,
And gain and grandeur load the tainted gales;
Few know the toiling statesman's fear or care,
Th' insidious rival and the gaping heir.[3]
  Once more, Democritus,[4] arise on earth,
50 With cheerful wisdom and instructive mirth,
See motley life in modern trappings dressed,
And feed with varied fools th' eternal jest:
Thou who couldst laugh where want enchained caprice,

---

[2] **traitor in the Tow'r:** Refers to four Scottish lords who were imprisoned for supporting the Jacobite rebellion of 1745, when "Bonnie Prince Charlie" led an invasion of England.
[3] **gaping heir:** Refers to the great personal hostility between Frederick, Prince of Wales, and his father, George II.
[4] **Democritus:** From the fifth century B.C., known as the "laughing philosopher" of Greece.

Toil crushed conceit, and man was of a piece;
55   Where wealth unloved without a mourner died;
And scarce a sycophant was fed by pride;
Where ne'er was known the form of mock debate,
Or seen a new-made mayor's unwieldy state;
Where change of fav'rites made no change of laws,
60   And senates heard before they judged a cause;
How wouldst thou shake at Britain's modish tribe,
Dart the quick taunt, and edge the piercing gibe?
Attentive truth and nature to descry,
And pierce each scene with philosophic eye.
65   To thee were solemn toys or empty show,
The robes of pleasure and the veils of woe:
All aid the farce, and all thy mirth maintain,
Whose joys are causeless, or whose griefs are vain.
     Such was the scorn that filled the sage's mind,
70   Renewed at ev'ry glance on humankind;
How just that scorn ere yet thy voice declare,
Search every state, and canvass ev'ry pray'r.
     Unnumbered suppliants crowd preferment's gate,
Athirst for wealth, and burning to be great;
75   Delusive Fortune hears th' incessant call,
They mount, they shine, evaporate and fall.
On ev'ry stage the foes of peace attend,
Hate dogs their flight, and insult mocks their end.
Love ends with hope, the sinking statesman's door
80   Pours in the morning worshipper no more;
For growing names the weekly scribbler lies,
To growing wealth the dedicator flies,
From every room descends the painted face,
That hung the bright Palladium⁵ of the place,
85   And smoked in kitchens, or in auctions sold,
To better features yields the frame of gold;
For now no more we trace in ev'ry line
Heroic worth, benevolence divine:
The form distorted justifies the fall,
90   And detestation rids th' indignant wall.
     But will not Britain hear the last appeal,
Sign her foes' doom, or guard her fav'rites' zeal?
Through Freedom's sons no more remonstrance rings,
Degrading nobles and controlling kings;
95   Our supple tribes repress their patriot throats,
And ask no questions but the price of votes;

---

⁵ **Palladium:** The preservation of Troy depended on the image of Pallas Athene.

With weekly libels and septennial ale,
Their wish is full to riot and to rail.
   In full-blown dignity, see Wolsey [6] stand,
100 Law in his voice, and fortune in his hand:
To him the church, the realm, their pow'rs consign,
Through him the rays of regal bounty shine,
Turned by his nod the stream of honour flows,
His smile alone security bestows:
105 Still to new heights his restless wishes tow'r,
Claim leads to claim, and pow'r advances pow'r;
Till conquest unresisted ceased to please,
And rights submitted left him none to seize.
At length his sov'reign frowns—the train of state
110 Mark the keen glance, and watch the sign to hate.
Where'er he turns he meets a stranger's eye,
His suppliants scorn him, and his followers fly;
At once is lost the pride of awful state,
The golden canopy, the glitt'ring plate,
115 The regal palace, the luxurious board,
The liv'ried army, and the menial lord.
With age, with cares, with maladies oppressed,
He seeks the refuge of monastic rest.
Grief aids disease, remembered folly stings,
120 And his last sighs reproach the faith of kings.
   Speak thou, whose thoughts at humble peace repine,
Shall Wolsey's wealth, with Wolsey's end be thine?
Or liv'st thou now, with safer pride content,
The wisest justice on the banks of Trent?
125 For why did Wolsey, near the steeps of fate,
On weak foundations raise th' enormous weight?
Why but to sink beneath misfortune's blow,
With louder ruin to the gulfs below?
   What gave great Villiers [7] to th' assassin's knife,
130 And fixed disease on Harley's closing life?
What murdered Wentworth,[8] and what exiled Hyde,[9]
By kings protected and to kings allied?
What but their wish indulged in courts to shine,
And pow'r too great to keep, or to resign?
135   When first the college rolls receive his name,

---

[6] **Wolsey:** Thomas Wolsey (1465?–1530) was cardinal under Henry VIII. He was the king's closest advisor, but he became too powerful and was eventually executed.
[7] **Villiers:** George Villiers, Duke of Buckingham, murdered in 1628. He was a well-known figure whom the king loved.
[8] **Wentworth:** Thomas Wentworth, Earl of Strafford, was executed in 1641 as a Royalist.
[9] **Hyde:** Robert Harley, Earl of Oxford, spent his last years in bad health after being imprisoned in 1715.

The young enthusiast quits his ease for fame;
Through all his veins the fever of renown
Burns from the strong contagion of the gown;
O'er Bodley's dome° his future labours spread,   library in Oxford
140 And Bacon's[10] mansion trembles o'er his head.
Are these thy views? proceed, illustrious youth,
And virtue guard thee to the throne of truth!
Yet should thy soul indulge the gen'rous heat,
Till captive Science yields her last retreat;
145 Should Reason guide thee with her brightest ray,
And pour on misty doubt resistless day;
Should no false kindness lure to loose delight,
Nor praise relax, nor difficulty fright;
Should tempting Novelty thy cell refrain,
150 And Sloth effuse her opiate fumes in vain;
Should Beauty blunt on fops her fatal dart,
Nor claim the triumph of a lettered heart;
Should no disease thy torpid veins invade,
Nor Melancholy's phantoms haunt thy shade;
155 Yet hope not life from grief or danger free,
Nor think the doom of man reversed for thee:
Deign on the passing world to turn thine eyes,
And pause awhile from letters to be wise;
There mark what ills the scholar's life assail,
160 Toil, envy, want, the patron, and the jail.
See nations slowly wise, and meanly just,
To buried merit raise the tardy bust.
If dreams yet flatter, once again attend,
Hear Lydiat's life, and Galileo's end.[11]
165 Nor deem, when Learning her last prize bestows,
The glitt'ring eminence exempt from foes;
See when the vulgar 'scape, despised or awed,
Rebellion's vengeful talons seize on Laud.[12]
From meaner minds though smaller fines content,
170 The plundered palace or sequestered rent;
Marked out by dangerous parts he meets the shock,
And fatal Learning leads him to the block:
Around his tomb let Art and Genius weep,
But hear his death, ye blockheads, hear and sleep.

---

[10] **Bacon:** Refers to Roger Bacon (1214–1294). There was a tradition that the great thinker's study was built over a bridge. If a greater man than Bacon passed under the bridge, it would collapse.
[11] **Lydiat's . . . Galileo's end:** Thomas Lydiat (1572–1646), a priest and historian who was imprisoned by the Puritans because of his Royalist leanings. Galileo struggled with the Church and the Inquisition about his scientific discoveries and theories. He was blind toward the end of his life.
[12] **Laud:** An English archbishop charged with high treason and executed in 1645.

175   The festal blazes, the triumphal show,
      The ravished standard, and the captive foe,
      The senate's thanks, the gazette's pompous tale,
      With force resistless o'er the brave prevail.
      Such bribes the rapid Greek o'er Asia whirled,
180   For such the steady Romans shook the world;
      For such in distant lands the Britons shine,
      And stain with blood the Danube or the Rhine;[13]
      This pow'r has praise, that virtue scarce can warm,
      Till fame supplies the universal charm.
185   Yet Reason frowns on war's unequal game,
      Where wasted nations raise a single name,
      And mortgaged states their grandsires' wreaths regret,
      From age to age in everlasting debt;
      Wreaths which at last the dear-bought right convey
190   To rust on medals, or on stones decay.
            On what foundation stands the warrior's pride?
      How just his hopes let Swedish Charles[14] decide;
      A frame of adamant, a soul of fire,
      No dangers fright him, and no labours tire;
195   O'er love, o'er fear, extends his wide domain,
      Unconquered lord of pleasure and of pain;
      No joys to him pacific sceptres yield,
      War sounds the trump, he rushes to the field;
      Behold surrounding kings their pow'r combine,
200   And one capitulate, and one resign;[15]
      Peace courts his hand, but spreads her charms in vain;
      'Think nothing gained,' he cries, 'till naught remain,
      On Moscow's walls till Gothic standards fly,
      And all be mine beneath the polar sky.'
205   The march begins in military state,
      And nations on his eye suspended wait;
      Stern Famine guards the solitary coast,
      And Winter barricades the realms of frost;
      He comes, not want and cold his course delay;—
210   Hide, blushing Glory, hide Pultowa's[16] day:
      The vanquished hero leaves his broken bands,
      And shows his miseries in distant lands;
      Condemned a needy supplicant to wait,

---

[13] **Danube . . . Rhine:** These are great European rivers.
[14] **Swedish Charles:** Charles XII of Sweden (1682–1718), a ruler who conquered Denmark, Saxony, and Poland. He was defeated by the Russians.
[15] **resign:** Refers to two of Charles XII's enemies, Frederick IV of Denmark and August II of Poland.
[16] **Pultowa:** Charles XII was beaten by Peter the Great of Russia at Poltava, Ukraine, in 1709.

While ladies interpose, and slaves debate.
215   But did not Chance at length her error mend?
Did no subverted empire mark his end?
Did rival monarchs give the fatal wound?
Or hostile millions press him to the ground?
His fall was destined to a barren strand,
220   A petty fortress, and a dubious hand;[17]
He left the name, at which the world grew pale,
To point a moral, or adorn a tale.
     All times their scenes of pompous woes afford,
From Persia's tyrant to Bavaria's lord.
225   In gay hostility, and barbarous pride,
With half mankind embattled at his side,
Great Xerxes[18] comes to seize the certain prey,
And starves exhausted regions in his way;
Attendant Flatt'ry counts his myriads o'er,
230   Till counted myriads soothe his pride no more;
Fresh praise is tried till madness fires his mind,
The waves he lashes, and enchains the wind;
New pow'rs are claimed, new pow'rs are still bestowed,
Till rude resistance lops the spreading god;
235   The daring Greeks deride the martial show,
And heap their valleys with the gaudy foe;
Th' insulted sea with humbler thoughts he gains,
A single skiff to speed his flight remains;
Th' incumbered oar scarce leaves the dreaded coast
240   Through purple billows and a floating host.
     The bold Bavarian, in a luckless hour,
Tries the dread summits of Caesarian power,
With unexpected legions bursts away,
And sees defenceless realms receive his sway;
245   Short sway! fair Austria spreads her mournful charms,
The queen, the beauty, sets the world in arms;
From hill to hill the beacon's rousing blaze
Spreads wide the hope of plunder and of praise;
The fierce Croatian, and the wild Hussar,°   a cavalryman
250   With all the sons of ravage crowd the war;
The baffled prince in honour's flatt'ring bloom
Of hasty greatness finds the fatal doom,

---

[17] **dubious hand:** Charles was reportedly killed by an aide.
[18] **Bavaria's lord . . . Xerxes:** Charles Albert (1697–1745) of Bavaria hoped to lead the Roman Empire himself. Xerxes was the King of Persia who invaded ancient Greece and was defeated at Salamis in 480 B.C.

His foes' derision, and his subjects' blame,
And steals to death from anguish and from shame.
255   'Enlarge my life with multitude of days,
In health, in sickness,' thus the suppliant prays;
Hides from himself his state, and shuns to know
That life protracted is protracted woe.
Time hovers o'er, impatient to destroy,
260   And shuts up all the passages of joy:
In vain their gifts the bounteous seasons pour,
The fruit autumnal, and the vernal flow'r,
With listless eyes the dotard views the store,
He views, and wonders that they please no more;
265   Now pall the tasteless meats, and joyless wines,
And Luxury with sighs her slave resigns.
Approach, ye minstrels, try the soothing strain,
Diffuse the tuneful lenitives of pain:
No sounds, alas, would touch th' impervious ear,
270   Though dancing mountains witnessed Orpheus near;
Nor lute nor lyre his feeble pow'rs attend,
Nor sweeter music of a virtuous friend,
But everlasting dictates crowd his tongue,
Perversely grave, or positively wrong.
275   The still-returning tale, and ling'ring jest,
Perplex the fawning niece and pampered guest,
While growing hopes scarce awe the gath'ring sneer,
And scarce a legacy can bribe to hear;
The watchful guests still hint the last offence,
280   The daughter's petulance, the son's expense,
Improve his heady rage with treach'rous skill,
And mould his passions till they make his will.
        Unnumbered maladies his joints invade,
Lay siege to life and press the dire blockade;
285   But unextinguished av'rice still remains,
And dreaded losses aggravate his pains;
He turns, with anxious heart and crippled hands,
His bonds of debt, and mortgages of lands;
Or views his coffers with suspicious eyes,
290   Unlocks his gold, and counts it till he dies.
        But grant, the virtues of a temp'rate prime
Bless with an age exempt from scorn or crime;
An age that melts with unperceived decay,
And glides in modest innocence away;
295   Whose peaceful day benevolence endears,
Whose night congratulating conscience cheers;

The gen'ral fav'rite as the gen'ral friend:
Such age there is, and who shall wish its end?
    Yet ev'n on this her load Misfortune flings,
300   To press the weary minutes' flagging wings:
New sorrow rises as the day returns,
A sister sickens, or a daughter mourns.
Now kindred merit fills the sable bier,
Now lacerated friendship claims a tear.
305   Year chases year, decay pursues decay,
Still drops some joy from with'ring life away;
New forms arise, and diff'rent views engage,
Superfluous lags the vet'ran on the stage,
Till pitying Nature signs the last release,
310   And bids afflicted worth retire to peace.
    But few there are whom hours like these await,
Who set unclouded in the gulfs of fate.
From Lydia's monarch should the search descend,
By Solon[19] cautioned to regard his end,
315   In life's last scene what prodigies surprise,
Fears of the brave, and follies of the wise?
From Marlb'rough's eyes the streams of dotage flow,
And Swift expires a driv'ler and a show.[20]
    The teeming° mother, anxious for her race,   pregnant
320   Begs for each birth the fortune of a face:
Yet Vane[21] could tell what ills from beauty spring,
And Sedley[22] cursed the form that pleased a king.
Ye nymphs of rosy lips and radiant eyes,
Whom pleasure keeps too busy to be wise,
325   Whom joys with soft varieties invite,
By day the frolic; and the dance by night,
Who frown with vanity, who smile with art,
And ask the latest fashion of the heart,
What care, what rules your heedless charms shall save,

---

[19] **Lydia's monarch . . . By Solon:** Croesus, the wealthy king of Lydia, was told by Solon, the Athenian law-giver, that no man was happy until he had finished his life happily.
[20] **Marlb'rough's . . . show:** John Churchill (1650–1722) was Duke of Marlborough, a great military leader who experienced two strokes that left him paralyzed. At the time of his death in 1722, at the age of seventy-two, Marlborough was not in his "dotage," however; nor is the comment on Swift's death more accurate unless Johnson subscribed to the apocryphal legend that Swift died insane.
[21] **Vane:** Anne Vane was the mistress of Frederick, Prince of Wales.
[22] **Sedley:** Sir Charles Sedley. His daughter, Catherine, was the mistress of the Duke of York, who became James II. She became Countess of Dorchester in 1686. Sir Charles, her father, was furious and supported the Glorious Revolution to overthrow James II.

330 Each nymph your rival, and each youth your slave?
Against your fame with fondness hate combines,
The rival batters, and the lover mines.
With distant voice neglected Virtue calls,
Less heard and less, the faint remonstrance falls;
335 Tired with contempt, she quits the slipp'ry reign,
And Pride and Prudence take her seat in vain.
In crowd at once; where none the pass defend,
The harmless freedom, and the private friend.
The guardians yield, by force superior plied;
340 By Int'rest, Prudence; and by Flatt'ry, Pride.
Now Beauty falls betrayed, despised, distressed,
And hissing Infamy proclaims the rest.
    Where then shall hope and fear their objects find?
Must dull suspense corrupt the stagnant mind?
345 Must helpless man, in ignorance sedate,
Roll darkling down the torrent of his fate?
Must no dislike alarm, no wishes rise,
No cries attempt the mercies of the skies?
Enquirer, cease, petitions yet remain,
350 Which heav'n may hear, nor deem religion vain.
Still raise for good the supplicating voice,
But leave to heav'n the measure and the choice,
Safe in his pow'r, whose eyes discern afar
The secret ambush of a specious pray'r.
355 Implore his aid, in his decisions rest,
Secure whate'er he gives, he gives the best.
Yet when the sense of sacred presence fires,
And strong devotion to the skies aspires,
Pour forth thy fervours for a healthful mind,
360 Obedient passions, and a will resigned;
For love, which scarce collective man can fill;
For patience sov'reign o'er transmuted ill;
For faith, that panting for a happier seat,
Counts death kind Nature's signal of retreat:
365 These goods for man the laws of heav'n ordain,
These goods he grants, who grants the pow'r to gain;
With these celestial wisdom calms the mind,
And makes the happiness she does not find.

PHILIP FRENEAU (1752–1832)

To Sir Toby[1]   (1784; 1792)

A Sugar Planter in the Interior Parts of Jamaica, Near the City of San Jago De La Vega, (Spanish Town) 1784

> "The motions of his spirit are black as night,
> And his affections dark as Erebus."
> —SHAKESPEARE

If there exists a hell—the case is clear—
Sir Toby's slaves enjoy that portion here:
Here are no blazing brimstone lakes—'tis true;
But kindled rum too often burns as blue;
5 In which some fiend, whom nature must detest,
Steeps Toby's brand, and marks poor Cudjoe's breast.[2]
　　Here whips on whips excite perpetual fears,
And mingled howlings vibrate on my ears:
Here nature's plagues abound, to fret and tease,
10 Snakes, scorpions, despots, lizards, centipedes–
No art, no care escapes the busy lash;
All have their dues—and all are paid in cash—
The eternal driver keeps a steady eye
On a black herd, who would his vengeance fly,
15 But chained, imprisoned, on a burning soil,
For the mean avarice of a tyrant toil!
The lengthy cart-whip guards this monster's reign—
And cracks, like pistols, from the fields of cane.
　　Ye powers! who formed these wretched tribes, relate,
20 What had they done, to merit such a fate!
Why were they brought from Eboe's[3] sultry waste,
To see that plenty which they must not taste—
Food, which they cannot buy, and dare not steal;
Yams and potatoes—many a scanty meal!—
25 　　One, with a gibbet wakes his negro's fears,
One to the windmill nails him by the ears;
One keeps his slave in darkened dens, unfed,
One puts the wretch in pickle ere he's dead:
This, from a tree suspends him by the thumbs,

---

[1] **Sir Toby:** In the West Indies, the poet encountered the savagery of slavery and became an early anti-slavery crusader.
[2] **Cudjoe's breast:** A "cudge" was a slave who had been branded by his owner.
[3] **Eboe's:** A small kingdom near the river Senegal, according to the poet.

30   That, from his table grudges even the crumbs!
         O'er yond' rough hills a tribe of females go,
     Each with her gourd,° her infant, and her hoe;   cup
     Scorched by a sun that has no mercy here,
     Driven by a devil, whom men call overseer—
35   In chains, twelve wretches to their labors haste;
     Twice twelve I saw, with iron collars graced!—
         Are such the fruits that spring from vast domains?
     Is wealth, thus got, Sir Toby, worth your pains!—
     Who would your wealth on terms, like these, possess,
40   Where all we see is pregnant with distress—
     Angola's[4] natives scourged by ruffian hands,
     And toil's hard product shipped to foreign lands.
         Talk not of blossoms, and your endless spring;
     What joy, what smile, can scenes of misery bring?—
45   Though Nature, here, has every blessing spread,
     Poor is the laborer—and how meanly fed!—
         Here Stygian° paintings light and shade renew,   hellish
     Pictures of hell, that Virgil's pencil drew:[5]
     Here, surly Charons[6] make their annual trip,
50   And ghosts arrive in every Guinea ship,
     To find what beasts these western isles afford,
     Plutonian[7] scourges, and despotic lords:—
         Here, they, of stuff determined to be free,
     Must climb the rude cliffs of the Liguanee;[8]
55   Beyond the clouds, in sculking haste repair,
     And hardly safe from brother traitors there.—

PHILLIS WHEATLEY (ca. 1753–1784)

To Mæcenas[1] (1773)

Mæcenas, you, beneath the myrtle° shade,   a ground plant
Read o'er what poets sung, and shepherds play'd.
What felt those poets but you feel the same?

---

[4] **Angola's:** Angola was a Portuguese province in West Africa.
[5] **Virgil's pencil drew:** Refers to Virgil's *Aeneid* (Book VI), where Aeneas descends into the underworld to consult with his father.
[6] **Charons:** Charon ferried the dead across the river Styx in Greek mythology.
[7] **Plutonian:** Pluto reigned in Hell.
[8] **Liguanee:** Highest plateau of Kingston, Jamaica.
[1] **Mæcenas:** Wheatley addresses the subject of the poem, Mæcenas, who was a close ally of Caesar Augustus, the Roman Emperor. He was also a man who supported poets, including Horace and Virgil. Wheatley praises Mæcenas as the equal of the poets he generously supported.

Does not your soul possess the sacred flame?
5   Their noble strains your equal genius shares
In softer language, and diviner airs.

While *Homer* paints lo! circumfus'd in air,
Celestial Gods in mortal forms appear;
Swift as they move hear each recess rebound,
10   Heav'n quakes, earth trembles, and the shores resound.
Great Sire of verse, before my mortal eyes,
The lightnings blaze across the vaulted skies,
And, as the thunder shakes the heav'nly plains,
A deep-felt horror thrills through all my veins.
15   When gentler strains demand thy graceful song,
The length'ning line moves languishing along.
When great *Patroclus* courts *Achilles'*[2] aid,
The grateful tribute of my tears is paid;
Prone on the shore he feels the pangs of love,
20   And stern *Pelides*[3] tend'rest passions move.

Great *Maro's*[4] strain in heav'nly numbers flows,
The *Nine*° inspire, and all the bosom glows.   the Muses
O could I rival thine and *Virgil's* page,
Or claim the *Muses* with the *Mantuan*° Sage;   Virgil
25   Soon the same beauties should my mind adorn,
And the same ardors in my soul should burn:
Then should my song in bolder notes arise,
And all my numbers pleasingly surprize;
But here I sit, and mourn a grov'ling mind,
30   That fain would mount, and ride upon the wind.

Not you, my friend, these plaintive strains become,
Not you, whose bosom is the *Muses* home;
When they from tow'ring *Helicon*[5] retire,
They fan in you the bright immortal fire,
35   But I less happy, cannot raise the song,
The fault'ring music dies upon my tongue.

The happier *Terence*[6] all the choir inspir'd,
His soul replenish'd, and his bosom fir'd;

[2] **Patroclus . . . Achilles:** Patroclus was a dear friend of Achilles in Homer's *Iliad*.
[3] **Pelides:** Achilles was the son of Pelides. Here, the name refers to Achilles himself.
[4] **Maro's:** The last name of Virgil, the great Roman poet. His full name: Publius Virgilius Maro.
[5] **Helicon:** A sacred mountain in ancient Greece, a home of the Muses.
[6] **Terence:** Roman playwright who lived in Africa.

But say, ye *Muses*, why this partial grace,
40   To one alone of *Afric's* sable° race;   black
From age to age transmitting thus his name
With the first glory in the rolls of fame?

     Thy virtues, great *Mæcenas*! shall be sung
In praise of him, from whom those virtues sprung;
45   While blooming wreaths around thy temples spread,
I'll snatch a laurel from thine honour'd head,
While you indulgent smile upon the deed.

     As long as *Thames* in streams majestic flows,
Or *Naiads*° in their oozy beds repose,   river gods
50   While Phœbus reigns above the starry train,
While bright *Aurora*° purples o'er the main,   dawn
So long, great Sir, the muse thy praise shall sing,
So long thy praise shall make *Parnassus*[7] ring:
Then grant, *Mæcenas*, thy paternal rays,
55   Hear me propitious, and defend my lays.°   songs

GEORGE GORDON, LORD BYRON (1788–1824)

from English Bards and Scotch Reviewers (1809)

Oh! Southey! Southey![1] cease thy varied song!
A bard may chant too often and too long:
As thou art strong in verse, in mercy, spare!
A fourth, alas! were more than we could bear.
5   But if, in spite of all the world can say,
Thou still wilt verseward plod thy weary way;
If still in Berkley ballads[2] most uncivil,
Thou wilt devote old women to the devil,
The babe unborn thy dread intent may rue:
10   "God help thee," Southey, and thy readers too.

     Next comes the dull disciple of thy school,
That mild apostate from poetic rule,

---

[7] **Parnassus:** Mountain near Delphi sacred to the Muses.
[1] **Southey:** Robert Southey (1774–1843) was an English poet often identified with the Lake District.
[2] **Berkley ballads:** Robert Southey wrote a ballad called "The Old Woman of Berkeley," in which an old gentlewoman is carried away by the Devil, Beelzebub, on a "high trotting horse."

The simple Wordsworth,[3] framer of a lay
As soft as evening in his favorite May,
15   Who warns his friend "to shake off toil and trouble,
And quit his books for fear of growing double;"
Who, both by precept and example, shows
That prose is verse, and verse is merely prose;
Convincing all, by demonstration plain,

20   Poetic souls delight in prose insane;
And Christmas stories tortured into rhyme
Contain the essence of the true sublime.
Thus, when he tells the tale of Betty Foy,
The idiot mother of "an idiot boy;"
25   A moon-struck, silly lad, who lost his way,
And, like his bard, confounded night with day;
So close on each pathetic part he dwells,
And each adventure so sublimely tells,
That all who view the "idiot in his glory"
30   Conceive the bard the hero of the story.

Shall gentle Coleridge[4] pass unnoticed here,
To turgid ode and tumid stanza dear?
Though themes of innocence amuse him best,
Yet still obscurity's a welcome guest.
35   If Inspiration should her aid refuse
To him who takes a pixy for a muse,
Yet none in lofty numbers can surpass
The bard who soars to elegize an ass.[5]
So well the subject suits his noble mind,
40   He brays the laureat of the long-ear'd kind.

Oh! wonder-working Lewis! monk, or bard,[6]
Who fain wouldst make Parnassus a churchyard!
Lo! wreaths of yew, not laurel, bind thy brow,
Thy muse a sprite, Apollo's sexton thou!
45   Whether on ancient tombs thou tak'st thy stand,
By gibb'ring spectres hail'd, thy kindred band;
Or tracest chaste descriptions on thy page,
To please the females of our modest age;

---

[3] **Wordsworth:** William Wordsworth, the poet.
[4] **Coleridge:** Samuel Taylor Coleridge, who collaborated with Wordsworth on *Lyrical Ballads* (1798).
[5] **ass:** Refers to a poem by Coleridge in which he calls an ass, or donkey, his brother.
[6] **Lewis! monk, or bard:** Refers to Mathew Lewis (1775–1818), known as Monk Lewis because of his book, *The Monk* (1796).

All hail, M. P.!⁷ from whose infernal brain
50 Thin-sheeted phantoms glide, a grisly train;
     At whose command "grim women" throng in crowds,
     And kings of fire, of water, and of clouds,
     With "small gray men," "wild yagers," and what not,
     To crown with honor thee and Walter Scott;⁸
55 Again all hail! if tales like thine may please,
     St. Luke alone can vanquish the disease;
     Even Satan's self with thee might dread to dwell,
     And in thy skull discern a deeper hell.

                              . . .

     Health to immortal Jeffrey!⁹ once, in name,
60 England could boast a judge almost the same;
     In soul so like, so merciful, yet just,
     Some think that Satan has resign'd his trust,
     And given the spirit to the world again,
     To sentence letters, as he sentenced men.
65 With hand less mighty, but with heart as black,
     With voice as willing to decree the rack;
     Bred in the courts betimes, though all that law
     As yet hath taught him is to find a flaw;
     Since well instructed in the patriot school
70 To rail at party, though a party tool,
     Who knows, if chance his patrons should restore
     Back to the sway they forfeited before,
     His scribbling toils some recompense may meet,
     And raise this Daniel to the judgment-seat?
75 Let Jeffrey's shade indulge the pious hope,
     And greeting thus, present him with a rope:
     "Heir to my virtues! man of equal mind!
     Skill'd to condemn as to traduce mankind,
     This cord receive, for thee reserved with care,
80 To wield in judgment, and at length to wear."

                              . . .

     To the famed throng now paid the tribute due,
     Neglected genius! let me turn to you.
     Come forth, oh Campbell!¹⁰ give thy talents scope;

---

⁷ **M.P.:** A joking poem of the period famously referred to Mathew "Monk" Lewis as an M.P., or Member of Parliament.
⁸ **Scott:** Sir Walter Scott (1771–1832), the Scottish novelist and poet.
⁹ **Jeffrey:** Francis Jeffrey (1773–1850) was a Scottish reviewer and editor who founded the influential *Edinburgh Review*.
¹⁰ **Campbell:** Thomas Campbell (1777–1844), Scottish poet.

Who dares aspire if thou must cease to hope?
85 And thou, melodious Rogers![11] rise at last,
Recall the pleasing memory of the past;
Arise! let blest remembrance still inspire,
And strike to wonted tones thy hallow'd lyre;
Restore Apollo to his vacant throne,
90 Assert thy country's honor and thine own.
What! must deserted Poesy still weep
Where her last hopes with pious Cowper[12] sleep?
Unless, perchance, from his cold bier she turns,
To deck the turf that wraps her minstrel, Burns![13]

. . .

95 There be who say, in these enlighten'd days,
That splendid lies are all the poet's praise;
That strain'd invention, ever on the wing,
Alone impels the modern bard to sing:
'Tis true, that all who rhyme—nay, all who write,
100 Shrink from that fatal word to genius—trite;
Yet Truth sometimes will lend her noblest fires,
And decorate the verse herself inspires:
This fact in Virtue's name let Crabbe[14] attest;
Though nature's sternest painter, yet the best.

JOHN KEATS (1795–1821)

from Endymion (1818)

Book I

A thing of beauty is a joy for ever:
Its loveliness increases; it will never
Pass into nothingness; but still will keep
A bower quiet for us, and a sleep
5 Full of sweet dreams, and health, and quiet breathing.
Therefore, on every morrow, are we wreathing.
A flowery band to bind us to the earth,
Spite of despondence, of the inhuman dearth
Of noble natures, of the gloomy days,

---

[11] **Rogers:** Samuel Rogers (1763–1855), English poet.
[12] **Cowper:** William Cowper (1731–1800), English poet.
[13] **Burns:** Robert Burns (1759–1796), Scottish poet, an early Romantic.
[14] **Crabbe:** George Crabbe (1754–1832), English poet.

10 Of all the unhealthy and o'er-darkened ways
Made for our searching: yes, in spite of all,
Some shape of beauty moves away the pall
From our dark spirits. Such the sun, the moon,
Trees old, and young, sprouting a shady boon
15 For simple sheep; and such are daffodils
With the green world they live in; and clear rills
That for themselves a cooling covert make
Gainst the hot season; the mid forest brake,°   ferns
Rich with a sprinkling of fair musk-rose blooms:
20 And such too is the grandeur of the dooms
We have imagined for the mighty dead;
All lovely tales that we have heard or read:
An endless fountain of immortal drink,
Pouring unto us from the heaven's brink.

25   Nor do we merely feel these essences
For one short hour; no, even as the trees
That whisper round a temple become soon
Dear as the temple's self, so does the moon,
The passion poesy, glories infinite,
30 Haunt us till they become a cheering light
Unto our souls, and bound to us so fast,
That, whether there be shine, or gloom o'ercast,
They alway must be with us, or we die.

        Therefore, 'tis with full happiness that I
35 Will trace the story of Endymion.[1]
The very music of the name has gone
Into my being, and each pleasant scene
Is growing fresh before me as the green
Of our own vallies: so I will begin
40 Now while I cannot hear the city's din;
Now while the early budders are just new,
And run in mazes of the youngest hue
About old forests; while the willow trails
Its delicate amber; and the dairy pails
45 Bring home increase of milk. And, as the year
Grows lush in juicy stalks, I'll smoothly steer
My little boat, for many quiet hours,
With streams that deepen freshly into bowers.
Many and many a verse I hope to write,

---

[1] **Endymion:** The subject of this poem, a Greek youth. The poem tells the story of his love for the goddess Cynthia.

50 Before the daisies, vermeil° rimm'd and white,   red
Hide in deep herbage; and ere yet the bees
Hum about globes of clover and sweet peas,
I must be near the middle of my story.
O may no wintry season, bare and hoary,
55 See it half finish'd: but let Autumn bold,
With universal tinge of sober gold,
Be all about me when I make an end.
And now at once, adventuresome, I send
My herald thought into a wilderness:
60 There let its trumpet blow, and quickly dress
My uncertain path with green, that I may speed
Easily onward, thorough flowers and weed.
　　Upon the sides of Latmos[2] was outspread
A mighty forest; for the moist earth fed
65 So plenteously all weed-hidden roots
Into o'er-hanging boughs, and precious fruits.
And it had gloomy shades, sequestered deep,
Where no man went; and if from shepherd's keep
A lamb stray'd far a-down those inmost glens,
70 Never again saw he the happy pens
Whither his brethren, bleating with content,
Over the hills at every nightfall went.
Among the shepherds,'twas believed ever,
That not one fleecy lamb which thus did sever
75 From the white flock, but pass'd unworried
By angry wolf, or pard with prying head,
Until it came to some unfooted plains
Where fed the herds of Pan:° aye great his gains   god of nature
Who thus one lamb did lose. Paths there were many,
80 Winding through palmy fern, and rushes fenny,
And ivy banks; all leading pleasantly
To a wide lawn, whence one could only see
Stems thronging all around between the swell
Of turf and slanting branches: who could tell
85 The freshness of the space of heaven above,
Edg'd round with dark tree tops? through which a dove
Would often beat its wings, and often too
A little cloud would move across the blue.

　　Full in the middle of this pleasantness
90 There stood a marble altar, with a tress
Of flowers budded newly; and the dew

---

[2] **Latmos:** Mountain in ancient Greece, now in Turkey.

Had taken fairy phantasies to strew
Daisies upon the sacred sward° last eve,   field
And so the dawned light in pomp receive.
95   For 'twas the morn: Apollo's upward fire
Made every eastern cloud a silvery pyre
Of brightness so unsullied, that therein
A melancholy spirit well might win
Oblivion, and melt out his essence fine
100 Into the winds: rain-scented eglantine
Gave temperate sweets to that well-wooing sun;
The lark was lost in him; cold springs had run
To warm their chilliest bubbles in the grass;
Man's voice was on the mountains; and the mass
105 Of nature's lives and wonders puls'd tenfold,
To feel this sun-rise and its glories old.

Now while the silent workings of the dawn
Were busiest, into that self-same lawn
All suddenly, with joyful cries, there sped
110 A troop of little children garlanded;
Who gathering round the altar, seem'd to pry
Earnestly round as wishing to espy
Some folk of holiday: nor had they waited
For many moments, ere their ears were sated
115 With a faint breath of music, which ev'n then
Fill'd out its voice, and died away again.
Within a little space again it gave
Its airy swellings, with a gentle wave,
To light-hung leaves, in smoothest echoes breaking
120 Through copse-clad vallies,—ere their death, o'er-taking
The surgy murmurs of the lonely sea.

And now, as deep into the wood as we
Might mark a lynx's eye, there glimmered light
Fair faces and a rush of garments white,
125 Plainer and plainer showing, till at last
Into the widest alley they all past,
Making directly for the woodland altar.
O kindly muse! let not my weak tongue faulter
In telling of this goodly company,
130 Of their old piety, and of their glee:
But let a portion of ethereal dew
Fall on my head, and presently unmew
My soul; that I may dare, in wayfaring,
To stammer where old Chaucer° us'd to sing.   Geoffrey Chaucer

135   Leading the way, young damsels danced along,
Bearing the burden of a shepherd song;
Each having a white wicker over brimm'd
With April's tender younglings: next, well trimm'd,
A crowd of shepherds with as sunburnt looks
140 As may be read of in Arcadian° books;   region in ancient Greece
Such as sat listening round Apollo's pipe,
When the great deity, for earth too ripe,
Let his divinity o'erflowing die
In music, through the vales of Thessaly°:   in Greece
145 Some idly trail'd their sheep-hooks on the ground,
And some kept up a shrilly mellow sound
With ebon-tipped flutes: close after these,
Now coming from beneath the forest trees,
A venerable priest full soberly,
150 Begirt with ministring looks: always his eye
Stedfast upon the matted turf he kept,
And after him his sacred vestments swept.
From his right hand there swung a vase, milk-white,
Of mingled wine, out-sparkling generous light;
155 And in his left he held a basket full
Of all sweet herbs that searching eye could cull:
Wild thyme, and valley-lillies whiter still
Than Leda's love, and cresses from the rill.
His aged head, crowned with beechen wreath,
160 Seem'd like a poll of ivy in the teeth
Of winter hoar. Then came another crowd
Of shepherds, lifting in due time aloud
Their share of the ditty. After them appear'd,
Up-followed by a multitude that rear'd
165 Their voices to the clouds, a fair wrought car,
Easily rolling so as scarce to mar
The freedom of three steeds of dapple brown:
Who stood therein did seem of great renown
Among the throng. His youth was fully blown,
170 Showing like Ganymede[3] to manhood grown;
And, for those simple times, his garments were
A chieftain king's: beneath his breast, half bare,
Was hung a silver bugle, and between
His nervy knees there lay a boar-spear keen.
175 A smile was on his countenance; he seem'd,
To common lookers on, like one who dream'd

---

[3] **Ganymede:** A beautiful young boy who became the love of Zeus.

Of idleness in groves Elysian:°   heavenly
But there were some who feelingly could scan
A lurking trouble in his nether lip,
180   And see that oftentimes the reins would slip
Through his forgotten hands: then would they sigh,
And think of yellow leaves, of owlets' cry,
Of logs piled solemnly.—Ah, well-a-day,
Why should our young Endymion pine away!

185   Soon the assembly, in a circle rang'd,
Stood silent round the shrine: each look was chang'd
To sudden veneration: women meek
Beckon'd their sons to silence; while each cheek
Of virgin bloom paled gently for slight fear.
190   Endymion too, without a forest peer,
Stood, wan, and pale, and with an awed face,
Among his brothers of the mountain chace.
In midst of all, the venerable priest
Eyed them with joy from greatest to the least,
195   And, after lifting up his aged hands,
Thus spake he: "Men of Latmos! shepherd bands!
Whose care it is to guard a thousand flocks:
Whether descended from beneath the rocks
That overtop your mountains; whether come
200   From vallies where the pipe is never dumb;
Or from your swelling downs, where sweet air stirs
Blue hare-bells lightly, and where prickly furze
Buds lavish gold; or ye, whose precious charge
Nibble their fill at ocean's very marge,
205   Whose mellow reeds are touch'd with sounds forlorn
By the dim echoes of old Triton's horn: [4]
Mothers and wives! who day by day prepare
The scrip, with needments, for the mountain air;
And all ye gentle girls who foster up
210   Udderless lambs, and in a little cup
Will put choice honey for a favoured youth:
Yea, every one attend! for in good truth
Our vows are wanting to our great god Pan.°   god of nature
Are not our lowing heifers sleeker than
215   Night-swollen mushrooms? Are not our wide plains
Speckled with countless fleeces? Have not rains
Green'd over April's lap? No howling sad

---

[4] **Triton's horn:** Triton was a sea god, the son of Poseidon, who blew his horn to warn sailors of danger.

Sickens our fearful ewes; and we have had
Great bounty from Endymion our lord.
220 The earth is glad: the merry lark has pour'd
His early song against yon breezy sky,
That spreads so clear o'er our solemnity."

     Thus ending, on the shrine he heap'd a spire
Of teeming sweets, enkindling sacred fire;
225 Anon he stain'd the thick and spongy sod
With wine, in honour of the shepherd-god.
Now while the earth was drinking it, and while
Bay leaves were crackling in the fragrant pile,
And gummy frankincense was sparkling bright
230 'Neath smothering parsley, and a hazy light
Spread greyly eastward, thus a chorus sang:

     "O thou, whose mighty palace roof doth hang
From jagged trunks, and overshadoweth
Eternal whispers, glooms, the birth, life, death
235 Of unseen flowers in heavy peacefulness;
Who lov'st to see the hamadryads dress
Their ruffled locks where meeting hazels darken;
And through whole solemn hours dost sit, and hearken
The dreary melody of bedded reeds—
240 In desolate places, where dank moisture breeds
The pipy hemlock to strange overgrowth;
Bethinking thee, how melancholy loth
Thou wast to lose fair Syrinx°—do thou now,   a spirit
By thy love's milky brow!
245 By all the trembling mazes that she ran,
Hear us, great Pan!

     "O thou, for whose soul-soothing quiet, turtles
Passion their voices cooingly 'mong myrtles,
What time thou wanderest at eventide
250 Through sunny meadows, that outskirt the side
Of thine enmossed realms: O thou, to whom
Broad leaved fig trees even now foredoom
Their ripen'd fruitage; yellow girted bees
Their golden honeycombs; our village leas
255 Their fairest blossom'd beans and poppied corn;
The chuckling linnet its five young unborn,
To sing for thee; low creeping strawberries
Their summer coolness; pent up butterflies
Their freckled wings; yea, the fresh budding year
260 All its completions—be quickly near,

By every wind that nods the mountain pine,
O forester divine!

"Thou, to whom every faun and satyr flies
For willing service; whether to surprise
265 The squatted hare while in half sleeping fit;
Or upward ragged precipices flit
To save poor lambkins from the eagle's maw;
Or by mysterious enticement draw
Bewildered shepherds to their path again;
270 Or to tread breathless round the frothy main,
And gather up all fancifullest shells
For thee to tumble into Naiads' cells,
And, being hidden, laugh at their out-peeping;
Or to delight thee with fantastic leaping,
275 The while they pelt each other on the crown
With silvery oak apples, and fir cones brown—
By all the echoes that about thee ring,
Hear us, O satyr king!

"O Hearkener to the loud clapping shears
280 While ever and anon to his shorn peers
A ram goes bleating: Winder of the horn,
When snouted wild-boars routing tender corn
Anger our hunstmen: Breather round our farms,
To keep off mildews, and all weather harms:
285 Strange ministrant of undescribed sounds,
That come a swooning over hollow grounds,
And wither drearily on barren moors:
Dread opener of the mysterious doors
Leading to universal knowledge—see,
290 Great son of Dryope,[5]
The many that are come to pay their vows
With leaves about their brows!

"Be still the unimaginable lodge
For solitary thinkings; such as dodge
295 Conception to the very bourne of heaven,
Then leave the naked brain: be still the leaven,
That spreading in this dull and clodded earth
Gives it a touch ethereal—a new birth:
Be still a symbol of immensity;

---

[5] **Son of Dryope:** Dryope was turned into a lotus plant by a treacherous nymph, and so nothing was left of her but her face. Her poor infant was left with a plant for a mother.

300   A firmament reflected in a sea;
      An element filling the space between;
      An unknown—but no more: we humbly screen
      With uplift hands our foreheads, lowly bending,
      And giving out a shout most heaven rending,
305   Conjure thee to receive our humble Pæan,°   praise
      Upon thy Mount Lycean!"

          Even while they brought the burden to a close,
      A shout from the whole multitude arose,
      That lingered in the air like dying rolls
310   Of abrupt thunder, when Ionian° shoals   Greek
      Of dolphins bob their noses through the brine.
      Meantime, on shady levels, mossy fine,
      Young companies numbly began dancing
      To the swift treble pipe, and humming string.
315   Aye, those fair living forms swam heavenly
      To tunes forgotten—out of memory:
      Fair creatures! whose young children's children bred
      Thermopylæ° its heroes—not yet dead,   famous Greek battle
      But in old marbles ever beautiful.
320   High genitors, unconscious did they cull
      Time's sweet first-fruits—they danc'd to weariness.
      And then in quiet circles did they press
      The hillock turf, and caught the latter end
      Of some strange history, potent to send
325   A young mind from its bodily tenement.
      Or they might watch the quoit-pitchers, intent
      On either side; pitying the sad death
      Of Hyacinthus, when the cruel breath
      Of Zephyr[6] slew him,—Zephyr penitent,
330   Who now, ere Phœbus° mounts the firmament,   the sun
      Fondles the flower amid the sobbing rain.
      The archers too, upon a wider plain,
      Beside the feathery whizzing of the shaft,
      And the dull twanging bowstring, and the raft
335   Branch down sweeping from a tall ash top,
      Call'd up a thousand thoughts to envelope
      Those who would watch. Perhaps, the trembling knee

---

[6] **Hyacinthus . . . Zephyr:** Hyacinthus was a beautiful boy loved by Apollo, who threw a discus that
was diverted by the jealous Zyphyr—the West Wind—so that it killed the boy. This is a sad tale of love
frustrated by jealousy of another.

And frantic gape of lonely Niobe,[7]
Poor, lonely Niobe! when her lovely young
340   Were dead and gone, and her caressing tongue
Lay a lost thing upon her paly lip,
And very, very deadliness did nip
Her motherly cheeks. Arous'd from this sad mood
By one, who at a distance loud halloo'd,
345   Uplifting his strong bow into the air,
Many might after brighter visions stare:
After the Argonauts,[8] in blind amaze
Tossing about on Neptune's° restless ways,   sea god
Until, from the horizon's vaulted side,
350   There shot a golden splendour far and wide,
Spangling those million poutings of the brine
With quivering ore: 'twas even an awful shine
From the exaltation of Apollo's° bow;   god of love
A heavenly beacon in their dreary woe.
355   Who thus were ripe for high contemplating,
Might turn their steps towards the sober ring
Where sat Endymion and the aged priest
'Mong shepherds gone in eld, whose looks increas'd
The silvery setting of their mortal star.
360   There they discours'd upon the fragile bar
That keeps us from our homes ethereal;
And what our duties there: to nightly call
Vesper, the beauty-crest of summer weather;
To summon all the downiest clouds together
365   For the sun's purple couch; to emulate
In ministring the potent rule of fate
With speed of fire-tail'd exhalations;
To tint her pallid cheek with bloom, who cons
Sweet poesy by moonlight: besides these,
370   A world of other unguess'd offices.
Anon they wander'd, by divine converse,
Into Elysium; vieing to rehearse
Each one his own anticipated bliss.
One felt heart-certain that he could not miss

---

[7] **Niobe:** Niobe had fourteen children. She bragged about her seven sons and seven daughters at a ceremony in honor of Leto, a goddess who only had two children—Apollo, god of prophecy and music, and Artemis, virgin goddess of the wild. Leto did not take the insult lightly, and in retaliation, sent Apollo and Artemis to Earth to slaughter all of Niobe's children.
[8] **Argonauts:** The Greek hero Jason asked Argus, a master shipbuilder, to build him a massive ship with fifty oars. Then he sent envoys to all the palaces in Greece, asking for volunteers to help capture the Golden Fleece. The ship was called the *Argo*, and the fifty volunteers, called Argonauts, included Heracles and Orpheus.

375 His quick gone love, among fair blossom'd boughs,
Where every zephyr-sigh pouts, and endows
Her lips with music for the welcoming.
Another wish'd, mid that eternal spring,
To meet his rosy child, with feathery sails,
380 Sweeping, eye-earnestly, through almond vales:
Who, suddenly, should stoop through the smooth wind,
And with the balmiest leaves his temples bind;
And, ever after, through those regions be
His messenger, his little Mercury.
385 Some were athirst in soul to see again
Their fellow huntsmen o'er the wide champaign°   country
In times long past; to sit with them, and talk
Of all the chances in their earthly walk;
Comparing, joyfully, their plenteous stores
390 Of happiness, to when upon the moors,
Benighted, close they huddled from the cold,
And shar'd their famish'd scrips.° Thus all out-told   scraps
Their fond imaginations,—saving him
Whose eyelids curtain'd up their jewels dim,
395 Endymion: yet hourly had he striven
To hide the cankering venom, that had riven
His fainting recollections. Now indeed
His senses had swoon'd off: he did not heed
The sudden silence, or the whispers low,
400 Or the old eyes dissolving at his woe,
Or anxious calls, or close of trembling palms,
Or maiden's sigh, that grief itself embalms:
But in the self-same fixed trance he kept,
Like one who on the earth had never stept.
405 Aye, even as dead still as a marble man,
Frozen in that old tale Arabian.°   *The Arabian Nights*

Who whispers him so pantingly and close?
Peona, his sweet sister: of all those,
His friends, the dearest. Hushing signs she made,
410 And breath'd a sister's sorrow to persuade
A yielding up, a cradling on her care.
Her eloquence did breathe away the curse:
She led him, like some midnight spirit nurse
Of happy changes in emphatic dreams,
415 Along a path between two little streams,—
Guarding his forehead, with her round elbow,
From low-grown branches, and his footsteps slow
From stumbling over stumps and hillocks small;
Until they came to where these streamlets fall.

420 With mingled bubblings and a gentle rush,
Into a river, clear, brimful, and flush
With crystal mocking of the trees and sky.
A little shallop, floating there hard by,
Pointed its beak over the fringed bank;
425 And soon it lightly dipt, and rose, and sank,
And dipt again, with the young couple's weight,—
Peona guiding, through the water straight,
Towards a bowery island opposite;
Which gaining presently, she steered light
430 Into a shady, fresh, and ripply cove,
Where nested was an arbour, overwove
By many a summer's silent fingering;
To whose cool bosom she was used to bring
Her playmates, with their needle broidery,
435 And minstrel memories of times gone by.
    So she was gently glad to see him laid
Under her favourite bower's quiet shade,
On her own couch, new made of flower leaves,
Dried carefully on the cooler side of sheaves
440 When last the sun his autumn tresses shook,
And the tann'd harvesters rich armfuls took.
Soon was he quieted to slumbrous rest:
But, ere it crept upon him, he had prest
Peona's busy hand against his lips,
445 And still, a sleeping, held her finger-tips
In tender pressure. And as a willow keeps
A patient watch over the stream that creeps
Windingly by it, so the quiet maid
Held her in peace: so that a whispering blade
450 Of grass, a wailful gnat, a bee bustling
Down in the blue-bells, or a wren light rustling
Among sere leaves and twigs, might all be heard.

    O magic sleep! O comfortable bird,
That broodest o'er the troubled sea of the mind
455 Till it is hush'd and smooth! O unconfin'd
Restraint! imprisoned liberty! great key
To golden palaces, strange minstrelsy,
Fountains grotesque, new trees, bespangled caves,
Echoing grottos, full of tumbling waves
460 And moonlight; aye, to all the mazy world
Of silvery enchantment!—who, upfurl'd
Beneath thy drowsy wing a triple hour,
But renovates and lives?—Thus, in the bower,
Endymion was calm'd to life again.

465 Opening his eyelids with a healthier brain,
He said: "I feel this thine endearing love
All through my bosom: thou art as a dove
Trembling its closed eyes and sleeked wings
About me; and the pearliest dew not brings
470 Such morning incense from the fields of May,
As do those brighter drops that twinkling stray
From those kind eyes,—the very home and haunt
Of sisterly affection. Can I want
Aught else, aught nearer heaven, than such tears?
475 Yet dry them up, in bidding hence all fears
That, any longer, I will pass my days
Alone and sad. No, I will once more raise
My voice upon the mountain-heights; once more
Make my horn parley from their foreheads hoar:
480 Again my trooping hounds their tongues shall loll
Around the breathed boar: again I'll poll
The fair-grown yew tree, for a chosen bow:
And, when the pleasant sun is setting low,
Again I'll linger in a sloping mead
485 To hear the speckled thrushes, and see feed
Our idle sheep. So be thou cheered, sweet,
And, if thy lute is here, softly intreat
My soul to keep in its resolved course."

    Hereat Peona,[9] in their silver source,
490 Shut her pure sorrow drops with glad exclaim,
And took a lute, from which there pulsing came
A lively prelude, fashioning the way
In which her voice should wander. 'Twas a lay
More subtle cadenced, more forest wild
495 Than Dryope's lone lulling of her child;
And nothing since has floated in the air
So mournful strange. Surely some influence rare
Went, spiritual, through the damsel's hand;
For still, with Delphic emphasis, she spann'd
500 The quick invisible strings, even though she saw
Endymion's spirit melt away and thaw
Before the deep intoxication.
But soon she came, with sudden burst, upon
Her self-possession—swung the lute aside,
505 And earnestly said: "Brother, 'tis vain to hide

---

[9] **Peona:** Sister of Endymion.

That thou dost know of things mysterious,
Immortal, starry; such alone could thus
Weigh down thy nature. Hast thou sinn'd in aught
Offensive to the heavenly power? Caught
510 A Paphian dove upon a message sent?
Thy deathful bow against some deer-herd bent
Sacred to Dian?° Haply, thou hast seen   Diana, a goddess
Her naked limbs among the alders green;
And that, alas! is death. No, I can trace
515 Something more high perplexing in thy face!"

    Endymion look'd at her, and press'd her hand,
And said, "Art thou so pale, who wast so bland
And merry in our meadows? How is this?
Tell me thine ailment: tell me all amiss!—
520 Ah! thou hast been unhappy at the change
Wrought suddenly in me. What indeed more strange?
Or more complete to overwhelm surmise?
Ambition is so sluggard: 'tis no prize,
That toiling years would put within my grasp,
525 That I have sighed for: with so deadly gasp
No man e'er panted for a mortal love.
So all have set my heavier grief above
These things which happen. Rightly have they done:
I, who still saw the horizontal sun
530 Heave his broad shoulder o'er the edge of the world,
Out-facing Lucifer, and then had hurl'd
My spear aloft, as signal for the chace—
I, who, for very sport of heart, would race
With my own steed from Araby; pluck down
535 A vulture from his towery perching; frown
A lion into growling, loth retire—
To lose, at once, all my toil-breeding fire,
And sink thus low! but I will ease my breast
Of secret grief, here in this bowery nest.

540   "This river does not see the naked sky,
Till it begins to progress silverly
Around the western border of the wood,
Whence, from a certain spot, its winding flood
Seems at the distance like a crescent moon:
545 And in that nook, the very pride of June,
Had I been used to pass my weary eves;
The rather for the sun unwilling leaves
So dear a picture of his sovereign power,
And I could witness his most kingly hour,

550   When he doth tighten up the golden reins,
And paces leisurely down amber plains
His snorting four. Now when his chariot last
Its beams against the zodiac-lion cast,
There blossom'd suddenly a magic bed
555   Of sacred ditamy, and poppies red:
At which I wondered greatly, knowing well
That but one night had wrought this flowery spell;
And, sitting down close by, began to muse
What it might mean. Perhaps, thought I, Morpheus,°   *god of sleep*
560   In passing here, his owlet pinions shook;
Or, it may be, ere matron Night uptook
Her ebon urn, young Mercury,° by stealth,   *messenger god*
Had dipt his rod in it: such garland wealth
Came not by common growth. Thus on I thought,
565   Until my head was dizzy and distraught.
Moreover, through the dancing poppies stole
A breeze, most softly lulling to my soul;
And shaping visions all about my sight
Of colours, wings, and bursts of spangly light;
570   The which became more strange, and strange, and dim,
And then were gulph'd in a tumultuous swim:
And then I fell asleep. Ah, can I tell
The enchantment that afterwards befel?
Yet it was but a dream: yet such a dream
575   That never tongue, although it overteem
With mellow utterance, like a cavern spring,
Could figure out and to conception bring
All I beheld and felt. Methought I lay
Watching the zenith, where the milky way
580   Among the stars in virgin splendour pours;
And travelling my eye, until the doors
Of heaven appear'd to open for my flight,
I became loth and fearful to alight
From such high soaring by a downward glance:
585   So kept me stedfast in that airy trance,
Spreading imaginary pinions wide.
When, presently, the stars began to glide,
And faint away, before my eager view:
At which I sigh'd that I could not pursue,
590   And dropt my vision to the horizon's verge;
And lo! from opening clouds, I saw emerge
The loveliest moon, that ever silver'd o'er
A shell for Neptune's goblet: she did soar
So passionately bright, my dazzled soul
595   Commingling with her argent spheres did roll

Through clear and cloudy, even when she went
At last into a dark and vapoury tent—
Whereat, methought, the lidless-eyed train
Of planets all were in the blue again.
600   To commune with those orbs, once more I rais'd
My sight right upward: but it was quite dazed
By a bright something, sailing down apace,
Making me quickly veil my eyes and face:
Again I look'd, and, O ye deities,
605   Who from Olympus° watch our destinies!   home of the gods
Whence that completed form of all completeness?
Whence came that high perfection of all sweetness?
Speak, stubborn earth, and tell me where, O where
Hast thou a symbol of her golden hair?
610   Not oat-sheaves drooping in the western sun;
Not—thy soft hand, fair sister! let me shun
Such follying before thee—yet she had,
Indeed, locks bright enough to make me mad;
And they were simply gordian'd up and braided,
615   Leaving, in naked comeliness, unshaded,
Her pearl round ears, white neck, and orbed brow;
The which were blended in, I know not how,
With such a paradise of lips and eyes,
Blush-tinted cheeks, half smiles, and faintest sighs,
620   That, when I think thereon, my spirit clings
And plays about its fancy, till the stings
Of human neighbourhood envenom all.
Unto what awful power shall I call?
To what high fane?°—Ah! see her hovering feet,   temple
625   More bluely vein'd, more soft, more whitely sweet
Than those of sea-born Venus, when she rose
From out her cradle shell. The wind out-blows
Her scarf into a fluttering pavillion;
'Tis blue, and over-spangled with a million
630   Of little eyes, as though thou wert to shed,
Over the darkest, lushest blue-bell bed,
Handfuls of daisies.'—'Endymion, how strange!
Dream within dream!'—'She took an airy range,
And then, towards me, like a very maid,
635   Came blushing, waning, willing, and afraid,
And press'd me by the hand: Ah! 'twas too much;
Methought I fainted at the charmed touch,
Yet held my recollections, even as one
Who dives three fathoms where the waters run
640   Gurgling in beds of coral: for anon,
I felt upmounted in that region

Where falling stars dart their artillery forth,
And eagles struggle with the buffeting north
That balances the heavy meteor-stone;—
645   Felt too, I was not fearful, nor alone,
But lapp'd and lull'd along the dangerous sky.
Soon, as it seem'd, we left our journeying high,
And straightway into frightful eddies swoop'd;
Such as aye muster where grey time has scoop'd
650   Huge dens and caverns in a mountain's side;
There hollow sounds arous'd me, and I sigh'd
To faint once more by looking on my bliss—
I was distracted; madly did I kiss
The wooing arms which held me, and did give
655   My eyes at once to death: but 'twas to live,
To take in draughts of life from the gold fount
Of kind and passionate looks; to count, and count
The moments, by some greedy help that seem'd
A second self, that each might be redeem'd
660   And plunder'd of its load of blessedness.
Ah, desperate mortal! I e'en dar'd to press
Her very cheek against my crowned lip,
And, at that moment, felt my body dip
Into a warmer air: a moment more,
665   Our feet were soft in flowers. There was store
Of newest joys upon that alp. Sometimes
A scent of violets, and blossoming limes,
Loiter'd around us; then of honey cells,
Made delicate from all white-flower bells;
670   And once, above the edges of our nest,
An arch face peep'd,—an Oread° as I guess'd.   *mountain spirit or nymph*

"Why did I dream that sleep o'er-power'd me
In midst of all this heaven? Why not see,
Far off, the shadows of his pinions dark,
675   And stare them from me? But no, like a spark
That needs must die, although its little beam
Reflects upon a diamond, my sweet dream
Fell into nothing—into stupid sleep.
And so it was, until a gentle creep,
680   A careful moving caught my waking ears,
And up I started: Ah! my sighs, my tears,
My clenched hands:—for lo! the poppies hung
Dew-dabbled on their stalks, the ouzel sung
A heavy ditty, and the sullen day
685   Had chidden herald Hesperus° away,   *Venus*
With leaden looks: the solitary breeze

Bluster'd, and slept, and its wild self did teaze
With wayward melancholy; and I thought,
Mark me, Peona! that sometimes it brought
690 Faint fare-thee-wells, and sigh-shrilled adieus!—
Away I wander'd—all the pleasant hues
Of heaven and earth had faded: deepest shades
Were deepest dungeons; heaths and sunny glades
Were full of pestilent light; our taintless rills
695 Seem'd sooty, and o'er-spread with upturn'd gills
Of dying fish; the vermeil rose had blown
In frightful scarlet, and its thorns out-grown
Like spiked aloe.° If an innocent bird   a plant
Before my heedless footsteps stirr'd, and stirr'd
700 In little journeys, I beheld in it
A disguis'd demon, missioned to knit
My soul with under darkness; to entice
My stumblings down some monstrous precipice:
Therefore I eager followed, and did curse
705 The disappointment. Time, that aged nurse,
Rock'd me to patience. Now, thank gentle heaven!
These things, with all their comfortings, are given
To my down-sunken hours, and with thee,
Sweet sister, help to stem the ebbing sea
Of weary life."
710   Thus ended he, and both
Sat silent: for the maid was very loth
To answer; feeling well that breathed words
Would all be lost, unheard, and vain as swords
Against the enchased crocodile, or leaps
715 Of grasshoppers against the sun. She weeps
And wonders; struggles to devise some blame;
To put on such a look as would say, *Shame*
On this poor weakness! but, for all her strife,
She could as soon have crush'd away the life
720 From a sick dove. At length, to break the pause,
She said with trembling chance: "Is this the cause?
This all? Yet it is strange, and sad, alas!
That one who through this middle earth should pass
Most like a sojourning demi-god, and leave
725 His name upon the harp-string, should achieve
No higher bard than simple maidenhood,
Singing alone, and fearfully,—how the blood
Left his young cheek; and how he used to stray
He knew not where; and how he would say, *nay*,
730 If any said 'twas love: and yet 'twas love;
What could it be but love? How a ring-dove

Let fall a spring of yew tree in his path;
And how he died: and then, that love doth scathe
The gentle heart, as northern blasts do roses;
735 And then the ballad of his sad life closes
With sighs, and an alas!—Endymion!
Be rather in the trumpet's mouth,—anon
Among the winds at large—that all my hearken!
Although, before the crystal heavens darken,
740 I watch and dote upon the silver lakes
Pictur'd in western cloudiness, that takes
The semblance of gold rocks and bright gold sands,
Islands, and creeks, and amber-fretted strands
With horses prancing o'er them, palaces
745 And towers of amethyst,—would I so teaze
My pleasant days, because I could not mount
Into those regions? The Morphean fount
Of that fine element that visions, dreams,
And fitful whims of sleep are made of, streams
750 Into its airy channels with so subtle,
So thin a breathing, not the spider's shuttle,
Circled a million times within the space
Of a swallow's nest-door, could delay a trace,
A tinting of its quality: how light
755 Must dreams themselves be; seeing they're more slight
Than the mere nothing that engenders them!
Then wherefore sully the entrusted gem
Of high and noble life with thoughts so sick?
Why pierce high-fronted honour to the quick
760 For nothing but a dream?" Hereat the youth
Look'd up: a conflicting of shame and ruth
Was in his plaited brow: yet, his eyelids
Widened a little, as when Zephyr bids
A little breeze to creep between the fans
765 Of careless butterflies: amid his pains
He seem'd to taste a drop of manna-dew,
Full palatable; and a colour grew
Upon his cheek, while thus he lifeful spake.

"Peona! ever have I long'd to slake
770 My thirst for the world's praises: nothing base,
No merely slumberous phantasm, could unlace
The stubborn canvas for my voyage prepar'd—
Though now 'tis tatter'd; leaving my bark bar'd
And sullenly drifting: yet my higher hope
775 Is of too wide, too rainbow-large a scope,
To fret at myriads of earthly wrecks.

Wherein lies happiness? In that which becks
Our ready minds to fellowship divine,
A fellowship with essence; till we shine,
780 Full alchemiz'd, and free of space. Behold
The clear religion of heaven! Fold
A rose leaf round thy finger's taperness,
And soothe thy lips: hist, when the airy stress
Of music's kiss impregnates the free winds,
785 And with a sympathetic touch unbinds
Æolian magic from their lucid wombs:
Then old songs waken from enclouded tombs;
Old ditties sigh above their father's grave;
Ghosts of melodious prophecyings rave
790 Round every spot where trod Apollo's foot;
Bronze clarions awake, and faintly bruit,
Where long ago a giant battle was;
And, from the turf, a lullaby doth pass
In every place where infant Orpheus[10] slept.
795 Feel we these things?—that moment have we stept
Into a sort of oneness, and our state
Is like a floating spirit's. But there are
Richer entanglements, enthralments far
More self-destroying, leading, by degrees,
800 To the chief intensity: the crown of these
Is made of love and friendship, and sits high
Upon the forehead of humanity.
All its more ponderous and bulky worth
Is friendship, whence there ever issues forth
805 A steady splendour; but at the tip-top,
There hangs by unseen film, an orbed drop
Of light, and that is love: its influence,
Thrown in our eyes, genders a novel sense,
At which we start and fret; till in the end,
810 Melting into its radiance, we blend,
Mingle, and so become a part of it,—
Nor with aught else can our souls interknit
So wingedly: when we combine therewith,
Life's self is nourish'd by its proper pith,
815 And we are nurtured like a pelican brood.
Aye, so delicious is the unsating food,
That men, who might have tower'd in the van

---

[10] **Orpheus:** A great musician, often identified with poets. He was later famous for going into Hades to retrieve his dead wife; he failed to bring her back when he looked back toward her at the wrong moment.

Of all the congregated world, to fan
And winnow from the coming step of time
820   All chaff of custom, wipe away all slime
Left by men-slugs and human serpentry,
Have been content to let occasion die,
Whilst they did sleep in love's elysium.
And, truly, I would rather be struck dumb,
825   Than speak against this ardent listlessness:
For I have ever thought that it might bless
The world with benefits unknowingly;
As does the nightingale, upperched high,
And cloister'd among cool and bunched leaves—
830   She sings but to her love, nor e'er conceives
How tiptoe Night holds back her dark-grey hood.
Just so may love, although 'tis understood
The mere commingling of passionate breath,
Produce more than our searching witnesseth:
835   What I know not: but who, of men, can tell
That flowers would bloom, or that green fruit would swell
To melting pulp, that fish would have bright mail,
The earth its dower of river, wood, and vale,
The meadows runnels, runnels pebble-stones,
840   The seed its harvest, or the lute its tones,
Tones ravishment, or ravishment its sweet
If human souls did never kiss and greet?

"Now, if this earthly love has power to make
Men's being mortal, immortal; to shake
845   Ambition from their memories, and brim
Their measure of content: what merest whim,
Seems all this poor endeavour after fame,
To one, who keeps within his stedfast aim
A love immortal, an immortal too.
850   Look not so wilder'd; for these things are true,
And never can be born of atomies
That buzz about our slumbers, like brain-flies,
Leaving us fancy-sick. No, no, I'm sure,
My restless spirit never could endure
855   To brood so long upon one luxury,
Unless it did, though fearfully, espy
A hope beyond the shadow of a dream.
My sayings will the less obscured seem,
When I have told thee how my waking sight
860   Has made me scruple whether that same night
Was pass'd in dreaming. Hearken, sweet Peona!
Beyond the matron-temple of Latona,

Which we should see but for these darkening boughs,
Lies a deep hollow, from whose ragged brows
865 Bushes and trees do lean all round athwart
And meet so nearly, that with wings outraught,
And spreaded tail, a vulture could not glide
Past them, but he must brush on every side.
Some moulder'd steps lead into this cool cell,
870 Far as the slabbed margin of a well,
Whose patient level peeps its crystal eye
Right upward, through the bushes, to the sky.
Oft have I brought thee flowers, on their stalks set
Like vestal primroses, but dark velvet
875 Edges them round, and they have golden pits:
'Twas there I got them, from the gaps and slits
In a mossy stone, that sometimes was my seat,
When all above was faint with mid-day heat.
And there in strife no burning thoughts to heed,
880 I'd bubble up the water through a reed;
So reaching back to boy-hood: make me ships
Of moulted feathers, touchwood, alder chips,
With leaves stuck in them; and the Neptune be
Of their petty ocean. Oftener, heavily,
885 When love-lorn hours had left me less a child,
I sat contemplating the figures wild
Of o'er-head clouds melting the mirror through.
Upon a day, while thus I watch'd, by flew
A cloudy Cupid, with his bow and quiver;
890 So plainly character'd, no breeze would shiver
The happy chance: so happy, I was fain
To follow it upon the open plain,
And, therefore, was just going; when, behold!
A wonder, fair as any I have told—
895 The same bright face I tasted in my sleep,
Smiling in the clear well. My heart did leap
Through the cool depth.—It moved as if to flee—
I started up, when lo! refreshfully
There came upon my face in plenteous showers
900 Dew-drops, and dewy buds, and leaves, and flowers,
Wrapping all objects from my smothered sight,
Bathing my spirit in a new delight.
Aye, such a breathless honey-feel of bliss
Alone preserved me from the drear abyss
905 Of death, for the fair form had gone again.
Pleasure is oft a visitant; but pain
Clings cruelly to us, like the gnawing sloth

On the deer's tender haunches: late, and loth,
'Tis scar'd away by slow returning pleasure.
910 How sickening, how dark the dreadful leisure
Of weary days, made deeper exquisite,
By a fore-knowledge of unslumbrous night!
Like sorrow came upon me, heavier still,
Than when I wander'd from the poppy hill:
915 And a whole age of lingering moments crept
Sluggishly by, ere more contentment swept
Away at once the deadly yellow spleen.
Yes, thrice have I this fair enchantment seen;
Once more been tortured with renewed life.
920 When last the wintry gusts gave over strife
With the conquering sun of spring, and left the skies
Warm and serene, but yet with moistened eyes
In pity of the shatter'd infant buds,—
That time thou didst adorn, with amber studs,
925 My hunting cap, because I laugh'd and smil'd,
Chatted with thee, and many days exil'd
All torment from my breast;—'twas even then,
Straying about, yet, coop'd up in the den
Of helpless discontent,—hurling my lance
930 From place to place, and following at chance,
At last, by hap, through some young trees it struck,
And, plashing among bedded pebbles, stuck
In the middle of a brook,—whose silver ramble
Down twenty little falls, through reeds and bramble.
935 Tracing along, it brought me to a cave,
Whence it ran brightly forth, and white did lave
The nether sides of mossy stones and rock,—
'Mong which it gurgled blythe adieus, to mock
Its own sweet grief at parting. Overhead,
940 Hung a lush screen of drooping weeds, and spread
Thick, as to curtain up some wood-nymph's home.
'Ah! impious mortal, whither do I roam?'
Said I, low voic'd: 'Ah, whither! 'Tis the grot
Of Proserpine, when Hell, obscure and hot,
945 Doth her resign; and where her tender hands
She dabbles, on the cool and sluicy sands:
Or 'tis the cell of Echo, where she sits,
And babbles thorough silence, till her wits
Are gone in tender madness, and anon,
950 Faints into sleep, with many a dying tone
Of sadness. O that she would take my vows,
And breathe them sighingly among the boughs,

To sue her gentle ears for whose fair head,
Daily, I pluck sweet flowerets from their bed,
955   And weave them dyingly—send honey-whispers
Round every leaf, that all those gentle lispers
May sigh my love unto her pitying!
O charitable Echo! hear, and sing
This ditty to her!—tell her'—so I stay'd
960   My foolish tongue, and listening, half afraid,
Stood stupefied with my own empty folly,
And blushing for the freaks of melancholy.
Salt tears were coming, when I heard my name
Most fondly lipp'd, and then these accents came:
965   'Endymion! the cave is secreter
Than the isle of Delos.[11] Echo hence shall stir
No sighs but sigh-warm kisses, or light noise
Of thy combing hand, the while it travelling cloys
And trembles through my labyrinthine hair.'
970   At that oppress'd I hurried in.—Ah! where
Are those swift moments? Whither are they fled?
I'll smile no more, Peona; nor will wed
Sorrow the way to death; but patiently
Bear up against it: so farewell, sad sigh;
975   And come instead demurest meditation,
To occupy me wholly, and to fashion
My pilgrimage for the world's dusky brink.
No more will I count over, link by link,
My chain of grief: no longer strive to find
980   A half-forgetfulness in mountain wind
Blustering about my ears: aye, thou shalt see,
Dearest of sisters, what my life shall be;
What a calm round of hours shall make my days.
There is a paly flame of hope that plays
985   Where'er I look: but yet, I'll say 'tis naught—
And here I bid it die. Have not I caught,
Already, a more healthy countenance?
By this the sun is setting; we may chance
Meet some of our near-dwellers with my car."

990   This said, he rose, faint-smiling like a star
Through autumn mists, and took Peona's hand:
They stept into the boat, and launch'd from land.

---

[11] **Delos:** A Greek island, known for its mysteries.

FRANCES E. W. HARPER (1825–1911)

Bury Me in a Free Land (1864)

Make me a grave where'er you will,
In a lowly plain or a lofty hill;
Make it among earth's humblest graves,
But not in a land where men are slaves.

5 I could not rest, if around my grave
I heard the steps of a trembling slave;
His shadow above my silent tomb
Would make it a place of fearful gloom.

I could not sleep, if I heard the tread
10 Of a coffle-gang to the shambles led,[1]
And the mother's shriek of wild despair
Rise, like a curse, on the trembling air.

I could not rest, if I saw the lash
Drinking her blood at each fearful gash;
15 And I saw her babes torn from her breast,
Like trembling doves from their parent nest.

I'd shudder and start, if I heard the bay
Of a bloodhound seizing his human prey;
And I heard the captive plead in vain,
20 As they bound, afresh, his galling chain.

If I saw young girls from their mother's arms.
Bartered and sold for their youthful charms,
My eye would flash with a mournful flame,
My death-pale cheek grow red with shame.

25 I would sleep, dear friends, where bloated Might
Can rob no man of his dearest right;
My rest shall be calm in any grave
Where none can call his brother a slave.

I ask no monument, proud and high,
30 To arrest the gaze of the passers by;
All that my yearning spirit craves
Is—*Bury me not in a land of slaves!*

---

[1] **coffle-gang . . . led:** A gang of slaves led to the selling block.

SARA TEASDALE (1884–1933)

There Will Come Soft Rains (1920)
(War Time)

There will come soft rains and the smell of the ground,
And swallows circling with their shimmering sound;

And frogs in the pools singing at night,
And wild plum-trees in tremulous white;

5   Robins will wear their feathery fire
Whistling their whims on a low fence-wire;

And not one will know of the war, not one
Will care at last when it is done.

Not one would mind, neither bird nor tree
10   If mankind perished utterly;

And Spring herself, when she woke at dawn,
Would scarcely know that we were gone.

WILFRED OWEN (1893–1918)

Strange Meeting (1918; 1920)

It seemed that out of battle I escaped
Down some profound dull tunnel, long since scooped
Through granites which titanic wars had groined.

Yet also there encumbered sleepers groaned,
5   Too fast in thought or death to be bestirred.
Then, as I probed them, one sprang up, and stared

With piteous recognition in fixed eyes,
Lifting distressful hands, as if to bless.
And by his smile, I knew that sullen hall,—
10   By his dead smile I knew we stood in Hell.

With a thousand pains that vision's face was grained;
Yet no blood reached there from the upper ground,
And no guns thumped, or down the flues made moan.
"Strange friend," I said, "here is no cause to mourn."

15   "None," said the other, "save the undone years,
The hopelessness. Whatever hope is yours,
Was my life also; I went hunting wild
After the wildest beauty in the world,
Which lies not calm in eyes, or braided hair,
20   But mocks the steady running of the hour,
And if it grieves, grieves richlier than here.
For by my glee might many men have laughed,
And of my weeping something had been left,
Which must die now. I mean the truth untold,
25   The pity of war, the pity war distilled.
Now men will go content with what we spoiled,
Or, discontent, boil bloody, and be spilled.
They will be swift with swiftness of the tigress.
None will break ranks, though nations trek from progress.
30   Courage was mine, and I had mystery,
Wisdom was mine, and I had mastery:
To miss the march of this retreating world
Into vain citadels that are not walled.
Then, when much blood had clogged their chariot-wheels,
35   I would go up and wash them from sweet wells,
Even with truths that lie too deep for taint.
I would have poured my spirit without stint
But not through wounds; not on the cess of war.
Foreheads of men have bled where no wounds were.

40   "I am the enemy you killed, my friend.
I knew you in this dark: for so you frowned
Yesterday through me as you jabbed and killed.
I parried; but my hands were loath and cold.
Let us sleep now. . . ."

JEAN TOOMER (1894–1967)

Reapers (1923)

Black reapers with the sound of steel on stones
Are sharpening scythes. I see them place the hones
In their hip-pockets as a thing that's done,
And start their silent swinging, one by one.
5   Black horses drive a mower through the weeds,
And there, a field rat, startled, squealing bleeds,
His belly close to ground. I see the blade,
Blood-stained, continue cutting weeds and shade.

E. E. CUMMINGS (1894–1962)

"maggie and milly and molly and may" (1958)

maggie and milly and molly and may
went down to the beach(to play one day)

and maggie discovered a shell that sang
so sweetly she couldn't remember her troubles,and

5   milly befriended a stranded star
whose rays five languid fingers were;

and molly was chased by a horrible thing
which raced sideways while blowing bubbles:and

may came home with a smooth round stone
10   as small as a world and as large as alone.

For whatever we lose(like a you or a me)
it's always ourselves we find in the sea

W. H. AUDEN (1907–1973)

from New Year Letter[1] (1940)

Under the familiar weight
Of winter, conscience and the State,
In loose formations of good cheer,
Love, language, loneliness and fear,
5   Towards the habits of next year,
Along the streets the people flow,
Singing or sighing as they go:
Exalté, piano,[2] or in doubt,
All our reflections turn about
10   A common meditative norm,
Retrenchment, Sacrifice, Reform.

Twelve months ago in Brussels, I
Heard the same wishful-thinking sigh

---

[1] Note Auden's modification of the traditional pentameter line. He uses tetrameter, a four-beat line, but retains many of the effects of the heroic couplet.
[2] *Exalté . . . piano:* Musical terms, meaning "exalted" or "softly."

As round me, trembling on their beds,
15   Or taut with apprehensive dreads,
The sleepless guests of Europe lay
Wishing the centuries away,
And the low mutter of their vows
Went echoing through her haunted house,
20   As on the verge of happening
There crouched the presence of The Thing.
All formulas were tried to still
The scratching on the window-sill,
All bolts of custom made secure
25   Against the pressure on the door,
But up the staircase of events
Carrying his special instruments,
To every bedside all the same
The dreadful figure swiftly came.

30   Yet Time can moderate his tone
When talking to a man alone,
And the same sun whose neutral eye
All florid August from the sky
Had watched the earth behave and seen
35   Strange traffic on her brown and green,
Obedient to some hidden force
A ship abruptly change her course,
A train make an unwonted stop,
A little crowd smash up a shop,
40   Suspended hatreds crystallise
In visible hostilities,
Vague concentrations shrink to take
The sharp crude patterns generals make,
The very morning that the war
45   Took action on the Polish floor,
Lit up America and on
A cottage in Long Island shone
Where BUXTEHUDE[3] as we played
One of his *passacaglias*[4] made
50   Our minds a *civitas* of sound
Where nothing but assent was found,
For art had set in order sense
And feeling and intelligence,
And from its ideal order grew
55   Our local understanding too.

[3] **Buxtehude:** Dietrich Buxtehude (1637–1707) was a Danish organist and composer.
[4] *passacaglias:* A slow, stately Spanish dance.

To set in order—that's the task
Both Eros° and Apollo° ask;   god of love / god of light
For Art and Life agree in this
That each intends a synthesis,
60   That order which must be the end
That all self-loving things intend
Who struggle for their liberty,
Who use, that is, their will to be.
Though order never can be willed
65   But is the state of the fulfilled,
For will but wills its opposite
And not the whole in which they fit,
The symmetry disorders reach
When both are equal each to each,
70   Yet in intention all are one,
Intending that their wills be done
Within a peace where all desires
Find each in each what each requires,
A true *Gestalt*[5] where indiscrete
75   Perceptions and extensions meet.
Art in intention is mimesis
But, realised, the resemblance ceases;
Art is not life and cannot be
A midwife to society,
80   For art is a *fait accompli*.°   finished task
What they should do, or how or when
Life-order comes to living men
It cannot say, for it presents
Already lived experience
85   Through a convention that creates
Autonomous completed states.
Though their particulars are those
That each particular artist knows,
Unique events that once took place
90   Within a unique time and space,
In the new field they occupy,
The unique serves to typify,
Becomes, though still particular,
An algebraic formula,
95   An abstract model of events
Derived from past experiments,
And each life must itself decide
To what and how it be applied.

---

[5] **Gestalt:** A unified whole. This refers to a popular tradition of modern psychology.

Great masters who have shown mankind
100   An order it has yet to find,
What if all pedants say of you
As personalities be true?
All the more honour to you then
If, weaker than some other men,
105   You had the courage that survives
Soiled, shabby, egotistic lives,
If poverty or ugliness,
Ill-health or social unsuccess
Hunted you out of life to play
110   At living in another way;
Yet the live quarry all the same
Were changed to huntsmen in the game,
And the wild furies of the past,
Tracked to their origins at last,
115   Trapped in a medium's artifice,
To charity, delight, increase.
Now large, magnificent, and calm,
Your changeless presences disarm
The sullen generations, still
120   The fright and fidget of the will,
And to the growing and the weak
Your final transformations speak,
Saying to dreaming "I am deed,"
To striving "Courage. I succeed,"
125   To mourning "I remain. Forgive,"
And to becoming "I am. Live."

They challenge, warn and witness. Who
That ever has the rashness to
Believe that he is one of those
130   The greatest of vocations chose,
Is not perpetually afraid
That he's unworthy of his trade,
As round his tiny homestead spread
The grand constructions of the dead,
135   Nor conscious, as he works, of their
Complete uncompromising stare,
And the surveillance of a board
Whose warrant cannot be ignored?
O often, often must he face,
140   Whether the critics blame or praise,
Young, high-brow, popular or rich,
That summary tribunal which
In a perpetual session sits,

And answer, if he can, to its
145   Intense interrogation. Though
Considerate and mild and low
The voices of the questioners,
Although they delegate to us
Both prosecution and defence,
150   Accept our rules of evidence
And pass no sentence but our own,
Yet, as he faces them alone,
O who can show convincing proof
That he is worthy of their love?
155   Who ever rose to read aloud
Before that quiet attentive crowd
And did not falter as he read,
Stammer, sit down, and hang his head?
Each one, so liberal is the law,
160   May choose whom he appears before,
Pick any influential ghost
From those whom he admires the most.
So, when my name is called, I face,
Presiding coldly on my case,
165   That lean hard-bitten pioneer
Who spoiled a temporal career
And to the supernatural brought
His passion, senses, will and thought,
By *Amor Rationalis*° led   rational love
170   Through the three kingdoms of the dead,
In concrete detail saw the whole
Environment that keeps the soul,
And grasped in its complexity
The Catholic ecology,
175   Described the savage fauna he
In Malebolge's⁶ fissure found,
And fringe of blessed flora round
A juster nucleus than Rome,
Where love had its creative home.
180   Upon his right appears, as I
Reluctantly must testify
And weigh the sentence to be passed,
A choleric enthusiast,
Self-educated WILLIAM BLAKE
185   Who threw his spectre in the lake,

---

⁶ **Malebolge:** A character in Dante's *Inferno*.

Broke off relations in a curse
With the Newtonian Universe,
But even as a child would pet
The tigers VOLTAIRE never met,
190 Took walks with them through Lambeth,[7] and
Spoke to Isaiah in the Strand,[8]
And heard inside each mortal thing
Its holy emanation sing,
While to his left upon the bench,
195 Muttering that terror is not French,
Frowns the young RIMBAUD[9] guilt demands,
The adolescent with red hands,
Skilful, intolerant and quick,
Who strangled an old rhetoric.
200 The court is full; I catch the eyes
Of several I recognize,
For as I look up from the dock
Embarrassed glances interlock.
There DRYDEN[10] sits with modest smile,
205 The master of the middle style,
Conscious CATULLUS[11] who made all
His gutter-language musical,
Black TENNYSON[12] whose talents were
For an articulate despair,
210 Trim, dualistic BAUDELAIRE,[13]
Poet of cities, harbours, whores,
Acedia, gaslight and remorse,
HARDY[14] whose Dorset gave much joy
To one unsocial English boy,
215 And RILKE[15] whom *die Dinge* bless,
The Santa Claus of loneliness.
And many others, many times,
For I relapse into my crimes,
Time and again have slubbered through
220 With slip and slapdash what I do,

[7] **Lambeth:** A part of London.
[8] **the Strand:** A main street in London.
[9] **Rimbaud:** Arthur Rimbaud was a French poet of the nineteenth century,
[10] **Dryden:** John Dryden was an English poet of the eighteenth century.
[11] **Catullus:** Ancient Roman poet of love.
[12] **Tennyson:** Famous Victorian English poet.
[13] **Baudelaire:** Charles Baudelaire was a French poet of the nineteenth century.
[14] **Hardy:** Thomas Hardy, late Victorian novelist and poet.
[15] **Rilke:** Ranier Maria Rilke, a German poet who lived at the beginning of the twentieth century. *Die Dinge* means "the things."

Adopted what I would disown,
The preacher's loose immodest tone;
Though warned by a great sonneteer
Not to sell cheap what is most dear,
225   Though horrible old KIPLING[16] cried
"One instant's toil to Thee denied
Stands all eternity's offence,"
I would not give them audience.
Yet still the weak offender must
230   Beg still for leniency and trust
His power to avoid the sin
Peculiar to his discipline.

The situation of our time
Surrounds us like a baffling crime.
235   There lies the body half-undressed
We all had reason to detest,
And all are suspects and involved
Until the mystery is solved
And under lock and key the cause
240   That makes a nonsense of our laws.
O Who is trying to shield Whom?
Who left a hairpin in the room?
Who was the distant figure seen
Behaving oddly on the green?
245   Why did the watchdog never bark?
Why did the footsteps leave no mark?
Where were the servants at that hour?
How did a snake get in the tower?
Delayed in the democracies
250   By departmental vanities,
The rival sergeants run about
But more to squabble than find out,
Yet where the Force has been cut down
To one inspector dressed in brown,
255   He makes the murderer whom he pleases
And all investigation ceases.
Yet our equipment all the time
Extends the area of the crime
Until the guilt is everywhere,
260   And more and more we are aware,
However miserable may be
Our parish of immediacy,

---

[16] **Kipling:** Rudyard Kipling, the poet and story writer, who died in 1936.

How small it is, how, far beyond,
Ubiquitous within the bond
265   Of one impoverishing sky,
Vast spiritual disorders lie.
Who, thinking of the last ten years,
Does not hear howling in his ears
The Asiatic cry of pain,
270   The shots of executing Spain,
See stumbling through his outraged mind
The Abyssinian, blistered, blind,
The dazed uncomprehending stare
Of the Danubian despair,
275   The Jew wrecked in the German cell,
Flat Poland frozen into hell,
The silent dumps of unemployed
Whose *areté* has been destroyed,
And will not feel blind anger draw
280   His thoughts towards the Minotaur,
To take an early boat for Crete
And rolling, silly, at its feet
Add his small tidbit to the rest?
It lures us all; even the best,
285   *Les hommes de bonne volonté*,[17] feel
Their politics perhaps unreal
And all they have believed untrue,
Are tempted to surrender to
The grand apocalyptic dream
290   In which the persecutors scream
As on the evil Aryan lives
Descends the night of the long knives,[18]
The bleeding tyrant dragged through all
The ashes of his capitol.

295   Though language may be useless, for
No words men write can stop the war
Or measure up to the relief
Of its immeasurable grief,
Yet truth, like love and sleep, resents
300   Approaches that are too intense,
And often when the searcher stood
Before the Oracle, it would
Ignore his grown-up earnestness

---

[17] *Les hommes de bonne volonté*: Men of good will.
[18] **night of the long knives**: Hitler's night of intimidating the Jews and others who opposed him in 1934.

But not the child of his distress,
305 For through the Janus of a joke
The candid psychopompos spoke.
May such heart and intelligence
As huddle now in conference
Whenever an impasse occurs
310 Use the Good Offices of verse;
May an Accord be reached, and may
This *aide-mémoire*° on what they say,   memory aid
This private minute for a friend,
Be the dispatch that I intend;
315 Although addressed to a Whitehall,
Be under Flying Seal to all
Who wish to read it anywhere,
And, if they open it, *En Clair*.[19]

NORMAN MacCAIG (1910–1996)

Summer Farm (1955)

Straws like tame lightnings lie about the grass
And hang zigzag on hedges. Green as glass
The water in the horse-trough shines.
Nine ducks go wobbling by in two straight lines.

5 A hen stares at nothing with one eye,
Then picks it up. Out of an empty sky
A swallow falls and, flickering through
The barn, dives up again into the dizzy blue.

I lie, not thinking, in the cool, soft grass,
10 Afraid of where a thought might take me—as
This grasshopper with plated face
Unfolds his legs and finds himself a space.

Self under self, a pile of selves I stand
Threaded on time, and with metaphysic hand
15 Lift the farm like a lid and see
Farm within farm, and in the centre, me.

---

[19] **Whitehall . . . *En Clair*:** "A Whitehall" would represent a person in the government; "under a Flying Seal" means, perhaps, by airmail; and "En Clair" is in ordinary, clear language, and so accessible to all.

ROBERT LOWELL (1917–1977)

"To Speak of Woe That Is in Marriage" (1959)

> "It is the future generation that presses into being by means of
> these exuberant feelings and supersensible soap bubbles of ours."
> —SCHOPENHAUER

"The hot night makes us keep our bedroom windows open.
Our magnolia blossoms. Life begins to happen.
My hopped up husband drops his home disputes,
and hits the streets to cruise for prostitutes,
5   free-lancing out along the razor's edge.
This screwball might kill his wife, then take the pledge.
Oh the monotonous meanness of his lust. . . .
It's the injustice . . . he is so unjust—
whiskey-blind, swaggering home at five.
10   My only thought is how to keep alive.
What makes him tick? Each night now I tie
ten dollars and his car key to my thigh. . . .
Gored by the climacteric of his want,
he stalls above me like an elephant."

MONA VAN DUYN (1921–2004)

The Stream (1982)
for my mother

Four days with you, my father three months dead.
You can't tell months from years, but you feel sad,

and you hate the nursing home. I've arranged a lunch
for the two of us, and somehow you manage to pinch

5   the pin from Madrid I bought you closed at the neck
of your best red blouse, put on new slacks, and take

off your crocheted slippers to put on shiny shoes,
all by yourself. "I don't see how you could close

that pin. You look so nice!" "Well, I tried and tried,
10   and worked till I got it. They didn't come," you said.

"Mother, I'm sorry, this is the wrong day,
our lunch is tomorrow. Here's a big kiss anyway

for dressing up for me. The nurse will come in
tomorrow and help you put on your clothes and pin."

15   "These last few days her mind has certainly cleared.
Of course the memory's gone," your doctor said.

Next day they bathed you, fixed your hair and dressed
you up again, got a wheelchair and wheeled you past

the fat happy babbler of nonsense who rolled her chair
20   all day in the hall, the silent stroller who wore

a farmer's cap and bib overalls with rows
of safety pins on the bib, rooms of old babies

in cribs, past the dining hall, on down to a sunny
lounge in the other wing. "Where can I pee,

25   if I have to pee? I don't like it here, I'm afraid.
Where's my room? I'm going to faint," you said.

But they came with the lunch and card table and chairs
and bustled and soothed you and you forgot the fears

and began to eat. The white tablecloth, the separate
30   plate for salad, the silvery little coffee pot,

the covers for dishes must have made you feel
you were in a restaurant again after all

those shut-in years. (Dad would never spend the money,
but long ago you loved to eat out with me.)

35   You cleaned your soup bowl and dishes, one by one,
and kept saying, "This is fun! This is *fun!*"

The cake fell from your trembly fork, so I fed
it to you. "Do you want mine, too?" "Yes," you said,

"and I'll drink your milk if you don't want it." (You'd
40   lost twelve pounds already by refusing your food.)

I wheeled you back. "Well, I never did *that* before!
Thank you, Jane." "We'll do it again." "Way down *there*,"

you marveled. You thanked me twice more. My eyes were wet.
"You're welcome, Mother. You'll have a good nap now, I'll bet."

45   I arranged for your old companion, who came twice a day,
to bring you milkshakes, and reached the end of my stay.

On the last night I helped you undress. Flat dugs°   breasts
like antimacassars° lay on your chest, your legs   armchair covers

and arms beetle-thin swung from the swollen belly
50   (the body no more misshapen, no stranger to see,

after all, at the end than at the beloved beginning).
You chose your flowered nightgown as most becoming.

You stood at the dresser, put your teeth away,
washed your face, smoothed on Oil of Olay,

55   then Avon night cream, then put Vicks in your nose,
then lay on the bed. I sat beside your knees

to say goodbye for a month. "You know I'll call
every Sunday and write a lot. Try to eat well—"

Tears stopped my voice. With a girl's grace you sat up
60   and, as if you'd done it lifelong, reached out to cup

my face in both your hands, and, as easily
as if you'd said it lifelong, you said, "Don't cry,

don't cry. You'll never know how much I love you."
I kissed you and left, crying. It felt true.

65   I forgot to tell them that you always sneaked your meat,
you'd bragged, to the man who ate beside you. One night

at home, my heart ringing with what you'd said,
then morning, when the phone rang to say you were dead.

I see your loving look wherever I go.
70   What is love? Truly I do not know.

Sometimes, perhaps, instead of a great sea,
it is a narrow stream running urgently

far below ground, held down by rocky layers,
the deeds of mother and father, helpless sooth-sayers

75   of how our life is to be, weighted by clay,
the dense pressure of thwarted needs, the replay

of old misreadings, by hundreds of feet of soil,
the gifts and wounds of the genes, the short or tall

shape of our possibilities, seeking
80   and seeking a way to the top, while above, running

and stumbling this way and that on the clueless ground,
another seeker clutches a dowsing-wand

which bends, then lifts, dips, then straightens, everywhere,
saying to the dowser, it is there, it is not there,

85   and the untaught dowser believes, does not believe,
and finally simply stands on the ground above,

till a sliver of stream finds a crack and makes its way,
slowly, too slowly, through rock and earth and clay.

Here at my feet I see, after sixty years,
90   the welling water—to which I add these tears.

TONY HARRISON (1937–   )

A Kumquat for John Keats (1981)

Today I found the right fruit for my prime,
not orange, not tangelo, and not lime,
nor moon-like globes of grapefruit that now hang
outside our bedroom, nor tart lemon's tang
5   (though last year full of bile and self-defeat
I wanted to believe no life was sweet)
nor the tangible sunshine of the tangerine,
and no incongruous citrus ever seen
at greengrocers' in Newcastle or Leeds
10   mis-spelt by the spuds° and mud-caked swedes,°   potatoes / turnips

a fruit an older poet might substitute
for the grape John Keats thought fit to be Joy's fruit,
when, two years before he died, he tried to write
how Melancholy dwelled inside Delight,[1]

15   and if he'd known the citrus that I mean
that's not orange, lemon, lime or tangerine,
I'm pretty sure that Keats, though he had heard
"of candied apple, quince and plum and gourd"[2]
instead of "grape against the palate fine"[3]

20   would have, if he'd known it, plumped for mine,
this Eastern citrus scarcely cherry size
he'd bite just once and then apostrophize
and pen one stanza how the fruit had all
the qualities of fruit before the Fall,

25   but in the next few lines be forced to write
how Eve's apple tasted at the second bite,
and if John Keats had only lived to be,
because of extra years, in need like me,
at 42 he'd help me celebrate

30   that Micanopy[4] kumquat that I ate
whole, straight off the tree, sweet pulp and sour skin—
or was it sweet outside, and sour within?
For however many kumquats that I eat
I'm not sure if it's flesh or rind that's sweet,

35   and being a man of doubt at life's mid-way
I'd offer Keats some kumquats and I'd say:
You'll find that one part's sweet and one part's tart:
say where the sweetness or the sourness start.

      I find I can't, as if one couldn't say
40   exactly where the night became the day,
which makes for me the kumquat taken whole
best fruit, and metaphor, to fit the soul
of one in Florida at 42 with Keats
crunching kumquats, thinking, as he eats

45   the flesh, the juice, the pith, the pips, the peel,
that this is how a full life ought to feel,
its perishable relish prick the tongue,
when the man who savours life 's no longer young,
the fruits that were his futures far behind.

---

[1] **Delight:** See John Keats's "Ode to a Nightingale."
[2] **gourd:** From Keats's "The Eve of St. Agnes," line 265.
[3] **palate fine:** From Keats's "Ode to Melancholy," line 28.
[4] **Micanopy:** A town in Florida.

50   Then it's the kumquat fruit expresses best
    how days have darkness round them like a rind,
    life has a skin of death that keeps its zest.

    History, a life, the heart, the brain
    flow to the taste buds and flow back again.
55   That decade or more past Keats's span
    makes me an older not a wiser man,
    who knows that it's too late for dying young,
    but since youth leaves some sweetnesses unsung,
    he's granted days and kumquats to express
60   Man's Being ripened by his Nothingness.
    And it isn't just the gap of sixteen years,
    a bigger crop of terrors, hopes and fears,
    but a century of history on this earth
    between John Keats's death and my own birth—
65   years like an open crater, gory, grim,
    with bloody bubbles leering at the rim;
    a thing no bigger than an urn explodes
    and ravishes all silence, and all odes,
    Flora[5] asphyxiated by foul air
70   unknown to either Keats or Lemprière,[6]
    dehydrated Naiads, Dryad[7] amputees
    dragging themselves through slagscapes with no trees,
    a shirt of Nessus[8] fire that gnaws and eats
    children half the age of dying Keats . . .

75   Now were you twenty five or six years old
    when that fevered brow at last grew cold?
    I've got no books to hand to check the dates.
    My grudging but glad spirit celebrates
    that all I've got to hand's the kumquats, John,
80   the fruit I'd love to have your verdict on,
    but dead men don't eat kumquats, or drink wine,
    they shiver in the arms of Proserpine,[9]
    not warm in bed beside their Fanny Brawne,[10]
    nor watch her pick ripe grapefruit in the dawn
85   as I did, waking, when I saw her twist,

---

[5] **Flora:** Goddess of flowers.
[6] **Lemprière:** Author of *The Classical Dictionary,* a classic of the eighteenth century.
[7] **Naiads, Dryad:** Wood nymphs and water nymphs.
[8] **Nessus:** Once put on, this shirt of fire cannot be removed. It consumes the wearer.
[9] **Proserpine:** Goddess of the underworld.
[10] **Fanny Brawne:** Keats's lover.

with one deft movement of a sunburnt wrist,
the moon, that feebly lit our last night's walk
past alligator swampland, off its stalk.
I thought of moon-juice juleps[11] when I saw,

90   as if I'd never seen the moon before,
the planet glow among the fruit, and its pale light
make each citrus on the tree its satellite.

Each evening when I reach to draw the blind
stars seem the light zest squeezed through night's black rind;

95   the night's peeled fruit the sun, juiced of its rays,
first stains, then streaks, then floods the world with days,
days, when the very sunlight made me weep,
days, spent like the nights in deep, drugged sleep,
days in Newcastle by my daughter's bed,

100   wondering if she, or I, weren't better dead,
days in Leeds, grey days, my first dark suit,
my mother's wreaths stacked next to Christmas fruit,
and days, like this in Micanopy. Days!

As strong sun burns away the dawn's grey haze

105   I pick a kumquat and the branches spray
cold dew in my face to start the day.
The dawn's molasses make the citrus gleam
still in the orchards of the groves of dream.
The limes, like Galway after weeks of rain,

110   glow with a greenness that is close to pain,
the dew-cooled surfaces of fruit that spent
all last night flaming in the firmament.
The new day dawns. O days! My spirit greets
the kumquat with the spirit of John Keats.

115   O kumquat, comfort for not dying young,
both sweet and bitter, bless the poet's tongue!
I burst the whole fruit chilled by morning dew
against my palate. Fine, for 42!

I search for buzzards as the air grows clear

120   and see them ride fresh thermals overhead.
Their bleak cries were the first sound I could hear
when I stepped at the start of sunrise out of doors,
and a noise like last night's bedsprings on our bed
from Mr Fowler sharpening farmers' saws.

---

[11] **juleps:** A sweet alcoholic drink flavored with mint.

ROBERT PINSKY (1940–   )

From the Childhood of Jesus (1990)

One Saturday morning he went to the river to play.
He modeled twelve sparrows out of the river clay

And scooped a clear pond, with a dam of twigs and mud.
Around the pond he set the birds he had made,

5 Evenly as the hours. Jesus was five. He smiled,
As a child would who had made a little world

Of clear still water and clay beside a river.
But a certain Jew came by, a friend of his father,

And he scolded the child and ran at once to Joseph,
10 Saying, "Come see how your child has profaned the Sabbath,

Making images at the river on the Day of Rest."
So Joseph came to the place and took his wrist

And told him, "Child, you have offended the Word."
Then Jesus freed the hand that Joseph held

15 And clapped his hands and shouted to the birds
To go away. They raised their beaks at his words

And breathed and stirred their feathers and flew away.
The people were frightened. Meanwhile, another boy,

The son of Annas the scribe, had idly taken
20 A branch of driftwood and leaning against it had broken

The dam and muddied the little pond and scattered
The twigs and stones. Then Jesus was angry and shouted,

"Unrighteous, impious, ignorant, what did the water
Do to harm you? Now you are going to wither

25 The way a tree does, you shall bear no fruit
And no leaves, you shall wither down to the root."

At once, the boy was all withered. His parents moaned,
The Jews gasped, Jesus began to leave, then turned

And prophesied, his child's face wet with tears:
30   "Twelve times twelve times twelve thousands of years

Before these heavens and this earth were made,
The Creator set a jewel in the throne of God

With Hell on the left and Heaven to the right,
The Sanctuary in front, and behind, an endless night

35   Endlessly fleeing a Torah° written in flame.   Jewish Bible
And on that jewel in the throne, God wrote my name."

Then Jesus left and went into Joseph's house.
The family of the withered one also left the place,

Carrying him home. The Sabbath was nearly over.
40   By dusk, the Jews were all gone from the river.

Small creatures came from the undergrowth to drink
And foraged in the shadows along the bank.

Alone in his cot in Joseph's house, the Son
Of Man was crying himself to sleep. The moon

45   Rose higher, the Jews put out their lights and slept,
And all was calm and as it had been, except

In the agitated household of the scribe Annas,
And high in the dark, where unknown even to Jesus

The twelve new sparrows flew aimlessly through the night,
50   Not blinking or resting, as if never to alight.

CHAPTER 10

THE PROUD FULL SAIL OF HIS GREAT VERSE
—William Shakespeare
An Anthology of the Sonnet

The **sonnet** is one of the most revered forms of English poetry, and has been put to excellent use by most of the great poets of the language, including Shakespeare, John Donne, John Milton, William Wordsworth, William Butler Yeats, Robert Frost, Robert Lowell, and Seamus Heaney. Traditionally defined as a poem of fourteen lines written in iambic pentameter with a particular rhyming pattern, the sonnet has proven itself an instrument of great tonal and intellectual possibilities from the thirteenth century to the present time.

The form was invented in Italy, where cycles of sonnets became popular in the late Middle Ages. The Italian poets Dante and Petrarch established the form, and the so-called **Petrarchan sonnet** is still one of the most common patterns for the English sonnet. In its early Italian form, the sonnet was written in lines that contained eleven syllables (hendecasyllabics) and rhymed as follows: abba abba cdecde. The first eight lines are called the **octet,** the last six lines the **sestet.** Generally speaking, the octet frames a question or presents a deep image; the sestet comments on, answers, or develops the imagery presented in the octet.

In the sixteenth century, when the Italian (Petrarchan) form of the sonnet first emerged in England, the rhyming and stanza patterns shifted. The Petrarchan sonnet in English is highly flexible, and rhyming patterns will vary. The meter is usually a five-beat line, often iambic pentameter, and the rhyme scheme is simplified: abba abba cdcdcd. It is obviously much easier to rhyme in Italian than English—even the telephone book rhymes in Italy! So it made good sense to simplify the rhyme scheme. The **Elizabethan** or **Shakespearean sonnet,** a variation on the scheme, rhymes as follows: abab cdcd efef gg. The poem drives toward a final couplet, which is used to sum up the point of the poem or provide same sort of counterpoint. In Shakespeare's capable hands, this kind of sonnet became a vehicle for some of the most sublime poetry ever written in English.

Because its form admits countless variations, poets have long experimented with the shape of the sonnet. Thomas Wyatt, an early sonneteer, preferred the Italian form, unlike many of his Elizabethan counterparts. Cycles of sonnets came into fashion in the Italian mode, and these were often sequences of love poems that chronicled the ups and downs of a relationship. The sonnets in the cycle called *Astrophil and Stella* by Sir Philip Sidney leaned toward the Italian model, with octaves. The Elizabethan variant, with quatrains and a couplet, was favored by Michael Drayton and, of course, Shakespeare. Edmund Spenser, who wrote a sequence of love sonnets called *Amoretti,* created a hybrid form of the sonnet, drawing on both the Italian and Elizabethan models. His poems have the rhyme scheme: ababbcbc cdcd ee. This form proved rather awkward, and few poets have followed in Spenser's wake.

One of the most famous sonnets in the Petrachan mode is "On His Blindness" by the seventeenth-century poet John Milton (p. 809). Milton's sonnet is masterful work, a poem of huge emotional force that uses the form quite efficiently. Note that the last six lines, the sestet, is rhymed by Milton (who had closely studied the Italian models) in the Italian way: cdecde. The crucial thing to look for in a sonnet, whatever its form, is its "turning point" or "volta." In Milton's poem, it occurs after the octet, in the ninth line. Milton has been complaining about his blindness; then suddenly Patience (or wisdom) answers the great question posed by the poet-speaker in the octet: "Doth God exact day-labour, light denied?" The last six lines, the sestet, provide a luminous response to that question. In Shakespearean sonnets, there is often no obvious turning point, although many shifts may occur.

The sonnet ebbed in popularity after the seventeenth century. It reemerged with a flourish during the nineteenth century, when it became a popular form once again, attracting writers like Charlotte Smith, Wordsworth, Shelley, Keats, and many others. Wordsworth's "Composed Upon Westminster Bridge" (p. 811), Keats's "On First Looking into Chapman's Homer" (p. 813), and Shelley's "Ozymandias" (p. 812), count among the crown jewels of English poetry. During the Victorian era, Elizabeth Barrett Browning revived the love sonnet, becoming one of the most popular sonneteers of all time. In the same period, the Jesuit poet Gerard Manley Hopkins invented the so-called "sprung" sonnet, which employs a kind of stressed rhythm that only counts the strong beats (usually five per line) and crowds in any number of unstressed beats. These wild-eared sonnets are remarkable, if somewhat idiosyncratic examples of the form. They writhe and thrash on the page, and readers should read them aloud to appreciate their rich and strange sound.

Among the modern poets, Yeats, Hardy, Frost, and Wilfred Owen contributed hugely to the development of the form. Edna St. Vincent Millay added a large number of magnificent sonnets. More recent examples of the form include a sequence of experimental sonnets by John Berryman, who cast aside many of the traditional requirements for the form, retaining only its overall "feel." Robert Lowell also created a form of fractured sonnet, and his last years were devoted to this peculiar but affecting form. In the hands of Berryman and Lowell, the sonnet takes on an almost diary-like quality.

Wherever one looks in anthologies of poetry in English, the sonnet appears, in myriad patterns, capable of endless modifications, always alluring to the poet's eye and ear. The themes of the sonnet vary immensely, although often they are devoted to erotic love or religious devotion. The form itself seems to draw from talented poets an urge toward compression and a deeply spiritual music.

ADDITIONAL EXAMPLES OF THE SONNET IN THIS BOOK

- Henry Howard, Earl of Surrey, "Love, That Doth Reign and Live Within My Thought" (p. 1038)

- Edmund Spenser, "Sonnet 68" (p. 1245)

- Samuel Daniel, "Sonnet 2 from *Delia*" (p. 802)

- Michael Drayton, "Since there's no help, come let us kiss and part" (p. 1039)

- Sir Philip Sidney, "Stella, think not that I by verse seek fame" from *Astrophil and Stella* (p. 1418)

- William Shakespeare, Sonnet 130 and Sonnet 151 (p. 1042)

- John Milton, "On the Late Massacre in Piedmont" (p. 1108)

- Rupert Brooke, "The Soldier" (p. 1127)

- Robert Frost, "Design," "The Oven Bird," and "The Silken Tent" (pp. 1259, 1360, and 1070)

- Robert Lowell, "To Speak of Woe That Is in Marriage" (p. 787)

SIR THOMAS WYATT (1503–1542)

My Galley, Charged with Forgetfulness[1] (1557)

My galley, chargèd with forgetfulness,
Thorough sharp seas in winter nights doth pass
'Tween rock and rock; and eke° mine en'my, alas,   also
That is my lord, steereth with cruelness;
5   And every owre° a thought in readiness,   oar
     As though that death were light in such a case.
     An endless wind doth tear the sail apace
Of forced sighs and trusty fearfulness.
     A rain of tears, a cloud of dark disdain,
10 Hath done the weared cords great hinderance;
Wreathèd with error and eke with ignorance.
The stars be hid that led me to this pain;
Drownèd is Reason that should me comfort,
     And I remain despairing of the port.

NICHOLAS BRETON (ca. 1545–ca. 1626)

Oh That My Heart Could Hit Upon a Strain (1602)

Oh that my heart could hit upon a strain
Would strike the music of my soul's desire;
Or that my soul could find that sacred vein
That sets the consort of the angels' choir.
5   Or that that spirit of especial grace
That cannot stoop beneath the state of heaven
Within my soul would take his settled place
With angels' *Ens,*[1] to make his glory even.
Then should the name of my most gracious King,
10 And glorious God, in higher tunes be sounded
Of heavenly praise, than earth hath power to sing,
Where heaven, and earth, and angels, are confounded.
     And souls may sing while all heart strings are broken;
     His praise is more than can in praise be spoken.

---

[1] **My Galley . . . Forgetfulness:** This poem is based on Petrarch's *Rime 189.*
[1] **Ens:** An entity, a being; also, essence.

EDMUND SPENSER (ca. 1552–1599)

from Amoretti (ca. 1594)

XXII "This holy season, fit to fast and pray"

This holy season, fit to fast and pray,
Men to devotion ought to be inclined:
Therefore, I likewise, on so holy day,
For my sweet saint some service fit will find.
5   Her temple fair is built within my mind,
In which her glorious image placèd is;
On which my thoughts do day and night attend,
Like sacred priests that never think amiss.
There I to her, as th' author of my bliss,
10   Will build an altar to appease her ire;
And on the same my heart will sacrifice,
Burning in flames of pure and chaste desire:
        The which vouchsafe, O goddess, to accept,
        Amongst thy dearest relics to be kept.

LXVII "Like as a huntsman after weary chase"

Like as a huntsman after weary chase,
Seeing the game from him escaped away,
Sits down to rest him in some shady place,
With panting hounds beguilèd of their prey:
5   So, after long pursuit and vain assay,
When I all weary had the chase forsook,
The gentle deer returned the self-same way,
Thinking to quench her thirst at the next brook:
There she, beholding me with milder look,
10   Sought not to fly, but fearless still did bide;
Till I in hand her yet half trembling took,
And with her own good-will her firmly tied.
        Strange thing, meseemed, to see a beast so wild,
        So goodly won, with her own will beguiled.

LXXI "I joy to see how, in your drawen work"

I joy to see how, in your drawen work,[1]
Yourself unto the bee ye do compare;
And me unto the spider, that doth lurk
In close await, to catch her unaware:
5   Right so yourself were caught in cunning snare
Of a dear foe, and thrallèd to his love;

---

[1] **drawen work:** I.e., embroidery.

In whose strait bands ye now captivèd are
So firmly, that ye never may remove.
But as your work is woven all above
10   With woodbind flowers and fragrant eglantine,
So sweet your prison you in time shall prove,
With many dear delights bedeckèd fine.
     And all thenceforth eternal peace shall see
     Between the spider and the gentle bee.

LXXV "One day I wrote her name upon the strand"

One day I wrote her name upon the strand;
But came the waves, and washèd it away:
Again, I wrote it with a second hand;
But came the tide, and made my pains his prey.
5   Vain man, said she, that dost in vain assay
A mortal thing so to immortalize;
For I myself shall like to this decay,
And eke my name be wipèd out likewise.
Not so, quoth I; let baser things devise
10   To die in dust, but you shall live by fame:
My verse your virtues rare shall eternize,
And in the heavens write your glorious name.
     Where, whenas death shall all the world subdue,
     Our love shall live, and later life renew.

SIR PHILIP SIDNEY (1554–1586)

from Astrophil and Stella (1591)

39

Come sleep, Oh sleep, the certain knot of peace,
The baiting place of wit, the balm of woe,
The poor man's wealth, the prisoner's release,
Th'indifferent judge between the high and low;
5   With shield of proof shield me from out the prease°   multitude
Of those fierce darts Despair at me doth throw;
Oh make in me those civil wars to cease;
I will good tribute pay, if thou do so.
Take thou of me smooth pillows, sweetest bed,
10   A chamber deaf to noise and blind to light,
A rosy garland and a weary head;
And if these things, as being thine by right,
Move not thy heavy grace, thou shalt in me,
Livelier than elsewhere, Stella's image see.

SAMUEL DANIEL (ca. 1562–1619)

from Delia (1592)
Let Others Sing of Knights and Paladins[1]

Let others sing of knights and paladins
In agèd accents and untimely words;
Paint shadows in imaginary lines,
Which well the reach of their high wits records:
5   But I must sing of thee, and those fair eyes.
Authentic shall my verse in time to come;
When yet th'unborn shall say, 'Lo where she lies,
Whose beauty made him speak that else was dumb.'
These are the arks, the trophies I erect,
10   That fortify thy name against old age;
And these thy sacred virtues must protect
Against the dark, and time's consuming rage.
    Though th'error of my youth in them appear,
    Suffice they show I lived and loved thee dear.

MICHAEL DRAYTON (1563–1631)

from Idea (1619)

Sonnet I "Like an adventurous seafarer am I"

Like an adventurous seafarer am I,
Who hath some long and dang'rous voyage been,
And called to tell of his discovery,
How far he sailed, what countries he had seen;
5   Proceeding from the port whence he put forth,
Shows by his compass how his course he steered,
When east, when west, when south, and when by north,
As how the pole to every place was reared,
What capes he doubled, of what continent,
10   The gulfs and straits that strangely he had passed,
Where most becalmed, where with foul weather spent,
And on what rocks in peril to be cast!
    Thus, in my love, time calls me to relate
    My tedious travels and oft-varying fate.

---

[1] **Paladins:** I.e., chivalrous defenders, heroes.

Sonnet VIII "There's nothing grieves me but that age should haste"

There's nothing grieves me but that age should haste,
That in my days I may not see thee old;
That where those two clear sparkling eyes are placed
Only two loop-holes then I might behold.
5   That lovely archèd, ivory, polished brow
Defaced with wrinkles, that I might but see;
Thy dainty hair, so curled and crispèd now
Like grizzled moss upon some agèd tree;
Thy cheek, now flush with roses, sunk and lean;
10   Thy lips, with age as any wafer thin;
Thy pearly teeth out of thy head so clean
That, when thou feedst, thy nose shall touch thy chin.
       These lines that now thou scornst, which should delight thee,
       Then would I make thee read, but to despite thee.

WILLIAM SHAKESPEARE (1564–1616)

from Sonnets (ca. 1595; 1609)

1 "From fairest creatures we desire increase"

From fairest creatures we desire increase,
That thereby beauty's rose might never die,
But as the riper should by time decease,
His tender heir might bear his memory;
5   But thou, contracted° to thine own bright eyes,   betrothed
Feed'st thy light's flame with self-substantial fuel,
Making a famine where abundance lies,
Thyself thy foe, to thy sweet self too cruel.
Thou that art now the world's fresh ornament
10   And only herald to the gaudy spring
Within thine own bud buriest thy content,
And, tender churl, mak'st waste in niggarding.
       Pity the world, or else this glutton be:
       To eat the world's due, by the grave and thee.

18 "Shall I compare thee to a summer's day?"

Shall I compare thee to a summer's day?
Thou art more lovely and more temperate.
Rough winds do shake the darling buds of May,
And summer's lease hath all too short a date.
5   Sometime too hot the eye of heaven shines,
And often is his gold complexion dimmed,

And every fair from fair sometime declines,
By chance or nature's changing course untrimmed;° divested
But thy eternal summer shall not fade
10   Nor lose possession of that fair thou ow'st,[1]
Nor shall death brag thou wander'st in his shade
When in eternal lines to time thou grow'st.
      So long as men can breathe or eyes can see,
      So long lives this, and this gives life to thee.

20 "A woman's face with nature's own hand painted"

A woman's face with nature's own hand painted
Hast thou, the master-mistress of my passion;
A woman's gentle heart, but not acquainted
With shifting change as is false women's fashion;
5   An eye more bright than theirs, less false in rolling,° roving
Gilding the object whereupon it gazeth;
A man in hue, all hues in his controlling,
Which steals men's eyes and women's souls amazeth.
And for a woman wert thou first created,
10   Till nature as she wrought thee fell a-doting,
And by addition me of thee defeated
By adding one thing to my purpose nothing.
      But since she pricked thee out for women's pleasure,
      Mine be thy love and thy love's use their treasure.

29 "When, in disgrace with fortune and men's eyes"

When, in disgrace with fortune and men's eyes,
I all alone beweep my outcast state,
And trouble deaf heaven with my bootless° cries, futile
And look upon myself and curse my fate,
5   Wishing me like to one more rich in hope,
Featured like him, like him with friends possessed,
Desiring this man's art and that man's scope,
With what I most enjoy contented least:
Yet in these thoughts myself almost despising,
10   Haply I think on thee, and then my state,
Like to the lark at break of day arising
From sullen earth, sings hymns at heaven's gate;
      For thy sweet love remembered such wealth brings
      That then I scorn to change my state with kings'.

---

[1] **ow'st:** I.e., own, but also, owe.

30 "When to the sessions of sweet silent thought"

When to the sessions of sweet silent thought
I summon up remembrance of things past,
I sigh the lack of many a thing I sought,
And with old woes new wail my dear time's waste.
5   Then can I drown an eye unused to flow
For precious friends hid in death's dateless° night,   endless
And weep afresh love's long-since-cancelled woe,
And moan th'expense of many a vanished sight.
Then can I grieve at grievances foregone,
10   And heavily from woe to woe tell o'er
The sad account of fore-bemoanèd moan,
Which I new pay as if not paid before.
     But if the while I think on thee, dear friend,
     All losses are restored, and sorrows end.

55 "Not marble nor the gilded monuments"

Not marble nor the gilded monuments
Of princes shall outlive this powerful rhyme,
But you shall shine more bright in these contents
Than unswept stone besmeared with sluttish time.
5   When wasteful war shall statues overturn,
And broils root out the work of masonry,
Nor Mars[2] his sword nor war's quick fire shall burn
The living record of your memory.
'Gainst death and all oblivious enmity
10   Shall you pace forth; your praise shall still find room
Even in the eyes of all posterity
That wear this world out to the ending doom.
     So, till the judgement that yourself arise,
     You live in this, and dwell in lovers' eyes.

71 "No longer mourn for me when I am dead"

No longer mourn for me when I am dead
Than you shall hear the surly sullen bell
Give warning to the world that I am fled
From this vile world with vilest worms to dwell.
5   Nay, if you read this line, remember not
The hand that writ it; for I love you so
That I in your sweet thoughts would be forgot
If thinking on me then should make you woe.

---

[2] **Mars:** The Roman god of war (Ares in the Greek tradition).

O, if, I say, you look upon this verse

10   When I perhaps compounded am with clay,
Do not so much as my poor name rehearse,
But let your love even with my life decay,
    Lest the wise world should look into your moan
    And mock you with me after I am gone.

74 *"But be contented when that fell arrest"*

But be contented when that fell arrest
Without all bail shall carry me away.
My life hath in this line some interest,
Which for memorial still with thee shall stay.

5   When thou reviewest this, thou dost review
The very part was consecrate to thee.
The earth can have but earth, which is his due;
My spirit is thine, the better part of me.
So then thou hast but lost the dregs of life,

10   The prey of worms, my body being dead,
The coward conquest of a wretch's knife,
Too base of thee to be rememberèd.
    The worth of that is that which it contains,
    And that is this, and this with thee remains.

91 *"Some glory in their birth, some in their skill"*

Some glory in their birth, some in their skill,
Some in their wealth, some in their body's force,
Some in their garments (though new-fangled ill),
Some in their hawks and hounds, some in their horse,

5   And every humour hath his adjunct pleasure
Wherein it finds a joy above the rest.
But these particulars are not my measure;
All these I better in one general best.
Thy love is better than high birth to me,

10   Richer than wealth, prouder than garments' cost,
Of more delight than hawks or horses be,
And having thee of all men's pride I boast,
    Wretched in this alone: that thou mayst take
    All this away, and me most wretched make.

132 *"Thine eyes I love, and they, as pitying me"*

Thine eyes I love, and they, as pitying me—
Knowing thy heart torment me with disdain—
Have put on black, and loving mourners be,
Looking with pretty ruth upon my pain;

5   And truly, not the morning sun of heaven

Better becomes the gray cheeks of the east,
Nor that full star that ushers in the even
Doth half that glory to the sober west,
As those two mourning eyes become thy face.
10   O, let it then as well beseem thy heart
To mourn for me, since mourning doth thee grace,
And suit thy pity like in every part.
    Then will I swear beauty herself is black,
    And all they foul that thy complexion lack.

SIR ROBERT AYTOUN (1570–1638)

Upone Tabacco

Forsaken of all comforts but these two,
My faggott[1] and my Pipe, I sitt and Muse
On all my crosses, and almost accuse
The heavens for dealing with me as they do.
5   Then hope steps in and with a smyling brow
Such chearfull expectations doth infuse
As makes me think ere long I cannot chuse
But be some Grandie, whatsoever I'm now.
But having spent my pipe, I then perceive
10   That hopes and dreams are Couzens, both deceive.
Then make I this conclusion in my mind,
Its all one thing, both tends unto one Scope
To live upon Tabacco and on hope,
The one's but smoake, the other is but wind.

JOHN DONNE (1572–1631)

from Holy Sonnets (ca. 1609, 1617; pub. 1633, 1899)

*Sonnet XIV "Batter my heart, three-personed
God; for you"*

Batter my heart, three-personed God; for you
As yet but knock, breathe, shine, and seek to mend;
That I may rise, and stand, o'erthrow me, and bend

---

[1] **faggott:** I.e., fagot, a bundle; perhaps a pouch of tobacco.

      Your force, to break, blow, burn, and make me new.
5   I, like an usurped town to another due,
      Labour to admit you, but oh, to no end:
      Reason your viceroy in me, me should defend,
      But is captived, and proves weak or untrue;
      Yet dearly I love you, and would be loved fain,°   with pleasure
10   But am betrothed unto your enemy:
      Divorce me, untie, or break that knot again,
      Take me to you, imprison me, for I
      Except you enthral me, never shall be free,
      Nor ever chaste, except you ravish me.

Sonnet XVIII *"Show me, dear Christ, thy spouse so bright and clear"*

      Show me, dear Christ, thy spouse[1] so bright and clear.
      What, is it she which on the other shore
      Goes richly painted? or which robbed and tore
      Laments and mourns in Germany and here?
5   Sleeps she a thousand, then peeps up one year?
      Is she self truth and errs? now new, now outwore?
      Doth she, and did she, and shall she evermore
      On one, on seven, or on no hill appear?[2]
      Dwells she with us, or like adventuring knights
10   First travail we to seek and then make love?
      Betray° kind husband thy spouse to our sights,   reveal
      And let mine amorous soul court thy mild dove,
      Who is most true and pleasing to thee then
      When she's embraced and open to most men.

Sonnet XIX *"Oh, to vex me, contraries meet in one"*

      Oh, to vex me, contraries meet in one:
      Inconstancy unnaturally hath begot
      A constant habit; that when I would not
      I change in vows, and in devotïon.
5   As humorous is my contritïon
      As my profane love, and as soon forgot:
      As riddlingly distempered, cold and hot,

---

[1] **thy spouse:** An allusion to the true church, also known as "the Bride of Christ" (Matthew 25:1–13) and referred to as "she" in this poem. Donne makes a distinction between the Roman Catholic churches "on the other shore" (e.g., in France, Spain, Italy) and the Protestant Church in Germany and "here" (England).
[2] **On one . . . appear:** The hill of Solomon's famous temple, Mount Moriah; the Seven Hills of Rome; "no hill" perhaps refers to the church in Geneva.

As praying, as mute; as infinite, as none.
I durst not view heaven yesterday; and today
10 In prayers and flattering speeches I court God:
Tomorrow I quake with true fear of his rod.
So my devout fits come and go away
Like a fantastic ague: save that here
Those are my best days, when I shake with fear.

GEORGE HERBERT (1593–1633)

Sin (I) (1633)

Lord, with what care hast thou begirt us round!
    Parents first season us: then schoolmasters
    Deliver us to laws; they send us bound
To rules of reason, holy messengers,
5 Pulpits and Sundays, sorrow dogging sin,
    Afflictions sorted, anguish of all sizes,
    Fine nets and stratagems to catch us in,
Bibles laid open, millions of surprises,
Blessings beforehand, ties of gratefulness,
10   The sound of glory ringing in our ears:
    Without, our shame; within, our consciences;
Angels and grace, eternal hopes and fears.
    Yet all these fences and their whole array
    One cunning bosom-sin blows quite away.

JOHN MILTON (1608–1674)

On His Blindness (1673)

When I consider how my light is spent,
    Ere half my days, in this dark world and wide,
    And that one talent which is death to hide
    Lodged with me useless, though my soul more bent
5 To serve therewith my maker, and present
    My true account, lest he returning chide,
    'Doth God exact day-labour, light denied?'
    I fondly ask; but patience to prevent
That murmur soon replies, 'God doth not need
10   Either man's work or his own gifts; who best
    Bear his mild yoke, they serve him best, his state

Is kingly. Thousands at his bidding speed
    And post o'er land and ocean without rest:
    They also serve who only stand and wait.'

ANNE SEWARD (1742–1809)

Sonnet (1789)

Ingratitude, how deadly is the smart°   pain
    Thou giv'st, inhabiting the form we love!
    How light compared all other sorrows prove!
    Thou shed'st a night of woe—from whence depart
5 The gentle beams of patience, that the heart
    Midst lesser ills illume. Thy victims rove,
    Unquiet as the ghost that haunts the grove
    Where murder spilt the life-blood. O! thy dart
Kills more than life—ev'n all that makes it dear;
10   Till we 'the sensible of pain' would change
    For frenzy, that defies the bitter tear;
Or wish in kindred callousness to range
    Where moon-eyed Idiocy, with fallen lip,
    Drags the loose knee and intermitting step.

CHARLOTTE SMITH (1749–1806)

Sonnet Written in the Church Yard at Middleton in Sussex (1789)

Pressed by the moon, mute arbitress of tides,
    While the loud equinox its power combines,
    The sea no more its swelling surge confines,
But o'er the shrinking land sublimely rides.
5 The wild blast, rising from the western cave,
    Drives the huge billows from their heaving bed,
    Tears from their grassy tombs the village dead,
And breaks the silent sabbath of the grave!
With shells and sea-weed mingled, on the shore
10   Lo! their bones whiten in the frequent wave;
    But vain to them the winds and waters rave;
They hear the warring elements no more:
While I am doomed—by life's long storm oppressed,
To gaze with envy on their gloomy rest.

WILLIAM WORDSWORTH (1770–1850)

Scorn Not the Sonnet (ca. 1802; 1827)

Scorn not the sonnet! Critic, you have frowned
Mindless of its just honours. With this key
Shakespeare unlocked his heart, the melody
Of this small lute gave ease to Petrarch's wound;
5   A thousand times this pipe did Tasso sound;
With it Camöens soothed an exile's grief.[1]
The sonnet glittered a gay myrtle-leaf
Amid the cypress with which Dante crowned
His visionary brow—a glow-worm lamp.
10   It cheered mild Spenser, called from Faery-land
To struggle through dark ways, and, when a damp
Fell round the path of Milton, in his hand
The thing became a trumpet, whence he blew
Soul-animating strains—alas, too few!

WILLIAM WORDSWORTH (1770–1850)

Composed Upon Westminster Bridge (1803)

Earth has not any thing to shew more fair:
Dull would he be of soul who could pass by
A sight so touching in its majesty:
This City now doth like a garment wear
5   The beauty of the morning; silent, bare,
Ships, towers, domes, theatres, and temples lie
Open unto the fields, and to the sky;
All bright and glittering in the smokeless air.
Never did sun more beautifully steep
10   In his first splendor valley, rock, or hill;

---

[1] **Tasso . . . exile's grief:** Toquato Tasso (1544–1595), one of the major literary figures of the Italian Renaissance, wrote numerous sonnets. His work influenced many English poets, most notably Spenser and Byron. Luís de Camöens (1554–1580), was a Portuguese poet who was exiled to Macao for writing satirical verse. Eventually, he returned to Lisbon, but died several years later in abject poverty. Like the other poets mentioned in Wordsworth's poem, Camöens was a master of the sonnet form.

Ne'er saw I, never felt, a calm so deep!
The river glideth at his own sweet will:
Dear God! the very houses seem asleep;
And all that mighty heart is lying still!

MARY TIGHE (1772–1810)

Written at Scarborough   (1799)

As musing pensive in my silent home
    I hear far off the sullen ocean's roar,
    Where the rude wave just sweeps the level shore
Or bursts upon the rocks with whitening foam,
5   I think upon the scenes my life has known—
    On days of sorrow, and some hours of joy;
    Both which alike Time could so soon destroy!
And now they seem a busy dream alone;
While on the earth exists no single trace
10 Of all that shook my agitated soul,
    As on the beach new waves for ever roll
And fill their past forgotten brother's place;
    But I, like the worn sand, exposed remain
    To each new storm which frets the angry main.

PERCY BYSSHE SHELLEY (1792–1822)

Ozymandias[1]   (1817; 1818)

I met a traveller from an antique land
Who said: 'Two vast and trunkless legs of stone
Stand in the desert. Near them on the sand,
Half sunk, a shattered visage lies, whose frown,
5 And wrinkled lip, and sneer of cold command,
Tell that its sculptor well those passions read
Which yet survive (stamped on these lifeless things)

---

[1] **Ozymandias:** The Greek name of the Egyptian king Ramses II (thirteenth century B.C.), who allegedly erected a giant statue of himself.

The hand that mocked them and the heart that fed.
And on the pedestal these words appear:
10   "My name is Ozymandias, King of Kings;
Look on my works, ye Mighty, and despair!"
Nothing beside remains. Round the decay
Of that colossal wreck, boundless and bare
The lone and level sands stretch far away.'

JOHN KEATS (1795–1821)

On First Looking into Chapman's Homer [1] (1816)

Much have I travell'd in the realms of gold,
  And many goodly states and kingdoms seen;
  Round many western islands have I been
Which bards in fealty to Apollo hold.
5   Oft of one wide expanse had I been told
  That deep-brow'd Homer ruled as his demesne°;   realm
  Yet did I never breathe its pure serene
Till I heard Chapman speak out loud and bold:
Then felt I like some watcher of the skies
10   When a new planet swims into his ken;
Or like stout Cortez [2] when with eagle eyes
  He star'd at the Pacific—and all his men
Look'd at each other with a wild surmise—
  Silent, upon a peak in Darien.

JOHN KEATS (1795–1821)

When I Have Fears that I May Cease to Be (1818; 1848)

When I have fears that I may cease to be
  Before my pen has gleaned my teeming brain,
Before high-piléd books, in charactery,
  Hold like rich garners the full ripened grain;

---

[1] **Chapman's Homer:** George Chapman translated Homer's *Odyssey* in 1616. See p. 704.
[2] **Cortez:** Hernando Cortez (1460–1521), a Spanish explorer and conquistador, devastated the Aztec Empire in Central America.

5   When I behold, upon the night's starred face,
         Huge cloudy symbols of a high romance,
     And think that I may never live to trace
         Their shadows, with the magic hand of chance;
     And when I feel, fair creature of an hour,
10   That I shall never look upon thee more,
     Never have relish in the fairy power
         Of unreflecting love—then on the shore
     Of the wide world I stand alone, and think
     Till love and fame to nothingness do sink.

ELIZABETH BARRETT BROWNING (1806–1861)

from Sonnets from the Portuguese (1846; 1850)

13 "And wilt thou have me
fashion into speech"

     And wilt thou have me fashion into speech
     The love I bear thee, finding words enough,
     And hold the torch out, while the winds are rough,
     Between our faces, to cast light on each?—
5   I drop it at thy feet. I cannot teach
     My hand to hold my spirit so far off
     From myself—me—that I should bring thee proof
     In words, of love hid in me out of reach.
     Nay, let the silence of my womanhood
10   Commend my woman-love to thy belief,—
     Seeing that I stand unwon, however wooed,
     And rend the garment of my life, in brief,
     By a most dauntless, voiceless fortitude,
     Lest one touch of this heart convey its grief.

24 "Let the world's sharpness,
like a clasping knife"

     Let the world's sharpness, like a clasping knife,
     Shut in upon itself and do no harm
     In this close hand of Love, now soft and warm,
     And let us hear no sound of human strife
5   After the click of the shutting. Life to life—
     I lean upon thee, Dear, without alarm,
     And feel as safe as guarded by a charm
     Against the stab of worldlings, who if rife
     Are weak to injure. Very whitely still
10   The lilies of our lives may reassure

Their blossoms from their roots, accessible
Alone to heavenly dews that drop not fewer,
Growing straight, out of man's reach, on the hill.
God only, who made us rich, can make us poor.

CAROLINE NORTON (1808–1877)

Be Frank with Me (1830)

Be frank with me, and I accept my lot;
    But deal not with me as a grieving child,
Who for the loss of that which he hath not
    Is by a show of kindness thus beguiled!
5   Raise not for me, from its enshrouded tomb,
    The ghostly likeness of a hope deceased;
Nor think to cheat the darkness of my doom
    By wavering doubts how far thou art released.
This dressing pity in the garb of love,
10   This effort of the heart to seem the same,
These sighs and lingerings (which nothing prove
    But that thou leavest me with a kind of shame),
Remind me more, by their most vain deceit,
Of the dear loss of all which thou dost counterfeit.

JONES VERY (1817–1862)

The Columbine (1850)

    Still, still my eye will gaze long fixed on thee,
    Till I forget that I am called a man,
    And at thy side fast-rooted seem to be,
    And the breeze comes my cheek with thine to fan.
5   Upon this craggy hill our life shall pass,
    A life of summer days and summer joys,
    Nodding our honey-bells mid pliant grass
    In which the bee half hid his time employs;
    And here we'll drink with thirsty pores the rain,
10   And turn dew-sprinkled to the rising sun,
    And look when in the flaming west again
    His orb across the heaven its path has run;
    Here left in darkness on the rocky steep,
My weary eyes shall close like folding flowers in sleep.

FREDERICK GODDARD TUCKERMAN (1821–1873)

Sonnet (1860)

And so, as this great sphere (now turning slow
Up to the light from that abyss of stars,
Now wheeling into gloom through sunset bars)—
With all its elements of form and flow,
5   And life in life; where crowned, yet blind, must go
The sensible king,—is but an Unity
Compressed of motes impossible to know;
Which worldlike yet in deep analogy,
Have distance, march, dimension, and degree;
10   So the round earth—which we the world do call—
Is but a grain in that that mightiest swells,
Whereof the stars of light are particles,
As ultimate atoms of one infinite Ball,
On which God moves, and treads beneath his feet the All!

GEORGE MEREDITH (1828–1909)

from Modern Love[1] (1862)

I "By this he knew she wept with waking eyes"

By this he knew she wept with waking eyes:
That, at his hand's light quiver by her head,
The strange low sobs that shook their common bed,
Were called into her with a sharp surprise,
5   And strangled mute, like little gaping snakes,
Dreadfully venomous to him. She lay
Stone-still, and the long darkness flowed away
With muffled pulses. Then, as midnight makes
Her giant heart of Memory and Tears
10   Drink the pale drug of silence, and so beat
Sleep's heavy measure, they from head to feet
Were moveless, looking through their dead black years,
By vain regret scrawled over the blank wall.
Like sculptured effigies they might be seen

---

[1] Note that Meredith experiments with a 16-line form that might be considered an extension of the sonnet. He is certainly using the notion of the sonnet sequence here.

15 Upon their marriage-tomb, the sword between;
    Each wishing for the sword that severs all.

VI "It chanced his lips did meet her forehead cool"

It chanced his lips did meet her forehead cool.
She had no blush, but slanted down her eye.
Shamed nature, then, confesses love can die:
And most she punishes the tender fool
5 Who will believe what honours her the most!
Dead! is it dead? She has a pulse, and flow
Of tears, the price of blood-drops, as I know,
For whom the midnight sobs around Love's ghost,
Since then I heard her, and so will sob on.
10 The love is here; it has but changed its aim.
O bitter barren woman! what's the name?
The name, the name, the new name thou hast won?
Behold me striking the world's coward stroke!
That will I not do, though the sting is dire.
15 —Beneath the surface this, while by the fire
They sat, she laughing at a quiet joke.

XVII "At dinner, she is hostess, I am host"

At dinner, she is hostess, I am host.
Went the feast ever cheerfuller? She keeps
The Topic over intellectual deeps
In buoyancy afloat. They see no ghost.
5 With sparkling surface-eyes we ply the ball:
It is in truth a most contagious game:
HIDING THE SKELETON, shall be its name.
Such play as this, the devils might appal!
But here's the greater wonder; in that we
10 Enamoured of an acting nought can tire,
Each other, like true hypocrites, admire;
Warm-lighted looks, Love's ephemerioe,
Shoot gaily o'er the dishes and the wine.
We waken envy of our happy lot.
15 Fast, sweet, and golden, shows the marriage-knot.
Dear guests, you now have seen Love's corpse-light shine.

XXIII " 'Tis Christmas weather, and a country house"

'Tis Christmas weather, and a country house
Receives us: rooms are full: we can but get
An attic-crib. Such lovers will not fret
At that, it is half-said. The great carouse
5 Knocks hard upon the midnight's hollow door,

But when I knock at hers, I see the pit.
Why did I come here in that dullard fit?
I enter, and lie couched upon the floor.
Passing, I caught the coverlet's quick beat:—
10 Come, Shame, burn to my soul! and Pride, and Pain—
Foul demons that have tortured me, enchain!
Out in the freezing darkness the lambs bleat.
The small bird stiffens in the low starlight.
I know not how, but shuddering as I slept,
15 I dreamed a banished angel to me crept:
My feet were nourished on her breasts all night.

XLVII "We saw the swallows gathering in the sky"

We saw the swallows gathering in the sky,
And in the osier°-isle we heard them noise.   willow
We had not to look back on summer joys,
Or forward to a summer of bright dye:
5 But in the largeness of the evening earth
Our spirits grew as we went side by side.
The hour became her husband and my bride.
Love that had robbed us so, thus blessed our dearth!
The pilgrims of the year waxed very loud
10 In multitudinous chatterings, as the flood
Full brown came from the West, and like pale blood
Expanded to the upper crimson cloud.
Love that had robbed us of immortal things,
This little moment mercifully gave,
15 Where I have seen across the twilight wave
The swan sail with her young beneath her wings.

CHRISTINA G. ROSSETTI (1830–1894)

Remember (1849; 1862)

Remember me when I am gone away,
    Gone far away into the silent land;
    When you can no more hold me by the hand,
Nor I half turn to go yet turning stay.
5 Remember me when no more day by day
    You tell me of our future that you planned:
    Only remember me; you understand
It will be late to counsel then or pray.
Yet if you should forget me for a while

10   And afterwards remember, do not grieve:
         For if the darkness and corruption leave
         A vestige of the thoughts that once I had,
         Better by far you should forget and smile
            Than that you should remember and be sad.

THOMAS HARDY (1840–1928)

Hap (1866; 1898)

         If but some vengeful god would call to me
         From up the sky, and laugh: "Thou suffering thing,
         Know that thy sorrow is my ecstasy,
         That thy love's loss is my hate's profiting!"
5   Then would I bear it, clench myself, and die,
         Steeled by the sense of ire unmerited;
         Half-eased in that a Powerfuller than I
         Had willed and meted me the tears I shed.

         But not so. How arrives it joy lies slain,
10   And why unblooms the best hope ever sown?
         —Crass Casualty obstructs the sun and rain,
         And dicing Time for gladness casts a moan. . . .
         These purblind Doomsters had as readily strown
         Blisses about my pilgrimage as pain.

GERARD MANLEY HOPKINS (1844–1889)

"I wake and feel the fell of dark, not day" (ca. 1885; 1918)

         I wake and feel the fell of dark, not day.
         What hours, O what black hours we have spent
         This night! what sights you, heart, saw; ways you went!
         And more must, in yet longer light's delay.

5   With witness I speak this. But where I say
         Hours I mean years, mean life. And my lament
         Is cries countless, cries like dead letters sent
         To dearest him that lives alas! away.

I am gall, I am heartburn. God's most deep decree
10   Bitter would have me taste: my taste was me;
Bones built in me, flesh filled, blood brimmed the curse.

Selfyeast of spirit a dull dough sours. I see
The lost are like this, and their scourge to be
As I am mine, their sweating selves; but worse.

GERARD MANLEY HOPKINS (1844–1889)

Carrion Comfort (1885; 1918)

Not, I'll not, carrion comfort, Despair, not feast on thee;
Not untwist—slack they may be—these last strands of man
In me ór, most weary, cry *I can no more.* I can;
Can something, hope, wish day come, not choose not to be.
5   But ah, but O thou terrible, why wouldst thou rude on me
Thy wring-world right foot rock? lay a lionlimb against me? scan
With darksome devouring eyes my bruisèd bones? and fan,
O in turns of tempest, me heaped there; me frantic to avoid thee and flee?

     Why? That my chaff might fly; my grain lie, sheer and clear.
10   Nay in all that toil, that coil, since (seems) I kissed the rod,
Hand rather, my heart lo! lapped strength, stole joy, would laugh, chéer.
Cheer whom though? the hero whose heaven-handling flung me, fóot tród
Me? or me that fought him? O which one? is it each one? That night,
          that year
Of now done darkness I wretch lay wrestling with (my God!) my God.

GERARD MANLEY HOPKINS (1844–1889)

"Thou art indeed just, Lord, if I contend" (1889; 1893)

Justus quidem tu es, Domine, si disputem tecum; verumtamen
justa loquar ad te: Quare via impiorum prosperatur? &c.[1]

---

[1] **Justus quidem . . . prosperatur? &c.:** "Thou indeed, O Lord, art just, if I plead with thee, but yet I will speak what is just to thee: Why doth the way of the wicked prosper: why is it well with all them that transgress, and do wickedly?" (from the Latin Vulgate version of Jeremiah 12:1). The "&c" means that the entire book of Jeremiah bears relevance to the poem.

Thou art indeed just, Lord, if I contend
With thee; but, sir, so what I plead is just.
Why do sinners' ways prosper? and why must
Disappointment all I endeavour end?

5   Wert thou my enemy, O thou my friend,
How wouldst thou worse, I wonder, than thou dost
Defeat, thwart me? Oh, the sots° and thralls of lust   intoxication
Do in spare hours more thrive than I that spend,

Sir, life upon thy cause. See, banks and brakes
10   Now, leavèd how thick! lacèd they are again
With fretty chervil,[2] look, and fresh wind shakes

Them; birds build—but not I build; no, but strain,
Time's eunuch,[3] and not breed one work that wakes.
Mine, O thou lord of life, send my roots rain.

WILLIAM BUTLER YEATS   (1865–1939)

Leda and the Swan[1]   (1923; 1928)

A sudden blow: the great wings beating still
Above the staggering girl, her thighs caressed
By the dark webs, her nape caught in his bill,
He holds her helpless breast upon his breast.

5   How can those terrified vague fingers push
The feathered glory from her loosening thighs,
And how can body, laid in that white rush,
But feel the strange heart beating where it lies?

A shudder in the loins engenders there
10   The broken wall, the burning roof and tower
And Agamemnon[2] dead.
                              Being so caught up,

---

[2] **chervil:** An aromatic herb of the parsley family.
[3] **eunuch:** A castrated man who serves as a harem attendant in certain Asian courts. Here, a keeper, a guardian.
[1] **Leda and the Swan:** According to the Greek myth, Zeus, the most powerful of the Olympian gods, fell in love with a mortal girl, Leda. Disguised as a swan, he raped her and as a result she bore a daughter, Helen, who later became the cause for the Trojan War.
[2] **Agamemnon:** The leader of the Greek forces in the Trojan War and brother of Menelaus, the rightful husband of Helen.

So mastered by the brute blood of the air,
Did she put on his knowledge with his power
Before the indifferent beak could let her drop?

ROBERT FROST (1874–1963)

Mowing (1913)

There was never a sound beside the wood but one,
And that was my long scythe whispering to the ground.
What was it it whispered? I knew not well myself;
Perhaps it was something about the heat of the sun,
5   Something, perhaps, about the lack of sound—
And that was why it whispered and did not speak.
It was no dream of the gift of idle hours,
Or easy gold at the hand of fay or elf:
Anything more than the truth would have seemed too weak
10   To the earnest love that laid the swale in rows,
Not without feeble-pointed spikes of flowers
(Pale orchises), and scared a bright green snake.
The fact is the sweetest dream that labor knows.
My long scythe whispered and left the hay to make.

CLAUDE McKAY (1889–1948)

The Harlem Dancer (1922)

Applauding youths laughed with young prostitutes
And watched her perfect, half-clothed body sway;
Her voice was like the sound of blended flutes
Blown by black players upon a picnic day.
5   She sang and danced on gracefully and calm,
The light gauze hanging loose about her form;
To me she seemed a proudly-swaying palm
Grown lovelier for passing through a storm.
Upon her swarthy neck black shiny curls
10   Luxuriant fell; and tossing coins in praise,
The wine-flushed, bold-eyed boys, and even the girls,
Devoured her shape with eager, passionate gaze;
But looking at her falsely-smiling face,
I knew her self was not in that strange place.

EDNA ST. VINCENT MILLAY (1892–1950)

Sonnet II "Time does not bring relief; you all have lied" (1917)

Time does not bring relief; you all have lied
   Who told me time would ease me of my pain!
   I miss him in the weeping of the rain;
I want him at the shrinking of the tide;
5   The old snows melt from every mountain-side,
   And last year's leaves are smoke in every lane;
   But last year's bitter loving must remain
Heaped on my heart, and my old thoughts abide!

There are a hundred places where I fear
10   To go,—so with his memory they brim!
And entering with relief some quiet place
Where never fell his foot or shone his face
I say, "There is no memory of him here!"
   And so stand stricken, so remembering him!

EDNA ST. VINCENT MILLAY (1892–1950)

Sonnet XLIII "What lips my lips have kissed, and where, and why" (1920)

What lips my lips have kissed, and where, and why,
I have forgotten, and what arms have lain
Under my head till morning; but the rain
Is full of ghosts tonight, that tap and sigh
5   Upon the glass and listen for reply,
And in my heart there stirs a quiet pain
For unremembered lads that not again
Will turn to me at midnight with a cry.
Thus in winter stands the lonely tree,
10   Nor knows what birds have vanished one by one,
Yet knows its boughs more silent than before:
I cannot say what loves have come and gone,
I only know that summer sang in me
A little while, that in me sings no more.

EDNA ST. VINCENT MILLAY (1892–1950)

Sonnet XI "Not in a silver casket cool with pearls" (1931)

Not in a silver casket cool with pearls
Or rich with red corundum or with blue,
Locked, and the key withheld, as other girls
Have given their loves, I give my love to you;
5   Not in a lovers'-knot, not in a ring
Worked in such fashion, and the legend plain—
Semper fidelis,[1] where a secret spring
Kennels a drop of mischief for the brain:
Love in the open hand, no thing but that,
10   Ungemmed, unhidden, wishing not to hurt,
As one should bring you cowslips in a hat
Swung from the hand, or apples in her skirt,
I bring you, calling out as children do:
"Look what I have!—And these are all for you."

WILFRED OWEN (1893–1918)

Anthem for Doomed Youth (1917; 1920)

What passing-bells for these who die as cattle?
    —Only the monstrous anger of the guns.
    Only the stuttering rifles' rapid rattle
Can patter out their hasty orisons.°   prayers
5   No mockeries now for them; no prayers nor bells;
    Nor any voice of mourning save the choirs,—
The shrill, demented choirs of wailing shells;
    And bugles calling for them from sad shires.

What candles may be held to speed them all?
10   Not in the hands of boys but in their eyes
Shall shine the holy glimmers of goodbyes.
    The pallor of girls' brows shall be their pall;
Their flowers the tenderness of patient minds,
And each slow dusk a drawing-down of blinds.

---

[1] *Semper fidelis:* Always faithful (Latin).

E. E. CUMMINGS (1894–1962)

"the Cambridge ladies who live in furnished souls" (1922)

the Cambridge ladies who live in furnished souls
are unbeautiful and have comfortable minds
(also,with the church's protestant blessings
daughters,unscented shapeless spirited)
5   they believe in Christ and Longfellow,[1] both dead,
are invariably interested in so many things—
at the present writing one still finds
delighted fingers knitting for the is it Poles?
perhaps.   While permanent faces coyly bandy
10   scandal of Mrs. N and Professor D
. . . .the Cambridge ladies do not care,above
Cambridge if sometimes in its box of
sky lavender and cornerless,the
moon rattles like a fragment of angry candy

LOUISE BOGAN (1897–1970)

Sub Contra (1923)

Notes on the tuned frame of strings
Plucked or silenced under the hand
Whimper lightly to the ear,
Delicate and involute,
5   Like the mockery in a shell.
Lest the brain forget the thunder
The roused heart once made it hear,—
Rising as that clamor fell,—
Let there sound from music's root
10   One note rage can understand,
A fine noise of riven things.
Build there some thick chord of wonder;
Then, for every passion's sake,
Beat upon it till it break.

---

[1] **Longfellow:** Henry Wadsworth Longfellow (1807–1882), an American poet, whose work was deeply
traditionalist in its style and choice of subjects.

COUNTEE CULLEN (1903–1946)

From the Dark Tower (1927)
To Charles S. Johnson[1]

We shall not always plant while others reap
The golden increment of bursting fruit,
Not always countenance, abject and mute,
That lesser men should hold their brothers cheap;
5   Not everlastingly while others sleep
Shall we beguile their limbs with mellow flute,
Not always bend to some more subtle brute;
We were not made eternally to weep.

The night whose sable breast relieves the stark,
10   White stars is no less lovely being dark,
And there are buds that cannot bloom at all
In light, but crumple, piteous, and fall;
So in the dark we hide the heart that bleeds,
And wait, and tend our agonizing seeds.

LOUIS MacNEICE (1907–1963)

Sunday Morning

Down the road someone is practising scales,
The notes like little fishes vanish with a wink of tails,
Man's heart expands to tinker with his car
For this is Sunday morning, Fate's great bazaar;
5   Regard these means as ends, concentrate on this Now,

And you may grow to music or drive beyond Hindhead anyhow,
Take corners on two wheels until you go so fast
That you can clutch a fringe or two of the windy past,
That you can abstract this day and make it to the week of time
10   A small eternity, a sonnet self-contained in rhyme.

---

[1] **Charles S. Johnson:** Charles S. Johnson (1893–1956) was a distinguished social scientist and editor of the journal *Opportunity: A Journal of Negro Life.* He served as the first African-American president of Fisk University.

But listen, up the road, something gulps, the church spire
Open its eight bells out, skulls' mouths which will not tire
To tell how there is no music or movement which secures
Escape from the weekday time. Which deadens and endures.

ELIZABETH BISHOP (1911–1979)

Sonnet (1979)

Caught—the bubble
in the spirit-level,
a creature divided;
and the compass needle
5   wobbling and wavering,
undecided.
Freed—the broken
thermometer's mercury
running away;
10 and the rainbow-bird
from the narrow bevel
of the empty mirror,
flying wherever
it feels like, gay!

JOHN BERRYMAN (1914–1972)

9 "Great citadels whereon the gold sun falls" (1967)

Great citadels whereon the gold sun falls
Miss you O Chris sequestered to the West
Which wears you Mayday lily[1] at its breast,
Part and not part, proper to balls and brawls,
5   Plains, cities, or the yellow shore, not false
Anywhere, free, native and Danishest[2]
Profane and elegant flower,—whom suggest
Frail and not frail, blond rocks and madrigals.

---

[1] **Mayday lily:** The Lily of the Valley (which blooms in May, hence Mayday) is considered a symbol of Christ.
[2] **Danishest:** A derivation of Danish; possibly an allusion to Hamlet, the Prince of Denmark.

Once in the car (cave of our radical love)
10 Your darker hair I saw than golden hair
Above your thighs whiter than white-gold hair,
And where the dashboard lit faintly your least
Enlarged scene, O the midnight bloomed . . the East
Less gorgeous, wearing you like a long white glove!

JOHN BERRYMAN (1914–1972)

115 "As usual I'm up before the sun" (1967)

As usual I'm up before the sun
begins to warm this intolerable place
and I have stared all night upon your face
but am not wiser thereby. Everyone
5 rattles his weakness or his thing undone,
I shake you like a rat. Open disgrace
yawns all before me: have I left a trace,
a spoor? Clouding it over, I look for my gun.

She's hidden it. I won't sing on of that.
10 Whiskey is bracing. Failures are my speed,
I thrive on ends, the dog is at the door
in heat, the neighbourhood is male except one cat
and they thresh on my stoop. Prevent my need,
Someone, and come & find me on the floor.

ROBERT LOWELL (1917–1977)

Reading Myself (1973)

Like thousands, I took just pride and more than just,
struck matches that brought my blood to a boil;
I memorized the tricks to set the river on fire—
somehow never wrote something to go back to.
5 Can I suppose I am finished with wax flowers
and have earned my grass on the minor slopes of Parnassus[1]. . . .
No honeycomb is built without a bee

---

[1] **Parnassus:** A mountain in Greece sacred to Apollo, god of poetry, and the Muses.

adding circle to circle, cell to cell,
the wax and honey of a mausoleum—
10   this round dome proves its maker is alive;
the corpse of the insect lives embalmed in honey,
prays that its perishable work live long
enough for the sweet-tooth bear to desecrate—
this open book . . . my open coffin.

GEORGE MACKAY BROWN   (1921–1996)

The Old Women   (1959)

Go sad or sweet or riotous with beer
Past the old women gossiping by the hour,
They'll fix on you from every close and pier
An acid look to make your veins run sour.

5   'No help,' they say, 'his grandfather that's dead
Was troubled with the same dry-throated curse,
And many a night he made the ditch his bed.
This blood comes welling from the same cracked source.'

On every kind of merriment they frown.
10   But I have known a gray-eyed sober boy
Sail to the lobsters in a storm and drown.
Over his body dripping on the stones
Those same old hags would weave into their moans
An undersong of terrible holy joy.

JACK GILBERT   (1925–   )

Haunted Importantly   (1994)

It was in the transept [1] of the church, winter in
the stones, the dim light brightening on her,
when Linda said, Listen. Listen to this, she said.
When he put his ear against the massive door,
5   there were spirits singing inside. He hunted for it

---

[1] **transept:** Either of the lateral arms of a cruciform church (i.e., church laid out in the shape of a cross).

afterward. In Madrid, he heard a bell begin somewhere
in the night rain. Worked his way through
the tangle of alleys, the sound deeper and more
powerful as he got closer. Short of the plaza,
10   it filled all of him and he turned back. No need,
he thought, to see the bell. It was not the bell
he was trying to find, but the angel lost
in our bodies. The music that thinking is.
He wanted to know what he heard, not to get closer.

TED BERRIGAN (1934–1983)

A Final Sonnet (1967)
for Chris

How strange to be gone in a minute!   A man
Signs a shovel and so he digs   Everything
Turns into writing a name for a day
                         Someone
5   is having a birthday and someone is getting
married and someone is telling a joke   my dream
a white tree   I dream of the code of the west
But this rough magic I here abjure   and
When I have required some heavenly music   which even
10   now
I do   to work mine end upon *their* senses
That this aery charm is for   I'll break
My staff   bury it certain fathoms in the earth
And deeper than did ever plummet sound
15   I'll drown my book.
It is 5:15 a.m.   Dear Chris, hello.

SEAMUS HEANEY (1939–   )

The Forge (1969)

All I know is a door into the dark.
Outside, old axles and iron hoops rusting;
Inside, the hammered anvil's short-pitched ring,
The unpredictable fantail of sparks
5   Or hiss when a new shoe toughens in water.
The anvil must be somewhere in the centre,

Horned as a unicorn, at one end square,
Set there immoveable: an altar
Where he expends himself in shape and music.
10   Sometimes, leather-aproned, hairs in his nose,
He leans out on the jamb, recalls a clatter
Of hoofs where traffic is flashing in rows;
Then grunts and goes in, with a slam and flick
To beat real iron out, to work the bellows.

WANDA COLEMAN (1946–   )

American Sonnet (10) (1993)

after Lowell[1]

our mothers wrung hell and hardtack from row
          and boll. fenced others'
gardens with bones of lovers. embarking
          from Africa in chains
5   reluctant pilgrims stolen by Jehovah's[2] light
          planted here the bitter
seed of blight and here eternal torches mark
          the shame of Moloch's[3] mansions
built in slavery's name. our hungered eyes
10   do see/refuse the dark
illuminate the blood-soaked steps of each
          historic gain. a yearning
yearning to avenge the raping of the womb
          from which we spring

RITA DOVE (1952–   )

History (1995)

Everything's a metaphor, some wise
guy said, and his woman nodded, wisely.
Why was this such a discovery
to him? Why did history

---

[1] **Lowell:** Robert Lowell (1917–1977), American poet. Late in his career, Lowell wrote numerous free verse sonnets.
[2] **Jehovah:** The Jewish god of the Old Testament.
[3] **Moloch's:** A malicious deity in the Old Testament, who demanded human sacrifices and other cruel practices.

5   happen only on the outside?
    She'd watched an embryo track an arc
    across her swollen belly from the inside
    and knew she'd best
    think *knee,* not *tumor* or *burrowing mole,* lest
10 it emerge a monster. Each craving marks
    the soul: splashed white upon a temple the dish
    of ice cream, coveted, broken in a wink,
    or the pickle duplicated just behind the ear. *Every wish*
    will find its symbol, the woman thinks.

MARK JARMAN (1952–   )

Unholy Sonnet (1998)

Breath like a house fly batters the shut mouth.
The dream begins, turns over, and goes flat.
The virus cleans the attic and heads south.
Somebody asks, "What did you mean by that?"
5   But nobody says, "Nothing," in response.
The body turns a last cell into cancer.
The ghost abandons all of his old haunts.
Silence becomes the question and the answer.
And then—banal epiphany—and then,
10 Time kick starts and the deaf brain hears a voice.
The eyes like orphans find the world again.
Day washes down the city streets with noise.
And oxygen repaints the blood bright red.
How good it is to come back from the dead!

SHERMAN ALEXIE (1966–   )

Sonnet: Tattoo Tears (1996)

1.

No one will believe this story I'm telling, so it must be true.

2.

It's true: the Indian woman with three tears tattooed under her left eye folded under the weight of her own expectations, after her real tears failed to convince. No disfigurement is small and three tears leave you without choices, without hope or grace. The Indian woman with three tears tattooed under her left eye shot or stabbed her husband and went to prison for murder. In this, I cannot find the slightest measure of music. My hands are empty when I wave Hello, Old Friends to the cancellation of air, to the inversion of possibilities, to the strange animals haunting my dreams.

3.

Strange animals haunt my dreams, animals formed wholly by color, animals chasing me through the gallop of my imagination. But it wasn't Gallup streets I ran through, afraid, and it wasn't Spokane or Seattle, and maybe I wasn't coming nearer to the childhood I forgive most often when I lie in bed all day, refusing to stand and leave the safety of inertia. Most often, the animals have faces, familiar, like each was a cousin by marriage or a promise of destruction, like my ancestors had chosen me for a twentieth-century vision.

4.

A twentieth-century vision: my sister in San Francisco, early '70s, with a single tear tattooed under her right eye. She is pregnant, her dreams protected by the cardboard box she carries as defense. It's a small kind of medicine. Years later, I search for her in the newsreels, the black-and-white photographs, the glossary of a textbook, look for some definition of her disappearance.

5.

Disappear, child, like a coin in the hands of another reservation magician. Disappear, mother, into a cable television memory, 40 channels of commercials selling the future. What was I thinking, sending cash by mail, $19.95 for a knife that could cut concrete and oranges into halves? Disappear, father, as you close your eyes to sleep in the drive-in theater. What did you tell me? *Movies are worthless. They're just sequels to my life.* Disappear, brother, into the changing river, salmontravelling beneath the uranium mine, all of it measured now by half-lives and miles-between-dams. Disappear, sister, like a paper cut, like a rock thrown through a window, like a Fourth of July firework.

6.

It's the Fourth of July and every Indian looks into the sky. Tears explode from their eyes, louder and brighter than a bottle rocket. Tears lick their cheeks like a Jimi Hendrix solo. Tears fall until they build a new bridge across the Bering Strait. Tears fill up a chipped cup and Big Mom makes it into instant coffee. Tears echo, tears confuse the local weatherman, tears the size of golf balls, tears canned and distributed by the BIA, tears pulled into a hypodermic and mainlined. Tears sprayed onto a slice of white bread and eaten. Tears tattooed under the eyes of Indians who believe everything their mirrors whisper.

7.

Whispering slowly, a pair of panty hose rolled over an ankle sounds like a promise, like a memory fitted tightly over the skin: my sister in the mirror braided her hair into wild ponies, pulled the Goodwill panty hose over her legs and let me rub my cheek against her calves while she waited for some Indian boy or other. What did she used to say? Every weekend can be a powwow if you know what kind of music to play.

8.

What kind of music do you play when drums aren't enough?

9.

The drums aren't loud enough, so the deaf fancydancer stands still, scratching at the tears tattooed under both his eyes. Then, a beer truck roars by outside, shakes the earth like a drum, and the deaf fancydancer two-steps to a horsepowered song.

10.

The jukebox in the bar is horsepowered. The street lights making shadows on the basketball court are horsepowered. Seymour's new drum is diesel, gets great gas mileage but stutters when it climbs hills. On the top of Wellpinit Mountain, I watch for fires, listen to a radio powered by the ghosts of 1,000 horses, shot by the United States Cavalry a century ago, last week, yesterday. My cousins paint red tears under their horses' eyes just before they run at Playfair Race Track. Last I heard, my cousins are still waiting for any of their horses to finish, to emerge from the dust and gallop toward a new beginning.

11.

If I begin this story with the last word, the last spark of flame left from the trailer fire, will you remember everything that came before? If I show you the photograph of my sister just emerged from the sweat house, steam rising from her body like horses, a single tear tattooed under the right eye, can you pretend to miss her? If I tell you her body was found in the ash, the soft edge of the earth, will you believe she attempted escape but couldn't lift her head from the pillow? If I show you the photograph of my sister in her coffin, hair cut short by the undertaker who never knew she called her hair *Wild Ponies,* will you imagine you loved her?

12.

Imagination is the only weapon on the reservation.

13.

The reservation waits for no one. Acre by acre, it roars past history, forgiving and forgetting nothing. There are moments here which can explain your whole life. For instance, the beer can wedged between bars in the cattle guard predicts the next car wreck, but it also sounds like an ocean of betrayal if picked up and held to the ear.

14.

Listen: truth is a strange animal haunting my dreams, my waking. In the reservation Kmart, forty televisions erupt in a twentieth-century vision: 500 years of bad situation comedies. Measured by the half hour, the Indian woman with three tears tattooed under her left eye disappears into the scenery, into the crowd of another Fourth of July celebration. The soundtrack of her life whispers some kind of music, but it isn't drums because drums are never enough. Can you hear canned laughter roaring out of her horse-powered stereo on the shelf next to her life? What can I tell you about the beginning of her story that would help you imagine how much of the reservation she had tattooed across her skin?

CHAPTER 11

AGAINST THE DYING OF THE LIGHT

—Dylan Thomas

An Anthology of the Villanelle

In the early Renaissance in France and Italy, many poets began to experiment with shapes and sounds to create elaborate new forms. These poetic innovations include the **rondeau**, the **ballade**, the **pantoum**, the **villanelle**, and the **sestina**. These are all intricate, short forms, with stanzas and complicated rhyme schemes. They often employ recurring lines, called **refrains.** Of these complex forms, only the sestina and the villanelle have attracted more than a handful of poets writing in English.

The villanelle, which first appears in the late fifteenth century, is among the oddest forms. One of the first examples of the form was written by the French poet Jean Passerat (p. 837). English poets generally ignored the form until the late nineteenth century, when it was often used as a vehicle for light verse.

The form consists of six stanzas that rhyme as follows: aba aba aba aba aba abaa. The first five stanzas are three-line stanzas or triolets. The final stanza is a quatrain. The meter is usually iambic pentameter or some form of pentameter, although this may vary (Oscar Wilde, p. 838, favored a four-beat line). The first and third lines of the first stanza become, alternately, the last lines of the second, third, fourth, and fifth stanzas. These two lines become a concluding couplet in the final quatrain.

For a writer of villanelles, the challenge is to make the first and third lines of the first stanza memorable and flexible, capable of modulation, and able to stand as a "conclusion" to the poem as well. The intent is that the sense of the refrain lines will gradually change and grow over the course of the poem, as the context enlarges. Poets often vary the refrain slightly to conform to the evolving meaning of the poem. This also makes the poem less predictable.

While not as rich or elastic as the sonnet, the villanelle has nevertheless proved itself a valuable addition to English poetic forms, and it has had a lively history. Perhaps the best known villanelle in the language is by Dylan Thomas—his powerful "Do Not Go Gentle into That Good Night" (p. 842). This poem is about the impending death of the speaker's father and is addressed to him, urging him to "Rage, rage against the dying of the light." The poem is written in a muscular sprung rhythm that Thomas borrowed from Gerard Manley Hopkins, whom he admired greatly and imitated to good effect. In the manner of Hopkins, it is thick with alliteration, leaping harshly from consonant to consonant. The music of the poem is grand, sorrowful, and evocative.

One might expect a form like the villanelle to die out, given its strangely artificial texture, but the opposite seems to have happened. W.H. Auden wrote quite an attractive and clever villanelle (p. 840), as did Theodore Roethke in "The Waking" (p. 841). "One Art" by Elizabeth Bishop (p. 841) is widely judged to be one of her finest poems. As you read it, notice how Bishop keeps enlarging the sense of loss, as the thing lost by the speaker in the poem grows in significance, building to a painful, even harrowing, last line, about a lost love. A wide range of contemporary poets have been attracted to the form, and they have used it for their own purposes. The villanelle is a strange instrument, capable of unique sounds; though limited in range, it remains pliable in its own way. As a form, it repays close study.

JEAN PASSERAT (1534–1602)
trans. Jay Parini

Villanelle

I've lost her now, my turtle-dove.
How can that be her song I hear?
I'll follow after my dear love.

You miss someone you really love?
5   Ah, how I do. She's gone, I fear.
I've lost her, my own turtle-dove.

If your love's true as God above,
then so was mine. Is that now clear?
I'll follow after her, my love.

10   I've heard you sighing for your love.
My own sighs mingle with my tears.
I've lost my only turtle-dove.

So lovely was my darling dove,
none other gives me any cheer.
15   I'll follow after her, my love.

O death, if you must now reprove me,
Take me: I have lost all fear,
as I have lost my turtle-dove.
I must fly after her, my love.

OSCAR WILDE (1854–1900)

Theocritus:[1] a Villanelle   (1881)

O Singer of Persephone![2]
    In the dim meadows desolate
Dost thou remember Sicily?

Still through the ivy flits the bee
5   Where Amaryllis[3] lies in state;
O Singer of Persephone!

Simætha calls on Hecate[4]
    And hears the wild dogs at the gate;
Dost thou remember Sicily?

10 Still by the light and laughing sea
    Poor Polypheme[5] bemoans his fate:
O Singer of Persephone!

And still in boyish rivalry
    Young Daphnis[6] challenges his mate:
15 Dost thou remember Sicily?

Slim Lacon[7] keeps a goat for thee,
    For thee the jocund shepherds wait,
O Singer of Persephone!
Dost thou remember Sicily?

---

[1] **Theocritus:** Greek pastoral poet (third century B.C.).
[2] **Persephone:** The wife of Hades and queen of the underworld. She was abducted by Hades and given the seed of the Pomegranate to eat; this obliged her to stay forever in the kingdom of the dead. However, Demeter, Persephone's mother and the goddess of fertility, was so disconcerted by the disappearance of her daughter that she caused severe droughts. In the end, Persephone was allowed to spend six months of every year with her mother in the land of the living and six months with her husband Hades in the underworld. Persephone is frequently invoked in pastoral poetry, as she has come to symbolize the cyclical character of nature, where death and resurrection are complementary processes.
[3] **Amaryllis:** A conventional name in pastoral poetry. See Milton's "Lycidas" in Chapter 2.
[4] **Simætha calls on Hecate:** A reference to the treatise *Pharmakeutriai* (*The Witches*) by the Greek poet Theocritus. Hecate is the lover of a young woman, Simætha. When one day he abandons her, Simætha attempts to bring him back by the power of magic spells.
[5] **Polypheme:** I.e., Polyphemus, the Cyclops who was blinded by Odysseus. Unlike Homer, who presents Polyphemus as a ruthless monster in the *Odyssey,* Ovid, in his *Metamorphoses,* casts him in a far more congenial (and humorous) light as a singer of pastorals recounting his unrequited love for Galatea. In this villanelle, Wilde probably had in mind Ovid's Polyphemus.
[6] **Daphnis:** According to the Greek myth, the god Apollo fell madly in love with the young girl Daphnis. He pursued her relentlessly, but since she would not submit to his desires, Apollo decided to rape her. At the moment he trapped her, Daphnis prayed to the gods to save her, and as a result, she was turned into a Laurel Tree. In his grief, Apollo plucked a branch from the tree and put it on his head to wear it as a crown. The story of Daphnis and Apollo is the subject of many pastoral lyrics.
[7] **Lacon:** A shepherd in the poems of Theocritus.

EDWIN ARLINGTON ROBINSON (1869–1935)

Villanelle of Change (1891)

Since Persia fell at Marathon,[1]
    The yellow years have gathered fast:
Long centuries have come and gone.

And yet (they say) the place will don
5   A phantom fury of the past,
Since Persia fell at Marathon;

And as of old, when Helicon[2]
    Trembled and swayed with rapture vast
(Long centuries have come and gone),

10   This ancient plain, when night comes on,
    Shakes to a ghostly battle-blast,
Since Persia fell at Marathon.

But into soundless Acheron[3]
    The glory of Greek shame was cast:
15   Long centuries have come and gone,

The suns of Hellas[4] have all shone,
    The first has fallen to the last:—
Since Persia fell at Marathon,
Long centuries have come and gone.

WILLIAM EMPSON (1906–1984)

Villanelle (1935)

It is the pain, it is the pain, endures.
Your chemic beauty burned my muscles through.
Poise of my hands reminded me of yours.

---

[1] **Marathon:** In the Battle of Marathon (490 B.C.), the allied Greek forces defeated the army of the
Persian king Darius I.
[2] **Helicon:** Mount Helicon in Greece was the legendary home of the Muses.
[3] **Acheron:** The river of woe. One of the five rivers of the underworld.
[4] **Hellas:** The Greek name for Greece.

What later purge from this deep toxin cures?
5   What kindness now could the old salve renew?
It is the pain, it is the pain, endures.

The infection slept (custom or change inures)
And when pain's secondary phase was due
Poise of my hands reminded me of yours.

10   How safe I felt, whom memory assures,
Rich that your grace safely by heart I knew.
It is the pain, it is the pain, endures.

My stare drank deep beauty that still allures.
My heart pumps yet the poison draught of you.
15   Poise of my hands reminded me of yours.

You are still kind whom the same shape immures.
Kind and beyond adieu. We miss our cue.
It is the pain, it is the pain, endures.
Poise of my hands reminded me of yours.

W. H. AUDEN (1907–1973)

If I Could Tell You   (1940)

Time will say nothing but I told you so,
Time only knows the price we have to pay;
If I could tell you I would let you know.

If we should weep when clowns put on their show,
5   If we should stumble when musicians play,
Time will say nothing but I told you so.

There are no fortunes to be told, although,
Because I love you more than I can say,
If I could tell you I would let you know.

10   The winds must come from somewhere when they blow,
There must be reasons why the leaves decay;
Time will say nothing but I told you so.

Perhaps the roses really want to grow,
The vision seriously intends to stay;
15   If I could tell you I would let you know.

Suppose the lions all get up and go,
And all the brooks and soldiers run away;
Will Time say nothing but I told you so?
If I could tell you I would let you know.

THEODORE ROETHKE (1908–1963)

The Waking (1953)

I wake to sleep, and take my waking slow.
I feel my fate in what I cannot fear.
I learn by going where I have to go.

We think by feeling. What is there to know?
5   I hear my being dance from ear to ear.
I wake to sleep, and take my waking slow.

Of those so close beside me, which are you?
God bless the Ground! I shall walk softly there,
And learn by going where I have to go.

10   Light takes the Tree; but who can tell us how?
The lowly worm climbs up a winding stair;
I wake to sleep, and take my waking slow.

Great Nature has another thing to do
To you and me; so take the lively air,
15   And, lovely, learn by going where to go.

This shaking keeps me steady. I should know.
What falls away is always. And is near.
I wake to sleep, and take my waking slow.
I learn by going where I have to go.

ELIZABETH BISHOP (1911–1979)

One Art (1976)

The art of losing isn't hard to master;
so many things seem filled with the intent
to be lost that their loss is no disaster.

Lose something every day. Accept the fluster
5   of lost door keys, the hour badly spent.
The art of losing isn't hard to master.

Then practice losing farther, losing faster:
places, and names, and where it was you meant
to travel. None of these will bring disaster.

10   I lost my mother's watch. And look! my last, or
next-to-last, of three loved houses went.
The art of losing isn't hard to master.

I lost two cities, lovely ones. And, vaster,
some realms I owned, two rivers, a continent.
15   I miss them, but it wasn't a disaster.

—Even losing you (the joking voice, a gesture
I love) I shan't have lied. It's evident
the art of losing's not too hard to master
though it may look like (*Write* it!) like disaster.

DYLAN THOMAS (1914–1953)

Do Not Go Gentle into That Good Night (1952)

Do not go gentle into that good night,
Old age should burn and rave at close of day;
Rage, rage against the dying of the light.

Though wise men at their end know dark is right,
5   Because their words had forked no lightning they
Do not go gentle into that good night.

Good men, the last wave by, crying how bright
Their frail deeds might have danced in a green bay,
Rage, rage against the dying of the light.

10   Wild men who caught and sang the sun in flight,
And learn, too late, they grieved it on its way,
Do not go gentle into that good night.

Grave men, near death, who see with blinding sight
Blind eyes could blaze like meteors and be gay,
15   Rage, rage against the dying of the light.

And you, my father, there on the sad height,
Curse, bless, me now with your fierce tears, I pray.
Do not go gentle into that good night.
Rage, rage against the dying of the light.

HAYDEN CARRUTH (1921–   )

Saturday at the Border (1995)

"Form follows function follows form . . . , etc."
—DR. J. ANTHONY WADLINGTON

Here I am writing my first villanelle
At seventy-two, and feeling old and tired—
"Hey, Pops, why dontcha give us the old death knell?"—

And writing it what's more on the rim of hell
5 In blazing Arizona when all I desired
Was north and solitude and not a villanelle,

Working from memory and not remembering well
How many stanzas and in what order, wired
On Mexican coffee, seeing the death knell

10 Of sun's salvos upon these hills that yell
Bloody murder silently to the much admired
Dead-blue sky. One wonders if a villanelle

Can do the job. Granted, old men now must tell
Our young world how these bigots and these retired
15 Bankers of Arizona are ringing the death knell

For everyone, how ideologies compel
Children to violence. Artifice acquired
For its own sake is war. Frail villanelle,

Have you this power? And must I go and sell
20 Myself? "Wow," they say, and "cool"—this hired
Old poetry guy with his spaced-out death knell.

Ah, far from home and God knows not much fired
By thoughts of when he thought he was inspired,
He writes by writing what he must. Death knell
25 Is what he's found in his first villanelle.

DONALD JUSTICE (1925–2004)

In Memory of the Unknown Poet, Robert Boardman Vaughn (1987)

> But the essential advantage for a poet is not, to
> have a beautiful world with which to deal: it is
> to be able to see beneath both beauty and ugliness;
> to see the boredom, and the horror, and the glory.
> —T. S. ELIOT

It was his story. It would always be his story.
It followed him; it overtook him finally—
The boredom, and the horror, and the glory.

Probably at the end he was not yet sorry,
5   Even as the boots were brutalizing him in the alley.
It was his story. It would always be his story,

Blown on a blue horn, full of sound and fury,
But signifying, O signifying magnificently
The boredom, and the horror, and the glory.

10   I picture the snow as falling without hurry
To cover the cobbles and the toppled ashcans completely.
It was his story. It would always be his story.

Lately he had wandered between St. Mark's Place and the Bowery,[1]
Already half a spirit, mumbling and muttering sadly.
15   O the boredom, and the horror, and the glory.

All done now. But I remember the fiery
Hypnotic eye and the raised voice blazing with poetry.
It was his story and would always be his story—
The boredom, and the horror, and the glory.

---

[1] **St. Mark's Place and the Bowery:** Locations in New York City.

MAXINE KUMIN (1925–   )

The Nuns of Childhood: Two Views (1992)

1.

O where are they now, your harridan nuns
who thumped on young heads with a metal thimble
and punished with rulers your upturned palms:

three smacks for failing in long division,
5   one more to instill the meaning of *humble*.
As the twig is bent, said your harridan nuns.

Once, a visiting bishop, serene
at the close of a Mass through which he had shambled,
smiled upon you with upturned palms.

10   "Because this is my feast day," he ended,
"You may all have a free afternoon." In the scramble
of whistles and cheers one harridan nun,

fiercest of all the parochial coven,
Sister Pascala, without preamble
15   raged, "I protest!" and rapping on palms

at random, had bodily to be restrained.
O God's perfect servant is kneeling on brambles
wherever they sent her, your harridan nun,
enthroned as a symbol with upturned palms.

2.

20   O where are they now, my darling nuns
whose heads were shaved under snowy wimples,
who rustled drily inside their gowns,

disciples of Oxydol,[1] starch and bluing,
their backyard clothesline a pious example?
25   They have flapped out of sight, my darling nuns.

---

[1] **Oxydol:** A detergent brand.

Seamless as fish, made all of one skin,
their language secret, these gentle vestals
were wedded to Christ inside their gowns.

O Mother Superior Rosarine
30   on whose lap the privileged visitor lolled
—I at age four with my darling nuns,

with Sister Elizabeth, Sister Ann,
am offered to Jesus, the Jewish child-
next-door, who worships your ample black gown,

35   your eyebrows as thick as mustachioed twins,
your rimless glasses, your ring of pale gold—
who can have stolen my darling nuns?
Who rustles drily inside my gown?

SYLVIA PLATH (1932–1963)

Admonitions (before 1956)

Oh never try to knock on rotten wood
    or play another card game when you've won;
never try to know more than you should.

The magic golden apples all look good
5   although the wicked witch has poisoned one.
Oh never try to knock on rotten wood.

From here the moon seems smooth as angel-food,
    from here you can't see spots upon the sun;
never try to know more than you should.

10   The suave dissembling cobra wears a hood
    and swaggers like a proper gentleman;
oh never try to knock on rotten wood.

While angels wear a wakeful attitude
    disguise beguiles and mortal mischief's done:
15   never try to know more than you should.

For deadly secrets strike when understood
    and lucky stars all exit on the run:
never try to knock on rotten wood,
never try to know more than you should.

MARILYN HACKER (1942–   )

Villanelle: Late Summer   (1976)

I love you and it makes me rather dull
when everyone is voluble and gay.
The conversation hits a certain lull.

I moon, rattled as china in a bull
5   shop, wanting to go, wanting to stay.
I love you and it makes me rather dull.

You might think I had cotton in my skull.
And why is one in Staithes and not in Hay?[1]
The conversation hits a certain lull.

10   You took a fretful, unoriginal
and unrelaxing friend on holiday.
I love you and it makes me rather dull.

A sheepish sky, with puffs of yellow wool,
watches the tide interrogate the day.
15   The conversation hits a certain lull.

And I am grimly silent, swollen full
of unsaid things. I certainly can't say
"I love you." And it makes me rather dull.
The conversation hits a certain lull.

WENDY COPE (1945–   )

Lonely Hearts   (1997)

Can someone make my simple wish come true?
Male biker seeks female for touring fun.
Do you live in North London? Is it you?

Gay vegetarian whose friends are few,
5   I'm into music, Shakespeare and the sun.
Can someone make my simple wish come true?

---

[1] **Staithes . . . Hay:** Staithes is a town in Yorkshire, England. Hay is a town in Wales.

Executive in search of something new—
Perhaps bisexual woman, arty, young.
Do you live in North London? Is it you?

10   Successful, straight and solvent? I am too—
Attractive Jewish lady with a son.
Can someone make my simple wish come true?

I'm Libran, inexperienced and blue—
Need slim non-smoker, under twenty-one.
15   Do you live in North London? Is it you?

Please write (with photo) to Box 152
Who knows where it may lead once we've begun?
Can someone make my simple wish come true?
Do you live in North London? Is it you?

WENDY COPE (1945–   )

Reading Scheme   (1997)

Here is Peter. Here is Jane. They like fun.
Jane has a big doll. Peter has a ball.
Look, Jane, look! Look at the dog! See him run!

Here is Mummy. She has baked a bun.
5   Here is the milkman. He has come to call.
Here is Peter. Here is Jane. They like fun!

Go Peter! Go Jane! Come, milkman, come!
The milkman likes Mummy. She likes them all.
Look, Jane, look! Look at the dog! See him run!

10   Here are the curtains. They shut out the sun.
Let us peep! On tiptoe Jane! You are small!
Here is Peter. Here is Jane. They like fun!

I hear a car Jane. The milkman looks glum.
Here is Daddy in his car. Daddy is tall.
15   Look, Jane, look! Look at the dog! See him run!

Daddy looks very cross. Has he a gun?
Up milkman! Up milkman! Over the wall!
Here is Peter. Here is Jane. They like fun!
Look, Jane, look! Look at the dog! See him run!

MARILYN NELSON (1946–   )

Daughters, 1900 (1990)

Five daughters, in the slant light on the porch,
are bickering. The eldest has come home
with new truths she can hardly wait to teach.

5   She lectures them: the younger daughters search
the sky, elbow each others' ribs, and groan.
Five daughters, in the slant light on the porch

and blue-sprigged dresses, like a stand of birch
saplings whose leaves are going yellow-brown
with new truths. They can hardly wait to teach,

10   themselves, to be called "Ma'am," to march
high-heeled across the hanging bridge to town.
Five daughters. In the slant light on the porch

Pomp lowers his paper for a while, to watch
the beauties he's begotten with his Ann:
15   these new truths they can hardly wait to teach.

The eldest sniffs, "A lady doesn't scratch."
The third snorts back, "Knock, knock: nobody home."
The fourth concedes, "Well, maybe not in *church* . . ."
Five daughters in the slant light on the porch.

JAY PARINI (1948–   )

After the Terror (2003)

Everything has changed, though nothing has.
They've changed the locks on almost every door,
and windows have been bolted just in case.

It's business as usual, someone says.
5   Is anybody left to mind the store?
Everything has changed, though nothing has.

The same old buildings huddle in the haze,
with faces at the windows, floor by floor,
the windows they have bolted just in case.

10   No cause for panic, they maintain, because
the streets go places they have been before.
Everything has changed, though nothing has.

We're still a country that is ruled by laws.
The system's working, and it's quite a bore
15   that windows have been bolted just in case.

Believe in victory and all that jazz.
Believe we're better off, that less is more.
Everything has changed, though nothing has.
The windows have been bolted just in case.

JOHN YAU (1950–   )

Chinese Villanelle (1979)

I have been with you, and I have thought of you
Once the air was dry and drenched with light
I was like a lute filling the room with description

We watched glum clouds reject their shape
5   We dawdled near a fountain, and listened
I have been with you, and I have thought of you

Like a river worthy of its gown
And like a mountain worthy of its insolence . . .
Why am I like a lute left with only description

10   How does one cut an axe handle with an axe
What shall I do to tell you all my thoughts
When I have been with you, and thought of you

A pelican sits on a dam, while a duck
Folds its wings again; the song does not melt
15   I remember you looking at me without description

Perhaps a king's business is never finished,
Though "perhaps" implies a different beginning
I have been with you, and I have thought of you
Now I am a lute filled with this wandering description

MARY JO SALTER (1954–   )

Video Blues   (1999)

My husband has a crush on Myrna Loy,[1]
and likes to rent her movies, for a treat.
It makes some evenings harder to enjoy.

The list of actresses who might employ
5   him as their slave is too long to repeat.
(My husband has a crush on Myrna Loy,

Carole Lombard, Paulette Goddard, coy
Jean Arthur[2] with that voice as dry as wheat . . .)
It makes some evenings harder to enjoy.

10   Does he confess all this just to annoy
a loyal spouse? I know I can't compete.
My husband has a crush on Myrna Loy.

And can't a woman have her dreamboats? Boy,
I wouldn't say my life is incomplete,
15   but some evening I could certainly enjoy

two hours with Cary Grant[3] as *my* own toy.
I guess, though, we were destined not to meet.
My husband has a crush on Myrna Loy,
which makes some evenings harder to enjoy.

---

[1] **Myrna Loy:** A legendary Hollywood actress (1905–1993), who was oftentimes cast in the role of a dark, seductive woman. Her acting credits include *Double Wedding* (1937), *The Best Years of Our Lives* (1946), and *Mr. Blandings Builds His Dream House* (1948).
[2] **Carole Lombard . . . Jean Arthur:** Famous Hollywood actresses.
[3] **Cary Grant:** A Hollywood actor (1904–1986) born in England. Some of his acting credits include *She Done Him Wrong* (1933) and Hitchcock's *North by Northwest* (1959).

JACQUELINE OSHEROW (1955–   )

Villanelle from a Sentence in a Poet's Brief Biography (1999)

In '42 he was conscripted to work on trains.
An odd thing to mention in a poet's biography.
In '42? In Czechoslovakia? Trains?

I'm trying to figure out what this entry means,
5   If he sees himself as victimized or guilty.
In '42 he was conscripted to work on trains.

Dutch workers refused to run their trains;
They found out that work makes you free.
In '42, in Czechoslovakia, trains

10   Weren't that busy. They didn't start the deportations[1]
In earnest until 1943.
In '42 he was conscripted to work on trains

But the next line says after the war, which means
That he was still at it in '43,
15   '44, '45 . . . . In Czechoslovakia, trains

(What did he do? Run switches? Check the lines?)
Were as instrumental, let's face it, as Zyklon B.[2]
In '42 he was conscripted to work on trains.
In '42. In Czechoslovakia. Trains.

---

[1] **Deportations:** I.e., the deportations of Jews to concentration camps during World War II.
[2] **Zyklon B:** Also known as Cyclon B, a powerful fumigant that contains the lethal compound hydrocyanic acid (HCN). During World War II, the Nazis used it in gas chambers to exterminate millions of people, primarily Jews.

THE UNDECODED MESSAGES

— John Ashbery

An Anthology of the Sestina

One of the most intricate forms of poetry is the **sestina**, which has a distinguished history in English, French, and Italian poetry. The form consists of thirty-nine lines: six 6-line stanzas and a 3-line conclusion called an envoy or *envoi*. In English, these lines are often (but not always) in some form of pentameter. There are no specific rhymes in a sestina; rather, the six final words of each stanza are repeated according to a specific pattern, and so repetition takes the place of rhyme. The crucial six words must also appear in the final three lines, with two of them occurring in each line.

The pattern of the repeating words in each stanza has varied over time. In its original form, which was used by the French troubadour poets such as Arnaut Daniel (often cited as the inventor of the form), the repeating scheme goes like this: abcdef faebdc cfdabe ecbfad deacfb bdfeca. The repeating words then occurred in the middle and at the end of the lines in the final stanza, which in effect became a kind of summary of the poem. The pattern of repetition in the final 3-line stanza is as follows: bedcfa

The sestina was popular among Italian and French poets during the twelfth century, and it eventually attracted both Dante and Petrarch. The form fell out of use, but was revived in the sixteenth century in France by Pontus de Tyard and in England by Sir Philip Sidney (p. 854). The form more or less died out in English until the late nineteenth and twentieth centuries. Rudyard Kipling (p. 858) and Ezra Pound (p. 860) were modern advocates of the form, contributing memorable sestinas to the tradition. Many contemporary poets have accepted the challenge posed by this form, as shown in this chapter.

Every poetic form is a kind of instrument, representing a discreet range of tones and intellectual possibilities. The sestina, being a kind of poetic spiral, has a lovely shape, and the repeating words create their own insistent music. Key to the sestina's magic is that a poet must choose six words that work together to create an argument, even a story. The repetitious nature of the form is significant. One hears the poet-speaker sounding these words over and over, enlarging the context for these words. But to what effect? The answer will be different in each case.

Given its complex shape, the sestina attracts poets who want to structure the reality of their poem in intricate ways. Ideally, the complicated form of the poem enhances the theme; with subject and form working together, a splendidly rich and nuanced music may be produced. Certainly, some of the most beautiful and complex poems in the English language have been sestinas.

SIR PHILIP SIDNEY (1554–1586)

Sestina (1593)

Farewell, Oh sun, Arcadia's[1] clearest light;
Farewell, Oh pearl, the poor man's plenteous treasure;
Farewell, Oh golden staff, the weak man's might;
Farewell, Oh joy, the joyful's only pleasure;
5   Wisdom, farewell, the skilless man's direction;
Farewell, with thee farewell, all our affection.

For what place now is left for our affection,
Now that of purest lamp is quenched the light
Which to our dark'ned minds was best direction?
10 Now that the mine is lost of all our treasure;
Now death hath swallowed up our worldly pleasure,
We orphans made, void of all public might!

Orphans, indeed, deprived of father's might,
For he our father was in all affection,
15 In our well-doing placing all his pleasure,
Still studying how to us to be a light;
As well he was in peace a safest treasure,
In war his wit and word was our direction.

Whence, whence, alas, shall we seek our direction,
20 When that we fear our hateful neighbour's might,
Who long have gaped to get Arcadians' treasure?
Shall we now find a guide of such affection,
Who for our sakes will think all travail light,
And make his pain to keep us safe his pleasure?

---

[1] **Arcadia's:** A region in ancient Greece. Because Arcadia was relatively isolated from the rest of the known civilized world, its inhabitants led simple, pastoral lives.

25 No, no; forever gone is all our pleasure,
For ever wandering from all good direction,
For ever blinded of our clearest light,
For ever lamèd of our surèd might,
For ever banished from well placed affection,
30 For ever robbed of all our royal treasure.

Let tears for him therefore be all our treasure,
And in our wailful naming him our pleasure;
Let hating of our selves be our affection,
And unto death bend still our thought's direction;
35 Let us against our selves employ our might,
And putting out our eyes seek we our light.

Farewell, our light; farewell, our spoilèd treasure;
Farewell, our might; farewell, our daunted pleasure;
Farewell, direction; farewell, all affection.

BARNABE BARNES (1570–1609)

Sestina (1593)

Then first with locks dishevellèd and bare,
Strait girded, in a cheerful calmy night;
Having a fire made of green cypress wood,
And with male frankincense on altar kindled,
5 I call on threefold Hecate[1] with tears,
And here, with loud voice invocate the furies[2]

For their assistance: to me with their furies,
Whilst snowy steeds in coach bright Phoebe[3] bear.
Ay me, Parthenophe[4] smiles at my tears!
10 I neither take my rest by day, or night,
Her cruel loves in me such heat have kindled.
Hence, goat, and bring her to me raging wood!

---

[1] **threefold Hecate:** The Greek goddess of crossroads, usually depicted as having three heads: one of a
snake, one of a dog, and one of a horse. She is also frequently perceived as the goddess of witchcraft.
[2] **furies:** In Greek and Roman mythology, three dreadful winged goddesses (Alecto, Megaera, and
Tisiphone), who punish the doers of unavenged crimes.
[3] **Phoebe:** Refers to one of the original Titans of Greek myth, associated with the moon.
[4] **Parthenophe:** From a sequence of sonnets by Barnabe Barnes, *Parthenophe and Parthenophil*
(1592), recounting the story of Parthenophil and his mistress Parthenophe.

Hecate, tell which way she comes through the wood.
This wine about this altar, to the furies
15   I sprinkle, whiles the cypress boughs be kindled,
This brimstone earth within her bowels bare,
And this blue incense sacred to the night.
This hand, perforce, from this bay this branch tears.

So be she brought which pitied not my tears,
20   And as it burneth with the cypress wood
So burn she with desire by day and night.
You gods of vengeance, and revengeful furies,
Revenge, to whom I bend on my knees bare!
Hence, goat, and bring her with love's outrage kindled!

25   Hecate, make signs, if she with love come kindled;
Think on my passions, Hecate, and my tears.
This rosemary (whose branch she chiefly bare,
And lovèd best), I cut both bark and wood,
Broke with this brazen axe, and in love's furies,
30   I tread on it, rejoicing in this night,

And saying, 'Let her feel such wounds this night!'
About this altar, and rich incense kindled,
This lace and vervain[5] to love's bitter furies
I bind, and strow, and with sad sighs and tears
35   About I bear her image, raging wood.
Hence, goat, and bring her from her bedding bare!

Hecate, reveal if she like passions bear.
I knit three true-lover's knots (this is love's night)
Of three discoloured silks, to make her wood,
40   But she scorns Venus[6] till her loves be kindled,
And till she find the grief of sighs and tears:
Sweet Queen of Loves, for mine unpitied furies,

Alike torment her with such scalding furies!
And this turtle, when the loss she bare
45   Of her dear make, in her kind did shed tears,
And mourning did seek him all day and night:
Let such lament in her for me be kindled,
And mourn she still, till she run raging wood.

---

[5] **vervain:** Any of various New World plants with beautifully colored flowers.
[6] **Venus:** The Roman goddess of love and beauty (Aphrodite in the Greek tradition).

Hence, goat, and bring her to me raging wood!
50 These letters, and these verses to the furies,
Which she did write, all in this flame be kindled:
Me, with these papers, in vain hope she bare,
That she to day would turn mine hopeless night.
These as I rent and burn, so fury tears

55 Her hardened heart, which pitied not my tears.
The wind-shaked trees make murmur in the wood,
The waters roar at this thrice-sacred night,
The winds come whisking still to note her furies:
Trees, woods, and winds, a part in my plaints bare,
60 And knew my woes, now joy to see her kindled—

See where she comes, with loves enraged and kindled!
The pitchy clouds in drops send down their tears,
Owls scritch, dogs bark, to see her carried bare;
Wolves yowl and cry, bulls bellow through the wood,
65 Ravens croak. Now, now, I feel love's fiercest furies!
See'st thou that black goat, brought this silent night

Through empty clouds by th' daughters of the night?
See how on him she sits, with love-rage kindled,
Hither perforce brought with avengeful furies?
70 Now I wax drowsy, now cease all my tears,
Whilst I take rest and slumber near this wood:
Ah me! Parthenophe naked and bare!

Come, blessed goat, that my sweet lady bare!
Where hast thou been, Parthenophe, this night?
75 What—cold? Sleep by this fire of cypress wood
Which I much longing for thy sake have kindled.
Weep not! Come, loves, and wipe away her tears.
At length yet, wilt thou take away my furies?

Ay me, embrace me! See those ugly furies!
80 Come to my bed, lest they behold thee bare,
And bear thee hence—they will not pity tears,
And these still dwell in everlasting night.
Ah, love's sweet love sweet fires for us hath kindled,
But not inflamed with frankincense or wood.

85 The furies, they shall hence into the wood,
Whiles Cupid[7] shall make calmer his hot furies,

---

[7] **Cupid:** The Roman god of love (Eros in the Greek tradition).

And stand appeasèd at our fires kindled.
Join, join, Parthenophe! Thyself unbare,
None can perceive us in the silent night.
90   Now will I cease from sighs, laments, and tears;

And cease Parthenophe, sweet, cease thy tears.
Bear golden apples thorns in every wood,
Joy heavens, for we conjoin this heavenly night;
Let alder trees bear apricocks (die furies!),
95   And thistles pears, which prickles lately bare.
Now both in one with equal flame be kindled.

Die, magic boughs, now die, which late were kindled!
Here is mine heaven; loves drop instead of tears.
It joins! it joins! ah, both embracing bare!
100   Let nettles bring forth roses in each wood;
Last ever-verdant, woods! Hence, former furies!
Oh die, live, joy! What? Last continual, night!

Sleep Phoebus still with Thetis![8] Rule still, night!
I melt in love, love's marrow flame is kindled:
105   Here will I be confirmed in love's sweet furies.
I melt! I melt! Watch, Cupid, my love-tears:
If these be furies, oh let me be wood!
If all the fiery element I bare,

'Tis now acquitted. Cease your former tears,
110   For as she once with rage my body kindled,
So in hers am I burièd this night.

RUDYARD KIPLING (1865–1936)

Sestina of the Tramp-Royal[1]

Speakin' in general, I 'ave tried 'em all—
The 'appy roads that take you o'er the world.

---

[8] **Sleep Phoebus still with Thetis:** According to Greek mythology, Phoebus was the sun-god and Thetis, a sea-goddess. Here, the speaker pleads for the sun not to rise from its ocean bed.
[1] **Sestina . . . Royal:** Kipling wrote this poem in Cockney dialect, which typically omits the "h" sound from words.

Speakin' in general, I 'ave found them good
For such as cannot use one bed too long,
5   But must get 'ence, the same as I 'ave done,
An' go observin' matters till they die.

What do it matter where or 'ow we die,
So long as we've our 'ealth to watch it all—
The different ways that different things are done,
10   An' men an' women lovin' in this world;
Takin' our chances as they come along,
An' when they ain't, pretendin' they are good?

In cash or credit—sno, it aren't no good;
You 'ave to 'ave the 'abit or you'd die,
15   Unless you lived your life but one day long,
Nor didn't prophesy nor fret at all,
But drew your tucker some'ow from the world,
An' never bothered what you might ha' done.

But, Gawd, what things are they I 'aven't done?
20   I've turned my 'and to most, an' turned it good,
In various situations round the world—
For 'im that doth not work must surely die;
But that's no reason man should labour all
'Is life on one same shift—life's none so long.

25   Therefore, from job to job I've moved along.
Pay couldn't 'old me when my time was done,
For something in my 'ead upset it all,
Till I 'ad dropped whatever 'twas for good,
An', out at sea, be'eld the dock-lights die,
30   An' met my mate—the wind that tramps the world!

It's like a book, I think, this bloomin' world,
Which you can read and care for just so long,
But presently you feel that you will die
Unless you get the page you're readin' done,
35   An' turn another—likely not so good;
But what you're after is to turn 'em all.

Gawd bless this world! Whatever she 'ath done—
Excep' when awful long—I've found it good.
So write, before I die, " 'E liked it all!"

EZRA POUND (1885–1972)

Sestina: Altaforte (1909)

Loquitur: En *Bertrans de Born. Dante Alighieri put this man in hell*
for that he was a stirrer up of strife. Eccovi! Judge ye! Have I dug
him up again? The scene is at his castle, Altaforte. "Papiols" is his
jongleur. "The Leopard," the device *of Richard Cœur de Lion.*[1]

I

Damn it all! all this our South stinks peace.
You whoreson dog, Papiols, come! Let's to music!
I have no life save when the swords clash.
But ah! when I see the standards gold, vair,[2] purple, opposing
5   And the broad fields beneath them turn crimson,
Then howl I my heart nigh mad with rejoicing.

II

In hot summer have I great rejoicing
When the tempests kill the earth's foul peace,
And the lightnings from black heav'n flash crimson,
10   And the fierce thunders roar me their music
And the winds shriek through the clouds mad, opposing,
And through all the riven skies God's swords clash.

III

Hell grant soon we hear again the swords clash!
And the shrill neighs of destriers[3] in battle rejoicing,
15   Spiked breast to spiked breast opposing!
Better one hour's stour° than a year's peace   battle
With fat boards, bawds, wine and frail music!
Bah! there's no wine like the blood's crimson!

IV

And I love to see the sun rise blood-crimson.
20   And I watch his spears through the dark clash
And it fills all my heart with rejoicing

---

[1] **Loquitur . . . de Lion:** *Loquitur:* he speaks (Italian); *En:* Sir; Bertrans de Born: a medieval knight and troubadour, famous for his poems about war; *Eccovi:* Here you are! (Italian); *device:* heraldic emblem; Richard Cœur de Lion: King Richard the Lion Hearted (1157–1199).
[2] **vair:** Gray and white fur. In medieval Europe, it was used for trimming garments.
[3] **destriers:** War horses.

And pries wide my mouth with fast music
When I see him so scorn and defy peace,
His lone might 'gainst all darkness opposing.

V

25   The man who fears war and squats opposing
My words for stour, hath no blood of crimson
But is fit only to rot in womanish peace
Far from where worth's won and the swords clash
For the death of such sluts I go rejoicing;
30   Yea, I fill all the air with my music.

VI

Papiols, Papiols, to the music!
There's no sound like to swords swords opposing,
No cry like the battle's rejoicing
When our elbows and swords drip the crimson
35   And our charges 'gainst "The Leopard's" rush clash.
May God damn for ever all who cry "Peace!"

VII

And let the music of the swords make them crimson!
Hell grant soon we hear again the swords clash!
Hell blot black for alway the thought "Peace"!

ELIZABETH BISHOP (1911–1979)

Sestina (1965)

September rain falls on the house.
In the failing light, the old grandmother
sits in the kitchen with the child
beside the Little Marvel Stove,
5   reading the jokes from the almanac,
laughing and talking to hide her tears.

She thinks that her equinoctial[1] tears
and the rain that beats on the roof of the house

---

[1] **equinoctial:** Related to the climate of the equinoctial line (the equator), occasionally marked by
hard rain and thunderstorms.

were both foretold by the almanac,
10   but only known to a grandmother.
The iron kettle sings on the stove.
She cuts some bread and says to the child,

It's time for tea now; but the child
is watching the teakettle's small hard tears
15   dance like mad on the hot black stove,
the way the rain must dance on the house.
Tidying up, the old grandmother
hangs up the clever almanac

on its string. Birdlike, the almanac
20   hovers half open above the child,
hovers above the old grandmother
and her teacup full of dark brown tears.
She shivers and says she thinks the house
feels chilly, and puts more wood in the stove.

25   *It was to be,* says the Marvel Stove.
I know what I know, says the almanac.
With crayons the child draws a rigid house
and a winding pathway. Then the child
puts in a man with buttons like tears
30   and shows it proudly to the grandmother.

But secretly, while the grandmother
busies herself about the stove,
the little moons fall down like tears
from between the pages of the almanac
35   into the flower bed the child
has carefully placed in the front of the house.

Time to plant tears, says the almanac.
The grandmother sings to the marvellous stove
and the child draws another inscrutable house.

ANTHONY HECHT (1923–   )

The Book of Yolek (1990)

> *Wir haben ein Gesetz,*
> *Und nach dem Gesetz soll er sterben.* [1]

The dowsed coals fume and hiss after your meal
Of grilled brook trout, and you saunter off for a walk
Down the fern trail, it doesn't matter where to,
Just so you're weeks and worlds away from home,
5   And among midsummer hills have set up camp
In the deep bronze glories of declining day.

You remember, peacefully, an earlier day
In childhood, remember a quite specific meal:
A corn roast and bonfire in summer camp.
10   That summer you got lost on a Nature Walk;
More than you dared admit, you thought of home;
No one else knows where the mind wanders to.

The fifth of August, 1942.
It was morning and very hot. It was the day
15   They came at dawn with rifles to The Home
For Jewish Children, cutting short the meal
Of bread and soup, lining them up to walk
In close formation off to a special camp.

How often you have thought about that camp,
20   As though in some strange way you were driven to,
And about the children, and how they were made to walk,
Yolek who had bad lungs, who wasn't a day
Over five years old, commanded to leave his meal
And shamble between armed guards to his long home.

25   We're approaching August again. It will drive home
The regulation torments of that camp
Yolek was sent to, his small, unfinished meal,
The electric fences, the numeral tattoo,
The quite extraordinary heat of the day
30   They all were forced to take that terrible walk.

---

[1] *Wir haben . . . sterben:* "We have a law, and by the law he ought to die." From the German translation of John 19.7. The poem is based on "Yanosz Korczak's Last Walk" by Hannah Mortkowitz-Olczakowa, which recounts events surrounding the Jewish Holocaust during World War II.

Whether on a silent, solitary walk
Or among crowds, far off or safe at home,
You will remember, helplessly, that day,
And the smell of smoke, and the loudspeakers of the camp.
35   Wherever you are, Yolek will be there, too.
His unuttered name will interrupt your meal.

Prepare to receive him in your home some day.
Though they killed him in the camp they sent him to,
He will walk in as you're sitting down to a meal.

DONALD JUSTICE (1925–2004)

Sestina: Here in Katmandu[1] (1956)

We have climbed the mountain,
There's nothing more to do.
It is terrible to come down
To the valley
5   Where, amidst many flowers,
One thinks of snow,

As, formerly, amidst snow,
Climbing the mountain,
One thought of flowers,
10   Tremulous, ruddy with dew,
In the valley.
One caught their scent coming down.

It is difficult to adjust, once down,
To the absence of snow.
15   Clear days, from the valley,
One looks up at the mountain.
What else is there to do?
Prayerwheels, flowers!

Let the flowers
20   Fade, the prayerwheels run down.
What have these to do
With us who have stood atop the snow

---

[1] **Katmandu:** The capital of Nepal, a country in the eastern Himalaya mountains.

Atop the mountain,
Flags seen from the valley?

25   It might be possible to live in the valley,
To bury oneself among flowers,
If one could forget the mountain,
How, setting out before dawn,
Blinded with snow,
30   One knew what to do.

Meanwhile it is not easy here in Katmandu,
Especially when to the valley
That wind which means snow
Elsewhere, but here means flowers,
35   Comes down,
As soon it must, from the mountain.

JOHN ASHBERY (1927–   )

Farm Implements and Rutabagas[1]
in a Landscape (1970)

The first of the undecoded messages read: "Popeye[2] sits in thunder,
Unthought of. From that shoebox of an apartment,
From livid curtain's hue, a tangram[3] emerges: a country."
Meanwhile the Sea Hag was relaxing on a green couch: "How
          pleasant
5   To spend one's vacation *en la casa de Popeye,*[4] she scratched
Her cleft chin's solitary hair. She remembered spinach

And was going to ask Wimpy if he had bought any spinach.
"M'love," he intercepted, "the plains are decked out in thunder
Today, and it shall be as you wish," He scratched

---

[1] **Rutabagas:** A plant (*Brassica napus* var. *napobrassica*) with an edible root; Swedish turnip.
[2] **Popeye:** A popular cartoon character, Popeye the sailor is best known for eating spinach that endows him with superhuman strength. This comes in handy especially when he has to confront Brutus, the antagonist intent on stealing the heart of his darling, Olive Oyle. Some other cartoon characters include Wimpy, Popeye's absentminded friend; Swee'pea, the adopted baby with astonishing fighting abilities; the Sea Hag, a dreadful witch devising schemes to kill Popeye; and Alice the Goon, a hairy creature that can mumble only "Goon-talk."
[3] **tangram:** A type of Chinese puzzle consisting of a square divided into five triangles, a rhomboid and a square.
[4] ***en la casa de Popeye:*** "In Popeye's house" (Spanish).

10   The part of his head under his hat. The apartment
      Seemed to grow smaller. "But what if no pleasant
      Inspiration plunge us now to the stars? *For this is my country.*"

      Suddenly they remembered how it was cheaper in the country.
      Wimpy was thoughtfully cutting open a number 2 can of spinach
15   When the door opened and Swee'pea crept in. "How pleasant!"
      But Swee'pea looked morose. A note was pinned to his bib. "Thunder
      And tears are unavailing," it read. "Henceforth shall Popeye's
            apartment
      Be but remembered space, toxic or salubrious, whole or scratched."

      Olive came hurtling through the window; its geraniums scratched
20   Her long thigh. "I have news!" she gasped. "Popeye, forced as you
            know to flee the country
      One musty gusty evening, by the schemes of his wizened, duplicate
            father, jealous of the apartment
      And all that it contains, myself and spinach
      In particular, heaves bolts of loving thunder
      At his own astonished becoming, rupturing the pleasant

25   Arpeggio[5] of our years. No more shall pleasant
      Rays of the sun refresh your sense of growing old, nor the scratched
      Tree-trunks and mossy foliage, only immaculate darkness and
            thunder."
      She grabbed Swee'pea. "I'm taking the brat to the country."
      "But you can't do that—he hasn't even finished his spinach,"
30   Urged the Sea Hag, looking fearfully around at the apartment.

      But Olive was already out of earshot. Now the apartment
      Succumbed to a strange new hush. "Actually it's quite pleasant
      Here," thought the Sea Hag. "If this is all we need fear from spinach
      Then I don't mind so much. Perhaps we could invite Alice the
            Goon over"—she scratched
35   One dug pensively—"but Wimpy is such a country
      Bumpkin, always burping like that." Minute at first, the thunder

      Soon filled the apartment. It was domestic thunder,
      The color of spinach. Popeye chuckled and scratched
      His balls: it sure was pleasant to spend a day in the country.

---

[5] **Arpeggio:** Musical tones of a chord played in rapid succession, rather than simultaneously.

JULIA ALVAREZ (1950–   )

Bilingual Sestina (1995)

Some things I have to say aren't getting said
in this snowy, blond, blue-eyed, gum-chewing English:
dawn's early light sifting through *persianas*[1] closed
the night before by dark-skinned girls whose words
5 evoke *cama, aposento, sueños* in *nombres*[2]
from that first world I can't translate from Spanish.

Gladys, Rosario, Altagracia—the sounds of Spanish
wash over me like warm island waters as I say
your soothing names: a child again learning the *nombres*
10 of things you point to in the world before English
turned *sol, tierra, cielo, luna* to vocabulary words—
sun, earth, sky, moon. Language closed

like the touch-sensitive *morivivi*[3] whose leaves closed
when we kids poked them, astonished. Even Spanish
15 failed us back then when we saw how frail a word is
when faced with the thing it names. How saying
its name won't always summon up in Spanish or English
the full blown genie from the bottled *nombre*.

Gladys, I summon you back by saying your *nombre*.
20 Open up again the house of slatted windows closed
since childhood, where *palabras*[4] left behind for English
stand dusty and awkward in neglected Spanish.
Rosario, muse of *el patio*,[5] sing in me and through me say
that world again, begin first with those first words

25 you put in my mouth as you pointed to the world—
not Adam, not God, but a country girl numbering
the stars, the blades of grass, warming the sun by saying,
¡Qué calor![6] as you opened up the morning closed
inside the night until you sang in Spanish,
30 *Estas son las mañanitas*,[7] and listening in bed, no English

---

[1] *persianas:* Shutters (Spanish).
[2] *cama, aposento, sueños* in *nombres: Cama*: bed; *aposento*: sleep; *sueños*: dreams; *nombres*: names (Spanish).
[3] *morivivi:* I died, I lived (Spanish). A tropical plant that turns black and shrivels when touched, but revives later.
[4] *palabras:* Words (Spanish).
[5] *el patio:* Playground (Spanish).
[6] *Qué calor:* It's hot! (Spanish).
[7] *Estas son las mañanitas:* These are the morning songs (Spanish).

yet in my head to confuse me with translations, no English
doubling the world with synonyms, no dizzying array of words
—the world was simple and intact in Spanish—
luna, sol, casa, luz, flor,[8] as if the *nombres*
35   were the outer skin of things, as if words were so close
one left a mist of breath on things by saying

their names, an intimacy I now yearn for in English—
words so close to what I mean that I almost hear my Spanish
heart beating, beating inside what I say *en inglés.*

ALBERTO RÍOS (1952–)

Nani[1] (1982)

Sitting at her table, she serves
the sopa de arroz[2] to me
instinctively, and I watch her,
the absolute *mamá,* and eat words
5   I might have had to say more
out of embarrassment. To speak,
now-foreign words I used to speak,
too, dribble down her mouth as she serves
me albondigas.[3] No more
10   than a third are easy to me.
By the stove she does something with words
And looks at me only with her
back. I am full. I tell her
I taste the mint, and watch her speak
15   smiles at the stove. All my words
make her smile. Nani never serves
herself, she only watches me
with her skin, her hair. I ask for more.

I watch the *mamá* warming more
20   tortillas for me. I watch her
fingers in the flame for me.

---

[8] *luna, sol, casa, luz, flor: Luna:* moon; *sol:* sun; *casa:* house; *luz:* light; *flor:* flower (Spanish).
[1] **Nani:** Grandma (Spanish).
[2] **sopa de arroz:** Soup of rice (Spanish).
[3] **albondigas:** Meatballs (Spanish).

Near her mouth, I see a wrinkle speak
of a man whose body serves
the ants like she serves me, then more words
25   from more wrinkles about children, words
about this and that, flowing more
easily from these other mouths. Each serves
as a tremendous string around her,
holding her together. They speak
30   nani was this and that to me
and I wonder just how much of me
will die with her, what were the words
I could have been, was. Her insides speak
through a hundred wrinkles, now, more
35   than she can bear, steel around her,
shouting, then, What is this thing she serves?

She asks me if I want more.
I own no words to stop her.
Even before I speak, she serves.

DAVID WOJAHN (1953–   )

Floating Houses (1982)

The night mist leaves us yearning for a new location
to things impossibly stationary,
the way they'd once float houses
made from dismantled ships, brass and timber,
5   from Plymouth, Massachusetts, across the sound
to White Horse Beach. You were only a boy.

Years later, gazing out to the red buoys
of the harbor, you sought those houses, each the location
of your childhood's end. Jon, I make this all sound
10   too complex. Our view of time is stationary,
a long prediction of remorse. We're drinking in timber,
camping above Tucson, Arizona. Below, the houses

are vague points of light, describing a grief you've housed
since watching those buildings careen on water, a boy
15   too sullen for your father. So the aspens creak like timber
in an aging sloop. The others sleep. You locate
the figure of your son, small and stationary,
but tell me he'll die young, body unsound,

a childhood diabetic. The bourbon makes you sound

20   entranced—to think one day you'll return to the house
to find that you've outlived him, maybe the radio station
playing some popular song. Outliving the boy,
you'll outlive yourself. Drunk, we've lost our location.
I shine my flashlight to find the others. The timbre

25   of your voice grows slack. Leaves and timber
rustle in the promise of rain, in the sound
of distant thunder that, like death, has no location.
Below, relentless clouds will cover houses.
The campfire sputters, then grows, buoyed

30   by wind, our bodies the only things stationary.

Because of death, our small, unstationary
lives become narration—a child is lost in timber
in a fable when night approaches. The boy
can't even see his hands. Only owl-cry, the sound

35   of his heart. But soon the aspens part, the houses
of his village appear, their location

precise and consoling. He's stationary, not a sound
from below. Beyond the timber, floating houses.
And there his papa's lantern, a light the boy can locate.

CHAPTER 13

THE MASS AND MAJESTY OF THIS WORLD
—W. H. Auden

An Anthology of Stanzas

Poems are often divided into clusters of lines called **stanzas,** a term derived from the Italian word meaning "rooms." In this sense, a poem may be considered a house of words with many rooms. We are used to looking at a poem and seeing stanzas, which are used to divide the argument or content of the poem into dramatically useful clusters. Often a stanza will contain a single image, make a strong point, or indicate a phase of the narrative. As you read the poems in this chapter, notice how the shape of the stanza plays into the overall impression the poem makes, how its meaning is enhanced by the division into stanzas, and what it means to separate a poem into bunches of lines.

One of the most basic techniques for identifying a kind of poem is by looking at its stanza formations. The range of possibilities is vast, but there are obvious markers and easily identified stanza shapes. Some of these stanzaic arrangements, as in Spenser's "Epithalamion" (p. 877), a wedding poem, are quite complex. Others, as in the examples here from George Herbert (p. 888) and Emily Dickinson (p. 899), are relatively simple, although each poet achieves complex effects within the simple stanza format. It should be noticed that the choice of stanza form by the poet strongly contributes to the nature of the poem. Dickinson uses a form called **common measure,** a quatrain in which the length of the lines varies from four to three feet, alternately. Many church hymns follow this pattern, as do many songs. (Indeed, most of Emily Dickinson's poems can be sung to the tune of "The Yellow Rose of Texas"—or "Amazing Grace.")

The ballad stanza, of course, is famously unique, although there are many examples of stanza variation within that form. For the ode, the possibilities for stanza variation are even more striking, especially in poems (such as "Alexander's Feast" by John Dryden, p. 396) that follow in the tradition of Pindar, the Greek poet who invented a primary form of the ode. Even sonnets make heavy use of stanza formations, with the two basic forms of the sonnet falling into a two-stanza arrangement (the Italian sonnet) or a four-stanza arrangement (the Elizabethan sonnet).

In Chapter 9, we looked at heroic couplets, written in iambic pentameter and rhyming on the end-words: aa bb cc dd. These may or may not be divided into stanzas, separating the poem into two-line sections.

Usually, the couplets are not separated, and so the shape of any given stanza may be arbitrary, or the poem may not be divided into "little rooms" at all. Quite often, poets (such as Andrew Marvell in "To His Coy Mistress," p. 1559) prefer a four-beat or tetrameter line instead of the pentameter of the heroic couplet.

The three-line stanza is called a **tercet**, and it has been a fairly common form. Dante, the great Italian poet, chose this form for his epic, *The Divine Comedy,* contriving a system of interlocking rhymes called **terza rima**. In this pattern, the first and third lines of each section rhyme, while the second line rhymes with the first and third lines in the following section. The pattern goes like this: aba bcb cdc ded efe. Of course, Italian is a language rich in rhymes, so Dante was able to create a long poem with many chiming vowels. This is much harder to do in English, and so good examples of *terza rima* are very scarce. The form is really quite inappropriate in English and has attracted only poetic acrobats.

In contrast, the four-line stanza, the **quatrain**, may be considered the most common stanza shape in English verse. If the lines rhyme abab, this is called an **heroic quatrain**—an extremely common shape. The ballad stanza is a related form, although the rhyming is abcb. If the rhyming words are the middle two words and the first and fourth line, this is called **rhyme enclosure** or **brace rhyme**, with a rhyme scheme of abba. Sometimes there is a triple rhyme on the first, second, and fourth lines. The odd man out is the third line, which often starts off the rhyming in the next stanza, as in "Stopping by Woods on a Snowy Evening" by Robert Frost (p. 1587). Occasionally, one sees a double couplet, which rhymes aabb ccdd eeff.

The quintain and sextain, with five or six lines per stanza, respectively, are far less common. John Keats preferred the sextain form for his odes—see "Ode on a Grecian Urn," p. 421.) The possibility for complex rhyming patterns increases as the number of lines per stanza multiplies, and this fact has not been lost on poets, who have often reveled in the possibilities of stanza complication and patterning.

Three of the most well-known stanza patterns are **rhyme royal** (a seven-line stanza also called the *Chaucerian stanza*), **ottava rima** (an eight-line stanza known as an *octet* or an *octave*), and the **Spenserian stanza**, which consists of nine lines. Rhyme royal rhymes as follows: ababbcc. Ottava rima, which was extremely popular in Italy, rhymes as: abababcc. Edmund Spenser developed the stanza that bears his name in *The Faerie Queene* (p. 264). It consists of eight lines of iambic pentameter followed by a single hexameter line, and rhymes as follows: ababbcbcc.

There are infinite variations on all of these patterns, and poets have delighted in finding new combinations, varying the rhyme and meter, and adding an extra metrical foot here or deleting one there.

Although free verse has become the dominant form of poetry for modern and contemporary poets, stanzas continue to play a role in shaping poems. For example, Wallace Stevens's "Sunday Morning" (p. 669) uses stanzas to great effect in a poem in blank verse.

In all, poets have employed stanzas in a variety of ways to create subtle effects, to complicate meaning, and to make their poems memorable and meaningful. Readers should become familiar with some of the major shapes that stanzas can take, and note the different impressions and effects produced by these various forms. As the vast majority of poems in this book make use of stanzas, it would be impractical to list all of the other examples here.

ANONYMOUS (ca. thirteenth century)

The Singing Maid

> Now springes the spray,
> All for love I am so seek°   sick
> That slepen I ne may.
>
> Als I me rode this endre° day   entire
> 5 O' my pleyinge,°   playing
> Seih° I whar a litel° may   saw / little
> Began to singe,
> 'The clot him clinge!
> Way es him i' love-longinge
> 10 Shall libben° ay!'   live
>
> Son I herde that mirye° note,   merry
> Thider I drogh:°   drew
> I fonde hire in an herber swot°   working in a garden
> Under a bogh,°   bough
> 15 With joye inogh.°   enough
> Son I asked, 'Thou mirye may,
> Why singes tou ay?'
>
> Than answerde that maiden swote°   sweet
> Midde° wordes fewe,   middle
> 20 'My lemman° me haves bihot°   sweetheart / beheld
> Of love trewe:
> He chaunges anewe.
> Yiif° I may, it shall him rewe°   if / upset; rue
> By this day!'

JOHN LYDGATE (ca. 1370–1449)

The Duplicity of Women   (1449)

This worlde is full of variaunce°   variety
In everything, who taketh hede:°   heed
That feith and trust and all constaunce
Exiled ben, this is no drede;°   dread
5   And, save oonly in womanhede,°   womanhood
I can see no sikernesse.°   sickness/ill
But, for all that, yet, as I rede,
Bewar° alway of doublenesse.   beware

Also these freshe somer floures,°   summer flowers
10   White and rede, blew and grene,
Ben sodeinly with winter shoures
Made feint and fade, withoute wene:°   waning
That trust is noon, as ye may sene,°   sense
In nothing, nor no stedfastnesse,
15   Except in women, thus I mene.
Yet ay bewar of doublenesse.

The croked° moone—this is no tale—   crooked
Som while is shene and bright of hewe,°   hue
And, after that, ful derk and pale,
20   And every monith chaungeth newe:
That whoso the verray sothe° knewe,   the truth
Alle thinge is bilte on brotilnesse,°   fickleness
Save that women ay be trewe—
Yet ay bewar of doublenesse.

25   The see eke° with his sterne wawes   each
Eche day floweth new agein,
And by concourse of his lawes
The ebbe followeth in certein;
After gret drought ther cometh a reine,°   rain
30   That, farewell! here, all stabelnesse,
Save that women be hool° and pleine—   whole
Yet ay bewar of doublenesse.

Fortune's whele gooth° rounde about   goes
A thousande times day and night,
35   Whos course stondeth ever in doute,

For to transmewe she is so light.
For which adverteth in your sight
The untrust of worldly fikelnesse,
Save women, which of kindely right
40   Ne have no tache of doublenesse.

. . .

Wherfore, whoso hem° accuse   him
Of any double entencioun,°   intention
To speke, roune, outher to muse,
To pinche at her condicioun,°   condition
45   Alle is but fals collusioun,
I dar right welle the sothe expresse:
They have no bette proteccioun°   protection
But shroude hem under doublenesse.

. . .

Sampson had experience
50   That women weren full trew founde,
Whan Dalida,° of innocence,   Delilah
With sheres° gan his hede° to rounde.   shears / head
To speke also of Rosamounde,
And Cleopatra's[1] feithfulnesse,
55   The stories pleinly will confounde
Men that apeche° her doublenesse.   apprehend

. . .

          L'envoi.

O! ye women, which ben inclined,
By influence of youre nature,
60   To ben as pure as golde ifined,
In your trouthe for to endure
Arme yourselfe in stronge armure,
Leste men assaile youre sikernesse:
Sette on youre brest, yourself t'assure,
65   A mighty shelde of doublenesse.

---

[1] **Rosamounde . . . Cleopatra:** These were both women known for their passionate loves.

SIR EDWARD DYER   (ca. 1543–1607)

My Mind to Me a Kingdom Is   (1588)

My mind to me a kingdom is,
    Such present joys therein I find,
That it excels all other bliss
    That world affords or grows by kind.
5   Though much I want which most would have,
Yet still my mind forbids to crave.

No princely pomp, no wealthy store,
    No force to win the victory,
No wily wit to salve a sore,
10   No shape to feed a loving eye;
To none of these I yield as thrall,
For why my mind doth serve for all.

I see how plenty suffers oft,
    And hasty climbers soon do fall;
15   I see that those which are aloft
    Mishap doth threaten most of all;
They get with toil, they keep with fear:
Such cares my mind could never bear.

Content I live, this is my stay,
20   I see no more than may suffice;
I press to bear no haughty sway;
    Look, what I lack my mind supplies.
Lo! thus I triumph like a king,
Content with that my mind doth bring.

25   Some have too much, but still do crave;
    I have little, and seek no more.
They are but poor, though much they have.
    And I am rich with little store.
They poor, I rich; they beg, I give;
30   They lack, I leave; they pine, I live.

I laugh not at another's loss;
    I grudge not at another's gain;
No worldly waves my mind can toss;
    My state at one doth still remain.
35   I fear no foe, I fawn no friend;
I loathe not life, nor dread my end.

Some weigh their pleasure by their lust,
    Their wisdom by their rage of will;
Their treasure is their only trust,
40   A cloakèd craft their store of skill:
But all the pleasure that I find
Is to maintain a quiet mind.

My wealth is health and perfect ease,
    My conscience clear my choice defence;
45 I neither seek by bribes to please,
    Nor by deceit to breed offence.
Thus do I live; thus will I die;
Would all did so as well as I!

EDMUND SPENSER   (ca. 1552–1599)

Epithalamion   (1595)

Ye learned sisters which have oftentimes
Beene to me ayding, others to adorne:
Whom ye thought worthy of your gracefull rymes,
That even the greatest° did not greatly scorne   Queen Elizabeth I
5   To heare theyr names sung in your simple layes,
But joyed in theyr prayse.
And when ye list your owne mishaps to mourne,
Which death, or love, or fortunes wreck did rayse,
Your string could soone to sadder tenor turne,
10 And teach the woods and waters to lament
Your dolefull dreriment.
Now lay those sorrowfull complaints aside,
And having all your heads with girland crownd,
Helpe me mine owne loves prayses to resound,
15 Ne let the same of any be envide
So Orpheus did for his owne bride,
So I unto my selfe alone will sing,
The woods shall to me answer and my Eccho° ring.   echo

Early before the worlds light giving lampe,
20 His golden beame upon the hils doth spred,
Having disperst the nights unchearefull dampe,
Doe ye awake, and with fresh lusty hed,
Go to the bowre of my beloved love,
My truest turtle dove,

25 Bid her awake; for Hymen° is awake,   god of marriage
    And long since ready forth his maske to move,
    With his bright Tead° that flames with many a flake,   torch
    And many a bachelor to waite on him,
    In theyr fresh garments trim.
30 Bid her awake therefore and soone her dight,
    For lo the wished day is come at last,
    That shall for al the paynes and sorrowes past,
    Pay to her usury of long delight:
    And whylest she doth her dight,
35 Doe ye to her of joy and solace sing,
    That all the woods may answer and your eccho ring.

    Bring with you all the Nymphes that you can heare
    Both of the rivers and the forrests greene:
    And of the sea that neighbours to her neare,
40 Al with gay girlands goodly wel beseene.
    And let them also with them bring in hand,
    Another gay girland°   garland
    For my fayre love of lillyes and of roses,
    Bound truelove wize with a blew silke riband.
45 And let them make great store of bridale poses,
    And let them eeke bring store of other flowers
    To deck the bridale bowers.
    And let the ground whereas her foot shall tread,
    For feare the stones her tender foot should wrong
50 Be strewed with fragrant flowers all along,
    And diapred° lyke the discolored mead.   variegated
    Which done, doe at her chamber dore awayt,
    For she will waken strayt,°   straight
    The whiles doe ye this song unto her sing,
55 The woods shall to you answer and your Eccho ring.

    Ye Nymphes of Mulla[1] which with carefull head,
    The silver scaly trouts doe tend full well,
    And greedy pikes which use therein to feed,
    (Those trouts and pikes all others doo excell)
60 And ye likewise which keepe the rushy lake,
    Where none doo fishes take,
    Bynd up the locks the which hang scatterd light,
    And in his waters which your mirror make,
    Behold your faces as the christall bright,
65 That when you come whereas my love doth lie,

---

[1] **Mulla:** A stream running through Spenser's estate in Ireland.

No blemish she may spie.
And eke ye lightfoot mayds which keepe the deere,
That on the hoary mountayne use to towre,
And the wylde wolves which seeke them to devoure,
70 With your steele darts doo chace from comming neer
Be also present heere,
To helpe to decke her and to help to sing,
That all the woods may answer and your eccho ring.

Wake now, my love, awake; for it is time.
75 The Rosy Morne long since left Tithones[2] bed,
All ready to her silver coche to clyme,
And Phoebus° gins to shew his glorious hed.   sun god
Hark how the cheerefull birds do chaunt theyr laies
And carroll of loves praise.
80 The merry Larke hir mattins sings aloft,
The thrush replyes, the Mavis° descant playes,   thrush
The Ouzell° shrills, the Ruddock° warbles soft,   a water bird / robin
So goodly all agree with sweet consent,
To this dayes merriment.
85 Ah my deere love, why doe ye sleepe thus long,
When meeter were that ye should now awake,
T'awayt the comming of your joyous make,°   mate
And hearken to the birds lovelearned song,
The deawy leaves among.
90 For they of joy and pleasance to you sing,
That all the woods them answer and theyr eccho ring.

My love is now awake out of her dreame,
And her fayre eyes, like stars that dimmed were
With darksome cloud, now shew theyr goodly beams
95 More bright then Hesperus° his head doth rere.   Evening star
Come now, ye damzels, daughters of delight,
Helpe quickly her to dight,
But first come, ye fayre houres which were begot
In Joves° sweet paradice, of Day and Night,   Jove's; God's
100 Which doe the seasons of the yeare allot,
And al that ever in this world is fayre
Doe make and still repayre.
And ye three handmayds of the Cyprian Queene,[3]
The which doe still adorne her beauties pride,
105 Helpe to addorne my beautifullest bride:

---

[2] **Tithones:** Tithonus married Aurora, goddess of dawn.
[3] **three handmayds of the Cyprian Queene:** The three Graces, attendants of Venus.

And as ye her array, still throw betweene
Some graces to be seene,
And as ye use to Venus, to her sing,
The whiles the woods shal answer and your eccho ring.

110 Now is my love all ready forth to come;
Let all the virgins therefore well awayt,
And ye fresh boyes that tend upon her groome
Prepare your selves; for he is comming strayt.
Set all your things in seemely good aray
115 Fit for so joyfull day,
The joyfulst day that ever sunne did see.
Faire Sun, shew forth thy favourable ray,
And let thy lifull heat not fervent be
For feare of burning her sunshyny face,
120 Her beauty to disgrace.
O fayrest Phoebus,° father of the Muse,   Apollo
If ever I did honour thee aright,
Or sing the thing, that mote thy mind delight,
Doe not thy servants simple boone refuse,
125 But let this day, let this one day, be myne,
Let all the rest be thine.
Then I thy soverayne prayses loud wil sing,
That all the woods shal answer and theyr eccho ring.

Harke how the Minstrels gin to shrill aloud
130 Their merry Musick that resounds from far,
The pipe, the tabor, and the trembling Croud,
That well agree withouten breach or jar.
But most of all the Damzels doe delite,
When they their tymbrels smyte,
135 And thereunto doe daunce and carrol sweet,
That all the senses they doe ravish quite,
The whyles the boyes run up and downe the street,
Crying aloud with strong confused noyce,
As if it were one voyce.
140 Hymen, io, Hymen,[4] Hymen, they do shout,
That even to the heavens theyr shouting shrill
Doth reach, and all the firmament doth fill,
To which the people standing all about,
As in approvance doe thereto applaud
145 And loud advance her laud,

---

[4] **Hymen, io, Hymen:** Ritual chant at Roman weddings.

And evermore they Hymen, Hymen sing,
That al the woods them answer and theyr eccho ring.

Loe where she comes along with portly pace
Lyke Phoebe from her chamber of the East,
150 Arysing forth to run her mighty race,
Clad all in white, that seemes a virgin best.
So well it her beseemes that ye would weene
Some angell she had beene.
Her long loose yellow locks lyke golden wyre,
155 Sprinckled with perle, and perling flowres a tweene,
Doe lyke a golden mantle her attyre,
And being crowned with a girland greene,
Seeme lyke some mayden Queene.
Her modest eyes abashed to behold
160 So many gazers, as on her do stare,
Upon the lowly ground affixed are.
Ne dare lift up her countenance too bold,
But blush to heare her prayses sung so loud,
So farre from being proud.
165 Nathlesse doe ye still loud her prayses sing.
That all the woods may answer and your eccho ring.

Tell me, ye merchants daughters, did ye see
So fayre a creature in your towne before,
So sweet, so lovely, and so mild as she,
170 Adornd with beautyes grace and vertues store,
Her goodly eyes lyke Saphyres shining bright,
Her forehead yvory white,
Her cheekes lyke apples which the sun hath rudded,
Her lips lyke cherryes charming men to byte,
175 Her brest like to a bowle of creame uncrudded,
Her paps lyke lyllies budded,
Her snowie necke lyke to a marble towre,
And all her body like a pallace fayre,
Ascending uppe with many a stately stayre,
180 To honors seat and chastities sweet bowre.
Why stand ye still, ye virgins, in amaze,
Upon her so to gaze,
Whiles ye forget your former lay to sing,
To which the woods did answer and your eccho ring.

185 But if ye saw that which no eyes can see,
The inward beauty of her lively spright,
Garnisht with heavenly guifts of high degree,
Much more then would ye wonder at that sight,

And stand astonisht lyke to those which red
190 Medusaes[5] mazeful hed.
There dwels sweet love and constant chastity,
Unspotted fayth and comely womanhood,
Regard of honour and mild modesty,
There vertue raynes as Queene in royal throne,
195 And giveth lawes alone.
The which the base affections doe obay,
And yeeld theyr services unto her will,
Ne thought of thing uncomely ever may
Thereto approch to tempt her mind to ill.
200 Had ye once seene these her celestial threasures,
And unrevealed pleasures,
Then would ye wonder and her prayses sing,
That al the woods should answer and your eccho ring.

Open the temple gates unto my love,
205 Open them wide that she may enter in,
And all the postes adorne as doth behove,
And all the pillours deck with girlands trim,
For to recyve this Saynt with honour dew,
That commeth in to you.
210 With trembling steps and humble reverence,
She commeth in, before th'almighties vew,
Of her, ye virgins, learne obedience,
When so ye come into those holy places,
To humble your proud faces:
215 Bring her up to th'high altar, that she may
The sacred ceremonies there partake,
The which do endlesse matrimony make,
And let the roring Organs loudly play
The praises of the Lord in lively notes,
220 The whiles with hollow throates
The Choristers the joyous Antheme sing,
That al the woods may answer and their eccho ring.

Behold whiles she before the altar stands
Hearing the holy priest that to her speakes
225 And blesseth her with his two happy hands,
How the red roses flush up in her cheekes,
And the pure snow with goodly vermill stayne,°   red color stained
Like crimsin dyde in grayne,

---

[5] **Medusaes:** Medusa's—a monster whose hair was many snakes.

That even th'Angels which continually
230 About the sacred Altare doe remaine,
Forget their service and about her fly,
Ofte peeping in her face that seemes more fayre,
The more they on it stare.
But her sad eyes still fastened on the ground,
235 Are governed with goodly modesty,
That suffers not one looke to glaunce awry,
Which may let in a little thought unsownd.
Why blush ye, love, to give to me your hand,
The pledge of all our band?
240 Sing ye, sweet Angels, Alleluya sing,
That all the woods may answer and your eccho ring.

Now al is done; bring home the bride againe,
Bring home the triumph of our victory,
Bring home with you the glory of her gaine,
245 With joyance bring her and with jollity.
Never had man more joyfull day then this,
Whom heaven would heape with blis.
Make feast therefore now all this live long day,
This day for ever to me holy is,
250 Poure out the wine without restraint or stay,
Poure not by cups, but by the belly full,
Poure out to all that wull,
And sprinkle all the postes and wals with wine,
That they may sweat, and drunken be withall.
255 Crowne ye God Bacchus [6] with a coronall,
And Hymen also crowne with wreathes of vine,
And let the Graces [7] daunce unto the rest;
For they can doo it best:
The whiles the maydens doe theyr caroll sing,
260 To which the woods shal answer and theyr eccho ring.

Ring ye the bels, ye yong men of the towne,
And leave your wonted labors for this day:
This day is holy; doe ye write it downe,
That ye for ever it remember may.
265 This day the sunne is in his chiefest hight,
With Barnaby the bright,
From whence declining daily by degrees,

---

[6] **Bacchus:** God of wine and revelry.
[7] **the Graces:** In Greek myth, the three graces were women who represented charm, beauty, and openness.

He somewhat loseth of his heat and light,
When once the Crab behind his back he sees.[8]
270   But for this time it ill ordained was,
To chose the longest day in all the yeare,
And shortest night, when longest fitter weare:
Yet never day so long, but late would passe.
Ring ye the bels, to make it weare away,
275   And bonefiers make all day,
And daunce about them, and about them sing,
That all the woods may answer, and your eccho ring.

Ah when will this long weary day have end,
And lende me leave to come unto my love?
280   How slowly do the houres theyr numbers spend!
How slowly does sad Time his feathers move!
Hast thee, O fayrest Planet,° to thy home   the sun
Within the Westerne fome:
Thy tyred steedes long since have need of rest.
285   Long though it be, at last I see it gloome,
And the bright evening star with golden creast
Appeare out of the East.
Fayre childe of beauty, glorious lampe of love,
That all the host of heaven in rankes doost lead,
290   And guydest lovers through the nightes dread,
How chearefully thou lookest from above,
And seemst to laugh atweene thy twinkling light
As joying in the sight
Of these glad many which for joy doe sing,
295   That all the woods them answer and their eccho ring.

Now ceasse, ye damsels, your delights forepast;
Enough is it, that all the day was youres:
Now day is doen, and night is nighing fast:
Now bring the Bryde into the brydall boures.
300   Now night is come, now soone her disaray,
And in her bed her lay;
Lay her in lillies and in violets,
And silken courteins over her display,
And odourd sheetes, and Arras coverlets.
305   Behold how goodly my faire love does ly
In proud humility;

---

[8] **With Barnaby . . . he sees:** June 11 was St. Barnabas' day, the longest day of the year (according to old calendars). The sun on that day entered the sign of the Crab (Cancer).

Like unto Maia,° when as Jove her tooke,   daughter of Atlas
In Tempe, lying on the flowry gras,
Twixt sleepe and wake, after she weary was,
310   With bathing in the Acidalian brooke.°   fountain of the Graces
Now it is night, ye damsels may be gon,
And leave my love alone,
And leave likewise your former lay to sing:
The woods no more shal answere, nor your eccho ring.

315   Now welcome night, thou night so long expected,
That long daies labour doest at last defray,
And all my cares, which cruell love collected,
Hast sumd in one, and cancelled for aye:
Spread thy broad wing over my love and me,
320   That no man may us see,
And in thy sable mantle us enwrap,
From feare of perrill and foule horror free.
Let no false treason seeke us to entrap,
Nor any dread disquiet once annoy
325   The safety of our joy:
But let the night be calme and quietsome,
Without tempestuous storms or sad afray:
Lyke as when Jove with fayre Alcmena lay,
When he begot the great Tirynthian groome:[9]
330   Or lyke as when he with thy selfe did lie,
And begot Majesty.
And let the mayds and yongmen cease to sing:
Ne let the woods them answer, nor theyr eccho ring.

Let no lamenting cryes, nor dolefull teares,
335   Be heard all night within nor yet without:
Ne let false whispers, breeding hidden feares,
Breake gentle sleepe with misconceived dout.
Let no deluding dreames, nor dreadful sights
Make sudden sad affrights;
340   Ne let housefyres, nor lightnings helpelesse harmes,
Ne let the Pouke,° nor other evill sprights,   Puck, a folklore demon
Ne let mischivous witches with theyr charmes,
Ne let hob Goblins, names whose sence we see not,
Fray us with things that be not.
345   Let not the shriech Oule,° nor the Storke be heard,   owl

---

[9] **fayre Alcmena . . . groome:** Jupiter disguised himself as her husband and slept with Alcmena, begetting Hercules (who is here called "the great Tirynthian groome").

Nor the night Raven that still deadly yels,
Nor damned ghosts cald up with mighty spels,
Nor griesly vultures make us once affeard,
Ne let th'unpleasant Quyre° of Frogs still croking   choir
350   Make us to wish theyr choking.
Let none of these theyr drery accents sing;
Ne let the woods them answer, nor theyr eccho ring.

But let stil Silence trew night watches keepe,
That sacred peace may in assurance rayne,
355   And tymely sleep, when it is tyme to sleepe,
May poure his limbs forth on your pleasant playne,
The whiles an hundred little winged loves,
Like divers fethered doves,
Shall fly and flutter round about your bed,
360   And in the secret darke, that none reproves,
Their prety stealthes shal worke, and snares shal spread
To filch away sweet snatches of delight,
Conceald through covert night.
Ye sonnes of Venus, play your sports at will,
365   For greedy pleasure, carelesse of your toyes,
Thinks more upon her paradise of joyes,
Then what ye do, albe it good or ill.
All night therefore attend your merry play,
For it will soone be day:
370   Now none doth hinder you, that say or sing,
Ne will the woods now answer, nor your Eccho ring.

Who is the same, which at my window peepes?
Or whose is that faire face, that shines so bright,
Is it not Cinthia,° she that never sleepes,   Artemis, goddess of childbirth
375   But walkes about high heaven al the night?
O fayrest goddesse, do thou not envy
My love with me to spy:
For thou likewise didst love, though now unthought,
And for a fleece of woll which privily
380   The Latmian shephard° once unto thee brought,   Endymion
His pleasures with thee wrought.
Therefore to us be favorable now;
And sith of wemens labours thou hast charge,
And generation goodly dost enlarge,
385   Encline thy will t'effect our wishfull vow,
And the chast wombe informe with timely seed,
That may our comfort breed:
Till which we cease our hopefull hap to sing,
Ne let the woods us answer, nor our Eccho ring.

390 And thou, great Juno,° which with awful might   protector of marriage
   The lawes of wedlock still dost patronize,
   And the religion of the faith first plight
   With sacred rites hast taught to solemnize:
   And eeke for comfort often called art
395 Of women in their smart,
   Eternally bind thou this lovely band,
   And all thy blessings unto us impart.
   And thou, glad Genius,° in whose gentle hand   spirit of fertility
   The bridale bowre and geniall bed remaine,
400 Without blemish or staine,
   And the sweet pleasures of theyr loves delight
   With secret ayde doest succour and supply,
   Till they bring forth the fruitfull progeny,
   Send us the timely fruit of this same night.
405 And thou, fayre Hebe,° and thou, Hymen free,   handmaid of the gods
   Grant that it may so be.
   Til which we cease your further prayse to sing,
   Ne any woods shal answer, nor your Eccho ring.

   And ye high heavens, the temple of the gods,
410 In which a thousand torches flaming bright
   Doe burne, that to us wretched earthly clods
   In dreadful darknesse lend desired light;
   And all ye powers which in the same remayne,
   More then we men can fayne,
415 Poure out your blessing on us plentiously
   And happy influence upon us raine,
   That we may raise a large posterity,
   Which from the earth, which they may long possesse,
   With lasting happinesse,
420 Up to your haughty pallaces may mount,
   And for the guerdon of theyr glorious merit
   May heavenly tabernacles there inherit,
   Of blessed Saints for to increase the count.
   So let us rest, sweet love, in hope of this,
425 And cease till then our tymely joyes to sing,
   The woods no more us answer, nor our eccho ring.

   Song, made in lieu of many ornaments,
   With which my love should duly have bene dect,
   Which cutting off through hasty accidents,
430 Ye would not stay your dew time to expect,
   But promist both to recompens,
   Be unto her a goodly ornament,
   And for short time an endlesse moniment.

JOHN DONNE (1572–1631)

The Good Morrow (1633)

I wonder by my troth,° what thou and I   pledge
    Did, till we loved? Were we not weaned till then,
But sucked on country pleasures, childishly?
    Or snorted we in the seven sleepers' den?[1]
5   'Twas so; but this, all pleasures fancies be.
If ever any beauty I did see,
Which I desired, and got, 'twas but a dream of thee.

And now good morrow to our waking souls,
    Which watch not one another out of fear;
10   For love, all love of other sights controls,
    And makes one little room, an every where.
Let sea-discoverers to new worlds have gone,
Let maps to others, worlds on worlds have shown:
Let us possess one world, each hath one, and is one.

15   My face in thine eye, thine in mine appears,
    And true plain hearts do in the faces rest:
Where can we find two better hemispheres
    Without sharp north, without declining west?
Whatever dies, was not mixed equally;
20   If our two loves be one, or, thou and I
Love so alike that none do slacken, none can die.

GEORGE HERBERT (1593–1633)

Artillery (1633)

As I one evening sat before my cell,
Methought° a star did shoot into my lap.   I thought
I rose and shook my clothes, as knowing well
That from small fires comes oft no small mishap;
5   When suddenly I heard one say,
    "Do as thou usest, disobey,
    Expel good motions from thy breast,
Which have the face of fire, but end in rest."

---

[1] **seven sleepers' den:** Refers to seven young Christians from Ephesus who escaped persecution by going into a cave, where they slept safely for two hundred years.

I, who had heard of music in the spheres,
10   But not of speech in stars, began to muse;
But turning to my God, whose ministers
The stars and all things are: "If I refuse,
        Dread Lord," said I, "so oft my good,
        Then I refuse not ev'n with blood
15   To wash away my stubborn thought;
For I will do or suffer what I ought.

"But I have also stars and shooters too,
Born where thy servants both artilleries use.
My tears and prayers night and day do woo
20   And work up to thee; yet thou dost refuse.
        Not but I am (I must say still)
        Much more obliged to do thy will
        Than thou to grant mine; but because
Thy promise now hath ev'n set thee thy laws.

25   "Then we are shooters both, and thou dost deign°   dare
To enter combat with us, and contest
With thine own clay. But I would parley fain:°   willingly suggest
Shun not my arrows, and behold my breast.
        Yet if thou shunnest, I am thine:
30   I must be so, if I am mine.
        There is no articling° with thee: arguing
I am but finite, yet thine infinitely."

HENRY VAUGHAN (1622–1695)

They Are All Gone into the World of Light (1655)

They are all gone into the world of light!
    And I alone sit ling'ring here;
Their very memory is fair and bright,
    And my sad thoughts doth clear.

5   It glows and glitters in my cloudy breast
    Like stars upon some gloomy grove,
Or those faint beams in which this hill is dressed,
    After the sun's remove.

I see them walking in an air of glory,
10   Whose light doth trample on my days:
My days, which are at best but dull and hoary,
    Mere glimmering and decays.

O holy hope! and high humility,
  High as the heavens above!
15 These are your walks, and you have showed them me
    To kindle my cold love.

Dear, beauteous death! the jewel of the just,
  Shining nowhere but in the dark;
What mysteries do lie beyond thy dust,
20   Could man outlook that mark?

He that hath found some fledged bird's nest may know
  At first sight, if the bird be flown;
But what fair well or grove he sings in now,
    That is to him unknown.

25 And yet, as angels in some brighter dreams
  Call to the soul when man doth sleep:
So some strange thoughts transcend our wonted themes,
    And into glory peep.

If a star were confined into a tomb
30   Her captive flames must needs burn there;
But when the hand that locked her up gives room,
    She'll shine through all the sphere.

O Father of eternal life, and all
  Created glories under thee!
35 Resume thy spirit from this world of thrall
    Into true liberty.

Either disperse these mists, which blot and fill
  My perspective (still) as they pass,
Or else remove me hence unto that hill
40   Where I shall need no glass.

THOMAS TRAHERNE (ca. 1637–1674)

Wonder (ca. 1665; 1903)

How like an angel came I down!
  How bright are all things here!
When first among his works I did appear
  Oh, how their glory me did crown!
5 The world resembled his eternity,

In which my soul did walk;
And everything that I did see
Did with me talk.

The skies in their magnificence,
10   The lively, lovely air,
Oh, how divine, how soft, how sweet, how fair!
The stars did entertain my sense,
And all the works of God, so bright and pure,
So rich and great did seem,
15   As if they ever must endure
In my esteem.

A native health and innocence
Within my bones did grow;
And while my God did all his glories show,
20   I felt a vigor in my sense
That was all Spirit. I within did flow
With seas of life, like wine;
I nothing in the world did know
But° 'twas divine.   except that

25   Harsh ragged objects were concealed;
Oppressions, tears, and cries,
Sins, griefs, complaints, dissensions, weeping eyes
Were hid, and only things revealed
Which heavenly spirits and the angels prize.
30   The state of innocence
And bliss, not trades° and poverties,   commerce
Did fill my sense.

The streets were paved with golden stones,
The boys and girls were mine,
35 Oh, how did all their lovely faces shine!
The sons of men were holy ones,
In joy and beauty they appeared to me,
And everything I found,
While like an angel I did see,
40   Adorned the ground.

Rich diamond and pearl and gold
In every place was seen;
Rare splendors, yellow, blue, red, white, and green,
Mine eyes did everywhere behold.
45 Great wonders clothed with glory did appear,
Amazement was my bliss,

That and my wealth met everywhere;
    No joy to this!

    Cursed and devised proprieties,°   *polite customs*
50   With envy, avarice,
And fraud, those fiends that spoil even paradise,
    Flew from the splendor of mine eyes;
And so did hedges, ditches, limits, bounds:
    I dreamed not aught of those,
55   But wandered over all men's grounds,
        And found repose.

    Proprieties themselves were mine,
        And hedges ornaments;
Walls, boxes, coffers, and their rich contents
60   To make me rich combine.
Clothes, ribbons, jewels, laces, I esteemed
        My joys by others worn:
For me they all to wear them seemed
        When I was born.

APHRA BEHN (ca. 1640–1689)

The Disappointment[1] (1680)

I

One day the amorous *Lysander,*[2]
By an impatient passion swayed,
Surprised fair *Cloris,* that loved maid,
Who could defend her self no longer
5   All things did with his love conspire;
The gilded planet of the day,[3]
In his gay chariot drawn by fire,
Was now descending to the sea,
And left no light to guide the world,
10   But what from *Cloris'* brighter eyes was hurled.

---

[1] **The Disappointment:** Behn's poem on impotence was not uncommon; both George Etherege and the Earl of Rochester, Behn's contemporaries, wrote poems with a similar topic. Even Ovid addresses sexual disfunction in his *Amores.*
[2] **Lysander:** Lysander and Cloris were traditional names for lovers in pastoral poetry.
[3] **The gilded . . . day:** Reference to the sun. In Greek mythology, the sun was Apollo's chariot, flown across the sky each day.

II

In a lone thicket made for love,
Silent as yielding maids' consent,
She with a charming languishment,
Permits his force, yet gently strove;°   strained
15 Her hands his bosom softly meet,
But not to put him back designed,
Rather to draw 'em on inclined;
Whilst he lay trembling at her feet,
Resistance 'tis in vain to show;
20 She wants° the power to say—*Ah! What d'ye do?*   lacks

III

Her bright eyes sweet, and yet severe,
Where love and shame confusedly strive,
Fresh vigor to *Lysander* give;
And breathing faintly in his ear,
25 She cried—*Cease, cease—your vain desire,*
Or I'll call out—What would you do?
My dearer honor ev'n to you
I cannot, must not give—retire,
Or take this life, whose chiefest part
30 *I gave you with the conquest of my heart.*

IV

But he as much unused to fear,
As he was capable of love,
The blessed minutes to improve,
Kisses her mouth, her neck, her hair;
35 Each touch her new desire alarms,
His burning trembling hand he prest
Upon her swelling snowy brest,
While she lay panting in his arms.
All her unguarded beauties lie
40 The spoils and trophies of the enemy.

V

And now without respect or fear,
He seeks the object of his vows,
(His love no modesty allows)
By swift degrees advancing—where
45 His daring hand that altar seized,
Where gods of love do sacrifice:
That awful° throne, that paradise   awe-inspiring
Where rage is calmed, and anger pleased;

That fountain where delight still flows,
50   And gives the universal world repose.

VI

Her balmy lips incountring° his,   encountering
Their bodies, as their souls, are joyned;
Where both in transports unconfined
Extend themselves upon the moss.
55   *Cloris* half dead and breathless lay;
Her soft eyes cast a humid light,
Such as divides the day and night;
Or falling stars, whose fires decay:
And now no signs of life she shows,
60   But what in short-breathed sighs returns and goes.

VII

He saw how at her length she lay;
He saw her rising bosom bare;
Her loose thin robes, through which appear
A shape designed for love and play;
65   Abandoned by her pride and shame,
She does her softest joys dispense,
Off'ring her virgin-innocence
A victim to loves sacred flame;
While the o'er-ravished shepherd lies
70   Unable to perform the sacrifice.

VIII

Ready to taste a thousand joys,
The too transported hapless swain°   lover
Found the vast pleasure turned to pain;
Pleasure which too much love destroys:
75   The willing garments by he laid,
And heaven all opened to his view,
Mad to possess, himself he threw
On the defenseless lovely maid.
But Oh what envying gods conspire
80   To snatch his power, yet leave him the desire!

IX

Nature's support, (without whose aid
She can no human being give)
It self now wants the art to live;
Faintness its slackened nerves invade:
85   In vain th' enragèd youth essayed°   tried

To call its fleeting vigor back,
No motion 'twill from motion take;
Excess of love his love betrayed;
In vain he toils, in vain commands;
90   The insensible fell weeping in his hand.

                          X

In this so amorous cruel strife,
Where love and fate were too severe,
The poor *Lysander* in despair
Renounced his reason with his life:
95   Now all the brisk and active fire
That should the nobler part inflame,
Served to increase his rage and shame,
And left no spark for new desire:
Not all her naked charms could move
100   Or calm that rage that had debauched his love.

                          XI

Cloris returning from the trance
Which love and soft desire had bred,
Her timorous hand she gently laid
(Or° guided by design or chance)   whether
105   Upon that Fabulous *Priapus*,[4]
That potent god, as poets feign;
But never did young shephedess,
Gath'ring of fern upon the plain,
More nimbly draw her fingers back,
110   Finding beneath the verdant leaves a snake;

                          XII

Than *Cloris* her fair hand withdrew,
Finding that god of her desires
Disarmed of all his awful fires,
And cold as flowers bathed in the morning dew.
115   Who can the Nymph's confusion guess?
The blood forsook the hinder place,
And strewed with blushes all her face,
Which both disdain and shame exprest:
And from *Lysander's* arms she fled,
120   Leaving him fainting on the gloomy bed.

---

[4] **Priapus:** God of male fertility, used here as an expression for penis.

XIII

Like lightning through the grove she hies,
Or *Daphne* from the *Delphick God,*[5]
No print upon the grassy road
She leaves, t' instruct pursuing eyes.
125   The wind that wantoned in her hair,
And with her ruffled garments played,
Discovered in the flying maid
All that the gods e'er made, if fair.
So *Venus,* when her love was slain,
130   With fear and haste flew o'er the fatal plain.[6]

XIV

The Nymph's resentments none but I
Can well imagine or condole:
But none can guess *Lysander's* soul,
But those who swayed his destiny.
135   His silent griefs swell up to storms,
And not one god his fury spares;
He cursed his birth, his fate, his stars;
But more the shepherdess's charms,
Whose soft bewitching influence
140   Had damn'd him to the hell of impotence.

WILLIAM WORDSWORTH (1770–1850)

"Strange fits of passion I have known" (1800)

Strange fits of passion I have known,
And I will dare to tell,
But in the lover's ear alone,
What once to me befel.

5   When she I lov'd, was strong and gay
And like a rose in June,
I to her cottage bent my way,
Beneath the evening moon.

---

[5] **Daphne . . . God:** In Greek mythology, the nymph Daphne escaped the advances of Apollo.
[6] **So Venus . . . plain:** Adonis, the lover of Venus, was killed by a wild boar. Although Venus rushed to his aid, she was unable to prevent his death.

Upon the moon I fix'd my eye,
10   All over the wide lea;
My horse trudg'd on, and we drew nigh
Those paths so dear to me.

And now we reach'd the orchard plot,
And, as we climb'd the hill,
15   Towards the roof of Lucy's cot
The moon descended still.

In one of those sweet dreams I slept,
Kind Nature's gentlest boon!
And, all the while, my eyes I kept
20   On the descending moon.

My horse mov'd on; hoof after hoof
·   He rais'd and never stopp'd:
When down behind the cottage roof
At once the planet dropp'd.

25   What fond and wayward thoughts will slide
Into a Lover's head—
'O mercy!' to myself I cried,
'If Lucy should be dead!'

OLIVER WENDELL HOLMES (1809–1894)

The Chambered Nautilus[1]   (1858)

This is the ship of pearl, which, poets feign,
          Sails the unshadowed main,
          The venturous bark that flings
On the sweet summer wind its purpled wings
5   In gulfs enchanted, where the Siren[2] sings,
          And coral reefs lie bare,
Where the cold sea-maids rise to sun their streaming hair.

Its webs of living gauze no more unfurl;
          Wrecked is the ship of pearl!

---

[1] **Nautilus:** The chambered or pearly nautilus is a member of the cephalopod class of mollusks.
[2] **Siren:** The beautiful Sirens sang to Odysseus, tempting him to hurl himself overboard; he put wax into his ears and tied himself to the mast so he would not abandon ship.

10   And every chambered cell,
Where its dim dreaming life was wont to dwell,
As the frail tenant shaped his growing shell,
        Before thee lies revealed,
Its irised ceiling rent, its sunless crypt unsealed!

15   Year after year beheld the silent toil
        That spread his lustrous coil;
        Still, as the spiral grew,
He left the past year's dwelling for the new,
Stole with soft step its shining archway through,
20   Built up its idle door,
Stretched in his last-found home, and knew the old no more.

Thanks for the heavenly message brought by thee,
        Child of the wandering sea,
        Cast from her lap, forlorn!
25   From thy dead lips a clearer note is born
Than ever Triton[3] blew from wreathéd horn!
        While on mine ear it rings,
Through the deep caves of thought I hear a voice that sings:

Build thee more stately mansions, O my soul,
30   As the swift seasons roll!
        Leave thy low-vaulted past!
Let each new temple, nobler than the last,
Shut thee from heaven with a dome more vast,
        Till thou at length art free,
35   Leaving thine outgrown shell by life's unresting sea!

MATTHEW ARNOLD (1822–1888)

The Scholar Gipsy (1853)

Go, for they call you, shepherd, from the hill;
    Go, shepherd, and untie the wattled cotes!
      No longer leave thy wistful flock unfed,
    Nor let thy bawling fellows rack their throats,
5   Nor the cropped herbage shoot another head.
      But when the fields are still,

---

[3] **Triton:** A sea god, son of Poseidon.

And the tired men and dogs all gone to rest,
   And only the white sheep are sometimes seen
   Cross and recross the strips of moon-blanched green,
10   Come, shepherd, and again begin the quest!

Here, where the reaper was at work of late—
   In this high field's dark corner, where he leaves
     His coat, his basket, and his earthen cruse,
   And in the sun all morning binds the sheaves,
15   Then here, at noon, comes back his stores to use—
      Here will I sit and wait,
   While to my ear from uplands far away
     The bleating of the folded flocks is borne,
     With distant cries of reapers in the corn—
20   All the live murmur of a summer's day.

Screened is this nook o'er the high, half-reaped field,
   And here till sun-down, shepherd! will I be.
     Through the thick corn the scarlet poppies peep,
   And round green roots and yellowing stalks I see
25   Pale pink convolvulus in tendrils creep;
      And air-swept lindens yield
   Their scent, and rustle down their perfumed showers
     Of bloom on the bent grass where I am laid,
     And bower me from the August sun with shade;
30   And the eye travels down to Oxford's towers.

EMILY DICKINSON (1830–1886)

"My Life had stood—a Loaded Gun—" (ca. 1863; 1929)

My Life had stood—a Loaded Gun—
In Corners—till a Day
The Owner passed—identified—
And carried Me away—

5   And now We roam in Sovereign Woods—
And now We hunt the Doe—
And every time I speak for Him—
The Mountains straight reply—

And do I smile, such cordial light
10   Upon the Valley glow—

It is as a Vesuvian face[1]
Had let its pleasure through—

And when at Night—Our good Day done—
I guard My Master's Head—
15   'Tis better than the Eider-Duck's
Deep Pillow—to have shared—

To foe of His—I'm deadly foe—
None stir the second time—
On whom I lay a Yellow Eye—
20   Or an emphatic Thumb—

Though I than He—may longer live
He longer must—then I—
For I have but the power to kill,
Without—the power to die—

WILLIAM BUTLER YEATS (1865–1939)

Among School Children (1927)

I

I walk through the long schoolroom questioning;
A kind old nun in a white hood replies;
The children learn to cipher and to sing,
To study reading books and histories,
5   To cut and sew, be neat in everything
In the best modern way—the children's eyes
In momentary wonder stare upon
A sixty-year-old smiling public man.

II

I dream of a Ledaean[1] body, bent
10   Above a sinking fire, a tale that she
Told of a harsh reproof, or trivial event
That changed some childish day to tragedy—
Told, and it seemed that our two natures blent

---

[1] **Vesuvian face:** A face like Mount Vesuvius in Italy—a famous volcano.
[1] **Ledaean:** As in Leda, a figure from classical mythology who was raped by Zeus who had taken the form of a swan. She was the mother of Helen of Troy.

Into a sphere from youthful sympathy,
15 Or else, to alter Plato's parable,[2]
Into the yolk and white of the one shell.

III

And thinking of that fit of grief or rage
I look upon one child or t'other there
And wonder if she stood so at that age—
20 For even daughters of the swan can share
Something of every paddler's heritage—
And had that colour upon cheek or hair,
And thereupon my heart is driven wild:
She stands before me as a living child.

IV

25 Her present image floats into the mind—
Did Quattrocento[3] finger fashion it
Hollow of cheek as though it drank the wind
And took a mess of shadows for its meat?
And I though never of Ledaean kind
30 Had pretty plumage once—enough of that,
Better to smile on all that smile, and show
There is a comfortable kind of old scarecrow.

V

What youthful mother, a shape upon her lap
Honey of generation had betrayed,
35 And that must sleep, shriek, struggle to escape
As recollection or the drug decide,
Would think her son, did she but see that shape
With sixty or more winters on its head,
A compensation for the pang of his birth,
40 Or the uncertainty of his setting forth?

VI

Plato thought nature but a spume that plays
Upon a ghostly paradigm of things;
Solider Aristotle played the taws
Upon the bottom of a king of kings;[4]

---

[2] **Plato's parable:** In *The Symposium*, Plato puts forward a parable about the origins of sexual desire. Heterosexual lovers, according to this myth, were originally part of a race of hermaphroditic creatures who were split in two; hence, they search the globe in pursuit of their lost other half.
[3] **Quattrocento:** Painters of the Renaissance or fourteenth century in Italy.
[4] **king of kings:** Refers to Alexander the Great, who was tutored by Aristotle as a child.

45   World-famous golden-thighed Pythagoras[5]
     Fingered upon a fiddle-stick or strings
     What a star sang and careless Muses heard:
     Old clothes upon old sticks to scare a bird.

                              VII

     Both nuns and mothers worship images,
50   But those the candles light are not as those
     That animate a mother's reveries,
     But keep a marble or a bronze repose.
     And yet they too break hearts—O Presences
     That passion, piety or affection knows,
55   And that all heavenly glory symbolise—
     O self-born mockers of man's enterprise;

                             VIII

     Labour is blossoming or dancing where
     The body is not bruised to pleasure soul,
     Nor beauty born out of its own despair,
60   Nor blear-eyed wisdom out of midnight oil.
     O chestnut-tree, great rooted blossomer,
     Are you the leaf, the blossom or the bole?
     O body swayed to music, O brightening glance,
     How can we know the dancer from the dance?

EDWIN ARLINGTON ROBINSON (1869–1935)

Mr. Flood's Party (1920)

     Old Eben Flood, climbing alone one night
     Over the hill between the town below
     And the forsaken upland hermitage
     That held as much as he should ever know
5   On earth again of home, paused warily.
     The road was his with not a native near;
     And Eben, having leisure, said aloud,
     For no man else in Tilbury Town to hear:

     "Well, Mr. Flood, we have the harvest moon
10   Again, and we may not have many more;

---

[5] **Pythagoras:** Early Greek philosopher and mathematician. He developed a music scale.

The bird is on the wing, the poet says,[1]
And you and I have said it here before.
Drink to the bird." He raised up to the light
The jug that he had gone so far to fill,
15   And answered huskily: "Well, Mr. Flood,
Since you propose it, I believe I will."

Alone, as if enduring to the end
A valiant armor of scarred hopes outworn,
He stood there in the middle of the road
20   Like Roland's ghost [2] winding a silent horn.
Below him, in the town among the trees,
Where friends of other days had honored him,
A phantom salutation of the dead
Rang thinly till old Eben's eyes were dim.

25   Then, as a mother lays her sleeping child
Down tenderly, fearing it may awake,
He set the jug down slowly at his feet
With trembling care, knowing that most things break;
And only when assured that on firm earth
30   It stood, as the uncertain lives of men
Assuredly did not, he paced away,
And with his hand extended paused again:

"Well, Mr. Flood, we have not met like this
In a long time; and many a change has come
35   To both of us, I fear, since last it was
We had a drop together. Welcome home!"
Convivially returning with himself,
Again he raised the jug up to the light;
And with an acquiescent quaver said:
40   "Well, Mr. Flood, if you insist, I might.

"Only a very little, Mr. Flood—
For auld lang syne.[3] No more, sir; that will do."
So, for the time, apparently it did,
And Eben evidently thought so too;
45   For soon amid the silver loneliness

---

[1] **The bird . . . says:** Paraphrase from *The Rubáiyát* of Omar Khayyám, translated by the poet Edward FitzGerald (1809–1883).
[2] **Roland's ghost:** Roland sounded his horn before dying in the medieval French poem *Song of Roland* (ca. 1000).
[3] **auld lang syne:** Scottish: "old long since." The title and refrain of a nostalgic song penned by Scottish poet Robert Burns (1759–1796).

Of night he lifted up his voice and sang,
Secure, with only two moons listening,
Until the whole harmonious landscape rang—

"For auld lang syne." The weary throat gave out,
50   The last word wavered, and the song was done.
He raised again the jug regretfully
And shook his head, and was again alone.
There was not much that was ahead of him,
And there was nothing in the town below—
55   Where strangers would have shut the many doors
That many friends had opened long ago.

ROBERT GRAVES (1895–1985)

To Juan at the Winter Solstice   (1945)

There is one story and one story only
That will prove worth your telling,
Whether as learned bard or gifted child;
To it all lines or lesser gauds belong
5   That startle with their shining
Such common stories as they stray into.

Is it of trees you tell, their months and virtues,
Or strange beasts that beset you,
Of birds that croak at you the Triple° will?   three-headed goddess
10   Or of the Zodiac and how slow it turns
Below the Boreal Crown,
Prison of all true kings that ever reigned?[1]

Water to water, ark again to ark,
From woman back to woman:
15   So each new victim treads unfalteringly
The never altered circuit of his fate,
Bringing twelve peers as witness
Both to his starry rise and starry fall.

---

[1] For a thorough understanding of these references, it would help to look at *The White Goddess* (1948),
a handbook of Graves's private mythology. Graves believed strongly in the idea of a female muse.

Or is it of the Virgin's silvery beauty,
20   All fish below the thighs?
She in her left hand bears a leafy quince;
When, with her right she crooks a finger, smiling,
How may the King hold back?
Royally then he barters life for love.

25   Or of the undying snake from chaos hatched,
Whose coils contain the ocean,
Into whose chops with naked sword he springs,
Then in black water, tangled by the reeds,
Battles three days and nights,
30   To be spewed up beside her scalloped shore?

Much snow is falling, winds roar hollowly,
The owl hoots from the elder,
Fear in your heart cries to the loving-cup:
Sorrow to sorrow as the sparks fly upward.
35   The log groans and confesses:
There is one story and one story only.

Dwell on her graciousness, dwell on her smiling,
Do not forget what flowers
The great boar trampled down in ivy time.
40   Her brow was creamy as the crested wave,
Her sea-blue eyes were wild
But nothing promised that is not performed.

HART CRANE   (1899–1932)

from Voyages   (1926)

I.

Above the fresh ruffles of the surf
Bright striped urchins flay each other with sand.
They have contrived a conquest for shell shucks,
And their fingers crumble fragments of baked weed
5   Gaily digging and scattering.

And in answer to their treble interjections
The sun beats lightning on the waves,
The waves fold thunder on the sand;
And could they hear me I would tell them:

10 O brilliant kids, frisk with your dog,
    Fondle your shells and sticks, bleached
    By time and the elements; but there is a line
    You must not cross nor ever trust beyond it
    Spry cordage of your bodies to caresses
15 Too lichen-faithful from too wide a breast.
    The bottom of the sea is cruel.

II.

    —And yet this great wink of eternity,
    Of rimless floods, unfettered leewardings,°   movement away from the wind
    Samite° sheeted and processioned where   a richly woven fabric
20 Her undinal° vast belly moonward bends,   like water nymphs or undines
    Laughing the wrapt inflections of our love;

    Take this Sea, whose diapason knells
    On scrolls of silver snowy sentences,
    The sceptred terror of whose sessions rends
25 As her demeanors motion well or ill,
    All but the pieties of lovers' hands.

    And onward, as bells off San Salvador
    Salute the crocus lustres of the stars,
    In these poinsettia meadows of her tides,—
30 Adagios° of islands,[1] O my Prodigal,   slow movements in music
    Complete the dark confessions her veins spell.

    Mark how her turning shoulders wind the hours,
    And hasten while her penniless rich palms
    Pass superscription of bent foam and wave,—
35 Hasten, while they are true, — sleep, death, desire,
    Close round one instant in one floating flower.

    Bind us in time, O Seasons clear, and awe.
    O minstrel galleons of Carib fire,
    Bequeath us to no earthly shore until
40 Is answered in the vortex of our grave
    The seal's wide spindrift gaze toward paradise.

---

[1] Crane's note on "adagios of islands": "when . . . I speak of 'adagios of islands,' the reference is to the motion of a boat through islands clustered thickly, the rhythm of the motion, etc."

PATRICK KAVANAGH   (1904–1967)

To the Man After the Harrow   (1942)

Now leave the check-reins slack,
The seed is flying far today—
The seed like stars against the black
Eternity of April clay.

5   This seed is potent as the seed
Of knowledge in the Hebrew Book,
So drive your horses in the creed
Of God the Father as a stook.°   haystack; a stubble

Forget the men on Brady's Hill.
10   Forget what Brady's boy may say.
For destiny will not fulfil
Unless you let the harrow play.

Forget the worm's opinion too
Of hooves and pointed harrow-pins,
15   For you are driving your horses through
The mist where Genesis begins.

W. H. AUDEN   (1907–1973)

The Shield of Achilles   (1952)

She looked over his shoulder
   For vines and olive trees,
Marble well-governed cities
   And ships upon untamed seas,
5   But there on the shining metal
   His hands had put instead
An artificial wilderness
   And a sky like lead.

A plain without a feature, bare and brown,
10   No blade of grass, no sign of neighborhood,
Nothing to eat and nowhere to sit down,
   Yet, congregated on its blankness, stood
   An unintelligible multitude,

A million eyes, a million boots in line,
15 Without expression, waiting for a sign.

Out of the air a voice without a face
    Proved by statistics that some cause was just
In tones as dry and level as the place:
    No one was cheered and nothing was discussed;
20   Column by column in a cloud of dust
They marched away enduring a belief
Whose logic brought them, somewhere else, to grief.

        She looked over his shoulder
            For ritual pieties,
25   White flower-garlanded heifers,
            Libation and sacrifice,
        But there on the shining metal
            Where the altar should have been,
        She saw by his flickering forge-light
30   Quite another scene.

Barbed wire enclosed an arbitrary spot
    Where bored officials lounged (one cracked a joke)
And sentries sweated for the day was hot:
    A crowd of ordinary decent folk
35   Watched from without and neither moved nor spoke
As three pale figures were led forth and bound
To three posts driven upright in the ground.

The mass and majesty of this world, all
    That carries weight and always weighs the same
40 Lay in the hands of others; they were small
    And could not hope for help and no help came:
    What their foes liked to do was done, their shame
Was all the worst could wish; they lost their pride
And died as men before their bodies died.

45   She looked over his shoulder
            For athletes at their games,
        Men and women in a dance
            Moving their sweet limbs
        Quick, quick, to music,
50   But there on the shining shield
        His hands had set no dancing-floor
            But a weed-choked field.

A ragged urchin, aimless and alone,
    Loitered about that vacancy; a bird
55 Flew up to safety from his well-aimed stone:
    That girls are raped, that two boys knife a third,
    Were axioms to him, who'd never heard
Of any world where promises were kept,
Or one could weep because another wept.

60   The thin-lipped armorer,
        Hephaestos,° hobbled away,   *god of fire, patron of blacksmiths*
      Thetis of the shining breasts
        Cried out in dismay
      At what the god had wrought
65   To please her son, the strong
      Iron-hearted man-slaying Achilles
        Who would not live long.

DYLAN THOMAS   (1914–1953)

Fern Hill [1]   (1946)

Now as I was young and easy under the apple boughs
About the lilting house and happy as the grass was green,
    The night above the dingle° starry,   *valley*
      Time let me hail and climb
5   Golden in the heydays of his eyes,
And honoured among wagons I was prince of the apple towns
And once below a time I lordly had the trees and leaves
      Trail with daisies and barley
    Down the rivers of the windfall light.

10 And as I was green and carefree, famous among the barns
About the happy yard and singing as the farm was home,
    In the sun that is young once only,
      Time let me play and be
    Golden in the mercy of his means,

---

[1] **Fern Hill:** A house in the country owned by the poet's aunt. He spent many happy summers there.

15   And green and golden I was huntsman and herdsman, the calves
     Sang to my horn, the foxes on the hills barked clear and cold,
          And the sabbath rang slowly
          In the pebbles of the holy streams.

     All the sun long it was running, it was lovely, the hay
20   Fields high as the house, the tunes from the chimneys, it was air
          And playing, lovely and watery
               And fire green as grass.
          And nightly under the simple stars
     As I rode to sleep the owls were bearing the farm away,
25   All the moon long I heard, blessed among stables, the nightjars°   night birds
          Flying with the ricks,° and the horses   haystacks
               Flashing into the dark.

     And then to awake, and the farm, like a wanderer white
     With the dew, come back, the cock on his shoulder: it was all
30   Shining, it was Adam and maiden,
               The sky gathered again
          And the sun grew round that very day.
     So it must have been after the birth of the simple light
     In the first, spinning place, the spellbound horses walking warm
35   Out of the whinnying green stable
               On to the fields of praise.

     And honoured among foxes and pheasants by the gay house
     Under the new made clouds and happy as the heart was long,
          In the sun born over and over,
40   I ran my heedless ways,
          My wishes raced through the house high hay
     And nothing I cared, at my sky blue trades, that time allows
     In all his tuneful turning so few and such morning songs
          Before the children green and golden
45   Follow him out of grace.

     Nothing I cared, in the lamb white days, that time would take me
     Up to the swallow thronged loft by the shadow of my hand,
          In the moon that is always rising,
               Nor that riding to sleep
50   I should hear him fly with the high fields
     And wake to the farm forever fled from the childless land.
     Oh as I was young and easy in the mercy of his means,
          Time held me green and dying
          Though I sang in my chains like the sea.

W. D. SNODGRASS (1926–   )

April Inventory (1957)

The green catalpa tree has turned
All white; the cherry blooms once more.
In one whole year I haven't learned
A blessed thing they pay you for.
5   The blossoms snow down in my hair;
The trees and I will soon be bare.

The trees have more than I to spare.
The sleek, expensive girls I teach,
Younger and pinker every year,
10   Bloom gradually out of reach.
The pear tree lets its petals drop
Like dandruff on a tabletop.

The girls have grown so young by now
I have to nudge myself to stare.
15   This year they smile and mind me how
My teeth are falling with my hair.
In thirty years I may not get
Younger, shrewder, or out of debt.

The tenth time, just a year ago,
20   I made myself a little list
Of all the things I'd ought to know,
Then told my parents, analyst,
And everyone who's trusted me
I'd be substantial, presently.

25   I haven't read one book about
A book or memorized one plot.
Or found a mind I did not doubt.
I learned one date. And then forgot.
And one by one the solid scholars
30   Get the degrees, the jobs, the dollars.

And smile above their starchy collars.
I taught my classes Whitehead's notions;[1]

---

[1] **Whitehead's notions:** Alfred North Whitehead (1861–1947), a British philosopher.

One lovely girl, a song of Mahler's.[2]
Lacking a source-book or promotions,
35   I showed one child the colors of
A luna moth and how to love.

I taught myself to name my name,
To bark back, loosen love and crying;
To ease my woman so she came,
40   To ease an old man who was dying.
I have not learned how often I
Can win, can love, but choose to die.

I have not learned there is a lie
Love shall be blonder, slimmer, younger;
45   That my equivocating eye
Loves only by my body's hunger;
That I have forces, true to feel,
Or that the lovely world is real.

While scholars speak authority
50   And wear their ulcers on their sleeves,
My eyes in spectacles shall see
These trees procure and spend their leaves.
There is a value underneath
The gold and silver in my teeth.

55   Though trees turn bare and girls turn wives,
We shall afford our costly seasons;
There is a gentleness survives
That will outspeak and has its reasons.
There is a loveliness exists,
60   Preserves us, not for specialists.

JOHN ASHBERY (1927–   )

Song (1970)

The song tells us of our old way of living,
Of life in former times. Fragrance of florals,
How things merely ended when they ended,
Of beginning again into a sigh. Later

---

[2] **Mahler's:** Gustav Mahler (1860–1911), an Austrian composer.

5   Some movement is reversed and the urgent masks
Speed toward a totally unexpected end
Like clocks out of control. Is this the gesture
That was meant, long ago, the curving in

Of frustrated denials, like jungle foliage
10   And the simplicity of the ending all to be let go
In quick, suffocating sweetness? The day
Puts toward a nothingness of sky

Its face of rusticated brick. Sooner or later,
The cars lament, the whole business will be hurled down.
15   Meanwhile we sit, scarcely daring to speak,
To breathe, as though this closeness cost us life.

The pretensions of a past will some day
Make it over into progress, a growing up,
As beautiful as a new history book
20   With uncut pages, unseen illustrations,

And the purpose of the many stops and starts will be made clear:
Backing into the old affair of not wanting to grow
Into the night, which becomes a house, a parting of the ways
Taking us far into sleep. A dumb love.

ANNE SEXTON (1928–1974)

In the Deep Museum (1962)

My God, my God, what queer corner am I in?
Didn't I die, blood running down the post,
lungs gagging for air, die there for the sin
of anyone, my sour mouth giving up the ghost?
5   Surely my body is done? Surely I died?
And yet, I know, I'm here. What place is this?
Cold and queer, I sting with life. I lied.
Yes, I lied. Or else in some damned cowardice
my body would not give me up. I touch
10   fine cloth with my hand and my cheeks are cold.
If this is hell, then hell could not be much,
neither as special nor as ugly as I was told.

What's that I hear, snuffling and pawing its way
toward me? Its tongue knocks a pebble out of place

15   as it slides in, a sovereign. How can I pray?
      It is panting; it is an odor with a face
      like the skin of a donkey. It laps my sores.
      It is hurt, I think, as I touch its little head.
      It bleeds. I have forgiven murderers and whores
20   and now I must wait like old Jonah, not dead
      nor alive, stroking a clumsy animal. A rat.
      His teeth test me; he waits like a good cook,
      knowing his own ground. I forgive him that,
      as I forgave my Judas the money he took.

25   Now I hold his soft red sore to my lips
      as his brothers crowd in, hairy angels who take
      my gift. My ankles are a flute. I lose hips
      and wrists. For three days, for love's sake,
      I bless this other death. Oh, not in air—
30   in dirt. Under the rotting veins of its roots,
      under the markets, under the sheep bed where
      the hill is food, under the slippery fruits
      of the vineyard, I go. Unto the bellies and jaws
      of rats I commit my prophecy and fear.
35   Far below The Cross, I correct its flaws.
      We have kept the miracle. I will not be here.

THOM GUNN (1929–2004)

On the Move (1957)

> "Man, you gotta Go."

     The blue jay scuffling in the bushes follows
     Some hidden purpose, and the gust of birds
     That spurts across the field, the wheeling swallows,
     Have nested in the trees and undergrowth.
5   Seeking their instinct, or their poise, or both,
     One moves with an uncertain violence
     Under the dust thrown by a baffled sense
     Or the dull thunder of approximate words.

     On motorcycles, up the road, they come:
10   Small, black, as flies hanging in heat, the Boys,
     Until the distance throws them forth, their hum
     Bulges to thunder held by calf and thigh.
     In goggles, donned impersonality,

In gleaming jackets trophied with the dust,
15 They strap in doubt—by hiding it, robust—
And almost hear a meaning in their noise.

Exact conclusion of their hardiness
Has no shape yet, but from known whereabouts
They ride, direction where the tyres press.
20 They scare a flight of birds across the field:
Much that is natural, to the will must yield.
Men manufacture both machine and soul,
And use what they imperfectly control
To dare a future from the taken routes.

25 It is a part solution, after all.
One is not necessarily discord
On earth; or damned because, half animal,
One lacks direct instinct, because one wakes
Afloat on movement that divides and breaks.
30 One joins the movement in a valueless world,
Choosing it, till, both hurler and the hurled,
One moves as well, always toward, toward.

A minute holds them, who have come to go:
The self-defined, astride the created will
35 They burst away; the towns they travel through
Are home for neither bird nor holiness,
For birds and saints complete their purposes.
At worst, one is in motion; and at best,
Reaching no absolute, in which to rest,
40 One is always nearer by not keeping still.

SYLVIA PLATH (1932–1963)

Lady Lazarus[1] (1962)

I have done it again.
One year in every ten
I manage it——

---

[1] **Lazarus:** This title is an ironic play on the figure of Lazarus, whom Jesus raised from the dead.

A sort of walking miracle, my skin
5   Bright as a Nazi lampshade,
My right foot

A paperweight,
My face a featureless, fine
Jew linen.

10   Peel off the napkin
O my enemy.
Do I terrify?——

The nose, the eye pits, the full set of teeth?
The sour breath
15   Will vanish in a day.

Soon, soon the flesh
The grave cave ate will be
At home on me

And I a smiling woman.
20   I am only thirty.
And like the cat I have nine times to die.

This is Number Three.
What a trash
To annihilate each decade.

25   What a million filaments.
The peanut-crunching crowd
Shoves in to see

Them unwrap me hand and foot——
The big strip tease.
30   Gentlemen, ladies

These are my hands
My knees.
I may be skin and bone,

Nevertheless, I am the same, identical woman.
35   The first time it happened I was ten.
It was an accident.

The second time I meant
To last it out and not come back at all.
I rocked shut

40 As a seashell.
They had to call and call
And pick the worms off me like sticky pearls.

Dying
Is an art, like everything else.
45 I do it exceptionally well.

I do it so it feels like hell.
I do it so it feels real.
I guess you could say I've a call.

It's easy enough to do it in a cell.
50 It's easy enough to do it and stay put.
It's the theatrical

Comeback in broad day
To the same place, the same face, the same brute
Amused shout:

55 'A miracle!'
That knocks me out.
There is a charge

For the eyeing of my scars, there is a charge
For the hearing of my heart——
60 It really goes.

And there is a charge, a very large charge
For a word or a touch
Or a bit of blood

Or a piece of my hair or my clothes.
65 So, so, Herr Doktor.
So, Herr Enemy.

I am your opus,
I am your valuable,
The pure gold baby

70 That melts to a shriek.
I turn and burn.
Do not think I underestimate your great concern.

Ash, ash—
You poke and stir.
75 Flesh, bone, there is nothing there——

A cake of soap,
A wedding ring,
A gold filling.

Herr God, Herr Lucifer
80 Beware
Beware.

Out of the ash
I rise with my red hair
And I eat men like air.

AUDRE LORDE (1934–1992)

Memorial I (1976)

If you come as softly
as wind within the trees
you may hear what I hear
see what sorrow sees.

5   If you come as lightly
as the threading dew
I shall take you gladly
nor ask more of you.

You may sit beside me
10 silent as a breath
and only those who stay dead
shall remember death.

If you come I will be silent
nor speak harsh words to you—
15 I will not ask you why, now,
nor how, nor what you knew.

But we shall sit here softly
beneath two different years
and the rich earth between us
20   shall drink our tears.

CHARLES SIMIC (1938–   )

Classic Ballroom Dances (1980)

Grandmothers who wring the necks
Of chickens; old nuns
With names like Theresa, Marianne,
Who pull schoolboys by the ear;

5   The intricate steps of pickpockets
Working the crowd of the curious
At the scene of an accident; the slow shuffle
Of the evangelist with a sandwich-board;

The hesitation of the early morning customer
10   Peeking through the window-grille
Of a pawnshop; the weave of a little kid
Who is walking to school with eyes closed;

And the ancient lovers, cheek to cheek,
On the dancefloor of the Union Hall,
15   Where they also hold charity raffles
On rainy Monday nights of an eternal November.

MICHAEL COLLIER (1953–   )

Argos (2000)

If you think Odysseus too strong and brave to cry,
that the god-loved, god-protected hero
when he returned to Ithaka disguised,
intent to check up on his wife

5   and candidly apprize the condition of his kingdom,
steeled himself resolutely against surprise
and came into his land cold-hearted, clear-eyed,
ready for revenge—then you read Homer as I did,

10 too fast, knowing you'd be tested for plot
and major happenings, skimming forward to the massacre,
the shambles engineered with Telémakhos°   son of Odysseus
by turning beggar and taking up the challenge of the bow.

Reading this way you probably missed the tear
Odysseus shed for his decrepit dog, Argos,
15 who's nothing but a bag of bones asleep atop
a refuse pile outside the palace gates. The dog is not

a god in earthly clothes, but in its own disguise
of death and destitution is more like Ithaka itself.
And if you returned home after twenty years
20 you might weep for the hunting dog

you long ago abandoned, rising from the garbage
of its bed, its instinct of recognition still intact,
enough will to wag its tail, lift its head, but little more.
Years ago you had the chance to read that page more closely

25 but instead you raced ahead, like Odysseus, cocksure
with your plan. Now the past is what you study,
where guile and speed give over to grief so you might stop,
and desiring to weep, weep more deeply.

BRAD LEITHAUSER (1953–   )

The Buried Graves (1986)

From the pier, at dusk, the dim
    Billowing arms of kelp
Seem the tops of trees, as though
        Not long ago
5 A summer wood stood here, before a dam
    Was built, a valley flooded.

Such a forest would release
    Its color only slowly,
And the leafy branches sway, as they'd
10   More lightly swayed
Under a less distant sun and far less
    Even weather. Now, deeper down,

Those glimmers of coral might
    Be the lots of some hard-luck
15 Town, or—depositing on the dead
      A second bed—
A submerged cemetery. . . . To this mute,
  Envisioned, birdless wood would

Come a kind of autumn, a tame
20   Sea-season, with foliage tumbling
Through a weighty, trancelike fall;
      And come, as well,
Soon in the emptying fullness of time,
  A mild but an endless winter.

GREG DELANTY (1958–   )

The Alien (2003)

I'm back again scrutinising the Milky Way
    of your ultrasound, scanning the dark
      matter, the nothingness, that now the heads say
    is chockablock with quarks & squarks,
5 gravitons & gravitini, photons & photinos. Our sprout,

who art there inside the spacecraft
    of your ma, the time capsule of this printout,
      hurling & whirling towards us, it's all daft
    on this earth. Our alien who art in the heavens,
10 our Martian, our little green man, we're anxious

to make contact, to ask divers questions
    about the heavendom you hail from, to discuss
      the whole shebang of the beginning&end,
    the pre-big-bang untime before you forget the why
15 and lie of thy first place. And, our friend,

to say Welcome, that we mean no harm, we'd die
    for you even, that we pray you're not here
      to subdue us, that we'd put away
    our ray guns, missiles, attitude and share
20 our world with you, little big head, if only you stay.

BRIAN HENRY (1972–   )

Break It on Down

In due course one admits the sex was magnificent

Borrowed from fandangos of chance

Markers soak through your sweatered chest

Frost heaves burst from the back yard's muddle

5   To meet and discuss the status of hands

You wept when you gleaned what he meant

My sentiments exactly heading west

Though not often enmeshed in such a meddle

The formal entourage retiring too early

10   Beyond the borders of suburban power outages

That cluster of hawks swoops toward the deer

For carcasses are all that we all that we

Bless the conceptual artist for his brazen images

Know there is no knowing here

CHAPTER 14

I CHANT A NEW CHANT
—Walt Whitman
An Anthology of Free Verse

There is no such thing as "free verse." That is, no verse is really "free" of all strictures and requirements, even those imposed by rhythm. But free verse is usually defined as poetry that has no set meters or rhymes. The number of "beats" or feet per line will vary from line to line, with an emphasis on the cadence of each line. The line normally expands to a breath unit, governed by the sense of evolving cadence in the stanza or section of the poem in which the line occurs. The term **free verse** comes from *vers libre,* a concept employed by nineteenth-century French poets such as Arthur Rimbaud and Jules LaForge, who wished to break free of the very strict tradition of the French *alexandrine* (a metrical line of six poetic feet or twelve syllables that dominated French poetry for centuries). Poets working in free verse still adhere to many of the techniques and forms that are commonly held within the traditions of poetry in English. But along with this disciplined under-standing of the traditions, there is a freedom from constraint in this poetry, a freedom to go wherever inspiration leads.

It was the translators of the *King James Bible* (1611) who pio-neered the use of free verse in English with their versions of the Psalms (p. 927) and the Song of Solomon. These poetic passages were based, not on any metrical system, but on cadences and parallelism. Paral-lelism is a technique in which certain phrases and sentence formations are echoed in other passages. John Milton, in his long verse play *Samson Agonistes* (1671), experimented with free verse in the chorus sections (as in the following, where some fairly regular lines of blank verse mix with other meters, and where rhyme is used only occasionally):

> *Chor.* Just are the ways of God,
> And justifiable to Men;
> Unless there be who think not God at all,
> If any be, they walk obscure;
> 5   For of such Doctrine never was there School,
> But the heart of the Fool,
> And no man therein Doctor but himself.
> Yet more there be who doubt his ways not just,
> As to his own edicts, found contradicting,

10 Then give the rains to wandering thought,
    Regardless of his glories diminution;
    Till by their own perplexities involv'd
    They ravel more, still less resolv'd,
    But never find self-satisfying solution.
15   As if they would confine th' interminable,
    And tie him to his own prescript,
    Who made our Laws to bind us, not himself.
    And hath full right to exempt
    Whom so it pleases him by choice
20 From National obstruction, without taint
    Of sin, or legal debt;
    For with his own Laws he can best dispense.

This experiment in free verse struck few chords, although William Blake, writing in the late eighteenth century, would use free verse cadences in his longer poems, such as *The Marriage of Heaven and Hell* (p. 929). This poem opens with a remarkable passage, called "The Argument":

Rintrah roars & shakes his fires in the burden'd air;
Hungry clouds swag on the deep

Once meek, and in a perilous path,
The just man kept his course along
5   The vale of death.
Roses are planted where thorns grow.
And on the barren heath
Sing the honey bees.

Then the perilous path was planted:
10 And a river, and a spring
On every cliff and tomb;
And on the bleached bones
Red clay brought forth.

Till the villain left the paths of ease,
15 To walk in perilous paths, and drive
The just man into barren climes.
Now the sneaking serpent walks
In mild humility.
And the just man rages in the wilds
20 Where lions roam.

Rintrah roars & shakes his fires in the burden'd air;
Hungry clouds swag on the deep.

Blake managed to free himself of the constraints of traditional metrics in many of his longer poems, and he appears to have influenced the great originator of modern free verse in English, Walt Whitman. Whitman's revolutionary work in *Leaves of Grass* (1855), especially the famous opening of "Song of Myself," suggests something of his immense freedom and control over the verse line:

> I CELEBRATE myself, and sing myself,
> And what I assume you shall assume,
> For every atom belonging to me as good belongs to you.
>
> I loafe and invite my soul,
> 5   I lean and loafe at my ease observing a spear of summer grass.
>
> My tongue, every atom of my blood, form'd from this soil, this air,
> Born here of parents born here from parents the same, and their parents the same,
> I, now thirty-seven years old in perfect health begin,
> Hoping to cease not till death.
>
> 10   Creeds and schools in abeyance,
> Retiring back a while sufficed at what they are, but never forgotten,
> I harbor for good or bad, I permit to speak at every hazard,
> Nature without check with original energy.

While a few other nineteenth-century poets such as Matthew Arnold (in "Dover Beach," p. 1594) experimented with free verse, it was Ezra Pound and T. S. Eliot who brought this kind of poetry into common currency in the twentieth century. Eliot and Pound were both influenced by the earlier work of the French poets Rimbaud and LaForge, and Pound's experimentation with Imagism, a school of poetry devoted to the concrete image, also helped to foster an interest in free verse. This revolution in meter was so successful that most poetry written after the time of Eliot and Pound has been composed in free verse, although not all of this poetry rises to their high level in accomplishment. Robert Frost famously said he would rather "play tennis with the net down" than write free verse; nevertheless, many (if not most) of the most interesting and provocative poets of the modern era, including William Carlos Williams, D. H. Lawrence, and e. e. cummings, have written poetry of a high order in free verse form. Most significant poets writing after World War II have been masters of free verse, as seen in the examples here by Theodore Roethke, Robert Lowell, Allen Ginsberg, Adrienne Rich, Seamus Heaney, and Anne Carson.

When reading free verse, notice that each line does have a rhythm, even a meter; the point is that the poet varies the meter from line to line, working with the cadence of the passage, often working in a stanza form to shape a larger rhetorical sweep. The ideal line of free verse unfolds, like a leaf, organically, assuming its own apparently inevitable shape, length, and weight. All of the usual organizing principles of poetry still apply to free verse, which often draws on the rhythms of metrical poetry but varies them, as the cadences in *The Waste Land* (p. 102) are, in certain sections, closely modeled on the cadences of blank verse.

Rhyme often appears in free verse poems, but it occurs within the line (assonance), as slant rhyme, or occasionally at the end. Rhyme becomes a form of echo or repetition, irregularly applied, yet very effective and important as a technique. Rhythms also occur; they are inevitable in poetry. But rhythm becomes a kind of pulse, a distinct throb in the line, in the stanza, or in the poem as a whole.

ADDITIONAL EXAMPLES OF FREE VERSE IN THIS BOOK

- Walt Whitman, "Song of Myself" (p. 84)

- Matthew Arnold, "Dover Beach" (p. 1594)

- T. S. Eliot, *The Waste Land* (p. 102) and "The Love Song of J. Alfred Prufrock" (p. 581)

- Ezra Pound, from *The Cantos* [Canto I] (p. 93)

- D. H. Lawrence, "Snake" (p. 1360)

- William Carlos Williams, "The Young Housewife" (p. 986)

- Langston Hughes, "Theme for English B" (p. 352)

- Theodore Roethke, "An Elegy for Jane" (p. 221)

- Sylvia Plath, "Daddy" (p. 234)

- Robert Penn Warren, "Heart of Autumn" (p. 1448)

- A. R. Ammons, "So I Said I Am Ezra" (p. 646)

- Allen Ginsberg, from *Howl* (p. 956)

- John Ashbery, "At North Farm" (p. 648)

- Charles Wright, "Sitting Outside at the End of Autumn" (p. 1320)

- Seamus Heaney, "Digging" (p. 1005)

- Mary Oliver, "The House" (p. 999)

- Nikki Giovanni, "Beautiful Black Men" (p. 1090)

- Jorie Graham, "The Geese" (p. 1404)

ANONYMOUS

Psalm 23, *from* The Bible
King James Version
A Psalm of David

The LORD *is* my shepherd; I shall not want.
2   He maketh me to lie down in green pastures: he leadeth me beside
      the still waters.
3   He restoreth my soul: he leadeth me in the paths of righteousness
      for his name's sake.
4   Yea, though I walk through the valley of the shadow of death, I will
      fear no evil: for thou *art* with me; thy rod and thy staff
      they comfort me.
5   Thou preparest a table before me in the presence of mine enemies:
      thou anointest my head with oil; my cup runneth over.
6   Surely goodness and mercy shall follow me all the days of my life:
      and I will dwell in the house of the LORD for ever.

ANONYMOUS

Psalm 100, *from* The Bible
King James Version
A Psalm of praise

Make a joyful noise unto the LORD, all ye lands.
2   Serve the LORD with gladness: come before his presence with singing.
3   Know ye that the LORD he *is* God: *it is* he *that* hath made us, and
      not we ourselves; *we are* his people, and the sheep of his pasture.
4   Enter into his gates with thanksgiving, *and* into his courts with praise:
      be thankful unto him, *and* bless his name.
5   For the LORD *is* good; his mercy *is* everlasting; and his truth *endureth*
      to all generations.

ANONYMOUS

Psalm 121, *from* The Bible
King James Version
A Song of degrees

I will lift up mine eyes unto the hills, from whence cometh my help.
2   My help *cometh* from the LORD, which made heaven and earth.
3   He will not suffer thy foot to be moved: he that keepeth thee will
      not slumber.

4   Behold, he that keepeth Israel shall neither slumber nor sleep.
5   The LORD *is* thy keeper: the LORD *is* thy shade upon thy right hand.
6   The sun shall not smite thee by day, nor the moon by night.
7   The LORD shall preserve thee from all evil: he shall preserve thy soul.
8   The LORD shall preserve thy going out and thy coming in from this
         time forth, and even for evermore.

CHRISTOPHER SMART (1722–1771)

from Jubilate Agno, Section VII, (lines 55–61) and (123–132) (1763; 1939)

For I pray God to bless POLLY[1] in the blessing of Naomi
     and assign her to the house of David.
For I am in charity with the French who are my
     foes and Moabites because of the Moabitish woman.[2]
For my Angel is always ready at a pinch to help
     me out and to keep me up.
For CHRISTOPHER must slay the Dragon with a
     PHEON's° head.   broad arrow
5   For they have separated me and my bosom, whereas
         the right comes by setting us together.[3]
For Silly fellow! Silly fellow! is against me
     and belongeth neither to me nor my family.

For I pray the Lord JESUS that cured the LUNATICK to
     be merciful to all my brethren and sisters in these houses.
For they work me with their harping-irons,° which is   harpoons
     a barbarous instrument, because I am more unguarded
     than others.
For the blessing of God hath been on my epistles,
     which I have written for the benefit of others.
10   For I bless God that the CHURCH OF ENGLAND is one
         of the SEVEN ev'n the candlestick of the Lord.[4]

---

[1] **Polly:** Pet name for Smart's daughter Marianne.
[2] **Moabitish woman:** For Smart, "Moabite" means Roman Catholic. The Moabitish woman likely represents his Roman Catholic wife Nancy, who wanted to raise their daughter in the Catholic church, rather than Smart's Anglican tradition.
[3] **separated . . . together:** Here, Smart refers to separation from his wife, due to his confinement in the Bethnal Green asylum.
[4] **SEVEN . . . Lord:** In Revelation 1.20, St. John addresses the seven churches of Asia Minor, symbolized by seven gold candlesticks.

For the ENGLISH TONGUE shall be the language of
    the WEST.
For I pray Almighty CHRIST to bless the MAGDALEN
    HOUSE[5] & to forward a National purification.
For I have the blessing of God in the three POINTS
    of manhood, of the pen, of the sword, & of chivalry.[6]
For I am inquisitive in the Lord, and defend the
    philosophy of the scripture against vain deceit.
15   For the nets come down from the eyes of the Lord
    to fish up men to their salvation.
For I have a greater compass both of mirth and
    melancholy than another.

WILLIAM BLAKE (1757–1827)

The Marriage of Heaven and Hell (1793)

The Argument

Rintrah[1] roars & shakes his fires in the burdend air;
Hungry clouds swag on the deep

Once meek, and in a perilous path,
The just man kept his course along
5   The vale of death.
Roses are planted where thorns grow.
And on the barren heath
Sing the honey bees.

Then the perilous path was planted:
10   And a river, and a spring
On every cliff and tomb;
And on the bleached bones
Red clay[2] brought forth.

Till the villain left the paths of ease,
15   To walk in perilous paths, and drive
The just man into barren climes.

---

[5] **MAGDALEN HOUSE:** An asylum for prostitutes in London, first opened in 1758.
[6] **three . . . chivalry:** Here, Smart refers to elements of Freemason ceremony and tradition.
[1] **Rintrah:** In Blake's personal mythology, an angry prophet, like Elijah, who precedes the formation of a new natural and social cycle.
[2] **Red clay:** In Hebrew, literal meaning of "Adam."

Now the sneaking serpent walks
In mild humility.
And the just man rages in the wilds
20   Where lions roam.

Rintrah roars & shakes his fires in the burdend air;
Hungry clouds swag on the deep.

[Plate 3]

As a new heaven is begun, and it is now thirty-three years since its
advent: the Eternal Hell revives. And lo! Swedenborg is the Angel
sitting at the tomb;[3] his writings are the linen clothes folded up.
Now is the dominion of Edom, & the return of Adam into Paradise;[4]
see Isaiah XXXIV & XXXV Chap.
5   Without Contraries is no progression. Attraction and Repul-
sion, Reason and Energy, Love and Hate, are necessary to Human
existence.
        From these contraries spring what the religious call Good &
Evil. Good is the passive that obeys Reason. Evil is the active
10   springing from Energy.
        Good is Heaven. Evil is Hell.

[Plate 4]

The Voice of the Devil

All Bibles or sacred codes. have been the causes of the following
Errors:
        1. That Man has two real existing principles Viz: a Body & a Soul.
        2. That Energy, calld Evil. is alone from the Body. & that Reason.
5   calld Good. is alone from the Soul.
        3. That God will torment Man in Eternity for following his
Energies.
        But the following Contraries to these are True:
        1. Man has no Body distinct from his Soul for that calld Body
10   is a portion of Soul discernd by the five Senses. the chief inlets of
Soul in this age.
        2. Energy is the only life and is from the Body and Reason is the
bound or outward circumference of Energy.
        3. Energy is Eternal Delight.

---

[3] **thirty-three . . . tomb:** Emanuel Swedenborg was a Swedish theologian who wrote that the Last
Judgment would begin in 1757, the year of Blake's birth. Written in 1793, thirty-three years after his
birth, *The Marriage of Heaven and Hell* adopts a critical view of Swedenborg's thinking. The poem
can be seen as an intellectual satire in which Blake's rebellious thought (associated with the devil) is
placed in conversation with Swedenborg, who represents an angelic perspective.
[4] **the return . . . Paradise:** Adam's return to paradise occurs only in Blake's imagination, not in
Biblical tradition.

[Plate 5]

Those who restrain desire, do so because theirs is weak enough to be restrained; and the restrainer or reason usurps its place & governs the unwilling.

And being restraind it by degrees becomes passive till it is only the shadow of desire.

5   The history of this is written in Paradise Lost.[5] & the Governor or Reason is call'd Messiah.

And the original Archangel or possessor of the command of the heavenly host, is calld the Devil or Satan and his children are call'd Sin & Death.

10   But in the Book of Job Miltons Messiah is call'd Satan.

For this history has been adopted by both parties.

It indeed appear'd to Reason as if Desire was cast out. but the Devils account is, that the Messi[PL 6]ah fell. & formed a heaven of what he stole from the Abyss

15   This is shewn in the Gospel, where he prays to the Father to send the comforter or Desire that Reason may have Ideas to build on, the Jehovah of the Bible being no other than he, who dwells in flaming fire.

Know that after Christs death, he became Jehovah.

20   But in Milton; the Father is Destiny, the Son, a Ratio° of the five senses. & the Holy-ghost, Vacuum!

reduction of reason

Note. The reason Milton wrote in fetters when he wrote of Angels & God, and at liberty when of Devils & Hell, is because he was a true Poet and of the Devils party without knowing it

A Memorable Fancy

25   As I was walking among the fires of hell, delighted with the enjoyments of Genius; which to Angels look like torment and insanity. I collected some of their Proverbs: thinking that as the sayings used in a nation, mark its character, so the Proverbs of Hell, shew the nature of Infernal wisdom better than any description of buildings or garments.

30   When I came home; on the abyss of the five senses, where a flat sided steep frowns over the present world. I saw a mighty Devil folded in black clouds, hovering on the sides of the rock, with cor[PL 7]roding fires he wrote the following sentence now perceived by the minds of men, & read by them on earth.

35   How do you know but ev'ry Bird that cuts the airy way,
         Is an immense world of delight, clos'd by your senses five?

---

[5] **The history . . . Paradise Lost:** A reflection of Blake's aesthetic reading, not Milton's intention.

Proverbs of Hell

In seed time learn, in harvest teach, in winter enjoy.
Drive your cart and your plow over the bones of the dead.
The road of excess leads to the palace of wisdom.
40   Prudence is a rich ugly old maid courted by Incapacity.
He who desires but acts not, breeds pestilence.
The cut worm forgives the plow.
Dip him in the river who loves water.
A fool sees not the same tree that a wise man sees.
45   He whose face gives no light, shall never become a star.
Eternity is in love with the productions of time.
The busy bee has no time for sorrow.
The hours of folly are measur'd by the clock, but of wisdom: no
clock can measure.
All wholsom food is caught without a net or a trap.
50   Bring out number weight & measure in a year of dearth.
No bird soars too high. if he soars with his own wings.
A dead body revenges not injuries.
The most sublime act is to set another before you.
If the fool would persist in his folly he would become wise.
55   Folly is the cloke of knavery.
Shame is Prides cloke.

[Plate 8]

Prisons are built with stones of Law, Brothels with bricks of
Religion.
The pride of the peacock is the glory of God.
The lust of the goat is the bounty of God.
The wrath of the lion is the wisdom of God.
5   The nakedness of woman is the work of God.
Excess of sorrow laughs. Excess of joy weeps.
The roaring of lions, the howling of wolves, the raging of the
stormy sea, and the destructive sword. are portions of eternity too
great for the eye of man.
The fox condemns the trap, not himself.
10   Joys impregnate. Sorrows bring forth.
Let man wear the fell of the lion. woman the fleece of the sheep.
The bird a nest, the spider a web, man friendship.
The selfish smiling fool. & the sullen frowning fool. shall be both
thought wise. that they may be a rod.
What is now proved was once, only imagin'd.
15   The rat, the mouse, the fox, the rabbet; watch the roots, the lion,
the tyger, the horse, the elephant, watch the fruits.
The cistern contains: the fountain overflows.

One thought. fills immensity.

Always be ready to speak your mind, and a base man will avoid you.

Every thing possible to be believ'd is an image of truth.

20　The eagle never lost so much time. as when he submitted to learn of the crow.

[Plate 9]

The fox provides for himself. but God provides for the lion.

Think in the morning, Act in the noon, Eat in the evening, Sleep in the night.

He who has sufferd you to impose on him knows you.

As the plow follows words, so God rewards prayers.

5　The tygers of wrath are wiser than the horses of instruction

Expect poison from the standing water.

You never know what is enough unless you know what is more than enough.

Listen to the fools reproach! it is a kingly title!

The eyes of fire, the nostrils of air, the mouth of water, the beard of earth.

10　The weak in courage is strong in cunning.

The apple tree never asks the beech how he shall grow, nor the lion. the horse; how he shall take his prey.

The thankful receiver bears a plentiful harvest.

If others had not been foolish. we should be so.

The soul of sweet delight. can never be defil'd.

15　When thou seest an Eagle, thou seest a portion of Genius. lift up thy head!

As the catterpiller chooses the fairest leaves to lay her eggs on, so the priest lays his curse on the fairest joys.

To create a little flower is the labour of ages.

Damn. braces: Bless relaxes.

The best wine is the oldest. the best water the newest.

20　Prayers plow not! Praises reap not!

Joys laugh not! Sorrows weep not!

[Plate 10]

The head Sublime, the heart Pathos,° the genitals Beauty, the hands & feet Proportion.　　　　　　　　　　　feeling of pity

As the air to a bird or the sea to a fish, so is contempt to the contemptible.

5　The crow wish'd every thing was black, the owl, that every thing was white.

Exuberance is Beauty.

If the lion was advised by the fox. he would be cunning.

Improvement makes strait roads, but the crooked roads
10   without Improvement, are roads of Genius.

Sooner murder an infant in its cradle than nurse unacted desires.

Where man is not nature is barren.

Truth can never be told so as to be understood, and not be believ'd.

Enough! or Too much.

[Plate 11]⁶

The ancient Poets animated all sensible objects with Gods or Geniuses, calling them by the names and adorning them with the properties of woods, rivers, mountains, lakes, cities, nations, and whatever their enlarged & numerous senses could perceive.
5   And particularly they studied the genius of each city & country. placing it under its mental deity.

Till a system was formed, which some took advantage of & enslav'd the vulgar by attempting to realize or abstract the mental dieties from their objects: thus began Priesthood.
10   Choosing forms of worship from poetic tales.

And at length they pronounced that the Gods had orderd such things.

Thus men forgot that All deities reside in the human breast.

[Plate 12]

A Memorable Fancy

The Prophets Isaiah and Ezekiel dined with me, and I asked them how they dared so roundly to assert. that God spake to them; and whether they did not think at the time, that they would be misunderstood, & so be the cause of imposition.
5   Isaiah answer'd. I saw no God. nor heard any, in a finite organical perception; but my senses discover'd the infinite in every thing, and as I was then perswaded. & remain confirm'd; that the voice of honest indignation is the voice of God, I cared not for consequences but wrote.
10   Then I asked: does a firm perswasion that a thing is so, make it so?

He replied. All poets believe that it does, & in ages of imagination this firm perswasion removed mountains; but many are not capable of a firm perswasion of any thing.

Then Ezekiel said. The philosophy of the east taught the first
15   principles of human perception   some nations held one principle for the origin & some another, we of Israel taught that the Poetic

---

⁶ **Plate 11:** Describes the transformation of poetry into scripture.

Genius (as you now call it) was the first principle and all the others merely derivative, which was the cause of our despising the Priests & Philosophers of other countries, and prophecying
20   that all Gods [PL 13] would at last be proved. to originate in ours & to be the tributaries of the Poetic Genius, it was this. that our great poet King David desired so fervently & invokes so patheticly, saying by this he conquers enemies & governs kingdoms; and we so loved our God. that we cursed in his name all the deities of
25   surrounding nations, and asserted that they had rebelled; from these opinions the vulgar came to think that all nations would at last be subject to the jews.

This said he, like all firm perswasions, is come to pass, for all
30   nations believe the jews code and worship the jews god, and what greater subjection can be

I heard this with some wonder, & must confess my own conviction. After dinner I ask'd Isaiah to favour the world with his lost works, he said none of equal value was lost. Ezekiel said the
35   same of his.

I also asked Isaiah what made him go naked and barefoot three years? he answerd, the same that made our friend Diogenes the Grecian.[7]

I then asked Ezekiel. why he eat dung, & lay so long on his
40   right & left side? he answerd. the desire of raising other men into a perception of the infinite   this the North American tribes practise. & is he honest who resists his genius or conscience. only for the sake of present ease or gratification?

[Plate 14]

The ancient tradition that the world will be consumed in fire at the end of six thousand years is true. as I have heard from Hell.

For the cherub with his flaming sword is hereby commanded to leave his guard at the tree of life, and when he does, the whole
5   creation will be consumed, and appear infinite. and holy whereas it now appears finite & corrupt.

This will come to pass by an improvement of sensual enjoyment.

But first the notion that man has a body distinct from his soul, is to be expunged; this I shall do, by printing in the infernal
10   method, by corrosives, which in Hell are salutary and medicinal, melting apparent surfaces away, and displaying the infinite which was hid.

If the doors of perception were cleansed every thing would appear to man as it is: infinite.

---

[7] **Diogenes the Grecian:** Diogenes (412–323 B.C.), a Cynic Greek philosopher.

15   For man has closed himself up, till he sees all things thro' narrow chinks of his cavern.

[Plate 15]

A Memorable Fancy

I was in a Printing house in Hell & saw the method in which knowledge is transmitted from generation to generation.

In the first chamber was a Dragon-Man, clearing away the rubbish from a caves mouth; within, a number of Dragons were hollowing the cave,

5   In the second chamber was a Viper folding round the rock & the cave, and others adorning it with gold silver and precious stones.

In the third chamber was an Eagle with wings and feathers of air, he caused the inside of the cave to be infinite, around were numbers of Eagle like men, who built palaces in the immense cliffs.

10   In the fourth chamber were Lions of flaming fire raging around & melting the metals into living fluids.

In the fifth chamber were Unnam'd forms, which cast the metals into the expanse.

15   There they were receiv'd by Men who occupied the sixth chamber, and took the forms of books & were arranged in libraries.

[Plate 16]

The Giants who formed this world into its sensual existence and now seem to live in it in chains; are in truth. the causes of its life & the sources of all activity, but the chains are, the cunning of weak and tame minds. which have power to resist energy. according to the proverb, the weak in courage is strong in cunning.

5   Thus one portion of being, is the Prolific. the other, the Devouring: to the devourer it seems as if the producer was in his chains, but it is not so, he only takes portions of existence and fancies that the whole.

10   But the Prolific would cease to be Prolific unless the Devourer as a sea received the excess of his delights.[8]

Some will say, Is not God alone the Prolific? I answer, God only Acts & Is, in existing beings or Men.

These two classes of men are always upon earth, & they should be enemies; whoever tries [PL 17] to reconcile them seeks to destroy existence.

Religion is an endeavour to reconcile the two.

---

[8] **Thus . . . delights:** Key passage tracing the marriage of angel and devil, where each is dependent on the other.

Note. Jesus Christ did not wish to unite but to separate them, as
in the Parable of sheep and goats! & he says I came not to send
20   Peace but a Sword.

Messiah or Satan or Tempter was formerly thought to be one of
the Antediluvians[9] who are our Energies.

A Memorable Fancy

An Angel came to me and said. O pitiable foolish young man!
O horrible! O dreadful state! consider the hot burning dungeon
25   thou art preparing for thyself to all eternity, to which thou art
going in such career.

I said. perhaps you will be willing to shew me my eternal lot &
we will contemplate together upon it and see whether your lot or
mine is most desirable

30   So he took me thro' a stable & thro' a church & down into the
church vault at the end of which was a mill: thro' the mill we
went, and came to a cave. down the winding cavern we groped
our tedious way till a void boundless as a nether sky appeard
beneath us & we held by the roots of trees and hung over this
35   immensity; but I said, if you please we will commit ourselves to
this void, and see whether providence is here also, if you will not
I will? but he answerd. do not presume O young-man but as we
here remain behold thy lot which will soon appear when the darkness passes away

40   So I remaind with him sitting in the twisted [PL 18] root of an
oak. he was suspended in a fungus which hung with the head
downward into the deep:

By degrees we beheld the infinite Abyss, fiery as the smoke of
a burning city; beneath us at an immense distance was the sun,
45   black but shining[;] round it were fiery tracks on which revolv'd
vast spiders, crawling after their prey; which flew or rather swum
in the infinite deep, in the most terrific shapes of animals sprung
from corruption. & the air was full of them, & seemd composed of
them; these are Devils. and are called Powers of the air, I now
50   asked my companion which was my eternal lot? he said, between
the black & white spiders

But now, from between the black & white spiders a cloud and
fire burst and rolled thro the deep blackning all beneath, so that
the nether deep grew black as a sea & rolled with a terrible noise:
55   beneath us was nothing now to be seen but a black tempest, till
looking east between the clouds & the waves, we saw a cataract
of blood mixed with fire and not many stones throw from us

---

[9] **Antediluvians:** Giant race that existed on earth before the Flood.

appeard and sunk again the scaly fold of a monstrous serpent. at
last to the east, distant about three degrees appeard a fiery crest
60   above the waves slowly it reared like a ridge of golden rocks till
we discoverd two globes of crimson fire. from which the sea fled
away in clouds of smoke, and now we saw, it was the head of
Leviathan.° his forehead was divided into streaks of green & pur-   a huge mythical
ple like those on a tygers forehead: soon we saw his mouth & red   beast
65   gills hang just above the raging foam tinging the black deep with
beams of blood, advancing toward [PL 19] us with all the fury of
a spiritual existence.

My friend the Angel climb'd up from his station into the mill; I
remain'd alone, & then this appearance was no more, but I found
70   myself sitting on a pleasant bank beside a river by moon light
hearing a harper who sung to the harp. & his theme was, The man
who never alters his opinion is like standing water, & breeds reptiles of the mind.

But I arose, and sought for the mill, & there I found my Angel,
75   who surprised asked me, how I escaped?

I answerd. All that we saw was owing to your metaphysics: for
when you ran away, I found myself on a bank by moonlight hearing a harper, But now we have seen my eternal lot, shall I shew
you yours? he laughd at my proposal: but I by force suddenly
80   caught him in my arms, & flew westerly thro' the night, till we were
elevated above the earths shadow: then I flung myself with him
directly into the body of the sun, here I clothed myself in white, &
taking in my hand Swedenborgs volumes sunk from the glorious
clime, and passed all the planets till we came to saturn, here I
85   staid to rest & then leap'd into the void, between saturn & the
fixed stars.

Here said I! is your lot, in this space, if space it may be calld,
Soon we saw the stable and the church, & I took him to the altar
and open'd the Bible, and lo! it was a deep pit, into which I
90   descended driving the Angel before me, soon we saw seven houses
of brick,[10] one we enterd; in it were a [PL 20] number of monkeys,
baboons, & all of that species chaind by the middle, grinning and
snatching at one another, but witheld by the shortness of their
chains: however I saw that they sometimes grew numerous, and
95   then the weak were caught by the strong and with a grinning
aspect, first coupled with & then devourd, by plucking off first one
limb and then another till the body was left a helpless trunk. this
after grinning & kissing it with seeming fondness they devourd

---

[10] **seven houses of brick:** In St. John's Revelation, the seven churches addressed in Asia.

too; and here & there I saw one savourily picking the flesh off of
100 his own tail; as the stench terribly annoyd us both we went into
the mill, & I in my hand brought the skeleton of a body, which in
the mill was Aristotles Analytics.[11]

So the Angel said: thy phantasy has imposed upon me & thou
oughtest to be ashamed.
105 I answerd: we impose on one another, & it is but lost time to
converse with you whose works are only Analytics.

Opposition is true Friendship.

[Plate 21]

I have always found that Angels have the vanity to speak of themselves as the only wise; this they do with a confident insolence
sprouting from systematic reasoning:

Thus Swedenborg boasts that what he writes is new; tho' it is
5 only the Contents or Index of already publish'd books.

A man carried a monkey about for a shew, & because he was
a little wiser than the monkey, grew vain, and conceiv'd himself
as much wiser than seven men. It is so with Swedenborg; he shews
the folly of churches & exposes hypocrites, till he imagines that all
10 are religious. & himself the single [PL 22] one on earth that ever
broke a net.

Now hear a plain fact: Swedenborg has not written one new
truth: Now hear another: he has written all the old falshoods.

And now hear the reason. He conversed with Angels who are
15 all religious, & conversed not with Devils who all hate religion, for
he was incapable thro' his conceited notions.

Thus Swedenborgs writings are a recapitulation of all superfi-
cial opinions, and an analysis of the more sublime, but no further.

Have now another plain fact: Any man of mechanical talents
20 may from the writings of Paracelsus or Jacob Behmen, produce
ten thousand volumes of equal value with Swedenborg's. and
from those of Dante or Shakespear, an infinite number.[12]

But when he has done this, let him not say that he knows better than his master, for he only holds a candle in sunshine.

A Memorable Fancy

25 Once I saw a Devil in a flame of fire. who arose before an Angel
that sat on a cloud. and the Devil utterd these words.

---

[11] **Aristotles Analytics:** Aristotle's writings on logic.
[12] **Paracelsus . . . an infinite number:** Paracelsus (c. 1490–1541) was a German physician and
alchemist. "Behmen" refers to Jakob Böhme (1575–1624), a mystical philosopher and theologian. To
Blake, these writers were amateurs compared to Dante and Shakespeare.

The worship of God is. Honouring his gifts in other men each according to his genius. and loving the [PL 23] greatest men best, those who envy or calumniate great men hate God, for there is no
30   other God.

The Angel hearing this became almost blue but mastering himself he grew yellow, & at last white pink & smiling, and then replied,

Thou Idolater, is not God One? & is not he visible in Jesus Christ?
35   and has not Jesus Christ given his sanction to the law of ten commandments and are not all other men fools, sinners, & nothings?

The Devil answer'd; bray a fool in a morter with wheat. yet shall not his folly be beaten out of him: if Jesus Christ is the greatest man, you ought to love him in the greatest degree; now hear how
40   he has given his sanction to the law of ten commandments: did he not mock at the sabbath, and so mock the sabbaths God? murder those who were murderd because of him? turn away the law from the woman taken in adultery? steal the labor of others to support him? bear false witness when he omitted making a defence before
45   Pilate? covet when he pray'd for his disciples, and when he bid them shake off the dust of their feet against such as refused to lodge them? I tell you, no virtue can exist without breaking these ten commandments: Jesus was all virtue, and acted from im[PL 24]pulse: not from rules.
50   When he had so spoken: I beheld the Angel who stretched out his arms embracing the flame of fire & he was consumed and arose as Elijah.

Note. This Angel, who is now become a Devil, is my particular friend: we often read the Bible together in its infernal or diabolical
55   sense which the world shall have if they behave well

I have also: The Bible of Hell: which the world shall have whether they will or no.

One Law for the Lion & Ox is Oppression.

[Plate 25]

A Song of Liberty

1. The Eternal Female groand! it was heard over all the Earth:
2. Albions° coast is sick silent; the American meadows faint!   England
3. Shadows of Prophecy shiver along by the lakes and the rivers and mutter across the ocean! France rend down thy dungeon;
5   4. Golden Spain burst the barriers of old Rome;
5. Cast thy keys O Rome into the deep down falling, even to eternity down falling,
6. And weep!
7. In her trembling hands she took the new born terror howling;

10   8. On those infinite mountains of light now barr'd out by the atlantic sea;[13] the new born fire stood before the starry king!

9. Flag'd with grey brow'd snows and thunderous visages the jealous wings wav'd over the deep.

10. The speary hand burned aloft, unbuckled was the shield,
15   forth went the hand of jealousy among the flaming hair, and [PL 26] hurl'd the new born wonder thro' the starry night.

11. The fire, the fire, is falling!

12. Look up! look up! O citizen of London. enlarge thy countenance; O Jew, leave counting gold! return to thy oil and wine; O African! black African! (go, winged thought widen his forehead.)
20   13. The fiery limbs, the flaming hair, shot like the sinking sun into the western sea.

14. Wak'd from his eternal sleep, the hoary° element roaring fled   grey-haired
away:

15. Down rushd beating his wings in vain the jealous king: his
25   grey brow'd councellors, thunderous warriors, curl'd veterans, among helms, and shields, and chariots horses, elephants: banners, castles, slings and rocks,

16. Falling, rushing, ruining! buried in the ruins, on Urthona's[14] dens.

17. All night beneath the ruins, then their sullen flames faded
30   emerge round the gloomy king,

18. With thunder and fire: leading his starry hosts thro' the waste wilderness [PL 27] he promulgates his ten commands, glancing his beamy eyelids over the deep in dark dismay,

19. Where the son of fire in his eastern cloud, while the morn-
35   ing plumes her golden breast,

20. Spurning the clouds written with curses, stamps the stony law to dust, loosing the eternal horses from the dens of night, crying

Empire is no more! and now the lion & wolf shall cease.

Chorus

Let the Priests of the Raven of dawn, no longer in deadly black,
40   with hoarse note curse the sons of joy. Nor his accepted brethren whom, tyrant, he calls free; lay the bound or build the roof. Nor pale religious letchery call that virginity, that wishes but acts not!

For every thing that lives is Holy.

---

[13] **infinite . . . sea:** Lost continent of Atlantis.
[14] **Urthona:** Literally translated, "Earth-owner." In Blake's later poems, Urthona is a symbol of creative power.

CARL SANDBURG (1878–1967)

Chicago (1916)

Hog Butcher for the World,
Tool Maker, Stacker of Wheat,
Player with Railroads and the Nation's Freight Handler;
Stormy, husky, brawling,
5   City of the Big Shoulders:

They tell me you are wicked and I believe them, for I have seen
     your painted women under the gas lamps luring the farm boys.
And they tell me you are crooked and I answer: Yes, it is true I
     have seen the gunman kill and go free to kill again.
And they tell me you are brutal and my reply is: On the faces of
     women and children I have seen the marks of wanton hunger.
And having answered so I turn once more to those who sneer at
     this my city, and I give them back the sneer and say to them:
10   Come and show me another city with lifted head singing so
     proud to be alive and coarse and strong and cunning.
Flinging magnetic curses amid the toil of piling job on job, here is
     a tall bold slugger set vivid against the little soft cities;
Fierce as a dog with tongue lapping for action, cunning as a savage
     pitted against the wilderness,
       Bareheaded,
       Shoveling,
15   Wrecking,
       Planning,
       Building, breaking, rebuilding,
Under the smoke, dust all over his mouth, laughing with white
     teeth,
Under the terrible burden of destiny laughing as a young man
     laughs,
20   Laughing even as an ignorant fighter laughs who has never lost a
     battle,
Bragging and laughing that under his wrist is the pulse, and under
     his ribs the heart of the people,
           Laughing!
Laughing the stormy, husky, brawling laughter of Youth, half-naked,
     sweating, proud to be Hog Butcher, Tool Maker, Stacker of
     Wheat,
25   Player with Railroads and Freight Handler to the Nation.

WILLIAM CARLOS WILLIAMS (1883–1963)

The Dance (1962)

In Brueghel's great picture,[1] The Kermess,
the dancers go round, they go round and
around, the squeal and the blare and the
tweedle of bagpipes, a bugle and fiddles
5   tipping their bellies (round as the thick-
sided glasses whose wash they impound)
their hips and their bellies off balance
to turn them. Kicking and rolling
about the Fair Grounds, swinging their butts, those
10   shanks must be sound to bear up under such
rollicking measures, prance as they dance
in Brueghel's great picture, The Kermess.

WILLIAM CARLOS WILLIAMS (1883–1963)

Portrait of a Lady (1934)

Your thighs are appletrees
whose blossoms touch the sky.
Which sky? The sky
where Watteau hung a lady's
5   slipper. Your knees
are a southern breeze—or
a gust of snow. Agh! what
sort of man was Fragonard?[1]
—as if that answered
10   anything. Ah, yes—below
the knees, since the tune
drops that way, it is
one of those white summer days,
the tall grass of your ankles
15   flickers upon the shore—

---

[1] **Brueghel's great picture:** Pieter Brueghel (1525–1569), a Flemish painter known for his portrayal of landscapes.
[1] **Watteau . . . Fragonard:** Jean-Antoine Watteau (1684–1721), a French artist famous for his pictures of theater, ballet, and outdoor gatherings. Williams refers here, however, to "The Swing" by French artist Jean Honoré Fragonard (1732–1806), a painting that portrays a girl on a swing whose kicked-off slipper is suspended in mid-air.

Which shore?—
the sand clings to my lips—
Which shore?
Agh, petals maybe. How
20   should I know?
Which shore? Which shore?
I said petals from an appletree.

D. H. LAWRENCE (1885–1930)

Bavarian Gentians[1] (1932)

Not every man has gentians in his house
in soft September, at slow, sad Michaelmas.[2]

Bavarian gentians, big and dark, only dark
darkening the day-time, torch-like with the smoking blueness of
        Pluto's gloom,
5   ribbed and torch-like, with their blaze of darkness spread blue
down flattening into points, flattened under the sweep of white day
torch-flower of the blue-smoking darkness, Pluto's dark-blue daze,
black lamps from the halls of Dis,[3] burning dark blue,
giving off darkness, blue darkness, as Demeter's pale lamps give
        off light,
10   lead me then, lead the way.

Reach me a gentian, give me a torch!
let me guide myself with the blue, forked torch of this flower
down the darker and darker stairs, where blue is darkened on
        blueness
even where Persephone goes, just now, from the frosted September
15   to the sightless realm where darkness is awake upon the dark
and Persephone herself is but a voice
or a darkness invisible enfolded in the deeper dark
of the arms Plutonic, and pierced with the passion of dense gloom,
among the splendour of torches of darkness, shedding darkness
        on the lost bride and her groom.

---

[1] **Gentians:** Blue flowers.
[2] **Michaelmas:** September 29, the Feast of St. Michael.
[3] **Dis:** Roman name for Pluto, god of the underworld. Pluto stole Persephone from Demeter, goddess
of the natural earth, yet allowed her to return to the living earth each summer.

H. D. (HILDA DOOLITTLE) (1886–1961)

Sea Rose (1916)

Rose, harsh rose,
marred and with stint of petals,
meagre flower, thin,
sparse of leaf,

5   more precious
than a wet rose
single on a stem—
you are caught in the drift.

Stunted, with small leaf,
10   you are flung on the sand,
you are lifted
in the crisp sand
that drives in the wind.

Can the spice-rose
15   drip such acrid fragrance
hardened in a leaf?

ROBINSON JEFFERS (1887–1962)

Boats in a Fog (1924)

Sports and gallantries, the stage, the arts, the antics of dancers,
The exuberant voices of music,
Have charm for children but lack nobility; it is bitter earnestness
That makes beauty; the mind
5   Knows, grown adult.
              A sudden fog-drift muffled the ocean,
A throbbing of engines moved in it,
At length, a stone's throw out, between the rocks and the vapor,
One by one moved shadows
10   Out of the mystery, shadows, fishing-boats, trailing each other,
Following the cliff for guidance,
Holding a difficult path between the peril of the sea-fog
And the foam on the shore granite.
One by one, trailing their leader, six crept by me,
15   Out of the vapor and into it,
The throb of their engines subdued by the fog, patient and cautious,

Coasting all round the peninsula
Back to the buoys in Monterey harbor. A flight of pelicans
Is nothing lovelier to look at;
20   The flight of the planets is nothing nobler; all the arts lose virtue
Against the essential reality
Of creatures going about their business among the equally
Earnest elements of nature.

E. E. CUMMINGS (1894–1962)

"Buffalo Bill's/defunct" (1923)

Buffalo Bill's[1]
defunct
          who used to
          ride a watersmooth-silver
5   stallion
and break onetwothreefourfive pigeonsjustlikethat
                                        Jesus
he was a handsome man
                    and what i want to know is
10   how do you like your blueeyed boy
Mister Death

JEAN TOOMER (1894–1967)

Harvest Song (1923)

I am a reaper whose muscles set at sundown. All my oats are cradled.
But I am too chilled, and too fatigued to bind them. And I hunger.

I crack a grain between my teeth. I do not taste it.
I have been in the fields all day. My throat is dry. I hunger.

5   My eyes are caked with dust of oatfields at harvest-time.
I am a blind man who stares across the hills, seeking stacked fields
          of other harvesters.

---

[1] **Buffalo Bill's:** Buffalo Bill (1846–1917), a famous United States showman known for his Wild West Show.

It would be good to see them . . crook'd, split, and iron-ringed
  handles of the scythes. It would be good to see them,
  dust-caked and blind. I hunger.

(Dusk is a strange feared sheath their blades are dulled in.)
10 My throat is dry. And should I call, a cracked grain like the oats . . .
  eoho—

I fear to call. What should they hear me, and offer me their grain,
  oats, or wheat, or corn? I have been in the fields all day. I fear
  I could not taste it. I fear knowledge of my hunger.

My ears are caked with dust of oatfields at harvest-time.
15 I am a deaf man who strains to hear the calls of other harvesters
  whose throats are also dry.

It would be good to hear their songs . . reapers of the sweet-stalked
  cane, cutters of the corn . . even though their throats cracked
  and the strangeness of their voices deafened me.

I hunger. My throat is dry. Now that the sun has set and I am chilled,
  I fear to call. (Eoho, my brothers!)

20 I am a reaper. (Eoho!) All my oats are cradled. But I am too fatigued
  to bind them. And I hunger. I crack a grain. It has no taste to
  it. My throat is dry . . .

O my brothers, I beat my palms, still soft, against the stubble of my
  harvesting. (You beat your soft palms, too.) My pain is sweet.
  Sweeter than the oats or wheat or corn. It will not bring me
  knowledge of my hunger.

W. H. AUDEN (1907–1973)

Musée des Beaux Arts[1] (1938)

About suffering they were never wrong,
The Old Masters: how well they understood
Its human position; how it takes place
While someone else is eating or opening a window or just
            walking dully along;

---

[1] **Musée des Beaux Arts:** The Museum of Fine Arts (French).

5   How, when the aged are reverently, passionately waiting
For the miraculous birth, there always must be
Children who did not specially want it to happen, skating
On a pond at the edge of the wood:
They never forgot
10   That even the dreadful martyrdom must run its course
Anyhow in a corner, some untidy spot
Where the dogs go on with their doggy life and the torturer's horse
Scratches its innocent behind on a tree.

In Brueghel's *Icarus*,[2] for instance: how everything turns away
15   Quite leisurely from the disaster; the ploughman may
Have heard the splash, the forsaken cry,
But for him it was not an important failure; the sun shone
As it had to on the white legs disappearing into the green
Water; and the expensive delicate ship that must have seen
20   Something amazing, a boy falling out of the sky,
Had somewhere to get to and sailed calmly on.

THEODORE ROETHKE (1908–1963)

Orchids (1948)

They lean over the path,
Adder-mouthed,°   snake-mouthed
Swaying close to the face,
Coming out, soft and deceptive,
5   Limp and damp, delicate as a young bird's tongue;
Their fluttery fledgling lips
Move slowly,
Drawing in the warm air.

---

[2] **Brueghel's *Icarus*:** Pieter Bruegel (ca. 1525–1569), also known as Pieter Bruegel the Elder (to distinguish from his son, also a painter), was perhaps the greatest Flemish painter of the sixteenth century. His masterpiece, *Landscape with the Fall of Icarus* depicts a serene countryside with a plowman and a shepherd in the foreground and ships sailing in the nearby bay. Though the painting is named after him, Icarus appears on the horizon only as a small dot, a pair of legs protruding from the green water. *Note:* Icarus was the son of Daedalus, the famous architect who was imprisoned in the Labyrinth by king Minos. In order to escape, Daedalus devised wings for himself and his son. Advised by his father not to fly too close to the sun, Icarus nonetheless ignored the warnings, the wax holding his wings together melted, and he fell into the sea to his death.

And at night,
10   The faint moon falling through whitewashed glass,
The heat going down
So their musky smell comes even stronger,
Drifting down from their mossy cradles:
So many devouring infants!
15   Soft luminescent fingers,
Lips neither dead nor alive,
Loose ghostly mouths
Breathing.

CZESLAW MILOSZ   (1911–2004)
trans. by the author

On Angels   (1969)

All was taken away from you: white dresses,
wings, even existence.
Yet I believe you,
messengers.

5   There, where the world is turned inside out,
a heavy fabric embroidered with stars and beasts,
you stroll, inspecting the trustworthy seams.

Short is your stay here:
now and then at a matinal° hour, if the sky is clear,   morning
10   in a melody repeated by a bird,
or in the smell of apples at the close of day
when the light makes the orchards magic.

They say somebody has invented you
but to me this does not sound convincing
15   for humans invented themselves as well.

The voice—no doubt it is a valid proof,
as it can belong only to radiant creatures,
weightless and winged (after all, why not?),
girdled with the lightning.

20   I have heard that voice many a time when asleep
and, what is strange, I understood more or less
an order or an appeal in an unearthly tongue:

day draws near
another one
25   do what you can.

JOHN BERRYMAN (1914–1972)

from The Dream Songs
"Life, friends, is boring . . ." (1964)

Life, friends, is boring. We must not say so.
After all, the sky flashes, the great sea yearns,
we ourselves flash and yearn,
and moreover my mother told me as a boy
5   (repeatingly) 'Ever to confess you're bored
means you have no

Inner Resources.' I conclude now I have no
inner resources, because I am heavy bored.
Peoples bore me,
10   literature bores me, especially great literature,
Henry bores me, with his plights & gripes
as bad as achilles,

who loves people and valiant art, which bores me.
And the tranquil hills, & gin, look like a drag
15   and somehow a dog
has taken itself & its tail considerably away
into mountains or sea or sky, leaving
behind: me, wag.

ROBERT LOWELL (1917–1977)

Grandparents (1959)

They're altogether otherworldly now,
those adults champing for their ritual Friday spin
to pharmacist and five-and-ten in Brockton.
Back in my throw-away and shaggy span
5   of adolescence, Grandpa still waves his stick
like a policeman;
Grandmother, like a Mohammedan, still wears her thick
lavender mourning and touring veil;

the Pierce Arrow[1] clears its throat in a horse stall.
10   Then the dry road dust rises to whiten
the fatigued elm leaves—
the nineteenth century, tired of children, is gone.
They're all gone into a world of light; the farm's my own.

The farm's my own!
15   Back there alone,
I keep indoors, and spoil another season.
I hear the rattly little country gramophone
racking its five foot horn:
"O Summer Time!"
20   Even at noon here the formidable
Ancien Régime[2] still keeps nature at a distance. Five
green shaded light bulbs spider the billiards-table;
no field is greener than its cloth,
where Grandpa, dipping sugar for us both,
25   once spilled his demitasse.[3]
His favorite ball, the number three,
still hides the coffee stain.
Never again
to walk there, chalk our cues,
30   insist on shooting for us both.
Grandpa! Have me, hold me, cherish me!
Tears smut my fingers. There
half my life-lease later,
I hold an *Illustrated London News*—;
35   disloyal still,
I doodle handlebar
mustaches on the last Russian Czar.

PHILIP LARKIN   (1922–1985)

Days   (1953)

What are days for?
Days are where we live.
They come, they wake us

---

[1] **Pierce Arrow:** A luxury automobile produced in the United States from 1901 to 1938, known for its elegance and prestige.
[2] ***Ancien Régime*:** A political or social system no longer in power.
[3] **demitasse:** Black coffee in a small cup.

Time and time over.
5   They are to be happy in:
Where can we live but days?

Ah, solving that question
Brings the priest and the doctor
In their long coats
10 Running over the fields.

JAMES SCHUYLER   (1923–1991)

A Man in Blue   (1969)

Under the French horns of a November afternoon
a man in blue is raking leaves
with a wide wooden rake (whose teeth are pegs
or rather, dowels). Next door
5   boys play soccer: "You got to start
over!" sort of. A round attic window
in a radiant gray house waits like a kettledrum.
"You got to start . . ." The Brahmsian[1] day
lapses from waltz to march. The grass,
10 rough-cropped as Bruno Walter's[2] hair,
is stretched, strewn and humped beneath a sycamore
wide and high as an idea of heaven
in which Brahms turns his face like a bearded thumb
and says, "There is something I must tell you!"
15 to Bruno Walter. "In the first movement
of my Second, think of it as a family
planning where to go next summer
in terms of other summers. A material ecstasy,
subdued, recollective." Bruno Walter
20 in a funny jacket with a turned-up collar
says, "Let me sing it for you."
He waves his hands and through the vocalese-shaped[3] spaces

---

[1] **Brahmsian:** Johannes Brahms (1833–1897), a German composer of classical music.
[2] **Bruno Walter's:** Bruno Walter (1876–1962), a German composer and conductor. Born in Berlin, he immigrated to the United States in 1939.
[3] **vocalese-shaped:** Musical style in which a singer adds words to a jazz tune.

of naked elms he draws a copper beech
ignited with a few late leaves. He bluely glazes
25   a rhododendron "a sea of leaves" against gold grass.
There is a snapping from the brightwork
of parked and rolling cars.
There almost has to be a heaven! so there could be
a place for Bruno Walter
30   who never needed the cry of a baton.
Immortality—
in a small, dusty, rather gritty, somewhat scratchy
Magnavox from which a forte
drops like a used Brillo pad?
35   Frayed. But it's hard to think of the sky as a thick glass floor
with thick-soled Viennese boots tromping about on it.
It's a whole lot harder thinking of Brahms
in something soft, white and flowing.
"Life," he cries (here, in the last movement),
40   "is something more than beer and skittles!"[4]
"And the something more
is a whole lot better than beer and skittles,"
says Bruno Walter,
darkly, under the sod. I don't suppose it seems so dark
45   to a root. Who are these men in evening coats?
What are these thumps?
Where is Brahms?
And Bruno Walter?
Ensconced in resonant plump easy chairs
50   covered with scuffed brown leather
in a pungent autumn that blends leaf smoke
(sycamore, tobacco, other),
their nobility wound in a finale
like this calico cat
55   asleep, curled up in a breadbasket,
on a sideboard where the sun falls.

---

[4] **Life . . . skittles:** Skittles, a game like bowling, where a player attempts to knock over nine pins in as few rolls as possible. The phrase "more than beer and skittles" figuratively suggests that life is more than unmixed enjoyment.

GERALD STERN (1925–   )

On the Island (1977)

After cheating each other for eighteen years
this husband and this wife are trying to do something with the three
days they still have left before they go back to the city;
and after cheating the world for fifty years these two old men
5 touch the rosy skin under their white hair and try to remember
the days of solid brass and real wood
before the Jews came onto the island.
They are worried about the trees in India
and the corruption in the Boy Scouts
10 and the climbing interest rate,
but most of all they spend their time remembering
the beach the way it was in the early thirties
when all the big hotels here were shaped like Greek churches.

Me, I think about salt
15 and how my life will one day be clean and simple
if only I can reduce it all to salt,
how I will no longer lie down like a tired dog,
whispering and sighing before I go to sleep,
how I will be able to talk to someone
20 without going from pure joy to silence
and touch someone
without going from truth to concealment.

Salt is the only thing that lasts on this island.
It gets into the hair, into the eyes, into the clothes,
25 into the wood, into the metal.
Everything is going to disappear here but the salt.
The flags will go, the piers,
the gift shops, the golf courses, the clam bars,
and the telephone poles and the rows of houses and the string of
            cars.

30 I like to think of myself turned to salt
and all that I love turned to salt;
I like to think of coating whatever is left
with my own tongue and fingers.
I like to think of floating again in my first home,
35 still remembering the warm rock
and its slow destruction,
still remembering the first conversion to blood
and the forcing of the sea into those cramped vessels.

A. R. AMMONS   (1926–2001)

Grassy Sound   (1960)

It occurred to me there are no
    sharp corners
        in the wind
and I was very glad to think
5   I had so close
      a neighbor
to my thoughts but decided to
    sleep before
        inquiring

10 The next morning I got up early
    and after yesterday had come
        clear again went
down to the salt marshes
    to talk with
15   the straight wind there
I have observed I said
    your formlessness
      and am

enchanted to know how
20   you manage loose to be
        so influential

The wind came as grassy sound
    and between its
        grassy teeth
25 spoke words said with grass
    and read itself
        on tidal creeks as on
the screens of oscilloscopes°   electrical monitor
    A heron opposing
30   it rose wing to wind

turned and glided to another creek
    so I named a body of water
        Grassy Sound
and came home dissatisfied there
35   had been no
      direct reply
but rubbed with my soul an
    apple to eat
        till it shone

ALLEN GINSBERG (1926–1997)

from Howl (1956)
For Carl Solomon

I

I saw the best minds of my generation destroyed by madness, starv-
        ing hysterical naked,
dragging themselves through the negro streets at dawn looking for
        an angry fix,
angelheaded hipsters burning for the ancient heavenly connec-
        tion to the starry dynamo in the machinery of night,
who poverty and tatters and hollow-eyed and high sat up smoking
        in the supernatural darkness of cold-water flats floating across
        the tops of cities contemplating jazz,

5   who bared their brains to Heaven under the El° and saw Moham-   elevated train
        medan angels staggering on tenement roofs illuminated,
who passed through universities with radiant cool eyes hallucinat-
        ing Arkansas and Blake-light tragedy[1] among the scholars of
        war,
who were expelled from the academies for crazy & publishing
        obscene odes on the windows of the skull,
who cowered in unshaven rooms in underwear, burning their
        money in wastebaskets and listening to the Terror through the
        wall,
who got busted in their pubic beards returning through Laredo
        with a belt of marijuana for New York,

10   who ate fire in paint hotels or drank turpentine in Paradise Alley,[2]
        death, or purgatoried their torsos night after night
with dreams, with drugs, with waking nightmares, alcohol and
        cock and endless balls,
incomparable blind streets of shuddering cloud and lightning in
        the mind leaping toward poles of Canada & Paterson,[3] illumi-
        nating all the motionless world of Time between,
Peyote[4] solidities of halls, backyard green tree cemetery dawns,
        wine drunkenness over the rooftops, storefront boroughs of
        teahead joyride neon blinking traffic light, sun and moon and
        tree vibrations in the roaring winter dusks of Brooklyn, ashcan
        rantings and kind king light of mind,
who chained themselves to subways for the endless ride from Bat-

---

[1] **Blake-light tragedy:** Refers to William Blake (1757–1827), an English visionary poet who, according
to Ginsberg, once appeared to him in a vision in his Harlem apartment.
[2] **Paradise Alley:** Slum courtyard in New York City.
[3] **Paterson:** In New Jersey, the city of Ginsberg's birth.
[4] **Peyote:** Hallucinogen derived from a small, spineless cactus.

tery to holy Bronx[5] on benzedrine until the noise of wheels
and children brought them down shuddering mouth-wracked
and battered bleak of brain all drained of brilliance in the
drear light of Zoo,

15 who sank all night in submarine light of Bickford's[6] floated out and
sat through the stale beer afternoon in desolate Fugazzi's,[7] listening to the crack of doom on the hydrogen jukebox,

who talked continuously seventy hours from park to pad to bar to
Bellevue[8] to museum to the Brooklyn Bridge,

a lost battalion of platonic conversationalists jumping down the
stoops off fire escapes off windowsills off Empire State out of
the moon,

yacketayakking screaming vomiting whispering facts and memories and anecdotes and eyeball kicks and shocks of hospitals
and jails and wars,

whole intellects disgorged in total recall for seven days and nights
with brilliant eyes, meat for the Synagogue cast on the pavement,

20 who vanished into nowhere Zen New Jersey leaving a trail of am-
biguous picture postcards of Atlantic City[9] Hall,

suffering Eastern sweats and Tangerian bone-grindings and
migraines of China under junk-withdrawal in Newark's bleak
furnished room,

who wandered around and around at midnight in the railroad
yard wondering where to go, and went, leaving no broken
hearts,

who lit cigarettes in boxcars boxcars boxcars racketing through
snow toward lonesome farms in grandfather night,

who studied Plotinus Poe St. John of the Cross[10] telepathy and bop
kaballa[11] because the cosmos instinctively vibrated at their
feet in Kansas,

25 who loned it through the streets of Idaho seeking visionary indian
angels who were visionary indian angels,

who thought they were only mad when Baltimore gleamed in
supernatural ecstasy,[12]

---

[5] **Battery . . . Bronx:** Endpoints of a New York City subway line; the Bronx is the location of the zoo.
[6] **Bickford's:** Chain of cafeterias open twenty-four hours a day, where Ginsberg once held a job
mopping floors.
[7] **Fugazzi's:** Bar near New York City's Greenwich Village.
[8] **Bellevue:** Public hospital and receiving center for mental patients.
[9] **Atlantic City:** Beach town in southeastern New Jersey, known for its gambling.
[10] **Plotinus . . . Cross:** Plotinus (205–270), mystic philosopher. Edgar Allen Poe (1809–1894), poet
and author of supernatural tales. St. John of the Cross (1542–1591), Spanish mystic and poet, author
of *The Dark Night of the Soul.*
[11] **bop kaballa:** Bop refers to a style of jazz popular in the 1940s, while the Kaballa refers to a tradition
of Hebrew mysticism.
[12] **Baltimore . . . ecstasy:** Baltimore is the site of Edgar Allen Poe's home and grave.

who jumped in limousines with the Chinaman of Oklahoma on the impulse of winter midnight streetlight smalltown rain,

who lounged hungry and lonesome through Houston seeking jazz or sex or soup, and followed the brilliant Spaniard to converse about America and Eternity, a hopeless task, and so took ship to Africa,

who disappeared into the volcanoes of Mexico leaving behind nothing but the shadow of dungarees and the lava and ash of poetry scattered in fireplace Chicago,

30 who reappeared on the West Coast investigating the F.B.I. in beards and shorts with big pacifist eyes sexy in their dark skin passing out incomprehensible leaflets,

who burned cigarette holes in their arms protesting the narcotic tobacco haze of Capitalism,

who distributed Supercommunist pamphlets in Union Square weeping and undressing while the sirens of Los Alamos[13] wailed them down, and wailed down Wall,[14] and the Staten Island ferry also wailed,

who broke down crying in white gymnasiums naked and trembling before the machinery of other skeletons,

who bit detectives in the neck and shrieked with delight in policecars for committing no crime but their own wild cooking pederasty and intoxication,

35 who howled on their knees in the subway and were dragged off the roof waving genitals and manuscripts,

who let themselves be fucked in the ass by saintly motorcyclists, and screamed with joy,

who blew and were blown by those human seraphim, the sailors, caresses of Atlantic and Caribbean love,

who balled in the morning in the evenings in rosegardens and the grass of public parks and cemeteries scattering their semen freely to whomever come who may,

who hiccupped endlessly trying to giggle but wound up with a sob behind a partition in a Turkish Bath when the blonde & naked angel came to pierce them with a sword,

40 who lost their loveboys to the three old shrews of fate[15] the one eyed shrew of the heterosexual dollar the one eyed shrew that winks out of the womb and the one eyed shrew that does nothing but sit on her ass and snip the intellectual golden threads of the craftsman's loom,

---

[13] **Los Alamos:** Town in New Mexico, chosen in 1942 as a nuclear research site, where the first atomic bombs were produced.

[14] **wailed down Wall:** Refers to Wall Street, the financial center in New York City, but also to the Wailing Wall in Jerusalem, a landmark of prayer and mourning.

[15] **three . . . fate:** Known as the Moirae, the three goddesses of fate in Greek mythology spin the thread of life, allot its length, and sever it at life's end.

who copulated ecstatic and insatiate with a bottle of beer a sweet-
heart a package of cigarettes a candle and fell off the bed, and
continued along the floor and down the hall and ended fainting on the wall with a vision of ultimate cunt and come elud-
ing the last gyzym of consciousness,

who sweetened the snatches of a million girls trembling in the
sunset, and were red eyed in the morning but prepared to
sweeten the snatch of the sunrise, flashing buttocks under
barns and naked in the lake,

who went out whoring through Colorado in myriad stolen night-
cars, N.C.,[16] secret hero of these poems, cocksman and Adonis
of Denver—joy to the memory of his innumerable lays of girls
in empty lots & diner backyards, moviehouses' rickety rows,
on mountaintops in caves or with gaunt waitresses in familiar
roadside lonely petticoat upliftings & especially secret gas-
station solipsisms of johns, & hometown alleys too,

who faded out in vast sordid movies, were shifted in dreams, woke
on a sudden Manhattan, and picked themselves up out
of basements hung-over with heartless Tokay° and horrors of   Hungarian wine
Third Avenue iron dreams & stumbled to unemployment
offices,

45   who walked all night with their shoes full of blood on the snow-
bank docks waiting for a door in the East River to open to a
room full of steamheat and opium,

who created great suicidal dramas on the apartment cliff-banks of
the Hudson under the wartime blue floodlight of the moon &
their heads shall be crowned with laurel in oblivion,

who ate the lamb stew of the imagination or digested the crab at
the muddy bottom of the rivers of Bowery,[17]

who wept at the romance of the streets with their pushcarts full of
onions and bad music,

who sat in boxes breathing in the darkness under the bridge, and
rose up to build harpsichords in their lofts,

50   who coughed on the sixth floor of Harlem crowned with flame
under the tubercular sky surrounded by orange crates of
theology,

who scribbled all night rocking and rolling over lofty incantations
which in the yellow morning were stanzas of gibberish,

who cooked rotten animals lung heart feet tail borsht° & tortillas   Russian soup
dreaming of the pure vegetable kingdom,

who plunged themselves under meat trucks looking for an egg,

who threw their watches off the roof to cast their ballot for Eternity

---

[16] **N.C.:** Neal Cassady (1926–1968), friend and lover of the author.
[17] **Bowery:** Street in Manhattan, associated with alcoholics and drifters.

outside of Time, & alarm clocks fell on their heads every day for the next decade,

55 who cut their wrists three times successively unsuccessfully, gave up and were forced to open antique stores where they thought they were growing old and cried,

who were burned alive in their innocent flannel suits on Madison Avenue[18] amid blasts of leaden verse & the tanked-up clatter of the iron regiments of fashion & the nitroglycerine shrieks of the fairies of advertising & the mustard gas of sinister intelligent editors, or were run down by the drunken taxicabs of Absolute Reality,

who jumped off the Brooklyn Bridge this actually happened and walked away unknown and forgotten into the ghostly daze of Chinatown soup alleyways & firetrucks, not even one free beer,

who sang out of their windows in despair, fell out of the subway window, jumped in the filthy Passaic,[19] leaped on negroes, cried all over the street, danced on broken wineglasses barefoot smashed phonograph records of nostalgic European 1930's German jazz finished the whiskey and threw up groaning into the bloody toilet, moans in their ears and the blast of colossal steam-whistles,

who barreled down the highways of the past journeying to each other's hotrod-Golgotha[20] jail-solitude watch or Birmingham jazz incarnation,

60 who drove crosscountry seventytwo hours to find out if I had a vision or you had a vision or he had a vision to find out Eternity.

who journeyed to Denver, who died in Denver, who came back to Denver & waited in vain, who watched over Denver & brooded & loned in Denver and finally went away to find out the Time, & now Denver is lonesome for her heroes,

who fell on their knees in hopeless cathedrals praying for each other's salvation and light and breasts, until the soul illuminated its hair for a second,

who crashed through their minds in jail waiting for impossible criminals with golden heads and the charm of reality in their hearts who sang sweet blues to Alcatraz,

who retired to Mexico to cultivate a habit, or Rocky Mount to

---

[18] **innocent . . . Avenue:** Madison Avenue is the center of New York's advertising business. *The Man in the Gray Flannel Suit* was a best-selling novel by Sloan Wilson. Both references suggest the conformity of the 1950s.

[19] **Passaic:** River that flows through Paterson, New Jersey; a source of inspiration for both Ginsberg and William Carlos Williams (1883–1963).

[20] **Golgotha:** Hill near Jerusalem, where Jesus was crucified.

tender Buddha or Tangiers[21] to boys or Southern Pacific to
the black locomotive or Harvard to Narcissus to Woodlawn[22]
to the daisy-chain or grave,

65   who demanded sanity trials accusing the radio of hypnotism &
were left with their insanity & their hands & a hung jury,

who threw potato salad at CCNY lecturers on Dadaism[23] and subsequently presented themselves on the granite steps of the
madhouse with shaven heads and harlequin speech of suicide, demanding instantaneous lobotomy,

and who were given instead the concrete void of insulin metrasol
electricity hydrotherapy psychotherapy occupational therapy
pingpong & amnesia,

who in humorless protest overturned only one symbolic pingpong
table, resting briefly in catatonia,

returning years later truly bald except for a wig of blood, and tears
and fingers, to the visible madman doom of the wards of the
madtowns of the East,

70   Pilgrim State's Rockland's and Greystone's[24] foetid halls, bickering
with the echoes of the soul, rocking and rolling in the midnight solitude-bench dolmen°-realms of love, dream of life a
nightmare, bodies turned to stone as heavy as the moon,

                                           prehistoric
                                           monument

with mother finally ******, and the last fantastic book flung out of
the tenement window, and the last door closed at 4 AM and
the last telephone slammed at the wall in reply and the last furnished room emptied down to the last piece of mental furniture, a yellow paper rose twisted on a wire hanger in the
closet, and even that imaginary, nothing but a hopeful little bit
of hallucination—

ah, Carl, while you are not safe I am not safe, and now you're really
in the total animal soup of time—

and who therefore ran through the icy streets obsessed with a
sudden flash of the alchemy of the use of the ellipse the cata-
log the meter & the vibrating plane,

who dreamt and made incarnate gaps in Time & Space through
images juxtaposed, and trapped the archangel of the soul
between 2 visual images and joined the elemental verbs and
set the noun and dash of consciousness together jumping with
sensation of Pater Omnipotens Aeterna Deus[25]

---

[21] **Tangiers:** City in northern Morocco.

[22] **Woodlawn:** Cemetery in the Bronx.

[23] **Dadaism:** Movement based on the presence of the absurd and accidental in artistic creation. CCNY
is an acronym for the City College of New York.

[24] **Pilgrim . . . Greystone's:** Three mental hospitals near New York City.

[25] **Pater Omnipotens Aeterna Deus:** "All-powerful Father, Eternal God," a phrase invoked by Impres-
sionist painter Paul Cézanne to describe the effect of nature on him.

75 to recreate the syntax and measure of poor human prose and
        stand before you speechless and intelligent and shaking with
        shame, rejected yet confessing out the soul to conform to the
        rhythm of thought in his naked and endless head,
    the madman bum and angel beat in Time, unknown, yet putting
        down here what might be left to say in time come after death,
    and rose reincarnate in the ghostly clothes of jazz in the goldhorn
        shadow of the band and blew the suffering of America's
        naked mind for love into an eli eli lamma lamma sabacthani[26]
        saxophone cry that shivered the cities down to the last radio
    with the absolute heart of the poem of life butchered out of their
        own bodies good to eat a thousand years.

JAMES WRIGHT (1927–1980)

Autumn Begins in Martins Ferry, Ohio (1963)

In the Shreve High football stadium,
I think of Polacks nursing long beers in Tiltonsville,
And gray faces of Negroes in the blast furnace at Benwood,
And the ruptured night watchman of Wheeling Steel,
5 Dreaming of heroes.

All the proud fathers are ashamed to go home.
Their women cluck like starved pullets,
Dying for love.

Therefore,
10 Their sons grow suicidally beautiful
At the beginning of October,
And gallop terribly against each other's bodies.

---

[26] **eli . . . sabacthani:** "My God, my God, why have you forsaken Me?" In Matthew 27:46, the last words of Christ.

PHILIP LEVINE (1928–   )

Salami (1972)

Stomach of goat, crushed
sheep balls, soft full
pearls of pig eyes,
snout gristle, fresh earth,
5 worn iron of trotter,° slate   foot of a pig
of Zaragoza, dried cat heart,
cock claws. She grinds
them with one hand and
with the other fists
10 mountain thyme, basil,
paprika, and knobs of garlic.
And if a tooth of stink thistle
pulls blood from the round
blue marbled hand
15 all the better for
this ruby of Pamplona,
this bright jewel of Vich,
this stained crown
of Solsona,[1] this
20 salami.
                The daughter
of mismatched eyes,
36 year old infant smelling
of milk. Mama, she cries, mama,
25 but mama is gone,
and the old stone cutter
must wipe the drool
from her jumper. His puffed fingers
unbutton and point her
30 to toilet. Ten, twelve hours
a day, as long as the winter sun
holds up he rebuilds
the unvisited church
of San Martín. Cheep cheep
35 of the hammer high above
the town, sparrow cries

---

[1] **Zaragoza . . . Solsona:** Pamplona, Vich, and Solsona are all cities in Spain.

lost in the wind or lost
in the mind. At dusk he leans
to the coal dull wooden Virgin
40   and asks for blessings on
the slow one and peace
on his grizzled head, asks
finally and each night
for the forbidden, for
45   the knowledge of every
mysterious stone, and
the words go out on
the overwhelming incense
of salami.
50   A single crow
passed high over the house,
I wakened out of nightmare.
The winds had changed,
the Tramontana² was tearing
55   out of the Holy Mountains
to meet the sea winds
in my yard, burning and
scaring the young pines.
The single poplar wailed
60   in terror. With salt,
with guilt, with the need
to die, the vestments
of my life flared, I
was on fire, a stranger
65   staggering through my house
butting walls and falling
over furniture, looking
for a way out. In the last room
where moonlight slanted
70   through a broken shutter
I found my smallest son
asleep or dead, floating
on a bed of colorless light.
When I leaned closer
75   I could smell the small breaths
going and coming, and each
bore its prayer for me,
the true and earthy prayer
of salami.

---

² **Tramontana:** Cold wind that blows south from the mountains into the Western Mediterranean.

ADRIENNE RICH (1929–   )

Diving into the Wreck (1973)

First having read the book of myths,
and loaded the camera,
and checked the edge of the knife-blade,
I put on
5   the body-armor of black rubber
the absurd flippers
the grave and awkward mask.
I am having to do this
not like Cousteau[1] with his
10   assiduous team
aboard the sun-flooded schooner
but here alone.

There is a ladder.
The ladder is always there
15   hanging innocently
close to the side of the schooner.
We know what it is for,
we who have used it.
Otherwise
20   it is a piece of maritime floss
some sundry equipment.

I go down.
Rung after rung and still
the oxygen immerses me
25   the blue light
the clear atoms
of our human air.
I go down.
My flippers cripple me,
30   I crawl like an insect down the ladder
and there is no one
to tell me when the ocean
will begin.

First the air is blue and then
35   it is bluer and then green and then
black I am blacking out and yet

---

[1] **Cousteau:** Jacques Cousteau (1910–1997) was a French oceanographer and author.

my mask is powerful
it pumps my blood with power
the sea is another story
40   the sea is not a question of power
I have to learn alone
to turn my body without force
in the deep element.

And now: it is easy to forget
45   what I came for
among so many who have always
lived here
swaying their crenellated° fans   notched, indented
between the reefs
50   and besides
you breathe differently down here.

I came to explore the wreck.
The words are purposes.
The words are maps.
55   I came to see the damage that was done
and the treasures that prevail.
I stroke the beam of my lamp
slowly along the flank
of something more permanent
60   than fish or weed

the thing I came for:
the wreck and not the story of the wreck
the thing itself and not the myth
the drowned face always staring
65   toward the sun
the evidence of damage
worn by salt and sway into this threadbare beauty
the ribs of the disaster
curving their assertion
70   among the tentative haunters.

This is the place.
And I am here, the mermaid whose dark hair
streams black, the merman in his armored body
We circle silently
75   about the wreck
we dive into the hold.
I am she: I am he

whose drowned face sleeps with open eyes
whose breasts still bear the stress
80   whose silver, copper, vermeil° cargo lies   gilded metal, or scarlet
obscurely inside barrels
half-wedged and left to rot
we are the half-destroyed instruments
that once held to a course
85   the water-eaten log
the fouled compass

We are, I am, you are
by cowardice or courage
the one who find our way
90   back to this scene
carrying a knife, a camera
a book of myths
in which
our names do not appear.

DIANE DI PRIMA (1934–   )

Backyard (1975)

where angels turned into honeysuckle & poured nectar into my mouth
where I french-kissed the roses in the rain
where demons tossed me a knife to kill my father in the stark
                    simplicity of the sky
where I never cried
5   where all the roofs were black
where no one opened the venetian blinds
O Brooklyn! Brooklyn!
where fences crumbled under the weight of rambling roses
and naked plaster women bent eternally white over birdbaths
10   the icicles on the chains of the swings tore my fingers
& the creaking tomato plants tore my heart as they wrapped their
                    roots around fish heads rotting beneath them
& the phonograph too creaked Caruso come down from the skies;
                    Tito Gobbi in gondola; Gigli ridiculous in soldier
                    uniform; Lanza frenetic[1]

---

[1] **phonograph . . . frenetic:** Enrico Caruso (1873–1921), Tito Gobbi (1915–1984), Beniamino Gigli
(1890–1957), and Mario Lanza (1921–1959) were all famous Italian opera singers.

& the needle tore at the records & my fingers
tore poems into little pieces & watched the sky
15 where clouds torn into pieces & livid w/neon or rain
scudded away from Red Hook,[2] away from Gowanus Canal, away
from Brooklyn Navy Yard where everybody worked, to fall to pieces
                over Clinton Street
and the plaster saints in the yard never looked at the naked women
                in the birdbaths
and the folks coming home from work in pizza parlor or furniture
                store, slamming wrought iron gates to come
                upon brownstone houses,
20 never looked at either: they saw that the lawns were dry
were eternally parched beneath red gloomy sunsets we viewed from
                a thousand brownstone stoops
leaning together by thousands on the same
wrought-iron bannister, watching the sun impaled
on black St. Stephen's steeple

CHARLES WRIGHT (1935–   )

Laguna Blues (1981)

It's Saturday afternoon at the edge of the world.
White pages lift in the wind and fall.
Dust threads, cut loose from the heart, float up and fall.
Something's off-key in my mind.
5 Whatever it is, it bothers me all the time.

It's hot, and the wind blows on what I have had to say.
I'm dancing a little dance.
The crows pick up a thermal[1] that angles away from the sea.
I'm singing a little song.
10 Whatever it is, it bothers me all the time.

It's Saturday afternoon and the crows glide down,
Black pages that lift and fall.
The castor beans and the pepper plant trundle their weary heads.
Something's off-key and unkind.
15 Whatever it is, it bothers me all the time.

---

[2] **Red Hook:** Neighborhood in Brooklyn, New York.
[1] **thermal:** Current of warm air, used by birds to gain height.

C. K. WILLIAMS (1936–   )

On Learning of a Friend's Illness (1983)
For James Wright

The morning is so gray that the grass is gray and the side of the
          white horse grazing
is as gray and hard as the harsh, insistent wind gnawing the iron
          surface of the river,
while far off on the other shore, the eruptions from the city seem
          for once more docile and benign
than the cover of nearly indistinguishable clouds they unfurl to
          insinuate themselves among.

5   It is a long while since the issues of mortality have taken me this
          way. Shivering,
I tramp the thin, bitten track to the first rise, the first descent, and,
          toiling up again,
I startle out of their brushy hollow the whole herd of wild-eyed,
          shaggy, unkempt mares,
their necks, rumps, withers, even faces begrimed with patches of
          the gluey, alluvial[1] mud.

All of them at once, their nostrils flared, their tails flung up over
          their backs like flags,
10 are suddenly in flight, plunging and shoving along the narrow
          furrow of the flood ditch,
bursting from its mouth, charging headlong toward the wires at
          the pasture's end,
banking finally like one great, graceful wing to scatter down the
          hillside out of sight.

Only the oldest of them all stays with me, and she, sway-backed,
          over at the knees,
blind, most likely deaf, still, when I move towards her, swings her
          meager backside to me,
15 her ears flattening, the imperturbable opals of her eyes gazing
          resolutely over the bare,
scruffy fields, the scattered pines and stands of third-growth oak I
          called a forest once.

---

[1] **alluvial:** Refers to a deposit of earth left by the flow of water over land not typically submerged.

I slip up on her, hook her narrow neck, haul her to me, hold her
      for a moment, let her go.
I hardly can remember anymore what there ever was out here
      that keeps me coming back
to watch the land be amputated by freeways and developments,
      and the mares, in their sanctuary,
20 thinning out, reverting, becoming less and less approachable,
      more and more the symbols of themselves.

How cold it is. The hoofprints in the hardened muck are frozen
      lakes, their rims atilt,
their glazed opacities skewered with straw, muddled with the
      ancient and ubiquitous manure.
I pick a morsel of it up: scentless, harmless, cool, as desiccated as
      an empty hive,
it crumbles in my hand, its weightless, wingless filaments taken
      from me by the wind and strewn

25 in a long, surprising arc that wavers once then seems to burst into
      a rain of dust.
No comfort here, nothing to say, to try to say, nothing for anyone.
      I start the long trek back,
the horses nowhere to be seen, the old one plodding wearily
      away to join them,
the river, bitter to look at, and the passionless earth, and the
      grasses rushing ceaselessly in place.

CHARLES SIMIC (1938–   )

Fear (1971)

Fear passes from man to man
Unknowing,
As one leaf passes its shudder
To another.

5 All at once the whole tree is trembling
And there is no sign of the wind.

SEAMUS HEANEY (1939–   )

Punishment (1975)

I can feel the tug
of the halter° at the nape   hangman's rope
of her neck, the wind
on her naked front.

5   It blows her nipples
to amber beads,
it shakes the frail rigging
of her ribs.

I can see her drowned
10 body in the bog,
the weighing stone,
the floating rods and boughs.

Under which at first
she was a barked sapling
15 that is dug up
oak-bone, brain-firkin:°   barrel

her shaved head
like a stubble of black corn,
her blindfold a soiled bandage,
20 her noose a ring

to store
the memories of love.
Little adulteress,
before they punished you

25 you were flaxen-haired,
undernourished, and your
tar-black face was beautiful.
My poor scapegoat,

I almost love you
30 but would have cast, I know,
the stones of silence.
I am the artful voyeur

of your brain's exposed
and darkened combs,
35   your muscles' webbing
and all your numbered bones:

I who have stood dumb
when your betraying sisters,
cauled° in tar,   hooded
40   wept by the railings,

who would connive
in civilized outrage
yet understand the exact
and tribal, intimate revenge.

ANNE CARSON (1950–   )

Lazarus (1st draft)   (2000)

Inside the rock on which we live, another rock.
So they believe.
What is a Lamb of God? People use this phrase.
I don't know.
5   I watch my sister, fingers straying absently about her mustache,
no help there.
Leaves stir through the house like souls, they stream
from the porch,
catch in the speaking holes, glow and are gone.
10 Remember
what Prince Andrei[1] said when they told him Moscow had burnt
right down to the ground.
He said *Really?*
A man who had been to the war! had seen our lives are just blind arrows flying.
15 There he sat
on his cot all the same, trying to get the string to the bowhorn.
Actions go on in us,
nothing else goes on. While a blurred and breathless hour
repeats, repeats.

---

[1] **Prince Andrei:** Prince Andrei Nikolayevich Bolkonsky, a character in Leo Tolstoy's *War and Peace.*

RITA DOVE (1952–   )

Dusting[1] (1986)
from *Thomas and Beulah*

Every day a wilderness—no
shade in sight. Beulah
patient among knicknacks,
the solarium a rage
5   of light, a grainstorm
as her gray cloth brings
dark wood to life.

Under her hand scrolls
and crests gleam
10   darker still. What
was his name, that
silly boy at the fair with
the rifle booth? And his kiss and
the clear bowl with one bright
15   fish, rippling
wound!

Not Michael—
something finer. Each dust
stroke a deep breath and
20   the canary in bloom.
Wavery memory: home
from a dance, the front door
blown open and the parlor
in snow, she rushed
25   the bowl to the stove, watched
as the locket of ice
dissolved and he
swam free.

That was years before
30   Father gave her up
with her name, years before
her name grew to mean

---

[1] **Dusting:** From a longer narrative whose main characters are African Americans born at the beginning of the twentieth century. *Thomas and Beulah* tells the same story from two contrasting perspectives.

Promise, then
Desert-in-Peace.
35 Long before the shadow and
sun's accomplice, the tree.

Maurice.

LI-YOUNG LEE (1957–   )

Night Mirror (2001)

Li-Young, don't feel lonely
when you look up
into great night and find
yourself the far face peering
5 hugely out from between
a star and a star. All that space
the nighthawk plunges through,
homing, all that distance beyond embrace,
what is it but your own infinity.

10 And don't be afraid
when, eyes closed, you look inside you
and find night is both
the silence tolling after stars
and the final word
15 that founds all beginning, find night,

abyss and shuttle,
a finished cloth
frayed by the years, then gathered
in the songs and games
20 mothers teach their children.

Look again
and find yourself changed
and changing, now the bewildered honey
fallen into your own hands,
25 now the immaculate fruit born of hunger.
Now the unequaled perfume of your dying.
And time? Time is the salty wake
of your stunned entrance upon
no name.

Section II

Themes

CHAPTER 15

LOVE'S AUSTERE AND LONELY OFFICES

—Robert Hayden

An Anthology of Poems about Family

Wallace Stevens once suggested that a poet's subject is his or her "sense of the world," so it should come as no surprise that poets often write about their families. Poetry deals with intimate experiences, and these experiences define a poet's sense of reality. As this selection of poems about family suggests, some of the finest poems in the language have dealt with this kind of intimacy—or lack of it.

The poems in this chapter are immensely various, calling up odd or commonplace relationships among members of a family and meditating on the responsibilities of love, as in Wendell Berry's "Marriage" (p. 998). In "I Go Back to May 1937" (p. 1009), Sharon Olds contemplates the early relationship between her parents in a wrenching poem. In "A Martian Sends a Postcard Home" (p. 1012), Craig Raine imagines what human relationships might look like from the point of view of a visitor from outer space, thus calling attention to the inherent oddness of human behavior in communal or family contexts.

Thus, we have Robert Hayden, in "Those Winter Sundays" (p. 990), remembering how his father would rise early and set the family day in motion. Fathers seem to play a huge role in many of these poems, as when Seamus Heaney remembers his father in "Digging," drawing a parallel between the work his father and grandfather did with a spade and the work he does with his pen. "I'll dig with it," he says. Another poem about fathers and sons is Alastair Reid's "Daedalus" (p. 992), an affecting poem written about a young boy from his father's point of view.

Theodore Roethke, on the other hand, writes about his own father—a German florist who owned a huge greenhouse in Saginaw, Michigan—with guarded affection, even fear, remembering the "whiskey on his breath" as the father danced his small son around the kitchen with the pots and pans flying. The boy's mother looks on with exasperation: "My mother's countenance / Could not unfrown itself." "My Papa's Waltz" (p. 989) is about this perilous dance, written in a three-beat, waltzing rhythm.

Among the most beautiful poems in English is Yeats's "A Prayer for My Daughter" (p. 983). Written in elegant stanzas, the poet—already in late middle age when his child was born—paces upon the battlements of the tower where he lived, wishing the best for his newborn child, hoping that one day she may occupy a house where all is "accustomed" and "ceremonious." While the poem now seems a little old-fashioned, even sexist, it remains a memorable piece of writing, one that reveals a powerful sense of a father's love for his daughter.

Each of the poems in this section is deeply felt, written in a straight-forward way that will engage the reader's attention from the outset. Each presents a small portrait of relationships, implying wider contexts—as in Douglas Dunn's remarkable "Men of Terry Street" (p. 1008), which summons a whole community that is now lost in time. In one of the oddest and most affecting poems in the selection, "Virgo Descending" (p. 1001), Charles Wright imagines a household lost in the earth, buried, quite literally, but resurrected, with all its power and ferocious sense of entanglement.

As Ezra Pound notes in the excerpt from *The Cantos* (p. 987), "What thou lovest well remains." There is something about relationships between members of a family or among close friends that seems beyond speech. Poets, of course, cannot resist the challenge of expressing the elusive. In these poems, there is considerable success at saying things that might not be spoken of often, or well, in the course of a life. These poets put words to the most intimate and delicate of issues, framing experience in unique and memorable ways.

ADDITIONAL POEMS ABOUT FAMILY IN THIS BOOK

ANONYMOUS

I Have a Young Sister   (fifteenth century)

I have a yong sister
    Fer° beyond the sea;   far
Manye be the druries
    That she sente me.

5   She sente me the cherry
        Withouten any stone,
    And so she did the dove
        Withouten any bone.

    She sente me the brere°   briar
10   Withouten any rinde;°   bark
    She bade me love my lemman°   dearest
        Without longing.

    How should any cherry
        Be withoute stone?
15   And how should any dove
        Be withoute bone?

    How should any brere
        Be withoute rind?
    How should I love my lemman
20   Without longing?

    When the cherry was a flowr,
        Then hadde it no stone.
    When the dove was an ey,°   egg
        Then hadde it no bone.

25   When the briar was unbred,
        Then hadde it no rinde.
    When the maiden hath that she loveth,
        She is without longinge.

SIR JOHN HARINGTON   (ca. 1561–1612)

To His Wife, For Striking Her Dog   (1618)

Your little dog, that barked as I came by,
I strake by hap so hard I made him cry;
And straight you put your finger in your eye,

And louring° sat. I asked the reason why.   scowling
5   'Love me, and love my dog,' thou didst reply.
    'Love as both should be loved.'—'I will,' said I,
    And sealed it with a kiss. Then by and by,
    Cleared were the clouds of thy fair frowning sky.
    Thus small events, greater masteries may try.
10   For I, by this, do at their meaning guess,
        That beat a whelp° afore° a lioness.   puppy / before

ROBERT HERRICK (1591–1674)

Upon a Child That Died (1648)

Here she lies, a pretty bud,
Lately made of flesh and blood,
Who as soon fell fast asleep
As her little eyes did peep.
5   Give her strewings,[1] but not stir
The earth that lightly covers her.

JOHN MILTON (1608–1674)

On His Dead Wife (1658; 1673)

Methought I saw my late espousèd saint
    Brought to me like Alcestis from the grave,
    Whom Jove's great son to her glad husband gave,
    Rescued from death by force, though pale and faint.[1]
5   Mine, as whom washed from spot of childbed taint
    Purification in the old Law° did save,   Old Testament
    And such as yet once more I trust to have
    Full sight of her in heaven without restraint,
Came vested all in white, pure as her mind.
10   Her face was veiled, yet to my fancied sight
    Love, sweetness, goodness, in her person shined
So clear as in no face with more delight.
    But O as to embrace me she inclined,
    I waked, she fled, and day brought back my night.

---

[1] **strewings:** Flowers cast on a grave.
[1] **Alcestis . . . faint:** In Greek mythology, Alcestis was a princess famous for her love of her husband
Admetus. When he fell ill, Alcestis agreed to die in his place, but was saved from Hades at the last
minute by Hercules.

ANNE BRADSTREET (ca. 1612–1672)

To My Dear and Loving Husband (1678)

If ever two were one, then surely we.
If ever man were loved by wife, then thee;
If ever wife was happy in a man,
Compare with me, ye women, if you can.
5   I prize thy love more than whole mines of gold,
Or all the riches that the east doth hold.
My love is such that rivers cannot quench,
Nor ought but love from thee give recompense.
Thy love is such I can no way repay:
10   The heavens reward thee manifold, I pray.
Then while we live, in love let's so persévere
That, when we live no more, we may live ever.

JOANNA BAILLIE (1762–1851)

A Mother to Her Waking Infant (1790)

Now in thy dazzling half-oped eye,
Thy curlèd nose and lip awry,
Thy up-hoist arms and noddling head,
And little chin with crystal spread,
5   Poor helpless thing! what do I see,
    That I should sing of thee?

From thy poor tongue no accents come,
Which can but rub thy toothless gum;
Small understanding boasts thy face,
10   Thy shapeless limbs nor step nor grace;
A few short words thy feats may tell,
    And yet I love thee well.

When sudden wakes the bitter shriek,
And redder swells thy little cheek;
15   When rattled keys thy woes beguile,
And through the wet eye gleams the smile,
Still for thy weakly self is spent
    Thy little silly plaint.

But when thy friends are in distress,
20   Thou'lt laugh and chuckle ne'er the less;
Nor e'en with sympathy be smitten,

Though all are sad but thee and kitten;
Yet little varlet° that thou art,   scoundrel
   Thou twitchest at the heart.

25   The rosy cheek so soft and warm;
Thy pinky hand and dimpled arm;
Thy silken locks that scantly peep,
With gold-tipped ends, where circles deep
Around thy neck in harmless grace
30   So soft and sleekly hold their place,
Might harder hearts with kindness fill,
   And gain our right good will.

Each passing clown bestows his blessing,
Thy mouth is worn with old wives' kissing;
35   E'en lighter looks the gloomy eye
Of surly sense, when thou art by;
And yet I think whoe'er they be,
   They love thee not like me.

Perhaps when time shall add a few
40   Short years to thee, thou'lt love me too.
Then wilt thou through life's weary way
Become my sure and cheering stay:
Wilt care for me, and be my hold,
   When I am weak and old.

45   Thou'lt listen to my lengthened tale,
And pity me when I am frail—
But see, the sweepy spinning fly
Upon the window takes thine eye.
Go to thy little senseless play—
50   Thou dost not heed my lay.°   song

WALT WHITMAN (1819–1892)

Old Salt Kossabone (1888)

Far back, related on my mother's side,
Old Salt Kossabone, I'll tell you how he died:
(Had been a sailor all his life—was nearly 90—lived with his
        married grandchild, Jenny;
House on a hill, with view of bay at hand, and distant cape, and
        stretch to open sea;)

5   The last of afternoons, the evening hours, for many a year his
          regular custom,
In his great arm chair by the window seated,
(Sometimes, indeed, through half the day,)
Watching the coming, going of the vessels, he mutters to himself—
          And now the close of all:
One struggling outbound brig, one day, baffled for long—cross-
          tides and much wrong going,
10   At last at nightfall strikes the breeze aright, her whole luck veering,
And swiftly bending round the cape, the darkness proudly entering,
          cleaving, as he watches,
"She's free—she's on her destination"—these the last words—
          when Jenny came, he sat there dead,
Dutch Kossabone, Old Salt, related on my mother's side, far back.

WILLIAM BUTLER YEATS   (1865–1939)

A Prayer for My Daughter   (1919; 1921)

Once more the storm is howling, and half hid
Under this cradle-hood and coverlid
My child sleeps on. There is no obstacle
But Gregory's wood and one bare hill
5   Whereby the haystack- and roof-levelling wind,
Bred on the Atlantic, can be stayed;
And for an hour I have walked and prayed
Because of the great gloom that is in my mind.

I have walked and prayed for this young child an hour
10   And heard the sea-wind scream upon the tower,[1]
And under the arches of the bridge, and scream
In the elms above the flooded stream;
Imagining in excited reverie
That the future years had come,
15   Dancing to a frenzied drum,
Out of the murderous innocence of the sea.

May she be granted beauty and yet not
Beauty to make a stranger's eye distraught,
Or hers before a looking-glass, for such,
20   Being made beautiful overmuch,

---

[1] **the tower:** Thoor Ballylee, a Norman tower on the Gregory Estate where Yeats was living.

Consider beauty a sufficient end,
Lose natural kindness and maybe
The heart-revealing intimacy
That chooses right, and never find a friend.

25   Helen being chosen found life flat and dull
And later had much trouble from a fool,[2]
While that great Queen, that rose out of the spray,
Being fatherless could have her way
Yet chose a bandy-leggèd smith for man.[3]
30   It's certain that fine women eat
A crazy salad with their meat
Whereby the Horn of Plenty is undone.

In courtesy I'd have her chiefly learned;
Hearts are not had as a gift but hearts are earned
35   By those that are not entirely beautiful;
Yet many, that have played the fool
For beauty's very self, has charm made wise,
And many a poor man that has roved,
Loved and thought himself beloved,
40   From a glad kindness cannot take his eyes.

May she become a flourishing hidden tree
That all her thoughts may like the linnet° be,   finch
And have no business but dispensing round
Their magnanimities of sound,
45   Nor but in merriment begin a chase,
Nor but in merriment a quarrel.
O may she live like some green laurel
Rooted in one dear perpetual place.

My mind, because the minds that I have loved,
50   The sort of beauty that I have approved,
Prosper but little, has dried up of late,
Yet knows that to be choked with hate
May well be of all evil chances chief.
If there's no hatred in a mind
55   Assault and battery of the wind
Can never tear the linnet from the leaf.

---

[2] **Helen . . . fool:** Helen of Troy, known for her legendary beauty, married Menelaus, brother of the Greek leader Agamemnon. Her affair with Paris of Troy resulted in an epic battle between Greece and Troy, following which she was reunited with her husband Menelaus.
[3] **While . . . man:** In classical mythology, Venus, goddess of love, was born from the sea and married Vulcan, the blacksmith, who made thunderbolts for the gods.

An intellectual hatred is the worst,
So let her think opinions are accursed.
Have I not seen the loveliest woman born[4]
60   Out of the mouth of Plenty's horn,
Because of her opinionated mind
Barter that horn and every good
By quiet natures understood
For an old bellows full of angry wind?

65   Considering that, all hatred driven hence,
The soul recovers radical innocence
And learns at last that it is self-delighting,
Self-appeasing, self-affrighting,
And that its own sweet will is Heaven's will;
70   She can, though every face should scowl
And every windy quarter howl
Or every bellows burst, be happy still.

And may her bridegroom bring her to a house
Where all's accustomed, ceremonious;
75   For arrogance and hatred are the wares
Peddled in the thoroughfares.
How but in custom and in ceremony
Are innocence and beauty born?
Ceremony's a name for the rich horn,
80   And custom for the spreading laurel tree.

ROBERT FROST (1874–1963)

"Out, Out—" (1916)

The buzz saw snarled and rattled in the yard
And made dust and dropped stove-length sticks of wood,
Sweet-scented stuff when the breeze drew across it.
And from there those that lifted eyes could count
5   Five mountain ranges one behind the other
Under the sunset far into Vermont.
And the saw snarled and rattled, snarled and rattled,
As it ran light, or had to bear a load.
And nothing happened: day was all but done.

---

[4] **loveliest woman born:** Maud Gonne, Yeats's lifelong, hopeless love, married Major John McBride in 1903. Yeats was critical of her militant support of Irish liberation.

10 Call it a day, I wish they might have said
To please the boy by giving him the half hour
That a boy counts so much when saved from work.
His sister stood beside them in her apron
To tell them "Supper." At the word, the saw,
15 As if to prove saws knew what supper meant,
Leaped out at the boy's hand, or seemed to leap—
He must have given the hand. However it was,
Neither refused the meeting. But the hand!
The boy's first outcry was a rueful laugh,
20 As he swung toward them holding up the hand,
Half in appeal, but half as if to keep
The life from spilling. Then the boy saw all—
Since he was old enough to know, big boy
Doing a man's work, though a child at heart—
25 He saw all spoiled. "Don't let him cut my hand off—
The doctor, when he comes. Don't let him, sister!"
So. But the hand was gone already.
The doctor put him in the dark of ether.
He lay and puffed his lips out with his breath.
30 And then—the watcher at his pulse took fright.
No one believed. They listened at his heart.
Little—less—nothing!—and that ended it.
No more to build on there. And they, since they
Were not the one dead, turned to their affairs.

WILLIAM CARLOS WILLIAMS (1883–1963)

The Young Housewife (1938)

At ten A.M. the young housewife
moves about in negligee behind
the wooden walls of her husband's house.
I pass solitary in my car.

5 Then again she comes to the curb
to call the ice-man, fish-man, and stands
shy, uncorseted, tucking in
stray ends of hair, and I compare her
to a fallen leaf.

10 The noiseless wheels of my car
rush with a crackling sound over
dried leaves as I bow and pass smiling.

EZRA POUND   (1885–1972)

from Canto LXXXI
"What thou lovest well remains"   (1948)

What thou lovest well remains,
                    the rest is dross
What thou lov'st well shall not be reft from thee
What thou lov'st well is thy true heritage
Whose world, or mine or theirs
                    or is it of none?
5   First came the seen, thus the palpable
        Elysium,[1] though it were in the halls of hell,
What thou lovest well is thy true heritage
What thou lov'st well shall not be reft from thee

The ant's a centaur in his dragon world.
10 Pull down thy vanity, it is not man
Made courage, or made order, or made grace,
        Pull down thy vanity, I say pull down.
Learn of the green world what can be thy place
In scaled invention or true artistry,
Pull down thy vanity,
                    Paquin pull down!
15 The green casque has outdone your elegance.

"Master thyself, then others shall thee beare"[2]
        Pull down thy vanity
Thou art a beaten dog beneath the hail,
A swollen magpie in a fitful sun,
20 Half black half white
Nor knowst'ou wing from tail
Pull down thy vanity
                How mean thy hates
Fostered in falsity,
25   Pull down thy vanity,
Rathe° to destroy, niggard in charity,   quick
Pull down thy vanity,
                I say pull down.

---

[1] **Elysium:** In Greek mythology, the after-death abode of those favored by the gods.
[2] **Master . . . beare:** Here Pound refers to Chaucer's "Ballade of Good Counsel": "Subdue thyself, and others thee shall hear."

HART CRANE (1899–1932)

My Grandmother's Love Letters (1920)

There are no stars to-night
But those of memory.
Yet how much room for memory there is
In the loose girdle of soft rain.

5   There is even room enough
For the letters of my mother's mother,
Elizabeth,
That have been pressed so long
Into a corner of the roof
10   That they are brown and soft,
And liable to melt as snow.

Over the greatness of such space
Steps must be gentle.
It is all hung by an invisible white hair.
15   It trembles as birch limbs webbing the air.

And I ask myself:

"Are your fingers long enough to play
Old keys that are but echoes:
Is the silence strong enough
20   To carry back the music to its source
And back to you again
As though to her?"

Yet I would lead my grandmother by the hand
Through much of what she would not understand;
25   And so I stumble. And the rain continues on the roof
With such a sound of gently pitying laughter.

LANGSTON HUGHES (1902–1967)

Mother to Son (1922)

Well, son, I'll tell you:
Life for me ain't been no crystal stair.

It's had tacks in it,
And splinters,
5   And boards torn up,
And places with no carpet on the floor—
Bare.
But all the time
I'se been a-climbin' on,
10   And reachin' landin's,
And turnin' corners,
And sometimes goin' in the dark
Where there ain't been no light.
So, boy, don't you turn back.
15   Don't you set down on the steps.
'Cause you finds it's kinder hard.
Don't you fall now—
For I'se still goin', honey,
I'se still climbin',
20   And life for me ain't been no crystal stair.

THEODORE ROETHKE   (1908–1963)

My Papa's Waltz   (1948)

The whiskey on your breath
Could make a small boy dizzy;
But I hung on like death:
Such waltzing was not easy.

5   We romped until the pans
Slid from the kitchen shelf;
My mother's countenance
Could not unfrown itself.

The hand that held my wrist
10   Was battered on one knuckle;
At every step you missed
My right ear scraped a buckle.

You beat time on my head
With a palm caked hard by dirt,
15   Then waltzed me off to bed
Still clinging to your shirt.

ROBERT HAYDEN (1913–1982)

Those Winter Sundays (1962)

Sundays too my father got up early
and put his clothes on in the blueblack cold,
then with cracked hands that ached
from labor in the weekday weather made
5   banked fires blaze. No one ever thanked him.

I'd wake and hear the cold splintering, breaking.
When the rooms were warm, he'd call,
and slowly I would rise and dress,
fearing the chronic angers of that house,

10   speaking indifferently to him,
who had driven out the cold
and polished my good shoes as well.
What did I know, what did I know
of love's austere and lonely offices?

WILLIAM STAFFORD (1914–1993)

Our Kind (1982)

Our mother knew our worth—
not much. To her, success
was not being noticed at all.
"If we can stay out of jail,"
5   she said, "God will be proud of us."

"Not worth a row of pins,"
she said, when we looked at the album:
"Grandpa?—ridiculous."
Her hearing was bad, and that
10   was good: "None of us ever says much."

She sent us forth equipped
for our kind of world, a world of
our betters, in a nation so strong
its greatest claim is no boast,
15   its leaders telling us all, "Be proud"—

But over their shoulders, God and
our mother, signaling: "Ridiculous."

GWENDOLYN BROOKS   (1917–2000)

The Bean Eaters   (1960)

They eat beans mostly, this old yellow pair.
Dinner is a casual affair.
Plain chipware on a plain and creaking wood,
Tin flatware.

5   Two who are Mostly Good.
Two who have lived their day,
But keep on putting on their clothes
And putting things away.

And remembering . . .
10   Remembering, with twinklings and twinges,
As they lean over the beans in their rented back room that
      is full of beads and receipts and dolls and cloths,
      tobacco crumbs, vases and fringes.

GWENDOLYN BROOKS   (1917–2000)

The Vacant Lot   (1945)

Mrs. Coley's three-flat brick
Isn't here any more.
All done with seeing her fat little form
Burst out of the basement door;
5   And with seeing her African son-in-law
(Rightful heir to the throne)
With his great white strong cold squares of teeth
And his little eyes of stone;
And with seeing the squat fat daughter
10   Letting in the men
When majesty has gone for the day—
And letting them out again.

ALASTAIR REID (1926–   )

Daedalus[1] (1988)

My son has birds in his head.

I know them now. I catch
the pitch of their calls, their shrill
cacophonies, their chitterings, their coos.
5   They hover behind his eyes and come to rest
on a branch, on a book, grow still,
claws curled, wings furled.
His is a bird world.

I learn the flutter of his moods,
10 his moments of swoop and soar.
From the ground I feel him try
the limits of the air—
sudden lift, sudden terror—
and move in time to cradle
15 his quivering, feathered fear.
At evening, in the tower,
I see him to sleep and see
the hooding-over of eyes,
the slow folding of wings.
20 I wake to his morning twitterings,
to the *croomb* of his becoming.

He chooses his selves—wren, hawk,
swallow or owl—to explore
the trees and rooftops of his heady wishing.
25 Tomtit, birdwit.
Am I to call him down, to give him
a grounding, teach him gravity?
Gently, gently.
Time tells us what we weigh, and soon enough
30 his feet will reach the ground.
Age, like a cage, will enclose him.
So the wise men said.

My son has birds in his head.

---

[1] **Daedalus:** In Greek mythology, an inventor who built wings for himself and his son Icarus in order
to escape the Labyrinth of Minos.

PHILIP LEVINE (1928–   )

Later Still (1972)

Two sons are gone.
The end of winter, and the almond blooms
near the back fence. The plum, slower,
unfolds under a streaked sky. The words become,
5   like prayer, a kind of nonsense
which becomes the thought of our lives.

In middle age we came
to the nine years war, the stars raged
in our horoscopes and the land
10   turned inwards biting for its heart.

Now in February the pussy willow
furs in the chill wind. In March
the sudden peach, cherry, lilac, in summer
the drumming gourd, corn, grape, and later still
15   the ghostly milkweed and the last laugh.

ANNE SEXTON (1928–1974)

Housewife (1962)

Some women marry houses.
It's another kind of skin; it has a heart,
a mouth, a liver and bowel movements.
The walls are permanent and pink.
5   See how she sits on her knees all day,
faithfully washing herself down.
Men enter by force, drawn back like Jonah[1]
into their fleshy mothers.
A woman *is* her mother.
10   That's the main thing.

---

[1] **Jonah:** Old Testament prophet who was saved from a storm by a whale who held him in its stomach for three days.

ADRIENNE RICH (1929–   )

Snapshots of a Daughter-in-Law   (1960; 1963)

1.

You, once a belle in Shreveport,
with henna-colored hair, skin like a peachbud,
still have your dresses copied from that time,
and play a Chopin prelude
5   called by Cortot: *"Delicious recollections*
float like perfume through the memory."[1]

Your mind now, moldering like wedding-cake,
heavy with useless experience, rich
with suspicion, rumor, fantasy,
10   crumbling to pieces under the knife-edge
of mere fact. In the prime of your life.

Nervy, glowering, your daughter
wipes the teaspoons, grows another way.

2.

Banging the coffee-pot into the sink
15   she hears the angels chiding, and looks out
past the raked gardens to the sloppy sky.
Only a week since They said: *Have no patience.*

The next time it was: *Be insatiable.*
Then: *Save yourself; others you cannot save.*
20   Sometimes she's let the tapstream scald her arm,
a match burn to her thumbnail,

or held her hand above the kettle's snout
right in the woolly steam. They are probably angels,
since nothing hurts her anymore, except
25   each morning's grit blowing into her eyes.

3.

A thinking woman sleeps with monsters.
The beak that grips her, she becomes. And Nature,
that sprung-lidded, still commodious

---

[1] *Delicious . . . memory:* Comment made by French pianist Alfred Cortot (1877–1962) concerning
"Prelude No. 7, Andantino, A Major," by Polish composer Frederic Chopin (1810–1849).

steamer-trunk of *tempora* and *mores*[2]
30   gets stuffed with it all: the mildewed orange-flowers,
the female pills, the terrible breasts
of Boadicea[3] beneath flat foxes' heads and orchids.

Two handsome women, gripped in argument,
each proud, acute, subtle, I hear scream
35   across the cut glass and majolica°   earthenware
like Furies[4] cornered from their prey:
The argument *ad feminam*,[5] all the old knives
that have rusted in my back, I drive in yours,
ma semblable, ma soeur![6]

4.

40   Knowing themselves too well in one another:
their gifts no pure fruition, but a thorn,
the prick filed sharp against a hint of scorn . . .
Reading while waiting
for the iron to heat,
45   writing, *My Life had stood—a Loaded Gun—*[7]
in that Amherst pantry while the jellies boil and scum,
or, more often,
iron-eyed and beaked and purposed as a bird,
dusting everything on the whatnot every day of life.

5.

50   *Dulce ridens, dulce loquens,*[8]
she shaves her legs until they gleam
like petrified mammoth-tusk.

6.

When to her lute Corinna sings[9]
neither words nor music are her own;

---

[2] *tempora* **and** *mores*: "Times and customs" (Latin). From the Roman orator Cicero's phrase, "O tempora! O mores!"

[3] **Boadicea:** First century British queen who led her people in an unsuccessful rebellion against Roman rule.

[4] **Furies:** In Greek mythology, female spirits of retribution.

[5] *ad feminam*: Rich's feminine version of the Latin phrase *ad hominem*, "against the man."

[6] *ma semblable, ma soeur*: Here, Rich feminizes the last line of Baudelaire's "Au Lecteur": "*Hypocrite lecteur!—mon semblable—mon frère!*" (French, "Hypocrite reader!—my likeness!—my brother!").

[7] *My life . . . Gun*: "Emily Dickinson, *Complete Poems*, ed. T. H. Johnson, 1960, p. 39" [Rich's note]. Dickinson spent her entire life in Amherst, Massachusetts.

[8] *Dulce ridens, dulce loquens*: "Sweetly laughing, sweetly speaking" (Latin). (From the *Odes* of Horace, 22.23–24).

[9] **When . . . sings:** From a poem by Thomas Campion (1567–1620).

55 only the long hair dipping
    over her cheek, only the song
    of silk against her knees
    and these
    adjusted in reflections of an eye.

60 Poised, trembling and unsatisfied, before
    an unlocked door, that cage of cages,
    tell us, you bird, you tragical machine—
    is this *fertilisante douleur?*[10] Pinned down
    by love, for you the only natural action,
65 are you edged more keen
    to prise the secrets of the vault? has Nature shown
    her household books to you, daughter-in-law,
    that her sons never saw?

7.

    "To have in this uncertain world some stay
70 *which cannot be undermined, is*
    of the utmost consequence."[11]
                            Thus wrote
    a woman, partly brave and partly good,
    who fought with what she partly understood.
    Few men about her would or could do more,
75 hence she was labeled harpy, shrew and whore.

8.

    "You all die at fifteen," said Diderot,[12]
    and turn part legend, part convention.
    Still, eyes inaccurately dream
    behind closed windows blankening with steam.
80 Deliciously, all that we might have been,
    all that we were—fire, tears,
    wit, taste, martyred ambition—
    stirs like the memory of refused adultery
    the drained and flagging bosom of our middle years.

---

[10] *fertilisante douleur*: "Fertilizing sorrow" (French).
[11] *"To . . . consequence."*: "From Mary Wollstonecraft, *Thoughts on the Education of Daughters*, London, 1787" [Rich's note].
[12] *"You . . . Diderot*: Denis Diderot (1713–1784), a French philosopher and author. "'You all die at fifteen': 'Vous mourez toutes a quinze ans,' from the *Lettres à Sophie Volland*, quoted by Simone de Beauvoir in *Le Deuxième Sexe*, Vol. II, pp. 123–24" [Rich's note].

9.

85 *Not that it is done well, but*
that it is done at all?[13] Yes, think
of the odds! or shrug them off forever.
This luxury of the precocious child,
Time's precious chronic invalid,—
90 would we, darlings, resign it if we could?
Our blight has been our sinecure:
mere talent was enough for us—
glitter in fragments and rough drafts.

Sigh no more, ladies.
                                    Time is male
95 and in his cups drinks to the fair.
Bemused by gallantry, we hear
our mediocrities over-praised,
indolence read as abnegation,
slattern thought styled intuition,
100 every lapse forgiven, our crime
only to cast too bold a shadow
or smash the mold straight off.

For that, solitary confinement,
tear gas, attrition shelling.
105 Few applicants for that honor.

10.

                              Well,
she's long about her coming, who must be
more merciless to herself than history.
Her mind full to the wind, I see her plunge
110 breasted and glancing through the currents,
taking the light upon her
at least as beautiful as any boy
or helicopter,[14]
                    poised, still coming,

---

[13] **Not . . . all?:** Reference to a conversation between Samuel Johnson and James Boswell.
[14] **I see . . . helicopter:** "She comes down from the remoteness of ages from Thebes, from Crete, from Chichén-Itzá; and she is also the totem set deep in the African jungle; she is a helicopter and she is a bird; and there is this, the greatest wonder of all: under her tinted hair the forest murmur becomes a thought, and words issue from her breasts" (Simone de Beauvoir, *The Second Sex,* trans. H. M. Parshley [New York, 1953], p. 279).

115　her fine blades making the air wince

but her cargo
no promise then:
delivered
palpable
120　ours.

WENDELL BERRY (1934–)

Marriage (1968)
　　　to Tanya

How hard it is for me, who live
in the excitement of women
and have the desire for them
in my mouth like salt. Yet
5　you have taken me and quieted me.
You have been such light to me
that other women have been
your shadows. You come near me
with the nearness of sleep.
10　And yet I am not quiet.
It is to be broken. It is to be
torn open. It is not to be
reached and come to rest in
ever. I turn against you,
15　I break from you, I turn to you.
We hurt, and are hurt,
and have each other for healing.
It is healing. It is never whole.

SONIA SANCHEZ (1934–)

Summer Words of a Sistuh Addict (1969)

the first day i shot dope
was on a sunday.
　　　　　　　i had just come
home from church

5   got mad at my motha
cuz she got mad at me. u dig?
                   went out. shot up
behind a feelen against her.
                        it felt good.
10 gooder than dooing it. yeah.
                   it was nice.
i did it. uh huh. i did it.   uh. huh.
i want to do it again. it felt so gooooood.
                   and as the sistuh
15   sits in her silent /
                   remembered / high
                   someone leans for
                   ward gently asks her:
                   sistuh.
20   did u
                   finally
                   learn how to hold yo / mother?
and the music of the day
                        drifts in the room
25 to mingle with the sistuh's young tears.
          and we all sing.

MARY OLIVER (1935–   )

The House (1963)

Because we lived our several lives
Caught up within the spells of love,
Because we always had to run
Through the enormous yards of day
5   To do all that we hoped to do,
We did not hear, beneath our lives,
The old walls falling out of true,
Foundations shifting in the dark.
When seedlings blossomed in the eaves,
10   When branches scratched upon the door
And rain came splashing through the halls,
We made our minor, brief repairs,
And sang upon the crumbling stairs
And danced upon the sodden floors.

15 For years we lived at peace, until
The rooms themselves began to blend
With time, and empty one by one,
At which we knew, with muted hearts,
That nothing further could be done,
20 And so rose up, and went away,
Inheritors of breath and love,
Bound to that final black estate
No child can mend or trade away.

GRACE SCHULMAN (1935–   )

Home Movie (1994)

Just then the squeaky camera caught
a sun crystal that haloed trees,
blurred fences, light dousing the light,
then twitched, and quivered into focus,

5 as I entered the child I was,
primped for the film in a ruffled smock,
touching the big hepaticas
I'd never seen in Central Park,

then pivoting to see my mother's
10 long arms arc through foamy water,
stroke by feathery stroke, and soar,
her white cap lost then found in glare,

and I, gasping in pride, in awe,
recalled a newsreel's dreadful flare
15 as warplanes fired at refugees,
mother and son, *people like us*,

then watched her rise up at the shore,
step to a tango, snap a towel,
and ran to her, eyes wide with all
20 I'd know of perfect form—and fear.

CHARLES WRIGHT (1935–   )

Virgo[1] **Descending** (1975)

Through the viridian° (and black of the burnt match),   green
Through ox-blood and ochre, the ham-colored clay,
Through plate after plate, down
Where the worm and the mole will not go,
5   Through ore-seam and fire-seam,
My grandmother, senile and 89, crimpbacked, stands
Like a door ajar on her soft bed,
The open beams and bare studs of the hall
Pink as an infant's skin in the floating dark;
10   Shavings and curls swing down like snowflakes across her face.

My aunt and I walk past. As always, my father
Is planning rooms, dragging his lame leg,
Stroke-straightened and foreign, behind him,
An aberrant 2-by-4 he can't fit snug.
15   I lay my head on my aunt's shoulder, feeling
At home, and walk on.
Through arches and door jambs, the spidery wires
And coiled cables, the blueprint takes shape:
My mother's room to the left, the door closed;
20   My father's room to the left, the door closed—

Ahead, my brother's room, unfinished;
Behind, my sister's room, also unfinished.
Buttresses, winches, block-and-tackle: the scale of everything
Is enormous. We keep on walking. And pass
25   My aunt's room, almost complete, the curtains up,
The lamp and the medicine arranged
In their proper places, in arm's reach of where the bed will go . . .
The next one is mine, now more than half done,
Cloyed by the scent of jasmine,
30   White-gummed and anxious, their mouths sucking the air dry.

Home is what you lie in, or hang above, the house
Your father made, or keeps on making,
The dirt you moisten, the sap you push up and nourish . . .

---

[1] **Virgo:** The sixth sign of the Zodiac. The sun falls in Virgo between August 23 and September 22.

I enter the living room, it, too, unfinished, its far wall
35 Not there, opening on to a radiance
I can't begin to imagine, a light
My father walks from, approaching me,
Dragging his right leg, rolling his plans into a perfect curl.
That light, he mutters, that damned light.
40 We can't keep it out. It keeps on filling your room.

LUCILLE CLIFTON (1936–)

the lost baby poem (1972)

the time i dropped your almost body down
down to meet the waters under the city
and run one with the sewage to the sea
what did i know about waters rushing back
5 what did i know about drowning
or being drowned

you would have been born into winter
in the year of the disconnected gas
and no car   we would have made the thin
10 walk over genesee hill into the canada wind
to watch you slip like ice into strangers' hands
you would have fallen naked as snow into winter
if you were here i could tell you these
and some other things

15 if i am ever less than a mountain
for your definite brothers and sisters
let the rivers pour over my head
let the sea take me for a spiller
of seas   let black men call me stranger
20 always   for your never named sake

later i'll say
i spent my life
loving a great man

later
25 my life will accuse me
of various treasons

not black enough
too black

30   eyes closed when they should have been open
     eyes open when they should have been closed

will accuse me for unborn babies
and dead trees

later
when i defend again and again
35   with this love
     my life will keep silent
     listening to
     my body breaking

SANDRA M. GILBERT (1936–   )

Simplicity
for Elliot

Wishing to praise
the simple, the univocal, the one
word that falls like a ripe fruit
into an infinite well,
5   I watch

that easy old couple, limber
sixty-year olds,
strolling, maybe just finished jogging,
under plum trees.
10   Over their mild

gray heads the air
is pink with blossoms
accomplishing themselves;
under their tan, accomplished Keds
15   the sidewalk's pink with petals.

She turns to him and speaks, a word
that fills and falls like another petal,
easy, simple:
a word of thirst? —*milk? wine?*—
20   a word of love? —*good run?*

whatever,
it befalls him

light as the stroke of a branch,
clear as color,
25   and he nods, smiles.

I want to learn that word, I want
to hold that word under my tongue
like a sip of milk,
I want to inhale that word
30   the way that gray-haired woman, now,

turns back to the tree
and inhales the lucid perfume
of a blossom that promises
ripeness, night, the sweetness
35   of the plum.

MICHAEL S. HARPER (1938–   )

Grandfather (1974)

In 1915 my grandfather's
neighbors surrounded his house
near the dayline he ran
on the Hudson
5   in Catskill, NY
and thought they'd burn
his family out
in a movie they'd just seen
and be rid of his kind:
10   the death of a lone black
family is *the Birth
of a Nation*,[1]
or so they thought.
His 5′ 4″ waiter gait
15   quenched the white jacket smile
he'd brought back from watered
polish of my father
on the turning seats,
and he asked his neighbors

---

[1] *the Birth of a Nation:* Directed by D. W. Griffith, a 1915 film that portrays the Southern United States during Reconstruction, casting African Americans as savage and violent. The film depicts the "birth" of the Ku Klux Klan.

20 up on his thatched porch
for the first blossom of fire
that would burn him down.
They went away, his nation,
spittooning their torched necks
25 in the shadows of the riverboat
they'd seen, posse decomposing;
and I see him on Sutter
with white bag from your
restaurant, challenged by his first
30 grandson to a foot-race
he will win in white clothes.

I see him as he buys galoshes
for his railed yard near Mineo's
metal shop, where roses jump
35 as the el circles his house
toward Brooklyn, where his rain fell;
and I see cigar smoke in his eyes,
chocolate Madison Square Garden chews
he breaks on his set teeth,
40 stitched up after cancer,
the great white nation immovable
as his weight wilts
and he is on a porch
that won't hold my arms,
45 or the legs of the race run
forwards, or the film
played backwards on his grandson's eyes.

SEAMUS HEANEY (1939–   )

Digging (1966)

Between my finger and my thumb
The squat pen rests; snug as a gun.

Under my window, a clean rasping sound
When the spade sinks into gravelly ground:
5 My father, digging. I look down

Till his straining rump among the flowerbeds
Bends low, comes up twenty years away
Stooping in rhythm through potato drills
Where he was digging.

10 The coarse boot nestled on the lug, the shaft
Against the inside knee was levered firmly.
He rooted out tall tops, buried the bright edge deep
To scatter new potatoes that we picked,
Loving their cool hardness in our hands.

15 By God, the old man could handle a spade.
Just like his old man.

My grandfather cut more turf in a day
Than any other man on Toner's bog.
Once I carried him milk in a bottle
20 Corked sloppily with paper. He straightened up
To drink it, then fell to right away
Nicking and slicing neatly, heaving sods
Over his shoulder, going down and down
For the good turf. Digging.

25 The cold smell of potato mould, the squelch and slap
Of soggy peat, the curt cuts of an edge
Through living roots awaken in my head.
But I've no spade to follow men like them.

Between my finger and my thumb
30 The squat pen rests.
I'll dig with it

TED KOOSER (1939–   )

Dishwater

Slap of the screen door, flat knock
of my grandmother's boxy black shoes
on the wooden stoop, the hush and sweep
of her knob-kneed, cotton-aproned stride
5 out to the edge and then, toed in
with a furious twist and heave,
a bridge that leaps from her hot red hands
and hangs there shining for fifty years
over the mystified chickens,
10 over the swaying nettles, the ragweed,
the clay slope down to the creek,
over the redwing blackbirds in the tops.

JAMES WELCH (1940–   )

Plea to Those Who Matter   (1971)

You don't know I pretend my dumb.
My songs often wise, my bells could chase
the snow across these whistle-black plains.
Celebrate. The days are grim. Call your winds
5   to blast these bundled streets and patronize
my past of poverty and 4-day feasts.

Don't ignore me. I'll build my face a different way,
a way to make you know that I am no longer
proud, my name not strong enough to stand alone.
10   If I lie and say you took me for a friend,
patched together in my thin bones,
will you help me be cunning and noisy as the wind?

I have plans to burn my drum, move out
and civilize this hair. See my nose? I smash it
15   straight for you. These teeth? I scrub my teeth
away with stones. I know you help me now I matter.
And I—I come to you, head down, bleeding from my smile,
happy for the snow clean hands of you, my friends.

SIMON ORTIZ (1941–   )

Juanita, Wife of Manuelito[1]   (1976)

after seeing a photograph of her in Dine Baa-Hani[2]

I can see by your eyes
the gray in them like by Sonsela Butte,
the long ache
that comes about when I think
5   about where the road climbs
up onto the Roof Butte.
I can see
the whole sky
when it is ready to rain

---

[1] **Manuelito:** Manuelito (1818–1893), Navajo war and political leader.
[2] **Dine Baa-Hani:** An American Indian newspaper.

10 over Whiskey Creek,
  and a small girl
  driving her sheep
  and she looks so pretty
  her hair tied up
15 with a length of yarn.

  I can see
  by the way you stare
  out of a photograph
  that you are a stern woman
20 informed by the history
  of a long walk
  and how it must have felt
  to leave the canyons
  and the mountains of your own land.

25 I can see, Navajo woman,
  that it is possible for dreams
  to occur, the prayers full of the mystery
  of children, laughter, the dances,
  my own humanity, so it can last unto forever.

30 That is what I want to teach my son.

DOUGLAS DUNN (1942–   )

Men of Terry Street (1969)

  They come in at night, leave in the early morning.
  I hear their footsteps, the ticking of bicycle chains,
  Sudden blasts of motorcycles, whimpering of vans.
  Somehow I am either in bed, or the curtains are drawn.

5 This masculine invisibility makes gods of them,
  A pantheon of boots and overalls.
  But when you see them, home early from work
  Or at their Sunday leisure, they are too tired

  And bored to look long at comfortably.
10 It hurts to see their faces, too sad or too jovial.
  They quicken their step at the smell of cooking,
  They hold up their children and sing to them.

SHARON OLDS (1942–   )

I Go Back to May 1937 (1997)

I see them standing at the formal gates of their colleges,
I see my father strolling out
under the ochre sandstone arch, the
red tiles glinting like bent
5   plates of blood behind his head, I
see my mother with a few light books at her hip
standing at the pillar made of tiny bricks with the
wrought-iron gate still open behind her, its
sword-tips black in the May air,
10   they are about to graduate, they are about to get married,
they are kids, they are dumb, all they know is they are
innocent, they would never hurt anybody.
I want to go up to them and say Stop,
don't do it—she's the wrong woman,
15   he's the wrong man, you are going to do things
you cannot imagine you would ever do,
you are going to do bad things to children,
you are going to suffer in ways you never heard of,
you are going to want to die. I want to go
20   up to them there in the late May sunlight and say it,
her hungry pretty blank face turning to me,
her pitiful beautiful untouched body,
his arrogant handsome blind face turning to me,
his pitiful beautiful untouched body,
25   but I don't do it. I want to live. I
take them up like the male and female
paper dolls and bang them together
at the hips like chips of flint as if to
strike sparks from them, I say
30   Do what you are going to do, and I will tell about it.

NIKKI GIOVANNI (1943–   )

Always There Are the Children

and always   there are the children

there will be children in the heat of day
there will be children in the cold of winter

children   like a quilted blanket
5   are welcomed in our old age

children   like a block of ice to a desert sheik
are a sign of status in our youth

we feed the children with our culture
that they might understand our travail

10   we nourish the children on our gods
that they may understand respect

we urge the children on the tracks
that our race will not fall short

but children are not ours
15   nor we theirs   they are future   we are past

how do we welcome the future
not with the colonialism of the past
        for that is our problem
not with the racism of the past
20   for that is their problem
not with the fears of our own status
        for history is lived not dictated

we welcome the young of all groups
as our own with the solid nourishment
25   of food and warmth
we prepare the way with the solid
nourishment of self-actualization

we implore all the young to prepare for the young
because always there will be children

ELLEN BRYANT VOIGT (1943–   )

Claiming Kin (1976)

Insistent as a whistle, her voice up
the stairs pried open the blanket's
tight lid and piped me
down to the pressure cooker's steam and rattle.
5   In my mother's kitchen, the hot iron spit

on signal, the vacuum cleaner whined
and snuffled. Bright face
and a snazzy apron, clicking her long spoons,
how she commandeered the razzle-dazzle!

10   In the front room I dabbed
the company chairs with a sullen rag.
Pale lump blinking at the light,
I could hear her sing in her shiny kingdom,
the sound drifted out like a bottled message.
15   It was the voice of a young girl,
who stopped to gather cool moss,
forgetting the errand, spilling the cornmeal,
and cried and cried in her bearish papa's ear.

At night, while I flopped like a fish
20   on grandma's spool bed, up from her bed
and my wheezing father she rose to the holly,
flat-leaf and Virginia Creeper.
Soft ghost, plush as a pillow,
she wove and fruited against the black hours:
25   red berries and running cedar, green signatures
on the table, on the mantel.

Mother, this poem is from your middle
child who, like your private second self
rising at night to wander the dark house,
30   grew in the shady places:
a green plant in a brass pot,
rootbound, without blossoms.

EAVAN BOLAND (1944–   )

Woman in Kitchen (1982)

Breakfast over, islanded by noise,
She watches the machines go fast and slow.
She stands among them as they shake the house.
They move. Their destination is specific.
5   She has nowhere definite to go.
She might be a pedestrian in traffic.

White surfaces retract. White
Sideboards light the white of walls.

Cups wink white in their saucers.
10   The light of the day bleaches as it falls
On cups and sideboards. She could use
The room to tap if she lost her sight.

Machines jigsaw everything she knows.
And she is everywhere among their furor;
15   The tropic of the dryer tumbling clothes.
The round lunar window of the washer.
The kettle in the toaster is a kingfisher
Swooping for trout above the river's mirror.

The wash done, the kettle boiled, the sheets
20   Spun and clean, the dryer stops dead.
The silence is death. It starts to bury
The room in white spaces. She turns to spread
A cloth on the board and irons sheets
In a room white and quiet as a mortuary.

CRAIG RAINE (1944–   )

A Martian Sends a Postcard Home (1979)

Caxtons[1] are mechanical birds with many wings
and some are treasured for their markings—

they cause the eyes to melt
or the body to shriek without pain.

5   I have never seen one fly, but
sometimes they perch on the hand.

Mist is when the sky is tired of flight
and rests its soft machine on ground:

then the world is dim and bookish
10   like engravings under tissue paper.

Rain is when the earth is television.
It has the property of making colours darker.

---

[1] **Caxtons:** Here, books printed by William Caxton (ca. 1422–1491), the first publisher to print books
in English.

Model T is a room with the lock inside—
a key is turned to free the world

15   for movement, so quick there is a film
to watch for anything missed.

But time is tied to the wrist
or kept in a box, ticking with impatience.

In homes, a haunted apparatus sleeps,
20   that snores when you pick it up.

If the ghost cries, they carry it
to their lips and soothe it to sleep

with sounds. And yet, they wake it up
deliberately, by tickling with a finger.

25   Only the young are allowed to suffer
openly. Adults go to a punishment room

with water but nothing to eat.
They lock the door and suffer the noises

alone. No one is exempt
30   and everyone's pain has a different smell.

At night, when all the colours die,
they hide in pairs

and read about themselves—
in colour, with their eyelids shut.

THOMAS LUX (1946–   )

Upon Seeing an Ultrasound Photo
of an Unborn Child (1990)

Tadpole, it's not time yet to nag you
about college (though I have some thoughts
on that), baseball (ditto), or abstract
principles. Enjoy your delicious,
5   soupy womb-warmth, do some rolls and saults
(it'll be too crowded soon), delight in your early

dreams—which no one will attempt to analyze.
For now: may your toes blossom, your fingers
lengthen, your sexual organs grow (too soon
10   to tell which yet) sensitive, your teeth
form their buds in their forming jawbone, your already
booming heart expand (literally
now, metaphorically later); O your spine,
eyebrows, nape, knees, fibulae,
15   lungs, lips . . . But your soul,
dear child: I don't see it here, when
does that come in, whence? Perhaps God,
and your mother, and even I—we'll all contribute
and you'll learn yourself to coax it
20   from wherever: your soul, which holds your bones
together and lets you live
on earth.—Fingerling, sidecar, nubbin,
I'm waiting, it's me, Dad,
I'm out here. You already know
25   where Mom is. I'll see you more directly
upon arrival. You'll recognize
me—I'll be the tall-seeming, delighted
blond guy, and I'll have
your nose.

RACHEL HADAS (1948–   )

The Red Hat (1998)

It started before Christmas. Now our son
officially walks to school alone.
Semi-alone, it's accurate to say:
I or his father track him on the way.
5   He walks up on the east side of the West End,
we on the west side. Glances can extend
(and do) across the street; not eye contact.
Already ties are feeling and not fact.
Straus Park is where these parallel paths part;
10   he goes alone from there. The watcher's heart
stretches, elastic in its love and fear,
toward him as we see him disappear,
striding briskly. Where two weeks ago,
holding a hand, he'd dawdle, dreamy, slow,
15   he now is hustled forward by the pull
of something far more powerful than school.

The mornings we turn back to are no more
than forty minutes longer than before,
but they feel vastly different—flimsy, strange,
20   wavering in the eddies of this change,
empty, unanchored, perilously light
since the red hat vanished from our sight

NTOZAKE SHANGE (1948–   )

Bocas:[1] A Daughter's Geography   (1983)

i have a daughter/ mozambique
i have a son/ angola
our twins
salvador & johannesburg[2]/ cannot speak
5   the same language
but we fight the same old men/ in the new world

we are so hungry for the morning
we're trying to feed our children the sun
but a long time ago/ we boarded ships/ locked in
10   depths of seas our spirits/ kisst the earth
on the atlantic side of nicaragua costa rica
our lips traced the edges of cuba puerto rico
charleston & savannah/ in haiti[3]
we embraced &
15   made children of the new world
but old men spit on us/ shackled our limbs
but for a minute
our cries are the panama canal/ the yucatan[4]
we poured thru more sea/ more ships/ to manila[5]
20   ah ha we're back again
everybody in manila awready speaks spanish

----

[1] **Bocas:** Mouths (Spanish).
[2] **mozambique . . . johannesburg:** Mozambique and Angola are African nations long impacted by civil war. Johannesburg, in South Africa, is a hotbed of poverty and racial inequality; Salvador, in Brazil, was involved in slavery and has a strong African heritage.
[3] **kisst . . . haiti:** All the cities and countries listed were destination points for the Western Hemisphere slave trade.
[4] **panama canal/ the yucatan:** The Panama Canal connects the Atlantic and Pacific oceans; Yucatan is a peninsula in southeastern Mexico.
[5] **manila:** Capital of the Philippines, where African slaves were oppressed by Spanish rulers.

the old men sent for the archbishop of canterbury
"can whole continents be excommunicated?"
"what wd happen to the children?"
25 "wd their allegiance slip over the edge?"
"dont worry bout lumumba/ don't even think bout
ho chi minh[6]/ the dead cant procreate"
so say the old men

but i have a daughter/ la habana
30 i have a son/ guyana[7]
our twins
santiago & brixton[8]/ cannot speak
the same language
yet we fight the same old men
35 the ones who think helicopters rhyme with hunger
who think patrol boats can confiscate a people
the ones whose dreams are full of none of our
children
they see mae west & harlow[9] in whittled white cafes
40 near managua/ listening to primitive rhythms in
jungles near pétionville[10]
with bejeweled benign natives
ice skating in abidjan[11]
unaware of the rest of us in chicago
45 all the dark urchins
rounding out the globe/ primitively whispering
the earth is not flat old men

there is no edge
no end to the new world
50 cuz i have a daughter/ trinidad
i have a son/ san juan[12]
our twins

---

6 **lumumba . . . ho chi minh:** Patrice Lumumba (1925–1961), original prime minister of Congo (modern-day Zaire, now named Democratic Republic of the Congo), who died under inexplicable circumstances. Ho Chi Minh (1860–1969), Vietnamese nationalist and first prime minister of North Vietnam.
7 **la habana . . . guyana:** La Habana, "Havana," is the capital of Cuba. Guyana is a nation in northeast South America.
8 **santiago & brixton:** Santiago is the capital city of Chile, and Brixton is an impoverished, racially diverse section of London.
9 **mae west & harlow:** Mae West (1892?–1980) and Jean Harlow (1911–1937), American actresses.
10 **pétionville:** City in Haiti.
11 **abidjan:** Former capital of the Ivory Coast.
12 **trinidad . . . san juan:** Trinidad is an island in the Caribbean, and San Juan is the capital of Puerto Rico.

capetown & palestine[13]/ cannot speak the same
language/ but we fight the same old men
55   the same men who thought the earth waz flat
go on over the edge/ go on over the edge old men
you'll see us in luanda.[14] or the rest of us
in chicago
rounding out the morning/
60   we are feeding our children the sun

JULIA ALVAREZ (1950–   )

Papi Working (1995)

The long day spent listening
to homesick hearts,
the tick tock of the clock—
the way Americans mark time,
5   long hours, long days.
Often they came only to hear him
say *nada* in their mother tongue.
I found nothing wrong.
To dole out *jarabe* for the children's coughs,
10   convince the *doña* to stay off that leg.

In his white *saco* Mami ironed out,
smoothing the tired wrinkles
till he was young again,
he spent his days, long days
15   tending to the ills of immigrants,
his own heart heavy with what was gone,
this new country like a pill
that slowly kills but keeps you
from worse deaths.
20   *What was to be done?*

They came to hear him say
nada in their mother tongue.

---

[13] **capetown & palestine:** Capetown is the capital of South Africa; Palestine is a historical region that covers parts of modern-day Israel, Egypt, and Jordan, and also the nation of the Palestinian people.
[14] **luanda:** The capital of Angola, and historically a focal-point of the Brazilian slave trade.

ALAN SHAPIRO (1952–   )

Cold Wood (1991)
—for Simone

One night I heard my parents calling
my name out softly through the dark house;
their voices nothing but a mild
greeting I didn't know I longed for

5   till I heard it, so far away
in the quiet that the sheets
I slid from and my softest step
were loud enough to make it vanish

from me as it drew me on, from bed
10   to hall, to landing, halfway
downstairs to where the bannister
between floors straightened before

descending toward their room. I paused,
my hand cold on the slippery wood.
15   Their calling still too far, too fugitive
to be down there. And it came to me

they must have flown up through the stairwell,
beyond the window, to the tree
where the leaves shivered the streetlights
20   into branching stars and tangling comet trails

whose shadows slid down the wall
over the bannister and through my hand.
Yes, they had dreamed themselves up there—
to sing my name, birds in the heaven-tree.

25   But my hand was heavy on the cold wood.
And the whole house heavy with listening
was falling away from the twined stars
shrinking to the wavering edge of sight

and then beyond it, till all of the night,
30   the black orient spaces were between me
and their voices, which were now just the trace
of voices, the trace of my happy name.

GARY SOTO (1952–   )

The Family in Spring (1991)

Family won't go away. I keep pulling up to them,
Brown faces inside a steamy station wagon.
When I was a boy my uncle flipped pennies
And let me lose, then gave them to me,
5   Small pile with no sack. I've done the same.
At my nephew's first communion party
I let him close his eyes and choose three times
From my wallet. Two singles is what he got, and a five.
I like my nephew. He missed the twenty and ten.
10   I talked with my mother, who is like those pennies
And bills, bitter with the acid of fingers.
Grandma is ill, she told me three times.
I told her I was doing OK only once.
I told her I had gone to New York. Carolyn
15   And I had painted the hallway
And put up new curtains. The cat ran
Away and our second car, the Chevy, was up on blocks.
This was a son speaking to his mother,
Son with the stilts of childhood not pulled down.
20   We sat and watched the leaves on a tree,
Fiddled with our napkins. Mariko
Brought me three inches of punch in a paper cup.
We'll turn on each other in smaller company.
I got up to leave. My family said
25   Their good-byes at a distance, crushed napkins
In their hands.
And went home to call in the backyard
For our lost kitten. Barney, Spike, Midnight.
We never settled on a name.
30   Now it was lost, a few houses away
For all we knew. When the cat didn't come,
I looked at the Chevy that was droopy eyed from
A wreck, and slammed the hood shut.
I then took my family to dinner because my nephew
35   Pulled the wrong bills.

That was last April. The weather then is
Today's weather, blue with some wind and leaves.
April or September, I sometimes think
I'd like to start a new family,

40   Join a household of three kids, not one.
      It's not a matter of love. I'm happy here,
      With wife and daughter, and I could
      Also be happy elsewhere. I suppose
      I want more, and I suppose
45   I'm wrong in the head. How strange,
      But for years I didn't wear my wedding band,
      And now it's on my finger, wink of light.
      Now I'm noticing rings. It's the left hand,
      The wink of gold, that says you're married,
50   That and the two kids in the car,
      And the car itself, which is plain,
      Or if not plain, then the color white.
      A few weeks ago at Safeway I watched a woman
      Write out a check for a great pile of groceries.
55   The wink was there, and a daughter, maybe thirteen,
      A little older perhaps, with just enough
      Purple dye in her hair to make her OK at school.
      I bought my tuna, milk, and a head of lettuce,
      And hurried out in time to see them pull away.
60   The car was a plain white Honda.
      Even in the parking lot, the woman's eyes
      Were on the dashboard, careful about going too fast.

      My wife is a Japanese Methodist.
      I went on a retreat with her only last Saturday
65   Where the woman in the white Honda showed up.
      Her ring finger winked a star of gold.
      When everyone's finger winked,
      I knew I was in the right place. We ate
      A lot, sat in lounge chairs, talked baseball scores.
70   No one complained. No one talked out of line,
      Drank too much, or bragged. I liked these people.
      They were kind and good, and sensible.
      I thought, The one with the white Honda
      Is nicer than me. All of them are nicer than me.
75   For a moment I felt a glow inside,
      The blush of happiness with my second beer,
      And was helping with the barbecue when I began
      To realize that I would never be
      As nice as they. This disturbed me,
80   That they were nicer and didn't care
      How much better they were than me.
      I joined my wife who was sitting
      On the lounge chair. I ate my potato salad
      And looked around for a place to throw my ribs.

85   Guilt, then repentance, is one way to Heaven.
It's Catholic, I suppose. You have one bad thought,
Then another, and suddenly you're in the confessional
Starting over on your knees. I ate my potato salad,
Tried to like them. The Japanese are the people
90   Who'll get everything the second time around.
I joined the game of volleyball on a new lawn.
I was smiling too much, too little, then not at all.

SANDRA CISNEROS (1954–   )

My Wicked Wicked Ways (1987)

This is my father.
See? He is young.
He looks like Errol Flynn.[1]
He is wearing a hat
5   that tips over one eye,
a suit that fits him good,
and baggy pants.
He is also wearing
those awful shoes,
10   the two-toned ones
my mother hates.

Here is my mother.
She is not crying.
She cannot look into the lens
15   because the sun is bright.
The woman,
the one my father knows,
is not here.
She does not come till later.

20   My mother will get very mad.
Her face will turn red
and she will throw one shoe.
My father will say nothing.
After a while everyone

---

[1] **Errol Flynn:** Errol Flynn (1909–1959), Australian-born Hollywood actor whose autobiography was entitled *My Wicked, Wicked Ways.*

25 will forget it.
Years and years will pass.
My mother will stop mentioning it.

This is me she is carrying.
I am a baby.
30 She does not know
I will turn out bad.

CORNELIUS EADY (1954–   )

Too Young to Know

One day, my father chopped down
The old apricot tree
Which used to live in my parents backyard.
My father deflected my anger at him
5 With a look I heard Muddy Waters sing:
Y'all too young to know.

When I went to my mother
For the truth,
I only heard
10 What he must have told her:
A vague story about roots
    and basement pipes,
A vague story about branches
    and kitchen windows,
15 Punctuated by a shrug which meant:
He just does what he does.

The blues don't know nothing about trees
Unless, of course,
It's enlisted the moon
20 To drag some shadows around,
Unless, of course,
Something jumps up
Out of a hollow log,
A worry you didn't need
25 To cross your path.

My father's gone,
The tree's a stump,

And I'm still too young to know
If one day, I'll glance
30   out my window
At the sycamore,
And cluck my teeth.

LOUISE ERDRICH (1954–   )

Family Reunion (1984)

Ray's third new car in half as many years.
Full cooler in the trunk, Ray sogging the beer
as I solemnly chauffeur us through the bush
and up the backroads, hardly cowpaths and hub-deep in mud.
5   All day the sky lowers, clears, lowers again.
Somewhere in the bush near Saint John
there are uncles, a family, one mysterious brother
who stayed on the land when Ray left for the cities.
One week Ray is crocked. We've been through this before.
10   Even, as a little girl, hands in my dress,
Ah punka, you's my Debby, come and ki me.

Then the road ends in a yard full of dogs.
Them's Indian dogs, Ray says, lookit how they know me.
And they do seem to know him, like I do. His odor—
15   rank beef of fierce turtle pulled dripping from Metagoshe,[1]
and the inflammable mansmell: hair tonic, ashes, alcohol.
Ray dances an old woman up in his arms.
Fiddles reel in the phonograph and I sink apart
in a corner, start knocking the Blue Ribbons[2] down.
20   Four generations of people live here.
No one remembers Raymond Twobears.

So what. The walls shiver, the old house caulked with mud
sails back into the middle of Metagoshe.
A three-foot-long snapper is hooked on a fishline,
25   so mean that we do not dare wrestle him in
but tow him to shore, heavy as an old engine.

---

[1] **rank . . . Metagoshe:** Lake Metagoshe and the Turtle Mountains are located in northern North Dakota.
[2] **Blue Ribbons:** In other words, beers.

Then somehow Ray pries the beak open and shoves
down a cherry bomb. Lights the string tongue.

Headless and clenched in its armor, the snapper
30   is lugged home in the trunk for tomorrow's soup.
Ray rolls it beneath a bush in the backyard and goes in
to sleep his own head off. Tomorrow I find
that the animal has dragged itself off.
I follow torn tracks up a slight hill and over
35   into a small stream that deepens and widens into a marsh.

Ray finds his way back through the room into his arms.
When the phonograph stops, he slumps hard in his hands
and the boys and their old man fold him into the car
where he curls around his bad heart, hearing how it knocks
40   and rattles at the bars of his ribs to break out.

Somehow we find our way back. Uncle Ray
sings an old song to the body that pulls him
toward home. The gray fins that his hands have become
screw their bones in the dashboard. His face
45   has the odd, calm patience of a child who has always
let bad wounds alone, or a creature that has lived
for a long time underwater. And the angels come
lowering their slings and litters.

CATHY SONG (1955–   )

The Youngest Daughter (1983)

The sky has been dark
for many years.
My skin has become as damp
and pale as rice paper
5   and feels the way
mother's used to before the drying sun
parched it out there in the fields.

    Lately, when I touch my eyelids,
my hands react as if
10   I had just touched something
hot enough to burn.

My skin, aspirin colored,
tingles with migraine. Mother
has been massaging the left side of my face
15 especially in the evenings
when the pain flares up.

This morning
her breathing was graveled,
her voice gruff with affection
20 when I wheeled her into the bath.
She was in a good humor,
making jokes about her great breasts,
floating in the milky water
like two walruses,
25 flaccid and whiskered around the nipples.
I scrubbed them with a sour taste
in my mouth, thinking:
six children and an old man
have sucked from these brown nipples.

30 I was almost tender
when I came to the blue bruises
that freckle her body,
places where she has been injecting insulin
for thirty years. I soaped her slowly,
35 she sighed deeply, her eyes closed.
It seems it has always
been like this: the two of us
in this sunless room,
the splashing of the bathwater.

40 In the afternoons
when she has rested,
she prepares our ritual of tea and rice,
garnished with a shred of gingered fish,
a slice of pickled turnip,
45 a token for my white body.
We eat in the familiar silence.
She knows I am not to be trusted,
even now planning my escape.
As I toast to her health
50 with the tea she has poured,
a thousand cranes curtain the window,
fly up in a sudden breeze.

SHERMAN ALEXIE (1966–   )

Indian Boy Love Song (#2) (1992)

I never spoke
the language
of the old women

visiting my mother
5   in winters so cold
they could freeze
the tongue whole.

I never held my head
to their thin chests
10 believing in the heart.

Indian women, forgive me.
I grew up distant
and always afraid.

CHAPTER 16

BE NOT AFRAID OF MY BODY

—Walt Whitman

An Anthology of Poems on Love and Longing

There is nothing quite like the experience of erotic love, named after the Greek god of love, the son of Aphrodite. Most of us fall in love at some point, with a man or woman; some of us want to write about that experience. It is, in fact, the rare lover who has not put pen to paper, trying to frame his or her experience in language.

Some of the best poems ever written fall into the category of erotic poetry: poems that deal with sexual feelings, with human desire, the wish to possess a beloved, with unrequited love, with love gone sour, with nostalgic feelings for love long passed. Every aspect of love and longing has found its expression in a poem, somewhere, in some language.

In one of his lesser love poems, not included here, John Donne wrote:

> I am two fools, I know,
> For loving, and for saying so
> In whining poetry.

But there is nothing wrong with whining in poetry about love, although in poetry the whining usually sounds better than a shriek or squeal. It certainly does not amount to a whine, except in rare instances.

This selection of poems about erotic love ranges across centuries, from the Latin poet Ovid's highly sexual poem of seduction from his *Amores* through some wonderful medieval poems, such as "Alison"; the forbidden longings of a queen are here, as are the tender acknowledgments of familiar love between a husband and wife.

William Shakespeare must be considered the premier English poet on the subject of love, which preoccupied him in many of his plays and poems. His famous sequence of sonnets is partly written from the point of view of a lover to his "dark lady"; there also seems to be a homoerotic aspect to some of the poems. Many of these sonnets, such as Sonnet 130—"My mistress's eyes are nothing like the sun" (p. 1043)—rank high on any list of great love poems. Indeed, it would be easy to compile an entire anthology of love poems by Shakespeare alone, and hardly any page in the book would fail to inspire. We have had to restrict ourselves here to a few obvious samples from the Bard because of space limitations.

John Donne, despite his little whine above, was another of the fine love poets of the English language, as seen in "The Sun Rising" (p. 1049) and "The Ecstasy" (p. 1047). Donne, who was also a priest and theologian, was clearly a passionate man who loved God and women with equal fervor. His poems of erotic love have inspired many later poets on the subject, and they have often been read aloud on wedding days.

Wit in love poetry is always refreshing, and "Delight in Disorder" (p. 1053) by Robert Herrick is a splendid example of this:

> A sweet disorder in the dress
> Kindles in clothes a wantonness:
> A lawn about the shoulders thrown
> Into a fine distraction:
> 5   An erring lace, which here and there
> Enthrals the crimson stomacher:
> A cuff neglectful, and thereby
> Ribbands to flow confusedly:
> A winning wave, deserving note,
> 10 In the tempestuous petticoat:
> A careless shoe-string, in whose tie
> I see a wild civility:
> Do more bewitch me than when art
> Is too precise in every part.

Who could resist such energy and good humor? Leafing through love poems over the centuries, readers will note that sexual desire often has a humorous aspect, as in Roethke's "I Knew a Woman" (p. 1078) and Joy Harjo's "He Told Me His Name Was Sitting Bull" (p. 1096). These poems, in different ways, reach back to Herrick, who took such delight in the disorder of his lover's dress, or undress. Roethke's "I Knew a Woman" moves artfully from erotic love to divine love—a direction in which all love aspires. In fact, when contemplating the possibility of erotic love, we should always keep Roethke's last, wonderful lines from this poem in mind:

> Let seed be grass, and grass turn into hay:
> I'm martyr to a motion not my own;
> What's freedom for? To know eternity.
> I swear she cast a shadow white as stone.
> 5   But who would count eternity in days?
> These old bones live to learn her wanton ways:
> (I measure time by how a body sways.)

Some of the most vivid poems about love focus on feelings of betrayal or rejection. All of us have been marked in some way by the scorn or indifference of people we have passionately loved, and many readers have found at least a companion in misery in some of the more cynical and bitter poems collected here. "No Second Troy" by William Butler Yeats (p. 1069) ranks high among such poems, dripping as it is with cynicism. The poem begins with a rhetorical question that is full of bitterness and rage:

> Why should I blame her that she filled my days
> With misery, or that she would of late
> Have taught to ignorant men most violent ways,
> Or hurled the little streets upon the great,
> 5   Had they but courage equal to desire?

As you will guess, Yeats does blame the woman in the poem. Indeed, he can barely contain his fury.

Many of the finest love poems of the modern era are included here: Robert Frost's "To Earthward" and "The Silken Tent" (pages 1069 and 1070), D. H. Lawrence's "Gloire de Dijon" (p. 1074), e. e. cummings's "All in green went my love riding" (p. 1075), and Edna St. Vincent Millay's "Love Is Not All: It Is Not Meat nor Drink" (p. 1074). These are poems that exhibit a stunning control and power. Note, for example, that "The Silken Tent" (which is also a sonnet) consists of a single sentence, elaborately strung. A curious reader might wish to explore the biographical details of these poets' lives, available in biographies as well as published letters and diaries; the concision with which these poets expressed the obvious tumult of their lives becomes all the more remarkable when put in context. That said, a reader should keep in mind that not every love poem is addressed to a particular (or even real) lover; these poems have come to be so memorable because generations of readers find personal resonance and meaning in their expressions of love and longing.

Homoerotic feelings are also expressed in many of these poems, from the time of Sappho to the present. W. H. Auden, Frank O'Hara, Adrienne Rich, and Carl Phillips write in this tradition, although they do so in very different ways. Indeed, Auden's famous "Lullaby" (p. 1077) might well be considered a poem about a brief, but intense homosexual affair. The crucial point is that the speaker in the poem addresses a beloved who will certainly be gone by the morning:

> But in my arms till break of day
> Let the living creature lie,
> Mortal, guilty, but to me
> The entirely beautiful.

Poems that praise the human body, offering frank celebrations of the human anatomy, are often humorous as well as rapturous. Readers delight in "homage to my hips" (p. 1086) by Lucille Clifton, "Breasts"

(p. 1087) by Charles Simic, and "Beautiful Black Men" (p. 1090) by Nikki Giovanni. Clifton, Simic, and Giovanni write without shame about the body, and these cannot in any way be considered sexist poems. They are, quite simply, sexy poems.

Some complex poems about marriage are included in this chapter, including Theodore Roethke's "Wish for a Young Wife" (p. 1079), "The Ache of Marriage" by Denise Levertov (p. 1080), and Ai's "Twenty-Year Marriage" (p. 1092). These are memorable poems about a venerable institution in which erotic love has been, over the centuries, contained and explored in countless ways.

In all, these poems offer a brief tour of sexual desire in its many aspects. Some of these poems are straightforward, such as Galway Kinnell's beautiful "After Making Love We Hear Footsteps" (p. 1083) or Robert Pinsky's "First Early Mornings Together" (p. 1089). Others, such as "Living in Sin" by Adrienne Rich (p. 1083) or "Dear Nobody's Business" by James Galvin (p. 1095), treat the complications of erotic love. But even the complications are delicious. Human beings will always want to make love, and to make poems about making love.

ADDITIONAL POEMS ABOUT LOVE AND LONGING IN THIS BOOK

- Anonymous, "I Have a Gentle Cock" (p. 1341)
- John Lidgate, "The duplicity of women" (p. 874)
- Edmund Spenser, from *Amoretti* (p. 1245)
- Thomas Wyatt, "Is It Possible" (p. 606)
- Sir Philip Sidney, Sonnet 39 from *Astrophil and Stella* (p. 81)
- William Shakespeare, "It Was a Lover and His Lass" (p. 612)
- John Donne, "The Good Morrow" (p. 888)
- Robert Burns, "Bonie Doon" (p. 625)
- Edgar Allan Poe, "Annabel Lee" (p. 495)
- William Butler Yeats, "Song of Wandering Aengus" (p. 1598)
- William Carlos Williams, "This Is Just to Say" (p. 1607)
- Edna St. Vincent Millay, "What lips my lips have kissed" (p. 823)
- Elizabeth Bishop, "One Art" (p. 841)
- Theodore Roethke, "Elegy for Jane" (p. 221)
- James Dickey, "Cherrylog Road" (p. 364)
- David Mason, "Spooning" (p. 370)

CATULLUS (ca. 84 B.C.–54 B.C.)
trans. Horace Gregory

"Come, Lesbia, let us live and love"

Come, Lesbia, let us live and love,
nor give a damn what sour old men say.
The sun that sets may rise again
but when our light has sunk into the earth,
5   it is gone forever.
            Give me a thousand kisses,
then a hundred, another thousand,
another hundred
            and in one breath
10   still kiss another thousand,
another hundred.
            O then with lips and bodies joined
many deep thousands;
            confuse
15   their number,
            so that poor fools and cuckolds (envious
even now) shall never
learn our wealth and curse us
with their
20   evil eyes.

OVID (43 B.C.–17 A.D.)
trans. Jay Parini[1]

from Amores

An afternoon in sultry summer.
After swimming, I slept on the long divan,
dreaming of a tall brown girl.

Nearby, a din of waves
5   blasted in the jaws of rocks.
The green sea wrestled with itself
like a muscular beast in the white sun.

A tinkle of glasses woke me: Corinna!
She entered with fruit and wine.
10   I remember the motion of her hair
like seaweed across her shoulders.

---

[1] This is an adaptation, not a literal translation.

Her dress: a green garment.
She wore it after swimming.
It pressed to the hollows of her body
15   and was beautiful as skin.

I tugged at the fringe, politely.
She poured out wine to drink.
"Shy thing," I whispered.

She held the silence with her breath,
20   her eyes to the floor, pretending,
then smiling: a self-betrayal.

In a moment she was naked.
I pulled her down beside me,
lively, shaking like an eel—
25   loose-limbed and slippery-skinned.
She wriggled in my arms at play.

When I kissed her closer
she was wet beneath me and wide as the sea.

I could think of nothing but the sun,
30   how it warmed my spine as
I hugged her, shuddering all white light,
white thighs. Need more be said
but that we slept as if
the world had died together with that day?

35   These afternoons are rare.

ANONYMOUS

Alison (thirteenth century)

Betwene Mersh° and Averil,°	March / April
When spray° beginneth to springe,	twig
The lutel° fowl hath hire will	little
On hire lud to singe.	
5 Ich° libbe° in love-longinge	I / live
For semlokest° of alle thinge—	fairest
He° may me blisse bringe;	She
Ich am in hire baundoun.°	bound

An hendy hap ich habbe ihent![1]
10 Ichot° from Hevene it is me sent. I know
From alle wimmen my love is lent,
And light on Alisoun.[2]

On hew hire her° is fair inogh, hair
Hire browe browne, hire eye blake;
15 With lossum chere[3] he on me logh,
With middle° small and well imake. waist
Bote he me wolle° to hire take, will
For to ben hire owen make,° mate
Longe to liven ichulle° forsake, I will
20 And feye fallen adoun.[4]

Nightes when I wende° and wake— turn
Forthy mine wonges waxeth won—[5]
Levedy,° all for thine sake, Lady
Longinge is ilent° me on. has come
25 In world nis non so witer mon[6]
That all hire bounte telle con°: can
Hire swire° is whittore° then the swon, neck / whiter
And fairest may° in toun. maid

Ich am for wowing all forwake,
30 Wery so water in wore,[7]
Lest eny reve° me my make, rob
Ich habbe iyirned yore.[8]
Betere is tholien while sore
Then mournen evermore.
35 Geynest under gore,
Herkne to my roun![9]

---

[1] **An hendy . . . ihent:** I.e., fair fortune has come my way.
[2] **From alle wimmen . . . Alisoun:** I.e., my love has been withdrawn from all other women and settled on Alison.
[3] **lossum chere:** I.e., lovely face.
[4] **And feye fallen adoun:** I.e., I will fall to my doom.
[5] **Forthy mine wonges waxeth won:** I.e., then my cheeks grow pale.
[6] **In world . . . mon:** I.e., there is not so wise a man anywhere in the world.
[7] **Ich am . . . water in wore:** I.e., I am awake with desire, / like water in a troubled pool.
[8] **Ich habbe iyirned yore:** I.e., I have yearned after for so long.
[9] **Geynest . . . roun:** I.e., Kindest of women, hear my song.

THOMAS HOCCLEVE (ca. 1369–1426)

A description of his ugly lady (fifteenth century)

Of my lady well me rejoise I may!
Hir golden forheed is full narw° and smal;   narrow
Hir browes been lik to dim, reed coral;
And as the jeet hir yen glistren ay.

5   Hir bowgy cheekes been as softe as clay,
With large jowes and substancial.

Hir nose a pentice[1] is that it ne shal
Reine in hir mouth thogh she uprightes lay.

Hir mouth is nothing scant with lippes gray;
10   Hir chin unnethe may be seen at al.

Hir comly body shape as a footbal,
And she singeth full like a papejay.[2]

ANONYMOUS

"I sing of a maiden" (fifteenth century)

I sing of a maiden
That is makeles:[1]
King of alle kinges
To here sone she ches.°   chose

5   He cam also stille
Ther his moder was,
As dew in Aprille
That falleth on the grass.

He cam also stille
10   To his moderes bowr,
As dew in Aprille
That falleth on the flowr.

---

[1] **pentice:** A covered walk between buildings. Used here as a metaphor.
[2] **papejay:** A parrot.
[1] **makeles:** I.e., without an equal; without a mate.

He cam also stille
Ther his moder lay,
15   As dew in Aprille
That falleth on the spray.

Moder and maiden
Was never non but she:
Well may swich a lady
20   Godes moder be.

ANONYMOUS

"Men only pretend" (fifteenth century)

Whatso men sayn,
Love is no pain
To them, certain,
But varians[1]:
5   For they constrain
Ther hertes to fein,
Ther mouthes to plain,°   utter
Ther displesauns.

Which is, indede,
10   But feined drede,
So God me spede,
And doubleness:
Ther othes to bede,°   offer
Ther lives to lede,
15   And profer mede—
Newfangleness!

For, when they pray,
Ye shall have nay,
Whatso they say—
20   Beware for shame!
For every day
They waite ther pray
Wherso they may,
And make but game.

---

[1] **But varians:** I.e., without variation.

25   Then, semeth me,
      Ye may well se
      They be so fre
      In every place,
      It were pite
30   But they shold be
      Begeled, parde,
      Withouten grace.

WILLIAM DUNBAR (ca. 1460–1525)

In Prais of Wemen (ca. 1510)

Now of wemen this I say for me,		
Of erthly thingis nane may bettir be;		
Thay should haif wirschep° and grit° honoring		worship / great
Of men, aboif all othir erthly thing;		
5 Rycht° grit dishonour upoun him self he takkis		right
In word or deid quha° evir wemen lakkis;°		who / faults; lacks
Sen that of wemen cumin all are we,		
Wemen are wemen and sa° will end and de.°		so / die
Wo° wirth° the fruct wald put the tre to nocht,[1]		Woe / come to
10 And wo wirth him rycht so that sayis ocht°		anything
Of womanheid that may be ony lak		
Or sic grit shame upone him for to tak.		
Thay us consaif° with pane, and by thame fed		take to themselves
Within thair breistis thair we be boun to bed;		
15 Grit pane and wo, and murnyng° mervellus,		mourning
Into thair birth thay suffir sair° for us;		sore
Than meit and drynk to feid us get we nane,		
Bot that we sowk° out of thair breistis bane.		suck
Thay are the confort that we all haif heir,		
20 Thair may no man be till us half so deir;		
Thay are our verry nest of nurissing;		
In lak of thame quha can say ony thing,		
That fowll his nest he fylis,° and for thy°		flees / that
Exylit° he should be of all gud cumpany;		excellence
25 Thair should na wyis man gif audience,		
To sic ane without intelligence.		
Christ to his fader he had nocht ane man;		

---

[1] **fruct . . . nocht:** I.e., Who with the fruit would put the tree to nothing.

Se quhat° wirschep wemen should haif than.   what
That Sone is Lord, that Sone is King of kingis,
30   In heaven and earth his majestie ay ringis.
Sen scho[2] hes borne him in hir halines,
And he is well and grund° of all gudnes,   ground
All wemen of us should haif honoring,
Service and luve, aboif all othir thing.

THOMAS WYATT (1503–1542)

They Flee from Me

They flee from me that sometime did me seek
    With naked foot stalking in my chamber.
I have seen them gentle tame and meek
    That now are wild and do not remember
5   That sometime they put themselves in danger
To take bread at my hand; and now they range
Busily seeking with a continual change.

Thanked be fortune, it hath been otherwise
    Twenty times better; but once in special,
10   In thin array after a pleasant guise,
    When her loose gown from her shoulders did fall,
    And she me caught in her arms long and small;
And therewithal sweetly did me kiss,
And softly said, *Dear heart, how like you this?*

15   It was no dream, I lay broad waking.
    But all is turned thorough my gentleness
Into a strange fashion of forsaking;
    And I have leave to go of her goodness
    And she also to use newfangleness.
20   But since that I so kindely am served,
I would fain know what she hath deserved.

---

[2] **scho:** She, i.e., the Virgin Mary.

HENRY HOWARD, EARL OF SURREY (ca. 1517–1547)
trans. from Petrarch, Rime 140

Love, That Doth Reign and Live Within My Thought[1] (1557)

Love, that doth reign and live within my thought,
And built his seat within my captive breast,
Clad in the arms wherein with me he fought,
Oft in my face he doth his banner rest.
5   But she that taught me love and suffer pain,
My doubtful hope and eke° my hot desire   also
With shamefast look to shadow and refrain,
Her smiling grace converteth straight to ire.
And coward Love, then, to the heart apace
10   Taketh his flight, where he doth lurk and plain,°   complain
His purpose lost, and dare not show his face.
For my lord's guilt thus faultless bide I pain,
Yet from my lord shall not my foot remove:
Sweet is the death that taketh end by love.

QUEEN ELIZABETH TUDOR I (1533–1603)

On Monsieur's Departure (1565)

I grieve and dare not show my discontent,
I love and yet am forced to seem to hate,
I do, yet dare not say I ever meant,
I seem stark mute but inwardly to prate.°   preen
5   I am and not, I freeze and yet am burned.
Since from myself another self I turned.

My care is like my shadow in the sun,
Follows me flying, flies when I pursue it,
Stands and lies by me, doth what I have done.
10   His too familiar care doth make me rue it.
No means I find to rid him from my breast,
Till by the end of things it be supprest.

Some gentler passion slide into my mind,
For I am soft and made of melting snow;
15   Or be more cruel, love, and so be kind.
Let me or float or sink, be high or low.
Or let me live with some more sweet content,
Or die and so forget what love ere meant.

---

[1] **Love . . . Thought:** This poem is a translation of Petrarch's *Rime* 140.

GEORGE GASCOIGNE (ca. 1535–1577)

And If I Did What Then? (1573)

"And if I did what then?
Are you aggrieved therefore?
The sea hath fish for every man,
And what would you have more?"

5   Thus did my mistress once
Amaze my mind with doubt,
And popped a question for the nonce
To beat my brains about.

Whereto I thus replied:
10 "Each fisherman can wish
That all the sea at every tide
Were his alone to fish.

And so did I, in vain;
But since it may not be,
15 Let such fish there as find the gain,
And leave the loss for me.

And with such luck and loss
I will content myself,
Till tides of turning time may toss
20 Such fishers on the shelf.

And when they stick on sands,
That every man may see,
Then will I laugh and clap my hands,
As they do now at me."

MICHAEL DRAYTON (1563–1631)

Sonnet LXI (1619)

Since there's no help, come let us kiss and part—
Nay, I have done: you get no more of me;
And I am glad, yea glad with all my heart,
That thus so cleanly I myself can free.
5 Shake hands for ever, cancel all our vows,
And when we meet at any time again,
Be it not seen in either of our brows

That we one jot of former love retain.
Now at the last gasp of love's latest breath,
10   When, his pulse failing, passion speechless lies,
When faith is kneeling by his bed of death,
And innocence is closing up his eyes,
    Now if thou wouldst, when all have given him over,
    From death to life thou mightst him yet recover.

WILLIAM SHAKESPEARE (1564–1616)

from Two Gentlemen of Verona
Act IV, Scene 2 (Host) (ca. 1590; 1623)

Who is Silvia? what is she,
That all our swains commend her?
Holy, fair and wise is she;
The heaven such grace did lend her,
5   That she might admired be.
Is she kind as she is fair?
For beauty lives with kindness.
Love doth to her eyes repair,
To help him of his blindness,
10   And, being help'd, inhabits there.
Then to Silvia let us sing,
That Silvia is excelling;
She excels each mortal thing
Upon the dull earth dwelling:
15   To her let us garlands bring.

WILLIAM SHAKESPEARE (1564–1616)

from Love's Labour's Lost
Act III, Scene 1 (Biron) (ca. 1595)

And I, forsooth, in love! I, that have been love's whip;
A very beadle to a humorous sigh;
A critic, nay, a night-watch constable;
A domineering pedant o'er the boy;
5   Than whom no mortal so magnificent!
This whimpled, whining, purblind, wayward boy;

This senior-junior, giant-dwarf, Dan Cupid;[1]
Regent of love-rhymes, lord of folded arms,
The anointed sovereign of sighs and groans,
10   Liege of all loiterers and malcontents,
Dread prince of plackets, king of codpieces,[2]
Sole imperator and great general
Of trotting 'paritors:—O my little heart:—
And I to be a corporal of his field,
15   And wear his colours like a tumbler's hoop!
What, I! I love! I sue! I seek a wife!
A woman, that is like a German clock,
Still a-repairing, ever out of frame,
And never going aright, being a watch,
20   But being watch'd that it may still go right!
Nay, to be perjured, which is worst of all;
And, among three, to love the worst of all;
A wightly wanton with a velvet brow,
With two pitch-balls stuck in her face for eyes;
25   Ay, and by heaven, one that will do the deed
Though Argus[3] were her eunuch and her guard:
And I to sigh for her! to watch for her!
To pray for her! Go to; it is a plague
That Cupid will impose for my neglect
30   Of his almighty dreadful little might.
Well, I will love, write, sigh, pray, sue and groan:
Some men must love my lady and some Joan.

WILLIAM SHAKESPEARE (1564–1616)

from Twelfth Night
Act I, Scene 1 (Duke Orsino)   (ca. 1602; 1623)

If music be the food of love, play on;
Give me excess of it, that, surfeiting,
The appetite may sicken, and so die.
That strain again! it had a dying fall:

---

[1] **Dan Cupid:** Cupid is the Roman god of love. Dan was formerly used as a title of honor for respected men.
[2] **plackets, king of codpieces:** Placket: a slit in a woman dress or skirt. Codpiece: a pouch at the crotch of breeches worn by men in fifteenth and sixteenth centuries.
[3] **Argus:** In Greek mythology, a giant with 100 eyes, who was the guardian of Io.

5 O, it came o'er my ear like the sweet sound,
That breathes upon a bank of violets,
Stealing and giving odour! Enough; no more:
'Tis not so sweet now as it was before.
O spirit of love! how quick and fresh art thou,
10 That, notwithstanding thy capacity
Receiveth as the sea, nought enters there,
Of what validity and pitch soe'er,
But falls into abatement and low price,
Even in a minute: so full of shapes is fancy
15 That it alone is high fantastical.

WILLIAM SHAKESPEARE (1564–1616)

Sonnet 130 (ca. 1595; 1609)

My mistress' eyes are nothing like the sun;
    Coral is far more red than her lips' red;
If snow be white, why then her breasts are dun;
    If hairs be wires, black wires grow on her head.
5 I have seen roses damask'd, red and white,
    But no such roses see I in her cheeks,
And in some perfumes is there more delight
    Than in the breath that from my mistress reeks.
I love to hear her speak, yet well I know
10   That music hath a far more pleasing sound.
I grant I never saw a goddess go;
    My mistress when she walks treads on the ground.
      And yet, by heav'n, I think my love as rare
      As any she belied with false compare.

WILLIAM SHAKESPEARE (1564–1616)

Sonnet 151 (ca. 1595; 1609)

Love is too young to know what conscience is;
Yet who knows not conscience is born of love?
Then, gentle cheater, urge not my amiss,
Lest guilty of my faults thy sweet self prove:
5 For, thou betraying me, I do betray

My nobler part to my gross body's treason;
My soul doth tell my body that he may
Triumph in love; flesh stays no further reason,
But rising at thy name doth point out thee
10   As his triumphant prize. Proud of this pride,
He is contented thy poor drudge to be,
To stand in thy affairs, fall by thy side.
No want of conscience hold it that I call
Her 'love' for whose dear love I rise and fall.

ANONYMOUS (late sixteenth century)

"Love me little, love me long" (ca. 1570)

Love me little, love me long,
Is the burden of my song.
Love that is too hot and strong
      Burneth soon to waste.
5   Still, I would not have thee cold,
Not too backward, nor too bold;
Love that lasteth till 'tis old
      Fadeth not in haste.
            Love me little, love me long,
10   *Is the burden of my song.*

If thou lovest me too much,
It will not prove as true as touch;
Love me little, more than such,
      For I fear the end.
15   I am with little well content,
And a little from thee sent
Is enough, with true intent
      To be steadfast friend.
            Love me little, love me long,
20   *Is the burden of my song.*

Say thou lov'st me while thou live;
I to thee my love will give,
Never dreaming to deceive
      Whiles that life endures.
25   Nay, and after death, in sooth,
I to thee will keep my truth,
As now, when in my May of youth;
      This my love assures.

> *Love me little, love me long,*
30   *Is the burden of my song.*

Constant love is moderate ever,
And it will through life persever;
Give me that, with true endeavor
     I will it restore.
35   A suit of durance let it be,
For all weathers that for me,
For the land or for the sea,
     Lasting evermore.
       Love me little, love me long,
40   *Is the burden of my song.*

Winter's cold, or summer's heat,
Autumn's tempests on it beat,
It can never know defeat,
     Never can rebel.
45   Such the love that I would gain,
Such the love, I tell thee plain,
Thou must give, or woo in vain;
     So to thee, farewell!
       Love me little, love me long,
50   *Is the burden of my song.*

THOMAS CAMPION (1567–1620)

My Sweetest Lesbia[1] (1601)

My sweetest Lesbia, let us live and love,
And though the sager sort our deeds reprove,
Let us not weigh them. Heaven's great lamps do dive
Into their west, and straight again revive,
5   But soon as once set is our little light,
Then must we sleep one ever-during night.

If all would lead their lives in love like me,
Then bloody swords and armor should not be;
No drum nor trumpet peaceful sleeps should move,
10   Unless alarm came from the camp of love.

---

[1] **Lesbia:** See also Catullus's poem "Come, Lesbia" at the beginning of this chapter.

But fools do live, and waste their little light,
And seek with pain their ever-during night.

When timely death my life and fortune ends,
Let not my hearse be vexed with mourning friends,
15   But let all lovers, rich in triumph, come
And with sweet pastimes grace my happy tomb;
And Lesbia, close up thou my little light,
And crown with love my ever-during night.

THOMAS CAMPION (1567–1620)

Rose-cheeked Laura (1602)

Rose-cheeked Laura, come,
Sing thou smoothly with thy beauty's
Silent music, either other
         Sweetly gracing.

5   Lovely forms do flow
From concent divinely framed;
Heav'n is music, and thy beauty's
         Birth is heavenly.

These dull notes we sing
10   Discords need for helps to grace them;
Only beauty purely loving
         Knows no discord,

But still moves delight,
Like clear springs renewed by flowing,
15   Ever perfect, ever in them-
         Selves eternal.

JOHN DONNE (1572–1631)

The Canonization (1633)

For God's sake hold your tongue, and let me love;
    Or chide my palsy, or my gout,
My five grey hairs or ruined fortune flout,
With wealth your state, your mind with arts improve,

5   Take you a course, get you a place,
         Observe his honour, or his grace,
   Or the king's real, or his stampèd face
         Contémplate; what you will, approve,
             So you will let me love.

10   Alas, alas, who's injured by my love?
         What merchant's ships have my sighs drowned?
   Who says my tears have overflowed his ground?
   When did my colds a forward spring remove?
         When did the heats which my veins fill
15   Add one more to the plaguy° bill?   vexatious
   Soldiers find wars, and lawyers find out still
         Litigious men, which quarrels move,
             Though she and I do love.

   Call us what you will, we're made such by love;
20   Call her one, me another fly:
   We're tapers too, and at our own cost die.
   And we in us find the eagle and the dove;[1]
         The phoenix riddle hath more wit
         By us: we two being one, are it;
25   So to one neutral thing both sexes fit.
         We die and rise the same, and prove
             Mysterious by this love.

   We can die by it, if not live by love,
         And if unfit for tombs and hearse
30   Our legend be, it will be fit for verse;
   And if no piece of chronicle we prove,
         We'll build in sonnets pretty rooms;
         As well a well wrought urn becomes
   The greatest ashes, as half-acre tombs;
35   And by these hymns, all shall approve
            Us canonized for love.

   And thus invoke us: 'You whom reverend love
         Made one another's hermitage;
   You, to whom love was peace, that now is rage;
40   Who did the whole world's soul contract, and drove

---

[1] **the eagle and the dove:** The dove symbolizes the Holy Ghost, while the eagle has been adopted as an emblem by many countries. Here, Donne possibly suggests that his love is representative of both religion and government (church and state).

    Into the glasses of your eyes
      (So made such mirrors, and such spies,
  That they did all to you epitomize)
      Countries, towns, courts: beg from above
45   A pattern of your love!'

JOHN DONNE (1572–1631)

The Ecstasy (1633)

  Where, like a pillow on a bed,
    A pregnant bank swelled up, to rest
  The violet's reclining head,
    Sat we two, one another's best.

5 Our hands were firmly cemented
    With a fast balm, which thence did spring;
  Our eye-beams twisted, and did thread
    Our eyes upon one double string;

  So to entergraft° our hands, as yet   engraft
10   Was all our means to make us one,
  And pictures on our eyes to get
    Was all our propagation.

  As 'twixt two equal armies Fate
    Suspends uncertain victory,
15 Our souls (which to advance their state
    Were gone out) hung 'twixt her and me.

  And whilst our souls negotiate there,
    We like sepulchral statues lay;
  All day the same our postures were,
20   And we said nothing all the day.

  If any, so by love refined
    That he soul's language understood,
  And by good love were grown all mind,
    Within convenient distance stood,

25 He (though he knew not which soul spake,
    Because both meant, both spake the same)
  Might thence a new concoction take,
    And part far purer than he came.

This ecstasy doth unperplex
30   (We said) and tell us what we love,
We see by this, it was not sex,
        We see, we saw not what did move:

But as all several souls contain
        Mixture of things, they know not what,
35 Love these mixed souls doth mix again,
        And makes both one, each this and that.

A single violet transplant,
        The strength, the colour, and the size,
(All which before was poor and scant)
40   Redoubles still, and multiplies.

When love with one another so
        Interinanimates two souls,
That abler soul, which thence doth flow,
        Defects of loneliness controls.

45 We then, who are this new soul, know
        Of what we are composed, and made,
For the atomies of which we grow
        Are souls, whom no change can invade.

But, O alas! so long, so far
50   Our bodies why do we forbear?
They are ours, though they are not we; we are
        The intelligences, they the sphere.[1]

We owe them thanks, because they thus
        Did us, to us, at first convey,
55 Yielded their forces, sense, to us,
        Nor are dross to us, but allay.

On man heaven's influence works not so,
        But that it first imprints the air;
So soul into the soul may flow,
60   Though it to body first repair.

As our blood labours to beget
        Spirits, as like souls as it can;

---

[1] **intelligences, they the sphere:** The nine orders of angels or "intelligences" were believed to govern the nine heavenly spheres of Ptolemic astronomy.

Because such fingers need to knit
    That subtle knot, which makes us man;

65 So must pure lovers' souls descend
    To affections, and to faculties,
Which sense may reach and apprehend,
    Else a great Prince in prison lies.

To our bodies turn we then, that so
70   Weak men on love revealed may look;
Love's mysteries in souls do grow,
    But yet the body is his book.

And if some lover, such as we,
    Have heard this dialogue of one,
75 Let him still mark us, he shall see
    Small change, when we're to bodies gone.

JOHN DONNE (1572–1631)

The Sun Rising (1633)

    Busy old fool, unruly sun,
        Why dost thou thus
Through windows and through curtains call on us?
Must to thy motions lovers' seasons run?
5   Saucy pedantic wretch, go chide
    Late schoolboys and sour prentices;
Go tell court huntsmen that the king will ride;
    Call country ants to harvest offices:
Love, all alike, no season knows, nor clime,
10 Nor hours, days, months, which are the rags of time.

    Thy beams, so reverend and strong
        Why shouldst thou think?
I could eclipse and cloud them with a wink,
But that I would not lose her sight so long:
15   If her eyes have not blinded thine,
    Look, and tomorrow late tell me
Whether both th' Indias of spice and mine
Be where thou leftst them, or lie here with me.
Ask for those kings whom thou sawst yesterday,
20 And thou shalt hear, all here in one bed lay.

She's all states, and all princes, I;
        Nothing else is.
Princes do but play us; compared to this,
All honour's mimic; all wealth alchemy.
25   Thou, sun, art half as happy as we,
        In that the world's contracted thus;
Thine age asks ease, and since thy duties be
To warm the world, that's done in warming us.
Shine here to us, and thou art everywhere:
30   This bed thy centre is, these walls, thy sphere.

BEN JONSON (1572–1637)

from The Sad Shepherd
Though I Am Young (1641)

Though I am young and cannot tell
    Either what Death or Love is well,
Yet I have heard they both bear darts,
    And both do aim at human hearts.
5   And then again, I have been told
    Love wounds with heat, as Death with cold;
So that I fear they do but bring
    Extremes to touch, and mean one thing.

    As in a ruin we it call
10   One thing to be blown up or fall;
Or to our end like way may have
    By a flash of lightning or a wave;
So Love's inflamed shaft or brand
    May kill as soon as Death's cold hand;
15   Except Love's fires the virtue have
    To fright the frost out of the grave.

AURELIAN TOWNSHEND (ca. 1583–ca. 1651)

Upon Kind and True Love (1656)

'Tis not how witty, nor how free,
Nor yet how beautiful she be,
But how much kind and true to me.

Freedom and wit none can confine,
5   And beauty like the sun doth shine,
But kind and true are only mine.

Let others with attention sit,
To listen, and admire her wit:
That is a rock where I'll not split.
10   Let others dote upon her eyes,
And burn their hearts for sacrifice;
Beauty's a calm where danger lies.

But kind and true have been long tried
A harbour where we may confide
15   And safely there at anchor ride.
From change of winds there we are free,
And need not fear storm's tyranny,
Nor pirate, though a prince he be.

MARY WROTH (ca. 1587–ca. 1651)

from Urania
Song (1621)

Love what art thou? A vain thought
     In our minds by phant'sie wrought,
     Idle smiles did thee beget
     While fond wishes made the net
5   Which so many fools have caught;

Love what art thou? light, and fair,
     Fresh as morning, clear as th'air,
     But too soon thy evening change
     Makes thy worth with coldness range;
10   Still thy joy is mixed with care.

Love what art thou? A sweet flow'r
     Once full blown, dead in an hour,
     Dust in wind as staid remains
     As thy pleasure, or our gains
15   If thy humor change to lour.°   gloom

Love what art thou? childish, vain,
     Firm as bubbles made by rain;

        Wantonness thy greatest pride,
        These foul faults thy virtues hide,
20   But babes can no staidness gain.

Love what art thou? causeless curse,
        Yet alas these not the worst,
        Much more of thee may be said
        But thy law I once obeyed
25   Therefore say no more at first.

ROBERT HERRICK (1591–1674)

To the Virgins, To Make Much of Time (1648)

Gather ye rosebuds while ye may,
    Old Time is still a flying;
And this same flower that smiles today,
    Tomorrow will be dying.

5 The glorious lamp of heaven, the sun,
    The higher he's a getting;
The sooner will his race be run,
    And nearer he's to setting.

That age is best which is the first,
10   When youth and blood are warmer;
But being spent, the worse, and worst
    Times, still succeed the former.

Then be not coy, but use your time,
    And while ye may, go marry;
15 For having lost but once your prime,
    You may for ever tarry.

ROBERT HERRICK (1591–1674)

Upon Julia's Clothes (1648)

Whenas in silks my Julia goes,
Then, then (methinks) how sweetly flows
That liquefaction of her clothes.

Next, when I cast mine eyes and see
5 That brave vibration each way free,
Oh how that glittering taketh me!

ROBERT HERRICK (1591–1674)

Upon Julia's Breasts (1648)

Display thy breasts, my Julia, there let me
Behold that circummortal[1] purity;
Between whose glories, there my lips I'll lay,
Ravished in that fair *Via Lactea.*[2]

ROBERT HERRICK (1591–1674)

Delight in Disorder (1648)

A sweet disorder in the dress
Kindles in clothes a wantonness.
A lawn[1] about the shoulders thrown
Into a fine distractiòn;
5 An erring lace, which here and there
Enthralls the crimson stomacher;[2]
A cuff neglectful, and thereby
Ribbons to flow confusedly;
A winning wave, deserving note,
10 In the tempestuous petticoat;
A careless shoestring, in whose tie
I see a wild civility;
Do more bewitch me than when art
Is too precise in every part.

[1] **circummortal:** A term coined by Herrick, literally "encompassing the mortal," though the more accurate reading would be "immortal." Herrick perhaps tried to depict at one and the same time the round quality of Julia's breasts and their abstract, immortal nature.
[2] ***Via Lactea:*** The Milky Way (Latin). Note how the English translation completes the rhyme scheme aabb, making "Way" rhyme with "lay."
[1] **lawn:** A light, transparent garment.
[2] **stomacher:** An ornament worn under the front of the bodice.

ROBERT HERRICK (1591–1674)

Corinna's Going A-Maying (1648)

Get up! get up for shame! the blooming morn
Upon her wings presents the god unshorn.[1]
　　See how Aurora[2] throws her fair
　　Fresh-quilted colors through the air:
5 　　Get up, sweet slug-a-bed, and see
　　The dew bespangling herb and tree.
Each flower has wept and bowèd toward the east
Above an hour since, yet you not dressed;
　　Nay, not so much as out of bed?
10 　　When all the birds have matins° said,　　　　　　　　　morning prayers
　　And sung their thankful hymns, 'tis sin,
　　Nay, profanation to keep in,
Whenas a thousand virgins on this day
Spring, sooner than the lark, to fetch in May.

15 Rise, and put on your foliage, and be seen
To come forth, like the springtime, fresh and green,
　　And sweet as Flora.[3] Take no care
　　For jewels for your gown or hair;
　　Fear not; the leaves will strew
20 　　Gems in abundance upon you;
Besides, the childhood of the day has kept,
Against you come, some orient pearls unwept;
　　Come and receive them while the light
　　Hangs on the dew-locks of the night,
25 　　And Titan[4] on the eastern hill
　　Retires himself, or else stands still
Till you come forth. Wash, dress, be brief in praying:
Few beads[5] are best when once we go a-Maying.

Come, my Corinna, come; and, coming mark
30 How each field turns a street, each street a park
　　Made green and trimmed with trees; see how
　　Devotion gives each house a bough

---

[1] **god unshorn:** I.e., Apollo, the sun god, whose hair was never cut.
[2] **Aurora:** The Greek goddess of dawn.
[3] **Flora:** The Greek goddess of flowers.
[4] **Titan:** I.e., the sun.
[5] **beads:** Referring to the beads of the rosary used in prayer.

Or branch: each porch, each door ere this,
An ark, a tabernacle[6] is,
35   Made up of whitethorn neatly interwove,
As if here were those cooler shades of love.
      Can such delights be in the street
      And open fields, and we not see 't?
      Come, we'll abroad; and let's obey
40   The proclamation made for May,
And sin no more, as we have done, by staying;
But, my Corinna, come, let's go a-Maying.

There's not a budding boy or girl this day
But is got up and gone to bring in May;
45   A deal of youth, ere this, is come
      Back, and with whitethorn laden home.
      Some have dispatched their cakes and cream
      Before that we have left to dream;
And some have wept, and wooed, and plighted troth,
50   And chose their priest, ere we can cast off sloth.
      Many a green-gown has been given,
      Many a kiss, both odd and even,
      Many a glance, too, has been sent
      From out the eye, love's firmament;
55   Many a jest told of the keys betraying
This night, and locks picked; yet we're not a-Maying.

Come, let us go while we are in our prime,
And take the harmless folly of the time.
      We shall grow old apace, and die
60   Before we know our liberty.
      Our life is short, and our days run
      As fast away as does the sun;
And, as a vapor or a drop of rain
Once lost, can ne'er be found again;
65   So when or you or I are made
      A fable, song, or fleeting shade,
      All love, all liking, all delight
      Lies drowned with us in endless night.
Then while time serves, and we are but decaying,
70   Come, my Corinna, come, let's go a-Maying.

---

[6] **tabernacle:** The ark where God's Covenant was kept. Here, the meaning is a holy place.

THOMAS CAREW (ca. 1598–ca. 1640)

Song. To My Inconstant Mistress (1640)

When thou, poor excommunicate
    From all the joys of love, shalt see
The full reward and glorious fate
    Which my strong faith shall purchase me,
5   Then curse thine own inconstancy.

A fairer hand than thine shall cure
    That heart which thy false oaths did wound,
And to my soul a soul more pure
    Than thine shall by Love's hand be bound,
10   And both with equal glory crowned.

Then shalt thou weep, entreat, complain
    To Love, as I did once to thee;
When all thy tears shall be as vain
    As mine were then, for thou shalt be
15   Damned for thy false apostasy.

SIR JOHN SUCKLING (1609–1642)

Song (1638)

Why so pale and wan, fond° lover?   *foolish*
    Prithee,° why so pale?   *pray thee*
Will, when looking well can't move her,
    Looking ill prevail?
5   Prithee, why so pale?

Why so dull and mute, young sinner?
    Prithee, why so mute?
Will, when speaking well can't win her,
    Saying nothing do 't?
10   Prithee, why so mute?

Quit, quit, for shame; this will not move,
    This cannot take her.
If of herself she will not love,
    Nothing can make her:
15   The devil take her!

RICHARD CRASHAW (1613–1649)

Wishes: To His (Supposed) Mistress (1641)

Whoe'er she be,
That not impossible she
That shall command my heart and me;

Where'er she lie,
5   Locked up from mortal eye
In shady leaves of destiny

Till that ripe birth
Of studied fate stand forth,
And teach her fair steps to our Earth;

10   Till that divine
Idea take a shrine
Of crystal flesh, through which to shine;

Meet you her, my wishes,
Bespeak her to my blisses,
15   And be ye called my absent kisses.

I wish her beauty
That owes not all his duty
To gaudy tire or glistering shoe-tie;

Something more than
20   Taffeta or tissue can,
Or rampant feather, or rich fan;

More than the spoil
Of shop, or silkworm's toil,
Or a bought blush, or a set smile;

25   A face that's best
By its own beauty dressed,
And can alone command the rest;

A face made up
Out of no other shop
30   Than what nature's white hand sets ope;

A cheek where youth
And blood, with pen of truth,
Write what the reader sweetly ru'th;

A cheek where grows
35 More than a morning rose:
Which to no box his being owes;

Lips where all day
A lover's kiss may play,
Yet carry nothing thence away;

40 Looks that oppress
Their richest tires, but dress
And clothe their simplest nakedness;

Eyes that displace
The neighbour diamond, and outface
45 The sunshine by their own sweet grace;

Tresses that wear
Jewels but to declare
How much themselves more precious are;

Whose native ray
50 Can tame the wanton day
Of gems, that in their bright shades play—

Each ruby there,
Or pearl that dare appear,
Be its own blush, be its own tear;

55 A well-tamed heart,
For whose more noble smart
Love may be long choosing a dart;

Eyes that bestow
Full quivers on love's bow,
60 Yet pay less arrows than they owe;

Smiles that can warm
The blood, yet teach a charm,
That chastity shall take no harm;

Blushes that bin
65 The burnish of no sin,
Nor flames of aught too hot within;

Joys that confess
Virtue their mistress,
And have no other head to dress;

70 Fears, fond and flight
    As the coy bride's, when night
    First does the longing lover right;

    Tears quickly fled
    And vain, as those are shed
75 For a dying maidenhead;

    Days that need borrow
    No part of their good morrow
    From a forespent night of sorrow;

    Days that, in spite
80 Of darkness, by the light
    Of a clear mind are day all night;

    Nights sweet as they,
    Made short by lover's play
    Yet long by the absence of the day;

85 Life that dares send
    A challenge to his end,
    And, when it comes, say, 'Welcome, friend.'

    Sydnaean[1] showers
    Of sweet discourse, whose powers
90 Can crown old winter's head with flowers;

    Soft silken hours,
    Open suns, shady bowers;
    'Bove all, nothing within that lours;

    Whate'er delight
95 Can make day's forehead bright,
    Or give down to the wings of night;

    In her whole frame
    Have nature all the name,
    Art and ornament the shame;

100 Her flattery,
     Picture and poesy:
     Her counsel her own virtue be;

---

[1] **Sydnaean:** I.e., a reference to the poet Sir Philip Sidney, who wrote numerous love lyrics.

I wish her store
Of worth may leave her poor
105 Of wishes; and I wish—no more.

Now if time knows
That her whose radiant brows
Weave them a garland of my vows;

Her whose just bays
110 My future hopes can raise,
A trophy to her present praise;

Her that dares be
What these lines wish to see:
I seek no further: it is she.

115 'Tis she, and here
Lo! I unclothe and clear
My wishes' cloudy character.

May she enjoy it
Whose merit dare apply it,
120 But modesty dares still deny it.

Such worth as this is
Shall fix my flying wishes,
And determine them to kisses.

Let her full glory,
125 My fancies, fly before ye:
Be ye my fictions, but her story.

RICHARD LOVELACE (1618–ca. 1657)

To Althea, from Prison: Song (1649)

When love with unconfinèd wings
    Hovers within my gates,
And my divine Althea brings
    To whisper at the grates;
5 When I lie tangled in her hair,
    And fettered to her eye,
The gods that wanton in the air
    Know no such liberty.

When flowing cups run swiftly round,
10   With no allaying Thames,
Our careless heads with roses bound,
        Our hearts with loyal flames;
When thirsty grief in wine we steep,
        When healths and draughts go free,
15 Fishes that tipple in the deep
        Know no such liberty.

When, like committed linnets, I
        With shriller throat shall sing
The sweetness, mercy, majesty
20   And glories of my king;
When I shall voice aloud how good
        He is, how great should be,
Enlargèd winds that curl the flood
        Know no such liberty.

25 Stone walls do not a prison make,
        Nor iron bars a cage;
Minds innocent and quiet take
        That for an hermitage:
If I have freedom in my love,
30   And in my soul am free,
Angels alone that soar above
        Enjoy such liberty.

JOHN WILMOT, EARL OF ROCHESTER   (1648–1680)

A Song of a Young Lady: To Her Ancient Lover   (1691)

Ancient person, for whom I
All the flattering youth defy,
Long be it ere thou grow old,
Aching, shaking, crazy cold;
5   But still continue as thou art,
Ancient person of my heart.

On thy withered lips and dry,
Which like barren furrows lie,
Brooding kisses I will pour,
10 Shall thy youthful heat restore.
Such kind showers in autumn fall,
And a second spring recall;

Nor from thee will ever part,
Ancient person of my heart.

15 Thy nobler part, which but to name
In our sex would be counted shame,
By age's frozen grasp possessed,
From his ice shall be released,
And, soothed by my reviving hand,
20 In former warmth and vigour stand.
All a lover's wish can reach,
For thy joy my love shall teach;
And for thy pleasure shall improve
All that art can add to love.
25 Yet still I love thee without art,
Ancient person of my heart.

MATHEW PRIOR (1664–1721)

A True Maid (1718)

'No, no; for my virginity,
    When I lose that,' says Rose, 'I'll die':
'Behind the elms last night,' cried Dick,
    'Rose, were you not extremely sick?'

ELIZABETH TOLLET (1694–1754)

Winter Song (1755)

Ask me no more, my truth to prove,
What I would suffer for my love.
With thee I would in exile go
To regions of eternal snow,
5 O'er floods by solid ice confined,
Through forest bare with northern wind:
While all around my eyes I cast,
Where all is wild and all is waste.
If there the tim'rous stag you chase,
10 Or rouse to fight a fiercer race,
Undaunted I thy arms would bear,
And give thy hand the hunter's spear.
When the low sun withdraws his light,
And menaces an half-year's night,

15   The conscious moon and stars above
      Shall guide me with my wand'ring love.
      Beneath the mountain's hollow brow,
      Or in its rocky cells below,
      Thy rural feast I would provide,
20   Nor envy palaces their pride.
      The softest moss should dress thy bed,
      With savage spoils about thee spread:
      While faithful love the watch should keep,
      To banish danger from thy sleep.

ROBERT BURNS   (1759–1796)

A Red, Red Rose   (1796)

      O my luve's like a red, red rose,
          That's newly sprung in June;
      O my luve's like the melodie
          That's sweetly played in tune.

5   As fair art thou, my bonnie lass,
          So deep in luve am I;
      And I will luve thee still, my dear,
          Till a' the seas gang dry.

      Till a' the seas gang dry, my dear,
10   And the rocks melt wi' the sun:
      O I will love thee still, my dear,
          While the sands o' life shall run.

      And fare thee weel, my only luve,
          And fare thee weel awhile!
15   And I will come again, my luve,
          Though it were ten thousand mile.

CHARLOTTE DACRE   ("Rosa Matilda") (1782–1842)

The Kiss   (1805)

      The greatest bliss
          Is in a kiss—
      A kiss of love refin'd,
          When springs the soul

5   Without controul,
And blends the bliss with mind.

For if desire
Alone inspire,
The kiss not *me* can charm;
10   The eye must beam
With *chasten'd* gleam
That would *my* soul disarm.

What fond delight
Does love excite
15   When sentiment takes part!
The falt'ring sigh,
Voluptuous eye,
And palpitating heart.

Ye fleet too fast—
20   Sweet moments, last
A little longer mine!
Like Heaven's bow
Ye fade—ye go;
Too tremulously fine!

GEORGE GORDON, LORD BYRON (1788–1824)

She Walks in Beauty (1815)

1

She walks in beauty, like the night
Of cloudless climes and starry skies;
And all that's best of dark and bright
Meet in her aspect and her eyes:
5   Thus mellow'd to that tender light
Which heaven to gaudy day denies.

2

One shade the more, one ray the less,
Had half impair'd the nameless grace
Which waves in every raven tress,
10   Or softly lightens o'er her face;
Where thoughts serenely sweet express
How pure, how dear their dwelling place.

3

And on that cheek, and o'er that brow,
    So soft, so calm, yet eloquent,
15   The smiles that win, the tints that glow,
    But tell of days in goodness spent,
A mind at peace with all below,
    A heart whose love is innocent!

ELIZABETH BARRETT BROWNING   (1806–1861)

from **Sonnets from the Portuguese, 43**   (1846; 1850)

How do I love thee? Let me count the ways.
I love thee to the depth and breadth and height
My soul can reach, when feeling out of sight
For the ends of Being and ideal Grace.
5   I love thee to the level of everyday's
Most quiet need, by sun and candle-light.
I love thee freely, as men strive for Right;
I love thee purely, as they turn from Praise.
I love thee with the passion put to use
10   In my old griefs, and with my childhood's faith.
I love thee with a love I seemed to lose
With my lost saints,—I love with the breath,
Smiles, tears, of all my life!—and, if God choose,
I shall but love thee better after death.

EDGAR ALLAN POE   (1809–1849)

To Helen   (1823; 1831)

Helen, thy beauty is to me
    Like those Nicéan barks[1] of yore,
That gently, o'er a perfumed sea,
    The weary, way-worn wanderer bore
5   To his own native shore.

---

[1] **Nicéan barks:** I.e., Nicaean ships. Nicaea: a city in the Byzantium Empire (present-day Turkey).

On desperate seas long wont to roam,
    Thy hyacinth hair, thy classic face,
Thy Naiad[2] airs have brought me home
    To the glory that was Greece
10 And the grandeur that was Rome.

Lo! in yon brilliant window-niche
    How statue-like I see thee stand,
    The agate lamp within thy hand!
Ah! Psyche,[3] from the regions which
15   Are Holy Land!

WALT WHITMAN (1819–1892)

As Adam Early in the Morning (1861; 1867)

As Adam early in the morning,
Walking forth from the bower refresh'd with sleep,
Behold me where I pass, hear my voice, approach,
Touch me, touch the palm of your hand to my body as I pass,
5 Be not afraid of my body.

EMILY DICKINSON (1830–1886)

"Wild Nights—Wild Nights!" (ca. 1861; 1891)

Wild Nights—Wild Nights!
Were I with thee
Wild Nights should be
Our luxury!

5 Futile—the Winds—
To a Heart in port—

---

[2] **Naiad:** A lake nymph in classical mythology.
[3] **Psyche:** According to the myth, the god of love, Cupid, fell madly in love with Psyche, a girl of unusual beauty, whom he eventually married. Because Psyche was a mortal, she was forbidden to see her lover's face. One night however, she couldn't resist the temptation and brought in a lamp to look at her unknown husband. A drop of hot oil from the lamp fell on Cupid's body, he awoke, and fled his wife.

Done with the Compass—
Done with the Chart!

Rowing in Eden—
10   Ah, the Sea!
Might I but moor—Tonight—
In Thee!

EMILY DICKINSON (1830–1886)

"I cannot live with You—" (ca. 1862; 1890)

I cannot live with You—
It would be Life—
And Life is over there—
Behind the Shelf

5   The Sexton keeps the Key to—
Putting up
Our Life—His Porcelain—
Like a Cup—

Discarded of the Housewife—
10   Quaint—or Broke—
A newer Sevres[1] pleases—
Old Ones crack—

I could not die—with You—
For One must wait
15   To shut the Other's Gaze down—
You—could not—

And I—Could I stand by
And see You—freeze—
Without my Right of Frost—
20   Death's privilege?

Nor could I rise—with You—
Because Your Face
Would put out Jesus'—
That New Grace

---

[1] **Sevres:** A fine, elaborately decorated French porcelain.

25   Glow plain—and foreign
      On my homesick Eye—
      Except that You than He
      Shone closer by—

      They'd judge Us—How—
30   For You—served Heaven—You know,
      Or sought to—
      I could not—

      Because You saturated Sight—
      And I had no more Eyes
35   For sordid excellence
      As Paradise

      And were You lost, I would be—
      Though My Name
      Rang loudest
40   On the Heavenly fame—

      And were You—saved—
      And I—condemned to be
      Where You were not—
      That self—were Hell to Me—

45   So We must meet apart—
      You there—I—here—
      With just the Door ajar
      That Oceans are—and Prayer—
      And that White Sustenance—
50   Despair—

THOMAS HARDY   (1840–1928)

Neutral Tones   (1898)

      We stood by a pond that winter day,
      And the sun was white, as though chidden of God,
      And a few leaves lay on the starving sod;
            —They had fallen from an ash, and were gray.

5   Your eyes on me were as eyes that rove
      Over tedious riddles of years ago;
      And some words played between us to and fro
            On which lost the more by our love.

The smile on your mouth was the deadest thing
10   Alive enough to have strength to die;
      And a grin of bitterness swept thereby
            Like an ominous bird a-wing. . . .

      Since then, keen lessons that love deceives,
      And wrings with wrong, have shaped to me
15   Your face, and the God-curst sun, and a tree,
            And a pond edged with grayish leaves.

WILLIAM BUTLER YEATS (1865–1939)

No Second Troy (1910)

      Why should I blame her that she filled my days
      With misery, or that she would of late
      Have taught to ignorant men most violent ways,
      Or hurled the little streets upon the great,
5   Had they but courage equal to desire?
      What could have made her peaceful with a mind
      That nobleness made simple as a fire,
      With beauty like a tightened bow, a kind
      That is not natural in an age like this,
10   Being high and solitary and most stern?
      Why, what could she have done, being what she is?
      Was there another Troy for her to burn?

ROBERT FROST (1874–1963)

To Earthward (1923)

      Love at the lips was touch
      As sweet as I could bear;
      And once that seemed too much;
      I lived on air

5   That crossed me from sweet things,
      The flow of—was it musk
      From hidden grapevine springs
      Downhill at dusk?

      I had the swirl and ache
10   From sprays of honeysuckle

That when they're gathered shake
Dew on the knuckle.

I craved strong sweets, but those
Seemed strong when I was young;
15 The petal of the rose
It was that stung.

Now no joy but lacks salt,
That is not dashed with pain
And weariness and fault;
20 I crave the stain

Of tears, the aftermark
Of almost too much love,
The sweet of bitter bark
And burning clove.

25 When stiff and sore and scarred
I take away my hand
From leaning on it hard
In grass and sand,

The hurt is not enough:
30 I long for weight and strength
To feel the earth as rough
To all my length.

ROBERT FROST (1874–1963)

The Silken Tent (1942)

She is as in a field a silken tent
At midday when a sunny summer breeze
Has dried the dew and all its ropes relent,
So that in guys it gently sways at ease,
5 And its supporting central cedar pole,
That is its pinnacle to heavenward
And signifies the sureness of the soul,
Seems to owe naught to any single cord,
But strictly held by none, is loosely bound
10 By countless silken ties of love and thought
To everything on earth the compass round,
And only by one's going slightly taut

In the capriciousness of summer air
Is of the slightest bondage made aware.

AMY LOWELL (1874–1925)

The Taxi (1914)

When I go away from you
The world beats dead
Like a slackened drum.
I call out for you against the jutted stars
5   And shout into the ridges of the wind.
Streets coming fast,
One after the other,
Wedge you away from me,
And the lamps of the city prick my eyes
10   So that I can no longer see your face.
Why should I leave you,
To wound myself upon the sharp edges of the night?

WILLIAM CARLOS WILLIAMS (1883–1963)

Rain (1930)

As the rain falls
so does
            your love

bathe every
5   open
object of the world—

In houses
the priceless dry
                rooms
10   of illicit love
where we live
hear the wash of the
                    rain—

There
15   paintings

and fine
       metalware
woven stuffs—
all the whorishness
20   of our
       delight
sees
from its window

the spring wash
25   of your love
       the falling
rain—

The trees
are become
30   beasts fresh-risen
from the sea—
water

trickles
from the crevices of
35   their hides—

So my life is spent
       to keep out love
with which
she rains upon

40   the world

of spring

    drips

so spreads

    the words

45   far apart to let in

       her love

And running in between

the drops

    the rain

50   is a kind physician

                          the rain
of her thoughts over

the ocean
              every

55   where

          walking with
invisible swift feet
over

          the helpless
60   waves—
Unworldly love
that has no hope
                          of the world

                          and that
65   cannot change the world
to its delight—

          The rain
falls upon the earth
and grass and flowers

70   come
          perfectly

into form from its
                          liquid

clearness

75   But love is
unworldly

              and nothing
comes of it but love
following
80   and falling endlessly
from
          her thoughts

D. H. LAWRENCE (1885–1930)

Gloire de Dijon[1] (1917)

When she rises in the morning
I linger to watch her;
She spreads the bath-cloth underneath the window
And the sunbeams catch her
5   Glistening white on the shoulders,
While down her sides the mellow
Golden shadow glows as
She stoops to the sponge, and her swung breasts
Sway like full-blown yellow
10   Gloire de Dijon roses.

She drips herself with water, and her shoulders
Glisten as silver, they crumple up
Like wet and falling roses, and I listen
For the sluicing of their rain-dishevelled petals.
15   In the window full of sunlight
Concentrates her golden shadow
Fold on fold, until it glows as
Mellow as the glory roses.

EZRA POUND (1885–1972)

Alba (1916)

As cool as the pale wet leaves
                    of lily-of-the-valley
She lay beside me in the dawn.

EDNA ST. VINCENT MILLAY (1892–1950)

"Love is not all: it is not meat nor drink" (1931)

Love is not all: it is not meat nor drink
Nor slumber nor a roof against the rain;
Nor yet a floating spar to men that sink
And rise and sink and rise and sink again;

---

[1] **Gloire de Dijon:** A variety of roses.

5   Love cannot fill the thickened lung with breath,
Nor clean the blood, nor set the fractured bone;
Yet many a man is making friends with death
Even as I speak, for lack of love alone.
It well may be that in a difficult hour,
10   Pinned down by pain and moaning for release,
Or nagged by want past resolution's power,
I might be driven to sell your love for peace,
Or trade the memory of this night for food.
It well may be. I do not think I would.

E. E. CUMMINGS (1894–1962)

"All in green went my love riding" (1923)

All in green went my love riding
on a great horse of gold
into the silver dawn.

four lean hounds crouched low and smiling
5   the merry deer ran before.

Fleeter be they than dappled dreams
the swift sweet deer
the red rare deer.

Horn at hip went my love riding
10   riding the echo down
into the silver dawn.

four lean hounds crouched low and smiling
the level meadows ran before.

Softer be they than slippered sleep
15   the lean lithe deer
the fleet flown deer.

Four fleet does at a gold valley
the famished arrows sang before.

Bow at belt went my love riding
20   riding the mountain down into the silver dawn.

four lean hounds crouched low and smiling
the sheer peaks ran before.

Paler be they than daunting death
the sleek slim deer
25   the tall tense deer.

Four tall stags at a green mountain
the lucky hunter sang before.

All in green went my love riding
on a great horse of gold
30   into the silver dawn.

four lean hounds crouched low and smiling
my heart fell dead before.

ROBERT GRAVES (1895–1985)

She Tells Her Love While Half Asleep (1945)

She tells her love while half asleep,
   In the dark hours,
     With half-words whispered low:
As Earth stirs in her winter sleep
5   And puts out grass and flowers
   Despite the snow,
     Despite the falling snow.

LOUIS ZUKOFSKY (1904–1978)

Non Ti Fidar[1] (1949)

   in opera poetry must be the obedient daughter of music
                         —MOZART

The hand a shade of moonlight on the pillow
And that a shadowed white would seem above or below
Their heads ear to ear, hearing water
Not like the word, the flickflack of the eye opening on it
5   With what happiness

---

[1] **Non Ti Fidar:** "Don't trust him" (Italian). A line from the libretto of Mozart's acclaimed opera *Don Giovanni* (1787), which tells the story of the seducer by that same name (known as Don Juan in the English-speaking world).

Where the word is the obedient daughter of music
And Don Giovanni's shapely seat and heart live in hell[2]
Lovable as its fire
As all loves that breathe and kiss
10   Simply by life
Rocking to sleep and flame:
Until mine own voice tired, the sound
A quiet wasting summer's breath

Babylon his flood is stilled
15   Babel her tower doeth tie my tongue
In the willow path that it hath swilled
My spirit, His case, and young.

W. H. AUDEN (1907–1973)

Lullaby (1937)

Lay your sleeping head, my love,
Human on my faithless arm;
Time and fevers burn away
Individual beauty from
5   Thoughtful children, and the grave
Proves the child ephemeral:
But in my arms till break of day
Let the living creature lie,
Mortal, guilty, but to me
10   The entirely beautiful.

Soul and body have no bounds:
To lovers as they lie upon
Her tolerant enchanted slope
In their ordinary swoon,
15   Grave the vision Venus[1] sends
Of supernatural sympathy,
Universal love and hope;
While an abstract insight wakes
Among the glaciers and the rocks
20   The hermit's carnal ecstasy.

---

[2] **Don Giovanni's . . . hell:** At the end of the opera, Don Giovanni is pulled down to hell by a statue of a man he has killed.
[1] **Venus:** The Roman goddess of love and beauty.

Certainty, fidelity
On the stroke of midnight pass
Like vibrations of a bell
And fashionable madmen raise
25   Their pedantic boring cry:
Every farthing of the cost,
All the dreaded cards foretell,
Shall be paid, but from this night
Not a whisper, not a thought,
30   Not a kiss nor look be lost.

Beauty, midnight, vision dies:
Let the winds of dawn that blow
Softly round your dreaming head
Such a day of welcome show
35   Eye and knocking heart may bless,
Find our mortal world enough;
Noons of dryness find you fed
By the involuntary powers,
Nights of insult let you pass
40   Watched by every human love.

THEODORE ROETHKE (1908–1963)

I Knew a Woman (1958)

I knew a woman, lovely in her bones,
When small birds sighed, she would sigh back at them;
Ah, when she moved, she moved more ways than one:
The shapes a bright container can contain!
5   Of her choice virtues only gods should speak,
Or English poets who grew up on Greek
(I'd have them sing in chorus, cheek to cheek).

How well her wishes went! She stroked my chin,
She taught me Turn, and Counter-turn, and Stand;
10   She taught me Touch, that undulant white skin;
I nibbled meekly from her proffered hand;
She was the sickle; I, poor I, the rake,
Coming behind her for her pretty sake
(But what prodigious mowing we did make).

15   Love likes a gander, and adores a goose:
Her full lips pursed, the errant note to seize;

She played it quick, she played it light and loose;
My eyes, they dazzled at her flowing knees;
Her several parts could keep a pure repose,
20 Or one hip quiver with a mobile nose
(She moved in circles, and those circles moved).

Let seed be grass, and grass turn into hay:
I'm martyr to a motion not my own;
What's freedom for? To know eternity.
25 I swear she cast a shadow white as stone.
But who would count eternity in days?
These old bones live to learn her wanton ways:
(I measure time by how a body sways).

THEODORE ROETHKE (1908–1963)

Wish for a Young Wife (1964)

My lizard, my lively writher,
May your limbs never wither,
May the eyes in your face
Survive the green ice
5 Of envy's mean gaze;
May you live out your life
Without hate, without grief,
And your hair ever blaze,
In the sun, in the sun,
10 When I am undone,
When I am no one.

J. V. CUNNINGHAM (1911–1985)

Ars Amoris[1] (1947)

Speak to her heart.
That manic force
When wits depart
Forbids remorse.

5 Dream with her dreaming
Until her lust

---

[1] **Ars Amoris:** The Art of Love (Latin).

Seems to her seeming
An act of trust.

Do without doing.
10   Love's wilful potion
Veils the ensuing,
And brief, commotion.

ROBERT LOWELL (1917–1977)

Dolphin (1973)

My Dolphin,[1] you only guide me by surprise,
captive as Racine, the man of craft,
drawn through his maze of iron composition
by the incomparable wandering voice of Phèdre.[2]
5   When I was troubled in mind, you made for my body
caught in its hangman's-knot of sinking lines,
the glassy bowing and scraping of my will. . . .
I have sat and listened to too many
words of the collaborating muse,
10   and plotted perhaps too freely with my life,
not avoiding injury to others,
not avoiding injury to myself—
to ask compassion . . . this book, half fiction,
an eelnet made by man for the eel fighting—

15   my eyes have seen what my hand did.

DENISE LEVERTOV (1923–1997)

The Ache of Marriage (1964)

The ache of marriage:

thigh and tongue, beloved,
are heavy with it,
it throbs in the teeth

---

[1] **Dolphin:** This poem addresses Lowell's third wife, Caroline Blackwood.
[2] **Racine . . . Phèdre:** Jean Baptiste Racine (1639–1699), a French playwright and one of the greatest tragedians of the French classical period. His play *Phèdre* (1677) tells the story of the illicit love, guilt, and desire of a mother for her stepson. Lowell translated some works by Racine late in his career.

5   We look for communion
     and are turned away, beloved,
     each and each

     It is leviathan[1] and we
     in its belly
10   looking for joy, some joy
     not to be known outside it

     two by two in the ark of
     the ache of it.

FRANK O'HARA   (1926–1966)

Homosexuality

So we are taking off our masks, are we, and keeping
our mouths shut? as if we'd been pierced by a glance!

The song of an old cow is not more full of judgment
than the vapors which escape one's soul when one is sick;

5   so I pull the shadows around me like a puff
     and crinkle my eyes as if at the most exquisite moment

     of a very long opera, and then we are off!
     without reproach and without hope that our delicate feet

     will touch the earth again, let alone "very soon."
10   It is the law of my own voice I shall investigate.

     I start like ice, my finger to my ear, my ear
     to my heart, that proud cur at the garbage can

     in the rain. It's wonderful to admire oneself
     with complete candor, tallying up the merits of each

15   of the latrines. 14th Street is drunken and credulous,
     53rd tries to tremble but is too at rest. The good

     love a park and the inept a railway station,
     and there are the divine ones who drag themselves up

---

[1] **leviathan:** A great fish, possibly a whale, that swallowed the biblical prophet Jonah.

and down the lengthening shadow of an Abyssinian[1] head
20   in the dust, trailing their long elegant heels of hot air

crying to confuse the brave "It's a summer day,
and I want to be wanted more than anything else in the world."

ALASTAIR REID (1926–   )

The Figures on the Frieze

Darkness wears off and, dawning into light,
they find themselves unmagically together.
He sees the stains of morning in her face.
She shivers, distant in his bitter weather.

5   Diminishing of legend sets him brooding.
Great goddess-figures conjured from his book
blur what he sees with bafflement of wishing.
Sulky, she feels his fierce, accusing look.

Familiar as her own, his body's landscape
10   seems harsh and dull to her habitual eyes.
Mystery leaves, and, mercilessly flying,
the blind fiends come, emboldened by her cries.

Avoiding simple reach of hand for hand
(which would surrender pride) by noon they stand
15   withdrawn from touch, reproachfully alone,
small in each other's eyes, tall in their own.

Wild with their misery, they entangle now
in baffling agonies of why and how.
Afternoon glimmers, and they wound anew,
20   flesh, nerve, bone, gristle in each other's view.

"What have you done to me?" From each proud heart,
new phantoms walk in the deceiving air.
As the light fails, each is consumed apart,
he by his ogre vision, she by her fire.

---

[1] **Abyssinian:** I.e., Ethiopian, from East Africa.

25 When night falls, out of a despair of daylight,
    they strike the lying attitudes of love,
    and through the perturbations of their bodies,
    each feels the amazing, murderous legends move.

GALWAY KINNELL (1927–   )

After Making Love We Hear Footsteps   (1980)

For I can snore like a bullhorn
or play loud music
or sit up talking with any reasonably sober Irishman
and Fergus will only sink deeper
5   into his dreamless sleep, which goes by all in one flash,
    but let there be that heavy breathing
    or a stifled come-cry anywhere in the house
    and he will wrench himself awake
    and make for it on the run—as now, we lie together,
10 after making love, quiet, touching along the length of our bodies,
    familiar touch of the long-married,
    and he appears—in his baseball pajamas, it happens,
    the neck opening so small
    he has to screw them on, which one day may make him wonder
15 about the mental capacity of baseball players—
    and flops down between us and hugs us and snuggles himself to sleep,
    his face gleaming with satisfaction at being this very child.

    In the half darkness we look at each other
    and smile
20 and touch arms across his little, startlingly muscled body—
    this one whom habit of memory propels to the ground of his making,
    sleeper only the mortal sounds can sing awake,
    this blessing love gives again into our arms.

ADRIENNE RICH (1929–   )

Living in Sin   (1955)

She had thought the studio would keep itself;
no dust upon the furniture of love.
Half heresy, to wish the taps less vocal,

the panes relieved of grime. A plate of pears,
5   a piano with a Persian shawl, a cat
stalking the picturesque amusing mouse
had risen at his urging.
Not that at five each separate stair would writhe
under the milkman's tramp; that morning light
10   so coldly would delineate the scraps
of last night's cheese and three sepulchral bottles;
that on the kitchen shelf among the saucers
a pair of beetle-eyes would fix her own—
envoy from some village in the moldings . . .
15   Meanwhile, he, with a yawn,
sounded a dozen notes upon the keyboard,
declared it out of tune, shrugged at the mirror,
rubbed at his beard, went out for cigarettes;
while she, jeered by the minor demons,
20   pulled back the sheets and made the bed and found
a towel to dust the table-top,
and let the coffee-pot boil over on the stove.
By evening she was back in love again,
though not so wholly but throughout the night
25   she woke sometimes to feel the daylight coming
like a relentless milkman up the stairs.

ADRIENNE RICH (1929–   )

from Twenty-One Love Poems (1976)

III

Since we're not young, weeks have to do time
for years of missing each other. Yet only this odd warp
in time tells me we're not young.
Did I ever walk the morning streets at twenty,
5   my limbs streaming with a purer joy?
did I lean from any window over the city
listening for the future
as I listen here with nerves tuned for your ring?
And you, you move toward me with the same tempo.
10   Your eyes are everlasting, the green spark
of the blue-eyed grass of early summer,
the green-blue wild cress washed by the spring.
At twenty, yes: we thought we'd live forever.
At forty-five, I want to know even our limits.

15   I touch you knowing we weren't born tomorrow,
     and somehow, each of us will help the other live,
     and somewhere, each of us must help the other die.

                              XII

     Sleeping, turning in turn like planets
     rotating in their midnight meadow:
     a touch is enough to let us know
     we're not alone in the universe, even in sleep:
5   the dream-ghosts of two worlds
     walking their ghost-towns, almost address each other.
     I've wakened to your muttered words
     spoken light- or dark-years away
     as if my own voice had spoken.
10   But we have different voices, even in sleep,
     and our bodies, so alike, are yet so different
     and the past echoing through our bloodstreams
     is freighted with different language, different meanings—
     though in any chronicle of the world we share
15   it could be written with new meaning
     we were two lovers of one gender,
     we were two women of one generation.

                              XIII

     The rules break like a thermometer,
     quicksilver spills across the charted systems,
     we're out in a country that has no language
     no laws, we're chasing the raven and the wren
5   through gorges unexplored since dawn
     whatever we do together is pure invention
     the maps they gave us were out of date
     by years . . . we're driving through the desert
     wondering if the water will hold out
10   the hallucinations turn to simple villages
     the music on the radio comes clear—
     neither *Rosenkavalier* nor *Götterdämmerung*[1]
     but a woman's voice singing old songs
     with new words, with a quiet bass, a flute
15   plucked and fingered by women outside the law.

---

[1] ***Rosenkavalier* nor *Götterdämmerung*:** *Der Rosenkavalier* (The Knight of the Rose): an opera by
Richard Strauss. *Götterdämerung* (The Ring): an opera by Richard Wagner.

(THE FLOATING POEM, UNNUMBERED)

Whatever happens with us, your body
will haunt mine—tender, delicate
your lovemaking, like the half-curled frond
of the fiddlehead fern in forests
5   just washed by sun. Your traveled, generous thighs
between which my whole face has come and come—
the innocence and wisdom of the place my tongue has found there—
the live, insatiate dance of your nipples in my mouth—
your touch on me, firm, protective, searching
10   me out, your strong tongue and slender fingers
reaching where I had been waiting years for you
in my rose-wet cave—whatever happens, this is.

XVIII

Rain on the West Side Highway,
red light at Riverside:
the more I live the more I think
two people together is a miracle.
5   You're telling the story of your life
for once, a tremor breaks the surface of your words.
The story of our lives becomes our lives.
Now you're in fugue across what some I'm sure
Victorian poet[2] called the *salt estranging sea.*
10   Those are the words that come to mind.
I feel estrangement, yes. As I've felt dawn
pushing toward daybreak. Something: a cleft of light—?
Close between grief and anger, a space opens
where I am Adrienne alone. And growing colder.

LUCILLE CLIFTON   (1936–   )

homage to my hips   (1980)

these hips are big hips.
they need space to
move around in.
they don't fit into little
5   petty places. these hips

---

[2] **Victorian poet:** I.e., Matthew Arnold.

are free hips.
they don't like to be held back.
these hips have never been enslaved,
they go where they want to go
10   they do what they want to do.
these hips are mighty hips.
these hips are magic hips.
i have known them
to put a spell on a man and
15   spin him like a top!

CHARLES SIMIC (1938–   )

Breasts (1974)

I love breasts, hard
Full breasts, guarded
By a button.

They come in the night.
5   The bestiaries of the ancients
Which include the unicorn
Have kept them out.

Pearly, like the east
An hour before sunrise,
10   Two ovens of the only
Philosopher's stone
Worth bothering about.

They bring on their nipples
Beads of inaudible sighs,
15   Vowels of delicious clarity
For the little red schoolhouse of our mouths.

Elsewhere, solitude
Makes another gloomy entry
In its ledger, misery
20   Borrows another cup of rice.

They draw nearer: Animal
Presence. In the barn
The milk shivers in the pail.

I like to come up to them
25 From underneath, like a kid
Who climbs on a chair
To reach a jar of forbidden jam.

Gently, with my lips,
Loosen the button.
30 Have them slip into my hands
Like two freshly poured beer-mugs.

I spit on fools who fail to include
Breasts in their metaphysics,
Star-gazers who have not enumerated them
35 Among the moons of the earth . . .

They give each finger
Its true shape, its joy:
Virgin soap, foam
On which our hands are cleansed.

40 And how the tongue honors
These two sour buns,
For the tongue is a feather
Dipped in egg-yolk.

I insist that a girl
45 Stripped to the waist
Is the first and last miracle,

That the old janitor on his deathbed
Who demands to see the breasts of his wife
For one last time
50 Is the greatest poet who ever lived.

O my sweet yes, my sweet no,
Look, everyone is asleep on the earth.

Now, in the absolute immobility
Of time, drawing the waist
55 Of the one I love to mine,

I will tip each breast
Like a dark heavy grape
Into the hive
Of my drowsy mouth.

ROBERT PINSKY (1940–   )

First Early Mornings Together (1975)

Waking up over the candy store together
We hear birds waking up below the sill
And slowly recognize ourselves, the weather,
The time, and the birds that rustle there until

5   Down to the street as fog and quiet lift
The pigeons from the wrinkled awning flutter
To reconnoiter, mutter, stare and shift
Pecking by ones or twos the rainbowed gutter.

SHARON OLDS (1942–   )

Topography (1987)

After we flew across the country we
got in bed, laid our bodies
delicately together, like maps laid
face to face, East to West, my
5   San Francisco against your New York, your
Fire Island against my Sonoma, my
New Orleans deep in your Texas, your Idaho
bright on my Great Lakes, my Kansas
burning against your Kansas your Kansas
10   burning against my Kansas, your Eastern
Standard Time pressing into my
Pacific Time, my Mountain Time
beating against your Central Time, your
sun rising swiftly from the right my
15   sun rising swiftly from the left your
moon rising slowly from the left my
moon rising slowly from the right until
all four bodies of the sky
burn above us, sealing us together,
20   all our cities twin cities,
all our states united, one
nation, indivisible, with liberty and justice for all.

NIKKI GIOVANNI (1943–   )

Beautiful Black Men   (1968)

(With compliments and apologies to all not mentioned by name)

i wanta say just gotta say something
bout those beautiful beautiful beautiful outasight
black men
with they afros
5   walking down the street
is the same ol danger
but a brand new pleasure

sitting on stoops, in bars, going to offices
running numbers, watching for their whores
10   preaching in churches, driving their hogs
walking their dogs, winking at me
in their fire red, lime green, burnt orange
royal blue tight tight pants that hug
what i like to hug

15   jerry butler, wilson pickett, the impressions
temptations, mighty mighty sly
don't have to do anything but walk
on stage
and i scream and stamp and shout
20   see new breed men in breed alls
dashiki[1] suits with shirts that match
the lining that complements the ties
that smile at the sandals
where dirty toes peek at me
25   and i scream and stamp and shout
for more beautiful beautiful beautiful
black men with outasight afros

---

[1] **dashiki:** A loose, colorful African shirt.

LOUISE GLÜCK (1943–   )

Happiness (1980)

A man and woman lie on a white bed.
It is morning. I think
Soon they will waken.
On the bedside table is a vase
5   of lilies; sunlight
pools in their throats.
I watch him turn to her
as though to speak her name
but silently, deep in her mouth—
10   At the window ledge,
once, twice,
a bird calls.
And then she stirs; her body
fills with his breath.

15   I open my eyes; you are watching me.
Almost over this room
the sun is gliding.
Look at your face, you say,
holding your own close to me
20   to make a mirror.
How calm you are. And the burning wheel
passes gently over us.

OLIVE SENIOR (1943–   )

Tropic Love (1994)

Gardening in the Tropics you hear poetry
in some unexpected places. Sitting on my
verandah last night I overheard two people
passing by. The woman said:

5   You don't bring me flowers anymore
—or anything for the children.
My heart has turned to stone
but I cannot put that in the pot.
Love me and my family or leave me
10   to sit by the roadside to sell,

by the riverside taking in washing,
by milady's fire cooking for my living.
I'm a woman with heavy responsibilities.
With my lot I'm prepared to be contented.
15 With your sweet words, Lover, tempt me
not, if you've come empty-handed.

AI (1947–   )

Twenty-Year Marriage (1973)

You keep me waiting in a truck
with its one good wheel stuck in the ditch,
while you piss against the south side of a tree.
Hurry. I've got nothing on under my skirt tonight.
5   That still excites you, but this pickup has no windows
and the seat, one fake leather thigh,
pressed close to mine is cold.
I'm the same size, shape, make as twenty years ago,
but get inside me, start the engine;
10 you'll have the strength, the will to move.
I'll pull, you push, we'll tear each other in half.
Come on, baby, lay me down on my back.
Pretend you don't owe me a thing
and maybe we'll roll out of here,
15 leaving the past stacked up behind us;
old newspapers nobody's ever got to read again.

GREGORY ORR (1947–   )

We Must Make a Kingdom of It (1986)

So that a colony will breed here,
love rubs together two words:
"I" and "she." How the long bone
of the personal pronoun
5   warms its cold length against her fur.

                    *

She plants the word "desire"
that makes the very air
amorous, that causes the light,

from its tall stalk, to bend down
10 until it almost kisses the ground.

*

It was green, I saw it—tendril
flickering from dry soil
like a grass snake's tongue;
call it "flame"—light
15 become life, what the word
wants, what the earth
in its turning
yearns for: to writhe and rise up,
even to fly briefly
20 like the shovelful over
the gravedigger's shoulder.

T. R. HUMMER (1950–   )

Courtly Love (1990)

The candle in the bathroom burns all night
And water in the clawfoot bathtub cools.
It is simple as that. It is clear
This man and woman are lonely and love each other.

5 Let's say each washed the other clean,
Each lay the other naked
And half asleep on the thick white rug
In the high-ceilinged room of the empty old house

Where I can't help making them lie,
10 Where in the word *night*
Outside the casement windows
Rain on oak limbs suddenly turns to ice—

As if any of this were more
Than something someone thought of saying,
15 More than a dream of lost words
We are living through,

The story that goes on being
Mumbled behind the thick,
Old-fashioned plaster of the walls
20 Of a mind we all share, that tries

Again and again to wring out of me
What those older, other lovers
Must have done when they woke stiff
And dew-cold in a forest

25   With the king her husband's unexpected sword
Between them like the bitter body
Of a child—he rode up while they slept
And laid it there in memory

Of certain honorable truths. But not enough
30   Remains of the unlikely off-center ballad
They had to sing to make sense of
Except the white façade

Of this house in mid-Ohio
That fronts a streetful of pickups hissing
35   Their all-weather tires on the ice,
Conditionally real as the bathroom floor

Where the ancient heraldic lion-footed tub
Spreads its porcelain claws
Beside the blanked-out bodies
40   Of the two who stir on the white rug now in candlelight,

Dreaming maybe, or—as if the flesh
Of the Western world has a right
To print its darkening
Story on the white page of itself—

45   In pain a little, a little bruised
Where touch turned to a desperate holding on.

CYN ZARCO (1950–   )

Saxophonetyx (1982)

I've heard all about musicians
they take love/don't give love
'cause they're savin it for the music
Got to be so one night I was watching him
5   take a solo and when he closed his eyes
everyone in the club closed their eyes

The first thing I saw was my shoes
float out of his horn

my favorite leopard-skin high-heel shoes
10   the left foot then the right one
followed by my black silk stockings
with the seam down the back
my best hat and all that
were floating in the air like half-notes
15   as if they belonged to nobody
least of all to me

I tried to close my eyes
but I couldn't
out flew my blue silk scarf
20   my alarm clock
my alligator suitcase
even the last month's phone bill

He kept on playing that horn
as if none of this even happened
25   and when I slowly closed my eyes
I saw his fingers wrap around my waist
my spine turn into saxophone keys
my mouth become his mouthpiece
and there was nothing left in the room
30   but mercy

JAMES GALVIN (1951–   )

Dear Nobody's Business (2003)

What did you expect
Threadbare me to do
With nothing to deflect
The gale of your remove?

5   The scanty sacred secret
Tries to thumb a ride
Through drubbed, irresolute,
And famously slippery light.

Like a spooky spark from an anvil
10   The sun makes a teary streak
Across the almost tranquil,
Which is the almost bleak.

What is threadbare me to do
When wind cleaves your summer dress
15   To almost all of you?

JOY HARJO (1951–   )

He Told Me His Name Was Sitting Bull[1]   (1975)

the great-grandson of the old chief
and he reached across my arm
to fill his glass
from the pitcher
5   that is his excuse to sit closer

"where you from"
     he is from southwest oklahoma
     i am from the northeast part

"i have been looking for you for six
10   hundred miles," he tells me
and the grassy plains near anadarko
he spreads out for me
in the brown hills of his eyes
     i smile   hiding my teeth
15   between the branches of oaks
in tahlequah hills

"come with me" he squeezes my arm
the sioux horseman rides away across
                    my shoulder
20   i shake my head
and drown his horse in the water
of the illinois river
the young warrior drops his hand
but he never surrenders
25   his name
               will follow me on the interstate
all the way into the center of oklahoma

---

[1] **Sitting Bull:** A famous Sioux leader (ca.1834–1890), who defeated General George Custer at the Battle of the Little Bighorn in 1876.

SANDRA CISNEROS (1954–   )

You Bring Out the Mexican in Me (1994)

You bring out the Mexican in me.
The hunkered thick dark spiral.
The core of a heart howl.
The bitter bile.
5   The tequila *lágrimas*[1] on Saturday all
through next weekend Sunday.
You are the one I'd let go the other loves for,
surrender my one-woman house.
Allow you red wine in bed,
10   even with my vintage lace linens.
Maybe. Maybe.

For you.

You bring out the Dolores del Río[2] in me.
The Mexican spitfire in me.
15   The raw *navajas*,[3] glint and passion in me.
The raise Cain and dance with the rooster-footed devil in me.
The spangled sequin in me.
The eagle and serpent in me.
The *mariachi*[4] trumpets of the blood in me.
20   The Aztec love of war[5] in me.
The fierce obsidian of the tongue in me.
The *berrinchuda, bien-cabrona*[6] in me.
The Pandora's curiosity[7] in me.
The pre-Columbian death and destruction in me.
25   The rainforest disaster, nuclear threat in me.
The fear of fascists in me.
Yes, you do. Yes, you do.

---

[1] *lágrimas:* Tears (Spanish).
[2] **Dolores del Río:** A Mexican-born actress (1905–1983), who began her career in Hollywood before going back to Mexico to become one of the most revered movie stars in her home country. Some of her acting credits include *Joanna* (1925), *María Candelaria* (1944), and *Las Abandonadas* (1944).
[3] *navajas:* Razors (Spanish).
[4] *mariachi:* A Mexican musician.
[5] **Aztec love of war:** The Aztecs, who lived on the territory of present-day Mexico, were one of the most advanced civilizations in the New World. However, they also were known for offering human sacrifices (usually prisoners of war) to their blood-thirsty god Huitzilopochtli. By some estimates, the Aztecs sacrificed 20,000 people each year. In 1519, their culture was decimated by Spaniard Hernan Cortez and his conquistadors.
[6] *berrinchuda, bien-cabrona:* Literally, "temperamental, good-looking bitch" (Spanish).
[7] **Pandora's curiosity:** According to the Greek myth, the first woman created by the gods as a punishment for Prometheus's theft of fire. Entrusted with a box containing all the evils of human life, she opened it out of curiosity and thereby released its contents into the world.

You bring out the colonizer in me.
The holocaust of desire in me.

30   The Mexico City '85[8] earthquake in me.
The Popocatepetl/Ixtaccíhuatl[9] in me.
The tidal wave of recession in me.
The Agustín Lara[10] hopeless romantic in me.
The *barbacoa taquitos*[11] on Sunday in me.

35   The cover the mirrors with cloth in me.

Sweet twin. My wicked other,
I am the memory that circles your bed nights,
that tugs you taut as moon tugs ocean.
I claim you all mine,

40   arrogant as Manifest Destiny.[12]
I want to rattle and rent you in two.
I want to defile you and raise hell.
I want to pull out the kitchen knives,
dull and sharp, and whisk the air with crosses.

45   *Me sacas lo mexicana en mi,*[13]
like it or not, honey.

You bring out the Uled-Nayl[14] in me.
The stand-back-white-bitch in me.
The switchblade in the boot in me.

50   The Acapulco[15] cliff diver in me.
The *Flecha Roja*[16] mountain disaster in me.
The *dengue*[17] fever in me.
The *¡Alarma!*[18] murderess in me.
I could kill in the name of you and think

55   it worth it. Brandish a fork and terrorize rivals,
female and male, who loiter and look at you,
languid in your light. Oh,

---

[8] **Mexico City '85:** On September 19, 1985, a devastating earthquake hit Mexico City, killing more than 10,000 people and injuring tens of thousands more.

[9] **Popocatepetl/Ixtaccíhuatl:** Active twin volcanoes near Mexico City.

[10] **Agustín Lara:** A popular Mexican composer and musician (1900–1970), known also for his numerous love affairs.

[11] *barbacoa taquitos:* I.e., barbeque taco (Spanish).

[12] **Manifest Destiny:** A phrase coined by politicians in the middle of the nineteenth century to explain continental expansion by the United States, particularly the annexation of Texas.

[13] *Me sacas lo mexicana en mi:* "You bring out the Mexican in me" (Spanish).

[14] **Uled-Nayl:** Exotic dancers.

[15] **Acapulco:** A famous, luxurious resort in Mexico.

[16] *Flecha Roja:* Literally, The Red Arrow (Spanish); name of a bus service running between Acapulco and Zihuatanejo in Mexico. The "mountain disaster" perhaps refers to a traffic accident along the line.

[17] *dengue:* An acute tropical disease transmitted by mosquito bites.

[18] *¡Alarma!:* I.e., a call for help; alarm (Spanish).

I am evil. I am the filth goddess Tlazoltéotl.[19]
I am the swallower of sins.
60   The lust goddess without guilt.
The delicious debauchery. You bring out
the primordial exquisiteness in me.
The nasty obsession in me.
The corporal and venial sin in me.
65   The original transgression in me.

Red ocher. Yellow ocher. Indigo. Cochineal.[20]
Piñón.[21] Copal. Sweetgrass. Myrrh.
All you saints, blessed and terrible,
Virgen de Guadalupe, diosa Coatlicue,[22]
70   I invoke you.

Quiero ser tuya.[23] Only yours. Only you.
Quiero amarte. Atarte. Amarrarte.[24]
Love the way a Mexican woman loves. Let
me show you. Love the only way I know how.

CARL PHILLIPS (1959–   )

As from a Quiver of Arrows (1998)

What do we do with the body, do we
burn it, do we set it in dirt or in
stone, do we wrap it in balm, honey,
oil, and then gauze and tip it onto
5   and trust it to a raft and to water?

What will happen to the memory of his
body, if one of us doesn't hurry now
and write it down fast? Will it be
salt or late light that it melts like?
10   Floss, rubber gloves, a chewed cap

---

[19] **Tlazoltéotl:** The Aztec goddess of the earth and fertility. According to the legend, at the end of a man's life, she comes and cleanses the soul by eating its filth.
[20] **Cochineal:** A vivid red.
[21] *Piñón:* Pine kernel; nut (Spanish).
[22] *Virgen de Guadalupe, diosa Coatlicue:* "Virgin of Guandeloupe [the islands in the West-Indies first discovered by Columbus in 1493 and later colonized by the French in 1635], goddess Coatlicue [Aztec goddess of earth and fire]." (Spanish).
[23] *Quiero ser tuya:* "Love is yours" (Spanish).
[24] *Quiero amarte. Atarte. Amarrarte:* "Love binds. Fetters. Moors" (Spanish).

to a pen elsewhere—how are we to
regard his effects, do we throw them
or use them away, do we say they are
relics and so treat them like relics?
15   Does his soiled linen count? If so,

would we be wrong then, to wash it?
There are no instructions whether it
should go to where are those with no
linen, or whether by night we should
20   memorially wear it ourselves, by day

reflect upon it folded, shelved, empty.
Here, on the floor behind his bed is
a bent photo—why? Were the two of
them lovers? Does it mean, where we
25   found it, that he forgot it or lost it

or intended a safekeeping? Should we
attempt to make contact? What if this
other man too is dead? Or alive, but
doesn't want to remember, is human?
30   Is it okay to be human, and fall away

from oblation and memory, if we forget,
and can't sometimes help it and sometimes
it is all that we want? How long, in
dawns or new cocks, does that take?
35   What if it is rest and nothing else that

we want? Is it a findable thing, small?
In what hole is it hidden? Is it, maybe,
a country? Will a guide be required who
will say to us how? Do we fly? Do we
40   swim? What will I do now, with my hands?

CHAPTER 17

IF I SHOULD DIE, THINK ONLY THIS OF ME

—Rupert Brooke

An Anthology of Poems about Wars and Rumors of Wars

In the Gospel of St. Matthew, we read: "And ye shall hear of wars and rumors of wars: see that ye be not troubled: for all these things come to pass, but the end is not yet" (Matthew 24:6). Indeed, there have always been wars as well as rumors about impending wars. Human beings seem programmed to destroy each other on the battlefield, or, more recently, in guerrilla wars where the arena is ill-defined. They do so for many reasons, although often they celebrate what they call "freedom," which usually means freedom from having to heed the wishes of another secular or religious power.

Poets have always written about war, sometimes with great eloquence. Two of the greatest epics of the ancient world, *The Iliad* by Homer and *The Aeneid* by Virgil, are book-length poems that deal with conflicts. Homer writes about the tragedy of the Trojan War, the death of Achilles, the sorrow that befalls soldiers and citizens on both sides of the conflict. Virgil's epic of the founding of Rome begins, famously: "Arms and the man I sing."

War brings out the full range of human emotion, dealing as it does with injury and death, with the grief and loneliness of warriors, with the fear of battle, with the exhilaration of victory and the sadness of defeat. War poetry may be pro-war or anti-war. It may focus on some aspect of battle, or it may confront the aftermath of war, as T. S. Eliot does indirectly in *The Waste Land* (p. 102) or Ezra Pound does more directly in this powerful extract from *Hugh Selwyn Mauberley* (p. 1118), where he writes about men who

> walked eye-deep in hell
> believing in old men's lies, then unbelieving
> came home, home to a lie,
> home to many deceits,
> 5   home to old lies and new infamy.

Some of the most inspiring (but ultimately sad and unconvincing) poems are those that poets write before the battle really begins, or before the poet learns about the real cost of war. One thinks, for example, of Tennyson's "Hands All Round," published in the London *Examiner* in 1852, not long before the Crimean War:

Gigantic daughter of the West,
We drink to thee across the flood,
We know thee most, we love thee best,
For art thou not of British blood?
5   Should war's mad blast again be blown,
Permit not thou the tyrant powers
To fight thy mother here alone,
But let thy broadsides roar with ours.
    Hands all round!
10   God the tyrant's cause confound!
To our great kinsmen of the West, my friends,
And the great name of England, round and round.

O rise, our strong Atlantic sons,
When war against our freedom springs!
15   O speak to Europe through your guns!
They *can* be understood by kings.
You must not mix our Queen with those
That wish to keep their people fools;
Our freedom's foemen are her foes,
20   She comprehends the race she rules.
    Hands all round!
God the tyrant's cause confound!
To our dear kinsmen of the West, my friends,
And the great cause of Freedom, round and round.

The "great cause of Freedom" has always been the rallying cry of national leaders, who must somehow convince young men to march into battle, inspiring them to sacrifice life and limb.

Rupert Brooke gladly, and rather poignantly, accepts this call to sacrifice in "The Soldier" (p. 1127), a beautiful sonnet in which he saw himself as willing to happily give up his life for England:

If I should die, think only this of me:
That there's some corner of a foreign field
That is for ever England.

Sadly enough, Brooke died soon after writing this, a victim of World War I.

The selection of poems about war that follows runs the gamut, including poems from the ancient Chinese poets Lao-Tzu, Su Wu, and Wang Han through Shakespeare, Milton, Whitman, Melville, Hardy, and the modern poets. For reasons that have never really been understood, World War I seems to have yielded the strongest poems about war, and most of these are anti-war poems, such as those by Siegfried Sassoon (p. 1125 and p. 1126), Isaac Rosenberg (p. 1129 and p. 1130), Wilfred Owen (p. 1132 and p. 1133), and Robert Graves.

A handful of remarkable poems did emerge from World War II, such as Richard Eberhart's "The Fury of Aerial Bombardment" (p. 1135), W. H.

Auden's "September 1, 1939" (p. 1137), and Edith Sitwell's "Still Falls the Rain" (p. 1128). Henry Reed, Alun Lewis, Keith Douglas, Karl Shapiro, and Sidney Keyes also wrote moving poems about war, and their best examples are included in this chapter. Whether or not these match in quality the poems of the previous world war must be left to readers to judge.

Among the contemporary examples included here are poems about wars in Korea, Vietnam, El Salvador, and elsewhere by a range of contemporary poets, such as Hayden Carruth and W. S. Merwin. These poems mostly fall into the category of "anti-war poem," for the obvious reason that few sensitive men or women seem to have returned from a theater of war with good feelings about what they witnessed. A sense of the injustice and absurdity, the cruelty and waste of war dominate these poems.

War poetry might well be considered a subgenre of political poetry, but it stands firmly on its own. Some of these poems must be counted among the strongest ever composed in the English language. They fire their verbal artillery across our heads, and we can only bow our heads and pray, knowing full well the truth of W. H. Auden's great line: "We must love one another or die."

ADDITIONAL POEMS ABOUT WARS AND RUMORS OF WAR IN THIS BOOK

- Anonymous, *Beowulf* (p. 46 and p. 1494)
- James Thompson, "Rule Britannia" (p. 1180)
- T. S. Eliot, *The Waste Land* (p. 102)
- Ezra Pound, from *The Cantos* [Canto I] (p. 93)
- Felicia Dorothea Hemans, "England's Dead" (p. 176)
- Matthew Arnold, "Dover Beach" (p. 1594)
- Rudyard Kipling, "Recessional" (p. 1184)
- William Butler Yeats, "Easter 1916" (p. 1187) and "An Irish Airman Forsees His Death" (p. 581)
- Wilfred Owen, "Strange Meeting" (p. 776) and "Anthem for Doomed Youth" (p. 824)
- W. H. Auden, "Epitaph on a Tyrant" (p. 1191)
- Wendell Berry, "Against the War in Vietnam" (p. 1215)
- Robert Bly, "Romans Angry about the Inner World" (p. 1195)
- Charles Simic, "Sunday Papers" (p. 1224)
- Marilyn Hacker, "Elegy for a Soldier" (p. 242)
- Jay Parini, "After the Terror" (p. 849)
- Peter Balakian, "After the Survivors Are Gone" (p. 1229)

LAO-TZU (551–479 B.C.)
trans. Stephen Mitchell

"Weapons are the tools of violence"

Weapons are the tools of violence;
all decent men detest them.

Weapons are the tools of fear;
a decent man will avoid them
5 except in the direst necessity
and, if compelled, will use them
only with the utmost restraint.
Peace is his highest value.
If the peace has been shattered,
10 how can he be content?
His enemies are not demons,
but human beings like himself.
He doesn't wish them personal harm.
Nor does he rejoice in victory.
15 How could he rejoice in victory
and delight in the slaughter of men?

He enters a battle gravely,
with sorrow and with great compassion,
as if he were attending a funeral.

SU WU (ca. second century A.D.)
trans. Kenneth Rexroth (1905–1982)

Drafted

They married us when they put
Up our hair. We were just twenty
And fifteen. And ever since,
Our love has never been troubled.
5 Tonight we have the old joy
In each other, although our
Happiness will soon be over.
I remember the long march
That lies ahead of me, and
10 Go out and look up at the stars,
To see how the night has worn on.

Betelgeuse and Antares[1]
Have both gone out. It is time
For me to leave for far off
15   Battlefields. No way of knowing
If we will ever see each
Other again. We clutch each
Other and sob, our faces
Streaming with tears. Goodbye, dear.
20   Protect the Spring flowers of
Your beauty. Think of the days
When we were happy together.
If I live I will come back.
If I die, remember me always.

WANG HAN (687–726)
trans. Arthur Sze

Song of Liang-chou

The grape wine is beautiful
as light shines into the cup at night.
I would like to drink
but the lute urges me to mount my horse.
5   Sir, if I am lying drunk on the battlefield,
please do not laugh.
Since ancient times,
how many soldiers ever returned?

ANONYMOUS

A carol of Agincourt[1]   (fifteenth century)

Deo gracias, Anglia,
Redde pro victoria.[2]

Oure kinge went forth to Normandy
With grace and might of chivalry.

---

[1] **Betelgeuse and Antares:** Bright stars in the evening sky.
[1] **Agincourt:** Battle in which Henry V and the English defeated the French in 1415.
[2] **Deo . . . victoria:** Latin, "Return thanks to God, England, for victory."

Ther God for him wrought mervelusly:
Wherfore Englonde may calle and cry.
5   'Deo gracias'.

He sette a sege,° the sothe° for to say,   siege / truth
To Harflu towne with ryal array:³
That towne he wan and made affray°   panic
That Fraunce shall riwe° till Domesday.   rue
10   'Deo gracias'.

Than went oure kinge with alle his hoste°   army
Thorwe Fraunce, for alle the Frenshe boste:
He spared, no drede, of lest ne moste,⁴
Till he come to Agincourt coste.°   region
15   'Deo gracias'.

Than, forsoth, that knight comely°   handsome
In Agincourt feld° he faught manly.   field
Thorw grace of God most mighty
He had bothe the felde and the victory.
20   'Deo gracias'.

There dukis and erlis, lorde and barone,
Were take and slaine, and that well sone,°   quickly
And summe were ladde° into Lundone   led
With joye and merthe and grete renone.°   pomp
25   'Deo gracias'.

Now gracious God he save oure kinge,
His peple and alle his well-willinge:°   friends
Yef him gode life and gode ending,
That we with merth mowe° safely singe,   may
30   'Deo gracias'.

---

³ **To Harflu . . . array:** Before the Battle at Agincourt, Henry captured the French port of Harfleur.
⁴ **He . . . moste:** I.e., he spared, no doubt, neither the least nor the greatest.

WILLIAM SHAKESPEARE (1564–1616)

from Henry V
Act III, Scene 1 (King Henry V)   (ca. 1599; 1623)

Once more unto the breach, dear friends, once more;
Or close the wall up with our English dead.
In peace there's nothing so becomes a man
As modest stillness and humility:
5   But when the blast of war blows in our ears,
Then imitate the action of the tiger;
Stiffen the sinews, summon up the blood,
Disguise fair nature with hard-favour'd rage;
Then lend the eye a terrible aspect;
10   Let pry through the portage of the head
Like the brass cannon; let the brow o'erwhelm it
As fearfully as doth a galled rock
O'erhang and jutty his confounded base,
Swill'd with the wild and wasteful ocean.
15   Now set the teeth and stretch the nostril wide,
Hold hard the breath and bend up every spirit
To his full height. On, on, you noblest English.
Whose blood is fet° from fathers of war-proof!   fetched
Fathers that, like so many Alexanders,°   heroes
20   Have in these parts from morn till even fought
And sheathed their swords for lack of argument:
Dishonour not your mothers; now attest
That those whom you call'd fathers did beget you.
Be copy now to men of grosser blood,
25   And teach them how to war. And you, good yeoman,
Whose limbs were made in England, show us here
The mettle of your pasture; let us swear
That you are worth your breeding; which I doubt not;
For there is none of you so mean and base,
30   That hath not noble lustre in your eyes.
I see you stand like greyhounds in the slips,
Straining upon the start. The game's afoot:
Follow your spirit, and upon this charge
Cry 'God for Harry, England, and Saint George!'

JOHN MILTON (1608–1674)

On the Late Massacre in Piemont[1] (1673)

Avenge, O Lord, thy slaughter'd saints, whose bones
     Lie scatter'd on the Alpine mountains cold,
     Ev'n them who kept thy truth so pure of old,
     When all our fathers worshipp'd stocks° and stones;[2]   idols
5 Forget not: in thy book record their groans
     Who were thy sheep and in their ancient fold
     Slain by the bloody Piemontese that roll'd
     Mother with infant down the rocks. Their moans
The vales redoubl'd to the hills, and they
10   To Heav'n. Their martyr'd blood and ashes sow
     O'er all th' Italian fields where still doth sway
The triple tyrant;[3] that from these may grow
     A hundred-fold, who having learnt thy way
Early may fly the Babylonian woe.[4]

SIR JOHN SUCKLING (1609–1642)

A Soldier (1659)

I am a man of war and might,
And know thus much, that I can fight,
Whether I am in the wrong or right,
        Devoutly.

5 No woman under heaven I fear,
New oaths I can exactly swear,
And forty healths my brain will bear
        Most stoutly.

I cannot speak, but I can do
10 As much as any of our crew,
And, if you doubt it, some of you
        May prove me.

---

[1] **Piemont:** On Easter Sunday of 1655, the duke of Savory attacked a Protestant Waldensian sect in the Piedmont of North Italy, killing seventeen hundred members of the sect.
[2] **stocks and stones:** Originally part of the Catholic church, the Waldenses were critical of the materialistic traditions of the Church.
[3] **The triple tyrant:** The pope's tiara has three crowns.
[4] **Babylonian woe:** Protestants often connected the Papal Court to Babylon, an ancient city of luxury.

I dare be bold thus much to say,
If that my bullets do but play,
15   You would be hurt so night and day,
                    Yet love me.

RICHARD LOVELACE (1618– ca. 1657)

To Lucasta, Going to the Wars (1649)

Tell me not, sweet, I am unkind,
      That from the nunnery
Of thy chaste breast and quiet mind
      To war and arms I fly.

5   True, a new mistress now I chase,
      The first foe in the field;
And with a stronger faith embrace
      A sword, a horse, a shield.

Yet this inconstancy is such
10   As you too shall adore;
I could not love thee, dear, so much,
      Loved I not honour more.

LUCY TERRY (1730–1821)

The Bars° Fight (ca. 1750)   meadows

August 'twas the twenty-fifth
Seventeen hundred forty-six
The Indians did in ambush lay
Some very valient men to slay
5   The names of whom I'll not leave out
Samuel Allen like a hero fout°   fought
And though he was so brave and bold
His face no more shall we behold
Eleazer Hawks was killed outright
10   Before he had time to fight
Before he did the Indians see
Was shot and killed immediately
Oliver Amsden he was slain

Which caused his friends much grief and pain
15   Simeon Amsden they found dead
Not many rods off from his head.
Adonijah Gillet, we do hear
Did lose his life which was so dear
John Saddler fled across the water
20   And so escaped the dreadful slaughter
Eunice Allen see the Indians comeing
And hoped to save herself by running
And had not her petticoats stopt her
The awful creatures had not cotched her
25   And tommyhawked her on the head
And left her on the ground for dead.
Young Samuel Allen, Oh! lack-a-day
Was taken and carried to Canada.

HERMAN MELVILLE (1819–1891)

The College Colonel (1866)

He rides at their head;
    A crutch by his saddle just slants in view,
One slung arm is in splints you see,
    Yet he guides his strong steed—how coldly too.

5   He brings his regiment home,
        Not as they filed two years before;
But a remnant half-tattered, and battered, and worn,
Like castaway sailors, who, stunned
        By the surf's loud roar,
10   Their mates dragged back and seen no more,—
Again and again breast the surge,
        And at last crawl, spent, to shore.

A still rigidity and pale,
        An Indian aloofness, lones his brow;
15   He has lived a thousand years
Compressed in battle's pains and prayers,
        Marches and watches slow.

There are welcoming shouts and flags;
        Old men off hat to the Boy,
20   Wreaths from gay balconies fall at his feet,
        But to him—there comes alloy.

It is not that a leg is lost,
    It is not that an arm is maimed,
It is not that the fever has racked,—
25   Self he has long disclaimed.

But all through the Seven Days' Fight,[1]
    And deep in the Wilderness grim,
And in the field-hospital tent,
    And Petersburg crater,[2] and dim
30 Lean brooding in Libby,[3] there came—
    Ah heaven!—what *truth* to him!

HERMAN MELVILLE (1819–1891)

The Portent (1859; 1866)

Hanging from the beam,
    Slowly swaying (such the law),
Gaunt the shadow on your green,
    Shenandoah![1]
5 The cut is on the crown
    (Lo, John Brown[2]),
And the stabs shall heal no more.

Hidden in the cap
    Is the anguish none can draw;
10 So your future veils its face,
    Shenandoah!
But the streaming beard is shown
    (Weird John Brown),
The meteor of the war.

[1] **Seven Days' Fight:** In the Civil War, a brief battle near Richmond, Virginia, fought from June 25 to July 1, 1862. Both the Union and Confederate sides suffered heavy casualties as a result of the engagement.
[2] **Petersburg crater:** In 1864, Union troops exploded a mine outside of Petersburg, Virginia. The resulting confusion, however, allowed the Confederates to retaliate and claim victory over the Union troops.
[3] **Libby:** Famous Civil War prison near Richmond, Virginia.
[1] **Shenandoah:** Valley in Virginia, site of Civil War battles in 1862 and 1864.
[2] **John Brown:** Famous abolitionist who was executed in 1859 for leading a raid against the United States armory in Harpers Ferry, Virginia.

WALT WHITMAN (1819–1892)

Cavalry Crossing a Ford (1865; 1871)

A line in long array where they wind betwixt green islands,
They take a serpentine course, their arms flash in the sun—hark to the
     musical clank,
Behold the silvery river, in it the splashing horses loitering stop to drink,
Behold the brown-faced men, each group, each person a picture,
     the negligent rest on the saddles,
5   Some emerge on the opposite bank, others are just entering the ford—
     while,
Scarlet and blue and snowy white,
The guidon flags[1] flutter gayly in the wind.

WALT WHITMAN (1819–1892)

Vigil Strange I Kept on the Field One Night (1865; 1867)

Vigil strange I kept on the field one night;
When you my son and my comrade dropt at my side that day,
One look I but gave which your dear eyes return'd with a look I shall
     never forget,
One touch of your hand to mine O boy, reach'd up as you lay on the
     ground,
5   Then onward I sped in the battle, the even-contested battle,
Till late in the night reliev'd to the place at last again I made my way,
Found you in death so cold dear comrade, found your body son of
     responding kisses, (never again on earth responding,)
Bared your face in the starlight, curious the scene, cool blew the
     moderate night-wind,
Long there and then in vigil I stood, dimly around me the
     battlefield spreading,
10 Vigil wondrous and vigil sweet there in the fragrant silent night,
But not a tear fell, not even a long-drawn sigh, long, long I gazed,
Then on the earth partially reclining sat by your side leaning my
     chin in my hands,
Passing sweet hours, immortal and mystic hours with you dearest
     comrade—not a tear, not a word,
Vigil of silence, love and death, vigil for you my son and my soldier,

---

[1] **guidon flags:** Small flags used to direct the movement of a cavalry of infantry.

15 As onward silently stars aloft, eastward new ones upward stole,
Vigil final for you brave boy, (I could not save you, swift was your
             death,
I faithfully loved you and cared for you living, I think we shall
             surely meet again,)
Till at latest lingering of the night, indeed just as the dawn appear'd,
My comrade I wrapt in his blanket, envelop'd well his form,
20 Folded the blanket well, tucking it carefully over head and carefully
             under feet,
And there and then and bathed by the rising sun, my son in his
             grave, in his rude-dug grave I deposited,
Ending my vigil strange with that, vigil of night and battle-field dim,
Vigil for boy of responding kisses, (never again on earth responding,)
Vigil for comrade swiftly slain, vigil I never forget, how as day brighten'd,
25 I rose from the chill ground and folded my soldier well in his blanket,
And buried him where he fell.

THOMAS HARDY (1840–1928)

Channel Firing (1914)

That night your great guns, unawares,
Shook all our coffins as we lay,
And broke the chancel window-squares,
We thought it was the Judgment-day

5 And sat upright. While drearisome
Arose the howl of wakened hounds:
The mouse let fall the altar-crumb,
The worms drew back into the mounds,

The glebe cow[1] drooled. Till God called, "No;
10 It's gunnery practice out at sea
Just as before you went below;
The world is as it used to be:

"All nations striving strong to make
Red war yet redder. Mad as hatters
15 They do no more for Christés sake
Than you who are helpless in such matters.

---

[1] **glebe cow:** A cow grazed on the glebe, a piece of land adjoining a rectory.

"That this is not the judgment-hour
For some of them's a blessed thing,
For if it were they'd have to scour
20   Hell's floor for so much threatening. . . .

"Ha, ha. It will be warmer when
I blow the trumpet (if indeed
I ever do; for you are men,
And rest eternal sorely need)."

25   So down we lay again. "I wonder,
Will the world ever saner be,"
Said one, "than when He sent us under
In our indifferent century!"

And many a skeleton shook his head.
30   "Instead of preaching forty year,"
My neighbour Parson Thirdly said,
"I wish I had stuck to pipes and beer."

Again the guns disturbed the hour,
Roaring their readiness to avenge,
35   As far inland as Stourton Tower,
And Camelot, and starlit Stonehenge.[2]

A. E. HOUSMAN (1859–1936)

Here Dead Lie We Because We Did Not Choose (1936)

Here dead lie we because we did not choose
      To live and shame the land from which we sprung.
Life, to be sure, is nothing much to lose;
      But young men think it is, and we were young.

---

[2] **Stourton . . . Stonehenge:** Stourton Tower is part of an estate in Wiltshire, England. Camelot is the site of King Arthur's court, and Stonehenge is a group of megalithic monuments in Wiltshire.

WILLIAM BUTLER YEATS (1865–1939)

The Second Coming[1]   (1921)

Turning and turning in the widening gyre[2]
The falcon cannot hear the falconer;
Things fall apart; the centre cannot hold;
Mere anarchy is loosed upon the world,
5   The blood-dimmed tide is loosed, and everywhere
The ceremony of innocence is drowned;
The best lack all conviction, while the worst
Are full of passionate intensity.

Surely some revelation is at hand;
10   Surely the Second Coming is at hand.
The Second Coming! Hardly are those words out
When a vast image out of *Spiritus Mundi*[3]
Troubles my sight: somewhere in sands of the desert
A shape with lion body and the head of a man,
15   A gaze blank and pitiless as the sun,
Is moving its slow thighs, while all about it
Reel shadows of the indignant desert birds.
The darkness drops again; but now I know
That twenty centuries[4] of stony sleep
20   Were vexed to nightmare by a rocking cradle,
And what rough beast, its hour come round at last,
Slouches toward Bethlehem[5] to be born?

---

[1] **The Second Coming:** Written in 1919, the poem reflects Yeats's position on the Black and Tan War in which British troops were sent to Ireland to curtail republican forces. The title is derived from two biblical sources: Christ's prediction of his second coming in Matthew 24 and John's prophecy of the coming of the Antichrist in 1 John 2.

[2] **the widening gyre:** The shape of the falcon's flight, but also, in Yeats's personal mythology, a gyre widening to its maximum, at which point time will turn on itself and a new era of history will be born through violence.

[3] ***Spiritus Mundi:*** For Yeats, divine inspiration.

[4] **twenty centuries:** The twenty centuries of the Christian era.

[5] **Bethlehem:** Christ's birthplace, yet also, Yeats suggests, the birthplace of the Antichrist who will usher in a new era.

STEPHEN CRANE (1871–1900)

from War is Kind (1899)

Do not weep, maiden, for war is kind.
Because your lover threw wild hands toward the sky
And the affrighted steed ran on alone,
Do not weep.
5   War is kind.

Hoarse, booming drums of the regiment
Little souls who thirst for fight,
These men were born to drill and die
The unexplained glory flies above them
10   Great is the battle-god, great, and his kingdom—
A field where a thousand corpses lie.

Do not weep, babe, for war is kind.
Because your father tumbled in the yellow trenches,
Raged at his breast, gulped and died,
15   Do not weep.
War is kind.

Swift, blazing flag of the regiment
Eagle with crest of red and gold,
These men were born to drill and die
20   Point for them the virtue of slaughter
Make plain to them the excellence of killing
And a field where a thousand corpses lie.

Mother whose heart hung humble as a button
On the bright splendid shroud of your son,
25   Do not weep.
War is kind.

CARL SANDBURG (1878–1967)

Grass (1918)

Pile the bodies high at Austerlitz and Waterloo.
Shovel them under and let me work—
                I am the grass; I cover all.

And pile them high at Gettysburg
5   And pile them high at Ypres and Verdun.[1]
Shovel them under and let me work.
Two years, ten years, and passengers ask the conductor:
                What place is this?
                Where are we now?

10   I am the grass.
                Let me work.

WALLACE STEVENS   (1879–1955)

from **Notes toward a Supreme Fiction**   (1947)

Soldier, there is a war between the mind
And sky, between thought and day and night. It is
For that the poet is always in the sun,

Patches the moon together in his room
5   To his Virgilian cadences, up down,
Up down. It is a war that never ends.

Yet it depends on yours. The two are one.
They are a plural, a right and left, a pair,
Two parallels that meet if only in

10   The meeting of their shadows or that meet
In a book in a barrack, a letter from Malay.[1]
But your war ends. And after it you return

With six meats and twelve wines or else without
To walk another room . . . Monsieur and comrade,
15   The soldier is poor without the poet's lines,

His petty syllabi, the sounds that stick,
Inevitably modulating, in the blood.
And war for war, each has its gallant kind.

How simply the fictive hero becomes the real;
20   How gladly with proper words the soldier dies,
If he must, or lives on the bread of faithful speech.

---

[1] **Austerlitz . . . Verdun:** Sandburg lists sites of major battles in the Napoleonic Wars, the Civil War, and World War I.
[1] **Malay:** Malaya, a peninsula in the South China Sea.

EZRA POUND (1885–1972)

from **Hugh Selwyn Mauberley** (1920)

IV

These fought in any case,
and some believing,
          pro domo,[1] in any case . . .

Some quick to arm,
5   some for adventure,
some from fear or weakness,
some from fear or censure,
some for love of slaughter, in imagination,
learning later . . .
10 some in fear, learning love of slaughter;

Died some, pro patria,
          non "dulce" non "et decor" . . .[2]
walked eye-deep in hell
believing in old men's lies, then unbelieving
15 came home, home to a lie,
home to many deceits,
home to old lies and new infamy;
usury age-old and age-thick
and liars in public places.

20 Daring as never before, wastage as never before.
Young blood and high blood,
fair cheeks, and fine bodies;

fortitude as never before
frankness as never before,
25 disillusions as never told in the old days,
hysterias, trench confessions,
laughter out of dead bellies.

V

There died a myriad,
And of the best, among them,

---

[1] **pro domo:** Latin, "for the home."
[2] **pro patria..."et decor":** Pound modifies a phrase from Horace (65 B.C.–8 B.C.), *Odes* 3.2.13: *"Dulce et decorum est pro partria mori"*—"It is sweet and fitting to die for one's country."

30   For an old bitch gone in the teeth,
      For a botched civilization,

      Charm, smiling at the good mouth,
      Quick eyes gone under earth's lid,

      For two gross of broken statues,
35   For a few thousand battered books.

H. D. (HILDA DOOLITTLE)   (1886–1961)

R.A.F.[1]   (1941)

I

      He said, I'm just out of hospital,
      but I'm still flying.

      I answered, *of course,*
      angry, prescient, knowing

5   what fire lay behind his wide stare,
      what fury of desire

      impelled him,
      pretending not to notice

      his stammer
10   and that now, in his agony to express himself

      his speech failed
      altogether,

      and his eyes seemed to gather
      in their white-heat,

15   all the fires of the wind,
      fire of sleet,

      snow like white-fire pellets,
      congealed radium, planets

---

[1] **R.A.F.:** Britain's Royal Air Force.

like snow-flakes:
20 and I thought,

the sun
is only a round platform

for his feet
to rest upon.

                          II

25 So I knew his name,
the coming-one

from a far star,
I knew he would come again,

though I did not know
30 he would come so soon;

he stood by my desk
in my room

where I write this;
he did not wear

35 his blue tunic with the wings,
nor his cap with the crown;

his flying-helmet,
and his cumbersome trappings

were unfamiliar,
40 like a deep-sea diver.

                          III

I had said,
I want to thank you,

he had said,
for what?

45 I had said,
it is very difficult

to say what I want,
I mean—I want

personally to thank you
50   for what you have done;

he had said,
I did nothing,

it was the others;
I went on,

55   for a moment infected with his stammer
but persistent,

I will think of you
when they come over,

I mean—I understand—I know—
60   I was there the whole time

in the Battle
of Britain.[2]

IV

He came again,
he did not speak;

65   I thought; he stands by my desk
in the dark,

he is emissary,
maybe he will speak later,

(does he still stammer?)
70   I remembered

how I had thought
this field, that meadow

is branded for eternity
(whatever becomes of our earth)

75   with the mark
of the new cross,

---

[2] **Battle of Britain:** In World War II, a crucial battle fought in 1940 in the skies over Britain from July 10 through October 31 with the German airforce.

the flying shadow
of high wings,

moving
80   over the grass.

V

Fortunately, there was no time
for lesser intimacy

than this—
instantaneous flash,

85   recognition, premonition, vision;
fortunately, there was no time,

for the two-edged drawn-swords
of our two separate twin-beings

to dull; no danger of rust;
90   the Archangel's own fine blade

so neatly divided us,
in the beginning.

VI

He was huddled
in the opposite corner,

95   bare-headed, curiously slumped forward
as if he were about to fall over;

the compartment was crowded,
I was facing forward;

I said, put your feet up here
100   and I wedged myself tighter

and dozed off in the roar
and the train rumble.

VII

In the train jolt
our knees brushed

105   and he murmured, sorry:
he was there;

I knew in the half-daze,
in the drug and drift,

the hypnotic sway
110 of the train, that we were very near;

we could not have been nearer,
and my mind winged away;

our minds are winged,
though our feet are clay.

VIII

115 True, I had travelled the world over,
but I had found no beauty, no wonder

to equal the cliff-edge,
the line of a river

we had just passed,
120 no picture nor colour in glass

to equal the fervour
of sea-blue, emerald, violet,

the stone-walls, prehistoric circles
and dolmens

125 that I had just left
in Cornwall.[3]

IX

True, we are cold, shivering,
and we ponder on many things,

waiting for the war to be over;
130 and I wonder,

has he come for me?
is this my particular winged messenger?

or was it tact,
a code of behaviour,

---

[3] **Cornwall:** Rural county in southwestern England.

135   was it only a sort of politeness,
       did he "drop in," as it were,

       to explain
       why he had not come sooner?

                        X

       My thoughts in the train,
140   rushed forward, backward,

       I was in the lush tall grass
       by the burning beeches,

       I followed the avenue, out of Tregonning,
       across the fields to the other house,

145   Trenoweth,[4]
       where friends were staying;

       there was the camellia-bush,
       the stone-basin with the tiny lilies

       and the pink snails; I remembered
150   the Scilly Islands off the coast,

       and other islands,
       the isles of Greece

       whose stone thresholds (nor Karnak)[5]
       were older

155   than the sun-circles I had just left;
       I thought of Stonehenge,

       I thought,
       we will be saved yet.

                        XI

       He could not know my thoughts,
160   but between us,

---

[4] **Tregonning . . . Trenoweth:** Tregonning and Trenoweth are both in Cornwall.
[5] **Karnak:** Village in Egypt, once part of the ancient Egyptian capital Thebes.

the shuttle sped,
passed back,

the invisible web,
bound us;

165   whatever we thought or said,
we were people who had crossed over,

we had already crashed,
we were already dead.

XII

If I dare recall
170   his last swift grave smile,

I award myself
some inch of ribbon

for valour,
such as he wore,

175   for I am stricken
as never before,

by the thought
of ineptitude, sloth, evil

that prosper,
180   while such as he fall.

SIEGFRIED SASSOON   (1886–1967)

Everyone Sang   (1919)

Everyone suddenly burst out singing;
And I was filled with such delight
As prisoned birds must find in freedom,
Winging wildly across the white
5   Orchards and dark-green fields; on—on—and out of sight.

Everyone's voice was suddenly lifted;
And beauty came like the setting sun:

My heat was shaken with tears; and horror
Drifted away . . . O, but Everyone
10   Was a bird; and the song was wordless; the singing will never be done.

SIEGFRIED SASSOON (1886–1967)

The Rear-Guard (1918)

(Hindenburg Line, April 1917)[1]

Groping along the tunnel, step by step,
He winked his prying torch with patching glare
From side to side, and sniffed the unwholesome air.

Tins, boxes, bottles, shapes too vague to know,
5   A mirror smashed, the mattress from a bed;
And he, exploring fifty feet below
The rosy gloom of battle overhead.

Tripping, he grabbed the wall; saw some one lie
Humped at his feet, half-hidden by a rug,
10   And stooped to give the sleeper's arm a tug.
"I'm looking for headquarters." No reply.
"God blast your neck!" (For days he'd had no sleep.)

"Get up and guide me through this stinking place."
Savage, he kicked a soft, unanswering heap,
15   And flashed his beam across the livid face
Terribly glaring up, whose eyes yet wore
Agony dying hard ten days before;
And fists of fingers clutched a blackening wound.

Alone he staggered on until he found
20   Dawn's ghost that filtered down a shafted stair
To the dazed, muttering creatures underground
Who hear the boom of shells in muffed sound.
At last, with sweat of horror in his hair,
He climbed through darkness to the twilight air,
25   Unloading hell behind him step by step.

---

[1] **Hindenburg Line, April 1917:** The Hindenburg Line was the strongest line of defense trenches on Germany's western front. April of 1917 was a difficult period for the British troops in France.

RUPERT BROOKE (1887–1915)

The Soldier (1914)

If I should die, think only this of me:
    That there's some corner of a foreign field
That is for ever England. There shall be
    In that rich earth a richer dust concealed;
5 A dust whom England bore, shaped, made aware,
    Gave, once, her flowers to love, her ways to roam,
A body of England's, breathing English air,
    Washed by the rivers, blest by suns of home.

And think, this heart, all evil shed away,
10   A pulse in the eternal mind, no less
      Gives somewhere back the thoughts by England given;
Her sights and sounds; dreams happy as her day;
    And laughter, learnt of friends; and gentleness,
      In hearts at peace, under an English heaven.

MARIANNE MOORE (1887–1972)

"Keeping Their World Large" (1951)

> All too literally, their flesh and their spirit are our shield
>   —NEW YORK TIMES, *JUNE 7, 1944*

I should like to see that country's tiles, bedrooms,
stone patios
      and ancient wells: Rinaldo
Caramonica's the cobbler's, Frank Sblendorio's
5   and Dominick Angelastro's country—
      the grocer's, the iceman's, the dancer's—the
beautiful Miss Damiano's; wisdom's

    and all angels' Italy, this Christmas Day
this Christmas year.
10   A noiseless piano, an
innocent war, the heart that can act against itself. Here,
      each unlike and all alike, could
        so many—stumbling, falling, multiplied
    till bodies lay as ground to walk on—

15   "If Christ and the apostles died in vain,
I'll die in vain with them"
      against this way of victory.

That forest of white crosses!
        My eyes won't close to it.
20   All laid like animals for sacrifice—
like Isaac on the mount,[1]
                were their own sacrifice.

        Marching to death, marching to life?
"Keeping their world large,"
25   whose spirits and whose bodies
all too literally were our shield,
        are still our shield.

        They fought the enemy,
we fight fat living and self-pity.
30   Shine, o shine,
        unfalsifying sun, on this sick scene.

EDITH SITWELL (1887–1964)

Still Falls the Rain (1942)

The Raids, 1940.[1] *Night and Dawn*

Still falls the Rain—
Dark as the world of man, black as our loss—
Blind as the nineteen hundred and forty nails
Upon the Cross.

5   Still falls the Rain
With a sound like the pulse of the heart that is changed to the
                hammerbeat
In the Potter's Field,[2] and the sound of the impious feet

On the Tomb:
                Still falls the Rain
10   In the Field of Blood where the small hopes breed and the human
                brain
Nurtures its greed, that worm with the brow of Cain.

---

[1] **Isaac on the mount:** As a test of faith, God asked Abraham to sacrifice his son Isaac on the altar.
(See Genesis 22.)
[1] **The Raids, 1940:** In the Battle of Britain, Germany frequently launched bombing raids over England.
[2] **Potter's Field:** In Jerusalem, a cemetery where foreigners are buried. It was supposedly bought with
blood money discarded by Judas.

Still falls the Rain
At the feet of the Starved Man hung upon the Cross.
Christ that each day, each night, nails there, have mercy on us—
15 On Dives and on Lazarus.[3]
Under the Rain the sore and the gold are as one.

Still falls the Rain—
Still falls the Blood from the Starved Man's wounded Side:
He bears in His Heart all wounds—those of the light that died,
20 The last faint spark
In the self-murdered heart, the wounds of the sad uncomprehending
        dark,
The wounds of the baited bear—[4]
The blind and weeping bear whom the keepers beat
On his helpless flesh . . . the tears of the hunted hare.

25 Still falls the Rain—
Then—O Ile leape up to my God: who pulles me doune—[5]
See, see where Christ's blood streames in the firmament:
It flows from the Brow we nailed upon the tree
Deep to the dying, to the thirsting heart
30 That holds the fires of the world—dark-smirched with pain
As Caesar's laurel crown.[6]

Then sounds the voice of One who like the heart of man
Was once a child who among beasts has lain—
'Still do I love, still shed my innocent light, my Blood, for thee.'

ISAAC ROSENBERG (1890–1918)

Break of Day in the Trenches (1916; 1922)

The darkness crumbles away.
It is the same old druid[1] Time as ever,
Only a live thing leaps my hand,
A queer sardonic rat,

---

[3] **On Dives and on Lazarus:** See Luke 16:19–31.
[4] **baited bear:** Medieval spectacle where a bear chained to a post is attacked by dogs.
[5] **O Ile . . . doune:** In Marlowe's *Dr. Faustus,* Faust's cry when he realizes he is damned for his agreement with Mephistopheles.
[6] **laurel crown:** In Roman times, a symbol of victory.
[1] **druid:** Member of an ancient Celtic religious order.

5   As I pull the parapet's poppy[2]
     To stick behind my ear.
     Droll rat, they would shoot you if they knew
     Your cosmopolitan sympathies.
     Now you have touched this English hand
10   You will do the same to a German
     Soon, no doubt, if it be your pleasure
     To cross the sleeping green between.
     It seems you inwardly grin as you pass
     Strong eyes, fine limbs, haughty athletes,
15   Less chanced than you for life,
     Bonds to the whims of murder,
     Sprawled in the bowels of the earth,
     The torn fields of France.
     What do you see in our eyes
20   At the shrieking iron and flame
     Hurled through still heavens?
     What quaver—what heart aghast?
     Poppies whose roots are in man's veins
     Drop, and are ever dropping;
25   But mine in my ear is safe—
     Just a little white with the dust.

ISAAC ROSENBERG (1890–1918)

Dead Man's Dump (1917; 1922)

     The plunging limbers[1] over the shattered track
     Racketed with their rusty freight,
     Stuck out like many crowns of thorns,
     And the rusty stakes like sceptres old
5   To stay the flood of brutish men
     Upon our brothers dear.

     The wheels lurched over sprawled dead
     But pained them not, though their bones crunched,
     Their shut mouths made no moan,
10   They lie there huddled, friend and foeman,
     Man born of man, and born of woman,

---

[2] **parapet's poppy:** A parapet was a wall that protected a trench in World War I. Poppies are a common flower in Europe.
[1] **limbers:** Vehicles for hauling a gun.

And shells go crying over them
From night till night and now.

Earth has waited for them
15   All the time of their growth
Fretting for their decay:
Now she has them at last!
In the strength of their strength
Suspended—stopped and held.

20   What fierce imaginings their dark souls lit
Earth! have they gone into you?
Somewhere they must have gone,
And flung on your hard back
Is their souls' sack,
25   Emptied of God-ancestralled essences.
Who hurled them out? Who hurled?

None saw their spirits' shadow shake the grass,
Or stood aside for the half used life to pass
Out of those doomed nostrils and the doomed mouth,
30   When the swift iron burning bee
Drained the wild honey of their youth.

What of us, who flung on the shrieking pyre,
Walk, our usual thoughts untouched,
Our lucky limbs as on ichor² fed,
35   Immortal seeming ever?
Perhaps when the flames beat loud on us,
A fear may choke in our veins
And the startled blood may stop.

The air is loud with death,
40   The dark air spurts with fire
The explosions ceaseless are.
Timelessly now, some minutes past,
These dead strode time with vigorous life,
Till the shrapnel called "an end!"
45   But not to all. In bleeding pangs
Some borne on stretchers dreamed of home,
Dear things, war-blotted from their hearts.

A man's brains splattered on
A stretcher-bearer's face;

---

² **ichor:** In Greek mythology, the fluid flowing through the veins of the gods.

50 His shook shoulders slipped their load,
But when they bent to look again
The drowning soul was sunk too deep
For human tenderness.

They left this dead with the older dead,
55 Stretched at the cross roads.
Burnt black by strange decay,
Their sinister faces lie
The lid over each eye,
The grass and coloured clay
60 More motion have than they,
Joined to the great sunk silences.

Here is one not long dead;
His dark hearing caught our far wheels,
And the choked soul stretched weak hands
65 To reach the living world the far wheels said,
The blood-dazed intelligence beating for light,
Crying through the suspense of the far torturing wheels
Swift for the end to break,
Or the wheels to break,
70 Cried as the tide of the world broke over his sight.

Will they come? Will they ever come?
Even as the mixed hoofs of the mules,
The quivering-bellied mules,
And the rushing wheels all mixed
75 With his tortured upturned sight,
So we crashed round the bend,
We heard his weak scream,
We heard his very last sound,
And our wheels grazed his dead face.

WILFRED OWEN   (1893–1918)

Dulce et Decorum Est[1]   (1917; 1920)

Bent double, like old beggars under sacks,
Knock-kneed, coughing like hags, we cursed through sludge,

---

[1] **Dulce et Decorum Est:** Latin, "It is sweet and meet to die for one's country. Sweet! And decorous!"
(Translation by the author.) From the *Odes* of Horace (3.2.13).

Till on the haunting flares we turned our backs
And towards our distant rest began to trudge.
5   Men marched asleep. Many had lost their boots
But limped on, blood-shod. All went lame; all blind;
Drunk with fatigue; deaf even to the hoots
Of tired, outstripped Five-Nines² that dropped behind.

Gas! GAS! Quick, boys!—An ecstasy of fumbling,
10   Fitting the clumsy helmets just in time;
But someone still was yelling out and stumbling,
And flound'ring like a man in fire or lime . . .
Dim, through the misty panes and thick green light,
As under a green sea, I saw him drowning.

15   In all my dreams, before my helpless sight,
He plunges at me, guttering, choking, drowning.

If in some smothering dreams you too could pace
Behind the wagon that we flung him in,
And watch the white eyes writhing in his face,
20   His hanging face, like a devil's sick of sin;
If you could hear, at every jolt, the blood
Come gargling from the froth-corrupted lungs,
Obscene as cancer, bitter as the cud
Of vile, incurable sores on innocent tongues,—
25   My friend,³ you would not tell with such high zest
To children ardent for some desperate glory,
The old Lie: Dulce et decorum est
Pro patria mori.

WILFRED OWEN (1893–1918)

Futility (1918; 1920)

Move him into the sun—
Gently its touch awoke him once,
At home, whispering of fields half-sown.
Always it woke him, even in France,
5   Until this morning and this snow.

---

² **Five-Nines:** 5.9-inch caliber shells.
³ **My friend:** The poem was originally dedicated to Jesse Pope, author of *Jessie Pope's War Poems* (1915).

If anything might rouse him now
The kind old sun will know.

Think how it wakes the seeds—
Woke once the clays of a cold star.
10 Are limbs, so dear achieved, are sides
Full-nerved, still warm, too hard to stir?
Was it for this the clay grew tall?
—O what made fatuous sunbeams toil
To break earth's sleep at all?

E. E. CUMMINGS (1894–1962)

"i sing of Olaf glad and big" (1931)

i sing of Olaf glad and big
whose warmest heart recoiled at war:
a conscientious object-or

his wellbelovéd colonel(trig°   clean-cut
5   westpointer most succinctly bred)
took erring Olaf soon in hand;
but—though an host of overjoyed
noncoms°(first knocking on the head   military officer
him)do through icy waters roll
10 that helplessness which others stroke
with brushes recently employed
anent this muddy toiletbowl,
while kindred intellects evoke
allegiance per blunt instruments—
15 Olaf(being to all intents
a corpse and wanting any rag
upon what God unto him gave)
responds,without getting annoyed
"I will not kiss your fucking flag"

20 straightway the silver bird[1] looked grave
(departing hurriedly to shave)

but—though all kinds of officers
(a yearning nation's blueeyed pride)
their passive prey did kick and curse

---

[1] **silver bird:** Insignia of an Army colonel.

25 until for wear their clarion
    voices and boots were much the worse,
    and egged the firstclassprivates on
    his rectum wickedly to tease
    by means of skilfully applied
30 bayonets roasted hot with heat—
    Olaf(upon what were once knees)
    does almost ceaselessly repeat
    "there is some shit I will not eat"

    our president,being of which
35 assertions duly notified
    threw the yellowsonofabitch
    into a dungeon,where he died

    Christ(of His mercy infinite)
    i pray to see;and Olaf,too

40 preponderatingly because
    unless statistics lie he was
    more brave than me:more blond than you.

RICHARD EBERHART (1904–   )

The Fury of Aerial Bombardment (1947)

    You would think the fury of aerial bombardment
    Would rouse God to relent; the infinite spaces
    Are still silent. He looks on shock-pried faces.
    History, even, does not know what is meant.

5   You would feel that after so many centuries
    God would give man to repent; yet he can kill
    As Cain could, but with multitudinous will,
    No farther advanced than in his ancient furies.

    Was man made stupid to see his own stupidity?
10 Is God by definition indifferent, beyond us all?
    Is the eternal truth man's fighting soul
    Wherein the Beast ravens in its own avidity?

    Of Van Wettering I speak, and Averill,
    Names on a list, whose faces I do not recall
15 But they are gone to early death, who late in school
    Distinguished the belt feed lever from the belt holding pawl.

W. H. AUDEN (1907–1973)

The Quarry (1932)

O what is that sound which so thrills the ear
    Down in the valley drumming, drumming?
Only the scarlet soldiers, dear,
    The soldiers coming.

5   O what is that light I see flashing so clear
    Over the distance brightly, brightly?
Only the sun on their weapons, dear,
    As they step lightly.

O what are they doing with all that gear,
10   What are they doing this morning, this morning?
Only their usual manoeuvres, dear,
    Or perhaps a warning.

O why have they left the road down there,
    Why are they suddenly wheeling, wheeling?
15   Perhaps a change in their orders, dear.
    Why are you kneeling?

O haven't they stopped for the doctor's care,
    Haven't they reined their horses, their horses?
Why, they are none of them wounded, dear,
20   None of these forces.

O is it the parson they want, with white hair,
    Is it the parson, is it, is it?
No, they are passing his gateway, dear,
    Without a visit.

25   O it must be the farmer who lives so near.
    It must be the farmer so cunning, so cunning?
They have passed the farmyard already, dear,
    And now they are running.

O where are you going? Stay with me here!
30   Were the vows you swore deceiving, deceiving?
No, I promised to love you, dear,
    But I must be leaving.

O it's broken the lock and splintered the door,
    O it's the gate where they're turning, turning;
35   Their boots are heavy on the floor
    And their eyes are burning.

W. H. AUDEN (1907–1973)

September 1, 1939[1] (1939)

I sit in one of the dives
On Fifty-Second Street
Uncertain and afraid
As the clever hopes expire
5   Of a low dishonest decade:
Waves of anger and fear
Circulate over the bright
And darkened lands of the earth,
Obsessing our private lives;
10   The unmentionable odour of death
Offends the September night.

Accurate scholarship can
Unearth the whole offence
From Luther[2] until now
15   That has driven a culture mad,
Find what occurred at Linz,[3]
What huge imago made
A psychopathic god:
I and the public know
20   What all schoolchildren learn,
Those to whom evil is done
Do evil in return.

Exiled Thucydides[4] knew
All that a speech can say
25   About Democracy,
And what dictators do,
The elderly rubbish they talk
To an apathetic grave;
Analysed all in his book,
30   The enlightenment driven away,
The habit-forming pain,
Mismanagement and grief:
We must suffer them all again.

---

[1] **September 1, 1939:** Date of the German invasion of Poland and the beginning of World War II.
[2] **Luther:** Martin Luther (1483–1546), a German theologian who began the Protestant Reformation.
[3] **Linz:** City in northwest Austria where Hitler spent his formative years.
[4] **Thucydides:** Thucydides (460 B.C.–395 B.C.), an ancient Greek historian who recorded a history of the Peloponnesian War.

Into this neutral air
35   Where blind skyscrapers use
Their full height to proclaim
The strength of Collective Man,
Each language pours its vain
Competitive excuse:
40   But who can live for long
In an euphoric dream;
Out of the mirror they stare,
Imperialism's face
And the international wrong.

45   Faces along the bar
Cling to their average day:
The lights must never go out,
The music must always play,
All the conventions conspire
50   To make this fort assume
The furniture of home;
Lest we should see where we are,
Lost in a haunted wood,
Children afraid of the night
55   Who have never been happy or good.

The windiest militant trash
Important Persons shout
Is not so crude as our wish:
What mad Nijinsky wrote
60   About Diaghilev [5]
Is true of the normal heart;
For the error bred in the bone
Of each woman and each man
Craves what it cannot have,
65   Not universal love
But to be loved alone.

From the conservative dark
Into the ethical life
The dense commuters come,
70   Repeating their morning vow,
'I *will* be true to the wife,
I'll concentrate more on my work',

---

[5] **What . . . Diaghilev:** Vaslav Nijinsky (1890–1950) was a Russian dancer considered by many to be
the best dancer of the twentieth century. Sergei Diaghilev (1872–1929) was the founder of Russian ballet.

And helpless governors wake
To resume their compulsory game:
75 Who can release them now,
Who can reach the deaf,
Who can speak for the dumb?

All I have is a voice
To undo the folded lie,
80 The romantic lie in the brain
Of the sensual man-in-the-street
And the lie of Authority
Whose buildings grope the sky:
There is no such thing as the State
85 And no one exists alone;
Hunger allows no choice
To the citizen or the police;
We must love one another or die.

Defenceless under the night
90 Our world in stupor lies;
Yet, dotted everywhere,
Ironic points of light
Flash out wherever the Just
Exchange their messages:
95 May I, composed like them
Of Eros and of dust,
Beleaguered by the same
Negation and despair,
Show an affirming flame.

A. D. HOPE (1907–2000)

Inscription for a War (1971)

>   Stranger, go tell the Spartans
>   we died here obedient to their commands.
>   —INSCRIPTION AT THERMOPYLAE[1]

Linger not, stranger; shed no tear;
Go back to those who sent us here.

---

[1] **Thermopylae:** A mountain pass in Greece, named for its hot water springs. Leonides and the Spartans attempted to defend the pass from a Persian army led by Xerxes, but the Persians used espionage to infiltrate the Greek lines.

We are the young they drafted out
To wars their folly brought about.

5   Go tell those old men, safe in bed,
We took their orders and are dead.

KARL SHAPIRO (1913–2000)

Troop Train (1944)

It stops the town we come through. Workers raise
Their oily arms in good salute and grin.
Kids scream as at a circus. Business men
Glance hopefully and go their measured way.
5   And women standing at their dumbstruck door
More slowly wave and seem to warn us back,
As if a tear blinding the course of war
Might once dissolve our iron in their sweet wish.

Fruit of the world, O clustered on ourselves
10 We hang as from a cornucopia
In total friendliness, with faces bunched
To spray the streets with catcalls and with leers.
A bottle smashes on the moving ties
And eyes fixed on a lady smiling pink
15 Stretch like a rubber-band and snap and sting
The mouth that wants the drink-of-water kiss.

And on through crummy continents and days,
Deliberate, grimy, slightly drunk we crawl,
The good-bad boys of circumstance and chance,
20 Whose bucket-helmets bang the empty wall
Where twist the murdered bodies of our packs
Next to the guns that only seem themselves.
And distance like a strap adjusted shrinks,
Tightens across the shoulder and holds firm.

25 Here is a deck of cards; out of this hand
Dealer, deal me my luck, a pair of bulls,
The right draw to a flush, the one-eyed jack.
Diamonds and hearts are red but spades are black,
And spades are spades and clubs are clovers—black.
30 But deal me winners, souvenirs of peace.

This stands to reason and arithmetic,
Luck also travels and not all come back.

Trains lead to ships and ships to death or trains,
And trains to death or trucks, and trucks to death,
35   Or trucks lead to the march, the march to death,
Or that survival which is all our hope;
And death leads back to trucks and trains and ships,
But life leads to the march, O flag! at last
The place of life found after trains and death—
40   Nightfall of nations brilliant after war.

RANDALL JARRELL (1914–1965)

The Death of the Ball Turret Gunner[1]   (1945)

From my mother's sleep I fell into the State,
And I hunched in its belly till my wet fur froze.
Six miles from earth, loosed from its dream of life,
I woke to black flak and the nightmare fighters.
5   When I died they washed me out of the turret with a hose.

RANDALL JARRELL (1914–1965)

Eighth Air Force[1]   (1945)

If, in an odd angle of the hutment,°   camp
A puppy laps the water from a can
Of flowers, and the drunk sergeant shaving
Whistles *O Paradiso!*[2]—shall I say that man
5   Is not as men have said: a wolf to man?

---

[1] **The Death . . . Gunner:** "A ball turret was a plexiglass sphere set into the belly of a B-17 or B-24, and inhabited by two .50 caliber machine-guns and one man, a short small man. When this gunner tracked with his machine-guns a fighter attacking his bomber from below, he revolved with the turret; hunched upside-down in his little sphere, he looked like the foetus in the womb. The fighters which attacked him were armed with cannon firing explosive shells. The hose was a steam hose" [Jarrell's note].
[1] **Eighth Air Force:** "A poem about the air force which bombed the Continent from England. The man who lies counting missions has one to go before being sent home. The phrases from the Gospels compare such criminals and scapegoats as these with that earlier criminal and scapegoat about whom the Gospels were written" [Jarrell's note]. For Gospel references, see John 19 and Matthew 27.
[2] *O Paradiso!*: Typical aria in an opera.

The other murderers troop in yawning;
Three of them play Pitch, one sleeps, and one
Lies counting missions, lies there sweating
Till even his heart beats: One; One; One.
10   *O murderers!* . . . Still, this is how it's done:

This is a war. . . . But since these play, before they die,
Like puppies with their puppy; since, a man,
I did as these have done, but did not die—
I will content the people as I can
15   And give up these to them: Behold the man!

I have suffered, in a dream, because of him,
Many things; for this last saviour, man,
I have lied as I lie now. But what is lying?
Men wash their hands, in blood, as best they can:
20   I find no fault in this just man.

HENRY REED (1914–1986)

from **Lessons of War** (1942; 1946)

1. Naming of Parts

Today we have naming of parts. Yesterday,
We had daily cleaning. And tomorrow morning,
We shall have what to do after firing. But today,
Today we have naming of parts. Japonica[1]
5   Glistens like coral in all of the neighbouring gardens,
          And today we have naming of parts.

This is the lower sling swivel. And this
Is the upper sling swivel, whose use you will see,
When you are given your slings. And this is the piling swivel,
10   Which in your case you have not got. The branches
Hold in the gardens their silent, eloquent gestures,
          Which in our case we have not got.

This is the safety-catch, which is always released
With an easy flick of the thumb. And please do not let me
15   See anyone using his finger. You can do it quite easy

---

[1] **Japonica:** The flowering quince, a shrub with red flowers.

If you have any strength in your thumb. The blossoms
Are fragile and motionless, never letting anyone see
    Any of them using their finger.

And this you can see is the bolt. The purpose of this
20 Is to open the breech, as you see. We can slide it
Rapidly backwards and forwards: we call this
Easing the spring.[2] And rapidly backwards and forwards
The early bees are assaulting and fumbling the flowers:
    They call it easing the Spring.

25 They call it easing the Spring: it is perfectly easy
If you have any strength in your thumb: like the bolt,
And the breech, and the cocking-piece, and the point of balance,
Which in our case we have not got; and the almond-blossom
Silent in all of the gardens and the bees going backwards and forwards,
30   For today we have naming of parts.

WILLIAM STAFFORD (1914–1993)

At the Bomb Testing Site (1966)

At noon in the desert a panting lizard
waited for history, its elbows tense,
watching the curve of a particular road
as if something might happen.

5 It was looking for something farther off
than people could see, an important scene
acted in stone for little selves
at the flute end of consequences.

There was just a continent without much on it
10 under a sky that never cared less.
Ready for a change, the elbows waited.
The hands gripped hard on the desert.

---

[2] **Easing the spring:** "Ease springs," a military command that orders soldiers to move the bolt of their rifle and eject leftover bullets in the magazine.

ALUN LEWIS (1915–1944)

All Day It Has Rained (1940; 1941)

All day it has rained, and we on the edge of the moors
Have sprawled in our bell-tents, moody and dull as boors,
Groundsheets and blankets spread on the muddy ground
And from the first grey wakening we have found
5   No refuge from the skirmishing fine rain
And the wind that made the canvas heave and flap
And the taut wet guy-ropes ravel out and snap.
All day the rain has glided, wave and mist and dream,
Drenching the gorse and heather, a gossamer stream
10 Too light to stir the acorns that suddenly
Snatched from their cups by the wild south-westerly
Pattered against the tent and our upturned dreaming faces.
And we stretched out, unbuttoning our braces,
Smoking a Woodbine,° darning dirty socks,   cigarette
15 Reading the Sunday papers—I saw a fox
And mentioned it in the note I scribbled home;—
And we talked of girls, and dropping bombs on Rome,
And thought of the quiet dead and the loud celebrities
Exhorting us to slaughter, and the herded refugees;
20 —Yet thought softly, morosely of them, and as indifferently
As of ourselves or those whom we
For years have loved, and will again
Tomorrow maybe love; but now it is the rain
Possesses us entirely, the twilight and the rain.

25 And I can remember nothing dearer or more to my heart
Than the children I watched in the woods on Saturday
Shaking down burning chestnuts for the schoolyard's merry play,
Or the shaggy patient dog who followed me
By Sheet and Steep and up the wooded scree°   embankment
30 To the Shoulder o' Mutton where Edward Thomas brooded long
On death and beauty—till a bullet stopped his song.[1]

---

[1] **To . . . song:** The "Shoulder o' Mutton" is a hill in Hampshire, England—part of the landscape that inspired the British poet Edward Thomas (1878–1917), who was killed in France during World War I.

GWENDOLYN BROOKS   (1917–2000)

Negro Hero   (1945)

to suggest Dorie Miller

I had to kick their law into their teeth in order to save them.
However I have heard that sometimes you have to deal
Devilishly with drowning men in order to swim them to shore.
Or they will haul themselves and you to the trash and the fish beneath.
5   (When I think of this, I do not worry about a few
Chipped teeth.)

It is good I gave glory, it is good I put gold on their name.
Or there would have been spikes in the afterward hands.
But let us speak only of my success and the pictures in the
            Caucasian dailies
10   As well as the Negro weeklies. For I am a gem.
(They are not concerned that it was hardly The Enemy my fight
           was against
But them.)

It was a tall time. And of course my blood was
Boiling about in my head and straining and howling and singing
           me on.
15   Of course I was rolled on wheels of my boy itch to get at the gun
Of course all the delicate rehearsal shots of my childhood massed
           in mirage before me.
Of course I was child
And my first swallow of the liquor of battle bleeding black air dying
           and demon noise
Made me wild.

20   It was kinder than that, though, and I showed like a banner my
           kindness.
I loved. And a man will guard when he loves.
Their white-gowned democracy was my fair lady.
With her knife lying cold, straight, in the softness of her sweet-flowing
           sleeve.
But for the sake of the dear smiling mouth and the stuttered
           promise I toyed with my life.
25   I threw back!—I would not remember
Entirely the knife.

Still—am I good enough to die for them, is my blood bright enough
           to be spilled,

Was my constant back-question—are they clear
On this? Or do I intrude even now?
30   Am I clean enough to kill for them, do they wish me to kill
For them or is my place while death licks his lips and strides to them
In the galley still?

(In a southern city a white man said
Indeed, I'd rather be dead;
35   Indeed, I'd rather be shot in the head
Or ridden to waste on the back of a flood
Than saved by the drop of a black man's blood.)

Naturally, the important thing is, I helped to save them, them and a
        part of their democracy.
Even if I had to kick their law into their teeth in order to do that for
        them.
40   And I am feeling well and settled in myself because I believe it was
        a good job,
Despite this possible horror: that they might prefer the
Preservation of their law in all its sick dignity and their knives
To the continuation of their creed
And their lives.

KEITH DOUGLAS (1920–1944)

Gallantry (1943; 1949)

The Colonel[1] in a casual voice
spoke into the microphone a joke
Which through a hundred earphones broke
into the ears of a doomed race.

5   Into the ears of the doomed boy, the fool
whose perfectly mannered flesh fell
in opening the door for a shell
as he had learnt to do at school.

Conrad luckily survived the winter:
10   he wrote a letter to welcome

---

[1] **The Colonel:** "Lt.-Col. J. D. Player, killed in Tunisisa, Enfiadaville, February, 1943, left £3,000 to the Beaufort Hunt, and directed that the incumbent of the living in his gift should be a 'man who approves of hunting, shooting, and all manly sports, which are the backbone of the nation' " [Douglas's note on manuscript for "Aristocrats"].

the auspicious spring: only his silken
intentions severed with a single splinter.

Was George fond of little boys?
We always suspected it,
15   but who will say: since George was hit
we never mention our surmise.

It was a brave thing the Colonel said,
but the whole sky turned too hot
and the three heroes never heard what
20   it was, gone deaf with steel and lead.

But the bullets cried with laughter,
the shells were overcome with mirth,
plunging their heads in steel and earth —
(the air commented in a whisper).

HAYDEN CARRUTH (1921–   )

On a Certain Engagement South of Seoul[1]

A long time, many years, we've had these wars.
When they were opened, one can scarcely say.
We were high school students, no more than sophomores,

When Italy broke her peace on a dark day,[2]
5   And that was not the beginning. The following years
Grew crowded with destruction and dismay.

When I was nineteen, once the surprising tears
Stood in my eyes and stung me, for I saw
A soldier in a newsreel clutch his ears

10   To hold his face together. Those that paw
The public's bones to eat the public's heart
Said far too much, of course. The sight, so raw

And unbelievable, of people blown apart
Was enough to change us without that bark and whine.
15   We grew disconsolate. Each had his chart

---

[1] **Seoul:** Capital and largest city in South Korea.
[2] **When . . . day:** Italy entered World War II on the side of Germany and invaded France on June 4, 1940.

To mark on the kitchen wall the battle-line,
But many were out of date. The radio
Droned through the years, a faithful anodyne.

Yet the news of this slight encounter somewhere below
20   Seoul stirs my remembrance: we were a few,
Sprawled on the stiff grass of a small plateau,

Afraid. No one was dead. But we were new—
We did not know that probably none would die.
Slowly, then, all vision went askew.

25   My clothing was outlandish; earth and sky
Were metallic and horrible. We were unreal,
Strange bodies and alien minds; we could not cry

For even our eyes seemed to be made of steel;
Nor could we look at one another, for each
30   Was a sign of fear, and we could not conceal

Our hatred for our friends. There was no speech.
We sat alone, all of us, trying to wake
Some memory of the selves beyond our reach.

That place was conquered. The nations undertake
35   Another campaign now, in another land,
A stranger land perhaps. And we forsake

The miseries there that we can't understand
Just as we always have. Yet still my glimpse
Of a scene on the distant field can make my hand

40   Tremble again. How quiet we are. One limps,
One cannot walk at all, or one is all right,
But one has this experience that crimps

Forgetfulness, especially at night.
Is this a bond? Does this make us brothers?
45   Or does it bring our hatred back? I might

Have known, but now I do not know. Others
May know. I know when I walk out-of-doors
I have a sorrow not wholly mine, but another's.

SIDNEY KEYES (1922–1943)

War Poet (1942; 1943)

I am the man who looked for peace and found
My own eyes barbed.
I am the man who groped for words and found
An arrow in my hand.
5   I am the builder whose firm walls surround
A slipping land.
When I grow sick or mad
Mock me not nor chain me:
When I reach for the wind
10   Cast me not down:
Though my face is a burnt book
And a wasted town.

DENISE LEVERTOV (1923–1997)

Life at War (1967)

The disasters numb within us
caught in the chest, rolling
in the brain like pebbles. The feeling
resembles lumps of raw dough

5   weighing down a child's stomach on baking day.
Or Rilke[1] said it, 'My heart. . .
Could I say of it, it overflows
with bitterness . . . but no, as though

its contents were simply balled into
10   formless lumps, thus
do I carry it about.'
The same war

continues.
We have breathed the grits of it in, all our lives,

---

[1] **Rilke:** Rainer Maria Rilke (1875–1926), a German mystical poet.

15   our lungs are pocked with it,
the mucous membrane of our dreams
coated with it, the imagination
filmed over with the gray filth of it:

the knowledge that humankind,

20   delicate Man, whose flesh
responds to a caress, whose eyes
are flowers that perceive the stars,

whose music excels the music of birds,
whose laughter matches the laughter of dogs,
25   whose understanding manifests designs
fairer than the spider's most intricate web,

still turns without surprise, with mere regret
to the scheduled breaking open of breasts whose milk
runs out over the entrails of still-alive babies,
30   transformation of witnessing eyes to pulp-fragments,
implosion of skinned penises into carcass-gulleys.

We are the humans, men who can make;
whose language imagines *mercy*,
lovingkindness; we have believed one another
35   mirrored forms of a God we felt as good—

who do these acts, who convince ourselves
it is necessary; these acts are done
to our own flesh; burned human flesh
is smelling in Viet Nam as I write.

40   Yes, this is the knowledge that jostles for space
in our bodies along with all we
go on knowing of joy, of love;

our nerve filaments twitch with its presence
day and night,
45   nothing we say has not the husky phlegm of it in the saying,
nothing we do has the quickness, the sureness,
the deep intelligence living at peace would have.

W. S. MERWIN (1927–   )

The Asians Dying (1967)

When the forests have been destroyed their darkness remains
The ash the great walker follows the possessors
Forever
Nothing they will come to is real
5   Nor for long
Over the watercourses
Like ducks in the time of the ducks
The ghosts of the villages trail in the sky
Making a new twilight

10   Rain falls into the open eyes of the dead
Again again with its pointless sound
When the moon finds them they are the color of everything

The nights disappear like bruises but nothing is healed
The dead go away like bruises
15   The blood vanishes into the poisoned farmlands
Pain the horizon
Remains
Overhead the seasons rock
They are paper bells
20   Calling to nothing living

The possessors move everywhere under Death their star
Like columns of smoke they advance into the shadows
Like thin flames with no light
They with no past
25   And fire their only future

PHILIP LEVINE (1928–   )

On the Murder of Lieutenant José del Castillo by the Falangist Bravo Martinez, July 12, 1936[1] (1976)

When the Lieutenant of the Guardia de Asalto
heard the automatic go off, he turned
and took the second shot just above
the sternum, the third tore away
5   the right shoulder of his uniform,
the fourth perforated his cheek. As he
slid out of his comrade's hold
toward the gray cement of the Ramblas
he lost count and knew only
10 that he would not die and that the blue sky
smudged with clouds was not heaven
for heaven was nowhere and in his eyes
slowly filling with their own light.
The pigeons that spotted the cold floor
15 of Barcelona rose as he sank below
the waves of silence crashing
on the far shores of his legs, growing
faint and watery. His hands opened
a last time to receive the benedictions
20 of automobile exhaust and rain
and the rain of soot. His mouth,
that would never again say "I am afraid,"
closed on nothing. The old grandfather
hawking daisies at his stand pressed
25 a handkerchief against his lips
and turned his eyes away before they held
the eyes of a gunman. The shepherd dogs
on sale howled in their cages
and turned in circles. There is more
30 to be said, but by someone who has suffered
and died for his sister the earth
and his brothers the beasts and the trees.

---

[1] **On the Murder . . . 1936:** Minor incident from the Spanish Civil War (1936–1939), fought between the right-wing nationalists and the left-wing republicans.

The Lieutenant can hear it, the prayer
that comes on the voices of water, today
35   or yesterday, from Chicago or Valladolid,[2]
and hangs like smoke above this street
he won't walk as a man ever again.

GEOFFREY HILL (1932–   )

The Distant Fury of Battle   (1955; 1959)

Grass resurrects to mask, to strangle
Words glossed on stone, lopped stone-angel;
But the dead maintain their ground—
That there's no getting round—

5   Who in places vitally rest,
Named, anonymous; who test
Alike the endurance of yews
Laurels, moonshine, stone, all tissues;

With whom, under licence and duress,
10   There are pacts made, if not peace.
Union with the stone-wearing dead
Claims the born leader, the prepared

Leader, the devourers and all lean men.
Some, finally, learn to begin.
15   Some keep to the arrangement of love
(Or similar trust) under whose auspices move

Most subjects, toward the profits of this
Combine of doves and witnesses.
Some, dug out of hot-beds, are brought bare,
20   Not past conceiving but past care.

---

[2] **Valladolid:** Beautiful, historically rich city in Spain.

PETER SCUPHAM (1933–)

Guard-Room (1983)

The New Guard forms, is present and correct,
Stamping its dolly boots, slapping its rifles.
We dress according to the ancient lights.

I am their Corporal; at my conscription
5   They take their stint of turn and turn about,
Conjuring for me their forgotten faces.

Lights out in barrack-blocks: Alma, Dettingen.[1]
The sky has moved into its winter quarters
Over this coarse plain, bruising to the heel.

10   The sentry's breath disperses a still plume.
We have dismissed the sun to his great arc;
The pendulum moves deep and slow beneath us.

Should some goodfellow come to bless this house,
He must be challenged, were it the Prince himself.
15   Even our shadows have offended us.

My lubber-fiends deploy and stretch their arms
To the one bar of our electric fire
Whose raw scrape intensifies the cold.

The Guard-room mirror plays its monkey tricks
20   And small hours crawl towards the edge of light,
A sticky silt brimming our mouths and eyes.

We are the tutelars, our field-dew consecrate,
A smear of cigarette-ash on the floor.
Even this dull ground needs a libation:

25   This staging-post for Somme and Passchendaele.[2]
The Square whitens towards our armistice;
In France, their markers steady the parade.

---

[1] **Alma, Dettingen:** The Battle of Alma (1854) in the Crimean War, and the Battle of Dettingen (1743) in the War of the Austrian Succession.
[2] **Somme and Passchendaele:** The Battle of the Somme (1916) and the Battle of Passchendaele (1917) were major conflicts in World War I.

C. K. WILLIAMS (1936–   )

The Hearth (2003)
February 2003

1.

Alone after the news on a bitter
evening in the country, sleet slashing
the stubbled fields, the river ice;
I keep stirring up the recalcitrant fire,

5   but when I throw my plastic coffee cup
in with new kindling it perches intact
on a log for a strangely long time,
as though uncertain what to do,

until, in a somehow reluctant, almost
10   creaturely way, it dents, collapses
and decomposes to a dark slime
untwining itself on the stone hearth.

I once knew someone who was caught in a fire
and made it sound something like that.
15   He'd been loading a bomber and a napalm shell
had gone off; flung from the flames,

at first he felt nothing and thought
he'd been spared, but then came the pain,
then the hideous dark—he'd been blinded,
20   and so badly charred he spent years

in recovery: agonizing debridements,
grafts, learning to speak through a mouth
without lips, to read Braille with fingers
lavaed with scar, to not want to die—

25   though that never happened. He swore,
even years later, with a family,
that if he were back there, this time allowed
to put himself out of his misery, he would.

2.

There was dying here tonight, after
dusk, by the road: an owl,

eyes fixed and flared, breast
so winter-white he seemed to shine

5 a searchlight on himself, helicoptered
near a wire fence, then suddenly
banked, plunged and vanished
into the swallowing dark with his prey.

Such an uncomplicated departure;
10 no detonation, nothing to mourn;
if the creature being torn from its life
made a sound, I didn't hear it.

But in fact I wasn't listening, I was thinking,
as I often do these days, of war;
15 I was thinking of my children, and their children,
of the more than fear I feel for them,

and then of radar, rockets, shrapnel,
cities razed, soil poisoned
for a thousand generations; of suffering so vast
20 it nullifies everything else.

I stood in the wind in the raw cold
wondering how those with power over us
can effect such things, and by what
cynical reasoning pardon themselves.

25 The fire's ablaze now, its glow
on the windows makes the night even darker,
but it barely keeps the room warm.
I stoke it again, and crouch closer.

CHAPTER 18

WHAT IS POSSIBLE
—Adrienne Rich

An Anthology of Poetry and Politics

Matthew Arnold, the Victorian poet, once noted that "poetry is at bottom a criticism of life." The degree to which one can say that poetry is political is, perhaps, another matter. Poets have long paid attention to the social dimensions of their art, debating its effectiveness, but always concerned about the relationship between poetry and the world around it.

Poetry has been a forum for political expression from ancient times to the present, a means of speaking truth to power. This tradition is a rich one, with many possibilities for range and tone, subject and approach. Yet certain questions often arise: What right do poets have to speak out for anyone? Why do they imagine themselves, as the Romantic poet Percy Bysshe Shelley wrote in *A Defence of Poetry*, "the unacknowledged legislators of the world"? Isn't this just pretension on the part of poets, who rarely have a wide audience for their work? Many critics would agree with W. H. Auden, who once suggested that "poetry makes nothing happen."

One good argument for political poetry is contained in a poem by Wallace Stevens called "Of Modern Poetry" (p. 1442). Stevens argues that poetry has "to be living." It has "to face the men of the time and to meet / The women of the time. It has to think about war / And it has to find what will suffice." A poet has to find language that will "suffice," that will prove adequate to the experience of the reader in the modern world. This remains, of course, a challenge.

To discover "what will suffice," poets have no choice but to listen and watch closely, making judgments that often have political ramifications. Whatever their party affiliations and political sympathies, poets have usually been sensitive to the demands of their own times—responsive to the cruelties, injustices, and absurdities that confront them in their daily lives. In "North American Time," Adrienne Rich puts it like this:

try sitting at a typewriter
one calm summer evening
at a table by a window
in the country, try pretending
5   your time does not exist

that you are simply you
that the imagination simply strays
like a great moth, unintentional
try telling yourself
10   you are not accountable
to the life of your tribe
the breath of your planet

In other words, poets cannot simply choose to separate themselves from the life of their times. They are, to a degree, responsible for the language, if not the life, of their nation. It has always been part of a poet's job description to point to things wrong and right about the human condition in its present manifestation. A poet's way of saying may have few listeners, but those who really listen do so acutely; the words of true poems cut deep and resonate down the centuries.

Poets create a kind of bedrock language for each generation, a form of meditated speech against which all other language must measure itself. Thus, poets face a huge challenge every time they put pen to paper. They must speak for themselves, first and foremost; but they must also speak for those around them, those without a voice, without the training to speak as precisely as poets can speak.

Although poetry often addresses political issues, readers of this anthology will notice that many of the important poems written over the past thousand years or so have had nothing overtly political about them. Poets write about desire, they mourn losses, they tease each other and their friends, they celebrate the daily activities that make life possible in a difficult world. But a certain strand of poetry—a major strand, at that— deals with issues that could be called political. In each generation, a few strong poets step forward to marry political concerns with poetic practice in memorable ways.

Edmund Spenser, the great English poet who wrote *The Faerie Queene,* was living in Ireland in the sixteenth century, part of the occupying force from England, and he noted that there were "amongst the Irish a certain kind of people called Bards." He said their profession was "to set fourth the praises and dispraises of men in their poems and rhymes." The English invasion of Ireland was bloody and painful for the ordinary people of that island; the Irish bards formed part of the resistance against the occupation, and their work gave courage to those committed to the long struggle against imperialism. In this, they created a kind of model for the rebel-poet who steps forward and raises a voice against something that is to them offensive.

In American literature, a significant number of major poets have taken up the challenge of writing poetry in response to politics. One of the more radical was Walt Whitman. "I hear it was charged against me that I sought to destroy institutions," he wrote in "Calamus." "But really I am neither for nor against institutions." He supported only one institution: "The institution of the dear love of comrades." As the critic Jerome Loving has observed, Whitman "introduced politics into poetry in *Leaves of Grass* by invoking the concerns of middle America"—jobs, confusion about slavery, spirituality (as opposed to mere religiosity), democracy. Whitman's poems appeal directly, and passionately, to the impulses of his readers.

African-American poets and other poets of color have raised their voices against, and called attention to the specific injustices of racism and oppression. Langston Hughes took a bold and activist stance during the first part of the twentieth century. His work has been vividly carried forward by later poets of color, including Audre Lorde, Amiri Baraka, June Jordan, Ai, and Rita Dove, all of whom are included in this chapter.

Readers will, I think, be struck by the variety of approaches taken by poets over the centuries in work that raises political issues and concerns. They do so with varying degrees of directness, but the effect is often stunning. This is poetry in the noble tradition of ancient rhetoric, which may be defined as the art of persuasion. Whatever the argument of the poem, whatever the cause that moves the poet, the language of the poem must be consistently sharp, intelligently shaped, and eloquent. If poetry "makes nothing happen" in any large political sense, it certainly can move the hearts and minds of readers. This is often enough and will, as Wallace Stevens would say, "suffice." When enough people believe a certain thing, whatever that may be, change becomes possible, even inevitable. In this sense, poetry contributes to the creation of culture; it helps to establish the conditions for change, which makes its value inestimable.

ADDITIONAL POEMS ABOUT POLITICS IN THIS BOOK

- Walt Whitman, "Song of Myself" (p. 84)

- John Milton, "On the Late Massacre in Piedmont" (p. 1108)

- Jonathan Swift, "A Satirical Elegy on the Death of a Late Famous General" (p. 151)

- Phillis Wheatley, "To Mæcenas" (p. 746)

- Frances E. W. Harper, "The Slave Mother" (p. 498) and "Bury Me in a Free Land" (p. 775)

- Thomas Hardy, "Channel Firing" (p. 1113)

- Langston Hughes, "The Ballad of the Landlord" (p. 517)

- W. H. Auden, "September 1, 1939" (p. 1137)

- Dudley Randall, "The Ballad of Birmingham" (p. 523)

- William Carlos Williams, "To a Poor Old Woman" (p. 639)
- Robert Hayden, "The Middle Passage" (p. 359)
- William Stafford, "At the Bomb Testing Site" (p. 1143)
- Robert Creeley, "America" (p. 442)

TU FU (712–770)
trans. Arthur Sze

Spring View

The nation is broken, but hills and rivers remain.
Spring is in the city, grasses and trees are thick.
Touched by the hard times, flowers shed tears.
Grieved by separations, birds are startled in their hearts.

5   The beacon fires burned for three consecutive months.
A letter from home would be worth ten thousand pieces of gold.
As I scratch my white head, the hairs become fewer:
so scarce that I try in vain to fasten them with a pin.

THOMAS WYATT (1503–1542)

Mine Own John Poins[1] (1536)

Mine own John Poins, since ye delight to know
    The cause why that homeward I me draw,
    And flee the press of courts whereso they go,[2]
Rather than to live thrall, under the awe
5   Of lordly looks, wrapped within my cloak,

---

[1] **John Poins:** Wyatt's friend and member of Henry VIII's court.
[2] **And flee . . . go:** In Renaissance England, the royal court frequently relocated in elaborate processions.

To will and lust learning to set a law;
It is not for because I scorn and mock
   The power of them, to whom fortune hath lent
   Charge over us, of right, to strike the stroke:[3]
10   But true it is that I have always meant
   Less to esteem them than the common sort,
   Of outward things that judge in their intent,
Without regard what doth inward resort.
   I grant sometime that of glory the fire
15   Doth touch my heart: me list not° to report   I care not
Blame by honor and honor to desire.
   But how may I this honor now attain
   That cannot dye the color black a liar?[4]
My Poins, I cannot frame me tune to feign,
20   To cloak the truth, for praise without desert,°   undeservedly
   Of them that list all vice for to retain.
I cannot honor them that sets their part
   With Venus and Bacchus[5] all their life long;
   Nor hold my peace of them although I smart.
25   I cannot crouch nor kneel to do so great a wrong,
   To worship them, like God on earth alone,
   That are as wolves these sely° lambs among.   blameless
I cannot with my words complain and moan,
   And suffer naught; nor smart without complaint,
30   Nor turn the word that from my mouth is gone.
I cannot speak and look like a saint,
   Use wiles° for wit or make deceit a pleasure,   craftiness
   And call craft counsel, for profit still to paint;°   flatter
I cannot wrest the law to fill the coffer
35   With innocent blood to feed myself fat,
   And do most hurt where most help I offer.
I am not he that can allow° the state   accept
   Of high Caesar and damn Cato to die,
   That with his death did 'scape out of the gate
40 From Caesar's hands (if Livy do not lie)[6]
   And would not live where liberty was lost:
   So did his heart the common weal apply.[7]

---

[3] **of right . . . stroke:** I.e., rightfully allowed to lead and punish us.
[4] **That . . . liar:** A common Renaissance proverb held that "black will take no other hue."
[5] **Venus and Bacchus:** In classical mythology, Venus was the Roman goddess of love, and Bacchus was the Roman god of wine.
[6] **I am not . . . lie:** According to the Roman historian Livy, Cato the Younger committed suicide rather than submit to Caesar's tyranny.
[7] **the common weal apply:** I.e., practice the common good.

I am not he such eloquence to boast,
    To make the crow singing as the swan,[8]
45   Nor call the lion of coward beasts the most
That cannot take a mouse as the cat can:
    And he that dieth for hunger of the gold
    Call him Alexander;[9] and say that Pan
Passeth Apollo in music manifold;[10]
50   Praise Sir Thopas for a noble tale,
    And scorn the story that the Knight told.[11]
Praise him for counsel that is drunk of ale;
    Grin when he laugheth that beareth all the sway,
    Frown when he frowneth and groan when he is pale;
55 On others' lust to hang both night and day:
    None of these points would ever frame in me;
    My wit is naught—I cannot learn the way.
And much the less of things that greater be,
    That asken help of colors of device[12]
60   To join the mean° with each extremity,   middle
With the nearest virtue to cloak alway the vice:
    And as to purpose likewise it shall fall,
    To press° the virtue that it may not rise;   to press down
As drunkenness good fellowship to call;
65   The friendly foe with his double face
    Say he is gentle and courteous therewithal;
And say that favel° hath a goodly grace   flattery
    In eloquence; and cruelty to name
    Zeal of justice and change in time and place;
70 And he that suff'reth offense without blame
    Call him pitiful; and him true and plain
    That raileth° reckless to every man's shame.   rants
Say he is rude that cannot lie and feign;
    The lecher a lover; and tyranny
75   To be the right of a prince's reign.
I cannot, I. No, no, it will not be.
    This is the cause that I could never yet
    Hang on their sleeves that weigh as thou mayst see

---

[8] **singing as the swan:** According to legend, the swan supposedly sang before it died.
[9] **Call him Alexander:** Alexander the Great (356 B.C.–323 B.C.) preferred glory to riches.
[10] **Pan passeth Apollo in music manifold:** Pan played simple melodies on his flute, while Apollo strummed divine melodies on his lyre.
[11] **Praise . . . told:** In Chaucer's *Canterbury Tales*, Sir Thopas tells an intentionally dull parody that is preempted by the Host, while "The Knight's Tale" is held as a noble and worthwhile story.
[12] **colors of device:** Language that "colors" or taints.

A chip° of chance more than a pound of wit.   bit
80   This maketh me at home to hunt and hawk
And in foul weather at my book to sit.
In frost and snow then with my bow to stalk,
No man doth mark whereso I ride or go;
In lusty leas° at liberty I walk,   meadows
85   And of these news I feel nor weal° nor woe,   joy
Save that a clog[13] doth hang yet at my heel:
No force° for that for it is ordered so,   matter
That I may leap both hedge and dike full well.
I am not now in France to judge the wine,
90   With sav'ry sauce those delicates to feel;[14]
Nor yet in Spain where one must him incline
Rather than to be, outwardly to seem.
I meddle not with wits that be so fine,
Nor Flanders' cheer[15] letteth° not my sight to deem   impedes
95   Of black and white, nor taketh my wit away
With beastliness, they beasts do so esteem;
Nor am I not where Christ is given in prey
For money, poison, and treason at Rome,
A common practice used night and day:
100   But here I am in Kent and Christendom
Among the Muses where I read and rhyme;
Where if thou list, my Poins, for to come,
Thou shalt be judge how I do spend my time.

HENRY HOWARD, EARL OF SURREY (ca. 1517–1547)

"Thassyryans king[1] in peas° with fowle desyre"   peace

Thassyryans king in peas with fowle desyre
And filthye lustes that staynd his regall harte
In warr that should sett pryncelye hertes afyre
vaynquyshd dyd yelde for want of marcyall° arte   martial
5   The dent of swordes from kysses semed straunge
and harder then hys ladyes syde his targe

---

[13] **clog:** A heavy object attached to a prisoner's foot to impede movement.
[14] **those delicates to feel:** I.e., to taste exquisite foods.
[15] **Flanders' cheer:** The Flemish were notorious for drinking.
[1] **Thassyryans king:** King of Thessaly, in ancient Greece.

from glotton feastes to sowldyers fare a chaunge
his helmet far above a garlandes charge
who scace° the name of manhode dyd retayne°   scarce / retain
10   Drenched in slouthe° and womanishe delight   sloth
Feble of sprete unpacyent° of payne   unpatient
when he hadd lost his honor and hys right
Prowde tyme of welthe in stormes appawld with drede
murdred hym self to shew some manfull dede

GEORGE PUTTENHAM (ca. 1529–ca. 1590)

Her Majestie resembled to the crowned pillar. Ye must
read upward.

Is   blisse   with   immortalitie
    Her trymest top of all ye see,
5   Garnish   the   crowne
        Her   just   renowne
        Chapter   and   head
        Parts   that   maintain
        And   womanhead
10   Her   mayden   raigne
        In   te   gri   tie:
        In   ho   nour   and
        With   ve   ri   tie;°   truth
        Her   roundnes   stand.
15   Strengthen   the   state.
        By   their   increase
        With   out   de   bate
        Concord   and   peace
        Of   her   sup   port,
20   They   be   the   base
        With   stedfastnesse
        Vertue   and   grace
        Stay   and   comfort
        Of   Al   bi   ons°   rest,   England's
25   The   sounde   Pillar
        And   seene   a   farre
        Is   plainely   exprest
    Tall   stately   and   strayt
By   this   no   ble   pour   trayt

FULKE GREVILLE, LORD BROOKE (1554–1628)

from Caelica (1633)

XC

The Turkish government allows no law,
Men's lives and states depend on his behest;
We think subjection there a servile awe,
Where nature finds both honour, wealth and rest.
5   Our Christian freedom is, we have a law,
Which even the heathen think no power should wrest;
Yet proves it crooked as power lists to draw,
The rage or grace that lurks in prince's breasts.
    Opinion bodies may to shadows give,
10   But no burnt zone it is, where people live.

CI

Man's youth it is a field of large desires,
Which pleas'd within, doth all without them please,
For in this love of men live those sweet fires,
That kindle worth and kindness unto praise,
5   And where self-love most from her selfness gives,
        Man greatest in himself, and others lives.

Old age again which deems this pleasure vain,
Dull'd with experience of unthankfulness,
Scornful of fame, as but effects of pain,
10 Folds up that freedom in her narrowness,
        And for it only loves her own dreams best,
        Scorn'd and contemned is of all the rest.

Such working youth there is again in state,
Which at the first with justice, piety,
15 Fame, and reward, true instruments of fate,
Strive to improve this frail humanity:
        By which as kings enlarge true worth in us,
        So crowns again are well enlarged thus.

But states grow old, when princes turn away
20 From honour, to take pleasure for their ends;
For that a large is, this a narrow way,
That wins a world, and this a few dark friends;
        The one improving worthiness spreads far,
        Under the other good things prisoners are.

25   Thus sceptres shadow-like, grow short or long,
       As worthy, or unworthy princes reign,
       And must contract, cannot be large or strong,
       If man's weak humours real power restrain,
          So that when power and nature do oppose,
30   All but the worst men are assur'd to lose.

       For when respect, which is the strength of states,
       Grows to decline by kings' descent within
       That power's baby-creatures dare set rates
       Of scorn upon worth, honour upon sin;
35   Then though kings, player-like, act glory's part,
       Yet all within them is but fear and art.

WILLIAM BIRCH (1558–1571)

from **A songe betwene the Quenes majestie[1] and Englande**

E   Come over the born bessy,
      come over the born bessy
         Swete bessy come over to me
      And I shall the take,
5   and my dere lady make
         Before all other that ever I see.

B   My thinke I hear a voice,
      at whom I do rejoyce
         and aunswer the now I shall
10   Tel me I say,
      what art thou that biddes me com away
         and so earnestly doost me call.

E   I am thy lover faire,
      hath chose the to mine heir
15   and my name is mery Englande
      Therefore come away,
      and make no more delaye
         Swete bessie give me thy hande.

---

[1] **Quenes majestie:** Elizabeth I (1533–1603) was known as the virgin queen of England.

B Here is my hand,
20   my dere lover Englande
            I am thine both with mind and hart
        For ever to endure,
        thou maiest be sure
            Untill death us two depart.

25   E Lady this long space,
        have I loved thy grace
            more then I durste well saye
        Hoping at the last,
        when all stormes were past
30   For to see this joyfull daye.

B yet my lover England,
        ye shall understand
            How Fortune on me did lowre
        I was tombled and tost,
35   from piller to post
            and prisoner in the Towre.

E Dere Lady we do know,
        how that tirauntes° not a fewe   tyrants
            went about for to seke thy bloude
40   And contrarie to right,
        they did what they might
            That now bare two faces in one hood.

B Then was I caried to wodstock,
        and kept close under lock
45   That no man mighte with me speake
        And against all reason,
        they accused me of treason
            And tirably thei did me threate.

E Oh my lover faire,
50   my dearlinge and mine heire
            Full sore for the I did lament
        But no man durst speak,
        but thei wuld him threat
            and quickly make him repent.

55   B Then was I deliverd their hands,
        but was faine to put in bands
            and good suerties for my forth comminge
        Not from my house to departe,

nor no where els to sterte

60   as though I had ben away runninge.

E why dere Lady I trow,
those mad men did not knowe
    That ye were doughter unto Kinge Hary
And a princesse of birth,
65   one of the noblest on earth
    and sister unto Quene Mary.

B yes, yet I must forgeve,
al such as do live
    if they wil hereafter amend
70   And for those that are gone,
God forgeve them every one
    and his mercy on them extend. . . .

E Oh swete virgin pure,
longe may ye endure
75   To reigne over us in this lande
For your workes do accord,
ye are the handmaid of the lord
    For he hath blessed you with his hand.

B My swete realme be obedient,
80   To gods holy commaundement
        and my procedinges embrace
And for that that is abused,
shalbe better used
    and that within shorte space.

WILLIAM SHAKESPEARE (1564–1616)

from Julius Caesar
Act I, Scene 2 (Cassius) (ca. 1599; 1623)

I cannot tell what you and other men
Think of this life; but, for my single self,
I had as lief not be[1] as live to be
In awe of such a thing as I myself.

---

[1] **I had as lief not be:** I.e., I had rather be dead.

5   I was born free as Caesar; so were you:
    We both have fed as well, and we can both
    Endure the winter's cold as well as he:
    For once, upon a raw and gusty day,
    The troubled Tiber² chafing with° her shores,   raging against
10 Caesar said to me 'Darest thou, Cassius, now
    Leap in with me into this angry flood,
    And swim to yonder point?' Upon the word,
    Accoutred° as I was, I plunged in   dressed in armor
    And bade him follow; so indeed he did.
15 The torrent roar'd, and we did buffet it
    With lusty sinews, throwing it aside
    And stemming° it with hearts of controversy;   approaching
    But ere we could arrive the point proposed,
    Caesar cried 'Help me, Cassius, or I sink!'
20 I, as Aeneas,³ our great ancestor,
    Did from the flames of Troy upon his shoulder
    The old Anchises bear, so from the waves of Tiber
    Did I the tired Caesar. And this man
    Is now become a god, and Cassius is
25 A wretched creature and must bend his body,
    If Caesar carelessly but nod on him.
    He had a fever when he was in Spain,
    And when the fit was on him, I did mark
    How he did shake: 'tis true, this god did shake;
30 His coward lips did from their colour fly,
    And that same eye whose bend° doth awe the world   glance
    Did lose his lustre: I did hear him groan:
    Ay, and that tongue of his that bade the Romans
    Mark him and write his speeches in their books,
35 Alas, it cried 'Give me some drink, Titinius,'
    As a sick girl. Ye gods, it doth amaze me
    A man of such a feeble temper should
    So get the start of° the majestic world   advantage of
    And bear the palm° alone.   be victorious

---

² **Tiber:** River that flows through Rome.
³ **Aeneas:** Legendary Trojan warrior who carried his father, Anchises, from the burning ruins of Troy.

WILLIAM SHAKESPEARE (1564–1616)

from Richard II
Act II, Scene 1 (John of Gaunt) (1597)

This royal throne of kings, this scepter'd isle,
This earth of majesty, this seat of Mars,[1]
This other Eden, demi-paradise,
This fortress built by Nature for herself
5 Against infection and the hand of war,
This happy breed of men, this little world,
This precious stone set in the silver sea,
Which serves it in the office° of a wall,   function
Or as a moat defensive to a house,
10 Against the envy of less happier lands,
This blessed plot, this earth, this realm, this England,
This nurse, this teeming womb of royal kings,
Fear'd by their breed° and famous by their birth,   inherited glory
Renowned for their deeds as far from home,
15 For Christian service and true chivalry,
As is the sepulchre in stubborn Jewry,[2]
Of the world's ransom, blessed Mary's Son,
This land of such dear souls, this dear dear land,
Dear for her reputation through the world,
20 Is now leased out, I die pronouncing it,
Like to a tenement or pelting° farm: worthless
England, bound in with the triumphant sea
Whose rocky shore beats back the envious siege
Of watery Neptune,[3] is now bound in with shame,
25 With inky blots and rotten parchment bonds:
That England, that was wont to conquer others,
Hath made a shameful conquest of itself.
Ah, would the scandal vanish with my life,
How happy then were my ensuing death!

---

[1] **Mars:** The Roman god of war.
[2] **in stubborn Jewry:** Judea was resistant to Christianity.
[3] **Neptune:** Roman god of the sea.

MARY SIDNEY, COUNTESS OF PEMBROKE
(1568–1621)

To the Thrice-Sacred Queen Elizabeth[1]
(1599; 1962)

1

Even now that care,° which on thy crown attends   responsibility
And with thy happy greatness daily grows,
Tells me, thrice-sacred Queen, my muse[2] offends,
And of respect to thee the line out goes.
5   One instant will or willing can she lose
I say not reading, but receiving rhymes,
On whom in chief dependeth to dispose°   settle
What Europe acts in these most active times?

2

Yet dare I so, as humbleness may dare,
10   Cherish some hope they° shall acceptance find;   the poems
Not weighing less thy state, lighter thy care,
But knowing more thy grace, abler thy mind.
What heavenly powers thee highest throne assigned,
Assigned thee goodness suiting that degree,
15   And by thy strength thy burthen so defined,
To others toil, is exercise to thee.

3

Cares, though still° great, cannot be greatest still,   constantly
Business must ebb, though leisure never flow;
Then these the posts[3] of duty and goodwill
20   Shall press° to offer what their senders owe,   hurry
Which once in two, now in one subject go,[4]
The poorer left, the richer reft° away,   heisted
Who better might (O might, ah word of woe)
Have given for me what I for him defray.°   pay

---

[1] **To the Thrice-Sacred Queen Elizabeth:** The poem was originally attached to a translation of the Psalms, a joint effort of Mary Sidney and her brother Philip.
[2] **my muse:** In Greek mythology, the Muses were the nine daughters of Zeus responsible for artistic inspiration.
[3] **posts:** Letters. Here Sidney refers to the poems that transmit the poet's "duty" and "goodwill."
[4] **Which . . . go:** Sir Philip Sidney wrote the translation of the first forty-three psalms. After his death, Mary completed the remaining translations.

4

25 How can I name whom sighing signs extend,
And not unstop my tears' eternal spring?
But he did warp, I weaved this web to end;[5]
The stuff not ours, our work no curious thing,
Wherein yet well we thought the Psalmist King[6]
30 Now English denizened, though Hebrew born,
Would to thy music undispleasèd sing,
Oft having worse, without repining,° worn;   complaining

5

And I the cloth° in both our names present,   poems
A livery robe[7] to be bestowed by thee;
35 Small parcel of that undischargèd° rent,   unpaid
From which nor pains nor payments can us free.
And yet enough to cause our neighbors see
We will° our best, though scanted° in our will;   want to do / limited
And those nigh° fields where sown thy favors be   neighboring
40 Unwealthy do, not else unworthy, till.

6

For in our work what bring we but thine own?
What English is, by many names is thine,
There humble laurels[8] in thy shadows grown
To garland others would themselves repine.
45 Thy breast the cabinet,° thy seat° the shrine,   room / throne
Where muses hang their vowèd° memories;   sacred
Where wit,° where art, where all that is divine   intelligence
Conceivèd best, and best defended lies.

7

Which if men did not (as they do) confess,
50 And wronging worlds would otherwise consent,
Yet here who minds so meet° a patroness   suitable
For authors' state° or writings' argument?   finances
A King should only to a Queen be sent;

---

[5] **But . . . end:** To completion; in weaving, the warp threads are set horizontally, and the woof threads
are woven crosswise through them.
[6] **Psalmist King:** King David, author of the Psalms.
[7] **livery robe:** A suit of clothes given by a noble to his servants. Here Sidney suggests that the Queen
will award her a livery robe to recognize that the poet is, in a sense, one of her servants.
[8] **laurels:** In ancient times, crowns of laurels were awarded as recognition of poetic accomplishment.

God's lovèd choice unto his chosen love;
55 Devotion to devotion's president;[9]
What all applaud, to her whom none reprove.

8

And who sees ought, but sees how justly square°   fit
His haughty ditties° to thy glorious days?   songs
How well beseeming° thee his triumphs are?   resembling
60 His hope, his zeal, his prayer, plaint, and praise,
Needless thy person to their height to raise;
Less need to bend them down to thy degree;
These holy garments° each good soul assays,°   psalms / tries on
Some sorting all, all sort to none but thee.

9

65 For even thy rule is painted° in his reign;   represented
Both clear in right; both nigh° by wrong oppressed;[10]   almost
And each at length (man crossing God in vain)
Possessed of place, and each in peace possessed.
Proud Philistines did interrupt his rest,
70 The foes of heaven no less have been thy foes;[11]
He with great conquest, thou with greater blessed;
Thou sure to win, and he secure to lose.

10

Thus hand in hand with him thy glories walk;
But who can trace them where alone they go?
75 Of thee two hemispheres on honor talk,
And lands and seas thy trophies jointly show.
The very winds did on thy party blow,
And rocks in arms thy foemen eft defy.[12]
But soft my muse, thy pitch° is earthly low;   rank
80 Forbear° this heaven where only eagles fly.   avoid

---

[9] **A King . . . president:** Lines 53–56 link King David with Queen Elizabeth.
[10] **oppressed:** Defeated (rather than its modern meaning). King David's succession to the throne of Israel was impeded by Saul, who attempted to have David murdered. Elizabeth's claim to the throne was disputed because of the uncertain legality of Henry VIII's second marriage to Anne Boleyn, Elizabeth's mother.
[11] **thy foes:** The Spanish, who were enemies of Elizabeth in the same way the Philistines were enemies of King David.
[12] **The very . . . defy:** Favorable winds assured the British victory over the Spanish Armada in 1588. The Spanish fleet suffered additional losses when storms knocked their ships against the western coast of Ireland.

11

Kings on a Queen enforced their states to lay;
Mainlands for empire waiting on an isle;
Men drawn by worth a woman to obey;
One moving all, herself unmoved the while;
85   Truth's restitution, vanity exile,[13]
Wealth sprung of want, war held without annoy,
Let subject be of some inspired style,
Till then the object of her subjects' joy.

12

Thy utmost can but offer to her sight
90   Her handmaids' task, which most her will endears,
And pray unto thy pains life from that light
Which lively lightsome,° court and kingdom cheers,   bright
What° wish she may (far past her living peers   who
And rival still to Judah's faithful king)
95   In more than he and more triumphant years,
Sing what God doth, and do what men may sing.

ANNE DOWRICHE (1589–1596)

from The French Historie   (1589)

So him at first *De Nance*[1] commanded was to kill;
But he most stoutlie did refuse this guiltlesse blood to spill.
    "Shall I, said he, consent to doo this fearfull thing
"To shed this blood, because I am commanded by the King?
5   "No, God forbid, I know I have a soule to save;
"So bloodie spot, to save my life my name shall never have.
"I know there is a day, a day that Saints desire;
"When of our deeds the king above a reckoning will require.
"*Obaie the King*; that's true, in things that honest be:
10   "When I obey in wicked hests,° wo worth the time to me. . . .   commands
"A murder to be done the King doth now request,
"My God commands the contrary: now which to chuse wer best?
"The King doth threaten death, and God doth threaten hell,
"If for the King I should forsake my God, should I doo well?

---

[13] **vanity exile:** Elizabeth restored the Protestant faith to England after the rule of Mary Tudor, a
Catholic. "Vanity exile," then, might refer to the banishment of lavish Catholic rituals.
[1] **De Nance:** Someone from a town in France.

JOHN MILTON   (1608–1674)

To the Lord General Cromwell   (1652; 1694)

Cromwell,[1] our chief of men, who through a cloud
   Not of war only, but detractions rude,
   Guided by faith and matchless fortitude
   To peace and truth thy glorious way hast ploughed,[2]
5   And on the neck of crowned fortune proud[3]
   Hast reared God's trophies and his work pursued,
   While Darwen stream with blood of Scots imbrued,
   And Dunbar field resounds thy praises loud.
And Worcester's laureate wreath; yet much remains
10   To conquer still; peace hath her victories
   No less renowned than war, new foes arise
Threatened to bind our souls with secular chains:
   Help us to save free conscience from the paw
   Of hireling wolves whose gospel is their maw.

KATHERINE FOWLER PHILIPS   (1632–1664)

On the 3. of *September,* 1651[1]   (1651)

As when the glorious Magazine of Light
Approches to his Canopy of Night,
He with new splendour clothes his dying Rays,
And double brightness to his Beams conveys;
5   And (as to brave and check his ending fate)
Puts on his highest looks in's lowest state,
Drest in such terrour as to make us all
Be *Anti-Persians,* and adore his Fall;
Then quits the world depriving it of Day,
10   While every Herb and Plant does droop away:
So when our gasping *English* Royalty
Perceiv'd her Period was now drawing nigh,
She summons her whole strength to give one blow,

---

[1] **Cromwell:** Oliver Cromwell (1588–1658), English general and statesman who led the parliamentary forces during the English Civil War.
[2] **To peace . . . ploughed:** In 1651, Parliament issued a coin inscribed with the words "Truth and Peace," to show confidence in Cromwell's victories over the Scots at "Darwen," "Dunbar," and "Worcester."
[3] **neck . . . proud:** In 1649, Charles I was beheaded.
[1] **3. of September, 1651:** Date of the Battle of Worcester, where Charles II was defeated and forced into exile.

To raise her self, or pull down others too.
15   Big with revenge and hope she now spake more
Of terror than in many months before;
And musters her Attendants, or to save
Her from, or else attend her to, the Grave:
Yet but enjoy'd the miserable fate
20   Of setting Majesty, to die in State.
Unhappy Kings, who cannot keep a Throne,
Nor be so fortunate to fall alone!
Their weight sinks others: *Pompey*[2] could not fly,
But half the World must bear him company;
25   And captiv'd *Sampson*[3] could not life conclude,
Unless attended with a multitude.
Who'd trust to Greatness now, whose food is air,
Whose ruine sudden, and whose end despair?
Who would presume upon his Glorious Birth,
30   Or quarrel for a spacious share of Earth,
That sees such Diadems become so cheap,
And Heros tumble in a common heap?
Oh give me Vertue then, which sums up all,
And firmly stands when Crowns and Scepters fall.

ANONYMOUS

The Character of a Roundhead[1]   (1641)

What creature's this with his short hairs,
His little band and huge long ears,
   That this new faith hath founded?
The Puritans were never such,
5   The Saints themselves had ne'er so much;
   Oh, such a knave's a roundhead.

What's he that doth the bishops hate,
And count their calling reprobate,
   'Cause by the Pope propounded,
10   And says a zealous cobbler's better
Than he that studieth every letter?
   Oh, such a knave's a roundhead.

---

[2] **Pompey**: Pompey (106 B.C.–48 B.C.), Roman general defeated by Caesar and exiled to Egypt, where he was later murdered.
[3] **Sampson**: Old Testament Judge of Israel who was betrayed to the Philistines by his mistress Delilah.
[1] **Roundhead**: A Puritan supporter of Oliver Cromwell (1588–1658) during the English Civil War.

What's he that doth high treason say,
As often as his yea and nay,
15   And wish the king confounded,
And dare maintain that Master Pym[2]
Is fitter for the crown than him?
     Oh, such a rogue's a roundhead.

What's he that if he chance to hear
20   A piece of London's Common-Prayer,
     Doth think his conscience wounded;
And goes five miles to preach and pray,
And lies with's sister by the way?
     Oh, such a rogue's a roundhead.

25   What's he that met a holy sister,
And in a haycock gently kissed her?
     Oh! then his zeal abounded:
Close underneath a shady willow,
Her bible served her for her pillow,
30   And there they got a roundhead.

JONATHAN SWIFT (1667–1745)

The Character of Sir Robert Walpole[1] (1731; 1789)

With favour and fortune fastidiously° blest,   proudly
He's loud in his laugh and he's coarse in his Jest;
Of favour and fortune unmerited vain,
A sharper in trifles, a dupe in the main.
5   Achieving of nothing, still promising wonders,
By dint of experience improving in Blunders;
Oppressing true merit, exalting the base,
And selling his Country to purchase his peace.
A Jobber of Stocks by retailing false news,
10   A prater at Court in the Stile of the Stews;
Of Virtue and worth by profession a giber,[2]

---

[2] **Master Pym:** John Pym (ca. 1583–1643), prominent leader of Parliament during the English Civil War.
[1] **Sir Robert Walpole:** Robert Walpole (1676–1745), Chancellor of the Exchequer and effective prime minister from 1721 to 1742. Swift's primary antagonist, Walpole, is portrayed in Swift's work as an incompetent manipulator of men and money.
[2] **A Jobber of Stocks . . . giber:** In each of these cases Walpole's character is attacked. He is a false reporter of stock values, working as a "jobber" or intermediary between buyers and sellers at the Stock Exchange. The "Stile of the Stews" is the language of the brothels. A giber is a fellow who makes gibes or taunts.

Of Juries and senates the bully and briber.
Tho' I name not the wretch you know who I mean,
T'is the Cur dog of Britain and spaniel of Spain.[3]

JONATHAN SWIFT (1667–1745)

Prometheus (1724)

On Wood[1] the Patentee's Irish Halfpence

As, when the squire and tinker, Wood,
Gravely consulting Ireland's good,
Together mingled in a mass
Smith's dust, and copper, lead and brass;
5   The mixture thus by chemic art,
United close in every part,
In fillets rolled, or cut in pieces,
Appeared like one continuous species,
And by the forming engine struck,
10   On all the same *impression* stuck.

   So, to confound this hated coin,
All parties and religions join;
Whigs, Tories, trimmers, Hanoverians,
Quakers, conformists, presbyterians,
15   Scotch, Irish, English, French unite
With equal interest, equal spite,
Together mingled in a lump,
Do all in one opinion jump;
And everyone begins to find
20   The same impression on his *mind*.

   A strange event! whom gold incites,
To blood and quarrels, brass unites:
So goldsmiths say, the coarsest stuff
Will serve for solder well enough;
25   So, by the kettle's loud alarm,
The bees are gathered to a swarm:
So by the brazen trumpet's bluster,

---

[3] **T'is . . . Spain:** Swift suggests that Walpole is the lapdog of England and too soft on Spain.
[1] **Wood:** William Wood (1671–1730), Irish ironmaster who received a patent to coin Irish halfpence from Robert Walpole's government in 1722. Wood received the patent by bribing court officials.

Troops of all tongues and nations muster:
And so the harp of Ireland brings,
30   Whole crowds about its brazen strings.

There is a chain let down from Jove,[2]
But fastened to his throne above;
So strong, that from the lower end,
They say, all human things depend:
35   This chain, as ancient poets hold,
When Jove was young, was made of gold.
Prometheus[3] once this chain purloined,
Dissolved, and into money coined;
Then whips me on a chain of brass,
40   (Venus[4] was bribed to let it pass.)

Now while this brazen chain prevailed,
Jove saw that all devotion failed;
No temple to his godship raised;
No sacrifice on altars blazed:
45   In short, such dire confusions followed,
Earth must have been in chaos swallowed.
Jove stood amazed, but looking round,
With much ado the cheat he found;
'Twas plain he could no longer hold
50   The world in any chain but gold;
And to the god of wealth his brother,
Sent Mercury[5] to get another.

Prometheus on a rock was laid,
Tied with the chain himself had made;
55   On icy Caucasus[6] to shiver,
While vultures eat his growing liver.

Ye powers of Grub Street,[7] make me able,
Discreetly to apply this fable.
Say, who is to be understood
60   By that old thief Prometheus? Wood.
For Jove, it is not hard to guess him,

---

[2] **Jove:** In classical mythology, ruler of the Roman gods.
[3] **Prometheus:** Titan who stole the sacred fire from Zeus and the gods. As punishment, he was tied to a rock, where an eagle gnawed on his liver, until Hercules killed the eagle.
[4] **Venus:** The Roman goddess of love.
[5] **Mercury:** In classical mythology, a messenger of the gods.
[6] **Caucasus:** Range of mountains between the Black and Caspian seas.
[7] **Grub Street:** World of literary hacks.

I mean His Majesty, God bless him.
This thief and blacksmith was so bold,
He strove to steal that chain of gold,
65   Which links the subject to the king:
And change it for a brazen string.
But sure, if nothing else must pass
Between the King and us but brass,
Although the chain will never crack,
70   Yet our devotion may grow slack.

But Jove will soon convert I hope,
This brazen chain into a rope;
With which Prometheus shall be tied,
And high in air for ever ride;
75   Where, if we find his liver grows,
For want of vultures, we have crows.

JAMES THOMSON (1700–1748)

Rule, Britannia (1740)

When Britain first, at heaven's command,
    Arose from out the azure main,
This was the charter of the land,
    And guardian angels sung this strain—
5   'Rule, Britannia, rule the waves;
        Britons never will be slaves.'

The nations, not so blest as thee,
    Must in their turns to tyrants fall;
While thou shalt flourish great and free,
10   The dread and envy of them all.
            'Rule,' &c.

Still more majestic shalt thou rise,
    More dreadful from each foreign stroke;
As the loud blast that tears the skies
15   Serves but to root thy native oak.
            'Rule,' &c.

Thee haughty tyrants ne'er shall tame;
    All their attempts to bend thee down
Will but arouse thy generous flame,

20   But work their woe and thy renown.
      'Rule,' &c.

To thee belongs the rural reign;
    Thy cities shall with commerce shine;
All thine shall be the subject main,
25   And every shore it circles thine.
      'Rule,' &c.

The Muses, still with freedom found,
    Shall to thy happy coast repair:
Blest isle! with matchless beauty crowned,
30   And manly hearts to guard the fair.
      'Rule, Britannia, rule the waves;
      Britons never will be slaves.'

ANNA LAETITIA AIKIN BARBAULD (1743–1825)

The Rights of Woman (ca. 1795; 1825)

Yes, injured Woman! rise, assert thy right!
Woman! too long degraded, scorned, oppressed;
O born to rule in partial Law's despite,
Resume thy native empire o'er the breast!

5   Go forth arrayed in panoply divine,
That angel pureness which admits no stain;
Go, bid proud Man his boasted rule resign
And kiss the golden sceptre of thy reign.

Go, gird thyself with grace, collect thy store
10   Of bright artillery glancing from afar;
Soft melting tones thy thundering cannon's roar,
Blushes and fears thy magazine of war.

Thy rights are empire; urge no meaner claim,—
Felt, not defined, and if debated, lost;
15   Like sacred mysteries, which withheld from fame,
Shunning discussion, are revered the most.

Try all that wit and art suggest to bend
Of thy imperial foe the stubborn knee;
Make treacherous Man thy subject, not thy friend;
20   Thou mayst command, but never canst be free.

Awe the licentious and restrain the rude;
Soften the sullen, clear the cloudy brow:
Be, more than princes' gifts, thy favours sued;—
She hazards all, who will the least allow.

25 But hope not, courted idol of mankind,
On this proud eminence secure to stay;
Subduing and subdued, thou soon shalt find
Thy coldness soften, and thy pride give way.

Then, then, abandon each ambitious thought;
30 Conquest or rule thy heart shall feebly move,
In Nature's school, by her soft maxims taught
That separate rights are lost in mutual love.

WILLIAM BLAKE (1757–1827)

And Did Those Feet (1804; ca. 1808)

And did those feet in ancient time
Walk upon England's mountains green?
And was the holy Lamb of God
On England's pleasant pastures seen?

5 And did the Countenance Divine
Shine forth upon our clouded hills?
And was Jerusalem builded here
Among these dark satanic mills?

Bring me my bow of burning gold!
10 Bring me my arrows of desire!
Bring me my spear—oh clouds unfold!
Bring me my chariot of fire!

I will not cease from mental fight,
Nor shall my sword sleep in my hand,
15 Till we have built Jerusalem,
In England's green and pleasant land.

RALPH WALDO EMERSON   (1803–1882)

Concord Hymn   (1876)

Sung at the Completion of the Battle Monument,[1] *July 4, 1837*

By the rude bridge that arched the flood,
    Their flag to April's breeze unfurled,
Here once the embattled farmers stood
    And fired the shot heard round the world.

5   The foe long since in silence slept;
    Alike the conqueror silent sleeps;
And Time the ruined bridge has swept
    Down the dark stream which seaward creeps.

On this green bank, by this soft stream,
10   We set to-day a votive stone;
That memory may their deed redeem,
    When, like our sires, our sons are gone.

Spirit, that made those heroes dare
    To die, and leave their children free,
15   Bid Time and Nature gently spare
    The shaft we raise to them and thee.

ARTHUR HUGH CLOUGH   (1819–1861)

from Amours De Voyage   (1849; 1858)

(Canto II; 2)

Claude to Eustace

Dulce it is, and *decorum*,[1] no doubt, for the country to fall,—to
Offer one's blood an oblation to Freedom, and die for the Cause; yet
Still, individual culture is also something, and no man
Finds quite distinct the assurance that he of all others is called on,
5   Or would be justified, even, in taking away from the world that

---

[1] **Battle Monument:** Built to commemorate the battles of Lexington and Concord, the first battles of the American Revolutionary War.
[1] **Dulce it is, and decorum:** From the Latin phrase, *"Dulce et decorum est pro patria mori"*—"It is sweet and fitting to die for one's country."

Precious creature, himself. Nature sent him here to abide here,
Else why sent him at all? Nature wants him still, it is likely.
On the whole, we are meant to look after ourselves; it is certain
Each has to eat for himself, digest for himself, and in general
10   Care for his own dear life, and see to his own preservation;
Nature's intentions, in most things uncertain, in this are decisive;
Which, on the whole, I conjecture the Romans will follow, and I shall.
      So we cling to our rocks like limpets; Ocean may bluster,
Over and under and round us; we open our shells to imbibe our
15   Nourishment, close them again, and are safe, fulfilling the purpose
Nature intended,—a wise one, of course, and a noble, we doubt not.
Sweet it may be and decorous, perhaps, for the country to die; but,
On the whole, we conclude the Romans won't do it, and I shan't.

RUDYARD KIPLING (1865–1936)

Recessional (1897)

1897[1]

God of our fathers, known of old,
      Lord of our far-flung battle-line,
Beneath whose awful Hand we hold
      Dominion over palm and pine—
5   Lord God of Hosts, be with us yet,
Lest we forget—lest we forget!

The tumult and the shouting dies;
      The Captains and the Kings depart:
Still stands Thine ancient sacrifice,
10   An humble and a contrite heart.
Lord God of Hosts, be with us yet,
Lest we forget—lest we forget!

Far-called, our navies melt away;
      On dune and headland sinks the fire:[2]
15   Lo, all our pomp of yesterday
      Is one with Nineveh and Tyre![3]
Judge of the Nations, spare us yet,
Lest we forget—lest we forget!

---

[1] **1897:** Year of Queen Victoria's Diamond Jubilee, acknowledging the sixtieth year of her reign.
[2] **On dune . . . fire:** On the anniversary of Victoria's accession, bonfires were lit on high elevations throughout the British empire.
[3] **Nineveh and Tyre:** Ancient cities of grandeur that later faded into insignificance.

	If, drunk with sight of power, we loose

20   If, drunk with sight of power, we loose
      Wild tongues that have not Thee in awe,
Such boastings as the Gentiles use,
      Or lesser breeds without the Law—
Lord God of Hosts, be with us yet,
Lest we forget—lest we forget!

25   For heathen heart that puts her trust
      In reeking tube and iron shard,
All valiant dust that builds on dust,
      And guarding, calls not Thee to guard,
For frantic boast and foolish word—
30   Thy mercy on Thy People, Lord!

RUDYARD KIPLING (1865–1936)

The White Man's Burden (1899)

1899
(The United States and the
Philippine Islands)[1]

Take up the White Man's burden—
      Send forth the best ye breed—
Go bind your sons to exile
      To serve your captives' need;
5   To wait in heavy harness
      On fluttered folk and wild—
Your new-caught, sullen peoples,
      Half devil and half child.

Take up the White Man's Burden—
10   In patience to abide,
To veil the threat of terror
      And check the show of pride;
By open speech and simple,
      An hundred times made plain,
15   To seek another's profit,
      And work another's gain.

Take up the White Man's burden—
      The savage wars of peace—

---

[1] **The United . . . Islands:** Kipling wrote the poem in 1899 as an appeal to the United States to develop the Philippine Islands, recently acquired following the Spanish-American war.

Fill full the mouth of Famine
20   And bid the sickness cease;
And when your goal is nearest
        The end for others sought,
Watch Sloth and heathen Folly
        Bring all your hope to nought.

25   Take up the White Man's burden—
        No tawdry rule of kings,
But toil of serf and sweeper—
        The tale of common things.
The ports ye shall not enter,
30   The roads ye shall not tread,
Go make them with your living,
        And mark them with your dead!

Take up the White Man's burden—
        And reap his old reward:
35   The blame of those ye better,
        The hate of those ye guard—
The cry of hosts ye humour
        (Ah, slowly!) toward the light:—
'Why brought ye us from bondage,
40   Our loved Egyptian night?'

Take up the White Man's burden—
        Ye dare not stoop to less—
Nor call too loud on Freedom
        To cloak your weariness;
45   By all ye cry or whisper,
        By all ye leave or do,
The silent, sullen peoples
        Shall weigh your Gods and you.

Take up the White Man's burden—
50   Have done with childish days—
The lightly proffered laurel,[2]
        The easy, ungrudged praise,
Comes now, to search your manhood
        Through all the thankless years,
55   Cold-edged with dear-bought wisdom,
        The judgment of your peers!

---

[2] **laurel:** A traditional symbol of victory.

WILLIAM BUTLER YEATS (1865–1939)

Easter 1916[1] (1916)

I have met them at close of day
Coming with vivid faces
From counter or desk among grey
Eighteenth-century houses.
5   I have passed with a nod of the head
Or polite meaningless words,
Or have lingered awhile and said
Polite meaningless words,
And thought before I had done
10   Of a mocking tale or a gibe
To please a companion
Around the fire at the club,
Being certain that they and I
But lived where motley is worn:
15   All changed, changed utterly:
A terrible beauty is born.

That woman's days were spent
In ignorant good-will,
Her nights in argument
20   Until her voice grew shrill.
What voice more sweet than hers
When, young and beautiful,
She rode to harriers?[2]
This man had kept a school
25   And rode our wingèd horse;[3]
This other[4] his helper and friend
Was coming into his force;
He might have won fame in the end,
So sensitive his nature seemed,
30   So daring and sweet his thought.
This other man I had dreamed
A drunken, vainglorious lout.[5]
He had done most bitter wrong

---

[1] **Easter 1916:** An Irish Nationalist uprising began on Easter Sunday, 1916, in Dublin, despite attempts by the British to thwart the event.
[2] **She rode to harriers:** Countess Markiewicz, nee Constance Gore-Booth (1868–1927) played a key role in the Easter rebellion.
[3] **This man . . . horse:** Patrick Pearse (1879–1916), Irish writer and headmaster of St. Edna's School. The "winged horse" is Pegasus, a symbol of poetic inspiration.
[4] **This other:** Thomas MacDonagh (1878–1916), a school-teacher.
[5] **This other . . . lout:** Major John MacBride, the husband of Maud Gonne, Yeats's life-long, hopeless love.

To some who are near my heart,
35   Yet I number him in the song;
He, too, has resigned his part
In the casual comedy;
He, too, has been changed in his turn,
Transformed utterly:
40   A terrible beauty is born.

Hearts with one purpose alone
Through summer and winter seem
Enchanted to a stone
To trouble the living stream.
45   The horse that comes from the road,
The rider, the birds that range
From cloud to tumbling cloud,
Minute by minute they change;
A shadow of cloud on the stream
50   Changes minute by minute;
A horse-hoof slides on the brim,
And a horse plashes within it;
The long-legged moor-hens dive,
And hens to moor-cocks call;
55   Minute by minute, they live:
The stone's in the midst of all.

Too long a sacrifice
Can make a stone of the heart.
O when may it suffice?
60   That is Heaven's part, our part
To murmur name upon name,
As a mother names her child
When sleep at last has come
On limbs that had run wild.
65   What is it but nightfall?
No, no, not night but death;
Was it needless death after all?
For England may keep faith
For all that is done and said.
70   We know their dream; enough
To know they dreamed and are dead;
And what if excess of love
Bewildered them till they died?
I write it out in a verse—
75   MacDonagh and MacBride
And Connolly and Pearse
Now and in time to be,

Wherever green is worn,
Are changed, changed utterly:
80   A terrible beauty is born.

ROBERT FROST   (1874–1963)

The Gift Outright   (1942)

The land was ours before we were the land's.
She was our land more than a hundred years
Before we were her people. She was ours
In Massachusetts, in Virginia,
5   But we were England's, still colonials,
Possessing what we still were unpossessed by,
Possessed by what we now no more possessed.
Something we were withholding made us weak
Until we found out that it was ourselves
10   We were withholding from our land of living,
And forthwith found salvation in surrender.
Such as we were we gave ourselves outright
(The deed of gift was many deeds of war)
To the land vaguely realizing westward,
15   But still unstoried, artless, unenhanced,
Such as she was, such as she would become.

ROBINSON JEFFERS   (1887–1962)

Shine, Perishing Republic   (1924)

While this America settles in the mold of its vulgarity, heavily
            thickening to empire,
And protest, only a bubble in the molten mass, pops and sighs out,
            and the mass hardens,
I sadly smiling remember that the flower fades to make fruit, the
            fruit rots to make earth.
out of the mother; and through the spring exultances, ripeness and
            decadence; and home to the mother.
5   You making haste haste on decay: not blameworthy; life is good,
            be it stubbornly long or suddenly
A mortal splendor: meteors are not needed less than mountains:
            shine, perishing republic.

But for my children, I would have them keep their distance from
      the thickening center; corruption
Never has been compulsory, when the cities lie at the monster's
      feet there are left the mountains.

And boys, be in nothing so moderate as in love of man, a clever
      servant, insufferable master.
10   There is the trap that catches noblest spirits, that caught—they
      say—God, when he walked on earth.

CLAUDE McKAY (1889–1948)

America (1921)

Although she feeds me bread of bitterness,
And sinks into my throat her tiger's tooth,
Stealing my breath of life, I will confess
I love this cultured hell that tests my youth!
5   Her vigor flows like tides into my blood,
Giving me strength erect against her hate.
Her bigness sweeps my being like a flood.
Yet as a rebel fronts a king in state,
I stand within her walls with not a shred
10 Of terror, malice, not a word of jeer.
Darkly I gaze into the days ahead,
And see her might and granite wonders there,
Beneath the touch of Time's unerring hand,
Like priceless treasures sinking in the sand.

E. E. CUMMINGS (1894–1962)

"next to of course god america i" (1926)

"next to of course god america i
love you land of the pilgrims' and so forth oh
say can you see by the dawn's early my
country 'tis of centuries come and go
5   and are no more what of it we should worry
in every language even deafanddumb

thy sons acclaim your glorious name by gorry
by jingo by gee by gosh by gum
why talk of beauty what could be more beaut-
10   iful than these heroic happy dead
who rushed like lions to the roaring slaughter
they did not stop to think they died instead
then shall the voice of liberty be mute?"

He spoke.   And drank rapidly a glass of water

LANGSTON HUGHES (1902–1967)

Harlem   (1951)

What happens to a dream deferred?

Does it dry up
like a raisin in the sun?
Or fester like a sore—
5   And then run?
Does it stink like rotten meat?
Or crust and sugar over—
like a syrupy sweet?

Maybe it just sags
10   like a heavy load.

Or does it explode?

W. H. AUDEN (1907–1973)

Epitaph on a Tyrant   (1939)

Perfection, of a kind, was what he was after,
And the poetry he invented was easy to understand;
He knew human folly like the back of his hand,
And was greatly interested in armies and fleets;
5   When he laughed, respectable senators burst with laughter,
And when he cried the little children died in the streets.

MURIEL RUKEYSER (1913–1980)

Poem (1968)

I lived in the first century of world wars.
Most mornings I would be more or less insane,
The newspapers would arrive with their careless stories,
The news would pour out of various devices
5 Interrupted by attempts to sell products to the unseen.
I would call my friends on other devices;
They would be more or less mad for similar reasons.
Slowly I would get to pen and paper,
Make my poems for others unseen and unborn.

10 In the day I would be reminded of those men and women
Brave, setting up signals across vast distances,
Considering a nameless way of living, of almost unimagined values.
As the lights darkened, as the lights of night brightened,
We would try to imagine them, try to find each other.
15 To construct peace, to make love, to reconcile
Waking with sleeping, ourselves with each other,
Ourselves with ourselves. We would try by any means
To reach the limits of ourselves, to reach beyond ourselves,
To let go the means, to wake.

20 I lived in the first century of these wars.

JOHN BERRYMAN (1914–1972)

The Soviet Union (1970)

There was that business in Siberia, in '19.
That was disgusting.
My God if John Adams[1] had foreseen that
he would have renounced his immortality.

5 It was despicable.   My friends, forgive us.
It was done by our fearful invasive fathers.
I have a Russian image: in the Crimea,[2] a train is stalled:

---

[1] **John Adams:** John Adams (1735–1826), second president of the United States.
[2] **Crimea:** Ukrainian peninsula between the Black Sea and the Sea of Azov.

She's in labour, lanterns are swinging,
they couldn't help her.   She hemorrhaged, among the peasants,

10   grimaced; & went away.
And Nikolay struck down in the advance
seeing the others going on

thought Am I wounded? Maybe I will die!
ME, Nikolay Rostov, whom everybody *loved* so?

15   You murdered Babel,
we murdered Martin Luther King;[3] redskins, blacks.
You have given a bitter time to Jews.
Maybe one of our Negroes was a Babel.

Trotsky[4] struggled: over the railway system
20   and which troops were when to be where.
When he addressed the Petrograd[5] Soviet
their vascular systems ran vodka.

Lenin wrote: Stalin is a boor,[6]
& should not continue as Secretary.
25   Lenin, that great man, dying off there,
with only her (that great woman) to talk to.

Stalin was mad at midnight: & criminal. But that Georgian had high
                even heroic qualities,
He stayed you through the horrible advance
of the German divisions.   He had faith.
30   Smolensk; & then in the South.

An Odessa Jew, a bespectacled intellectual small man,
who rode with the revolutionary Cossacks,[7]
was murdered in one of your prisons or your camps.
Man is vicious.   We forgive you.

---

[3] **Babel . . . Martin Luther King:** In Genesis, a tower built by Noah's descendants with the aspiration
to reach heaven; God confused their languages to teach them humility. Martin Luther King, Jr.
(1929–1968), a United States civil rights leader.
[4] **Trotsky:** Leon Trotsky (1879–1940), Russian revolutionist and Communist theorist. He was ousted
from the Communist Party by Stalin, and later assassinated in Mexico.
[5] **Petrograd:** Second largest city in Russia. Smolensk and Odessa were cities in the Soviet Union as well.
[6] **Lenin wrote: Stalin is a boor:** Lenin and Stalin, the first leaders of the Communist Soviet Union.
[7] **Cossacks:** An elite cavalry corps in Czarist Russia.

MARGARET WALKER (1915–1998)

For My People (1942)

For my people everywhere singing their slave songs repeatedly:
    their dirges and their ditties and their blues and jubilees, pray-
    ing their prayers nightly to an unknown god, bending their
    knees humbly to an unseen power;

5   For my people lending their strength to the years, to the gone years
    and the now years and the maybe years, washing ironing cook-
    ing scrubbing sewing mending hoeing plowing digging planting
    pruning patching dragging along never gaining never reaping
    never knowing and never understanding;

10   For my playmates in the clay and dust and sand of Alabama back-
    yards playing baptizing and preaching and doctor and jail and
    soldier and school and mama and cooking and playhouse and
    concert and store and hair and Miss Choomby and company;

For the cramped bewildered years we went to school to learn to
15   know the reasons why and the answers to and the people who
    and the places where and the days when, in memory of the
    bitter hours when we discovered we were black and poor and
    small and different and nobody cared and nobody wondered
    and nobody understood;

20   For the boys and girls who grew in spite of these things to be man
    and woman, to laugh and dance and sing and play and drink
    their wine and religion and success, to marry their playmates
    and bear children and then die of consumption and anemia
    and lynching;

25   For my people thronging 47th Street in Chicago and Lenox Avenue
    in New York and Rampart Street in New Orleans, lost disin-
    herited dispossessed and happy people filling the cabarets
    and taverns and other people's pockets needing bread and
    shoes and milk and land and money and something—some-
30   thing all our own;

For my people walking blindly spreading joy, losing time being lazy,
    sleeping when hungry, shouting when burdened, drinking
    when hopeless, tied and shackled and tangled among our-
    selves by the unseen creatures who tower over us omnisciently
35   and laugh;

For my people blundering and groping and floundering in the dark
of churches and schools and clubs and societies, associations
and councils and committees and conventions, distressed
and disturbed and deceived and devoured by money-hungry
40   glory-craving leeches, preyed on by facile force of state and
fad and novelty, by false prophet and holy believer;

For my people standing staring trying to fashion a better way from
confusion, from hypocrisy and misunderstanding, trying to
fashion a world that will hold all the people, all the faces, all
45   the adams and eves and their countless generations;

Let a new earth rise. Let another world be born. Let a bloody peace
be written in the sky. Let a second generation full of courage
issue forth; let a people loving freedom come to growth. Let a
beauty full of healing and a strength of final clenching be the
50   pulsing in our spirits and our blood. Let the martial songs be
written, let the dirges disappear. Let a race of men now rise
and take control.

ROBERT BLY (1926–   )

Romans Angry about the Inner World (1967)

What shall the world do with its children?
There are lives the executives
Know nothing of:
A leaping of the body
5   The body rolling—I have felt it—
And we float
Joyfully toward the dark places.
But the executioners
Move toward Drusia. They tie her legs
10   On the iron horse. "Here is a woman
Who has seen our Mother
In the other world." Next they warm
The hooks. The two Romans had put their trust
In the outer world. Irons glowed
15   Like teeth. They wanted her
To assure them. She refused. Finally
They took burning
Pine sticks, and pushed them
Into her sides. Her breath rose

20   And she died. The executioners
     Rolled her off onto the ground.
     A light snow began to fall from the clear sky
     And covered the mangled body.
     And the executives, astonished, withdrew.
25   The inner world is a thorn
     In the ear of a tiny beast!
     The fingers of the executive are too thick
     To pull it out.
     It is a jagged stone
30   Flying toward us out of the darkness.

ALLEN GINSBERG (1926–1997)

America[1] (1956)

America I've given you all and now I'm nothing.
America two dollars and twentyseven cents January 17, 1956.
I can't stand my own mind.
America when will we end the human war?
5   Go fuck yourself with your atom bomb.
I don't feel good don't bother me.
I won't write my poem till I'm in my right mind.
America when will you be angelic?
When will you take off your clothes?
10   When will you look at yourself through the grave?
When will you be worthy of your million Trotskyites?[2]
America why are your libraries full of tears?
America when will you send your eggs to India?
I'm sick of your insane demands.
15   When can I go into the supermarket and buy what I need with my
         good looks?
America after all it is you and I who are perfect not the next world.
Your machinery is too much for me.
You made me want to be a saint.
There must be some other way to settle this argument.

---

[1] **America:** Published in 1956, shortly after Senator Joseph McCarthy's anti-communist witch-hunts were discredited, Ginsberg's "America" was sent out to an America distrustful of political dissent.
[2] **Trotskyites:** The Trotskyites were aggressive American communists; the Wobblies (line 27) were members of the Industrial Workers of the World, a left-leaning labor organization active during the early twentieth century.

20   Burroughs[3] is in Tangiers I don't think he'll come back it's sinister.
      Are you being sinister or is this some form of practical joke?
      I'm trying to come to the point.
      I refuse to give up my obsession.
      America stop pushing I know what I'm doing.
25   America the plum blossoms are falling.
      I haven't read the newspapers for months, everyday somebody
            goes on trial for murder.
      America I feel sentimental about the Wobblies.
      America I used to be a communist when I was a kid I'm not sorry.
      I smoke marijuana every chance I get.
30   I sit in my house for days on end and stare at the roses in the closet.
      When I go to Chinatown I get drunk and never get laid.
      My mind is made up there's going to be trouble.
      You should have seen me reading Marx.[4]
      My psychoanalyst thinks I'm perfectly right.
35   I won't say the Lord's Prayer.
      I have mystical visions and cosmic vibrations.
      America I still haven't told you what you did to Uncle Max after he
            came over from Russia.

      I'm addressing you.
      Are you going to let your emotional life be run by Time Magazine?
40   I'm obsessed by Time Magazine.
      I read it every week.
      Its cover stares at me every time I slink past the corner candystore.
      I read it in the basement of the Berkeley Public Library.
      It's always telling me about responsibility. Businessmen are serious.
            Movie producers are serious. Everybody's serious but me.
45   It occurs to me that I am America.
      I am talking to myself again.

      Asia is rising against me.
      I haven't got a chinaman's chance.
      I'd better consider my national resources.
50   My national resources consist of two joints of marijuana millions
            of genitals an unpublishable private literature that goes 1400
            miles an hour and twentyfive-thousand mental institutions.
      I say nothing about my prisons nor the millions of underprivileged
            who live in my flowerpots under the light of five hundred suns.

---

[3] **Burroughs:** William Burroughs (1914–1997), a Beat author. Addicted to heroin for over a decade, Burroughs left the United States for Mexico, and later Tangiers, to avoid prosecution.
[4] **Marx:** Karl Marx (1818–1883), founder of modern communism and author, with Frederich Engels, of *The Communist Manifesto* (1848).

I have abolished the whorehouses of France, Tangiers is the next
    to go.
My ambition is to be President despite the fact that I'm a Catholic.[5]
America how can I write a holy litany in your silly mood?
55   I will continue like Henry Ford my strophes° are as individual as   stanzas
    his automobiles more so they're all different sexes.
America I will sell you strophes $2500 apiece $500 down on your
    old strophe
America free Tom Mooney[6]
America save the Spanish Loyalists
America Sacco & Vanzetti must not die
60   America I am the Scottsboro boys.[7]
America when I was seven momma took me to Communist Cell
    meetings they sold us garbanzos a handful per ticket a ticket
    costs a nickel and the speeches were free everybody was
    angelic and sentimental about the workers it was all so
    sincere you have no idea what a good thing the party was in
    1935 Scott Nearing was a grand old man a real mensch
    Mother Bloor made me cry I once saw Israel Amter plain.[8]
    Everybody must have been a spy.
America you don't really want to go to war.
America it's them bad Russians.
Them Russians them Russians and them Chinamen. And them
    Russians.
65   The Russia wants to eat us alive. The Russia's power mad. She wants
    to take our cars from out our garages.
Her wants to grab Chicago. Her needs a Red Readers' Digest. Her
    wants our auto plants in Siberia. Him big bureaucracy
    running our filling-stations.
That no good. Ugh. Him make Indians learn read. Him need big
    black niggers. Hah. Her make us all work sixteen hours a day.
    Help.
America this is quite serious.
America this is the impression I get from looking in the television set.
70   America is this correct?

---

[5] **My ambition . . . Catholic:** Here Ginsberg refers to the Catholic John F. Kennedy's presidential campaign.
[6] **Tom Mooney:** Tom Mooney (1882–1942), a labor organizer imprisoned on perjured evidence that suggested his participation in the bombing of a San Francisco parade. In another labor case, Nicola Sacco and Bartholomeo Vanzetti (line 59) were sentenced to death for the murder of a shoe factory accountant and security guard.
[7] **the Spanish Loyalists . . . Scottsboro boys:** In the 1930s, the American Communist Party generated support for the Spanish Loyalists who fought for the socialist government of Spain against General Francisco Franco's Fascist revolution. The Communist Party also supported the "Scottsboro boys," eight African Americans sentenced to death after an unjust rape trial in Scottsboro, Alabama.
[8] **Scott Nearing . . . plain:** Scott Nearing, an influential socialist economist, left the Communist Party in the 1930s. Ella Reeve Bloor and Israel Amter were leaders of the New York chapter of the Communist Party.

I'd better get right down to the job.
It's true I don't want to join the Army or turn lathes in precision
      parts factories, I'm nearsighted and psychopathic anyway.
America I'm putting my queer shoulder to the wheel.

ADRIENNE RICH (1929–   )

from An Atlas of the Difficult World   (1991)

II

Here is a map of our country:
here is the Sea of Indifference, glazed with salt
This is the haunted river flowing from brow to groin
we dare not taste its water
5   This is the desert where missiles are planted like corms
This is the breadbasket of foreclosed farms
This is the birthplace of the rockabilly boy
This is the cemetery of the poor
who died for democracy   This is a battlefield
10   from a nineteenth-century war   the shrine is famous
This is the sea-town of myth and story   when the fishing fleets
went bankrupt   here is where the jobs were   on the pier
processing frozen fishsticks   hourly wages and no shares
These are other battlefields   Centralia   Detroit[1]
15   here are the forests primeval   the copper   the silver lodes
These are the suburbs of acquiescence   silence rising fumelike
         from the streets
This is the capital of money and dolor whose spires
flare up through air inversions whose bridges are crumbling
whose children are drifting blind alleys pent
20   between coiled rolls of razor wire
I promised to show you a map you say but this is a mural
then yes let it be   these are small distinctions
where do we see it from is the question

IV

Late summers, early autumns, you can see something that binds
the map of this country together: the girasol, orange gold-petalled
with her black eye, laces the roadsides from Vermont to California

---

[1] **Centralia Detroit:** Centralia, a lumber town in Washington State where the Lumberman's Association initiated violence against the left-leaning Industrial Workers of the World in November 1911. Detroit, Michigan, has been frequently visited by racial and labor-related violence.

runs the edges of orchards, chain-link fences
5   milo fields and malls, schoolyards and reservations
truckstops and quarries, grazing ranges, graveyards
of veterans, graveyards of cars hulked and sunk, her tubers the
jerusalem artichoke
that has fed the Indians, fed the hobos, could feed us all.
Is there anything in the soil, cross-country, that makes for
10   a plant so generous?   *Spendthrift* we say, as if
accounting nature's waste.   Ours darkens
the states to their strict borders, flushes
down borderless streams, leaches from lakes to the curdled foam
down by the riverside.

15   Waste.   Waste.   The watcher's eye put out, hands of the builder
severed, brain of the maker starved
those who could bind, join, reweave, cohere, replenish
now at risk in this segregate republic
locked away out of sight and hearing, out of mind, shunted aside
those needed to teach, advise, persuade, weigh arguments
20   those urgently needed for the work of perception
work of the poet, the astronomer, the historian, the architect of new streets
work of the speaker who also listens
meticulous delicate work of reaching the heart of the desperate
woman, the desperate man
—never-to-be-finished, still unbegun work of repair—it cannot be
done without them
25   and where are they now?

XI

One night on Monterey Bay[2] the death-freeze of the century:
a precise, detached calliper-grip holds the stars and the quarter-moon
in arrest: the hardiest plants crouch shrunken, a "killing frost"
on bougainvillea, Pride of Madeira,[3] roseate black-purple succulents bowed
5   juices sucked awry in one orgy of freezing
slumped on their stems like old faces evicted from cheap hotels
—*into the streets of the universe, now!*

Earthquake and drought followed by freezing followed by war.[4]
Flags are blossoming now where little else is blossoming
10   and I am bent on fathoming what it means to love my country.

---

[2] **Monterey Bay:** Inlet of the Pacific Ocean in California.
[3] **Pride of Madeira:** Tropical vine with white blossoms.
[4] **Earthquake . . . war:** After a five-year dry spell, an earthquake struck California on October 17, 1989.
The winter of 1990–1991 witnessed a period of record-breaking freezing weather, and the Gulf War
began in January of 1991.

The history of this earth and the bones within it?
Soils and cities, promises made and mocked, plowed contours of
        shame and of hope?
Loyalties, symbols, murmurs extinguished and echoing?
Grids of states stretching westward, underground waters?
15   Minerals, traces, rumors I am made from, morsel, minuscule fibre,
        one woman
like and unlike so many, fooled as to her destiny, the scope of her task?
One citizen like and unlike so many, touched and untouched in
        passing
—each of us now a driven grain, a nucleus, a city in crisis
some busy constructing enclosures, bunkers, to escape the common
        fate
20   some trying to revive dead statues to lead us, breathing their breath
        against marble lips
some who try to teach the moment, some who preach the moment
some who aggrandize, some who diminish themselves in the face of
        half-grasped events
—power and powerlessness run amuck, a tape reeling backward in
        jeering, screeching syllables—
some for whom war is new, others for whom it merely continues the
        old paroxysms of time
25   some marching for peace who for twenty years did not march for
        justice
some for whom peace is a white man's word and a white man's
        privilege
some who have learned to handle and contemplate the shapes of
        powerlessness and power
as the nurse learns hip and thigh and weight of the body he has to
        lift and sponge, day upon day
as she blows with her every skill on the spirit's embers still burning
        by their own laws in the bed of death.
30   A patriot is not a weapon.   A patriot is one who wrestles for the soul
        of her country
as she wrestles for her own being, for the soul of his country
(gazing through the great circle at Window Rock into the sheen of
        the Viet Nam Wall)[5]
as he wrestles for his own being.   A patriot is a citizen trying to wake
from the burnt-out dream of innocence, the nightmare
35   of the white general and the Black general posed in their camouflage,[6]

---

[5] **Window Rock . . . Viet Nam Wall:** Window Rock, sacred capital of the Navajo Nation in Arizona.
The Vietnam Veterans Memorial, completed in 1982, is made of black granite walls inscribed with the
names of fifty-eight thousand troops killed or lost in Vietnam.
[6] **white . . . camouflage:** Generals H. Norman Schwarzkopf and Colin Powell, commanding generals
during the Gulf War.

to remember her true country, remember his suffering land: remember
that blessing and cursing are born as twins and separated at birth to
          meet again in mourning
that the internal emigrant is the most homesick of all women and of
          all men
that every flag that flies today is a cry of pain.
40   Where are we moored?
          What are the bindings?
          What behooves us?

ADRIENNE RICH (1929–   )

Cartographies of Silence (1975; 1978)

                    1.

A conversation begins
with a lie. And each

speaker of the so-called common language feels
the ice-floe split, the drift apart

5   as if powerless, as if up against
a force of nature

A poem can begin
with a lie. And be torn up.

A conversation has other laws
10   recharges itself with its own

false energy. Cannot be torn
up. Infiltrates our blood. Repeats itself.

Inscribes with its unreturning stylus
the isolation it denies.

                    2.

The classical music station
playing hour upon hour in the apartment

the picking up and picking up
and again picking up the telephone

5   The syllables uttering
       the old script over and over

       The loneliness of the liar
       living in the formal network of the lie

       twisting the dials to drown the terror
10   beneath the unsaid word

                              3.

       The technology of silence
       The rituals, etiquette

       the blurring of terms
       silence not absence

5   of words or music or even
       raw sounds

       Silence can be a plan
       rigorously executed

       the blueprint to a life

10   It is a presence
       it has a history   a form

       Do not confuse it
       with any kind of absence

                              4.

       How calm, how inoffensive these words
       begin to seem to me

       though begun in grief and anger
       Can I break through this film of the abstract

5   without wounding myself or you
       there is enough pain here

       This is why the classical or the jazz music station plays?
       to give a ground of meaning to our pain?

5.

The silence that strips bare:
In Dreyer's *Passion of Joan*[1]

Falconetti's face, hair shorn, a great geography
mutely surveyed by the camera

5   If there were a poetry where this could happen
not as blank spaces or as words

stretched like a skin over meanings
but as silence falls at the end

of a night through which two people
10   have talked till dawn

6.

The scream
of an illegitimate voice

It has ceased to hear itself, therefore
it asks itself

5   How do I exist?

This was the silence I wanted to break in you
I had questions but you would not answer

I had answers but you could not use them
This is useless to you and perhaps to others

7.

It was an old theme even for me:
Language cannot do everything—

chalk it on the walls where the dead poets
lie in their mausoleums

5   If at the will of the poet the poem
could turn into a thing

---

[1] **Dreyer's *Passion of Joan*:** Carl Theodore Dreyer (1889–1968), innovative, early filmmaker who produced *The Passion of Joan of Arc* (1928).

a granite flank laid bare, a lifted head
alight with dew

If it could simply look you in the face
10   with naked eyeballs, not letting you turn

till you, and I who long to make this thing,
were finally clarified together in its stare

                              8.

No. Let me have this dust,
these pale clouds dourly lingering, these words

moving with ferocious accuracy
like the blind child's fingers

5   or the newborn infant's mouth
violent with hunger

No one can give me, I have long ago
taken this method

whether of bran pouring from the loose-woven sack
10   or of the bunsen-flame turned low and blue

If from time to time I envy
the pure annunciations to the eye

the *visio beatifica*[2]
if from time to time I long to turn

15   like the Eleusinian[3] hierophant
holding up a simple ear of grain

for return to the concrete and everlasting world
what in fact I keep choosing

are these words, these whispers, conversations
20   from which time after time the truth breaks moist and green.

---

[2] *visio beatifica:* Latin, "the view of blessedness"
[3] **Eleusinian:** Resembling Eleusius, a small town north of Athens, home to the Eleusinian Mysteries, a cult dedicated to Demeter and Persephone.

ADRIENNE RICH (1929–   )

The Phenomenology of Anger (1972; 1973)

1. The freedom of the wholly mad
to smear & play with her madness
write with her fingers dipped in it
the length of a room

5   which is not, of course, the freedom
you have, walking on Broadway
to stop & turn back or go on
10 blocks; 20 blocks

but feels enviable maybe
10   to the compromised

curled in the placenta of the real
which was to feed & which is strangling her.

2. Trying to light a log that's lain in the damp
as long as this house has stood:
15   even with dry sticks I can't get started
even with thorns.
I twist last year into a knot of old headlines
—this rose won't bloom.

How does a pile of rags the machinist wiped his hands on
20   feel in its cupboard, hour upon hour?
Each day during the heat-wave
they took the temperature of the haymow.
I huddled fugitive
in the warm sweet simmer of the hay

25   muttering: *Come.*

3. Flat heartland of winter.
The moonmen come back from the moon
the firemen come out of the fire.
Time without a taste: time without decisions.

30   Self-hatred, a monotone in the mind.
The shallowness of a life lived in exile
even in the hot countries.
Cleaver,[1] staring into a window full of knives.

---

[1] **Cleaver:** Eldridge Cleaver (1935–1998), member of the Black Panther Party who split the party line by refusing to advocate violence.

4. White light splits the room.
35 Table.   Window.   Lampshade.   You.
My hands, sticky in a new way.
Menstrual blood
seeming to leak from your side.

Will the judges try to tell me
40 which was the blood of whom?

5. Madness.   Suicide.   Murder.
Is there no way out but these?
The enemy, always just out of sight
snowshoeing the next forest, shrouded
45 in a snowy blur, abominable snowman
—at once the most destructive
and the most elusive being
gunning down the babies at My Lai[2]
vanishing in the face of confrontation.

50 The prince of air and darkness
computing body counts, masturbating
in the factory
of facts.

6. Fantasies of murder: not enough:
55 to kill is to cut off from pain
but the killer goes on hurting

Not enough. When I dream of meeting
the enemy, this is my dream:

white acetylene
60 ripples from my body
effortlessly released
perfectly trained
on the true enemy

raking his body down to the thread
65 of existence
burning away his lie
leaving him in a new
world; a changed
man

---

[2] **My Lai:** South Vietnamese village whose inhabitants were massacred by the American army in
March, 1968.

70   7. I suddenly see the world
as no longer viable:
you are out there burning the crops
with some new sublimate
This morning you left the bed
75   we still share
and went out to spread impotence
upon the world

I hate you.
I hate the mask you wear, your eyes
80   assuming a depth
they do not possess, drawing me
into the grotto of your skull
the landscape of bone
I hate your words
85   they make me think of fake
revolutionary bills
crisp imitation parchment
they sell at battlefields.

Last night, in this room, weeping
90   I asked you: *what are you feeling?*
do you feel anything?

Now in the torsion of your body
as you defoliate the fields we lived from
I have your answer.

95   8. Dogeared earth. Wormeaten moon.
A pale cross-hatching of silver
lies like a wire screen on the black
water. All these phenomena
are temporary.

100   I would have loved to live in a world
of women and men gaily
in collusion with green leaves, stalks,
building mineral cities, transparent domes,
little huts of woven grass
105   each with its own pattern—
a conspiracy to coexist
with the Crab Nebula, the exploding
universe, the Mind—

9. *The only real love I have ever felt*
110 *was for children and other women.*
Everything else was lust, pity,
self-hatred, pity, lust.
This is a woman's confession.
Now, look again at the face
115 of Botticelli's Venus, Kali,
the Judith of Chartres[3]
with her so-called smile.

10. how we are burning up our lives
testimony:
120   the subway
hurtling to Brooklyn
her head on her knees
asleep or drugged

la vía del tren subterráneo
es peligrosa [4]

125   many sleep
the whole way
others sit
staring holes of fire into the air
others plan rebellion:
130   night after night
awake in prison, my mind
licked at the mattress like a flame
till the cellblock went up roaring

Thoreau setting fire to the woods

135 Every act of becoming conscious
(it says here in this book)
is an unnatural act

---

[3] **Now . . . Chartres:** Sandro Botticelli (1445–1510), Italian painter of the *Birth of Venus*. "Kali," a
Hindu goddess and wife of Shiva. Chartres Cathedral in France has a window that portrays Judith's
decapitation of Assyrian General Holofernes.
[4] *la . . . peligrosa:* Spanish, "the subway track is dangerous."

EDWARD KAMAU BRATHWAITE (1930–   )

Prelude   (1967)

Drum skin whip
lash, master sun's
cutting edge of
heat, taut
5   surfaces of things
I sing
I shout
I groan
I dream
10 about

Dust glass grit
the pebbles of the desert:
sands shift:
across the scorched
15 world water ceases
to flow.
The hot
wheel'd caravan's
carcases
20 rot.
Camels wrecked
in their own
shit
resurrect butter-
25 flies that
dance in the noon
without hope
without hope
of a morning.

30 Soon
rock
elephant-
hided boulders
dragged in now
35 dry river
beds, death's
valleys.
Here clay

cool coal clings
40 to glass, creates
clinks, silica glitters,
children of stars.
Here cool
dew falls
45 in the evening
black
birds blink
on the tree
stump ravished
50 with fire
ruined with its
gold.

Build now
the new
55 villages, you
must mix spittle
with dirt, dung
to saliva and
sweat: round
60 mud walls will rise
in the dawn
walled cities
arise
from savanna and
65 rock river bed:
O Kano Bamako
Gao

But populations of flies
arise from the cattle
70 towns: blood sucking
Try—
Panosoma. Milk
curdles in
udder in
75 nipple in
mouth. Flies
nibble and ulcer:
tight silver-
backed swarms bringing
80 silence, the slender

proboscis of rot.
In the hot
harmattan,

dead bodies settle
85 and quiver
given up to the blanket
that covers and warms
from the heat of the final
cold; until suddenly burst,
90 the buzzing black zones that were
silence, swirl through the
sunlight, the left fest-
ering flesh they had covered
runnelled and holed like dust
95 under raindrops, soil
under rain.

But no
rain comes
while the flesh
100 rots, while the flies
swarm. But across the
dried out gut of the river-
bed, look!
The trees are
105 cool, there
leaves are
green, there
burns the dream
of a fountain,
110 garden of odours,
soft alleyways.

So build build
again the new
villages: you
115 must mix spittle
with dirt, dung
to saliva and
sweat, making
mortar. Leaf
120 work for the
roof and vine
tendrils.
But square frames

crack, wood
125   rots, smooth mortar
too remains mortal,
trapped in its own salt,
its unstable foundations of water.
So grant, God
130   that this house will stand
the four winds
the seasons' alterations
the explorations of the worm.

Grant, God,
135   a clear release from thieves,
from robbers and from those that plot
and poison while they dip
into our dish.
Grant, too, warm fires, good
140   wives and grateful children.

But the too warm fire flames.
Flames burn, scorch, crack,
consume the dry leaves of the hot
house. Flames trick the seasons,
145   worms, our neighbours' treacheries,
our bars, our bolts, our prayers,
our dogs, our God. Flame,
that red idol, is our power's
founder: flames fashion wood; with powder,
150   iron. Long iron
runs to swords,
to spears, to burnished points
that stall the wild, the eyes, the whinneyings.

Flame is our god, our last defence, our peril.

155   Flame burns the village down.

CHRISTOPHER OKIGBO (1932–1967)

Come Thunder (1967)

Now that the triumphant march has entered the last street corners,
Remember, O dancers, the thunder among the clouds . . .

Now that laughter, broken in two, hangs tremulous between the teeth,
Remember, O dancers, the lightning beyond the earth . . .

5   The smell of blood already floats in the lavender-mist of the afternoon.
The death sentence lies in ambush along the corridors of power;
And a great fearful thing already tugs at the cables of the open air,
A nebula immense and immeasurable, a night of deep waters—
An iron dream unnamed and unprintable, a path of stone.

10   The drowsy heads of the pods in barren farmlands witness it,
The homesteads abandoned in this century's brush fire witness it:
The myriad eyes of deserted corn cobs in burning barns witness it:
Magic birds with the miracle of lightning flash on their feathers . . .

The arrows of God tremble at the gates of light,
15   The drums of curfew pander to a dance of death;

And the secret thing in its heaving
Threatens with iron mask
The last lighted torch of the century . . .

AMIRI BARAKA (1934–   )

A New Reality Is Better Than a New Movie! (1972)

How will it go, crumbling earthquake, towering inferno, juggernaut,[1]
    volcano, smashup.
in reality, other than the feverish nearreal fantasy of the capitalist
    flunky film hacks
tho they sense its reality breathing a quake inferno scar on their
    throat even snorts of
100% pure cocaine cant cancel the cold cut of impending death to
    this society. On all the
5   screens of america, the joint blows up every hour and a half for two
    dollars an fifty cents.
They have taken the niggers out to lunch, for a minute, made us
    partners (nigger charlie) or
surrogates (boss nigger) for their horror. But just as superafrikan
    mobutu cannot leopardskinhat his
way out of responsibility for lumumba's death,[2] nor even with his
    incredible billions rockefeller

---

[1] **towering inferno, juggernaut:** *The Towering Inferno*, a movie about a skyscraper aflame. "Juggernaut," a massive force that crushes everything in its path.
[2] **mobutu . . . death:** Soko Mobutu was given power to rule Zaire by the United States CIA after Patrice Lumumba was murdered in 1961.

cannot even save his pale ho's titties in the crushing weight of
    things as they really are.
10 How will it go, does it reach you, getting up, sitting on the side of
    the bed, getting ready
to go to work. Hypnotized by the machine, and the cement floor,
    the jungle treachery of trying
to survive with no money in a money world, of making the boss
    100,000 for every 200 dollars
you get, and then having his brother get you for the rent, and if you
    want to buy the car you
helped build, your downpayment paid for it, the rest goes to buy his
    old lady a foam rubber
15 rhinestone set of boobies for special occasions when kissinger[3]
    drunkenly fumbles with
her blouse, forgetting himself.
If you dont like it, what you gonna do about it. That was the question
    we asked each other, &
still right regularly need to ask. You dont like it? Whatcha gonna do,
    about it??
The real terror of nature is humanity enraged, the true technicolor
    spectacle that hollywood
20 cant record. They cant even show you how you look when you go to
    work or when you come back.
They cant even show you thinking or demanding the new socialist
    reality, its the ultimate tidal
wave. When all over the planet, men and women, with heat in their
    hands, demand that society
be planned to include the lives and self determination of all the
    people ever to live. That is
the scalding scenario with a cast of just under two billion that they
    dare not even whisper.
25 Its called, "We Want It All . . . The Whole World!"

WENDELL BERRY (1934–   )

Against the War in Vietnam (1968)

Believe the automatic righteousness
of whoever holds an office. Believe
the officials who see without doubt

---

[3] **kissinger:** Henry Kissinger (1923–   ), Secretary of State under Richard Nixon, was a bachelor.

that peace is assured by war, freedom
5   by oppression. The truth preserved by lying
becomes a lie. Believe or die.

In the name of ourselves we ride
at the wheels of our engines,
in the name of Plenty devouring all,
10 the exhaust of our progress falling
deadly on villages and fields
we do not see. We are prepared
for millions of little deaths.

Where are the quiet plenteous dwellings
15 we were coming to, the neighborly holdings?
We see the American freedom defended
with lies, and the lies defended
with blood, the vision of Jefferson[1]
served by the agony of children,
20 women cowering in holes.

AUDRE LORDE (1934–1992)

Power (1976)

The difference between poetry and rhetoric
is being ready to kill
yourself
instead of your children.

5   I am trapped on a desert of raw gunshot wounds
and a dead child dragging his shattered black
face off the edge of my sleep
blood from his punctured cheeks and shoulders
is the only liquid for miles
10 and my stomach
churns at the imagined taste while
my mouth splits into dry lips

---

[1] **Jefferson:** Thomas Jefferson (1743–1826), third president of the United States and author of the
Declaration of Independence.

without loyalty or reason
thirsting for the wetness of his blood

15   as it sinks into the whiteness
of the desert where I am lost
without imagery or magic
trying to make power out of hatred and destruction
trying to heal my dying son with kisses

20   only the sun will bleach his bones quicker.

A policeman who shot down a ten year old in Queens
stood over the boy with his cop shoes in childish blood
and a voice said "Die you little motherfucker" and
there are tapes to prove it. At his trial

25   this policeman said in his own defense
"I didn't notice the size nor nothing else
only the color". And
there are tapes to prove that, too.

Today that 37 year old white man

30   with 13 years of police forcing
was set free
by eleven white men who said they were satisfied
justice had been done
and one Black Woman who said

35   "They convinced me" meaning
they had dragged her 4′10″ Black Woman's frame
over the hot coals
of four centuries of white male approval
until she let go

40   the first real power she ever had
and lined her own womb with cement
to make a graveyard for our children.

I have not been able to touch the destruction
within me.

45   But unless I learn to use
the difference between poetry and rhetoric
my power too will run corrupt as poisonous mold
or lie limp and useless as an unconnected wire
and one day I will take my teenaged plug

50   and connect it to the nearest socket
raping an 85 year old white woman
who is somebody's mother
and as I beat her senseless and set a torch to her bed
a greek chorus will be singing in 3/4 time

55   "Poor thing. She never hurt a soul. What beasts they are."

JUNE JORDAN (1936–2002)

Poem about My Rights (1980)

Even tonight and I need to take a walk and clear
my head about this poem about why I can't
go out without changing my clothes my shoes
my body posture my gender identity my age
5   my status as a woman alone in the evening /
alone on the streets / alone not being the point /
the point being that I can't do what I want
to do with my own body because I am the wrong
sex the wrong age the wrong skin and
10   suppose it was not here in the city but down on the beach /
or far into the woods and I wanted to go
there by myself thinking about God / or thinking
about children or thinking about the world / all of it
disclosed by the stars and the silence:
15   I could not go and I could not think and I could not
stay there
alone
as I need to be
alone because I can't do what I want to do with my own
20   body and
who in the hell set things up
like this
and in France they say if the guy penetrates
but does not ejaculate then he did not rape me
25   and if after stabbing him if after screams if
after begging the bastard and if even after smashing
a hammer to his head if even after that if he
and his buddies fuck me after that
then I consented and there was
30   no rape because finally you understand finally
they fucked me over because I was wrong I was
wrong again to be me being me where I was / wrong
to be who I am
which is exactly like South Africa
35   penetrating into Namibia penetrating into
Angola[1] and does that mean I mean how do you know if

---

[1] **South Africa . . . Angola:** Namibia, Angola, and Zimbabwe (line 40) are all African nations north of
South Africa. Pretoria (line 37) is the administrative capital of South Africa.

Pretoria ejaculates what will be the evidence look like the
proof of the monster jackboot ejaculation on Blackland
and if
40 after Namibia and if after Angola and if after Zimbabwe
and if after all of my kinsmen and women resist even to
self-immolation of the villages and if after that
we lose nevertheless what will the big boys say will they
claim my consent:
45 Do You Follow Me: We are the wrong people of
the wrong skin on the wrong continent and what
in the hell is everybody being reasonable about
and according to the *Times* this week
back in 1966 the C.I.A. decided that they had this problem
50 and the problem was a man named Nkrumah so they
killed him and before that it was Patrice Lumumba[2]
and before that it was my father on the campus
of my Ivy League school and my father afraid
to walk into the cafeteria because he said he
55 was wrong the wrong age the wrong skin the wrong
gender identity and he was paying my tuition and
before that
it was my father saying I was wrong saying that
I should have been a boy because he wanted one / a
60 boy and that I should have been lighter skinned and
that I should have had straighter hair and that
I should not be so boy crazy but instead I should
just be one / a boy and before that
it was my mother pleading plastic surgery for
65 my nose and braces for my teeth and telling me
to let the books loose to let them loose in other
words
I am very familiar with the problems of the C.I.A.
and the problems of South Africa and the problems
70 of Exxon Corporation and the problems of white
America in general and the problems of the teachers
and the preachers and the F.B.I. and the social
workers and my particular Mom and Dad / I am very
familiar with the problems because the problems
75 turn out to be
me

---

[2] **back . . . Lumumba:** Ghanaian leader Kwame Nkrumah was removed from office in 1966;
Lumumba, the prime minister of Zaire, was murdered in 1961.

I am the history of rape
I am the history of the rejection of who I am
I am the history of the terrorized incarceration of
80   my self
I am the history of battery assault and limitless
armies against whatever I want to do with my mind
and my body and my soul and
whether it's about walking out at night
85   or whether it's about the love that I feel or
whether it's about the sanctity of my vagina or
the sanctity of my national boundaries
or the sanctity of my leaders or the sanctity
of each and every desire
90   that I know from my personal and idiosyncratic
and indisputably single and singular heart
I have been raped
be-
cause I have been wrong the wrong sex the wrong age
95   the wrong skin the wrong nose the wrong hair the
wrong need the wrong dream the wrong geographic
the wrong sartorial I
I have been the meaning of rape
I have been the problem everyone seeks to
100   eliminate by forced
penetration with or without the evidence of slime and /
but let this be unmistakable this poem
is not consent I do not consent
to my mother to my father to the teachers to
105   the F.B.I. to South Africa to Bedford-Stuy
to Park Avenue³ to American Airlines to the hardon
idlers on the corners to the sneaky creeps in
cars
I am not wrong: Wrong is not my name
110   My name is my own my own my own
and I can't tell you who the hell set things up like this
but I can tell you that from now on my resistance
my simple and daily and nightly self-determination
may very well cost you your life

---

³ **Bedford-Stuy . . . Park Avenue:** Bedford-Stuyvesant is an impoverished Black ghetto in Brooklyn, while Park Avenue is a wealthy street in New York City.

MARGE PIERCY (1936–   )

Barbie Doll (1971)

This girlchild was born as usual
and presented dolls that did pee-pee
and miniature GE stoves and irons
and wee lipsticks the color of cherry candy.
5   Then in the magic of puberty, a classmate said:
You have a great big nose and fat legs.

She was healthy, tested intelligent,
possessed strong arms and back,
abundant sexual drive and manual dexterity.
10   She went to and fro apologizing.
Everyone saw a fat nose on thick legs.

She was advised to play coy,
exhorted to come on hearty,
exercise, diet, smile and wheedle.
15   Her good nature wore out
like a fan belt.
So she cut off her nose and her legs
and offered them up.

In the casket displayed on satin she lay
20   with the undertaker's cosmetics painted on,
a turned-up putty nose,
dressed in a pink and white nightie.
Doesn't she look pretty? everyone said.
Consummation at last.
25   To every woman a happy ending.

MARGE PIERCY (1936–   )

The Moon Is Always Female (1980)

The moon is always female and so
am I although often in this vale
of razorblades I have wished I could
put on and take off my sex like a dress
5   and why not? Do men wear their sex

always? The priest, the doctor, the teacher
all tell us they come to their professions
neuter as clams and the truth is
when I work I am pure as an angel
10   tiger and clear is my eye and hot
my brain and silent all the whining
grunting piglets of the appetites.
For we were priests to the goddesses
to whom were fashioned the first altars
15   of clumsy stone on stone and leaping animal
in the wombdark caves, long before men
put on skirts and masks to scare babies.
For we were healers with herbs and poultices
with our milk and careful fingers
20   long before they began learning to cut up
the living by making jokes at corpses.
For we were making sounds from our throats
and lips to warn and encourage the helpless
young long before schools were built
25   to teach boys to obey and be bored and kill.

I wake in a strange slack empty bed
of a motel, shaking like dry leaves
the wind rips loose, and in my head
is bound a girl of twelve whose female
30   organs all but the numb womb are being
cut from her with a knife. Clitoridectomy,
whatever Latin name you call it, in a quarter
of the world girl children are so maimed
and I think of her and I cannot stop.
35   And I think of her and I cannot stop.

If you are a woman you feel the knife in the words.
If you are a man, then at age four or else
at twelve you are seized and held down
and your penis is cut off. You are left
40   your testicles but they are sewed to your
crotch. When your spouse buys you, you
are torn or cut open so that your precious
semen can be siphoned out, but of course
you feel nothing. But pain. But pain.

45   For the uses of men we have been butchered
and crippled and shut up and carved open

under the moon that swells and shines
and shrinks again into nothingness, pregnant
and then waning toward its little monthly
50   death. The moon is always female but the sun
is female only in lands where females
are let into the sun to run and climb.

A woman is screaming and I hear her.
A woman is bleeding and I see her
55   bleeding from the mouth, the womb, the breasts
in a fountain of dark blood of dismal
daily tedious sorrow quite palatable
to the taste of the mighty and taken for granted
that the bread of domesticity be baked
60   of our flesh, that the hearth be built
of our bones of animals kept for meat and milk,
that we open and lie under and weep.
I want to say over the names of my mothers
like the stones of a path I am climbing
65   rock by slippery rock into the mists.
Never even at knife point have I wanted
or been willing to be or become a man.
I want only to be myself and free.

I am waiting for the moon to rise. Here
70   I squat, the whole country with its steel
mills and its coal mines and its prisons
at my back and the continent tilting
up into mountains and torn by shining lakes
all behind me on this scythe of straw,
75   a sand bar cast on the ocean waves, and I
wait for the moon to rise red and heavy
in my eyes. Chilled, cranky, fearful
in the dark I wait and I am all the time
climbing slippery rocks in a mist while
80   far below the waves crash in the sea caves;
I am descending a stairway under the groaning
sea while the black waters buffet me
like rockweed to and fro.

I have swum the upper waters leaping
85   in dolphin's skin for joy equally into the necessary air and the tumult of the powerful wave.
I am entering the chambers I have visited.

I have floated through them sleeping and sleep-
walking and waking, drowning in passion
90   festooned with green bladderwrack° of misery.   seaweed
I have wandered these chambers in the rock
where the moon freezes the air and all hair
is black or silver. Now I will tell you
what I have learned lying under the moon
95   naked as women do: now I will tell you
the changes of the high and lower moon.
Out of necessity's hard stones we suck
what water we can and so we have survived,
women born of women. There is knowing
100   with the teeth as well as knowing with
the tongue and knowing with the fingertips
as well as knowing with words and with all
the fine flickering hungers of the brain.

CHARLES SIMIC (1938–   )

Sunday Papers (2001)

The butchery of the innocent
Never stops. That's about all
We can ever be sure of, love,
Even more sure than the roast
5   You are bringing out of the oven.

It's Sunday. The congregation
Files slowly out of the church
Across the street. A good many
Carry Bibles in their hands.
10   It's the vague desire for truth
And the mighty fear of it
That makes them turn up
Despite the glorious spring weather.

In the hallway, the old mutt
15   Just now had the honesty
To growl at his own image in the mirror,
Before lumbering off to the kitchen
Where the lamb roast sat
In your outstretched hands
20   Smelling of garlic and rosemary.

JAMES WELCH (1940–2003)

The Man from Washington (1976)

The end came easy for most of us.
Packed away in our crude beginnings
in some far corner of a flat world,
we didn't expect much more
5   than firewood and buffalo robes
to keep us warm. The man came down,
a slouching dwarf with rainwater eyes,
and spoke to us. He promised
that life would go on as usual,
10   that treaties would be signed, and everyone—
man, woman and child—would be inoculated
against a world in which we had no part,
a world of money, promise and disease.

DEREK MAHON (1941–   )

The Snow Party (1975)
for Louis Asekoff

Bashō,[1] coming
To the city of Nagoya,[2]
Is asked to a snow party.

There is a tinkling of china
5   And tea into china;
There are introductions.

Then everyone
Crowds to the window
To watch the falling snow.

10   Snow is falling on Nagoya
And farther south
On the tiles of Kyōto.

Eastward, beyond Irago,
It is falling
15   Like leaves on the cold sea.

---

[1] **Bashō:** Matsuo Bashō (1644–1694), a Japanese poet.
[2] **Nagoya:** Japanese city on the Pacific coast. Kyōto and Irago are Japanese cities as well.

Elsewhere they are burning
Witches and heretics
In the boiling squares,

Thousands have died since dawn
20 In the service
Of barbarous kings;

But there is silence
In the houses of Nagoya
And the hills of Ise.

OLIVE SENIOR (1943–   )

Stowaway (1994)

There's this much space between me and
            discovery
a hairline fracture getting wider with
            each wave.
5   I feel it, though I cannot see to
            hold
my thoughts together—they're
            running loose
all over; someone's bound
10   to trip,
I know it. One day light will enter
            this grave.
Till then, I let my thoughts go.
            Dangerously
15 unstrung, I dive deeper into this
            fault, this
undeclared passage. Without soundings
            there's no telling
how unfathomable the fall, how
20   attainable
the littoral. Surfacing
            I'll dangle
on a single hope: that my eyes
            be blinded
25 only by the promised land.

AI (1947–   )

Killing Floor (1979)

1. Russia, 1927

On the day the sienna-skinned man
held my shoulders between his spade-shaped hands,
easing me down into the azure water of Jordan,[1]
I woke ninety-three million miles from myself,
5   Lev Davidovich Bronstein,[2]
shoulder-deep in the Volga,
while the cheap dye of my black silk shirt darkened the water.

My head wet, water caught in my lashes.
Am I blind?
10   I rub my eyes, then wade back to shore,
undress and lie down,
until Stalin comes from his place beneath the birch tree.
He folds my clothes
and I button myself in my marmot coat,
15   and together we start the long walk back to Moscow.
He doesn't ask, *what did you see in the river?*,
but I hear the hosts of a man drowning in water and holiness,
the castrati voices[3] I can't recognize,
skating on knives, from trees, from air
20   on the thin ice of my last night in Russia.
Leon Trotsky. Bread.
I want to scream, but silence holds my tongue
with small spade-shaped hands
and only this comes, so quietly
25   Stalin has to press his ear to my mouth:
I have only myself. Put me on the train.
I won't look back.

---

[1] **Jordan:** River that flows through the Holy Land; its waters are believed to be sacred. The Volga (line 6) is Russia's largest river.
[2] **Lev Davidovich Bronstein:** (1879–1940), Russian revolutionary who was a Communist Party leader until Lenin's death in 1924, at which point he lost power to Stalin. Bronstein was expelled from the Communist Party in 1927.
[3] **castrati voices:** High-pitched voices of male singers castrated in their youth to save their soprano voices.

2. Mexico, 1940

At noon today, I woke from a nightmare:
my friend Jacques ran toward me with an ax,
as I stepped from the train in Alma-Ata.[4]
He was dressed in yellow satin pants and shirt.
5   A marigold in winter.
When I held out my arms to embrace him,
he raised the ax and struck me at the neck,
my head fell to one side, hanging only by skin.
A river of sighs poured from the cut.

3. Mexico, August 20, 1940[5]

The machine-gun bullets
hit my wife in the legs,
then zigzagged up her body.
I took the shears, cut open her gown
5   and lay on top of her for hours.
Blood soaked through my clothes
and when I tried to rise, I couldn't.

I wake then. Another nightmare.
I rise from my desk, walk to the bedroom
10   and sit down at my wife's mirrored vanity.
I rouge my cheeks and lips,
stare at my bone-white, speckled egg of a face:
lined and empty.
I lean forward and see Jacques's reflection.
15   I half-turn, smile, then turn back to the mirror.
He moves from the doorway,
lifts the pickax
and strikes the top of my head.
My brain splits.
20   The pickax keeps going
and when it hits the tile floor,
it flies from his hands,
a black dove on whose back I ride,
two men, one cursing,
25   the other blessing all things:
Lev Davidovich Bronstein,
I step from Jordan without you.

---

[4] **Alma-Ata:** City in Russia; Jacques van den Dreschd feigned friendship with Trotsky in Mexico until attempting to take his life in May 1940.
[5] **August 20, 1940:** Date of Trotsky's assassination at the hands of van den Dreschd.

CAROLYN FORCHÉ (1950–   )

The Colonel (1981)

What you have heard is true. I was in his house. His wife carried a tray
of coffee and sugar. His daughter filed her nails, his son went out for the
night. There were daily papers, pet dogs, a pistol on the cushion beside
him. The moon swung bare on its black cord over the house. On the
5   television was a cop show. It was in English. Broken bottles were
embedded in the walls around the house to scoop the kneecaps from a
man's legs or cut his hands to lace. On the windows there were gratings
like those in liquor stores. We had dinner, rack of lamb, good wine, a gold
bell was on the table for calling the maid. The maid brought green
10 mangoes, salt, a type of bread. I was asked how I enjoyed the country.
There was a brief commercial in Spanish. His wife took everything away.
There was some talk then of how difficult it had become to govern. The
parrot said hello on the terrace. The colonel told it to shut up, and pushed
himself from the table. My friend said to me with his eyes: say nothing.
15 The colonel returned with a sack used to bring groceries home. He spilled
many human ears on the table. They were like dried peach halves. There
is no other way to say this. He took one of them in his hands, shook it in
our faces, dropped it into a water glass. It came alive there. I am tired of
fooling around he said. As for the rights of anyone, tell your people they
20 can go fuck themselves. He swept the ears to the floor with his arm and
held the last of his wine in the air. Something for your poetry, no? he said.
Some of the ears on the floor caught this scrap of his voice. Some of the
ears on the floor were pressed to the ground.

PETER BALAKIAN (1951–   )

After the Survivors Are Gone (1996)

I tried to imagine the Vilna ghetto,[1]
to see a persimmon tree after the flash at Nagasaki.[2]
Because my own tree had been hacked,
I tried to kiss the lips of Armenia.[3]

---

[1] **Vilna ghetto:** Ghetto established for Jews in Lithuania after the Nazi invasion in World War II.
Almost all of the Jews residing in the ghetto were killed in Nazi concentration camps.
[2] **Nagasaki:** The United States dropped an atomic bomb on Nagasaki, Japan, in 1945.
[3] **Armenia:** Small, land-locked republic in southwestern Asia that has been oppressed and invaded by
its neighbors for the past 2500 years.

5   At the table and the altar
we said some words written ages ago.
Have we settled for just the wine and bread,
for candles lit and snuffed?

Let us remember how the law has failed us.
10   Let us remember the child naked,
waiting to be shot on a bright day
with tulips blooming around the ditch.

We shall not forget the earth,
the artifact, the particular song,
15   the dirt of an idiom—
things that stick in the ear.

RITA DOVE (1952–   )

Parsley[1] (1983)

1. The Cane° Fields   sugar cane

There is a parrot imitating spring
in the palace, its feathers parsley green.
Out of the swamp the cane appears

to haunt us, and we cut it down. El General
5   searches for a word; he is all the world
there is. Like a parrot imitating spring,

we lie down screaming as rain punches through
and we come up green. We cannot speak an R—
out of the swamp, the cane appears

10   and then the mountain we call in whispers *Katalina.*
The children gnaw their teeth to arrowheads.
There is a parrot imitating spring.

El General has found his word: *perejil.*
Who says it, lives. He laughs, teeth shining
15   out of the swamp. The cane appears

---

[1] **Parsley:** "On October 2, 1937, Rafael Trujillo (1891–1961), dictator of the Dominican Republic, ordered 20,000 blacks killed because they could not pronounce the letter r in *perejil*, the Spanish word for parsley" [Dove's note].

in our dreams, lashed by wind and streaming.
And we lie down. For every drop of blood
there is a parrot imitating spring.
Out of the swamp the cane appears.

2. The Palace

The word the general's chosen is parsley.
It is fall, when thoughts turn
to love and death; the general thinks
of his mother, how she died in the fall
5   and he planted her walking cane at the grave
and it flowered, each spring stolidly forming
four-star blossoms. The general

pulls on his boots, he stomps to
her room in the palace, the one without
10   curtains, the one with a parrot
in a brass ring. As he paces he wonders
Who can I kill today. And for a moment
the little knot of screams
is still. The parrot, who has traveled

15   all the way from Australia in an ivory
cage, is coy as a widow, practising
spring. Ever since the morning
his mother collapsed in the kitchen
while baking skull-shaped candies
20   for the Day of the Dead,[2] the general
has hated sweets. He orders pastries
brought up for the bird; they arrive

dusted with sugar on a bed of lace.
The knot in his throat starts to twitch;
25   he sees his boots the first day in battle
splashed with mud and urine
as a soldier falls at his feet amazed—
how stupid he looked!—at the sound
of artillery. I *never thought it would sing*
30   the soldier said, and died. Now

the general sees the fields of sugar
cane, lashed by rain and streaming.

---

[2] **Day of the Dead:** All Souls' Day, November 2. A holiday blending Aztec and Catholic ritual, honoring the spirits of the dead.

He sees his mother's smile, the teeth
gnawed to arrowheads. He hears
35 the Haitians sing without R's
as they swing the great machetes:
Katalina, they sing, *Katalina*,

mi madle, mi amol en muelte.[3] God knows
his mother was no stupid woman; she
40 could roll an R like a queen. Even
a parrot can roll an R! In the bare room
the bright feathers arch in a parody
of greenery, as the last pale crumbs
disappear under the blackened tongue. Someone

45 calls out his name in a voice
so like his mother's, a startled tear
splashes the tip of his right boot.
My mother, my love in death.
The general remembers the tiny green sprigs
50 men of his village wore in their capes
to honor the birth of a son. He will
order many, this time, to be killed

for a single, beautiful word.

GARY SOTO (1952–   )

The Map (1978)

When the sun's whiteness closes around us
Like a noose,

It is noon, and Molina squats
In the uneven shade of an oleander.[1]

5 He unfolds a map and, with a pencil,
Blackens Panama[2]

---

[3] *mi . . . muelte:* Spanish, "my mother, my love in death."
[1] **oleander:** White poisonous plant.
[2] **Panama:** The place locations in the following lines are all countries, cities, and rivers in Latin America.

Into a bruise;
He dots rain over Bogotá, the city of spiders,

And x's in a mountain range that climbs
10   Like a thermometer

Above the stone fence
The old never thought to look over.

A fog presses over Lima.
Brazil is untangled of its rivers.

15   Where there is a smudge,
Snow has stitched its cold into the field.

Where the river Orinoco cuts east,
A new river rises nameless

From the open grasses,
20   And Molina calls it his place of birth.

DIONNE BRAND (1953–   )

Blues Spiritual for Mammy Prater (1990)

> *On looking at the photograph of Mammy Prater, an ex-slave, 115
> years old when her photograph was taken*

she waited for her century to turn
she waited until she was one hundred and fifteen
years old to take a photograph
to take a photograph and to put those eyes in it
5   she waited until the technique of photography was
suitably developed
to make sure the picture would be clear
to make sure no crude daguerreotype[1] would lose

---

[1] **daguerreotype:** Early form of photograph, made from an image on a silver plate and developed in mercury vapor. "Talbotype" (line 34) was another early form of photograph.

her image
10 would lose her lines and most of all her eyes
and her hands
she knew the patience of one hundred and fifteen years
she knew that if she had the patience,
to avoid killing a white man
15 that I would see this photograph
she waited until it suited her
to take this photograph and to put those eyes in it.

in the hundred and fifteen years which it took her to
wait for this photograph she perfected this pose
20 she sculpted it over a shoulder of pain,
a thing like despair which she never called
this name for she would not have lasted
the fields, the ones she ploughed
on the days that she was a mule, left
25 their etching on the gait of her legs
deliberately and unintentionally
she waited, not always silently, not always patiently,
by the time she sat in her black dress, white collar,
white handkerchief, her feet had turned to marble,
30 her heart burnished red,
and her eyes.

she waited one hundred and fifteen years
until the science of photography passed tin and
talbotype for a surface sensitive enough
35 to hold her eyes
she took care not to lose the signs
to write in those eyes what her fingers could not script
a pact of blood across a century, a decade and more
she knew then that it would be me who would find
40 her will, her meticulous account, her eyes,
her days when waiting for this photograph
was all that kept her sane
she planned it down to the day,
the light,
45 the superfluous photographer
her breasts,
her hands
this moment of
my turning the leaves of a book,
50 noticing, her eyes.

SANDRA CISNEROS (1954–   )

14 de julio (1987)

Today, *catorce de julio,*
a man kissed a woman in the rain.
On the corner of Independencia y Cinco de Mayo.
A man kissed a woman.

5   Because it is Friday.
Because no one has to go to work tomorrow.
Because, in direct opposition to Church and State,
a man kissed a woman
oblivious to the consequence of sorrow.

10   A man kisses a woman unashamed,
within a universe of two I'm certain.
Beside the sea of taxicabs on Cinco de Mayo.
In front of an open-air statue.
On an intersection busy with tourists and children.
15   Every day little miracles like this occur.

A man kisses a woman in the rain
and I am envious of that simple affirmation.
I who timidly took and timidly gave—
you who never admitted a public grace.
20   We of the half-dark who were unbrave.

BROTHER WILL HAIRSTON

Alabama Bus[1] (1956)

Stop that Alabama bus   I don't wanna ride
Stop that Alabama bus   I don't wanna ride
Stop that Alabama bus   I don't wanna ride
Lord an Alabama boy   'cause I don't wanna ride

---

[1] **Alabama Bus:** In December 1955, civil rights leader Martin Luther King, Jr. (1929–1968) led a
boycott against public bus transportation in Montgomery, Alabama.

5   Stop that Alabama bus   I don't wanna ride
        Stop that Alabama bus   I don't wanna ride
        Stop that Alabama bus   I don't wanna ride
        Lord an Alabama boy   'cause I don't wanna ride

        Lord, there come a bus don't have no load
10   You know, they tell me that a human being stepped on board
        You know, they tell me that the man stepped on the bus
        You know, they tell me that the driver began to fuss
        He said, Lookit here, man, you from the Negro race
        And don't you know you sitting in the wrong place?
15   The driver told the man, I know you paid your dime
        But if you don't move you gonna pay a fine
        The man told the driver, My feets are hurting
        The driver told the man to move behind the curtain

        Stop that Alabama bus   I don't wanna ride
20   Stop that Alabama bus   I don't wanna ride
        Stop that Alabama bus   I don't wanna ride
        Lord an Alabama boy   'cause I don't wanna ride

        I wanna tell you 'bout the Reverend Martin Luther King
        You know, they tell me that the people began to sing
25   You know, the man God sent out in the world
        You know, they tell me that the man had a mighty nerve
        You know, the poor man didn't have a bus to rent
        You know, they tell me, Great God, he had *a mighty spent*
        And he reminded me of Moses in Israel land
30   He said, A man ain't nothing but a man
        He said, Lookit here, Alabama, don't you see
        He says, A all of my people gonna follow me
        You know, they tell me Reverend King was very hurt
        He says, A all of my people gonna walk to work
35   They said, Lookit here, boy, you hadn't took a thought
        So, don't you know you broke the anti-boycott law
        They tell me Reverend King said, Treat us right
        You know, in the Second World War my father lost his sight
        You know, they tell me Abraham signed the pledge one night
40   He said that all of these men should have their equal rights
        You know, they had the trial and Clayton Powell[2] was there
        You know, they tell me Clayton Powell asked the world for prayer

---

[2] **Clayton Powell:** Adam Clayton Powell, Jr. (1908–1972), civil rights leader and congressional representative from Harlem, in New York City.

You know, they sent down there to go his bail
You know they PUT REVEREND KING IN A ALABAMA JAIL

45   Stop that Alabama bus   I don't wanna ride
        Stop that Alabama bus   I don't wanna ride
        Stop that Alabama bus   I don't wanna ride
        Lord an Alabama boy   'cause I don't wanna ride

        Stop that Alabama bus   I don't wanna ride
50   Stop that Alabama bus   I don't wanna ride
        Stop that Alabama bus   I don't wanna ride
        Lord an Alabama boy   'cause I don't wanna ride

You know, they tell me Reverend King was *a violence 'bide*
A when all the buses passed, and no body will ride
55 You know, they tell me that the Negroes was ready to go
They had a walked along the streets until their feets was sore
You know, they tell me Reverend King had spreaded the word
'Bout an Alabama bus ride, so I heard
You know, they spent a lot of money since King go on
60 You know, in nineteen and twenty-nine that man was born
You know, the five hundred dollars aren't very heavy
You know, the poor man was born the fifteenth of January

        Stop that Alabama bus   I don't wanna ride
        Stop that Alabama bus   I don't wanna ride
65   Stop that Alabama bus   I don't wanna ride
        Lord an Alabama boy   but I don't wanna ride

SHERMAN ALEXIE (1966–   )

The Powwow at the End of the World (1996)

I am told by many of you that I must forgive and so I shall
after an Indian woman puts her shoulder to the Grand Coulee
        Dam[1]
and topples it. I am told by many of you that I must forgive
and so I shall after the floodwaters burst each successive dam

---

[1] **Grand Coulee Dam:** Massive hydroelectric dam built on the Columbia River in Washington. The
dam flooded lands around the river and destroyed the spawning grounds of salmon, devastating a
Native American culture in which the Columbia River played a central role. Electricity from the dam
helped produce uranium at the Hanford site as part of the atomic bomb development project.

5 downriver from the Grand Coulee. I am told by many of you
that I must forgive and so I shall after the floodwaters find
their way to the mouth of the Columbia River as it enters the
       Pacific
and causes all of it to rise. I am told by many of you that I must
       forgive
and so I shall after the first drop of floodwater is swallowed by that
       salmon
10 waiting in the Pacific. I am told by many of you that I must forgive
       and so I shall
after that salmon swims upstream, through the mouth of the
       Columbia
and then past the flooded cities, broken dams and abandoned
       reactors
of Hanford. I am told by many of you that I must forgive and so I
       shall
after that salmon swims through the mouth of the Spokane River
15 as it meets the Columbia, then upstream, until it arrives
in the shallows of a secret bay on the reservation where I wait
       alone.
I am told by many of you that I must forgive and so I shall after
that salmon leaps into the night air above the water, throws
a lightning bolt at the brush near my feet, and starts the fire
20 which will lead all of the lost Indians home. I am told
by many of you that I must forgive and so I shall
after we Indians have gathered around the fire with that salmon
who has three stories it must tell before sunrise: one story will
       teach us
how to pray; another story will make us laugh for hours;
25 the third story will give us reason to dance. I am told by many
of you that I must forgive and so I shall when I am dancing
with my tribe during the powwow at the end of the world.

CHAPTER 19

BATTER MY HEART, THREE-PERSONED GOD
—John Donne
An Anthology of Poems about First and Last Things

Poets often write about birth and death, taking on these central issues in the life of a human being. Their work becomes a kind of scripture, helping readers to understand their lives, process the difficulties that beset a life, and contemplate the meaning of their existence. Of course, poets and writers are fallible, and their work bears all the marks of human frailty as well as the nobility of human aspirations.

"We work in the dark—and do what we can," wrote Henry James, the novelist. "We give what we have. Our doubt is our passion and our passion is our task. The rest is the madness of art." Poets, it must be said, are specialists in the madness of art, testing the limits of language in order to test the limits of reality. They look for God wherever they can: in nature, in themselves, in friends and loved ones. They work, as James said, in the dark, but what they create is a small lamp that burns in the night, that gives comfort and hope to readers.

Wallace Stevens once suggested that a poet is "the priest of the invisible." What he meant, perhaps, is that poets do not usually content themselves with what has been already observed and written. They look around corners, in thickets where the ordinary hiker fears to tread. In all of this, they remain aware that poetry is not religion, even though it (like religion) often deals with first and last things. They confront the great questions of human existence: Where did I come from? Why am I here? Where am I going? What does it all mean?

This chapter presents poems—both well-known and less familiar—in which poets ponder the imponderables. There is, of course, a long tradition of traditional religious poetry, and some of the greatest poets have written poems that both explore and express their faith. The examples here by Edmund Spenser, Robert Southwell, John Donne, George Herbert, Isaac Watts, Charles Wesley, and Gerard Manley Hopkins—all Christian poets—might be considered poems in this line. These poets celebrate the divine, often referring quite explicitly to Christ himself or to tenets of Christian theology.

Some of the poets included in this selection might be called—rather loosely—mystics. Henry Vaughan, writing in seventeenth-century England, certainly drew on the traditions of mystical writing, and his poems are full of astonishing moments: "I saw eternity the other night/Like a great ring of pure and endless light" (p. 1251). Such claims are breathtaking in their immensity. William Blake was certainly a mystic in his idiosyncratic way: a poet in search of God, but willing to create that God in his own image. Blake forged an intensely private and complicated mythology, a kind of parallel universe of signs and symbols. Although he considered himself a Christian, he was an unusual one, a visionary of the highest order.

Emily Dickinson was obsessed by first and last things. She wrote a myriad of poems about death and the mystery of being. The two poems of hers included in this chapter are startling examples of her best work. Both are about death, and the uncertainty of what that means. In "I heard a Fly buzz—when I died" (p. 1256), the speaker imagines the final moments of consciousness with an eerie serenity. In "Because I could not stop for Death" (p. 1256), she portrays Death as a person coming to pick her up for a little ride out of town. Dickinson was among the most original of all poets, and her view of reality challenges readers to rethink basic premises of their beliefs.

In exploring the limits of faith and the extent to which faith is tested, many poets write movingly about doubt. Yet we should not dismiss doubt as simply "nonbelief." As the Christian theologian Paul Tillich once wrote: "Doubt is not the opposite of faith; it is one element of faith." Some of the poems included here that explore doubt in interesting ways are "Design" by Robert Frost (p. 1259) and "Church Going" by Philip Larkin (p. 1264). These are central in modern and contemporary poetry. In the first, Frost contemplates the possibility that God is responsible for evil in the world, thus making him a rather malevolent creator. The poem's argument follows from the "argument from design" made by medieval theologians, who suggested that God designed the world in such a way that his presence would be evident to all. In its commingling of purity and "blight," it may well be the most frightening poem in the English language. In Larkin's poem, the English poet presents a highly secular speaker who visits a church when nobody is there. A man without explicit faith himself, he nevertheless acknowledges the importance of the building and what it symbolizes:

A serious house on serious earth it is,
In whose blent air all our compulsions meet,
Are recognised, and robed as destinies.

Wallace Stevens thought consistently about spiritual matters, writing from the point of view of an atheist who nevertheless yearned for God. He believed that, in an age of disbelief, it was the poet's job to provide the satisfactions of belief. His poetry became more and more spiritual, and one of his most affecting poems is "Final Soliloquy of the Interior Paramour" (p. 1259), a comforting poem that rises in the end to the level of secular scripture:

We say God and the imagination are one . . .
How high that highest candle lights the dark.

Out of this same light, out of the central mind,
We make a dwelling in the evening air,
5   In which being there together is enough.

The contemporary poets included here—including William Stafford, Howard Nemerov, A. R. Ammons, Charles Wright, Charles Simic, Mary Oliver, and Louise Erdrich—each make a journey to the interior, searching for meaning in a world that seems apparently random, godless, pointless. Each of these poets finds the satisfactions of belief in the world itself and in the language of poetry, which is the embodiment of spirit. Such an attitude, so dependent on the human imagination to create and sustain the world, would never please the more traditional poets of religion. Indeed, it was T. S. Eliot, a devout Christian poet, who put these reservations succinctly: "We know too much and are convinced of too little. Our literature is a substitute for religion, and so is our religion." Yet poetry has become a kind of secular alternative to religion since the time of the Romantics, and there can be little doubt that many poets have addressed spiritual questions with rigor and commitment to whatever truths that they can discover.

ADDITIONAL POEMS ABOUT FIRST AND LAST THINGS IN THIS BOOK

- Anonymous, "How Death Comes" (p. 603)

- Chidiock Tichborne, "Elegy" (p. 136)

- George Herbert, "Love Unknown" (p. 1528)

- John Milton, from *Paradise Lost* (p. 657)

- John Keats, "Ode on a Grecian Urn" (p. 421)

- Gerard Manley Hopkins, "Carrion Comfort" (p. 820) and "Thou Art Indeed Just, Lord" (p. 820)

- Walt Whitman, "When I Heard the Learn'd Astronomer" (p. 1299)

- Thomas Hardy, "Hap" (p. 819)

- Robert Frost, "Fire and Ice" (p. 636) and "Nothing Gold Can Stay" (p. 636)

- Wallace Stevens, "The Emperor of Ice-Cream" (p. 207) and "The Snow Man" (p. 1606)

T'AO YUAN MING (TAO CHIN) (365–427)
trans. Kenneth Rexroth

I Return to the Place I Was Born

From my youth up I never liked the city.
I never forgot the mountains where I was born.
The world caught me and harnessed me
And drove me through dust, thirty years away from home.
5   Migratory birds return to the same tree.
Fish find their way back to the pools where they were hatched.
I have been over the whole country,
And have come back at last to the garden of my childhood.
My farm is only ten acres.
10   The farm house has eight or nine rooms.
Elms and willows shade the back garden.
Peach trees stand by the front door.
The village is out of sight.
You can hear dogs bark in the alleys,
15   And cocks crow in the mulberry trees.
When you come through the gate into the court
You will find no dust or mess.
Peace and quiet live in every room.
I am content to stay here the rest of my life.
20   At last I have found myself.

LI PO (701–762)
trans. Arthur Sze

Night Thoughts

The moonlight falls by my bed.
I wonder if there's frost on the ground.
I raise my head to look at the moon,
then ease down, thinking of home.

ANONYMOUS

Despise the world   (fifteenth century)

Why is the world beloved, that fals is and vein,
Sithen° that hise welthes° ben uncertein?   since / blessings

Also soone slideth his power away
As doith a brokil pot that freish is and gay.

5   Truste ye rather to letters writen in th'is°   the ice
Than to this wretched world, that full of sinne is.

It is fals in his beheste° and right disceiveable;   promise
It hath begiled manye men, it is so unstable.

It is rather to beleve the waveringe wind
10   Than the chaungeable world, that maketh men so blind.

Whether thou slepe othere° wake thou shalt finde it fals,   or
Bothe in his bisynesses and in his lustes als.

Telle me where is Salamon,[1] sumtime a kinge riche?
Or Sampson[2] in his strenkethe, to whom was no man liche.

15   Or the fair man, Absolon,[3] merveilous in chere?
Or the duke, Jonatas,[4] a well-beloved fere°?   friend

---

[1] **Salamon:** I.e., Solomon, the great king of the Jews, son of David. His profligate lifestyle, however, embittered him to God and his kingdom was lost after his death.
[2] **Sampson:** I.e., Samson, a Biblical hero, whose legendary strength helped him win numerous battles against the Philistines. He was betrayed by his wife, who cut his hair (the source of his strength).
[3] **Absolon:** I.e., Absalom, one of the sons of David, murdered his half-brother Amnon as a revenge for the raping Tamar (Absalom's sister). Later, he took arms against David, but was eventually defeated and killed in battle.
[4] **Jonatas:** Perhaps Jonathan, son of Saul, who became a loyal companion of David and later ceded his right to the throne in favor of his friend. He was eventually killed in battle together with his father and brothers.

Where is become Cesar,[5] that lord was of al?
Or the riche man cloithd in purpur and in pal?

Telle me where is Tullius,[6] in eloquence so swete?
20   Or Aristotle the philisophre with his wit so grete?

Where ben these worithy that weren here toforen°?   before
Boithe kinges and bishopes her° power is all loren.°   their / lost

All these grete princes with her power so hiye
Ben vanished away in twinkeling of an iye.

25   The joye of this wretched world is a short feeste:
It is likned to a shadewe that abideth leeste.

And yit it draweth man from Heveneriche° blis,   Heavenly
And ofte time maketh him to sinne and do amis.

Thou that art but wormes mete, powder and dust,
30   To enhance thysilf in pride sette not thy lust.

For thou woost not today that thou shalt live tomorewe,
Therfore do thou evere weel, and thanne shalt thou not sorewe.

It were full joyful and swete lordship to have,
If so that lordship miyite° a man fro deeth save.   could

35   But, for as miche° a man muste die at the laste,   much
It is no worship but a charge lordship to taste.

Calle nothing thine owen, therfore, that thou maist her lese:°   lose
That the world hath lent thee, eft he wolde it sese![7]

Sette thine herte in Heven above and thenke what joye is there,
40   And thus to despise the world I rede° that thou lere.°   advise / learn

---

[5] **Cesar:** I.e., Julius Caesar, who was assassinated by Brutus in 44 B.C.
[6] **Tullius:** I.e., Marcus Tullius Cicero (106 B.C.–43 B.C.), an accomplished Roman poet, philosopher, and rhetorician.
[7] **eft he wolde it sese:** I.e., he intends to take it back.

EDMUND SPENSER   (ca. 1552–1599)

from Amoretti   (1595)

LXVIII

Most glorious Lord of life, that on this day[1]
Didst make Thy triumph over death and sin,
And, having harrowed hell, didst bring away
Captivity thence captive, us to win:
5   This joyous day, dear Lord, with joy begin;
And grant that we, for whom Thou diddest die,
Being with Thy dear blood clean washed from sin,
May live for ever in felicity!
And that Thy love we weighing worthily,
10 May likewise love Thee for the same again;
And for Thy sake, that all like dear didst buy,
With love may one another entertain.
    So let us love, dear love, like as we ought:
    Love is the lesson which the Lord us taught.

ROBERT SOUTHWELL   (ca. 1561–1595)

The Burning Babe[1]   (1602)

As I in hoary winter's night stood shivering in the snow,
Surpris'd I was with sudden heat which made my heart to glow;
And lifting up a fearful eye to view what fire was near,
A pretty Babe all burning bright did in the air appear;
5   Who, scorched with excessive heat, such floods of tears did shed
As though his floods should quench his flames which with his tears
        were fed.
"Alas!" quoth he, "but newly born, in fiery heats I fry,
Yet none approach to warm their hearts or feel my fire but I!
My faultless breast the furnace is, the fuel wounding thorns,
10 Love is the fire, and sighs the smoke, the ashes shame and scorns;
The fuel Justice layeth on, and Mercy blows the coals,
The metal in this furnace wrought are men's defiled souls,
For which, as now on fire I am to work them to their good,
    So will I melt into a bath to wash them in my blood."
15   With this he vanish'd out of sight and swiftly shrunk away,
    And straight I called unto mind that it was Christmas day.

---

[1] **on this day:** I.e., Easter.
[1] **The Burning Babe:** I.e., Jesus Christ.

WILLIAM SHAKESPEARE (1564–1616)

Sonnet 146
"Poor soul, the centre of my sinful earth" (ca. 1595; 1609)

Poor soul, the centre of my sinful earth,
Fool'd by these rebel powers that thee array,
Why dost thou pine within and suffer dearth,
Painting thy outward walls so costly gay?
5   Why so large cost, having so short a lease,
Dost thou upon thy fading mansion spend?
Shall worms, inheritors of this excess,
Eat up thy charge? Is this thy body's end?
Then, soul, live thou upon thy servant's loss,
10   And let that pine to aggravate thy store;
Buy terms divine in selling hours of dross;
Within be fed, without be rich no more:
    So shalt thou feed on Death, that feeds on men,
    And Death once dead, there's no more dying then.

WILLIAM SHAKESPEARE (1564–1616)

from Hamlet
Act III, Scene 1 (Hamlet) (1600; 1623)

To be, or not to be: that is the question:
Whether 'tis nobler in the mind to suffer
The slings and arrows of outrageous fortune,
Or to take arms against a sea of troubles,
5   And by opposing end them? To die: to sleep;
No more; and, by a sleep to say we end
The heart-ache and the thousand natural shocks
That flesh is heir to, 'tis a consummation
Devoutly to be wish'd. To die, to sleep;
10   To sleep: perchance to dream: ay, there's the rub;
For in that sleep of death what dreams may come
When we have shuffled off this mortal coil,
Must give us pause. There's the respect
That makes calamity of so long life;

15 For who would bear the whips and scorns of time,
    The oppressor's wrong, the proud man's contumely,
    The pangs of dispriz'd love, the law's delay,
    The insolence of office, and the spurns
    The patient merit of the unworthy takes,
20 When he himself might his quietus make
    With a bare bodkin°? who would fardels° bear,   *dagger / burdens*
    To grunt and sweat under a weary life,
    But that the dread of something after death,
    The undiscover'd country from whose bourn
25 No traveller returns, puzzles the will,
    And makes us rather bear those ills we have
    Than fly to others that we know not of?
    Thus conscience does make cowards of us all;
    And thus the native hue of resolution
30 Is sicklied o'er with the pale cast of thought,
    And enterprises of great pith and moment
    With this regard their currents turn awry,
    And lose the name of action.

WILLIAM SHAKESPEARE (1564–1616)

from Measure for Measure
Act III, Scene 1 (Claudio) (ca. 1604; 1623)

    Aye, but to die, and go we know not where;
    To lie in cold obstruction and to rot;
    This sensible warm motion to become
    A kneaded clod; and the delighted spirit
5   To bathe in fiery floods, or to reside
    In thrilling region of thick-ribbed ice;
    To be imprison'd in the viewless winds,
    And blown with restless violence round about
    The pendant world; or to be worse than worst
10 Of those that lawless and incertain thoughts
    Imagine howling: 'tis too horrible!
    The weariest and most loathed worldly life
    That age, ache, penury and imprisonment
    Can lay on nature is a paradise
15 To what we fear of death.

WILLIAM SHAKESPEARE (1564–1616)

from Macbeth
Act V, Scene 3 (Macbeth)   (ca. 1606; 1623)

I have liv'd long enough: my way of life
Is fall'n into the sear, the yellow leaf;
And that which should accompany old age,
As honour, love, obedience, troops of friends,
5   I must not look to have; but, in their stead,
Curses, not loud but deep, mouth-honour, breath,
Which the poor heart would fain deny, and dare not.

JOHN DONNE (1572–1631)

from Holy Sonnets   (1633)
Sonnet X

Death be not proud, though some have callèd thee
Mighty and dreadful, for thou art not so;
For those whom thou thinkst thou dost overthrow
Die not, poor death, nor yet canst thou kill me;
5   From rest and sleep, which but thy pictures be,
Much pleasure, then from thee, much more must flow,
And soonest our best men with thee do go,
Rest of their bones, and soul's delivery.
Thou art slave to fate, chance, kings, and desperate men,
10   And dost with poison, war, and sickness dwell;
And poppy or charms can make us sleep as well
And better than thy stroke; why swellst thou then?
One short sleep past, we wake eternally,
And death shall be no more: death thou shalt die.

GEORGE HERBERT (1593–1633)

Easter Wings (1633)

Lord, who createdst man in wealth and store,
　　Though foolishly he lost the same,
　　　　Decaying more and more,
　　　　　　Till he became
5　　　　　　Most poor:
　　　　　　With thee
　　　　　O let me rise
　　　As larks, harmoniously,
　　And sing this day thy victories:
10　Then shall the fall further the flight in me.

My tender age in sorrow did begin:
　　And still with sicknesses and shame
　　　　Thou didst so punish sin
　　　　　That I became
15　　　　　　Most thin.
　　　　　　With thee
　　　　　Let me combine
　　　And feel this day thy victory:
　　For, if I imp my wing on thine,
20　Affliction shall advance the flight in me.

GEORGE HERBERT (1593–1633)

The Pulley (1633)

　　　When God at first made man,
　Having a glass of blessings standing by,
　Let us (said he) pour on him all we can:
　Let the world's riches, which dispersèd lie,
5　　　Contract into span.[1]

---

[1] **Contract into span:** The distance between the thumb and the little finger of a spread hand; i.e., a very small space.

So strength first made a way;
Then beauty flowed, then wisdom, honour, pleasure:
When almost all was out, God made a stay,
Perceiving that alone of all his treasure
10   Rest in the bottom lay.

For if I should (said he)
Bestow this jewel also on my creature,
He would adore my gifts instead of me,
And rest in nature, not the God of nature:
15   So both should losers be.

Yet let him keep the rest,
But keep them with repining restlessness:
Let him be rich and weary, that at least,
If goodness lead him not, yet weariness
20   May toss him to my breast.

GEORGE HERBERT (1593–1633)

The Altar (1633)

A BROKEN ALTAR, Lord, thy servant rears,
Made of a heart, and cémented with tears:
  Whose parts are as thy hand did frame;
  No workman's tool hath touched the same.
5   A HEART alone
          Is such a stone
          As nothing but
          Thy power doth cut.
          Wherefore each part
10   Of my hard heart
          Meets in this frame,
          To praise thy name:
  That, if I chance to hold my peace,
  These stones to praise thee may not cease.
15 O let thy blessed SACRIFICE be mine,
And sanctify this ALTAR to be thine.

HENRY VAUGHAN (1622–1695)

The World (I) (1650)

I saw eternity the other night
Like a great ring of pure and endless light,
    All calm as it was bright,
And round beneath it, time in hours, days, years
5   Driven by the spheres
Like a vast shadow moved, in which the world
    And all her train were hurled:
The doting lover in his quaintest strain
      Did there complain,
10 Near him, his lute, his fancy, and his flights,
      Wit's sour delights,
With gloves and knots, the silly snares of pleasure;
      Yet his dear treasure
All scattered lay, while he his eyes did pour
15   Upon a flower.
The darksome statesman hung with weights and woe
Like a thick midnight-fog moved there so slow
    He did nor stay, nor go;
Condemning thoughts (like sad eclipses) scowl
20   Upon his soul,
And clouds of crying witnesses without
      Pursued him with one shout.
Yet digged the mole, and lest his ways be found
      Worked under ground,
25 Where he did clutch his prey (but one did see
      That policy):
Churches and altars fed him, perjuries
      Were gnats and flies,
It rained about him blood and tears; but he
30   Drank them as free.
The fearful miser on a heap of rust
Sat pining all his life there, did scarce trust
    His own hands with the dust;
Yet would not place one piece above, but lives
35   In fear of thieves.
Thousands there were as frantic as himself
      And hugged each one his pelf;°   riches
The downright epicure placed heaven in sense
      And scorned pretence,
40 While others slipped into a wide excess
      Said little less;

The weaker sort slight, trivial wares enslave
      Who think them brave;
And poor, despisèd truth sat counting by
45   Their victory.
Yet some, who all this while did weep and sing,
And sing and weep, soared up into the ring,
      But most would use no wing.
O fools (said I) thus to prefer dark night
50   Before true light,
To live in grots and caves, and hate the day
      Because it shows the way,
The way which from this dead and dark abode
      Leads up to God,
55 A way where you might tread the sun, and be
      More bright than he.
But as I did their madness so discuss
      One whispered thus,
'This ring the bride-groom did for none provide
60   But for his bride.'

John ii 16–17
All that is in the world, the lust of the flesh, the lust of the eyes, and
the pride of life, is not of the father but is of the world.
    And the world passeth away, and the lusts thereof, but he that
doth the will of God abideth for ever.

ISAAC WATTS (1674–1748)

When I Survey the Wondrous Cross (1707)

When I survey the wondrous cross
on which the Prince of glory died,
my richest gain I count but loss,
and pour contempt on all my pride.

5   Forbid it, Lord, that I should boast,
save in the cross of Christ my God:
all the vain things that charm me most,
I sacrifice them to his blood.

See, from his head, his hands, his feet,
10 sorrow and love flow mingled down!

Did e'er such love and sorrow meet,
or thorns compose so rich a crown?

Were the whole realm of nature mine,
that were a present far too small;
15 love so amazing, so divine,
demands my soul, my life, my all.

CHARLES WESLEY (1707–1788)

"Come on, my partners in distress" (1749)

1

Come on, my partners in distress,
My comrades through the wilderness,
    Who still your bodies feel;
Awhile forget your griefs and fears,
5 And look beyond this vale of tears
    To that celestial hill.

2

Beyond the bounds of time and space
Look forward to that heavenly place,
    The saints' secure abode;
10 On faith's strong eagle pinions rise,
And force your passage to the skies,
    And scale the mount of God.

3

Who suffer with our Master here,
We shall before his face appear,
15   And by his side sit down;
To patient faith the prize is sure,
And all that to the end endure
    The cross, shall wear the crown.

4

Thrice blessed bliss-inspiring hope!
20 It lifts the fainting spirits up,
    It brings to life the dead;
Our conflicts here shall soon be past,
And you and I ascend at last
    Triumphant with our head.

5

25 That great mysterious Deity
    We soon with open face shall see;
        The beatific sight
    Shall fill heaven's sounding courts with praise,
    And wide diffuse the golden blaze
30   Of everlasting light.

6

    The Father shining on his throne,
    The glorious, co-eternal Son,
        The Spirit, one and seven,[1]
    Conspire our rapture to complete,
35 And lo! we fall before his feet,
        And silence heightens heaven.

7

    In hope of that ecstatic pause,
    Jesu, we now sustain the cross,
        And at thy footstool fall,
40 Till thou our hidden life reveal,
    Till thou our ravished spirits fill,
        And God is all in all.

WILLIAM BLAKE (1757–1827)

The Divine Image (1789)

    To Mercy, Pity, Peace, and Love,
    All pray in their distress,
    And to these virtues of delight
    Return their thankfulness.

5   For Mercy, Pity, Peace, and Love,
    Is God our father dear,
    And Mercy, Pity, Peace, and Love,
    Is man, his child and care.

    For Mercy has a human heart,
10 Pity, a human face,

---

[1] **one and seven:** God's seven spirits, according to the book of Revelation.

And Love, the human form divine,
And Peace, the human dress.

Then every man of every clime
That prays in his distress,
15   Prays to the human form divine
Love, Mercy, Pity, Peace.

And all must love the human form,
In heathen, Turk or Jew:
Where Mercy, Love, and Pity dwell
20   There God is dwelling too.

MATTHEW ARNOLD (1822–1888)

To Marguerite: Continued (1852)

Yes! in the sea of life enisled,°   *in an island*
   With echoing straits between us thrown,
   Dotting the shoreless watery wild,
   We mortal millions live *alone.*
5   The islands feel the enclasping flow,
   And then their endless bounds they know.

   But when the moon their hollows lights,
   And they are swept by balms of spring,
   And in their glens, on starry nights,
10 The nightingales divinely sing;
   And lovely notes, from shore to shore,
   Across the sounds and channels pour—

Oh! then a longing like despair
Is to their farthest caverns sent;
15 For surely once, they feel, we were
Parts of a single continent!
Now round us spreads the watery plain—
Oh might our marges meet again!

Who order'd, that their longing's fire
20 Should be, as soon as kindled, cool'd?
Who renters vain their deep desire?—
A God, a God their severance ruled!
And bade betwixt their shores to be
The unplumb'd, salt, estranging sea.

EMILY DICKINSON (1830–1886)

"I heard a Fly buzz—when I died—"
(ca. 1862; 1890)

I heard a Fly buzz—when I died—
The Stillness in the Room
Was like the Stillness in the Air—
Between the Heaves of Storm—

5   The Eyes around—had wrung them dry—
And Breaths were gathering firm
For that last Onset—when the King
Be witnessed—in the Room—

I willed my Keepsakes—Signed away
10 What portion of me be
Assignable—and then it was
There interposed a Fly—

With Blue—uncertain stumbling Buzz—
Between the light—and me—
15 And then the Windows failed—and then
I could not see to see—

EMILY DICKINSON (1830–1886)

"Because I could not stop for Death"
(ca. 1863; 1890)

Because I could not stop for Death—
He kindly stopped for me—
The Carriage held but just Ourselves—
And Immortality.

5   We slowly drove—He knew no haste
And I had put away
My labor and my leisure too,
For His Civility—

We passed the School, where Children strove
10 At Recess—in the Ring—
We passed the Fields of Gazing Grain—
We passed the Setting Sun—

Or rather—He passed Us—
The Dews drew quivering and chill—
15 For only Gossamer, my Gown—
My Tippet—only Tulle—

We paused before a House that seemed
A Swelling of the Ground—
The Roof was scarcely visible—
20 The Cornice—in the Ground—

Since then—'tis Centuries—and yet
Feels shorter than the Day
I first surmised the Horses' Heads
Were toward Eternity—

GERARD MANLEY HOPKINS (1844–1889)

Pied Beauty (1877; 1918)

Glory be to God for dappled things—
   For skies of couple-colour as a brinded cow;
     For rose-moles all in stipple upon trout that swim;
Fresh-firecoal chestnut-falls; finches' wings;
5   Landscape plotted and pieced—fold, fallow, and plough;
     And áll trádes, their gear and tackle and trim.

All things counter, original, spare, strange;
   Whatever is fickle, freckled (who knows how?)
     With swíft, slów; sweet, sóur; adázzle, dím;
10 He fathers-forth whose beauty is pást chánge:
     Praise him.

FRANCIS THOMPSON (1859–1907)

from The Hound of Heaven (1893)

I fled Him, down the nights and down the days;
   I fled Him, down the arches of the years;
I fled Him, down the labyrinthine ways
   Of my own mind; and in the mist of tears
5 I hid from Him, and under running laughter.
     Up vistaed hopes I sped;

And shot, precipitated,
Adown Titanic glooms of chasmèd fears,
From those strong Feet that followed, followed after.
10   But with unhurrying chase,
          And unperturbèd pace,
     Deliberate speed, majestic instancy,
          They beat—and a Voice beat
          More instant than the Feet—
15   "All things betray thee, who betrayest Me."

          I pleaded, outlaw-wise,
By many a hearted casement, curtained red,
     Trellised with intertwining charities;
(For, though I knew His love Who followèd,
20   Yet was I sore adread
Lest, having Him, I must have naught beside,)
But, if one little casement parted wide,
     The gust of His approach would clash it to:
     Fear wist not to evade, as Love wist to pursue.
25 Across the margent of the world I fled,
          And troubled the gold gateways of the stars,
          Smiting for shelter on their clangèd bars;
               Fretted to dulcet jars
And silvern chatter the pale ports o' the moon.
30 I said to Dawn: Be sudden—to Eve: Be soon;
     With thy young skiey blossoms heap me over
          From this tremendous Lover—
Float thy vague veil about me, lest He see!

          *   *   *

          Now of that long pursuit
35   Comes on at hand the bruit;
     That Voice is round me like a bursting sea:
          "And is thy earth so marred,
          Shattered in shard on shard?
     Lo, all things fly thee, for thou fliest Me!
40   Strange, piteous, futile thing!
Wherefore should any set thee love apart?
Seeing none but I makes much of naught" (He said),
"And human love needs human meriting:
          How hast thou merited—
45 Of all man's clotted clay the dingiest clot?
          Alack, thou knowest not
How little worthy of any love thou art!
Whom wilt thou find to love ignoble thee,
          Save Me, save only Me?

50   All which I took from thee I did but take,
        Not for thy harms,
    But just that thou might'st seek it in My arms.
        All which thy child's mistake
    Fancies as lost, I have stored for thee at home:
55   Rise, clasp My hand, and come!"

      Halts by me that footfall:
      Is my gloom, after all,
    Shade of His hand, outstretched caressingly?
        "Ah, fondest, blindest, weakest,
60   I am He Whom thou seekest!
    Thou dravest love from thee, who dravest Me."

ROBERT FROST (1874–1963)

Design (1936)

    I found a dimpled spider, fat and white,
    On a white heal-all, holding up a moth
    Like a white piece of rigid satin cloth—
    Assorted characters of death and blight
5   Mixed ready to begin the morning right,
    Like the ingredients of a witches' broth—
    A snow-drop spider, a flower like a froth,
    And dead wings carried like a paper kite.

    What had that flower to do with being white,
10   The wayside blue and innocent heal-all?
    What brought the kindred spider to that height,
    Then steered the white moth thither in the night?
    What but design of darkness to appall?—
    If design govern in a thing so small.

WALLACE STEVENS (1879–1955)

Final Soliloquy of the Interior Paramour (1954)

    Light the first light of evening, as in a room
    In which we rest and, for small reason, think
    The world imagined is the ultimate good.

This is, therefore, the intensest rendezvous.
5   It is in that thought that we collect ourselves,
Out of all the indifferences, into one thing:

Within a single thing, a single shawl
Wrapped tightly round us, since we are poor, a warmth,
A light, a power, the miraculous influence.

10 Here, now, we forget each other and ourselves.
We feel the obscurity of an order, a whole,
A knowledge, that which arranged the rendezvous.

Within its vital boundary, in the mind.
We say God and the imagination are one . . .
15 How high that highest candle lights the dark.

Out of this same light, out of the central mind,
We make a dwelling in the evening air,
In which being there together is enough.

E. E. CUMMINGS (1894–1962)

"when god lets my body be" (1922)

when god lets my body be

From each brave eye shall sprout a tree
fruit that dangles therefrom

the purpled world will dance upon
5   Between my lips which did sing

a rose shall beget the spring
that maidens whom passion wastes

will lay between their little breasts
My strong fingers beneath the snow

10 Into strenuous birds shall go
my love walking in the grass

their wings will touch with her face
and all the while shall my heart be

With the bulge and nuzzle of the sea

CHARLES REZNIKOFF (1894–1976)

Padua 1717

The sentences we studied are rungs upon the ladder Jacob saw;[1]
the law itself is nothing but the road;
I have become impatient of what the rabbis said,
and try to listen to what the angels say.
5 I have left Padua and am in Jerusalem at last, my friend;
for, as our God was never of wood or bone,
our land is not of stones or earth.

COUNTEE CULLEN (1903–1946)

Yet Do I Marvel (1925)

I doubt not God is good, well-meaning, kind,
And did He stoop to quibble could tell why
The little buried mole continues blind,
Why flesh that mirrors Him must some day die,
5 Make plain the reason tortured Tantalus[1]
Is baited by the fickle fruit, declare
If merely brute caprice dooms Sisyphus[2]
To struggle up a never-ending stair.
Inscrutable His ways are, and immune
10 To catechism by a mind too strewn
With petty cares to slightly understand
What awful brain compels His awful hand.
Yet do I marvel at this curious thing:
To make a poet black, and bid him sing!

---

[1] **the ladder Jacob saw:** According to the Bible, in a vision, Jacob saw a ladder leading from earth to heaven.
[1] **Tantalus:** According to Greek mythology, a king who was condemned in Hades to stand up to his neck in water, thirsty, but never able to drink.
[2] **Sisyphus:** A mythical king who was condemned for eternity to roll a boulder up a mountain, only to have it roll back when he approached the top.

R. S. THOMAS (1913–2000)

Kneeling (1968)

Moments of great calm,
Kneeling before an altar
Of wood in a stone church
In summer, waiting for the God
5   To speak; the air a staircase
For silence; the sun's light
Ringing me, as though I acted
A great rôle. And the audiences
Still; all that close throng
10 Of spirits waiting, as I,
For the message.
                    Prompt me, God;
But not yet. When I speak,
Though it be you who speak
15 Through me, something is lost.
The meaning is in the waiting.

WILLIAM STAFFORD (1914–1993)

Traveling through the Dark (1960)

Traveling through the dark I found a deer
dead on the edge of the Wilson River road.
It is usually best to roll them into the canyon:
that road is narrow; to swerve might make more dead.

5   By glow of the tail-light I stumbled back of the car
and stood by the heap, a doe, a recent killing;
she had stiffened already, almost cold.
I dragged her off; she was large in the belly.

My fingers touching her side brought me the reason—
10 her side was warm; her fawn lay there waiting,
alive, still, never to be born.
Beside that mountain road I hesitated.

The car aimed ahead its lowered parking lights;
under the hood purred the steady engine.
15 I stood in the glare of the warm exhaust turning red;
around our group I could hear the wilderness listen.

I thought hard for us all—my only swerving—,
then pushed her over the edge into the river.

WILLIAM STAFFORD   (1914–1993)

Meditation   (1983)

Animals full of light
walk through the forest
toward someone aiming a gun
loaded with darkness.

5   That's the world: God
holding still
letting it happen again,
and again and again.

HOWARD NEMEROV   (1920–1991)

Easter   (1980)

Even this suburb has overcome Death.
Overnight, by a slow explosion, or
A rapid burning, it begins again
Bravely disturbing the brown ground
5   With grass and even more elaborate
Unnecessaries such as daffodils
And tulips, till the whole sordid block
Of houses turned so inward on themselves,
So keeping of a winter's secret sleep,
10   Looks like a lady's hat, improbably
Nodding with life, with bluejays hooting
And pigeons caracoling[1] up among
The serious chimney pots, and pairs
Of small birds speeding behind the hedges
15   Readying to conceal them soon. Here,
Even here, Death has been vanquished again,
What was a bramble of green barbed wire
Becomes forsythia, as the long war
Begins again, not by our doing or desiring.

---

[1] **caracoling:** To turn slightly to the right or left.

PHILIP LARKIN (1922–1985)

Church Going (1954)

Once I am sure there's nothing going on
I step inside, letting the door thud shut.
Another church: matting, seats, and stone,
And little books; sprawlings of flowers, cut
5   For Sunday, brownish now; some brass and stuff
Up at the holy end; the small neat organ;
And a tense, musty, unignorable silence,
Brewed God knows how long. Hatless, I take off
My cycle-clips in awkward reverence,

10 Move forward, run my hand around the font.
From where I stand, the roof looks almost new—
Cleaned, or restored? Someone would know: I don't.
Mounting the lectern, I peruse a few
Hectoring large-scale verses, and pronounce
15 'Here endeth' much more loudly than I'd meant.
The echoes snigger briefly. Back at the door
I sign the book, donate an Irish sixpence,
Reflect the place was not worth stopping for.

Yet stop I did: in fact I often do,
20 And always end much at a loss like this,
Wondering what to look for; wondering, too,
When churches fall completely out of use
What we shall turn them into, if we shall keep
A few cathedrals chronically on show,
25 Their parchment, plate and pyx[1] in locked cases,
And let the rest rent-free to rain and sheep.
Shall we avoid them as unlucky places?

Or, after dark, will dubious women come
To make their children touch a particular stone;
30 Pick simples° for a cancer; or on some   medicinal herb
Advised night see walking a dead one?
Power of some sort or other will go on
In games, in riddles, seemingly at random;
But superstition, like belief, must die,
35 And what remains when disbelief has gone?
Grass, weedy pavement, brambles, buttress, sky,

---

[1] **pyx:** A box where communion wafers are kept.

A shape less recognisable each week,
A purpose more obscure. I wonder who
Will be the last, the very last, to seek
40   This place for what it was; one of the crew
That tap and jot and know what rood-lofts were?
Some ruin-biber, randy for antique,
Or Christmas-addict, counting on a whiff
Of gown-and-bands and organ-pipes and myrrh?
45   Or will he be my representative,

Bored, uninformed, knowing the ghostly silt
Dispersed, yet tending to this cross of ground
Through suburb scrub because it held unspilt
So long and equably what since is found
50   Only in separation—marriage, and birth,
And death, and thoughts of these—for which was built
This special shell? For, though I've no idea
What this accoutred frowsty barn is worth,
It pleases me to stand in silence here;

55   A serious house on serious earth it is,
In whose blent air all our compulsions meet,
Are recognised, and robed as destinies.
And that much never can be obsolete,
Since someone will forever be surprising
60   A hunger in himself to be more serious,
And gravitating with it to this ground,
Which, he once heard, was proper to grow wise in,
If only that so many dead lie round.

PHILIP LARKIN   (1922–1985)

Aubade   (1977)

I work all day, and get half-drunk at night.
Waking at four to soundless dark, I stare.
In time the curtain-edges will grow light.
Till then I see what's really always there:
5   Unresting death, a whole day nearer now,
Making all thought impossible but how
And where and when I shall myself die.
Arid interrogation: yet the dread

Of dying, and being dead,
10   Flashes afresh to hold and horrify.

The mind blanks at the glare. Not in remorse
—The good not done, the love not given, time
Torn off unused—nor wretchedly because
An only life can take so long to climb
15   Clear of its wrong beginnings, and may never;
But at the total emptiness for ever,
The sure extinction that we travel to
And shall be lost in always. Not to be here,
Not to be anywhere,
20   And soon; nothing more terrible, nothing more true.

This is a special way of being afraid
No trick dispels. Religion used to try,
That vast moth-eaten musical brocade
Created to pretend we never die,
25   And spacious stuff that says *No rational being*
Can fear a thing it will not feel, not seeing
That this is what we fear—no sight, no sound,
No touch or taste or smell, nothing to think with,
Nothing to love or link with,
30   The anaesthetic from which none come round.

And so it stays just on the edge of vision,
A small unfocused blur, a standing chill
That slows each impulse down to indecision.
Most things may never happen: this one will,
35   And realisation of it rages out
In furnace-fear when we are caught without
People or drink. Courage is no good:
It means not scaring others. Being brave
Lets no one off the grave.
40   Death is no different whined at than withstood.

Slowly light strengthens, and the room takes shape.
It stands plain as a wardrobe, what we know,
Have always known, know that we can't escape,
Yet can't accept. One side will have to go.
45   Meanwhile telephones crouch, getting ready to ring
In locked-up offices, and all the uncaring
Intricate rented world begins to rouse.
The sky is white as clay, with no sun.
Work has to be done.
50   Postmen like doctors go from house to house.

RICHARD HUGO   (1923–1982)

Degrees of Gray in Philipsburg[1]   (1973)

You might come here Sunday on a whim.
Say your life broke down. The last good kiss
you had was years ago. You walk these streets
laid out by the insane, past hotels
5   that didn't last, bars that did, the tortured try
of local drivers to accelerate their lives.
Only churches are kept up. The jail
turned seventy this year. The only prisoner
is always in, not knowing what he's done.

10   The principal supporting business now
is rage. Hatred of the various grays
the mountain sends, hatred of the mill,
the Silver Bill repeal, the best liked girls
who leave each year for Butte. One good
15   restaurant and bars can't wipe the boredom out.
The 1907 boom, eight going silver mines,
a dance floor built on springs—
all memory resolves itself in gaze,
in panoramic green you know the cattle eat
20   or two stacks high above the town,
two dead kilns, the huge mill in collapse
for fifty years that won't fall finally down.

Isn't this your life? That ancient kiss
still burning out your eyes? Isn't this defeat
25   so accurate, the church bell simply seems
a pure announcement: ring and no one comes?
Don't empty houses ring? Are magnesium
and scorn sufficient to support a town,
not just Philipsburg, but towns
30   of towering blondes, good jazz and booze
the world will never let you have
until the town you came from dies inside?

Say no to yourself. The old man, twenty
when the jail was built, still laughs
35   although his lips collapse. Someday soon,

---

[1] **Philipsburg:** A town in Montana.

he says, I'll go to sleep and not wake up.
You tell him no. You're talking to yourself.
The car that brought you here still runs.
The money you buy lunch with,
40   No matter where it's mined, is silver
And the girl who serves you food
Is slender and her red hair lights the wall.

A. R. AMMONS (1926–2001)

Hymn (1956)

I know if I find you I will have to leave the earth
and go on out
       over the sea marshes and the brant in bays
and over the hills of tall hickory
5   and over the crater lakes and canyons
and on up through the spheres of diminishing air
past the blackset noctilucent° clouds   luminous
              where one wants to stop and look
way past all the light diffusions and bombardments
10   up farther than the loss of sight
              into the unseasonal undifferentiated empty stark

And I know if I find you I will have to stay with the earth
inspecting with thin tools and ground eyes
trusting the microvilli sporangia and simplest
              coelenterates[1]
15   and praying for a nerve cell
with all the soul of my chemical reactions
and going right on down where the eye sees only traces

You are everywhere partial and entire
You are on the inside of everything and on the outside

20   I walk down the path down the hill where the sweetgum
has begun to ooze spring sap at the cut

---

[1] **microvilli sporangia . . . coelenterates:** Microvilli: small hair-like structures, projecting from certain epithelial cells. Sporangia: organisms which produce spores, e.g., fungi, algae, mosses, and ferns. Coelenterates: any of the various invertebrate animals from the phylum Cnidaria, such as hydras and jellyfish.

and I see how the bark cracks and winds like no other bark
chasmal to my ant-soul running up and down
and if I find you I must go out deep into your far resolutions
25   and if I find you I must stay here with the separate leaves

PETER SCUPHAM (1933–   )

First Things, Last Things (1994)

And it was first, after the mess and straining,
Runs of hot water, new-bread smells of linen,
Ripples of light, and I think there would be flowers,
To bring, from throat and loosened tongue
5   The urgent vocables of love and fear,

Which might be only the ungiven names
For what was warm, cold. The night, the night,
A face pressed against the press of milk,
And, under a smile stretched from her smiling,
10   The suck and sob of things . . .

In between, the long brocade of lies,
Truths, half-truths, webs of such distinction
That every face he knew could grow to fit them,
Though there were flowers with a myriad names
15   Dying easily on dying grasses.

And it was last, and the retreat of words
Drained from the bed, as Matthew Arnold's sea[1]
Drained, still drains over the smoothened shingle.
Again, flowers: the new-bread smells of linen,
20   The urgent vocables of love and fear

When hands that never touched were quick to touch,
Touched to the quick. There were no names for things,
Because, in that communion of shades
Which sang in paradox with angel-voices
25   The dark was entered easily as the light.

---

[1] **Matthew Arnold's sea:** See Arnold's "Dover Beach" in Chapter 25.

WOLE SOYINKA (1934–   )

Night

Your hand is heavy, Night, upon my brow,
I bear no heart mercuric like the clouds, to dare
Exacerbation from your subtle plough.

Woman as a clam, on the sea's crescent
5   I saw your jealous eye quench the sea's
Fluorescence, dance on the pulse incessant

Of the waves. And I stood, drained
Submitting like the sands, blood and brine
Coursing to the roots. Night, you rained

10   Serrated shadows through dank leaves
Till, bathed in warm suffusion of your dappled cells
Sensations pained me, faceless, silent as night thieves.

Hide me now, when night children haunt the earth
I must hear none! These misted calls will yet
15   Undo me; naked, unbidden, at Night's muted birth.

MARY OLIVER (1935–   )

When Death Comes (1992)

When death comes
like the hungry bear in autumn;
when death comes and takes all the bright coins from his purse

to buy me, and snaps the purse shut;
5   when death comes
like the measle-pox;

when death comes
like an iceberg between the shoulder blades,

I want to step through the door full of curiosity, wondering:
10   what is it going to be like, that cottage of darkness?

And therefore I look upon everything
as a brotherhood and a sisterhood,

and I look upon time as no more than an idea,
and I consider eternity as another possibility,

15   and I think of each life as a flower, as common
as a field daisy, and as singular,

and each name a comfortable music in the mouth,
tending, as all music does, toward silence,

and each body a lion of courage, and something
20   precious to the earth.

When it's over, I want to say: all my life
I was a bride married to amazement.
I was the bridegroom, taking the world into my arms.

When it's over, I don't want to wonder
25   if I have made of my life something particular, and real.
I don't want to find myself sighing and frightened,
or full of argument.

I don't want to end up simply having visited this world.

CHARLES WRIGHT (1935–   )

Him (1977)

His sorrow hangs like a heart in the star-flowered boundary tree.
It mirrors the endless wind.

He feeds on the lunar differences and flies up at the dawn.

When he lies down, the waters will lie down with him,
5   And all that walks and all that stands still, and sleep through the thunder.

It's for him that the willow bleeds.

Look for him high in the flat black of the northern Pacific sky,
Released in his suit of lights,
                              lifted and laid clear.

CHARLES SIMIC (1938–   )

Charon's[1] Cosmology (1977)

With only his dim lantern
To tell him where he is
And every time a mountain
Of fresh corpses to load up

5   Take them to the other side
Where there are plenty more
I'd say by now he must be confused
As to which side is which

I'd say it doesn't matter
10   No one complains he's got
Their pockets to go through
In one a crust of bread in another a sausage

Once in a long while a mirror
Or a book which he throws
15   Overboard into the dark river
Swift and cold and deep

JAMES TATE (1943–   )

A Radical Departure (1976)

Bye!

I'm going to a place so thoroughly remote
you'll never hear from me again.

No train ship plane or automobile
5   has ever pierced its interior

I'm not even certain it's still there
or ever was
the maps are very vague about it

---

[1] **Charon:** In Greek mythology, the boatman who ferries the dead across the river Styx to Hades (the underworld).

some say here some say there
10   but most have let the matter drop

Yes of course it requires courage
I'll need two bottles of vintage champagne every day
to keep the morale high

and do you mind if I take your wife?
15   Well, I guess this is it
we'll see ourselves to the door

Where are we . . . ?

J. D. McCLATCHY (1945–   )

Aden[1] (2002)

Rimbaud dying[2]

His room. His room is a burning aquarium.
The moon has set. The click of prayer beads
Soothes someone's panic downstairs.
Any minute now the sun's evil eye
5   Will peer through the packing-crate shutters
To settle on a scale hung from the ceiling.

The indifferent day stretches out on rawhide
And chews its qat.[3] The bandage is sweating,
His leg is sweating, his knee now swollen
10   To the size of a skull. Angels in his veins
Weep for their empty sabbath and loot his sorrows.
Stalls in the Market of Silence open next door.

The world is happening again without him.
Grit's blown up onto the trussed sharks.

---

[1] **Aden:** A former British colony, now a city on the territory of Yemen.
[2] **Rimbaud dying:** Arthur Rimbaud (1854–1891), one of the most influential French poets of the nineteenth century, abandoned his craft at the age of 21 and left for Africa and the Middle East to become an explorer, mercenary, and a gun runner. Later in his life he developed synovitis in the right knee, a condition which required that his leg be amputated. The surgery, however, did not help him, as he died of cancer that same year. During his adolescence, Rimbaud was notorious for his excessive drinking and dissolute lifestyle.
[3] **qat:** A shrub cultivated in the Middle East and Africa for its aromatic leaves, which were used as a stimulant when chewed or brewed as tea.

15   Two subalterns in topees[4] are arguing.
     Dhows at the wharf, gharries[5] at the curb,
     Mongrels and hawkers and slops in the shade.
     The black boy beside him whispers "*Mektoub*."[6]

     Where is forgiveness? A hand is stroking
20   His head, the fingers like albino carp
     Gliding aimlessly through his hair,
     Brushing sometimes against the fever-weed.
     Where is forgiveness? Sleep with your eyes open,
     Sleep on the stone you have made of your heart.

25   Here at the end—Death clumsy as an old priest—
     Some words, some oil, a thin broth of memory . . .
     Lying at night in a waving wheatfield, face to face
     With the sky's black icon. The stars are moving too.
     They rustle like a silk in whose pleats are kept
30   The changes: flesh to flame, ash to air.

THOMAS LUX (1946–   )

The Perfect God (1990)

     The perfect god puts forth no dogma, cant,
     or laws that dim the soul. He lets you sleep
     and eat and work and love and treats you like
     a man, woman. He needs no slaves; the self-
5   appointed, meek but cruel—they annoy him.
     There are old books he didn't write but likes

     for their rhythms and truths some of the stories tell.
     He likes, loves these books, I said, but is bored
     by exegesis too literal, wild.
10   Prose, poems, sometimes suffer the same fate,
     but this also bores him and he won't, can't,
     or does not care, or dare, to interfere

     with either. The perfect god is sad, hurt,
     when humans fear their lives—those solitudes

---

[4] **topee:** A pith helmet worn for protection against the sun.
[5] **dhows . . . gharries:** Dhow: A sailing vessel with one mast used in Arabia and the Indian Ocean.
Gharry: a horse-drawn carriage used in Egypt and India.
[6] **Mektoub:** It has been written, i.e., it is Allah's will (Arabic).

15   so small beside the tundra, polar caps,
      Congo River (whose every curve he loves),
      the empty, equatorial bliss. He likes,
      loves what's vast, which seems to us so blank.

      He loves what's sane, serene, and fiercely calm,
20   which he didn't invent but understands.
      The perfect god—and god, yes, is perfect—
      is impassive, patient, aloof, alert,
      and needs not our praise nor our blame.
      And needs not our praise nor our blame.

LORNA GOODISON (1947–   )

In the Mountains of the Moon, Uganda (1995)

      In the mountains of the moon, Uganda
      God wept fresh tears when God's gracious heart
      conceived of what it would mean
      for willing souls to make the journey of peril
5   back to Her/Him.

      From these twin streams of compassion
      the Nile was born.
      And your soul has followed its course
      winding, bending back upon itself
10   forcing you to bend too.

      Who can walk to where the Nile begins or ends?
      You with a will of iron and a head as hard.
      For no one can convince you not to follow
      to its ending
15   what God wept to create in the beginning.

CHASE TWICHELL (1950–   )

Passing Clouds (1998)

      One sip of self-understanding
      and I'm drunk as the wind slurring
      its words on the field.

Once in a while the cloud bank splits,
5   and I glimpse the perfect sky,
there all the time behind the mind's cumulus.

Like all intoxicants, self-knowledge
darkens the mind. It's a good thing surprise still
pierces that darkness with its white shoots.

10   When I cut the young maples,
light ploughed a garden in the field.
Now my stakes and string claim a square of shade.

The apples lie where they fall, hard and green
until the animals come to feed on them,
15   or the hungry frost.

MICHAEL COLLIER (1953–   )

A Real-Life Drama (2000)

This dog standing in the middle of the street,
tail stiff, fur bushy with fear, and a pedigree rabbit,
its neck broken and bleeding beneath his paws,
might have been forgiven or simply taken away

5   and shot under different circumstances
and no one would have said much, except his owner
who'd gone out into the yard at the start
of the commotion, having been involved

at other times with the dog's truancies, and yelled,
10   "Bosco, Bosco, goddamnit!" but unavailing,
and everyone understanding that once more Bosco
had been taken over by the dark corner of his nature.

But this other sentiment we shared as well: the man
who'd raised the rabbit shouldn't husband something
15   so rare and beautiful he couldn't keep it
from the likes of Bosco.

LOUISE ERDRICH (1954–   )

Fooling God (1970)

I must become small and hide where he cannot reach.
I must become dull and heavy as an iron pot.
I must be tireless as rust and bold as roots
growing through the locks on doors
5   and crumbling the cinder blocks
of the foundations of his everlasting throne.
I must be strange as pity so he'll believe me.
I must be terrible and brush my hair
so that he finds me attractive.
10   Perhaps if I invoke Clare, the patron saint of television.
Perhaps if I become the images
passing through the cells of a woman's brain.

I must be very large and block his sight.
I must be sharp and impetuous as knives.
15   I must insert myself into the bark of his apple trees,
and cleave the bones of his cows. I must be the marrow
that he drinks into his cloud-wet body.
I must be careful and laugh when he laughs.
I must turn down the covers and guide him in.
20   I must fashion his children out of Play-Doh, blue, pink, green.
I must pull them from between my legs
and set them before the television.

I must hide my memory in a mustard grain
so that he'll search for it over time until time is gone.
25   I must lose myself in the world's regard and disparagement.
I must remain this person and be no trouble.
None at all. So he'll forget.
I'll collect dust out of reach,
a single dish from a set, a flower made of felt,
30   a tablet the wrong shape to choke on.

I must become essential and file everything
under my own system,
so we can lose him and his proofs and adherents.
I must be a doubter in a city of belief
35   that hails his signs (the great footprints
long as limousines, the rough print on the wall).
On the pavement where his house begins
fainting women kneel. I'm not among them
although they polish the brass tongues of his lions
40   with their own tongues
and taste the everlasting life.

EARTH'S THE RIGHT PLACE FOR LOVE

CHAPTER 20

—Robert Frost

An Anthology of Poems on the Nature of Nature

"Nature is the symbol of the spirit," wrote Ralph Waldo Emerson in his seminal book, *Nature* (1836). Emerson, a poet and essayist, understood that poets survey the natural world—its rivers and trees, its fields and streams—for signs of spiritual life, and that a deep correspondence exists between the natural world and the human mind. Indeed, "the whole of nature is a metaphor of the human mind," he asserted.

Poets have always written about the natural world, finding a wealth of material in its landscapes and weather, its flora and fauna. The early Chinese poets, in particular, were attentive to landscapes and the shifts in weather, which seemed to mirror shifts in the poet's mood. They read the natural world closely, as in "Sunset," a lovely poem by Tu Fu (712–770 A.D.) that is as much about the end of a life as about the physical end of the day:

> Sunset glitters on the beads
> Of the curtains. Spring flowers
> Bloom in the valley. The gardens
> Along the river are filled
> 5 With perfume. Smoke of cooking
> Fires drifts over the slow barges.
> Sparrows hop and tumble in
> The branches. Whirling insects
> Swarm in the air. Who discovered
> 10 That one cup of thick wine
> Will dispel a thousand cares?

(translated by Kenneth Rexroth)

The stillness at the center of Chinese nature poetry is breathtaking, and it calms the reader. This is true of a good deal of nature poetry, which in the West reaches back to the pastoral verse of Greece and Rome.

In Greek poetry the tradition of pastoral verse begins with Theocritus, who wrote in the third century B.C. His intensely lyrical poems about the Sicilian countryside were meant for a sophisticated audience in Alexandria, and they stood to illustrate the differences in tempo and quality of life between country and city. W. W. Greg, a scholar, writes: "What does appear to be a constant element in the pastoral as known to literature is the recognition of a contract, implicit or expressed, between pastoral life and some more complex type of civilization."

Pastoral poems (from the Latin word *pastor,* meaning "shepherd") feature shepherds with names like Daphnis and Chloe. They roam the countryside, keeping watch over their flocks, engaged in wooing, discussing the corruption of civil societies and urban life, and meditating on the brevity of life and the meaning of death. Virgil, the great Roman poet, imitated Greek bucolic (another word for pastoral) poetry in his **eclogues,** which were stylized poems featuring shepherds in conversation. Virgil's rustic scenery and humble shepherds provided a stark contrast to his contemporary Romans, whose culture was decadent and egotistical. In the best of pastoral verse, the contrast between country and city is not shallow and overly simple; an equilibrium between country and city life strikes these poets as ideal, although the yearning for a rustic life remains at the center of their work. William Empson, a poet and critic, discussed these matters in *English Pastoral Poetry* (1938):

> The essential trick of the old pastoral, which was felt to imply a beautiful relation between rich and poor, was to make simple people express strong feelings . . . in learned and fashionable language. . . . From seeing the two sorts of people combined like this you thought better of both; the best parts of both were used. The effect was in some degree to combine in the reader or author the merits of the two sorts; he was made to mirror in himself more completely the effective elements of the society he lived in.

In other words, these writers of pastoral verse were extremely sophisticated, and they wrote for a well-educated audience, which meant an audience in the city.

During the Renaissance in England, an attempt was made by extremely learned poets to imitate Greek and Latin poets in the pastoral mode; the results were highly artificial, as in Edmund Spenser's *Shepheard's Calender* (1579). More interesting examples of the pastoral revival can be found in Christopher Marlowe's "The Passionate Shepherd to His Love" (p. 1550) and Sir Walter Ralegh's "The Nymph's Reply to the Shepherd" (p. 1551).

Pastoral poetry tends to take as its subject love and loss. Often, these poems were elegies for a lost friend or important figure. The pastoral elegy was fairly strict in its form, with an invocation of the muse and a progression through various stages of lament. Examples of the pastoral elegy in English are Shelley's tribute to his friend John Keats "Adonais" (p. 161) and Matthew Arnold's "Thrysis" (p. 194). These are both learned elegies, evoking their Greek and Roman models effectively for an audience that would have been familiar with both.

Pastoral poetry, as a tradition, underlies the modern tradition of nature poetry, which finds its best early examples in Wordsworth, John Clare, Whitman, and other poets of the nineteenth century. Certainly, most critics consider Wordsworth the father of modern nature poetry. He was deeply attracted to nature, and his verse is suffused with natural imagery. Well before Emerson, Wordsworth read nature as a symbol of the spirit, always finding in the natural world a place where he could retreat for solitude and spiritual sustenance, as he wrote in "Tintern Abbey":

                                    For I have learned
       To look on nature, not as in the hour
       Of thoughtless youth; but hearing oftentimes
       The still, sad music of humanity,
       Nor harsh nor grating, though of ample power
5   To chasten and subdue. And I have felt
       A presence that disturbs me with the joy
       Of elevated thoughts; a sense sublime
       Of something far more deeply interfused,
       Whose dwelling is the light of setting suns,
10   And the round ocean and the living air,
       And the blue sky, and in the mind of man;
       A motion and a spirit, that impels
       All thinking things, all objects of all thought,
       And rolls through all things.

This magical "sense of something far more deeply interfused" permeates the nature poetry of the twentieth century, from Frost and D. H. Lawrence to Robinson Jeffers, Theodore Roethke, Charles Wright, and Mary Oliver. These are all spiritual poets who cast their thoughts upon nature and discover, in the details of nature, a spiritual reality. Some of the poetry in this section merely presents a vivid sense of nature, as in "Corsons Inlet" by A. R. Ammons (p. 1310) or "Death of a Naturalist" by Seamus Heaney (p. 1322). We would not wish to make great claims for this work as having a spiritual aspect, but nature shines through it, grounding the poems in a sense of place.

The sense of place is largely what governs most of the poems included in this chapter. And *place* means more than mere geographical setting. It is a state of mind as well, a construct made of words and intended to *stand in* for nature. The old tension between the rustic world and the sophisticated reader who wants to discover this world in language continues to play a part in this poetry. Nature poets, consciously or unconsciously, understand this, and their work pulls into play the most complex forms and techniques of poetry to create verbal constructs that will get the job done.

Never imagine that a nature poet is just some talented and well-spoken farmer, a rustic who happens to delight in the natural world.

Poems are made of words, not mud and straw, not sticks and stones. These words nevertheless evoke a world of mud and straw, of sticks and stones. The reality of this language is undeniable; but it remains language. Nature—that elusive thing—lies at the center of this work, of course. It may also be true, as Wordsworth once noted, that nature never did "betray the heart that loved her." Yet it will not serve the reader well to make easy, unqualified assumptions. Poets point to the natural world with language much as a man points to the beautiful moon. Foolishly, the man's dog barks at his finger, losing sight of the moon.

ADDITIONAL POEMS ABOUT NATURE IN THIS BOOK

- Ch'u Ch'uang I, "A Mountain Spring" (p. 601)
- Ch'u Ch'uang I, "Evening in the Garden Clear After Rain" (p. 601)
- Wang Wei, "Autumn Twilight in the Mountains" (p. 602)
- Tu Fu, "Spring Rain" (p. 602)
- William Shakespeare, "Under the Greenwood Tree" (p. 611)
- Christopher Marlowe, "The Passionate Shepherd to His Love" (p. 1550)
- Sir Walter Ralegh, "The Nymph's Reply to the Shepherd" (p. 1551)
- John Milton, "Lycidas" (p. 142)
- Percy Bysshe Shelley, "Adonais" (p. 161)
- Percy Bysshe Shelley, "Ode to the West Wind" (p. 419)
- Gerard Manley Hopkins, "Pied Beauty" (p. 1257)
- Matthew Arnold, "Thrysis" (p. 194)
- Robert Frost, "Birches" (p. 666)
- Robert Frost, "The Road Not Taken" (p. 1600)
- Robert Frost, "Directive" (p. 667)
- William Carlos Williams, "Willow Poem" (p. 639)
- W. H. Auden, "In Praise of Limestone" (p. 439)
- Dylan Thomas, "Fern Hill" (p. 909)
- James Wright, "Lying in a Hammock at William Duffy's Farm in Pine Island, Minnesota" (p. 649)
- John Ashbery, "Farm Implements and Rutabagas in a Landscape" (p. 865)
- Charles Wright, "Yard Work" (p. 1460)
- Charles Simic, "Summer Morning" (p. 1321)
- Gary Soto, "Field Poem" (p. 654)
- Robert Hass, "Meditation at Lagunitas" (p. 1464)

CHUANG TZU (399 B.C.–295 B.C.)
trans. Thomas Merton

The Breath of Nature (ca. fourth century B.C.)

When great Nature sighs, we hear the winds
Which, noiseless in themselves,
Awaken voices from other beings,
Blowing on them.
5   From every opening
Loud voices sound. Have you not heard
This rush of tones?

There stands the overhanging wood
On the steep mountain:
10   Old trees with holes and cracks
Like snouts, maws, and ears,
Like beam-sockets, like goblets,
Grooves in the wood, hollows full of water:
You hear mooing and roaring, whistling,
15   Shouts of command, grumblings,
Deep drones, sad flutes.
One call awakens another in dialogue.
Gentle winds sing timidly,
Strong ones blast on without restraint.
20   Then the wind dies down. The openings
Empty out their last sound.
Have you not observed how all then trembles and subsides?

Yu replied: I understand:
The music of earth sings through a thousand holes.
25   The music of man is made on flutes and instruments.
What makes the music of heaven?

Master Ki said:
Something is blowing on a thousand different holes.
Some power stands behind all this and makes the sounds die down.
30   What is this power?

T'AO CH'IEN (365–427)
trans. Arthur Sze

Returning to Fields and Gardens (I)

When I was young, I did not fit in
with others, and simply loved the hills and mountains.
By mistake, I fell into the dusty net
and before I knew it, it was thirty years!
5   The caged bird longs for the old forest.
The fish in the pond misses the old depths.
I cultivate land along the southern wilds,
and, keeping to simplicity, return to fields and gardens.
Ten acres now surround my house;
10   it is thatched, and has eight, nine rooms.
Elms and willows shade the back eaves.
Peach and plum trees are lined out the front hall.
The distant village is hazy, hazy: and
slender, slender, the smoke hanging over houses.
15   Dogs bark in the deep lane, and a rooster
crows on top of a mulberry tree.
My house untouched by the dust of the world—
ample leisure in these bare rooms.
I was held so long inside a narrow bird-
20   cage, but now, at last, can return to nature.

T'AO CH'IEN (365–427)
trans. Arthur Sze

Returning to Fields and Gardens (II)

I plant beans below the southern hill:
there grasses flourish and bean sprouts are sparse.
At dawn, I get up, clear out a growth of weeds,
then go back, leading the moon, a hoe over my shoulder.

5   Now the path is narrow, grasses and bushes are high.
Evening dew moistens my clothes;
but so what if my clothes are wet—
I choose not to avoid anything that comes.

RIHAKU (eighth century)
trans. Ezra Pound

Taking Leave of a Friend

Blue mountains to the north of the walls,
White river winding about them;
Here we must make separation
and go out through a thousand miles of dead grass.

5   Mind like a floating wide cloud,
Sunset like the parting of old acquaintances
Who bow over their clasped hands at a distance.
Our horses neigh to each other as we are departing.

HENRY HOWARD, EARL OF SURREY (ca. 1517–1547)

The Soote Season[1] (1557)

The soote° season, that bud and bloom forth brings,	sweet
With green hath clad the hill and eke° the vale;	also
The nightingale with feathers new she sings;	
The turtle° to her make° hath told her tale.	turtledove / mate
5 Summer is come, for every spray now springs;	
The hart hath hung his old head on the pale;[2]	
The buck in brake° his winter coat he flings,	the bushes
The fishes float with new repairèd scale;	
The adder all her slough away she slings,	
10 The swift swallow pursueth the flies small;	
The busy bee her honey now she mings.°	releases
Winter is worn, that was the flowers' bale.°	bane
And thus I see among these pleasant things,	
Each care decays, and yet my sorrow springs.	

---

[1] **The Soote Season:** Howard's adaptation of Petrarch's *Rime* 310.
[2] **hath hung . . . pale:** I.e., has hung his antlers on the fence.

WILLIAM SHAKESPEARE (1564–1616)

When Daisies Pied (ca. 1595)

Spring

	When daisies pied° and violets blue	colored
	And lady-smocks° all silver-white	cuckoo-flowers
	And cuckoo-buds of yellow hue	
	Do paint the meadows with delight,	
5	The cuckoo then, on every tree,	
	Mocks married men;[1] for thus sings he,	
	Cuckoo;	
	Cuckoo, cuckoo: Oh word of fear,	
	Unpleasing to a married ear!	
10	When shepherds pipe on oaten straws,	
	And merry larks are plowmen's clocks,	
	When turtles tread,° and rooks, and daws,	turtledoves mate
	And maidens bleach their summer smocks,	
	The cuckoo then, on every tree,	
15	Mocks married men, for thus sings he,	
	Cuckoo;	
	Cuckoo, cuckoo: Oh word of fear,	
	Unpleasing to a married ear!	

Winter

	When icicles hang by the wall	
	And Dick the shepherd blows his nail[2]	
	And Tom bears logs into the hall,	
	And milk comes frozen home in pail.	
5	When blood is nipped and ways be foul,	
	Then nightly sings the staring owl,	
	Tu-who;	
	Tu-whit, tu-who: a merry note,	
	While greasy Joan doth keel° the pot.	stir
10	When all aloud the wind doth blow,	
	And coughing drowns the parson's saw,°	sermon
	And birds sit brooding in the snow,	
	And Marian's nose looks red and raw,	
	When roasted crabs° hiss in the bowl,	crab apples (for ale)

---

1. **Mocks married men:** "Cuckoo" sounds like "cuckold," a man whose wife has committed adultery.
2. **blows his nail:** I.e., blows on his hands to stay warm.

15 Then nightly sings the staring owl,
                    Tu-who;
    Tu-whit, tu-who: a merry note
    While greasy Joan doth keel the pot.

WILLIAM SHAKESPEARE (1564–1616)

"When daffodils begin to peer" (ca. 1609; 1623)

When daffodils begin to peer,
    With heigh! the doxy,° over the dale,   beggar
Why, then comes in the sweet o' the year;
    For the red blood reigns in the winter's pale.[1]

5   The white sheet bleaching on the hedge,[2]
    With heigh! the sweet birds, O, how they sing!
Doth set my pugging tooth on edge,
    For a quart of ale is a dish for a king.

The lark, that tirra-lirra chants,
10   With heigh! with heigh! the thrush and the jay,
Are summer songs for me and my aunts,[3]
    While we lie tumbling in the hay.

THOMAS NASHE (1567–1601)

from Summer's Last Will (1600)
Spring, the Sweet Spring

Spring, the sweet spring, is the year's pleasant king,
Then blooms each thing, then maids dance in a ring,
Cold doth not sting, the pretty birds do sing:
    Cuckoo, jug-jug, pu-we, to-witta-woo![1]

---

[1] **The red . . . pale:** I.e., the skin is turned pale in the winter.
[2] **The white . . . hedge:** In Shakespeare's day, it was a typical practice to dry clothing on the hedges.
[3] **aunts:** Slang term for women who take beggars for lovers.
[1] **Cuckoo . . . woo:** Song of the cuckoo, nightingale, lapwing, and owl.

5   The palm and may² make country houses gay,
     Lambs frisk and play, the shepherds pipe all day,
     And we hear aye birds tune this merry lay:
          Cuckoo, jug-jug, pu-we, to-witta-woo!

     The fields breathe sweet, the daisies kiss our feet,
10   Young lovers meet, old wives a-sunning sit,
     In every street these tunes our ears do greet:
          Cuckoo, jug-jug, pu-we, to-witta-woo!
               Spring, the sweet spring!

ANDREW MARVELL   (1621–1678)

The Garden   (1681)

     How vainly men themselves amaze
     To win the palm, the oak, or bays,¹
     And their uncessant labours see
     Crowned from some single herb or tree,
5   Whose short and narrow vergèd shade
     Does prudently their toils upbraid,
     While all flow'rs and all trees do close°   unite
     To weave the garlands of repose.

     Fair quiet, have I found thee here,
10   And innocence thy sister dear!
     Mistaken long, I sought you then
     In busy companies of men.
     Your sacred plants,° if here below,   cuttings
     Only among the plants will grow.
15   Society is all but rude,
     To° this delicious solitude.   compared to

     No white nor red² was ever seen
     So am'rous as this lovely green.
     Fond lovers, cruel as their flame,
20   Cut in these trees their mistress' name.
     Little, alas, they know, or heed,
     How far these beauties hers exceed!

---

² **The palm and may:** I.e., palm leaves and hawthorn blossoms.
¹ **the palm . . . bays:** Wreaths presented for accomplishment in athletics, civics, and poetics, respectively.
² **white nor red:** Colors typically used to depict female beauty in the Petrarchan tradition of love poetry.

Fair trees! wheres'e'er your barks I wound,
No name shall but your own be found.

25 When we have run our passion's heat,°   course
Love hither makes his best retreat.
The gods, that mortal beauty chase,
Still in a tree did end their race.[3]
Apollo hunted Daphne so,
30 Only that she might laurel grow:
And Pan did after Syrinx speed,
Not as a nymph, but for a reed.

What wondrous life in this I lead!
Ripe apples drop about my head;
35 The luscious clusters of the vine
Upon my mouth do crush their wine;
The nectarine and curious° peach   wonderful
Into my hands themselves do reach;
Stumbling on melons, as I pass,
40 Ensnared with flowers, I fall on grass.

Meanwhile the mind, from pleasures less,
Withdraws into its happiness:
The mind, that ocean where each kind
Does straight its own resemblance find;[4]
45 Yet it creates, transcending these,
Far other worlds, and other seas,
Annihilating all that's made
To a green thought in a green shade.

Here at the fountain's sliding foot,
50 Or at some fruit-tree's mossy root,
Casting the body's vest[5] aside,
My soul into the boughs does glide:
There like a bird it sits, and sings,
Then whets, and combs its silver wings;
55 And, till prepared for longer flight,
Waves in its plumes the various° light.   iridescent

---

[3] **in a tree . . . race:** According to Ovid, the nymphs Daphne and Syrinx both avoided the unwanted
love of their pursuers by being transformed into a laurel tree (Daphne) and reeds (Syrinx) with the
help of Apollo and Pan.
[4] **The mind . . . find:** The mind was thought to be a counterpart of the ocean in the same way that
every land creature was thought to have a corresponding sea creature.
[5] **the body's vest:** I.e., the body itself.

Such was that happy garden-state,
While man there walked without a mate:
After a place so pure, and sweet,
60   What other help could yet be meet!
But 'twas beyond a mortal's share
To wander solitary there:
Two paradises 'twere in one
To live in paradise alone.

65   How well the skilful gardener drew
Of flowers and herbs this dial new;
Where from above the milder sun
Does through a fragrant zodiac run;
And, as it works, the industrious bee
70   Computes its time as well as we.
How could such sweet and wholesome hours
Be reckoned but with herbs and flowers!

HENRY VAUGHAN (1622–1695)

The Waterfall (1655)

With what deep murmurs through time's silent stealth
Doth thy transparent, cool and watery wealth
      Here flowing fall,
      And chide, and call,
5   As if his liquid, loose retínue[1] stayed
Ling'ring, and were of this steep place afraid,
      The common pass
      Where, clear as glass,
      All must descend
10   Not to an end:
But quickened by this deep and rocky grave,
Rise to a longer course more bright and brave.[2]

Dear stream! dear bank, where often I
Have sat, and pleased my pensive eye,
15   Why, since each drop of thy quick° store   living
Runs thither, whence it flowed before,

---

[1] **loose retínue:** Those in service; i.e., the water above the precipice is linked to Time's ("his") followers.
[2] **But quickened . . . brave:** To Vaughan, the course of the water mirrors Christ's resurrection in the Christian tradition.

Should poor souls fear a shade or night,
Who came (sure) from a sea of light?
Or since those drops are all sent back
20   So sure to thee that none doth lack,
Why should frail flesh doubt any more
That what God takes he'll not restore?
O useful element and clear!
My sacred wash and cleanser here,
25   My first consigner[3] unto those
Fountains of life where the lamb goes!
What sublime truths and wholesome themes
Lodge in thy mystical, deep streams!
Such as dull man can never find
30   Unless that Spirit lead his mind,
Which first upon thy face did move,
And hatched all with his quickening love.[4]
As this loud brook's incessant fall
In streaming rings restagnates° all,   becomes stagnant
35   Which reach by course the bank, and then
Are no more seen, just so pass men.
O my invisible estate,
My glorious liberty, still late!
Thou art the channel my soul seeks,
40   Not this with cataracts° and creeks.   waterfalls

WILLIAM WORDSWORTH (1770–1850)

Nutting (1800)

It seems a day,
(I speak of one from many singled out)
One of those heavenly days which cannot die,
When forth I sallied from our cottage-door,
5   And with a wallet o'er my shoulder slung,
A nutting crook in hand, I turn'd my steps
Towards the distant woods, a Figure quaint,
Trick'd out in proud disguise of Beggar's weeds
Put on for the occasion, by advice
10   And exhortation of my frugal Dame.

---

[3] **consigner:** One who delivers goods; i.e., the baptismal font ("cleanser here") delivers the speaker to eternal life ("where the Lamb goes").
[4] **Which first . . . love:** A reference to creation; see Genesis 1.2: "And the Spirit of God moved upon the face of the waters."

Motley accoutrement! of power to smile
At thorns, and brakes, and brambles, and, in truth,
More ragged than need was. Among the woods,
And o'er the pathless rocks, I forc'd my way
15   Until, at length, I came to one dear nook
Unvisited, where not a broken bough
Droop'd with its wither'd leaves, ungracious sign
Of devastation, but the hazels rose
Tall and erect, with milk-white clusters hung,
20   A virgin scene!—A little while I stood,
Breathing with such suppression of the heart
As joy delights in; and with wise restraint
Voluptuous, fearless of a rival, eyed
The banquet, or beneath the trees I sate
25   Among the flowers, and with the flowers I play'd;
A temper known to those, who, after long
And weary expectation, have been bless'd
With sudden happiness beyond all hope.—
—Perhaps it was a bower beneath whose leaves
30   The violets of five seasons re-appear
And fade, unseen by any human eye,
Where fairy water-breaks do murmur on
For ever, and I saw the sparkling foam,
And with my cheek on one of those green stones
35   That, fleec'd with moss, beneath the shady trees,
Lay round me scatter'd like a flock of sheep,
I heard the murmur and the murmuring sound,
In that sweet mood when pleasure loves to pay
Tribute to ease, and, of its joy secure
40   The heart luxuriates with indifferent things,
Wasting its kindliness on stocks and stones,
And on the vacant air. Then up I rose,
And dragg'd to earth both branch and bough, with crash
And merciless ravage; and the shady nook
45   Of hazels, and the green and mossy bower
Deform'd and sullied, patiently gave up
Their quiet being: and unless I now
Confound my present feelings with the past,
Even then, when from the bower I turn'd away,
50   Exulting, rich beyond the wealth of kings
I felt a sense of pain when I beheld
The silent trees and the intruding sky.—

Then, dearest Maiden! move along these shades
In gentleness of heart, with gentle hand
55   Touch,—for there is a Spirit in the woods.

ISABELLA LICKBARROW (1784–1847)

On Esthwaite Water [1] (1814)

O'er Esthwaite's lake, serene and still,
    At sunset's silent peaceful hour
Scarce moved the zephyr's softest breath,
    Or sighed along its reedy shore.

5   The lovely landscape on its sides,
    With evening's softening hues impressed,
Shared in the general calm, and gave
    Sweet visions of repose and rest.

Inverted on the waveless flood,
10   A spotless mirror smooth and clear,
Each fair surrounding object shone
    In softer beauty imaged there.

Brown hills and woods of various shades,
    Orchards and sloping meadows green,
15   Sweet rural seats and sheltered farms,
    Were in the bright reflector seen.

E'en lofty Tilberthwaite from far
    His giant shadow boldly threw,
His ruggéd, dark, high-towering head
20   On Esthwaite's tranquil breast to view.

Struck with the beauty of the scene,
    I cried, 'Oh may my yielding breast
Retain but images of peace
    Like those, sweet lake, on thine impressed!

25   Ne'er may it feel a ruder gale
    Than that which o'er thy surface spreads,
When sportive zephyrs briskly play,
    And whisper through thy bordering reeds—

When, dancing in the solar beam,
30   Thy silvery waves the margin seek

---

[1] **Esthwaite Water:** Small lake in England's Lake District.

With gently undulating flow,
    And there in softest murmurs break.'

Vain wish—o'er Esthwaite's tranquil lake
    A stronger gale full frequent blows,
35 The soothing prospect disappears,
    The lovely visions of repose!

GEORGE GORDON, LORD BYRON (1788–1824)

from Childe Harold's Pilgrimage III (1816; 1817)
Lake Leman[1]

68

Lake Leman woos me with its crystal face,
    The mirror where the stars and mountains view
    The stillness of their aspect in each trace
    Its clear depth yields of their far height and hue.
5   There is too much of man here, to look through
    With a fit mind the might which I behold;
    But soon in me shall loneliness renew
    Thoughts hid, but not less cherished than of old,
Ere mingling with the herd had penned me in their fold.

69

To fly from, need not be to hate, mankind:
    All are not fit with them to stir and toil,
    Nor is it discontent to keep the mind
    Deep in its fountain, lest it over-boil
5   In the hot throng, where we become the spoil
    Of our infection, till too late and long
    We may deplore and struggle with the coil,
    In wretched interchange of wrong for wrong
Midst a contentious world, striving where none are strong.

70

There, in a moment, we may plunge our years
    In fatal penitence, and in the blight

---

[1] **Lake Leman:** Lake near Geneva, Switzerland, where Byron spent the summer of 1816.

       Of our own soul turn all our blood to tears,
       And colour things to come with hues of night!
5   The race of life becomes a hopeless flight
       To those that walk in darkness—on the sea
       The boldest steer but where their ports invite—
       But there are wanderers o'er eternity
Whose bark drives on and on, and anchored ne'er shall be.

71

Is it not better, then, to be alone,
       And love Earth only for its earthly sake—
       By the blue rushing of the arrowy Rhone,[2]
       Or the pure bosom of its nursing Lake
5   Which feeds it as a mother who doth make
       A fair but froward infant her own care,
       Kissing its cries away as these awake—
       Is it not better thus our lives to wear,
Than join the crushing crowd, doomed to inflict or bear?

72

I live not in myself, but I become
       Portion of that around me, and to me
       High mountains are a feeling, but the hum
       Of human cities torture! I can see
5   Nothing to loathe in Nature, save to be
       A link reluctant in a fleshly chain,
       Classed among creatures, when the soul can flee,
       And with the sky, the peak, the heaving plain
Of ocean, or the stars, mingle—and not in vain.

73

And thus I am absorbed, and this is life:
       I look upon the peopled desert past,
       As on a place of agony and strife,
       Where, for some sin, to sorrow I was cast,
5   To act and suffer, but remount at last
       With a fresh pinion—which I feel to spring,
       Though young, yet waxing vigorous as the blast
       Which it would cope with, on delighted wing
Spurning the clay-cold bonds which round our being cling.

---

[2] **Rhone:** Major French river that flows into the Mediterranean near Marseilles.

74

And when, at length, the mind shall be all free
    From what it hates in this degraded form,
    Reft of its carnal life, save what shall be
    Existent happier in the fly and worm—
5   When elements to elements conform
    And dust is as it should be, shall I not
    Feel all I see less dazzling but more warm?
    The bodiless thought? The spirit of each spot,
Of which, even now, I share at times the immortal lot?

75

Are not the mountains, waves, and skies, a part
    Of me and of my soul, as I of them?
    Is not the love of these deep in my heart
    With a pure passion? Should I not contemn
5   All objects, if compared with these—and stem
    A tide of suffering, rather than forego
    Such feelings for the hard and worldly phlegm
    Of those whose eyes are only turned below,
Gazing upon the ground with thoughts which dare not glow? . . .

85

Clear, placid Leman! thy contrasted lake,
    With the wild world I dwelt in, is a thing
    Which warns me, with its stillness, to forsake
    Earth's troubled waters for a purer spring.
5   This quiet sail is as a noiseless wing
    To waft me from distraction. Once I loved
    Torn ocean's roar, but thy soft murmuring
    Sounds sweet as if a sister's voice reproved
That I with stern delights should e'er have been so moved.

86

It is the hush of night, and all between
    Thy margin and the mountains, dusk, yet clear
    (Mellowed and mingling, yet distinctly seen),
    Save darkened Jura,[3] whose capped heights appear
5   Precipitously steep—and drawing near,
    There breathes a living fragrance from the shore,

---

[3] **Jura:** A range of mountains between Switzerland and France.

Of flowers yet fresh with childhood; on the ear
Drops the light drip of the suspended oar,
Or chirps the grasshopper one good-night carol more.

87

He is an evening reveller, who makes
    His life an infancy, and sings his fill!
    At intervals, some bird from out the brakes
    Starts into voice a moment, then is still.
5   There seems a floating whisper on the hill—
    But that is fancy!—for the starlight-dews
    All silently their tears of love instill,
    Weeping themselves away, till they infuse
Deep into Nature's breast the spirit of her hues.

88

Ye stars, which are the poetry of Heaven!
    If in your bright leaves we would read the fate
    Of men and empires, 'tis to be forgiven
    That in our aspirations to be great,
5   Our destinies o'erleap their mortal state,
    And claim a kindred with you—for ye are
    A beauty and a mystery, and create
    In us such love and reverence from afar
That fortune, fame, power, life, have named themselves a star.

89

All Heaven and Earth are still—though not in sleep,
    But breathless, as we grow when feeling most,
    And silent, as we stand in thoughts too deep—
    All Heaven and Earth are still! From the high host
5   Of stars, to the lulled lake and mountain-coast,
    All is concentred in a life intense
    Where not a beam, nor air, nor leaf is lost,
    But hath a part of being, and a sense
Of that which is of all creator and defense.

90

Then stirs the feeling infinite, so felt
    In solitude, where we are least alone—
    A truth which through our being then doth melt,
    And purifies from self: it is a tone,
5   The soul and source of music, which makes known
    Eternal harmony . . .

JOHN CLARE (1793–1864)

from The Shepherd's Calendar (ca. 1824; 1827)

>   Loud is the Summer's busy song,
>   The smallest breeze can find a tongue,
>   While insects of each tiny size
>   Grow teasing with their melodies,
> 5 Till noon burns with its blistering breath
>   Around, and day dies still as death.
>   The busy noise of man and brute
>   Is on a sudden lost and mute;
>   Even the brook that leaps along
> 10 Seems weary of its bubbling song,
>   And, so soft its waters creep,
>   Tired silence sinks in sounder sleep.
>   The cricket on its banks is dumb,
>   The very flies forget to hum;
> 15 And, save the wagon rocking round,
>   The landscape sleeps without a sound.
>   The breeze is stopped, the lazy bough
>   Hath not a leaf that dances now;
>   The tottergrass upon the hill,
> 20 And spiders' threads, are standing still;
>   The feathers dropped from moorhen's wing,
>   Which to the water's surface cling,
>   Are steadfast, and as heavy seem
>   As stones beneath them in the stream;
> 25 Hawkweed and groundsel's fanning downs
>   Unruffled keep their seedy crowns;
>   And in the oven-heated air,
>   Not one light thing is floating there,
>   Save that to the earnest eye
> 30 The restless heat seems twittering by!
>   Noon swoons beneath the heat it made,
>   And flowers e'en wither in the shade,
>   Until the sun slopes in the west,
>   Like weary traveller, glad to rest,
> 35 On pillowed clouds of many hues;
>   Then Nature's voice its joy renews,
>   And chequered field and grassy plain
>   Hum, with their summer songs again,
>   A requiem to the day's decline,
> 40 Whose setting sunbeams coolly shine,
>   As welcome to day's feeble powers
>   As falling dews to thirsty flowers.

RALPH WALDO EMERSON (1803–1882)

The Snow-Storm (1847)

Announced by all the trumpets of the sky,
Arrives the snow, and, driving o'er the fields,
Seems nowhere to alight: the whited air
Hides hills and woods, the river, and the heaven,
5   And veils the farmhouse at the garden's end.
The sled and traveler stopped, the courier's feet
Delayed, all friends shut out, the housemates sit
Around the radiant fireplace, enclosed
In a tumultuous privacy of storm.

10   Come see the north wind's masonry.
Out of an unseen quarry evermore
Furnished with tile, the fierce artificer
Curves his white bastions with projected roof
Round every windward stake, or tree, or door.
15   Speeding, the myriad-handed, his wild work
So fanciful, so savage, nought cares he
For number or proportion. Mockingly,
On coop or kennel he hangs Parian[1] wreaths;
A swan-like form invests the hidden thorn;
20   Fills up the farmer's lane from wall to wall,
Maugre° the farmer's sighs; and, at the gate,   in spite of
A tapering turret overtops the work.
And when his hours are numbered, and the world
Is all his own, retiring, as he were not,
25   Leaves, when the sun appears, astonished Art
To mimic in slow structures, stone by stone,
Built in an age, the mad wind's night-work,
The frolic architecture of the snow.

---

[1] **Parian:** Resembling Greek marble from the island of Paros.

WALT WHITMAN (1819–1892)

When I Heard the Learn'd Astronomer (1865)

When I heard the learn'd astronomer,
When the proofs, the figures, were ranged in columns before me,
When I was shown the charts and diagrams, to add, divide, and
      measure them,
When I sitting heard the astronomer where he lectured with much
      applause in the lecture-room,
5   How soon unaccountable I became tired and sick,
Till rising and gliding out I wander'd off by myself,
In the mystical moist night-air, and from time to time,
Look'd up in perfect silence at the stars.

THOMAS HARDY (1840–1928)

A Light Snow-Fall after Frost (1925)

On the flat road a man at last appears:
    How much his whitening hairs
Owe to the settling snow's mute anchorage,
And how much to a life's rough pilgrimage,
5   One cannot certify.

    The frost is on the wane,
And cobwebs hanging close outside the pane
Pose as festoons° of thick white worsted there,   decorative curtains
Of their pale presence no eye being aware
10   Till the rime made them plain.

    A second man comes by;
His ruddy beard brings fire to the pallid scene:
    His coat is faded green;
    Hence seems it that his mien
15   Wears something of the dye
Of the berried holm-trees that he passes nigh.

The snow-feathers so gently swoop that though
    But half an hour ago
The road was brown, and now is starkly white,
20 A watcher would have failed defining quite
    When it transformed it so.

A. E. HOUSMAN (1859–1936)

Loveliest of Trees, the Cherry Now   (1896)

Loveliest of trees, the cherry now
Is hung with bloom along the bough,
And stands about the woodland ride
Wearing white for Eastertide.

5 Now, of my threescore years and ten,
Twenty will not come again,
And take from seventy springs a score,
It only leaves me fifty more.

And since to look at things in bloom
10 Fifty springs are little room,
About the woodlands I will go
To see the cherry hung with snow.

WILLIAM BUTLER YEATS (1865–1939)

The Lake Isle of Innisfree[1]   (1890)

I will arise and go now, and go to Innisfree,
And a small cabin build there, of clay and wattles° made: framework
Nine bean-rows will I have there, a hive for the honey-bee,
And live alone in the bee-loud glade.

5 And I shall have some peace there, for peace comes dropping slow,
Dropping from the veils of the morning to where the cricket sings;
There midnight's all a glimmer, and noon a purple glow,
And evening full of the linnet's wings.

I will arise and go now, for always night and day
10 I hear lake water lapping with low sounds by the shore;
While I stand on the roadway, or on the pavements grey,
I hear it in the deep heart's core.

---

[1] **Innisfree:** A small island in Lough Gill in western Ireland.

ROBERT FROST (1874–1963)

The Most of It (1942)

He thought he kept the universe alone;
For all the voice in answer he could wake
Was but the mocking echo of his own
From some tree-hidden cliff across the lake.
5   Some morning from the boulder-broken beach
He would cry out on life, that what it wants
Is not its own love back in copy speech,
But counter-love, original response.
And nothing ever came of what he cried
10   Unless it was the embodiment that crashed
In the cliff's talus on the other side,
And then in the far-distant water splashed,
But after a time allowed for it to swim,
Instead of proving human when it neared
15   And someone else additional to him,
As a great buck it powerfully appeared,
Pushing the crumpled water up ahead,
And landed pouring like a waterfall,
And stumbled through the rocks with horny tread,
20   And forced the underbrush—and that was all.

CARL SANDBURG (1878–1967)

Fog (1916)

The fog comes
on little cat feet.
It sits looking
over harbor and city
5   on silent haunches
and then moves on.

EDWARD THOMAS (1878–1917)

Rain (1916; 1917)

Rain, midnight rain, nothing but the wild rain
On this bleak hut, and solitude, and me
Remembering again that I shall die

And neither hear the rain nor give it thanks
5   For washing me cleaner than I have been
Since I was born into this solitude.
Blessed are the dead that the rain rains upon:
But here I pray that none whom once I loved
Is dying tonight or lying still awake
10   Solitary, listening to the rain,
Either in pain or thus in sympathy
Helpless among the living and the dead,
Like a cold water among broken reeds,
Myriads of broken reeds all still and stiff,
15   Like me who have no love which this wild rain
Has not dissolved except the love of death,
If love it be towards what is perfect and
Cannot, the tempest tells me, disappoint.

WALLACE STEVENS (1879–1955)

Anecdote of the Jar (1923)

I placed a jar in Tennessee,
And round it was, upon a hill.
It made the slovenly wilderness
Surround that hill.

5   The wilderness rose up to it,
And sprawled around, no longer wild.
The jar was round upon the ground
And tall and of a port in air.

It took dominion everywhere.
10   The jar was gray and bare.
It did not give of bird or bush,
Like nothing else in Tennessee.

D. H. LAWRENCE (1885–1930)

Trees in the Garden (1932)

Ah in the thunder air
How still the trees are!

And the lime-tree, lovely and tall, every leaf silent
Hardly looses even a last breath of perfume.

5   And the ghostly, creamy coloured little tree of leaves
White, ivory white among the rambling greens
How evanescent, variegated elder, she hesitates on the green grass
As if, in another moment, she would disappear
With all her grace of foam!

10   And the larch that is only a column, it goes up too tall to see:
And the balsam-pines that are blue with the grey-blue blueness of
              things from the sea,
And the young copper beech, its leaves red-rosy at the ends
How still they are together, they stand so still
In the thunder air, all strangers to one another
15   As the green grass glows upwards, strangers in the garden.

ROBINSON JEFFERS (1887–1962)

Carmel Point[1] (1954)

The extraordinary patience of things!
This beautiful place defaced with a crop of suburban houses—
How beautiful when we first beheld it,
Unbroken field of poppy and lupin walled with clean cliffs;
5   No intrusion but two or three horses pasturing,
Or a few milch cows rubbing their flanks on the outcrop rock-heads—
Now the spoiler has come: does it care?
Not faintly. It has all time. It knows the people are a tide
That swells and in time will ebb, and all
10   Their works dissolve. Meanwhile the image of the pristine beauty
Lives in the very grain of the granite,
Safe as the endless ocean that climbs our cliff.—As for us:
We must uncenter our minds from ourselves;
We must unhumanize our views a little, and become confident
15   As the rock and ocean that we were made from.

---

[1] **Carmel Point:** On the Pacific Ocean in California.

EDNA ST. VINCENT MILLAY (1892–1950)

Ragged Island (pub. 1954)

There, there where those black spruces crowd
To the edge of the precipitous cliff,
Above your boat, under the eastern wall of the island;
And no wave breaks; as if
5   All had been done, and long ago, that needed
Doing; and the cold tide, unimpeded
By shoal or shelving ledge, moves up and down,
Instead of in and out;
And there is no driftwood there, because there is no beach;
10   Clean cliff going down as deep as clear water can reach;

No driftwood, such as abounds on the roaring shingle,[1]
To be hefted home, for fires in the kitchen stove;
Barrels, banged ashore about the boiling outer harbor;
Lobster-buoys, on the eel-grass of the sheltered cove:

15   There, thought unbraids itself, and the mind becomes single.
There you row with tranquil oars, and the ocean
Shows no scar from the cutting of your placid keel;
Care becomes senseless there; pride and promotion
Remote; you only look; you scarcely feel.

20   Even adventure, with its vital uses,
Is aimless ardour now; and thrift is waste.

Oh, to be there, under the silent spruces,
Where the wide, quiet evening darkens without haste
Over a sea with death acquainted, yet forever chaste.

E. E. CUMMINGS (1894–1962)

"in Just-" (1922)

in Just-
spring   when the world is mud-
luscious the little
lame balloonman

---

[1] **shingle:** Seashore covered with stones.

5   whistles   far   and wee

    and eddieandbill come
    running from marbles and
    piracies and it's
    spring

10   when the world is puddle-wonderful

    the queer
    old balloonman whistles
    far   and   wee
    and bettyandisbel come dancing

15   from hop-scotch and jump-rope and

    it's
    spring
    and
       the

20   goat-footed

    balloonMan   whistles
    far
    and
    wee

LOUISE BOGAN (1897–1970)

Night (1968)

    The cold remote islands
    And the blue estuaries
    Where what breathes, breathes
    The restless wind of the inlets,
5   And what drinks, drinks
    The incoming tide;

    Where shell and weed
    Wait upon the salt wash of the sea,
    And the clear nights of stars
10   Swing their lights westward
    To set behind the land;

Where the pulse clinging to the rocks
Renews itself forever;
Where, again on cloudless nights,

15 The water reflects
The firmament's partial setting;

— O remember
In your narrowing dark hours
That more things move

20 Than blood in the heart.

LANGSTON HUGHES (1902–1967)

The Negro Speaks of Rivers (1926)
(To W. E. B. Du Bois)[1]

I've known rivers:
I've known rivers ancient as the world and older than the
        flow of human blood in human veins.
My soul has grown deep like the rivers.

5 I bathed in the Euphrates when dawns were young.
I built my hut near the Congo and it lulled me to sleep.
I looked upon the Nile and raised the pyramids above it.
I heard the singing of the Mississippi when Abe Lincoln
        went down to New Orleans, and I've seen its muddy
10   bosom turn all golden in the sunset.

I've known rivers:
Ancient, dusky rivers.

My soul has grown deep like the rivers.

---

[1] **W. E. B. Du Bois:** Du Bois (1868–1963), an American historian, educator, and civil rights activist
who was a founder of the NAACP.

LOUIS MACNEICE (1907–1963)

The Sunlight on the Garden[1] (1938)

The sunlight on the garden
Hardens and grows cold,
We cannot cage the minute
Within its nets of gold,
5   When all is told
We cannot beg for pardon.

Our freedom as free lances
Advances towards its end;
The earth compels, upon it
10   Sonnets and birds descend;
And soon, my friend,
We shall have no time for dances.

The sky was good for flying
Defying the church bells
15   And every evil iron
Siren and what it tells:
The earth compels,
We are dying, Egypt, dying[2]

And not expecting pardon,
20   Hardened in heart anew,
But glad to have sat under
Thunder and rain with you,
And grateful too
For sunlight on the garden.

---

[1] **The Sunlight on the Garden:** The author's farewell to his first wife, formerly the best dancer in Oxford.
[2] **dying, Egypt, dying:** From *Antony and Cleopatra* 4.15.41: "I am dying, Egypt, dying."

THEODORE ROETHKE (1908–1963)

A Field of Light (1948)

1

Came to lakes; came to dead water,
Ponds with moss and leaves floating,
Planks sunk in the sand.

A log turned at the touch of a foot;
5   A long weed floated upward;
An eye tilted.

Small winds made
A chilly noise;
The softest cove
10   Cried for sound.

Reached for a grape
And the leaves changed;
A stone's shape
Became a clam.

15   A fine rain fell
On fat leaves;
I was there alone
In a watery drowse.

2

Angel within me, I asked,
Did I ever curse the sun?
Speak and abide.

Under, under the sheaves,
5   Under the blackened leaves,
Behind the green viscid trellis,
In the deep grass at the edge of field,
Along the low ground dry only in August,—

Was it dust I was kissing?
10   A sigh came far.
Alone, I kissed the skin of a stone;
Marrow-soft, danced in the sand.

3

The dirt left my hand, visitor.
I could feel the mare's nose.
A path went walking.
The sun glittered on a small rapids.
5   Some morning thing came, beating its wings.
The great elm filled with birds.

Listen, love,
The fat lark sang in the field;
I touched the ground, the ground warmed by the killdeer,
10   The salt laughed and the stones;
The ferns had their ways, and the pulsing lizards,
And the new plants, still awkward in their soil,
The lovely diminutives.
I could watch! I could watch!
15   I saw the separateness of all things!
My heart lifted up with the great grasses;
The weeds believed me, and the nesting birds.
There were clouds making a rout of shapes crossing a windbreak
         of cedars,
And a bee shaking drops from a rain-soaked honeysuckle.
20   The worms were delighted as wrens.
And I walked, I walked through the light air;
I moved with the morning.

R. S. THOMAS (1913–2000)

The Moor (1966)

It was like a church to me.
I entered it on soft foot,
Breath held like a cap in the hand.
It was quiet.
5   What God was there made himself felt,
Not listened to, in clean colours
That brought a moistening of the eye,
In movement of the wind over grass.

There were no prayers said. But stillness
10   Of the heart's passions—that was praise

Enough; and the mind's cession
Of its kingdom. I walked on,
Simple and poor, while the air crumbled
And broke on me generously as bread.

WILLIAM STAFFORD (1914–1993)

At Cove on the Crooked River (1962)

At Cove at our camp in the open canyon
it was the kind of place where you might look out
some evening and see trouble walking away.

And the river there meant something
5   always coming from snow and flashing around boulders
after shadow-fish lurking below the mesa.

We stood with wet towels over our heads for shade,
looking past the Indian picture rock and the kind of trees
that act out whatever has happened to them.

10   Oh civilization, I want to carve you like this,
decisively outward the way evening comes
over that kind of twist in the scenery

When people cramp into their station wagons
and roll up the windows, and drive away.

A. R. AMMONS (1926–2001)

Corsons Inlet[1] (1965)

I went for a walk over the dunes again this morning
to the sea,
then turned right along
        the surf

---

[1] **Corsons Inlet:** In southeast New Jersey.

5   rounded a naked headland
               and returned

      along the inlet shore:

      it was muggy sunny, the wind from the sea steady and high.
      crisp in the running sand,
10   some breakthroughs of sun
         but after a bit

      continuous overcast:

      the walk liberating, I was released from forms,
      from the perpendiculars
15   straight lines, blocks, boxes, binds
      of thought
      into the hues, shadings, rises, flowing bends and blends
               of sight:

                    I allow myself eddies of meaning:
20   yield to a direction of significance
      running
      like a stream through the geography of my work:
         you can find
      in my sayings
25   swerves of action
                     like the inlet's cutting edge:
            there are dunes of motion,
      organizations of grass, white sandy paths of remembrance
      in the overall wandering of mirroring mind:

30   but Overall is beyond me: is the sum of these events
      I cannot draw, the ledger I cannot keep, the accounting
      beyond the account:

      in nature there are few sharp lines: there are areas of
      primrose
35   more or less dispersed;
      disorderly orders of bayberry; between the rows
      of dunes,
      irregular swamps of reeds,
      though not reeds alone, but grass, bayberry, yarrow, all . . .
40   predominantly reeds:

      I have reached no conclusions, have erected no boundaries,
      shutting out and shutting in, separating inside

from outside: I have
drawn no lines:

45   as

manifold events of sand
change the dune's shape that will not be the same shape
tomorrow.

so I am willing to go along, to accept
50   the becoming
thought, to stake off no beginnings or ends, establish
            no walls:

by transitions the land falls from grassy dunes to creek
to undercreek: but there are no lines, though
55   change in that transition is clear
            as any sharpness: but "sharpness" spread out,
allowed to occur over a wider range
than mental lines can keep:

the moon was full last night: today, low tide was low:
60   black shoals of mussels exposed to the risk
of air
and, earlier, of sun,
waved in and out with the waterline, waterline inexact,
caught always in the event of change:
65   a young mottled gull stood free on the shoals
            and ate
to vomiting: another gull, squawking possession, cracked a crab,
picked out the entrails, swallowed the soft-shelled legs, a ruddy
turnstone running in to snatch leftover bits:

70   risk is full: every living thing in
siege: the demand is life, to keep life: the small
white blacklegged egret, how beautiful, quietly stalks and spears
            the shallows, darts to shore
                        to stab—what? I couldn't
75   see against the black mudflats—a frightened
            fiddler crab?

            the news to my left over the dunes and
reeds and bayberry clumps was
            fall: thousands of tree swallows
80   gathering for flight:
            an order held
            in constant change: a congregation

rich with entropy: nevertheless, separable, noticeable
      as one event,
85   not chaos: preparations for
flight from winter,
cheet, cheet, cheet, cheet, wings rifling the green clumps,
beaks
at the bayberries
90   a perception full of wind, flight, curve,
      sound:
    the possibility of rule as the sum of rulelessness:
the "field" of action
with moving, incalculable center:

95   in the smaller view, order tight with shape:
blue tiny flowers on a leafless weed: carapace of crab:
snail shell:
      pulsations of order
      in the bellies of minnows: orders swallowed,
100 broken down, transferred through membranes
to strengthen larger orders: but in the large view, no
lines or changeless shapes: the working in and out, together
      and against, of millions of events: this,
            so that I make
105   no form
            formlessness:

orders as summaries, as outcomes of actions override
or in some way result, not predictably (seeing me gain
the top of a dune,
110 the swallows
could take flight—some other fields of bayberry
      could enter fall
      berryless) and there is serenity:

      no arranged terror: no forcing of image, plan,
115 or thought:
no propaganda, no humbling of reality to precept:

terror pervades but is not arranged, all possibilities
of escape open: no route shut, except in
    the sudden loss of all routes:

120   I see narrow orders, limited tightness, but will
not run to that easy victory:
      still around the looser, wider forces work:
      I will try

to fasten into order enlarging grasps of disorder, widening
125   scope, but enjoying the freedom that
Scope eludes my grasp, that there is no finality of vision,
that I have perceived nothing completely,
            that tomorrow a new walk is a new walk.

ALLEN GINSBERG (1926–1997)

Reflections at Lake Louise (1980)

I

At midnight the teacher lectures on his throne
Gongs, bells, wooden fish, tingling brass
Transcendent Doctrines, non-meditation, old dog barks
Past present future burn in Candleflame
5   incense fills intellects—
Mornings I wake, forgetting my dreams,
dreary hearted, lift my body out of bed
shave, wash, sit, bow down to the ground for hours.

II

Which country is real, mine or the teacher's?
Going back & forth I cross the Canada border, unguarded,
            guilty, smuggling 10,000 thoughts.

III

Sometimes my guru seems a Hell King, sometimes a King in Eternity,
            sometimes a newspaper story, sometimes familiar eyed
                father, lonely mother, hard working—
Poor man! to give me birth who may never grow up
5   and earn my own living.

IV

Now the sky's clearer, clouds lifted, a patch of blue
shows above Mt. Victoria. I should go walking to the Plain of
                the Six Glaciers[1]
but I have to eat Oryoki style,[2] prostrate hours in the basement,
                study for

---

[1] **Mt. Victoria . . . Glaciers:** Lake Louise, Mt. Victoria, and the Plain of the Six Glaciers are all found in Banff National Park in northwest Canada.
[2] **Oryoki style:** In the Zen tradition, a formal way of eating.

If I had a heart attack on the path around the lake would I be
                                 ready to face my mother?
Noon

V

Scandal in the Buddhafields
        The lake's covered with soft ice inches thick.
Naked, he insulted me under the glacier!
        He raped my mind on the wet granite cliffs!
He misquoted me in the white mists all over the *Nation*.[3]
Hurrah! the Clouds drift apart!
        Big chunks of blue sky fall down!
Mount Victoria stands with a mouth full of snow.

VI

I wander this path along little Lake Louise, the teacher's too busy
                              to see me,
my dharma friends think I'm crazy, or worse, a lonely neurotic,
                              maybe
Alone in the mountains, same as in snowy streets of New York.

VII

Trapped in the Guru's Chateau surrounded by 300 disciples
I could go home to Cherry Valley, Manhattan, Nevada City
to be a farmer forever, die in Lower East Side slums, sit with no
        lightbulbs in the forest,
Return to my daily mail Secretary, *Hard Times*,[4] Junk mail and
        love letters, get wrinkled old in Manhattan
Fly out and sing poetry, bring home windmills, grow tomatoes and
                              Marijuana
chop wood, do Zazen,[5] obey my friends, muse in Gary's Maidu[6]
        Territory, study acorn mush,
Here I'm destined to study the Higher Tantras and be a slave to
        Enlightenment.
Where can I go, how choose? Either way my life stands before me,
mountains rising over the white lake 6 a.m., mist drifting
between water and sky.

---

[3] the *Nation:* A liberal news magazine.
[4] *Hard Times:* Novel by Charles Dickens.
[5] **Zazen:** Form of Zen meditation.
[6] **Gary's Maidu:** The Maidu Indians of Nevada County, studied by the poet Gary Snyder (1930–   ).

GALWAY KINNELL (1927–   )

Blackberry Eating (1980)

I love to go out in late September
among the fat, overripe, icy, black blackberries
to eat blackberries for breakfast,
the stalks very prickly, a penalty
5   they earn for knowing the black art
of blackberry-making; and as I stand among them
lifting the stalks to my mouth, the ripest berries
fall almost unbidden to my tongue,
as words sometimes do, certain peculiar words
10   like *strengths* or *squinched,*
many-lettered, one-syllabled lumps,
which I squeeze, squinch open, and splurge well
in the silent, startled, icy, black language
of blackberry-eating in late September.

JAMES WRIGHT (1927–1980)

Trying to Pray (1963)

This time, I have left my body behind me, crying
In its dark thorns.
Still,
There are good things in this world.
5   It is dusk.
It is the good darkness
Of women's hands that touch loaves.
The spirit of a tree begins to move.
I touch leaves.
10   I close my eyes, and think of water.

ADRIENNE RICH (1929–   )

What Kind of Times Are These

There's a place between two stands of trees where the grass grows uphill
and the old revolutionary road breaks off into shadows
near a meeting-house abandoned by the persecuted
who disappeared into those shadows.

5 I've walked there picking mushrooms at the edge of dread, but don't
        be fooled,
this isn't a Russian poem, this is not somewhere else but here,
our country moving closer to its own truth and dread,
its own ways of making people disappear.

I won't tell you where the place is, the dark mesh of the woods
10 meeting the unmarked strip of light—
ghost-ridden crossroads, leafmold paradise:
I know already who wants to buy it, sell it, make it disappear.

And I won't tell you where it is, so why do I tell you
anything? Because you still listen, because in times like these
15 to have you listen at all, it's necessary
to talk about trees.

TED HUGHES (1930–1998)

Thistles (1967)

Against the rubber tongues of cows and the hoeing hands of men
Thistles spike the summer air
Or crackle open under a blue-black pressure.

Every one a revengeful burst
5 Of resurrection, a grasped fistful
Of splintered weapons and Icelandic frost thrust up

From the underground stain of a decayed Viking.
They are like pale hair and the gutturals of dialects.
Every one manages a plume of blood.

10 Then they grow grey, like men.
Mown down, it is a feud. Their sons appear,
Stiff with weapons, fighting back over the same ground.

CHRISTOPHER OKIGBO (1932–1967)

Eyes Watch the Stars (1961)

Eyes open on the beach,
eyes open, of the prodigal;
upward to heaven shoot
where stars will fall from.

5   Which secret I have told into no ear;
              into a dughole to hold,
              not to drown with —
    Which secret I have planted into beachsand;
                    now breaks
10 salt-white surf on the stones and me,
              and lobsters and shells in
              iodine smell—
              maid of the salt-emptiness,
              sophisticreamy, native,

15 whose secret I have covered up with beachsand.

         Shadow of rain
         over sunbeaten beach,
         shadow of rain
         over man with woman.

WENDELL BERRY (1934–   )

Enriching the Earth (1970)

    To enrich the earth I have sowed clover and grass
    to grow and die. I have plowed in the seeds
    of winter grains and of various legumes,
    their growth to be plowed in to enrich the earth.
5   I have stirred into the ground the offal
    and the decay of the growth of past seasons
    and so mended the earth and made its yield increase.
    All this serves the dark. I am slowly falling
    into the fund of things. And yet to serve the earth,
10 not knowing what I serve, gives a wideness
    and a delight to the air, and my days
    do not wholly pass. It is the mind's service,
    for when the will fails so do the hands
    and one lives at the expense of life.
15 After death, willing or not, the body serves,
    entering the earth. And so what was heaviest
    and most mute is at last raised up into song.

N. SCOTT MOMADAY (1934–   )

Headwaters (1976)

Noon in the intermountain plain:
There is scant telling of the marsh —
A log, hollow and weather-stained,
An insect at the mouth, and moss —
5   Yet waters rise against the roots,
Stand brimming to the stalks. What moves?
What moves on this archaic force
Was wild and welling at the source.

MARK STRAND (1934–   )

A Piece of the Storm (2001)
For Sharon Horvath

From the shadow of domes in the city of domes,
A snowflake, a blizzard of one, weightless, entered your room
And made its way to the arm of the chair where you, looking up
From your book, saw it the moment it landed. That's all
5   There was to it. No more than a solemn waking
To brevity, to the lifting and falling away of attention, swiftly,
A time between times, a flowerless funeral. No more than that
Except for the feeling that this piece of the storm,
Which turned into nothing before your eyes, would come back,
10   That someone years hence, sitting as you are now, might say:
"It's time. The air is ready. The sky has an opening."

MARY OLIVER (1935–   )

Skunk Cabbage (1983)

And now as the iron rinds over
the ponds start dissolving,
you come, dreaming of ferns and flowers
and new leaves unfolding,
5   upon the brash

turnip-hearted skunk cabbage
slinging its bunched leaves up
through the chilly mud.
You kneel beside it. The smell
10   is lurid and flows out in the most
unabashed way, attracting
into itself a continual spattering
of protein. Appalling its rough
green caves, and the thought
15   of the thick root nested below, stubborn
and powerful as instinct!
But these are the woods you love,
where the secret name
of every death is life again—a miracle
20   wrought surely not of mere turning
but of dense and scalding reenactment. Not
tenderness, not longing, but daring and brawn
pull down the frozen waterfall, the past.
Ferns, leaves, flowers, the last subtle
25   refinements, elegant and easeful, wait
to rise and flourish.
What blazes the trail is not necessarily pretty.

CHARLES WRIGHT (1935–   )

Sitting Outside at the End of Autumn (1995)

Three years ago, in the afternoons,
                    I used to sit back here and try
To answer the simple arithmetic of my life,
But never could figure it—
5   This object and that object
Never contained the landscape
                    nor all of its implications,
This tree and that shrub
Never completely satisfied the sum or quotient
10   I took from or carried to,
                    nor do they do so now,
Though I'm back here again, looking to calculate,
Looking to see what adds up.

Everything comes from something,
15   only something comes from nothing,

Lao Tzu[1] says, more or less.
Eminently sensible, I say,
Rubbing this tiny snail shell between my thumb and two fingers.
Delicate as an earring,
20   it carries its emptiness like a child
It would be rid of.
I rub it clockwise and counterclockwise, hoping for anything
Resplendent in its vocabulary or disguise—
But one and one make nothing, he adds,
25   endless and everywhere,
The shadow that everything casts.

CHARLES SIMIC (1938–   )

Summer Morning (1971)

I love to stay in bed
All morning,
Covers thrown off, naked,
Eyes closed, listening.

5   Outside they are opening
Their primers
In the little school
Of the corn field.

There's a smell of damp hay,
10   Of horses, laziness,
Summer sky and eternal life.

I know all the dark places
Where the sun hasn't reached yet,
Where the last cricket
15   Has just hushed; anthills
Where it sounds like it's raining;
Slumbering spiders spinning wedding dresses.

I pass over the farmhouses
Where the little mouths open to suck,
20   Barnyards where a man, naked to the waist,

---

[1] **Lao Tzu:** Famous Chinese philosopher of the fourth century B.C.; author of the Dao de Jing.

Washes his face and shoulders with a hose,
Where the dishes begin to rattle in the kitchen.

The good tree with its voice
Of a mountain stream
25   Knows my steps.
It, too, hushes.

I stop and listen:
Somewhere close by
A stone cracks a knuckle,
30   Another rolls over in its sleep.

I hear a butterfly stirring
Inside a caterpillar,
I hear the dust talking
Of last night's storm.

35   Further ahead, someone
Even more silent
Passes over the grass
Without bending it.

And all of a sudden!
40   In the midst of that quiet,
It seems possible
To live simply on this earth.

SEAMUS HEANEY (1939–   )

Death of a Naturalist (1966)

All year the flax-dam festered in the heart
Of the townland; green and heavy-headed
Flax had rotted there, weighted down by huge sods.
Daily it sweltered in the punishing sun.
5   Bubbles gargled delicately, bluebottles
Wove a strong gauze of sound around the smell.
There were dragonflies, spotted butterflies,
But best of all was the warm thick slobber
Of frogspawn that grew like clotted water
10   In the shade of the banks. Here, every spring
I would fill jampotfuls of the jellied
Specks to range on window-sills at home,

On shelves at school, and wait and watch until
The fattening dots burst into nimble-
15 Swimming tadpoles. Miss Walls would tell us how
The daddy frog was called a bullfrog
And how he croaked and how the mammy frog
Laid hundreds of little eggs and this was
Frogspawn. You could tell the weather by frogs too
20 For they were yellow in the sun and brown
In rain.

   Then one hot day when fields were rank
With cowdung in the grass the angry frogs
Invaded the flax-dam; I ducked through hedges
To a coarse croaking that I had not heard
25 Before. The air was thick with a bass chorus.
Right down the dam gross-bellied frogs were cocked
On sods; their loose necks pulsed like sails. Some hopped:
The slap and plop were obscene threats. Some sat
Poised like mud grenades, their blunt heads farting.
30 I sickened, turned, and ran. The great slime kings
Were gathered there for vengeance and I knew
That if I dipped my hand the spawn would clutch it.

BILLY COLLINS (1941–   )

Morning (1998)

Why do we bother with the rest of the day,
the swale of the afternoon,
the sudden dip into evening,

then night with his notorious perfumes,
5 his many-pointed stars?

This is the best—
throwing off the light covers,
feet on the cold floor,
and buzzing around the house on espresso—

10 maybe a splash of water on the face,
a palmful of vitamins—
but mostly buzzing around the house on espresso,

dictionary and atlas open on the rug,
the typewriter waiting for the key of the head,
15   a cello on the radio,

and, if necessary, the windows—
trees fifty, a hundred years old
out there,
heavy clouds on the way
20   and the lawn steaming like a horse
in the early morning.

SYDNEY LEA (1942–   )

Late Season (1990)

This was the last I'd trouble the ducks this season:
there'd be skim-ice on the slues
and later, snow come down from Canada, horizontal.
There might be some luck, a little . . .
5   no, more. It was already there, beforehand:
dirt road near dawn, canoe
snubbed in the pickup's bed,

and in my lap the great good head
of my dog, the blood in his graying muzzle
10   a pulse in my leg as we bucked the ruts.
And, come down from a Canada even farther,
music, local notices, news of the weather—
the radio's early report. I imagined the struggle
of a farmer there. Up like me. *Good mutt,*
15   I whispered. I scratched

the retriever's neck.
It was warm.   Reception good.   The farmer leaned
in mind into winds that they say
can straighten a tow-chain out behind a tractor.
20   I liked driving tractor-slow, imagining that weather.
Plenty of time. Down here, whatever the wind,
I could count for now on a milder day.
I was forty-five.   I liked how the a.m. signal

said something about what it was to be fuddled,
25   or rather how static fell away when your object was clear:
getting from house to barn and back in a gale;
getting the decoys out before you froze;
getting into the proper kinds of clothes
to meet a day.   Getting it right.   A cold time of year,
30   but for now I was snug behind the wheel,
and already I could envision

the redleg Blackduck blown down and past in migration,
the reach of a wave from the farther shore of the river
toward me, where I'd sit, alone but for the dog.
35   Wave like a single important announcement.
A blind of fragile reeds, and all around it
the signs of how we must seek to save forever
what we receive of what goes by: a buck
who has left his ghostly track in slush and mud;

40   gleam of low sun in old blood;
spent shells, drifting clumps of insubstantial feather,
gone in a moment, abiding in the mind;
feel of a dog companion's eager breathing
turned to frost on your cheek, then melting to nothing.
45   Later the awful snow would come to the river,
and later the careful blind no longer stand,

nor dog, nor duck, nor I, nor Canada farmer.

LINDA GREGG (1942–   )

A Flower No More Than Itself (1991)

She was there on the mountain,
still as the fig tree and the failed wheat.
Only the lizards and a few goats moved.
Everything stunned by heat and silence.
5   I would get to the top of the terraced starkness
with my ankles cut by thistles and all of me
drained by the effort in the fierce light.
I would put the pomegranate and the anise
and a few daisies on the great rock

10   where the fountain was long ago.
     Too tired to praise. And found each time
     tenderness and abundance in the bareness.
     Went back down knowing I would sleep clean.
     That She would be awake all year with sun
15   and dirt and rain. Pride Her life.
     All nature Her wealth. Sound of owls Her pillow.

ALFRED CORN (1943–   )

Grass (1979)

     At this range, it's really monumental—
     Tall spears and tilted spears, most
     Blunted by the last mowing.
     A few cloverleafs (leaves?)
5   And infant plantains fight
     For their little plot of ground.
     Wing-nuts or boomerangs, the maple seeds
     Try to and really can't take root.
     There's always more going on
10   Than anyone has the wit to notice:
     Look at those black ants, huge,
     In their glistening exoskeletons.
     Algebraically efficient,
     They're dismembering a dragonfly—
15   Goggle-eyed at being dead
     And having its blue-plated chassis,
     Its isinglass° delicately   mica
     Leaded wings put in pieces.
     When you get right down to it,
20   The earth's a jungle.
     The tough grass grows over and around it all,
     A billion green blades, each one
     Sharply creased down the spine.
     Now that I've gotten up to go,
25   It's nothing but a green background
     With a body-shaped dent left behind.
     As the grass stretches and rises,
     That will go, too.

LOUISE GLÜCK (1943–   )

The Pond (1975)

Night covers the pond with its wing.
Under the ringed moon I can make out
your face swimming among minnows and the small
echoing stars. In the night air
5   the surface of the pond is metal.

Within, your eyes are open. They contain
a memory I recognize, as though
we had been children together. Our ponies
grazed on the hill, they were gray
10   with white markings. Now they graze
with the dead who wait
like children under their granite breastplates,
lucid and helpless:

The hills are far away. They rise up
15   blacker than childhood.
What do you think of, lying so quietly
by the water? When you look that way I want
to touch you, but do not, seeing
as in another life we were of the same blood.

LINDA McCARRISTON (1943–   )

Riding Out at Evening (1984)

At dusk, everything blurs and softens.
From here out over the long valley,
the fields and hills pull up
the first slight sheets of evening,
5   as, over the next hour,
heavier, darker ones will follow.

Quieted roads, predictable deer
browsing in a neighbor's field, another's
herd of heifers, the kitchen lights
10   starting in many windows. On horseback
I take it in, neither visitor
nor intruder, but kin passing, closer

and closer to night, its cold streams
rising in the sugarbush and hollow.

15   Half-aloud, I say to the horse,
or myself, or whoever: let fire not come
to this house, nor that barn,
nor lightning strike the cattle.
Let dogs not gain the gravid doe, let the lights
20   of the rooms convey what they seem to.

And who is to say it is useless
or foolish to ride out in the falling light
alone, wishing, or praying,
for particular good to particular beings
25   on one small road in a huge world?
The horse bears me along, like grace,
making me better than what I am,
and what I think or say or see
is whole in these moments, is neither
30   small nor broken. For up, out of
the inscrutable earth, have come my body
and the separate body of the mare:
flawed and aching and wronged. Who then
is better made to say *be well, be glad,*

35   or who to long that we, as one,
might course over the entire valley,
over all valleys, as a bird in a great embrace
of flight, who presses against her breast,
in grief and tenderness,
40   the whole weeping body of the world?

ELLEN BRYANT VOIGT (1943–)

The Lotus Flowers (1983)

The surface of the pond was mostly green—
bright green algae reaching out from the banks,
then the mass of water lilies, their broad round leaves
rim to rim, each white flower spreading
5   from the center of a green saucer.
We teased and argued, choosing the largest,
the sweetest bloom, but when the rowboat
lumbered through and rearranged them

we found the plants were anchored, the separate
10   muscular stems descending in the dense water—
only the most determined put her hand
into that frog-slimed pond
to wrestle with a flower. Back and forth
we pumped across the water, in twos and threes,
15   full of brave adventure. On the marshy shore,
the others hollered for their turns,
or at the hem of where we pitched the tents
gathered firewood—
                              this was wilderness,
20   although the pond was less than half an acre
and we could still see the grand magnolias
in the village cemetery, their waxy,
white conical blossoms gleaming in the foliage.
A dozen girls, the oldest only twelve, two sisters
25   with their long braids, my shy neighbor,
someone squealing without interruption—
all we didn't know about the world buoyed us
as the frightful water sustained and moved the flowers
tethered at a depth we couldn't see.

30   In the late afternoon, before they'd folded
into candles on the dark water,
I went to fill the bucket at the spring.
Deep in the pines, exposed tree roots
formed a natural arch, a cave of black loam.
35   I raked off the skin of leaves and needles,
leaving a pool so clear and shallow
I could count the pebbles
on the studded floor. The sudden cold
splashing up from the bucket to my hands
40   made me want to plunge my hand in—
and I held it under, feeling the shock that wakes
and deadens, watching first my fingers,
then the ledge beyond me,
the snake submerged and motionless,
45   the head propped on its coils the way a girl
crosses her arms before her on the sill
and rests her chin there.
                              Lugging the bucket
back to the noisy clearing, I found nothing changed,
50   the boat still rocked across the pond,
the fire straggled and cracked as we fed it
branches and debris into the night,
leaning back on our pallets—

spokes in a wheel—learning the names of the many
55   constellations, learning how each fixed
cluster took its name:
not from the strongest light, but from the pattern
made by stars of lesser magnitude,
so like the smaller stars we rowed among.

RICHARD KENNEY (1948–   )

In April   (1984)

In April, in New England, the earth ball yields
under its own mass, gives in to dead
gravity, loses tone, relinquishing
the rigor of the last freeze like slack skin
5   fallen from the cheekbones of the Canadian Shield.[1]
Even Yankees start to soften, thumb the dread
almanacs, shed mackinaws, maxims
sour in the mouth, and offer up halting, truculent
hearts like flushed chameleons—in that radical
10   instant god-struck as Ikhnaton[2] or cold Incan
warlocks in their own mountains were, when power
flowed out of the sky again. It makes me think
of the reindeer men winding down from the shielings,
the high slopes of summer, following spoor

15   down forty thousand years, the sun cupped
in their frightened minds like a cinder—
smell them, seared fat, still. Von Humboldt, Lewis,
Clark, Amundsen[3]—we shared ancient values
then as I stood, in my twelfth year, ankle
20   deep in the drowning sluiceway of our gravel
road. I watched the winter off in rivulets.
Those waters might have been birth-waters, torn loose
all at once as the snowveils bled back to wrinkled
tatters in the shade of the forest; like great unraveling
25   nets, they dropped their catch. I imagined distinct,
torn wings, the earth littered with wings of cicadas,

---

[1] **Canadian Shield:** Vast region of northern Canada.
[2] **Ikhnaton:** Ikhnaton (ca. 1372 B.C.–1354 B.C.), an Egyptian king who held that the sun, named Aton, was god.
[3] **Von Humboldt . . . Amundsen:** List of famous explorers.

all the thousands of hours held perfect, incorruptible,
since the first heavy snows of mid-December.

In April, between the Champlain Valley and the Connecticut
River, a single mountain roadside remains
arrested forever: in indistinct, random patterns
of matted foliage and straw, I saw a delicate
arrangement of brown hair, exposed bone—a single
instant, discrete as a snowflake on a neuron
imperishable among millions in the gray moraine
of long accumulation (I can still feel that new
sun on my damp back like a mild alkaline
burn, intense and shallow—I saw the pick-up-sticks
complexity the earth assumed, and thought *Isn't*
the sun the same as life? and, grown fearful, yearned
for the first time for the brittle light, the fixed,
stupefying conservation of form that had been winter.)

I fell back in that starving light of past time
when a white-tailed deer fell over on its ribs
and froze; here was the first dead juvenescence°   youth
of spring, stillbirth, when winterkill drops
across the season like stone. How plausible,
the ancient stone planet reborn each year a stone,
a watch-fob charm spun down some lazy, oval
fall through time, until a soft Pleistocene[4]
wind drifted the mind of the first man whose lime-
dusted doppelgänger's form faced him like this: eyes full
to their pink rims with snow, the dead thought
and fish-stare still—behind the retinas, like loam,
the flat brain keeps the antique taproot of the
fear that spring is nothing more than a thaw.

We stand, imagining the strobe of afternoons
since earth began, the unregenerate gray
ground slacking weight all around us, once
more unfreezing, to be frozen again and thrown
back again in twigs and slag snow, and nowhere grace
or quick or leaf, the least flush or fragrance—
Then in some cold bedroom—as finely dreamt
as riffling cotton sleeves, and all the plant stems
like new copper by the road—a seine, a spill

---

[4] **Pleistocene:** Prehistoric era of human evolution.

of hair will fall and touch the face to simple
recognition, then: that blind instant caught,
in the absence of desire, out of the confusing sun,
when two of our species reach thoughtlessly
70   to groom one another, to smooth the other's skin.

LESLIE SILKO (1948–   )

Indian Song: Survival (1981)

We went north
         to escape winter
climbing pale cliffs
            we paused   to sleep at the river.

5   Cold water   river cold from the north
I sink my body in the shallow
            sink into sand and cold river water.

You sleep in the branches of
           pale river willows above me.
10   I smell you in the silver leaves, mountain lion man
           green willows aren't sweet enough to hide you.

I have slept with the river   and
           he is warmer than any man.
At sunrise
15   I heard ice on the cattails.

Mountain lion, with dark yellow eyes
           you nibble moonflowers
           while we wait.
I don't ask why do you come
20   on this desperation journey north.

I am hunted for my feathers
I hide in spider's web
          hanging   in a thin gray tree
            above the river.

25   In the night   I hear music
          song of branches   dry leaves scraping the moon.
Green spotted frogs sing to the river
          and I know he is waiting.

Mountain lion shows me the way
30   path of mountain wind
                climbing higher
                        up
                        up to Cloudy Mountain.

It is only a matter of time, Indian
35   you can't sleep with the river forever.
Smell winter and know.

I swallow black mountain dirt
            while you catch hummingbirds
                trap them with wildflowers
40   pollen and petals
                    fallen from the Milky Way.

You lie beside me in the sunlight
            warmth around us and
            you ask me if I still smell winter.
45   Mountain forest wind travels east and I answer:
                taste me,
                    I am the wind
                touch me,
                    I am the lean gray deer
50   running on the edge of the rainbow.

CAROLYN FORCHÉ (1950–   )

The Garden Shukkei-en[1] (1994)

By way of a vanished bridge we cross this river
as a cloud of lifted snow would ascend a mountain.

She has always been afraid to come here.

It is the river she most
5   remembers, the living
and the dead both crying for help.

---

[1] **Garden Shukkei-en:** A traditional, Japanese style garden in Hiroshima. *Shukkei-en* literally means "shrink scenery garden," and the seventeenth-century garden displays life-sized scenery in miniature form.

A world that allowed neither tears nor lamentation.

The *matsu* trees brush her hair as she passes
beneath them, as do the shining strands of barbed wire.

10   Where this lake is, there was a lake,
where these black pine grow, there grew black pine.

Where there is no teahouse I see a wooden teahouse
and the corpses of those who slept in it.

On the opposite bank of the Ota,[2] a weeping willow
15   etches its memory of their faces into the water.

Where light touches the face, the character for heart is written.

She strokes a burnt trunk wrapped in straw:
I was weak and my skin hung from my fingertips like cloth

Do you think for a moment we were human beings to them?

20   She comes to the stone angel holding paper cranes.
Not an angel, but a woman where she once had been,
who walks through the garden Shukkei-en
calling the carp to the surface by clapping her hands.

Do Americans think of us?

25   So she began as we squatted over the toilets:
If you want, I'll tell you, but nothing I say will be enough.

We tried to dress our burns with vegetable oil.

Her hair is the white froth of rice rising up kettlesides, her mind also.
In the postwar years she thought deeply about how to live.

30   The common greeting *dozo-yiroshku* is please take care of me.
All *hibakusha*[3] still alive were children then.

A cemetery seen from the air is a child's city.

I don't like this particular red flower because
it reminds me of a woman's brain crushed under a roof.

---

[2] **Ota:** A river in Hiroshima.
[3] *hibakusha*: Survivors of the atomic bombs dropped on Hiroshima and Nagasaki.

35   Perhaps my language is too precise, and therefore difficult to understand?

We have not, all these years, felt what you call happiness.
But at times, with good fortune, we experience something close.
As our life resembles life, and this garden the garden.
And in the silence surrounding what happened to us

40   it is the bell to awaken God that we've heard ringing.

CHASE TWICHELL (1950–   )

Pine   (1998)

The first night at the monastery,
a moth lit on my sleeve by firelight,
long after the first frost.

A short stick of incense burns
5   thirty minutes, fresh thread of pine
rising through the old pine of the hours.

Summer is trapped under the thin
glass on the brook, making
the sound of an emptying bottle.

10   Before the long silence,
the monks make a long soft rustling,
adjusting their robes.

The deer are safe now. Their tracks
are made of snow. The wind has dragged
15   its branches over their history.

JAMES GALVIN (1951–   )

Nature, Beside Herself   (2003)

Nothing is at one with nature,
Not wind or wind-tried trees,
Not striving grass,
Not famished coyotes or lovesick whales.

5   How do I know?
    Interviews.
    Without the part
    Where I point out the obvious—
    The *not with us*—there's no such thing as nature,
10 Is there?
    It's just another everywhere where
    We loiter
    Outside in order
    To side-glance in.

PAUL MULDOON (1951–   )

Why Brownlee Left (1980)

Why Brownlee left, and where he went,
Is a mystery even now.
For if a man should have been content
It was him; two acres of barley,
5   One of potatoes, four bullocks,°   bulls
A milker, a slated farmhouse.
He was last seen going out to plough
On a March morning, bright and early.

By noon Brownlee was famous;
10 They had found all abandoned, with
The last rig[1] unbroken, his pair of black
Horses, like man and wife,
Shifting their weight from foot to
Foot, and gazing into the future.

LOUISE ERDRICH (1954–   )

The Woods

At one time your touches were clothing enough.
Within these trees now I am different.
Now I wear the woods.

---

[1] **rig:** Ridge left between two plow furrows.

I lower a headdress of bent sticks and secure it.
5   I strap to myself a breastplate of clawed, roped bark.
I fit the broad leaves of sugar maples
to my hands, like mittens of blood.

Now when I say *come,*
and you enter the woods,
10   hunting some creature like the woman I was,
I surround you.

Light bleeds from the clearing. Roots rise.
Fluted molds burn blue in the falling light,
and you also know
15   the loneliness that you taught me with your body.

When you lie down in the grave of a slashed tree,
I cover you, as I always did.
Only this time you do not leave.

JOHN BURNSIDE   (1955–   )

Home Farm   (1994)

I am thinking of hedges and orchards,
the paths I could walk in the dark
from field to field

and a silence about the house
5   like a wider self,
a lifelong, unlaboured attunement,

rehearsing the names of crossroads,
breeds of sheep, varieties of pear,
words to exchange with a neighbour for no good cause

10   but the making and sharing of sounds,
the subtle replacement of meaning
with pauses and gestures,

a form of courtesy, the marking out of bounds
we do not choose, and take so long to measure.

CHAPTER 21

THY FEARFUL SYMMETRY
—William Blake

An Anthology of Poems
on Animals and Beasts

In "The Tyger," William Blake asks an essential question of the beast: "What immortal hand or eye / Could frame thy fearful symmetry?" Each living creature is a unique blast of creativity by some immortal hand. Poets have always understood this, and they have been drawn to animals as subjects in part because they represent a "made" thing, like a poem. As a result, poets have compiled a strange and luminous bestiary in their work.

It should be obvious that sometimes animals in poems are simply animals, and sometimes they represent more than that. Animals are often symbols, and the nature of the literary symbol is such that no single interpretation can capture its complete meaning. One would, for example, be at a loss to state in simple terms what Blake intended in "The Tyger." It's a poem full of hard questions, such as these:

> When the stars threw down their spears,
> And watered heaven with their tears,
> Did he smile his work to see?
> Did he who made the lamb make thee?

This is clearly a poem about creation, one that asks crucial questions about the nature of the imagination. Blake wonders whether the God who made the lamb, an innocent creature, also made the vicious and unrelenting tiger. In a sense, Blake's poem introduces the question of evil, much as Robert Frost does in his poem "Design" (p. 1259).

Other poems in this chapter are about nothing more than the animal itself, as in "To a Mouse" by Robert Burns (p. 1345). It would be far-fetched to assume that this simple and humorous poem had more complex meanings. A few other poems here also seem—for the most part—to be about the animal, rather than assigning any symbolic or mythical meaning to the creature. Yet many of these poems reach beyond their immediate circumstances, and the animal at the center of the poem summons a wider range of experience and impressions, as in "To a Nightingale," an ode by Keats (p. 1352). This poem is largely about the experience of escape, as with dreams or drugs; the speaker—the "I" of the poem—wishes to extricate himself from his life, from suffering he cannot easily tolerate. As we know from his letters, Keats believed that a poet must have what he called "negative capability," a talent for entering into the consciousness of other creatures and forgetting himself. Such an experience occurs in this poem. The poet abandons his "sole self" to join the nightingale, whose lovely song is moving, yet somehow beyond human language. Compare this transformative imagination with William Butler Yeats's "Sailing to Byzantium" (p. 1439), in which the speaker projects himself into a mythical paradise of perfect, perpetual, yet artificial song.

We may also compare these poems with "The Oven Bird" by Robert Frost (p. 1360). "There is a singer everyone has heard, / Loud, a mid-summer and a mid-wood bird, / Who makes the solid tree trunks sound again," says the poet. This is no nightingale. Frost's bird sings in the middle of the woods in the middle of summer and, presumably, in the middle of the day. Yet the bird "frames in all but words" a heady question: "what to make of a diminished thing." This sad thing is the world past its peak, a time when "early petal-fall is past," and the beautiful flowers of spring and early summer have been washed away. Frost also alludes to "that other fall we name the fall." He refers here to the Fall of Man and original sin, which has led to the diminished thing we call the modern world. In essence, Frost uses this bird as a mouthpiece for himself.

Many of the animals described here take on a strange, almost otherworldly, quality, as in "Snake" by D. H. Lawrence (p. 1360). The snake forms a contrast to the poet himself, who is a character in the poem:

> A snake came to my water-trough
> On a hot, hot day, and I in pyjamas for the heat,
> To drink there.
>
> In the deep, strange-scented shade of the great dark carob-tree
> 5   I came down the steps with my pitcher
> And must wait, must stand and wait, for there he was at the trough
>   before me.
>
> He reached down from a fissure in the earth-wall in the gloom
> And trailed his yellow-brown slackness soft-bellied down, over the
>   edge of the stone trough
> And rested his throat upon the stone bottom,
> 10 And where the water had dripped from the tap, in a small clearness,
> He sipped with his straight mouth,
> Softly drank through his straight gums, into his slack long body,
> Silently.

The snake appears malevolent, much like the serpent that tempted Eve in the Garden of Eden; yet Lawrence worships this creature, identifying with its primitive life-force, with its rippling intensity, its alertness, its need for water and sunlight. The snake becomes a dark, luminous symbol of life itself.

In the same way, Ted Hughes writes about animals as embodiments of creation's irresistible dark forces. Hughes, one of the strongest of modern British poets, focuses his relentless attention on animals in many of his best poems, and we could have filled this entire section with poems by him. He identifies closely with these animals: birds and beasts of prey, for the most part. The hawk, in particular, caught his imagination, as a bird of power and great intensity, as in "Hawk Roosting" (p. 1388) and "Hawk in the Rain" (p. 1519). Similarly, Hughes celebrates the brutal energies of aggressive fish, as in "Pike" (p. 1390). The pike is at once terrifying and beautiful; it is also cannibalistic, eating its own kind. The poet describes two of them, "six pounds each, over two feet long, / High and dry and dead in the willow-herb— / One jammed past its gills down the other's gullet."

Animals and beasts, as emblems and as themselves, have fascinated other contemporary poets as well. Among the oddest of the poems here is "Animals Are Passing from Our Lives" by Philip Levine (p. 1383), in which the poet identifies thoroughly with a pig who refuses to be led to the slaughter. The tone of this poem—the attitude of the poet toward the material—is worth considering at length. Levine attributes a defiance to the pig that we admire, but with certain reservations. There is an edge of ambivalence here, in the poet, that transfers to the reader.

In all, each poet uses the fish, fowl, or beast at the center of his or her poem as an emblem, a symbol for all that is wild, untamed, unbearable, earthly, exhilarating. These are vivid poems, and they speak to the human need to makes allies in the wild and natural world, to recognize that we— as human beings—are animals as well, subject to the same drives and energies, the same will, the same violent and unchecked powers.

ADDITIONAL POEMS ABOUT ANIMALS IN THIS BOOK

- Christopher Smart, "When I Consider My Cat Jeoffrey" (p. 1571)
- Edgar Allan Poe, "The Raven" (p. 318)
- William Butler Yeats, "Leda and the Swan" (p. 821)
- Robert Frost, "The Most of It" (p. 1301)
- John Crowe Ransom, "Janet Waking" (p. 215)
- Elizabeth Bishop, "The Moose" (p. 354)
- Robert Penn Warren, "Heart of Autumn" (p. 1448)
- William Stafford, "Traveling Through the Dark" (p. 1262)
- Ted Hughes, "Hawk in the Rain" (p. 1519)
- Erica Jong, "Jubilate Canis" (p. 1574)
- Louise Glück, "Messengers" (p. 1543)
- Edward Hirsch, "Wild Gratitude" (p. 1575)

ANONYMOUS

The Cuckoo Song (ca. thirteenth century)

Sing, cuccu, nu.° Sing, cuccu.   now
Sing, cuccu. Sing, cuccu, nu.

Sumer is i-cumen in—
    Lhude° sing, cuccu!   loudly
5 Groweth sed and bloweth° med°   blooms / meadow
    And springth the wude° nu.   wood
        Sing, cuccu!

Awe° bleteth after lomb,   Ewe
    Lhouth° after calve cu,°   Lows / low
10 Bulluc sterteth,° bucke verteth°   starts / farts
    Murie° sing, cuccu!   Merrily
      Cuccu, cuccu.
    Wel singes thu, cuccu.
    Ne swik° thu naver° nu!   cease / never

ANONYMOUS

I Have a Gentle Cock (fifteenth century)

I have a gentle° cock,   noble
    Croweth me day;
He doth me risen early
    My matins° for to say.   prayers

5 I have a gentle cock,
    Comen he is of great;°   great ancestry
His comb is of red coral,
    His tail is of jet.°   black

I have a gentle cock,
10 Comen he is of kind;°   fine stock
His comb is of red coral,
    His tail is of inde.°   indigo

His legges be of azure,
    So gentle and so small;

15   His spurres are of silver white
            Into the wortewale.[1]

        His eyen are of crystal,
            Locked all in amber;
        And every night he percheth him
20   In my lady's chamber.

JOHN DONNE (1572–1631)

The Flea[1] (1633)

        Mark but this flea, and mark in this,
        How little that which thou deniest me is;
        It sucked me first, and now sucks thee,
        And in this flea, our two bloods mingled be;
5   Thou know'st that this cannot be said
        A sin, nor shame nor loss of maidenhead,[2]
            Yet this enjoys before it woo,
            And pampered swells with one blood made of two,[3]
            And this, alas, is more then we would do.

10   Oh stay, three lives in one flea spare,
        Where we almost, yea more than married are.
        This flea is you and I, and this
        Our marriage bed, and marriage temple is;
        Though parents grudge, and you, w'are met,
15   And cloisered in these living walls of jet.[4]
            Though use° make you apt to kill me,   custom
            Let not to that, self murder added be,
            And sacrilege, three sins in killing three.

        Cruel and sudden, hast thou since
20   Purpled thy nail, in blood of innocence?
        Wherein could this flea guilty be,
        Except in that drop which it sucked from thee?

---

[1] **Into the wortewale:** In other words, down to the bottom of the spurs, or claws.
[1] **The Flea:** In Renaissance erotic poems, the flea is envied by a male narrator for its opportunity to contact and be killed by his lady. In this period, both "die" and "kill" were slang terms for orgasm.
[2] **loss of maidenhead:** In other words, loss of virginity. (The maidenhead is the hymen.)
[3] **And pampered . . . two:** In the Renaissance, blood was thought to blend during sexual intercourse, leading to pregnancy.
[4] **And . . . jet:** Here, the "living walls of jet" refer to the flea's body.

Yet thou triumph'st, and say'st that thou
Find'st not thy self, nor me the weaker now;
25   'Tis true, then learn how false, fears be;
        Just so much honor, when thou yield'st to me,
        Will waste, as this flea's death took life from thee.

ANONYMOUS

The Silver Swan[1] (1612)

The silver swan, who living had no note,
When death approached, unlocked her silent throat;
Leaning her breast against the reedy shore,
Thus sung her first and last, and sung no more:
5   "Farewell, all joys; Oh death, come close mine eyes;
More geese than swans now live, more fools than wise."

RICHARD LOVELACE (1618–ca. 1657)

The Grasshopper: To My Noble Friend, Mr Charles Cotton[1]: Ode (1649)

O thou that swingst upon the waving hair
    Of some well-fillèd oaten beard,[2]
Drunk every night with a delicious tear°   water
    Dropped thee from heaven, where now th'art reared,

5   The joys of earth and air are thine entire,
        That with thy feet and wings dost hop and fly;
    And when thy poppy° works thou dost retire   sleeping potion
        To thy carved acorn bed to lie.

    Up with the day, the sun thou welcom'st then,
10   Sportst in the gilt plats° of his beams,   braids
    And all these merry days mak'st merry men,
        Thyself, and melancholy streams.

---

[1] **The Silver Swan:** From *First Set of Madrigals and Motets* (1612) by Orlando Gibbons.
[1] **The Grasshopper . . . Cotton:** Lovelace embellishes the ant and grasshopper fable, where the sensible ant prepares for the winter while the carefree grasshopper shirks his responsibility. Charles Cotton was a scholar and friend of Lovelace.
[2] **beard:** I.e., grain.

But ah, the sickle! Golden ears are cropped;
    Ceres and Bacchus[3] bid good-night;
15 Sharp frosty fingers all your flow'rs have topped,
    And what scythes spared, winds shave off quite.

Poor verdant fool! And now green ice![4] Thy joys,
    Large and as lasting as thy perch of grass,
Bid us lay in 'gainst winter rain, and poise
20   Their floods with an o'erflowing glass.

Thou best of men and friends! We will create
    A genuine summer in each other's breast;
And spite of this cold time and frozen fate
    Thaw us a warm seat to our rest.

25 Our sacred hearths shall burn eternally
    As Vestal flames:[5] the north wind, he
Shall strike his frost-stretched wings, dissolve and fly
    This Etna[6] in epitome.

Dropping December shall come weeping in,
30   Bewail the usurping of his reign;
But when in showers of old Greek we begin,
    Shall cry he hath his crown again.[7]

Night as clear Hesper[8] shall our tapers whip
    From the light casements where we play,
35 And the dark hag from her black mantle strip,
    And stick there everlasting day.[9]

Thus richer than untempted kings are we,
    That asking nothing, nothing need:
Though lord of all what seas embrace, yet he
40   That wants himself is poor indeed.

---

[3] **Ceres and Bacchus:** In other words, the grain and grape. Ceres is the goddess of the harvest, and Bacchus is the god of wine.

[4] **And now green ice!:** Here, Lovelace suggests that the grasshopper has frozen.

[5] **Vestal flames:** Vestal virgins, attendants of the Roman goddess Vesta, tended an eternal fire on her altar.

[6] **Etna:** Mount Etna, a volcano in Sicily, whose flames are an emblem of friendship.

[7] **old Greek . . . again:** In the classical world, those who drank Greek wine often wore festive crowns.

[8] **Hesper:** Hesperus, the morning star.

[9] **tapers . . . day:** The "dark hag" is Hecate, daughter of the Night. Lovelace suggests that burning candles through the night will remove her black cloak, or "mantle."

WILLIAM BLAKE (1757–1827)

The Tyger (1794)

Tyger, tyger, burning bright
In the forests of the night,
What immortal hand or eye
Could frame thy fearful symmetry?

5   In what distant deeps or skies
Burnt the fire of thine eyes?
On what wings dare he aspire?
What the hand dare seize the fire?

And what shoulder, and what art,
10   Could twist the sinews of thy heart?
And when thy heart began to beat,
What dread hand? And what dread feet?

What the hammer? What the chain?
In what furnace was thy brain?
15   What the anvil? What dread grasp
Dare its deadly terrors clasp?

When the stars threw down their spears,
And watered heaven with their tears,
Did he smile his work to see?
20   Did he who made the lamb make thee?

Tyger, tyger burning bright
In the forests of the night,
What immortal hand or eye
Dare frame thy fearful symmetry?

ROBERT BURNS (1759–1796)

To a Mouse, On Turning Her Up in Her Nest with the Plough, November 1785 (1786)

Wee, sleeket,° cowran', tim'rous beastie,   *sleek*
O, what a panic's in thy breastie!
Thou need na start awa sae hasty
      Wi' bickering brattle°—   *scurry*
5   I wad be laith to rin an' chase thee
      Wi' murd'ring pattle.°   *plowstaff*

I'm truly sorry man's dominion
Has broken Nature's social union,
An' justifies that ill opinion
      Which makes thee startle
At me, thy poor earth-born companion
      An' fellow-mortal!

I doubt na, whyles, but thou may thieve—
What then? poor beastie, thou maun° live!   must
A daimen°-icker° in a thrave   chance / corn-ear
      'S a sma' request;
I'll get a blessin' wi' the lave,°   remainder
      An' never miss't!

Thy wee-bit housie, too, in ruin—
Its silly° wa's the win's are strewin'—   fragile
An' naething, now, to big° a new ane   build
      O' foggage° green!   mosses
An' bleak December's winds ensuin',
      Baith snell° an' keen!   sour

Thou saw the fields laid bare an' wast,
An' weary winter comin' fast,
An' cozie here, beneath the blast,
      Thou thought to dwell—
Till crash! the cruel coulter° past   plow
      Out thro' thy cell.

That wee-bit heap o' leaves an' stibble,
Has cost thee monie a weary nibble!
Now thou's turn'd out, for a' thy trouble,
      But° house or hald,°   With no / hold
To thole° the winter's sleety dribble   bear
      An' cranreuch° cauld!   hoarfrost

But Mousie, thou art no thy-lane°   not alone
In proving foresight may be vain:
The best laid schemes o' mice an' men
      Gang° aft agley,°   go / awry
An' lea'e us nought but grief an' pain,
      For promis'd joy!

Still, thou art blest compar'd wi' me:
The present only toucheth thee,

Line numbers: 10, 15, 20, 25, 30, 35, 40

45   But och! I backward cast my e'e
     On prospects drear—
An' forward, though I canna see,
     I guess an' fear!

PERCY BYSSHE SHELLEY (1792–1822)

To a Skylark (1820)

Hail to thee, blithe Spirit!
     Bird thou never wert,
That from Heaven, or near it,
     Pourest thy full heart
5   In profuse strains of unpremeditated art.

Higher still and higher
     From the earth thou springest
Like a cloud of fire;
     The blue deep thou wingest,
10   And singing still dost soar, and soaring ever singest.

In the golden lightning
     Of the sunken sun,
O'er which clouds are bright'ning,
     Thou dost float and run;
15   Like an unbodied joy whose race is just begun.

The pale purple even
     Melts around thy flight;
Like a star of Heaven,
     In the broad day-light
20   Thou art unseen, but yet I hear thy shrill delight,

Keen as are the arrows
     Of that silver sphere,
Whose intense lamp narrows
     In the white dawn clear
25   Until we hardly see, we feel that it is there.

All the earth and air
     With thy voice is loud,

As, when night is bare,
 From one lonely cloud
30 The moon rains out her beams, and Heaven is overflow'd.

What thou art we know not;
 What is most like thee?
From rainbow clouds there flow not
 Drops so bright to see
35 As from thy presence showers a rain of melody.

Like a Poet hidden
 In the light of thought,
Singing hymns unbidden,
 Till the world is wrought
40 To sympathy with hopes and fears it heeded not:

Like a high-born maiden
 In a palace-tower,
Soothing her love-laden
 Soul in secret hour
45 With music sweet as love, which overflows her bower:

Like a glow-worm golden
 In a dell of dew,
Scattering unbeholden
 Its aërial hue
50 Among the flowers and grass, which screen it from the view:

Like a rose embower'd
 In its own green leaves,
By warm winds deflower'd,
 Till the scent it gives
55 Makes faint with too much sweet those heavy-winged thieves:

Sound of vernal showers
 On the twinkling grass,
Rain-awaken'd flowers,
 All that ever was
60 Joyous, and clear, and fresh, thy music doth surpass.

Teach us, Sprite or Bird,
 What sweet thoughts are thine:
I have never heard
 Praise of love or wine
65 That panted forth a flood of rapture so divine.

Chorus Hymeneal,°   for a wedding
   Or triumphal chant,
Match'd with thine would be all
   But an empty vaunt,
70 A thing wherein we feel there is some hidden want.

What objects are the fountains
   Of thy happy strain?
What fields, or waves, or mountains?
   What shapes of sky or plain?
75 What love of thine own kind? what ignorance of pain?

With thy clear keen joyance
   Languor cannot be:
Shadow of annoyance
   Never came near thee:
80 Thou lovest: but ne'er knew love's sad satiety.

Waking or asleep,
   Thou of death must deem
Things more true and deep
   Than we mortals dream,
85 Or how could thy notes flow in such a crystal stream?

We look before and after,
   And pine for what is not:
Our sincerest laughter
   With some pain is fraught;
90 Our sweetest songs are those that tell of saddest thought.

Yet if we could scorn
   Hate, and pride, and fear;
If we were things born
   Not to shed a tear,
95 I know not how thy joy we ever should come near.

Better than all measures
   Of delightful sound,
Better than all treasures
   That in books are found,
100 Thy skill to poet were, thou scorner of the ground!

Teach me half the gladness
   That thy brain must know,
Such harmonious madness

From my lips would flow
105   The world should listen then, as I am listening now.

JOHN CLARE   (1793–1864)

Badger   (ca. 1835; 1920)

When midnight comes a host of dogs and men
Go out and track the badger to his den,
And put the sack within the hole, and lie
Till the old grunting badger passes by.
5   He comes and hears—they let the strongest loose.
The old fox hears the noise and drops the goose.
The poacher shoots and hurries from the cry,
And the old hare half wounded buzzes by.
They get a forked stick to bear him down
10   And clap the dogs and take him to the town,
And bait him all the day with many dogs,
And laugh and shout and fright the scampering hogs.
He runs along and bites at all he meets:
They shout and hollo down the noisy streets.

15   He turns about to face the loud uproar
And drives the rebels to their very door.
The frequent stone is hurled where'er they go;
When badgers fight, then every one's a foe.
The dogs are clapt and urged to join the fray;
20   The badger turns and drives them all away.
Though scarcely half as big, demure and small,
He fights with dogs for hours and beats them all.
The heavy mastiff, savage in the fray,
Lies down and licks his feet and turns away.
25   The bulldog knows his match and waxes cold,
The badger grins and never leaves his hold.
He drives the crowd and follows at their heels
And bites them through—the drunkard swears and reels.

The frighted women take the boys away,
30   The blackguard laughs and hurries on the fray.
He tries to reach the woods, an awkward race,
But sticks and cudgels° quickly stop the chase.   clubs
He turns agen and drives the noisy crowd
And beats the many dogs in noises loud.
35   He drives away and beats them every one,

And then they loose them all and set them on.
He falls as dead and kicked by boys and men,
Then starts and grins and drives the crowd again;
Till kicked and torn and beaten out he lies
40 And leaves his hold and cackles, groans, and dies.

WILLIAM CULLEN BRYANT (1794–1878)

To a Waterfowl (1815; 1818)

    Whither, 'midst falling dew,
While glow the heavens with the last steps of day,
Far, through their rosy depths, dost thou pursue
    Thy solitary way?

5   Vainly the fowler's eye
Might mark thy distant flight, to do thee wrong,
As, darkly seen against the crimson sky,
    Thy figure floats along.

    Seek'st thou the plashy brink
10 Of weedy lake, or marge of river wide,
Or where the rocking billows rise and sink
    On the chaféd ocean side?

    There is a Power, whose care
Teaches thy way along that pathless coast,—
15 The desert and illimitable air,
    Lone wandering, but not lost,

    All day thy wings have fanned,
At that far height, the cold thin atmosphere;
Yet stoop not, weary, to the welcome land,
20   Though the dark night is near.

    And soon that toil shall end,
Soon shalt thou find a summer home, and rest,
And scream among thy fellows; reeds shall bend,
    Soon, o'er thy sheltered nest.

25   Thou'rt gone, the abyss of heaven
Hath swallowed up thy form, yet, on my heart
Deeply hath sunk the lesson thou hast given,
    And shall not soon depart.

He, who, from zone to zone,
30   Guides through the boundless sky thy certain flight,
In the long way that I must trace alone,
     Will lead my steps aright.

JOHN KEATS (1795–1821)

Ode to a Nightingale (1819; 1820)

I

My heart aches, and a drowsy numbness pains
  My sense, as though of hemlock[1] I had drunk,
Or emptied some dull opiate to the drains
  One minute past, and Lethe-wards[2] had sunk.
5 'Tis not through envy of thy happy lot,
  But being too happy in thine happiness—
    That thou, light-wingéd dryad° of the trees,   wood nymph
      In some melodious plot
    Of beechen green, and shadows numberless,
10   Singest of summer in full-throated ease.

II

Oh, for a draught of vintage that hath been
  Cooled a long age in the deep-delvéd earth,
Tasting of Flora and the country green,
  Dance, and Provençal song, and sunburnt mirth.[3]
15 Oh for a beaker full of the warm South,
  Full of the true, the blushful Hippocrene,[4]
    With beaded bubbles winking at the brim,
      And purple-stainéd mouth;
That I might drink, and leave the world unseen,
20   And with thee fade away into the forest dim—

---

[1] **hemlock:** Poison derived from an Eurasian herb.
[2] **Lethe-wards:** In Hades, the Lethe is the river whose waters, when consumed, allow the dead to forget their life on earth.
[3] **Flora . . . mirth:** In Roman mythology, Flora is the goddess of blossoming flowers. Provençal song refers to the troubadours of Provence, in southern France, known for their love lyrics.
[4] **Hippocrene:** Water from Mt. Helicon in ancient Greece, home of the nine Muses responsible for artistic inspiration.

III

Fade far away, dissolve, and quite forget
    What thou among the leaves hast never known,
The weariness, the fever, and the fret
    Here, where men sit and hear each other groan—
25 Where palsy shakes a few, sad, last, grey hairs,
    Where youth grows pale, and spectre-thin, and dies;
      Where but to think is to be full of sorrow
        And leaden-eyed despairs,
    Where beauty cannot keep her lustrous eyes
30   Or new love pine at them beyond tomorrow.

IV

Away! Away! For I will fly to thee,
    Not charioted by Bacchus and his pards,[5]
But on the viewless wings of poesy,
    Though the dull brain perplexes and retards.
35 Already with thee! Tender is the night,
    And haply the Queen-Moon is on her throne,
      Clustered around by all her starry fays;°   *fairies*
        But here there is no light,
    Save what from heaven is with the breezes blown
40   Through verdurous glooms and winding mossy ways.

V

I cannot see what flowers are at my feet,
    Nor what soft incense hangs upon the boughs,
But, in embalméd darkness, guess each sweet
    Wherewith the seasonable month endows
45 The grass, the thicket, and the fruit-tree wild;
    White hawthorn, and the pastoral eglantine;°   *wild rose*
      Fast fading violets covered up in leaves;
        And mid-May's eldest child,
    The coming musk-rose, full of dewy wine,
50   The murmurous haunt of flies on summer eves.

VI

Darkling° I listen, and for many a time   *In the dark*
    I have been half in love with easeful death,
Called him soft names in many a muséd rhyme,
    To take into the air my quiet breath.

---

[5] **Bacchus and his pards:** Bacchus, the Roman god of wine, rode in a chariot drawn by leopards.

55 Now more than ever seems it rich to die,
    To cease upon the midnight with no pain,
        While thou art pouring forth thy soul abroad
            In such an ecstasy!
        Still wouldst thou sing, and I have ears in vain—
60   To thy high requiem become a sod.

VII

Thou wast not born for death, immortal bird!
    No hungry generations tread thee down;
The voice I hear this passing night was heard
    In ancient days by emperor and clown—
65 Perhaps the self-same song that found a path
        Through the sad heart of Ruth,[6] when, sick for home,
            She stood in tears amid the alien corn;
                The same that oft-times hath
        Charmed magic casements, opening on the foam
70   Of perilous seas, in fairy lands forlorn.

VIII

Forlorn—the very word is like a bell
    To toll me back from thee to my sole self!
Adieu! The fancy cannot cheat so well
    As she is famed to do, deceiving elf!
75 Adieu! adieu! Thy plaintive anthem fades
        Past the near meadows, over the still stream,
            Up the hillside; and now 'tis buried deep
                In the next valley-glades:
        Was it a vision, or a waking dream?
80   Fled is that music! Do I wake or sleep?

ALFRED, LORD TENNYSON (1809–1892)

The Eagle (ca. 1833; 1851)

Fragment

He clasps the crag with crooked hands;
Close to the sun in lonely lands,
Ring'd with the azure world, he stands.

---

[6] **sad heart of Ruth:** In the Old Testament, Ruth was a Moabite amongst Israelites who found a husband while gleaning the barley fields in Judah. (See Ruth 2.1-2.)

The wrinkled sea beneath him crawls;
5   He watches from his mountain walls,
And like a thunderbolt he falls.

HERMAN MELVILLE (1819–1891)

The Maldive Shark (1888)

About the Shark, phlegmatical one,
Pale sot° of the Maldive sea,[1]   drunkard
The sleek little pilot-fish, azure and slim,
How alert in attendance be.
5   From his saw-pit of mouth, from his charnel of maw,°   stomach
They have nothing of harm to dread,
But liquidly glide on his ghastly flank
Or before his Gorgonian head;[2]
Or lurk in the port of serrated teeth
10 In white triple tiers of glittering gates,
And there find a haven when peril's abroad,
An asylum in jaws of the Fates!
They are friends; and friendly they guide him to prey,
Yet never partake of the treat—
15 Eyes and brains to the dotard lethargic and dull,
Pale ravener of horrible meat.

WALT WHITMAN (1819–1892)

The Dalliance° of the Eagles (1880; 1881)   flirtation

Skirting the river road, (my forenoon walk, my rest,)
Skyward in air a sudden muffled sound, the dalliance of the eagles,
The rushing amorous contact high in space together,
The clinching interlocking claws, a living, fierce, gyrating wheel,
5   Four beating wings, two beaks, a swirling mass tight grappling,
In tumbling turning clustering loops, straight downward falling,

---

[1] **Maldive sea:** In the Indian Ocean, the area around the Maldive Islands that stretches from the tip of India to the equator.
[2] **Gorgonian head:** In Greek mythology, the Gorgons were vicious female monsters with wretched faces and serpent hair who turned anyone looking upon them into stone.

Till o'er the river pois'd, the twain yet one, a moment's lull,
A motionless still balance in the air, then parting, talons loosing,
Upward again on slow-firm pinions slanting, their separate diverse flight,
10   She hers, he his, pursuing.

WALT WHITMAN (1819–1892)

A Noiseless Patient Spider (1868; 1881)

A noiseless patient spider,
I mark'd where on a little promontory it stood isolated,
Mark'd how to explore the vacant vast surrounding,
It launch'd forth filament, filament, filament, out of itself,
5   Ever unreeling them, ever tirelessly speeding them.

And you O my soul where you stand,
Surrounded, detached, in measureless oceans of space,
Ceaselessly musing, venturing, throwing, seeking the spheres to
          connect them,
Till the bridge you will need be form'd, till the ductile anchor hold,
10   Till the gossamer thread you fling catch somewhere, O my soul.

EMILY DICKINSON (1830–1886)

"A narrow Fellow in the Grass" (ca. 1865; 1866)

A narrow Fellow in the Grass
Occasionally rides—
You may have met Him—did you not
His notice sudden is—

5   The Grass divides as with a Comb—
A spotted shaft is seen—
And then it closes at your feet
And opens further on—

He likes a Boggy Acre
10   A Floor too cool for Corn—
Yet when a Boy, and Barefoot—
I more than once at Noon
Have passed, I thought, a Whip lash

Unbraiding in the Sun
15   When stooping to secure it
It wrinkled, and was gone—

Several of Nature's People
I know, and they know me—
I feel for them a transport
20   Of cordiality—

But never met this Fellow
Attended, or alone
Without a tighter breathing
And Zero at the Bone—

THOMAS HARDY (1840–1928)

The Darkling Thrush   (1900)

I leant upon a coppice gate
    When Frost was spectre-gray,
And Winter's dregs made desolate
    The weakening eye of day.
5   The tangled bine-stems[1] scored the sky
    Like strings of broken lyres,
And all mankind that haunted nigh
    Had sought their household fires.

The land's sharp features seemed to be
10   The Century's corpse outleant,
His crypt the cloudy canopy,
    The wind his death-lament.
The ancient pulse of germ and birth
    Was shrunken hard and dry,
15   And every spirit upon earth
    Seemed fervourless as I.

At once a voice arose among
    The bleak twigs overhead
In a full-hearted evensong
20   Of joy illimited;

---

[1] **bine-stems:** Twigs from a climbing plant.

An aged thrush, frail, gaunt, and small,
    In blast-beruffled plume,
Had chosen thus to fling his soul
    Upon the growing gloom.

25 So little cause for carolings
    Of such ecstatic sound
Was written on terrestrial things
    Afar or nigh around,
That I could think there trembled through
30   His happy good-night air
Some blessed Hope, whereof he knew
    And I was unaware.

GERARD MANLEY HOPKINS (1844–1889)

The Windhover:[1] (1918)
    To Christ our Lord

I caught this morning morning's minion,° King-   *darling*
    dom of daylight's dauphin,° dapple-dawn-drawn Falcon, in his riding   *prince*
    Of the rolling level underneath him steady air, and striding
High there, how he rung upon the rein of a wimpling° wing   *rippling*
5 In his ecstasy! then off, off forth on swing,
    As a skate's heel sweeps smooth on a bow-bend: the hurl and gliding
    Rebuffed the big wind. My heart in hiding
Stirred for a bird,—the achieve of, the mastery of the thing!

Brute beauty and valour and act, oh, air, pride, plume here
10   Buckle! AND the fire that breaks from thee then, a billion
    Times told lovelier, more dangerous, O my chevalier!

    No wonder of it: shéer plód makes plough down sillion[2]
Shine, and blue-bleak embers, ah my dear,
    Fall, gall themselves, and gash gold-vermilion.

---

[1] **The Windhover:** A kestrel, or European falcon.
[2] **sillion:** A ridge between two furrows.

WILLIAM BUTLER YEATS (1865–1939)

Long-legged Fly (1939)

That civilisation may not sink,
Its great battle lost,
Quiet the dog, tether the pony
To a distant post.
5   Our master Caesar[1] is in the tent
Where the maps are spread,
His eyes fixed upon nothing,
A hand under his head.

Like a long-legged fly upon the stream
10   *His mind moves upon silence.*

That the topless towers be burnt
And men recall that face,
Move most gently if move you must
In this lonely place.
15   She[2] thinks, part woman, three parts a child,
That nobody looks; her feet
Practise a tinker shuffle
Picked up on a street.

Like a long-legged fly upon the stream
20   *His mind moves upon silence.*

That girls at puberty may find
The first Adam in their thought,
Shut the door of the Pope's chapel,
Keep those children out.
25   There on that scaffolding reclines
Michael Angelo.[3]
With no more sound than the mice make
His hand moves to and fro.

Like a long-legged fly upon the stream
30   *His mind moves upon silence.*

---

[1] **Caesar:** Julius Caesar (100 B.C.–44 B.C.), Roman military general and politician who conquered Gaul and ruled the Roman world.
[2] **She:** Helen of Troy, a tragic figure from Homer's *Iliad*.
[3] **Michael Angelo:** Michelangelo (1475–1564) painted a series of biblical scenes on the ceiling of the Sistine Chapel, built by Pope Sixtus IV.

G. K. CHESTERTON (1874–1936)

The Donkey (1920)

"The tattered outlaw of the earth,
    Of ancient crooked will;
Starve, scourge, deride me: I am dumb,
    I keep my secret still.

5   "Fools! For I also had my hour;
    One far fierce hour and sweet:
There was a shout about my ears,
    And palms before my feet."

ROBERT FROST (1874–1963)

The Oven Bird[1] (1916)

There is a singer everyone has heard,
Loud, a mid-summer and a mid-wood bird,
Who makes the solid tree trunks sound again.
He says that leaves are old and that for flowers
5   Mid-summer is to spring as one to ten.
He says the early petal-fall is past,
When pear and cherry bloom went down in showers
On sunny days a moment overcast;
And comes that other fall we name the fall.
10 He says the highway dust is over all.
The bird would cease and be as other birds
But that he knows in singing not to sing.
The question that he frames in all but words.
Is what to make of a diminished thing.

D. H. LAWRENCE (1885–1930)

Snake (1923)

A snake came to my water-trough
On a hot, hot day, and I in pyjamas for the heat,
To drink there.

---

[1] **Oven Bird:** The warbler, a small songbird.

In the deep, strange-scented shade of the great dark carob-tree[1]
5 I came down the steps with my pitcher
And must wait, must stand and wait, for there he was at the trough
       before me.

He reached down from a fissure in the earth-wall in the gloom
And trailed his yellow-brown slackness soft-bellied down, over the
       edge of the stone trough
And rested his throat upon the stone bottom,
10 And where the water had dripped from the tap, in a small clearness,
He sipped with his straight mouth,
Softly drank through his straight gums, into his slack long body,
Silently.

Someone was before me at my water-trough,
15 And I, like a second comer, waiting.

He lifted his head from his drinking, as cattle do,
And looked at me vaguely, as drinking cattle do,
And flickered his two-forked tongue from his lips, and mused a moment,
And stooped and drank a little more,
20 Being earth-brown, earth-golden from the burning bowels of the earth
On the day of Sicilian July, with Etna[2] smoking.

The voice of my education said to me
He must be killed,
For in Sicily the black, black snakes are innocent, the gold are
       venomous.

25 And voices in me said, If you were a man
You would take a stick and break him now, and finish him off.

But must I confess how I liked him,
How glad I was he had come like a guest in quiet, to drink at my
       water-trough
And depart peaceful, pacified, and thankless,
30 Into the burning bowels of this earth?

Was it cowardice, that I dared not kill him?
Was it perversity, that I longed to talk to him?
Was it humility, to feel so honoured?
I felt so honoured.

---

[1] **carob-tree:** Mediterranean evergreen with edible pods.
[2] **Etna:** Mount Etna, a large volcano in Sicily.

35   And yet those voices:
      If you were not afraid, you would kill him!

      And truly I was afraid, I was most afraid,
      But even so, honoured still more
      That he should seek my hospitality
40   From out the dark door of the secret earth.

      He drank enough
      And lifted his head, dreamily, as one who has drunken,
      And flickered his tongue like a forked night on the air, so black;
      Seeming to lick his lips,
45   And looked around like a god, unseeing, into the air,
      And slowly turned his head,
      And slowly, very slowly, as if thrice adream,
      Proceeded to draw his slow length curving round
      And climb again the broken bank of my wall-face.

50   And as he put his head into that dreadful hole,
      And as he slowly drew up, snake-easing his shoulders, and entered
                    farther,
      A sort of horror, a sort of protest against his withdrawing into that
                    horrid black hole,
      Deliberately going into the blackness, and slowly drawing himself after,
      Overcame me now his back was turned.

55   I looked round, I put down my pitcher,
      I picked up a clumsy log
      And threw it at the water-trough with a clatter.

      I think it did not hit him,
      But suddenly that part of him that was left behind convulsed in
                    undignified haste,
60   Writhed like lightning, and was gone
      Into the black hole, the earth-lipped fissure in the wall-front,
      At which, in the intense still noon, I stared with fascination.

      And immediately I regretted it.
      I thought how paltry, how vulgar, what a mean act!
65   I despised myself and the voices of my accursed human education.

      And I thought of the albatross,[3]
      And I wished he would come back, my snake.

---

[3] **albatross:** In Coleridge's "Rime of the Ancient Mariner," a sailor brings bad luck to his ship after
killing an albatross, a traditional symbol of good fortune.

For he seemed to me again like a king,
Like a king in exile, uncrowned in the underworld,
70   Now due to be crowned again.

And so, I missed my chance with one of the lords
Of life.
And I have something to expiate;
A pettiness.

H. D. (HILDA DOOLITTLE) (1886–1961)

Birds in Snow (1931)

See,
how they trace
across the very-marble
of this place,
5   bright sevens and printed fours,
elevens and careful eights,
abracadabra
of a mystic's lore
or symbol
10   outlined
on a wizard's gate;

like plaques of ancient writ
our garden flags now name
the great and very-great;
15   our garden flags acclaim
in carven hieroglyph,
here king and kinglet lie,
here prince and lady rest,
mystical queens sleep here
20   and heroes that are slain

in holy righteous war;
hieratic, slim and fair,
the tracery written here,
proclaims what's left unsaid
25   in Egypt of her dead.

ROBINSON JEFFERS (1887–1962)

Birds and Fishes (pub. 1963)

Every October millions of little fish come along the shore,
Coasting this granite edge of the continent
On their lawful occasions: but what a festival for the sea-fowl.
What a witches' sabbath[1] of wings
5   Hides the dark water. The heavy pelicans shout. "Haw!" like Job's
              friend's warhorse[2]
And dive from the high air, the cormorants[3]
Slip their long black bodies under the water and hunt like wolves
Through the green half-light. Screaming, the gulls watch,
Wild with envy and malice, cursing and snatching. What hysterical
              greed!
10   What a filling of pouches! the mob
Hysteria is nearly human—these decent birds!—as if they were
              finding
Gold in the street. It is better than gold,
It can be eaten: and which one in all this fury of wild-fowl pities
              the fish?
No one certainly. Justice and mercy
15   Are human dreams, they do not concern the birds nor the fish
              nor eternal God.
However—look again before you go.
The wings and wild hungers, the wave-worn skerries, the bright
              quick minnows
Living in terror to die in torment—
Man's fate and theirs—and the island rocks and immense ocean
              beyond, and Lobos[4]
20   Darkening above the bay: they are beautiful?
That is their quality: not mercy, not mind, not goodness, but the
              beauty of God.

---

[1] **witches' sabbath:** Meeting of occult characters and devil worshippers at midnight.
[2] **Job's friend's warhorse:** In Job 39:25, God describes the strength of the horse: "He saith among the trumpets, Ha ha; and he smelleth the battle afar off, the thunder of the captains, and the shouting."
[3] **cormorants:** Long-necked seabirds.
[4] **Lobos:** Point Lobos, below Carmel, California.

ROBINSON JEFFERS (1887–1962)

Hurt Hawks (1928)

I

The broken pillar of the wing jags from the clotted shoulder,
The wing trails like a banner in defeat,
No more to use the sky forever but live with famine
And pain a few days: cat nor coyote
5   Will shorten the week of waiting for death, there is game without
        talons.
He stands under the oak-bush and waits
The lame feet of salvation; at night he remembers freedom
And flies in a dream, the dawns ruin it.
He is strong and pain is worse to the strong, incapacity is worse.
10   The curs° of the day come and torment him   mongrel dogs
At distance, no one but death the redeemer will humble that head,
The intrepid readiness, the terrible eyes.
The wild God of the world is sometimes merciful to those
That ask mercy, not often to the arrogant.
15   You do not know him, you communal people, or you have
        forgotten him;
Intemperate and savage, the hawk remembers him;
Beautiful and wild, the hawks, and men that are dying, remember
        him.

II

I'd sooner, except the penalties, kill a man than a hawk; but the
        great redtail
Had nothing left but unable misery
20   From the bones too shattered for mending, the wing that trailed
        under his talons when he moved.
We had fed him six weeks, I gave him freedom,
He wandered over the foreland hill and returned in the evening,
        asking for death,
Not like a beggar, still eyed with the old
Implacable arrogance. I gave him the lead gift in the twilight.
        What fell was relaxed.
25   Owl-downy, soft feminine feathers; but what
Soared: the fierce rush: the night-herons by the flooded river cried
        fear at its rising
Before it was quite unsheathed from reality.

MARIANNE MOORE (1887–1972)

The Pangolin[1] (1936)

Another armored animal—scale
  lapping scale with spruce-cone regularity until they
form the uninterrupted central
  tail-row! This near artichoke with head and legs and grit-equipped
5   gizzard,
the night miniature artist engineer is,
    yes, Leonardo da Vinci's replica—
     impressive animal and toiler of whom we seldom hear.
    Armor seems extra. But for him,
10   the closing ear-ridge—
     or bare ear lacking even this small
     eminence and similarly safe

contracting nose and eye apertures
  impenetrably closable, are not; a true ant-eater,
15 not cockroach-eater, who endures
  exhausting solitary trips through unfamiliar ground at night,
  returning before sunrise; stepping in the moonlight,
    on the moonlight peculiarly, that the outside
     edges of his hands may bear the weight and save the claws
20   for digging. Serpentined about
    the tree, he draws
     away from danger unpugnaciously,
     with no sound but a harmless hiss; keeping

the fragile grace of the Thomas-
25   of-Leighton Buzzard Westminster Abbey wrought-iron vine,[2] or
rolls himself into a ball that has
  power to defy all effort to unroll it; strongly intailed, neat
  head for core, on neck not breaking off, with curled-in feet.
    Nevertheless he has sting-proof scales; and nest
30   of rocks closed with earth from inside, which he can thus
     darken.
    Sun and moon and day and night and man and beast
    each with a splendor
     which man in all his vileness cannot
35   set aside; each with an excellence!

---

[1] **The Pangolin:** An ant-eater.
[2] **Thomas . . . vine:** "A fragment of ironwork in Westminster Abbey" [Moore's note].

"Fearful yet to be feared," the armored
    ant-eater met by the driver-ant does not turn back, but
engulfs what he can, the flattened sword-
    edged leafpoints on the tail and artichoke set leg- and body-plates
40   quivering violently when it retaliates
        and swarms on him. Compact like the furled fringed frill
          on the hat-brim of Gargallo's hollow iron[3] head of a
    matador, he will drop and will
        then walk away
45   unhurt, although if unintruded on,
          he cautiously works down the tree, helped

by his tail. The giant-pangolin-
    tail, graceful tool, as a prop or hand or broom or ax, tipped like
an elephant's trunk with special skin,
50   is not lost on this ant- and stone-swallowing uninjurable
    artichoke which simpletons thought a living fable
        whom the stones had nourished, whereas ants had done
          so. Pangolins are not aggressive animals; between
    dusk and day they have the not unchain-like machine-like
55   form and frictionless creep of a thing
        made graceful by adversities, con-

versities. To explain grace requires
    a curious hand. If that which is at all were not forever,
why would those who graced the spires
60   with animals and gathered there to rest, on cold luxurious
    low stone seats—a monk and monk and monk—between the thus
        ingenious roof supports, have slaved to confuse
          grace with a kindly manner, time in which to pay a debt,
    the cure for sins, a graceful use
65   of what are yet
          approved stone mullions branching out across
          the perpendiculars? A sailboat

was the first machine. Pangolins, made
    for moving quietly also, are models of exactness,
70   on four legs; on hind feet plantigrade,
    with certain postures of a man. Beneath sun and moon, man slaving
    to make his life more sweet, leaves half the flowers worth having,
        needing to choose wisely how to use his strength;
        a paper-maker like the wasp; a tractor of foodstuffs,

---

[3] **Gargallo's hollow iron:** Pablo Gargallo (1881–1934), Spanish sculptor whose preferred medium was iron.

75   like the ant; spidering a length
            of web from bluffs
                above a stream; in fighting, mechanicked
                like the pangolin; capsizing in

disheartenment. Bedizened or stark
80   naked, man, the self, the being we call human, writing-
master to this world, griffons a dark
        "Like does not like like that is obnoxious"; and writes error with four
            r's. Among animals, *one* has sense of humor.
                Humor saves a few steps, it saves years. Unignorant,
85   modest and unemotional, and all emotion,
            he has everlasting vigor,
                power to grow,
                    though there are few creatures who can make one
                    breathe faster and make one erecter.

90 Not afraid of anything is he,
                and then goes cowering forth, tread paced to meet an obstacle
        at every step. Consistent with the
            formula—warm blood, no gills, two pairs of hands and a few hairs—
                that
95   is a mammal; there he sits on his own habitat,
                serge-clad, strong-shod. The prey of fear, he, always
                    curtailed, extinguished, thwarted by the dusk, work partly
                        done,
                says to the alternating blaze,
100   "Again the sun!
                    anew each day; and new and new and new,
                    that comes into and steadies my soul."

EDWIN MUIR (1887–1959)

The Horses (1956)

Barely a twelvemonth after
The seven days war that put the world to sleep,
Late in the evening the strange horses came.
By then we had made our covenant with silence,
5   But in the first few days it was so still
We listened to our breathing and were afraid.
On the second day
The radios failed; we turned the knobs; no answer.

On the third day a warship passed us, heading north,
10 Dead bodies piled on the deck. On the sixth day
A plane plunged over us into the sea. Thereafter
Nothing. The radios dumb;
And still they stand in corners of our kitchens,
And stand, perhaps, turned on, in a million rooms
15 All over the world. But now if they should speak,
If on a sudden they should speak again,
If on the stroke of noon a voice should speak,
We would not listen, we would not let it bring
That old bad world that swallowed its children quick
20 At one great gulp. We would not have it again.
Sometimes we think of the nations lying asleep,
Curled blindly in impenetrable sorrow,
And then the thought confounds us with its strangeness.
The tractors lie about our fields; at evening
25 They look like dank sea-monsters couched and waiting.
We leave them where they are and let them rust:
'They'll moulder away and be like other loam'.
We make our oxen drag our rusty ploughs,
Long laid aside. We have gone back
30 Far past our fathers' land.
                              And then, that evening
Late in the summer the strange horses came.
We heard a distant tapping on the road,
A deepening drumming; it stopped, went on again
35 And at the corner changed to hollow thunder.
We saw the heads
Like a wild wave charging and were afraid.
We had sold our horses in our fathers' time
To buy new tractors. Now they were strange to us
40 As fabulous steeds set on an ancient shield
Or illustrations in a book of knights.
We did not dare go near them. Yet they waited,
Stubborn and shy, as if they had been sent
By an old command to find our whereabouts
45 And that long-lost archaic companionship.
In the first moment we had never a thought
That they were creatures to be owned and used.
Among them were some half-a-dozen colts
Dropped in some wilderness of the broken world,
50 Yet new as if they had come from their own Eden.
Since then they have pulled our ploughs and borne our loads,
But that free servitude still can pierce our hearts.
Our life is changed; their coming our beginning.

EDNA ST. VINCENT MILLAY (1892–1950)

The Buck in the Snow (1928)

White sky, over the hemlocks bowed with snow,
Saw you not at the beginning of evening the antlered buck and his doe
Standing in the apple-orchard? I saw them. I saw them suddenly go,
Tails up, with long leaps lovely and slow,
5   Over the stone-wall into the wood of hemlocks bowed with snow.

Now lies he here, his wild blood scalding the snow.

How strange a thing is death, bringing to his knees, bringing to his antlers
The buck in the snow.
How strange a thing,—a mile away by now, it may be,
10   Under the heavy hemlocks that as the moments pass
Shift their loads a little, letting fall a feather of snow—
Life, looking out attentive from the eyes of the doe.

RICHARD EBERHART (1904–   )

The Groundhog

In June, amid the golden fields,
I saw a groundhog lying dead.
Dead lay he; my senses shook,
And mind outshot our naked frailty.
5   There lowly in the vigorous summer
His form began its senseless change,
And made my senses waver dim
Seeing nature ferocious in him.
Inspecting close his maggots' might
10   And seething cauldron of his being,
Half with loathing, half with a strange love,
I poked him with an angry stick.
The fever arose, became a flame
And Vigour circumscribed the skies,
15   Immense energy in the sun,
And through my frame a sunless trembling.
My stick had done nor good nor harm.
Then stood I silent in the day
Watching the object, as before;
20   And kept my reverence for knowledge
Trying for control, to be still,

To quell the passion of the blood;
Until I had bent down on my knees
Praying for joy in the sight of decay.
25   And so I left; and I returned
In Autumn strict of eye, to see
The sap gone out of the groundhog,
But the bony sodden hulk remained.
But the year had lost its meaning,
30   And in intellectual chains
I lost both love and loathing,
Mured up in the wall of wisdom.
Another summer took the fields again
Massive and burning, full of life,
35   But when I chanced upon the spot
There was only a little hair left,
And bones bleaching in the sunlight
Beautiful as architecture;
I watched them like a geometer,
40   And cut a walking stick from a birch.
It has been three years, now.
There is no sign of the groundhog.
I stood there in the whirling summer,
My hand capped a withered heart,
45   And thought of China and of Greece,
Of Alexander in his tent;
Of Montaigne in his tower,
Of Saint Theresa in her wild lament.[1]

STANLEY KUNITZ (1905–   )

The Snakes of September (1985)

All summer I heard them
rustling in the shrubbery,
outracing me from tier
to tier in my garden,
5   a whisper among the viburnums,°   shrubs
a signal flashed from the hedgerow,
a shadow pulsing

---

[1] **Of Alexander . . . lament:** Eberhart refers to three types of human activity: Alexander the Great who conquered the world, Montaigne who wrote and thought critically about human affairs, and St. Theresa of Avila, a mystic who founded a religious order.

in the barberry thicket.
Now that the nights are chill
10   and the annuals spent,
I should have thought them gone,
in a torpor of blood
slipped to the nether world
before the sickle frost.
15   Not so. In the deceptive balm
of noon, as if defiant of the curse
that spoiled another garden,
these two appear on show
through a narrow slit
20   in the dense green brocade
of a north-country spruce,
dangling head-down, entwined
in a brazen love-knot.
I put out my hand and stroke
25   the fine, dry grit of their skins.
After all,
we are partners in this land,
co-signers of a covenant.
At my touch the wild
30   braid of creation
trembles.

ROBERT PENN WARREN (1905–1989)

Evening Hawk (1975)

From plane of light to plane, wings dipping through
Geometries and orchids that the sunset builds,
Out of the peak's black angularity of shadow, riding
The last tumultuous avalanche of
5   Light above pines and the guttural gorge,
The hawk comes.

           His wing
Scythes down another day, his motion
Is that of the honed steel-edge, we hear
10   The crashless fall of stalks of Time.

The head of each stalk is heavy with the gold of our error.

Look! Look! he is climbing the last light
Who knows neither Time nor error, and under
Whose eye, unforgiving, the world, unforgiven, swings
15 Into shadow.

        Long now,
The last thrush is still, the last bat
Now cruises in his sharp hieroglyphics. His wisdom
Is ancient, too, and immense. The star
20 Is steady, like Plato,[1] over the mountain.

If there were no wind we might, we think, hear
The earth grind on its axis, or history
Drip in darkness like a leaking pipe in the cellar.

NORMAN MacCAIG (1910–1996)

Frogs (1966)

FROGS sit more solid
than anything sits. In mid-leap they are
parachutists falling
in a free fall. They die on roads
5 with arms across their chests and
heads high.

I love frogs that sit
like Buddha, that fall without
parachutes, that die
10 like Italian tenors.

Above all, I love them because,
pursued in water, they never
panic so much that they fail
to make stylish triangles
15 with their ballet dancer's
legs.

---

[1] **Plato:** Plato (427 B.C.–347 B.C.) was an ancient Greek philosopher who held that physical objects
were impermanent depictions of static ideas.

ROBERT HAYDEN (1913–1982)

A Plague of Starlings (1970)

(Fisk Campus)[1]

Evenings I hear
the workmen fire
into the stiff
magnolia leaves,
5   routing the starlings
gathered noisy and
befouling there.

Their scissoring
terror like glass
10   coins spilling breaking
the birds explode
into mica sky
raggedly fall
to ground rigid
15   in clench of cold.

The spared return,
when the guns are through,
to the spoiled trees
like choiceless poor
20   to a dangerous
dwelling place,
chitter and quarrel
in the piercing dark
about the killed.

25   Morning, I pick
my way past death's
black droppings:
on campus lawns
and streets
30   the troublesome
starlings
frost-salted lie,
troublesome still.

---

[1] **Fisk Campus:** Fisk University in Nashville, Tennessee, where the author was a faculty member from 1946 to 1968.

And if not careful
35   I shall tread
upon carcasses
carcasses when I
go mornings now
to lecture on
40   what Socrates,
the hemlock hour nigh,
told sorrowing
Phaedo and the rest
about the migratory
45   habits of the soul.[2]

CHARLES BUKOWSKI (1920–1994)

the mockingbird (1972)

the mockingbird had been following the cat
all summer
mocking mocking mocking
teasing and cocksure;
5   the cat crawled under rockers on porches
tail flashing
and said something angry to the mockingbird
which I didn't understand.

yesterday the cat walked calmly up the driveway
10   with the mockingbird alive in its mouth,
wings fanned, beautiful wings fanned and flopping,
feathers parted like a woman's legs,
and the bird was no longer mocking,
it was asking, it was praying
15   but the cat
striding down through centuries
would not listen.
I saw it crawl under a yellow car
with the bird
20   to bargain it to another place.

summer was over.

---

[2] **Socrates . . . soul:** Socrates (470 B.C.–399 B.C.), an Athenian philosopher and teacher executed with hemlock poison after he refused to denounce his teachings. According to his student Plato's dialog, Socrates speaks to Phaedo and others moments before his death.

GEORGE MACKAY BROWN (1921–1996)

The Hawk (1970)

On Sunday the hawk fell on Bigging
    And a chicken screamed
    Lost in its own little snowstorm.
And on Monday he fell on the moor
5   And the Field Club
    Raised a hundred silent prisms.°   binocular lenses
And on Tuesday he fell on the hill
    And the happy lamb
    Never knew why the loud collie straddled him.
10   And on Wednesday he fell on a bush
    And the blackbird
    Laid by his little flute for the last time.
And on Thursday he fell on Cleat
    And peerie Tom's rabbit
15   Swung in a single arc from shore to hill.
And on Friday he fell on a ditch
    But the rampant rat,
    That eye and that tooth, quenched his flame.
And on Saturday he fell on Bigging
20   And Jock lowered his gun
    And nailed a small wing over the corn.

JAMES DICKEY (1923–1997)

The Heaven of Animals (1961)

Here they are. The soft eyes open.
If they have lived in a wood
It is a wood.
If they have lived on plains
5   It is grass rolling
Under their feet forever.

Having no souls, they have come,
Anyway, beyond their knowing.
Their instincts wholly bloom
10   And they rise.
The soft eyes open.

To match them, the landscape flowers,
Outdoing, desperately

Outdoing what is required:
15   The richest wood,
The deepest field.

For some of these,
It could not be the place
It is, without blood.
20   These hunt, as they have done,
But with claws and teeth grown perfect,

More deadly than they can believe.
They stalk more silently,
And crouch on the limbs of trees,
25   And their descent
Upon the bright backs of their prey

May take years
In a sovereign floating of joy.
And those that are hunted
30   Know this as their life,
Their reward: to walk

Under such trees in full knowledge
Of what is in glory above them,
And to feel no fear,
35   But acceptance, compliance.
Fulfilling themselves without pain

At the cycle's center,
They tremble, they walk
Under the tree,
40   They fall, they are torn,
They rise, they walk again.

CAROLYN KIZER (1925–   )

The Great Blue Heron (1958)

M.A.K., September, 1880–September, 1955

As I wandered on the beach
I saw the heron standing
Sunk in the tattered wings
He wore as a hunchback's coat.

5 Shadow without a shadow,
Hung on invisible wires
From the top of a canvas day,
What scissors cut him out?
Superimposed on a poster
10 Of summer by the strand
Of a long-decayed resort,
Poised in the dusty light
Some fifteen summers ago;
I wondered, an empty child,
15 "Heron, whose ghost are you?"

I stood on the beach alone,
In the sudden chill of the burned.
My thought raced up the path.
Pursuing it, I ran
20 To my mother in the house
And led her to the scene.
The spectral bird was gone.
But her quick eye saw him drifting
Over the highest pines
25 On vast, unmoving wings.
Could they be those ashen things,
So grounded, unwieldy, ragged,
A pair of broken arms
That were not made for flight?
30 In the middle of my loss
I realized she knew:
My mother knew what he was.

O great blue heron, now
That the summer house has burned
35 So many rockets ago,
So many smokes and fires
And beach-lights and water-glow
Reflecting pin-wheel and flare:
The old logs hauled away,
40 The pines and driftwood cleared
From that bare strip of shore
Where dozens of children play;
Now there is only you
Heavy upon my eye.
45 Why have you followed me here,
Heavy and far away?
You have stood there patiently
For fifteen summers and snows,

Denser than my repose,
50 Bleaker than any dream,
Waiting upon the day
When, like gray smoke, a vapor
Floating into the sky,
A handful of paper ashes,
55 My mother would drift away.

ALASTAIR REID (1926–)

Curiosity (1988)

may have killed the cat. More likely,
the cat was just unlucky, or else curious
to see what death was like, having no cause
to go on licking paws, or fathering
5 litter on litter of kittens, predictably.

Nevertheless, to be curious
is dangerous enough. To distrust
what is always said, what seems,
to ask odd questions, interfere in dreams,
10 smell rats, leave home, have hunches,
does not endear cats to those doggy circles
where well-smelt baskets, suitable wives, good lunches
are the order of things, and where prevails
much wagging of incurious heads and tails.

15 Face it. Curiosity
will not cause us to die—
only lack of it will.
Never to want to see
the other side of the hill
20 or that improbable country
where living is an idyll
(although a probable hell)
would kill us all.
Only the curious
25 have if they live a tale
worth telling at all.

Dogs say cats love too much, are irresponsible,
are dangerous, marry too many wives,
desert their children, chill all dinner tables
30 with tales of their nine lives.

Well, they are lucky. Let them be
nine-lived and contradictory,
curious enough to change, prepared to pay
the cat-price, which is to die
35 and die again and again,
each time with no less pain.
A cat-minority of one
is all that can be counted on
to tell the truth; and what cats have to tell
40 on each return from hell
is this: that dying is what the living do,
that dying is what the loving do,
and that dead dogs are those who never know
that dying is what, to live, each has to do.

GALWAY KINNELL (1927–   )

The Bear (1968)

1

In late winter
I sometimes glimpse bits of steam
coming up from
some fault in the old snow
5 and bend close and see it is lung-colored
and put down my nose
and know
the chilly, enduring odor of bear.

2

I take a wolf's rib and whittle
10 it sharp at both ends
and coil it up
and freeze it in blubber and place it out
on the fairway of the bears.

And when it has vanished
15 I move out on the bear tracks,
roaming in circles
until I come to the first, tentative, dark
splash on the earth.

And I set out
20 running, following the splashes

of blood wandering over the world.
At the cut, gashed resting places
I stop and rest,
at the crawl-marks
25   where he lay out on his belly
to overpass some stretch of bauchy ice
I lie out
dragging myself forward with bear-knives in my fists.

3

On the third day I begin to starve,
30   at nightfall I bend down as I knew I would
at a turd sopped in blood,
and hesitate, and pick it up,
and thrust it in my mouth, and gnash it down,
and rise
35   and go on running.

4

On the seventh day,
living by now on bear blood alone,
I can see his upturned carcass far out ahead, a scraggled,
steamy hulk,
40   the heavy fur riffling in the wind.

I come up to him
and stare at the narrow-spaced, petty eyes,
the dismayed
face laid back on the shoulder, the nostrils
45   flared, catching
perhaps the first taint of me as he
died.

I hack
a ravine in his thigh, and eat and drink,
50   and tear him down his whole length
and open him and climb in
and close him up after me, against the wind,
and sleep.

5

And dream
55   of lumbering flatfooted
over the tundra,
stabbed twice from within,

splattering a trail behind me,
splattering it out no matter which way I lurch,
60   no matter which parabola of bear transcendence,
which dance of solitude I attempt,
which gravity-clutched leap,
which trudge, which groan.

6

Until one day I totter and fall—
65   fall on this
stomach that has tried so hard to keep up,
to digest the blood as it leaked in,
to break up
and digest the bone itself: and now the breeze
70   blows over me, blows off
the hideous belches of ill-digested bear blood
and rotted stomach
and the ordinary, wretched odor of bear,

blows across
75   my sore, lolled tongue a song
or screech, until I think I must rise up
and dance. And I lie still.

7

I awaken I think. Marshlights
reappear, geese
80   come trailing again up the flyway.
In her ravine under old snow the dam-bear
lies, licking
lumps of smeared fur
and drizzly eyes into shapes
85   with her tongue. And one
hairy-soled trudge stuck out before me,
the next groaned out,
the next,
the next,
90   the rest of my days I spend
wandering: wondering
what, anyway,
was that sticky infusion, that rank flavor of blood, that poetry, by
            which I lived?

W. S. MERWIN (1927–   )

The Animals (1967)

All these years behind windows
With blind crosses sweeping the tables

And myself tracking over empty ground
Animals I never saw

5 I with no voice

Remembering names to invent for them
Will any come back will one

Saying yes

Saying look carefully yes
10 We will meet again

PHILIP LEVINE (1928–   )

Animals Are Passing from Our Lives (1968)

It's wonderful how I jog
on four honed-down ivory toes
my massive buttocks slipping
like oiled parts with each light step.

5 I'm to market. I can smell
the sour, grooved block, I can smell
the blade that opens the hole
and the pudgy white fingers

that shake out the intestines
10 like a hankie. In my dreams
the snouts drool on the marble,
suffering children, suffering flies,

suffering the consumers
who won't meet their steady eyes

15 for fear they could see. The boy
    who drives me along believes

    that any moment I'll fall
    on my side and drum my toes
    like a typewriter or squeal
20 and shit like a new housewife

    discovering television,
    or that I'll turn like a beast
    cleverly to hook his teeth
    with my teeth. No. Not this pig.

ROBERT PACK (1929–   )

Elk in Winter (2004)

    Laden with snow
        the moonlit high pines
    Loom above their shadows
        in the undulating drifts,
5   And in the watcher's mind
        a strange serenity
    Pervades the silence
        of the windless scene,
    As if permanent winter seals the woods
10   from further change
    And sets the mood the watcher now
        considers his reward
    For seeing rounded moonlit forms
        with luminescent curves
15 And sweeping shades of blue.
        As silence deepens
    Into deeper thought, the watcher,
        unresistant to the spell
    His watching adds to the still woods,
20   hears footfalls softly
    Crunching in the shadowed snow,
        step upon sure unhurried step,
    As marching elk, perhaps a hundred
        in a staggered line,
25 Their nostrils smoking over glowing eyes,
        push through on an ancestral path

To where elk go in wintertime
    beyond the watcher's gaze.
The watcher sees the elk as a tableaux,[1]
30   held in abeyance in his mind,
Because he senses some vague correspondence
    in their unrushed passing
Through the shadows of the pines
    and his hushed witness to the scene,
35   As if he could be anyone who came upon
    tall elk in moonlight,
Moving beneath loose shades of evergreens.
    And yet the watcher must
Acknowledge that awareness
40   of a half-formed wish
to dwell forever in his watcher's mood
    distracts him into reverie
And thus disturbs his merging
    with the moonlit atmosphere
45   So that the silver scene can have
    no correspondence to himself
Other than that strong stomping elk
    have somewhere else to go
And feel no haste in getting there.
50   He ponders that the wish
To lose himself in thinking of the passing elk
    defeats its goal
By mirroring his roused and wishful self
    and thus revives the gloom
55   Of contemplating his own murmured life
    or what is left of it.
His life, his self-reflecting life,
    with children gone into another mist,
And parents having crossed
60   the last shore of the roaring brink,
Is it too precious to be dwelt upon
    with all his ghosts now
Numbered in the name of loss?
    The shudder of that thought
65   Flows backwards and recedes, and now
    the last of the cascading elk,
In what had seemed an endless line,
    passes from view;
The watcher sees himself

---

[1] **tableaux:** French, "painting."

70   beneath a steadfast tree,
His face in moonlight almost featureless,
        despite its worn-out care,
And does not know how long in silence
        he's been standing there.

A. K. RAMANUJAN (1929–1993)

Snakes (1966)

No, it does not happen
when I walk through the woods.
But, walking in museums of quartz
or the aisles of bookstacks,
5   looking at their geometry
without curves
and the layers of transparency
that make them opaque,
dwelling on the yellower vein
10   in the yellow amber
or touching a book that has gold
on its spine,
                I think of snakes.

The twirls of their hisses
15   rise like the tiny dust-cones on slow-noon roads
winding through the farmers' feet.
Black lorgnettes[1] are etched on their hoods,
ridiculous, alien, like some terrible aunt,
a crest among tiles and scales
20   that moult with the darkening half
of every moon.

A basketful of ritual cobras
comes into the tame little house,
their brown-wheat glisten ringed with ripples.
25   They lick the room with their bodies, curves
uncurling, writing a sibilant alphabet of panic
on my floor. Mother gives them milk
in saucers. She watches them suck

---

[1] **lorgnettes:** Spectacles held to the eyes with a long handle.

and bare the black-line design
30 etched on the brass of the saucer.
The snakeman wreathes their writhing
round his neck
for father's smiling
money. But I scream.

35 Sister ties her braids
with a knot of tassel.
But the weave of her knee-long braid has scales,
their gleaming held by a score of clean new pins.
I look till I see her hair again.
40 My night full of ghosts from a sadness
in a play, my left foot listens to my right footfall,
a clockwork clicking in the silence
within my walking.
                         The clickshod heel suddenly strikes
45 and slushes on a snake: I see him turn,
the green white of his belly
measured by bluish nodes, a water-bleached lotus stalk
plucked by a landsman hand. Yet panic rushes
my body to my feet, my spasms wring
50 and drain his fear and mine. I leave him sealed,
a flat-head whiteness on a stain.
                                          Now
frogs can hop upon this sausage rope,
flies in the sun will mob the look in his eyes,

55 and I can walk through the woods.

GREGORY CORSO (1930–2001)

The Mad Yak (1958)

I am watching them churn the last milk
      they'll ever get from me.
They are waiting for me to die;
They want to make buttons out of my bones.
5 Where are my sisters and brothers?
That tall monk there, loading my uncle,
      he has a new cap.
And that idiot student of his—
      I never saw that muffler before.

10   Poor uncle, he lets them load him.
     How sad he is, how tired!
     I wonder what they'll do with his bones?
     And that beautiful tail!
     How many shoelaces will they make of that!

TED HUGHES   (1930–1998)

Hawk Roosting   (1960)

I sit in the top of the wood, my eyes closed.
Inaction, no falsifying dream
Between my hooked head and hooked feet:
Or in sleep rehearse perfect kills and eat.

5   The convenience of the high trees!
    The air's buoyancy and the sun's ray
    Are of advantage to me;
    And the earth's face upward for my inspection.

    My feet are locked upon the rough bark.
10 It took the whole of Creation
    To produce my foot, my each feather:
    Now I hold Creation in my foot

    Or fly up, and revolve it all slowly—
    I kill where I please because it is all mine.
15 There is no sophistry in my body:
    My manners are tearing off heads—

    The allotment of death.
    For the one path of my flight is direct
    Through the bones of the living.
20 No arguments assert my right:

    The sun is behind me.
    Nothing has changed since I began.
    My eye has permitted no change.
    I am going to keep things like this.

TED HUGHES   (1930–1998)

The Horses   (1957)

I climbed through woods in the hour-before-dawn dark.
Evil air, a frost-making stillness,

Not a leaf, not a bird—
A world cast in frost. I came out above the wood

5   Where my breath left tortuous statues in the iron light.
But the valleys were draining the darkness

Till the moorline—blackening dregs of the brightening grey—
Halved the sky ahead. And I saw the horses:

Huge in the dense grey—ten together—
10   Megalith-still.[1] They breathed, making no move,

With draped manes and tilted hind-hooves,
Making no sound.

I passed: not one snorted or jerked its head.
Grey silent fragments

15   Of a grey silent world.

I listened in emptiness on the moor-ridge.
The curlew's[2] tear turned its edge on the silence.

Slowly detail leafed from the darkness. Then the sun
Orange, red, red, erupted

20   Silently, and splitting to its core tore and flung cloud,
Shook the gulf open, showed blue,

And the big planets hanging.
I turned,

Stumbling in the fever of a dream, down towards
25   The dark woods, from the kindling tops,

---

[1] **Megalith-still:** A megalith is a memorial (such as Stonehenge) where large stones form part of a prehistoric structure.
[2] **curlew's:** A curlew is a large, migratory bird.

And came to the horses.
There, still they stood,
But now steaming and glistening under the flow of light,

Their draped stone manes, their tilted hind-hooves
30   Stirring under a thaw while all around them

The frost showed its fires. But still they made no sound.
Not one snorted or stamped,

Their hung heads patient as the horizons,
High over valleys, in the red levelling rays—

35   In din of the crowded streets, going among the years, the faces,
May I still meet my memory in so lonely a place

Between the streams and the red clouds, hearing curlews,
Hearing the horizons endure.

TED HUGHES   (1930–1998)

Pike   (1960)

Pike, three inches long, perfect
Pike in all parts, green tigering the gold.
Killers from the egg: the malevolent aged grin.
They dance on the surface among the flies.

5   Or move, stunned by their own grandeur
Over a bed of emerald, silhouette
Of submarine delicacy and horror.
A hundred feet long in their world.

In ponds, under the heat-struck lily pads—
10   Gloom of their stillness:
Logged on last year's black leaves, watching upwards.
Or hung in an amber cavern of weeds

The jaws' hooked clamp and fangs
Not to be changed at this date;
15   A life subdued to its instrument;
The gills kneading quietly, and the pectorals.

Three we kept behind glass,
Jungled in weed: three inches, four,
And four and a half: fed fry to them—
20   Suddenly there were two. Finally one.

With a sag belly and the grin it was born with.
And indeed they spare nobody.
Two, six pounds each, over two feet long,
High and dry and dead in the willow-herb—

25   One jammed past its gills down the other's gullet:
The outside eye stared: as a vice locks—
The same iron in this eye
Though its film shrank in death.

A pond I fished, fifty yards across,
30   Whose lilies and muscular tench[1]
Had outlasted every visible stone
Of the monastery that planted them—

Stilled legendary depth:
It was as deep as England. It held
35   Pike too immense to stir, so immense and old
That past nightfall I dared not cast

But silently cast and fished
With the hair frozen on my head
For what might move, for what eye might move.
40   The still splashes on the dark pond,

Owls hushing the floating woods
Frail on my ear against the dream
Darkness beneath night's darkness had freed,
That rose slowly towards me, watching.

---

[1] **tench:** Thick, freshwater fish.

GARY SNYDER (1930–   )

Lines on a Carp (1986)

old fat fish of everlasting life
in rank brown pools discarded by the river
soft round-mouth nudging mud
among the reeds, beside the railroad track

5   you will not hear the human cries
but pines will grow between those ties
before you turn your belly to the sun

JAY MACPHERSON (1931–   )

The Swan (1957)

White-habited, the mystic Swan
Walks her rank° cloister as the night draws down,   overgrown
In sweet communion with her sister shade,
Matchless and unassayed.

5   The tower of ivory sways,
Gaze bends to mirrored gaze:
This perfect arc embraces all her days.
And when she comes to die,
The treasures of her silence patent lie:
10 'I am all that is and was and shall be,
My garment may no man put by.'

WENDELL BERRY (1934–   )

Sparrow (1964)

A sparrow is
his hunger organized.
Filled, he flies
before he knows he's going to.
5   And he dies by the
same movement: filled
with himself, he goes

by the eye-quick
reflex of his flesh
10   out of sight,
leaving his perfect
absence without a thought.

MARY OLIVER (1935–   )

The Hermit Crab (1990)

Once I looked inside
    the darkness
        of a shell folded like a pastry,
            and there was a fancy face—

5   or almost a face—
        it turned away
            and frisked up its brawny forearms
                so quickly

against the light
10   and my looking in
            I scarcely had time to see it,
                gleaming

under the pure white roof
    of old calcium.
15   When I set it down, it hurried
                along the tideline

of the sea,
    which was slashing along as usual,
        shouting and hissing
20   toward the future,

turning its back
    with every tide on the past,
        leaving the shore littered
            every morning

25   with more ornaments of death—
        what a pearly rubble
            from which to choose a house
                like a white flower—

and what a rebellion
30   to leap into it
       and hold on,
         connecting everything,

the past to the future—
    which is of course the miracle—
35   which is the only argument there is
       against the sea.

C. K. WILLIAMS (1936–   )

Doves (2003)

So much crap in my head,
so many rubbishy facts,
so many half-baked
theories and opinions,
5   so many public figures
I care nothing about
but who stick like pitch;
so much political swill.

So much crap, yet
10   so much I don't know
and would dearly like to:
I recognize nearly none
of the birdsongs of dawn—
all I'm sure of is
15   the maddeningly vapid *who,*
who-who of the doves.

And I don't have half
the names of the flowers
and trees, and still less
20   of humankind's myths,
the benevolent ones,
from the days before ours;
water-plashed wastes,
radiant intercessions.

25   So few poems entire,
such a meager handful
of precise recollections of paintings:

detritus instead, junk,
numbers I should long ago
30   have erased, inane
"information," I'll doubtlessly
take with me to the grave.

So much crap, and yet,
now, morning, that first
35   sapphire dome of glow,
the glow! The first sounds
of being awake, *the sounds!*—
a wind whispering, but even
trucks clanking past,
40   even the idiot doves.

And within me, along
with the garbage, faces, faces
and voices, so many
lives woven into mine,
45   such improbable quantities
of memory; so much already
forgotten, lost, pruned away—
the doves though, the doves!

JOSEPH BRODSKY (1940–1996)
trans. by the author and Alan Myers

The Hawk's Cry in Autumn   (1975)

Wind from the northwestern quarter is lifting him high above
the dove-gray, crimson, umber, brown
Connecticut Valley. Far beneath,
chickens daintily pause and move
5   unseen in the yard of the tumbledown
farmstead, chipmunks blend with the heath.

Now adrift on the airflow, unfurled, alone,
all that he glimpses—the hills' lofty, ragged
ridges, the silver stream that threads
10   quivering like a living bone
of steel, badly notched with rapids,
the townships like strings of beads

strewn across New England. Having slid down to nil
thermometers—those household gods in niches—

15 freeze, inhibiting thus the fire
of leaves and churches' spires. Still,
no churches for him. In the windy reaches,
undreamt of by the most righteous choir,

he soars in a cobalt-blue ocean, his beak clamped shut,
20 his talons clutched tight into his belly
—claws balled up like a sunken fist—
sensing in each wisp of down the thrust
from below, glinting back the berry
of his eyeball, heading south-southeast

25 to the Rio Grande, the Delta, the beech groves and farther still:
to a nest hidden in the mighty groundswell
of grass whose edges no fingers trust,
sunk amid forest's odors, filled
with splinters of red-speckled eggshell,
30 with a brother or a sister's ghost.

The heart overgrown with flesh, down, feather, wing,
pulsing at feverish rate, nonstopping,
propelled by internal heat and sense,
the bird goes slashing and scissoring
35 the autumnal blue, yet by the same swift token,
enlarging it at the expense

of its brownish speck, barely registering on the eye,
a dot, sliding far above the lofty
pine tree; at the expense of the empty look
40 of that child, arching up at the sky,
that couple that left the car and lifted
their heads, that woman on the stoop.

But the uprush of air is still lifting him
higher and higher. His belly feathers
45 feel the nibbling cold. Casting a downward gaze,
he sees the horizon growing dim,
he sees, as it were, the features
of the first thirteen colonies whose

chimneys all puff out smoke. Yet it's their total within his sight
50 that tells the bird of his elevation,
of what altitude he's reached this trip.
What am I doing at such a height?
He senses a mixture of trepidation
and pride. Heeling over a tip

55   of wing, he plummets down. But the resilient air
bounces him back, winging up to glory,
to the colorless icy plane.
His yellow pupil darts a sudden glare
of rage, that is, a mix of fury
60   and terror. So once again
he turns and plunges down. But as walls return
rubber balls, as sins send a sinner to faith, or near,
he's driven upward this time as well!
He! whose innards are still so warm!
65   Still higher! Into some blasted ionosphere![1]
That astronomically objective hell

of birds that lacks oxygen, and where the milling stars
play millet served from a plate or a crescent.
What, for the bipeds, has always meant
70   height, for the feathered is the reverse.
Not with his puny brain but with shriveled air sacs
he guesses the truth of it: it's the end.

And at this point he screams. From the hooklike beak
there tears free of him and flies *ad luminem*[2]
75   the sound Erinyes[3] make to rend
souls: a mechanical, intolerable shriek,
the shriek of steel that devours aluminum;
"mechanical," for it's meant

for nobody, for no living ears:
80   not man's, not yelping foxes',
not squirrels' hurrying to the ground
from branches; not for tiny field mice whose tears
can't be avenged this way, which forces
them into their burrows. And only hounds

85   lift up their muzzles. A piercing, high-pitched squeal,
more nightmarish than the D-sharp grinding
of the diamond cutting glass,
slashes the whole sky across. And the world seems to reel
for an instant, shuddering from this rending.
90   For the warmth burns space in the highest as

---

[1] **ionosphere:** The outer region of the Earth's atmosphere.
[2] *ad luminem:* Latin, "toward the light."
[3] **Erinyes:** In classical mythology, snake-haired monsters who pursued unpunished criminals.

badly as some iron fence down here
brands incautious gloveless fingers.
We, standing where we are, exclaim
"There!" and see far above the tear
95 that is a hawk, and hear the sound that lingers
in wavelets, a spider skein

swelling notes in ripples across the blue vault of space
whose lack of echo spells, especially in October,
an apotheosis of pure sound.
100 And caught in this heavenly patterned lace,
starlike, spangled with hoarfrost powder,
silver-clad, crystal-bound,

the bird sails to the zenith, to the dark-blue high
of azure. Through binoculars we foretoken
105 him, a glittering dot, a pearl.
We hear something ring out in the sky,
like some family crockery being broken,
slowly falling aswirl,

yet its shards, as they reach our palms, don't hurt
110 but melt when handled. And in a twinkling
once more one makes out curls, eyelets, strings,
rainbowlike, multicolored, blurred
commas, ellipses, spirals, linking
heads of barley, concentric rings—

115 the bright doodling pattern the feather once possessed,
a map, now a mere heap of flying
pale flakes that make a green slope appear
white. And the children, laughing and brightly dressed,
swarm out of doors to catch them, crying
120 with a loud shout in English, "Winter's here!"

JAMES WELCH (1940–2003)

Day after Chasing Porcupines (1976)

Rain came. Fog out of the slough° and horses   swamp
asleep in the barn. In the fields, sparrow hawks
glittered through the morning clouds.

No dreamers knew the rain. Wind ruffled quills
5 in the mongrel's nose. He sighed cautiously,
kicked further beneath the weathered shed and slept.

Timid chickens watched chickens in the puddles.
Watching the chickens, yellow eyes harsh
below the wind-drifting clouds, sparrow hawks.

10   Horses stamped in the barn. The mongrel whimpered
in his dream, wind ruffled his mongrel tail,
the lazy cattails and the rain.

BILLY COLLINS (1941–   )

Dog (1991)

I can hear him out in the kitchen,
his lapping the night's only music,
head bowed over the waterbowl
like an illustration in a book for boys.

5   He enters the room with such etiquette,
licking my bare ankle as if he understood
the Braille of the skin.

Then he makes three circles around himself,
flattening his ancient memory of tall grass
10   before dropping his weight with a sigh on the floor.

This is the spot where he will spend the night,
his ears listening for the syllable of his name,
his tongue hidden in his long mouth
like a strange naked hermit in a cave.

EAMON GRENNAN (1941–   )

Lizards in Sardinia[1] (1978)

I miss our lizards. The one who watched us
lunch on the rocks, half of him
sandstone brown, the other half neat rings
of neon avocado. He moved his head

---

[1] **Sardinia:** In the Mediterranean Sea, an island west of Italy.

5   in wary jerks, like a small bird. Unblinking,
his stillness turned him stone. When he
shifted, whiptail, his whole length flowed
like water. Those reptile eyes of his
took in a world we couldn't see, as he paused
10 in the dragon-roar of sunlight
till his blood boiled again, then lit out for shadows
and an age of fragrance. The other one—
who'd lost his tail and stumped about, still
quick as a lizard—vanishing behind the trunk
15 of the eucalyptus. Two who scuttled circles,
tail of one clamped fast in the other's mouth:
courtship, you hoped, as they dervished
among the piebald, finger-slim, fallen leaves
and rustled into infinity—a flash,
20 an absence—minute leftovers with molten brains,
escapees when their sky-high brothers bowed
cloud-scraping heads and bit the dust, leaving
the wrecked armadas of their ribs
for us to wonder at. Or that plump one
25 I watched for a long time squatting beside me
at the edge of the steel and turquoise bay
you rose from dripping light and smiling
in my direction: unblemished emerald
down half his length, the rest opaque and
30 dull, we thought, till we saw the envelope
of old skin he was shedding, under which
jewel-bright he blazed our breath away—the image
of the one I dreamt when my father died, big
as an iguana and the colour of greaseproof paper
35 till I saw him gleam and be a newborn beast
of jade and flame, who stood there mildly casting
his old self off, and shining. Those afternoons
after we'd made love, I lay quite still
along your back, blood simmering, and saw
40 your splayed palms flatten on the white sheet
like a lizard's, while we listened—barely
breathing—to the wind whiffle the eucalyptus
leaves against the window, our new world
steadying around us, its weather settled.

WILLIAM MATTHEWS (1942–1997)

Photo of the Author with a Favorite Pig (1987)

Behind its snout like a huge button,
like an almost clean plate, the pig
looks candid compared to the author,

and why not? He has a way with words,
5   but the unspeakable pig, squat
and foursquare as a bathtub,

squints frankly. Nobody knows
the trouble it's seen, this rained-out
pork roast, this ham escaped into

10 its corpulent jokes, its body of work.
The author is skinny and looks serious:
what will he say next? The copious pig

has every appearance of knowing,
from his pert, coiled tail to the wispy tips
15 of his edible ears, but the pig isn't telling.

DAVE SMITH (1942–   )

Bats (1983)

Still in sleeping bags, the promised delivery
only words as usual, our lives upside down,
we are transients lost in thirteen rooms
built by a judge who died. The landlord says
5   they mean no harm, the bats, and still I wake
at the shrill whistling, the flutter overhead.

I fumble to a tall window open among maples.
A car crawling a hill splashes my face with light
spread fine by mist that had been summer rain,
10 a sweetness that drips from black-palmed leaves.
The breeze I feel is damp, edged with mown hay,

enough to make me think the thumps and titters
I hear might be the loving pleasure of parents
unguessed, a long quarrel ended, a thrilling

15 touch that trails to muffled play. Slight shadows,
these are bats, residents of the house elders
built to last, the vaulted attic tall as a man

holding them hung in rows daylong like words
unuttered above the yard where children romp.
20 Flashlight in hand, I pass through the parlor
papered in silk for marriages the judges made,
and stand beneath the hidden door. The truth is

nothing can drive them out or contravene those
fretful, homespinning voices we cannot help
25 fearing as if they were the all-knowing dead.
Yet if I had one chair to stand tall enough on
I would climb with my light and shaking voice
to see whatever has lodged in their wizened eyes.

Under a room I have never seen but know, I stand
30 like one of the unblessed at the edge of dawn.
Smelling mold, I hear a dog's hopeless howl
and think of the stillness in the deep heads
of creatures who hang in sleep that is like love

in the children we cannot keep forever, absolute.
35 Each one near me unfurls a homekeeping song no
darkness or deed can kill. With them all green
from the field clings beyond each flood of light.
As if I had never been out of this room, I listen.
The sound is like rain, leaves, or sheets settling.

LOUISE GLÜCK (1943–   )

Cottonmouth[1] Country (1968)

Fish bones walked the waves off Hatteras.[2]
And there were other signs
That Death wooed us, by water, wooed us
By land: among the pines
5 An uncurled cottonmouth that rolled on moss
Reared in the polluted air.

---

[1] **Cottonmouth:** A venomous, semiaquatic snake found in the southern United States.
[2] **Hatteras:** Cape Hatteras, a cape on North Carolina's Atlantic coast.

Birth, not death, is the hard loss.
I know. I also left a skin there.

HEATHER McHUGH (1948–   )

Animal Song (1987)

We're flattered they come so close,
amused they seem like us,
amazed they don't.
The animal we named
5 the sex fiend for
has no known family but ours.
The angels are distinguished by
what random birds in any small backyard
are largely made of. If we do not move

10 perhaps they may approach us,
in the spirit of
unearthing something.
Everywhere inside the ground
are avenues and townships
15 of another world, enormously minute.
And when we take upon ourselves
the calm and the largesse°   gift
of a blue sky no one knows
where starts or stops

20 then for a moment
we don't terrify the animals. It's rare
but it happens. So maybe someday, when the something
greater than our lives has come, we'll stop
our businesses of digging
25 little definitions for a hole. Perhaps we can recall
the language in which we were intimate—before the tower
and before the fall—before we called
the creature names. We'd have to
talk with it, remembering

30 how animal is soul, and not its opposite.

MICHAEL BLUMENTHAL (1949–   )

Squid (1984)

So this is love:

How you grimace at the sight
of these fish; how I pull
(forefinger, then thumb)
5   the fins and tails from the heads,
slice the tentacles from the accusing eyes.

And then how I pile the silvery ink sacs
into the sieve like old fillings, heap
the entrails and eyes on a towel in the corner;
10   and how you sauté the onions and garlic,
how they turn soft and transparent, lovely
in their own way, and how you turn to me
and say, simply, *isn't this fun, isn't it?*

And something tells me this all has to do
15   with love, perhaps even more than lust
or happiness have to do with love:
How the fins slip easily from the tails,
how I peel the membranes from the fins
and cones like a man peeling his body
20   from a woman after love, how these
ugly squid diminish in grotesqueness
and all nausea reduces, finally, to a hunger
for what is naked and approachable,

tangible and delicious.

JORIE GRAHAM (1950–   )

The Geese (1980)

Today as I hang out the wash I see them again, a code
as urgent as elegant,
tapering with goals.
For days they have been crossing. We live beneath these geese

5   as if beneath the passage of time, or a most perfect heading.
Sometimes I fear their relevance.

Closest at hand,
between the lines,

10
the spiders imitate the paths the geese won't stray from,
imitate them endlessly to no avail:
things will not remain connected,
will not heal,

and the world thickens with texture instead of history,
texture instead of place.
15
Yet the small fear of the spiders
binds and binds

the pins to the lines, the lines to the eaves, to the pincushion bush,
as if, at any time, things could fall further apart
and nothing could help them
20
recover their meaning. And if these spiders had their way,

chainlink over the visible world,
would we be in or out? I turn to go back in.
There is a feeling the body gives the mind
of having missed something, a bedrock poverty, like falling

25
without the sense that you are passing through one world,
that you could reach another
anytime. Instead the real
is crossing you,
your body an arrival
30
you know is false but can't outrun. And somewhere in between
these geese forever entering and
these spiders turning back,

this astonishing delay, the everyday, takes place.

PAUL MULDOON (1951–   )

Hedgehog (1973)

The snail moves like a
Hovercraft,[1] held up by a
Rubber cushion of itself,
Sharing its secret

---

[1] **Hovercraft:** A boat that floats on a cushion of air, thus hovering above the surface of the water.

5   With the hedgehog. The hedgehog
Shares its secret with no one.
We say, *Hedgehog, come out*
Of yourself and we will love you.

We mean no harm. We want
10   *Only to listen to what*
You have to say. We want
Your answers to our questions.

The hedgehog gives nothing
Away, keeping itself to itself.
15   We wonder what a hedgehog
Has to hide, why it so distrusts.

We forget the god
Under this crown of thorns.
We forget that never again
20   Will a god trust in the world.

MARY JO SALTER   (1954–   )

Kangaroo   (1999)

Like flustered actors
who don't know what to do
with their hands, they're hanging
around in awkward clusters,
5   paws dangling, ears pricked for a cue.

And then look properly
stunned when our typecast
tour bus, bumptious as a cousin
none of them invited, raises
10   a ruckus of flung stones and dust

and scrapes to a halt
before them, face to face.
If it isn't clear what a tour bus is,
they've seen its like before;
15   their startle softens to a stare

of seeming acceptance,
as if next time they'd sniff
our coming in advance. A twitch
from one, and all's a blank:
20   in unison they begin to bounce

across the empty
apron of the plain (where
every line has been forgotten
or not even thought of once
25   for millions of years), an unlikely

hop not happy-
go-lucky but utterly
matter-of-fact; then they stop up-
stage, for reasons none of us,
30   on the edge of our seats, can guess.

Yet it seems so human
when we happen upon (what
joy, it's blue) a kangaroo
standing back from the crowd:
35   her joey's tall enough to nurse

on its feet, while its head
and forearms are buried deep
in the pouch, like a woman
rummaging in her purse for something
40   nobody else can touch.

CHAPTER 22

THE POET'S EYE, IN FINE FRENZY ROLLING

–William Shakespeare

An Anthology of Poems on Poets and Poetry

In the minds of many poets, *poetry* represents life itself, the creative process, all that is meaningful and worth doing. It's no surprise, then, that poets do some of their best work on the subject of poetry. Indeed, as the eighteenth century poet and critic Samuel Johnson once said to his biographer James Boswell, the poet "must write as the interpreter of nature, and the legislator of mankind, and consider himself as presiding over the thoughts and manners of future generations." This is quite an assignment!

The tradition of *ars poetica* (which, in Latin, means "the art of poetry") goes back to Horace, the Roman poet who coined this phrase. His "Ars Poetica" is the first poem explicitly written on this subject. Horace writes the poem as an epistle, and it's full of advice to would-be poets, referring to art and artifice, arguing for unity of vision—a fusion of form and content. Horace regards the artificial limits of form as essential, as bestowing a certain kind of freedom on the poet:

> Exquisiteness alone is not enough.
> Entice the reader's heart with empathy.
> You must, whatever else you do, draw forth
> A smile or tear. If you would make me sad,
> 5   Be sad yourself . . .

(translated by Jay Parini)

This is excellent advice, and is echoed by Lord Byron in his "Hints from Horace" (1811):

> 'Tis not enough, ye bards, with all your art,
> To polish poems; they must touch the heart:
> Wherever the scene be laid, whate'er the song,
> Still let it bear the hearer's soul along;
> 5   Command your audience or to smile or weep,
> Whiche'er may please you—anything but sleep.
> The poet claims our tears; but, by his leave,
> Before I shed them, let me see him grieve.

Poets in all times and languages have written, overtly or covertly, about poems, about the poetic process, about the operations of the imagination. To poets, "poems are all that matter," as Robert Frost once observed.

The poems included in this chapter are all, in one way or another, "about" poetry, but they are also about what the poet believes to be the function and nature of poetry. Often a poet writes one of his or her signature poems when considering the nature of the poet's work in the world, as in "Lament for the Makaris" by William Dunbar (p. 1412), where he contemplates the "makers"—the word simply means poets—who have passed away.

Shakespeare, as might be expected, took up the subject of the poet's art many times in his poems and plays. The passage included here from *A Midsummer Night's Dream* (p. 1420) is, perhaps, the supreme statement about poetry, which "gives to airy nothing/A local habitation and a name." Poetry, he says, is about the embodiment of spirit, about transforming abstract ideas into concrete images. Poetry is about place and time, about the human mind in the act of finding what will suffice (as Wallace Stevens suggests in "Of Modern Poetry," p. 1442).

Many of these poems serve a didactic function, in that the poet feels an obligation to forcefully state his or her ideas about poetry, excluding poets and poetic traditions that lie beyond their scope or interest. "O Black and Unknown Bards" by James Weldon Johnson (p. 1440) presents a challenge to other African-American poets. The same might be said for "Esthete in Harlem" by Langston Hughes (p. 1448) or "For Black Poets Who Think of Suicide" by Etheridge Knight (p. 1458). Other poems that take a didactic tone are specifically about theories of poetry or "poetics." Yusef Komunyakaa (p. 1470) and August Kleinzahler (p. 1473) both write poems called "Poetics." These poems ask essential questions about the nature and function of poetic language. Charles Bernstein's "Of Time and the Line" (p. 1475) and David Lehman's "An Alternative to Speech" (p. 1473) are also about poetics, looking at different aspects of the relationship between language and time or language and poetic space. Less specifically, "Dismantling the Silence" by Charles Simic (p. 1462) digs into the philosophical basis for language and, of course, poetry.

Poets in the tradition of **ars poetica** also look inward, attempting to characterize their own poetic process and trying to locate the source of their imagination. This is certainly the case in "The Thought-Fox" by Ted Hughes (p. 1457), "Personal Helicon" by Seamus Heaney (p. 1463), and "Essay on What I Think about Most" by Anne Carson (p. 1477). These poems sometimes reveal considerable anxiety, as poets contemplate their relationship with one another and with their traditions. In Julia Alvarez's "On Not Shoplifting Louise Bogan's *The Blue Estuaries*" (p. 1474), for example, the word *shoplifting* has a literal as well as a figurative meaning.

In each of these poems, the poet asks: What is poetry? What is important to me? What is *real*? In his own oblique way, William Carlos Williams answers these questions in "The Red Wheelbarrow" (p. 1443), concluding that everything depends on concrete reality, on the image itself. But there are as many answers to these questions as there are poets. This selection demonstrates the astonishing variety and liveliness of this tradition.

ADDITIONAL POEMS ABOUT POETRY IN THIS BOOK

- Thomas Carew, "An Elegy upon the Death of the Dean of St. Paul's, Dr. John Donne" (p. 139)
- William Wordsworth, "Scorn Not the Sonnet" (p. 811)
- William Wordsworth, "The Solitary Reaper" (p. 1534)
- Percy Bysshe Shelley, "Adonais" (p. 161)
- John Keats, "Ode on a Grecian Urn" (p. 421)
- Emily Dickinson, "I dwell in Possibility" (p. 632)
- Robert Frost, "Mowing" (p. 822)
- Wallace Stevens, "The Idea of Order at Key West" (p. 436)
- Robert Graves, "To Juan and the Winter Solstice" (p. 904)
- W. H. Auden, "In Memory of W. B. Yeats" (p. 219)
- Frank O'Hara, "The Day Lady Died" (p. 227)
- Elizabeth Bishop, "One Art" (p. 841)
- Iain Chrichton Smith, "At the Scott Exhibition, Edinburgh Festival" (p. 229)
- Jack Gilbert, "Explicating the Twilight" (p. 645)
- Adrienne Rich, "Diving into the Wreck" (p. 965)
- Mark Strand, "In Memory of Joseph Brodsky" (p. 237)
- Charles Wright, "Sitting Outside at the End of Autumn" (p. 1320)
- Seamus Heaney, "The Forge" (p. 830)
- Seamus Heaney, "Digging" (p. 1005)
- Craig Raine, "A Martian Sends a Postcard Home" (p. 1012)
- Peter Balakian, "After the Survivors Are Gone" (p. 1229)

HORACE   (65 B.C.–8 B.C.)
trans. James Michie

from Odes Book III

Exegi Monumentum

More durable than bronze, higher than Pharaoh's
Pyramids is the monument I have made,
A shape that angry wind or hungry rain
Cannot demolish, nor the innumerable
5   Ranks of the years that march in centuries.
I shall not wholly die: some part of me
Will cheat the goddess of death, for while High Priest
And Vestal° climb our Capitol[1] in a hush,   chaste woman
My reputation shall keep green and growing.
10   Where Aufidus growls torrentially, where once,
Lord of a dry kingdom, Daunus[2] ruled
His rustic people, I shall be renowned
As one who, poor-born, rose and pioneered
A way to fit Greek rhythms to our tongue.
15   Be proud, Melpomene,[3] for you deserve
What praise I have, and unreluctantly
Garland my forehead with Apollo's laurel.[4]

OVID   (43 B.C.–17 A.D.)
trans. Allen Mandelbaum

from Metamorphoses

And now my work is done: no wrath of Jove[1]
nor fire nor sword nor time, which would erode
all things, has power to blot out this poem.
Now, when it wills, the fatal day (which has
5   only the body in its grasp) can end
my years, however long or short their span.

---

[1] **Capitol:** Ancient temple in Rome, considered to be a sign of Rome's power and eternal existence.
[2] **Aufidus . . . Daunus:** The Aufidus is a river in southern Italy; King Daunus is a mythical king from Horace's homeland.
[3] **Melpomene:** In mythology, the Greek muse of tragedy.
[4] **Apollo's laurel:** Moved by Eros, Apollo pursued the nymph Daphne. Annoyed, she begged for help from the river god Peneus, who turned her into a laurel tree when Apollo attempted to embrace her. Distraught, Apollo made the laurel his sacred tree.
[1] **Jove:** In classical mythology, god of the sky and ruler of the Roman gods.

But, with the better part of me, I'll gain
a place that's higher than the stars: my name,
indelible, eternal, will remain.
10   And everywhere that Roman power has sway,
in all domains the Latins gain, my lines
will be on people's lips; and through all time—
if poets' prophecies are ever right—
my name and fame are sure: I shall have life.

TU FU (712–770)
trans. Arthur Sze

Thoughts on a Night Journey

A slight wind stirs grasses along the bank.
A lone boat sails with a mast in the night.
The stars are pulled down to the vast plain,
and the moon bobs in the river's flow.

5   My name will never be famous in literature:
I have resigned office from sickness and age.
Drifting and drifting, what am I
but a solitary gull between earth and heaven?

WILLIAM DUNBAR (ca. 1460–ca. 1525)

Lament for the Makaris° (1508)   Poets

I that in heill° was and gladness,   health
Am troublit now with great seikness,
And feeblit with infirmity:
    Timor Mortis conturbat me.[1]

5   Our plesance here is all vain-glory
This false warld is bot transitory,
The flesh is brukill,° the Fiend is sle;°   fragile / sly
    Timor Mortis conturbat me.

---

[1] **Timor . . . me:** Latin, "the fear of death dismays me." From "The Office of the Dead," a well-known
fifteenth-century poem.

The state of man dois change and vary,
10   Now sound, now seik, now blyth,° now sary,°   happy / sorry
      Now dansand° merry, now like to die;   dance and be
          Timor Mortis conturbat me.

      No state in erd° here standis siccar;°   earth / securely
      As with the wind wavis the wicker,°   willow
15   Wavis this warldis vanitie;
          Timor Mortis conturbat me.

      Unto the deid gois all Estatis,[2]
      Princes, Prelatis,° and Potestatis,°   prelates / potenates
      Baith rich and puir° of all degree;   poor
20   *Timor Mortis conturbat me.*

      He takis the knichtis into the field,
      Enarmit under helm and shield;
      Victor he is at all mêlée;°   encounters
          Timor Mortis conturbat me.

25   That strang° unmerciful tyrand   strong
      Takis on the moderis breist soukand°   sucking
      The babe, full of benignite;°   tenderness
          Timor Mortis conturbat me.

      He takis the champion in the stour,°   battle
30   The capitane closit in the tour,°   tower
      The lady in bour° full of beautie;   bedroom
          Timor Mortis conturbat me.

      He sparis no lord for his puissance,°   power
      Na clerk for his intelligence;
35   His awful straik° may no man flee;   stroke
          Timor Mortis conturbat me.

      Art magicianis, and astrologis,°   astrologers
      Rethoris,° logicianis, and theologis,   rhetoricians
      Them helpis no conclusionis sle;
40   *Timor Mortis conturbat me.*

      In medicine the most practicianis,
      Leechis,° surigianis, and phisicianis,   doctors
      Them-self fra deid° may not supple;°   death / relieve
          Timor Mortis conturbat me.

---

[2] **Estatis:** Estates. Society was divided into three segments: the rulers, the religious order, and the laborers.

45   I see that makaris amang the lave°   *remainder*
      Playis here their pageant, syne° gois to grave;   *then*
      Sparit° is nocht° their facultie;   *spared / not*
         Timor Mortis conturbat me.

      He has done piteously devour
50   The noble Chaucer, of makaris flour,°   *flower*
      The Monk of Bery, and Gower, all three,[3]
         Timor Mortis conturbat me.

      The gude Sir Hew of Eglintoun,[4]
      And eik° Heriot, and Wintoun,   *also*
55   He has ta'en out of this countrie;
         Timor Mortis conturbat me.

      That scorpion fell has done infec'
      Maister John Clerk and James Affleck,
      Fra ballad-making and tragedie;
60   *Timor Mortis conturbat me.*

      Holland and Barbour he has bereavit;
      Alas! that he nought with us leavit
      Sir Mungo Lockhart of the Lea;
         Timor Mortis conturbat me.

65   Clerk of Tranent eke he has ta'en,
      That made the Aunteris° of Gawain;[5]   *adventures*
      Sir Gilbert Hay endit has he;
         Timor Mortis conturbat me.

      He has Blind Harry, and Sandy Traill
70   Slain with his shour° of mortal hail,   *shower*
      Whilk° Patrick Johnstoun micht nocht flee;   *which*
         Timor Mortis conturbat me.

      He has reft Merser endite,
      That did in luve so lively write,
75   So short, so quick, of sentence hie;°   *vigorous*
         Timor Mortis conturbat me.

---

[3] **noble Chaucer . . . three:** Three English poets: Geoffrey Chaucer (ca. 1343–1400), The Monk of Bery or John Lydgate (1370?–1451?), and John Gower (1325?–1408).
[4] **Sir Hew of Eglintoun:** The first in a list of Scottish poets.
[5] **Gawain:** A knight in King Arthur's court.

He has ta'en Roull of Aberdeen,
And gentle Roull of Corstorphin;
Two better fellowis did no man see;
80   *Timor Mortis conturbat me.*

In Dunfermline he has done roune°   round
With Maister Robert Henryson;
Sir John the Ross embraced has he;
Timor Mortis conturbat me.

85   And he has now ta'en, last of a',
Gude gentle Stobo and Quintin Shaw,
Of wham all wichtis° has pitie: creatures
Timor Mortis conturbat me.

Gude Maister Walter Kennedy
90   In point of deid lies verily,
Great ruth° it were that so suld be;   misfortune
Timor Mortis conturbat me.

Sen he has all my brether° ta'en,   brothers
He will nocht lat me live alane,
95   On force I maun° his next prey be;   must
Timor Mortis conturbat me.

Sen for the deid remead° is none,   remedy
Best is that we for deid dispone,°   prepare
Eftir our deid that live may we;
100 *Timor Mortis conturbat me.*

THOMAS WYATT (1503–1542)

My Lute Awake! (1557)

My lute awake! Perform the last
Labor that thou and I shall waste,
   And end that I have now begun;
For when this song is sung and past,
5   My lute be still, for I have done.

As to be heard where ear is none,
As lead to grave° in marble stone,   engrave
   My song may pierce her heart as soon?
Should we then sigh, or sing, or moan?
10   No, no, my lute, for I have done.

The rocks do not so cruelly
Repulse the waves continually
    As she my suit and affection.
So that I am past remedy:
15   Whereby my lute and I have done.

Proud of the spoil that thou hast got
Of simple hearts thorough° love's shot,[1]   through
    By whom, unkind, thou hast them won,
Think not he hath his bow forgot,
20   Although my lute and I have done.

Vengeance shall fall on thy disdain,
That makest but game on earnest pain;
    Think not alone under the sun
Unquit° to cause thy lovers plain,°   unrequited / lament
25   Although my lute and I have done.

Perchance thee lie withered and old,
The winter nights that are so cold,
    Plaining in vain unto the moon;
Thy wishes then dare not be told;
30   Care then who list,° for I have done.   likes

And then may chance thee to repent
The time that thou hast lost and spent
    To cause thy lovers sigh and swoon;
Then shalt thou know beauty but lent,
35   And wish and want as I have done.

Now cease, my lute, this is the last
Labor that thou and I shall waste,
    And ended is that we begun;
Now is this song both sung and past:
40   My lute be still, for I have done.

---

[1] **love's shot:** I.e., Cupid's arrow.

GEORGE GASCOIGNE (ca. 1535–1577)

Gascoigne's Lullaby (1573)

Sing lullaby, as women do,
Wherewith they bring their babes to rest,
And lullaby can I sing too,
As womanly as can the best.
5   With lullaby they still the child,
And if I be not much beguiled,
Full many wanton babes have I,
Which must be stilled with lullaby.

First, lullaby, my youthful years,
10   It is now time to go to bed,
For crooked age and hoary hairs
Have won the haven within my head.
With lullaby then, youth, be still,
With lullaby content they will,
15   Since courage quails° and comes behind,   shrinks
Go sleep, and so beguile thy mind.

Next, lullaby, my gazing eyes,
Which wonted were° to glance apace.   were accustomed
For every glass may now suffice
20   To show the furrows in my face.
With lullaby then wink[1] awhile,
With lullaby your looks beguile.
Let no fair face nor beauty bright
Entice you eft° with vain delight.   after

25   And lullaby, my wanton will,
Let reason's rule now rein thy thought,
Since all too late I find by skill°   experience
How dear I have thy fancies bought.
With lullaby now take thine ease,
30   With lullaby thy doubts appease.
For trust to this, if thou be still,
My body shall obey thy will.

Eke° lullaby, my loving boy,   also
My little Robin,[2] take thy rest.

---

[1] **wink:** I.e., shut your eyes.
[2] **My little Robin:** I.e., my penis.

35 Since age is cold and nothing coy,
Keep close thy coin, for so is best.
With lullaby be thou content,
With lullaby thy lusts relent.
Let others pay which° hath mo° pence;   who / more
40 Thou art too poor for such expense.

Thus, lullaby, my youth, mine eyes,
My will, my ware, and all that was.
I can no mo delays devise,
But welcome pain, let pleasure pass.
45 With lullaby now take your leave,
With lullaby your dreams deceive,
And when you rise with waking eye,
Remember Gascoigne's lullaby.

SIR PHILIP SIDNEY (1554–1589)

from Astrophil and Stella[1] (1582; 1591)
90 "Stella, think not that I by verse seek fame"

Stella, think not that I by verse seek fame,
Who seek, who hope, who love, who live but thee;
Thine eyes my pride, thy lips my history;
If thou praise not, all other praise is shame.
5   Nor so ambitious am I, as to frame
A nest for my young praise in laurel tree:[2]
In truth I sweare, I wish not there should be
Graved in mine epitaph a Poet's name:
Nay if I would, could I just title make,
10 That any laud to me thereof should grow,
Without my plumes from others' wings I take.
For nothing from my wit or will doth flow,
Since all my words thy beauty doth endite,[3]
And love doth hold my hand, and makes me write.

---

[1] **Astrophil and Stella:** "Starlover and Star," a sonnet sequence that hints at Sidney's relationship with Penelope Devereux, who married Lord Rich in 1581.
[2] **laurel tree:** The laurel is symbolic of poetic achievement.
[3] **endite:** A blending of "indict" (to proclaim) and "indite" (to inscribe).

SAMUEL DANIEL   (ca. 1562–1619)

from Delia   (1592)

Go wailing verse, the infants of my love,
Minerva-like,[1] brought forth without a Mother:
Present the image of the cares I prove,
Witness your Father's grief exceeds all other.
5   Sigh out a story of her cruel deeds,
With interrupted accents of despair:
A monument that whosoever reads,
May justly praise, and blame my loveless Fair.
Say her disdain hath dried up my blood,
10   And starved you, in succours° still denying: support
Press to her eyes, importune me some good;
Waken her sleeping pity with your crying.
Knock at that hard heart, beg till you have mov'd her;
And tell th'unkind, how dearly I have lov'd her.

MICHAEL DRAYTON   (1563–1631)

Idea VI[1]   (1619)

How many paltry, foolish, painted things,
That now in coaches trouble every street,
Shall be forgotten, whom no poet sings,
Ere they be well wrapp'd in their winding-sheet?
5   Where I to thee eternity shall give,
When nothing else remaineth of these days,
And queens hereafter shall be glad to live
Upon the alms of thy superfluous praise.
Virgins and matrons reading these my rhymes
10   Shall be so much delighted with thy story,

---

[1] **Minerva-like:** Minerva, the classical goddess of war and wisdom, emerged fully formed from the head of her father, Jove.
[1] **Idea:** A sequence of 59 sonnets that explore the embodiment of the Platonic ideals of virtue and beauty. The sequence was written with Drayton's lifelong devotion to Anne Goodyere, Lady Rainsford, in mind.

That they shall grieve they liv'd not in these times
To have seen thee, their sex's only glory.
So shalt thou fly above the vulgar throng,
Still to survive in my immortal song.

WILLIAM SHAKESPEARE (1564–1616)

from A Midsummer Night's Dream
Act V, Scene 1 (Theseus) (ca. 1596; 1623)

Lovers and madmen have such seething brains,
Such shaping fantasies,° that apprehend   imaginations
More than cool reason ever comprehends.
The lunatic, the lover, and the poet,
5   Are of imagination all compact:°   composed
One sees more devils than vast hell can hold,
That is, the madman; the lover, all as frantic,
Sees Helen's beauty in a brow of Egypt:[1]
The poet's eye, in fine frenzy rolling,
10   Doth glance from heaven to earth, from earth to heaven;
And, as imagination bodies forth
The forms of things unknown, the poet's pen
Turns them to shapes, and gives to airy nothing
A local habitation and a name.
15   Such tricks hath strong imagination,
That, if it would but apprehend some joy,
It comprehends some bringer° of that joy;   source
Or in the night, imagining some fear,
How easy is a bush suppos'd a bear!

---

[1] **Sees . . . Egypt:** I.e., sees Helen of Troy's beauty in a gypsy's face.

WILLIAM SHAKESPEARE (1564–1616)

from The Tempest
Act V, Scene 1 (Prospero)[1]   (ca. 1611; 1623)

Ye elves of hills, brooks, standing lakes, and groves;
And ye, that on the sands with printless foot
Do chase the ebbing Neptune[2] and do fly him
When he comes back; you demi-puppets, that
5   By moonshine do the green sour ringlets[3] make
Whereof the ewe not bites; and you, whose pastime
Is to make midnight mushrooms; that rejoice
To hear the solemn curfew,[4] by whose aid,—
Weak masters though ye be—I have bedimm'd
10   The noontide sun, call'd forth the mutinous winds,
And 'twixt the green sea and the azur'd vault°   the sky
Set roaring war: to the dread-rattling thunder
Have I given fire and rifted Jove's[5] stout oak
With his own bolt; the strong-bas'd promontory
15   Have I made shake; and by the spurs° pluck'd up   roots
The pine and cedar; graves at my command
Have wak'd their sleepers, op'd, and let them forth
By my so potent art. But this rough° magic   violent
I here abjure; and, when I have requir'd
20   Some heavenly music,—which even now I do,—
To work mine end upon their senses that
This airy charm is for, I'll break my staff,
Bury it certain° fathoms in the earth,   multiple
And, deeper than did ever plummet sound,
25   I'll drown my book.

---

[1] **Prospero:** Prospero's speech closely follows Arthur Golding's translation of Ovid's *Metamorphoses*.
The speaker in the *Metamorphoses* is Medea, who uses her witchcraft toward deceitful ends.
[2] **Neptune:** In Roman mythology, God of the sea.
[3] **ringlets:** Rings made in the grass by dancing fairies.
[4] **solemn curfew:** Bell rung at night to indicate that spirits are traveling about.
[5] **Jove's:** Jove is ruler of the Roman gods.

BEN JONSON   (1572–1637)

from To the Memory of my Beloved
Mr. William Shakespeare   (1623)

I, therefore, will begin. Soul of the Age!
    The applause, delight, the wonder of our Stage!
My Shakespeare, rise; I will not lodge thee by
    Chaucer, or Spenser, or bid Beaumont lie[1]
5 A little further, to make thee a room:
    Thou art a monument, without a tomb,
And art alive still, while thy book doth live,
    And we have wits to read and praise to give.
That I not mix thee so, my brain excuses;
10 I mean with great, but disproportioned Muses:[2]
For, if I thought my judgement were of years,
    I should commit° thee surely with thy peers,   connect
And tell how far thou didst our Lyly out-shine,
    Or sporting Kyd, or Marlowe's mighty line.[3]
15 And though thou hadst small Latin and less Greek,
    From thence to honour thee, I would not seek
For names; but call forth thundering Aeschylus,
    Euripides, and Sophocles to us,
Paccuvius, Accius, him of Cordova dead,[4]
20 To life again, to hear thy buskin° tread,   boot
And shake a stage; or, when thy socks were on,
    Leave thee alone, for the comparison
Of all that insolent Greece or haughty Rome
    Sent forth, or since did from their ashes come.
25 Triumph, my Britain, thou hast one to show
    To whom all scenes of Europe homage owe.
He was not of an age but for all time!
    And all the Muses still were in their prime
When, like Apollo, he came forth to warm
30 Our ears, or, like a Mercury,[5] to charm!

---

[1] **I . . . lie:** Chaucer (ca. 1343–1400), Spenser (ca. 1552–1599), and Beaumont (1584–1616) are all buried in Westminster Abbey, London, while Shakespeare is buried in the Holy Trinity Church, Stratford-on-Avon.
[2] **Muses:** Nine Greek goddesses responsible for artistic inspiration.
[3] **Lyly . . . line:** A list of Elizabethan dramatists: John Lyly (1554–1606), Thomas Kyd (1558–1594), and Christopher Marlowe (1564–1593).
[4] **but call forth . . . dead:** Aeschylus (524 B.C.–456 B.C.), Euripides (ca. 484 B.C.–406 B.C.), and Sophocles (496 B.C.–406 B.C.) were Greek dramatists. Marcus Pacuvius (second century B.C.), Lucius Accius (second century B.C.), and Seneca (first century A.D.) were all Roman tragedians.
[5] **Apollo . . . Mercury:** Apollo was the Greek god of light and music; Mercury, the messenger of the Roman god Jupiter, was associated with good luck and enchantment.

Nature herself was proud of his designs,
　　And joyed to wear the dressing of his lines!
Which were so richly spun and woven so fit
　　As, since, she will vouchsafe no other wit.
35　The merry Greek, tart Aristophanes,
　　Neat Terence, witty Plautus,[6] now not please,
But antiquated and deserted lie
　　As they were not of Nature's family.
Yet must I not give Nature all: thy Art,
40　My gentle Shakespeare, must enjoy a part.
For though the poet's matter Nature be,
　　His Art doth give the fashion.° And that he   form
Who casts to write a living line must sweat,
　　(Such as thine are) and strike the second heat
45　Upon the Muses' anvil: turn the same
　　(And himself with it) that he thinks to frame;
Or for the laurel he may gain a scorn,
　　For a good poet's made as well as born.
And such wert thou. . . .

THOMAS HEYWOOD   (ca. 1574–1641)

The Author to His Book   (1612)

The world's a theatre, the Earth a stage,
Which God and nature doth with actors fill:
Kings have their entrance in due equipage,
And some their parts play well and others ill.
5　The best no better are, in this theatre,
Where every humour's fitted in his kind:
This a true subject acts, and that a traitor,
The first applauded and the last confined;
This plays an honest man and that a knave,
10　A gentle person this, and he a clown;
One man is ragged and another brave:
All men have parts, and each man acts his own.
She a chaste lady acteth all her life,
A wanton courtesan another plays.
15　This covets marriage love, that, nuptial strife:

---

[6] **Aristophanes . . . Plautus:** Aristophanes (Greek), Terence (Roman), and Plautus (Roman) were
comic writers.

Both in continual action spend their days:
Some citizens, some soldiers born to adventure,
Shepherds and seamen. Then our play's begun
When we are born, and to the world first enter;
20   And all find *exits* when their parts are done.
If then the world a theatre present,
As by the roundness it appears most fit,
Built with star-galleries of high ascent,
In which Jehove° doth as spectator sit   Jehovah
25   And chief determiner to applaud the best,
And their endeavours crown with more than merit;
But by their evil actions dooms the rest
To end disgraced whilst others praise inherit,
      He that denies then theatres should be,
30   He may as well deny a world to me.

ROBERT HERRICK (1591–1674)

The Argument of His Book (1648)

I sing of brooks, of blossoms, birds, and bowers:
Of April, May, of June, and July-flowers.
I sing of May-poles, hock-carts, wassails,[1] wakes,
Of bridegrooms, brides, and of their bridal cakes.
5   I write of youth, of love, and have access
By these to sing of cleanly-wantonness.
I sing of dews, of rains, and piece by piece
Of balm, of oil, of spice, and amber-Greece.
I sing of time's trans-shifting; and I write
10   How roses first came red, and lilies white.
I write of groves, of twilights, and I sing
The court of Mab,[2] and of the fairy king.
I write of hell; I sing (and ever shall)
Of heaven, and hope to have it after all.

---

[1] **hock-carts, wassails:** Hock carts were used to carry in the final load of the harvest; to wassail was to drink to the health of others.
[2] **Mab:** Queen of the fairies.

JOHN MILTON   (1608–1674)

from Paradise Lost, Book 3   (1667)
"Invocation to Light"

Hail, holy Light, offspring of heaven first-born,
Or of the eternal co-eternal beam
May I express thee unblamed? since God is light,[1]
And never but in unapproachèd light
5   Dwelt from eternity, dwelt then in thee,
Bright effluence of bright essence increate.°   uncreated
Or hearst thou rather pure ethereal stream,
Whose fountain who shall tell? Before the sun,
Before the heavens thou wert, and at the voice
10 Of God, as with a mantle didst invest°   envelope
The rising world of waters dark and deep,
Won from the void and formless infinite.
Thee I revisit now with bolder wing,
Escaped the Stygian° pool, though long detained   hellish
15 In that obscure sojourn, while in my flight
Through utter and through middle darkness borne
With other notes than to the Orphean lyre[2]
I sung of chaos and eternal night,
Taught by the heavenly Muse[3] to venture down
20 The dark descent, and up to reascend,
Though hard and rare: thee I revisit safe,
And feel thy sovereign vital lamp; but thou
Revisitst not these eyes, that roll in vain
To find thy piercing ray, and find no dawn;
25 So thick a drop serene[4] hath quenched their orbs,
Or dim suffusion veiled. Yet not the more
Cease I to wander where the Muses haunt
Clear spring, or shady grove, or sunny hill,
Smit with the love of sacred song; but chief
30 Thee Sion[5] and the flowery brooks beneath
That wash thy hallowed feet, and warbling flow,

---

[1] **God is light:** See 1 John 1.5: "Then this is the message which we have heard of him, and declare unto you, that God is light, and in him is no darkness at all."
[2] **With other . . . lyre:** In Greek mythology, Orpheus descended into hell to charm Pluto and Persephone with song in hope of rescuing his wife Eurydice. Milton's "other notes" are epic, whereas those of Orpheus were lyric.
[3] **heavenly Muse:** The Muses were the nine daughters of Zeus charged with inspiring artistic creation; Milton's heavenly muse is a Judeo-Christian manifestation of the mythological muses.
[4] **drop serene:** Medical term for Milton's blindness.
[5] **Sion:** A version of Zion, an imaginary place of great tranquility; also used as a synonym for Jerusalem itself during ancient times.

Nightly I visit, nor sometimes forget
Those other two equalled with me in fate,
So were I equalled with them in renown,
35   Blind Thamyris and blind Maeonides,
And Tiresias and Phineus prophets old.[6]
Then feed on thoughts, that voluntary move
Harmonious numbers,° as the wakeful bird   verses
Sings darkling, and in shadiest covert hid
40   Tunes her nocturnal note. Thus with the year
Seasons return, but not to me returns
Day, or the sweet approach of even or morn,
Or sight of vernal bloom, or summer's rose,
Or flocks, or herds, or human face divine;
45   But cloud instead and ever-during dark
Surrounds me, from the cheerful ways of men
Cut off, and for the book of knowledge fair
Presented with a universal blank
Of nature's works to me expunged and razed,
50   And wisdom at one entrance quite shut out.
So much the rather thou celestial Light
Shine inward, and the mind through all her powers
Irradiate; there plant eyes, all mist from thence
Purge and disperse, that I may see and tell
55   Of things invisible to mortal sight.

ANNE BRADSTREET   (ca. 1612–1672)

The Author to Her Book   (1678)

Thou ill-formed offspring of my feeble brain,
Who after birth didst by my side remain,
Till snatched from thence by friends, less wise than true,
Who thee abroad, exposed to public view,
5   Made thee in rags, halting to th' press to trudge,
Where errors were not lessened (all may judge).
At thy return my blushing was not small,
My rambling brat (in print) should mother call,
I cast thee by as one unfit for light,
10   The visage was so irksome in my sight;
Yet being mine own, at length affection would

---

[6] **Blind Thamyris . . . old:** Thamyris was a blind poet in the *Iliad*, and Maeonides was Homer, author
of the *Iliad*. Tiresias and Phineus were ancient blind prophets.

Thy blemishes amend, if so I could.
I washed thy face, but more defects I saw,
And rubbing off a spot still made a flaw.
15   I stretched thy joints to make thee even feet,[1]
Yet still thou run'st more hobbling than is meet;
In better dress to trim thee was my mind,
But nought save homespun cloth i' th' house I find.
In this array 'mongst vulgars° may'st thou roam.   common people
20   In critic's hands beware thou dost not come,
And take thy way where yet thou art not known;
If for thy father asked, say thou hadst none;
And for thy mother, she alas is poor,
Which caused her thus to send thee out of door.

EDWARD TAYLOR   (ca. 1642–1729)

Housewifery   (ca. 1682; 1939)

Make me, O Lord, thy spinning wheel complete.[1]
    Thy holy word my distaff make for me.
Make mine affections thy swift flyers neat,
    And make my soul thy holy spool to be.
5   My conversation make to be thy reel,
        And reel the yarn thereon spun on thy wheel.

Make me thy loom then, knit therein this twine:
    And make thy holy spirit, Lord, wind quills.°   spools
Then weave the web thyself. The yarn is fine.
10   Thine ordinances make my fulling mills.[2]
        Then dye the same in heavenly colors choice,
        All pinked° with varnished° flowers of paradise.   decorated / lustrous

Then clothe therewith mine understanding, will,
    Affections, judgment, conscience, memory,
15   My words, and actions, that their shine may fill
        My ways with glory and thee glorify.
        Then mine apparel shall display before ye
        That I am clothed in holy robes for glory.

---

[1] **even feet:** In other words, even-metered feet, or to smooth out the lines.
[1] **thy spinning wheel complete:** In the first stanza, "distaff," "flyers," "spool," and "reel" are all parts of a spinning wheel.
[2] **fulling mills:** In a fulling mill, cloth is pressed between rollers and then cleansed with soap.

ANNE FINCH, COUNTESS OF WINCHILSEA (1661–1720)

The Introduction (1689; 1902)

Did I, my lines intend for public view,
How many censures, would their faults pursue,
Some would, because such words they do affect,
Cry they're insipid, empty, uncorrect.
5   And many have attained, dull and untaught,
The name of wit only by finding fault.
True judges might condemn their want of wit,
And all might say, they're by a woman writ.
Alas! a woman that attempts the pen,
10   Such an intruder on the rights of men,
Such a presumptuous creature, is esteemed,
The fault can by no virtue be redeemed.
They tell us we mistake our sex and way;
Good breeding, fashion, dancing, dressing, play
15   Are the accomplishments we should desire;
To write, or read, or think, or to inquire
Would cloud our beauty, and exhaust our time,
And interrupt the conquests of our prime;
Whilst the dull manage of a servile house
20   Is held by some our outmost° art, and use.   utmost
     Sure 'twas not ever thus, nor are we told
Fables, of women that excelled of old;
To whom, by the diffusive hand of Heaven
Some share of wit, and poetry was given.
25   On that glad day, on which the Ark returned,[1]
The holy pledge, for which the land had mourned,
The joyful tribes, attend it on the way,
The Levites do the sacred charge convey,
Whilst various instruments, before it play;
30   Here, holy virgins in the concert join
The louder notes, to soften, and refine,
And with alternate verse complete the hymn divine.
Lo! the young Poet,[2] after God's own heart,
By Him inspired, and taught the Muses art,
35   Returned from conquest, a bright chorus meets,
That sing his slain ten thousand in the streets.

---

[1] **the Ark returned:** After the Philistines captured the Ark of the Covenant, God forced them to return it to Jerusalem. As punishment for the transgressions of the Israelites, however, God withheld the Ark from Jerusalem for twenty years. It was later returned to Jerusalem by the Levites during the reign of King David.
[2] **the young Poet:** King David of Israel, author of many of the Psalms. During the reign of King Saul, before he became king, David defeated Goliath in a battle against the Philistines.

In such loud numbers they his acts declare,
Proclaim the wonders of his early war,
That Saul upon the vast applause does frown,
40   And feels its mighty thunder shake the crown.
What, can the threatened judgment now prolong?
Half of the kingdom is already gone;
The fairest half, whose influence guides the rest,
Have David's empire o'er their hearts confessed.
45   A woman[3] here, leads fainting Israel on,
She fights, she wins, she triumphs with a song,
Devout, majestic, for the subject fit,
And far above her arms,° exalts her wit;   military exploits
Then, to the peaceful, shady palm withdraws,
50   And rules the rescued nation, with her laws.
How are we fall'n, fall'n by mistaken rules?
And education's, more than nature's fools,
Debarred from all improvements of the mind,
And to be dull, expected and designed;
55   And if some one would soar above the rest,
With warmer fancy, and ambition pressed,
So strong th' opposing faction still appears,
The hopes to thrive can ne'er outweigh the fears,
Be cautioned then my Muse, and still retired;
60   Nor be despised, aiming to be admired;
Conscious of wants, still with contracted wing,
To some few friends, and to thy sorrows sing;
For groves of laurel[4] thou wert never meant;
Be dark enough thy shades, and be thou there content.

WILLIAM BLAKE   (1757–1827)

"Trembling I Sit"   (ca. 1805)
from Jerusalem

Trembling I sit day and night. My friends are astonished at me,
Yet they forgive my wanderings. I rest not from my great task—
To open the eternal worlds, to open the immortal eyes
Of Man inwards into the worlds of thought; into Eternity
5   Ever expanding in the bosom of God, the human imagination!

---

[3] **A woman:** Deborah, fourth judge of Israel, who persuaded her fellow judge Barak to encourage the Israelites to wage war against the Canaanites who enslaved them. After the Israelite victory, Deborah and Barak wrote a song of praise. (See Judges 5.)
[4] **groves of laurel:** The laurel was a symbol of poetic accomplishment.

MARY ROBINSON (1758–1800)

To the Poet Coleridge[1] (1800; 1806)

Rapt in the visionary theme,
    Spirit divine, with thee I'll wander,
Where the blue, wavy, lucid stream
    Mid forest-glooms shall slow meander!
5 With thee I'll trace the circling bounds
    Of thy new paradise, extended,
And listen to the varying sounds
    Of winds and foamy torrents blended.

Now by the source which labouring heaves
10 The mystic fountain, bubbling, panting,
While gossamer its network weaves
    Adown the blue lawn slanting—
I'll mark thy 'sunny dome' and view
Thy 'caves of ice', thy fields of dew,
15 Thy ever-blooming mead, whose flower
Waves to the cold breath of the moonlight hour!
Or when the day-star, peering bright
On the grey wing of parting night,
With more than vegetating power
20 Throbs, grateful to the burning hour,
As summer's whispered sighs unfold
Her million million buds of gold,
Then will I climb the breezy bounds
    Of thy new paradise, extended,
25 And listen to the different sounds
    Of winds and foamy torrents blended!

Spirit divine, with thee I'll trace
    Imagination's boundless space!
With thee, beneath thy 'sunny dome'
30 I'll listen to the minstrel's lay
    Hymning the gradual close of day,

---

[1] **To the Poet Coleridge:** See Samuel Taylor Coleridge's "Kubla Khan" on page 1433.

In 'caves of ice' enchanted roam,
Where on the glittering entrance plays
The moon's beam with its silvery rays,
35 Or when the glassy stream
   That through the deep dell° flows   valley
Flashes the noon's hot beam—
   The noon's hot beam that midway shows
Thy flaming temple, studded o'er
40 With all Peruvia's° lustrous store!   Peru's
There will I trace the circling bounds
   Of thy new paradise, extended,
And listen to the awful sounds
   Of winds and foamy torrents blended.

45 And now I'll pause to catch the moan
   Of distant breezes, cavern-pent;
Now, ere the twilight tints are flown,
   Purpling the landscape far and wide
   On the dark promontory's side
50   I'll gather wild-flowers dew-besprent
And weave a crown for thee,
Genius of Heaven-taught poesy!
While, opening to my wondering eyes
Thou bidst a new Creation rise,
55 I'll raptured trace the circling bounds
   Of thy rich paradise, extended,
And listen to the varying sounds
   Of winds and foamy torrents blended.

And now, with lofty tones inviting,
60 Thy nymph, her dulcimer swift-smiting,
Shall wake me in ecstatic measures,
Far, far removed from mortal pleasures,
In cadence rich, in cadence strong,
Proving the wondrous witcheries of song!
65 I hear her voice—thy 'sunny dome',
   Thy 'caves of ice', aloud repeat—
   Vibrations maddening, sweet,
Calling the visionary wanderer home!
She sings of thee, oh favoured child
70 Of minstrelsy, sublimely wild—
Of thee whose soul can feel the tone
Which gives to airy dreams a magic all their own!

WILLIAM WORDSWORTH (1770–1850)

The Glad Preamble (ca. 1799; 1850)

Oh, there is blessing in this gentle breeze,
That blows from the green fields, and from the clouds,
And from the sky; it beats against my cheek,
And seems half-conscious of the joy it gives.
5   Oh welcome messenger! Oh welcome friend!
A captive greets thee, coming from a house
Of bondage, from yon city's walls set free,
A prison where he hath been long immured.
Now I am free, enfranchised and at large,
10   May fix my habitation where I will.
What dwelling shall receive me? In what vale
Shall be my harbour? Underneath what grove
Shall I take up my home, and what sweet stream
Shall with its murmur lull me to my rest?
15   The earth is all before me—with a heart
Joyous, nor scared at its own liberty,
I look about, and should the guide I choose
Be nothing better than a wandering cloud
I cannot miss my way. I breathe again;
20   Trances of thought and mountings of the mind
Come fast upon me. It is shaken off—
As by miraculous gift 'tis shaken off—
That burden of my own unnatural self,
The heavy weight of many a weary day
25   Not mine, and such as were not made for me.
Long months of peace (if such bold word accord
With any promises of human life),
Long months of ease and undisturbed delight
Are mine in prospect. Whither shall I turn,
30   By road or pathway, or through open field,
Or shall a twig, or any floating thing
Upon the river, point me out my course?
    Enough that I am free, for months to come
May dedicate myself to chosen tasks—
35   May quit the tiresome sea and dwell on shore
If not a settler on the soil, at least
To drink wild waters, and to pluck green herbs,
And gather fruits fresh from their native tree.
Nay more—if I may trust myself, this hour
40   Hath brought a gift that consecrates my joy;

For I, methought, while the sweet breath of heaven
Was blowing on my body, felt within
A corresponding, mild, creative breeze,
A vital breeze, which travelled gently on
45   O'er things which it had made, and is become
A tempest, a redundant energy,
Vexing its own creation. 'Tis a power
That does not come unrecognized, a storm
Which, breaking up a long continued frost,
50   Brings with it vernal promises, the hope
Of active days, of dignity and thought,
Of prowess in an honourable field,
Pure passions, virtue, knowledge and delight,
The holy life of music and of verse.

SAMUEL TAYLOR COLERIDGE (1772–1834)

Kubla Khan[1] (1797; 1816)

In Xanadu did Kubla Khan
A stately pleasure-dome decree,
Where Alph the sacred river ran
Through caverns measureless to man
5   Down to a sunless sea.
So twice five miles of fertile ground
With walls and towers were girdled round—
And there were gardens bright with sinuous rills,
Where blossomed many an incense-bearing tree;
10   And here were forests ancient as the hills,
Enfolding sunny spots of greenery.

But oh, that deep romantic chasm, which slanted
Down the green hill athwart a cedarn cover!
A savage place, as holy and enchanted
15   As e'er beneath a waning moon was haunted

---

[1] **Kubla Khan:** The first *khan*, or ruler, of the Mongol dynasty in China. The place names in the poem are from the author's imagination.

By woman wailing for her demon lover!
And from this chasm, with ceaseless turmoil seething
As if this earth in fast thick pants were breathing,
A mighty fountain momently was forced,
20   Amid whose swift half-intermitted burst
Huge fragments vaulted, like rebounding hail
Or chaffy grain beneath the thresher's flail;
And mid these dancing rocks, at once and ever,
It flung up momently the sacred river.
25   Five miles meandering with a mazy motion
Through wood and dale the sacred river ran,
Then reached the caverns measureless to man
And sank in tumult to a lifeless ocean—
And mid this tumult Kubla heard from far
30   Ancestral voices prophesying war!

The shadow of the dome of pleasure
Floated midway on the waves,
Where was heard the mingled measure
From the fountain and the caves.
35   It was a miracle of rare device—
A sunny pleasure-dome with caves of ice!

A damsel with a dulcimer
In a vision once I saw:
It was an Abyssinian maid,
40   And on her dulcimer she played
Singing of Mount Abora.
Could I revive within me
Her symphony and song,
To such a deep delight 'twould win me,
45   That with music loud and long
I would build that dome in air—
That sunny dome, those caves of ice!
And all who heard should see them there,
And all should cry 'Beware! Beware!'
50   His flashing eyes, his floating hair!
Weave a circle round him thrice,
And close your eyes with holy dread,
For he on honey-dew hath fed
And drunk the milk of Paradise.

ELIZABETH BARRETT BROWNING (1806–1861)

from Aurora Leigh (1853–56; 1857)
from Book 5

Poets and the Present Age

The critics say that epics have died out
With Agamemnon and the goat-nursed gods;[1]
I'll not believe it. I could never deem,
As Payne Knight[2] did (the mythic mountaineer
5 Who travelled higher than he was born to live,
And showed sometimes the goitre[3] in his throat
Discoursing of an image seen through fog),
That Homer's heroes measured twelve feet high.
They were but men:—his Helen's hair turned gray
10 Like any plain Miss Smith's who wears a front;°   hairpiece
And Hector's infant whimpered at a plume[4]
As yours last Friday at a turkey-cock.
All actual heroes are essential men,
And all men possible heroes: every age,
15 Heroic in proportions, double-faced,
Looks backward and before, expects a morn
And claims an epos.°   epic poem
Ay, but every age
Appears to souls who live in 't (ask Carlyle)[5]
Most unheroic. Ours, for instance, ours:
20 The thinkers scout it, and the poets abound
Who scorn to touch it with a finger-tip:
A pewter age,—mixed metal, silver-washed;
An age of scum, spooned off the richer past,
An age of patches for old gaberdines,°   labor smocks
25 An age of mere transition, meaning nought
Except that what succeeds must shame it quite
If God please. That's wrong thinking, to my mind,
And wrong thoughts make poor poems.
Every age,

---

[1] **Agamemnon . . . gods:** In Greek mythology, Agamemnon returned from the Trojan war and was murdered by his wife, Clytemnestra. Zeus, the ruler of the Greek gods, was nursed by a goat.
[2] **Payne Knight:** Richard Payne Knight (1750–1824), an English philologist who argued that not all of the Elgin Marbles, sculptures brought from the Parthenon to England by Lord Elgin, were Greek.
[3] **goitre:** Goiter, an enlargement of the thyroid gland due to a lack of iodine in water.
[4] **Hector's . . . plume:** In the *Iliad,* Hector's son cries at the sight of his father's helmet.
[5] **ask Carlyle:** Thomas Carlyle (1795–1881), a British essayist who called for a renewed interest in heroism.

30   Through being beheld too close, is ill-discerned
      By those who have not lived past it. We'll suppose
      Mount Athos carved, as Alexander schemed,
      To some colossal statue of a man.[6]
      The peasants, gathering brushwood in his ear,
35   Had guessed as little as the browsing goats
      Of form or feature of humanity
      Up there,—in fact, had travelled five miles off
      Or ere the giant image broke on them,
      Full human profile, nose and chin distinct,
40   Mouth, muttering rhythms of silence up the sky
      And fed at evening with the blood of suns;
      Grand torso,—hand, that flung perpetually
      The largesse of a silver river down
      To all the country pastures. 'Tis even thus
45   With times we live in,—evermore too great
      To be apprehended near.
                     But poets should
      Exert a double vision; should have eyes
      To see near things as comprehensively
50   As if afar they took their point of sight,
      And distant things as intimately deep
      As if they touched them. Let us strive for this.
      I do distrust the poet who discerns.
      No character or glory in his times,
55   And trundles back his soul five hundred years,
      Past moat and drawbridge, into a castle-court,
      To sing—oh, not of lizard or of toad
      Alive i' the ditch there,—'twere excusable,
      But of some black chief, half knight, half sheep-lifter,
60   Some beauteous dame, half chattel and half queen,
      As dead as must be, for the greater part,
      The poems made on their chivalric bones;
      And that's no wonder: death inherits death.

      Nay, if there's room for poets in this world
65   A little overgrown (I think there is),
      Their sole work is to represent the age,
      Their age, not Charlemagne's,[7]—this live, throbbing age,
      That brawls, cheats, maddens, calculates, aspires,

---

[6] **We'll suppose . . . man:** According to legend, Alexander the Great (356 B.C.–323 B.C.) considered
the sculptor Dionocrates's proposal to carve Mount Athos into a statue of the conquerer.
[7] **Charlemagne's:** Charles the Great (742–814 A.D.), ruler of a European empire.

And spends more passion, more heroic heat,
70   Betwixt the mirrors of its drawing-rooms,
Than Roland[8] with his knights at Roncesvalles.
To flinch from modern varnish, coat or flounce,
Cry out for togas and the picturesque,
Is fatal,—foolish too. King Arthur's self
75   Was commonplace to Lady Guenever;
And Camelot to minstrels seemed as flat
As Fleet Street[9] to our poets.
                                    Never flinch,
But still, unscrupulously epic, catch
80   Upon the burning lava of a song
The full-veined, heaving, double-breasted Age:
That, when the next shall come, the men of that
May touch the impress with reverent hand, and say
"Behold,—behold the paps° we all have sucked!   breasts
85   This bosom seems to beat still, or at least
It sets ours beating: this is living art,
Which thus presents and thus records true life."

WALT WHITMAN   (1819–1892)

One's-Self I Sing   (1867; 1871)

One's-Self I sing, a simple separate person,
Yet utter the word Democratic, the word En-Masse.

Of physiology from top to toe I sing,
Not physiognomy alone nor brain alone is worthy for the Muse, I
          say the Form complete is worthier far,
5   The Female equally with the Male I sing.

Of Life immense in passion, pulse, and power,
Cheerful, for freest action form'd under the laws divine,
The Modern Man I sing.

---

[8] **Roland:** Hero of *Chanson de Roland*, a medieval epic.
[9] **Fleet Street:** Center of the publishing district in London; Camelot was King Arthur's castle.

EMILY DICKINSON (1830–1886)

"Tell all the Truth but tell it slant—"
(ca. 1868; 1945)

Tell all the Truth but tell it slant—
Success in Circuit lies
Too bright for our infirm Delight
The Truth's superb surprise
5   As Lightning to the Children eased
With explanation kind
The Truth must dazzle gradually
Or every man be blind—

EMILY DICKINSON (1830–1886)

"This is my letter to the World" (ca. 1862; 1890)

This is my letter to the World
That never wrote to Me—
The simple News that Nature told—
With tender Majesty

5   Her Message is committed
To Hands I cannot see—
For love of Her—Sweet—countrymen—
Judge tenderly—of Me

THOMAS HARDY (1840–1928)

I Looked Up from My Writing (1916)

I looked up from my writing,
    And gave a start to see,
As if rapt in my inditing,
    The moon's full gaze on me.

5   Her meditative misty head
    Was spectral in its air,
And I involuntarily said,
    'What are you doing there?'

'Oh, I've been scanning pond and hole
10   And waterway hereabout
For the body of one with a sunken soul
     Who has put his life-light out.

'Did you hear his frenzied tattle?
     It was sorrow for his son
15 Who is slain in brutish battle,
     Though he has injured none.

'And now I am curious to look
     Into the blinkered mind
Of one who wants to write a book
20   In a world of such a kind.'

Her temper overwrought me,
     And I edged to shun her view,
For I felt assured she thought me
     One who should drown him too.

WILLIAM BUTLER YEATS (1865–1939)

Sailing to Byzantium[1] (1927)

I

That is no country for old men. The young
In one another's arms, birds in the trees
—Those dying generations—at their song,
The salmon-falls, the mackerel-crowded seas,
5 Fish, flesh, or fowl, commend all summer long
Whatever is begotten, born, and dies.
Caught in that sensual music all neglect
Monuments of unageing intellect.

II

An aged man is but a paltry thing,
10 A tattered coat upon a stick, unless
Soul clap its hands and sing, and louder sing

---

[1] **Byzantium:** Ancient city, near modern-day Istanbul, famous for its art and architecture. For Yeats, the art of Byzantium represented the pursuit of artifice, or an art form born of the intellect and not from a desire to convey the life of "natural things." See notes for Yeats's "Byzantium" on page 1536.

For every tatter in its mortal dress,
Nor is there singing school but studying
Monuments of its own magnificence;
15   And therefore I have sailed the seas and come
To the holy city of Byzantium.

III

O sages standing in God's holy fire
As in the gold mosaic of a wall,
Come from the holy fire, perne in a gyre,[2]
20   And be the singing-masters of my soul.
Consume my heart away; sick with desire
And fastened to a dying animal
It knows not what it is; and gather me
Into the artifice of eternity.

IV

25   Once out of nature I shall never take
My bodily form from any natural thing,
But such a form as Grecian goldsmiths make
Of hammered gold and gold enamelling
To keep a drowsy Emperor awake;
30   Or set upon a golden bough to sing
To lords and ladies of Byzantium
Of what is past, or passing, or to come.

JAMES WELDON JOHNSON   (1871–1938)

O Black and Unknown Bards   (1908)

O Black and unknown bards of long ago,
How came your lips to touch the sacred fire?
How, in your darkness, did you come to know
The power and beauty of the minstrel's lyre?
5   Who first from midst his bonds lifted his eyes?
Who first from out the still watch, lone and long,
Feeling the ancient faith of prophets rise
Within his dark-kept soul, burst into song?

---

[2] **perne in a gyre:** Yeats creates the verb "perne" from the noun "pern," a weaver's bobbin or spool.
Here the speaker asks the sages to "perne," or descend in a spiral pattern, into the gyres of history.

Heart of what slave poured out such melody
10   As "Steal away to Jesus"?[1] On its strains
His spirit must have nightly floated free,
Though still about his hands he felt his chains.
Who heard great "Jordan roll"? Whose starward eye
Saw chariot "swing low"? And who was he
15   That breathed that comforting, melodic sigh,
"Nobody knows de trouble I see"?

What merely living clod, what captive thing,
Could up toward God through all its darkness grope,
And find within its deadened heart to sing
20   These songs of sorrow, love, and faith, and hope?
How did it catch that subtle undertone,
That note in music heard not with the ears?
How sound the elusive reed, so seldom blown,
Which stirs the soul or melts the heart to tears?

25   Not that great German master[2] in his dream
Of harmonies that thundered 'mongst the stars
At the creation, ever heard a theme
Nobler than "Go down, Moses." Mark its bars,
How like a mighty trumpet-call they stir
30   The blood. Such are the notes that men have sung,
Going to valorous deeds; such tones there were
That helped make history when Time was young.

There is a wide, wide wonder in it all,
That from degraded rest and service toil
35   The fiery spirit of the seer should call
These simple children of the sun and soil
O black slave singers, gone, forgot, unfamed,
You—you alone, of all the long, long line
Of those who've sung untaught, unknown, unnamed,
40   Have stretched out upward, seeking the divine.

You sang not deeds of heroes or of kings;
No chant of bloody war, no exulting pæan°   song
Of arms-won triumphs; but your humble strings
You touched in chord with music empyrean.°   of highest heaven
45   You sang far better than you knew; the songs

---

[1] **"Steal away to Jesus":** This, and other quotations in the poem, refer to Negro spirituals.
[2] **great German master:** Gottfried Wilhelm Leibniz (1646–1716), philosopher.

That for your listeners' hungry hearts sufficed
Still live,—but more than this to you belongs:
You sang a race from wood and stone to Christ.

ALICE MOORE DUNBAR NELSON (1875–1935)

I Sit and Sew (1920)

I sit and sew—a useless task it seems,
My hands grown tired, my head weighed down with dreams—
The panoply of war, the martial tred of men,
Grim-faced, stern-eyed, gazing beyond the ken
5   Of lesser souls, whose eyes have not seen Death,
Nor learned to hold their lives but as a breath—
But—I must sit and sew.

I sit and sew—my heart aches with desire—
That pageant terrible, that fiercely pouring fire
10   On wasted fields, and writhing grotesque things
Once men. My soul in pity flings
Appealing cries, yearning only to go
There in that holocaust of hell, those fields of woe—
But—I must sit and sew.

15   The little useless seam, the idle patch;
Why dream I here beneath my homely thatch,
When there they lie in sodden mud and rain,
Pitifully calling me, the quick ones and the slain?
You need me, Christ! It is no roseate dream
20   That beckons me—this pretty futile seam,
It stifles me—God, must I sit and sew?

WALLACE STEVENS (1879–1955)

Of Modern Poetry (1942)

The poem of the mind in the act of finding
What will suffice. It has not always had
To find: the scene was set; it repeated what

Was in the script.
5   Then the theatre was changed
To something else. Its past was a souvenir.
It has to be living, to learn the speech of the place.
It has to face the men of the time and to meet
The women of the time. It has to think about war
10   And it has to find what will suffice. It has
To construct a new stage. It has to be on that stage
And, like an insatiable actor, slowly and
With meditation, speak words that in the ear,
In the delicatest ear of the mind, repeat,
15   Exactly, that which it wants to hear, at the sound
Of which, an invisible audience listens,
Not to the play, but to itself, expressed
In an emotion as of two people, as of two
Emotions becoming one. The actor is
20   A metaphysician in the dark, twanging
An instrument, twanging a wiry string that gives
Sounds passing through sudden rightnesses, wholly
Containing the mind, below which it cannot descend,
Beyond which it has no will to rise.
25   It must
Be the finding of a satisfaction, and may
Be of a man skating, a woman dancing, a woman
Combing. The poem of the act of the mind.

WILLIAM CARLOS WILLIAMS   (1883–1963)

The Red Wheelbarrow   (1923)

so much depends
upon

a red wheel
barrow

5   glazed with rain
water

beside the white
chickens.

EZRA POUND (1885–1973)

A Pact (1916)

I make a pact with you, Walt Whitman—
I have detested you long enough.
I come to you as a grown child
Who has had a pig-headed father;
5   I am old enough now to make friends.
It was you that broke the new wood,
Now is a time for carving.
We have one sap and one root—
Let there be commerce between us.

MARIANNE MOORE (1887–1972)

Poetry[1] (1921)

I, too, dislike it: there are things that are important beyond all this fiddle.
    Reading it, however, with a perfect contempt for it, one discovers in
    it after all, a place for the genuine.
        Hands that can grasp, eyes
5   that can dilate, hair that can rise
            if it must, these things are important not because a

high-sounding interpretation can be put upon them but because they are
    useful. When they become so derivative as to become unintelligible,
    the same thing may be said for all of us, that we
10   do not admire what
        we cannot understand: the bat
            holding on upside down or in quest of something to

eat, elephants pushing, a wild horse taking a roll, a tireless wolf under
    a tree, the immovable critic twitching his skin like a horse that feels
15   a flea, the base-
    ball fan, the statistician—
        nor is it valid
            to discriminate against 'business documents and

---

[1] **Poetry:** Later in life, Moore cut this poem to three lines.

school-books';[2] all these phenomena are important. One must
      make a distinction
20   however: when dragged into prominence by half poets, the
      result is not poetry,
  nor till the poets among us can be
    'literalists of
    the imagination'[3]—above
      insolence and triviality and can present

25   for inspection, 'imaginary gardens with real toads in them', shall
      we have
  it. In the meantime, if you demand on the one hand,
  the raw material of poetry in
    all its rawness and
    that which is on the other hand
30   genuine, you are interested in poetry.

ARCHIBALD MACLEISH   (1892–1982)

Ars Poetica   (1926)

A poem should be palpable and mute
As a globed fruit,

Dumb
As old medallions to the thumb,

5   Silent as the sleeve-worn stone
Of casement ledges where the moss has grown—

A poem should be wordless
As the flight of birds.

                *

A poem should be motionless in time
10   As the moon climbs,

---

[2] **business documents and school-books:** "*Diary of Tolstoy* (Dutton), p. 84. 'Where the boundary between prose and poetry lies, I shall never be able to understand. The question is raised in manuals of style, yet the answer to it lies beyond me. Poetry is verse: prose is not verse. Or else poetry is everything with the exception of business documents and school-books" [Moore's note].

[3] **literalists of the imagination:** "Yeats: *Ideas of Good and Evil* (A. H. Bullen), p. 182. 'The limitation of [Blake's] view was from the very intensity of his vision; he was a too literal realist of the imagination, as others are of nature; and because he believed that the figures seen by the mind's eye, when exalted by inspiration, were "eternal existences," symbols of divine essences, he hated every grace of style that might obscure their lineaments' " [Moore's note].

Leaving, as the moon releases
Twig by twig the night-entangled trees,

Leaving, as the moon behind the winter leaves,
Memory by memory the mind—

15 A poem should be motionless in time
As the moon climbs.

                                        *

A poem should be equal to:
Not true.

For all the history of grief
20 An empty doorway and a maple leaf.

For love
The leaning grasses and two lights above the sea—

A poem should not mean
But be.

E. E. CUMMINGS (1894–1962)

"since feeling is first" (1926)

since feeling is first
who pays any attention
to the syntax of things
will never wholly kiss you;

5 wholly to be a fool
while Spring is in the world

my blood approves,
and kisses are a better fate
than wisdom
10 lady i swear by all flowers.   Don't cry
—the best gesture of my brain is less than
your eyelids' flutter which says

we are for each other:then
laugh,leaning back in my arms
15 for life's not a paragraph

And death i think is no parenthesis

HART CRANE (1899–1932)

The Broken Tower (1933)

The bell-rope that gathers God at dawn
Dispatches me as though I dropped down the knell
Of a spent day—to wander the cathedral lawn
From pit to crucifix, feet chill on steps from hell.

5 Have you not heard, have you not seen that corps
Of shadows in the tower, whose shoulders sway
Antiphonal carillons° launched before   bells
The stars are caught and hived in the sun's ray?

The bells, I say, the bells break down their tower;
10 And swing I know not where. Their tongues engrave
Membrane through marrow, my long-scattered score
Of broken intervals. . . . And I, their sexton° slave!   church officer

Oval encyclicals in canyons heaping
The impasse high with choir. Banked voices slain!
15 Pagodas, campaniles° with reveilles[1] outleaping—   bell towers
O terraced echoes prostrate on the plain! . . .

And so it was I entered the broken world
To trace the visionary company of love, its voice
An instant in the wind (I know not whither hurled)
20 But not for long to hold each desperate choice.

My word I poured. But was it cognate, scored
Of that tribunal monarch of the air
Whose thigh embronzes earth, strikes crystal Word[2]
In wounds pledged once to hope—cleft to despair?

25 The steep encroachments of my blood left me
No answer (could blood hold such a lofty tower
As flings the question true?)—or is it she
Whose sweet mortality stirs latent power?—

And through whose pulse I hear, counting the strokes
30 My veins recall and add, revived and sure

---

[1] **reveilles:** Signals sounded in the morning.
[2] **Word:** See John 1.14: "And the Word was made flesh, and dwelt among us."

The angelus[3] of wars my chest evokes:
What I hold healed, original now, and pure . . .

And builds, within, a tower that is not stone
(Not stone can jacket heaven)—but slip
35 Of pebbles—visible wings of silence sown
In azure circles, widening as they dip

The matrix of the heart, lift down the eye
That shrines the quiet lake and swells a tower . . .
The commodious, tall decorum of that sky
40 Unseals her earth, and lifts love in its shower.

LANGSTON HUGHES (1902–1967)

Esthete[1] in Harlem (1926)

Strange,
That in this nigger place
I should meet life face to face;
When, for years, I had been seeking
5 Life in places gentler-speaking,
Until I came to this vile street
And found Life stepping on my feet!

ROBERT PENN WARREN (1905–1989)

Heart of Autumn (1978)

Wind finds the northwest gap, fall comes.
Today, under gray cloud-scud and over gray
Wind-flicker of forest, in perfect formation, wild geese
Head for a land of warm water, the *boom,* the lead pellet.

5 Some crumple in air, fall. Some stagger, recover control,
Then take the last glide for a far glint of water. None
Knows what has happened. Now, today, watching
How tirelessly *V* upon *V* arrows the season's logic,

---

[3] **angelus:** Bell signal that announces the appropriate time for devotional prayer in the morning, at noon, and in the evening.
[1] **Esthete:** One who expresses great appreciation for the beauty of art and nature.

Do I know my own story? At least, they know
10   When the hour comes for the great wing-beat. Sky-strider,
Star-strider—they rise, and the imperial utterance,
Which cries out for distance, quivers in the wheeling sky.

That much they know, and in their nature know
The path of pathlessness, with all the joy
15   Of destiny fulfilling its own name.
I have known time and distance, but not why I am here.

Path of logic, path of folly, all
The same—and I stand, my face lifted now skyward,
Hearing the high beat, my arms outstretched in the tingling
20   Process of transformation, and soon tough legs,

With folded feet, trail in the sounding vacuum of passage,
And my heart is impacted with a fierce impulse
To unwordable utterance—
Toward sunset, at a great height.

W. H. AUDEN (1907–1973)

"The Truest Poetry Is the Most Feigning"[1] (1953)
(for Edgar Wind)

By all means sing of love but, if you do,
Please make a rare old proper hullabaloo:
When ladies ask *How much do you love me?*
The Christian answer is *così-così;*[2]
5   But poets are not celibate divines:
Had Dante[3] said so, who would read his lines?
Be subtle, various, ornamental, clever,
And do not listen to those critics ever
Whose crude provincial gullets crave in books
10   Plain cooking made still plainer by plain cooks,
As though the Muse preferred her half-wit sons;
Good poets have a weakness for bad puns.

---

[1] **"The . . . Feigning":** From Shakespeare's *As You Like It,* Act III, Scene iii.
[2] ***così-così:*** Italian, "so-so."
[3] **Dante:** Dante Alighieri (1265–1321), Italian poet and author of *The Divine Comedy.* In the poem, Beatrice, a sort of Muse, guides Dante through Paradise.

Suppose your Beatrice be, as usual, late,
And you would tell us how it feels to wait,
15   You're free to think, what may be even true,
You're so in love that one hour seems like two,
But write—*As I sat waiting for her call,*
Each second longer darker seemed than all
(Something like this but more elaborate still)
20   *Those raining centuries it took to fill*
That quarry whence Endymion's Love[4] *was torn;*
From such ingenious fibs are poems born.
Then, should she leave you for some other guy,
Or ruin you with debts, or go and die,
25   No metaphor, remember, can express
A real historical unhappiness;
Your tears have value if they make us gay;
O Happy Grief! is all sad verse can say.

The living girl's your business (some odd sorts
30   Have been an inspiration to men's thoughts):
Yours may be old enough to be your mother,
Or have one leg that's shorter than the other,
Or play Lacrosse or do the Modern Dance,
To you that's destiny, to us it's chance;
35   We cannot love your love till she take on,
Through you, the wonders of a paragon.
Sing her triumphant passage to our land,
The sun her footstool, the moon in her right hand,
And seven planets blazing in her hair,
40   Queen of the Night and Empress of the Air;
Tell how her fleet by nine king swans is led,
Wild geese write magic letters overhead
And hippocampi[5] follow in her wake
With Amphisboene,[6] gentle for her sake;
45   Sing her descent on the exulting shore
To bless the vines and put an end to war.

---

[4] **Endymion's Love:** Endymion, a handsome shepherd so loved by Selene, the moon goddess, that she asked Zeus to give him eternal life so that he would never leave her. Zeus blessed Endymion with eternal sleep, and every night Selene visited him where he was buried on Mt. Latmus.
[5] **hippocampi:** In Greek mythology, one of the half horse, half sea-monsters who pulled Poseidon's chariot.
[6] **Amphisboene:** In classical mythology, serpents with heads at each end of their bodies.

If half-way through such praises of your dear,
Riot and shooting fill the streets with fear,
And overnight as in some terror dream
50   Poets are suspect with the New Regime,
Stick at your desk and hold your panic in,
What you are writing may still save your skin:
Re-sex the pronouns, add a few details,
And, lo, a panegyric° ode which hails   formal
55   (How is the Censor, bless his heart, to know?)
The new pot-bellied Generalissimo.
Some epithets, of course, like *lily-breasted*
Need modifying to say, *lion-chested*,
A title *Goddess of wry-necks and wrens*
60   To *Great Reticulator of the fens*,
But in an hour your poem qualifies
For a State pension or His annual prize,
And you will die in bed (which He will not:
That public nuisance will be hanged or shot).
65   Though honest Iago,[7] true to form, will write
Shame! in your margins, *Toady! Hypocrite!*,
True hearts, clear heads will hear the note of glory
And put inverted commas round the story,
Thinking—*Old Sly-boots! We shall never know*
70   *Her name or nature. Well, it's better so.*

For given Man, by birth, by education,
Imago Dei[8] who forgot his station,
The self-made creature who himself unmakes,
The only creature ever made who fakes,
75   With no more nature in his loving smile
Than in his theories of a natural style,
What but tall tales, the luck of verbal playing,
Can trick his lying nature into saying
That love, or truth in any serious sense,
80   Like orthodoxy, is a reticence?

---

[7] **Iago:** Iago, villain in William Shakespeare's *Othello*, who tricked Othello into murdering his wife Desdemona.
[8] **Imago Dei:** Latin, "image of God."

J. V. CUNNINGHAM   (1911–1985)

For My Contemporaries   (1942)

How time reverses
The proud in heart!
I now make verses
Who aimed at art.

5   But I sleep well.
Ambitious boys
Whose big lines swell
With spiritual noise,

Despise me not,
10   And be not queasy
To praise somewhat:
Verse is not easy.

But rage who will.
Time that procured me
15   Good sense and skill
Of madness cured me.

DYLAN THOMAS   (1914–1953)

In My Craft or Sullen Art   (1945; 1946)

In my craft or sullen art
Exercised in the still night
When only the moon rages
And the lovers lie abed
5   With all their griefs in their arms,
I labour by singing light
Not for ambition or bread
Or the strut and trade of charms
On the ivory stages
10   But for the common wages
Of their most secret heart.

Not for the proud man apart
From the raging moon I write
On these spindrift pages

15 Nor for the towering dead
With their nightingales and psalms
But for the lovers, their arms
Round the griefs of the ages,
Who pay no praise or wages
20 Nor heed my craft or art.

ROBERT LOWELL (1917–1977)

Epilogue (1977)

Those blessèd structures, plot and rhyme—
why are they no help to me now
I want to make
something imagined, not recalled?
5 I hear the noise of my own voice:
The painter's vision is not a lens,
it trembles to caress the light.
But sometimes everything I write
with the threadbare art of my eye
10 seems a snapshot,
lurid, rapid, garish, grouped,
heightened from life,
yet paralyzed by fact.
All's misalliance.
15 Yet why not say what happened?
Pray for the grace of accuracy
Vermeer[1] gave to the sun's illumination
stealing like the tide across a map
to his girl solid with yearning.
20 We are poor passing facts,
warned by that to give
each figure in the photograph
his living name.

---

[1] **Vermeer:** Jan Vermeer (1632–1675), a Dutch painter recognized for his unique treatment of light.

GWENDOLYN BROOKS (1917–2000)

my dreams, my works, must wait till after hell (1945)

I hold my honey and I store my bread
In little jars and cabinets of my will.
I label clearly, and each latch and lid
I bid, Be firm till I return from hell.
5   I am very hungry. I am incomplete.
And none can tell when I may dine again.
No man can give me any word but Wait,
The puny light. I keep eyes pointed in;
Hoping that, when the devil days of my hurt
10 Drag out to their last dregs and I resume
On such legs as are left me, in such heart
As I can manage, remember to go home,
My taste will not have turned insensitive
To honey and bread old purity could love.

DENISE LEVERTOV (1923–1997)

The Dog of Art (1959)

That dog with daisies for eyes
who flashes forth
flame of his very self at every bark
is the Dog of Art.
5   Worked in wool, his blind eyes
look inward to caverns and jewels
which they see perfectly,
and his voice
measures forth the treasure
10 in music sharp and loud,
sharp and bright,
bright flaming barks,
and growling smoky soft, the Dog
of Art turns to the world
15 the quietness of his eyes.

LOUIS SIMPSON (1923–   )

American Poetry (1963)

Whatever it is, it must have
A stomach that can digest
Rubber, coal, uranium, moons, poems.

Like the shark, it contains a shoe.
5   It must swim for miles through the desert
Uttering cries that are almost human.

FRANK O'HARA (1926–1966)

Why I Am Not a Painter (1971)

I am not a painter, I am a poet.
Why? I think I would rather be
a painter, but I am not. Well,

for instance, Mike Goldberg[1]
5   is starting a painting. I drop in.
"Sit down and have a drink" he
says. I drink; we drink. I look
up. "You have SARDINES in it."
"Yes, it needed something there."
10   "Oh." I go and the days go by
and I drop in again. The painting
is going on, and I go, and the days
go by. I drop in. The painting is
finished. "Where's SARDINES?"
15   All that's left is just
letters, "It was too much," Mike says.

But me? One day I am thinking of
a color: orange. I write a line
about orange. Pretty soon it is a
20   whole page of words, not lines.
Then another page. There should be

---

[1] **Mike Goldberg:** Mike Goldberg (1924–   ), New York artist who painted the silk screens for
O'Hara's *Odes* (1960).

so much more, not of orange, of
words, of how terrible orange is
and life. Days go by. It is even in
25   prose, I am a real poet. My poem
is finished and I haven't mentioned
orange yet. It's twelve poems, I call
it ORANGES. And one day in a gallery
I see Mike's painting, called SARDINES.

ALASTAIR REID (1926–   )

A Lesson in Music (1963)

Play the tune again: but this time
with more regard for the movement at the source of it
and less attention to time. Time falls
curiously in the course of it.

5   Play the tune again: not watching
your fingering, but forgetting, letting flow
the sound till it surrounds you. Do not count
or even think. Let go.

Play the tune again: but try to be
10   nobody, nothing, as though the pace
of the sound were your heart beating, as though
the music were your face.

Play the tune again. It should be easier
to think less every time of the notes, of the measure.
15   It is all an arrangement of silence. Be silent, and then
play it for your pleasure.

Play the tune again; and this time, when it ends,
do not ask me what I think. Feel what is happening
strangely in the room as the sound glooms over
20   you, me, everything.

Now,
play the tune again.

JOHN ASHBERY (1927–   )

Late Echo (1979)

Alone with our madness and favorite flower
We see that there really is nothing left to write about.
Or rather, it is necessary to write about the same old things
In the same way, repeating the same things over and over
5   For love to continue and be gradually different.

Beehives and ants have to be reexamined eternally
And the color of the day put in
Hundreds of times and varied from summer to winter
For it to get slowed down to the pace of an authentic
10   Saraband[1] and huddle there, alive and resting.

Only then can the chronic inattention
Of our lives drape itself around us, conciliatory
And with one eye on those long tan plush shadows
That speak so deeply into our unprepared knowledge
15   Of ourselves, the talking engines of our day.

TED HUGHES (1930–1998)

The Thought-Fox (1957)

I imagine this midnight moment's forest:
Something else is alive
Beside the clock's loneliness
And this blank page where my fingers move.

5   Through the window I see no star:
Something more near
Though deeper within darkness
Is entering the loneliness:

Cold, delicately as the dark snow
10   A fox's nose touches twig, leaf;
Two eyes serve a movement, that now
And again now, and now, and now

Sets neat prints into the snow
Between trees, and warily a lame

---

[1] **Saraband:** Popular court dance of the seventeenth century.

15 Shadow lags by stump and in hollow
    Of a body that is bold to come

    Across clearings, an eye,
    A widening deepening greenness,
    Brilliantly, concentratedly,
20 Coming about its own business

    Till, with a sudden sharp hot stink of fox,
    It enters the dark hole of the head.
    The window is starless still; the clock ticks,
    The page is printed.

ETHERIDGE KNIGHT (1931–1991)

For Black Poets Who Think of Suicide (1968)

    Black Poets should live—not leap
    From steel bridges (Like the white boys do.
    Black Poets should *live*—not lay
    Their necks on railroad tracks (like the white boys do.
5   Black Poets should seek—but not search too much
    In sweet dark caves, nor hunt for snipe°   marsh birds
    Down psychic trails (like the white boys do.

    For Black Poets belong to Black People. Are
    The Flutes of Black Lovers. Are
10 The Organs of Black Sorrows. Are
    The Trumpets of Black Warriors.
    Let All Black poets die as trumpets,
    And be buried in the dust of marching feet.

LINDA PASTAN (1932–   )

Ethics (1981)

    In ethics class so many years ago
    our teacher asked this question every fall:
    if there were a fire in a museum
    which would you save, a Rembrandt[1] painting
5   or an old woman who hadn't many
    years left anyhow? Restless on hard chairs

---

[1] **Rembrandt:** Rembrandt van Rijn (1606–1669), an influential Dutch painter.

caring little for pictures or old age
we'd opt one year for life, the next for art
and always half-heartedly. Sometimes
10   the woman borrowed my grandmother's face
leaving her usual kitchen to wander
some drafty, half-imagined museum.
One year, feeling clever, I replied
why not let the woman decide herself?
15   Linda, the teacher would report, eschews
the burdens of responsibility.
This fall in a real museum I stand
before a real Rembrandt, old woman,
or nearly so, myself. The colors
20   within this frame are darker than autumn,
darker even than winter—the browns of earth,
though earth's most radiant elements burn
through the canvas. I know now that woman
and painting and season are almost one
25   and all beyond saving by children.

MARK STRAND (1934–   )

Eating Poetry (1968)

Ink runs from the corners of my mouth.
There is no happiness like mine.
I have been eating poetry.

The librarian does not believe what she sees.
5   Her eyes are sad
and she walks with her hands in her dress.

The poems are gone.
The light is dim.
The dogs are on the basement stairs and coming up.

10   Their eyeballs roll,
their blond legs burn like brush.
The poor librarian begins to stamp her feet and weep.
She does not understand.
When I get on my knees and lick her hand,
15   she screams.

I am a new man.
I snarl at her and bark.
I romp with joy in the bookish dark.

CHARLES WRIGHT (1935–   )

Yard Work (1996)

I think that someone will remember us in another time,
Sappho[1] once said—more or less—
Her words caught
Between the tongue's tip and the first edge of the invisible.

5 I hope so, myself now caught
Between the edge of the landscape and the absolute,
Which is the same place, and the same sound,
That she made.

Meanwhile, let's stick to business.
10 Everything else does, the landscape, the absolute, the invisible.
My job is yard work—
I take this inchworm, for instance, and move it from here to there.

SANDRA M. GILBERT (1936–   )

The Return of the Muse

You always knew you wrote for him, you said.
He is the father of my art, the one who watches all night,
chain-smoking, never smiling, never satisfied.
You liked him because he was carved from glaciers,
5 because you had to give him strong wine to make him human,
because he flushed once, like a November sunset,
when you pleased him.

But you didn't love him.
You thought that was part of the bargain.
10 He'd always be there like a blood relative,
a taciturn uncle or cousin,
if you didn't love him. You'd hand him poems,
he'd inspect them, smoke, sip, a business deal,
and that would be that.

15 Then he went away and you hardly noticed.
Except you were happy, you danced on the lawn,

---

[1] **Sappho:** Sixth-century B.C. lyric poet of Lesbos.

swelled like a melon, lay naked long mornings,
brushed your hair more than you needed.
Your breasts grew pink and silky,
20   you hummed, you sucked the pulp of oranges, you forgot
all about words.

         And when you were
absolutely ignorant,
         he came back,
25   his jacket of ice flashed white light,
his cap of pallor bent toward you, genteel, unsmiling.
He lit a cigarette, crossed his legs,
told you how clumsy you were.

Ah, then, love seized you like a cramp,
30   you doubled over in the twist of love.
You shrieked. You gave birth to enormous poems.

He looked embarrassed and said how bad they were.
They became beasts, they grew fangs and beards.
You sent them against him like an army.

35   He said they were all right
but added that he found you, personally,
unattractive.

         You howled with love,
you spun like a dervish with rage, you
40   kept on writing.

LES MURRAY (1938–   )

Poetry and Religion (1987)

Religions are poems. They concert
our daylight and dreaming mind, our
emotions, instinct, breath and native gesture

into the only whole thinking: poetry.
5   Nothing's said till it's dreamed out in words
and nothing's true that figures in words only.

A poem, compared with an arrayed religion,
may be like a soldier's one short marriage night
to die and live by. But that is a small religion.

10 Full religion is the large poem in loving repetition;
  like any poem, it must be inexhaustible and complete
  with turns where we ask Now why did the poet do that?

  You can't pray a lie, said Huckleberry Finn;
  you can't poe one either. It is the same mirror:
15 mobile, glancing, we call it poetry,

  fixed centrally, we call it a religion,
  and God is the poetry caught in any religion,
  caught, not imprisoned. Caught as in a mirror

  that he attracted, being in the world as poetry
20 is in the poem, a law against its closure.
  There'll always be religion around while there is poetry

  or a lack of it. Both are given, and intermittent,
  as the action of those birds—crested pigeon, rosella parrot—
  who fly with wings shut, then beating, and again shut.

CHARLES SIMIC (1938–   )

Dismantling the Silence (1971)

  Take down its ears first,
  Carefully, so they don't spill over.
  With a sharp whistle slit its belly open.
  If there are ashes in it, close your eyes
5 And blow them whichever way the wind is pointing.
  If there's water, sleeping water,
  Bring the root of a flower, that hasn't drunk for a month.

  When you reach the bones,
  And you haven't got a dog with you,
10 And you haven't got a pine coffin
  And a cart pulled by oxen to make them rattle,
  Slip them quickly under your skin.
  Next time you hunch your shoulders
  You'll feel them pressing against your own.

15 It is now pitch dark.
  Slowly and with patience

Search for its heart. You will need
To crawl far into the empty heavens
To hear it beat.

SEAMUS HEANEY (1939–   )

Personal Helicon (1966)
for Michael Longley

As a child, they could not keep me from wells
And old pumps with buckets and windlasses.
I loved the dark drop, the trapped sky, the smells
Of waterweed, fungus and dank moss.

5 One, in a brickyard, with a rotted board top.
I savoured the rich crash when a bucket
Plummeted down at the end of a rope.
So deep you saw no reflection in it.

A shallow one under a dry stone ditch
10 Fructified like any aquarium.
When you dragged out long roots from the soft mulch
A white face hovered over the bottom.

Others had echoes, gave back your own call
With a clean new music in it. And one
15 Was scaresome, for there, out of ferns and tall
Foxgloves, a rat slapped across my reflection.

Now, to pry into roots, to finger slime,
To stare, big-eyed Narcissus,[1] into some spring
Is beneath all adult dignity. I rhyme
20 To see myself, to set the darkness echoing.

---

[1] **Narcissus:** In Greek mythology, a beautiful young man who fell in love with his own reflection in a
pool of water.

JOSEPH BRODSKY (1940–1996)
trans. from the Russian by the author

A Polar Explorer (1977)

All the huskies are eaten. There is no space
left in the diary. And the beads of quick
words scatter over his spouse's sepia-shaded face
adding the date in question like a mole to her lovely cheek.
5   Next, the snapshot of his sister. He doesn't spare his kin:
what's been reached is the highest possible latitude!
And, like the silk stocking of a burlesque half-nude
queen, it climbs up his thigh: gangrene.

ROBERT HASS (1941–   )

Meditation at Lagunitas[1] (1979)

All the new thinking is about loss.
In this it resembles all the old thinking.
The idea, for example, that each particular erases
the luminous clarity of a general idea. That the clown-
5   faced woodpecker probing the dead sculpted trunk
of that black birch is, by his presence,
some tragic falling off from a first world
of undivided light. Or the other notion that,
because there is in this world no one thing
10   to which the bramble of *blackberry* corresponds,
a word is elegy to what it signifies.
We talked about it late last night and in the voice
of my friend, there was a thin wire of grief, a tone
almost querulous. After a while I understood that,
15   talking this way, everything dissolves: *justice,*
pine, hair, woman, you and *I.* There was a woman
I made love to and I remembered how, holding
her small shoulders in my hands sometimes,
I felt a violent wonder at her presence
20   like a thirst for salt, for my childhood river
with its island willows, silly music from the pleasure boat,
muddy places where we caught the little orange-silver fish
called *pumpkinseed.* It hardly had to do with her.
Longing, we say, because desire is full

---

[1] **Lagunitas:** Small town near San Francisco, California.

25 of endless distances. I must have been the same to her.
But I remember so much, the way her hands dismantled bread,
the thing her father said that hurt her, what
she dreamed. There are moments when the body is as numinous[2]
as words, days that are the good flesh continuing.
30 Such tenderness, those afternoons and evenings,
saying *blackberry, blackberry, blackberry.*

DAVE SMITH (1942–   )

The Roundhouse[1] Voices (1979)

In full flare of sunlight I came here, man-tall but thin
as a pinstripe, and stood outside the rusted fence
with its crown of iron thorns while
the soot cut into our lungs with tiny diamonds.
5 I walked through houses with my grain-lovely slugger
from Louisville[2] that my uncle bought and stood
in the sun that made its glove soft on my hand
until I saw my chance to crawl under and get past
anyone who would demand a badge and a name.

10 The guard hollered that I could get the hell from there quick
when I popped in his face like a thief. All I ever wanted
to steal was life and you can't get that easy
in the grind of a railyard. *You can't catch me
lardass, I can go left or right good as the Mick,*[3]
15 I hummed to him, holding my slugger by the neck
for a bunt laid smooth where the coal cars
jerked and let me pass between tracks
until, in a slide on ash, I fell safe and heard
the wheeze of his words: *Who the hell are you, kid?*

20 I hear them again tonight Uncle, hard as big brakeshoes,
when I lean over your face in the box of silk. The years
you spent hobbling from room to room alone crawl
up my legs and turn this house to another
house, round and black as defeat, where slugging

---

[2] **numinous:** Filled with a divine presence.
[1] **Roundhouse:** Circular railway building.
[2] **Louisville:** The "Louisville Slugger," a popular brand of baseball bats manufactured in Louisville, Kentucky.
[3] **the Mick:** Mickey Mantle (1931–1997), a famous baseball player.

25   comes easy when you whip the gray softball over
        the glass diesel globe. Footsteps thump on the stairs
        like that fat ball against bricks and when I miss
        I hear you warn me to watch the timing, to keep
        my eyes on your hand and forget the fence,

30   hearing also that other voice that keeps me out and away
        from you on a day worth playing good ball. Hearing
        Who the hell . . . I see myself, like a burning speck
        of cinder come down the hill and through a tunnel
        of porches like stands, running on deep ash,
35   and I give him the finger, whose face still gleams
        clear as a B & O[4] headlight, just to make him get up
        and chase me into a dream of scoring at your feet.
        At Christmas that guard staggered home sobbing,
        the thing in his chest tight as a torque wrench.
40   In the summer I did not have to run and now

        who is the one who dreams of a drink as he leans over
        tools you kept bright as a first-girl's promise? I
        have no one to run from or to, nobody to give
        my finger to as I steal his peace. Uncle, the light
45   bleeds on your gray face like the high barbed wire
        shadows I had to get through and maybe you don't remember
        you said to come back, to wait and you'd show me
        the right way to take a hard pitch
        in the sun that shudders on the ready man. I'm here

50   though this is a day I did not want to see. In the roundhouse
        the rasp and heel-click of compressors is still,
        soot lies deep in every greasy fingerprint.
        I called you from the pits and you did not come up
        and I felt the fear when I stood on the tracks
55   that are like stars which never lead us
        into any kind of light and I don't know who'll
        tell me now when the guard sticks his blind snoot
        between us: take off and beat the bastard out.
        Can you hear him over the yard, grabbing his chest,
60   cry out *Who the goddamn hell are you, kid?*

        I gave him every name in the book, Uncle, but he caught us
        and what good did all those hours of coaching do?
        You lie on your back, eyeless forever, and I think
        how once I climbed to the top of a diesel and stared

---

[4] **B & O:** Baltimore & Ohio, a railway line.

65   into that gray roundhouse glass where, in anger,
      you threw up the ball and made a star
      to swear at greater than the Mick ever dreamed.
      It has been years but now I know what followed there
      every morning the sun came up, not light
70   but the puffing bad-bellied light of words.

      All day I have held your hand, trying to say back that life,
      to get under that fence with words I lined
      and linked up and steamed into a cold room
      where the illusion of hope means skin torn in boxes
75   of tools. The footsteps come pounding into words
      and even the finger I give death is words
      that won't let us be what we wanted, each one
      chasing and being chased by dreams in a dark place.
      Words are all we ever were and they did us
80   no damn good. Do you hear that?

      Do you hear the words that, in oiled gravel, you gave me
      when you set my feet in the right stance to swing?
      They are coal-hard and they come in wings
      and loops like despair not even the Mick
85   could knock out of this room, words softer
      than the centers of hearts in guards or uncles,
      words skinned and numbed by too many bricks.
      I have had enough of them and bring them back here
      where the tick and creak of everything dies
90   in your tiny starlight and I stand down
      on my knees to cry, *Who the hell are you, kid?*

NIKKI GIOVANNI (1943–   )

Poetry (1979)

      poetry is motion graceful
      as a fawn
      gentle as a teardrop
      strong like the eye
5   finding peace in a crowded room

      we poets tend to think
      our words are golden
      though emotion speaks too

loudly to be defined
10   by silence

sometimes after midnight or just before
the dawn
we sit typewriter in hand
pulling loneliness around us
15   forgetting our lovers or children
who are sleeping
ignoring the weary wariness
of our own logic
to compose a poem
20   no one understands it
it never says "love me" for poets are
beyond love
it never says "accept me" for poems seek not
acceptance but controversy
25   it only says "i am" and therefore
i concede that you are too

a poem is pure energy
horizontally contained
between the mind
30   of the poet and the ear of the reader
if it does not sing discard the ear
for poetry is song
if it does not delight discard
the heart for poetry is joy
35   if it does not inform then close
off the brain for it is dead
if it cannot heed the insistent message
that life is precious

which is all we poets
40   wrapped in our loneliness
are trying to say

JAMES TATE (1943–   )

When the Nomads Come Over the Hill (1971)

When the nomads come over the hill
on the wheatstraw camels
the angel of joy crawls down a long hallway
and the green vegetables in the abandoned cart
5   pour into blue flames

old men by the fountain rise
and bid one another adieu
the bright sun is rinsed in blackest ink
snakes sleep on their backs
10   around the golden sundial
giant night hides in the storyteller's pupils
and the wind is divided
by a well-placed needle
when the nomads come over the hill
15   with their invisible language.

MICHAEL PALMER (1943–   )

Notes for Echo Lake 3 (1981)

Words that come in smoke and go.

Some things he kept, some he kept and lost. He loved the French
poets fell through the partly open door.

And I as it is, I as the one but less than one in it. I was the blue against
5   red and a voice that emptied, and I is that one with broken back.

While April is ours and dark, as something always stands for
what is: dying elm, headless man, winter—

salamander, chrysalis,

fire—

10   grammar and silence.

Or grammar against silence. Years later they found themselves talking in a crowd. Her white cat had been killed in the woods behind
her house. It had been a good possibly even a terrible winter. Ice
had coated the limbs of the hawthorn and lilac, lovely but dan-
15   gerous. Travel plans had been made then of necessity abandoned.
At different times entire weeks had seemed to disappear. She wondered what initially they had agreed not to discuss.

Some things he kept while some things he kept apart.

As Robert's call on Tuesday asking whether I knew that Zukofsky[1]
20   had died a couple of days before. The call came as I was reading
a copy of Larry Rivers' talk at Frank O'Hara's[2] funeral (July, 1966),

---

[1] **Zukofsky:** Louis Zukofsky (1904–1978), an American poet.
[2] **Larry Rivers' . . . O'Hara's:** Larry Rivers (1923–2002), American painter and sculptor. Frank O'Hara
(1926–1966), an American poet.

"He was a quarter larger than usual. Every few inches there was some sewing composed of dark blue thread. Some stitching was straight and three or four inches long, others were longer and semi-
25   circular . . ."

As Robert's call on Tuesday a quarter larger than usual asking whether I knew whether I knew. Blue thread every few inches, straight and semi-circular, and sand and wet snow. Blue snow a couple of days before. Whether I know whatever I know.

30   The letters of the words of our legs and arms. What he had seen or thought he'd seen within the eye, voices overheard rising and falling.

And if each conversation has no end, then composition is a plac- ing beside or with and is endless, broken threads of cloud driven from the west by afternoon wind.

35   The letters of the words of our legs and arms. In the garden he dreamt he saw four bearded men and listened to them discussing metaphor. They are standing at the points of the compass. They are standing at the points of the compass and saying nothing. They are sitting in the shade of a flowering tree. She is holding the child's body out toward
40   the camera. She is standing before the mirror and asking. She is offer- ing and asking. He-she is asking me a question I can't quite hear. Evenings they would walk along the shore of the lake.

Letters of the world. Bright orange poppy next to white rose next to blue spike of larkspur and so on. Artichoke crowding garlic and
45   sage. Hyssop, marjoram, orange mint, winter and summer savory, oregano, trailing rosemary, fuchsia, Dutch iris, day lily, lamb's tongue, lamb's ears, blackberry, feverfew, lemon verbena, sorrel, costmary, never reads it as it is, "poet living tomb of his/games."

Eyes eyeing what self never there, as things in metaphor cross, are
50   thrown across, a path he calls the path of names. In the film *La Jetée* she is thrown against time and is marking time:

> sun burns thru the roars
> dear eyes, *all eyes*, pageant
> bay inlet, garden casuarina, spittle-spawn
55   > (not laurel) nameless we name
> it, and sorrows dissolve—human

In silence he would mark time listening for whispered words. I began this in spring, head ready to burst, flowers, reddening sky, moon with a lobster, New York, Boston, return, thin coating of ice,
60   moon while dogs bark, moon dogs bark at, now it's late fall.

And now he told me it's time to talk.

Words would come in smoke and go, inventing the letters of the
voyage, would walk through melting snow to the corner store for
cigarettes, oranges and a newspaper, returning by a different route
65   past red brick townhouses built at the end of the Civil War. Or was
the question in the letters themselves, in how by chance the words
were spelled.

In the poem he learns to turn and turn, and prose seems always a
sentence long.

PAUL HOOVER (1946–   )

Poems We Can Understand (1983)

If a monkey drives a car
down a colonnade facing the sea
and the palm trees to the left are tin
we don't understand it.

5   We want poems we can understand.
We want a god to lead us,
renaming the flowers and trees,
color-coding the scene,

doing bird calls for guests.
10   We want poems we can understand,
no sullen drunks making passes
next to an armadillo, no complex nothingness

amounting to a song,
no running in and out of walls
15   on the dry tongue of a mouse,
no bludgeoness, no girl, no sea that moves

with all deliberate speed, beside itself
and blue as water, inside itself and still,
no lizards on the table becoming absolute hands.
20   We want poetry we can understand,

the fingerprints on mother's dress,
pain of martyrs, scientists.
Please, no rabbit taking a rabbit
out of a yellow hat, no tattooed back

25   facing miles of desert, no wind.
We don't understand it.

LORNA GOODISON (1947–   )

Jamaica 1980 (1986)

It trails always behind me
a webbed seine° with a catch of fantasy   fishnet
a penance I pay for being me
who took the order of poetry.
5   Always there with the gaping holes
and the mended ones, and the stand-in words.
But this time my Jamaica
my green-clad muse
this time your callings are of no use
10   I am spied on by your mountains
wire-tapped by your secret streams
your trees dripping blood-leaves
and jasmine selling tourist-dreams.

For all over this edenism
15   hangs the smell of necromancy
and each man eats his brother's flesh
Lord, so much of the cannibal left
in the jungle on my people's tongues.

We've sacrificed babies
20   and burnt our mothers
as payment to some viridian-eyed God dread
who works in cocaine under hungry men's heads.

And mine the task of writing it down
as I ride in shame round this blood-stained town.
25   And when the poem refuses to believe
and slimes to aloes in my hands
mine is the task of burying the dead
I the late madonna of barren lands.

YUSEF KOMUNYAKAA (1947–   )

Poetics (1979)

Beauty, I've seen you
pressed hard against the windowpane.
But the ugliness was unsolved
in the heart & mouth.
5   I've seen the quick-draw artist

crouch among the chrysanthemums.
Do I need to say more?

Everything isn't ha-ha
in this valley. The striptease
10   on stage at the Blue Movie
is your sweet little Sara Lee.
An argument of eyes
cut through the metaphor,
& I hear someone crying
15   among crystal trees & confetti.

The sack of bones in the magnolia,
what's more true than that?
Before you can see
her long pretty legs,
20   look into her unlit eyes.
A song of B-flat breath
staggers on death row. Real
men, voices that limp
behind the one-way glass wall.
25   I've seen the legless beggar
chopped down to his four wheels.

HEATHER McHUGH (1948–   )

What He Thought (1994)
for Fabbio Doplicher

We were supposed to do a job in Italy
and, full of our feeling for
ourselves (our sense of being
Poets from America) we went
5   from Rome to Fano, met
the mayor, mulled
a couple matters over (what's
cheap date, they asked us; what's
flat drink). Among Italian literati

10   we could recognize our counterparts:
the academic, the apologist,
the arrogant, the amorous,
the brazen and the glib—and there was one

administrator (the conservative), in suit
15   of regulation gray, who like a good tour guide

with measured pace and uninflected tone narrated
sights and histories the hired van hauled us past.
Of all, he was most politic and least poetic,
so it seemed. Our last few days in Rome
20   (when all but three of the New World Bards had flown)
I found a book of poems this
unprepossessing one had written: it was there
in the *pensione* room (a room he'd recommended)
where it must have been abandoned by
25   the German visitor (was there a bus of *them?*)
to whom he had inscribed and dated it a month before.
I couldn't read Italian, either, so I put the book
back into the wardrobe's dark. We last Americans

were due to leave tomorrow. For our parting evening then
30   our host chose something in a family restaurant, and there
we sat and chatted, sat and chewed,
till, sensible it was our last
big chance to be poetic, make
our mark, one of us asked
                              "What's poetry?
35   Is it the fruits and vegetables and
marketplace of Campo dei Fiori, or
the statue there?" Because I was

the glib one, I identified the answer
instantly, I didn't have to think—"The truth
40   is both, it's both," I blurted out. But that
was easy. That was easiest to say. What followed
taught me something about difficulty,
for our underestimated host spoke out,
all of a sudden, with a rising passion, and he said:

45   The statue represents Giordano Bruno,
brought to be burned in the public square
because of his offense against
authority, which is to say
the Church. His crime was his belief
50   the universe does not revolve around
the human being: God is no
fixed point or central government, but rather is
poured in waves through all things. All things
move. "If God is not the soul itself, He is
55   the soul of the soul of the world." Such was
his heresy. The day they brought him
forth to die, they feared he might
incite the crowd (the man was famous

for his eloquence). And so his captors
60 placed upon his face
an iron mask, in which

he could not speak. That's
how they burned him. That is how
he died: without a word, in front
65 of everyone.
                    And poetry—
                            (we'd all
put down our forks by now, to listen to
the man in gray; he went on
70 softly)—
                    poetry is what

he thought, but did not say.

DAVID LEHMAN (1948–   )

An Alternative to Speech (1986)

Sudden attack of aphasia, I hold my breath like smoke
And take credit for the brutal gifts
The darkness bestows. Do you have a friend
To lend me? Someone to visit me at midnight,
5 Pace back and forth on the rug, smoke his pipe and say
Not a word? From whom I may learn an alternative
To speech, recipes for staying hungry, instructions on staying awake,
If death isn't everything. My task
To give names to the darkest nothings,
10 Safety in numbers, the friendliest darkness,
Darkness afterwards, before the first door appears
At the end of a long blank corridor
And light slips under it, like a thief.

AUGUST KLEINZAHLER (1949–   )

Poetics (1985)

I have loved the air outside Shop-Rite Liquor
on summer evenings
better than the Marin hills at dusk
lavender and gold
5 stretching miles to the sea.

At the junction, up from the synagogue
a weeknight, necessarily
and with my father—
a sale on German beer.

10   Air full of living dust:
bus exhaust, air-borne grains of pizza crust
wounded crystals
appearing, disappearing
among streetlights and unsuccessful neon.

JULIA ALVAREZ (1950–   )

On Not Shoplifting Louise Bogan's
The Blue Estuaries (1995)

Connecticut College, fall 1968

Your book surprised me on the bookstore shelf—
swans gliding on a blueblack lake;
no blurbs by the big boys on back;
no sassy, big-haired picture
5   to complicate the achievement;
no mentors musing
over how they had discovered
you had it in you
before you even knew
10   you had it in you.
The swans posed on a placid lake,
your name blurred underwater
sinking to the bottom.

I had begun to haunt
15   the poetry shelf at the college store—
thin books crowded in by texts,
reference tomes and a spread
of magazines for persistent teens
on how to get their boys,
20   Chaucer-Milton-Shakespeare-Yeats.
Your name was not familiar,
I took down the book and read.

Page after page, your poems
were stirring my own poems—

25 words rose, breaking the surface,
    shattering an old silence.
    I leaned closer to the print
    until I could almost feel
    the blue waters drawn
30 into the tip of my pen.
    I bore down on the page,
    the lake flowed out again,
    the swans, the darkening sky.
    For a moment I lost my doubts,
35 my girl's voice, my coming late
    into this foreign alphabet.
    I read and wrote as I read.

    I wanted to own this moment.
    My breath came quickly, thinking it over—
40 I had no money, no one was looking.
    The swans posed on the cover,
    their question-mark necks arced
    over the dark waters.
    I was asking them what to do . . .

45 The words they swam over answered.
    I held the book closed before me
    as if it were something else,
    a mirror reflecting back
    someone I was becoming.
50 The swans dipped their alphabet necks
    in the blueblack ink of the lake.
    I touched their blank, downy sides, musing,
    and I put the book back.

CHARLES BERNSTEIN (1950–   )

Of Time and the Line (1991)

George Burns[1] likes to insist that he always
takes the straight lines; the cigar in his mouth
is a way of leaving space between the
lines for a laugh. He weaves lines together

---

[1] **George Burns:** George Burns (1896–1996), legendary American vaudeville comedian and actor.
Hennie Youngman was another American comedian.

5   by means of a picaresque narrative;
      not so Hennie Youngman, whose lines are strict-
      ly paratactic. My father pushed a
      line of ladies' dresses—not down the street
      in a pushcart but upstairs in a fact'ry
10   office. My mother has been more concerned
      with her hemline. Chairman Mao[2] put forward
      Maoist lines, but that's been abandoned (most-
      ly) for the East-West line of malarkey
      so popular in these parts. The prestige
15   of the iambic line has recently
      suffered decline, since it's no longer so
      clear who "I" am, much less who *you* are. When
      making a line, better be double sure
      what you're lining in & what you're lining
20   out & which side of the line you're on; the
      world is made up so (Adam didn't so much
      name as delineate). Every poem's got
      a prosodic lining, some of which will
      unzip for summer wear. The lines of an
25   imaginary are inscribed on the
      social flesh by the knifepoint of history.
      Nowadays, you can often spot a work
      of poetry by whether it's in lines
      or no; if it's in prose, there's a good chance
30   it's a poem. While there is no lesson in
      the line more useful than that of the pick-
      et line, the line that has caused the most ad-
      versity is the bloodline. In Russia
      everyone is worried about long lines;
35   back in the USA, it's strictly soup-
      lines. "Take a chisel to write," but for an
      actor a line's got to be cued. Or, as
      they say in math, it takes two lines to make
      an angle but only one lime to make
40   a Margarita.

---

[2] **Chairman Mao:** Mao Zedong (1893–1976), leader of the Chinese Communist party.

ANNE CARSON (1950–   )

Essay on What I Think about Most (2000)

Error.
And its emotions.
On the brink of error is a condition of fear.
In the midst of error is a state of folly and defeat.
5   Realizing you've made an error brings shame and remorse.
Or does it?

Let's look into this.
Lots of people including Aristotle[1] think error
an interesting and valuable mental event.
10   In his discussion of metaphor in the *Rhetoric*
Aristotle says there are 3 kinds of words.
Strange, ordinary and metaphorical.

"Strange words simply puzzle us;
ordinary words convey what we know already;
15   it is from metaphor that we can get hold of something new & fresh"
          (*Rhetoric*, 1410b10–13).
In what does the freshness of metaphor consist?
Aristotle says that metaphor causes the mind to experience itself

in the act of making a mistake.
He pictures the mind moving along a plane surface
20   of ordinary language
when suddenly
that surface breaks or complicates.
Unexpectedness emerges.

At first it looks odd, contradictory or wrong.
25   Then it makes sense.
And at this moment, according to Aristotle,
the mind turns to itself and says:
"How true, and yet I mistook it!"
From the true mistakes of metaphor a lesson can be learned.

30   Not only that things are other than they seem,
and so we mistake them,
but that such mistakenness is valuable.

---

[1] **Aristotle:** Aristotle (384 B.C.–322 B.C.), Greek philosopher influential to the shaping of Western thought.

Hold onto it, Aristotle says,
there is much to be seen and felt here.
35   Metaphors teach the mind

to enjoy error
and to learn
from the juxtaposition of *what is* and *what is not* the case.
There is a Chinese proverb that says,
40   Brush cannot write two characters with the same stroke.
And yet

that is exactly what a good mistake does.
Here is an example.
It is a fragment of ancient Greek lyric
45   that contains an error of arithmetic.
The poet does not seem to know
that $2 + 2 = 4$.

Alkman fragment 20:
         [?] made three seasons, summer
50   *and winter and autumn third*
         and fourth spring when
         there is blooming but to eat enough
         is not.

Alkman[2] lived in Sparta in the 7th century B.C.
55   Now Sparta was a poor country
and it is unlikely
that Alkman led a wealthy or well-fed life there.
This fact forms the background of his remarks
which end in hunger.

60   Hunger always feels
like a mistake.
Alkman makes us experience this mistake
with him
by an effective use of computational error.
65   For a poor Spartan poet with nothing

left in his cupboard
at the end of winter—

---

[2] **Alkman:** One of the nine lyric poets of Greece and founder of Doric lyric poetry.

along comes spring
like an afterthought of the natural economy,
70   fourth in a series of three,
unbalancing his arithmetic

and enjambing his verse.
Alkman's poem breaks off midway through an iambic metron
with no explanation
75   of where spring came from
or why numbers don't help us
control reality better.

There are three things I like about Alkman's poem.
First that it is small,
80   light
and more than perfectly economical.
Second that it seems to suggest colors like pale green
without ever naming them.

Third that it manages to put into play
85   some major metaphysical questions
(like Who made the world)
without overt analysis.
You notice the verb "made" in the first verse
has no subject: [?]

90   It is very unusual in Greek
for a verb to have no subject, in fact
it is a grammatical mistake.
Strict philologists will tell you
that this mistake is just an accident of transmission,
95   that the poem as we have it

is surely a fragment broken off
some longer text
and that Alkman almost certainly did
name the agent of creation
100   in the verses preceding what we have here.
Well that may be so.

But as you know the chief aim of philology
is to reduce all textual delight
to an accident of history.
105   And I am uneasy with any claim to know exactly

what a poet means to say.
So let's leave the question mark there

at the beginning of the poem
and admire Alkman's courage
110   in confronting what it brackets.
The fourth thing I like
about Alkman's poem
is the impression it gives

of blurting out the truth in spite of itself.
115   Many a poet aspires
to this tone of inadvertent lucidity
but few realize it so simply as Alkman.
Of course his simplicity is a fake.
Alkman is not simple at all,

120   he is a master contriver—
or what Aristotle would call an "imitator"
of reality.
Imitation (*mimesis* in Greek)
is Aristotle's collective term for the true mistakes of poetry.
125   What I like about this term

is the ease with which it accepts
that what we are engaged in when we do poetry is error,
the willful creation of error,
the deliberate break and complication of mistakes
130   out of which may arise
unexpectedness.

So a poet like Alkman
sidesteps fear, anxiety, shame, remorse
and all the other silly emotions associated with making mistakes
135   in order to engage
the fact of the matter.
The fact of the matter for humans is imperfection.

Alkman breaks the rules of arithmetic
and jeopardizes grammar
140   and messes up the metrical form of his verse
in order to draw us into this fact.
At the end of the poem the fact remains
and Alkman is probably no less hungry.

Yet something has changed in the quotient of our expectations.
145   For in mistaking them,
Alkman has perfected something.
Indeed he has
more than perfected something.
Using a single brushstroke.

DANA GIOIA (1950–   )

Unsaid (2001)

So much of what we live goes on inside—
The diaries of grief, the tongue-tied aches
Of unacknowledged love are no less real
For having passed unsaid. What we conceal
5   Is always more than what we dare confide.
Think of the letters that we write our dead.

JORIE GRAHAM (1950–   )

Mind (1980)

The slow overture of rain,
each drop breaking
without breaking into
the next, describes
5   the unrelenting, syncopated
mind. Not unlike
the hummingbirds
imagining their wings
to be their heart, and swallows
10   believing the horizon
to be a line they lift
and drop. What is it
they cast for? The poplars,
advancing or retreating,
15   lose their stature
equally, and yet stand firm,

making arrangements
in order to become
imaginary. The city
20 draws the mind in streets,
and streets compel it
from their intersections
where a little
belongs to no one. It is
25 what is driven through
all stationary portions
of the world, gravity's
stake in things. The leaves,
pressed against the dank
30 window of November
soil, remain unwelcome
till transformed, parts
of a puzzle unsolvable
till the edges give a bit
35 and soften. See how
then the picture becomes clear,
the mind entering the ground
more easily in pieces,
and all the richer for it.

JOY HARJO (1951–   )

The Creation Story (1994)

I'm not afraid of love
or its consequence of light.

It's not easy to say this
or anything when my entrails
5   dangle between paradise
and fear.

I am ashamed
I never had the words
to carry a friend from her death
10   to the stars
correctly.

Or the words to keep
my people safe

from drought
15   or gunshot.

The stars who were created by words
are circling over this house
formed of calcium, of blood

this house
20   in danger of being torn apart
by stones of fear.

If these words can do anything
if these songs can do anything
I say bless this house
25   with stars.

Transfix us with love.

MICHAEL COLLIER (1953–   )

The Snake (2000)

A cross of oak twigs marks the place
among the ferns and ivy where the children
dug the grave and coiled the baby python
in the dirt. Why feel regret and sadness
5   for a thing I would not touch?
Why be anything other than annoyed about the hundred bucks
it cost, on sale! And the accessories—
glass terrarium, heating pad, thermometer,
the driftwood pedestal, the strip of Astro Turf
10   that lined its floor, and the sun lamp—
that cost as much. Why lament a creature
who stared down the good but nervous meal of mouse
and starved itself? Why write except to notice
how love captures love or how my wife and children
15   could reach inside the artificial world
and lift the serpent with their hands
and hold it like a pliable divining rod
so they could drape it over their shoulders
and laugh a creepy kind of laugh I've never laughed
20   as the snake constricts around their necks,
its skin a loose diamond basket weave, its shape
a necklace or a noose.

GREG DELANTY (1958–   )

The Compositor (2004)

Perhaps it's the smell of printing ink
sets me off out of memory's jumbled font
or maybe it's the printer's lingo
as he relates how phrases came about.

5   How for instance *mind your p's & q's*
has as much to do with pints & quarts
and the printer's renown for drink
as it has with those descenders.

But I don't say anything about
10   how I discovered where *widows & orphans*
and *out of sorts* came from the day my father
unnoticed and unexpectedly set *30*

on the bottom of his compositor's page
and left me mystified about the origins
15   of that end, how to measure a line gauge
and how, since he was first to go,

he slowly and without a word
turned from himself into everyone
as we turn into that last zero
20   before finally passing on to the stoneman.

Section III

Contexts

DOOM IS DARK AND DEEPER

CHAPTER 23

— W. H. Auden

An Anthology of Alliterative Verse

The alliterative tradition in English poetry begins with the Anglo-Saxon poets. Anglo-Saxon (also known as Old English) was a variation of Old German with modifications and local inflections. In the Germanic languages, such as Old Norse, Old High German, and Old Saxon, there was no conscious use of rhyme as a device for patterning a poem. That is, unless you count **alliteration**—chiming on consonants— as a kind of rhyme. One can find long passages of alliterative poetry in most poems in the Germanic tradition, such as the *Elder Edda*, an ancient oral poem (like the Homeric epics) written down in Old Norse sometime between the eleventh and the fourteenth centuries, and the *Heliand*, written in Old Saxon sometime in the latter half of the ninth century.

The first great English epic, *Beowulf*, is thought to have been written sometime between 650 and 800 A.D., although it self-consciously seems to place itself within an even older tradition. It was one of many poems that made use of alliterative verse, with its characteristic surge from consonant to consonant. This is stressed poetry, which means that the reader counts only the hard or accented beats in a line. The line itself is divided into halves, called **distichs,** with a pause called a **caesura** in the middle of each line. Every half-line has two strong beats, called **lifts.** Two or even three of these lifts will usually alliterate. Often there will be two alliterations in the first half of the line, then one in the second.

Anglo-Saxon poets used various permutations of this system, which was largely based on stresses per line and alliterative patterns, although sometimes the nature of the vowel sound (its quantity, as grammarians say) came into play as well. This type of verse was highly musical, and it should be kept in mind that these poems were based on oral poetry: the poet, called a **scop**, or a shaper of words, often chanted the poem to the accompaniment of a harp-like instrument.

The Anglo-Saxon poets, much like the ancient Greek epic poets, relied on stock imagery: this is part of the oral tradition, making poems easier to remember and recite aloud. These stock images were called **kennings**, which are periphrastic expressions, as when a ship was called an "oar-steed" or when a battle was called "a storm of swords." Audiences at the time would have been familiar with these phrases, and would have known what they meant.

Apart from *Beowulf*, some of the other great poems in Anglo-
Saxon, all anonymous, are *The Seafarer, The Battle of Maldon, The Wife's
Lament*, and *The Wanderer*. These poems have remained highly influential, and have often been translated by modern and contemporary
poets from Ezra Pound to Seamus Heaney.

The Old English period lasted from about 450–1066 A.D., ending
abruptly with the invasion of William the Conqueror from Normandy, in
what is now France. With the infusion of a vast new Latinate vocabulary,
the English language changed dramatically, as did its poetry. Anglo-Saxon
itself fragmented into dialects, and these eventually melded into what is
called Middle English, which by the mid-fourteenth century had become
the language of England. Many fine, usually anonymous poems appeared
in alliterative form during this century: a period often referred to as the
alliterative revival. Among these poems were *The Pearl*, a Christian allegory of some intricacy and intellectual depth, *Sir Gawain and the Green
Knight* (p. 1494), a brilliant Arthurian poem, and *Morte Arthure*, another
poem about Arthur and his Round Table, not to be confused with *Le Morte
D'Arthur*, a work of prose that Sir Thomas Malory published in the late fifteenth century. Another fine poem of the alliterative revival was the moral
allegory called *Piers Plowman* by William Langland. This body of work is
distinguished, and it has compelled the attention of later poets and critics.

The alliterative tradition, per se, dwindled with the coming of the
Renaissance, a period when poets tended to look to France and Italy for
models, depending more and more on rhyme for stylistic effects and
stanza patterns. But we can sense the influence of alliterative verse in the
muscular language of John Donne and, at times, John Milton. In fact, English poetic meter has always been heavily dependent on stress as a
means of forming the poetic line. Much of the blank verse tradition, so
heavily influenced by Shakespeare, harkens back to the Anglo-Saxons,
and we can hear this line in Shakespeare's pulsing alliterative lyrics, as in:

> Full fathom five thy father lies;
> Of his bones are coral made;
> Those are pearls that were his eyes;
> Nothing of him that does fade,
> 5   But doth suffer a sea-change
> Into something rich and strange.
> Sea-nymphs hourly ring his knell:
> Ding-dong,
> Hark! Now I hear them—Ding-dong, bell.

We can hear the influence of the alliterative tradition in the work of
many poets of the nineteenth and twentieth centuries. A good example
is Gerard Manley Hopkins, the Victorian priest-poet, who consciously
based his **sprung rhythm**—a line of verse that is highly alliterative and
counts only stressed syllables in measuring out the meter—an Anglo-
Saxon meter. We see this operating in "God's Grandeur" (p. 1506). In

modern poetry, Ezra Pound and T. S. Eliot both experimented with alliterative verse, as did W. H. Auden, Dylan Thomas, and Robert Lowell. In
his long poem, *The Age of Anxiety*, Auden attempts to recover many of
the same elements of alliterative verse found in Anglo-Saxon poetry.
Thomas is, in fact, mainly known for his intensely alliterative style, represented in all its glory by "The Force That through the Green Fuse Drives
the Flower" (p. 1510). More recently, Richard Wilbur, Ted Hughes, and
Seamus Heaney have made inventive use of the alliterative tradition.

Seamus Heaney has devoted a good deal of time to Anglo-Saxon
poetry, translating the whole of *Beowulf* (p. 1492), much as Ezra Pound
translated *The Seafarer* (p. 1505). W. S. Merwin has recently translated the
Middle English alliterative poem, *Sir Gawain and the Green Knight* (p. 1494),
to good effect. That the alliterative tradition is alive and well should be
obvious to anyone familiar with contemporary poetry, and we have
included here a few very recent examples, such as Louise Glück's "Scilla"
(p. 1520) and Lucie Brock-Broido's "Of the Finished World" (p. 1522).

ADDITIONAL POEMS IN THE ALLITERATIVE TRADITION IN THIS BOOK

- Gerard Manley Hopkins, "Carrion Comfort" (p. 820)
- Gerard Manley Hopkins, "I Wake and Feel the Fell of Dark, Not Day" (p. 819)
- Gerard Manley Hopkins, "The Windhover" (p. 1358)
- Gerard Manley Hopkins, "Spring and Fall" (p. 1535)
- Dylan Thomas, "A Refusal to Mourn the Death, by Fire, of a Child in London" (p. 224)
- Dylan Thomas, "Do Not Go Gentle into that Good Night" (p. 842)
- Robert Penn Warren, "Evening Hawk" (p. 1372)
- Robert Penn Warren, "Heart of Autumn" (p. 1448)
- Theodore Roethke, "Orchids" (p. 948)
- Theodore Roethke, "Big Wind" (p. 353)
- Theodore Roethke, "Wish for a Young Wife" (p. 1079)
- Norman MacCaig, "Frogs" (p. 1373)
- Ted Hughes, "Pike" (p. 1390)
- Ted Hughes, "Hawk Roosting" (p. 1388)
- Galway Kinnell, "Blackberry Eating" (p. 1316)
- Seamus Heaney, "Digging" (p. 1005)
- Seamus Heaney, "Personal Helicon" (p. 1463)

ANONYMOUS
trans. Seamus Heaney (1939–   )

from **Beowulf**   (trans. 2000)

After these words, the prince of the Weather-Geats°   Beowulf
was impatient to be away and plunged suddenly:
without more ado, he dived into the heaving
depths of the lake. It was the best part of a day
5   before he could see the solid bottom.
Quickly the one who haunted those waters,
who had scavenged and gone her gluttonous rounds
for a hundred seasons, sensed a human
observing her outlandish lair from above.
10   So she lunged and clutched and managed to catch him
in her brutal grip; but his body, for all that,
remained unscathed: the mesh of the chain-mail
saved him on the outside. Her savage talons
failed to rip the web of his warshirt.
15   Then once she touched bottom, that wolfish swimmer
carried the ring-mailed prince to her court
so that for all his courage he could never use
the weapons he carried; and a bewildering horde
came at him from the depths, droves of sea-beasts
20   who attacked with tusks and tore at his chain-mail
in a ghastly onslaught. The gallant man
could see he had entered some hellish turn-hole
and yet the water did not work against him
because the hall-roofing held off
25   the force of the current; then he saw firelight,
a gleam and flare-up, a glimmer of brightness.

The hero observed that swamp-thing from hell,
the tarn-hag in all her terrible strength,
then heaved his war-sword and swung his arm:
30   the decorated blade came down ringing
and singing on her head. But he soon found
his battle-torch extinguished: the shining blade
refused to bite. It spared her and failed
the man in his need. It had gone through many
35   hand-to-hand fights, had hewed the armour
and helmets of the doomed, but here at last
the fabulous powers of that heirloom failed.
Hygelac's[1] kinsman kept thinking about

---

[1] **Hygelac's:** Hygelac, Beowulf's uncle and king of the Geats.

his name and fame: he never lost heart.
40 Then, in a fury, he flung his sword away.
The keen, inlaid, worm-loop-patterned steel
was hurled to the ground: he would have to rely
on the might of his arm. So must a man do
who intends to gain enduring glory
45 in a combat. Life doesn't cost him a thought.
Then the prince of War-Geats, warming to this fight
with Grendel's mother, gripped her shoulder
and laid about him in a battle frenzy:
he pitched his killer opponent to the floor
50 but she rose quickly and retaliated,
grappled him tightly in her grim embrace.
The sure-footed fighter felt daunted,
the strongest of warriors stumbled and fell.
So she pounced upon him and pulled out
55 a broad, whetted knife: now she would avenge
her only child. But the mesh of chain-mail
on Beowulf's shoulder shielded his life,
turned the edge and tip of the blade.
The son of Ecgtheow would have surely perished
60 and the Geats lost their warrior under the wide earth
had the strong links and locks of his war-gear
not helped to save him: holy God
decided the victory. It was easy for the Lord,
the Ruler of Heaven, to redress the balance
65 once Beowulf got back up on his feet.

Then he saw a blade that boded well,
a sword in her armoury, an ancient heirloom
from the days of the giants, an ideal weapon,
one that any warrior would envy,
70 but so huge and heavy of itself
only Beowulf could wield it in a battle.
So the Shieldings' hero, hard-pressed and enraged,
took a firm hold of the hilt and swung
the blade in an arc, a resolute blow
75 that bit deep into her neck-bone
and severed it entirely, toppling the doomed
house of her flesh; she fell to the floor.
The sword dripped blood, the swordsman was elated.

ANONYMOUS
trans. W. S. Merwin

from Sir Gawain and the Green Knight
(ca. late fourteenth century)

I

Since the siege and the assault upon Troy were finished,
The city destroyed and burned down to embers and ashes,
And the man who made the decoys that deceived them
Was tried for his treachery, though no man on earth was more true,
5   It was the noble Aeneas and his high-born kin
Who came to conquer provinces and become the lords
Of almost all the wealth of the Western Isles.
Noble Romulus went to Rome at once.
Proudly he set up that city at the beginning,
10   Giving it his own name, which it bears to this day.
Ticius to Tuscany, to begin building there.
Longobard builds high houses in Lombardy,
And far across the flood from France Felix Brutus
Is happy to settle the many hills and the whole breadth of Britain,
15   Where war and woe and wonder
          Have been known frequently,
          And by turns bliss and despair
          Have changed places suddenly.

And when this Britain was built by this noble knight,
20   Bold men were bred in it who loved fighting,
And they made trouble in the course of time.
More marvels have happened, often, in this land
Than in any other I know, since that first age.
But of all who lived here as kings of Britain
25   Arthur was ever the noblest, as I have heard tell.
So I intend to tell of one adventure that happened
Which some have considered a marvel to behold,
One of the wonders that are told about Arthur.
If you will listen for a little while to my lay
30   I shall tell it as I heard it in the hall, aloud,
          As it is set down
          In a strong story,
          With true letters written
          Together in the old way.

35   This King was staying at Camelot[1] at Christmastime
     With many fair lords and the most beautiful ladies
     And the whole high brotherhood of the Round Table
     In happy festivity and the high revels of the season.
     The men charged in tournaments again and again,
40   Noble knights jousting in high spirits;
     Then they rode to the court and danced to carols,
     And the feast went on like that a full fifteen days,
     With all the food and entertainment anyone could imagine.
     The laughter and merrymaking were a glory to hear,
45   A happy din all day and dancing at night,
     All on a high note in halls and chambers,
     With lords and ladies as they liked it best.
     They stayed there together with all the wealth in the world,
     The most famous knights under Christ himself,
50   And the most beautiful ladies who ever lived,
     And the finest of all was the King holding the court,
     All of these fair folk there in the hall in their first age,
             The most fortunate under heaven,
             The highest King, famous for his will,
55   Now it would be hard for anyone
             To name such a brave host on any hill.

     When the year had turned new only the night before
     The company that day was served double at the high table.
     When the King and his knights came into the hall,
60   The chanting in the chapel had come to an end
     And a loud cry went up from the clerics and the others
     Proclaiming Noel once more, calling out the word again,
     And then the nobles ran and got the gifts ready,
     Called out the New Year's presents, holding them high,
65   And they debated back and forth over the gifts.
     The ladies laughed loudly, all the ones who had lost,
     And the winner was not sorry, you can be sure.
     All this celebration went on until dinner time.
     When they had washed well, they went to sit at the table,
70   The most famous knights nearest the top, as was proper,
     And Guenever,[2] in high spirits, was seated in the middle of them,
     In the arrangement of the famous table, with them arrayed around her,

---

[1] **Camelot:** King Arthur's legendary castle.
[2] **Guenever:** The wife of King Arthur.

Fine silk, furthermore, in a canopy over her,
Of Toulouse red, and many Tharsian tapestries
75 Embroidered and set with the finest of jewels
That would have cost a great deal if someone had tried to buy them.
   The most beautiful there was the Queen,
   Flashing her gray eye.
   No one had ever seen
80   Anyone lovelier in his day.

Yet Arthur would not eat until they were all served.
He seemed full of the joy of youth, almost a boy.
He was happy with his life; he cared little
For lying in bed or sitting still for a long time,
85 His young blood so stirred him and his wild brain.
And there was a custom, besides, that he meant to keep,
That he had assumed in his noble way: he would not eat
On such a holiday until he had been told
A tale all new of some wonderful event,
90 Of some great marvel that he might believe
About kings, or arms, or other adventures,
Or unless someone came to ask for a proven knight
To join with him in jousting, putting his life in peril,
Risking life against life, each of them allowing
95 Fortune to grant the advantage to one of them.
This was the King's custom when he was holding court
At every great feast with his noble company
    in the castle.
   So with his proud face there
   Bravely he stands waiting
100   Bold in that New Year,
   And joins in the merrymaking.

So the King in his strength was standing there by himself
Talking of court trifles to those at the high table.
There sat good Gawain with Guenever beside him
105 And Agravaine of the hard hand on the other side of her,
Both of them the King's nephews and famous knights.
Bishop Bawdewyn was up at the head of the table,
And then Ywain beside him, who was the son of Urien.
These were seated on the dais, and lavishly served,
110 And many renowned knights were near them at the side tables.
Then came the first course, to the blaring of trumpets
With many brilliant banners hanging from them.
New kettledrums rumbled with the noble pipes
Wakening wild warblings with their loud sounds
115 And lifting many hearts high with their music.

In the midst of it rare and delicate dishes are served,
Mounds of fresh meat, and so many platters
That it was hard to find enough places
To set down the silver with the stews in it on the tablecloth.
120   Each one as he pleases
           Takes whatever he will.
           For every two there are twelve dishes,
           Good beer and bright wine both.

Now I will say no more about their service,
125 For all must know that no one lacked anything.
Another noise and a new one suddenly reached them
In less time than it takes to lift food to the lips.
Scarcely had the sound faded away again,
With the first course in the court properly served,
130 Than in at the hall door comes a frightening figure,
He must have been taller than anyone in the world:
From the neck to the waist so huge and thick,
And his loins and limbs so long and massive,
That I would say he was half a giant on earth.
135 At least I am sure he was the biggest of men.
Yet he sat with a matchless grace in the saddle.
His back and his chest and whole body were frightening
And both his belt and belly were trim and small
And all of his features were in proportion to the rest of him.
140   But more than anything
           His color amazed them:
           A bold knight riding,
           The whole of him bright green.

And all in green this knight and his garments
145 With a close-fitting coat that clung to his side,
A fine robe over it adorned on the inside
With furs cut to one color, an elegant lining
Trimmed brightly with white fur, and his hood also
That was caught back from his long locks and lay on his shoulders;
150 Neat, tight-tailored hose of that same green
Clung fast to his calf, and shining spurs below
Of bright gold, on silk bands enriched with stripes,
And so the knight rides with slippers on his feet
And all that he was wearing was indeed pure verdure
155 But the crossbars of his belt and the shining stones set
Resplendent here and there in his gleaming garments
All around him and his saddle, in silk embroidery—
It would be too hard to tell half of the details
That were there in fine stitches, with birds and butterflies

160 In a high green radiance with gold running through it.
    The tassels of his horse's trappings and the handsome crupper,
    The studs on the enameled bit and all the other metal,
    And the stirrups that he stood in were of the same color,
    And his saddle bow also and the rest of the fastenings,
165 It all kept glimmering and glinting with green stones.
    The horse that he was riding resplendent with the same hue as all
                    the rest.
            A green horse, hard to handle,
            A strong steed, huge and massive,
            Tossing the embroidered bridle,
170   The right horse for that knight to have.

    How splendid he looked, this knight in the green apparel,
    And his horse's hair was as lovely as his own.
    Fair waving locks tumbled around his shoulders,
    A beard big as a bush flowing over his breast,
175 And the full length of the noble hair of his head
    Had been cut in a circle above his elbows
    So that his arms were half hidden under it
    As by the tunic that covers a king's neck.
    The mane of that mighty horse looked much like that,
180 Its curls well combed and caught into many knots
    With gold cord wound around the bright green,
    For every strand of hair another of gold.
    His tail and his forelocks were enwound the same way,
    And both were bound with a band of bright green
185 And precious stones adorning them to the tip of his tail,
    Then laced up tightly in a twirled knot.
    There many bright shining bells of fine gold were ringing.
    No knight rides a horse like that anywhere on earth.
    Never before had one been seen in that hall by anyone.
190   Bright as lightning he shone,
            So they all said who saw him.
            It seemed that no man
            Could stand against him.

    Yet he wore no helmet and no chain mail either,
195 Nor any breastplate, nor brassarts on his arms,
    He had no spear and no shield for thrusting and striking,
    But in his hand he held a branch of holly
    That is greenest of all when the groves are bare,
    And an ax in the other hand, huge and monstrous,
200 A fearsome battle-ax to find words to tell of.
    The length of its head was at least a yard and a half,
    The point all hammered out of green steel and gold,

The blade brightly burnished, with a broad edge,
Shaped for shearing as well as sharp razors.
205   The grim knight gripped the stout handle of the weapon.
It was wrapped with iron to the shaft's end
And all engraved with green in graceful designs.
A lace was wound around it, fastened at the head,
Twining in many turns around the handle
210   With a fringe of fine tassels attached to it,
Rich embroidery above buttons of bright green.
This knight rides straight ahead into the hall,
Making for the high dais, undaunted by anything,
With no greeting to anyone, but his eyes high above them.
215   The first sound from him: "Where," he asked, "is
The head of this gathering? I would be glad
To set eyes on that knight, and I have something to say to him."
Over the knights he cast his eye
Riding up and down,
220   Stopping and looking hard to see
Who might have most renown.

They went on staring at the knight for some time,
Everyone wondering what it might mean
For a man and a horse to acquire such a color,
225   As green as the grass grows, and greener still, it seemed,
The green enamel glowing brighter on the gold.
All of them standing there stared and crept closer to him
With all the wonder in the world, to see what he would do.
For they had seen many marvels but never any like this,
230   So they all thought it might be a phantom or trick of magic,
So that many of the noble knights were afraid to answer,
And all were struck by his voice and stayed stone still,
And there was a silence like death through the great hall.
Not a sound rose out of them, as though they had all fallen asleep.
235   Not, I think, from fear only,
But some waiting for
Their King, out of courtesy,
To let him answer.

Then Arthur, addressing this wonder before the high dais,
240   Greeted him courteously, for nothing ever frightened him,
And said, "Knight, you are welcome indeed in this place.
My name is Arthur. I am the head of this house.
I pray you to have the grace to dismount and stay with us
And whatever you want we shall learn later."
245   "No, as I hope for help," the knight said, "from Him who sits on high,
It was never my mission to stay long in this house.

But because your fame, sire, is so exalted
And your castles and your knights are said to be
The best and strongest who ride in armor on horses,
250   The bravest and most noble anywhere in the world,
Worthy to contend with for the pure play of it,
And I have heard of the famous chivalry of this place,
All of that, I may tell you, brought me here at this time.
You may be assured by this branch that I bear here
255   That I am passing through in peace and not looking for enemies,
For if I had set out intent upon fighting
I have chain mail at home, and helmet too,
A shield and a sharp spear shining brightly,
And other weapons to wield also, to be sure.
260   But since I did not come for fighting, my clothes are softer.
But if you are as bold as knights everywhere say you are,
You will be so good as to grant me the request that I have the right
                   to ask."
              Arthur gave the knight
              This answer: "Courteous sir,
265   Whatever sport or fight
              You came for, you will find here."

"No, I tell you in good faith, it is not a fight I have come for.
These are nothing but beardless boys around this bench.
If I were buckled in armor on a big horse,
270   There is no man here strong enough to be worth riding against.
And so in this court I call for a Christmas game,
Since it is Yuletide and the New Year and all these brave men are here:
If anyone in this house thinks he has the courage
And is so bold in his blood and wild in his way of thinking
275   That he dares to exchange one heavy blow for another,
I shall make him a gift of this great battle-ax,
And a heavy one it is, this ax, to handle as he pleases,
And I shall await the first blow without armor, just as I sit here.
If any knight is brave enough to test my word,
280   Run up to me right now and take hold of this weapon.
I give it up for good, he can keep it as his own,
And I shall take a stroke from him on this floor, without flinching.
Then you must grant me the right to give him one in return without
                   resisting,
              But for that one he
285   May wait a year and a day.
              Now let me see
              What anyone here has to say."

If he had stunned them at first, then they were even more still,
All the courtiers in the hall, the high and the low.

290   The knight on his horse turned in his saddle,
      And wildly he flashed his red eyes around,
      Arched his bristling bright-green eyebrows,
      And waved his beard, waiting to see who would stand up.
      When no one would answer him, he gave a loud cough
295   And stretched as a lord might, and made ready to speak.
      "Well, is this Arthur's house," the knight said then,
      "That all the talk runs on through so many kingdoms?
      Where is your haughtiness now, where are your triumphs,
      Your belligerence and your wrath and your big words?
300   Now the revel and the renown of the Round Table
      Are overturned by a word of one man alone,
      All cowering in dread before a blow has been struck."
      With this he roars with such laughter that the lord was angry.
      Shame shot the blood into his white face and his cheeks.
305   Like the wind was his anger.
             It swept through everyone.
             The King, bold by nature,
             Went up to that huge man

      And said, "Knight, by heaven, your request is senseless.
310   What you ask is such madness you deserve to have it granted.
      No knight I know is afraid of your great words.
      Give me your ax now, in the name of God,
      And I shall grant the boon that you have requested."
      He strides toward him and grasps him by the hand.
315   Then proudly that other knight sets foot on the ground,
      Now Arthur has his ax, gripping the handle,
      And grimly swings it around, preparing to strike with it.
      The bold man stood towering before him,
      Taller than any in the house by a head and more.
320   With a grim look on his face he stood there and stroked his beard,
      And with unmoved expression he pulled down his tunic,
      No more daunted nor dismayed before that great stroke
      Than he would have been if a knight had brought him, at table, a
                drink of wine.
             Gawain, sitting next to the Queen,
325   Bowed to the King then:
             "I will keep my words plain.
             I ask for this battle to be mine."

      "If you please, glorious lord," Gawain said to the King,
      "I will turn from this table and stand by you there,
330   If I may do that without discourtesy,
      And without displeasing my liege lady,
      I would come to your counsel before your great court,
      For I think it not proper, according to our customs,

For such a request to be put so high in your hall
335 That you feel moved to reply to it yourself
When so many of the bravest are about you on the bench.
There are no better warriors, I believe, under heaven,
No better bodies on earth, when the battle begins.
I am the weakest, I know, and the least wise,
340 And cling least to my life, if anyone wants the truth,
But as you are my uncle whom I live to praise
And your blood is the sole virtue in my body,
And since this affair is so foolish, it does not befit you.
I have asked this of you first, and beg you to grant it,
345 And if my request is improper, I ask this great court not to blame me."
    All the court began whispering
    And all thought the same:
    Relieve the crowned King
    And let Gawain have the game.

350 Then the King commanded the knight to rise
And he leapt to his feet and turned gracefully,
Knelt before the King and took hold of the weapon.
The King let go of it and lifted his hand,
Gave him God's blessing and was glad to hope
355 That his heart and his hand would both be hardy.
"Take care, cousin," the King said, "how you make your cut,
And if you strike as you should, it seems certain to me
You will endure the blow he gives you in return."
Gawain goes to the knight with ax in hand
360 And the knight waits for him boldly, utterly undaunted.
Then the knight in green said to Sir Gawain,
"Let us repeat our agreement before we go further.
First, knight, I inquire of you what your name is,
And you tell me that truthfully, as I trust you will."
365 "In good faith," the good knight said, "my name is Gawain,
Who offer you this blow, whatever it leads to,
And twelve months from now I will take from you another
With what weapon you will, and not otherwise in the world."
    That other knight answers then,
370   "I welcome this stroke,
    Upon my life, Gawain,
    That you are about to make."

"By God," the Green Knight said, "I am glad
That I shall have from your hand what I asked for here,
375 And that you have repeated fully, in your own words,
The whole of the covenant I asked of the King:

Only now you must swear to me, upon your word,
That you will expect, for yourself, wherever you manage
To find me on earth, to be repaid in kind
380   For what you accord me today before this high company."
"Where shall I find you?" Gawain asked. "Where is your place?
I do not know where you live, by him that made me,
Nor do I know you, knight, nor your house nor your name.
Only tell me the truth about that, and what your name is,
385   And I shall use all my wits to make my way there,
And I swear to this on my word as a knight."
"That is enough for this New Year, no more need be said,"
The Green Knight said to the courteous Gawain.
"The truth is that when I have taken the blow,
390   And you have struck me soundly, I will tell you then
About my house and my home and my own name.
Then you will find out about me and how to keep our agreement,
And if I say nothing, so much the better for you,
And you may live long in your land and not have to look further—
but enough!
395   Pick up your grim tool now
             And let us see how you handle it."
             "Gladly, sir, I promise you,"
             Gawain said, stroking it.

The Green Knight takes his stand without lingering
400   And bends his head a little to show the skin.
He laid his long graceful locks across his crown,
Leaving the naked neck bare and ready.
Gawain gripped his ax and heaved it up high.
He set his left foot on the ground in front of him
405   And brought the blade down suddenly onto the bare skin
So that the sharp edge sundered the man's bones
And sank through the white flesh and sliced it in two
Until the bright steel of the bit sank into the ground.
The handsome head fell from the neck to the earth
410   And rolled out among their feet so that they kicked it.
The blood gushed from the body, glittering over the green,
And the knight never staggered or fell, for all that,
But he stepped forth as strong as ever, on unshaken legs,
And reached in roughly among the knights
415   To snatch up his lovely head and at once lift it high.
And then he turns to his horse and takes hold of the bridle,
Steps into the stirrup and swings himself up,
Holding his head in his hand by the hair,
And settles into the saddle as firmly as ever

420 With no trouble at all, though he sits there headless.
　　　　All around him the blood sprayed
　　　　As his gruesome body bled.
　　　　Many of them were afraid
　　　　When they heard what he said.

425 For he holds the head up high in his hand,
Turning the face toward the noblest on the platform,
And it raised its eyelids and opened its eyes wide
And said this much with its mouth, which you may hear now:
"Remember, Gawain, to get ready for what you agreed to,
430 And search carefully, knight, until you find me
As you have sworn to do in this hall where these knights heard you.
I charge you to make your way to the Green Chapel
To receive a stroke like the one you have given—you have earned it—
To be repaid promptly on New Year's morning.
435 Many men know me as the Knight of the Green Chapel,
So if you ask, you cannot fail to find me.
Come then, or you will rightly be called a coward."
With a terrible roar he turns the reins,
Rides out through the hall door, his head in his hand,
440 So that the flint flashes fire from his horse's hooves.
No one there knew what land he was going to
Any more than they knew where he had come from. What then?
　　　　Gawain and the King smile
　　　　And laugh about that green man.
445 　　　　All agreed that he was marvel
　　　　Enough for anyone.

In his heart Arthur, that noble king, was stunned.
He allowed no sign of it to show but said aloud,
Gently, courteously, to the beautiful Queen,
450 "Belovèd lady, do not be troubled by what happened today.
Things of this kind can occur at Christmastime,
With the performing of plays, the laughing and singing,
And carols and courtly dances of knights and ladies.
Just the same, I may well turn to my meal now,
455 For I have seen a wonder, I cannot deny it."
He glanced at Sir Gawain and, making light of it, said,
"Now, sir, hang up your ax, which has hewn enough,"
And it was done, above the dais, attached to a tapestry,
Where everyone might stare at it as a marvel
460 And try to find words for the wonder of it.
Then all those knights turned together to the table,
The King, and the good knight, and bold men served them
Double of all the fine dishes, whatever was most delicious.
There was all manner of food and also of minstrelsy.

465   They spent that day in pleasures until it came to an end on the earth.
         Now take thought, Sir Gawain,
         Of the danger before you,
         The risk to be run,
         Which you have taken upon you.

ANONYMOUS
trans. Ezra Pound (1885–1972)

The Seafarer[1] (ca. tenth century)

From the Anglo-Saxon

May I, for my own self, song's truth reckon,
Journey's jargon, how I in harsh days
Hardship endured oft.
Bitter breast-cares have I abided,
5   Known on my keel many a care's hold,
And dire sea-surge, and there I oft spent
Narrow nightwatch nigh the ship's head
While she tossed close to cliffs. Coldly afflicted,
My feet were by frost benumbed.
10   Chill its chains are; chafing sighs
Hew my heart round and hunger begot
Mere-weary° mood. Lest man know not   sea-weary
That he on dry land loveliest liveth,
List how I, care-wretched, on ice-cold sea,
15   Weathered the winter, wretched outcast
Deprived of my kinsmen;
Hung with hard ice-flakes, where hail-scur flew,
There I heard naught save the harsh sea
And ice-cold wave, at whiles the swan cries,
20   Did for my games, the gannet's° clamour,   seabird's
Sea-fowls' loudness was for me laughter,
The mews'° singing all my mead-drink.[2]   gulls'
Storms, on the stone-cliffs beaten, fell on the stern
In icy feathers; full oft the eagle screamed
25   With spray on his pinion.
                         Not any protector
May make merry man faring needy.
This he little believes, who aye in winsome life

---

[1] **The Seafarer:** Pound's translation of the first 100 lines of an 124-line Old English poem.
[2] **mead-drink:** Fermented milk and honey.

Abides 'mid burghers some heavy business,
30 Wealthy and wine-flushed, how I weary oft
Must bide above brine.
Neareth nightshade, snoweth from north,
Frost froze the land, hail fell on earth then,
Corn of the coldest. Nathless there knocketh now
35 The heart's thought that I on high streams
The salt-wavy tumult traverse alone.
Moaneth alway my mind's lust
That I fare forth, that I afar hence
Seek out a foreign fastness°.   place
40 For this there's no mood-lofty man over earth's midst,
Not though he be given his good, but will have in his youth greed;
Nor his deed to the daring, nor his king to the faithful
But shall have his sorrow for sea-fare
Whatever his lord will.
45 He hath not heart for harping, nor in ring-having
Nor winsomeness to wife, nor world's delight
Nor any whit else save the wave's slash,
Yet longing comes upon him to fare forth on the water.
Bosque° taketh blossom, cometh beauty of berries,   Grove
50 Fields to fairness, land fares brisker,
All this admonisheth man eager of mood,
The heart turns to travel so that he then thinks
On flood-ways to be far departing.
Cuckoo calleth with gloomy crying,
55 He singeth summerward, bodeth sorrow,
The bitter heart's blood. Burgher knows not—
He the prosperous man—what some perform
Where wandering them widest draweth.
So that but now my heart burst from my breastlock,
60 My mood 'mid the mere-flood,
Over the whale's acre, would wander wide.
On earth's shelter cometh oft to me,
Eager and ready, the crying lone-flyer,
Whets for the whale-path the heart irresistibly,
65 O'er tracks of ocean; seeing that anyhow
My lord deems to me this dead life
On loan and on land, I believe not
That any earth-weal eternal standeth
Save there be somewhat calamitous
70 That, ere a man's tide go, turn it to twain.
Disease or oldness or sword-hate
Beats out the breath from doom-gripped body.
And for this, every earl whatever, for those speaking after—
Laud of the living, boasteth some last word,
75 That he will work ere he pass onward,

Frame on the fair earth 'gainst foes his malice,
Daring ado,°...   acts
So that all men shall honour him after
And his laud beyond them remain 'mid the English,
80   Aye, for ever, a lasting life's-blast,
Delight 'mid the doughty.°   resolute
                         Days little durable,
And all arrogance of earthen riches,
There come now no kings nor Cæsars
Nor gold-giving lords like those gone.
85   Howe'er in mirth most magnified,
Whoe'er lived in life most lordliest,
Drear all this excellence, delights undurable!
Waneth the watch, but the world holdeth.
Tomb hideth trouble. The blade is layed low.
90   Earthly glory ageth and seareth.
No man at all going the earth's gait,
But age fares against him, his face paleth,
Grey-haired he groaneth, knows gone companions,
Lordly men, are to earth o'ergiven,
95   Nor may he then the flesh-cover, whose life ceaseth,
Nor eat the sweet nor feel the sorry,
Nor stir hand nor think in mid heart,
And though he strew the grave with gold,
His born brothers, their buried bodies
100 Be an unlikely treasure hoard.

EDWARD TAYLOR (ca. 1642–1729)

The Preface (1939)

     Infinity, when all things it beheld
In nothing, and of nothing all did build,
Upon what base was fixt the lathe, wherein
He turned this globe, and riggalled° it so trim?   made ring-like
5   Who blew the bellows of his furnace vast?
Or held the mould wherein the world was cast?
Who laid its corner-stone? Or whose command?
Where stand the pillars upon which it stands?
Who laced and filleted the Earth so fine,
10   With rivers like green ribbons smaragdine°?   emerald
Who made the seas its selvage°, and it locks   border
Like a gilt ball within a silver box?
Who spread its canopy? Or curtains spun?
Who in this bowling alley bowled the sun?

15   Who made it always when it rises set
      To go at once both down, and up to get?
      Who the curtain rods made for this tapestry?
      Who hung the twinkling lanthorns° in the sky?   lanterns
      Who? Who did this? Or who is he? Why, know
20   It's only might almighty this did do.
      His hand hath made this noble work, which stands
      His glorious handiwork not made by hands;
      Who spake all things from nothing, and with ease
      Can speak all things to nothing, if he please;
25   Whose little finger at his pleasure can
      Out mete ten thousand worlds with half a span;
      Whose might almighty can by half a looks
      Root up the rocks and rock the hills by th' roots;
      Can take this mighty world up in his hand,
30   And shake it like a squitchen° or a wand;   shield
      Whose single frown will make the heavens shake
      Like as an aspen leaf the wind makes quake.
      Oh, what a might is this, whose single frown
      Doth shake the world as it would shake it down!
35   Which all from nothing fet,° from nothing, all: fetched
      Hath all on nothing set, lets nothing fall.
      Gave all to nothing man indeed, whereby
      Through nothing man all might him glorify.
      In nothing then embossed the brightest gem,
40   More precious than all preciousness in them.
      But nothing man did throw down all by sin,
      And darkenèd that lightsome gem in him;
           That now his brightest diamond is grown
           Darker by far than any coalpit stone.

GERARD MANLEY HOPKINS (1844–1889)

God's Grandeur (1877; 1895)

The world is charged with the grandeur of God.
     It will flame out, like shining from shook foil;
     It gathers to a greatness, like the ooze of oil
Crushed.[1] Why do men then now not reck his rod?

---

[1] **like . . . Crushed:** Hopkins refers to olives, crushed for their oil.

5 Generations have trod, have trod, have trod;
    And all is seared with trade; bleared, smeared with toil;
    And wears man's smudge and shares man's smell: the soil
Is bare now, nor can foot feel, being shod.

    And for all this, nature is never spent;
10   There lives the dearest freshness deep down things;
    And though the last lights off the black West went
       Oh, morning, at the brown brink eastward, springs—
    Because the Holy Ghost over the bent
       World broods with warm breast and with ah! bright wings.

W. H. AUDEN (1907–1973)

The Wanderer[1] (1930)

Doom is dark and deeper than any sea-dingle.°   abyss
Upon what man it fall
In spring, day-wishing flowers appearing,
Avalanche sliding, white snow from rock-face,
5 That he should leave his house,
No cloud-soft hand can hold him, restraint by women;
But ever that man goes
Through place-keepers, through forest trees,
A stranger to strangers over undried sea,
10 Houses for fishes, suffocating water,
Or lonely on fell as chat,[2]
By pot-holed becks°   brooks
A bird stone-haunting, an unquiet bird.

There head falls forward, fatigued at evening,
15 And dreams of home,
Waving from window, spread of welcome,

---

[1] **The Wanderer:** Auden draws inspiration from an Old English poem also entitled "The Wanderer," translated by Richard Hoggart: "Often the solitary man prays for favor, for the mercy of the Lord, though, sad at heart, he must needs stir with his hands for a weary while the icy sea across the watery wastes, must journey the paths of exile; settled in truth is fate! So spoke the wanderer, mindful of hardships . . . He knows who put it to the test how cruel a comrade is sorrow for him who has few dear protectors; his is the path of exile, in no wise the twisted gold; a chill body, in no wise the riches of the earth; he thinks of retainers in hall and the receiving of treasure, of how in his youth his gold-friend was kind to him at the feast. The joy has all perished . . . Then the friendless man wakes again, sees before him the dark waves, the sea-birds bathing, spreading their feathers; frost and snow falling mingles with hail. Then heavier are the wounds in his heart, sore for his beloved; sorrow is renewed."
[2] **Or lonely on fell as chat:** A "chat" is a warbler, and "fell" suggests a moorland ridge.

Kissing of wife under single sheet;
But waking sees
Bird-flocks nameless to him, through doorway voices
20   Of new men making another love.

Save him from hostile capture,
From sudden tiger's leap at corner;
Protect his house,
His anxious house where days are counted
25   From thunderbolt protect,
From gradual ruin spreading like a stain;
Converting number from vague to certain,
Bring joy, bring day of his returning,
Lucky with day approaching, with leaning dawn.

DYLAN THOMAS (1914–1953)

The Force That through the Green Fuse Drives the Flower (1933; 1934)

The force that through the green fuse drives the flower
Drives my green age; that blasts the roots of trees
Is my destroyer.
And I am dumb to tell the crooked rose
5   My youth is bent by the same wintry fever.

The force that drives the water through the rocks
Drives my red blood; that dries the mouthing streams
Turns mine to wax.
And I am dumb to mouth unto my veins
10   How at the mountain spring the same mouth sucks.

The hand that whirls the water in the pool
Stirs the quicksand; that ropes the blowing wind
Hauls my shroud sail.
And I am dumb to tell the hanging man
15   How of my clay is made the hangman's lime.[1]

---

[1] **the hangman's lime:** To speed the process of decomposition, quicklime was placed in the graves of executed criminals.

The lips of time leech to the fountain head;
Love drips and gathers, but the fallen blood
Shall calm her sores.
And I am dumb to tell a weather's wind
20   How time has ticked a heaven round the stars.

And I am dumb to tell the lover's tomb
How at my sheet goes the same crooked worm.

GWENDOLYN BROOKS (1917–2000)

We Real Cool (1960)

THE POOL PLAYERS.
SEVEN AT THE GOLDEN SHOVEL.

We real Cool. We
Left school. We

5   Lurk late. We
Strike straight. We

Sing sin. We
Thin gin. We

Jazz June. We
10   Die soon.

ROBERT LOWELL (1917–1977)

The Quaker Graveyard in Nantucket (1946)
For Warren Winslow,[1] Dead at Sea

Let man have dominion over the fishes of the sea and the fowls of
the air and the beasts of the whole earth, and every creeping
creature that moveth upon the earth.[2]

---

[1] **Warren Winslow:** Lowell's cousin, lost at sea when his naval vessel sunk.
[2] **Let man . . . earth:** See Genesis 1.26.

I

A brackish reach of shoal off Madaket³—
The sea was still breaking violently and night
Had steamed into our North Atlantic Fleet,
When the drowned sailor clutched the drag-net. Light
5   Flashed from his matted head and marble feet,
He grappled at the net
With the coiled, hurdling muscles of his thighs:
The corpse was bloodless, a botch of reds and whites,
Its open, staring eyes
10 Were lustreless dead-lights
Or cabin-windows on a stranded hulk
Heavy with sand. We weight the body, close
Its eyes and heave it seaward whence it came,
Where the heel-headed dogfish barks its nose
15 On Ahab's⁴ void and forehead; and the name
Is blocked in yellow chalk.
Sailors, who pitch this portent at the sea
Where dreadnaughts° shall confess   battleships
Its hell-bent deity,
20 When you are powerless
To sand-bag this Atlantic bulwark, faced
By the earth-shaker,⁵ green, unwearied, chaste
In his steel scales: ask for no Orphean lute
To pluck life back.⁶ The guns of the steeled fleet
25 Recoil and then repeat
The hoarse salute.

II

Whenever winds are moving and their breath
Heaves at the roped-in bulwarks of this pier,
The terns and sea-gulls tremble at your death
30 In these home waters. Sailor, can you hear
The Pequod's sea wings, beating landward, fall
Headlong and break on our Atlantic wall

³ **Madaket:** A settlement on the western side of Nantucket Island, Massachusetts. Historically, Nantucket was the hub of the American whaling industry.
⁴ **Ahab's:** In Melville's *Moby-Dick* (1851), Captain Ahab sails from Nantucket on the *Pequod* in pursuit of the white whale.
⁵ **the earth-shaker:** In Greek mythology, Poseidon, god of the sea.
⁶ **Orphean lute . . . back:** In Greek mythology, Orpheus used his music to convince Persephone to allow his wife, Eurydice, to leave Hades and return to earth.

Off 'Sconset, where the yawing S-boats splash[7]
The bellbuoy, with ballooning spinnakers,
35 As the entangled, screeching mainsheet clears
The blocks: off Madaket, where lubbers lash
The heavy surf and throw their long lead squids
For blue-fish? Sea-gulls blink their heavy lids
Seaward. The winds' wings beat upon the stones,
40 Cousin, and scream for you and the claws rush
At the sea's throat and wring it in the slush
Of this old Quaker graveyard where the bones
Cry out in the long night for the hurt beast
Bobbing by Ahab's whaleboats in the East.

III

45 All you recovered from Poseidon died
With you, my cousin, and the harrowed brine
Is fruitless on the blue beard of the god,
Stretching beyond us to the castles in Spain,
Nantucket's westward haven. To Cape Cod
50 Guns, cradled on the tide,
Blast the eelgrass about a waterclock
Of bilge and backwash, roil the salt and sand
Lashing earth's scaffold, rock
Our warships in the hand
55 Of the great God, where time's contrition blues
Whatever it was these Quaker sailors lost
In the mad scramble of their lives. They died
When time was open-eyed,
Wooden and childish; only bones abide
60 There, in the nowhere, where their boats were tossed
Sky-high, where mariners had fabled news
Of IS, the whited monster.[8] What it cost
Them is their secret. In the sperm-whale's slick
I see the Quakers drown and hear their cry:
65 "If God himself had not been on our side,
If God himself had not been on our side,
When the Atlantic rose against us, why,
Then it had swallowed us up quick."

---

[7] **Off . . . splash:** Siasconset is a town on Eastern Nantucket. S-boats were racing sailboats once popular in New England.
[8] **IS, the whited monster:** Here, Lowell identifies Moby-Dick with God, who referred to himself as "I AM" in Exodus 3.14.

IV

    This is the end of the whaleroad⁹ and the whale
70   Who spewed Nantucket bones on the thrashed swell
    And stirred the troubled waters to whirlpools
    To send the Pequod packing off to hell:
    This is the end of them, three-quarters fools,
    Snatching at straws to sail
75   Seaward and seaward on the turntail whale,
    Spouting out blood and water as it rolls,
    Sick as a dog to these Atlantic shoals:
    Clamavimus, O depths.¹⁰ Let the sea-gulls wail

    For water, for the deep where the high tide
80   Mutters to its hurt self, mutters and ebbs.
    Waves wallow in their wash, go out and out,
    Leave only the death-rattle of the crabs,
    The beach increasing, its enormous snout
    Sucking the ocean's side.
85   This is the end of running on the waves;
    We are poured out like water. Who will dance
    The mast-lashed master of Leviathans¹¹
    Up from this field of Quakers in their unstoned graves?

V

    When the whale's viscera go and the roll
90   Of its corruption overruns this world
    Beyond tree-swept Nantucket and Woods Hole
    And Martha's Vineyard, Sailor, will your sword
    Whistle and fall and sink into the fat?
    In the great ash-pit of Jehoshaphat¹²
95   The bones cry for the blood of the white whale,
    The fat flukes arch and whack about its ears,
    The death-lance churns into the sanctuary, tears
    The gun-blue swingle,° heaving like a flail,   rod
    And hacks the coiling life out: it works and drags
100 And rips the sperm-whale's midriff into rags,
    Gobbets of blubber spill to wind and weather,

---

⁹ **whaleroad:** Old English epithet for the sea.
¹⁰ *Clamavimus,* O depths: Latin, "we have cried." See Psalm 130.1: "Out of the depths have I cried
unto thee, O Lord."
¹¹ **Leviathans:** A Leviathan is a great water monster from the Old Testament.
¹² **great . . . Jehoshaphat:** In Joel 3, the site of the Last Judgment.

Sailor, and gulls go round the stoven timbers
Where the morning stars sing out together
And thunder shakes the white surf and dismembers
105　The red flag hammered in the mast-head. Hide,
Our steel, Jonas Messias,[13] in Thy side.

VI

Our Lady of Walsingham[14]

There once the penitents took off their shoes
And then walked barefoot the remaining mile;
And the small trees, a stream and hedgerows file
110　Slowly along the munching English lane,
Like cows to the old shrine, until you lose
Track of your dragging pain.
The stream flows down under the druid tree,
Shiloah's[15] whirlpools gurgle and make glad
115　The castle of God. Sailor, you were glad
And whistled Sion by that stream. But see:

Our Lady, too small for her canopy,
Sits near the altar. There's no comeliness
At all or charm in that expressionless
120　Face with its heavy eyelids. As before,
This face, for centuries a memory,
Non est species, neque decor,[16]
Expressionless, expresses God: it goes
Past castled Sion. She knows what God knows,
125　Not Calvary's Cross nor crib at Bethlehem
Now, and the world shall come to Walsingham.

VII

The empty winds are creaking and the oak
Splatters and splatters on the cenotaph,°   empty tomb
The boughs are trembling and a gaff
130　Bobs on the untimely stroke

---

[13] **Jonas Messias:** The Old Testament prophet Jonah, who spent three days in the belly of a whale, is often linked with the Messiah. Here, Jonah is associated with Christ, who was stabbed in the side by a Roman centurion. (See Matthew 12.)
[14] **Our Lady of Walsingham:** Walsingham, a small town in England where a shrine was built in honor of the Virgin Mary in the eleventh century.
[15] **Shiloah's:** A stream in Jerusalem.
[16] *Non . . . decor:* Latin: "There is no beauty or charm."

Of the greased wash exploding on a shoal-bell
In the old mouth of the Atlantic. It's well;
Atlantic, you are fouled with the blue sailors,
Sea-monsters, upward angel, downward fish:
135   Unmarried and corroding, spare of flesh
Mart once of supercilious, wing'd clippers,
Atlantic, where your bell-trap guts its spoil
You could cut the brackish winds with a knife
Here in Nantucket, and cast up the time
140   When the Lord God formed man from the sea's slime
And breathed into his face the breath of life,
And blue-lung'd combers lumbered to the kill.
The Lord survives the rainbow of His will.

GEORGE MACKAY BROWN (1921–1996)

The Net (1971)

The first day from the weaving of the ling net
Three cod lay on the deck, gulping.
A careful gleam was put in their bellies.

The second day from the net weaving
5   A dogfish slapped the scuppers.
He barked at the women soundlessly.
Dog, wet or dry, is poor tooth-relish.

The third day from the net weaving
We handled a halibut on board.
10   The women sliced that turbulence in segments.
They wrung fierce blood in a stone jar.
(And still we tracked the gold beast into the west.)

The fourth day from the net weaving.

The fifth day from the net weaving
15   We gathered a mermaid into the mesh—
Njal said, a long-drowned sailor—
At least something with knuckle and rib and teeth.
Skald sullied harp with sickness.
The skull splayed streams of hair. And smiled. And sank.

20   The sixth day from the net weaving
A shark surged through the net.

The seventh day from the net weaving
Were bodkin,° twine, snicking teeth.   dagger
The shark had laid our thousand ordered holes
25   In one black knot and ravel.
The second net was tougher than the first.
The eighth day from the net weaving
Herring danced in, a thousand.

RICHARD WILBUR (1921–   )

Junk (1961)

Huru Welandes
        worc ne geswiceð
  monna ænigum
        ðara ðe Mimming can
  heardne gehealdan.
          —WALDERE[1]

An axe angles
       from my neighbor's ashcan;
It is hell's handiwork,
       the wood not hickory,
5   The flow of the grain
       not faithfully followed.
The shivered shaft
       rises from a shellheap
Of plastic playthings,
10   paper plates,
And the sheer shards
       of shattered tumblers
That were not annealed
       for the time needful.
15   At the same curbside,
       a cast-off cabinet
Of wavily-warped
       unseasoned wood
Waits to be trundled
20   in the trash-man's truck.

---

[1] **Waldere:** "The epigraph, taken from a fragmentary Anglo-Saxon poem, concerns the legendary smith Wayland, and may roughly be translated: 'Truly, Wayland's handiwork—the sword Mimming which he made—will never fail any man who knows how to use it bravely" [Wilbur's note].

Haul them off! Hide them!
                              The heart winces
For junk and gimcrack,
                              for jerrybuilt things
25 And the men who make them
                              for a little money,
Bartering pride
                      like the bought boxer
Who pulls his punches,
30   or the paid-off jockey
Who in the home stretch
                              holds in his horse.
Yet the things themselves
                              in thoughtless honor
35 Have kept composure,
                              like captives who would not
Talk under torture.
                      Tossed from a tailgate
Where the dump displays
40   its random dolmens,
Its black barrows
                      and blazing valleys,

They shall waste in the weather
                              toward what they were.
45 The sun shall glory
                      in the glitter of glass-chips,
Foreseeing the salvage
                      of the prisoned sand,
And the blistering paint
50   peel off in patches,
That the good grain
                      be discovered again.
Then burnt, bulldozed,
                      they shall all be buried
55 To the depth of diamonds,
                              in the making dark
Where halt Hephaestus[2]
                      keeps his hammer
And Wayland's work
60   is worn away.

---

[2] **Hephaestus:** In Greek mythology, the god of fire and metal-work.

TED HUGHES (1930–1998)

The Hawk in the Rain (1956)

I drown in the drumming ploughland, I drag up
Heel after heel from the swallowing of the earth's mouth,
From clay that clutches my each step to the ankle
With the habit of the dogged grave, but the hawk

5   Effortlessly at height hangs his still eye.
His wings hold all creation in a weightless quiet,
Steady as a hallucination in the streaming air.
While banging wind kills these stubborn hedges,

Thumbs my eyes, throws my breath, tackles my heart,
10   And rain hacks my head to the bone, the hawk hangs
The diamond point of will that polestars
The sea drowner's endurance: and I,

Bloodily grabbed dazed last-moment-counting
Morsel in the earth's mouth, strain towards the master-
15   Fulcrum of violence where the hawk hangs still.
That maybe in his own time meets the weather

Coming the wrong way, suffers the air, hurled upside down,
Fall from his eye, the ponderous shires crash on him,
The horizon trap him; the round angelic eye
20   Smashed, mix his heart's blood with the mire of the land.

SEAMUS HEANEY (1939–   )

Sunlight (1975)

There was a sunlit absence.
The helmeted pump in the yard
heated its iron,
water honeyed

5   in the slung bucket
and the sun stood
like a griddle cooling
against the wall

of each long afternoon.
10 So, her hands scuffled
over the bakeboard,
the reddening stove

sent its plaque of heat
against her where she stood
15 in a floury apron
by the window.

Now she dusts the board
with a goose's wing,
now sits, broad-lapped,
20 with whitened nails

and measling shins:
here is a space
again, the scone rising
to the tick of two clocks.

25 And here is love
like a tinsmith's scoop
sunk past its gleam
in the meal-bin.

LOUISE GLÜCK (1943–   )

Scilla (1992)

Not I, you idiot, not self, but we, we—waves
of sky blue like
a critique of heaven: why
do you treasure your voice
5 when to be one thing
is to be next to nothing?
Why do you look up? To hear
an echo like the voice
of god? You are all the same to us,
10 solitary, standing above us, planning
your silly lives: you go

where you are sent, like all things,
where the wind plants you,
one or another of you forever
15   looking down and seeing some image
of water, and hearing what? Waves,
and over waves, birds singing.

HENRY HART (1954–   )

Riddle (1990)

Rooted in fresh earth, I am a bush of flies,
feedroost for cowbirds, cumbersome backpresser
of sunlit horizons on stonewalled hills.
Bigboned, I am heavy as eight tackles.

5   Among wild strawberries and bluets
I flaunt my fragrance like a medieval king.
I print my forked signature in mud, stamp out
mice by plowing up their camouflage.

I rub my mark on fencepoles, gatebars,
10   hang talismanic scalps on every strand
of barbed wire to indicate my outposts.
With axeblade hooves I blaze new fields

with walkways, stipple grass with spoors,
make good ground for gardens. In March
15   farmers from the far barn drag me down
the tarred road with a chain in my nosering.

Moonstruck for nights, bolted behind doors,
battened to haybales and cows,
I limp out weeks later, weakkneed,
20   drooling a noose of foam.

Now I stand on green earth, legproud.
My cousin is the dragon, guardian
of treasure troves, ruiner of kingdoms.
My gold is the grass they envy.

LUCIE BROCK-BROIDO (1956–   )

Of the Finished World (2004)

Open the final book: November spills
Its lamplit light, the clenched astronomer

Hunched at table, considering his vexed
Celestial map, illegible as the flinch

5   Of needles falling on the blanched
Rye fields in pentagrams.

The harvest is done with itself, its ransack
Done. The wild-coated horses bunch

In the clot of darkness that falls on the land.
10   In the twice-ploughed field, picked

Clean, what is left of the bottle-gourds
Will freeze by night, a throttled hour

From here. On the freighted road, laden with
Old hunger and apocrypha, a heaven sloughs

15   Its midden things, things left of the unfinished
World, its most hideous & permanent

Impermanence. I was not awake
For any war to speak of.

                    In the finished world
20   I will be wind-awry, will be out

                    Of mind, in asylum
Where even the astronomer will no longer

Attend to the world undone.
How have I lived here so long?

CHAPTER 24

BEHOLD HER, SINGLE IN THE FIELD!

—William Wordsworth

An Anthology of Meditative Poetry

Meditative poetry often dwells on philosophical or spiritual matters. More specifically, the term refers to poetry inspired by the great meditative and religious poems of the seventeenth century. During that time, English poets were deeply influenced by the traditions of religious meditation that had been popular for centuries in Europe.

Among the many writers of handbooks for Christian meditation was St. Ignatius Loyola, who in 1536 published his *Spiritual Exercises*, which remains a central text for the training of Jesuit priests to this day. Meditation and prayer are related, but they are not the same thing. In essence, a practice of meditation is a regular devotional period in the day of a Christian, one in which the mind of the meditator prepares for contact with God. A good exercise in meditation, in the Ignatian tradition, leads naturally into prayer.

According to Ignatius, the meditator must call into play the "three powers of the soul," which are memory, the intellect, and the affective will. A specific meditation will mirror this tripartite aspect of the mind, and so meditative practice begins with what Ignatius calls "composition of place" (*compositio loci*). The meditator is asked to conjure concrete images, dwelling on a specific place or scene, using the memory to recall particular instances or images. In the second phase of the meditation, the meditator applies the intellect, which means making comparisons. Analogical thinking uses metaphor, saying this is like that, or this is not like that. It is the process of making distinctions, actively engaging the mind. In the third phase, having summoned the powers of memory and intellect, the will is called into play, and the meditator addresses God directly, as a friend. A conversation, or colloquy, occurs. Thus, prayer comes into play, as the mind and heart turn outward in affiliation with God.

We can see this pattern explicitly unfolding in the poems of John Donne, Robert Southwell, Edward Taylor, George Herbert, and Henry Vaughan—all Christian poets of the seventeenth century who were deeply influenced by the traditions of meditation, as critic Louis L. Martz explains in *The Poetry of Meditation* (1957). This tradition, as Martz shows, also had an impact on later poets, including the Romantics and Moderns. We see the most explicit use of the Ignatian tradition in Gerard Manley Hopkins, who was himself a Jesuit, trained in the *Spiritual Exercises* of Ignatius.

Let us consider one example of the secular use of this tradition. In "The Solitary Reaper" (p. 1534), Wordsworth begins by summoning a scene from memory, using vision to seize and keep the highly pictorial image in place.

> Behold her, single in the field,
> Yon solitary highland lass,
> Reaping and singing by herself—
> Stop here, or gently pass!
> 5   Alone she cuts and binds the grain,
> And sings a melancholy strain:
> O listen, for the vale profound
> Is overflowing with the sound!

With the image firmly established visually, the poet employs analogies, comparing this lovely singer to the nightingale and the cuckoo.

> No nightingale did ever chant
> So sweetly to reposing bands
> Of travellers in some shady haunt
> Among Arabian sands;
> 5   No sweeter voice was ever heard
> In springtime from the cuckoo-bird,
> Breaking the silence of the seas
> Among the farthest Hebrides.

Wordsworth then interrogates some hypothetical listeners who (perhaps) walk along with him in the countryside. It could also be that the poet is talking to himself here, asking rhetorical questions. This stanza broadens the meditation, connecting the poet with an audience, bringing them into the contemplative scene.

> Will no one tell me what she sings?
> Perhaps the plaintive numbers flow
> For old, unhappy, far-off things,
> And battles long ago:
> 5   Or is it some more humble lay,
> Familiar matter of today—
> Some natural sorrow, loss, or pain,
> That has been, and may be again?

The final stanza is that which Ignatius identifies with the affective will. In a religious meditation, this would become a prayer, a conversation with God. Here it becomes an outward turning, an attempt to generalize, to fuse the various emotional and intellectual elements of the poem.

> Whate'er the theme, the maiden sang
> As if her song could have no ending;
> I saw her singing at her work
> And o'er the sickle bending;
> 5 I listened till I had my fill
> And as I mounted up the hill
> The music in my heart I bore
> Long after it was heard no more.

The three-part template for the meditative poem is not necessarily so rigorous and prescriptive; later poets simply bring various aspects of the tradition into play, usually by summoning a concrete scene, then contemplating that scene, using the intellect. There is often, at the end of such poems, an outward turning, an attempt to find a **totalizing image**, one that brings the thought and feeling of the poem into juxtaposition, in a kind of summary way. (A good example of totalizing images would be the chestnut tree and the dancer at the end of "Among School Children" by William Butler Yeats, p. 900.)

We could also trace the influence of the great Eastern meditative traditions on poetry, but that is beyond the scope of this chapter and this anthology. Many Eastern traditions of meditation, beginning with Hinduism and Buddhism, have their own techniques and spiritual approaches to meditative practice that are reflected in the poetry of China, Japan, India, and other Eastern cultures. A number of English and American poets, such as Allen Ginsberg, Gary Snyder, and Charles Wright, have absorbed these traditions in their own ways, and their poems often reflect this interest and practice.

The meditative tradition is not one that many critics think about much, or often identify as such. But it remains a powerful force in poetry, and it informs—quite literally—so many lyrical poems, giving them structure and direction, guiding the hand of the poet in the subtle (even unconscious) ways that traditions operate.

ROBERT SOUTHWELL (ca. 1561–1595)

New Prince, New Pomp (1591)

Behold, a silly tender Babe
  In freezing winter night
In homely manger trembling lies,
  Alas, a piteous sight!

5   The inns are full; no man will yield
  This little pilgrim bed,
But forced he is with silly° beasts   lowly
  In crib to shroud his head.

Despise him not for lying there,
10   First, what he is inquire;
An orient pearl is often found
        In depth of dirty mire.

Weigh not his crib, his wooden dish,
        Nor beasts that by him feed;
15   Weigh not his Mother's poor attire,
        Nor Joseph's simple weed.°   garment

This stable is a Prince's court,
        This crib his chair of state;
The beasts are parcel of his pomp,
20   The wooden dish his plate.

The persons in that poor attire
        His royal liveries wear;
The Prince himself is come from heaven;
        This pomp is prizèd there.

25   With joy approach, O Christian wight,°   person
        Do homage to thy King;
And highly praise his humble pomp,
        Which he from heaven doth bring.

JOHN DONNE (1572–1631)

from Holy Sonnets (1618)

Spit in my face, you Jews, and pierce my side,
Buffet, and scoff, scourge, and crucify me,
For I have sinn'd, and sinne', and only He,
Who could do no iniquity, hath died.
5   But by my death can not be satisfied
My sins, which pass the Jews' impiety.
They kill'd once an inglorious man, but I
Crucify him daily, being now glorified.
O let me then His strange love still admire;
10   Kings pardon, but He bore our punishment;
And Jacob came clothed in vile harsh attire,
But to supplant, and with gainful intent;
God clothed Himself in vile man's flesh, that so
He might be weak enough to suffer woe.

JOHN DONNE (1572–1631)

from Holy Sonnets (1633)

At the round earth's imagin'd corners,[1] blow
Your trumpets, angels, and arise, arise
From death, you numberless infinities
Of souls, and to your scatter'd bodies go;
5   All whom the flood did, and fire shall o'erthrow,[2]
All whom war, dearth, age, agues, tyrannies,
Despair, law, chance hath slain, and you whose eyes
Shall behold God and never taste death's woe.[3]
But let them sleep, Lord, and me mourn a space,
10   For if above all these my sins abound,
'Tis late to ask abundance of thy grace
When we are there; here on this lowly ground
Teach me how to repent; for that's as good
As if thou'hadst seal'd my pardon with thy blood.

GEORGE HERBERT (1593–1633)

Love Unknown (1633)

Deare Friend, sit down, the tale is long and sad:
And in my faintings I presume your love
Will more complie then help. A Lord I had,
And have, of whom some grounds, which may improve,
5   I hold for two lives, and both lives in me.
To him I brought a dish of fruit one day,
And in the middle plac'd my heart. But he
(I sigh to say)
Lookt on a servant, who did know his eye
10   Better then you know me, or (which is one)
Then I my self. The servant instantly
Quitting the fruit, seiz'd on my heart alone,

---

[1] **At . . . corners:** See Revelation 7.1: "And after these things I saw four angels standing on the four corners of the earth, holding the four winds of the earth, that the wind should not blow on the earth, nor on the sea, nor on any tree."
[2] **fire shall o'erthrow:** See 2 Peter 3.10: "But the day of the Lord will come as a thief in the night; in which the heavens shall pass away with a great noise, and the elements shall melt with fervent heat, the earth also and the works that are therein shall be burned up."
[3] **never taste death's woe:** See Luke 9.27: "But I tell you of a truth, there be some standing here, which shall not taste of death, till they see the kingdom of God."

And threw it in a font, wherein did fall
A stream of bloud, which issu'd from the side
15   Of a great rock: I well remember all,
And have good cause: there it was dipt and dy'd,
And washt, and wrung: the very wringing yet
Enforceth tears. *Your heart was foul, I fear.*
Indeed 'tis true. I did and do commit
20   Many a fault more then my lease will bear;
Yet still askt pardon, and was not deni'd.
But you shall heare. After my heart was well,
And clean and fair, as I one even-tide
                              (I sigh to tell)
25   Walkt by my self abroad, I saw a large
And spacious fornace flaming, and thereon
A boyling caldron, round about whose verge
Was in great letters set *AFFLICTION.*
The greatnesse shew'd the owner. So I went
30   To fetch a sacrifice out of my fold,
Thinking with that, which I did thus present,
To warm his love, which I did fear grew cold.
But as my heart did tender it, the man,
Who was to take it from me, slipt his hand,
35   And threw my heart into the scalding pan;
My heart, that brought it (do you understand?)
The offerers heart. *Your heart was hard, I fear.*
Indeed it's true. I found a callous matter
Began to spread and to expatiate there:
40   But with a richer drug then scalding water
I bath'd it often, ev'n with holy bloud,
Which at a board, while many drunk bare wine,
A friend did steal into my cup for good,
Ev'n taken inwardly, and most divine
45   To supple hardnesses. But at the length
Out of the caldron getting, soon I fled
Unto my house, where to repair the strength
Which I had lost, I hasted to my bed.
But when I thought to sleep out all these faults
50   (I sigh to speak)
I found that some had stuff'd the bed with thoughts,
I would say *thorns.* Deare, could my heart not break,
When with my pleasures ev'n my rest was gone?
Full well I understood, who had been there:
55   For I had giv'n the key to none, but one:
It must be he. *Your heart was dull, I fear.*
Indeed a slack and sleepie state of minde
Did oft possesse me, so that when I pray'd,

Though my lips went, my heart did stay behinde.
60   But all my scores were by another paid,
Who took the debt upon him. *Truly, Friend,*
For ought I heare, your Master shows to you
More favour then you wot of. Mark the end.
The Font did onely, what was old, renew:
65   *The Caldron suppled, what was grown too hard:*
The Thorns did quicken, what was grown too dull:
All did but strive to mend, what you had marr'd.
Wherefore be cheer'd, and praise him to the full
Each day, each houre, each moment of the week,
70   *Who fain would have you be new, tender, quick.*

HENRY VAUGHAN (1622–1695)

I Walk'd the Other Day (1650)

I walk'd the other day, to spend my hour,
        Into a field,
Where I sometimes had seen the soil to yield
        A gallant flow'r;
5   But winter now had ruffled all the bow'r
        And curious store
    I knew there heretofore.

Yet I, whose search lov'd not to peep and peer
        I' th' face of things,
10   Thought with my self, there might be other springs
        Besides this here,
Which, like cold friends, sees us but once a year;
        And so the flow'r
        Might have some other bow'r.

15   Then taking up what I could nearest spy,
        I digg'd about
That place where I had seen him to grow out;
        And by and by
I saw the warm recluse alone to lie,
20   Where fresh and green
        He liv'd of us unseen.

Many a question intricate and rare
        Did I there strow;
But all I could extort was, that he now

25   Did there repair
Such losses as befell him in this air,
        And would ere long
        Come forth most fair and young.

This past, I threw the clothes quite o'er his head;
30   And stung with fear
Of my own frailty dropp'd down many a tear
        Upon his bed;
Then sighing whisper'd, "happy are the dead!
        What peace doth now
35   Rock him asleep below!"

And yet, how few believe such doctrine springs
        From a poor root,
Which all the winter sleeps here under foot,
        And hath no wings
40 To raise it to the truth and light of things;
        But is still trod
        By ev'ry wand'ring clod.

O Thou! whose spirit did at first inflame
        And warm the dead,
45 And by a sacred incubation[1] fed
        With life this frame,
Which once had neither being, form, nor name;
        Grant I may so
        Thy steps track here below,

50   That in these masques and shadows I may see
        Thy sacred way;
And by those hid ascents climb to that day,
        Which breaks from Thee,
Who art in all things, though invisibly!
55   Shew me thy peace,
        Thy mercy, love, and ease,

And from this care, where dreams and sorrows reign,
        Lead me above,
Where light, joy, leisure, and true comforts move
60   Without all pain;
There, hid in thee, shew me his life again,
        At whose dumb urn
        Thus all the year I mourn.

---

[1] **sacred incubation:** Here, Vaughan refers to the presence of the Holy Spirit at Creation. (See Genesis 1.2.)

EDWARD TAYLOR (ca. 1642–1729)

from Meditations

Meditation I. vi: Another Meditation at the Same Time
[as Meditation I. v: Cant. 2: 1: The Lily of the Valleys] **(1683; 1939)**

Am I thy gold? Or purse, Lord, for thy wealth,
    Whether in mine, or mint, refined for thee?
I'm counted so; but count me o'er thyself,
    Lest gold-washed face and brass in heart I be.
5   I fear my touchstone touches when I try
    Me, and my counted gold too overly.

Am I new minted by thy stamp indeed?
    Mine eyes are dim, I cannot clearly see.
Be thou my spectacles that I may read
10   Thine image and inscription stamped on me.
    If thy bright image do upon me stand,
    I am a golden angel in thy hand.

Lord, make my soul thy plate; thine image bright
    Within the circle of the same enfoil.
15   And on its brims in golden letters write
    Thy superscription in an holy style.
    Then I shall be thy money, thou my hoard:
    Let me thy angel be, be thou my Lord.

Meditation II. xviii: Heb. 13: 10: We Have
an Altar **(1696; 1939)**

A bran, a chaff, a very barley yawn,
    An husk, a shell, a nothing, nay yet worse,
A thistle, briar prickle, pricking thorn,
    A lump of lewdness, pouch of sin, a purse
5   Of naughtiness I am, yea what not, Lord?
    And wilt thou be mine altar? And my board?[1]

Mine heart's a park or chase of sins; mine head
    'S a bowling alley. Sins play ninehole[2] here.
Fancy's a green: sin, barley breaks in it led.
10   Judgement's a pingle:[3] blind man's buff's[4] played there.

---

[1] **my board:** The Lord's Table, or Communion table in church.
[2] **ninehole:** Game where nine holes are made in the ground, into which a ball is rolled.
[3] **pingle:** A small section of enclosed ground.
[4] **blind man's buff's:** Game where a blindfolded player attempts to identify the other players.

Sin plays at coursey⁵ park within my mind:
My will's a walk in which it airs what's blind.

Sure then I lack atonement. Lord me help.
Thy shittim° wood o'erlaid with wealthy brass   buckthorn
15   Was an atoning altar, and sweet smelt;
        But if o'erlaid with pure pure gold it was,
        It was an incense altar, all perfúmed
        With odours, wherein, Lord, thou thus was bloomed.

Did this e'erduring wood, when thus o'erspread
20   With these e'erlasting metals altarwise,
Type thy eternal plank of Godhead, wed
        Unto our mortal chip, its sacrifice?
        Thy deity mine altar, manhood thine,
        Mine offering on't for all men's sins, and mine?

25   This golden altar puts such weight into
        The sacrifices offered on 't, that it
O'erweighs the weight of all the sins that flow
        In thine elect. This wedge and beetle split
        The knotty logs of vengeance, too, to shivers;
30   And from their guilt and shame them clear delivers.

This holy altar by its heavenly fire
        Refines our offerings: casts out their dross
And sanctifies their gold by its rich tire
        And all their steams with holy odours boss.
35   Pillars of frankincense and rich perfúme
        They 'tone God's nostrils with, off from this loom.

Good news, good sirs, more good than comes within
        The canopy of angels: heaven's hall
Allows no better. This atones for sin,
40   My glorious God, whose grace here thickest falls.
        May I my barley yawn, bran, briar claw,
        Lay on't, a sacrifice? Or chaff or straw?

Shall I my sin pouch lay on thy gold bench,
        My offering, Lord, to thee? I've such alone,
45   But have no better; for my sins do drench
        My very best unto their very bone.

_____

⁵ **coursey:** Game where dogs pursue by sight instead of scent.

And shall mine offering, by thine altar's fire
Refined and sanctified, to God aspire?

Amen, ev'n so be it. I now will climb
50   The stairs up to thine altar, and on 't lay
Myself, and services, even for its shrine.
        My sacrifice brought thee accept, I pray.
        My morn and evening offerings I'll bring,
        And on this golden altar incense fling.

55   Lord, let thy deity mine altar be,
        And make thy manhood on 't my sacrifice.
For mine atonement, make them both for me
        My altar, to sanctify my gifts likewise,
        That so myself and service on 't may bring
60   Its worth along with them to thee, my King.

The thoughts whereof do make my tunes as fume
        From off this altar rise to thee, Most High,
And all their steams, stuffed with thy altar's blooms,
        My sacrifice of praise in melody.
65   Let thy bright angels catch my tune, and sing 't.
        That equals David's michtam,° which is in 't.   psalms

WILLIAM WORDSWORTH (1770–1850)

The Solitary Reaper (1805; 1807)

Behold her, single in the field,
Yon solitary highland lass,
Reaping and singing by herself—
Stop here, or gently pass!
5   Alone she cuts and binds the grain,
And sings a melancholy strain:
Oh listen, for the vale profound
Is overflowing with the sound!

No nightingale did ever chant
10   So sweetly to reposing bands
Of travellers in some shady haunt
Among Arabian sands;
No sweeter voice was ever heard
In springtime from the cuckoo-bird,

₁₅   Breaking the silence of the seas
     Among the farthest Hebrides.[1]

     Will no one tell me what she sings?
     Perhaps the plaintive numbers flow
     For old, unhappy, far-off things,
₂₀   And battles long ago;
     Or is it some more humble lay,
     Familiar matter of today—
     Some natural sorrow, loss, or pain,
     That has been, and may be again?

₂₅   Whate'er the theme, the maiden sang
     As if her song could have no ending;
     I saw her singing at her work
     And o'er the sickle bending;
     I listened till I had my fill,
₃₀   And as I mounted up the hill
     The music in my heart I bore
     Long after it was heard no more.

GERARD MANLEY HOPKINS (1844–1889)

Spring and Fall (1885)
To a Young Child

     Márgarét, are you gríeving
     Over Goldengrove[1] unleaving?
     Leáves, líke the thíngs of man, you
     With your fresh thoughts care for, can you?
₅   Áh! ás the heart grows older
     It will come to such sights colder
     By and by, nor spare a sigh
     Though worlds of wanwood leafmeal lie;[2]
     And yet you wíll weep and know why.
₁₀   Now no matter, child, the name:
     Sórrow's spríngs áre the same.

---

[1] **Hebrides:** A cluster of more than 500 islands off the western coast of Scotland.
[1] **Goldengrove:** Hopkins likely refers to Golden Grove, the estate just north of Liverpool where Anglican bishop Jeremy Taylor (1613–1667) wrote the devotional *The Golden Grove* (1655). Also, the name suggests a grove of golden leaves in autumn.
[2] **wanwood leafmeal lie:** A pale or dark forest, with its leaves lying scattered on the ground. (Hopkins coined the word "leafmeal" along the lines of "piecemeal.")

Nor mouth had, no nor mind, expressed
What heart heard of, ghost° guessed: soul
It ís the blight man was born for,
15 It is Margaret you mourn for.

WILLIAM BUTLER YEATS (1865–1939)

Byzantium[1] (1930)

The unpurged images of day recede;
The Emperor's drunken soldiery are abed;
Night resonance recedes, night-walkers' song
After great cathedral gong;
5   A starlit or a moonlit dome[2] disdains
All that man is,
All mere complexities,
The fury and the mire of human veins.

Before me floats an image, man or shade,
10 Shade more than man, more image than a shade;
For Hades' bobbin bound in mummy-cloth[3]
May unwind the winding path;
A mouth that has no moisture and no breath
Breathless mouths may summon;
15 I hail the superhuman;
I call it death-in-life and life-in-death.

Miracle, bird or golden handiwork,
More miracle than bird or handiwork,
Planted on the star-lit golden bough,
20 Can like the cocks of Hades crow,[4]
Or, by the moon embittered, scorn aloud

---

[1] **Byzantium:** In April 1930, Yeats described a "subject for a poem" in his diary: "Describe Byzantium as it is in the system towards the end of the first Christian millennium. A walking mummy. Flames at the street corners where the soul is purified, birds of hammered gold singing in the golden trees, in the harbour [dolphins] offering the backs to the wailing dead that they may carry them to Paradise." Byzantium is an ancient city, founded by the Greeks on the site of modern Istanbul, known for its art and architecture.
[2] **A starlit . . . dome:** The dome of St. Sophia in Istanbul.
[3] **For Hades' . . . cloth:** "Hades' bobbin" represents the soul, which is wound in a mummy-cloth of experience during life.
[4] **the cocks of Hades crow:** The cock is a symbol of rebirth and resurrection, often depicted on Roman gravestones.

In glory of changeless metal
Common bird or petal
And all complexities of mire or blood.

25 At midnight on the Emperor's pavement flit
Flames that no faggot feeds, nor steel has lit,
Nor storm disturbs, flames begotten of flame,
Where blood-begotten spirits come
And all complexities of fury leave,
30 Dying into a dance,
An agony of trance,
An agony of flame that cannot singe a sleeve.

Astraddle on the dolphin's mire and blood,
Spirit after spirit! The smithies° break the flood,   forges
35 The golden smithies of the Emperor!
Marbles of the dancing floor
Break bitter furies of complexity,
Those images that yet
Fresh images beget,
40 That dolphin-torn, that gong-tormented sea.

T. S. ELIOT (1888–1965)

Gerontion[1] (1919; 1920)

> Thou hast nor youth nor age
> But as it were an after dinner sleep
> Dreaming of both.[2]

Here I am, an old man in a dry month,
Being read to by a boy, waiting for rain.
I was neither at the hot gates
Nor fought in the warm rain
5 Nor knee deep in the salt marsh, heaving a cutlass,
Bitten by flies, fought.
My house is a decayed house,
And the Jew[3] squats on the window sill, the owner,

---

[1] **Gerontion:** From Greek *geron,* "little old man."
[2] **Thou . . . both:** From Shakespeare's *Measure for Measure* 3.1, where the Duke eases Claudio before his execution with a view of life as illusory and pointless.
[3] **the Jew:** In Eliot's view, a symbol of the displaced man.

Spawned in some estaminet° of Antwerp,   tavern
10 Blistered in Brussels, patched and peeled in London.
The goat coughs at night in the field overhead;
Rocks, moss, stonecrop, iron, merds.°   feces
The woman keeps the kitchen, makes tea,
Sneezes at evening, poking the peevish gutter.
15   I an old man,
A dull head among windy spaces.

Signs are taken for wonders. 'We would see a sign!'
The word within a word, unable to speak a word,
Swaddled with darkness.[4] In the juvescence° of the year   youth
20 Came Christ the tiger

In depraved May, dogwood and chestnut, flowering judas,
To be eaten, to be divided, to be drunk
Among whispers; by Mr. Silvero
With caressing hands, at Limoges[5]
25 Who walked all night in the next room;
By Hakagawa, bowing among the Titians;
By Madame de Tornquist, in the dark room
Shifting the candles; Fräulein von Kulp[6]
Who turned in the hall, one hand on the door. Vacant shuttles
30 Weave the wind. I have no ghosts,
An old man in a draughty house
Under a windy knob.°   hill

After such knowledge, what forgiveness? Think now
History has many cunning passages, contrived corridors
35 And issues, deceives with whispering ambitions,
Guides us by vanities. Think now
She gives when our attention is distracted
And what she gives, gives with such supple confusions
That the giving famishes the craving. Gives too late
40 What's not believed in, or if still believed,
In memory only, reconsidered passion. Gives too soon
Into weak hands, what's thought can be dispensed with

---

[4] **Signs . . . darkness:** See Lancelot Andrews's commentary on the gospels: "Signs are taken for wonders. 'Master, we would fain see a sign,' that is a miracle. And in this sense it [the Gospel] is a sign to wonder at" (*Works* 1.204).

[5] **Limoges:** City in southern France, known for its fine porcelain.

[6] **Hakagawa . . . Fräulein von Kulp:** Imaginary persons who value—perhaps overvalue—art (Titians) or mystery (the candles of a seance) or anything that is exotic in some sense.

Till the refusal propagates a fear. Think
Neither fear nor courage saves us. Unnatural vices
45   Are fathered by our heroism. Virtues
Are forced upon us by our impudent crimes.
These tears are shaken from the wrath-bearing tree.[7]

The tiger springs in the new year. Us he devours.[8] Think at last
We have not reached conclusion, when I
50   Stiffen in a rented house. Think at last
I have not made this show purposelessly
And it is not by any concitation°   agitation
Of the backward devils.
I would meet you upon this honestly.
55   I that was near your heart was removed therefrom
To lose beauty in terror, terror in inquisition.
I have lost my passion: why should I need to keep it
Since what is kept must be adulterated?
I have lost my sight, smell, hearing, taste and touch:
60   How should I use them for your closer contact?

These with a thousand small deliberations
Protract the profit of their chilled delirium,
Excite the membrane, when the sense has cooled,
With pungent sauces, multiply variety
65   In a wilderness of mirrors. What will the spider do,
Suspend its operations, will the weevil
Delay? De Bailhache, Fresca, Mrs. Cammel, whirled
Beyond the circuit of the shuddering Bear[9]
In fractured atoms. Gull against the wind, in the windy straits
70   Of Belle Isle, or running on the Horn.[10]
White feathers in the snow, the Gulf claims,
And an old man driven by the Trades°   trade winds
To a sleepy corner.
                              Tenants of the house,
75   Thoughts of a dry brain in a dry season.

---

[7] **the wrath-bearing tree:** In Eden, the tree of the knowledge of good and evil. (See Genesis 2 and 3.)
[8] **Us he devours:** The opposite of Communion, where the faithful "devour" the body and blood of
Christ. Here, Christ the tiger "devours" the faithful.
[9] **the shuddering Bear:** The Great Bear, a constellation in the northern sky.
[10] **Belle Isle . . . Horn:** Belle Isle is a small island between Labrador and Newfoundland. The Horn
refers to Tierra del Fuego, the southernmost tip of South America, or else the Horn of Africa.

T. S. ELIOT (1888–1965)

from Four Quartets, Burnt Norton (IV)

Time and the bell have buried the day,
The black cloud carries the sun away.
Will the sunflower turn to us, will the clematis
Stray down, bend to us; tendril and spray
5   Clutch and cling?
Chill
Fingers of yew be curled
Down on us? After the kingfisher's wing
Has answered light to light, and is silent, the light is still
10   At the still point of the turning world.

MARY OLIVER (1935–   )

Lilies (1990)

I have been thinking
about living
like the lilies
that blow in the fields.

5   They rise and fall
in the wedge of the wind,
and have no shelter
from the tongues of the cattle,

and have no closets or cupboards,
10   and have no legs.
Still I would like to be
as wonderful

as that old idea.
But if I were a lily
15   I think I would wait all day
for the green face

of the hummingbird
to touch me.
What I mean is,
20   could I forget myself

even in those feathery fields?
When van Gogh[1]
preached to the poor
of course he wanted to save someone—

25 most of all himself.
He wasn't a lily,
and wandering through the bright fields
only gave him more ideas

it would take his life to solve.
30 I think I will always be lonely
in this world, where the cattle
graze like a black and white river—

where the ravishing lilies
melt, without protest, on their tongues—
35 where the hummingbird, whenever there is a fuss,
just rises and floats away.

SEAMUS HEANEY (1939–   )

Exposure (1975)

It is December in Wicklow:[1]
Alders dripping, birches
Inheriting the last light,
The ash tree cold to look at.

5 A comet that was lost
Should be visible at sunset,
Those million tons of light
Like a glimmer of haws and rose-hips,

And I sometimes see a falling star.
10 If I could come on meteorite!
Instead I walk through damp leaves,
Husks, the spent flukes of autumn,

---

[1] **van Gogh:** Vincent van Gogh (1853–1890), a Dutch postimpressionist painter.
[1] **Wicklow:** County Wicklow, on the east coast of Ireland.

Imagining a hero
On some muddy compound,
His gift like a slingstone
Whirled for the desperate.

15

How did I end up like this?
I often think of my friends'
Beautiful prismatic counselling
And the anvil brains of some who hate me

20

As I sit weighing and weighing
My responsible *tristia*.°   sorrows
For what? For the ear? For the people?
For what is said behind-backs?

Rain comes down through the alders,
Its low conducive voices
Mutter about let-downs and erosions
And yet each drop recalls

25

The diamond absolutes.
I am neither internee nor informer;
An inner émigré, grown long-haired
And thoughtful; a wood-kerne²

30

Escaped from the massacre,
Taking protective colouring
From bole and bark, feeling
Every wind that blows;

35

Who, blowing up these sparks
For their meagre heat, have missed
The once-in-a-lifetime portent,
The comet's pulsing rose.

40

---

² **kerne:** An Irish foot-soldier.

LOUISE GLÜCK (1943–   )

Messengers (1975)

You have only to wait, they will find you.
The geese flying low over the marsh,
glittering in black water.
They find you.

5   And the deer—
how beautiful they are,
as though their bodies did not impede them.
Slowly they drift into the open
through bronze panels of sunlight.

10   Why would they stand so still
if they were not waiting?
Almost motionless, until their cages rust,
the shrubs shiver in the wind,
squat and leafless.

15   You have only to let it happen:
that cry—*release, release*—like the moon
wrenched out of earth and rising
full in its circle of arrows

until they come before you
20   like dead things, saddled with flesh,
and you above them, wounded and dominant.

THIS IS JUST TO SAY
—William Carlos Williams

An Anthology of Poets in Dialogue

Poetry comes from poetry. What this means is that poets rewrite the poetry of the past, adding their own voice to earlier voices, transforming what they encounter in very different ways. This is sometimes called **influence**, a general term used to suggest that poets read the works of earlier poets and often reflect the style or content of those they have admired.

In *The Anxiety of Influence*, critic Harold Bloom makes the point that poets either unconsciously or deliberately "misread" poets of the past, contending with them in an almost Freudian way: a son wrestling with the father, in Bloom's analysis. Apart from being rather sexist, this is only partially true. Poets actually pay homage to their predecessors, and many of them feel no strong impulse to misread or overcome their literary masters. The exact nature of a poet's reaction to his or her ancestors will vary in each instance, as the poem-sequences in this chapter will suggest.

Sometimes there is an element of contention, as when Eavan Boland, an Irish poet, answers a poem by Yeats (p. 1598) in which a beautiful girl is magically transformed into a fish. In Boland's poem (p. 1598), the woman actually turns herself into the fish, making herself the agent of her own transformation. This refutes the earlier poem in a way, although there is still a trace of homage in the actual choice of the subject, even in the quality of anger implicit in Boland's powerful revision.

Quite often a later poet's responses to an earlier poem are ironic, as in the rewritings of "This Is Just to Say" by William Carlos Williams (p. 1607). Kenneth Koch (p. 1607) remakes the poem in his own aesthetic, although his admiration for Williams is palpable, whereas the poet's wife, Flossie, writes with an almost sarcastic detachment, beginning her poem (p. 1608):

> Dear Bill: I've made a
> couple of sandwiches for you.
> In the ice-box you'll find
> blue-berries—a cup of grapefruit
> 5   a glass of cold coffee.

The poem ends with some humor: "See you later. Love. Floss. / Please switch off the telephone."

Poets often write to each other as if they were passing a ball back and forth, or exchanging notes. One of the most famous examples of poets talking to each other across the decades and centuries began with Christopher Marlowe's "The Passionate Shepherd to His Love" (p. 1550). Sir Walter Ralegh responded to this with "The Nymph's Reply to the Shepherd" (p. 1551). We could probably find many responses to these two poems. Several of the most famous are included here.

Throughout this book are found poems that have been translated by other poets. For example, in this chapter, Ezra Pound translates Li Po's "Song of Ch'ang-kan" (p. 1546) in his lovely "The River-Merchant's Wife: A Letter" (p. 1547). But note the differences between the original (itself a translation from the Chinese by Chinese-American poet Arthur Sze) and its "translation" by Ezra Pound. Translation is always an act of interpretation, a response of one poetic sensibility to another. Pound's poem is as much Pound as Li Po, and the two poems, while seeming the same, are remarkably distinct.

Poets frequently establish in a particular poem a tune or a tonal range that later poets find attractive and generative. These later poets attach themselves to the music of the earlier poem and create their own music from it, as when Erica Jong (p. 1574) and Edward Hirsch (p. 1575) hitched their wagons to the harmonies and playful tone of "My Cat Jeoffry" by Christopher Smart (p. 1571). A more complex chain of literary reactions followed from "The Armadillo" by Elizabeth Bishop (p. 1617). Before it was published, this poem was read by her friend, Robert Lowell, who found something in the tone and form of the poem that liberated him from his earlier style. He dedicated his poem "Skunk Hour" (p. 1618) to Bishop because "re-reading her suggested a way of breaking through the shell of my old manner." He noted that both poems "use short line stanzas, start with a drifting description and end with a single animal." Lowell's "Skunk Hour" would seem, on the surface, to have little in common with "The Armadillo," but the connections are there, and quite strong. Seamus Heaney, writing decades later, rewrote the Lowell poem in his own fashion in "The Skunk" (p. 1619), a fascinating example of literary homage.

Oblique connections between poems can still be generative for poets, who find something in an earlier poem that ignites their own thinking. Frost was a close reader of John Keats, and his "After Apple-Picking" (p. 1585)—certainly one of the greatest poems by Frost—picks up on themes initiated by Keats in "To Autumn" (p. 1584). Frost also harks back, quite explicitly, to a poem by Keats in "Take Something Like a Star" (p. 1582). The latter became a touchstone for Peter Davison, who wrote about Frost watching stars in "The Star Watcher" (p. 1583). Thus poem leads to poem.

Of course, parody is a familiar form of homage, the most direct example of literary influence. One of the most well-known examples of this tradition is "The Dover Bitch" by Anthony Hecht (p. 1595), a poem that alludes amusingly to "Dover Beach," a classic poem by Matthew Arnold (p. 1594). The transformation of the title points to a rather abrasive but witty form of parody. A less caustic strain of parodic writing begins with Andrew Marvell's "Picture of Little T. C. in a Prospect of Flowers" (p. 1564), a poem that has generated many imitations and parodies, several of which are included here, including "Picture of Little J. A. in a Prospect of Flowers," a distinguished contemporary example by John Ashbery (p. 1565).

Often the impulse to parody leads in unlikely directions, as when Billy Collins responds to Wordsworth's "Lines Written a Few Miles above Tintern Abbey" (p. 1576) in "Lines Composed Over Three Thousand Miles from Tintern Abbey" (p. 1580). In both cases, the famous original sparked the imagination of the contemporary poet, and the parodic impulse led to a poem of distinct originality.

Readers will find much to enjoy here: poems reflecting poems, distorting them, expanding on insights, extrapolating from their content or countermanding points. Poetry is an ongoing dialogue between poets, an extended conversation on which readers are allowed to eavesdrop. Poetry feeds on language, especially poetic language, without regard for intellectual property or the feelings of the poets whose work has been cannibalized. Indeed, it could be said that poets eat poetry, digest it, and use the nutrients in the language of other poets to create themselves in their work, to create the poetic tradition itself.

LI PO (701–762)
trans. Arthur Sze

Song of Ch'ang-kan

When my hair just began to cover my forehead,
I was plucking flowers, playing in front of the gate.
You came along riding a bamboo stick horse,
circling and throwing green plums.
5   Together we lived in Ch'ang-kan Village
never suspicious of our love.
At fourteen, I became your wife,
my shy face never opened.
I lowered my head, faced the dark wall,
10   to your thousand calls, never a response.
At fifteen, I became enlightened,
was willing to be dust with you, ashes with you.
Always preserving you in my heart,
why should I ascend the terrace to look for your return?
15   At sixteen, you traveled far, through

Chü-t'ang Gorge, by rocks and swirling waters . . .
And in the fifth month, they are impassable,
monkeys wailing to the sky . . .
By our door where you left footprints,
20   mosses, one by one, grew over;
too deep to be swept away!
Leaves fall early in the autumn wind.
In lunar August, yellow butterflies
hovered in pairs over the west garden grasses.
25   My heart hurt at this sight, beauty flickering . . .
Sooner or later, if you return through the Three Pa district,
send home first. I will meet you,
ignore the long distance, even to Long Wind Sands.

EZRA POUND (1885–1972)

The River-Merchant's Wife: A Letter (1915)

While my hair was still cut straight across my forehead
I played about the front gate, pulling flowers.
You came by on bamboo stilts, playing horse,
You walked about my seat, playing with blue plums.
5   And we went on living in the village of Chōkan:
Two small people, without dislike or suspicion.

At fourteen I married My Lord you.
I never laughed, being bashful.
Lowering my head, I looked at the wall.
10   Called to, a thousand times, I never looked back.

At fifteen I stopped scowling,
I desired my dust to be mingled with yours
Forever and forever and forever.
Why should I climb the lookout?

15   At sixteen you departed,
You went into far Ku-tō-en, by the river of swirling eddies,
And you have been gone five months.
The monkeys make sorrowful noise overhead.

You dragged your feet when you went out.
20   By the gate now, the moss is grown, the different mosses,
Too deep to clear them away!

The leaves fall early this autumn, in wind.
The paired butterflies are already yellow with August
Over the grass in the West garden;
25   They hurt me. I grow older.
If you are coming down through the narrows of the river Kiang,
Please let me know beforehand,
And I will come out to meet you
                    As far as Chō-fū-Sa.

                                                Rihaku

ANONYMOUS

Western Wind   (sixteenth century)

Westron winde, when will thou blow,
The smalle raine downe can raine?
Christ if my love were in my armes,
And I in my bed againe.

ROBERT PENN WARREN   (1905–1989)

Blow, West Wind   (1935)

I know, I know—though the evidence
Is lost, and the last who might speak are dead.
Blow, west wind, blow, and the evidence, O,

Is lost, and wind shakes the cedar, and O,
5   I know how the kestrel hung over Wyoming,
Breast reddened in sunset, and O, the cedar

Shakes, and I know how cold
Was the sweat on my father's mouth, dead.
Blow, west wind, blow, shake the cedar, I know

10   How once I, a boy, crouching at creekside,
Watched, in the sunlight, a handful of water
Drip, drip, from my hand. The drops—they were bright!

But you believe nothing, with the evidence lost.

SIR PHILIP SIDNEY (1554–1586)

from Astrophil and Stella (1682; 1691)
31 "With how sad steps, Oh Moon . . ."

With how sad steps, Oh Moon, thou climb'st the skies,
How silently, and with how wan a face!
What, may it be that even in heav'nly place
That busy archer[1] his sharp arrows tries?
5   Sure, if that long-with-love-acquainted eyes
Can judge of love, thou feel'st a lover's case;
I read it in thy looks: thy languished grace,
To me that feel the like, thy state descries.
Then even of fellowship, Oh Moon, tell me,
10   Is constant love deemed there but want of wit?
Are beauties there as proud as here they be?
Do they above love to be loved, and yet
Those lovers scorn whom that love doth possess?
Do they call virtue there ungratefulness?

PHILIP LARKIN (1922–1985)

Sad Steps (1968)

Groping back to bed after a piss
I part thick curtains, and am startled by
The rapid clouds, the moon's cleanliness.

Four o'clock: wedge-shadowed gardens lie
5   Under a cavernous, a wind-picked sky.
There's something laughable about this,

The way the moon dashes through clouds that blow
Loosely as cannon-smoke to stand apart
(Stone-coloured light sharpening the roofs below)

10   High and preposterous and separate—
Lozenge of love! Medallion of art!
O wolves of memory! Immensements! No,

---

[1] **That busy archer:** I.e., Cupid, the Greek god of love, who is commonly depicted with a bow and arrows.

One shivers slightly, looking up there.
The hardness and the brightness and the plain
15   Far-reaching singleness of that wide stare

Is a reminder of the strength and pain
Of being young; that it can't come again,
But is for others undiminished somewhere.

CHRISTOPHER MARLOWE (1564–1593)

The Passionate Shepherd to His Love (1599)

Come live with me and be my love,
And we will all the pleasures prove,
That hills and valleys, dales and fields,
And all the craggy mountains yields.

5   There we will sit upon the rocks,
And see the shepherds feed their flocks,
By shallow rivers to whose falls
Melodious birds sing madrigals.

And I will make thee beds of roses
10   With a thousand fragrant posies,
A cap of flowers, and a kirtle[1]
Embroidered all with leaves of myrtle;

A gown made of the finest wool
Which from our pretty lambs we pull;
15   Fair linèd slippers for the cold,
With buckles of the purest gold;

A belt of straw and ivy buds,
With coral clasps and amber studs:
And if these pleasures may thee move,
20   Come live with me and be my love.

The shepherds' swains shall dance and sing
For thy delight each May morning:
If these delights thy mind may move,
Then live with me and be my love.

---

[1] **kirtle:** A woman's dress or skirt.

SIR WALTER RALEGH   (ca. 1552–1618)

The Nymph's Reply to the Shepherd   (1600)

If all the world and love were young,
And truth in every shepherd's tongue,
These pretty pleasures might me move
To live with thee and be thy love.

5   Time drives the flocks from field to fold,
When rivers rage and rocks grow cold,
And Philomel[1] becometh dumb;
The rest complains of cares to come.

The flowers do fade, and wanton fields
10   To wayward winter reckoning yields;
A honey tongue, a heart of gall,
Is fancy's spring, but sorrow's fall.

Thy gowns, thy shoes, thy beds of roses,
Thy cap, thy kirtle,[2] and thy posies
15   Soon break, soon wither, soon forgotten,
In folly ripe, in reason rotten.

Thy belt of straw and ivy buds,
Thy coral clasps and amber studs,
All these in me no means can move
20   To come to thee and be thy love.

But could youth last and love still breed,
Had joys no date nor age no need,
Then these delights my mind might move
To live with thee and be thy love.

---

[1] **Philomel:** I.e., the nightingale.
[2] **kirtle:** A woman's dress or skirt.

JOHN DONNE (1572–1631)

The Bait (1633)

Come live with me, and be my love,
And we will some new pleasures prove
Of golden sands and crystal brooks,
With silken lines and silver hooks.

5 There will the river whispering run
Warmed by thy eyes, more than the sun.
And there the'enamoured fish will stay,
Begging themselves they may betray.

When thou wilt swim in that live bath,
10 Each fish, which every channel hath,
Will amorously to thee swim,
Gladder to catch thee, than thou him.

If thou, to be so seen, be'st loth,°   reluctant
By sun, or moon, thou darkenest both,
15 And if myself have leave to see,
I need not their light, having thee.

Let others freeze with angling reeds,
And cut their legs with shells and weeds,
Or treacherously poor fish beset,
20 With strangling snare or windowy net:

Let coarse bold hands, from slimy nest
The bedded fish in banks out-wrest,
Or curious traitors, sleavesilk flies
Bewitch poor fishes' wandering eyes.

25 For thee, thou need'st no such deceit,
For thou thyself art thine own bait:
That fish, that is not catched thereby,
Alas, is wiser far than I.

WILLIAM CARLOS WILLIAMS (1883–1963)

Raleigh Was Right (1944)

We cannot go to the country
for the country will bring us no peace
What can the small violets tell us
that grow on furry stems in
5   the long grass among lance shaped leaves?

Though you praise us
and call to mind the poets
who sung of our loveliness
it was long ago!
10   long ago! when country people
would plow and sow with
flowering minds and pockets at ease—
if ever this were true.

Not now. Love itself a flower
15   with roots in a parched ground.
Empty pockets make empty heads.
Cure it if you can but
do not believe that we can live
today in the country
20   for the country will bring us no peace.

C. DAY LEWIS (1904–1972)

"Come live with me and be my love" (1935)

Come, live with me and be my love,
And we will all the pleasures prove
Of peace and plenty, bed and board,
That chance employment may afford.

5   I'll handle dainties on the docks
And thou shalt read of summer frocks:
At evening by the sour canals
We'll hope to hear some madrigals.

Care on thy maiden brow shall put
10   A wreath of wrinkles, and thy foot

Be shod with pain: not silken dress
But toil shall tire thy loveliness.

Hunger shall make thy modest zone
And cheat fond death of all but bone—
15   If these delights thy mind may move,
Then live with me and be my love.

DOUGLAS CRASE (1944–   )

Covenant (1981)

To live with me and be
My love, proposing it
As if all the pleasures
Came to the same test,
5   Invites the love from living
In for life, deposing it
With an innocent lively
Tension of intent. And
To live with me *or* be
10   My love, selecting it
As if without the other's
Commerce the one could live,
Secures the life from loving
In live death, protecting it
15   With a deadly living
Waste of discontent. But
To love with me and live
My love, engaging it
One from the other neither
20   Leaving off, is to love
In the life of division
And live in loving it,
Where if loving only lives
It dies
25   But if living only will love
Then loving will live.

GREG DELANTY (1958–   )

Williams Was Wrong (2004)

Now I find peace in everything around me;
in the modest campion and the shoals of light
leaping across the swaying sea
and the gulls gliding out of sight.
5   The tops of wave-confettied rocks
slide into water and turn into seals.
They move to the lively reel
of the cove's clapping dance hall,
rising blithe yelps above the sea's music.
10   The ocean draws in and out like an accordion
and unseen lithe fingers play the strings
of joy on what the moment brings.
The seals close and part and close again.
Their awkward fins have turned to wings.

WILLIAM SHAKESPEARE (1564–1616)

from Macbeth
Act V, Scene 5 (Macbeth)   (1606; 1623)

To-morrow, and to-morrow, and to-morrow,
Creeps in this petty pace from day to day,
To the last syllable of recorded time;
And all our yesterdays have lighted fools
5   The way to dusty death. Out, out, brief candle!
Life's but a walking shadow, a poor player
That struts and frets his hour upon the stage,
And then is heard no more; it is a tale
Told by an idiot, full of sound and fury,
10   Signifying nothing.

JAMES TATE (1943–   )

Rooster (1979)

Tomorrow, since I have so few,
and Tomorrow, less dramatically,
and Tomorrow any number of times.
As for renouncing, isn't that
5 the oldest?

Rooster crowing: dark blue velvet
that knows itself too well—
empty wallet, busted heart—
Oh yes, my very good friend,
10 a voice searching for orchids,
that dances alone.

And then for that one hour
there are no familiar faces:
this lovely, misbegotten animal
15 created from odd bits of refuse
from minute to minute
splits us down the middle.

WILLIAM SHAKESPEARE (1564–1616)

Sonnet 116 "Let me not to the marriage of true minds" (ca. 1595; 1609)

Let me not to the marriage of true minds
Admit impediments. Love is not love
Which alters when it alteration finds,
Or bends with the remover to remove:
5 O, no! it is an ever-fixed mark,
That looks on tempests and is never shaken;

It is the star to every wandering bark,°   ship
Whose worth's unknown, although his height be taken.
Love's not Time's fool, though rosy lips and cheeks
10   Within his bending sickle's compass come;
Love alters not with his brief hours and weeks,
But bears it out even to the edge of doom.
     If this be error, and upon me prov'd,
     I never writ, nor no man ever lov'd.

WENDY COPE (1945–   )

Strugnell's Sonnets (VI)   (1997)

Let me not to the marriage of true swine
Admit impediments. With his big car
He's won your heart, and you have punctured mine.
I have no spare; henceforth I'll bear the scar.
5   Since women are not worth the booze you buy them
I dedicate myself to Higher Things.
If men deride and sneer, I shall defy them
And soar above Tulse Hill on poet's wings—
A brother to the thrush in Brockwell Park,[1]
10   Whose song, though sometimes drowned by rock guitars,
Outlives their din. One day I'll make my mark,
Although I'm not from Ulster[2] or from Mars,
And when I'm published in some classy mag
You'll rue the day you scarpered° in his Jag.[3]   left quickly

---

[1] **Tulse Hill . . . Brockwell Park:** Both Tulse Hill and Brockwell Park are part of London.
[2] **Ulster:** A historical region and ancient kingdom in Ireland. It now refers to Northern Ireland.
[3] **Jag:** I.e., Jaguar, an expensive car.

SIR ROBERT AYTOUN (1570–1638)

To His Coy Mistress

What others doth discourage and dismay
Is unto me a pastime and a play.
I sport in her denials and do know
Women love best that does love least in show.
5   Too sudden favours may abate delight;
When modest coyness sharps the appetite,
I grow the hotter for her cold neglect,
And more inflamed when she shows least respect.
Heat may arise from rocks, from flints so fire:
10 So from her coldness I do strike desire.
She, knowing this perhaps, resolves to try
My faith and patience, offering to deny
Whate'er I ask of her, that I may be
More taken with her, for her slighting me.
15 When fishes play with baits, best, anglers say,
To make them bite, is draw the bait away:
So dallies she with me till, to my smart,
Both bait and hook sticks fastened in my heart.
And now I am become her foolish prey;
20 And, that she knows I cannot break away,
Let her resolve no longer to be free
From Cupid's[1] bonds, and bind herself to me.
Nor let her vex me longer with despair
That they be cruel that be young and fair:
25 It is the old, the creasèd, and the black
That are unkind and for affection lack.
I'll tie her eyes with lines, her ears with moans;
Her marble heart I'll pierce with hideous groans
That neither eyes, ears, heart shall be at rest
30 Till she forsake her sire to love me best;
Nor will I raise my siege nor leave my field
Till I have made my valiant mistress yield.

---

[1] **Cupid's:** Belonging to Cupid, the Roman god of love.

ANDREW MARVELL (1621–1678)

To His Coy Mistress (1681)

Had we but world enough, and time,
This coyness, Lady, were no crime.
We would sit down, and think which way
To walk, and pass our long love's day.
5   Thou by the Indian Ganges' side
Shouldst rubies find: I by the tide
Of Humber[1] would complain. I would
Love you ten years before the Flood:
And you should, if you please, refuse
10   Till the conversion of the Jews.[2]
My vegetable love should grow
Vaster than empires, and more slow.
An hundred years should go to praise
Thine eyes, and on thy forehead gaze.
15   Two hundred to adore each breast;
But thirty thousand to the rest.
An age at least to every part,
And the last age should show your heart:
For, Lady, you deserve this state;
20   Nor would I love at lower rate.
    But at my back I always hear
Time's wingèd chariot hurrying near;
And yonder all before us lie
Deserts of vast eternity.
25   Thy beauty shall no more be found;
Nor, in thy marble vault, shall sound
My echoing song: then worms shall try
That long-preserved virginity:
And your quaint honour turn to dust;
30   And into ashes all my lust.
The grave's a fine and private place,
But none, I think, do there embrace.
    Now, therefore, while the youthful glue
Sits on thy skin like morning dew,
35   And while thy willing soul transpires

---

[1] **Indian Ganges . . . Humber:** The Ganges and the Humber rivers flow through India and England respectively.
[2] **before the Flood . . . conversion of the Jews:** I.e., from the beginning to the end of the world. The Flood, sent by God as a punishment for the wickedness of His people, is recounted in Genesis, the first book of the Bible. The conversion of the Jews is an event described in Revelation, the last book of the New Testament.

At every pore with instant fires,
Now let us sport us while we may;
And now, like amorous birds of prey,
Rather at once our time devour,
40   Than languish in his slow-chapped power.
Let us roll all our strength, and all
Our sweetness, up into one ball:
And tear our pleasures with rough strife
Thorough the iron grates of life.
45   Thus, though we cannot make our sun
Stand still, yet we will make him run.

JAY PARINI (1948–   )

To His Dear Friend, Bones (1982)

The arguments against restraint
in love, in retrospect, seem quaint;
I would have thought this obvious
to you, at least, whose serious
5   pursuit of intellectual grace
is not less equal to your taste
for all things richly formed. No good
will come of what we force. I should
be hesitant to say how long
10   this shy devotion has gone on,
how days beyond account have turned
to seasons as we've slowly learned
to speak a common tongue, to find
the world's erratic text defined
15   and stabilized. I should be vexed
to mention time at all, except
that, even as I write, a blear
October dampness feels like fear
externalized; I number days
20   in lots of thirty—all the ways
we have for counting breaths, so brief,
beside the measures of our grief
and joy. So let me obviate
this cold chronology and state
25   more simply what I mean: it's sure
enough, the grave will make obscure
whatever fierce, light moments love

affords. I should not have to prove
by metaphysical displays
30   of wit how numerous are the ways
in which it matters that we touch,
not merely with our hearts; so much
depends upon the skin, dear bones,
with all its various, humid tones,
35   the only barrier which contrives
to keep us in our separate lives.

JOHN DONNE (1572–1631)

A Valediction°: Forbidding Mourning (1633)   Farewell

As virtuous men pass mildly away,
    And whisper to their souls to go,
Whilst some of their sad friends do say,
    The breath goes now, and some say, no:

5   So let us melt, and make no noise,
    No tear-floods, nor sigh-tempests move,
'Twere profanation of our joys
    To tell the laity our love.

Moving of th' Earth brings harms and fears,
10   Men reckon what it did and meant;
But trepidation of the spheres,
    Though greater far, is innocent.

Dull sublunary lovers' love
    (Whose soul is sense) cannot admit
15 Absence, because it doth remove
    Those things which elemented it.

But we by a love so much refined
    That ourselves know not what it is,
Inter-assurèd of the mind,
20   Care less, eyes, lips, and hands to miss.

Our two souls therefore, which are one,
    Though I must go, endure not yet
A breach, but an expansion,
    Like gold to aery thinness beat.

25 If they be two, they are two so
          As stiff twin compasses are two;
    Thy soul the fixed foot makes no show
          To move, but doth, if th'other do.

    And though it in the centre sit,
30   Yet when the other far doth roam
    It leans, and hearkens after it,
          And grows erect as that comes home.

    Such wilt thou be to me, who must
          Like th' other foot obliquely run;
35 Thy firmness makes my circle just,
          And makes me end where I begun.

ADRIENNE RICH (1929–   )

A Valediction Forbidding Mourning (1970)

    My swirling wants. Your frozen lips.
    The grammar turned and attacked me.
    Themes, written under duress.
    Emptiness of the notations.

5   They gave me a drug that slowed the healing of wounds.

    I want you to see this before I leave:
    the experience of repetition as death
    the failure of criticism to locate the pain
    the poster in the bus that said:
10 *my bleeding is under control.*

    A red plant in a cemetery of plastic wreaths.

    A last attempt: the language is a dialect called metaphor.
    These images go unglossed: hair, glacier, flashlight.
    When I think of a landscape I am thinking of a time.
15 When I talk of taking a trip I mean forever.
    I could say: those mountains have a meaning
    but further than that I could not say.

    To do something very common, in my own way.

GEORGE HERBERT (1593–1633)

Virtue (1633)

Sweet day, so cool, so calm, so bright,
The bridal of the earth and sky:
The dew shall weep thy fall tonight;
        For thou must die.

5   Sweet rose, whose hue angry and brave
Bids the rash gazer wipe his eye:
Thy root is ever in its grave,
        And thou must die.

Sweet spring, full of sweet days and roses,
10   A box where sweets compacted lie:
My music shows ye have your closes,
        And all must die.

Only a sweet and virtuous soul,
Like seasoned timber, never gives;
15   But though the whole world turn to coal,
        Then chiefly lives.

WILLIAM MEREDITH (1919–   )

Airman's Virtue (1944)

After Herbert[1]

High plane for whom the winds incline,
   Who own but to your own recall,
There is a flaw in your design
   For you must fall.

5   High cloud whose proud and angry stuff
   Rose up in heat against earth's thrall,
The nodding law has time enough
   To wait your fall.

---

[1] **After Herbert:** I.e., the English poet George Herbert.

High sky, full of high shapes and vapors,
10   Against whose vault nothing is tall,
It is written that your torch and tapers
        Headlong shall fall.

Only an outward-aching soul
        Can hold in high disdain these ties
15 And fixing on a farther pole
        Will sheerly rise.

ANDREW MARVELL (1621–1678)

The Picture of Little T. C. in a Prospect[1]
of Flowers (1681)

See with what simplicity
This nymph begins her golden days!
In the green grass she loves to lie,
And there with her fair aspect tames
5   The wilder flowers, and gives them names;
But only with the roses plays,
        And them does tell
What color best becomes them, and what smell.

Who can foretell for what high cause
10 This darling of the gods was born?
Yet this is she whose chaster laws
The wanton Love[2] shall one day fear,
And, under her command severe,
See his bow broke and ensigns torn.
15   Happy who can
Appease this virtuous enemy of man!

O then let me in time compound
And parley with those conquering eyes,
Ere they have tried their force to wound;
20 Ere with their glancing wheels they drive
In triumph over hearts that strive,
And them that yield but more despise:
        Let me be laid
Where I may see thy glories from some shade.

---

[1] **The Picture . . . Prospect:** T. C. was perhaps Theophila Cornewall; Prospect: a background scene.
[2] **wanton Love:** I.e., Cupid, the Roman god of love, who is commonly depicted with a bow and arrows.

25 Meantime, whilst every verdant thing
   Itself does at thy beauty charm,
   Reform the errors of the spring;
   Make that the tulips may have share
   Of sweetness, seeing they are fair;
30 And roses of their thorns disarm;
   　　　But most procure
   That violets may a longer age endure.

   But, O young beauty of the woods,
   Whom nature courts with fruits and flowers,
35 Gather the flowers, but spare the buds,
   Lest Flora,[3] angry at thy crime
   To kill her infants in their prime,
   Do quickly make the example yours;
   　　　And ere we see,
40 Nip in the blossom all our hopes and thee.

JOHN ASHBERY (1927– 　)

The Picture of Little J. A.[1] in a Prospect of Flowers (1956)

> He was spoilt from childhood
> by the future, which he mastered
> rather early and apparently
> without great difficulty.
> 　　　　—BORIS PASTERNAK

I

Darkness falls like a wet sponge
And Dick gives Genevieve a swift punch
In the pajamas. "Aroint° thee, witch."　　　　　　　　　begone
Her tongue from previous ecstasy
5 Releases thoughts like little hats.

"He clap'd me first during the eclipse.
Afterwards I noted his manner

---

[3] **Flora:** The Roman goddess of flowers.
[1] **J.A.:** Perhaps John Ashbery.

Much altered. But he sending
At that time certain handsome jewels
10 I durst not seem to take offence."

In a far recess of summer
Monks are playing soccer.

II

So far is goodness a mere memory
Or naming of recent scenes of badness
15 That even these lives, children,
You may pass through to be blessed,
So fair does each invent his virtue.

And coming from a white world, music
Will sparkle at the lips of many who are
20 Beloved. Then these, as dirty handmaidens
To some transparent witch, will dream
Of a white hero's subtle wooing,
And time shall force a gift on each.

That beggar to whom you gave no cent
25 Striped the night with his strange descant.

III

Yet I cannot escape the picture
Of my small self in that bank of flowers:
My head among the blazing phlox
Seemed a pale and gigantic fungus.
30 I had a hard stare, accepting

Everything, taking nothing,
As though the rolled-up future might stink
As loud as stood the sick moment
The shutter clicked. Though I was wrong,
35 Still, as the loveliest feelings

Must soon find words, and these, yes,
Displace them, so I am not wrong
In calling this comic version of myself
The true one. For as change is horror,
40 Virtue is really stubbornness

And only in the light of lost words
Can we imagine our rewards.

CHARLES TOMLINSON (1927–   )

The Picture of J. T. in a Prospect of Stone (1963)

What should one
　　wish a child
　　　　and that, one's own
emerging
5　　　　from between
　　　　　　the stone lips
of a sheep-stile
　　that divides
　　　　village graves
10　and village green?
　　　　—Wish her
　　　　　　the constancy of stone.
—But stone
　　is hard.
15　　　　—Say, rather
it resists
　　the slow corrosives
　　　　and the flight
of time
20　　and yet it takes
　　　　the play, the fluency
from light.
　　　　—How would you know.
　　　　　　the gift you'd give
25　was the gift
　　she'd wish to have?
　　　　—Gift is giving,
gift is meaning:
　　first
30　　　　I'd give
then let her
　　live with it
　　　　to prove
its quality the better and
35　　thus learn
　　　　to love
what (to begin with)
　　she might spurn.
　　　　—You'd
40　moralize a gift?
　　　　—I'd have her
　　　　　　understand

the gift I gave her.
　　　—And so she shall
45　　　but let her play
her innocence away
　　emerging
　　　as she does
between
50　　her doom (unknown),
　　　her unmown green.

AMITTAI F. AVIRAM

Pictures of Maurice Among Funeral Flowers (1995; 2002)
For Maurice P. Quesnel, in memory.

Gather the flowers, but spare the buds.
　　　　　—MARVELL

1.

Your smile, the only thing that glimmered through
the heavy snow, that February night,
the only bright, new thing in all New Haven,
shone out your snorkel-hood, when I trudged out
5　onto my stoop, braced for the bar, to which
you, too, were headed. Seeing sincerity through
your wire-framed glasses, and a measureless smile,
I showed you in. And soon your glasses, fogged,
came off. And we forgot about the bar.

2.

I hadn't seen you in ages. It was time,
after the hundredth fight with my new lover,
to see your narrow half of a narrow room
in the East Village. But then, you cracked the hatch,
5　and up we climbed to freedom on the roof.
You and the air burst heady on my funk.°　　　　　depression
Our clothes came off again, and all your skin
said yes, like a silken flower, and mine cried yes,
caressing your petals, filling your pliant clasp.

3.

Something familiar about those white buttocks,
and then my eyes rose—it was you, head turned
gently over your shoulder, more to reveal

your profile, sloped—there, at the Fifty-Ninth
5   Street Pool, among the jocks and homeless men,
picture of innocence, voluptuous,
in a chance ray among shadows in the shower.
You looked surprised before you could quite place me,
waking, a little boy, from dreams of flowers.

4.

My watch advanced while you were disappeared
among the dunes behind us at Jones Beach.
I knew how you would burn. But when you came
back, spent, your hair shone redder with the blush
5   of joy—half in the deed, half in the report.
We'd heard the age was past for sport in bushes,
but who'd find blame in such triumphant colors,
the pink-flushed neck, the green eyes ever open
to taste, to sip, to drink from summer fruit.

5.

By days, your voice got thinner on the line;
the shadow-thought I kept of you got thin.
What did you look like, then? A shadowy sore
slowly enveloped you from the crotch upwards
5   and swallowed up the brightness, shade by shade,
making your voice flicker and cast its dim,
warm light around the little that was left.
You'd done what you were sent here for: you came,
and left, too soon, before we thought to look.

ALEXANDER POPE (1688–1744)

Impromptu (ca. 1715; 1741)
To Lady Winchilsea,
Occasioned by four Satirical Verses on Women Wits,
In *The Rape of the Lock*[1]

In vain you boast poetic names of yore,
And cite those Sapphos we admire no more:[2]

---

[1] **To Lady Winchilsea . . . Lock:** In Canto IV (lines 59–62) of *The Rape of the Lock* (see Chapter 1), Pope attacked female poets, and the work of Anne Finch, Countess of Winchilsea, in particular. Irked by his criticism, Anne Finch replied with her own verse, which she sent to Pope (the poem is, unfortunately, not preserved). Continuing the dialogue, Pope wrote "Impromptu."
[2] **Sapphos . . . no more:** A reference to the Ancient Greek female poet Sappho.

Fate doomed the fall of every female wit;
But doomed it then, when first Ardelia³ writ.
5   Of all examples by the world confessed,
I knew Ardelia could not quote the best;
Who, like her mistress on Britannia's throne,
Fights and subdues in quarrels not her own.⁴
To write their praise you but in vain essay;
10   Even while you write, you take that praise away.
Light to the stars the sun does thus restore,
but shines himself till they are seen no more.

ANNE FINCH, COUNTESS OF WINCHILSEA
(1661–1720)

The Answer   (1734)
(*To Pope's* Impromptu)

Disarmed with so genteel an air,
    The contest I give o'er;
Yet, Alexander, have a care,
    And shock the sex no more.
5   We rule the world our life's whole race,
    Men but assume that right;
First slaves to ev'ry tempting face,
    Then martyrs to our spite.
You of one Orpheus¹ sure have read,
10   Who would like you have writ
Had he in London town been bred,
    And polished to[o] his wit;
But he poor soul thought all was well,
    And great should be his fame,

---

³ **Ardelia:** Anne Finch wrote occasionally under this name.
⁴ **not her own:** A reference to the policies of Queen Anne, of which Pope strongly disapproved.
¹ **Orpheus:** According to the Greek myth, when his wife Eurydice died of snakebite, the singer Orpheus descended into the land of the dead to seek her out. With his fantastic music, he managed to charm Pluto and Proserpina, the rulers of the underworld, who agreed to let Eurydice go on the condition that Orpheus never looked back on his way out. However, the poet was tempted to see whether his wife was really following him and glanced over his shoulder—only to witness Eurydice disappear forever in the gloom. When he returned disconsolate to the land of the living, Orpheus continued to sing, enchanting the animals and even the stones around him. But the Maenads, women devoted to worshipping the god Dionysius, heard him and, enraged by his music (and probably Orpheus's lack of interest in them), they tore him to pieces, which afterwards they threw in the river Hebrus. His head, however, continued to sing even as it floated downstream.

15 When he had left his wife in hell,
        And birds and beasts could tame.
    Yet venturing then with scoffing rhymes
        The women to incense,
    Resenting heroines of those times
20   Soon punished his offense.
    And as the Hebrus rolled his skull,
        And harp besmeared with blood,
    They clashing as the waves grew full,
        Still harmonized the flood.
25 But you our follies gently treat,
        And spin so fine the thread,
    You need not fear his awkward fate,
        The lock[2] won't cost the head.
    Our admiration you command
30   For all that's gone before;
    What next we look for at your hand
        Can only raise it more.
    Yet sooth the Ladies I advise
        (As me too pride has wrought)
35 We're born to wit, but to be wise
        By admonitions taught.

CHRISTOPHER SMART (1722–1771)

from Jubilate Agno[1] (ca. 1760; 1939)
My Cat Jeoffry

For I will consider my Cat Jeoffry.
For he is the servant of the Living God duly and daily serving him.
For at the first glance of the glory of God in the East he worships in
        his way.
For is this done by wreathing his body seven times round with
        elegant quickness.
5   For then he leaps up to catch the musk, which is the blessing of
        God upon his prayer.
For he rolls upon prank to work it in.

---

[2] **lock:** A pun on Pope's "The Rape of the Lock," which prompted the exchange of poems between its author and Anne Finch.
[1] **Jubilate Agno:** Latin, "Rejoice in the Lamb" (i.e., Christ). While he was confined for insanity at St. Luke's madhouse, Smart wrote this long poem using for his model the Biblical psalms.

For having done duty and received blessing he begins to consider
     himself.
For this he performs in ten degrees.
For first he looks upon his fore-paws to see if they are clean.
10   For secondly he kicks up behind to clear away there.
For thirdly he works it upon stretch with the fore paws extended.
For fourthly he sharpens his paws by wood.
For fifthly he washes himself.
For sixthly he rolls upon wash.
15   For seventhly he fleas himself, that he may not be interrupted upon
     the beat.[2]
For eighthly he rubs himself against a post.
For ninthly he looks up for his instructions.
For tenthly he goes in quest of food.
For having considered God and himself he will consider his
     neighbour.
20   For if he meets another cat he will kiss her in kindness.
For when he takes his prey he plays with it to give it chance.
For one mouse in seven escapes by his dallying.
For when his day's work is done his business more properly begins.
For he keeps the Lord's watch in the night against the adversary.
25   For he counteracts the powers of darkness by his electrical skin and
     glaring eyes.
For he counteracts the Devil, who is death, by brisking about the life.
For in his morning orisons he loves the sun and the sun loves him.
For he is of the tribe of Tiger.
For the Cherub Cat is a term of the Angel Tiger.[3]
30   For he has the subtlety and hissing of a serpent, which in goodness
     he suppresses.
For he will not do destruction, if he is well-fed, neither will he spit
     without provocation.
For he purrs in thankfulness, when God tells him he's a good Cat.
For he is an instrument for the children to learn benevolence upon.
For every house is incompleat without him and a blessing is lacking
     in the spirit.
35   For the Lord commanded Moses concerning the cats at the
     departure of the Children of Israel from Egypt.
For every family had one cat at least in the bag.[4]
For the English Cats are the best in Europe.
For he is the cleanest in the use of his fore-paws of any quadrupede.

---

[2] **upon the beat:** I.e., while hunting.
[3] **Cherub . . . Tiger:** The cherubs were usually depicted as smaller, childlike versions of angels;
hence, the comparison between Jeoffry and the tiger.
[4] **For the Lord commanded . . . bag:** In Exodus, the Israelites take gold and silver, flocks and herds
with them. Smart adds the cats to the list.

For the dexterity of his defence is an instance of the love of God to
him exceedingly.

40 For he is the quickest to his mark of any creature.

For he is tenacious of his point.

For he is a mixture of gravity and waggery.

For he knows that God is his Saviour.

For there is nothing sweeter than his peace when at rest.

45 For there is nothing brisker than his life when in motion.

For he is of the Lord's poor and so indeed is he called by
benevolence perpetually—Poor Jeoffry! poor Jeoffry! the rat
has bit thy throat.

For I bless the name of the Lord Jesus that Jeoffry is better.

For the divine spirit comes about his body to sustain it in compleat
cat.

For his tongue is exceeding pure so that it has in purity what it
wants in music.

50 For he is docile and can learn certain things.

For he can set up with gravity which is patience upon approbation.

For he can fetch and carry, which is patience in employment.

For he can jump over a stick which is patience upon proof positive.

For he can spraggle upon waggle at the word of command.

55 For he can jump from an eminence into his master's bosom.

For he can catch the cork and toss it again.

For he is hated by the hypocrite and miser.

For the former is afraid of detection.

For the latter refuses the charge.

60 For he camels his back to bear the first notion of business.

For he is good to think on, if a man would express himself neatly.

For he made a great figure in Egypt for his signal services.

For he killed the Icneumon-rat[5] very pernicious by land.

For his ears are so acute that they sting again.

65 For from this proceeds the passing quickness of his attention.

For by stroking of him I have found out electricity.

For I perceived God's light about him both wax and fire.

For the Electrical fire is the spiritual substance, which God sends
from heaven to sustain the bodies both of man and beast.

For God has blessed him in the variety of his movements.

70 For, tho he cannot fly, he is an excellent clamberer.

For his motions upon the face of the earth are more than any other
quadrupede.

For he can tread to all the measures upon the music.

For he can swim for life.

For he can creep.

---

[5] **Icneumon-rat:** Possibly a creature related to the mongoose.

ERICA JONG (1941–   )

Jubilate Canis[1] (1979)

(With apologies to Christopher Smart)

For I will consider my dog Poochkin
(& his long-lost brothers, Chekarf & Dogstoyevsky).
For he is the reincarnation of a great canine poet.
For he barks in meter, & when I leave him alone
5   his yelps at the door are epic.
For he is white, furry, & resembles a bathmat.
For he sleeps at my feet as I write
& therefore is my greatest critic.
For he follows me into the bathroom
10   & faithfully pees on paper.
For he is *almost* housebroken.
For he eats the dogfood I give him
but also loves Jarlsburg and Swiss cheese.
For he disdains nothing that reeks—
15   whether feet or roses.
For to him, all smells are created equal by God—
both turds and perfumes.
For he loves toilet bowls no less than soup bowls.
For by watching him, I have understood democracy.
20   For by stroking him, I have understood joy.
For he turns his belly toward God
& raises his paws & penis in supplication.
For he hangs his pink tongue out of his mouth
like a festival banner for God.
25   For though he is male, he has pink nipples on his belly
like the female.
For though he is canine, he is more humane
than most humans.
For when he dreams he mutters in his sleep
30   like any poet.
For when he wakes he yawns & stretches
& stands on his hind legs to greet me.
For, after he shits, he romps and frolics
with supreme abandon.
35   For, after he eats, he is more contented
than any human.

---

[1] **Jubilate Canis:** I.e., "Rejoice in the Dog" (see the title of Smart's poem).

For in every room he will find the coolest corner,
& having found it, he has the sense to stay there.
For when I show him my poems,
40   he eats them.
For an old shoe makes him happier than a Rolls-Royce
makes a rock star.
For he has convinced me of the infinite wisdom
of dog-consciousness.
45   For, thanks to Poochkin, I praise the Lord
& no longer fear death.
For when my spirit flees my body through my nostrils,
may it sail into the pregnant belly
of a furry bitch,
50   and may I praise God always
as a dog.

EDWARD HIRSCH (1950–   )

Wild Gratitude (1984)

Tonight when I knelt down next to our cat, Zooey,
And put my fingers into her clean cat's mouth,
And rubbed her swollen belly that will never know kittens,
And watched her wriggle onto her side, pawing the air,
5   And listened to her solemn little squeals of delight,
I was thinking about the poet, Christopher Smart,
Who wanted to kneel down and pray without ceasing
In every one of the splintered London streets,

And was locked away in the madhouse at St. Luke's
10   With his sad religious mania, and his wild gratitude,
And his grave prayers for the other lunatics,
And his great love for his speckled cat, Jeoffry.
All day today—August 13, 1983—I remembered how
Christopher Smart blessed this same day in August, 1759,
15   For its calm bravery and ordinary good conscience.

This was the day that he blessed the Postmaster General
"And all conveyancers of letters" for their warm humanity,
And the gardeners for their private benevolence
And intricate knowledge of the language of flowers,
20   And the milkmen for their universal human kindness.
This morning I understood that he loved to hear—

As I have heard—the soft clink of milk bottles
On the rickety stairs in the early morning,[1]

And how terrible it must have seemed
25   When even this small pleasure was denied him.
But it wasn't until tonight when I knelt down
And slipped my hand into Zooey's waggling mouth
That I remembered how he'd called Jeoffry "the servant
Of the Living God duly and daily serving Him,"
30   And for the first time understood what it meant.
Because it wasn't until I saw my own cat

Whine and roll over on her fluffy back
That I realized how gratefully he had watched
Jeoffry fetch and carry his wooden cork
35   Across the grass in the wet garden, patiently
Jumping over a high stick, calmly sharpening
His claws on the woodpile, rubbing his nose
Against the nose of another cat, stretching, or
Slowly stalking his traditional enemy, the mouse,
40   A rodent, "a creature of great personal valour,"
And then dallying so much that his enemy escaped.

And only then did I understand
It is Jeoffry—and every creature like him—
Who can teach us how to praise—purring
45   In their own language,
Wreathing themselves in the living fire.

WILLIAM WORDSWORTH (1770–1850)

Lines Written a Few Miles above Tintern Abbey (1798)

On Revisiting the Banks of the Wye during a Tour, July 13, 1798

Five years have passed; five summers, with the length
Of five long winters! and again I hear
These waters, rolling from their mountain-springs
With a sweet inland murmur.—Once again
5   Do I behold these steep and lofty cliffs,

---

[1] **This was the day . . . early morning:** This stanza refers to other sections of Smart's long poem
Jubilate Agno, of which "When I Consider My Cat Jeoffry" is only a small part.

Which on a wild secluded scene impress
Thoughts of more deep seclusion; and connect
The landscape with the quiet of the sky.
The day is come when I again repose
10   Here, under this dark sycamore, and view
These plots of cottage-ground, these orchard-tufts,
Which, at this season, with their unripe fruits,
Among the woods and copses lose themselves,
Nor, with their green and simple hue, disturb
15   The wild green landscape. Once again I see
These hedge-rows, hardly hedge-rows, little lines
Of sportive wood run wild; these pastoral farms
Green to the very door; and wreathes of smoke
Sent up, in silence, from among the trees,
20   With some uncertain notice, as might seem,
Of vagrant dwellers in the houseless woods,
Or of some hermit's cave, where by his fire
The hermit sits alone.

                              Though absent long,
25   These forms of beauty have not been to me,
As is a landscape to a blind man's eye:
But oft, in lonely rooms, and mid the din
Of towns and cities, I have owed to them,
In hours of weariness, sensations sweet,
30   Felt in the blood, and felt along the heart,
And passing even into my purer mind
With tranquil restoration:—feelings too
Of unremembered pleasure; such, perhaps,
As may have had no trivial influence
35   On that best portion of a good man's life;
His little, nameless, unremembered acts
Of kindness and of love. Nor less, I trust,
To them I may have owed another gift,
Of aspect more sublime; that blessed mood,
40   In which the burthen of the mystery,
In which the heavy and the weary weight
Of all this unintelligible world
Is lighten'd:—that serene and blessed mood,
In which the affections gently lead us on,
45   Until, the breath of this corporeal frame,
And even the motion of our human blood
Almost suspended, we are laid asleep
In body, and become a living soul:
While with an eye made quiet by the power
50   Of harmony, and the deep power of joy,

We see into the life of things.

If this

Be but a vain belief, yet, oh! how oft,
In darkness, and amid the many shapes
55 Of joyless day-light; when the fretful stir
Unprofitable, and the fever of the world,
Have hung upon the beatings of my heart,
How oft, in spirit, have I turned to thee
O sylvan Wye! Thou wanderer through the woods,
60 How often has my spirit turned to thee!
And now, with gleams of half-extinguish'd thought,
With many recognitions dim and faint,
And somewhat of a sad perplexity,
The picture of the mind revives again:
65 While here I stand, not only with the sense
Of present pleasure, but with pleasing thoughts
That in this moment there is life and food
For future years. And so I dare to hope
Though changed, no doubt, from what I was, when first
70 I came among these hills; when like a roe
I bounded o'er the mountains, by the sides
Of the deep rivers, and the lonely streams,
Wherever nature led; more like a man
Flying from something that he dreads, than one
75 Who sought the thing he loved. For nature then
(The coarser pleasures of my boyish days,
And their glad animal movements all gone by,)
To me was all in all.—I cannot paint
What then I was. The sounding cataract
80 Haunted me like a passion: the tall rock,
The mountain, and the deep and gloomy wood,
Their colours and their forms, were then to me
An appetite: a feeling and a love,
That had no need of a remoter charm,
85 By thought supplied, or any interest
Unborrowed from the eye.—That time is past,
And all its aching joys are now no more,
And all its dizzy raptures. Not for this
Faint I, nor mourn nor murmur: other gifts
90 Have followed, for such loss, I would believe,
Abundant recompence. For I have learned
To look on nature, not as in the hour
Of thoughtless youth, but hearing oftentimes
The still, sad music of humanity,
95 Not harsh nor grating, though of ample power

To chasten and subdue. And I have felt
A presence that disturbs me with the joy
Of elevated thoughts; a sense sublime
Of something far more deeply interfused,
100 Whose dwelling is the light of setting suns,
And the round ocean, and the living air,
And the blue sky, and in the mind of man,
A motion and a spirit, that impels
All thinking things, all objects of all thought,
105 And rolls through all things. Therefore am I still
A lover of the meadows and the woods,
And mountains; and of all that we behold
From this green earth; of all the mighty world
Of eye and ear, both what they half-create,
110 And what perceive; well pleased to recognize
In nature and the language of the sense,
The anchor of my purest thoughts, the nurse,
The guide, the guardian of my heart, and soul
Of all my moral being.

115   Nor, perchance,
If I were not thus taught, should I the more
Suffer my genial spirits to decay:
For thou art with me, here, upon the banks
Of this fair river; thou, my dearest Friend,
120 My dear, dear Friend, and in thy voice I catch
The language of my former heart, and read
My former pleasures in the shooting lights
Of thy wild eyes. Oh! yet a little while
May I behold in thee what I was once,
125 My dear, dear Sister! And this prayer I make,
Knowing that Nature never did betray
The heart that loved her; 'tis her privilege,
Through all the years of this our life, to lead
From joy to joy: for she can so inform
130 The mind that is within us, so impress
With quietness and beauty, and so feed
With lofty thoughts, that neither evil tongues,
Rash judgments, nor the sneers of selfish men,
Nor greetings where no kindness is, nor all
135 The dreary intercourse of daily life,
Shall e'er prevail against us, or disturb
Our chearful faith that all which we behold
Is full of blessings. Therefore let the moon
Shine on thee in thy solitary walk;
140 And let the misty mountain winds be free

To blow against thee: and in after years,
When these wild ecstasies shall be matured
Into a sober pleasure, when thy mind
Shall be a mansion for all lovely forms,
145   Thy memory be as a dwelling-place
For all sweet sounds and harmonies; Oh! then,
If solitude, or fear, or pain, or grief,
Should be thy portion, with what healing thoughts
Of tender joy wilt thou remember me,
150   And these my exhortations! Nor, perchance,
If I should be, where I no more can hear
Thy voice, nor catch from thy wild eyes these gleams
Of past existence, wilt thou then forget
That on the banks of this delightful stream
155   We stood together; and that I, so long
A worshipper of Nature, hither came,
Unwearied in that service: rather say
With warmer love, oh! with far deeper zeal
Of holier love. Nor wilt thou then forget,
160   That after many wanderings, many years
Of absence, these steep woods and lofty cliffs,
And this green pastoral landscape, were to me
More dear, both for themselves, and for thy sake.

BILLY COLLINS (1941–   )

Lines Composed Over Three Thousand Miles from Tintern Abbey (1998)

I was here before, a long time ago,
and now I am here again
is an observation that occurs in poetry
as frequently as rain occurs in life.

5   The fellow may be gazing
over an English landscape,
hillsides dotted with sheep,
a row of tall trees topping the downs,

or he could be moping through the shadows
10   of a dark Bavarian forest,
a wedge of cheese and a volume of fairy tales
tucked into his rucksack.

But the feeling is always the same.
It was better the first time.
15   This time is not nearly as good.
I'm not feeling as chipper as I did back then.

Something is always missing—
swans, a glint on the surface of a lake,
some minor but essential touch.
20   Or the quality of things has diminished.

The sky was a deeper, more dimensional blue,
clouds were more cathedral-like,
and water rushed over rock
with greater effervescence.

25   From our chairs we have watched
the poor author in his waistcoat
as he recalls the dizzying icebergs of childhood
and mills around in a field of weeds.

We have heard the poets long dead
30   declaim their dying
from a promontory, a riverbank,
next to a haycock, within a copse.

We have listened to their dismay,
the kind that issues from poems
35   the way water issues forth from hoses,
the way the match always gives its little speech on fire.

And when we put down the book at last,
lean back, close our eyes,
stinging with print,
40   and slip in the bookmark of sleep,

we will be schooled enough to know
that when we wake up
a little before dinner
things will not be nearly as good as they once were.

45   Something will be missing
from this long, coffin-shaped room,
the walls and windows now
only two different shades of gray,

the glossy gardenia drooping
50   in its chipped terra-cotta pot.

And on the floor, shoes, socks,
the browning core of an apple.

Nothing will be as it was
a few hours ago, back in the glorious past
55 before our naps, back in that Golden Age
that drew to a close sometime shortly after lunch.

JOHN KEATS (1795–1821)

Bright Star (1819; 1838)

Bright star, would I were steadfast as thou art!
    Not in lone splendour hung aloft the night
And watching with eternal lids apart,
    Like Nature's patient sleepless eremite,°   hermit
5 The moving waters at their priestlike task
    Of pure ablution round earth's human shores;
Or gazing on the new soft-fallen mask
    Of snow upon the mountains and the moors.
No! Yet still steadfast, still unchangeable,
10   Pillowed upon my fair Love's ripening breast
To feel for ever its soft fall and swell,
    Awake for ever in a sweet unrest—
Still, still to hear her tender-taken breath,
And so live ever: or else swoon to death.

ROBERT FROST (1874–1963)

Take Something Like a Star (1949)

O Star (the fairest one in sight),
We grant your loftiness the right
To some obscurity of cloud—
It will not do to say of night,
5 Since dark is what brings out your light.
Some mystery becomes the proud.
But to be wholly taciturn
In your reserve is not allowed.
Say something to us we can learn
10 By heart and when alone repeat.

Say something! And it says, "I burn."
But say with what degree of heat.
Talk Fahrenheit, talk Centigrade.
Use language we can comprehend.
15   Tell us what elements you blend.
It gives us strangely little aid,
But does tell something in the end.
And steadfast as Keats' Eremite,[1]
Not even stooping from its sphere,
20   It asks a little of us here.
It asks of us a certain height,
So when at times the mob is swayed
To carry praise or blame too far,
We may take something like a star
25   To stay our minds on and be staid.

PETER DAVISON   (1928–   )

The Star Watcher   (1963)
(For R. F.)[1]

Stars had the look of dogs to him sometimes,
Sometimes of bears and more than once of flowers,
But stars were never strange to him because
Of where they stood. We knew him jealous
5   And in his younger days a little sly
About his place among the poesies;
Yet when his eyes showed envy or delight
They rested upon knowledge, not on distance.
All that he saw, up close or farther off,
10   Was capable of being understood,
Though not by him perhaps. He had enough
Of science in him to be optimistic,
Enough of tragedy to know the worst,
Enough of wit to keep on listening,
15   Or watching, when it came to stars. He knew,
Across the distance that their light might travel,
That nothing matters to the stars but matter,
Yet that their watchers have to learn the difference
Between the facts of knowledge and of love,

---

[1] **Keats' Eremite:** See "Bright Star" by John Keats.
[1] **R.F.:** Robert Frost.

20   Or of love's opposite, which might be hate.
      Therefore he taught, and, like the best of teachers,
      Often annoyed the students at his feet,
      Whether they learned too much or not enough,
      Whether or not they understood him wrong.
25   Two was his pleasure, and the balance held
      In love, in conversation, or in verse.
      With knuckles like burled hemlock roots, his hands
      Had, in his age, smooth palms as white as milk;
      And, through the massy cloudbanks of his brows,
30   His eyes burned shrewdly as emerging stars.

JOHN KEATS (1795–1821)

To Autumn (1819; 1820)

Season of mists and mellow fruitfulness,
      Close bosom-friend of the maturing sun,
Conspiring with him how to load and bless
      With fruit the vines that round the thatch-eaves run—
5   To bend with apples the mossed cottage-trees,
      And fill all fruit with ripeness to the core;
            To swell the gourd, and plump the hazel-shells
      With a sweet kernel; to set budding more,
And still more, later flowers for the bees,
10   Until they think warm days will never cease,
            For Summer has o'erbrimmed their clammy cells.

Who hath not seen thee oft amid thy store?
      Sometimes whoever seeks abroad may find
Thee sitting careless on a granary floor,
15   Thy hair soft-lifted by the winnowing wind;
Or on a half-reaped furrow, sound asleep,
      Drowsed with the fume of poppies, while thy hook
            Spares the next swath and all its twinéd flowers;
And sometimes like a gleaner thou dost keep
20   Steady thy laden head across a brook,
      Or by a cider-press, with patient look,
            Thou watchest the last oozings hours by hours.

Where are the songs of Spring? Aye, where are they?
      Think not of them, thou hast thy music too—

25   While barred clouds bloom the soft-dying day,
      And touch the stubble-plains with rosy hue.
Then in a wailful choir the small gnats mourn
      Among the river sallows, borne aloft
         Or sinking as the light wind lives or dies;
30   And full-grown lambs loud-bleat from hilly bourn;
      Hedge-crickets sing; and now, with treble soft,
      The redbreast whistles from a garden-croft,
         And gathering swallows twitter in the skies.

ROBERT FROST   (1874–1963)

After Apple-Picking   (1914)

My long two-pointed ladder's sticking through a tree
Toward heaven still,
And there's a barrel that I didn't fill
Beside it, and there may be two or three
5   Apples I didn't pick upon some bough.
But I am done with apple-picking now.
Essence of winter sleep is on the night,
The scent of apples: I am drowsing off.
I cannot rub the strangeness from my sight
10   I got from looking through a pane of glass
I skimmed this morning from the drinking trough
And held against the world of hoary grass.
It melted, and I let it fall and break.
But I was well
15   Upon my way to sleep before it fell,
And I could tell
What form my dreaming was about to take.
Magnified apples appear and disappear,
Stem end and blossom end,
20   And every fleck of russet showing clear.
My instep arch not only keeps the ache,
It keeps the pressure of a ladder-round.
I feel the ladder sway as the boughs bend.
And I keep hearing from the cellar bin
25   The rumbling sound
Of load on load of apples coming in.
For I have had too much

Of apple-picking: I am overtired
Of the great harvest I myself desired.
30 There were ten thousand thousand fruit to touch,
Cherish in hand, lift down, and not let fall.
For all
That struck the earth,
No matter if not bruised or spiked with stubble,
35 Went surely to the cider-apple heap
As of no worth.
One can see what will trouble
This sleep of mine, whatever sleep it is.
Were he not gone,
40 The woodchuck could say whether it's like his
Long sleep, as I describe its coming on,
Or just some human sleep.

THOMAS LOVELL BEDDOES (1803–1849)

The Phantom-Wooer (ca. 1847)

I

A ghost, that loved a lady fair,
Ever in the starry air
    Of midnight at her pillow stood;
And, with a sweetness skies above
5   The luring words of human love,
    Her soul the phantom wooed.
Sweet and sweet is their poisoned note,
The little snakes of silver throat,
In mossy skulls that nest and lie,
10 Ever singing 'die, oh! die.'

II

Young soul put off your flesh, and come
With me into the quiet tomb,
    Our bed is lovely, dark, and sweet;
The earth will swing us, as she goes,
15 Beneath our coverlid of snows,
    And the warm leaden sheet.
Dear and dear is their poisoned note,
The little snakes of silver throat,
In mossy skulls that nest and lie,
20 Ever singing 'die, oh! die.'

ROBERT FROST (1874–1963)

Stopping by Woods on a Snowy Evening (1923)

Whose woods these are I think I know.
His house is in the village, though;
He will not see me stopping here
To watch his woods fill up with snow.

5   My little horse must think it queer
To stop without a farmhouse near
Between the woods and frozen lake
The darkest evening of the year.

He gives his harness bells a shake
10   To ask if there is some mistake.
The only other sound's the sweep
Of easy wind and downy flake.

The woods are lovely, dark, and deep,
But I have promises to keep,
15   And miles to go before I sleep,
And miles to go before I sleep.

WALT WHITMAN (1819–1892)

Crossing Brooklyn Ferry[1] (1856)

1

Flood-tide below me! I see you face to face!
Clouds of the west—sun there half an hour high—I see you also face
    to face.

Crowds of men and women attired in the usual costumes, how
    curious you are to me!
On the ferry-boats the hundreds and hundreds that cross, returning
    home, are more curious to me than you suppose,
5   And you that shall cross from shore to shore years hence are more
    to me, and more in my meditations, than you might suppose.

---

[1] **Brooklyn Ferry:** I.e., New York City ferry that used to run between Brooklyn and Manhattan Island.

2

The impalpable sustenance of me from all things at all hours of the
    day,
The simple, compact, well-join'd scheme, myself disintegrated, every
    one disintegrated yet part of the scheme,
The similitudes of the past and those of the future,
The glories strung like beads on my smallest sights and hearings, on
    the walk in the street and the passage over the river,
10   The current rushing so swiftly and swimming with me far away,
The others that are to follow me, the ties between me and them,
The certainty of others, the life, love, sight, hearing of others.

Others will enter the gates of the ferry and cross from shore to shore,
Others will watch the run of the flood-tide,
15   Others will see the shipping of Manhattan north and west, and the
    heights of Brooklyn to the south and east,
Others will see the islands large and small;
Fifty years hence, others will see them as they cross, the sun half an
    hour high,
A hundred years hence, or ever so many hundred years hence, others
    will see them,
Will enjoy the sunset, the pouring-in of the flood-tide, the falling-back
    to the sea of the ebb-tide.

3

20   It avails not, time nor place—distance avails not,
I am with you, you men and women of a generation, or ever so many
    generations hence,
Just as you feel when you look on the river and sky, so I felt,
Just as any of you is one of a living crowd, I was one of a crowd,
Just as you are refresh'd by the gladness of the river and the bright
    flow, I was refresh'd,
25   Just as you stand and lean on the rail, yet hurry with the swift current,
    I stood yet was hurried,
Just as you look on the numberless masts of ships and the thick-
    stemm'd pipes of steamboats, I look'd.

I too many and many a time cross'd the river of old,
Watched the Twelfth-month sea-gulls, saw them high in the air floating
    with motionless wings, oscillating their bodies,
Saw how the glistening yellow lit up parts of their bodies and left
    the rest in strong shadow,
30   Saw the slow-wheeling circles and the gradual edging toward the
    south,
Saw the reflection of the summer sky in the water,

Had my eyes dazzled by the shimmering track of beams,
Look'd at the fine centrifugal spokes of light round the shape of my
    head in the sunlit water,
Look'd on the haze on the hills southward and south-westward,
35   Look'd on the vapor as it flew in fleeces tinged with violet,
Look'd toward the lower bay to notice the vessels arriving,
Saw their approach, saw aboard those that were near me,
Saw the white sails of schooners and sloops, saw the ships at anchor,
The sailors at work in the rigging or out astride the spars,
40   The round masts, the swinging motion of the hulls, the slender
    serpentine pennants,
The large and small steamers in motion, the pilots in their pilot-
    houses,
The white wake left by the passage, the quick tremulous whirl of the
    wheels,
The flags of all nations, the falling of them at sunset,
The scallop-edged waves in the twilight, the ladled cups, the
    frolicsome crests and glistening,
45   The stretch afar growing dimmer and dimmer, the gray walls of
    the granite storehouses by the docks,
On the river the shadowy group, the big steam-tug closely flank'd on
    each side by the barges, the hay-boat, the belated lighter,
On the neighboring shore the fires from the foundry chimneys
    burning high and glaringly into the night,
Casting their flicker of black contrasted with wild red and yellow
    light over the tops of houses, and down into the clefts of streets.

4

These and all else were to me the same as they are to you,
50   I loved well those cities, loved well the stately and rapid river,
The men and women I saw were all near to me,
Others the same—others who look back on me because I look'd
    forward to them,
(The time will come, though I stop here to-day and to-night.)

5

What is it then between us?
55   What is the count of the scores or hundreds of years between us?

Whatever it is, it avails not—distance avails not, and place avails not,
I too lived, Brooklyn of ample hills was mine,
I too walk'd the streets of Manhattan island, and bathed in the
    waters around it,
I too felt the curious abrupt questionings stir within me,
60   In the day among crowds of people sometimes they came upon me,

In my walks home late at night or as I lay in my bed they came
    upon me,
I too had been struck from the float forever held in solution,
I too had receiv'd identity by my body,
That I was I knew was of my body, and what I should be I knew I
    should be of my body.

6

65 It is not upon you alone the dark patches fall,
The dark threw its patches down upon me also,
The best I had done seem'd to me blank and suspicious,
My great thoughts as I supposed them, were they not in reality
    meagre?
Nor is it you alone who know what it is to be evil,
70 I am he who knew what it was to be evil,
I too knitted the old knot of contrariety,
Blabb'd, blush'd, resented, lied, stole, grudg'd,
Had guile, anger, lust, hot wishes I dared not speak,
Was wayward, vain, greedy, shallow, sly, cowardly, malignant,
75 The wolf, the snake, the hog, not wanting in me,
The cheating look, the frivolous word, the adulterous wish, not wanting,
Refusals, hates, postponements, meanness, laziness, none of these
    wanting,
Was one with the rest, the days and haps of the rest,
Was call'd by my nighest name by clear loud voices of young men
    as they saw me approaching or passing,
80 Felt their arms on my neck as I stood, or the negligent leaning of
    their flesh against me as I sat,
Saw many I loved in the street or ferry-boat or public assembly, yet
    never told them a word,
Lived the same life with the rest, the same old laughing, gnawing,
    sleeping,

Play'd the part that still looks back on the actor or actress,
The same old role, the role that is what we make it, as great as we like,
85 Or as small as we like, or both great and small.

7

Closer yet I approach you,
What thought you have of me now, I had as much of you—I laid in
    my stores in advance,
I consider'd long and seriously of you before you were born.

Who was to know what should come home to me?
90 Who knows but I am enjoying this?

Who knows, for all the distance, but I am as good as looking at you
    now, for all you cannot see me?

8

Ah, what can ever be more stately and admirable to me than mast-
    hemm'd Manhattan?
River and sunset and scallop-edg'd waves of flood-tide?
The sea-gulls oscillating their bodies, the hay-boat in the twilight,
    and the belated lighter?

95   What gods can exceed these that clasp me by the hand, and with
    voices I love call me promptly and loudly by my nighest name
    as I approach?
What is more subtle than this which ties me to the woman or man
    that looks in my face?
Which fuses me into you now, and pours my meaning into you?

We understand then do we not?
What I promis'd without mentioning it, have you not accepted?
100   What the study could not teach—what the preaching could not
    accomplish is accomplish'd, is it not?

9

Flow on, river! flow with the flood-tide, and ebb with the ebb-tide!
Frolic on, crested and scallop-edg'd waves!
Gorgeous clouds of the sunset! drench with your splendor me, or the
    men and women generations after me!
Cross from shore to shore, countless crowds of passengers!
105   Stand up, tall masts of Mannahatta! stand up, beautiful hills of
    Brooklyn!
Throb, baffled and curious brain! throw out questions and answers!
Suspend here and everywhere, eternal float of solution!
Gaze, loving and thirsting eyes, in the house or street or public
    assembly!

Sound out, voices of young men! loudly and musically call me by my
    nighest name!
110   Live, old life! play the part that looks back on the actor or actress!
Play the old role, the role that is great or small according as one
    makes it!
Consider, you who peruse me, whether I may not in unknown ways
    be looking upon you;
Be firm, rail over the river, to support those who lean idly, yet haste
    with the hasting current;
Fly on, sea-birds! fly sideways, or wheel in large circles high in the air;

115   Receive the summer sky, you water, and faithfully hold it till all down-
            cast eyes have time to take it from you!

Diverge, fine spokes of light, from the shape of my head, or any one's
            head, in the sunlit water!
Come on, ships from the lower bay! pass up or down, white-sail'd
            schooners, sloops, lighters!
Flaunt away, flags of all nations! be duly lower'd at sunset!
Burn high your fires, foundry chimneys! cast black shadows at night-
            fall! cast red and yellow light over the tops of the houses!

120   Appearances, now or henceforth, indicate what you are,
You necessary film, continue to envelop the soul,
About my body for me, and your body for you, be hung out divinest
            aromas,
Thrive, cities—bring your freight, bring your shows, ample and
            sufficient rivers,
Expand, being than which none else is perhaps more spiritual,
125   Keep your places, objects than which none else is more lasting.

You have waited, you always wait, you dumb, beautiful ministers,
We receive you with free sense at last, and are insatiate henceforward,
Not you any more shall be able to foil us, or withhold yourselves from
            us,
We use you, and do not cast you aside—we plant you permanently
            within us,
130   We fathom you not—we love you—there is perfection in you also,
You furnish your parts toward eternity,
Great or small, you furnish your parts toward the soul.

HART CRANE (1899–1932)

Proem: To Brooklyn Bridge[1] (1930)

How many dawns, chill from his rippling rest
The seagull's wings shall dip and pivot him,
Shedding white rings of tumult, building high
Over the chained bay waters Liberty—

---

[1] **Brooklyn Bridge:** In New York City, the bridge connects Brooklyn and Manhattan Island.

5 Then, with inviolate curve, forsake our eyes
 As apparitional as sails that cross
 Some page of figures to be filed away;
 —Till elevators drop us from our day . . .

 I think of cinemas, panoramic sleights
10 With multitudes bent toward some flashing scene
 Never disclosed, but hastened to again,
 Foretold to other eyes on the same screen;

 And Thee,[2] across the harbor, silver-paced
 As though the sun took step of thee, yet left
15 Some motion ever unspent in thy stride,—
 Implicitly thy freedom staying thee!

 Out of some subway scuttle, cell or loft
 A bedlamite speeds to thy parapets,
 Tilting there momently, shrill shirt ballooning,
20 A jest falls from the speechless caravan.

 Down Wall,[3] from girder into street noon leaks,
 A rip-tooth of the sky's acetylene;
 All afternoon the cloud-flown derricks turn . . .
 Thy cables breathe the North Atlantic still.

25 And obscure as that heaven of the Jews,
 Thy guerdon° . . . Accolade thou dost bestow   reward
 Of anonymity time cannot raise:
 Vibrant reprieve and pardon thou dost show.

 O harp and altar, of the fury fused,
30 (How could mere toil align thy choiring strings!)
 Terrific threshold of the prophet's pledge,
 Prayer of pariah, and the lover's cry,—

 Again the traffic lights that skim thy swift
 Unfractioned idiom, immaculate sigh of stars,
35 Beading thy path—condense eternity:
 And we have seen night lifted in thine arms.

---

[2] **Thee:** I.e., Brooklyn Bridge.
[3] **Down Wall:** Wall Street, in Manhattan, is half a mile south of Brooklyn Bridge.

Under thy shadow by the piers I waited;
Only in darkness is thy shadow clear.
The City's fiery parcels all undone,
40   Already snow submerges an iron year . . .

O Sleepless as the river under thee,
Vaulting the sea, the prairies' dreaming sod,
Unto us lowliest sometime sweep, descend
And of the curveship lend a myth to God.

MATTHEW ARNOLD   (1822–1888)

Dover Beach[1]   (1867)

The sea is calm to-night.
The tide is full, the moon lies fair
Upon the straits;—on the French coast the light
Gleams and is gone; the cliffs of England stand,
5   Glimmering and vast, out in the tranquil bay.
Come to the window, sweet is the night-air!
Only, from the long line of spray
Where the sea meets the moon-blanched land,
Listen! you hear the grating roar
10   Of pebbles which the waves draw back, and fling,
At their return, up the high strand,
Begin, and cease, and then again begin,
With tremulous cadence slow, and bring
The eternal note of sadness in.

15   Sophocles long ago
Heard it on the Ægæan,[2] and it brought
Into his mind the turbid ebb and flow
Of human misery; we
Find also in the sound a thought,
20   Hearing it by this distant northern sea.

The Sea of Faith
Was once, too, at the full, and round earth's shore

---

[1] **Dover Beach:** Located in southern England, it is the closest point of proximity to France and continental Europe. It is famous for its white cliffs, which gave England the name Albion.
[2] **Sophocles . . . Ægean:** Sophocles (496 B.C.–406 B.C.), author of *Oedipus Rex*, was one of the greatest and most famous of the Ancient Greek tragedians. Aegean: the sea east of Greece.

Lay like the folds of a bright girdle furled.
But now I only hear
25   Its melancholy, long, withdrawing roar,
Retreating, to the breath
Of the night-wind, down the vast edges drear
And naked shingles of the world.

Ah, love, let us be true
30   To one another! for the world, which seems
To lie before us like a land of dreams,
So various, so beautiful, so new,
Hath really neither joy, nor love, nor light,
Nor certitude, nor peace, nor help for pain;
35   And we are here as on a darkling plain
Swept with confused alarms of struggle and flight,
Where ignorant armies clash by night.

ANTHONY HECHT   (1923–2004)

The Dover Bitch   (1967)

A Criticism of Life?

For Andrews Wanning

So there stood Matthew Arnold and this girl
With the cliffs of England crumbling away behind them,
And he said to her, "Try to be true to me,
And I'll do the same for you, for things are bad
5   All over, etc., etc."
Well now, I knew this girl. It's true she had read
Sophocles[1] in a fairly good translation
And caught that bitter allusion to the sea,
But all the time he was talking she had in mind
10   The notion of what his whiskers would feel like
On the back of her neck. She told me later on
That after a while she got to looking out
At the lights across the channel, and really felt sad,
Thinking of all the wine and enormous beds
15   And blandishments in French and the perfumes.
And then she got really angry. To have been brought
All the way down from London, and then be addressed

---

[1] **Sophocles:** See note 2 in Arnold's "Dover Beach"

As a sort of mournful cosmic last resort
Is really tough on a girl, and she was pretty.
20 Anyway, she watched him pace the room
And finger his watch-chain and seem to sweat a bit,
And then she said one or two unprintable things.
But you mustn't judge her by that. What I mean to say is,
She's really all right. I still see her once in a while
25 And she always treats me right. We have a drink
And I give her a good time, and perhaps it's a year
Before I see her again, but there she is,
Running to fat, but dependable as they come.
And sometimes I bring her a bottle of *Nuit d'Amour.*[2]

A. E. HOUSMAN (1859–1936)

Epitaph on an Army of Mercenaries[1] (1915; 1922)

These, in the day when heaven was falling,
    The hour when earth's foundations fled,
Followed their mercenary calling
    And took their wages and are dead.
5 Their shoulders held the sky suspended;
    They stood, and earth's foundations stay;
What God abandoned, these defended,
    And saved the sum of things for pay.

HUGH MacDIARMID (1892–1978)

Another Epitaph on an Army of Mercenaries (1935)

It is a God-damned lie to say that these
Saved, or knew, anything worth any man's pride.
They were professional murderers and they took
Their blood money and impious risks and died.
5 In spite of all their kind some elements of worth
With difficulty persist here and there on earth.

---

[2] **Nuit d' Amour:** A variety of wine; literally, "Night Love" (French).
[1] **Army of Mercenaries:** Professional soldiers of the British army during World War I.

WILLIAM BUTLER YEATS (1865–1939)

The Choice (1932)

The intellect of man is forced to choose
Perfection of the life, or of the work,
And if it take the second must refuse
A heavenly mansion, raging in the dark.

5 And when the story's finished, what's the news?
In luck or out the toil has left its mark:
That old perplexity an empty purse,
Or the day's vanity, the night's remorse.

ANNIE FINCH (1956–   )

The Intellect of Woman (2003)

> "The intellect of man is forced to choose
> perfection of the life or of the work."
> —YEATS, "THE CHOICE"

The intellect of woman must not choose
perfection of the life, or of the work.
Perfection has a diamond for a muse
who scratches where she only needs to look.

5 And yet the intellect of woman fears
for imperfection's grandeur, in the sharp
delight that breaks her hearing through her ears,
the edge that cuts her vision through the dark.

So the intellect of woman will not mind
10 the sight of where the diamond's edge has moved.
Perfection's habit opens us to find
cuts in a window we have never loved.

WILLIAM BUTLER YEATS (1865–1939)

The Song of Wandering Aengus (1899)

I went out to the hazel wood,
Because a fire was in my head,
And cut and peeled a hazel wand,
And hooked a berry to a thread;
5   And when white moths were on the wing,
And moth-like stars were flickering out,
I dropped the berry in a stream
And caught a little silver trout.

When I had laid it on the floor
10   I went to blow the fire aflame,
But something rustled on the floor,
And some one called me by my name:
It had become a glimmering girl
With apple blossom in her hair
15   Who called me by my name and ran
And faded through the brightening air.

Though I am old with wandering
Through hollow lands and hilly lands,
I will find out where she has gone,
20   And kiss her lips and take her hands;
And walk among long dappled grass,
And pluck till time and times are done
The silver apples of the moon,
The golden apples of the sun.

EAVAN BOLAND (1944–   )

The Woman Turns Herself into a Fish (1990)

Unpod
the bag,
the seed.

Slap
5   the flanks back.
Flatten

paps.
Make finny,
scaled

10 and chill
the slack
and dimple

of the rump.
Pout
15 the mouth,

brow the eyes
and now
and now

eclipse
20 in these hips,
these loins,

the moon,
the blood
flux.

25 It's done.
I turn.
I flab upward.

blub-lipped,
hipless,
30 and I am

sexless,
shed
of ecstasy,

a pale
35 swimmer
sequin-skinned,

pearling eggs
screamlessly
in seaweed.

40 It's what
I set my heart on.
Yet,

ruddering
and muscling
45   in the sunless tons

of new freedoms,
still
I feel

a chill pull,
50   a brightening,
a light, a light:

and how
in my loomy cold,
my greens

55   still
she moons
in me.

ROBERT FROST (1874–1963)

The Road Not Taken (1916)

Two roads diverged in a yellow wood,
And sorry I could not travel both
And be one traveler, long I stood
And looked down one as far as I could
5   To where it bent in the undergrowth;

Then took the other, as just as fair,
And having perhaps the better claim,
Because it was grassy and wanted wear;
Though as for that, the passing there
10   Had worn them really about the same,

And both that morning equally lay
In leaves no step had trodden black.
Oh, I kept the first for another day!
Yet knowing how way leads on to way,
15   I doubted if I should ever come back.

I shall be telling this with a sigh
Somewhere ages and ages hence:
Two roads diverged in a wood, and I—
I took the one less traveled by,
20   And that has made all the difference.

ALAN JENKINS (1955–   )

The Road Less Travelled (2000)

I've never scaled the heights of Macchu Picchu[1] with a backpack
or trekked through India, breakfasting on hunger,
or listened in the African night to the insects' claptrap,
smoked a peace-pipe on Big Sur, or surfed Down Under.[2]

5   I never featured on the cork board in your kitchen
among the postcards from the friends who'd gone to Goa,[3]
Guatemala, Guam; among the glossy shots of lichen-
and liana-festooned temples, girls who grin *Aloa!*[4]

I never wrote, 'I have walked the sands of Dar-es-Salaam
10   and seen elephants drink from the great Zambezi';
'Moving on to Bogota'; 'Babar says *Salaam*[5]
from San Francisco'; 'Here in Maui the living's easy'.

(I always sent my greetings from a *caffe, camera* or *chambre*[6]
with a view of the Rose Window, Bridge of Sighs, Alhambra . . .)[7]

15   But if I stand on my roof-top in London, West Eleven
with my head in the clouds of Cloudesley Place, North One
I can get it clear: how one day you'll move earth and heaven
to have me here, but I'll have changed tack, I'll be gone

in search of some more fascinating place or person,
20   I'll have made a fresh start, with no thought, now, of failure,
it won't be my emotions that you play on (or rehearse on),
it won't be my tongue that tastes the coastline of Australia

---

[1] **Macchu Picchu:** An ancient site in Peru, once a cultural center of the Incas.
[2] **Big Sur . . . Down Under:** Big Sur: a coastal region in California. Down Under: another name for Australia.
[3] **Goa:** A region on the west coast of India.
[4] *Aloa:* Or Aloha, a greeting native to Hawaii, which, depending on the situation, can mean "I love you," "hello," or "goodbye."
[5] **Dar-es-Salaam . . . Salaam:** Dar-es-Salaam is a popular destination in Tanzania and the gateway to the game and safari parks in the region. Zambezi, a river running through central and eastern Africa. *Salaam:* a popular greeting in the Arab world ("peace" in Arabic).
[6] *caffe, camera . . . chambre:* Caffe: coffee shop (Italian). Camera: room (Italian). Chambre: room (French).
[7] **Rose Window . . . Alhambra:** Rose Window: perhaps referring to the circular stained-glass windows of Notre-Dame de Paris. The Bridge of Sighs is in Venice. Alhambra: an architectural complex from the fourteenth century in Granada, Spain.

in the birthmark on your thigh; it won't be me who brings you
tea in bed, or a cappuccino with the froth still on it,
25   or performs my 'Dance to Morning' for you, or sings you
'The Shadow of your Smile', or writes a double sonnet

to you, to your freckled breasts, your sturdy
dancer's legs and neat behind (or, if that's too wordy

for your answering machine, ghazals
30   to your eyes that are the colour of the clear green water
of Sardinia[8]), or puts on 'El cant dels ocells' by Casals[9]
and holds the phone up to the speaker, or holds your daughter
to the sunrise in a suburban garden with galahs
and kookaburras, holds her up as if I'd caught her
35   to hear the song of the Catalan birds, and Bala's.

ROBERT W. SERVICE (1874–1958)

The Cremation of Sam McGee (1907)

There are strange things done in the midnight sun
    By the men who moil for gold;
The Arctic trails have their secret tales
    That would make your blood run cold;
5   *The Northern Lights have seen queer sights,*
    But the queerest they ever did see
Was that night on the marge of Lake Lebarge
    I cremated Sam McGee.

Now Sam McGee was from Tennessee, where the cotton blooms
    and blows.
10   Why he left his home in the South to roam 'round the Pole, God only
    knows.
He was always cold, but the land of gold seemed to hold him like a
    spell;
Though he'd often say in his homely way that "he'd sooner live in
    hell."

---

[8] **Sardinia:** An exotic Italian island in the Mediterranean.
[9] **'El cant dels ocells' by Casals:** Literally, "The Song of the Birds," a composition by Pablo Casals
(1876–1973), the Catalan cellist and composer.

On a Christmas Day we were mushing our way over the Dawson
    trail.
Talk of your cold! through the parka's fold it stabbed like a driven
    nail.
15   If our eyes we'd close, then the lashes froze till sometimes we couldn't
    see;
It wasn't much fun, but the only one to whimper was Sam McGee.

And that very night, as we lay packed tight in our robes beneath the
    snow,
And the dogs were fed, and the stars o'erhead were dancing heel
    and toe,
He turned to me, and "Cap," says he, "I'll cash in this trip, I guess;
20   And if I do, I'm asking that you won't refuse my last request."

Well, he seemed so low that I couldn't say no; then he says with a
    sort of moan:
"It's the cursèe cold, and it's got right hold till I'm chilled clean
    through to the bone.
Yet 'taint being dead—it's my awful dread of the icy grave that
    pains;
So I want you to swear that, foul or fair, you'll cremate my last
    remains."

25   A pal's last need is a thing to heed, so I swore I would not fail;
And we started on at the streak of dawn; but God! he looked ghastly
    pale.
He crouched on the sleigh, and he raved all day of his home in
    Tennessee;
And before nightfall a corpse was all that was left of Sam McGee.

There wasn't a breath in that land of death, and I hurried, horror-
    driven,
30   With a corpse half hid that I couldn't get rid, because of a promise
    given;
It was lashed to the sleigh, and it seemed to say: "You may tax your
    brawn and brains,
But you promised true, and it's up to you to cremate those last
    remains."

Now a promise made is a debt unpaid, and the trail has its own
    stern code.
In the days to come, though my lips were dumb, in my heart how I
    cursed that load.
35   In the long, long night, by the lone firelight, while the huskies, round
    in a ring,

Howled out their woes to the homeless snows—O God! how I
    loathed the thing.

And every day that quiet clay seemed to heavy and heavier grow;
And on I went, though the dogs were spent and the grub was
    getting low;
The trail was bad, and I felt half mad, but I swore I would not give in;
40   And I'd often sing to the hateful thing, and it hearkened with a grin.

Till I came to the marge of Lake Lebarge, and a derelict there lay;
It was jammed in the ice, but I saw in a trice it was called the "Alice
    May."
And I looked at it, and I thought a bit, and I looked at my frozen chum;
Then "Here," said I, with a sudden cry, "is my cre-ma-tor-eum."

45   Some planks I tore from the cabin floor, and I lit the boiler fire;
Some coal I found that was lying around, and I heaped the fuel higher;
The flames just soared, and the furnace roared—such a blaze you
    seldom see;
And I burrowed a hole in the glowing coal, and I stuffed in Sam McGee.

Then I made a hike, for I didn't like to hear him sizzle so;
50   And the heavens scowled, and the huskies howled, and the wind
    began to blow.
It was icy cold, but the hot sweat rolled down my cheeks, and I
    don't know why;
And the greasy smoke in an inky cloak went streaking down the sky.

I do not know how long in the snow I wrestled with grisly fear;
But the stars came out and they danced about ere again I ventured
    near;
55   I was sick with dread, but I bravely said: "I'll just take a peep inside.
I guess he's cooked, and it's time I looked;" . . . then the door I opened
    wide.

And there sat Sam, looking cool and calm, in the heart of the
    furnace roar;
And he wore a smile you could see a mile, and he said: "Please close
    that door.
It's fine in here, but I greatly fear you'll let in the cold and storm—
60   Since I left Plumtree, down in Tennessee, it's the first time I've been
    warm."

There are strange things done in the midnight sun
    By the men who moil for gold;
The Arctic trails have their secret tales
    That would make your blood run cold;

65   *The Northern Lights have seen queer sights,*
        But the queerest they ever did see
      Was that night on the marge of Lake Lebarge
        I cremated Sam McGee.

W. S. MERWIN (1927–   )

The Drunk in the Furnace (1960)

        For a good decade
      The furnace stood in the naked gully, fireless
      And vacant as any hat. Then when it was
      No more to them than a hulking black fossil
5   To erode unnoticed with the rest of the junk-hill
      By the poisonous creek, and rapidly to be added
        To their ignorance.

        They were afterwards astonished
      To confirm, one morning, a twist of smoke like a pale
10   Resurrection, staggering out of its chewed hole,
      And to remark then other tokens that someone,
      Cosily bolted behind the eye-holed iron
      Door of the drafty burner, had there established
        His bad castle.

15   Where he gets his spirits
      It's a mystery. But the stuff keeps him musical:
      Hammer-and-anvilling with poker and bottle
      To his jugged bellowings, till the last groaning clang
      As he collapses onto the rioting
20   Springs of a litter of car-seats ranged on the grates,
        To sleep like an iron pig.[1]

        In their tar-paper church
      On a text about stoke-holes that are sated never
      Their Reverend lingers. They nod and hate trespassers.
25   When the furnace wakes, though, all afternoon
      Their witless offspring flock like piped rats[2] to its siren
      Crescendo, and agape on the crumbling ridge
        Stand in a row and learn.

---

[1] **iron pig:** A crude block poured from a smelting furnace.
[2] **piped rats:** A reference to the story of the Pied Piper, who lured rats out of the town with his piping.
When the residents refused to pay him, he lured their children.

WALLACE STEVENS (1879–1955)

The Snow Man (1923)

One must have a mind of winter
To regard the frost and the boughs
Of the pine-trees crusted with snow;

And have been cold a long time
5   To behold the junipers shagged with ice,
The spruces rough in the distant glitter

Of the January sun; and not to think
Of any misery in the sound of the wind,
In the sound of a few leaves,

10   Which is the sound of the land
Full of the same wind
That is blowing in the same bare place

For the listener, who listens in the snow,
And, nothing himself, beholds
15   Nothing that is not there and the nothing that is.

JOHN BURNSIDE (1955–   )

Variation on a Theme of Wallace Stevens (1994)

If I switched off the light
I would see him out in the yard,
tending a fire by the hedge,
raking the windfalls and leaves
5   from a different year,

a ghost in his smoke-coloured shirt
with his back to the house,
my double, from his looks: same age, same build,
the same clenched rage in his arms,
10   the same bright fear,

and I would be with him, looking at the dark,
but missing what he sees, or thinks he sees:
the sudden night, the blur of wind and rain,

the shadow in the woods that matches him
15   with nothing that is, and the nothing that is not there.

WILLIAM CARLOS WILLIAMS (1883–1963)

This Is Just to Say (1934)

I have eaten
the plums
that were in
the icebox

5   and which
you were probably
saving
for breakfast

Forgive me
10   they were delicious
so sweet
and so cold

KENNETH KOCH (1925–2002)

Variations on a Theme by William Carlos Williams (1962)

1

I chopped down the house that you had been saving to live in
        next summer.
I am sorry, but it was morning, and I had nothing to do
and its wooden beams were so inviting.

2

We laughed at the hollyhocks together
5   and then I sprayed them with lye.[1]
Forgive me. I simply do not know what I am doing.

---

[1] **lye:** A toxic liquid obtained by leaching wood ashes.

3

I gave away the money that you had been saving to live on for the
     next ten years.
The man who asked for it was shabby
and the firm March wind on the porch was so juicy and cold.

4

10 Last evening we went dancing and I broke your leg.
Forgive me. I was clumsy and
I wanted you here in the wards, where I am the doctor![2]

FLOSSIE WILLIAMS

Reply (1982)
(crumped on her desk)

Dear Bill: I've made a
couple of sandwiches for you.
In the ice-box you'll find
blue-berries—a cup of grapefruit
5 a glass of cold coffee.

On the stove is the tea-pot
with enough tea leaves
for you to make tea if you
prefer—Just light the gas—
10 boil the water and put it in the tea

Plenty of bread in the bread-box
and butter and eggs—
I didn't know just what to
make for you. Several people
15 called up about office hours—

See you later. Love. Floss.

Please switch off the telephone.

---

[2] **wards . . . doctor:** Apart from being a poet, Williams was also a professional obstetrician.

MARIANNE MOORE (1887–1972)

The Fish (1921)

wade
through black jade.
   Of the crow-blue mussel-shells, one keeps
   adjusting the ash-heaps;
5   opening and shutting itself like

an
injured fan.
   The barnacles which encrust the side
   of the wave, cannot hide
10   there for the submerged shafts of the

sun,
split like spun
   glass, move themselves with spotlight swiftness
   into the crevices—
15   in and out, illuminating

the
turquoise sea
   of bodies. The water drives a wedge
   of iron through the iron edge
20   of the cliff; whereupon the stars,

pink
rice-grains, ink-
   bespattered jelly-fish, crabs like green
   lilies, and submarine
25   toadstools, slide each on the other.

All
external
   marks of abuse are present on this
   defiant edifice—
30   all the physical features of

ac-
cident—lack
   of cornice, dynamite grooves, burns, and
   hatchet strokes, these things stand
35   out on it; the chasm-side is

dead.
Repeated
    evidence has proved that it can live
    on what can not revive
40   its youth. The sea grows old in it.

ELIZABETH BISHOP (1911–1979)

The Fish (1940; 1946)

I caught a tremendous fish
and held him beside the boat
half out of water, with my hook
fast in the corner of his mouth.
5   He didn't fight.
He hadn't fought at all.
He hung a grunting weight,
battered and venerable
and homely. Here and there
10 his brown skin hung in strips
like ancient wallpaper,
and its pattern of darker brown
was like wallpaper:
shapes like full-blown roses
15 stained and lost through age.
He was speckled with barnacles,
fine rosettes of lime,
and infested
with tiny white sea-lice,
20 and underneath two or three
rags of green weed hung down.
While his gills were breathing in
the terrible oxygen
—the frightening gills,
25 fresh and crisp with blood,
that can cut so badly—
I thought of the coarse white flesh
packed in like feathers,
the big bones and the little bones,
30 the dramatic reds and blacks
of his shiny entrails,

and the pink swim-bladder
like a big peony.
I looked into his eyes
35 which were far larger than mine
but shallower, and yellowed,
the irises backed and packed
with tarnished tinfoil
seen through the lenses
40 of old scratched isinglass.
They shifted a little, but not
to return my stare.
—It was more like the tipping
of an object toward the light.
45 I admired his sullen face,
the mechanism of his jaw,
and then I saw
that from his lower lip
—if you could call it a lip—
50 grim, wet, and weaponlike,
hung five old pieces of fish-line,
or four and a wire leader
with the swivel still attached,
with all their five big hooks
55 grown firmly in his mouth.
A green line, frayed at the end
where he broke it, two heavier lines,
and a fine black thread
still crimped from the strain and snap
60 when it broke and he got away.
Like medals with their ribbons
frayed and wavering,
a five-haired beard of wisdom
trailing from his aching jaw.
65 I stared and stared
and victory filled up
the little rented boat,
from the pool of bilge
where oil had spread a rainbow
70 around the rusted engine
to the bailer rusted orange,
the sun-cracked thwarts,
the oarlocks on their strings,
the gunnels—until everything
75 was rainbow, rainbow, rainbow!
And I let the fish go.

ALLEN TATE (1899–1979)

Ode to the Confederate Dead   (1928)

Row after row with strict impunity
The headstones yield their names to the element,
The wind whirrs without recollection;
In the riven troughs the splayed leaves
5   Pile up, of nature the casual sacrament
To the seasonal eternity of death;
Then driven by the fierce scrutiny
Of heaven to their election in the vast breath,
They sough the rumour of mortality.

10   Autumn is desolation in the plot
Of a thousand acres where these memories grow
From the inexhaustible bodies that are not
Dead, but feed the grass row after rich row.
Think of the autumns that have come and gone!—
15   Ambitious November with the humors of the year,
With a particular zeal for every slab,
Staining the uncomfortable angels that rot
On the slabs, a wing chipped here, an arm there:
The brute curiosity of an angel's stare
20   Turns you, like them, to stone,
Transforms the heaving air
Till plunged to a heavier world below
You shift your sea-space blindly
Heaving, turning like the blind crab.

25   Dazed by the wind, only the wind
          The leaves flying, plunge

You know who have waited by the wall
The twilight certainty of an animal,
Those midnight restitutions of the blood
30   You know—the immitigable pines, the smoky frieze
Of the sky, the sudden call: you know the rage,
The cold pool left by the mounting flood,
Of muted Zeno and Parmenides.[1]
You who have waited for the angry resolution

---

[1] **Zeno and Parmenides:** Zeno of Elea (495 B.C.–430 B.C.) was an ancient Greek philosopher, who formulated the paradox that change and motion are illusory. Parmenides: a pre-Socratic Greek philosopher (fifth century B.C.), who arrived at conclusions similar to those of Zeno.

35 Of those desires that should be yours tomorrow,
You know the unimportant shrift of death
And praise the vision
And praise the arrogant circumstance
Of those who fall
40 Rank upon rank, hurried beyond decision—
Here by the sagging gate, stopped by the wall.

Seeing, seeing only the leaves
Flying, plunge and expire

Turn your eyes to the immoderate past,
45 Turn to the inscrutable infantry rising
Demons out of the earth they will not last.
Stonewall, Stonewall, and the sunken fields of hemp,
Shiloh, Antietam, Malvern Hill, Bull Run.[2]
Lost in that orient of the thick and fast
50 You will curse the setting sun.

Cursing only the leaves crying
Like an old man in a storm

You hear the shout, the crazy hemlocks point
With troubled fingers to the silence which
55 Smothers you, a mummy, in time.

The hound bitch
Toothless and dying, in a musty cellar
Hears the wind only.

Now that the salt of their blood
60 Stiffens the saltier oblivion of the sea,
Seals the malignant purity of the flood,
What shall we who count our days and bow
Our heads with a commemorial woe
In the ribboned coats of grim felicity,
65 What shall we say of the bones, unclean,
Whose verdurous anonymity will grow?
The ragged arms, the ragged heads and eyes
Lost in these acres of the insane green?
The gray lean spiders come, they come and go;
70 In a tangle of willows without light
The singular screech-owl's tight

---

[2] **Shiloh, Antietam . . . Bull Run:** Famous battlegrounds of the American Civil War.

Invisible lyric seeds the mind
With the furious murmur of their chivalry.

      We shall say only the leaves
75   Flying, plunge and expire

We shall say only the leaves whispering
In the improbable mist of nightfall
That flies on multiple wing:
Night is the beginning and the end
80 And in between the ends of distraction
Waits mute speculation, the patient curse
That stones the eyes, or like the jaguar leaps
For his own image in a jungle pool, his victim.

What shall we say who have knowledge
85 Carried to the heart? Shall we take the act
To the grave? Shall we, more hopeful, set up the grave
In the house? The ravenous grave?

                Leave now
The shut gate and the decomposing wall:
90 The gentle serpent, green in the mulberry bush,
Riots with his tongue through the hush—
Sentinel of the grave who counts us all!

ROBERT LOWELL (1917–1977)

For the Union Dead (1964)

"Relinquunt Omnia Servare Rem Publicam."[1]

The old South Boston Aquarium stands
in a Sahara of snow now. Its broken windows are boarded.
The bronze weathervane cod has lost half its scales.
The airy tanks are dry.

---

[1] **Relinquunt . . . Publicam:** "They give up everything for the Republic" (Latin). This motto is inscribed on a bronze relief depicting Colonel Robert Gould Shaw (1837–1863) and the first all-black Civil War regiment (Lowell changed only the pronoun "he gives up" to "they give up"). Colonel Shaw and many of his troops were killed in the assault of Fort Wagner, South Carolina. The monument, which stands in the Boston Public Garden (The Boston Common), was designed by Augustus St. Gaudens (1848–1897) and dedicated in 1897.

5   Once my nose crawled like a snail on the glass;
my hand tingled
to burst the bubbles
drifting from the noses of the cowed, compliant fish.

My hand draws back. I often sigh still
10   for the dark downward and vegetating kingdom
of the fish and reptile. One morning last March,
I pressed against the new barbed and galvanized

fence on the Boston Common. Behind their cage,
yellow dinosaur steamshovels were grunting
15   as they cropped up tons of mush and grass
to gouge their underworld garage.

Parking spaces luxuriate like civic
sandpiles in the heart of Boston.
A girdle of orange, Puritan-pumpkin colored girders
20   braces the tingling Statehouse,

shaking over the excavations, as it faces Colonel Shaw
and his bell-cheeked Negro infantry
on St. Gaudens' shaking Civil War relief,
propped by a plank splint against the garage's earthquake.

25   Two months after marching through Boston,
half the regiment was dead;
at the dedication,
William James[2] could almost hear the bronze Negroes breathe.

Their monument sticks like a fishbone
30   in the city's throat.
Its Colonel is as lean
as a compass-needle.

He has an angry wrenlike vigilance,
a greyhound's gentle tautness;
35   he seems to wince at pleasure,
and suffocate for privacy.

He is out of bounds now. He rejoices in man's lovely,
peculiar power to choose life and die—

---

[2] **William James:** A famous nineteenth-century psychologist and philosopher, brother of the novelist Henry James.

when he leads his black soldiers to death,
40   he cannot bend his back.

On a thousand small town New England greens,
the old white churches hold their air
of sparse, sincere rebellion; frayed flags
quilt the graveyards of the Grand Army of the Republic.

45   The stone statues of the abstract Union Soldier
grow slimmer and younger each year—
wasp-waisted, they doze over muskets
and muse through their sideburns . . .

Shaw's father wanted no monument
50   except the ditch,
where his son's body was thrown
and lost with his "niggers."

The ditch is nearer.
There are no statues for the last war here;
55   on Boylston Street, a commercial photograph
shows Hiroshima boiling

over a Mosler Safe,[3] the "Rock of Ages"
that survived the blast. Space is nearer.
When I crouch to my television set,
60   the drained faces of Negro school-children rise like balloons.

Colonel Shaw
is riding on his bubble,
he waits
for the blesséd break.

65   The Aquarium is gone. Everywhere,
giant finned cars nose forward like fish;
a savage servility
slides by on grease.

---

[3] **Boylston Street . . . Mosler Safe:** Boylston: a major street in Boston. Mosler Safe: the safe of the Teikoho Bank built by the Mosler Company, was one of the only structures to survive the American nuclear bombing of Hiroshima on August 6, 1945. In the blast, 80,000 people were killed instantaneously and 97,000 more died of radiation-associated cancer.

ELIZABETH BISHOP (1911–1979)

The Armadillo (1965)[1]

For Robert Lowell

This is the time of year
when almost every night
the frail, illegal fire balloons appear.
Climbing the mountain height,

5   rising toward a saint
still honored in these parts,
the paper chambers flush and fill with light
that comes and goes, like hearts.

Once up against the sky it's hard
10   to tell them from the stars—
planets, that is—the tinted ones:
Venus going down, or Mars,

or the pale green one. With a wind,
they flare and falter, wobble and toss;
15   but if it's still they steer between
the kite sticks of the Southern Cross,

receding, dwindling, solemnly
and steadily forsaking us,
or, in the downdraft from a peak,
20   suddenly turning dangerous.

Last night another big one fell.
It splattered like an egg of fire
against the cliff behind the house.
The flame ran down. We saw the pair

25   of owls who nest there flying up
and up, their whirling black-and-white
stained bright pink underneath, until
they shrieked up out of sight.

The ancient owls' nest must have burned.
30   Hastily, all alone,
a glistening armadillo left the scene,
rose-flecked, head down, tail down,

---

[1] The poem was written much earlier, but not published with the dedication to Lowell until 1965.

and then a baby rabbit jumped out,
short-eared, to our surprise.
35   So soft!—a handful of intangible ash
with fixed, ignited eyes.

Too pretty, dreamlike mimicry!
O falling fire and piercing cry
and panic, and a weak mailed fist
40   *clenched ignorant against the sky!*

ROBERT LOWELL (1917–1977)

Skunk Hour (1959)
For Elizabeth Bishop

Nautilus Island's[1] hermit
heiress still lives through winter in her Spartan[2] cottage;
her sheep still graze above the sea.
Her son's a bishop. Her farmer
5   is first selectman in our village;
she's in her dotage.

Thirsting for
the hierarchic privacy
of Queen Victoria's century,[3]
10   she buys up all
the eyesores facing her shore,
and lets them fall.

The season's ill—
we've lost our summer millionaire,
15   who seemed to leap from an L. L. Bean[4]
catalogue. His nine-knot yawl
was auctioned off to lobstermen.
A red fox stain covers Blue Hill.

And now our fairy
20   decorator brightens his shop for fall;
his fishnet's filled with orange cork,

---

[1] **Nautilus Island's:** An island off the coast of Maine.
[2] **Spartan:** I.e., austerely furnished.
[3] **Queen Victoria's century:** I.e., the nineteenth century. Queen Victoria's reign spanned the length of almost seven decades between 1837 and 1901.
[4] **L. L. Bean:** A shopping catalogue of the clothing brand L.L. Bean.

orange, his cobbler's bench and awl;
there is no money in his work,
he'd rather marry.

25 One dark night,
my Tudor Ford climbed the hill's skull;
I watched for love-cars. Lights turned down,
they lay together, hull to hull,
where the graveyard shelves on the town. . . .
30 My mind's not right.

A car radio bleats,
"Love, O careless Love. . . ." I hear
my ill-spirit sob in each blood cell,
as if my hand were at its throat. . . .
35 I myself am hell;
nobody's here—

only skunks, that search
in the moonlight for a bite to eat.
They march on their soles up Main Street:
40 white stripes, moonstruck eyes' red fire
under the chalk-dry and spar spire
of the Trinitarian Church.

I stand on top
of our back steps and breathe the rich air—
45 a mother skunk with her column of kittens swills the garbage pail.
She jabs her wedge-head in a cup
of sour cream, drops her ostrich tail,
and will not scare.

SEAMUS HEANEY (1939–   )

The Skunk (1979)

Up, black, striped and damasked like the chasuble[1]
At a funeral mass, the skunk's tail
Paraded the skunk. Night after night
I expected her like a visitor.

---

[1] **chasuble:** A long sleeveless garment worn by a priest during services.

5   The refrigerator whinnied into silence.
My desk light softened beyond the verandah.
Small oranges loomed in the orange tree.
I began to be tense as a voyeur.

After eleven years I was composing
10   Love-letters again, broaching the word "wife"
Like a stored cask, as if its slender vowel
Had mutated into the night earth and air

Of California. The beautiful, useless
Tang of eucalyptus spelt your absence.
15   The aftermath of a mouthful of wine
Was like inhaling you off a cold pillow.

And there she was, the intent and glamorous,
Ordinary, mysterious skunk,
Mythologized, demythologized,
20   Snuffing the boards five feet beyond me.

It all came back to me last night, stirred
By the sootfall of your things at bedtime,
Your head-down, tail-up hunt in a bottom drawer
For the black plunge-line nightdress.

MURIEL RUKEYSER   (1913–1980)

Effort at Speech Between Two People   (1935)

:   Speak to me. Take my hand. What are you now?
I will tell you all. I will conceal nothing.
When I was three, a little child read a story about a rabbit
who died, in the story, and I crawled under a chair :
5   a pink rabbit : it was my birthday, and a candle
burnt a sore spot on my finger, and I was told to be happy.

:   Oh, grow to know me. I am not happy. I will be open:
Now I am thinking of white sails against a sky like music,
like glad horns blowing, and birds tilting, and an arm about me.
10   There was one I loved, who wanted to live, sailing.

:   Speak to me. Take my hand. What are you now?
When I was nine, I was fruitily sentimental,
fluid : and my widowed aunt played Chopin,

and I bent my head on the painted woodwork, and wept.
15   I want now to be close to you. I would
link the minutes of my days close, somehow, to your days.

  : I am not happy. I will be open.
I have liked lamps in evening corners, and quiet poems.
There has been fear in my life. Sometimes I speculate
20   On what a tragedy his life was, really.

  : Take my hand. Fist my mind in your hand. What are you now?
When I was fourteen, I had dreams of suicide,
and I stood at a steep window, at sunset, hoping toward death :
if the light had not melted clouds and plains to beauty,
25   if light had not transformed that day, I would have leapt.
I am unhappy. I am lonely. Speak to me.

  : I will be open. I think he never loved me:
he loved the bright beaches, the little lips of foam
that ride small waves, he loved the veer of gulls:
30   he said with a gay mouth: I love you. Grow to know me.

What are you now? If we could touch one another,
if these our separate entities could come to grips,
clenched like a Chinese puzzle . . . yesterday
I stood in a crowded street that was live with people,
35   and no one spoke a word, and the morning shone.
Everyone silent, moving. . . . Take my hand.
    Speak to me.

WILLIAM MEREDITH (1919–   )

Effort at Speech (1970)
For Muriel Rukeyser

Climbing the stairway gray with urban midnight,
Cheerful, venial, ruminating pleasure,
Darkness takes me, an arm around my throat and
        Give me your wallet.

5   Fearing cowardice more than other terrors,
Angry I wrestle with my unseen partner,
Caught in a ritual not of our own making,
        panting like spaniels.

Bold with adrenaline, mindless, shaking,

10   *God damn it, no!* I rasp at him behind me,
Wrenching the leather wallet from his grasp. It
                        breaks like a wishbone,

So that departing (routed by my shouting,
Not by my strength or inadvertent courage)

15   Half of the papers lending me a name are
                        gone with him nameless.

Only now turning, I see a tall boy running,
Fifteen, sixteen, dressed thinly for the weather.
Reaching the streetlight he turns a brown face briefly

20   phrased like a question.

I like a questioner watch him turn the corner
Taking the answer with him, or his half of it.
Loneliness, not a sensible emotion,
                        breathes hard on the stairway.

25   Walking homeward I fraternize with shadows,
Zigzagging with them where they flee the streetlights,
Asking for trouble, asking for the message
                        trouble had sent me.

All fall down has been scribbled on the street in

30   Garbage and excrement: so much for the vision
Others taunt me with, my untimely humor,
                        so much for cheerfulness.

Next time don't wrangle, give the boy the money,
Call across chasms what the world you know is.

35   *Luckless and lied to, how can a child master*
                        human decorum?

Next time a switchblade, somewhere he is thinking,
I should have killed him and took the lousy wallet.
Reading my cards he feels a surge of anger

40   blind as my shame.

Error from Babel mutters in the places,
Cities apart, where now we word our failures:
Hatred and guilt have left us without language
                        who might have held discourse.

ELLEN BRYANT VOIGT (1943–   )
for William Meredith

Effort at Speech (1992)

Nothing was as we'd thought, the sea
anemones not plants but animals,
flounder languishing on the sand
like infants waiting to be turned—
5   from the bottom we followed the spiral ramp
around and up, circling the tank.
Robert, barely out of the crib,
rode his father's shoulders, uttering
words or parts of words and pointing
10   ceaselessly toward the water, toward some
one of the many shapes in the water,
what he could not name, could not describe.
Starfish, monkfish—not fish—catfish,
sea hare, sea horse: we studied the plaques
15   for something to prompt him with,
but he tucked his head as if shamed.
So I left them at the school of the quick
yellow-with-black-stripes conventional,
passed the armored centenary
20   turtle going down as I went up,
seaweed, eels, elongate gun-gray suede
bodies of the prehistoric sharks
transversing the reef, and headed to the top,
thinking to look down through the multiple layers.
25   When it first came at me, it seemed more
creature of the air than of the sea,
huge, delta-winged, bat-winged,
head subsumed in the spread pectorals—
unless it was all head—a kite
30   gliding to the wall between us, veering
up, over, exposing its light belly,
"face" made by gill-slits opening,
the tail's long whip and poison spine.
Eagle Ray: Cordata, like the eagle;
35   it skated along the glass—
eagle scanning the sheer canyon wall,
bat trapped inside the cave,
no, like a mind at work, at play,
I felt I was seeing through the skull—
40   and then away.

GLOSSARY OF POETIC TERMS

Alliteration The repetition of consonant sounds to create a consistent pattern. In Robert Hayden's "A Plague of Starlings," the line "in clench of cold" is a taut example of alliteration, the "n" sound of *in/clench*, the hard "c" of *clench/cold*, the "l" in *clench/cold*.

Alliterative verse Poetry whose metrical structure is based upon correspondences between consonant sounds and the number of stresses in each line; Old English verse is primarily alliterative.

Allusion A literary technique in which an author refers to a person, place, or thing, real or fictional, outside of the text at hand. Successful allusions enrich the work by bringing in additional associations for the reader. An allusion to the Bible, for example, might allow an author to call up an entire worldview and moral code. The danger in using allusion is that the reader may not have read the texts to which the author is alluding. In some cases, this does not pose a major problem. Not infrequently, however, the success of a work of literature will hinge, in whole or in part, on the reader's ability to identify an allusion or allusions. Writers often allude to other works of literature, but in fact, they can allude to anything from any sphere of life, public or private.

Anapest A metrical foot of two unaccented syllables followed by one accented syllable: "unabridged" (adjective: *anapestic*).

Ars poetica From Latin, "the art of poetry"; a common theme among poets reflecting on their art and work.

Assonance The same vowel sound in words with different consonant endings, not to be confused with **rhyme** ("like/kind" is an example of assonance; "like/bike" is pure rhyme).

Avant-garde From the French "vanguard," applied (often self-consciously) to movements in art that deliberately challenge the status quo and propose a new direction.

Ballad A **narrative** poem, originally to be sung, that employs a regular, rhyming **stanza** format as a mnemonic device (an aid to memory).

Ballad stanza A ballad **stanza** usually consists of four lines, in which the second and fourth lines rhyme, or six lines, in which the first, fourth, and sixth lines rhyme. Poets will sometimes vary the pattern.

Beat movement A movement in American youth culture with its origins in the postwar 1950s, the Beats challenged social, political, and artistic conventions. Inspired by other art forms out of the mainstream of American culture (from jazz music to Buddhism), the Beat movement in literature drew from forms as diverse as haiku and Walt Whitman's free verse. Key Beat poets include Gregory Corso, Allen Ginsberg, and Kenneth Rexroth.

Black Arts movement A response in the 1960s by African-American poets and artists to the rising political consciousness and revolutionary zeal of African-American politics and culture. Key figures include Gwendolyn Brooks, Imamu Amiri Baraka, and Sonia Sanchez.

Black Mountain school   In America, an offshoot of the Beat movement associated with the experimental Black Mountain College in North Carolina. Poets of the Black Mountain school include Robert Creeley and Robert Duncan.

Blank verse   Unrhymed iambic pentameter, of which Shakespeare and Milton are masters.

Cacophony   This literally means "harsh sound." Poets will often create cacophonous effects by using alliteration, or clustering heavy stresses together, or by writing with abrupt, awkward rhythms. This does not mean, of course, that any one of these elements, or even all of them in combination, will automatically produce cacophony. It should also be noted that even the most cacophonous sounds should be pleasing in the sense that they should contribute to making the poem a more perfectly realized work.

Caesura   A pause in the middle of the four-beat line of alliterative Anglo-Saxon verse, or, more generally, any pause within the middle of a line.

Canon   A group of texts commonly held by a culture to be of utmost importance and of the very best quality.

Classical poetry   Verse written in ancient Greece (in Greek) and ancient Rome (in Latin) on which the conventions of Western European poetry are based.

Close reading   A careful examination of the language, form, themes, and literary and historical contexts of a poem.

Common measure   Also known as "hymn meter" for its prevalence in English-language hymn lyrics, consisting of quatrains of iambic tetrameter alternating with iambic trimeter and rhyming *abab*.

Conceit   An extended comparison, sometimes informing and reaching throughout an entire poem.

Confessional school   A mid-twentieth-century development, primarily American and associated with the poets Robert Lowell, Sylvia Plath, and Anne Sexton. Usually in blank verse, confessional poets explore their own lived experiences and feelings.

Consonance   Like alliteration, consonance is an effect involving the repetition of consonants. Unlike alliteration, however, consonance does not have to occur at the beginnings of words. The term can therefore be used to describe the relationship between any two identical consonants.

Conventions   The historically consistent elements that a reader has come to expect from a particular kind of poetry.

Couplet   The most basic unit of rhymed verse, in that the end of one line rhymes with the end of the line immediately following it. While couplets can be written in any meter, and with any line length, couplets in English are typically in iambic tetrameter or iambic pentameter. Two unrhymed lines grouped together as a stanza are usually referred to as a *distich*, rather than a *couplet*.

Cubism   In Modern art, especially painting, a fracturing of viewpoint and content; some modern poets adapted this sense of a multiplicity of viewpoints and perspectives for their verse.

Dactyl   A metrical foot of one stressed syllable followed by two unstressed syllables: merrily, tenderly, happily (adjective: *dactylic*).

Dimeter   A line consisting of two metrical feet.

Dramatic poetry   Not to be confused with a play written in verse (Shakespeare, for example), dramatic poetry uses the conventions of drama (monologue, soliloquy), but without the intention of ever being staged or performed.

Eclogue   A variant of **pastoral** poetry, usually in the form of a dialogue between two shepherds.

Elegy   From a Greek word that means "a poem written in couplets," or more simply a "song." The earliest Greek elegies were songs written for soldiers as they left for battle; in both the Greek and the later Roman tradition, elegies were strong expressions of emotion, but rarely if ever of mourning. In the English tradition, the elegy was adopted as a poem of mourning or lament. Although the meter and rhyme of the English elegy varies tremendously, the most beautiful elegies share a sense of great dignity and heightened emotion.

End-stopped   Lines of poetry whose grammatical or rhythmical sense comes to a halt at the end of the line.

Enjambment   Lines of poetry whose grammatical or rhythmical sense spills over from one line to the next.

Epic   A very long narrative poem that recounts and celebrates the accomplishments of a mythic hero, often involving supernatural or divine intervention.

Epigram   A brief, witty poem, often a pointed satire.

Epistle   A poem in the form of a letter.

Euphony   The term *euphony* literally means "pleasing sound." Although what is pleasing or not is to some degree a matter of taste, most listeners will agree about whether a series of sounds is musical or harsh. Poets will often use assonance, especially with long vowels, and alliteration, to create this sense of musicality. It's important to note that a line or phrase may sound euphonious in itself without necessarily being pleasing or effective in the larger context of the poem.

Experimentalist   Poetry that dispenses with the easy realism of already familiar work.

Feet   Lines of metrical poetry are divided into smaller units, usually two or three syllables long, called *feet*. Breaking the line down in this way allows for easier scansion, and makes it easier to determine the basic meter of the poem, although poets do not, generally speaking, compose one foot at a time.

Feminine rhyme   A rhyme is feminine when it consists of two syllables, one stressed and one unstressed. While not uncommon in English poetry, this type of rhyme is less common than masculine rhyme.

Feminist criticism   An approach to reading and studying poetry that is particularly attentive to the political and social contexts in which women have written—or have not been allowed or encouraged to write. Feminist critics have been especially important in the rediscovery of many women writers, and have also proposed particular ways of reading and understanding work from a distinctly or uniquely female point of view. Some feminist critics also suggest that there is a particularly feminine way of using language to encode a uniquely female experience.

Figurative reading   A deeper reading of a poem that searches out its subtler meanings and is especially attentive to metaphor. See **literal reading**.

Figure of speech   A use of language that departs from standard literal usage; **metaphor** and **simile** are examples.

Form   In poetry, the shape and arrangement of words, lines, and images that determines the **genre** of a poem.

Formalism   A way of reading and critiquing poetry that pays special attention to the poem's form and the poet's skill at using form in fresh, innovative ways.

Free verse   No verse is truly "free," in that to be recognized and read as poetry, a poem must have some inherent form and reflect some aspect of the poetic tradition. Free verse is poetry that does not conform rigidly to a particular form or **genre**, but still makes use of the figurative language and rhythmical sense of poetry.

Fugitive movement   An American group of poets in the 1920s associated with the magazine *The Fugitive*; the group later became known as Agrarians and included many Southern poets associated with Vanderbilt University.

Genre   A genre is a kind or type of poetry that conforms to certain **conventions** and expectations. Many contemporary writers play with the notion of genre, combining elements of different genres into distinctive new forms.

Haiku   A three-line poem in which the lines have syllable counts of 5–7–5, respectively. The form was invented in Japan, but has since become popular in English and other European languages. Obviously, there is not much room for narrative or explanation in a haiku; instead, the form depends on carefully chosen details—like the spare brush strokes in a Japanese ink drawing—to suggest more than it can directly say.

Harlem Renaissance   A movement of African-American writers, artists, musicians, and performers who lived in and around Harlem in New York City in the 1920s. Key poets of the Harlem Renaissance include Langston Hughes and Countee Cullen.

Heroic couplet   A pair of rhyming lines, usually of **iambic pentameter**.

Hexameter   A line of poetry with six "feet."

Iamb   A metrical foot, very common in English, in which the stress falls on the second syllable; "upstairs," "around the block" (adjective: *iambic*).

Images   The visual associations called up by a poet's use of description.

Imagism   An early twentieth-century school of poetry, associated with Ezra Pound and H. D. (Hilda Doolittle), focusing on the creation of a single, deep **image** within a poem.

Influence   Sometimes implicit, sometimes acknowledged and made explicit, nearly all poetry is engaged with and informed by the work of other poets. Some poets call attention to these influences (see Chapter 25); other poets struggle against influences and traditions that seem inadequate to the task at hand.

Irony   An effect that occurs when a statement or situation has two levels of meaning and there is a gap or contradiction between them. This difference can add richness and complexity to a work. In order for irony to work, the reader must recognize and appreciate that two levels of meaning are operating. In the case of verbal irony, a character or narrator says one thing while meaning something else. Situational irony exists when there is a difference between what appears to be the case (a man appears to be a model husband and father) and what is actually true (he is really a serial killer). While irony is often reserved for particular statements or situations in a work, the tone of an entire work may sometimes be ironic.

Language poets   A group of American poets working in the 1980s whose work reflects a radical skepticism about the ability of language to meaningfully express anything other than its own sounds.

Literal reading   Most of us approach a first reading of a poem from a literal level. We read newspapers at a literal level, too. When we read at a literal level, we are considering only the most obvious meanings of words and phrases, rather than any deeper **figurative** or connotative significance.

Lyric   From the Greek term for a single singer accompanied by a lyre, lyric is now applied very broadly to poetry that is profoundly subjective in its expression of a specific emotional experience. The adjective "lyric" is still applied to work that has a marked musical quality to it, a sense of melody and rhythm even if no actual "music" accompanies the text. (Of course, words written for the purpose of being sung to musical accompaniment are also called *lyrics*.)

Martian school   A group of British poets born in the 1940s whose mature work of the 1980s seems to perceive the world from an entirely original viewpoint, as a visitor from Mars might see it. Poet James Fenton first applied the term to fellow poet Craig Raine.

Masculine rhyme   A rhyme is masculine if it occurs on a stressed syllable that is also the last syllable of the line. The majority of rhymes in English poetry are of this kind, and are also an example of full rhyme.

Meditative poetry   Usually applied to the work of sixteenth- and seventeenth-century English metaphysical poets, meditative poetry connects the poetic person with a transcendent reality or God. More generally, meditative poetry depicts an intense engagement between the speaker of a poem and some concept, natural object, or belief; the engagement leads to a kind of self-revelation.

Metaphor   From the Greek "to carry across," a metaphor is a figure of speech that implies one thing but, by comparison, evokes another. When Sir Thomas Wyatt describes

> "My galley charged with forgetfulness / Through sharp seas in winter nights doth pass / 'Tween rock and rock. . . ." the imperiled ship (or galley) is a metaphor for the poet's struggling faith.

Meter   In a broad sense, meter refers to a recurring rhythmic pattern in a poem that establishes the internal structure of the lines, and, in some cases, of whole stanzas. It is also known as *measure*, since it nearly always involves the counting—and sometimes ordering—of some linguistic or syntactic element. Meter in English is primarily determined by stress, and secondarily by number of syllables. Any time we listen to poetry in English and hear a relatively steady, relatively repetitive beat, we are hearing meter in one of its forms.

Metonymy   A figure of speech in which a word associated with a larger concept is substituted for that larger concept itself.

Mimesis   An aesthetic theory which holds that art (including poetry) is an imitation of life.

Modernism   A movement in European and American culture following World War I, in which longstanding **conventions** and canons of artistic representation were radically challenged in response to the war's chaos. Perhaps the key Modernist text in poetry is T. S. Eliot's "The Waste Land."

Monologue   A speech given by a single character, either in a poem or in a play; the **persona** of the speaker is readily determined (either by a character's name and being in a performed play, or through other means in a poetic monologue), and the words spoken are those that the character would conceivably use if speaking to another character within the play or poem (as opposed to a soliloquy, which allows an audience to "eavesdrop" on a character's innermost thoughts).

Monometer   A line of verse containing just one "foot."

Multiculturalism   In the last decades of the twentieth century, a movement in American culture at large that recognizes racial, cultural, and religious diversity. In literature, the multiculturalist movement among editors, teachers, publishers, and writers themselves has challenged the traditional canon and sought to introduce the work of writers of color to a wider audience.

Narrative poetry   At its simplest, poetry that "tells a story," often using a chronological structure to relay events.

Neoclassical movement   Any movement in the arts that looks back to ancient Greece and Rome for models and inspiration. In poetry, a particularly neoclassical movement was in eighteenth-century England, where many writers translated directly from the Latin and Greek originals and adapted those forms for original English-language work (see the work of Alexander Pope).

New formalism   A contemporary movement in poetry associated with American poets born before World War II; these poets (Robert Pinsky, Anthony Hecht, John Hollander, and others) used traditional **conventions** of verse to explore modern concerns, issues, and experiences.

New York school   A group of American poets based in New York whose key work was produced between 1950 and 1970. The New York Poets (such as Frank O'Hara) were especially engaged with the jazzy rhythms of urban New York life in the postwar years.

Octameter   A line of verse with eight metrical "feet."

Ode   An extended lyric devoted to a single purpose and theme. The tone of the ode is serious, and the poem's speaker is often understood to be addressing a large audience upon a solemn or meaningful occasion. The ode is often associated with the eulogy and other formal expressions of reverence for the dead.

Onomatopoeia A poetic effect in which the sounds of the words mimic the sound of the thing or process they describe. Sometimes, we can see this in the case of individual words—the sound of the word *pop*, for example, resembles the sound itself. When writers move beyond single words to create whole phrases or lines that are onomatopoeic, they can employ any poetic device, including assonance, alliteration, or rhyme.

Originality An elusive, but immediately recognizable quality that allows for such tremendous variety and freshness in even the most conventionally rigorous of forms. A truly original poet seems at once to have absorbed the entirety of poetic tradition, and yet writes verse that no one else will ever be able to "imitate"—for example, T. S. Eliot, Emily Dickinson, or Walt Whitman.

Pastoral verse In the classical Greek and Roman traditions, poetry set in the countryside among shepherds (*pastor* in Latin) who speak of friendship, love, and loss. In the subsequent English and American traditions, pastoral poetry has come to mean verse that has to do with rural life (sometimes explicitly and directly set in contrast to urban life and concerns).

Pentameter A poetic line with five metrical feet. Pentameter is most "natural" to the English language and to much English-language poetry.

Performance poetry Also known as "spoken word" poetry, this freeform kind of verse is meant to be read (or recited) expressively by the poet in front of a responsive, sometimes participatory audience. Performance poetry is especially associated with urban areas such as New York City and San Francisco, and is an especially vibrant stage for multicultural and politically engaged poets.

Persona From the Greek word for "mask," the persona of a poem is the "who" of the poem, the voice or character created by a poet and given either an explicit identity or an implicit **point of view**.

Point of view The perspective from which a poem's speaker or **persona** is viewing, interpreting, and describing.

Postmodernism An international cultural movement whose origins are often located in the social and political upheavals of the 1960s. Postmodernism seeks to strip art of its **conventions**, to overturn **genres**, to challenge **canons**, and to more closely critique the relationship between art and structures of power and politics.

Quatrain After the couplet, the quatrain—a stanza consisting of four lines—is the most basic stanza form in English poetry, and one of the building blocks of such forms as the Shakespearean sonnet. It may be unrhymed or rhymed; if rhymed, it may have any of a number of rhyme schemes.

Rhyme Words with very different meanings yet very similar, almost identical, sounds make up the basics of rhyme and the fundamental pleasure of poetry to the ear. True rhyme matches both the vowel sound and the final consonant of two words: "dove/above" is a true rhyme. (See **assonance**, **consonance**, **sight rhyme**, and **slant rhyme**.) Because English, especially, is such a complex and nuanced language, the possibilities for all kinds of rhyme are infinite. At its most basic, the use of rhyme determines the shape of a stanza and the overall form or genre of a poem; rhyme works with meter to shape verse.

Romanticism   A late-eighteenth-century movement with origins in Germany and France and quick influence in England and America. Romantic poets believed in the primacy of the self and in self-expression; their verse is highly subjective and explores feelings and emotions in a way that was revolutionary for its time. In England, the Romantic poets and their associates were also deeply concerned with issues of social justice and industrialization.

San Francisco poetry renaissance   The West Coast version of the Beat movement, the San Francisco poetry renaissance was heralded by a reading given by Beat writers Jack Kerouac, Alan Ginsberg, Neal Cassady, Kenneth Rexroth, and their colleagues at the 6 Gallery on Fillmore Street in San Francisco on October 13, 1955; it was the first public reading of Ginsberg's great epic "Howl."

Scan   To read a poem with close attention to its metrical structure, often annotating the text to indicate individual "feet" and where the stresses fall.

Sestina   A complex form originated by medieval Provençal poets, the sestina has six six-line **stanzas** and a concluding three-line stanza. The last words of each of the first six lines of the poem must be repeated in a specific order at the ends of the lines of the next five six-line stanzas, and all six words must finally appear in the final three-line stanza.

Sight rhyme   When two words "look" like they ought to rhyme to the ear, but either shifts over time in pronunciation or a deliberate move by the poet doesn't allow for a clear aural rhyme (cough/plough, love/move).

Simile   A figure of speech in which two things are explicitly compared by using "is" or "like": "the darkness / of a shell folded like a pastry" (Mary Oliver, "The Hermit Crab").

Slam poetry   A particularly urban genre of performance poetry, slam poetry's origins are often traced to New York City's Nuyorican Poetry Café in the late 1980s. At a poetry slam, poets perform their work before an audience; unlike **performance poetry**, the audience shouts its approval (or disapproval). The poet whose work is best acclaimed wins the "slam."

Slant rhyme   A rhyme that is a kind of "near miss"—words echo each other without exactly corresponding. Consonants might match, as in "sack/sick"; this is **consonance**. When vowels match, as in "leap/weed," the effect is called **assonance**.

Sonnet   A poem in fourteen lines in iambic pentameter; the two most common rhyme schemes in English are the Petrarchan sonnet (a stanza of eight rhymed lines and a stanza of six differently rhymed lines) and the Shakespearean sonnet (three quatrains and a final couplet).

Spondee   A metrical foot composed of two equally accented syllables (adjective: *spondaic*).

Stanza   From the Italian word for "room," a distinct section of a poem. Each stanza of a poem is consistent in its meter, length, and rhyme scheme; stanzas can also be formed around a central image or idea.

Stress   Essentially the weight or emphasis placed on a syllable when it is spoken. No syllable is without any stress, but some will have more than others. In one way or another, stress forms the basis of most English meters.

Syllabics   Verse whose structure is determined by the number of syllables in the line. Marianne Moore's highly complex syllabic poetry is an especially good example of the form.

Symbol   Something that stands for something else; a rose for a woman, a dog for fidelity, a bare tree for an aging man.

Synecdoche   When a part of something represents the whole; "all hands on deck" means all sailors on deck—not just their hands.

Tenor   In **metaphor**, the tenor is the subject being illustrated by the comparison; the **vehicle** is the image that conveys the comparison. When A. K. Ramanujan describes snakes "writing a sibilant alphabet of panic / on my floor," the snakes' movement is the tenor and the alphabet is the vehicle (metaphorically, the movement of the snakes is compared to writing).

Tetrameter   A metrical line consisting of four feet.

Tone   The poet's stance toward the poem's subject.

Totalizing image   An ultimate **image**, often the last of a poem, that gathers the thematic elements of the poem into a single (often unifying) image. The final line of Shakespeare's Sonnet 94, "Lilies that fester smell far worse than weeds," is a particularly striking example.

Trimeter   A metrical line consisting of three feet.

Trochee   A metrical foot of one accented syllable followed by one unaccented syllable: "dismal," "Boston" (adjective *trochaic).*

Vehicle   In **metaphor**, the vehicle is the **image** that conveys a comparison to the subject being illustrated (the **tenor).** When A. K. Ramanujan describes snakes "writing a sibilant alphabet of panic / on my floor," the snakes' movement is the tenor and the alphabet is the vehicle (metaphorically, the movement of the snakes is compared to writing).

Villanelle   Originally French, this complex form of nineteen lines uses only two rhymes, but those rhymes are repeated according to a fixed pattern.

Voice   To say that a poem has an identifiable voice is to say that it sounds as though it were being spoken by a living individual. Each poem has a particular speaker (sometimes speakers), and the reader will interpret the poem based in part on what sort of person the speaker seems to be. Just as with the narrator of a piece of fiction, the reader will have to decide whether the speaker of a poem is reliable or unreliable. In theory, the number of different voices a poet can employ is limitless, and there is no reason why the same poet cannot be in one poem prophetic and in the next crudely comical. In some poems, there is little difference between the speaker of the poem and the author. It is always a mistake, however, to assume that the two are identical, since it is common practice for poets to write in voices other than their own.

Word choice   It is safe to say that word choice is one of the most fundamental aspects of any type of writing. Even when no one word draws attention to itself in a text, word choice is still crucial. One of the factors that both complicates and enriches word choice is the difference between denotation and connotation. Denotation is the literal dictionary meaning of a word, while connotation refers to the additional meaning or set of meanings associated with a word. An obvious example of this is the difference between the words *inexpensive* and *cheap*. On one level, both words simply mean that something doesn't cost much. On another level, however, *cheap* implies that the item in question is somehow inferior. Another consideration is the sound of a word. This is especially important for poets, who may need a word that fits a particular meter or rhyme scheme. In addition to choosing their words, authors must also decide on the best order in which to put them. The order of the parts of speech in English sentences is relatively fixed, but there is some variation, and writers can take advantage of these variations for expressive purposes.

CREDITS

Ai "Twenty-Year Marriage" from *Cruelty* by Ai. "Killing Floor" from *Killing Floor* by Ai. New York: W. W. Norton & Company.

Margaret Walker Alexander "For My People" by Margaret Walker Alexander from *This Is My Century: New and Collected Poems*. Reprinted by permission of The University of Georgia Press.

Sherman Alexie "Indian Boy Long Song (#2)" by Sherman Alexie reprinted from *The Business of Fancydancing* © 1992 by Sherman Alexie, by permission of Hanging Loose Press. "The Powwow at the End of the World" and "Sonnet: Tattoo Tears" by Sherman Alexie reprinted from *The Summer of Black Widows* © 1996 by Sherman Alexie, by permission of Hanging Loose Press.

Julia Alvarez "Papi Working," "Bilingual Sestina," and "On Not Shoplifting Louise Bogan's *The Blue Estuaries*" from *The Other Side/El Otro Lado*. Copyright © 1995 by Julia Alvarez. Published by Plume/Penguin, a division of Penguin Group (USA). Reprinted by permission of Susan Bergholz Literary Services, New York. All rights reserved.

A. R. Ammons "So I Said I Am Ezra" and "Corsons Inlet." Copyright © 1963 by A. R. Ammons, from *The Selected Poems, Expanded Edition* by A. R. Ammons. Copyright © 1987, 1977, 1975, 1974, 1972, 1971, 1970, 1966, 1965, 1964, 1955 by A. R. Ammons. Used by permission of W. W. Norton & Company, Inc. "Grassy Sound" and "Hymn" from *Collected Poems 1951–1971* by A. R. Ammons. Copyright © 1972 by A. R. Ammons. Used by permission of W. W. Norton & Company, Inc.

John Ashbery "Thoughts of a Young Girl" in *The Tennis Court Oath* © 1977 by John Ashbery and reprinted by permission of Wesleyan University Press. "Farm Implements and Rutabagas in a Landscape" and "Song" by John Ashbery from *The Double Dream of Spring*. "Late Echo" by John Ashbery from *As We Know*. "At North Farm" by John Ashbery from *A Wave*. "Picture of Little J. A. in a Prospect of Flowers" by John Ashbery from *Some Trees*.

Margaret Atwood "At the Tourist Center in Boston" by Margaret Atwood from *Selected Poems, 1966–1984*. Copyright © 1990 Margaret Atwood. Reprinted by permission of Oxford University Press.

W. H. Auden "In Memory of W. B. Yeats," copyright © 1940 & renewed 1968 by W. H. Auden, "In Praise of Limestone," copyright © 1951 by W. H. Auden, "Miss Gee," copyright © 1940 and renewed 1968 by W. H. Auden, "Hell," copyright © 1976 by Edward Mendelson, William Meredith and Monroe K. Spears, Executors of the Estate of W. H. Auden, "New Year Letter," copyright © 1941 & renewed 1969 by W. H. Auden, "If I Could Tell You," copyright © 1945 by W. H. Auden, "The Shield of Achilles," copyright © 1952 by W. H. Auden, "Musee des Beaux Arts," copyright © 1940 & renewed 1968 by W. H. Auden, "Lullaby (40 lines)," copyright © 1940 & 1968 by W. H. Auden, "The Quarry" ["Oh What is That Sound"], copyright © 1937 & renewed 1965 by W. H. Auden, "September 1, 1939," copyright © 1940 & renewed by W. H. Auden, "Epitaph on a Tyrant," copyright © 1940 & renewed 1968 by W. H. Auden, "The Truest Poetry Is the Most Feigning," copyright © 1954 by W. H. Auden, "The Wanderer," copyright

Amittai F. Aviram "Pictures of Maurice Among Funeral Flowers" from *Gents, Bad Boys and Barbarians* by Amittai F. Aviram. Reprinted by permission of the author, Amittai F. Aviram.

Peter Balakian "After the Survivors are Gone" by Peter Balakian from *New and Selected Poems*.

Amiri Baraka "A Poem for Black Hearts" by Amiri Baraka from *Selected Poetry of Amiri Baraka/Leroi Jones*. Copyright © by Amiri Baraka. Reprinted by permission of SLL/Sterling Lord Literistic, Inc. "A New Reality is Better Than a New Movie" from *Transbluesency* by Amiri Baraka. Copyright © by Amiri Baraka. Reprinted by permission of SLL/Sterling Lord Literistic, Inc.

Gwendolyn B. Bennett "To a Dark Girl" © by Gwendolyn B. Bennett.

Charles Bernstein "Of Time and the Line" from *Rough Trades*. Copyright © 1991 by Charles Bernstein. Reprinted with the permission of Green Integer Books, Los Angeles, www.greeninteger.com.

Ted Berrigan "A Final Sonnet" from *The Sonnets* by Ted Berrigan, copyright © 2000 by Alice Notley, Literary Executrix of the Estate of Ted Berrigan. Used by permission of Viking Penguin, a division of Penguin Group (USA) Inc.

Wendell Berry "Marriage," "Enriching the Earth," "Sparrow," and "Against the War in Vietnam" by Wendell Berry from *The Collected Poems*. NY: Farrar, Straus and Giroux.

John Berryman "An Elegy for W.C.W., the Lovely Man" and "Life, friends, is boring" by John Berryman from *The Dream Songs*. NY: Farrar, Straus and Giroux. "Sonnet 9" and "Sonnet 115" by John Berryman from *Berryman's Sonnets*. NY: Farrar, Straus and Giroux. "The Soviet Union" by John Berryman from *Love and Fame*. NY: Farrar, Straus and Giroux.

Elizabeth Bishop "The Moose," "Sestina," "One Art," "The Fish," "The Armadillo," and "Sonnet" by Elizabeth Bishop from *The Complete Poems*. NY: Farrar, Straus and Giroux.

Michael Blumenthal "Squid" by Michael Blumenthal. Copyright © Michael Blumenthal, from *Days We Would Rather Know* (Viking-Penguin, 1984). Reprinted by permission of the author.

Robert Bly "Romans Angry About the Inner World" from *The Light Around the Body* by Robert Bly. Copyright © 1967 by Robert Bly. Copyright renewed 1995 by Robert Bly. Reprinted by permission of HarperCollins Publishers Inc.

Louise Bogan "M., Singing," "Night," and "Sub Contra" from *The Blue Estuaries* by Louise Bogan. Copyright © 1968 by Louise Bogan. Copyright renewed 1996 by Ruth Limmer. Reprinted by permission of Farrar, Straus and Giroux, LLC.

Eavan Boland "The Woman Turns Herself into a Fish" from *Outside History: Selected Poems 1980–1990* by Eavan Boland. Copyright © 1990 by Eavan Boland. Used by permission of W. W. Norton & Company, Inc. "Woman in Kitchen." Copyright © 1982 by Eavan Boland, from *An Origin Like Water: Collected Poems 1967–1987* by Eavan Boland. Used by permission of W. W. Norton & Company, Inc.

"Stopping by Woods on a Snowy Evening," "The Road Not Taken," "Home Burial," "Mowing," "Out—Out," and "The Oven Bird" by Robert Frost. New York: Henry Holt and Company.

Tu Fu "Spring View" and "Thoughts on a Night Journey," translated by Arthur Sze, from *Silk Dragon: Translations from the Chinese*. Copyright © 2001 by Arthur Sze. Reprinted with the permission of Copper Canyon Press, P.O. Box 271, Port Townsend, WA 98368-0271. "Spring Rain" by Tu Fu, translated by Kenneth Rexroth from *Collected Shorter Poems*, copyright © 1956 by New Directions Publishing Corp. Reprinted by permission of New Directions Publishing Corp.

James Galvin "Dear Nobody's Business" and "Nature, Beside Herself" from *X*. Copyright © 2003 by James Galvin. Reprinted with the permission of BOA Editions, Ltd., www.BOAEditions.org.

Jack Gilbert "Explicating the Twilight" and "Haunted Importantly" from *The Great Fires: Poems 1982–1992* by Jack Gilbert, copyright © 1994 by Jack Gilbert. Used by permission of Alfred A. Knopf, a division of Random House, Inc.

Sandra M. Gilbert "Simplicity," "Elegy," and "The Return of the Muse" by Sandra M. Gilbert from *Kissing the Bread: New and Selected Poems, 1969–1999*. New York: W. W. Norton & Company.

Allen Ginsberg "To Aunt Rose" from *Collected Poems 1947–1980* by Allen Ginsberg. Copyright © 1958 by Allen Ginsberg. Reprinted by permission of HarperCollins Publishers Inc. "America" from *Collected Poems 1947–1980* by Allen Ginsberg. Copyright © 1956, 1959 by Allen Ginsberg. Reprinted by permission of HarperCollins Publishers Inc. "Reflections at Lake Louise" from *Collected Poems 1947–1980* by Allen Ginsberg. Copyright © 1984 by Allen Ginsberg. Reprinted by permission of HarperCollins Publishers Inc. "Howl" from *Collected Poems 1947–1980* by Allen Ginsberg. Copyright © 1955 by Allen Ginsberg. Reprinted by permission of HarperCollins Publishers Inc.

Dana Gioia "Guide to the Other Gallery" by Dana Gioia. Copyright © 1991 by Dana Gioia. Reprinted from *The Gods of Winter* with the permission of Graywolf Press, Saint Paul, Minnesota. "Unsaid" by Dana Gioia. Copyright © 2001 by Dana Gioia. Reprinted from *Interrogations at Noon* with the permission of Graywolf Press, Saint Paul, Minnesota.

Nikki Giovanni "Always There Are the Children" and "Poetry" from *The Women and the Men* by Nikki Giovanni. Copyright © 1970, 1974, 1975 by Nikki Giovanni. Reprinted by permission of HarperCollins Publishers Inc. "Beautiful Black Men" from *Black Feeling, Black Talk, Black Judgement* by Nikki Giovanni. Copyright © 1968, 1970 by Nikki Giovanni. Reprinted by permission of HarperCollins Publishers Inc.

Louise Glück "The Pond" and "Messengers" from *The House on Marshland* by Louise Glück. "Cottonmouth Country" by Louise Glück from *The First Four Books of Poems*. "Happiness" by Louise Glück from *Descending Figure*. "Scilla" by Louise Glück from *The Wild Iris*. NY: HarperCollins.

Lorna Goodison "Jamaica 1980" from *Guinea Woman* by Lorna Goodison. Reprinted by permission of Carcanet Press Limited. "In the Mountains of the Moon, Uganda" from *To Us, All Flowers are Roses: Poems*. Copyright © 1995 by

ing Group, form *The Collected Poems of Hugh MacDiarmid* by Hugh MacDiarmid. Copyright © 1948, 1962 by Christopher Murray Grieve. Copyright © 1967 by Macmillan Publishing Company.

Archibald MacLeish "Ars Poetica" from *Collected Poems, 1917–1982* by Archibald MacLeish. Copyright © 1985 by The Estate of Archibald MacLeish. Reprinted by permission of Houghton Mifflin Company. All rights reserved.

Louis MacNeice "Sunday Morning" and "The Sunlight on the Garden" by Louis MacNeice from *Collected Poems*. Reprinted by permission of David Higham Associates.

Jay MacPherson "The Swan" by Jay MacPherson from *Poems Twice Told: The Boatman and Welcoming Disaster* by Jay MacPherson. Copyright © 1981 by Oxford University Press. Reprinted by permission of Oxford University Press.

Derek Mahon "The Snow Party" by Derek Mahon from *Poems: 1962–1978.*

David Mason "Spooning" by David Mason from *The Buried Houses*. Reprinted with permission of the author and Story Line Press (www.storylinepress.com).

William Matthews "Photo of the Author with a Favorite Pig" from *Search Party: Collected Poems of William Matthews*, edited by Sebastian Matthews and Stanley Plumly. Copyright © 2004 by Sebastian Matthews and Stanley Plumly. Reprinted by permission of Houghton Mifflin Company. All rights reserved. "An Elegy for Bob Marley" by William Matthews from *A Happy Childhood*.

William Meredith "Airman's Virtue" and "Effort at Speech" are reprinted from *Effort at Speech: New and Selected Poems by William Meredith*, published by TriQuarterly Books/Northwestern University Press in 1997. Copyright © 1997 by William Meredith. All rights reserved; used by permission of Northwestern University Press and the author.

James Merrill "The Kimono" from *Collected Poems* by James Merrill and J. D. McClatchy and Stephen Yenser, editors, copyright © 2001 by the Literary Estate of James Merrill at Washington University. Used by permission of Alfred A. Knopf, a division of Random House, Inc.

Thomas Merton "The Breath of Nature" translated by Thomas Merton from *The Way of Chuang Tzu*, copyright © 1965 by The Abbey of Gethsemani. Reprinted by permission of New Directions Publishing Corp.

W. S. Merwin "The Asians Dying" and "The Animals" by W. S. Merwin. Copyright © 1993 by W. S. Merwin. Reprinted by permission from the Wylie Agency Inc. Excerpt from *Sir Gawain and the Green Knight* by W. S. Merwin, copyright © 2002 by W. S. Merwin. Used by permission of Alfred A. Knopf, a division of Random House, Inc. and the Wylie Agency Inc. "The Drunk in the Furnace" by W. S. Merwin. Copyright © 1960 by W. S. Merwin. Reprinted by permission from the Wylie Agency Inc. "For the Anniversary of My Death" by W. S. Merwin. Copyright © 1967 by W. S. Merwin. Reprinted by permission from the Wylie Agency Inc.

Linda McCarrison "Riding Out at Evening" by Linda McCarrison. Reprinted by permission from *Talking Soft Dutch* by Linda McCarrison. Copyright © 1984 Texas Tech University Press, 1-800-832-4042, www.ttup.ttu.edu.

Ntozake Shange   "Bocas" from *A Daughter's Geography* by Ntozake Shange. Copyright © 1991 by the author and reprinted by permission of St. Martin's Press, LLC.

Alan Shapiro   "Cold Wood" by Alan Shapiro from *Covenant*. Reprinted by permission of the author Alan Shapiro.

Karl Shapiro   "Troop Train" by Karl Shapiro from *Collected Poems*.

Chiang She Ch'uan   "A Mountain Spring" and "Evening in the Garden Clear After Rain" by Chiang She Ch'uan, translated by Kenneth Rexroth, from *One Hundred More Poems from the Chinese*, copyright © 1970 by Kenneth Rexroth. Reprinted by permission of New Directions Publishing Corp.

Leslie Marmon Silko   "Indian Song: Survival" by Leslie Marmon Silko. Copyright © 1975 by Leslie Marmon Silko. Reprinted with the permission of the Wylie Agency Inc.

Charles Simic   "Sunday Papers" from *Night Picnic*, copyright © 2001 by Charles Simic, reprinted by permission of Harcourt, Inc. This material may not be reproduced in any form or by any means without the prior written permission of the publisher. "Fork," "Classic Ballroom Dance," "Fear," "Breasts," "Charon's Cosmology," "Summer Morning," and "Dismantling the Silence" from *Selected Poems* by Charles Simic. Reprinted by permission of George Braziller, Inc.

Louis Simpson   "American Poetry" and "Early in the Morning" from *The Owner of the House: New Collected Poems 1940–2001*. Copyright © 2003 by Louis Simpson. Reprinted with the permission of BOA Editions, Ltd., www.BOAEditions.org.

Edith Sitwell   "Still Falls the Rain" by Edith Sitwell from *The Collected Poems*.

Dave Smith   "Bats" and "The Roundhouse Voices" by Dave Smith from *The House of the Judge*.

Iain Crichton Smith   "At the Scott Exhibition, Edinburgh Festival" by Iain Crichton Smith from *Love Poems & Elegies*. Victor Gollancz Ltd.

Stevie Smith   "Not Waving But Drowning" by Stevie Smith from *Collected Poems of Stevie Smith*, copyright © 1972 by Stevie Smith. Reprinted by permission of New Directions Publishing Corp.

W. D. Snodgrass   "April Inventory" by W. D. Snodgrass from *Heart's Needle*. Reprinted by permission of W. D. Snodgrass.

Gary Snyder   "The Snow on Saddle Mountain" by Gary Snyder from *The Back Country*. Copyright © 1968 by Gary Snyder. Reprinted by permission of New Directions Publishing Corp. "Mid-August at Sourdough Mountain Lookout" by Gary Snyder from *Rip Rap and Cold Mountain Poems*. Reprinted by permission of the publisher, Shoemaker & Hoard. "Lines on a Carp" by Gary Snyder from *New and Selected Poems*. NY: Pantheon Books.

Cathy Song   "The Youngest Daughter" by Cathy Song from *Picture Bride*. Reprinted by permission of Yale University Press.

Gary Soto   "Ode to the Yard Sale," "Field Poem," and "The Family in Spring" from *New and Selected Poems* by Gary Soto. Copyright © 1995 by Gary Soto.

CHRONOLOGICAL TABLE OF CONTENTS

INDEX